More praise for *Treasure Trove of Benefits and Variet*

"Nasrallah's extensive linguistic, cultural, and culinai
Anny Gaul in *Gastronomica*, Summer 2019.

"A formidable intertwined offering from a historian, translator, cook, cooking instructor and writer ..." Hala N. Barakat in *Madamasr*, August 25, 2018.

"For culinary enthusiasts as well as for those fascinated by Egypt's heritage ... a thrilling revelation." Aziza Sami in *Al-Ahram Weekly*, August 31, 2018.

"Nasrallah provides her readers not only with an annotated translation, but also details of texts and manuscripts, and excellent and detailed glossaries, helpfully divided into classes of food such as vegetables and legumes, fruits and nuts and so forth, as well as kitchen and cooking implements and culinary terms." Susan Weingarten in *Mediterranean Historical Review*, 33:2, 2018.

"The tremendous linguistic and contextual expertise that has gone into the preparation of this book has paid off. It is not only an invaluable historical document for the better understanding of the material culture and foodways of pre-modern Egyptian society, but also a fine example of thorough research and scholarly responsibility to one's material." Leyla Rouhi in *Al-Masāq*, 30/3 (2018).

"N. Nasrallah nous propose ici un travail exceptionnel. Sa minutie et son expérience passée de la traduction d'ouvrages culinaires confère à ce livre une valeur scientifique indéniable, mais aussi une dimension sociale, vivante de ce que fut la cuisine arabe médiévale." Veronique Pitchon in *BCAI* 33, 2019.

"Cet ouvrage contient tout ce que l'on peut attendre de la traduction d'un livre de cuisine médiéval : une traduction sérieuse ..., une présentation qui permette au lecteur, même non spécialiste, d'apprécier l'originalité du texte, des glossaires efficaces et une petite touche de gourmandise." Audrey Caire in *Arabica* 65, 2018.

Treasure Trove of Benefits and Variety at the Table: A Fourteenth-Century Egyptian Cookbook

كنز الفوائد في تنويع الموائد

Treasure Trove of Benefits and Variety at the Table

A Fourteenth-Century Egyptian Cookbook

English Translation, with an Introduction and Glossary by

Nawal Nasrallah

TUTA SUB AEGIDE PALLAS 1683

BRILL

LEIDEN | BOSTON

This paperback was originally published in hardback as Volume 148 in the series *Islamic History and Civilization*.

Cover illustration: Cooks preparing for a grand feast, folio from *Divan* of Jami, 52.20.4, detail (MET NY—Purchase, Joseph Pulitzer Bequest, 1952).

The Library of Congress has cataloged the hardcover edition as follows:

Names: Nasrallah, Nawal, translator.
Title: Treasure trove of benefits and variety at the table : a fourteenth-century Egyptian cookbook / English translation, with an introduction and glossary by Nawal Nasrallah.
Other titles: Kanz al-fawāʾid fī tanwīʿ al-mawāʾid. English
Description: Leiden ; Boston : Brill, [2018] | Series: Islamic history and civilization ; V. 148 | Includes bibliographical references and index.
Identifiers: LCCN 2017040760 (print) | LCCN 2017043260 (e-book) | ISBN 9789004349919 (E-book) | ISBN 9789004347298 (hardback : alk. paper)
Subjects: LCSH: Cooking, Arab—Early works to 1800. | Cooking, Egyptian—Early works to 1800.
Classification: LCC TX725.A7 (e-book) | LCC TX725.A7 K2913 2018 (print) | DDC 641.5962/09023—dc23
LC record available at https://lccn.loc.gov/2017040760

Typeface for the Latin, Greek, and Cyrillic scripts: "Brill". See and download: brill.com/brill-typeface.

ISBN 978-90-04-435623-8 (paperback, 2020)
ISBN 978-90-04-34729-8 (hardback, 2018)
ISBN 978-90-04-34991-9 (e-book, 2018)

This book is printed on acid-free paper and produced in a sustainable manner.

To Sara El-Sayed and Bassem Khalifa, pioneers of the Slow Food Movement in Egypt, for their commendable efforts to promote Egyptian food heritage through their organizational and documentary projects Nawaya (نوايا), Baladini (بلديني), Ma7ali (محلي), *and* Ma7sool (محصول). *And to our mutual friend Lena Alazawi, who introduced me to them.*

Contents

Preface XIII
Acknowledgments XV
List of Figures XVI
Notes on Translating the Text XX

Introduction 1
Part I: The Making of the *Kanz al-fawāʾid* 1
1 *The Text* 3
2 *The Provenance* 8
3 *Date and Sources* 13
4 *A Case of Abridged Borrowing*: Kanz al-fawāʾid *and* Zahr al-ḥadīqa 19
Part II: Medieval Egyptian Food Culture 20
5 *Diet and Formation of a Cuisine* 20
6 *What was Cooking in Medieval Cairo?* 26
7 *The Culture of Food and Cooking* 33
8 *Shopping and Eating Out* 38
Part III 44
9 *Medieval Egyptian Cooking as Reflected in the* Kanz al-fawāʾid 44
10 *Eating in Good Health* 53

Infinite Benefits of Variety at the Table, Containing Twenty-Three Chapters on Cooking Foods, by Various Knowing Experts

1 **Indispensable Instructions For Cooks** 66

2 **How to Knead Bread Dough and Bake It; and Making Varieties of Bread: Enhanced (*muṭayyab*), Seeded (*mubazzar*), Salted (*mamlūḥ*), and More** 79

3 **Measures Taken When Drinking Water, in a *muzammal*, and Chilled with Ice (*thalj maḍrūb*)** 83

4 **Qualities of Air-Cooled Water and What the Physicians Said About It** 84

5 Miscellany of Dishes 85

6 Making *murrī* (Liquid Fermented Sauce), and Preserving Sour Grape Juice (*mā' al-ḥiṣrim*) and Lemon Juice (*mā' al-laymūn*) 162

7 Eggs Cooked as Omelets and Other Dishes 171

8 Vegetarian Dishes (*muzawwarāt al-buqūl*) for the Nourishment of the Sick 184

9 All Kinds of Dishes Made with Different Varieties of Fish 193

10 Making All Kinds of Sweets (*ḥalwā*) 211

11 Digestive Stomachics (*juwārishnāt*), Electuaries (*maʿājin*), and Drinks (*ashriba*) Offered Before and After the Meal 250

12 Making *fuqqāʿ* (Foamy Beer), and Other Drinks 270

13 Dried-Apricot Compote (*naqūʿ al-mishmish*) 290

14 Making Preparations Which Relieve Nausea (*adwiyat al-qaraf*) 295

15 Making Mustard [Condiments], Mild and Pungent Hot 305

16 On Making Table Sauces (*ṣulūṣāt*) 315

17 Of Dishes Made with Dairy (*albān*): *kawāmikh* (Fermented Condiments), *jājaq* (Drained-Yogurt Condiment), Condiments with *kabar* (Capers), and *zaʿtar* (Thyme), *bīrāf* (Clotted Cream), and the Like 323

18 All Kinds of Pickled Turnips and Onions, Pickling Fruits and Vegetables of All Kinds, and Preserving Lemons, Damascus Citron and the Like, in Salt 340

19 Making Cold Dishes (*bawārid*) 378

20 On Aromatics (*ṭīb*), and the Properties of Toothpicks (*khilāl*) Made from Willow Wood (*ṣafṣāf*) and Egyptian Willow Twigs (*ʿīdān al-khilāf*) 392

21 Varieties of Aroma-Diffusing Incense, Which Fortify Spirit and Heart; Aromatizing Pills; Deodorants; and Other Preparations 403

22 Top Quality Perfumed Powders (*dharāʾir mulūkiyya*) and Other Preparations 421

23 Storing Fresh Fruits and Keeping Them to Use After Their Season 438

Glossary

1 Beverages for Pleasure and Health 457

2 Breads, Grains, Pasta, Noodles, and Sweet and Savory Pastries 465

3 Dairy 478

4 Desserts, Sweeteners, and Conserves for Pleasure and Health 481

5 Dishes and Prepared Foods: Main and Side Dishes, Snacks, Condiments, Pickles, Dips, and Table Sauces 492

6 Fats and Oils 503

7 Fruits and Nuts 506

8 Ingredients Used in Foods and Medicinal Preparations: Herbs, Spices, Aromatics, Minerals, Food Colors, and Seasoning Sauces 529

9 Kitchen and Cooking Implements, and Culinary Techniques and Terms 576

10 Meat 609

11 Medical Terms, Medicinal Preparations, and Personal Hygiene and Perfumes 619

12 Vegetables and Legumes 630

13 Weights and Measures 642

Appendix 647
Works Cited 675
General Index 683
Index of Ingredients, Dishes, Beverages, Aromatics, and other Preparations 687

Preface

With more than 820 recipes, the *Kanz al-fawāʾid fī tanwīʿ al-mawāʾid* is unique in its dizzying variety and aspiration to comprehensively present the Egyptian cuisine of the time. Its anonymous author/compiler presents an impressive volume and variety that make this fourteenth-century cookbook a brilliant showcase of not only recipes of dishes, but also recipes for distilled waters, incense, perfumed oils, handwashing compounds, and the like. Nowhere is this intent to dazzle more evident than in his choice of the book's title. It is truly a treasure trove.

Egyptian cuisine has been underrepresented in the culinary map of the medieval Arabo-Islamic world. The *Kanz al-fawāʾid* was written at a time when Baghdad was no longer the navel of the earth (*surrat al-arḍ*); Cairo, the 'mother of all nations' (*umm al-bilād*), had already replaced it as a flourishing metropolis, a cultural haven for diverse ethnicities and nationalities from surrounding regions. It was an interesting time, indeed, for a cookbook like the *Kanz* to reflect its diversity and broad sweep. And yet, the *Kanz* remained a little-known culinary manual until the Arabic edition came out in 1993, and now for the first time in an English translation.

The *Kanz* is a copious and valuable source whose culinary repertoire remarkably bridges the gap between ancient gastronomic riches and today's cuisine. In myriad ways, it enriches our knowledge of the history of medieval material culture in that region during one of its most active and propitious times. The *Kanz* has preserved for us the largest number of recipes of *ḥimmaṣ kassā*—eleven of them, which predates by centuries what we now know as *ḥummuṣ bi-ṭaḥīna*. It includes a recipe for cooking okra (*bāmiya*), which nowadays is the most common vegetable in the Egyptian diet. It is the only recipe for this vegetable which has survived from the entire medieval era. One of the *Kanz* recipes uses a tool, called *mifrāk*, which is a kind of stick blender nowadays used in Upper Egypt and Sudan. A similar blender was excavated from some ruins in Lower Egypt that date back to the beginning of the first millennium AD. Linguistically, the text of the *Kanz* is equally gratifying, particularly the colloquial aspect of it, which again predates by several centuries the first book on the Egyptian Arabic dialect, *Dafʿ al-iṣr ʿan kalām ahl Miṣr*, by the seventeenth-century lexicographer Yūsuf al-Maghribī.

To ensure an accurate and a meaningful reading of the text, I left no stone unturned; the translation of a book such as this deserves no less. The text has inevitably suffered from the familiar process of copying and recopying, which has resulted in several cases of recipes merged incoherently, or words copied inaccurately due to the copyist's unfamiliarity with ingredients—in some cases *ḥall* (حل) 'sugar syrup' is mistaken for *khall* (خل) 'vinegar.' In addition, there are instances in which the copyists exhibit incompetent linguistic skills, or simply copied dictated words mechanically. A word like ونصف, for instance, required some head scratching to realize that it was an ungrammatical rendering of the colloquial vocalization of وانسف 'and sift.' I even came across places where the copyist, most probably absentmindedly, kept the words as he heard them recited by readers with speech impediments, thus we encounter words like *ighmihā* (اغمها) for *irmihā* (ارمها) 'throw it.' I amended the text based on the corresponding recipes in the available copies of the *Kanz* manuscript, as well as comparable recipes in medieval sources. A section in the introduction to this translation discusses the various medieval sources that share recipes with the *Kanz*. Some amendments, however, were determined through context when external evidence is lacking.

The comprehensive introduction, the glossary, and the illustrations accompanying the book are all meant to initiate the readers into the world of the *Kanz*, particularly to familiarize them with ingredients, cooking techniques, and implements and gadgets—all of which facilitated the emergence of a complex and sophisticated cuisine. It is hoped that the twenty-two modern adaptations of *Kanz* recipes with their photos in the appendix will whet appetites and inspire further experimentations with the *Kanz* cookbook, where hundreds of recipes, including a good number of vegetarian ones, are truly worth discovering.

Acknowledgments

I am grateful to Brill for publishing this volume, my second with them. To my editors, Kathy van Vliet, for coming to the rescue whenever the need arose, and to Teddi Dols for her admirable diligence and inspiring persistence to bring this project to fruition. My thanks also extend to the insightful comments of the peer reviewers, who contributed to making this volume better, each in their own way; and to Valerie Turner, for her careful and thorough copy editing of the text, and Kim Fiona Plas, Production Editor, for her meticulous care and patience. I would also like to acknowledge the support and guidance generously offered by Professor David Waines, co-editor of the Arabic text of the *Kanz*. I am thankful to my friend Nadia Hassani, Laila Rizk, director of the National Library in Cairo, and Professors Paulina Lewicka and Liesbeth Zack for their assistance in providing the documents I needed for my research. The greatest debt of gratitude I owe to my husband Shakir Mustafa, for his unconditional support in every possible way all the years we've been together.

List of Figures

1 Title page of *Kanz* MS 2
2 Two pigeon cotes in al-Tawfīqiyya village in Egypt 11
3 Ancient Egyptian bounty: Fragment from the funerary offering scene, c. 1350 BC 22
4 Sugar cane, one of the crops brought to Egypt with the spread of Islam. Muḥammad al-Qazwīnī, *ʿAjāʾib al-makhlūqāt*, F1954.78v, detail 24
5 Sour orange (*nāranj*), one of the crops brought to Egypt with the spread of Islam. Al-ʿUmarī, *Masālik al-abṣār*, fol. 212r, detail 25
6 Serving food at a grand feast, folio from *Divan* of Jāmī, 52.20.4, detail 28
7 Cooks preparing for a grand feast, folio from *Divan* of Jāmī, 52.20.4, detail 30
8 Butchers, folio from *Divan* of Jāmī, 52.20.4, detail 40
9 Kneader covering mouth and nose with a face muffler. Folio from *Divan* of Jāmī, 52.20.4, detail 43
10 Grinding food in a mortar, folio from *Divan* of Jāmī, 52.20.4, detail 46
11 Cooking on a portable stove (*mustawqad*), detail from Arabic translation of *De Materia Medica* of Dioscorides, thirteenth century, 57.51.21 46
12 Cough medicine being prepared, folio from Arabic Translation of *De Materia Medica* of Dioscorides, thirteenth century, 13.152.6 55
13 Long-necked *fayyāsha* bottle, x.21.210 57
14 *Fol. 1v of Kanz* MS 60
15 Fol. 2r of *Kanz* MS 62
16 Collecting firewood, fol. 44r from *Manṭiq al-ṭayr*, 63.210.44, detail 67
17 Washing up dishes, folio from *Divan* of Jāmī 52.20.4, detail 68
18 Cutting boards and knives, folio from *Divan* of Jami 52.20.4, detail 69
19 Jar, c. thirteenth century, 48.113.15 76
20 Pomegranate tree, F1954.77r, Muḥammad al-Qazwīnī, *ʿAjāʾib al-makhlūqāt*, detail 87
21 Sumac, al-ʿUmarī, *Masālik al-abṣār*, fol. 179r 92
22 Mulberry, F1954.74v, Muḥammad al-Qazwīnī, *ʿAjāʾib al-makhlūqāt*, detail 98
23 Hazelnut, F1954.78r, Muḥammad al-Qazwīnī, *ʿAjāʾib al-makhlūqāt*, detail 106
24 Quince, al-ʿUmarī, *Masālik al-abṣār*, fol. 177r 111
25 Apples, F1954.74r, Muḥammad al-Qazwīnī, *ʿAjāʾib al-makhlūqāt*, detail 144

26 Apricots, F1954.80r, Muḥammad al-Qazwīnī, *ʿAjāʾib al-makhlūqāt*, detail 145
27 Pigeon, F1954.102v, Muḥammad al-Qazwīnī, *ʿAjāʾib al-makhlūqāt*, detail 146
28 Sparrow, F1954.103v, Muḥammad al-Qazwīnī, *ʿAjāʾib al-makhlūqāt*, detail 157
29 Distilling apparatus, Add. 25724, fol.36v, detail 166
30 Sour oranges, F1954.80v, Muḥammad al-Qazwīnī, *ʿAjāʾib al-makhlūqāt*, detail 167
31 Mint, F1954.83r, Muḥammad al-Qazwīnī, *ʿAjāʾib al-makhlūqāt*, detail 169
32 Rooster, F1954.100v Muḥammad al-Qazwīnī, *ʿAjāʾib al-makhlūqāt*, detail 178
33 Gourd, F1954.83v, Muḥammad al-Qazwīnī, *ʿAjāʾib al-makhlūqāt*, detail 186
34 Damask rose (*ward Jūrī/ward Shāmī*), Elizabeth Blackwell, *A Curious Herbal*, 1738, plate 82 219
35 Wild marjoram, Elizabeth Blackwell, *A Curious Herbal*, 1738, plate 280 224
36 *Utrujj* (Citron), F1954.72r, Muḥammad al-Qazwīnī, *ʿAjāʾib al-makhlūqāt*, detail 253
37 Endive, F1954.83v, Muḥammad al-Qazwīnī, *ʿAjāʾib al-makhlūqāt*, detail 258
38 Green glazed wide-mouthed jar (*barniyya*), thirteenth century 294
39 White mustard, Elizabeth Blackwell, *A Curious Herbal*, 1738, plate 29 312
40 *Bāṭiya*, F1954.47v, Muḥammad al-Qazwīnī, *ʿAjāʾib al-makhlūqāt*, detail 351
41 Olives, al-ʿUmarī, *Masālik al-abṣār*, fol. 171v 355
42 Lemons, al-ʿUmarī, *Masālik al-abṣār*, fol. 202v 363
43 Quince, al-ʿUmarī, *Masālik al-Abṣār*, fol. 177r, detail 367
44 Purslane, Elizabeth Blackwell, *A Curious Herbal*, 1738, plate 287 386
45 Dog-rose, F1954.83r, Muḥammad al-Qazwīnī, *ʿAjāʾib al-makhlūqāt*, detail 400
46 Incense burner, early fourteenth century, 17.190.1716 404
47 Pierced globe incense burner, diam. 6.25 in., early fourteenth century, 17.190.2095a, b 407
48 Ancient Egyptian *mifrāk* (hand mixer/blender), Graeco-Roman Period 416
49 Distilling apparatus, Add. 25724, fol. 36v 426

50 Figs, F1954.74v, Muḥammad al-Qazwīnī, *ʿAjāʾib al-makhlūqāt*, detail 445
51 Zodiac sign of Sagittarius, F1954.45r, Muḥammad al-Qazwīnī, *ʿAjāʾib al-makhlūqāt*, detail 447
52 Zodiac sign of Capricorn, F1954.45r, Muḥammad al-Qazwīnī, *ʿAjāʾib al-makhlūqāt*, detail 450
53 Spheroconical *fuqqāʿ* drinking vessel, unglazed earthenware, c. tenth century, 40.170.232 461
54 Cook making *rishtā*, detail from a detached folio, S1986.221 476
55 Olive tree, al-ʿUmarī, *Masālik al-abṣār*, fol. 171v, detail 504
56 Muskmelon, F1954.82v, Muḥammad al-Qazwīnī, *ʿAjāʾib al-makhlūqāt*, detail 506
57 Melon seller, fol. 49r from *Manṭiq al-ṭayr*, 63.210.44, detail 508
58 Plum tree, F1954.72v, Muḥammad al-Qazwīnī, *ʿAjāʾib al-makhlūqāt*, detail 510
59 Peach tree, F1954.76r, Muḥammad al-Qazwīnī, *ʿAjāʾib al-makhlūqāt*, detail 513
60 Banana tree, F1954.80v, Muḥammad al-Qazwīnī, *ʿAjāʾib al-makhlūqāt*, detail 517
61 *Umluj* (emblic myrobalan), Elizabeth Blackwell, *A Curious Herbal*, 1738, plate 400 525
62 *Utrujj* (citron), al-ʿUmarī, *Masālik al-abṣār*, fol. 142r, detail 526
63 *Baqdūnis* (Macedonian parsley), Elizabeth Blackwell, *A Curious Herbal*, 1738, plate 382 532
64 *Barnūf* (sticky fleabane), Elizabeth Blackwell, *A Curious Herbal*, 1738, plate 103 533
65 *Ḥulba* (fenugreek), Elizabeth Blackwell, *A Curious Herbal*, 1738, plate 384 539
66 *Karafs* (common parsley), Elizabeth Blackwell, *A Curious Herbal*, 1738, plate 172 542
67 *Kurrāth Nabaṭī* (leaf leeks) 547
68 *Kuzbara raṭba* (fresh cilantro leaves), Elizabeth Blackwell, *A Curious Herbal*, 1738, plate 176 548
69 *Lisān al-thawr* (borage), Elizabeth Blackwell, *A Curious Herbal*, 1738, plate 36 549
70 *Rijl al-ḥamāma* (alkanet), Elizabeth Blackwell, *A Curious Herbal*, 1738, plate 112 560
71 *Sadhāb* (rue), Elizabeth Blackwell, *A Curious Herbal*, 1738, plate 7 561
72 *Ẓufr* (onycha), F1954.71v, Muḥammad al-Qazwīnī, *ʿAjāʾib al-makhlūqāt*, detail 575

73 *Bustūqa*, F1902.190, c. twelfth century 577
74 *Fayyāsha*, long-necked glass bottle, c. fourteenth century 578
75 Bronze mortar, c. twelfth century, 13.81 580
76 *Kūz* (earthenware drinking cup), c. thirteenth century 583
77 Ancient Egyptian *mifrāk* (hand mixer/blender), Graeco-Roman Period 585
78 Silver spoons, fourteenth century, 07. 228.85a, b, d 585
79 Glass drinking beaker with fish motif, fourteenth century 587
80 Glass bottle, twelve century 589
81 Flat glass plate, fourteenth century 590
82 Plate, twelfth century 590
83 Lipped pan, fourteenth century 592
84 Set of bowls, fourteenth century 595
85 *Zibdiyya* (bowl), c. fourteenth century 595
86 Pot suspended on the fire, detail from Arabic Translation of *De Materia Medica* of Dioscorides 604
87 Cooking in liquid, detail from Arabic translation of *De Materia Medica* of Dioscorides, thirteenth century 607
88 Sheep to be slaughtered for the feast of Sada, fol. 22v from *Shahnama of Shah Tahmasp*, c. sixteenth century 609
89 Chicken, F1954.101r, Muḥammad al-Qazwīnī, *ʿAjāʾib al-makhlūqāt*, detail 611
90 Fat-tailed sheep, the source for the rendered cooking fat *alya*, F1954.89r, Muḥammad al-Qazwīnī, *ʿAjāʾib al-makhlūqāt*, detail 612
91 *Burj al-ḥamām* (pigeon cotes) 613
92 Preparing medicine from honey, folio from Arabic translation of *De Materia Medica* of Dioscorides, thirteenth century 620
93 Fresh *lūbiya* (black-eyed peas) 638
94 Measuring cup, sealed with a capacity of 50 cc (1.70 fluid ounces), which must have been used by pharmacists 644

Notes on Translating the Text

The English translation of *Kanz al-fawāʾid* is based on the edited text by Manuela Marín and David Waines (1993). My amendments were made with the help of other copies of the *Kanz* and several contemporary culinary sources that share recipes with it. Substantial changes are pointed out in footnotes. The obvious ones are silently executed.

Abbreviations of References to Manuscripts and Print Editions Frequently Used in the Translated Text

The Edited Text

1. *Kanz* = *Kanz al-fawāʾid*, edited text
2. C = *Kanz al-fawāʾid*, MS Cambridge U Library (basic copy)
3. CB = *Kanz al-fawāʾid*, MS Chester Beatty Library, Dublin
4. DK = *Kanz al-fawāʾid*, MS Dār al-Kutub, Cairo
5. Gotha = *Kanz al-fawāʾid*, MS Gotha Research Library
6. *Zahr* = *Zahr al-ḥadīqa fī l-aṭʿima al-anīqa* by Ibn Mubārak Shāh, MS Gotha Research Library.

Contemporary Sources That Share Recipes with the Kanz

1. Baghdādī = *Kitāb al-Ṭabīkh* by Ibn al-Karīm al-Kātib al-Baghdādī (Arabic edition)
2. Baghdādī BL = *Kitāb al-Ṭabīkh*, BL MS
3. al-Warrāq = *Kitāb al-Ṭabīkh* by Ibn Sayyār al-Warrāq (Arabic edition)
4. al-Warrāq, English trans. *Annals* = *Kitāb al-Ṭabīkh*, English translation, *Annals of the Caliphs' Kitchens*
5. al-Warrāq Istanbul MS = *Kitāb al-Ṭabīkh*, Topkapi Sarayi MS, Istanbul
6. *Waṣf* = *Kitāb Waṣf al-aṭʿima al-muʿtāda*, anonymous, MS 11 Ṣināʿa, Dār al-Kutub, Cairo (modern pagination)
7. *Wuṣla* = *Kitāb al-Wuṣla ilā l-ḥabīb fī waṣf al-ṭayyibāt wa-l-ṭīb* by Ibn al-ʿAdīm (Arabic edition)
8. *Wuṣla* SOAS = *Kitāb al-Wuṣla ilā l-ḥabīb*, SOAS London University MS

The Numbering System of the Recipes in the Translated Text

The edited Arabic text, based on C MS, contains 750 recipes. I have preserved the editors' numbering sequence. In addition, the editors opted to include 79 additional recipes in the appendix. Most of these occur in DK MS, and a few in CB MS. These I have inserted into the main text, approximately where they might have occurred. To avoid confusion, I have not enumerated them in the translated text. However, their numbers, as given in the appendix, are duly cited in the footnotes. My additions in the translated text are enclosed in square brackets.

I also use Gotha MS of *Kanz* (94 folios), which was not available to the editors when they prepared their edition. This copy is closer to DK MS than C MS, and has been helpful in amending the edited text. However, it contains the first ten chapters only.

On *Zahr al-ḥadīqa*

Upon examining the edited Arabic text of *Zahr al-ḥadīqa fī l-aṭʿima al-anīqa* by Ibn Mubārak Shāh (d. 1458), I discovered that it is, in fact, an abridged copy of the *Kanz al-fawāʾid*. Therefore, I used it to amend the text in several places. My references to it are all from its Gotha MS (38 folios).

Introduction

Part 1: The Making of the *Kanz al-fawāʾid*

Briefing his readers on the contents of his book, the anonymous author of the *Kanz al-fawāʾid* states that when he finished it, he chose to name it *Kanz al-fawāʾid fī tanwīʿ al-mawāʾid*. This indeed reveals a conscious acknowledgement on his part of putting together an inexhaustible gastronomic resource, a treasure trove (*kanz*) no less,[1] of dishes and drinks popular in his time, as well as preparations to aid their digestion, perfumed cleansing compounds, and much more. Altogether, in its twenty-three chapters, this compilation comprises more than 820 recipes, garnered from "various knowing experts."

Regrettably, none of the surviving five manuscripts of the *Kanz* establish its authorship. On the title page of the manuscript at the Library of Bankipore, however, the work is attributed to the renowned Abbasid Arabic translator of Greek texts and physician Abū Zayd Ḥunayn b. Isḥāq al-ʿIbādī (d. 873). This claim is certainly too far-fetched to consider.[2] The editors of the *Kanz*, Manuela Marín and David Waines, tentatively place the text in fourteenth-century Mamluk Egypt. Based on internal evidence, such as typical Egyptian material comprising the names of dishes, ingredients, and the like, they conclude that the book's Egyptian identity "seems reasonable." Nevertheless, they propose that a better understanding of the nature of its compilation might render revision of their conclusion necessary.[3]

The following sections investigate various aspects related to the text: the discovery of its manuscripts and the editing of the text; its composition and sources, which the compiler might have tapped into for his material; and the borrowings the text itself may have brought about. The *Kanz* was one of several cookbooks that survived from medieval times; indeed, Marín and Waines suggest a "family connection" and "extended family" relations with some of them.[4] The question of textual duplications and affinities with the "extended family" is further explored, and it is hoped that what follows will deepen our understanding of the text, and shed more light on some of the lingering issues, such as those of time and place.

1 Described as "encyclopedic" in character by Marín, "Beyond Taste" 206.

2 This information is found in the Catalogue of the Arabic Manuscripts at the Oriental Public Library in Bankipore, iv 8–10, see Marín and Waines, *Kanz* 2. I was unable to acquire a copy of this manuscript, due to the library's strict regulations.

3 Marín and Waines, *Kanz* 7–8.

4 Marín and Waines, *Kanz* 2–5.

 | DOI 10.1163/9789004349919_002

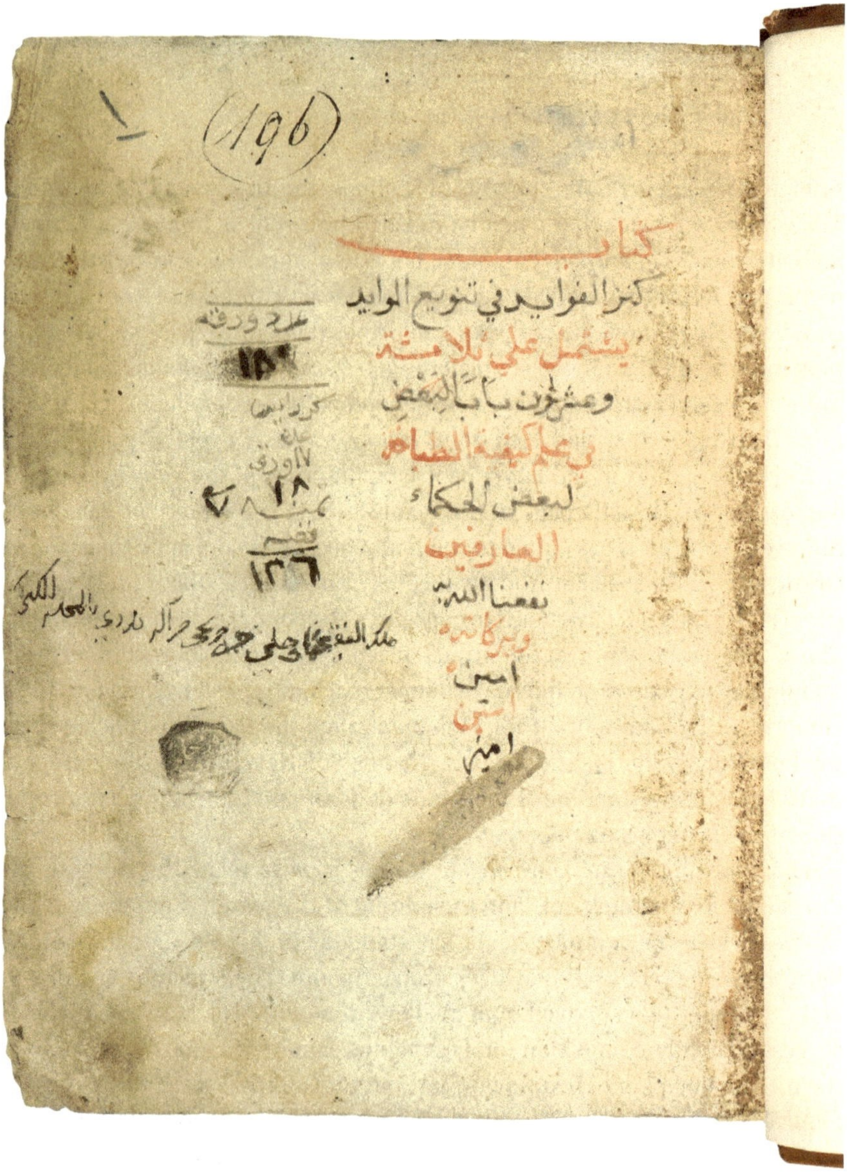

كتاب
كنز الفوايد في تنويع الموايد
يشتمل علي ثلاثة
وعشرين بابا البعض
في علم كيفية الطباخة
لبعض الحكماء
العارفين
نفعنا الله به
وبركاته
امين
امين
امين

FIGURE 1 *Title page of* Kanz MS *(Reproduced by the kind permission of the Syndics of Cambridge University Library).*

1 *The Text*

As early as 1947, the Lebanese scholar Ḥabīb Zayyāt drew attention to the existence of a copy of a manuscript entitled *Kanz al-fawāʾid* at the Royal Egyptian Library.[5] In the following year, Maxime Rodinson mentioned the existence of three manuscripts of this book in Dār al-Kutub in Cairo, and concluded that it "must have achieved some popularity." He says that the library's catalogue states that it deals with "the preparations of food and drinks as well as preserving in vinegar and household cleaning."[6] Almost half a century elapsed before it was edited and published in 1993. In the judgment of the editors, Manuela Marín and David Waines, the manuscript was "an important text with certain characteristics setting it off from other known medieval cookbooks within the same tradition."[7]

The editors established the existence of five manuscripts of the *Kanz*, today located in Cambridge University Library, Chester Beatty Library in Dublin, Dār al-Kutub of Cairo, Oriental Public Library at Bankipore, and Gotha Research Library. For their critical edition, they used the manuscripts at the libraries of Cambridge (C), Cairo (DK), and Dublin (CB). Although both C and DK are complete, they chose C for their basic text, largely because it has relatively fewer misreadings. They numbered the 750 edited recipes consecutively for easier reference. In cases of isolated recipes that C does not include but which exist in DK and CB, they provided them in an appendix, and numbered them separately 1–79. The 8,900 endnotes they provide document all the textual variations among the three manuscripts. The resulting edition is a thorough piece of work, for which the editors are to be commended.

At the time they edited the book they were unable to use the manuscript housed at Gotha Research Library because their requests for a microfilm were refused "during what was to be the final period of the ancient regime of East Germany," as they explain.[8] Fortunately, I managed to acquire a copy, and use it in my translation of the *Kanz* text.[9] Like the others, the Gotha manuscript is anonymous. In all the existing copies, the only place where our author speaks

5 Zayyāt, "*Fann al-ṭabkh*" 17. The manuscript is categorized as *ʿulūm maʿāshiyya* (everyday life affairs).

6 Rodinson, "Studies in Arabic Manuscripts" 104; see also his n. 3, where the date of this catalogue (فهرست الكتب العربية) is given as 1933. Rodinson's seminal study of Arabic culinary manuscripts was first published in 1948 in French. Zayyāt and the editors mention the presence of only one copy there, which is MS no. 18.

7 Marín and Waines, *Kanz* 1.

8 Marín and Waines, *Kanz* 2. Its shelf number is MS. orient. A1345.

9 I here extend my thanks to my friend Nadia Hassani for her help with the contacts and transactions.

in the first person is in the introductory section, where he surveys the contents of his composition and states that when he finished it all, he named it *Kanz al-fawāʾid fī tanwīʿ al-mawāʾid*. The Gotha manuscript also fails to shed light on the book's date or authorship. Its title page simply reads:

كتاب كنز الفوايد وتنويع الموايد لمؤلفه عفى الله عنه والمسلمين آمين

> *Book of the Treasure Trove of Benefits, and Variety at the Table*, by its author, may he and all Muslims be forgiven by God. Amen.

The Gotha copy has a total of 94 folios,[10] and contains only the first ten chapters of the book. These chapters have indeed proved to be quite useful in amending the edited text in many places.[11] In one instance it was particularly instrumental in filling a folio missing from the rest of the manuscripts.[12]

Gotha shows more affinities with DK than C, and it may have been copied from it. In the first long chapter, which is a guide to cooks and cooking, the copyist made the chapter easier to follow by writing the first word of each new topic in a different color, probably red. When the copyist reached the end of chapter 10, which is about desserts, he concludes it with a new recipe (source unknown) on making a sort of adulterated *samn* 'ghee' using milk instead of butter,[13] followed by the familiar explicit, which reads:

تم وكمل والله اعلم بالصواب واليه المرجع والمآب
وصلى الله على سيدنا محمد وعلى اله وصحبه
وسلم تسليما كثيرا دايما الى يوم الدين والحمد لله رب العالمين

The full version of the *Kanz* is a long text, which the editors acknowledge as being one of its "notable features."[14] It contains twenty-three chapters with a total of 750 recipes (plus the additional 79 recipes included in DK and CD), neatly and logically sequenced as follows:

10 Cf. number of folios in C, 175; CB, 88; and DK, 149.

11 All the amendments are stated in footnotes to the translated text.

12 See the translated text, recipe 20, n. 41.

13 See the translated text, p. 248.

14 Marín and Waines, *Kanz* 6.

1. The first four chapters deal with preliminaries: After a relatively long opening chapter on directions to cooks and good cooking, recipes of bread follow, and then two short chapters on drinking water.
2. Chapters 5 to 10 deal with foods prepared daily. Chapter 5, which describes the main dishes, is the longest in the book; it has 142 recipes. Related to this is chapter 6, which deals with liquid fermented sauces (*murrī*) and preserved sour juices used to season the dishes (16 recipes). Chapter 7 specializes in smaller dishes with eggs, such as omelets (37 recipes). To feed the sick, chapter 8 comes to the rescue with its *muzawwarāt* 'meatless dishes,' approved by physicians at the time (24 recipes). Fish dishes (36 recipes) follow, in chapter 9. After that, it is dessert time, where no less than 81 sweets are included in chapter 10.
3. Then comes the aftermath of eating, addressed in chapters 11 to 14. Varieties of digestive stomachics (*juwārishnāt*), electuaries (*maʿājīn*), and drinks (*ashriba*) are given (44 recipes). Next follows chapter 12 with its digestive beverages (42 recipes), and several preparations for apricot compote (6 recipes), also recommended after meals. In case none of these helps in washing down the foods consumed, there are 26 recipes with preparations to help combat vomiting and nausea of the surfeited digestive system.
4. Chapters 15 to 19 are about cold dishes, such as appetizers and condiments (17 recipes), table sauces (14 recipes), condiments with yogurt (33 recipes), pickles (75 recipes), and cold vegetable dishes (27 recipes). All these are useful as they can be prepared in advance and used when needed. Some of the pickles are even said to last more than a year.
5. Chapters 20 to 22 cover matters of hygiene and perfuming rituals. For washing the hands, 'flossing the teeth,' and anointing the body with perfumed oils, 16 preparations are made available. Next, 18 preparations follow, including aroma-diffusing incense to rid dining places of odors of food; and others, such as deodorants and breath-sweeteners. This part concludes with chapter 22, which contains 43 preparations for perfumed powders and distilled waters.
6. The last chapter is about storing fresh fruits and vegetables, a topic that should also concern skilled cooks. The thrill they get from surprising their guests with out of season produce and roses is priceless. Recipe 736 on storing fresh mulberries, for instance, ends with this exciting incentive, "You will blow their minds away with it, especially if offered when the sun is at the zodiac sign of Sagittarius." This chapter offers 32 recipes.

With a few exceptions, the recipes depicting the abundance of dishes mentioned above are earnestly executed and adequately explained, with an eye to detail, where needed.[15] For instance, if a recipe requires a stone mortar and it is not available, a brass one may be used, but it must be rust-free (recipe 19); or if a cook is working on finely chopped mustard greens, he is advised to mask both mouth and nose with a piece of cloth (recipe 518). The recipes sometimes suggest cheaper alternatives for the less prosperous, these include replacing honey or sugar syrup with cheaper sugar cane molasses (recipe 338). Amounts are mostly left to the discretion of the cook, especially for familiar dishes; but they are provided, by weight and sometimes parts, for drink preparations, for instance, or for a restorative dessert (recipe 288). Descriptive remarks, such as those related to consistencies, are also given.

In naming the dishes, most of them are prosaically described, for example, they are called after the main ingredient, or place name, or the way they are cooked, such as 'fried' and 'grilled.' Other dishes are more interestingly named, such as *yāqūtiyya* 'carnelian,' which is a stew dish cooked with red mulberries; or the Nubian lady, thus called for its blackish hue from the tiny black seeds of purslane (recipes 23, 66 respectively). In other cases, a dish may turn out to be something other than its name suggests. *Mishmishiyya*, for instance, which suggests a dish cooked with apricot (*mishmish*), as the name seemingly proclaims, is in fact a sweetened chicken dish, enhanced with marzipan 'apricots,' in the heart of each is a skinned almond, with a whole shelled pistachio stuck on top to make it look like its stem (recipe 73). It is in the realm of desserts that imagination is given full play; for example, delicate sandwich cookies are named chanteuses' cheeks (*khudūd al-aghānī*) and dainty cookies shaped like breasts are called virgins' breasts (*nuhūd al-ʿadhārī*), as in recipes 270 and 300 respectively.

As a practical culinary document, the *Kanz* is essentially an instructive text. The directions are mostly conveyed in the passive voice, beginning, for instance, with the formulaic يؤخذ 'to be taken.' However, the tone shifts repeatedly, even in the same recipe, to polite requests, such as تأخذ 'you take,' or تحتاج 'you need'; or to imperatives like لا تبطّل الوقيد 'do not stop fueling the fire'; with the occasional afterthought—'by the way, you will have done this before doing that'—jotted at the end. The overall effect of the text is more utilitarian than literary; it manages to communicate the cooking instructions, and reflects the

15 Admittedly, the *Kanz* manuscripts we have today are copies of copies; we have not seen the original manuscript. However, the initial and thorough editing by Marín and Waines, and my additional efforts, all documented in the annotated footnotes of the translated text, bring us closer to what the original manuscript might have been.

familiar language of a busy cook who often distractedly forgets a step or an ingredient, only to remember it as he wraps up his recipe.

The *Kanz* also displays the typical tendency, characteristic of pre-modern cooking manuals in general, to assume its users' familiarity with ingredients and the cooking techniques required in the recipe. We often come across the instruction 'as usual' (ويعمل كالعادة), which, while frustrating for modern readers, likely did not pose a problem for contemporary cooks. At any rate, cooking manuals like the *Kanz* were indeed expected to be used by household cooks, hired chefs, apprentices, and the like, who looked for good recipes for daily dishes and more unusual concoctions. Admittedly, some recipes involve lengthy descriptions, especially the complex ones, such as those for making beer, fermented sauces, and aromatics, or the recipe for sparrows stewed in an unusual glass pot; this occupies two pages of the edited text (recipe 149).

In the *Kanz* we often encounter a tendency to resort to a casual style which avoids the repetition of obvious ingredients (obvious to contemporaries at least), such as the names of familiar spices and herbs that were usually added to a given dish. In this case, they are referred to as *ḥawāʾij*, which is a generic term for 'the needed ingredients.' A handy verb like 'make' (عمل), frequently used in the *Kanz*, spares the recipe writer the headache of the nuances of the language; and hence it is used to cover a variety of actions like 'put,' 'add,' 'drizzle,' and even 'boil.'

Often, the recipes reveal a promotional tone aimed at motivating readers to try them. The *Kanz* compiler, for instance, assumes the reassuring position that he or someone else has tried or tasted them. For instance, in recipe 507 for *bīrāf* 'clotted cream,' the famous scholar and connoisseur, Aḥmad al-Tīfāshī,[16] is quoted at length describing the different ways it is served—some have it with ground white sugar and others with honey, and how he prefers to have it: "I eat it with sugar syrup, and I recommended [it] this way to my friends and they also liked it"; he adds that some people like to eat it with syrupy fritters (*mushabbaka*), and "I tried it and found it delicious."

The recipes often end with a word or two in their praise: they are delicious (*ṭayyib*), truly delicious (*ṭayyib ladhīdh*), utterly delicious (*ghāyat al-ṭība*), splendid (*ʿajīb*), and the like. Even better, some recipes belong to a 'celebrity' chef, as in recipe 273 for Ḥāfiẓiyya cookies, which are named after a slave girl of an Ayyubid king; or it is said that they used to be cooked especially for caliphs and sultans, as in recipe 12; or they were savored and gifted by a dignitary like

16 Scholar, poet, and geologist, he was originally from Tīfāsh in Tunisia. He traveled to Baghdad and Damascus, and then spent the rest of his life in Cairo, where he was buried in 1253.

al-Qāḍī l-Fāḍil, one of Sultan Saladin's favorite counselors (recipe DK, appendix 4, p. 81).

The overall impression we get from reading the recipes in the *Kanz* is that cooks from all walks of life are encouraged to try them—if you cannot afford bee honey in cooking a variety of desserts with dates, no problem, use the cheaper sugar cane molasses instead (recipe 338). A simple variety of pickled quince, "pickling quince, the commoners' way," uses sugar cane molasses and none of the nuts, spices, and aromatics like musk, used in other recipes (recipe 595). And, if a cook prefers to prepare a table sauce (*ṣalṣ*) the Turkish way, then garlic may replace sugar (recipe 490).

We can assume, too, that professional cooks also may have benefited from good cookbooks, like the *Kanz*, perhaps in other ways, besides as instructions on how to prepare delicious and creative dishes. Recipe 724, for instance, describes how to perform magic with fruits, by writing on them. Surprise your master, the recipe suggests, with a plate of lusciously ripe fruits with verses inscribed in green and you will be in his good graces.

2 *The Provenance*

There are numerous signs in the *Kanz* that point to its Egyptian provenance, beginning with the first chapter, where the weights of pulses and grains are given in the Egyptian measure *qadaḥ Miṣrī*. In recipe 31, we get the impression of a cookbook writer adjusting a borrowed recipe for his readers. The recipe uses the Iraqi *raṭl*, followed by the addition that it equals 130 *dirhams*; this was necessary because the Egyptian *raṭl* has 144 *dirhams*. This originally Iraqi recipe is found in al-Baghdādī's *Kitāb al-Ṭabīkh*,[17] where the measure is given in unspecified *raṭls*. In another recipe on preserving olives (recipe 557), the weight measure is the Levantine *mudd*, with its Egyptian equivalent given right after it. In addition, in several places, we come across the weight measure of *raṭl jarwī*, which is associated with Egypt.[18]

Many designative terms involving ingredients and dishes do indeed support the argument for an Egyptian provenance for the *Kanz*. The recipes repeatedly use Egyptian sugar and honey products, such as *sukkar Miṣrī* 'Egyptian sugar,' *ʿasal naḥl Miṣrī* 'Egyptian bee honey,' and *ʿasal mursal*, which is sugar cane syrup made by reducing sugar cane juice when it fails to crystallize. According to al-Nuwayrī, it is an exclusively Egyptian product, not known in the Levant.[19] Another case in point is a type of sugar cane molasses called *usṭarūs*, used

17 British Library MS, fol. 49r.

18 For more on this weight measure, see glossary 13, n. 5.

19 Al-Nuwayrī, *Nihāyat al-arab* viii 196.

in *Kanz* recipe 750. It is described by al-Nuwayrī, who calls it *usṭarūsh*,[20] and mentioned in al-Ḥajjār's fifteenth-century Egyptian battle of the dishes, *Kitāb al-Ḥarb al-maʿshūq*, where most interestingly it is written as *ushṭarūsh*, a dialectical vocalization we also encounter in *Kanz*.[21]

The recipes use *aruzz Wāḥī* and *tamr Wāḥī*, which are rice and date products of the oases in western Egypt, called Wāḥāt. Add to these the *zabīb Ṣaʿīdī* (raisins from Upper Egypt), and *biṭṭīkh ʿAbdulī*, a variety of melon that grows only in Egypt. The only okra recipe that survived from the medieval era appears in the *Kanz*. In medieval times, okra (*bāmiya*) was recognized as a vegetable indigenous to Egypt.[22]

Mulūkhiyya 'Jew's mallow' is a vegetable which has been closely associated with the Egyptian diet from ancient times. The *Kanz* offers four recipes: in one of them, it is wilted first and then chopped finely, as is still traditionally done in Egypt today. *Mulūkhiyya*, however, was also used in the Levant. The thirteenth-century Aleppan cookbook, *al-Wuṣla ilā-l-ḥabīb* (ii 560–2) has four recipes for it. But *mulūkhiyya* was indeed acknowledged as a widely-known vegetable in Egypt.[23]

Another plant, which the *Kanz* uses and which was an important crop in Egypt, is *qulqās* 'taro,' and the finger-like taro variety called *qulqās aṣābiʿ*. The latter was favored for its fine taste and texture.[24] Again, the Aleppan *al-Wuṣla* offers five recipes, while the *Kanz* offers more, and shows greater variety and uses for its cooking. We learn from the fourteenth-century *Waṣf al-aṭʿima al-muʿtāda*, believed to have been written in Egypt, that Egyptians used to fry taro in sesame oil and add it to dishes. The expression *Waṣf* uses is وهو عادة أهل مصر 'this is how the Egyptians usually prepare it.' Added to these are the varieties of dishes in chapter 5, of chicken served smothered in perfumed syrups and nuts. To ʿAbd al-Laṭīf al-Baghdādī (*Riḥla* 119), sweetened chicken was one of the unusual foods he encountered in Egypt.

---

20 Al-Nuwayrī, *Nihāyat al-arab* viii 202, describes it as an inferior sugar cane molasses produced at the sugar mills from the leftovers collected from cooked sugar. See glossary 4.

21 Al-Ḥajjār, *Kitāb al-Ḥarb al-maʿshūq* 105.

22 See Ibn al-Bayṭār, *al-Jāmiʿ* i 111; ʿAbd al-Laṭīf al-Baghdādī, *Riḥla* 60. Mehdawy and Hussain, *Pharaoh's Kitchen* 89, point out that the Pharaonic name for okra is *bano*.

23 Ibn al-Bayṭār, *al-Jāmiʿ* iv 459; and ʿAbd al-Laṭīf al-Baghdādī *Riḥla* 61. In fact, medieval physicians highly recommended that *mulūkhiyya* be finely chopped. See, for instance, *Jāmiʿ al-gharaḍ* 230, by the famous Syrian physician Ibn al-Quff (d. 1286).

24 Described in a similar manner by both ʿAbd al-Laṭīf al-Baghdādī, *Riḥla* 119, who saw it during his visit to Egypt in the thirteenth century; and the seventeenth-century Egyptian al-Shirbīnī, *Hazz al-quḥūf* 212.

The large number of fish dishes in the *Kanz* (36 recipes), many of which use fresh fish (*samak ṭarī*), are comparable only to those included in the augmented version of al-Warrāq's *Kitāb al-Ṭabīkh* (31 augmented recipes from the thirteenth century).[25] The latter is believed to have been written in Egypt. In contrast with these two is *al-Wuṣla*, whose provenance is believed to be Aleppo, a landlocked city in Syria. It does not have any recipes with fresh fish; only a few that deal with salt-cured anchovies (*ṣīr*) and small fish (*ṣaḥna*) condiments. They are all included in the *Kanz.*[26]

All the fish varieties specified in the *Kanz* recipes are indigenous to Egypt. *Absāriyya/bisāriyya* is the small sardine-like anchovy, named *ṣīr* when salt-cured. The flathead grey mullet, called *būrī*, is used fresh and salt cured. Reference to it as *samak al-baṭārikh* indicates that it is salt-dried with the eggs inside it. The seventeenth-century Egyptian al-Shirbīnī (*Hazz al-quḥūf* 251–3), calls this fish *fasīkh al-baṭārikh*. *Fasīkh* is still consumed in Egypt for the spring festival of ʿĪd Shamm al-Nasīm, which harkens back to the ancient Pharaonic new year festivals. *Labīs*, fresh water Nile carp, is mentioned in the opening chapter of the *Kanz.*[27] A refined preparation of salt-cured anchovies that we encounter only in the *Kanz* is called *ṣīr mushakshak* (recipe 244). This *mushakshak* is a genuinely Egyptian dish, whose counterpart in the Egyptian countryside is a much humbler fare, as described a few centuries later by al-Shirbīnī (*Hazz al-quḥūf* 218–9).

The Egyptians' love for pigeons, especially young plump ones (*firākh ḥamām*), is evident in the several preparations that use them as the main meat in the dish, or as a supplementary ingredient. The main source for their pigeons was from cotes, called *abrāj al-ḥamām*, which were built by peasants in rural areas.[28] Pigeon cotes were known in Egypt from ancient times, when "most villages and larger estates would have their own dovecotes"; they can still be seen today in rural Egypt along the Nile Delta.[29]

Another uniquely Egyptian food, which is not found in any other cookbooks, is *manfūsh* (recipe 299). It must have been a popular snack food and readily

25 Istanbul MS, fols. 60v–8v, where the recipes use types of fish native to Egypt, such as *balṭī*, *būrī*, *ṣīr*, *lūṭīs*, and *rāi*.

26 *Wuṣla* recipes, ii 694, 696; in *Kanz*, the identical recipes are 260 and 261.

27 *Kanz* editors, citing Hinds and Badawi, *A Dictionary of Egyptian Arabic*, Beirut 1986, point out that the names of the fishes, *labīs*, *ṣīr* and *būrī*, are Coptic in origin (editorial introduction, 7).

28 Described in detail in the seventeenth-century al-Shirbīnī, *Hazz al-quḥūf* 255.

29 Wilson, Egyptian *Food and Drink* 40; Kindersley, *Ultimate Food Journeys* 185, respectively. In the latter, stuffed pigeon (*ḥamām maḥshī*) is mentioned as the "unofficial national dish" of Egypt.

FIGURE 2 *Two pigeon cotes in al-Tawfiqiyya village in Egypt.*
PHOTO BY FARIS EL-GWELY, 2014 (https://commons.wikimedia.org/w/index.php?curid=34019681).

available in the Egyptian markets, as it was regulated by the food inspectors.[30] It is fried fluffy and brittle white bread sprinkled with sugar. We gather this information from references to it in fifteenth-century Egyptian literary sources.[31]

The linguistic aspect of the text reveals many of the features associated with the ungrammatical language of the uneducated, which the editors refer to as *laḥn al-ʿāmma*. They provide an extensive list of instances depicted in the *Kanz*,[32] such as the pronunciation of *th* as *t* (*thalj*/*talj*) 'ice'; *t* as *ṭ* (*zaʿtar*/*zaʿṭar*) 'thyme'; and *ḍ* as *d* (*amrāḍ*/*amrād*) 'sicknesses'; and vice versa (*mudaqqaqa*/*muḍaqqaqa*) 'meatball'; *ḍ* as *z* (*yaḍaʿ*/*yazaʿ*) 'put'; *s* as *ṣ* (*wa-nsif*/*wa-nṣif*) 'and sift' and (*khass*/*khaṣṣ*) 'lettuce'; and vice versa (*maṣbūgh*/*masbūgh*) 'colored'; or *s* as *sh* (*fustuq*/*fushtuq*) 'pistachio.'[33] As for vocabulary, the editors point out three colloquial expressions, بديت, بتاع, and متاع, to which may be added يشال في مطر لايرشح,[34] وتخليه في الصيف نهاراً تطلع تعمله بكرة واشربه العصر,[35] and ديّة 'this,' وديّه 'take it,' and وتطوّل روحك 'be patient.'[36]

---

30 Ibn al-Ukhuwwa, *Maʿālim al-qurba*, fol. 76r.

31 See Geries, *Mufākhara* 67; Ibn Sūdūn, *Nuzhat al-nufūs* 150, 179, 182, 188, 200, 221, 233; and al-Ḥajjār *Kitāb al-Ḥarb al-maʿshūq* 118. For more on these sources, see pp. 36–8 below. Note that *Kanz* editors in their Introduction, point 4.2, discuss the Egyptian provenance issues, albeit very briefly, of weights, types of fish, a fish condiment named after Alexandria (recipe 262), a reference to the Coptic months (recipe 607), and instances where there are "separate preparations for the Turkish and *baladī* classes." However, the yogurt condiment of *jājaq*, which they mention, should be excluded from the Egyptian evidence. First, a recipe for it does indeed occur in al-Warrāq's tenth-century Baghdadi cookbook (Chapter 39), and second, the *Kitāb al-Ḥarb al-maʿshūq* 100, they cite, describes it as a Kurdish specialty.

32 Marín and Waines, *Kanz* 8–11.

33 Most of these phonological idiosyncrasies are also featured in the seventeenth-century first lexicon of the Egyptian Arabic dialect *Dafʿ al-iṣr ʿan kalām ahl Miṣr* by Yūsuf al-Maghribī. For thorough linguistic analyses of this unique text, see the sixth chapter in Liesbeth Zack, *Egyptian Arabic in the Seventeenth Century: A Study and Edition of Yūsuf al-Maghribī's* Dafʿ al-iṣr ʿan kalām ahl Miṣr, particularly 77–112.

34 The recipe recommends keeping the liquid in stone jars so that it does not filter through.

35 Found in recipe 431 for a *sūbiya* drink, where the advice is that in the summer, the drink is made early in the morning and is ready to drink in the afternoon.

36 There is also an interesting instance, not necessarily Egyptian in nature, where it is uncertain whether the copyist absentmindedly jotted down the word as he heard it, or deliberately kept it just for the entertainment value. It is found in DK, n. 292 and in Gotha MS, fol. 8v, which I suspect is copied from it. The edited text clearly uses the verb *irmīthā* 'throw it,' whereas DK has *ighmihā*, and Gotha *ighmīthā*, as typically pronounced by a rhotacistic—one who has difficulty pronouncing the sound '*r*,' which usually comes out as '*gh*.' A rare window, indeed, into the world of medieval copyists at work. Interestingly,

Apparently, the Egyptian dialect was distinguished by specific features associated with it among other Arabic-speaking countries even from the early medieval times, as is illustrated in a wine recipe included in the tenth-century cookbook of al-Warrāq (in chapter 114).[37] This recipe is said to be done the Egyptian way (على رأي أهل مصر). Expressions like 'keep it soaking' (يقعد منقوع),[38] and the vocalization of the words *fals* (فلس) and *fulūs* (فلوس), an Egyptian coin and weight measure, as *falsh* (فلش) and *fulūsh* (فلوش), replacing the *s* sound with *sh* are unique to this recipe. Interestingly, the recipe also uses the expression يوعى في الجرار 'it is put in jars', which we encounter repeatedly in *Kanz* recipes dealing with emptying liquids into jars. This Egyptian wine recipe in al-Warrāq's cookbook is the only place it is used; otherwise, the verb used is the more familiar يجعل 'it is put.'

All things considered, it is possible that the above mentioned idiosyncratic vocalizations and colloquial expressions indeed reflected the medieval dialect. Admittedly, we do not know whether the *Kanz* was originally written this way or whether the linguistic 'deterioration' of the text crept into it at the hands of copyists and readers. Be that as it may, and taking into account all the notes related to content and language mentioned above, the book of *Kanz al-fawāʾid* was an Egyptian product.

3 *Date and Sources*

While translating the *Kanz*, I was pleasantly surprised by the discovery of several sources that share some of its contents. They were indeed helpful in amending parts of the text, although at the same time they raised questions regarding the possibilities and the nature of its composition. Similarities of some of the recipes in the *Kanz* with those from two other medieval cookbooks, namely, the thirteenth-century Aleppan *Kitāb al-Wuṣla ilā-l-ḥabīb*, and the fourteenth-century *Waṣf al-aṭʿima al-muʿtāda*, written in Egypt, have already been acknowledged by the editors, Marín and Waines. Such parallels, they speculate, might reveal a "family connection" among them, or they could be the result of the dependence of compilers/authors on "existing written

---

fifteenth-century *Nuzhat al-Nufūs* 300–3 by Egyptian Ibn Sūdūn, who exploited popular and 'pot' cultures of his time, includes a comic anecdote, whose main character is a rhotacistic.

37 English trans. *Annals* 462–3. Note that the ingredient *faṭṭāra*, as it occurs in al-Warrāq's edited text should be read as *quṭāra*, 'sugar cane molasses.'

38 In her study of al-Maghribī's lexicon mentioned in n. 33 above, Zack, points out that the verb قعد was and still is used in the Egyptian dialect as "an auxiliary verb expressing continuity ... to keep doing something" (*Egyptian Arabic in the Seventeenth Century*, 111).

specialized monographs of limited size ... to which was added other material from written/oral tradition and which to some extent possibly reflected regional tastes in the main dishes."[39] In the case of the *Kanz*, the latter possibility may explain what happened during its compilation.

In putting together such a massive volume with such a wide range of food categories, our anonymous author must have tapped into dozens of food-related books and manuals. These range from general cooking manuals on main dishes and desserts, to specialized pamphlets on drinks, condiments, fermented sauces, and pickling, to horticultural guides, as well as physicians' treatises with recipes for the sick, and perfumers' concoctions. An interesting illustration of this writing method can be detected at the end of chapter 6, which deals with preparing fermented sauces and preserved sour juices. At the end of this chapter, we read the following:

والحمد لله وحده وصلى الله على سيدنا محمد وعلى آله
وصحبه وسلم تسليما كثيرا دائما ابدا الى يوم الدين[40]

This is a typical explicit, which must have appeared, originally, at the end of a pamphlet dealing with fermented sauces and similar preparations, and which is not appropriate at this place in *Kanz*. Still, it was kept, perhaps inadvertently, by the original writer of the *Kanz*, and copied by C and DK. This explicit, however, is missing from CB and Gotha. Based on this, I am tempted to suggest that of the existing manuscripts, C and DK are the earliest, and that the subsequent copyists must have been attentive enough to notice that an explicit such as this was not original to the manuscript and not copy it.

In the following, I explore the sources, though in fact they may not turn out to be sources from which the *Kanz* borrowed, arranged chronologically. My aim is to enable us to better understand the text, and perhaps narrow down the possibilities for the time of its composition:

> **3.1 Yaʿqūb b. Isḥāq al-Kindī** (d. 873), prominent Abbasid scholar and physician, has a specialized volume on perfumed preparations called *al-Taraffuq fi-l-ʿiṭr*. The *Kanz* recipes 684–94 (on distilled waters in chapter 22) are duplicates of recipes found in this book.

39 Marín and Waines, *Kanz* 4–5. The *Waṣf* cookbook is an augmented version of al-Baghdādī's thirteenth-century cookbook.

40 *Kanz*, n. 2211. Whereas C includes the first line only, DK copies it all.

3.2. Ibn Sayyār al-Warrāq (mid tenth century), *Kitāb al-Ṭabīkh*, offers several parallel passages:

3.2.1. The third and fourth chapters of the *Kanz*, as well as segments 5 and 6 from the DK *Kanz* manuscript, are identical to al-Warrāq's chapter 110, and the opening of chapter 111 on properties of air-cooled water. They are similar in titles and contents, and only vary in a few minor stylistic details.

There is no indication of direct borrowing on the part of the *Kanz* compiler. I have recently discovered that ultimately, both al-Warrāq's book and the *Kanz* drew on a copy of ***Kitāb al-Manṣūrī*** by Abū Bakr al-Rāzī, the famous physician (d. 925), who wrote it for the Persian governor of Rayy. Al-Rāzī's chapter is on the humoral power of water (في قوة الماء), fols. 17r–8v. The opening statement of chapter 12 on *fuqqāʿ* 'foamy beer' in the *Kanz* is almost identical to al-Warrāq's chapter 112. It turns out that both quoted from the section on the humoral power of non-intoxicating drinks (في قوة الاشربة غير المسكرة) fol. 19r in the *Kitāb al-Manṣūrī*.

3.2.2. In chapter 8 of the *Kanz*, which deals with vegetarian dishes for the sick, recipes 205, 206, 207, and 224 correspond with al-Warrāq's recipes in chapter 108, where he mentions Ibn Māsawayh (d. 857), the Nestorian physician, as his source. The similarities include the title of the chapter and its content. Ibn Māsawayh's famous manual must have been the source for both.

3.2.3. In chapter 10 of the *Kanz*, on desserts, recipes 316, 318, and 319 are similar to al-Warrāq's recipes in chapters 94 and 97.[41] The *Kanz* versions, however, differ slightly in style and are somewhat simplified.

3.2.4. The title of chapter 15 of the *Kanz*, and the first recipe on making a mustard condiment are also found in al-Warrāq's chapter 38, which copies only one recipe and moves on to the following chapter. The *Kanz*, on the other hand, includes additional mustard recipes, apparently from similar manuals that specialized in condiments and share the same recipe.

3.2.5. Al-Warrāq's short chapter 128, which deals with the properties of toothpicks (*khilāl*), corresponds with the opening section of the *Kanz*, chapter 20, in title and content. Once again, both books must have derived this chapter from similar sources on oral and personal hygiene.

---

41 al-Warrāq, English trans. *Annals* 391, 392, and 402.

3.2.6. Al-Warrāq's last recipe in chapter 95, on how to serve fresh dates when not in season, is identical to *Kanz* recipe 740. It even cites the Abbasid caliph al-Ma'mūn (d. 833), who used to prefer them served on a platter with pieces of broken ice over them. Specialized manuals dealing with food preservation and storing fruits and vegetables were in demand then; the *Kanz* chapter includes 32 recipes. Clearly, al-Warrāq's Abbasid source was still in active circulation more than four hundred years after it was written.

3.3. In its recipes on personal hygiene, including handwashing preparations (recipes 639, 640, 645, 646, and 648), aromatic incense (recipe 661), and perfumed powders and distilled waters (recipes 695, 702, 706, and 707), the *Kanz* seems to have drawn on some specialized books dealing with such preparations, which must have been, originally, selected from *Ṭīb al-ʿarūs* by **Muḥammad b. Aḥmad al-Tamīmī** (d. ca. 1000).[42] Al-Tamīmī's original recipes are a little more elaborate, and involved adding additional ingredients to the compounds. The ones in the *Kanz* are simplified versions.

3.4. The opening segment of the *Kanz*, no. 204 of chapter 8 that deals with vegetarian recipes for the sick is also found in *Waṣf* 181–2 (see also 3.6 below), where it states that it is copied from chapter 41 of **Ibn ʿAbdūn's** book. Ibn ʿAbdūn, in fact, is none other than Ibn Buṭlān, the Christian physician of Baghdad, Abū Anīs al-Mukhtār b. ʿAbdūn b. Saʿdūn b. Buṭlān (d. 1066), whose works include *Taqwīm al-ṣiḥḥa*, *Daʿwat al-aṭibbāʾ*, and *Kunnāsh al-adīra wa-l-ruhbān*. Ibn ʿAbdūn's chapter 41 must have been widely circulated as a useful pamphlet of meatless recipes for the sick and fasting Christians.[43]

3.5. ***Al-Wuṣla ilā l-ḥabīb fī waṣf al-ṭayyibāt wa-l-ṭīb*** (Winning the beloved's heart with delectable dishes and perfumes) was allegedly compiled by the Aleppan historian Ibn al-ʿAdīm (d. 1262) around the mid thirteenth century.[44] Similarities between recipes in the *Kanz* and those in *al-Wuṣla* indeed abound, albeit they are scattered throughout the text. The corresponding recipes in the *Kanz* are as follows:

---

42 Al-Tamīmī, *Ṭīb al-ʿarūs*, page citations to this appear in the respective *Kanz* translated recipes, below.

43 I am grateful to Professor Paulina Lewicka for providing me with this chapter from Jadon, "The Arab Physician ibn Buṭlān" 317–30. See also Lewicka, *Food and Foodways* 37, n. 50.

44 See Ibn al-ʿAdīm, *Wuṣla* ii 421–3; Rodinson, "Studies in Arabic Manuscripts" 130.

3.5.1. Recipes in chapter 5 on main dishes 12, 34, 80, 96, 144, and 145; recipe 186 in chapter 7 on omelets; recipes 260 and 261 in chapter 9 on fish.

3.5.2. Recipes in chapter 10 on desserts: 268, 270, 274, 290, 291, 293–7; 299, 301–6; 309, 311; 320, 337, and 340–2.

3.5.3. Recipes in chapter 12 on beverages: 394–6, 401, 408, 420, 426.

3.5.4. Recipes in chapter 16 on condiments: 485–7, and 490.

3.5.5. Recipes in chapter 18 on pickles: 537–43, 545–6, 550, 563, 570–2, 576, 592, 596–8, 601, 604–7.

3.5.6. Recipes in chapter 19 on cold dishes: 613, 620, 622–4, 627–9, and 632–3.

3.5.7. Recipes in chapter 20 on handwashing preparations: 639–40, 642, 645–8, 651, and 653.

3.5.8. Recipes in chapter 21 on incense and other aromatics: 657–8, 660–2, 664–5, 667–8, and 670–3.

3.5.9. Recipes in chapter 22 on perfumed powders and distilled waters: 674–8, and 690–715.

Indeed, a considerable number of recipes were shared. And yet it is unlikely that *al-Wuṣla* might have been a direct source of borrowing for the *Kanz*. The *Kanz* does not show convincing signs of dependency on this source, given the disparities we see in focus and the configuration of their material. Whereas *al-Wuṣla* is more an ingredient-oriented cookbook, the *Kanz* is more traditionally organized into food categories, each of which comprises numerous recipes.

3.6. *Waṣf al-aṭʿima al-muʿtāda* (Recipes of the familiar dishes) is a fourteenth-century augmented version of al-Baghdādī's *Kitāb al-Ṭabīkh* that was written in Baghdad in 1226.[45] Less than half of it comprises al-Baghdādī's original recipes, the rest were added by the anonymous compiler.

The recipes *Kanz* shares with this volume are scattered throughout the book, but several of them are clustered in the *Kanz*, in chapter 5, which contains 142 recipes of main dishes. Several sources must have been used in accumulating this large chapter, with the result that some recipes show up again later in the chapter, often as variations, but also as duplicates, as is the case with recipes 7 and 136 of *sikbāj* 'sour vinegar stew.' The *Kanz*

45 The colophon of the copy I have of the *Waṣf* MS states that it was copied in 1914 from the MS possessed by Dār al-Kutub al-Khudaywiyya in Cairo, which was originally written in 1373. I am indebted to the director of the National Library in Cairo, Laila Rizk, for providing me with a copy of this manuscript (11 Ṣināʿa Taymūr).

shares with *al-Wuṣla*—and with al-Baghdādī by proxy—recipes 7–20, 23, 24, 26–35, 44, and 141. The same may be said about the chapter on desserts with its 81 recipes. The recipes that are shared with *Waṣf* are 274, 299, 300, 302, 305, and 340.

The rest of the corresponding recipes are scattered throughout the *Kanz*. Some specialized manuals may have been resorted to, such as manuals for digestives (recipes 378 and 420); manuals for beverages (recipes 394 and 420), manuals for making condiments (recipes 494–6), pickling manuals (recipe 568), and manuals of cold dishes (recipe 618).

Other than the shared recipes, the opening part of the book is a guide to cooks and good cooking, which we encounter in al-Baghdādī's cookbook, *Waṣf*, and *Kanz*. Al-Baghdādī's is the shortest, and that of the *Kanz* is the longest. This must have been a simple case of borrowing from a common source, perhaps it was written as a guide on proper cooking for chefs.

3.7. *Kanz* recipes 516 (fresh fennel with yogurt), and pickling recipes 547, 550, 570, 572, 575, 576, 588, 590, 591, 596, and 601, are all found in *ʿAlam al-malāḥa fī ʿilm al-filāḥa* by **al-Nābulusī** (d. 1731). It is a book on agriculture, which is a concise version of the copy by Raḍiyy al-Dīn al-Ghazzī l-ʿĀmirī (d. 1529), both from Syria. Since the *Kanz* was written before their time, we assume that both drew on similar sources dealing with yogurt condiments and food preservation.

3.8. Duplicate recipes appear in *Maṭāliʿ al-budūr* by **al-Ghuzūlī** (d. 1412)[46] and *Kanz* recipe 432 in chapter 12 on beverages, recipes 435–6 on apricot compote in chapter 13, and DK MS of *Kanz* in appendix 63 of handwashing preparation. Both must have used similar sources.

3.9. Related to al-Warrāq's tenth-century cookbook (see 3.2 above) is the **augmented version** of his book compiled in Egypt, and copied in 1297.[47] Interestingly, the *Kanz* recipes 470–2 in chapter 15 dealing with sauces served with fish correspond with al-Warrāq Istanbul MS, fols. 111r–v, with some stylistic differences and textual variants. Possibly, both drew on the same source—although not necessarily the same copy—perhaps it was a pamphlet that specialized in cold dishes and accompanying sauces.

The textual parallels between the *Kanz* and the sources listed above are indubitably apparent, but rather than offering us clues, which might help us detect the possible dependency of one upon another, the picture we get is rather that of works drawing on common culinary sources and independently concocted.

---

46 Al-Ghuzūlī, *Maṭāliʿ al-budūr* ii 88, 89, and 66, respectively.

47 Hereafter referred to as al-Warrāq Istanbul MS. See al-Warrāq, English trans. *Annals* 5–10.

The editors' tentative conclusion, that the book was written sometime in the fourteenth century in Mamluk Egypt, remains unchallenged. However, based on internal evidence, we can say with certainty that the book could not have been written before the lifetime of Aḥmad al-Tīfāshī.[48] *Kanz* recipe 507 includes a relatively long citation from al-Tīfāshī regarding his preferences for eating *bīrāf* 'clotted cream.' Equally certain is that the *Kanz* could not have been written after the lifetime of the Egyptian scholar Ibn Mubārak Shāh (1403–58). His cookbook, entitled *Zahr al-ḥadīqa fī-l-aṭʿima al-anīqa* (The best of the delectable dishes), has passed, thus far, as just another medieval cookbook with which the *Kanz* shares recipes, but a closer look reveals that it was indeed an abridged version of the *Kanz* itself.[49]

4 *A Case of Abridged Borrowing*: Kanz al-fawāʾid *and* Zahr al-ḥadīqa

Ibn Mubārak Shāh was a prominent Cairene scholar who lived during the first half of the fifteenth century.[50] His biographers do not allude to his *Zahr al-ḥadīqa fī-l-aṭʿima al-anīqa*, but apparently, it had its fair share of fame; enough for a copy to survive to this day.[51] It was executed after his death, as the opening sentence describes him as 'the deceased' (رحمه الله).

The *Zahr* presents a unique opportunity for modern readers to see how cookbooks might have been written then. If we did not know the *Kanz*, we would not have doubted Ibn Mubārak Shāh's absolute authorship of the book. He manipulates the text in accordance with his personal taste and budget. Whereas the approach in the *Kanz* is the more recipes the better; the *Zahr* is more concise, resulting in a short volume of no more than 38 folios; it includes a peppering of Ibn Mubārak Shāh's brief personal comments, justifications, and elaborations.

The overall components of the *Kanz* are mostly preserved. The entire chapter on guidelines for cooks has been kept, but in the chapters that follow, many of the *Kanz's* recipes and passages are shortened to avoid long-windedness. He repeatedly declares that he favors brevity; if a cook is good enough, he can improvise and create endless dishes of his own (fol. 7r). Often, he inserts

48 He was a well-known scholar, anthologist, geologist, and poet. Originally from Tifash in Tunisia, he settled in Cairo, and was buried there in 1253.

49 Lewicka, *Food and Foodways* 39, in her mention of fifteenth-century Ibn Mubārak Shāh's *Zahr al-ḥadīqa*, points out that "much of its contents seem to be copied from *Kanz*." However, no connection, as is being made here, is suggested.

50 His full name is Aḥmad b. Muḥammad al-Miṣrī Shihāb al-Dīn (1403–58).

51 The manuscript is in Gotha Research Library, shelf no. 1344. An Arabic edition was published in 2007 in Cairo. Unfortunately, it contains a fair number of misreadings, which could have been avoided had the editor, Muḥammad al-Shāghūl, been aware of its close connection with *Kanz*.

remarks based on his own cooking experience, as when he explains the culinary expression *yuhadda' wa-yurfa'* (let the pot simmer and then remove), and cautions against neglecting this important rule. He updates the names of dishes, as in fol. 8r, where he changes a dish in the *Kanz*, namely *fālūdhajiyya* to *māwardiyya*, explaining that the former was its older name (fol. 1v).

Ibn Mubārak Shāh maintains a personal tone, which is lacking in the *Kanz*. He must have been an amateur chef. To the recommended types of firewood, he adds dried stems of date clusters (*'arājīn al-balaḥ*), saying that he used to cook with them and enjoyed the pleasant smell of their smoke. In a recipe for beestings (*liba'*), he says the farmers who worked at an estate he once owned (*ḍay'a*) used to make it for him, but he never liked it until he taught them how to make it properly (fol. 24v). He chooses not to include any recipes on fermented condiments, because he does not like them, he explains (fol. 24r). On the preparations of table sauces and condiments, he says there are many ways of making them, but he protests that they are labor intensive and quite costly. He therefore gives the cheapest and the easiest recipes, and apologetically explains that he compiled this inventory of recipes for his own household slave girls to use, and that he had to accommodate it to his own limited budget (fol. 23v). He might have been frugal, but his household surely must have enjoyed good food.

It seems that Ibn Mubārak Shāh's original volume was tampered with between folio 30r, where the original *Kanz* ends, and folio 37v, where he chose to place the *Kanz* chapter on cold dishes, followed by the chapter on toothpicks, and a final chapter on aromatics (all abridged from the *Kanz*). In the space between these two folios, a series of recipes deals mostly with the familiar fare of main dishes. Some are not found elsewhere, but a good number of them are identical with those of *al-Wuṣla*. Given the uncharacteristically generic tone and the way these recipes disrupt the structure, it is highly likely that they were inserted by other hands, posthumously perhaps, to beef up an otherwise slim volume.

Part II: Medieval Egyptian Food Culture

5 *Diet and Formation of a Cuisine*

We remember the fish, which we did eat
in Egypt, freely. The cucumbers, the melons,
and the leeks; the onions, and the garlic.
(Numbers 11:5) The wandering Hebrews missing their familiar diet after the Exodus.

The ancient Egyptians left no culinary recipes, but food remains from their tombs and coffin murals that depict baking and other food-related activities testify to the sophisticated level of their cuisine, at least judging from the baking activities depicted. These depictions also reveal the abundance of their produce, such as Jew's mallow (*mulūkhiyya*), okra,[52] cucumber, onion, radishes, leeks, broad beans (*fūl*), peas, lentils, chickpeas, lupine (*turmus*), along with herbs and seeds like cumin and fenugreek; and fruits, like dates, grapes, figs, sycomore figs (*jummayz*), and pomegranates. Fish was the main source of meat; birds, especially ducks, pigeons kept in cotes, and quails captured as they rested in Egypt during their migration season. Red meat was obtained from oxen, deer, rams, goats, and rabbits. Cows were kept for their milk, from which dairy products with a long shelf life were made, such as salty cheese and *kishk*.[53]

When the Greek historian Herodotus visited Egypt in the fifth century BC, he marveled at its unparalleled wonders. He commented that the Egyptians were healthy because their seasons did not change. He saw them preserve fish and birds by salting them and drying them in the sun, and roasting or boiling the fresh ones. He also noticed the unusual direction of the flow of the Nile, which led him to the bizarre observation that Egyptians, like their Nile, do things the opposite way, such as women urinating standing up and men crouching down.[54] Aside from such nonsense, the Nile (indeed because of its northern flow), did affect the lives of the Egyptians from ancient times, and in a more profound way than even that noticed by Herodotus. It was their lifeblood.

Up until 1970, when the High Dam of Aswan was built, agricultural life in Egypt had been regulated by the annual flooding of the Nile; it began its rising cycle in the summer and reached its peak in the fall, flooding the vast areas along the river. When it receded, it left behind rich soil loaded with silt; this was used in cultivating the land and making good pottery. Their year was accordingly divided into three seasons: Inundation, Growth, and Harvest. There were years when the Nile did not live up to its promise or it overdid its bounties, resulting in periods of famine and suffering. Overall, this regular natural force, on which the peasants' year depended, regulated the lives of Egyptians from ancient times, resulting in enduring modes of daily activities.

---

52 Mehdawy and Hussain, *Pharaoh's Kitchen* 89, point out that the Pharaonic name for okra is *bano*.

53 It is a mixture of crushed wheat and yogurt, formed into lumps, dried in the sun, and stored. For the ancient Egyptian diet and culture, see Mehdawy and Hussein, *The Pharaoh's Kitchen*; Wilson, *Egyptian Food and Drink*; Manniche, *Ancient Egyptian Herbal*; and Riolo, *Egyptian Cuisine and Culture*.

54 Herodotus, *History* ii 35, 77.

FIGURE 3 *Ancient Egyptian bounty: Fragment from the funerary offering scene, c. 1350 BC.*

By the end of the Pharaonic rule around the turn of the first century CE, Egypt became a province of the Roman Empire and Byzantium. During this period, its indigenous population were largely Copts, believed to be descendants of the ancient dynastic times.[55] They were known for their conservative attitude toward their ways of life, which expectedly included food consumption, and thereby "paid little attention to Greek, Roman, or Hellenized Egyptian Elites and their lifestyles, their menu included."[56] At the time, Egypt was the indispensable granary of the empire, and its varieties of bread must have been quite familiar to Roman and Byzantine consumers. Alexandrian bread, for instance, was featured in the Roman cookbook *Apicius*, which was believed to have been compiled between the first and fourth centuries CE.[57] It is a luxurious bread, pithy, soft and, spongy, typical of breads baked in a *furn* 'brick oven,' which we often encounter later, in extant medieval Arabic cookbooks, including the *Kanz*.

In 641 CE, Egypt fell to the Arabs, who built the city of Fusṭāṭ to replace Alexandria as the new capital city. The first wave of settlers was mostly Arabs from southern Arabia. The indigenous Coptic population was still a majority, and the official language was Greek. Gradually, the number of Muslim Arab settlers increased and Arabic became the administrative language. Egypt was ruled by a succession of caliphates and dynasties. The first to start an independent state were the Tulunids (858–905); then the Ikhshidids (935–69); then the Fatimids (969–1171), who built Cairo next to Fusṭāṭ; then the Ayyubids (1171–1260); followed by the Mamluks (1260–1517), which was when our book, the *Kanz al-fawāʾid*, was written, sometime during the fourteenth century.

With the successions of caliphates and sultanates over a period of several centuries, Cairo became the 'mother of all nations' (*umm al-bilād*),[58] and replaced Baghdad, the 'navel of the earth' (*surrat al-arḍ*), as a flourishing metropolis. It became a cultural magnet and a haven for surrounding regions and peoples of multiple nationalities and ethnicities, including Turks, Kurds, Arabs of the southern Arabian Peninsula, Moroccans, Sudanese, Persians, and Iraqis (particularly after the attacks of the Mongols in western Asia), and many more.

Such a colorful multiplicity inevitably enriched the already bountiful local culinary repertoire of the region. This was, for instance, how we come to see

55 Parallel to this, the indigenous Nabateans of Iraq (Nabaṭ) were believed to be the descendants of the ancient Mesopotamians.

56 Lewicka, *Food and Foodways* 70. Lewicka's book is by far the most extensive study on medieval Cairene food and culture.

57 Grocock and Granger, *Apicius* 177.

58 Ibn al-Kindī, *Faḍāʾil Miṣr* 6.

FIGURE 4 *Sugar cane, one of the crops brought to Egypt with the spread of Islam. Muḥammad al-Qazwīnī,* ʿAjāʾib al-makhlūqāt, *F1954.78v, detail (Freer Gallery of Art and Arthur M. Sackler Gallery, Smithsonian Institution, Washington, DC: Purchase—Charles Lang Freer Endowment).*

traditional Moroccan recipes for *marwaziyya* and *kuskusū* in an Egyptian cookbook like the *Kanz*. To such ethno-regional diversities, we should also add the influence of Baghdadi cooking, which had matured and flourished during the rule of the Abbasids. Judging from the *Kanz al-fawāʾid* and the numerous allusions to foods and dishes in contemporary literature, the culinary traditions of Baghdad found their way to Egyptian kitchens.

Added to these, the spread of Islam brought about the introduction of new crops, such as eggplant, taro, rice, sugar cane, citrus fruits, and many more.[59] The fertile flooded lands along the Nile contributed to favorable conditions for growing these migrant crops. These were introduced to the already abundant crops growing there. Indeed, the unique agricultural situation in Egypt never failed to impress whoever visited Egypt during the medieval period or wrote about it. The Nile they said flowed from paradise. The land itself was no

59 For the spread of new crops in the Islamic world, see Watson, *Agricultural Innovation*.

FIGURE 5 *Sour orange* (nāranj)*, one of the crops brought to Egypt with the spread of Islam. Al-ʿUmarī,* Masālik al-abṣār, *fol. 212r, detail (BnF, Department of manuscripts, Arab 2771).*

less amazing with its four seasons: summer (Abīb, Masrā, and Tūt),[60] when the land was like a gleaming white pearl as a result of the rising and flooding of the Nile; the fall (Bāba, Hātūr, and Kayhak), when it looked like black musk, with the receding water and the black and fragrant soil. In winter (Ṭūba, Amshīr, and Barmahāt), it was emerald green with the growing crops; and in spring (Barmūda, Bishnis, and Buʾūna), the harvest season, it looked like golden amber.[61]

When the Persian scholar Nāṣir Khusrū visited Egypt during the Fatimid rule in the eleventh century,[62] he said the country produced large amounts of honey and sugar. He also observed that on a day in January, he saw red roses,

---

60 The text cited uses the names of the indigenous Coptic calendar, starting with Abīb (July). The Coptic New Year starts with Tūt (September), when the Nile reaches its highest point, in recognition of the role of the river in cultivating the land.

61 Ibn Iyās, *Badāʾiʿ al-zuhūr* i 38.

62 Nāṣir Khusrū (1003–77) was a well-known Persian poet, philosopher, scholar, and traveler who visited Fatimid Cairo during the reign of Caliph al-Mustanṣir Billāh (1029–94).

water lilies, narcissus, citron, oranges, lemons, apples, jasmine, quince, pomegranates, pears, melons, bananas, olives, fresh dates (*ruṭab*), grapes, sugar cane, eggplants, gourds, turnips, cabbages, green broad beans, common cucumbers (*khiyār*), snake cucumbers (*qiththā'*), onion, garlic, carrots, and beets (*banjar*). "Whoever wonders," he adds, "how can all these be found at the same time, some are spring products, some summer, and others winter, would not believe this, but I only commit to paper what I see with my own eyes."[63]

Trade with neighboring regions was quite active, especially with the Levant. Whatever was not economic to cultivate locally was imported via port cities like Alexandria, by means of ships along the Mediterranean shores. Products imported from the Levant included walnuts, pistachios, hazelnuts, apples, quince, and pears. Limited amounts of excellent olives grew in the Fayyūm district; otherwise, most olives were imported from the Levant. Egypt, on the other hand, exported its surplus of local products, such as salt-cured fish (*samak qadīd*), *ḥālūm* cheese (semi-hard white cheese, smooth in texture), *nayda* (a local variety of taffy), *zayt ḥārr* (oil of radish and turnip seeds), safflower, *bisillā* 'field peas,' lentils, and *sukkar mukarrar* 'refined sugar' to the Levant and other countries surrounding the Mediterranean. The importation of spices and other aromatics, moreover, had been carried out for centuries (1181–1484) by prosperous Egyptian merchants, called Kārimī. Their economic activities were mostly conducted via Yemen and Damascus. Yemen was their supply center. Merchandise was transported from India to Yemen and the Kārimī merchants then shipped the goods along the Nile to Fusṭāṭ and Alexandria, and then to other Mediterranean countries.[64]

6 *What was Cooking in Medieval Cairo?*

After Fusṭāṭ was built on the eastern bank of the Nile in 641, it gradually grew into a thriving city and an important commercial center that attracted migrants from all over the Islamic world. In the tenth century, the city of al-Qāhira 'Cairo' was built by the Fatimids north of Fusṭāṭ, initially for the ruling family and the elite. Fusṭāṭ was usually referred to as Miṣr. In the twelfth century, Fusṭāṭ suffered from famine and fire and continued to deteriorate over the next centuries. However, it persisted as an important industrial neighborhood adjoined to Cairo; today it is known as Miṣr al-Qadīma 'Old Egypt.'

When the Persian scholar Nāṣir Khusrū visited the city of Cairo in 1047, he was impressed by its spaciousness, and the cleanliness of its villas, which were well spaced from each other. The orchards between the palaces were watered

63 Khusrū, *Safarnāma* 118–9.

64 See Fischel, "Spice Trade"; see also Goitein, *Studies* 351–60.

from wells, by means of aqueducts. They also grew gardens on the roofs of their houses. In fact, Khusrū said, Cairenes could grow such gardens anywhere at any time of the year. Trees in large pots were easily purchased. These were mostly fruit-bearing trees, such as citron, pomegranate, apple, quince, roses, aromatic herbs, as well as all kinds of flowers. When the palaces overlooking the Nile needed water, they just filled buckets and lifted them with ropes. In the inner-city quarters, water was carried from the Nile by carriers (*saqqāʾīn*) on camels, or on their shoulders in narrow streets.[65]

The adjoining city of Fusṭāṭ, a mile south of Cairo, had a bustling population, businesses, sugar and paper factories, and busy wharfs. Living costs, in general, were said to be lower there than in Cairo. The housing quarters were distinguished by multistoried compound buildings. The street-level units were occupied by businesses, which were not connected to the living quarters. The upper levels were apartments and single rooms rented mostly by business owners, laborers, and artisans who preferred to stay close to the city center. These compounds were large enough to house up to 350 people, but were not equipped with proper kitchens.[66] Most people, therefore, were dependent on ready-cooked foods purchased from food markets.[67]

In normal conditions, Cairo was a thriving metropolis. Medieval histories left us lavish accounts of the luxurious lives led by the ruling classes and the elites. At the same time, we are told that even the very poor among the populace did not go hungry because bread was cheap and plenty.[68] Interestingly, the poor could receive nutritious and delicious food when they got sick and stayed at the *bīmāristān* 'hospital.' Meat, mainly poultry, fruits, and medications were generously offered free. There are stories that some poor people even faked illness just for the food.

There were also times when the public enjoyed the bounties of the royalty right in their palaces. During the times of the Tulunids, the kitchens of Amir Ibn Ṭūlūn (d. 884) prepared carry-out meals in pottery vessels each day, each containing a meat dish, and four breads, two of which would cover the dish, and the other two would be stuffed with *fālūdhaj* (a starch-based dessert). The palace doors would be opened and everyone was welcomed; the amir enjoyed watching them eat and carry away the palace food.[69]

---

65 Khusrū, *Safarnāma* 106.

66 Khusrū, *Safarnāma* 116–7. See Lewicka, *Food and Foodways* 88–95, for a discussion on the absence of kitchens in residential buildings in Cairo centers.

67 On this subject, see section 8 below.

68 Al-Maqrīzī, *Khiṭaṭ* ii 68.

69 Al-Maqrīzī, *Khiṭaṭ* i 872.

FIGURE 6 *Serving food at a grand feast, folio from* Divan *of Jāmī, 52.20.4, detail (MET NY—Purchase, Joseph Pulitzer Bequest, 1952).*

During the rule of Khumārawayh (d. 896), son of Ṭūlūn, it is said that the harem's cooks used to sell what was left of the food they cooked. It was not in perfect shape, it might have included a chicken missing a leg or with its breast meat split, a remaining chunk of a roasted lamb, *fālūdhaj* (a starch-based dessert) still in good condition, *lawzīnaj* (an almond confection), *qaṭāʾif* (syrupy pancakes), *Maʾmūniyya* (thick almond pudding), and the like, along with large breads. It was good food, cheap to buy, there was plenty of it, and it was always available. We are told that if someone had unexpected guests, he would immediately go the harem's gate and buy this food, the likes of which he could not have cooked, or afforded in the first place.[70]

We also read of Abū Bakr al-Mādrānī, an Egyptian tax clerk (*kātib kharāj*) during the rule of the Ikhshidids; he accumulated tremendous wealth. In medieval histories, his name was associated with a cookie called *ifṭin lahu*, with the explanation that al-Mādrānī used to entertain his guests and impress them with his wealth by offering them platters, all containing cookies stuffed with sugar except for one, which contained cookies stuffed with gold dinars. The host would reveal the secret code to the 'right' cookies by dropping a casual remark, 'mind the cookie' with a subtle gesture of his head,[71] and that was how the cookie got its name. Later, when professional confectioners started making

70 Al-Maqrīzī, *Khiṭaṭ* i 876.

71 Al-Maqrīzī, *Khiṭaṭ* i 917.

the cookie in the food markets, the name had already been corrupted to *ifṭilū*,[72] humbly filled with nuts, to be sure.

During the Fatimid caliphate, rulers shared meals with the populace during Ramadan, feast days, and special occasions, such as royal marriages and births. They also celebrated the Christian religious feasts with the Copts, such as the New Year festival of Nayrūz/Nawrūz, on the first day of Tūt 'September.' For the end of Ramadan feast, about a hundred palace cooks and confectioners made the traditional fare of *khushkanānaj*,[73] *basandūd* 'sandwich cookies,' *kaʿb al-ghazāl* (variety of taffy), *kaʿk* 'dry cookies,' and *bazmāward* 'pinwheel sandwiches,' to be distributed to everyone, high and low, in disposable containers (*awānī lā tustaʿād*).[74]

The formal Fatimid feasts, *simāṭ*s, were, in effect, displays of wealth, pomp, and power. To celebrate a religious festival, a magnificent *simāṭ* would be arranged for the caliph and his entourage; it was loaded with breads, grilled lambs, poultry, and more, until the food was the height of a tall man. The empty spaces in between were filled with small dishes of puddings, diced fried meat, all redolent with spicy aromas. Overall, about 500 types of dishes were arranged on this *simāṭ*. Timed with the arrival of the caliph to start the feast, were the entrance of two huge sugar palaces that had been made at the royal kitchens outside the palace, and were carried all the way along the streets that led to the palace for the public congregations to enjoy looking at. The sugar palaces would be placed at both ends of the *simāṭ*, on beautifully gilded gold paper, decked with sugar figurines arranged in rows. For their entertainment, the guests would watch a contest between two soldiers known for their fathomless appetites; they would devour a grilled lamb, ten sweetened chickens, and a 10-pound platter of halva, each. What was left of the food, which was still plenty, would then be taken out to a place, for the public to devour.[75]

Not all festivals were happy occasions. Whereas most of the Muslim populace in Egypt were Sunnis, the Fatimids were Shiis, who honored the martyrdom of al-Ḥusayn, grandson of the Prophet Muḥammad. On the day of ʿĀshūrāʾ (the tenth day of Muḥarram) much humbler *simāṭ*s were shared in a solemn manner, at humbler places. For this occasion, everyone was invited. The food consisted of bowls of cheese, plain yogurt, *salāʾiṭ* (large elongated

72 Ibn al-Ukhuwwa, *Maʿālim al-qurba*, fol. 75r.

73 Cookies stuffed with dates and nuts, like today's Levantine *maʿmūl* and Iraqi *kleicha*.

74 Al-Maqrīzī, *Khiṭaṭ* ii 201.

75 Al-Maqrīzī, *Khiṭaṭ* ii 114–5.

FIGURE 7 *Cooks preparing for a grand feast, folio from* Divan *of Jāmī, 52.20.4, detail (MET NY—Purchase, Joseph Pulitzer Bequest, 1952).*

breads baked in brick ovens called *furn*), and pickles.[76] All the bread would be made with barley, and was deliberately made to look dark. These would be followed with *ʿadas aswad* 'black lentils,' and then *ʿadas muṣaffā*;[77] bowls of bee honey would end the meal. This humbly shared meal was called *simāṭ al-ḥuzn* 'table of sorrow.'[78]

The fact that the Fatimids were Shiis also, sometimes, played a role in restricting the diet of the Egyptians. The Fatimid caliph al-Ḥākim bi-Amrillāh (d. 1021) was a Shii Ismāʿīlī whose rule was eccentric and oppressive. He prohibited the Egyptians from eating their beloved *mulūkhiyya* 'Jew's mallow' because it was favored by the Sunni Umayyad caliph Muʿāwiya (d. 680). He prevented them from eating *jirjīr* 'arugula,' because it was associated with the Prophet's wife ʿĀʾisha, who was favored by the Sunnis. He prohibited a popular dish cooked with meat and *qulqās* 'taro' called *al-Mutawakkiliyya* because it was named after the Abbasid caliph al-Mutawakkil (d. 861), who was a Sunni. He prevented people from imbibing *fuqqāʿ* 'foamy beer' because ʿAlī b. Abī Ṭālib, husband of the Prophet's daughter Fāṭima, and father of al-Ḥusayn, used to hate this beverage, because of its intoxicating properties.[79] He also prohibited fishermen from selling *dallīna*s (river mussels, *umm al-khulūl*). After al-Ḥākim's death, the Egyptians resumed eating their favorite foods, and *al-Mutawakkiliyya* acquired another name, *sitt al-shanaʿ*, or 'the best of the maligned dishes.'[80]

It is noteworthy that among the social strata of medieval Egypt, culinary distinctions were not principally perceived through the varieties of the dishes offered, as much as by the quality of these dishes and the amount of care and expertise involved in their preparation. Ibn Shāhīn al-Ẓāhirī (1468), for instance, enumerates 54 varieties of dishes that were usually cooked for the palace and other banquets. The *Kanz al-fawāʾid* includes recipes for most of these dishes, including even those that incorporated what were commonly considered the humble fare of the common people, such as *bāmiya* 'okra,' *mulūkhiyya* 'Jew's mallow,' *fūl* 'fava beans,' and *kishk*.[81] Dishes like *sanbūsak*, *harīsa*, *ṭabāhija* 'fried meat,' sweetened chicken, *bazmāward* 'pinwheel sandwiches,' *lawzīnaj*, *qaṭāʾif*,

---

76 Such foods are called *ḥawāḍir*. The term designates meatless foods, which are ready to eat whenever needed.

77 Porridge of strained lentil. See *Kanz* recipe 128.

78 Al-Maqrīzī, *Khiṭaṭ* ii 213–4.

79 Al-Maqrīzī, *Khiṭaṭ* iii 385. Note that not all *fuqqāʿ* was left long enough to ferment. Cf. *Kanz* recipes in chapter 12.

80 See *Kanz* recipes 88 and 89.

81 Dough of yogurt and cracked wheat, dried as clumps, and used to enhance broths.

fānīdh 'taffy,' *khushkanān* 'filled cookies,' *and basandūd* 'sandwich cookies' were prepared by all those who had kitchens; otherwise, they could be easily purchased from the myriad food markets. Cooking them well, however, involved greater expense and more knowledge of the culinary arts, and this was where the affluent excelled because they had the means.

Even among ordinary people, distinctions in the quality of home-cooked foods persisted. The Egyptian humorist Yūsuf al-Shirbīnī enlightens us on this in his mock commentary on Abū Shādūf's poem *Hazz al-quḥūf* (Jolting the yokels),[82] written mostly in the colloquial Egyptian dialect. Even though it was written in the first half of the seventeenth century, most of the dishes it describes applied to the previous centuries. Even a dish as basic as *mudammas* (simmered fava beans) could not escape the nuances of good cooking and the expenses it incurred. Cooked in the city (*ḥaḍar*), *mudammas* would look like gold, as soft as fully ripe dates, and appetizing to look at, because good fava beans were used, it was cooked in pure water, in a clean pot, and simmered on clean firewood, free of smoke. When served, it would be drizzled with ghee (*samn*) or good olive oil (*zayt ṭayyib*), offered with clean white wheat bread,[83] with leaf leeks, lemon or vinegar. *Mudammas* cooked in the countryside (*rīf*), on the other hand, would look discolored and smell of the dung fire it was left to simmer in. It would be served with corn or barley bread. The 'affluent' (*akābir*) among the peasants would splurge with a drizzle or two of oil of turnip seeds (*zayt ḥārr*).[84]

In medieval records, we often come across generalized statements regarding the foods of common Egyptians. They ate little meat, but consumed a lot of *dallīnas* 'river mussels' also known as *umm al-khulūl*, *ṣīr* 'anchovies,' *ṣaḥnāt* (a condiment of small crushed salt-cured fish), *ḥālūm* cheese, and bread. Their dessert was *nayda* (sugarless taffy made with germinated wheat), they snacked on *ḥimmaṣ* 'chickpeas,' and their wine was cheap *mizr*.[85] When the Nile flooded, they would catch and eat dormice. They considered them a delicacy and called them *sumānā al-ghayṭ* (field quails).[86]

---

82 As translated by Geert Jan van Gelder, *God's Banquet* 103.

83 There were different grades of wheat bread, the best was described as white wheat bread.

84 This oil was of inferior quality, used mainly for lighting. Al-Shirbīnī, *Hazz al-quḥūf* 202–4.

85 See glossary 1.

86 Al-Maqdisī, *Aḥsan al-taqāsīm* 75; and ʿAbd al-Laṭīf al-Baghdādī, *Riḥla* 122–3. In his account of his visit to Egypt, seventeenth-century Awliyā Chalabī described this variety of mice as funny-looking fat creatures that weighed approximately one pound. The natives ate their meat and sold their fur. They said their meat is easy to digest and a great aphrodisiac (Chalabī, *Riḥla* ii 35–6).

Prosperity in Egypt went hand in hand with the flood of the Nile, referred to as *wafāʾ al-Nīl*, and when it did not deliver, the consequences of famine and diseases were devastating. As always happens, the poor suffered the most when prices skyrocketed and food became scarce; and as always, some grew rich taking advantage of it. Such an incident took place when ʿAbd al-Laṭīf al-Baghdādī was in Cairo in the year 1199. His report on the ensuing human disaster is devastating, sometimes disturbing, and too graphic to believe. Based on his account, cannibalism spread; babies became the 'new meat'; in fact, no one was spared. Bakers used to buy houses just for their wood; and it was quite common for mothers to let their children loose in the crowd.[87]

7 *The Culture of Food and Cooking*

While medieval histories spared no ink describing the festive Fatimid foods and celebrations, or the details of the lavish expenses of the Mamluk sultans' kitchens, we know very little about who prepared all the magnificent sugar creations and the endless *simāṭ*s. The culinary 'shows' that characterized the age were, in effect, primarily shows of pomp and polish. Gone were the days of the Abbasids, when the caliphs and the elites were themselves patrons of the art of cooking; they opened their doors to talented cooks and poets from all walks of life; they themselves had cookbooks and gastronomic poems in their names; they even arranged for cooking contests, and much more. Abbasid records mention a huge number of books on cooking and dietetics. Except for a few, none of these survived.[88]

For medieval Egypt, the information we have at our disposal on the subject of food culture is not as rich. However, enough may be garnered to give us a picture, albeit one less colorful than that of the Abbasids. We know that at least one of the Ayyubid kings was interested in acquiring cookbooks. The title page of the augmented Egyptian copy of Ibn Sayyār al-Warrāq's Baghdadi cookbook states that it was owned by al-Malik al-Ṣāliḥ Najm al-Dīn Ayyūb (d. 1249).[89] The son of this king, al-Malik al-Saʿīd b. al-Malik al-Ṣāliḥ (d. 1284), who was known for his good taste in clothes and food, wrote a cookbook entitled *al-Maʾākil wa-alwānihā* (Foods and their varieties).[90] In addition, al-Maqrīzī mentions a cookbook entitled *al-Ṭaʿām wa-l-idām* (Dishes and

87 ʿAbd al-Laṭīf al-Baghdādī, *Riḥla* 133–42.

88 See, for instance, the introduction in al-Warrāq, English trans. *Annals*.

89 See al-Warrāq, English trans. *Annals* 7.

90 Al-Yūnīnī, *Dhayl mirʾāt al-zamān* 588.

appetizers) by the Fatimid historian al-Musabbiḥī (d. 1029), which contained 1,500 folios.[91] Neither cookbook survived.

Of the gourmet kings and sultans who practiced cooking as a hobby but had no literary aspirations, we know of al-Malik al-ʿĀdil (d. 1218), the youngest brother of Ṣalāḥ al-Dīn (Saladin), who was known for his gluttony. He loved all kinds of foods. He ate mostly at night, like a horse, and ended his meals with a large pound (*raṭl Shāmī*) of sugar halva (*khabīṣ al-sukkar*) as a digestive stomachic (*juwārish*). He lived a long life, and rarely got sick—except once when he overdid it with a load of melons. He loved to prepare his food with his own hands, even though each of his concubines had a kitchen in her abode.[92] The secret to his longevity was probably that he prepared his food himself.

The Mamluk sultan al-Ṣāliḥ Ṣāliḥ (d. 1354) was a handy man. He used to meet secretly with smiths, silk weavers, cooks, and others to learn their trades, and we are told that he was a fast learner. He once treated his mother Qutlūbak and a group of close friends to a lavish banquet. He wrapped an apron around his waist, cooked all the food, and then spread the table with the dishes himself. It is said that he spent a lot of money on this event.[93]

The Fatimid palace kitchens were like culinary schools, from which hundreds of slave girls 'graduated' with honors. At least, that is the impression we get from anecdotes and passing remarks on them. Al-Maqrīzī mentions these slave girls, trained as cooks, as an exclusively Egyptian commodity.[94] He says they were acclaimed as marvelous cooks. One of the Egyptian viziers had two slave girls; each of them perfected the cooking of 80 varieties of *taqālī*,[95] and this was aside from the rest of the dishes they knew.[96] When the ruler of Diyarbakir, Naṣr al-Dawla al-Kurdī (d. 1061) wanted his cooks to perfect the art of cooking, he dispatched them to Egypt so they could learn the tricks of the trade at the hands of the Fatimid cooks.[97] Indeed the fame of Fatimid cooks spread east and west. When the poet, *fāris*, and diplomat Usāma b. Munqidh (d. 1188) went to Antioch on a mission, he was invited to share a meal with a

91 Cited in Zayyāt, "*Fann al-ṭabkh*" 15. For extensive modern surveys in Arabic on the medieval Egyptian culinary culture, see ʿAbd al-ʿAzīz, *al-Maṭbakh al-sulṭānī*; and Maḥjūb and Durriyya, *al-Wuṣla ilā l-ḥabīb* i 298–412. See also Levanoni, Food and cooking 211–7.

92 Ibn Taghrī Birdī, *Nujūm* vi 150–1.

93 Al-Maqrīzī, *Sulūk* iv 206.

94 Described in Arabic as جوار طباخات اصل تعليمهن من قصور الخلفاء الفاطميين (al-Maqrīzī, *Khiṭaṭ* ii 68).

95 Sg., *taqliyya*. It is a moist fried dish of sliced meat with spices and herbs. For example, see *Kanz* recipe 101.

96 Ibn Iyās, *Badāʾiʿ al-zuhūr* i 574.

97 Cited in Zayyāt, "*Fann al-ṭabkh*" 14..

retired knight of the first crusade. He said the table was loaded with excellent food. When his host saw him hesitate, he reassured him that he himself would not eat the food of the Franks, and that his food was always prepared by his Egyptian cooks.[98] As for the female Ayyubid cooks, we only know of al-Ḥāfiẓiyya. A cookie immortalized in our cookbook *Kanz* (recipe 273) was named after her. She was the concubine of the Ayyubid king al-Malik al-ʿĀdil al-Kabīr (d. 1218).

Of the professional male cooks who succeeded in climbing the culinary ladder to become palace chefs, we have a somewhat detailed record of only one; al-Maqrīzī dedicates a separate entry to him.[99] His name was ʿAlī b. al-Ṭabbākh, which implies that he descended from a family of professional cooks. He served the Mamluk sultan al-Nāṣir b. Qalāwūn (d. 1341) for a long time, and accumulated tremendous wealth. His son Aḥmad worked with him. His ingenuity in making money was revealed by an anecdote that tells how he used to sell the accumulated heads and offal of the day's slaughtered animals outside the kitchens of the palace. After the death of the sultan, he lost his job and his wealth was confiscated.

In the events of the year 1463, Ibn Iyās tells how the butcher and cook al-Babbāwī rose from the humble status of a commoner (*ʿawām*) to become a vizier (*wazīr*) during the reign of the Circassian Mamluks. He was illiterate and did not handle his new position well. The educated at the time were furious that the position of vizier had reached this point, and they nicknamed him al-Zafūrī, from *zafar* (the unpleasant greasy odor of raw meat), because of his previous profession as a cook and butcher. Apparently, other Zafūrīs followed suit. His relative Qāsim Shaghīta also rose from being a baker and meat handler to a vizier during the rule of the Circassian mamluk sultan Qāytbay (d. 1496). Even though this one proved to be efficient, he still was a Zafūrī in the eyes of the educated.[100]

Besides its consumption, food was a subject worth writing about, and some among the cultured Egyptian class seem to have produced short compositions on food for their own entertainment and circulation. A good example is the small lighthearted volume entitled *Manhal al-laṭāyif fī al-kunāfa wa-l-qaṭāyif* (On *kunāfa* and *qaṭāyif*: A fountain of delight), in which Jalāl al-Dīn al-Suyūṭī (d. 1505) compiled whatever he knew had been composed on the popular

98 Usāma b. Munqidh, *Kitāb al-Iʿtibār* 48. See *Kanz* recipe 576, for another instance on the fame of the Fatimid palace slave-girl cooks.

99 Al-Maqrīzī, *Khiṭaṭ* iii 318–9.

100 Ibn Iyās, *Badāʾiʿ al-zuhūr* ii 415–6, iii 317.

pastries of *qaṭāʾif* (syrupy pancakes) and *kunāfa* (syrupy shredded pastry).[101] It included descriptive verses and witty riddles, which were amusing mental exercises enjoyed by all. Al-Suyūṭī was a renowned religious scholar (*ʿālim*) and historian with countless books in his name. As much as possible, he avoided the circles of the Mamluk elite. This was typical of many Arab/Muslim Egyptian men of letters at the time, and likely resulted from the inevitable cultural gap between the Mamluk Turks and the Egyptian civilians. Discussing the roots for this gap, Amalia Levanoni explains,

> The reign of the Mamluks was founded on continual recruitment of fresh human resources from the Eurasian steppes and therefore the Mamluk elite, despite long years of rule, was permanently composed of first-generation immigrants within a society with a deep-rooted Arab-Muslim culture.[102]

Generally, poets and other men of letters of mainstream Egyptian society did not expect to receive the favors and patronage they had in previous ages. Instead, they had to earn their living by working in the markets, and their names at the time were typically tagged by such epithets as al-Jazzār (butcher), al-Ḥammāmī (public-bath server), al-Khayyāṭ (tailor), al-ʿAṭṭār (dealer in perfumes, drugs, and spices), and so on. Abū l-Ḥusayn al-Jazzār (d. 1281) grew up in Fusṭāṭ and earned his living as a butcher, like the rest of his family. He is best known for his humorous poetry and prose work *Fawāʾid al-mawāʾid* (Guide to table manners), whose lessons are delivered sugared with humor, throughout.[103]

At the time, the popular literary genre was the *munāẓarāt* or *mufākharāt*, which were debates between objects loosely framed in a narrative form. Of the ones dealing with foods, we know of *Kitāb al-Ḥarb al-maʿshūq bayn laḥm al-ḍaʾn wa-ḥawāḍir al-sūq*,[104] which was written at some point in the fifteenth century by a certain Aḥmad b. Yaḥyā al-Ḥajjār, apparently, a Cairene. The allegory describes a heated battle between meat dishes, of the kind mostly cooked and enjoyed by the elite, and the meatless snack foods usually bought from marketplaces, such as different types of cheese, yogurt, pickles, vegetables, and the like. The battle ends with the defeat of the snack foods by King Mutton and his followers. According to the story, the triumphant dishes were devoured by

---

101 See glossary 2, s.v. *kunāfa*.

102 Levanoni, Food and cooking 221.

103 Al-Jazzār, *Fawāʾid al-mawāʾid*.

104 Translated by Joshua Finkel as "The delectable war between mutton and the refreshments of the market-place." See Finkel, King mutton.

the elite, whereas the meatless snacks, the losers, were dispatched to the common people.[105] The other debate takes place between rice and pomegranate seeds, *Mufākharat al-ruzz wa-l-ḥabb rummān*.[106] The symbolic political lessons of these works, if any were meant, might escape us today, but they are certainly goldmines to modern readers, linguistically and culturally. Our cookbook *Kanz al-fawāʾid* contains recipes for most of the dishes that were personified in these two works.

Once the men of letters turned to the public, the language of literary expression became increasingly colloquial, which was the language of the people. The first to use it in a more liberal manner was ʿAlī b. Sūdūn (d. 1463) in his *Nuzhat al-nufūs wa-muḍḥik al-ʿabūs*,[107] a satirical mix of prose and poetry. It offers a wealth of information on life in Mamluk Egypt, including many allusions to food and dishes. It would seem that Ibn Sūdūn was obsessed with food; and his inclination was, perhaps, a reflection of the poor economic conditions common Egyptians suffered at the time. His continuous craving for sugar and sweets was a humorous façade for his own affliction—he was a *ḥashīsh* addict. In his work, we learn a good deal about the most popular desserts consumed at the time. He describes what he once saw while under the influence: He swam in a tumultuous sea with a base of *ṣābūniyya* (starch *ḥalwā*) and sides of *Maʾmūniyya* (almond *ḥalwā*), the seawater was pure syrup, and its fishes were peeled bananas. At its shores, he saw nets of *zalābiya* (latticed fritters), so he took one and caught loads of fishes with it. He tried to pull in the net, but could not, so he took off his clothes and went down to them, and started eating them, alternating between bananas and *zalābiya*. His sweet dream continued with more sugary details.

Alarmed by the poor conditions his people lived in, he tells the story of a neighbor who used to sleep most of the time. When asked why he slept so much, the neighbor told him that once he dreamt that he was hungry, and while roaming the streets, he heard someone summoning people to a feast. He ran with the crowd, and what a sight he saw: a house built of all kinds of sweets and pastries, with fountains of syrup, and everyone was happy and laughing. Then a table was spread with whatever one craved, so, he said, he snatched a

---

105 For discussions of the allegory, see Gelder, *God's Banquet* 96–9; and Lewicka, *Food and Foodways* 57–64.

106 Anonymously written, sometime in the fifteenth century. See English translation, Geries, *Mufākhara*, 17–46, for a detailed discussion of the text.

107 'A diversion to the soul, which makes the gloomy laugh.' See a discussion of the work in Gelder, *God's Banquet* 90–6.

grilled chicken and pulled its thigh, and as he was about to put it in his mouth, he woke up. So he decided to sleep, hoping one day to resume his dream.[108]

In his *Khiṭaṭ*, al-Maqrīzī also comments on the spread of *ḥashīsha*; he calls it *ḥashīshat al-fuqarā'* (marijuana of the poor). He was told that it first began with the Sufis, who used it to repress their feelings of hunger. The poor also benefitted from it in this respect. They also said that its hot and dry properties dried semen and repressed sexual desires,[109] and this translated to a more virtuous life, fewer children, and less expense.

8 *Shopping and Eating Out*

Medieval Cairo bustled with a tremendous number of marketplaces (*aswāq*) that were so crowded shoppers had to develop ways to maneuver themselves through the never-ending flows of people. The markets normally remained active until the small hours of the night. Al-Maqrīzī reports that every day the Cairenes would throw out one thousand dinars' worth of disposable items in the trash and into the dumpster mounds outside the city. They threw out earthenware bowls (*shiqāf ḥumr*) used for selling yogurt, cheese, and serving food to the poor diners at cooks' shops. They threw out the thread and small mats usually placed underneath the cheese in the pottery bowls, and the paper and thread the grocers used to wrap the paper with when they sold cooking ingredients (*ḥawā'ij al-ṭa'ām*) like grains, pulses, and spices. These items were used to help shoppers carry their purchases safely home; as soon as they removed them from their parcels, they threw out the wrappers and disposable containers.

Besides walking, donkeys were the most common means of transportation to and from the markets. Vividly decorated donkeys were quite inexpensive, available to hire, and conveniently accessible to each neighborhood (*ḥāra*). They were used by all Cairene civilians, such as traders, peasants, artisans, and *'ulamā'* (religious scholars). Horses were only used by the military.[110]

For their daily quick shopping, people did not need to go to the large markets, as each neighborhood had its own shops, complete with a public bath and a bakery. Al-Maqrīzī mentions one affluent neighborhood, Ḥārat Burjuwān, which had its own sprawling marketplace. Its inhabitants boasted two public baths and two bakeries. It had butchers, who sold all kinds of meat; many stores selling cured olives, and sellers of cheese, bread, and yogurt. They had their own stew shops, grillers, sellers of cold dishes (*bawārid*), spice shops,

108 Ibn Sūdūn, *Nuzhat al-nufūs* 178–9.

109 Al-Maqrīzī, *Khiṭaṭ* ii 658–66.

110 Nāṣir Khusrū, *Safarnāma* 121.

and vegetable stalls. They even had a stall that sold nothing but herbs served fresh at the table (*ḥawāʾij al-māʾida*), such as parsley, rue, leeks, fresh fennel (*shamār*), and mint. Another shop sold sesame and cottonseed lighting oils. In that market, residents could shop for raw mutton as well as already cooked meat up until an hour before the break of dawn.[111]

A street like Bayn al-Qaṣrayn (between the two palaces) was a thoroughfare that people frequented for fun. It was a pleasure for the five senses. Both sides of this street were lined with all kinds of snack sellers, who sold foods such as succulent fried chicken, ducks, fried young pigeons, and sparrows to munch on, and other stalls that sold melon wedges and snack foods like cheese, and many more.[112]

The largest of the general marketplaces was al-Qaṣaba, which in its golden days contained 12,000 stalls, brimming with countless varieties of foods and drinks, and shoppers. It was a pleasure to be there, al-Maqrīzī says. Of the other markets, he describes the confectioners' (*sūq al-ḥalāwiyyīn*) as the most fun of all the markets. He describes a platter loaded with small dishes of yogurt, cheese, cucumbers, and bananas, all made with sugar. The confectioners made *ʿalālīq* especially for the religious festivals. These were sugar figurines shaped like horses, lions, and cats with threads attached to them to hang them from; some weighed a quarter of a pound, and others up to ten pounds. Children in Egypt were given these. It was also a pleasure, al-Maqrīzī adds, to see the mounds of *khushkanānaj* 'filled cookies,' *basandūd* 'sandwich cookies,' and colorful lollipops (*mushāsh*) prepared for the religious festival (*ʿīd*) at the end of Ramadan. These were made everywhere, in markets of Cairo and in rural areas alike.[113]

One of al-Maqrīzī's most nostalgic memories was of a beautiful Egyptian market that was destroyed by a huge fire in the spring of 1354; it was a stretch of about twenty stores, on both sides of the street, that sold *fuqqāʿ* 'foamy beer.' He says it had been a most beautiful sight. The stores were all built of colorful marble; they had fountains, which sprayed water on the marble, where the sealed beer jars (*kīzān al-fuqqāʿ*) were arranged in lines on both sides of the street for passersby to look at.[114]

Shopping for foods and ingredients in medieval Egyptian urban markets, especially in Cairo, required visits to several places, as the markets were highly specialized and there was a clear division of labor. The market-inspection

111 Al-Maqrīzī, *Khiṭaṭ* ii 583.

112 Al-Maqrīzī, *Khiṭaṭ* ii 427–8.

113 Al-Maqrīzī, *Khiṭaṭ* ii 592–3.

114 Al-Maqrīzī, *Khiṭaṭ* ii 435–6.

FIGURE 8
Butchers, folio from Divan *of Jāmī, 52.20.4, detail* (*MET NY—Purchase, Joseph Pulitzer Bequest, 1952*).

manuals (*kutub al-ḥisba*) that circulated then bear witness to this economic phenomenon. The most relevant were those of Ibn al-Ukhuwwa (d. 1329), who wrote a manual entitled *Maʿālim al-qurba fī aḥkām al-ḥisba*; Ibn Bassām (fourteenth century), who wrote the *Nihāyat al-rutba fī ṭalab al-ḥisba*;[115] and Ibn al-Ḥājj's *Madkhal*.[116]

The butchers (*jazzār*) who slaughtered the animals were often different from those who sold the meat (*qaṣṣāb*); the *farrānī* was the person who ran a commercial *furn* 'brick oven,' where he baked bread and grilled other foods for his neighborhood customers; while the *khabbāz* was specialized in selling bread, and often availed himself of the services of the *farrānī*. The *naqāniqī* specialized in making sausages for the market, whereas the *kubūdī* sold grilled livers. The *bawāridī* provided market customers with cold meatless dishes, which people consumed as snack foods and appetizers such as boiled vegetables, condiments with yogurt, omelets (*ʿujaj*), and the like. With regard to omelets, cooks were required to test the eggs before adding them to the pan by putting them in a large basin of water first, to test their freshness. The *rawwās* sold offal, like heads, trotters, and tripe, already cooked or raw. Vegetables were sold by the *khuḍarī*, and fruit by a *fākihānī*.

115 Ibn Bassām's volume (including its title) is based on the manual written by the Ayyubid al-Shayzarī (d. 1193). Ibn Bassām's, however, has additional material, which indeed reflects the new conditions of the marketplaces in his time.

116 He was an Egyptian scholar originally from Morocco, he died in Egypt in 1336.

The *ṭabbākh* was the one who dealt with dishes cooked in pots, such as stews, whereas the *harāʾisī* specialized only in porridges. The *sharāʾiḥī*, by contrast, served a special function for his customers: when they brought him the ingredients, his task was to cook them. There were also fryers (*qallāʾīn*), such as those of fish and *zalābiya* (lattice fritters).[117] The number of confectioners (*ḥalwāniyyīn*) in the markets was phenomenal; Ibn al-Ukhuwwa gives a list of more than sixty types of desserts, and these, he says, were only the most popular ones.[118] The potters, *fākhrāniyyīn* and *ghaḍḍārīn*, provided the markets with the utensils needed to cook and serve food. Besides the artisans, there were sellers of groceries (*bayyāʿīn*), and *saqqāʾīn*, who sold water in jars to households or, in cups, to passersby in the markets.

Poultry had its own market, called *sūq al-dajjājīn*, where chicken, along with geese, sparrows, and other birds were sold.[119] Most of the chicken available in Egypt was supplied by what were called *maʿmal al-farrūj* (a chicks' factory). These could be found throughout the country. This sort of factory housed many incubators (*ḥāḍina*) built to simulate the hens. ʿAbd al-Laṭīf al-Baghdādī, an eyewitness, described the place in detail.[120] In his account, he states that in every city there were several places where chicks were produced by artificial incubation. It was a lucrative industry. Each factory occupied a large courtyard containing ten to twenty incubators (*bayt al-tarqīd*), each of which was large enough to hold 1,000 eggs. The incubator, built to imitate the hen (complete with wings), was designed to provide the warmth like that of the hen for full twenty-two days. The workers responsible for taking care of the eggs turned them periodically, as hens do, and tested the warmth of the eggs by placing them on their eyelids, the way the hens did. The high season for this industry was during the months of Amshīr, Barmahāt, and Barmūda (February, March, and April). It seems to have been an occupation uniquely suited for the land and climate of Egypt. We are told that an Egyptian entrepreneur went to the Levant to start a similar business there. He built it in the summer and acquired the chicks, but when the fall came, they did not hatch. He lost his business and

117 Fish fryers were specifically instructed to reduce the smell of fish by keeping the place clean. Fish sellers in the fish market (*sūq al-samak*) were required to clean their places; and whatever they did not sell, they would preserve in salt and sell as salt-cured fish.

118 Ibn al-Ukhuwwa, *Maʿālim al-qurba*, fol. 75r–v.

119 Al-Maqrīzī, *Khiṭaṭ* ii 854–5.

120 ʿAbd al-Laṭīf al-Baghdādī, *Riḥla* 80–3.

went back to Egypt.[121] Egyptian dishes of *farārīj* 'young chicken' obtained from these incubators were deemed the greatest of all Egyptian foods.[122]

Pigeons, especially the young plump ones (*firākh al-ḥamām*), also known as *zaghālīl*, were purchased from the bird markets. The domesticated house pigeons were not usually used for food, rather the ones obtained from the pigeon cotes (*abrāj al-ḥamām*), commonly built by the peasants in rural areas, were used for eating. They were built like towers with holes, to which were attached pottery vessels (*qawādīs*). The wild pigeons (*ḥamām barrī*) would remain in the cotes long enough to hatch their eggs there.[123] Pigeons grown there were sold to the urban markets.

Another intriguing aspect of the food culture that developed in Egypt at that time involved the emergence of a system of standardization and inspection. Given the large number of food businesses and services offered in the city markets, the task of the market inspectors (sg. *muḥtasib*) must have been a colossal one, indeed. The manuals written at the time were meant to teach the inspectors the regulations for doing things the proper way, and techniques to detect cheaters and adulterators who left no stone (or I should say no ingredient), unturned in their pursuit of finding ways to deceive their customers. The *ḥisba* manuals abound with such examples. For instance, saffron threads were adulterated by increasing the bulk with chicken breasts that had been boiled and shredded into threads, and then dyed with saffron-water, dried and mixed with the real saffron.[124]

Personal hygiene was always emphasized in the *muḥtasib* manuals, especially for the bread makers. The kneaders were required to shave the hair on their hands, and wear clothes with tight fitting sleeves. They were supposed to cover their mouths and noses with face mufflers, lest they should sneeze or cough, and deposit their saliva and mucus in the dough. They were also required to wear headbands lest their perspiration fall into the dough. During the daytime, they were supposed to have people next to them with hand fans to shoo the flies away.

To make sure the roaster of whole sheep would not deliberately sell the meat before it was fully done (as this would make it heavier in the scales), the *muḥtasib* himself had to weigh the carcass before it was lowered into the *tannūr*, and write down the weight. When it came out of the oven, it must have lost at least a third of its pre-roast weight; otherwise, it would be returned to

---

121 Al-ʿUmarī, *Masālik* iii 286.

122 Ibn Iyās, *Badāʾiʿ al-zuhūr* 44.

123 Al-Shirbīnī, *Hazz al-quḥūf* 255.

124 Ibn al-Ukhuwwa, *Maʿālim al-qurba* fol. 81v.

FIGURE 9
Kneader covering mouth and nose with a face muffler. Folio from Divan *of Jāmī, 52.20.4, detail* (MET NY—*Purchase, Joseph Pulitzer Bequest, 1952*).

the oven.[125] The *farrānī* (brick oven operator) who baked foods (besides bread) brought by neighborhood households, had to have two separate ovens so that the bread would not smell like the roasting fish casseroles.

The daily meals of the city folks were not always prepared in the private kitchens of people's homes. Indeed, this was, for the most part, only possible for well-off families who could afford a large house, probably in the suburbs away from the congested city center, with a well-equipped kitchen and running water. Even in such households, the preference was often to send certain dishes out to the neighborhood *furn*, as is evident in our cookbook, the *Kanz al-fawāʾid*. Fish dishes, for instance, were sent out to the *furn* to keep the house free of the smell of fish, as in *Kanz* recipes 236 and 241. Such households would also prefer to make their bread with their own hands, using their own ingredients, and then dispatch them to be baked at the *furn*. The *ḥisba* manuals call this bread *khubz baytūtī* 'house bread,' to differentiate it from *khubz al-sūq* 'marketplace bread.'

Most city dwellers, however, depended, either partially or entirely, on the services offered by the food markets. For those who had small kitchens, the preference, perhaps, was to put the dish together in a *ṭājin* and send it to the *furn*. Otherwise, the *sharāʾiḥī* had a shop in the food market. He cooked in pots on direct heat. His customers would bring him the ingredients, and he would cook the dish for them. The fear of causing fires in chronically congested neighborhoods in the city was a major factor, as was the high cost of fuel.

125 Ibn al-Ukhuwwa, *Maʿālim al-qurba* fol. 62v.

The vast number of those who lived in the city center, however, did not have kitchens of their own, as they lived in rented units in multistoried housing complexes. Their only option was to avail themselves of the services offered by the numerous cookshops, stalls, and the roaming vendors who catered mainly to low income people. Their choices in the food markets were never boring, and overall, the food was tasty.[126]

Part III

9 *Medieval Egyptian Cooking as Reflected in the* Kanz al-fawāʾid

Preparing food in one's home required a kitchen and a good supply of clean water. As we have seen in the previous section, this was not always possible in a congested city center like Cairo. Among the public, such amenities were a privilege that only the well-to-do households could afford for two reasons: the high cost and the fear of fire.[127] It was in such households that a cookbook like the *Kanz al-fawāʾid* might have been put to good use. Or, perhaps it would be used in a household like that of Ibn Mubārak Shāh, a prominent Cairene scholar who lived during the first half of the fifteenth century. He was a frugal gourmet who claimed he wrote 'his' cookbook for his own slave girls to use.

The general terminology the recipes utilized suggests household conditions in which there were many hands to prepare the dishes, what with the various chores of pounding, sifting, mashing, stirring, squeezing, tending to the fire, and so on. For some food preparations, places in the house, other than the kitchen, were used; for example, small onions were wilted for twenty days in the highest roof of the house before they could be pickled (recipe 580); other ingredients required a breeze catcher, which is a shaft built in a wall for ventilation and to cool the indoor temperature. Ingredients were placed in front of its opening to keep them ventilated.[128] The last chapter in the *Kanz* that deals with storing fresh produce for out of season consumption was useful for those who had access to an estate or a farm in the countryside, perhaps. By contrast, preservation by pickling was a common annual activity in any given household, and the large number of recipes given in chapter 18 attests to its popularity.

For daily cooking activities, a variety of vessels and equipment were used. Depending on the dishes to be cooked, different sizes of pots and pans were

---

126 For the issue of eating out in medieval Cairo, see Lewicka, *Food and Foodways*, 88–100.

127 See Levanoni, Food and cooking 204.

128 *Kanz* recipe in DK, appendix 75, p. 409.

needed. The large ones were generally made of tinned copper or soapstone; these were used to make the main dishes of stews (*alwān kibār*), some of which were served as *tharīd* 'bread sop' in large wide bowls. The large pots were also used to make the different porridges of wheat, rice, and pulses. We learn from the Persian scholar Nāṣir Khusrū, who visited Egypt in the eleventh century, during the Fatimid rule, that some Egyptian households with limited means used to rent pots. He said he saw large copper pots from Damascus in the Egyptian markets; these were so polished that they looked as if they were made of gold. People told him that a woman owned 5,000 of these pots, which people would rent for a monthly charge of one *dirham*.[129] To these we may add the regular frying pan (*miqlā*) and the versatile *ṭājin*, which was a wide pan with low sides, made of pottery, soapstone, or tinned copper. It served as a frying pan as well as a casserole pan, and was used for baking dishes in the *furn* 'brick oven.'

A good cook needed several knives, each of which had its own function: a cleaver for splitting the bones without splintering them; a strong knife for disjointing the meat; a thin, very sharp knife for slicing the meat; and a separate knife and board for cutting onion and garlic. In addition, a wooden knife was required to carefully extract the juice vesicles of citron pulp without breaking them (*Kanz* recipe 360). Mortars and pestles were indispensable in medieval kitchens, what with all the grinding and crushing needed for fine cooking. Two types were required: the *hāwan*, which was made of metal, mostly brass, for dry ingredients; and the *jurn*, made of stone, for grinding meat and moist ingredients. Also, it was necessary to have several sieves and strainers, and different sizes of bowls, the most commonly used was the *zibdiyya*, and many more.[130]

No mention is made in the *Kanz* of a cooking stove (*mustawqad*).[131] The recipes only give instructions to set the pot on the fire (*yūḍaʿ* or *yunṣab*), or suspend the pan (*yuʿallaq*) on the fire. Coal was the preferred fuel to use, but generally, dry, non-sappy wood was also considered good because it did not create a lot of smoke. Portable braziers (*kawānīn*, sg. *kānūn*) must have been used for grilling purposes. A somewhat elaborate one was used specifically for smoking foods. As we gather from recipe 568, which deals with smoking olives,

129 Nāṣir Khusrū, *Safarnāma* 119.

130 See glossary 9.1, for kitchen equipment.

131 *Mustawqad* 'stove,' as described in al-Warrāq's tenth-century cookbook, "should be built as a rectangular trapezoid for easier access and better control of the fire burning in it. It should have outlets to drive out smoke and let in fresh air. A good stove should measure half a man's height" (English trans. *Annals* 87).

FIGURE 10
Grinding food in a mortar, folio from Divan *of Jāmī, 52.20.4, detail (MET NY—Purchase, Joseph Pulitzer Bequest, 1952).*

FIGURE 11 *Cooking on a portable stove* (mustawqad), *detail from Arabic translation of* De Materia Medica *of Dioscorides, thirteenth century, 57.51.21 (MET NY—Bequest of Cora Timken Burnett, 1956).*

it looked like a box with a perforated top, and a door that was kept closed during smoking.

For baking purposes, a *tannūr* or *furn* was built outside the house, location permitting. The *tannūr* was an immobile open-topped, bell-shaped clay oven. Besides baking flat breads in it, by sticking them to its heated inner sides, it was also used for roasting meat, or lowering a pot of chickpeas and water to simmer slowly in the remaining heat, as in *Kanz* recipe 377. The *furn* was another type of oven used in the *Kanz* recipes. The home built *furn* was a small brick dome oven, with a frontal opening and a flat floor, fueled from a separate compartment underneath it. Alternatively, fuel was burnt in the oven floor itself, and when heated, the ashes were removed and baking started. It was used for baking bread, trays of cookies (recipes 273 and 300), and other simpler tasks. The neighborhood *furn* was another place to bake home-prepared bread and trays of cookies, and casserole dishes of fish and the like (see chapter 9).[132]

Most of the recipes in the *Kanz* do not strike us as being overly demanding in terms of cost; sometimes they were adjusted to accommodate lesser privileged households. Recipe 413 for *fuqqāʿ* 'foamy beer' is described as easy to make and quite cheap, and in recipe 338, a cheaper alternative to fine white sugar is suggested, namely sugar cane molasses (*quṭāra*). In recipes that require expensive musk or civet, the instruction is to add as much as one can afford or desire (على قدر همتك).

In other instances, instructions are adjusted not to lower costs, but to satisfy the familiar palate of an ethnic group. In recipe 488 for a table sauce called *ṣalṣ*, the instruction is to add garlic if making it for a Turk; and not to add it if it is for a local person (*baladī*). In another sauce recipe (490), the suggestion is to sweeten it with sugar for the common people (*ʿawām*), and to use garlic if making it for Turks.[133] Such instructions might not have been useful for a household cook, but they certainly would have been to a hired cook, for instance, or a self-employed *sharāʾiḥī*, whose job was to cook dishes for customers

132 Writing about daily lives of the Egyptian peasants, the seventeenth-century al-Shirbīnī, *Hazz al-quḥūf* 194, mentions that the household *furn* is used for baking the daily bread and simmering pots of beans, as well as baking modest fish and pigeon *ṭājin*s. In Lane's account of nineteenth-century Egyptian customs and manners, a detailed description is given of a peasant's household in Lower Egypt; in it, the oven is said to "resemble … a wide bench or seat, and is about breast-high: it is constructed of brick and mud; the roof arched within, and flat on the top" (Lane, *Manners and Customs* 21). See also glossary 9.1, s.v. *furn*, *tannūr*.

133 Recipes 304 and 307 also give separate recipes for the Turks and the indigenes or locals, described as *baladī*.

who brought him the ingredients. Indeed, a book like the *Kanz al-fawāʾid* would have helped such cooks to enrich their repertoires and gain them more customers. In fact, they were required by the *muḥtasib* 'market inspector' to master cooking all varieties of dishes before they could open their businesses.[134] The possibility of such a slice of society reading cookbooks was quite feasible. As mentioned earlier, many literary men also had to work as butchers, bath servers, tailors and the like to support their families. Addressing an employed server, recipe 729 reads, "If you want to write words in green on apples, sour oranges (*nāranj*), or citron (*utrujj*), which will look beautiful, served in fruit platters, and for which you will be in your master's good graces, mix…."

The recommended initial stage of cooking red meat was called *taʿrīq*, literally 'sweating.' The meat, along with some rendered sheep-tail fat (*alya*), was sautéed until all the moisture evaporated. This was deemed an important step to rid the meat of undesirable greasy odors (*zafar*). The meat was then used as required. Another essential rule in cooking meat was to skim the froth using a perforated ladle. Spices and herbs were used in all the dishes,[135] each of which required its own set of seasonings. It is particularly notable that mastic gum is used in all the meat dishes in the *Kanz* recipes. Using mastic with savory dishes and particularly with meat was, indeed, uniquely Egyptian, and still is. One clue to this culinary practice can be found in Ibn al-Ḥājj's observation about Egyptian meat; he said it had a strong gamey smell, unlike meat in Iraq, the Maghrib, and the Hijaz. He even recommended that one's hands should be thoroughly washed after eating it.[136] Another reason could be the power of mastic to dispel putridity (*ʿafan*) for which Egypt was known due to the nature of its air and climate.[137]

We also notice that *murrī*, a liquid fermented sauce, which was ubiquitous in medieval Baghdadi cuisine, was only used in a limited way in Egyptian kitchens, even though we do find recipes for making it, as in chapter 6. Instead, what is ubiquitous in *Kanz* recipes is lemon juice, the sour juice of unripe grapes, or sour pomegranate seeds (*ḥabb rummān*). The reason for this may have stemmed, originally, from the quality of the water of the Nile that was used. Based on al-Maqrīzī's report, it was deemed too sweet to maintain good health, and to drive away its harms, Egyptians got into the custom of consuming

134 Ibn al-Ukhuwwa, *Maʿālim al-qurba* fol. 73r.

135 To enhance their flavor, spice seeds of coriander, cumin, caraway, and purslane, were often used toasted (*muḥammaṣ*), as in recipes 12, 66, 130, 151, 199, 237.

136 Ibn al-Ḥājj, *Madkhal* i 126.

137 See Dols, *Medieval Islamic Medicine*; Ibn Riḍwān's Arabic text 30.

vinegar and the juices of sour fruits, such as sour orange (*nāranj*) and lemon.[138] Or, it may have been related to the nature of Egypt itself, as expounded by the Egyptian physician Ibn Riḍwān (d. 1061), who described Egypt's air as putrid, humid, and hot, and recommended that Egyptians should consume foods and drinks with cold properties.[139]

The final stage of cooking a stew involved covering the pot, stopping the fuel of the fire, and letting the pot simmer for about an hour in the remaining heat. During this time, the aromas of the spices would have enough time to permeate the dish, and the oils and fats would separate and surface. By contrast, porridges had to be stirred all the time, on high heat, to prevent the grains from sticking to the bottom of the pot and burning (thus creating a stench).

For a dish like *kuskusū* 'couscous,' which was likely incorporated into the mainstream Egyptian repertoire with the arrival of the Moroccans, when the Fatimids ruled Egypt, a special pot was needed. This pot has a perforated bottom, and must be tightly fitted into the top of another pot in which the meat and vegetables simmer (recipe 123). Sometimes, the joining points of pots were sealed with dough to ensure tightness. A dish called *umm nārayn* (lit., 'mother of two fires'), required an unusual method of cooking: a sweet bread pudding was cooked between two sources of heat. Burning coals were placed on the lid of the pot cooking on top of the stove; this resulted in a browned top and bottom of the pudding (recipe 111).

The most interesting dish in the *Kanz*, which stands out for its novelty, is described in recipe 149 for stewed sparrows (*ʿaṣāfīr maṭbūkha*). We are told that this was a favorite among the Andalusian and Moroccan kings and viziers, as it was an aphrodisiac. They had it as a mezza dish during their drinking sessions, especially in autumn and winter. It is a long recipe with many details related to making the pot and the cooking process:

> The pot is to be made of thin glass, which is used for making bottles and glasses. However, it is not how thin or thick it is that makes it good, as much as the way it is made. It looks like a pot, no difference here, but the glassmaker (*zajjāj*) should apply the pontil (*būlīn*) to its bottom while it is still malleable and push it up to two thirds of its height, without letting it open at the top.

---

138 Al-Maqrīzī, *Khiṭaṭ* i 188; Ibn Iyās, *Badāʾiʿ al-zuhūr* 46.

139 Dols, *Medieval Islamic Medicine*; Ibn Riḍwān's Arabic text 27.

This pot is filled with cleaned sparrows (with heads attached), chickpeas, and coarsely chopped fresh vegetables, such as fresh fennel, leeks, green onion, and spices. It is then placed on a slow burning portable stove called *nāfikh nafsihi*,[140] fueled with clean coal. When the sparrows are cooked, the recipe continues,

> People at this point can start eating from this dish, as we mentioned earlier, while watching the cooking sparrows with heads attached moving up and down with all the white and black chickpeas in between and the greenness of the fennel heads and the herbs and vegetables, which is even more fantastic and delightful than eating it.

Medieval Egyptian cuisine was also distinguished by its sweet chicken dishes, so sweet that some are named after desserts, like thick starch-based puddings, such as *dajāja ḥulwiyya* and *dajāja fālūdhajiyya* (recipes 46 and 47). When the famous physician of Baghdad, ʿAbd al-Laṭīf al-Baghdādī, visited Egypt around the turn of the thirteenth century, he included them in his account of the local Egyptian foods with which he was not familiar.[141] In these dishes neither onion nor garlic are used; only coriander, cassia, and black pepper.

Delicious fish dishes are abundant in the *Kanz* (chapter 9). There are recipes for fresh (*ṭarī*) fish, salt-cured (*māliḥ*) small fish called *ṣīr*, and condiments of small crushed fishes (*ṣaḥna*); these were all popular and affordable. During the season of the flooding of the Nile, even children could catch fish for their families quite easily. Fish dishes, however, needed to be seasoned with sour ingredients and spiced to facilitate their digestion. Fish was fried, but first it was coated with flour to prevent the oil from splattering. However, the instruction in most baked fish dishes was to send them to the neighborhood commercial oven (*furn*). This was probably done because the commercial ovens were more efficient in controlling heat, and more importantly, to avoid the smell of baking fish in one's house.

In addition to the 'large dishes,' 'small dishes' were also served, either with other foods or to be enjoyed as small dishes and snacks to while away hunger. *Taqliyya*, for instance, was sliced meat fried with herbs and spices, cooked in a wide pot to facilitate the stirring of the ingredients. It was a very popular dish, and could be cooked in many ways. Omelets, by contrast, needed a frying pan with high sides and a long handle. Alternatively, they were boiled in a glass bottle. Once finished, the bottle was gently broken, resulting in a bottle-shaped omelet (*ʿujjat qanānī*). Such an omelet was certainly fun to look

---

140 The stove, which blows its fire by itself. See glossary 9.1, for details.

141 ʿAbd al-Laṭīf al-Baghdādī, *Riḥla* 119.

at and was usually used to garnish other dishes. Cold vegetable dishes were also welcomed as supplementary foods called *bawārid*. Chapter 19 contains many recipes for boiled vegetables, both seasoned and spiced. Added to these are chickpea dishes, especially *ḥimmaṣ kassā*, for which the *Kanz* contains the largest number of recipes. This was an elaborate preparation of boiled and mashed chickpeas, scrumptiously seasoned; it was a precursor of the much simpler modern version of *ḥummuṣ bi-ṭaḥīna*, commonly known in the West as hummus.

In addition, an exciting array of small dishes was also offered to herald the meal, excite the appetite, and aid digestion; all of these were served with bread. They ranged from the fermented condiments of *kāmakh*, yogurt condiments of *jājaq* and *akhlāṭ*, seasoned cheese of *ḥālūm* (Egyptian semi-hard white cheese) and *qanbarīs* 'cream cheese,' capers, pickles, cured olives, and the like (see chapters 17 and 18).

We also encounter, only in the *Kanz*, a delightful culinary tradition related to snacks. The *sukurdān* involves filling a large beautiful tray with varieties of delicious small dishes, and serving them as snacks to nibble on during social gatherings, especially those involving drinking alcoholic beverages. In fact, drinking sessions gave rise to the *sukurdān* ritual, even its name. The word is said to be a combination of the Arabic *sukr* 'imbibing alcoholic drinks,' and the Persian *dān* 'vessel.'[142] In the *Kanz*, the *sukurdān* is filled with apricot compote, pickles of carrot and quince, yogurt condiment of *jājaq*, and lemon preserved in salt.[143]

The *Kanz* does not provide recipes for plain bread, the kind usually served with the above dishes and condiments and generally distributed in stacks in between the dishes for diners to use as scoops. Instead, it offers general recommendations for good bread: it must be made with good fine white flour, kneaded thoroughly, and baked in a quiet oven so that it is evenly cooked, inside and out (chapter 2). In the course of the recipes, we learn about a bread called *kumāj*, which is round white bread that is thick, spongy and pithy, and baked in a commercial *furn* 'brick oven,' and the familiar thin sheets of *ruqāq* bread.[144]

---

142 Al-Khafājī, *Shifāʾ al-ghalīl* 182.

143 Al-Ḥajjār, *Kitāb al-Ḥarb al-maʿshūq* 102, offers another example of what such trays may be filled with, for instance, he mentions many varieties of pickles, cured olives and capers, lemon preserved in salt, varieties of salted fish dishes, such as Alexandrian *ṣaḥna*, salt-cured sparrows and fishes of batoids (*rāi*), anchovies (*ṣīr*), tilapia (*balṭī*), and Nile carp (*labīs*).

144 Ibn Riḍwān, the Egyptian physician, did not think much of Egyptian bread made with wheat grown in Egypt. Due to the humid and hot nature of the Egyptian region, he says

Interestingly, we see in the *Kanz* how a dish inherited from Abbasid times adjusted to the changing times and constrictions of space in the Egyptian households. This dish is *jūdhāba*, which was originally made by suspending a whole skewered lamb, or a smaller chunk of meat, in a *tannūr*. While roasting, all its fat and juices would drip into a casserole of a sweet bread pudding positioned underneath it. The dish was served by slicing the meat into thin shreds and offering it with the bread casserole. The *Kanz* (recipe 132) describes how to prepare the sweet bread casserole; as for the lamb part, the cook had the option of preparing it in the kitchen, and skipping the lamb. Apparently, the dish gradually became known as a sweet bread casserole called *Asyūṭiyya*, named after Asyūṭ in Upper Egypt (recipes 269 and 274). Recipe 44 offers more variety; in this version, a disjointed chicken is boiled and fried, then placed on rice cooked with milk, without sugar, but with a lot of chicken fat, then covered and left to simmer for an hour. The dish obviously evolved into a simpler fare.

Desserts usually followed the meal, and the *Kanz* offers no fewer than 80 recipes (chapter 10) for desserts. These range from the usual assortments of thick puddings of *ḥalāwa*, syrupy pastries of *kunāfa* and *qaṭā'if*, Zaynab's fingers, to *mukhannaqa* (lit., 'the throttled') made of thin strips of *kunāfa* cooked in syrup to resemble silk threads of throttled silk worm cocoons (recipe 297). We also find the lusciously sweet cheeks of the chanteuses (*khudūd al-aghānī*, recipe 270), fledgling locusts (*dhāt al-katifayn*, recipe 267), virgins' breasts (recipe 300), and colored lollipops (*mushāsh*) molded into figurines, and much more.

During the meal, only water was offered. As soon as meals were over, chilled sweet drinks and other digestive drinks, such as *aqsimā* and *sūbiya*, were served. The recommendation was to drink *fuqqā'* 'foamy beer' before the meal, as it was said to cause bloating. The drinks given in *Kanz* recipes are non-alcoholic, because they are not allowed to ferment (chapter 12). Such drinks were imbibed even during the month of Ramadan.

Related to food consumption, we find in the *Kanz* many preparations for washing the hands and perfuming and purging the ambience, including incense (*bakhūr*), potpourri (*lakhlakha*), distilled waters (*taṣʿīdāt*), and many more (chapters 20–22). Such preparations required many ingredients which were usually purchased from the perfume and spice dealers (*ʿaṭṭārīn*). The process of assembling these into the above-mentioned aromatic preparations did not require special culinary skills, but they did require good recipes so one knew the ingredients and their amounts; there are more than enough of these

---

it is not chewy in texture, and gets quite stale and crumbly after a day. See Dols, *Medieval Islamic Medicine*; Ibn Riḍwān, Arabic text 7.

recipes in the *Kanz*. There are 31 recipes for distilling waters in the *Kanz*, the assumption being that households were adequately equipped with the necessary distilling apparatuses.

People also supplied themselves with home-made foods when they traveled, and in our book, we do indeed have several recipes for travelers' provisions. These include fried fish (237); candy brittle (278); mustard condiment, carried as dried balls, and reconstituted with vinegar and sugar (483); date confection of *hays* (recipe 343);[145] granola (287, 304);[146] and sugar and lemon (425) prepared like flavored sugar, diluted with water and imbibed as needed, something like today's Kool-Aid.

10 *Eating in Good Health*

Although, as we might expect, the recipes in the *Kanz* describe familiar dishes of stews, porridges, desserts, and the like, which are consumed daily to feed the body and please the palate, we often encounter others that are tagged with health-related recommendations and benefits. Gourd pudding (314), for instance, is beneficial for moistening dry humoral properties (*tarṭīb*) and breaking up dense humors (*taḥlīl*). Jujube pudding (288) is heralded for a long list of benefits:

> It is recommended for weight gain. Its properties are moderately hot and high in moisture. It nourishes the thin and the weak, provides the bodily system with the needed moisture. It induces euphoria, lightens the skin color, softens the complexion, and gives it luster. It strengthens the hot stomach, and helps soften the bowels, and deflates winds. It is diuretic, and beneficial to kidneys and the bladder. It helps women gain weight quickly, which is something they care a lot about. It also helps reduce the density of their humors. However, it is harmful for the phlegmatic and the old.

By including such recipes, the *Kanz*, as a cookbook, undoubtedly presented its readers with a shared core of knowledge. This shared knowledge came from the Galenic medico-culinary tradition of the four humors, which dominated the thinking of the medieval Arabo-Islamic world. The theory held that all objects in nature were composed of four elements (*arkān*): fire, air, water, and

145 Recipe 321 is another preparation for *hays*, called *jimāliyya*, which could have derived its name from *jimāl* (camels), related to the custom of carrying food as a provision for travelers in camel caravans.

146 The recipes call it by the Turkish name, *qāwūt*, the Arabic name for which is *sawīq*.

earth; each of which possessed its own innate quality, (*mizāj*), of which there were four basic types: hot, cold, dry, and moist.[147] Humans had *akhlāṭ* (bodily humoral fluids): blood, phlegm, yellow bile, and black bile.

The theory postulated that all ingredients, with their various properties and innate powers, could be useful for general purposes, such as those described in the quotation above. They were also believed to have healing properties; they could correct imbalances in humors and bring them (and thus the patient) back to a healthy balanced state. Certainly, in cases of serious illnesses, curing patients was better left to physicians, but in times of malaise, simple home cures were used. In addition to being comforting and nourishing, light foods were manipulated, with the properties of their ingredients, to counterbalance symptoms; for example, the feverish were fed gourd dishes because of their cold properties. Such dishes were collectively called *muzawwarāt* 'fake' because they were made to simulate real dishes with meat. Recipes for such dishes were found in books on dietetics and medicine, written and approved by physicians. Some of the *muzawwarāt* recipes in *Kanz* chapter 8 belonged to the famous Baghdadi physician Ibn Buṭlān (d. 1066), and others were from Ibn Māsawayh (d. 857).

The home preparations provided in the *Kanz* were mostly aids to digestion, and ranged from digestive stomachics (*juwārishnāt*), electuaries (*maʿājīn*), and drinks (*ashriba*) offered before and after the meal, to preparations for treating nausea (*adwiyat al-qaraf*). A digestive stomachic (recipe 373), for instance, was recommended for its power to sweeten the breath, scent the stomach, invigorate digestion, induce euphoria, and disperse vapors in the head. Besides, even daily dipping sauces and condiments (*ṣibāgh* and *ṣulūṣāt*), which were offered in small bowls with the dishes, were believed to aid digestion and ward off harms.

Furthermore, the *Kanz* cites the repeated claims that specific dishes promote and invigorate coitus (*bāh*). This should also be expected, since one of the tenets of the Galenic theory was that the well-being of this aspect of the body was deemed essential for the welfare of the entire body. At any rate, whether motivated by health concerns or otherwise, aphrodisiac recipes were in great demand, and the *Kanz* offered plenty of them. The recipe for fish sauce (recipe 478), for instance, was promoted as mightily effective in this respect; it uses no less than the salt of scincus (*saqanqūr*), the equivalent of today's Viagra.

---

147 For a more detailed account of the Galenic theory of the humors, see glossary 11, s.v. *mizāj*; al-Warrāq, English trans. *Annals* 55–64; Dols, *Medieval Islamic Medicine* 3–14; Waines, "Dietetics in Medieval Islam" 228–40; and Waines, "'Luxury foods' in Medieval Islamic Societies" 571–80.

FIGURE 12 *Cough medicine being prepared, folio from Arabic Translation of* De Materia Medica *of Dioscorides, thirteenth century, 13.152.6* (*MET NY—Rogers Fund, 1913*).

Recipe 679 gives instructions for making a restorative powder called *dharūr al-māʾ ward*, which was sprinkled on one's food as needed. It was enthusiastically touted as having "amazing properties, boosting libido in the elderly, invigorating intercourse, and bringing joy."

Most of the ingredients and dishes thought of as aphrodisiacs possessed hot and moist properties. Chickpeas were at the top of the list. Omelet dishes and sparrows were similarly potent. The entirety of chapter 7 is dedicated to the former, and the last ten recipes of chapter 5 are all about sparrows. The last sparrow recipe, by far the longest in the *Kanz*, was said to be "one of the most exclusive dishes, which kings and dignitaries eat to boost libido."

An essential regimen for the maintenance of one's well-being was personal hygiene, and the *Kanz* does not neglect to include the required recipes and recommendations for good toothpicks (*khilāl*), and cleansing aromatic hand-washing preparations of *ushnān* and soap, attractively colored and shaped (chapter 20). Added to these are numerous aromatic preparations ranging from perfumed oils, purifying incense, to deodorants, pills to sweeten the breath, distilled waters, and perfumed powders. Perfumes were valued not merely for their pleasant scents, but also for their therapeutic and cleansing properties; they purged the air, cleared the head, and improved one's mood.

In recipe 671, an aromatic potpourri was to be put in a long-necked bottle, set on a very quiet fire, and placed in the way of the blowing breeze. The recipe says, "A wonderfully aromatic scent will emit from it." In recipe 672, aromatic incense was to be used by those sitting in corridors or toilets, "it is very good," the recipe assures. One can even have some fun with the aromatics. The instruction in recipe 666 calls for one to prepare, at home, a piece of cotton saturated with musk and rosewater; it continues,

> When you go to the bath with whomever you wish, once you get there, put this piece of cotton in the way of the water pouring into the tub. Put a piece of wood crosswise to keep the cotton from falling. The entire water [in the tub] will smell as if it were pure rosewater, and whoever takes water from this tub for his bath will not doubt that it is rosewater.

Aroma therapy, indeed!

FIGURE 13
Long-necked fayyāsha *bottle, x.21.210* (MET NY—*Museum accession*).

Infinite Benefits of Variety at the Table, Containing Twenty-Three Chapters on Cooking Foods, by Various Knowing Experts[1]

كنز الفوائد في تنويع الموائد

يشتمل على ثلاثة وعشرون بابا في علم كيفية الطباخة

لبعض الحكماء العارفين

---

1 *Kanz* (كنز) in the main title designates 'a treasure trove,' or indeed any accumulation of good things. The subtitle is added in C only. The ungrammatical Arabic ثلاثة وعشرون is copied here as it originally occurs in the manuscript. The title in Gotha is written as:

كتاب كنز الفوايد وتنويع الموايد لمؤلفه عفى الله عنه والمسلمين آمين

Book of the Treasure Trove of Benefits and Variety at the Table, by its author, may he and all Muslims be forgiven by God. Amen.

In DK, it is كتاب الفوائد في تنويع الموائد (Book of Benefits of Variety at the Table).

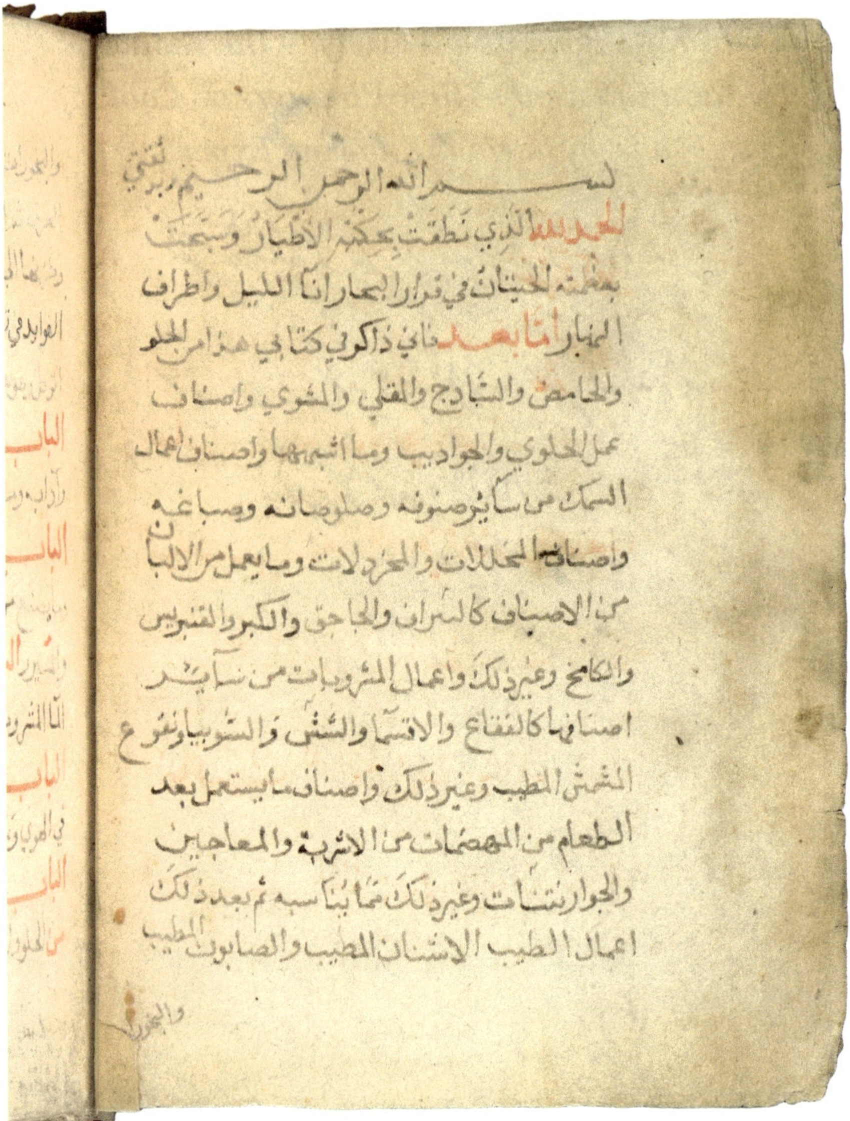
بسم الله الرحمن الرحيم وبه ثقتي
الحمد لله الذي نطقت بحكمته الأطيار وسبحت
بعظمته الحيتان في قرار البحار آناء الليل وأطراف
النهار أما بعد فاني ذاكر في كتابي هذا من الحلو
والحامض والبارد والمقلي والمشوي واصناف
عمل الحلوي والجواذيب وما اشبهها واصناف اعمال
السمك من سائر صنوفه وصلوصاته وصباغه
واصناف المخللات والمجردلات وما يعمل من الالبان
من الاصناف كالشيراز والجاجق والكبر والقنبريس
والكامخ وغير ذلك واعمال المشروبات من سائر
اصنافها كالفقاع والاقسما والشش والسوبيا ونوع
المشمش المطيب وغير ذلك واصناف ما يستعمل بعد
الطعام من المهضمات من الاشربة والمعاجين
والجوارشنات وغير ذلك مما يناسبه ثم بعد ذلك
اعمال الطيب الاشنان المطيب والصابون المطيب
والبخور

FIGURE 14 *Fol. 1v of* Kanz MS *(Reproduced by the kind permission of the Syndics of Cambridge University Library).*

بسم الله الرحمن الرحيم

الحمد لله الذي نطقت بحكمته الأطيار وسبّحت بعظمته الحيتان
في قرار البحار آناء الليل وأطراف النهار

In the name of God, the Compassionate, the Merciful. All praise is due to Him, whose divine mystery the birds enunciate, and whose greatness the fish in the depths of the sea glorify by day and night.

Now to our subject.[1] In my book here presented I describe how to make dishes commonly prepared these days,[2] including the sweet, the sour, and the plain ones (*sādhaj*);[3] the fried dishes (*maqlī*), and the roasted ones (*mashwī*); and [how to] make numerous types of sweets (*ḥalwā*), *jawādhīb*,[4] and the like. I also include a wide range of fish dishes, along with the table sauces (*ṣulūṣāt*) and the dipping sauces (*ṣibāgh*) which go with them.

Added to these are all varieties of pickles and mustard sauces; dairy foods, such as clotted cream (*bīrāf*), drained yogurt condiments (*jājaq*), capers (*kabar*), soft yogurt cheese (*qanbarīs*), fermented condiments (*kāmakh*), and similar ones; and dishes made with chicken eggs, such as omelets (*ʿujaj*), scrambled eggs (*mubaʿtharāt*), and the like.[5]

Then follow all kinds of drinks like foamy beers (*fuqqāʿ*), and other grain-based digestive beers and drinks like *aqsimā, shush*, and *sūbiyā*; along with the seasoned apricot compotes (*naqūʿ mishmish muṭayyab*). Then follow preparations of different types of digestives (*muhaḍḍimāt*) taken after the meals, such as tonic drinks (*ashriba*), electuaries (*maʿājīn*), digestive stomachics (*juwārishnāt*), and more.

---

1 The Arabic expression *amma baʿd* is a transitional phrase conventionally used to separate the incipit (the opening lines concerned with God's praises and glorification) from the main topic.

2 Addition in DK, n. 5; and Gotha, fol. 1v.

3 Descriptive of stews, which are neither sour nor sweet.

4 A dish of meat roasted in a *tannūr* (open-topped, bell-shaped clay oven), while suspended over a casserole of sweet bread pudding.

5 Addition in DK, n. 9; and Gotha, fol. 1v.

 | DOI 10.1163/9789004349919_003

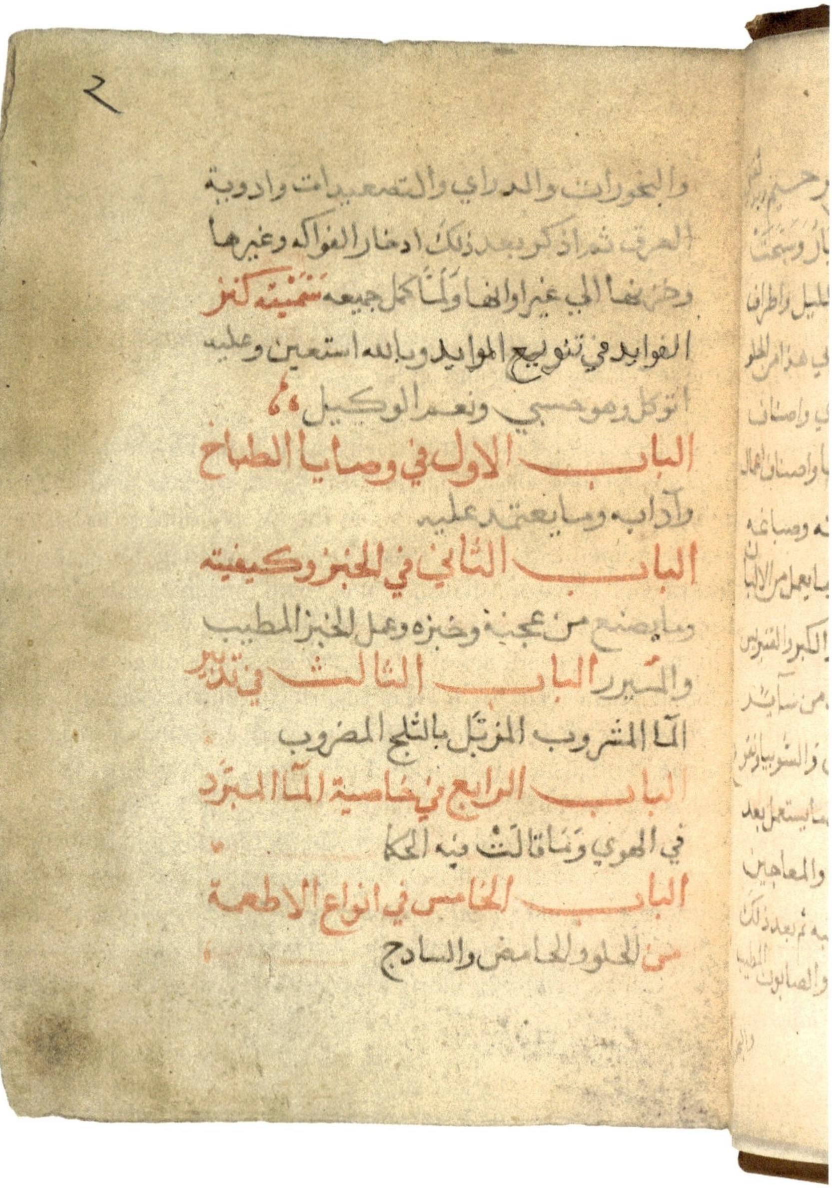
والبخورات والدراي والتصعيدات والادوية
العرق ثم اذكر بعد ذلك ادخار الفواكه وغيرها
وطبخها الى غير اوانها ولما كمل جميعه سميته كنز
الفوايد في تنويع الموايد وبالله استعين وعليه
اتوكل وهو حسبي ونعم الوكيل
الباب الاول في وصايا الطباخ
وآدابه ومايعتمد عليه
الباب الثاني في الخبز وكيفيته
ومايصنع من عجينه وخبزه وعمل الخبز المطيب
والمشير الباب الثالث في تدبير
الما المشروب المزمل بالثلج المضروب
الباب الرابع في خاصية الما المبرد
في الهوي وما قالت فيه الحكما
الباب الخامس في انواع الاطعمة
من الحلو والحامض والساذج

FIGURE 15 *Fol. 2r of* Kanz MS *(Reproduced by the kind permission of the Syndics of Cambridge University Library).*

Recipes for aromatic preparations follow, which include scented handwashing compounds (*ushnān muṭayyab*) and scented soap (*ṣābūn muṭayyab*), (**2r**) incense (*bakhūrāt*), perfumed powders (*dharāʾir*), distilled waters (*taṣʿīdāt*), and deodorants (*adwiyat al-ʿaraq*).

I then describe how to keep fruits and other produce fresh longer, and how to store them and use them when not in season. Once I finished writing the book, I gave it the name *Kanz al-fawāʾid fī tanwīʿ al-mawāʾid*, and may God assist me, for in Him I put my trust; sufficient unto me is He, the best to trust and rely on.

Chapter 1: Recommendations for cooks, and cooking guidelines and instructions.
Chapter 2: On bread, how it is kneaded and baked; and making cookies, enhanced (*khubz muṭayyab*) and seasoned with spice seeds (*khubz mubazzar*).
Chapter 3: Measures taken when drinking water, both *muzammal* (cooled in *muzammala*),[6] and chilled with crushed ice (*thalj maḍrūb*).
Chapter 4: Qualities of air-cooled water, and what the physicians said about it.
Chapter 5: All kinds of dishes: sweet (*ḥulw*), sour (*ḥāmiḍ*), and plain (*sādhaj*). (**2v**)
Chapter 6: Making *murrī* (liquid fermented sauce), and preserving the juice of sour unripe grapes (*māʾ al- ḥiṣrim*) and lemon juice (*māʾ al-laymūn*).
Chapter 7: Omelets (*ʿujaj*) and scrambled eggs (*mubaʿtharāt*) made with chicken eggs.
Chapter 8: Vegetarian dishes (*muzawwarāt al-buqūl*) for the nourishment of the sick.
Chapter 9: Making all kinds of fish dishes.
Chapter 10: Making all types of sweets (*ḥalwā*).[7]
Chapter 11: Digestive stomachics (*juwārishnāt*), electuaries (*maʿājīn*), and tonic drinks (*ashriba*) to be taken before and after the meal.
Chapter 12: Making *fuqqāʿ* (foamy beer), *aqsimā* (digestive drinks), *shush* (Yemeni grain-based beer), and other drinks.
Chapter 13: Making compote (*naqūʿ*) of sweet apricot (*mishmish lawzī*).[8] (**3r**)

---

6 *Muzammala* is a water-cooling green-enameled vessel that is insulated by wrapping it in sackcloth. I amended the edited word *murammal* (مرمل) to *muzammal* (مزمل) based on Gotha, where it is correctly copied (fol. 2r).

7 Gotha ends with this chapter, but adds a concluding recipe for making *samn* (ghee) from milk (fol. 94r); this is not found in any of the recipe sources available to us.

8 A variety of sweet apricots with sweet kernels, which taste like almonds.

Chapter 14: Making preparations which relieve nausea (*adwiyat al-qaraf*).

Chapter 15: Making mustard [sauce], mild (*laṭīf*), and hot and pungent (*ḥār ḥirrīf*).

Chapter 16: Making various types of table sauces (*ṣulūṣāt*).

Chapter 17: Foods made with dairy: *kawāmikh* (fermented condiments), *jājaq* (drained yogurt condiment), condiments with capers (*kabar*) and thyme (*zaʿtar*), *bīrāf* (clotted cream), and *qanbarīs* (soft yogurt cheese).

Chapter 18: Making all kinds of pickled turnip (*lift*), preserving olives, pickling fruits and other produce; preserving lemon (*laymūn*) and Damascus citron (*kabbād*) in salt;[9] and other similar varieties.

Chapter 19: Making cold dishes (*bawārid*) with vegetables and the like, and making *ḥimmaṣ kassā* (mashed chickpeas) and other varieties.[10] (**3v**)

Chapter 20: On toothpicks (*khilāl*); and aromatic compounds (*ṭīb*) which perfume and remove food odors [from mouth and hands], such as scented handwashing compounds (*ushnān muṭayyab*), scented soap (*ṣābūn muṭayyab*); and oils infused with scented smoke (*adhān mubakhkhara*) to remove greasy odors (*zafar*); and other preparations.

Chapter 21: Aroma diffusing incense (*bakhūrāt muṭayyaba*), which fortifies the spirit and heart; making deodorants (*adwiyat al-ʿaraq*); and pills (*ḥubūb*), which sweeten the breath, whet the appetite, strengthen the stomach, and invigorate coitus (*bāh*).

Chapter 22: Making top quality perfumed powder compounds (*dharāʾir*) and distilled waters (*miyāh muṣaʿʿda*), such as water of rose (*ward*), musk (*misk*), saffron (*zaʿfarān*), aloeswood (*ʿūd*), sandalwood (*ṣandal*), cloves (*qaranful*), camphor (*kāfūr*), spikenard (*sunbul*), and other waters extracted from citron (*utrujj*), myrtle (*ās*), blossoms of sour orange (*zahr al-nāranj*), and basil (*rayḥān*).[11]

Chapter 23: Storing fruits, such as peaches (*khawkh*), apricots (*mishmish*), (**4r**) grapes (*ʿinab*), quince (*safarjal*), cherry plums (*qarāṣiyā*), mulberries (*tūt*), apples (*tuffāḥ*), and the like, so that they may be used when not in season.

---

9 (Kharna sour orange hybrid, *Citrus aurantium* var. *khatta*). Al-Anṭākī, *Tadhkira* 50, identifies *kabbād* as a variety of *astabūn*. It is the fruit of a *nāranj* tree (sour orange, *Citrus aurantium*), which has been grafted with branches of the *utrujj* tree (true citron, *Citrus medica*). See glossary 7.

10 The predecessor of today's *ḥummuṣ bi-ṭaḥīna*.

11 DK, n. 48 adds the herb *nammām*, which is wild thyme.

Also, treating *ruṭab* and *busr* (fresh dates) to serve them out of season;[12] displaying fresh roses (*ward*) when not in season; and storing common cucumbers (*khiyār*), snake cucumbers (*qiththāʾ*),[13] *ʿajjūr* (variety of unripe melon),[14] eggplant (*bādhinjān*), and lemon (*laymūn*), to be used beyond their season.

12 *Busr* are ripe sweet dates, which are still firm and crunchy. *Ruṭab* are dates in the following stage of ripeness, when they start to soften and moisten.

13 *Cucumis melo* var. *flexuosus.*

14 *Cucumis melo* var. *chate*, chate of Egypt. See glossary 12.

CHAPTER 1

فى وصايا يلزم الطبّاخ معرفتها

Indispensable Instructions For Cooks[1]

The cook should be an agreeable person, who is well versed in the proper rules of cooking, and proficient in practicing it. He needs to keep his fingernails trimmed at all times. However, he should clip them neither too short and cause injuries, nor let them grow long enough to trap dirt underneath them.

Of the pots, the cook's best choice are those made of soapstone (*birām*),[2] and next are the earthenware ones (*fakhkhār*), and only when required, pots of tinned copper.[3] The worst to use are copper pots with worn-off tin coatings.

The cook needs to pick dry firewood (*ḥaṭab yābis*), which does not produce a great deal of smoke due to its wetness, such as wood of the olive tree and dry oak (*sindiyān*). Wood of oleander (*diflā*) and trees with milky sap (*ashjār yatūʿiyya/tuyūʿiyya*) and the like must be avoided.[4] Firewood from the fig tree and any wood high in moisture also must be avoided because it produces a lot of smoke.[5] The cook should be able to figure out the proper amount of fuel to use.

---

1 Versions of this chapter on cooking instructions are also found in two other medieval cookbooks, namely Baghdādī and *Waṣf.* The *Kanz*, however, is by far the longest. Baghdādī BL and Waṣf include almost one-fourth of it, and Baghdādī is even shorter than these two.

Gotha manuscript, which was not used by the editors, is identical with the edited text except for some copyist's stylistic changes and different readings—or misreadings—of some of the words. Besides, Gotha denotes changes in subject matter by writing the first word in a different color, which I follow using bold type. *Zahr*, which is an abridged version of *Kanz*, includes this introductory part in its entirety with the exception of some stylistic variations and minor omissions and additions. Here I amended the edited text with the help of all these versions.

2 Sg. *burma*.

3 *Dusūt nuḥās muʾannaka* were primarily used for making the thickened puddings (*ḥalāwāt*) because they could stand the rigorous stirring and beating involved in making them.

4 Fumes from the burning wood of trees with milky sap and oleander trees were considered harmful, even poisonous. See, for instance, Bīrūnī, *Ṣaydana* 381–2.

5 In these statements dealing with types of firewood, I use Baghdādī 11, and Baghdādī BL, fol. 5v, to amend the edited text. In the abridged version of *Kanz, Zahr al-ḥadīqa*, Ibn Mubārak Shāh adds that when the cook prepares food for his master he needs to use sweet-smelling firewood. He adds that he used to cook with the dried stems of date clusters (*ʿarājīn al-balaḥ*), and he enjoyed the pleasant smell of their smoke (*Zahr*, fol. 1 v).

 | DOI 10.1163/9789004349919_004

FIGURE 16 *Collecting firewood, fol. 44r from* Manṭiq al-ṭayr, *63.210.44, detail* (*MET NY—Fletcher Fund, 1963*).

Rock salt (*milḥ Andarānī*) is recommended; however, if this is not available, then any clean pure white salt, (**4v**) which is free of dirt and small stones, will do. The best salt is that which has been dissolved [in water] and then allowed to crystallize.[6] Use fresh seasoning spices (*abāzīr*). Coriander seeds (*kusfara*), cumin (*kammūn*), and caraway (*karāwiya*) should be dry and look greenish.[7] Choose the thick aromatic rolled bark of cassia (*dār Ṣīnī*), which has a sharp taste. Of mastic gum (*maṣṭakā'*), large and bright white grains should be chosen over the small ones. In addition, it should be free of any dust or dirt. Newly dried black peppercorns (*fulful*) rather than old ones should be used, and they ought to be large. Ginger (*zanjabīl*) should be free of any insect damage (*ghayr musawwas*). The cook must pick over the spices quite thoroughly and grind them only as needed; otherwise, they will lose their power.

Kitchen utensils and pots are to be cleaned with pure clay (*ṭīn ḥurr*) followed by potash (*ushnān*) and rose petals, both dried and ground.[8] Before ladling food into the bowls (*zabādī*), they need to be infused with the aromatic smoke of mastic gum and aloeswood (*yubakhkhar*). After the pots are washed, they must be wiped with crumbled leaves of *nāranj* (sour orange) and citron (*utrujj*).

6 The dissolved salt is strained to ensure the elimination of all impurities.

7 I amended the text slightly here and in the following sentences based on Baghdādī BL, fols. 5v–6r.

8 ثمّ 'followed by' is Baghdādī BL addition, fol. 6r.

FIGURE 17
Washing up dishes, folio from Divan *of Jāmī 52.20.4, detail* (*MET NY—Purchase, Joseph Pulitzer Bequest, 1952*).

For pounding meat, choose a mortar and pestle made of stone, and for spices, copper ones. For plain dishes (*sādhaj*), fried dishes (*qalāyā*), and sauceless dishes (*nawāshif*)—both the sweet and the sour—spices can be generously applied. However, with sour stews, spices must be used sparingly.

Essential Rules for Good Cooking: Any froth, scum, impurities, and whatever (**5r**) floats up to the surface when the meat boils must be removed. In addition, before boiling the meat, it must be washed in hot salted water, and all nodules (*ghudad*),[9] blood vessels (*ʿurūq*), and membranes (*aghshiya*) should be removed. When cooking plain dishes (*sawādhij*) and fried dishes (*qalāyā*), the meat to be used must be initially sweated[10] in some rendered sheep-tail fat,[11] and a bit of sesame oil (*shayraj*), as this is an essential step to remove the meat's undesirable greasy odors (*zafar*) before boiling it. After the food is fully cooked, the pot must be left on a very low fire [to settle] for a whole hour before serving it.[12]

9 They could be glands, lymph nodes, and any stiff growths found in meat, tallow, or between skin and meat; believed to be harmful because they are susceptible to infections. See, for instance, Yāqūt al-Ḥamawī, *Muʿjam al-udabāʾ* 783.

10 *Taʿrīq* (v. *ʿarraqa*) is a cooking technique which requires that the pieces of meat are first quickly fried in fat. In the process, the meat is frequently stirred and its juices ooze out (i.e., it sweats), this quickly evaporates, leaving behind the slightly browned meat and the fat.

11 *Duhn*, more commonly referred to as *alya*. As used in this cookbook, *duhn* is associated with animal fats and vegetable oils alike, excluding olive oil, which is always called *zayt*.

12 In Baghdādī BL, fol. 7r, it is 'one good hour' (ساعة واحدة جيدة); this emphasizes that the duration is to be taken literally, as one full hour, and not the vague 'for some time.'

FIGURE 18
Cutting boards and knives, folio from Divan *of Jami 52.20.4, detail* (MET NY—*Purchase, Joseph Pulitzer Bequest, 1952*).

Foods which turn out to be too salty (*māliḥ*) or astringent (*ʿafiṣ*) can be fixed by boiling them in fine-tasting plain water (*māʾ ḥulw*).[13] If too sour (*ḥāmiḍ*), they can be remedied by adding extra salt; and the insipid ones (*tafih*)[14] are remedied with spices. If meat is lean (*mahzūl*), boil it first before using it to cook liquid dishes. However, if it is to be roasted (*mashwī*), smear it with fat first; and while it is roasting, put a container with plain water underneath it. [As a rule,] take roasted meat out of the oven while it is still moist.

Do not neglect to trim [raw] meat thoroughly of all unwanted stuff. The cleaver (*sāṭūr*) used for cutting the meat must be sharpened first;[15] otherwise the bones will splinter (*yatashaḍḍā*). Do likewise with knives used for chopping the meat and slicing it thinly (*tashrīḥ*), lest it should acquire an unpleasant greasy odor (*zafar*). Clean the cutting board (*khiwān*) by scraping it regularly.[16] Each pot should have its own ladle (*mighrafa*), and a separate knife must be used for cutting onions and nothing else.

Keep the [inner] sides of the cooking pot clean by wiping them with [a piece of cloth moistened with] water so that nothing burns.[17] In addition, any

13 Lit., 'sweet water.'

14 Here I amended the word based on Baghdādī BL, fol. 7r, where it is clearly written as تفه. *Waṣf* 5, adds that foods that are pungent (*ḥirrīf*) and bitter (*murr*) can be remedied with vinegar; and the lean meat of male animals can be remedied by adding extra fat.

15 Here I replaced the edited خذ 'take,' which is irrelevant in this context, with حُدّ 'sharpen,' based on Baghdādī BL, fol. 7r, and *Waṣf* 5.

16 Here I replaced the edited بالخردل 'with mustard,' which is irrelevant in this context, with بالجرد 'scraping clean,' following Baghdādī BL, fol. 7r, and *Waṣf* 5. *Khiwān*, a low table, was used for serving food, but also as a cutting board for meat and vegetables.

17 If this is not done, the food particles sticking to the sides of the pot will burn, fall back into the cooking food, and spoil the dish. The last part of the sentence is an addition from Baghdādī BL, fol. 7v.

extra water which needs to be added to the cooking pot should be hot. Do not use a mortar, which smells unpleasantly of greasy odors of meat, to pound spices, (5v) nuts (*qulūb*), herbs, or vegetables to extract their juices (*ʿuṣārāt*). Do not ladle food until the pot has stopped boiling and settled, and the fire underneath it is no longer hot.

If too much salt was added to the pot, throw in a small piece of papyrus (*bardī*), which will completely absorb all extra salt. It will do the same thing to smoky odors in the pot. [Another thing to do] if the cooking food develops smoky odors (*dakhkhana*) is to throw hazelnut shells into the pot to absorb the smoke. Do the same thing if the cooking meat does not smell good (*muntin*). [To clean] tripe, it should not be scalded without using slaked lime (*jīr*). Just sprinkle it on the tripe, and it will strip it of all the dirt, and [it] will look as [white as] camphor (*kāfūr*).

Before ladling the food, wash your hands and deodorize them with aromatic smoke [such as that of sandalwood and ambergris] to rid them of the smell of onion. When you cook *qalāyā* (fried dishes) remember to fry the spices and the onion because this is an essential thing to do when cooking such dishes.[18] To cook tough and dense meat (*ghalīẓ*) well, let it first stay overnight [after slaughtering the animal],[19] and then boil it in salted water. Indeed, any slaughtered meat should be given time to cool down before cooking it. In any case, avoid cooking on fire fueled by wood which is not dry (*ḥaṭab raṭb*). The best fire to use should be the opposite of this, as mentioned earlier.[20]

IF you want the cooking meat to fall apart fast, add to the pot some sodium bicarbonate (*būraq*), wax (*shamʿ*), or stems of melon leaves or its peel.[21]

---

18 Here I amended the edited text using Baghdādī BL, fol. 8r.

19 Here I replaced the text's نبت اللحم الغليظة, which does not make sense, with Baghdādī BL, fol. 8r, and Waṣf 6, where it occurs as بيّت اللحوم الغليظة. The following sentence is an addition from these versions, too.

20 Here I amended the text following Baghdādī BL, fol. 8r; and *Waṣf* 6.

21 The text at this point does not specify which variety of *biṭṭīkh* to use, whether muskmelon or watermelon. However, further down in the text (p. 77), the peel of watermelon (*biṭṭīkh akhḍar*) is specified. Apparently, both peels would work. See glossary 7.

Here ends the introduction given in Baghdādī BL, fol. 8r. *Waṣf* 6 also stops here, but it resumes later in the book (40–2) to give instruction on cooking vegetables and grains.

Here, and in the following text, I use capitalized words in bold type to indicate the places where Gotha draws its readers' attention using a different color of ink.

When cooking *ashriba*:[22] while sitting close to the large brass pot (*dast*)[23] [that is boiling], have in front of you a bowl of water and a clean piece of white cloth. Whenever the rim of the pot or its [inner] sides get stained (**6r**), wipe it with the wetted piece of cloth so that the cooking syrup does not spoil or burn. **ALL FRUITS** added to the thickened sugar syrup (*jullāb maʿqūd*) to make *sharāb* must boil with it until it is fully cooked, after which its foam is to be skimmed off, and then continue cooking it until it has the consistency of *sharāb*.[24] However, *sharāb* of lemon (*laymūn*) and that of *ḥummāḍ* (citron pulp) must be cooked differently because their taste will change and spoil if they are kept boiling for too long. The syrup should be boiled [first] until it has the consistency of [syrup for] *mushāsh* (lollipops),[25] and then add the [juice of the] fruit to it, and continue boiling it for a short while, so that it may dissolve and blend, and thicken. Immediately remove the pot and empty it into big bowls (*jifān*, sg. *jafna*) or large wide-mouthed earthenware tubs (*mawājīr*, sg. *mājūr*) which have been rinsed with water. After it cools down, transfer it into large green-glazed wide-mouthed jars,[26] whose outside you need to wipe with sesame oil (*shayraj*). To keep the ants away, wipe off anything sweet that might have fallen on the floor in the place where you keep the jars.

KNOW THAT[27] *sikbāj* (sour vinegar stew) is the best way to cook beef; and dense veal is good for *harīsa* (wheat porridge). Fatty meat of *thanī* (yearling sheep) is suitable for *harīsa*, *aruzziyya* (rice porridge), *farīkiyya* (green-wheat porridge), *iṭriya* (dishes with dried thin noodles), and other similar dishes. Fatty meat of any kind tastes better in cooking than lean meat.[28] Fatty dense meat is the best choice for cooking *sikbāj* stew. In addition, arugula (*jirjīr*) is quite delicious eaten [raw] with it; (**6v**) radishes (*fujl*) go well with *kishkiyya*,[29]

---

22 Sg. *sharāb*, concentrated syrup, diluted and used as a drink.

23 Here I amended the edited text, replacing *nār* (نار) 'fire' with *bi-azaʾ* (بأزاء) 'close to,' incorrectly written as *bāzā* (بازا) in DK, n. 117.

24 Judging from the recipes in chapter 11, the final syrup is boiled down to honey-like consistency.

25 See Kanz recipe 284 below. I here read the DK, n. 124 *al-shāsh* (الشاش), irrelevant here, as *al-mushāsh* (المشاش) 'lollipops.' Besides, neither the edited text *al-shush* (الشش) 'sweet beer' nor Gotha, fol. 5r, *al-mishmish* (المشمش) 'apricot' are relevant here. These must be copyists' misreadings.

26 *Barānī*, sg. *barniyya*, see glossary 9.1.

27 Added in Gotha, fol. 5r.

28 Here I amended the sentence based on Gotha, fol. 5r.

29 A meat dish prepared with *kishk*, which is dried dough of crushed wheat and yogurt.

and mint (*naʿnaʿ*) with *ḥiṣrimiyya*.[30] Eggplant should only be used with sour dishes (*muḥammaḍāt*), unless it is cooked as *qalāyā* (fried dishes),[31] both dry and moist, excluding the main dishes (*alwān kibār*).[32]

GARLIC enhances the aroma and flavor of all the main dishes that are cooked as stews or those cooked with grains and pulses (*ḥubūb*) or vegetables (*buqūl*). **BLACK PEPPER** is added to all the main dishes and it is indeed the spice to use, particularly in *isbīdbājāt*,[33] *ṭabāhijāt*,[34] and all the dishes cooked with spices and herbs (*mubazzar*). The same can be said of **CASSIA** (*dār Ṣīnī*) and **GALANGAL** (*khūlanjān*), but they should be smashed (*yushaddakh*) well, so that they impart all their aroma and flavor [into the dish], thus only small amounts will be needed.

SPINACH (*isfānākh*) and arugula (*jirjīr*) are delicious in *summāqiyya* (sumac stew) and *narjisiyya*.[35] The tender inner leaves of chard and its stalks[36] go well with *kishkiyya* (meat dish with *kishk*).[37] Tender lettuce hearts (*qulūb al-khaṣṣ*) are also good with it.[38] Also add fresh thyme (*ṣaʿtar raṭb*),[39] use it dried if fresh is not available: just crumble it between your fingers and add it when you ladle the dish. **GOURDS** (*qarʿ*) go well with *sikbāj* (sour stew) and other dishes, but it is particularly good with *sikbāj*. Common parsley (*karafs*) and rue (*sadhāb*) are also good with it. Sour apples, juice of [unripe] grapes, and tarragon (*ṭarkhūn*) (7r) go well with *rummāniyya* (pomegranate stew).

Crushed gum arabic and flour of rice and chickpeas are used to thicken the dishes. If you want your *sikbāj* (sour vinegar stew) to be *qarīṣ* (aspic),[40] add

30 Stew soured with juice of unripe grapes (*ḥiṣrim*).

31 In this case, it can be cooked without sour agents.

32 Lit., 'large dishes.' The 'small dishes' are *alwān ṣighār*.

33 A variant of *isfidhbāja*, white stew.

34 These are succulent fried dishes of thinly sliced red meat.

35 A dish named after the narcissus flower, see *Kanz* recipes 95 and 203. In Gotha, fol. 5v, it is written as *rakhbīniyya*, which is meat stew flavored with *rakhbīn* (dried buttermilk).

36 *Qulūb al-silq* (lit., 'hearts of chard') and its *aḍlāʿ* (lit., 'ribs'), respectively.

37 *Kishk* is dried dough of crushed wheat and yogurt. See glossary 3.

38 *Khaṣṣ* is the dialectical vocalization of *khass*, now often associated with the Egyptian dialect (*ʿāmmiyya Miṣriyya*).

39 Here I replaced safflower (*ʿuṣfur*), which appears in the edited text, with thyme, based on Gotha, fol. 5v, as it is more likely to be used in such dishes.

40 The word may also mean 'very sour.' The context, however, suggests that the topic, at this point, is about thickening foods.

some crushed melon peel (*qishr al-biṭṭīkh*) [to the pot], and after you ladle the dish, sprinkle a bit of the milky sap of the fig tree (*laban al-tīn*) on it.[41] Alternatively, rub the *qaṣʿa* (large, wide serving bowl) before ladling the dish with the root of fresh cilantro (*kuzbara khaḍrā'*). This will make the *sikbāj* set.

Of pots, choose the smooth wide ones with high sides; for these are the safest to use [in cooking stews]. Choose similar pots when cooking *ṭabāhijāt* (succulent fried dishes of thinly sliced red meat) and *qalāyā* (fried meat dishes), so that you can stir the food, fry whatever needs to be fried, and dissolve whatever needs to be dissolved, with ease.[42]

DO NOT add olive oil (*zayt*) to the pot until after you have skimmed the foaming scum [of the cooking meat]. Use a perforated ladle (*mighrafa muthaqqaba*) for skimming it to let the liquid fat (*dasam*) drain down while the froth remains in the ladle. When cooking grains and pulses (*ḥubūb*), continue stirring until you remove the pot from the fire; otherwise, it will burn with a stench.[43]

IF the cooking meat turns out to be tough (*ghalīẓ*), add sodium bicarbonate (*būraq*) or crushed dried melon peel to the pot. If the meat is not so fresh and has an unpleasant greasy odor (*zufra*), pound walnuts finely and rub the meat with it quite well, and then add it to the pot. (7v) The meat will taste as though it were fresh, and the unpleasant greasy odor will disappear. In addition, the walnut oil will enhance the taste of the dish.

Cover the cooking pot with its lid to let the aromas of the spices permeate into the entire pot and to let the liquid fats and oils rise to the surface, but this should not be done before the flames of the burning fire underneath the pot have died down, leaving behind a smoldering fire (*jamr layyin*). If it is done otherwise, the food will absorb a disagreeable smoky taste (*tadakhkhana*).

Moreover, add salt only after the dish is done cooking, so that it is the last ingredient added to the pot. Salt itself does not need to be cooked, neither does it benefit from further cooking. If it is put in at the beginning of cooking and liquids are further added to the pot, there is a possibility that its amount may turn out to be either too much or too little. However, if it is added at the

---

41 Ibn al-Bayṭār, *al-Jamiʿ* i 201, mentions that the milky sap of fig trees can be used to tenderize tough meat and curdle milk into yogurt. See glossary 7, s.v. *tīn*.

42 The reference here is to chopped sheep-tail fat (*alya*), which is used generously in such dishes, and needs to be rendered.

43 The verb is *tashayyaṭa*, which was a common cooking mishap with pulses and grains. Here I amended the text based on *Zahr*, fol. 2v, where لا يحرك 'not to be stirred' is written as لايزال يحرك 'to be constantly stirred.'

end of cooking, after the pot has been given what it needs of liquids,[44] its amount will be just right. This is particularly important when cooking grains and pulses. No salt is to be added until they are fully cooked; otherwise, they will never be soft and tender, or they may take longer to cook. The same rule applies to dishes that require the addition of vinegar, even to already cooked fava beans (*bāqillā'*). If you make a cold dish (*bārida*) with them and pour the vinegar, even just a short while before eating them, they will toughen and taste as though they were raw.[45] Pour vinegar on fava beans the moment you want to eat them. In addition, spices should be added to the pot only after it has stopped boiling over and started to simmer.

AS FOR dishes cooked in liquid (*aṭbikha*), if the liquid turns out to be too much, reduce it by keeping it on the fire longer. However, if the pot dries out, or the liquid was not to your satisfaction, (**8r**) remedy this by adding water until the amount is right. However, you cannot do this with dishes of *harīsa* (wheat porridge), *aruzziyya* (rice porridge), or dishes with beans and grains, and whatever vegetables (*buqūl*) are cooked with them. This is because replenishing the water of such dishes after they are cooked spoils their flavor, even though they were good and tasty to begin with. Therefore, it is important that the cook should estimate the correct amount of water for the pot right from the beginning, so that it does not become so deficient later that it needs replenishing.

THE AIM of cooking is to put together balanced amounts of the dish's ingredients so that no one flavor overpowers the other. The right thing to do—and this must be heeded—is to thoroughly wash, with water, the onion you chop for any dishes you cook, before adding it to the pot. There should be a separate knife for cutting onion, which you rub with sweet olive oil before using it for this purpose.[46] This knife is to be used for cutting onion and garlic and nothing else. Sturdy knives must be used for disjointing the meat (*tafṣīl*), and thin and sharp ones for slicing it thinly (*tashrīḥ*). This will make such tasks easier for the cook. (**8v**)

Whenever eggplants and gourds are used, after cutting them, they must be kept in salted water for a whole hour before adding them to the pot. When eggplant is used in white dishes like *maḍīra* (stew with sour milk) or *ḥiṣrimiyya*

44 Here I replaced اشتَق, which is irrelevant in the given context, with استق from Gotha, fol. 6v. The grammatically correct form of the word is استقى 'had enough liquid.'

45 Here I amended the text by using the word *nayyan* (نيّا) 'raw,' in Gotha, fol. 6v.

46 *Zayt muṭayyab* or *ṭayyib* (sweet olive oil), is enhanced oil, which is free of any astringency or bitterness. See glossary 6.

(stew with sour unripe grapes), its outer skin and the calyx (*libās aqmāʿihi*) must be peeled off before drenching it in the salted water.

The cook must allocate a separate ladle for each dish, one not to be used with other dishes unless they are of the same variety, so that their tastes and flavors do not get mingled.

AS FOR *tharīd* (bread sop), the most delicious is made with the thin sheets of *ruqāq* bread, *jardaq* (thick and pithy round bread), *kaʿk* (dry cookies), or stale good flat bread (*khubz*) sopped in a sour, fatty, and sweetened stew (*maraq*). Especially delicious is *tharīd* sopped in liquid of *sikbāj* (sour vinegar stew). *Tharīd* must be given enough liquid and fat to saturate the bread—neither too much or too little, and set aside to give the bread enough time to absorb the liquid and soften. Then press the middle with [the back of] a ladle to make a dent,[47] and pour into it enough of the stew fat.[48]

IF *aruzziyya* (rice porridge) burns, **(9r)** add some rue (*sadhāb*) to the pot to get rid of the smell. If the cooking pot develops *zuhūma* (undesirable greasy odors), throw one or two whole walnuts into it, and leave them for an hour, and they will absorb all these odors. You can tell that this worked by sniffing the walnuts after you take them out of the pot—you will not be able to tolerate their unpleasant greasy smell. In addition, if a piece of cloth is drenched in water and put in the cooking pot, it will absorb all excess salt.[49] Likewise, the same is true with bran (*nukhāla*).[50] Also, if a ladle (*muqaʿʿara*) is heated to redness and put in the pot, it will absorb the salt.[51] If you want chickpeas to cook fast, just add some mustard [seeds] to the pot, and they will cook fast.

IF you want to keep [raw] meat fresh (*ṭarī*) for whenever you need it, take meat from the thigh, trim off its fat (*shaḥm*), remove the bone, slice it, salt it very well, and set it aside overnight. The following morning, wash it very well,

47 Gotha, fol. 6v, uses the verb بخش 'dent,' a dialectical variant of بخس, which sometimes occurs as بخص or بخز.

48 *Dasam* is liquid fats and oils that accumulate on the surface of the cooking pot after it has been allowed to simmer gently for an hour. It is skimmed off with a ladle and used for such purposes.

49 I amended the text based on Gotha, fol. 7v, by replacing the edited والجزاء ما, which is redundant in this context, with وكذا الما 'also, water.'

50 That is, if it is put in a piece of cloth and added to the pot.

51 Presumably, when the red-hot ladle is dipped into the pot, the liquid touching it will at once evaporate, leaving the salt attached to the ladle, which should be taken out immediately if this is to work.

FIGURE 19
Jar, c. thirteenth century, 48.113.15 (MET NY— H.O. Havemeyer Collection, Gift of Horace Havemeyer, 1948).

and spread it to dry out. Then, smear it with ghee (*samn*) and keep it in a large earthenware jar (*bustūqa*).[52] Keep the meat there as long as you wish, and take it out whenever you need it, and you will find it still fresh.

IF you want to keep meat fresh in hot weather without having to salt it, then take the meat (9v) and attach it to a pitchfork (*shawka*), and lower it into a well until it almost touches the surface of the water. Take it out whenever you need it, and it will still be fresh. In case the meat becomes smelly (*natana*) or does not smell fresh (*taghayyara*) and you still want to use it, cook it in a pot along with some whole walnuts, after piercing a hole all the way to the core of each one of them. They will absorb all the unwanted odors and their insides will stink even worse than carrion. In addition, an egg broken into the pot

52 In *Zahr*, fol. 3r, the ghee is also poured over the meat in the jar to submerge it.

will absorb the meat's bad odors. [Another way is to], boil a bit of fenugreek (*ḥulba*) with the smelly meat, and then pour off the liquid, and cook it in a fresh change of water. The meat will no longer smell bad and will taste so good that its eater cannot tell whether it was initially fresh or not. In case the meat just does not smell fresh (*mutaghayyir al-rāʾiḥa*), cut it into chunks and cook it in a pot along with broken pieces of hazelnut (*bunduq*). This will remove the smell.

IF you want foods to cook fast, take the peel of watermelon (*biṭṭīkh akhḍar*),[53] dry it, crush it, and store it. Whenever you want a dish to cook fast, add a small amount of it to the pot. IF you do not want the meat to lose its freshness in hot weather, attach it to a spit (*saffūd*) and lower it into a well until it almost touches the surface of the water, and the meat will not change. IF you do not want garlic bulbs to shrivel, (**10r**) burn their hairy roots (*kanāfish*). Your garlic will stay as long as you wish, without shriveling or spoiling.

IF you want to get rid of all the prickly fine bones (*shawk*) of *labīs* fish (Nile carp), grind some betel nut (*fawfal*). Then, on each side of the fish, make two deep gashes,[54] and sprinkle them with the betel nut. When you grill the fish, all the bones will fall apart.

IF you want to improve the smell of not-so-fresh meat (*murawwaḥ*), finely pound or crush fenugreek [seeds]. Season the meat with it,[55] and [wrap it] in a woolen cloth (*miʾzar*). Fill a pot with water, let it come to a full boil, and then put the [wrapped] cloth in the water and let it boil for a short while. If there is a lot of meat, change the water [and repeat]. This will rid the meat of the unpleasant smell. After that, you can use it in any dish you want.[56]

IF you want to boil turnip (*lift*), beans (*lūbiya*), wild mustard greens (*labsān*), cabbage (*kurunb*), or chard (*silq*) and keep them green, add a bit of natron (*naṭrūn*) to the water, and let it come to a rolling boil (*yashuqq*). Then add whichever [of the vegetables] you want to boil. Do not cover the pot; otherwise,

53 Cf. Anṭākī, *Tadhkira* 85, where the peel of *biṭṭīkh aṣfar* (muskmelon) is recommended. Apparently, peels of both varieties will work the same way.

54 In the edited text, فلخين seems to be a dialectical variant of فلجين, from فلج 'make long deep cut.'

55 Here I followed Gotha, fol. 8v, where the verb is clearly تتبّل 'spiced.'

56 At this point, *Waṣf* 40 resumes, till the end of this chapter. I used it to slightly amend the edited text.

all the vegetables will turn yellow. Besides, avoid overcooking the vegetables; (**10v**) take the pot off the fire while they are still firm. They will taste better cooked this way.

IF you want to boil spinach, wash it first and then put it in the pot without adding any water because the spinach will release a lot of liquid once it is heated. As for Jew's mallow (*mulūkhiyya*),[57] when you throw it[58] into the pot, do not cover it, and do not use a flaming fire underneath it, but let it cook slowly on the low heat.[59]

IF you need to cook pulses (*ḥubūb*),[60] like lentil (*ʿadas*), *bisillā* (large variety of grass pea), grass peas (*jullubān*), fava beans (*fūl*), mung beans (*māsh*), or chickpeas (*ḥimmaṣ*), do not buy them from the market already coarsely crushed (*madshūsh*). Instead, buy whatever you wish of these [pulses] whole. Coarsely crush them at home, sift out their skins, and rub them with sweet olive oil (*zayt ṭayyib*)—for each Egyptian *qadaḥ*[61] (2¼ pounds) of the pulses, use ½ *raṭl* (1 cup) of the oil. [Color them with] as much saffron as needed, and dry them out. Whenever you need to cook the pulses, bring water with a bit of salt to a boil, put some of it aside, and add to the pot whatever you want of the abovementioned pulses. The ratio [of water to pulses] is one and a half *ghumra* for each *qadaḥ* of pulses.[62] After the pulses are cooked, add whatever seasonings they need,[63] while stirring the pot all the time, as this will prevent the pot from burning with a stench (*tashyīṭ*). (**11r**)

---

57 Also, known as jute mallow (*Corchorus olitorius*).

58 The edited text clearly uses the verb *irmīthā* (throw it). However, in DK, n. 292, it occurs as *ighmihā*, and in Gotha, fol. 8v, as *ighmīthā*, both of which do not make sense in the given context. It is my guess that the copyist's reader must have been rhotacistic—one who has difficulty pronouncing the sound 'r'; which usually comes out as '*gh*'. The copyist must have mindlessly jotted down the word as he heard it, or he might have deliberately kept it for fun.

59 Here I replaced the edited تتهرأ 'falls apart' with تتهدأ 'slowly cooks' in *Waṣf* 41, as it is more compatible with the context.

60 The same word is used to designate grains.

61 For this Egyptian measure, see glossary 13.

62 *Ghumra*/*ghumr* is approx. 7 pounds/14 cups. Based on this, for each 2¼ pounds of pulses called for in the recipe, 21 cups of water are used. The boiling water that is set aside is used to complement the amount of water, as needed.

63 The word used is *ḥawāʾijuhu*, that is, the necessary ingredients. In *Waṣf* version 41, they are mentioned as cilantro pounded with garlic, white onion, and suet (*shaḥm*).

CHAPTER 2

في الاخباز وكيفية صفة عجنها وخبزها
وعمل الاخباز المطيبة المبزرة والمملوحة وغير ذلك

How to Knead Bread Dough and Bake It; and Making Varieties of Bread: Enhanced (*muṭayyab*), Seeded (*mubazzar*), Salted (*mamlūḥ*), and More

The best bread is made with fine white flour, recently ground (*ḥadīth*), and vigorously kneaded.[1] Water is added gradually until the dough is neither too soft nor too stiff. After it has risen, bake the dough on a quiet fire. A strong fire will burn the bread [from the outside] and it must be taken out while still doughy [from the inside]. If the fire is too low, the bread will come out insufficiently risen,[2] and dense (*lāẓī*).

When the bread is taken out of the oven, it must be left out in the air for a while [lit., 'an hour'] to allow its moisture to be absorbed and its steam to dissipate. After that, it will be good to eat.

Recipe for *khubz ṭayyib* (delicious bread)[3]

Take 1 *qadaḥ* (2¼ pounds) flour, 4 *ūqiyyas* (4 ounces) wheat starch (*nashā*), and 10 *ūqiyyas* (10 ounces) sugar. Add milk (*laban ḥalīb*), knead the mix, [divide it] and bake it, handling it gently. No water should be added in the making of this bread. It is wonderful, flavorful, and delicious.

1 The adjective used (*maʿrūk*) describes a vigorous way of kneading, which involves pressing and rubbing the dough, probably more effectively done with the heels of the hands because the dough is supposed to be stiff at the initial stage, and water is added gradually to the desired consistency. Throughout the chapter, the Arabic word for flour is the generic *daqīq*.

2 The word used in the recipe is *mamṣūṣ*, lit., 'thin.'

3 DK and Gotha manuscripts contain more recipes than the edited text. In this chapter, I follow the recipe sequence of Gotha, fols. 9v–10v, as it offers nine bread recipes. *Zahr* includes eight recipes. In DK, this recipe is in appendix 1.

 | DOI 10.1163/9789004349919_005

Recipe for *khubz al-abāzīr* (bread with seeds)[4]

Take good flour, and for each *raṭl* (1 pound/4 cups) use ⅓ *raṭl* (5 ounces) sesame oil (*shayraj*), 1 *ūqiyya* (1 ounce) sesame seeds, and a handful (*kaff*) of shelled pistachios and almonds. Knead them together [with some yeast and water]. After the dough rises, shape it into round discs, the thickness of each should be the width of two fingers put together. Bake them in the *furn* (brick oven), and when they are done, take them out and eat them with *ḥalwā* (thick pudding).

(1) Recipe for *aqrāṣ mamlūḥa* (salted cookies)[5]

Take as much flour as you need. For each *raṭl* (1 pound/4 cups), use ¼ *raṭl* (4 ounces/½ cup) sesame oil, and enough salt to give it a noticeably salty taste. Knead [the ingredients with yeast and water], and after the dough rises shape it into discs as you do with *khubz al-abāzīr* [above], but make them a little bit thinner, and bake them. After they develop a golden hue (*tawarrada*), take them out. These cookies are offered in case the eater's appetite dulls from having sweet foods. Therefore, they are to be served while having sweets.

Recipe for *irnīn* (stuffed cookies)[6]

Take as much flour as you need, and make dough with it like that of *khubz al-abāzīr* [above].[7] When the dough rises, have a wooden mold (*qālab khashab*) ready,[8] and make the dough into little round discs that would fit into it. Combine the sugar and ground almonds, and bind them together with rosewater. Stuff each disc with this mixture, combine the edges of the discs, seal them well, and bake them in the *furn* (brick oven) until they look golden (*tawarrada*).

Some people knead dried dates (*tamr*) with sesame oil—after they remove the stones, add some aromatic spices (*afāwīh ṭayyiba*),[9] and stuff the discs with it.[10]

---

4 This recipe appears in DK, appendix 2. It also occurs in *Waṣf* 172–3, which besides this one, includes the following two, in the same sequence.

5 In *Waṣf* 172–3, the name occurs as *aqrāṣ mumallaḥa*.

6 This recipe also appears in DK, appendix 3. A somewhat similar *irnīn* recipe can be found in *Wuṣla* ii 648–9, as well.

7 In Baghdādī's similar recipe, for each *raṭl* (1 pound) of flour, 3 *ūqiyyas* (3 ounces) of fresh sesame oil are used (79–80).

8 In Baghdādī's recipe, the mold is concave, compared to a small bowl (*ḥuqq*).

9 These are sweet-smelling spices, such as cardamom, nutmeg, mace, spikenard, cinnamon, and cloves.

10 The addition in *Zahr*, fol. 4r, reads, "If *ka'k* is stuffed with ground sugar and almonds combined with rosewater, the edges are brought together and sealed tightly, and each one is

Recipe for *ka'k* (dry cookies), which al-Qāḍī l-Fāḍil savored, and used to gift to dignitaries[11]

Take excellent sifted, finely milled white flour (*daqīq ʿalāma*), pistachios, and sugar—one part of each [by weight]. Finely grind the pistachios and sugar, mix them with the flour, and knead them together with chicken fat (*duhn al-dajāj*) and sheep-tail fat (*alya*) after you render it and enhance it (*yukhlaʿ*) with mastic gum (*maṣṭakā*), Ceylon cinnamon (*qarfa*), a bit of musk (*misk*) and camphor (*kāfūr*), and a squeeze of lime juice (*laymūn akhḍar*).[12] Shape it into discs (*aqrāṣ*).

Grease a tinned-copper tray (*ṭabaq nuḥās mubayyaḍ*) inside and out with sesame oil, and arrange the *kaʿk* discs on it. Put the tray in the remaining heat of the *furn* (brick oven) until the *kaʿk* is browned (*yaḥmarr*), and serve.

(2) *Kaʿk* recipe

Blend to moisten (*yulatt*) finely milled flour with ghee (*samn*) or sesame oil, along with musk and rosewater. Flatten the dough [until it is] thin with a rolling pin (*suwayq*).[13] Fry the pieces in sesame oil, and then dip them in sugar syrup (*jullāb*) flavored with a bit of musk and rosewater. Stack them on a plate, (**11v**) and as you do this, sprinkle each layer with coarsely crushed pistachios.

(3) Recipe for *kaʿk sukkarī* (sugar cookies)

[In the edited text, this is a repetition of the previous recipe, only the name is slightly different.]

(4) Recipe for *kaʿk sukkarī* (sugar cookies)

Take 1 *raṭl* (1 pound/4 cups) flour and 8 *ūqiyyas* (8 ounces/1 cup) sugar. Finely crush the sugar, blend it with the flour along with 2 *ūqiyyas* (2 ounces) sesame oil. Add to these 4 *ūqiyyas* (4 ounces/½ cup) water and knead it into a stiff

---

shaped into a *kubbā* (ball) or *khushkān*." The latter would be shaped into a crescent, more commonly known as *khushkanānaj* in Abbasid Baghdad. See glossary 2.

11 This recipe also appears in DK, appendix 4, and *Zahr*, fol. 4r. Al-Qāḍī l-Fāḍil ʿAbd al-Raḥīm b. ʿAlī b. al-Saʿīd al-ʿAsqalānī was a favorite counselor of the Ayyubid sultan Ṣalāḥ al-Dīn. He died in Cairo in 1200 (Zarkalī, *Aʿlām* 491–2). Gotha version يستطيبه 'savored it,' is replaced with يعمله 'made it,' in DK. To my knowledge, aside from this recipe, no extant records tie al-Qāḍī l-Fāḍil's name to cookery.

12 Al-Maqrīzī (1364–1442), *Khiṭaṭ* ii 69, mentions that both lime (*laymūn akhḍar*, lit., 'green lemon') and common lemon (*laymūn aṣfar*, lit., 'yellow lemon') were available in Egypt. Even though *akhḍar* may also designate freshness, the reference here points to lime.

13 It is to be assumed that the dough is then cut out into small discs.

dough. Shape it into *kaʿk*[14] and discs (*aqrāṣ*), and bake them on a copper tray. They will be splendid.

(5) Recipe for *kaʿk bi-l-ʿajwa* (date cookies)

For each *raṭl* (1 pound/4 cups) flour, use ½ *raṭl* (8 ounces/1 cup) sesame oil, 8 *ūqiyyas* (8 ounces/1 cup) *ʿajwa* (sweet and soft dried dates), along with rosewater, saffron, *aṭrāf ṭīb* (blend of aromatic spices),[15] black pepper, and ginger.[16]

(6) Recipe for *kaʿk maltūt* (cookies enriched with fat)[17]

Take excellent flour (*daqīq ʿalāma*), sesame oil, bitter ginger (*ʿirq kāfūr*), and mastic gum. Begin by mixing and moistening the flour with oil, and then knead it with water. Finely pound bitter ginger and mastic gum. Also, pound a small amount of *shayba* (usnea, a variety of lichen) after you soak it in water. Work all these into the dough, shape it into rings (*ḥalaq*) [and bake].

---

14 I.e., rings, which was the traditional shape of this type of cookies. See recipe 6 below, for instance.

15 See glossary 8 for a recipe of this blend of spices.

16 The recipe does not give directions. The dates with rosewater and spices are most probably used as a filling for the cookies. Cf. recipe for the stuffed cookies of *irnīn* above.

17 *Maltūt* is flour, enriched and moistened with fat; the process is similar to making today's pastry crusts.

CHAPTER 3

في تدبير الماء المشروب المزمّل وبالثلج المضروب

Measures Taken When Drinking Water, in a *muzammal*,[1] and Chilled with Ice (*thalj maḍrūb*)[2]

The physicians stated that those who seek good health should avoid drinking water first thing in the morning. They should not drink it during the meal or immediately after it, but wait until the upper part of the abdomen feels light. Meanwhile, they should drink just enough to abate feelings of thirst, and avoid having too much of it. It is only when the digesting food descends and the upper belly feels light that they can have their fill of water and any other drinks, God willing.

Ice-chilled water (*māʾ al-thalj*) should be taken in small amounts while having a meal, and only on a rare occasion. Drinking it in small quantities will not do harm. However, those with weak nervous systems or cold stomachs and livers should avoid ice-chilled water. In fact, it is not good for anyone who suffers from slow digestion, and feels weak and drained of energy. However, those who have a lot of flesh, whose blood is red and whose appetites are strong, should not be wary of it. They can have it whenever they wish, and even while eating, because it will do them very little harm.[3]

Drinking cold water first thing in the morning is recommended only for those suffering from acute heat (*iltihāb*) and fever. Even so, they should avoid drinking it in one large gulp. Rather, they need to have it in several small doses and breathe deeply between one sip and the other.

Water is good, and drinking it following these rules will benefit the body and keep it strong, God willing.

---

1 Cooled in a *muzammala*, which is a green-enameled water-cooling vessel that was insulated by wrapping it in sackcloth. I amend the edited word *murammal* (مرمل) to *muzammal* (مزمل), based on Gotha, fol. 2r, where it is correctly copied.

2 To amend the edited text in this chapter, I used Gotha, fols. 10v–1r; and al-Warrāq's chapter 110.

3 The following lines are also included in DK, appendix 5.

 | DOI 10.1163/9789004349919_006

CHAPTER 4

في خاصية الماء المبرّد في الهواء وما قالت فيه الحكماء

Qualities of Air-Cooled Water and What the Physicians Said About It[1]

Know that water preserves the body's innate moistures. It dilutes the nourishing bodily liquids and facilitates their absorption. It also reduces heat. Therefore, it suits people with fevers and those with hot temperaments more than wine (*sharāb*) does.

Know also that the best and the most beneficial water is the lightest in weight, the fastest to heat up or cool down, and the sweetest in taste. Water with an odious taste or smell is the worst. It is bad and not fit to drink. However, it might be useful medicinally. Murky water (*kadir*) causes blockages in the liver and stones in the kidneys.[2]

Salty water first causes diarrhea, then constipation, and if one drinks it all the time, it will cause putridity to settle in, the spleen to enlarge, and the temperament (*mizāj*) to spoil.[3] Drinking it propagates fevers.

Water chilled with ice (*mubarrad bi-l-thalj*), or water which is, by itself, cold, will cool down the liver immensely. However, only those prone to excess heat can have it first thing in the morning, as they will benefit greatly from it. Having it with the meal strengthens the stomach and arouses the appetite, provided it is taken only in small amounts.

As for chilled water that is too cold to enjoy, it causes flatulence, does not quench feelings of thirst, spoils the appetite, and weakens the body. Altogether, it is not good.

Boiled and tepid water nauseate and are only good for inducing vomiting (*ʿilāj*). When hot water is taken first thing in the morning, it cleanses the stomach of the previous day's excretions. It can also have a laxative power. However, having too much of it will exhaust the stomach (*yukhliq*).

---

1 To amend the edited text here, I use Gotha, fols. 11r–v, as it is more complete; with the help of al-Warrāq's chapter 111. See n. 2 in the previous chapter. Ultimately, both al-Warrāq's book and the *Kanz* drew on al-Rāzī, *Kitāb al-Manṣūrī* fols. 17r–8v.

2 The following two paragraphs also appear in DK, appendix 6.

3 See glossary 11, s.v. *mizāj*.

 | DOI 10.1163/9789004349919_007

CHAPTER 5

في أنواع الأطعمة

Miscellany of Dishes[1]

Know that some of the sour dishes are sweetened and others are kept sour. The sweetened sour ones are usually cooked with sugar, honey, or date syrup. It is fitting that all these dish varieties are put in one chapter. The following are such dishes.

(7) *Sikbāj* (sour vinegar stew)[2]

To make it, cut fatty meat into medium-size pieces, (**13r**) and put it in a pot with enough water to submerge it, with a bit of salt, aloeswood (*ʿūd*), and cassia (*dār Ṣīnī*). When it comes to a boil, remove the scum, and add to it coriander seeds (*kusbara yābisa*).

Now take white onion, bulbous leeks (*kurrāth Shāmī*) or Levantine shallots (*thūm Shāmī*),[3] carrots if in season, and eggplant. Peel them all. Cut the eggplant in a deep cross [almost to the stem, lengthwise], and boil it in salted water in a separate pot. Drain it well, and add it to the meat pot [along with the other vegetables]. Add some spices and herbs (*abāzīr*), and adjust the salt.

When the stew is almost cooked, take vinegar and date syrup or honey.[4] Use as much of them as needed to make a balanced sour and sweet seasoning sauce (*mizāj*), and add it to the pot. Let it cook for an hour, and then thicken it with a bit of wheat starch (*nashā*ʾ) or [ground] rice.

Now take skinned and split almonds, jujube (*ʿunnāb*), dried figs, and raisins (*zabīb*). Spread them on top of the cooking stew [do not stir them in]. Cover the pot and let it cook for an hour, after which, stop fueling the fire, wipe the [inner] sides of the pot with a clean cloth, sprinkle it with some rosewater, and

---

1 This is a very long chapter containing 142 recipes of main dishes. Note that the first part of this chapter (recipes 7–20) closely follows the second chapter in the *Waṣf* (several of the recipes are also found in Baghdādī). It is highly possible that both drew on similar sources unavailable to us today. Here I used the *Waṣf* to amend the edited text wherever needed.

2 This recipe is almost identical with recipe 136 below, which clearly indicates that the compiler of this book used several sources dealing with dishes, in which case repetition is expected and inevitable.

3 See glossary 8, s.v. *kurrāth*.

4 Here I follow *Zahr*, fol. 5r, replacing the edited 'and' with 'or.'

 | DOI 10.1163/9789004349919_008

leave it on the remaining heat of the fire to simmer, and then take the pot off the fire.

(8) *Ibrāhīmiyya*[5]

Cut the meat into medium chunks, and put it in a pot with enough water to submerge it. (**13v**) Throw into it a tied bundle of light linen containing coriander seeds, ginger, black pepper, and aloeswood, all finely ground. Also add pieces of cassia (*dār Ṣīnī*) and mastic gum. Slit three small onions cross-like [but leave intact], and add them. Then, pound more meat, shape it into balls (*kubab*), and throw them into the pot.

When the food boils, take out the cloth-bundle with the spices in it, and soak it in aged juice of unripe sour grapes (*māʾ ḥiṣrim ʿatīq*). If aged juice is not available, use fresh sour grapes (*ṭarī*), and extract their juice by hand, without boiling the grapes. Alternatively, use distilled vinegar.[6] Strain the liquid, thicken it (*yurabbā*) with sweet almonds, finely pounded, and pour it into the pot. Sweeten it with a bit of white sugar, [add enough] so that it does not taste overly sour.

Leave the pot on the fire to simmer. Wipe the [inner] sides of the pot with a clean cloth, sprinkle a little bit of rosewater on top, and then remove.

(9) *Jurjāniyya*[7]

Cut fatty meat into medium chunks and put it in a pot with enough water to submerge it. Add a bit of salt, too. Chop onion into small pieces, and when the pot comes to a boil, add the onion, along with coriander seeds, black pepper, ginger, and cassia (*dār Ṣīnī*), all finely ground. Some might also like to add shelled walnuts, from which the inner wooden membranes have been removed, (**14r**) that are cut into medium pieces. Stir the pot.

When the ingredients (*ḥawāʾij*) are cooked,[8] take equal amounts of [dried] pomegranate seeds and black raisins. Pound them thoroughly, and then rub and press them with water [to release their essence]. Strain them through a fine-meshed sieve (*munkhul ṣafīq*), and add [the liquid] to the pot. Also, add

---

5 White stew named after the Abbasid gourmet Prince Ibrāhīm b. al-Mahdī (d. 839). Ibn Mubārak Shāh (d. 1458) in *Zahr al-ḥadīqa*, fol. 5r, replaces *Ibrāhīmiyya* with *ṭaʿām ẓarīf* 'elegant food.'

6 For distilling, see glossary 9.2, s.v. *taṣʿīd*.

7 Named after Jurjān, a city in northern Persia.

8 *Ḥawāʾij*, often used in recipes, designates ingredients needed for cooking the dish in a given recipe.

FIGURE 20
Pomegranate tree, F1954.77r, Muḥammad al-Qazwīnī, ʿAjāʾib al-makhlūqāt, *detail (Freer Gallery of Art and Arthur M. Sackler Gallery, Smithsonian Institution, Washington, DC: Purchase—Charles Lang Freer Endowment Art).*

a bit of vinegar, which has been thickened (*yurabbā*) with finely pounded skinned sweet almonds.

When the pot comes to a boil, and it is almost cooked, sweeten it with a bit of sugar, adding just what it needs. Scatter a handful of jujube (*ʿunnāb*) on top, give the pot a light sprinkle of rosewater, put the lid back, and leave it to simmer (*tahdaʾ*) on the [smoldering] fire.

(10) *Rummāniyya mukhaththara* [*bi fustuq*] (pomegranate stew thickened with pistachios)[9]

Cut meat into pieces, and add it to the pot with some water. When it comes to a boil, remove the scum, and throw in meatballs of pounded meat (*kubab mudaqqaqa*), made as small as hazelnuts. Use a small amount of liquid in the pot [to begin with], so that when it is all done nothing remains but a small amount of a nice rich sauce.

Take sour pomegranate juice, balance it with rose petal jam made with sugar (*ward murabbā bi-l-sukkar*), and add it to the pot along with some mint leaves. Pound pistachios and thicken the stew with them. Add a bit of saffron

9 The addition of 'pistachio' is based on *Zahr*, fol. 5v.

for color, as well as all the components of *aṭrāf al-ṭīb*.[10] Sprinkle the pot with some rosewater with saffron steeped in it, and then remove.

(11) *Ḥummāḍiyya* (stew soured with citron pulp)

Cut fatty meat (**14v**) into pieces and put it in the pot with enough water to submerge it, with a bit of salt. Let it boil, then add spices such as coriander seeds, black pepper, ginger, and cloves, all finely pounded and tied in a clean piece of linen cloth. Also, add broken pieces of cassia (*dār Ṣīnī*).

Pound meat with some spices and shape it into balls, then add them to the pot after it boils. When the meatballs are cooked, take out the spice bundle.[11]

Take the pulp of large citrons (*ḥummāḍ al-utrujj*), remove the seeds, extract the juice by hand, and then mix with it juice of sour unripe grapes.[12] Add it to the pot, and let it cook for an hour. Take finely pounded skinned sweet almonds, as much as the dish needs, blend it with some water,[13] and add it to the pot. Sweeten the dish with some sugar or sugar syrup (*jullāb*) if you wish. Leave the pot on the [smoldering] fire to simmer for an hour. Sprinkle the top with rosewater, wipe the [inner] sides of the pot with a clean cloth, and then remove.

(12) *Another ḥummāḍiyya*[14]

Cut fattened chickens at the joints, and finely pound the meat of the thighs with a cleaver (*sāṭūr*), but do not [pound] their skins. Also, pound the breasts. (**15r**) Wash the rest of the chicken and add it to the pot along with its fat. Add some chopped onions to the pot and sprinkle it with water. Sweat (*yuʿarraq*) the chicken with spices,[15] namely, coriander, ginger, toasted and pounded cumin, and a piece of cassia (*dār Ṣīnī*); add a good amount of oil of sweet almonds as well. Let the chicken sweat very well with these. Add 1 *dirham* (3 grams/½ teaspoon) salt, and continue stirring the pot.

Add leaves or blossoms (*qiddāḥ*) of citron (*utrujj*) tied in a bundle. Take citron pulp, which has been cleaned of its peel and seeds, sprinkle it with rosewater, [extract the juice, and set it aside].

---

10 A spice mix. See glossary 8, for a recipe.

11 Here I amended the edited text based on its counterpart in *Waṣf* 9.

12 In *Waṣf*, the amount is a quarter of this amount of citron juice.

13 *Murabbā* (v. *yurabbā*) designates thickened liquids. The thickening ingredients used include ground nuts, rice, and bread crumbs. See n. 20 below for an alternative term.

14 Here I amended the edited text slightly based on its counterpart in *Wuṣla* ii 614.

15 *Taʿrīq* 'sweating' involves letting the meat release its moisture first, and then browning it in its juices and some added fat.

Next, take the bundle out of the pot; add the pounded thigh and breast meat. Sweat this meat [stirring all the time] until it absorbs the flavor of the spices. Add sour juice of unripe grapes mixed with rosewater, enough to cover the meat. Also, add mint and fresh thyme (*zaʿtar raṭb*). When the pot boils, add a small amount of fine-tasting [preserved] clear light-colored lemon juice (*māʾ al-laymūn al-abyaḍ al-ʿadhb*).[16] Also, add chopped onions.

When all of it is cooked, pound a suitable amount of sweet almonds and dissolve it (*yurabbā*) in rosewater [and set it aside].[17]

Take out the herbs [i.e., mint and thyme, and discard], and add the squeezed citron juice [which has been set aside].[18] When the pot comes to a simmer, **(15v)** balance its sourness with sugar syrup (*jullāb*) and coarsely pounded fine white sugar (*sukkar ṭabarzad*). Add [the prepared] almonds. Perfume the pot with rosewater and camphor (*kāfūr*), add enough to permeate the dish. Allow the pot to simmer [on the smoldering fire], and then remove. This is one of the dishes which used to be served to caliphs.

(13) *Kibrīkiyya* of meat (moderately sour meat stew)[19]

Cut the meat into pieces and put it in the pot, along with a bit of salt, a handful of skinned chickpeas, coriander and cilantro, chopped onion, and leaf leeks (*kurrāth*). Add enough water to submerge them all, bring the pot to a boil, and skim [off] the froth.

Add sesame oil, wine vinegar, *murrī* (liquid fermented sauce), and a bit of finely ground black pepper to the pot. Further cook it in the pot until it tastes good. Some people choose to sweeten it with a bit of sugar.

When the ingredients are cooked, add *aṭrāf al-ṭīb* (spice blend), with some black pepper and coriander. Let it simmer [on the smoldering fire], and then remove.

---

16 The Arabic phrase is ماء الليمون الابيض العذب. It is my guess that the lemon juice is preserved because of the way it is described. Preserved lemon juice, which is old, or which has not been stored properly, deteriorates in taste and becomes dark in color.

17 See n. 13 above.

18 In all *Kanz* versions, including *Zahr* and Gotha, the citron pulp is described as مزعتر/ مصعتر/ مزعطر 'seasoned with thyme,' which does not apply to the recipe. Here I follow the more correct reading of the word, which is معتصر 'juiced,' as it is written in *Wuṣla*.

19 Here I amended the edited *Kurunbiyya* (meat cooked with cabbage) using Gotha, fol. 14r. The name is a corruption of *dīkabrīka*, as it occurs in *Waṣf* 11, Baghdādī 15, and al-Warrāq's chapter 56.

(14) *Zīrbāj* (delicately sour golden stew)

Cut the meat into small pieces and put it in the pot with enough water to cover it. Add pieces of cassia (*dār Ṣīnī*), skinned chickpeas, and a bit of salt. Skim the froth from the pot when it comes to a boil. Then, add to it sesame oil, and wine vinegar as needed, along with a quarter of its weight in sugar. Also, add finely pounded skinned almonds dissolved in rosewater,[20] (**16r**) along with a small amount of coriander, ground black pepper, and mastic gum. Color the stew with saffron; and scatter on top of it all the skinned almonds which have been split by rubbing them by hand. Sprinkle the pot with a bit of rosewater, wipe its [inner] sides [with a clean cloth], and let it simmer on the [smoldering] fire.

For those who like to add chicken to it, take a scalded chicken (*masmūṭ*),[21] wash it, and cut it at the joints. When the pot comes to a light boil [at the initial stage], add the chicken to the meat, and let them cook together until it is done. For those who prefer the dish to be noticeably sweet, let them add more sugar, which can be replaced with honey.

(15) *Fustuqiyya* (stew with pistachios)

Cut the meat and [put it in the pot] with enough water to submerge it. [Bring it to a boil], remove the scum, and let it boil. When the meat is half cooked, add to it small meatballs (*kubab*), seasoned with all the components of *aṭrāf al-ṭīb* (spice blend).[22] Also, add cassia (*dār Ṣīnī*), mastic gum, salt, sesame oil, and mint to the pot.

When the pot is cooked and only a small amount of its liquid remains, remove the liquid [and set it aside]. Fry the meat [in the pot] with sheep-tail fat (*duhn*) and spices. Then return the liquid, and thicken it with pounded pistachios. After cooking is resumed, adjust the taste with lemon juice, and sprinkle the pot with a small amount of rosewater. Wipe the [inner] sides of the pot, let it simmer on the smoldering fire, and then remove. (**16v**)

Recipe for *mudaqqaqa Miṣriyya* (Egyptian dish of pounded meat)[23]

Take meat and pound it until it is the size of peppercorns. Put it in a pot with water, enough to cover it by twice its bulk. Let it boil, remove the scum, and throw in pounded cassia (*dār Ṣīnī*) and mastic, along with mint.

---

20 The verb used to designate the action of blending ground almonds with rosewater is *yudhāb* (يذاب) lit., 'dissolve.' In the previous recipes, the term used was *yurabbā*. See n. 13 above.

21 After slaughtering a chicken, it was first briefly dipped in boiling water to make the task of plucking the feathers quicker and easier.

22 See glossary 8, for a recipe.

23 Included in Gotha fol. 15r.

Let the pot boil until the meat is cooked, and then [take the liquid out and] strain it. Fry the meat, and return the broth to it, along with the chickpeas that were boiled with the meat. Chop and add Macedonian parsley (*baqdūnis*) and mint, along with spices (*abāzīr*).

When the pot boils, throw in rice that has been picked over and washed. Adjust the flavor by adding lemon juice, and let the pot simmer on the smoldering fire, and then remove.

(16) *Rībāsiyya* (sour rhubarb stew)

It is made with meat, which has been boiled and then sweated with some spices.[24] Add to it a small amount of finely chopped onion, and pour rhubarb juice on it. Also, add finely pounded sweet almonds which have been blended with water (*murabbā*). Crumble a sprig[25] of dried mint on top of it, let it simmer on a low fire, and then remove the pot.

(17) *Amīrbārīsiyya* (sour barberry stew)[26]

It is made like *summāqiyya* (a sour sumac dish),[27] just replace the sumac with (*amīr bārīs*) barberries, and instead of walnuts use finely crushed skinned almonds. Some people like to sweeten it with a little sugar.

[*Summāqiyya* (sour sumac stew)[28]

Take fatty meat, cut it into pieces, and boil it in water, enough to cover it by twice its bulk, adding cassia (*dār Ṣīnī*), mastic, and olive oil. Remove the scum, and throw in meatballs (*kubāb*) seasoned with spices. Also, add leeks (*qirṭ*),[29] rice (*aruzz*), and mint.

---

24 This cooking technique is called *taʿrīq*. See n. 15 above.

25 In the edited text, it occurs as *bāqa* (باقة) 'bunch,' in *Waṣf* as *ṭāqa* (طاقة) 'sprig,' and in C as *tāqa* (تاقة), which is probably a spoken Egyptian variant of the word. I chose *ṭāqa*, because a whole bunch of mint will impart an overwhelmingly minty flavor.

26 Sometimes more accurately called *barbārīs*. Another name for it is *zirishk*.

27 Up to this point in the *Kanz*, there has not been a recipe for *summāqiyya* (although there are a couple further in the chapter, recipes 55 and 56).

Both Baghdādī BL, fol. 18r, and *Waṣf* 18 include a recipe almost identical with this barberry recipe, but at this point, they have already given a couple of *summāqiyya* recipes. The compiler of the *Kanz* must have opted to overlook them, not realizing that this barberry recipe is dependent on them. I am providing a sumac recipe right after this one, to make it more coherent.

28 Recipe from *Waṣf* 16–7. See above note.

29 *Qirṭ* is another name for *kurrāth* 'leaf leeks,' as another *summāqiyya* recipe, *Waṣf* 18, explains.

وقال غيره
ومن العجائب والعجائب جمة قرب الجبيب وما اليه وصول
كالعيش افلا ما يكون من الظما والماء وظهورها
محمول
سُمَّاق حَشَن معروفة جِلَّة
تنبت بنفسها من غير عرس وسعي من الناس

FIGURE 21   Sumac, al-ʿUmarī, Masālik al-abṣār, fol. 179r (BnF, Department of manuscripts, Arab 2771).

When the meat is cooked, remove the liquid in the pot, fry the pieces of meat, and return the liquid, which should not be much.

Boil the sumac berries in water with a piece of bread in it. Strain the juice, and add it to the meat and meatballs. Arrange in the pot pieces of eggplant fried in sesame oil (*shayraj*) or sheep-tail fat (*duhn alya*), along with all kinds of spices, *aṭrāf al-ṭīb* (spice blend), mint, and tahini. Throw in shelled walnuts, skinned almonds, and crushed garlic. Let the pot simmer on a low fire, and then remove.]

(18) *Ḥiṣrimiyya* (sour stew with juice of unripe grapes)

Cut fatty meat into pieces, or use chicken cut at the joints. Throw it into the pot to sweat (*yuʿarraq*),[30] adding spices, namely, coriander and cumin.

This dish is best cooked with fine-tasting, aged juice of unripe grapes (*māʾ al-ḥiṣrim al-ʿatīq al-ʿadhb*). However, if fresh grapes are used, then it is better if the juice is pressed by hand rather than by cooking them first. Add a bit of salt and sprigs of mint and thyme to the extracted juice so that it can absorb their flavors. Set it aside, let it settle [and then collect the clear liquid]. Now, take the thick grape juice that has settled, add water to it, and press and mash it (*yumras*), and then strain it.

Add all the strained grape juices to the meat. That is, after you [initially boil the meat], remove the scum, add sesame oil to it and let it cook until [all the moisture evaporates and] nothing remains but the fats, and add onion chopped into small pieces. Now, add the grape juice, along with mint, rue (*sadhāb*), and some stalks of purslane (*baqla ḥamqāʾ*). (**17r**) When it is all cooked, add rose petal jam.

If the taste lacks acidity, strengthen it with lemon juice, and add a few drops of rosewater. If you like, add leeks or onion and carrots to it;[31] but boil them in a separate pot first and then add them.

You may also like to make it with Persian yogurt (*laban Fārisī*):[32] blend it with the grape juice and let it boil, and then add the meat [that has been boiled, skimmed and sweated with sesame oil, as mentioned above]. When this boils and the dish is half cooked, add the spices, [and let it simmer on the smoldering fire.]

---

30 This cooking technique is called *taʿrīq*. See n. 15 above.

31 I follow *Waṣf* 20, where the word occurs as carrot (جزر) and not walnut (جوز) in the edited text. Clearly, the recipe is dealing with vegetables. I also used the *Waṣf* to make small amendments in the edited text.

32 Another name for it is *laban shīrāz*, which is thick drained yogurt.

(19) Recipe for *nāranjiyya* (sour orange stew)[33]

Cut fatty meat into medium chunks and put it in the pot with enough water to submerge it. Bring it to a boil, remove the scum, and add salt as needed. Chop onion and large Levantine leeks (*kurrāth Shāmī*);[34] wash carrots, remove their hard cores, and chop them into small pieces, and add them all to the pot. Throw salt and the above-mentioned spices and sprigs of mint into the pot.[35] For those who want to add meatballs, pound red (i.e., lean) meat, shape it into medium-sized balls, and add them to the pot.

Take oranges, peel them and remove the white pith, cut them into halves, and squeeze their juice through a colander (*miṣfāt*) or a sieve (*munkhul*). The person who does the peeling should be different from the one who juices it.[36]

Now take safflower seeds (*ḥabb al-qurṭum*),[37] which have been picked over, washed, soaked in hot water for an hour, (17v) and finely crush them in a stone mortar (*hāwan*). If this is not available, then use a rust-free copper one instead. Extract their juice (*yustaḥlab*) by hand, and then strain it and add it to the pot. Crumble a few sprigs of dried mint; and wipe the [inner] sides of the pot with a clean cloth as usual. Leave the pot [on the smoldering fire] for an hour, and then remove it.

(20) Another *nāranjiyya*, outstanding (*ʿāl*)[38]

Boil meat in a small amount of water, remove the scum, and then add sesame oil, along with cassia (*dār Ṣīnī*) and mastic gum. When the meat is almost done, throw into the pot pounded chicken breast mixed with meat: for each chicken breast use 2 *ūqiyyas* (2 ounces) of meat.[39] However, before adding this [pounded] meat to the pot, it should be made into meatballs filled with pistachios, and then added. When all this is fully cooked, [drain the boiling liquid] and set it aside; and fry the meats.

---

33 I amended this recipe based on Baghdādī BL fols. 21v–2r; and *Waṣf* 26–7.

34 This is the large bulbous variety of leeks.

35 No spices are mentioned above. In fact, Baghdādī BL version is the only one that lists the spices. They are cumin, coriander, cassia sticks (*dār Ṣīnī*), black pepper, ginger, and mastic, all finely pounded.

36 This is stressed here because the peel is bitter.

37 This is also called *ḥabb al-ʿuṣfur*. They are added to thicken the stew.

38 I used the corresponding recipes in Baghdādī BL, fols. 21v–2r and *Waṣf* 27 to amend the edited text in several places.

39 The corresponding recipes in Baghdādī BL and *Waṣf* specify the Iraqi *ūqiyya*. The measuring units at that time differed from one region to the other. Such a recipe is a clear indication that al-Baghdādī's cookbook was used outside Iraq. The meat specified in these two sources is lamb (*laḥm kharūf*).

Extract some almond milk [by pounding the almonds with water, and straining the juice]. Take a good amount of it and add it to the fried meat and meatballs. Add meat broth (*māʾ al-laḥm*), use only a small amount. Then add sugar syrup (*jullāb*), mint, galangal (*khūlanjān*), and pieces of ginger. By the time everything is cooked, you will have already sectioned the peeled oranges, [removed the membranes], discarded the seeds, and divided juice vesicles into chunks (*fuṣūṣ*), and set them aside on a plate.[40]

Now add the orange prepared as we have just described to the pot, and let it simmer for an hour [on the smoldering fire]. Add to it [dried] mint, pistachios, and rosewater. [The pistachios] need to be pounded first.[41] (**18r**)

Sour *sanbūsak*[42]

Take fine lean [ground] meat, as much as you wish, boil it, spread it to drain,[43] and set it aside. Take *ḥawāʾij al-baql*, which is Macedonian parsley (*maqdūnis*),[44] as needed, and chop the leaves. Also, chop the core of an onion and mint. Split skinned almonds in half, and toast hazelnuts and crush it coarsely. Combine the meat and the rest of the prepared *ḥawāʾij* (ingredients), but the parsley needs to be lightly pounded [before adding it to the meat mix]. Color it with saffron, and spice it as we will mention.

Boil a small amount of vinegar with a bit of lime juice (*laymūn akhḍar*). The meat and the other ingredients (*ḥawāʾij*) should be added to the vinegar mix while it is still on the fire. So, when the vinegar heats up, add the meat and the other ingredients to it, and stir until the mix combines and blends well. Throw

---

40 The juice vesicles of the orange (and any other citrus fruits) are called *shaʿr* 'hair,' as in Baghdādī BL, and *shuʿayr*, as in *Waṣf*.

41 At this point in the edited text, the recipe continues for four lines, giving unrelated instructions. Upon examining Gotha, these lines belong to a *kishk* recipe (meat dish with *kishk*), given after a couple of recipes on *sanbūsak* (filled pastries, made with thin sheets of dough), which the edited text does not include at this point. Both Gotha, fol. 17r and *Zahr*, fol. 7r provide the entire *kishk* recipe (the former is more complete). The *Kanz* copyist must have accidentally skipped a folio, or just followed an already flawed copy. Here I provide the missing folio.

42 This recipe is only in Gotha, fols. 16v–7r; and *Waṣf* 44–5. I used the latter to amend the text. *Sanbūsak* are filled pastries made with thin sheets of dough, ancestors of the Ottoman *būreg*.

43 To drain hot cooked foods, they were spread on latticed trays made from date palm fronds or branches of willow tree (*khilāf*).

44 More commonly called *baqdūnis*. This addition appears in *Waṣf* only. Generally, *ḥawāʾij al-baql* are the familiar fresh herbs used in cooking the dishes, such as leaf leeks, mint, parsley, and cilantro.

in the spices,[45] and then remove the pot, and let it cool down. Make sure not to use too much vinegar.

When ready, take thin sheets of *ruqāq* bread or *kunāfa* (crepes),[46] cut them, as usual, and stuff them.[47] Prepare soft dough made with flour, and use it to seal the pieces, so that they do not open in the frying pan (*ṭājin*).[48] When you are done filling the pieces, take a large brass pot (*dast*), put enough sesame oil in it, fry the pieces, and then take them out [and serve].

Sweet sanbūsak[49]

[This] is done as mentioned above, except neither vinegar nor lemon is used. If you want to sweeten it with some sugar, then go ahead and do so.

Kishk[50]

For each 1½ *raṭls* (1½ pounds) of meat use 1 *raṭl kishk*, 1½ *ūqiyyas* (1½ ounces) garlic; 6 heads of onion; 2 *dirhams* (6 grams/approx. 1 teaspoon) each of caraway and black pepper; 4 sticks of cassia (*dār Ṣīnī*), and four lemons.

Fry the meat with one onion and a bit of black pepper. When it is nicely done, pound the garlic with olive oil and salt, add it to the pot, and stir. When the garlic is nicely cooked, pour water [on the meat and bring it to a boil]. Rinse the *kishk* twice, and then add enough water to submerge it, and press and mash it (*tamrusuhu*).

When the water in the meat pot starts boiling,[51] add the *kishk* to it, feed the fire, and continue stirring so that it does not stick to the pot (*lā yaʿluq*). Next, cut the onions but not all the way through,[52] and add them to the pot along with the spices (*abāzīr*), as well as caraway, mint, and cassia (*dār Ṣīnī*). Continue feeding the fire, and cook the dish until it is done, and tastes good.

---

45 These must be the familiar spices usually added to this type of dishes, see, for instance, recipe 127 below.

46 For more information on these types of thin breads, see glossary 2.

47 For more details on how these pastries are stuffed, see recipes 115, 116, 127.

48 A *ṭājin* is a low-sided pot; the word was sometimes used loosely to designate any frying pan. Notice that in the following sentence, the recipe mentions frying the pastries in a large brass pot '*dast*,' to indicate that the pastries are to be deep-fried.

49 This recipe only appears in Gotha, fol. 17r.

50 This recipe is in Gotha, fol. 17r; as well as *Zahr* 7r, and *Waṣf* 47, which I used here to amend Gotha recipe. This *kishk* stew is named after the ingredient *kishk*, dried clumps or discs of dough of crushed wheat and yogurt, used to enhance and enrich the sauce. See glossary 3.

51 At this point, we return to the edited text, where the recipe continues. See n. 41 above.

52 The expression is تقطع البصل صحيحا; it means that the onions should be sliced into large sections, but left intact.

Squeeze the juice of the four lemons on top of it, and let the pot simmer on the smoldering fire and fully cook, and then remove. It is splendid.

[Here begin recipes for dishes with very little sauce in them, called *nawāshif* (lit., 'dry') and *qalāyā* (fried), using diced and pounded meat, often shaped into meatballs.]

(21) Recipe for *qaliyya* (fried dish)

Finely pound meat and boil it in sumac juice (*mā' al-summāq*).[53] Boil with it meatballs made from another batch of pounded meat. Drain the meats, and add to them salt, pounded coriander, cassia (*dār Ṣīnī*), black pepper, and mastic gum; use enough to balance the taste. Crumble some sprigs of dried mint over them.

Now, take fresh sheep-tail fat (*alya*), chop it, render it (*tusla'*), and discard the solids (*shaḥm*).[54] Fry the meats in this fat (*duhn*), making sure it is enough so that they come out nice and moist.

When the meat is perfectly browned in the frying pan (*miqlā*), break some eggs on it, sunny side up (*'uyūn al-bayḍ*). Wipe the sides—I mean the sides of the frying pan—with a clean cloth, and sprinkle the dish with rosewater.

(22) Recipe for *makhfiyya* (lit., 'hidden')[55]

Chop fatty meat into small pieces. Render sheep-tail fat, discarding its solids (*ḥumam*). Fry the meat in it, adding salt and coriander. (**18v**) Pour off the fat in the pot, and set it aside. Add water to the meat, bring it to a boil, remove the scum, and throw in sprigs of cilantro (*kuzbara khaḍrā'*), grated sticks of cassia (*dār Ṣīnī*), a handful of coarsely crushed (*marḍūḍ*) skinned chickpeas, and two or three skinned and chopped onions.

Take as much trimmed meat (*laḥm aḥmar*) as needed, and finely pound it with salt and spices. Take the yolks out of boiled eggs, and stuff the pounded meat with it, to make meatballs (*kubab*). Boil these in the pot. When they are done cooking, return the fat that was set aside to the pot, sprinkle a bit of *murrī* (liquid fermented sauce),[56] adjust salt and spices, and let the pot simmer on a low fire for an hour. Sprinkle it with finely pounded cassia (*dār Ṣīnī*) and then remove. It is a wonderful dish (*ghāya*).

---

53 This is obtained by soaking sumac berries in hot water, or boiling them in water with a piece of bread, and then straining the resulting liquid.

54 More accurately called *ḥumam*. *Shaḥm* more commonly designates the solid fat 'suet.'

55 Here I amended the edited name of the dish following Gotha, fol. 17v; and *Waṣf* 67–8. The recipe also occurs in Baghdādī BL, fols. 46r–v, but with extra details.

56 This addition only appears in *Waṣf*.

FIGURE 22 *Mulberry, F1954.74v, Muḥammad al-Qazwīnī,* ʿAjāʾib al-makhlūqāt, *detail (Freer Gallery of Art and Arthur M. Sackler Gallery, Smithsonian Institution, Washington, DC: Purchase—Charles Lang Freer Endowment).*

(23) Recipe for *yāqūtiyya* (carnelian)[57]

Sweat the meat as usual;[58] adding whatever enhances its flavor, such as olive oil (*zayt*), cassia (*dār Ṣīnī*), mastic gum, and the like. Cut gourds (*yaqṭīn*) into chunks (*fuṣūṣ*), and add them to the pot. When it is almost done, throw in juice of red mulberry (*tūt aḥmar*), and sweeten it with honey (*ʿasal naḥl*), sugar (*sukkar*), or sugar syrup (*jullāb*). Let it cook well, and then crumble some sprigs of [dried] mint over it. Keep the pot on low heat to simmer for an hour, and then ladle and serve the dish.

(24) Recipe for *mudaqqaqa ḥāmiḍa* (sour pounded meat)[59]

Slice trimmed meat and pound it very well. (**19r**) Add salt to it, along with the familiar spices and a bit of finely chopped onion. Form it into meatballs, make as many as you need, and boil them in moderately salted water (*milḥ muʿtadil*). When the meatballs are cooked, drain them.

---

57 This is available in *Waṣf* 55, as well.

58 This initial step in cooking is called *taʿrīq*. See glossary 9.2.

59 *Mudaqqaqa* is usually used to designate dishes cooked with pounded/ground meat, which is left loose or shaped into patties or meatballs, as in this recipe. This recipe is also available in *Waṣf* 59–60.

Take some sheep-tail fat (*alya*); render it, discarding any remaining solid pieces of fat.[60] Throw the meatballs into this fat along with pieces of onion. For the souring agent, some may choose to sprinkle it with juice of citron pulp (*māʾ ḥummāḍ*), vinegar, juice of unripe grapes, or lemon juice. Alternatively, use a mixture of two of them. For those who like to color the dish with saffron, let them add it to the vinegar or lemon juice, as needed. Also, sprinkle some of the familiar spices on it. If you prefer, crumble sprigs of [dried] mint on it. Leave it on the smoldering fire to simmer, and then remove.[61]

(25) Recipe for *ḥiṣrimiyya* (meat with sour juice of unripe grapes)[62]
It is made with meat,[63] sheep-tail fat, and meatballs (*kubab*). They are boiled along with a handful of skinned chickpeas, until done. Then the salt and spices are adjusted. Sunny side up eggs, as many as needed, are spread on it, and cassia (*dār Ṣīnī*) is sprinkled all over. It is left on the smoldering fire to simmer, and then taken away.

(26) Recipe for *manbūsha* (stirred-up meat)[64]
Pound trimmed meat very well, and remove the veins.[65] Put the meat in a pot with enough water to cover it. When it boils, skim the froth, and add a handful of skinned and coarsely crushed chickpeas. When all of it is cooked, adjust the salt, and drain the meat. **(19v)**

Render some fresh sheep-tail fat, and discard the remaining solid fat. Put the meat in it and let it sweat (*yuʿarraq*), while adding the familiar spices.[66] Some people like to put eggs sunny side up on top of it. Sprinkle the dish with finely pounded cassia (*dār Ṣīnī*), and wipe the sides of the pot (*qidr*) with a clean cloth. Let it cook on low heat for an hour and then remove.

60 *Shaḥm* 'suet' is more accurately called *ḥumam* in *Waṣf* 59.

61 In *Zahr* 35, the recipe adds that it is essential to remove the blood vessels (*ʿurūq*) from the pounded meat. Because they are muscular and elastic in texture, they will not grind as well as meat does, and this will spoil the texture of the meatballs.

62 The recipe does not mention the juice of unripe grapes. However, judging from recipe 18 above for *ḥiṣrimiyya*, the meat is to be boiled with some of the juice to give it the desired sourness.

63 Judging from the rest of the recipes in this category, the meat is either pounded or chopped into small pieces.

64 Also in *Waṣf* 64–5; and Baghdādī BL, fol. 43r–v, where the recipe is given with more details. The dish is called this because the ground meat is stirred up and looks like dug-up earth.

65 See n. 61 above.

66 See glossary 9.2, s.v. *taʿrīq*. In Baghdādī BL, the verb is *yatawarrad* (nicely brown).

A frying pan (*miqlā*) ought to be used in cooking this dish, instead of a regular pot with high sides (*qidr*). Indeed, this should be the case with any fried (*qalāyā*) dishes, and those with very little sauce in them (*nawāshif*).

(27) Recipe for *dīnāriyya* ('gold coins' of meat patties and carrots)[67]

Cut fatty meat into small pieces. Sweat it in fat first and then boil it with enough water to cover it.[68] When it boils, skim the froth, and add 1 *dirham* (3 grams/½ teaspoon) salt, a stick of cassia (*dār Ṣīnī*), and some leaves of cilantro to the pot.

Pound as much trimmed meat as needed, shape it into discs like dinars, and boil them with the meat. When all the meat is fully cooked, [take it out of the pot,] fry it in rendered sheep-tail fat with some spices, and put it aside.

Take large carrots,[69] scrape their skins,[70] and cut them like *dinar*s [i.e., discs]. Throw them into the pot, along with a small handful of finely chopped skinned onion. Adjust salt and spices.

When the carrots are cooked al dente,[71] return [the chopped meat and] the meat patties to the pot. Slice some boiled eggs and arrange them on top of all of it, and give them a sprinkle of finely ground cassia (*dār Ṣīnī*). (**20r**) If you like, sprinkle the meat with a bit of *murrī* (liquid fermented sauce) before arranging the egg slices. Wipe the [inner] sides of the pot, and leave it [on the smoldering fire] to simmer.

(28) *Ruṭabiyya* (meat with fresh dates)

Cut trimmed meat into small pieces, boil it until it is done, and then strain it and fry it in freshly rendered sheep-tail fat. Adjust salt and spices. When the meat is thoroughly fried, arrange as many fresh dates (*ruṭab*) on top of it as needed. Leave it on the smoldering fire for an hour to simmer, and then remove.

It may also be cooked as follows: Take the stones out of the dates using a *misalla* (large needle), and replace them with skinned whole almonds [and add to the stew]. Also, add meatballs made with pounded trimmed meat. Elongate the meatballs to resemble the shape of dates. Stuff an almond in the middle of

---

67 Recipes 27–35 in the edited text are also found in *Waṣf* 68–75, which will be used to amend the text where needed. Baghdādī BL, on which *Waṣf* was largely based, also contains copies of these recipes, but the versions in the former are generally better written and have more detail.

68 On sweating the meat, see glossary 9.2, s.v. *taʿrīq*.

69 Only Baghdādī BL specifies that the carrots should be large.

70 The verb is clearly written as يحك in Gotha, fol. 18v, and ينحت in *Waṣf* and Baghdādī BL.

71 The Arabic is نضج الجزر وبقي فيه ادنى قوة.

each [and arrange them on top of the dish, as described above]. Sprinkle the surface with a little bit of rosewater, color it with a small amount of saffron, and let it simmer on the smoldering fire for an hour, and then remove.

(29) As for *tamriyya* (meat cooked with dried dates), it is made the same way [as described above, but using *tamr*] when fresh dates are not available.

(30) *Mudaqqaqa sādhaja* (plain pounded meat)[72]

Cut fatty meat into small pieces and put it in a pot with enough water to cover it [and bring it to a boil]. Take trimmed meat, finely pound it, add to it as much salt and spices as it can take, (**20v**) in addition to a handful of skinned and coarsely crushed chickpeas and another handful of washed rice (*aruzz*). Shape the meat into meatballs, and drop them into the pot; put as many as you like.

When the meat is fully cooked, season it with whatever salt and spices it needs. Take out most of the liquid in the pot, and add as much fat as needed. Sprinkle the surface with finely ground cassia (*dār Ṣīnī*), and after an hour of simmering on low heat, remove.

(31) *Khashkhāshiyya* (meat with poppy seeds)[73]

Cut trimmed meat into small slices. Render some fresh sheep-tail fat, and discard the remaining sediment (*shaḥm*).[74] Add the meat to the rendered fat, and continue stirring until it nicely browns (*yatawarrad*). Sprinkle on it ½ *dirham* (1½ grams/¼ teaspoon) salt, and the same amount of crushed coriander. Then, cover it with lukewarm water (*māʾ fātir*); and when it boils, skim the froth. Add a finely grated stick of cassia (*dār Ṣīnī*) and a bit of finely pounded ginger.

Now, add to the pot 1½ Iraqi *raṭl*s hot water (approx. 1½ pints/3 cups)—it [i.e., the Iraqi *raṭl*] equals 130 *dirhams*.[75] Also, add 150 *dirhams* (1¼ cups) sugar or bee honey. When the sugar dissolves, sprinkle a handful of poppy-seed flour on it, and stir well until the dish is cooked and thickened.

Throw 30 *dirhams* (approx. 3 ounces/¾ cup) fresh poppy seeds into the pot and stir the pot to mix the ingredients. Color it with saffron, sprinkle the

---

72 It is neither sweet nor sour. Here I slightly amended the edited recipe based on Baghdādī BL version, fol. 48r.

73 Here I amended the recipe at several places based on Baghdādī BL version, fol. 49r.

74 See n. 54 above.

75 The Egyptian *raṭl* equals 144 *dirhams*. This is an interesting instance of how a borrowed recipe was adjusted for its Egyptian users. The original recipe gives the weight by '*raṭl*' only.

surface with a bit of rosewater, (21r) and leave the pot on the smoldering fire to simmer for an hour, and then remove.

(32) Recipe for *ʿunnābiyya* (meat with jujubes)[76]

Cut trimmed meat into small pieces and boil it in water. Add meatballs made with lean pounded meat, each shaped like a jujube fruit. When all the meat is cooked, take it out, color it with saffron, and return it to the pot. Adjust the taste with salt and spices, and then drain the meat and throw it into freshly rendered sheep-tail fat.

Take fresh jujubes, as many as needed, and add them to the pot. Sprinkle [the surface] with a bit of rosewater, and wipe the [inner] sides of the pot with a cloth. Do not leave the pot on the fire until the jujubes become mushy (*yataharraʾ*). It should be taken away while they are still nicely firm to the touch (*maska laṭīfa*).

(33) Recipe for *fālūdhajiyya* (meat dish, which resembles *fālūdhaj*)[77]

Cut meat into small rectangular pieces, and after you sweat it,[78] cover it with water, [bring it to a boil], and skim the froth. When the meat is done, and all the liquid has evaporated, add sugar or honey, as much as needed. Also, add a handful of coarsely crushed skinned almonds. Color the dish with saffron and add rosewater. Continue stirring until it thickens.

Leave the pot on the [smoldering] fire to let it simmer. Ladle the dish, and arrange fried *sanbūsak* pastries, filled with almonds and sugar on top of it.[79]

If you perfume it with a little bit of camphor (*kāfūr*), sprinkled all over it, it will indeed be superb (*ghāya*).

***Bunduqiyya* (dish with hazelnut-like meatballs)**[80]

Cut trimmed meat into small pieces, cover it with water in a pot, and skim the froth when it starts boiling. Add a handful of coarsely crushed chickpeas to it.

---

76 See glossary 7, s.v. *ʿunnāb*.

77 *Fālūdhaj* is starch-based thick pudding; see glossary 4. Interestingly, in *Zahr*, fol. 8r, which is an abridged version of our edited text, Ibn Mubārak Shāh (d. 1458) gives the same recipe but calls it *māwardiyya* (rosewater-scented pudding). At the end of the recipe, he explains that in olden times it was called *fālūdhajiyya*.

78 In Gotha, fol. 20r, the word is clearly written as يعرق. On sweating the meat, see glossary 9.2, s.v. *taʿrīq*.

79 Here I amended the text based on *Waṣf* 72. For sweet *sanbūsak*, see recipe 115 below.

80 This recipe is available in Gotha, fol. 20r; DK, appendix 7; Baghdādī BL, fol. 50v; and *Waṣf* 72.

Make meatballs (*kubab*) with pounded trimmed meat seasoned with the familiar spices, and fill each meatball with some of the cooked chickpeas. Shape the meatballs like hazelnuts and throw them into the pot. When they are almost done, add 2 *dirhams* (6 grams/1 teaspoon) coriander, cumin, caraway, black pepper, mastic gum, and cassia (*dār Ṣīnī*), [all] finely pounded. Keep the pot on the smoldering fire to let it simmer, and then remove.

(34) Recipe for *mawziyya* (meat dish with bananas)[81]
Take trimmed meat (21v) from a fat sheep (*kharūf samīn*), and take a similar amount of its sheep-tail fat (*alya*). Put them in a pot with a bit of cassia (*dār Ṣīnī*), mastic gum, and coriander. Add enough water to cover the meat, bring it to a boil and remove the frothy scum (*zafar*). When the meat is almost done, pour off the liquid, and fry the meat in sheep-tail fat.

Pound one part pistachios, one part toasted hazelnuts, and two parts sugar. Mix and combine these with a bit of saffron steeped in rosewater. Take half of this mixture and throw it on top of the meat in the pot, and remove the fuel from the fire underneath the pot. Next, arrange slices of very ripe yellow bananas on top.[82] Cover the bananas with what remains of the mix of pistachios, hazelnuts, and sugar. Sprinkle a little bit of rosewater on it, cover the pot, let it simmer, and then remove and serve. Do not feed the fire [in this last stage].

(35) Recipe for *qaliyyat al-shawī* (fried roasted meat)[83]
Take the previous day's cold roasted meat and chop it into small pieces. Fry it in sesame oil (*shayraj*), and when the meat is cooked and its fat has melted, add whatever spices it needs. For those who want it sour (*muḥammaḍa*), sprinkle a bit of vinegar or lemon juice on it. For those who want to top it with eggs sunny side up, let them do so. Sprinkle a little bit of cassia (*dār Ṣīnī*), leave it for a while on a low fire, and then remove it.

(36) Recipe for *maṣlūqa* (boiled meat)
It is usually cooked in a new earthenware pot (*qidr fakhkhār*) or a tinned copper (*nuḥās mubayyaḍ*) pot. Add water equal to the amount of meat or chicken used. Throw some mastic gum and cassia (*dār Ṣīnī*) into the pot. (**22r**) Get a

81 A copy of this recipe can also be found in *Wuṣla* ii 612–3; and *Waṣf* 74. Here I used them to amend the edited text.

82 Here I amended the edited text, replacing لوز 'almond' with موز 'banana,' as it occurs in Gotha, fol. 20v; and *Waṣf* 74. In addition, the *Waṣf* and *Wuṣla* clearly call for very ripe yellow bananas (موز اصفر منتهي).

83 This recipe also appears in *Waṣf* 75–6.

lamb hock (*ʿurqūb*) from the butcher, and add it to the pot. Cover it [while cooking] so that the food does not become discolored from the smoke. Some people take the juice extract from finely crushed boiled almonds, and add it to the pot when it is taken off the heat.

Sprinkle a small amount of rosewater and add a couple of cilantro sprigs to it.

Recipe for *qamḥiyya* (meat dish with wheat berries)[84]

Wash wheat berries (*qamḥ*) very well and add them to the pot after the water in it has come to a full boil. Let it boil until you see that the wheat berries start splitting. Strain them and set them aside.

With a fresh change of water, cook the meat but do not add salt to it until you take it off the heat. Put the meat [and the boiled berries in a pot], cover the pot [to protect the cooking food from smoke], all the time, replenish with cold water whatever liquid is lost. Throw in dill, mastic gum, and cassia (*dār Ṣīnī*).

When you ladle the food, you should have [crushed] cumin and cassia ready [to sprinkle on the dishes]. Protect the pot from smoke [while cooking].

(37) Recipe for fried *shishbarak* (raviolis)[85]

Take very well kneaded dough. Make [pastries] shaped like *mukaffan* (rolls)[86] and *sanbūsak* (triangles), stuffed with the usual *sanbūsak* filling—sweet, sour, and plain. Fry them.

If you are cooking the dish with yogurt, take the dough and roll it out like *ṭuṭmāj* (thin sheets of fresh pasta),[87] and cut out circles with the rim of a clean cup (*kūz*). Stuff them, as mentioned above [they will look like half circles]. Boil some water for them, and when ready, throw them in, but do not let them stick to each other. When they are done, take them out with a *jāwlī*,[88] and put them in yogurt or [liquid of dried] pomegranate seeds [which have been steeped in hot water, and then mashed and drained].[89]

---

84 This recipe also appears in DK, appendix 8; Gotha, fol. 21r; and *Zahr*, fol. 8r.

85 Here I used the correct name for the dish, as given in Gotha, fol. 21r.

86 *Mukaffan* (lit., 'shrouded') is similar to today's *būreg*, rolled like cigars. To the medieval imagination, they looked like a shrouded body. In Baghdādī 77, there is a sweet recipe for *mukaffan*, where a sheet of flattened taffy is cut into squares, sprinkled with nuts and sugar, and rolled. For *sanbūsak* fillings, see pp. 95–6 above.

87 See glossary 2.

88 In Steingass Persian/English dictionary, it occurs as *chāwlī*. It is a winnowing fan made of reeds, known in Arabic as *minsaf*.

89 *Ḥabb al-rummān* 'pomegranate seeds' are used in dried form unless otherwise specified.

[The following recipes, 38–52, are cooked with chicken.]

(38) Recipe for *dajāj maṣlūq* (boiled chicken)

Slaughter the chicken, scald it, and clean it. Wash it several times with water, salt, and olive oil. Boil water, and when it is hot enough, put the chicken in it, after you have cut it at the joints. Remove the scum, and add a handful of coarsely crushed chickpeas, the white head of an onion, a sprig of dill, mastic gum, cassia (*dār Ṣīnī*), and sesame oil. (**22v**)

Remove the chicken brain and dissolve it in a small amount of the broth, and return it to the pot. Continue feeding the fire until the chicken is done, and then leave it on the smoldering fire to let it simmer, and then remove. It will be splendid.

Recipe for *dajāj maḥshī khāṣṣ* (excellent stuffed chicken)[90]

Boil the chicken until it is half done, and then color it with saffron and fry it in sesame oil. Take chopped Macedonian parsley (*baqdūnis*), toasted hazelnuts, crushed coriander seeds, olive oil, and tahini (*ṭaḥīna*). First, pound the herbs (*ḥawāʾij al-baql*) in a *hāwan* (mortar), and then the other ingredients (*ḥawāʾij*) [i.e., the hazelnuts and coriander]. Knead them all with lemon juice, olive oil, and tahini. Stuff the chicken with it. Sumac may be added to it, too.

Resume the cooking of the chicken once more. Take some of the stuffing and add a small amount of the chicken broth to it, [stir] and return it to the boiling pot [to enrich the sauce].

Recipe for *dajāj maḥshī ḥulw* (sweet stuffed chicken)[91]

Take sugar, pistachios or almonds, musk, and rosewater, and stuff a chicken with them, after [first] braising and coloring it with saffron.[92] Put the chicken in sauce made of sugar syrup (*jullāb*), honey, or rose-petal jam (*ward murabbā*), and [pounded] almonds, which have [all] been boiled until thickened. Whatever variations you make will be good.

(39) Recipe for chicken prepared as *bunduqiyya* (chicken cooked with hazelnuts)

Take 1 *raṭl* (1 pound) bee honey and 2 *ūqiyyas* (2 ounces) sugar, and boil them until thick in consistency. Stir in toasted hazelnuts. [Additionally,] you will

---

90 Given only in DK, appendix 9; and Gotha, fols. 21v–2r. I restructured the recipe in a few places to straighten out the meaning.

91 This was found only in Gotha, fol. 22r.

92 The Arabic word for braising is تطجين, which suggests an initial stage of frying the meat and then letting it slowly cook in a small amount of liquid. See glossary 9.2, s.v. *tatjīn*.

FIGURE 23 *Hazelnut, F1954.78r, Muḥammad al-Qazwīnī,* ʿAjāʾib al-makhlūqāt, *detail (Freer Gallery of Art and Arthur M. Sackler Gallery, Smithsonian Institution, Washington, DC: Purchase—Charles Lang Freer Endowment).*

have prepared small balls (*banādiq*) made with sugar, [pounded] almonds, musk, rosewater, and camphor. Add these to the [cooked] honey mix.

Fry a chicken (*yuṭajjan*), and stuff it with a mix of sugar, [pounded] toasted hazelnuts, rosewater, and saffron to color it. While the chicken is still hot, put it in the [prepared] honey mix. Season the pot with some aromatic spices, and then remove.

(40) *Dajāj zīrbāj* (delicately sour golden chicken stew)

After you boil a chicken in salted water seasoned with mastic gum and cassia (*dār Ṣīnī*), cut it at the joints or in half. However, it would be better if you leave it whole.

Sweat the chicken and brown it in fresh sesame oil,[93] adding coriander, mastic gum, and cassia. After that, sauce it (*yumraq*) with [a mix of] sugar, saffron, *aṭrāf al-ṭīb* (spice blend), and skinned sweet almonds, pounded and blended with water (*murabbā*).[94] Throw in a sprig of fresh mint.

93 For details on the technique of sweating meat, see glossary 9.2, s.v. *taʿrīq*.

94 See glossary 9.2, s.v. *yurabbā*.

(41) Recipe for *dajāja ḥāmiḍa* (sour chicken)

Chicken [is cooked as described above and] with a sauce of sumac liquid (*māʾ summāq*), [dried] pomegranate seeds (*ḥabb rummān*), juice of unripe grapes (*māʾ ḥiṣrim*) or lemon juice (*māʾ laymūn*). It is to be cooked with the spices usually used [in such dishes]. (**23r**)

(42) Recipe for *dajāja maṣūṣ* (chicken cooked with vinegar)[95]

Sweat chicken in sesame oil,[96] and throw on it a small amount of common parsley (*karafs*) leaves that have been stripped from their stems (*makhrūṭ*). Add as much vinegar as needed, color it with saffron [and continue cooking]. It will also be nice if eggs are arranged on it sunny side up.

(43) A recipe for *dajāja mamqūra* (fried chicken steeped in vinegar)[97]

Sweat the chicken in sesame oil and let it fry until it nicely browns (*yatawarrad*), and all the moisture is gone.[98] Add to it equal parts of *murrī* (liquid fermented sauce) and vinegar [and let it steep in them].

(44) Recipe for *jawādhib al-dajāj*[99]

Cut the chicken at the joints, and boil it in enough water to cover it. Throw in sesame oil, mastic gum, and cassia (*dār Ṣīnī*). When it is cooked, [take it out of the broth,] and fry it in sesame oil;[100] [set aside any remaining oil]. The broth of the boiled chicken will have reduced considerably.

Take rice, wash it in water, and throw it into the remaining broth, to which milk has been added. [However,] you should let them [the broth and milk] boil together before adding the rice, which will have been colored with saffron before adding it to the pot. Let the pot cook until the rice is done. Pour into the pot the frying oil that has been set aside. Arrange the chicken pieces all over

---

95 See glossary 5, s.v. *maṣūṣ*.

96 See glossary 9.2, s.v. *taʿrīq*.

97 Prepared this way, the chicken can stay good to eat as a cold dish for several days. See glossary 5, s.v. *mamqūr*.

98 Sweating the meat (*taʿrīq*) releases its moisture first, then it is browned in its juices and some added fat. The recipe stresses the importance of allowing all the moisture to evaporate because preparing the chicken this way was a method for the short-term preservation of meat.

99 This recipe is a good example of how dishes sometimes kept their names, but the way they were made evolved over time. See glossary 5, s.v. *jawādhib*. This recipe can also be found in *Waṣf* 77, which I used to slightly amend the edited text.

100 This addition is from *Waṣf* 77.

the top, and then cover the pot and leave it on low heat for an hour,[101] and then remove.

(45) Recipe for *dajāja fustuqiyya* (sweet chicken with pistachios)[102]

[This recipe requires] 1 *raṭl* (1 pound) sugar syrup (*jullāb*), and ½ *raṭl* (½ pound) pistachios. Boil [the dissolved sugar] on the fire until it thickens into syrup (*ḥall*).[103] [Briefly] boil pistachios [and remove the skins], pound it until it looks like *samīdh* (semolina),[104] and then put it in a large brass pot (*dast*), along with the thick syrup, and stir. Also, blend into them 2 *ūqiyya*s (2 ounces) wheat starch (*nashā*) and one egg white, (**23v**) and stir them all together. They will thicken the sauce [when added].

You will already have boiled a couple of chickens and fried them in sesame oil. Immerse them in the syrup in the pot, and then take them out and put them in a porcelain bowl (*zibdiyya*). Pour the syrup (*al-ḥall al-jullāb*) and rosewater all over them.

The same thing is done when cooking ***bunduqiyya*** (sweet chicken with hazelnuts). The hazelnuts are toasted first, [pounded,] and then sifted through a sieve (*ghirbāl*) [and cooked as above].[105]

(46) *Dajāja fālūdhajiyya* (chicken cooked like *fālūdhaj*),[106] and *khashkhāshiyya* (cooked with poppy seeds)

Sweat the chicken in sesame oil, and then return to it as much of the broth in which it was boiled as is needed. Then follow the same method described in cooking *fālūdhajiyya* and *khashkhāshiyya*.[107]

(47) Recipe for *dajāja ḥulwiyya* (sweet chicken)

Sweat the chicken as we mentioned [in the recipes above], and then return to it as much of the broth in which it was initially boiled as is needed. Throw

---

101 The Arabic for 'cover it' used in the edited text here is خمّره and اكمره in *Waṣf*.

102 This recipe is almost a duplicate of recipe 60 below. Here I used it to fill in some of the missing steps.

103 There is confusion in this recipe and some of the following ones regarding the word *ḥall* (حلّ). Internal evidence indicates that *ḥall* designates sugar-syrup, sometimes referred to as *ḥall jullāb*. Copyists in this book often mistake it for *khall* (خلّ) 'vinegar.' See glossary 4, s.v. *ḥall*.

104 Semolina, sandy in texture, is a product of durum wheat, *Triticum durum*, which is the hardest of hard wheat varieties. See glossary 2.

105 This dish is repeated, with some variations, in recipe 60, below.

106 Starch-based thickened pudding, see glossary 4.

107 The reference here is to recipes 31 and 33 above, cooked with red meat.

in the ingredients usually added to a *ḥulwiyya* dish, and cook it the same way described earlier.[108]

[**General tips:**] Do not cook chicken without cassia (*dār Ṣīnī*), black pepper, and a small amount of coriander. However, never use onion or garlic with it.

(48) A recipe for *farārīj mumazzaja* (seasoned young chickens)[109]

Fry the young chickens in sesame oil,[110] with some spices. Take them out of the skillet, and while still hot, dip them in [sauce] that has already been prepared, which is [a mix of] good vinegar, *murrī* (liquid fermented sauce), and lemon juice, mixed in balanced proportions.[111]

[**General tips:**][112] The best way to grill chicken, whichever way you choose to do it, is to fatigue it [before slaughtering it] by running after it until it can no longer run from exhaustion. Choose a fat chicken, and slaughter it (**24r**) after feeding it vinegar and rosewater. After that, scald it as usual, and prepare a mix of sesame oil, salt, and a bit of saffron for it. Grill the chicken on slow low heat, and baste [the grilling rotating chicken] with it [i.e., the oil mix]. It will come out marvelously tender and delicious.

---

108 There is no *ḥulwiyya* recipe mentioned earlier in this book. However, in *Waṣf*, which draws on a similar source or sources, two *ḥulwiyya* recipes do indeed exist. They are made with red meat; therefore, the assumption is that the recipe would be adjusted when used with chicken. One of them is called *farḥāna* (lit., 'the happy one'), which is sweetened with sugar syrup and garnished with pieces of *musayyar* (gourd paste, see recipe 280 below) and *ḥalwā qurāḍiyya*, which is pulled taffy (*fānīdh*, see glossary 4). Here is the other one:

"Sweat meat with sesame oil, coriander, cassia, onion [chopped], and a bit of salt. When all the liquid evaporates and only fat remains, make a sauce in the pot with water mixed with wine vinegar. Add skinned chickpeas. When all is cooked, sweeten the dish with sugar or honey, color it with saffron, and spread seeded raisins on top. Perfume the pot with rosewater, and then remove." (21, translation mine)

109 In Gotha, fol. 23r, and *Waṣf* 80, the word is clearly written as *mumazzaja*, which is used to designate dishes in which liquid seasonings are added to lend a balanced flavor to the dish.

110 The verb used is تطجّن. See glossary 9.2, s.v. *taṭjīn*.

111 Here I amended the text based on *Waṣf* 80.

112 The following lines are similar to recipe 139 below, with the exception of minor stylistic differences. In recipe 139, the dish is called *dajāj karnadāj*, which is chicken grilled by rotating it on an open camp-like fire. In other sources, the word for grilling by rotating also occurs as *kardhanāj* and *kardanāj*.

Recipe for *al-Mutawakkiliyya* (meat with taro)[113]
After cleaning and washing taro (*qulqās*), fry it in sesame oil until it cooks well and looks like smooth ointment (*marham*), and set it aside. Take the tender meat of a yearling sheep (*thanī*), cut it into pieces,[114] cover it with water, and cook it until well done.

Take the pot off the fire, set aside the broth, and return the meat to the pot. Scoop the fat from the top of the broth that was set aside and fry the meat with it, until it is browned.

Have a bowlful (*zibdiyya*) of finely pounded cilantro and hazelnuts ready, [and add them to the pot]. When [all the moisture evaporates], and only fat remains in the pot, throw in the taro, which has been fried in sesame oil. Let it cook for a short while, and then remove.

(49) Recipe for *rummāniyya bi-dajāj* (pomegranate stew with chicken)
Boil a fine plump chicken (*dajāj fā'iq*) in salted water, along with galangal (*khūlanjān*) and cassia (*dār Ṣīnī*), a stick of each, until it is almost done.[115]

When it is completely cooked, take fresh pomegranate seeds, both sweet and sour. Press them with a stone, put them in a sieve (*ghirbāl*) and press them down [to extract] the juice. Take half the juice and add it to the pot. Blend the second half with some [finely crushed] almonds, and add it to the pot [in the final stage] when it is simmering on the smoldering fire, to thicken the sauce. Season it with aromatic spices, rosewater, and camphor. Keep the pot on the smoldering fire to simmer, and then remove.

(50) A recipe for a chicken dish with cherry plums (*qarāṣiyā*)
Boil a fine plump chicken in water, along with a stick of galangal and [another one of] cassia (*dār Ṣīnī*). Cook until almost done.

Take fully ripe cherry plums, boil them and press down their juice through a sieve. Take half of what is extracted [from] the juice and add it to the pot, along with sugar and bee honey (*'asal naḥl*). Blend the rest of the juice with [finely ground] almonds and add it to the pot.

Season the pot with distilled rosewater and camphor. Let the pot simmer, and then ladle it and serve it.

---

113 Both DK, appendix 10, and Gotha, fol. 23v, have *Mutawakkiliyya* recipe (meat with *qulqās* 'taro') in the middle of chicken recipes. Cf. another *Mutawakkiliyya*, recipe 89 below. For more on the name of this dish, see glossary 5.

114 In Gotha, it is cut *mudarham* (like dirhams 'silver coins'), i.e., about 1-inch pieces.

115 This is a redundant instruction, unless the recipe is asking the cook to start preparing the pomegranate juice, so that it may be ready to use when the chicken is done.

FIGURE 24 *Quince, al-ʿUmarī,* Masālik al-abṣār, *fol. 177r (BnF, Department of manuscripts, Arab 2771).*

(51) Recipe for *safarjaliyya* (chicken with quinces)

Boil a fine plump chicken in water, salt (**24v**), a stick of galangal, and [another of] cassia (*dār Ṣīnī*). When it is almost cooked, take the quince, remove the seeds, and pound it until it is smooth. Strain its juice [through a sieve], and add it to the chicken.

Now take some more quince, peel it and take the pulp. Discard the seeds, and boil it thoroughly. Take the pulp and crush it on a stone along with skinned almonds, until it becomes as smooth as bone marrow (*mukh*).

The [quince juice] you have added to the chicken will be its seasoning sauce (*mizāj*). [As for] the pounded quince, spread it on the surface along with sugar, rosewater, musk, and camphor. Stir the pot so that the ingredients mix, and then let the pot simmer on the smoldering fire, and remove it.

Recipe for *ḥiṣrimiyya* (chicken with sour unripe grapes)[116]

Boil the chicken in water, with salt, galangal, and cassia (*dār Ṣīnī*). Boil fresh unripe grapes (*ḥiṣrim*), and press them down through a sieve. [Set aside the thick juice containing the sediment, and] take the clear juice, and spread it in the pot after the chicken is fully cooked.

Now, take [finely ground] pistachios and blend it with boiled *tuffāḥ rayḥānī*,[117] along with the thick juice of unripe grapes which you have set aside. Put this in another pot along with the chicken fat, [cook them to thicken the sauce,] and set it aside until the time comes for ladling the dish. [When ready to serve the food,] thicken this sauce again with whatever you wish [such as crushed nuts], and offer it [with the chicken].

(52) Recipe for *zīrbāj* (delicately sour golden chicken stew)

Boil the chicken until it is done. For each chicken, grind 1 *ūqiyya* (1 ounce/2 tablespoons) sugar and a similar amount of skinned almonds. Season them with a bit of camphor and stuff the chicken cavity with them [then set it aside].

For each two chickens used, take 1 *raṭl* (1 pint/2 cups) sugar syrup (*jullāb*), put it in a pot on the fire. Add 20 jujubes (*ʿunnāb*), ½ *ūqiyya* (½ ounce/1 tablespoon) skinned almonds (do not crush them), 1 *ūqiyya* raisins (*zabīb*), and a bit of wheat starch (*nashā*)—just enough to thicken the sauce.

Add vinegar to the pot, but not before you color the chicken with saffron. [So, you put the colored chicken into the pot], and add enough vinegar to give

---

116 Both DK, appendix 11, and Gotha, fols. 24r–v, have this recipe. The edited text does not include it.

117 An apple variety that must have been valued for its aroma, as the name seems to suggest.

it a sweet and sour taste (*mazāza*), similar to that of *sakanjabīn* drink.[118] (**25r**) Season the pot with a bit of camphor and *aṭrāf al-ṭīb* (spice blend). Let the pot simmer on the smoldering fire, and ladle it.

[Now back to dishes cooked with red meat.]

(53) Recipe for *kishkiyya* (meat and *kishk* dish)[119]

Take 5 *raṭl*s (5 pounds) fatty meat, cut it into large pieces and then wash it and put it in a clean pot on the fire. Throw in ½ *raṭl* (½ pound) white onion, ¼ *raṭl* fresh sesame oil, 10 *dirhams* (1 ounce/2 tablespoons) crushed rock salt (*milḥ Andarānī*), and 2 *dirhams* (6 grams/1 teaspoon) garlic. Pour enough water to cover [the ingredients], and let it boil until almost cooked.

Put *kishk* in a bowl (*zibdiyya*) and add enough yogurt (*laban ḥāmiḍ*) to cover it by a width of four fingers spread apart. When all the *kishk* disintegrates, whip it vigorously, pour it into the pot and let it boil. Add to the pot 10 whole boiled onions, and season it with 5 *dirhams* (15 grams/2½ teaspoons) coriander seeds, and 2 *dirhams* (6 grams/1 teaspoon) black pepper, both crushed. Also add one bunch of rue (*sadhāb*). Let the pot boil until cooked, stirring [occasionally], and then remove and ladle.

(54) Another *kishk* recipe, delicious[120]

Take fatty meat, cut it into medium-sized pieces, wash it, and chop fresh herbs (*abzār ruṭb*) on it. Add coriander and caraway.

(55) Recipe for *summāqiyya* (meat dish with sumac)[121]

(**25v**) Take meat ribs (*aḍlāʿ*) and wash them thoroughly. Soak sumac berries in hot water. After [the meat has finished sweating] and all its liquid is gone and its fat released,[122] strain the soaked sumac, and add enough of the liquid to cover the meat [and continue cooking].

Pound the meat to make *mudaqqaqa* (meatballs), mixing with it Macedonian parsley (*baqdūnis*), mint, and all kinds of spices. Also, chop chard stalks. When

---

118 Sometimes written as *sakanjabīl* 'oxymel drink.' See chapter 11 for recipes.

119 *Kishk* is dried dough of crushed wheat and yogurt. See glossary 3.

120 This is an incomplete recipe, unless we are to understand that the cook needs to follow the same instructions in the previous recipe. Cf. other *kishk* recipes below (pp. 124–5, and recipe 102).

121 I amended the text at several places based on Gotha, fols. 25r–6v.

122 There are some missing words, which I filled in to straighten the sense. On sweating the meat, see glossary 9.2, s.v. *taʿrīq*.

the meat is half cooked, throw in the prepared meatballs [and the cut chard stalks].

Now take walnuts and pound them,[123] skin some garlic cloves [add them to the walnuts] along with [chopped] mint. When the meat is done, [add the walnut mix to] thicken the sauce.

Now take lemons preserved in salt (*laymūn māliḥ*), remove their seeds [but keep them whole].[124] Chop parsley and mint and stuff them in the lemons. When all the ingredients have been added to the pot and it has simmered, and sauce is reduced, insert the lemons in the stew.[125] When you ladle the dish, make sure to include the lemons and the meatballs.

(56) Recipe for *summāqiyya* with taro (*qulqās*)

Cook the meat in a pot, and when it is half-done, add the taro, and let it cook until done. (**26r**) You will have prepared finely pounded sumac, put it in a bowl and set it aside, so that when the meat is cooked, [you can] sprinkle it with enough sumac to cover it.

If desired, add chard (*silq*), walnuts, garlic, and all kinds of spices and herbs (*tawābil*) to the pot. Also, if desired, the garlic may be kept whole.

Recipe for *tamriyya* (meat with dried dates)[126]

Cut meat into small pieces, wash it in hot water, and fry it well. Take good pressed dried dates (*tamr maʿjūn*), split them open and remove the stones. Take almonds, remove their skins by blanching them in boiling water, and toast them (*yuḥammaṣ*). Replace the date stones with these almonds.

Mix rosewater, a small amount of water, and 1 *ūqiyya* (1 ounce/2 tablespoons) sesame oil. Add this to the [meat] pot. Add the dates, and continue cooking until the sauce is somewhat reduced. When all of it is done, serve it.

Recipe for *rukhāmiyya* (marblelike meat dish)[127]

Boil the meat until it is cooked. If a lot of broth remains, take some of it out; if a little is left, just add milk to it. Now take rice, wash it, and add it to the pot along

123 *Waṣf* uses almonds instead.

124 Lemons preserved in salt are usually cut lengthwise at several places, but are kept whole. See the last three recipes in chapter 18 below.

125 The verb (يغرز) clearly indicates that the final stew will be shallow and thick in the pot, and the tops of stuffed lemons should be visible.

126 This recipe is found only in DK, appendix 12.

127 This recipe only appears in DK, appendix 13, and Gotha, fol. 26r. The dish is called so because of its color and smooth texture. Cf. recipes 64 and 72 below.

with mastic gum and cassia (*dār Ṣīnī*). For each *raṭl* (1 pint/2 cups) of milk, use 2 *ūqiyyas* (2 ounces) rice. When it is done cooking, ladle it onto a plate and eat it with honey, sugar, or sugar syrup (*jullāb*). It is a wonderful dish.

Recipe for *khayṭiyya* (rice with thread-like shreds of meat)[128]

Take trimmed meat (*laḥm aḥmar*), preferably from a yearling sheep.[129] Cut it into pieces and boil it until it falls apart. Pour off the liquid, take out the meat and loosen it into hair-like threads. Wash it thoroughly until it looks white and the water comes out clean.

Put milk on the fire. Wash rice and add it to [the milk]. Then pound another amount of rice, sift it, and sprinkle it over the milk bit by bit, while stirring the pot. For each *raṭl* (1 pound) of meat, use 4 *ūqiyyas* (4 ounces) rice, 3 *raṭls* (3 pints/6 cups) milk, 2 *raṭls* (2 pints/4 cups) water, and 2 *ūqiyyas* (2 ounces) pounded rice.

This dish is eaten with sugar syrup (*jullāb*).

Recipe for *mulūkhiyya* (meat dish with Jew's mallow)[130]

Wash the meat, cut it into pieces, and fry it until it is cooked, then add water to it. Wilt the Jew's mallow in the sun, and then chop it finely. Do not chop it without wilting it because it chops better this way.

Add the Jew's mallow to the water [and meat] in the pot. Grind coriander seeds, caraway, hot spices,[131] salt, and garlic. Grind them all and blend them in water, and then add them to the pot. When it is done cooking, keep it on the smoldering fire to simmer, and eat it.

[Now several recipes for sweetened chicken dishes follow.[132]]

---

128 This recipe only appears in DK, appendix 14; Gotha, fol. 26r; and *Zahr*, fol. 9r. The name of the dish is clearly written as *khayṭiyya* (خيطية) in Gotha and *Zahr*, and not *ḥinṭiyya* (حنطية) as in DK.

129 *Thanī*, described in Gotha as *zamānayn* (lit., 'which has been through two seasons').

130 This recipe only appears in DK, appendix 15; Gotha, fol. 26v; and *Zahr*, fol. 25r. Cf. recipe 134 below.

131 *Abāzīr ḥārra*, such as black pepper, cinnamon, and ginger.

132 Sweetened chicken dishes like the following seem to have been an Egyptian specialty at the time. See 'Abd al-Laṭīf al-Baghdādī, *Riḥla* 119. *Wuṣla* ii 542, which includes sweet chicken dishes like these, categorizes them as *ḥalāwat al-dajāj* 'chicken dessert.'

(57) *Khayṭiyya* (porridge with thread-like shreds of chicken breasts)[133]

When the chicken is cooked, take off the breasts and loosen their meat into threads.[134] Boil pistachios to remove the skins, and then pound and sift it through a sieve (*munkhul*). Put it [in a pot] and add white sugar to it. Also, add to it the chicken breast [threads], which you will have washed.

Boil the mix until it thickens (*yashtadd*) thoroughly. Pour in pistachio oil to moisten the mix, and then spread it in a thin layer (*yubsaṭ*) on plates.

(58) If you want the ***khayṭiyya*** to look white, then make it with almond milk (*mā' al-lawz*), use almond oil to moisten it, and eat it.

(59) Recipe for *sitt al-Nūba* (the 'Nubian lady')[135]

Take chicken, scald it [to pluck the feathers, and clean it] and then boil it for a third of the duration it usually takes to cook it fully. Fry it in sesame oil and set it aside on a plate.

Take almonds, which have already been skinned by scalding them in hot water. Toast them and grind them, and then extract the milk.[136] Put almond milk on the fire along with white sugar. Dissolve saffron [in water] and boil it with the almond milk and sugar until it looks thick.

Now take the chicken [and return it to the pot], and spread some jujubes and black raisins, (**26v**) which have been steeped in rosewater flavored with mastic gum, all over the surface. Also, take split pistachios, which have been skinned by scalding them in hot water, and sprinkle them all over the surface. Drizzle the dish with toasted almond oil, and serve.

(60) Recipe for *fustuqiyya* (chicken with pistachios)[137]

These are the measurements for a couple of chickens: 1 *raṭl* (1 pint/2 cups) sugar syrup (*ḥall jullāb*),[138] and ½ *raṭl* (½ pound) pistachios.

Cook the syrup (*ḥall*) until it thickens. Scald the pistachios in hot water to remove the skins, and then pound them and sift them through a fine sieve. Add

---

133 Cf. recipe 104 below.

134 Here I followed the imperative verb *nassil* (نسّل) 'loosen into threads,' as it occurs in Gotha, fol. 25v. In the edited text, the word *tushill* (تشل), might also be taken as a regional dialectical vocalization of the sound 's' as 'sh,' which occurs in several places in this cookbook.

135 Called so because of its darkish hue; here it is caused by the steeped black raisins used in the recipe. Cf. recipes 66 and 137 below.

136 Almond milk is extracted by adding water to the ground nuts and then straining it.

137 This recipe is almost identical to recipe 45 above.

138 The correct word is *ḥall* (حلّ) 'thick syrup' and not *khall* (خلّ) 'vinegar.' See n. 103 above.

it the pot and stir it with 1½ or 2 *ūqiyyas* (1½ or 2 ounces) fine-tasting wheat starch.[139] Also, vigorously stir in one egg white. These [two ingredients] will thicken the sauce.

You will have prepared two chickens, which have been cleaned, boiled, and fried in sesame oil. Dip them in the syrup pot, and then take them out and place them in a bowl or two. Pour the remaining syrup-pistachio sauce all over them. It is a wonderful dish.

(61) *Al-bunduqiyya* (chicken with hazelnuts)

For each *raṭl* (1 pint/2 cups) of sugar syrup (*jullāb*), use ½ *raṭl* (½ pound) hazelnuts. These are the measurements used when cooking two chickens.

Put the syrup (*ḥall*) on the fire to heat it up.[140] (27r) Alternatively, you may make the syrup [yourself] using sugar [and some water] and leave it on the fire until it acquires the consistency of syrup.[141]

Put the hazelnuts in a pan (*ṭājin*), toast them on the fire, remove the skins, pound them in a mortar, and then sift them through a fine sieve so that it looks like fine semolina.[142] Add it to the [cooking] syrup, and stir. Also, add 1½ *ūqiyyas* (1½ ounces) fine-tasting wheat starch (*nashā' qalb*) and 2 *ūqiyyas* (2 ounces) egg whites, and stir. These [two ingredients] will thicken the sauce.

You will have prepared two chickens as you did in the *fustuqiyya* recipe [above]: boil them and then after that fry them in sesame oil in a frying pan (*ṭājin*). When the syrup in the pot is thick enough, take the two chickens and dip them in the syrup.[143] Then take them out and put them in the bowls (*zabādī*), and pour the [remaining] syrup all over them, adding musk and rosewater as you like. Set them aside for about an hour so that [the syrup] sets and thickens.

(62) *Al-jullābiyya* (chicken with sugar syrup)

For each two chickens use 1 *raṭl* (1 pound) sugar syrup (*jullāb*).

Heat the syrup (*ḥall*) in a pot set on the fire.[144] Alternatively, you may put a *raṭl* of sugar on the fire and dissolve it with enough water, and cook it until

139 *Nashā' qalb*, extracted from hearts of wheat grains. See glossary 2.

140 See n. 103 above.

141 As this recipe shows, ready-made syrup was available to cooks. See recipe 63 below, where the cook is given the option of buying it from the market place (*sūq*).

142 *Samīdh al-daqīq*, granular sand-like flour made from durum wheat, *Triticum durum*. See glossary 2.

143 The intention is to dip the chickens in the syrup and not to cook them further.

144 The correct word is *ḥall* (حلّ) and not *khall* 'vinegar' (خلّ), see n. 103 above. In addition, as the text clearly shows, the words *jullāb* and *ḥall* are used synonymously.

it becomes the consistency of *jullāb*. Add to it 1½ *ūqiyyas* (1½ ounces) fine-tasting wheat starch[145] (27v) and one egg white, and stir them. These [two ingredients] will thicken the sauce.

Now, take two chickens, which have been boiled and fried in sesame oil, and when the syrup reaches the right consistency, add them to the pot. Then [take them out] and put them in bowls (*zabādī*), pour the syrup all over them, and flavor them with as much musk and rosewater as you like. Set them aside for about an hour until the syrup over the chicken sets and thickens. It is a wonderful dish.

Recipe for *laymūniyya* (lemon chicken)[146]

For two chickens, use 1 *raṭl* (1 pound) sugar syrup (*ḥall jullāb*) and ¼ *raṭl* (4 ounces) almonds.

Heat the syrup (*ḥall*) in a pot set on the fire. Alternatively, you may dissolve sugar in water and cook it until it becomes the right consistency.

Scald almonds, skin them, and after grinding them in a mortar, sift them through a sieve so that they look like *samīdh al-qamḥ* (semolina durum wheat, *Triticum durum*). Add it to the syrup and stir. Then squeeze the juice of 7 lemons, and strain the juice with a piece of cloth. Add it to the syrup, and stir the pot.

Next, add 1½ *ūqiyyas* (1½ ounces) fine-tasting wheat starch, one egg white, and a couple of mint sprigs, and stir. In addition, you will have prepared a couple of chickens as described in the recipes above, so that when the syrup reaches the right consistency, [you can] add them to the pot, then take them out and put them in bowls [with the syrup], adding as much musk and rosewater as you like. Set them aside for about an hour until the [syrup] sets and thickens. It is a wonderful dish.

(63) Recipe for *zīrbāj* (delicately sour golden chicken)[147]

For two chickens, use 1 *raṭl* (1 pound) sugar syrup (*jullāb*) and ½ *raṭl* (8 ounces) almonds.

[Either] put sugar in a pot [with some water] and dissolve it on the fire [and boil it down to syrup consistency, i.e., *jullāb*]; or if you wish, buy sugar syrup (*ḥall*) from the marketplace, and heat it up very well on the fire.[148]

---

145 *Nashā' qalb*, extracted from hearts of wheat grains. See glossary 2.

146 This recipe only appears in DK, appendix 16; Gotha, fol. 27v; and *Zahr*, fol. 9v.

147 A shortened version of this recipe is included in *Zahr*, fol. 10r, where the writer says that the same procedure mentioned in the earlier recipes is followed here. He explains that this abbreviated version should suffice for adept cooks.

148 See n. 103 regarding *ḥall*.

Scald almonds, and skin them and grind them in a mortar. Sift them through a sieve so that they look like *samīdh* (semolina of durum wheat), and then add them to the syrup in the pot, and stir. Also add 4 *ūqiyyas* (4 ounces/½ cup) fine-tasting wine vinegar (*khall khamr*), the best you can get, and stir the pot. However, before pouring it into the pot, throw 2 *dirhams* (6 grams/1 teaspoon) *zaʿfarān Janawī* (Genoese saffron) into it.[149] Add it to the pot, along with one egg white, and two sprigs of fresh mint (*naʿnāʿ akhḍar*). Do not add any other herbs.

Now, take (**28r**) the two chickens, which you have prepared as described in the earlier recipes, and dip them in the pot after the sauce has cooked nicely, and then take them out and put them in bowls (*zabādī*). [Pour all the remaining sauce in the pot on them.] Sprinkle them with as much musk and rosewater as you prefer, and set them aside for an hour or so until the syrup sets on them. It is a wonderful dish.

(64) *Rukhāmiyya* (meatless marblelike rice porridge)[150]

For each *qadaḥ* (2¼ pounds) rice, use 3 *raṭls* (6 cups) milk, a piece of ginger, a piece of Ceylon cinnamon (*qarfa*), and ¼ *dirham* (¾ grams/⅛ teaspoon) mastic gum.

Take half the milk and put it in a [soapstone] pot;[151] add a similar amount of water, and then throw in the cinnamon, ginger, and mastic gum. When they come to a boil, wash the rice and add it to the soapstone pot. Start adding it to the pot with the remaining 1½ *raṭls* of milk, little by little, while it is cooking on low fire. Continue feeding it with milk little by little and stirring it on a quiet fire, and continue stirring. It is best if charcoal (*faḥm*) is used.

So, when it is done cooking, let the pot simmer [on the remaining heat] for a while, and then remove it, lest it should absorb any smoke from the fire. Should this happen to any cooking food, take a bunch of sulfur-tipped sticks (*ḥuzmat kibrīt*), break off the [sulfured] tips [and discard them], and tie the sticks in a bundle and dip them into the pot.[152] They will pick up all traces of smoke. A hazelnut, which has been pierced and emptied of its kernel, will also pick up the smoke.

---

149 As copied in DK, n. 1024; otherwise, copied as *janūbī* (southern) in the edited text. It is good saffron imported from Genoa. In DK and *Zahr*, the saffron amount is 1 *dirham* (3 grams).

150 Cf. other *rukhāmiyya* recipes, p. 114 above, and recipe 72 below. Most probably, the dish is named for its color and smooth texture.

151 The pot is later specified as *burma* 'soapstone pot.'

152 This is a rare mention of matchsticks, with tips dipped in sulfur. They were used in medieval kitchens to light fire by striking them on a granite stone. See glossary 9.2, s.v. *ḥuzmat kibrīt*.

Now, when you ladle the dish onto plates,[153] drizzle sesame oil (*shayraj*) on top, and sprinkle sugar all over them. It will be wonderful.

(65) Recipe for *marwaziyya* (golden meat dish with dried fruits)[154]

1½ *raṭls* (1½ pounds) meat, 4 *ūqiyyas* (4 ounces) cherry plums (*qarāṣiyā*), ½ *raṭl* (½ pound) *baṣal ramlī*,[155] ¾ *dirham* (2¼ gram, ⅔ teaspoon) saffron,[156] 2½ *ūqiyyas* (2½ ounces) raisins (*zabīb*), 4 *ūqiyyas* (8 tablespoons) fine-tasting wine vinegar, 1½ *ūqiyyas* (1½ ounce) jujube (*ʿunnāb*), half a bunch of fresh mint, and as much *aṭrāf ṭīb* (spice blend) as needed.

Fry the meat with *abāzīr*,[157] and when it is done, add to it 1½ *raṭls* (3 cups) water. When it boils, chop the onion and wash it, once with salted water and once with water, and add it to the meat. (**28v**) Let the pot boil until the onion is half done.

Add the [dried] cherry plums, which will have been soaked in water, and then add the raisins and the jujubes. Let them cook until the raisins and the cherry plums are done. If you like, add 3 *ūqiyyas* (3 ounces) sugar, and let it boil. Next, add saffron dissolved [in some water], and continue boiling, and then add the vinegar. When the pot has boiled for a while, add the mint and *aṭrāf al-ṭīb*. Keep the pot on the remaining heat to simmer.

Recipe for *tamr-Hindiyya* (chicken with tamarind)[158]

Boil the chicken thoroughly, wipe it dry, and fry it in sesame oil. Stuff the cavities with almonds and sugar. For each chicken use 1 *ūqiyya* (1 ounce) almonds and 1 *ūqiyya* sugar, which you grind in a mortar (*hāwan*) with a bit of camphor and rosewater, and stuff the cavities with them.

Take sugar syrup (*jullāb*) and put it in a pot. For each 100 *dirhams* (300 grams) of *jullāb*, take 1 *ūqiyya* (1 ounce) tamarind. Press and mash it in hot or cold water, [strain it] and add it to the *jullāb* in the pot [and let them boil]. [Put the stuffed chickens in bowls,] drench them with the syrup, and allow them to settle.

---

153 *Aṣḥun* (sg. *ṣaḥn*).

154 Dozy, *Takmilat al-maʿājim* 1446, credibly traces the name of the dish to the Latin *amorusia* 'boiled meat' or 'bouillon.' He adds that the dish was also named *al-ʿāṣimī* in Granada. Here I amended the edited text based on Gotha, fols 28r–v; and *Waṣf* 116–7. See glossary 5, for more on this dish.

155 Onions grown in sandy soil, juicy and not pungent.

156 The weight "¾ *dirham*" is expressed as *niṣf wa-rubʿ dirham*, 'half and a quarter of a dirham.'

157 This is a general name for seasoning spices.

158 This recipe only appears in DK, appendix 17; Gotha, fols. 28v–9r; and *Zahr*, fol. 10r.

(66) Recipe for *sitt al-Nūba* (the 'Nubian lady')[159]

Boil the chicken and set it aside.[160] Next, take 1 *ūqiyya* (1 ounce) sugar, and finely pound it with a similar amount of almonds; season them with a bit of camphor and rosewater, [stuff the chicken with the mix], and put them in a bowl [and set them aside].[161]

For each chicken, use ½ *jarwī raṭl* (1 pound) of sugar syrup (*jullāb*) [and put it in a pot].[162] Take toasted purslane seeds (*bazr al-rijla*), pound them finely, and add them to the syrup [and let them boil]. Season the syrup with a bit of camphor and rosewater, drench the chicken with it, and allow it to settle.

(67) Recipe for *Ma'mūniyya* (rice porridge without meat)[163]

Grind the rice, and for each *qadaḥ* (2¼ pounds) of it, use one *jarwī raṭl* (2 pounds) of sugar syrup (*jullāb maḥlūl*),[164] or sugar cane molasses (*qaṭr*). Cook the syrup until it boils, and then gradually add the rice and gently stir it (**29r**). Continue adding hot water whenever you see it becoming dry, until it is done.

Color it with saffron, using ½ *dirham* (¼ teaspoon) for each *qadaḥ* [of rice]. Season it with camphor, musk, and rosewater. Keep the pot on the remaining heat to simmer, and serve.

(68) Recipe for *fustuqiyya* (chicken with pistachios)

Take shelled pistachios and finely pound some of them in a mortar along with some sugar. Add musk and camphor to it, and knead them all with a bit of rosewater. Stuff the cavity of a chicken with them. For each chicken, use 1 *ūqiyya* (1 ounce) sugar and a similar amount of almonds and pistachios.[165] [Stuff the chicken] after it is fried in 2 *ūqiyyas* (2 ounces) sesame oil until it is fully cooked and browned.

---

159 Named for its blackish hue from using the tiny black seeds of purslane. See 'Abd al-Laṭīf al-Baghdādī, *Riḥla* 119. He describes these dishes as typically Egyptian. Cf. recipes 59 above, and 137 below.

160 The chicken in such dishes is usually fried after boiling it.

161 In the edited text "and then put them in a bowl" does not make sense. Instead, I follow the example of recipe 52 above, where the boiled chicken is stuffed with a similar mix.

162 *Jarwī raṭl* is a medieval Egyptian measure of weight, it equals approximately 2 pounds. See glossary 13.

163 This dish is named after the Abbasid caliph al-Ma'mūn (d. 833). See glossary 5.

164 This was also called *ḥall jullāb*, as in recipe 60 above. See glossary 13, for details on *jarwī raṭl*.

165 Almonds are mentioned here only; otherwise it is a pistachio dish.

Now take sugar syrup (*jullāb*) and put it on the fire. Take the remaining pistachios, pound them finely, and add it to the syrup. Take chard leaves (*silq*) and pound them to extract their juice, which you add to the *jullāb* to change it to a green color. As soon as the syrup becomes green, put the chicken in a bowl (*zibdiyya*), drench it with the prepared syrup (*ḥall*),[166] and let it settle and then serve it.

Avoid using a lot of camphor lest the dish taste bitter. One small lump (*ḥabba*) should suffice.

Recipe for *khayṭiyya* (rice porridge with thread-like shreds of meat)[167]

Take 2 *qadaḥ*s (4½ pounds) of *Wāḥī* rice,[168] and wash it with water until it is completely clean, and then drain it. Now take 6 Egyptian *raṭl*s (12 cups) of water, which you boil with a lump of mastic gum and a piece of Ceylon cinnamon (*qarfa*)—leave it whole. Add rice to a pot and let it cook until it absorbs the liquid. Then feed it with 6 *raṭl*s (12 cups) of milk, adding it little by little until it is absorbed.

Next, add to the pot 2 *raṭl*s (2 pounds) of meat, which has been boiled and finely shredded [like threads]. Stir the pot vigorously so that the ingredients mix thoroughly. Remove the pot [from the fire], and then pour in sugar syrup (*jullāb*) or honey (*ʿasal al-naḥl*), and serve.

(69) *al-Laymūniyya* (meat with lemon juice)

Take the meat, put it in a pot [with water] and let it boil until half cooked. Add taro fingers (*qulqās aṣābiʿ*).[169] When it is fully cooked, (**29v**) sugar and lemon are added [as follows]: Set aside some of the meat broth in a bowl (*zibdiyya*) and then add sugar and lemon juice to the pot. Now, return some of the broth to the pot, the amount of which depends on how much sugar and lemon juice are used.

Thicken the stew by adding almonds or safflower seeds (*qurṭum*),[170] as much as needed to thicken the sauce. Do this while the pot is set on hot ashes (*ramād sukhn*); otherwise the sauce will curdle (*yuqaṭṭiʿ*). Add mastic and cassia (*dār Ṣīnī*).

---

166 On *ḥall*, see n. 103 above.

167 This recipe only appears in DK, appendix 18; Gotha, fol. 29v; and *Zahr*, fols. 10r–v.

168 Egyptian rice grown in the oases. See glossary 2, s.v. *aruzz Wāḥī*. The rice grains must be washed well to remove any remaining salt used in whitening them.

169 This variety of taro was believed to be tastier and more digestible than round taro.

170 Usually, they are finely crushed and dissolved in water before adding them to the pot.

(70) *al-Zīrbāj*[171]

It is made with meat and taro, like *laymūniyya* [above]. There should also be an onion, mastic gum, and cassia (*dār Ṣīnī*). When [the meat] is cooked, take white vinegar and sugar, and [continue] cooking it, as you did with *laymūniyya*.

Thicken it with almonds, and add all the spices of *aṭrāf al-ṭīb* (spice blend). The spices need to be pounded, and then added to the pot. [Generally,] all sweet and sour dishes should contain 1 *dirham* (3 grams/½ teaspoon) olive oil.[172]

(71) *al-Maʾmūniyya* (rice porridge without meat)[173]

For each *raṭl* (pint/2 cups) of milk, use 2 *ūqiyyas* (2 ounces) of pounded rice [combine and cook them]. Boil sugar syrup (*jullāb*), use enough to sweeten the dish. You will have already rendered sheep-tail fat (*alya*) for it. Add *jullāb* in batches, alternating with rendered fat until it throws up its fat [i.e., separates and surfaces].

[The following eight recipes are found in Gotha, some of them are in DK and *Zahr* as well, but only the *labaniyya* is in the edited text]

Recipe for *lubābiyya* (meat or chicken with bread crumbs)[174]

Take a chicken or meat, chop it into small pieces, boil it, and then fry it in sesame oil [set aside the broth]. Take bread crumbs (*lubāb*),[175] rub and pass them through a sieve (*ghirbāl*), and toast them until they look golden brown.

Put the meat or chicken broth [in a pot], add to it the bread crumbs, and [crushed] poppy seeds. Add to it some sugar syrup (*jullāb*), and let them cook until done. Also, put rendered sheep-tail fat (*alya*) in it and the [fried] meat or chicken. Also add saffron, musk, rosewater, and shelled and skinned whole pistachios.

---

171 This delicately flavored sweet and sour stew is usually cooked with saffron, cf. for instance, recipe 63 above.

172 *Zayt* (زيت), in Gotha, fol. 30r; and C, n. 1118. In the edited text, it is written as *zabīb* (زبيب) 'raisins.'

173 Cf. recipe 67 above.

174 This recipe can be found in DK, appendix 19 (erroneously written as *labaniyya* 'made with milk'; Gotha, fols. 30r–v; and *Zahr*, fol. 10v. Cf. recipe 78 below.

175 The following direction to rub and pass the crumbs through a sieve (يفرك من تحت الغربال) indicates that fresh crumbs should be used here.

al-Jurjāniyya (fried chicken in yogurt sauce)[176]

Boil the chicken and fry it in sesame oil. Take *laban rāʾib* or any other kind of yogurt,[177] and strain it through a piece of cloth. Pound mustard seeds, dissolve them in water, and extract their liquid (*yustaḥlab*). Add this liquid to the yogurt along with some sugar. Meanwhile, the chicken will have been kept in sugar syrup (*jullāb*) after frying it, so that it can absorb its sweetness. Put it in a bowl (*zibdiyya*), and pour the prepared yogurt all over it.

al-Qanbarīsiyya (meat with soft yogurt cheese)[178]

Wash the meat in hot water and then drain it very well and set it aside on a plate. Dilute *qanbarīs* [with some water], let it boil in a pot, and then add the meat along with mastic gum, cassia, and salt. [Let it cook until done], and then keep the pot on the smoldering fire until it settles.

al-Labaniyya (meat cooked in milk)

[This recipe is an exact copy of recipe 74 below.]

al-Kishk[179]

Chop meat and onion. [Put them in] cold water, along with cassia (*dār Ṣīnī*), galangal (*khūlanjān*), and a head of cauliflower (*bayḍa*) and cook.[180] When it has boiled twice,[181] add the eggplant, gourd (*qarʿ*), chard (*silq*), and purslane (*rijla*).

When the pot is almost cooked, ladle some of the broth into a bowl (*zibdiyya*), and throw some pounded *kishk* into it. When it completely dissolves, return the liquid to the pot. After that, refrain from stirring the pot, because if you do, and the bottom of the pot happens to be burnt [the dish will be spoiled by the burnt particles]. If the *kishk* is not sour enough, add a bit of unripe grape juice (*māʾ al-ḥiṣrim*) to it.

When it is fully cooked, add the usual spices, which are coriander, black pepper, cumin, thyme (*zaʿtar*), and pounded cassia (*dār Ṣīnī*) to it. Grind all

---

176 This recipe only appears in DK, appendix 20; and Gotha, fol. 30v. The dish is named after Jurjān, a city in northern Persia.

177 *Laban rāʾib* is made without rennet. See glossary 3.

178 This recipe only appears in DK, appendix 21; and Gotha, fol. 30v. *Qanbarīs* is soft yogurt cheese. See recipes 508 and 515 below.

179 This recipe only appears in Gotha, fol. 31r. *Kishk* is dried dough of crushed wheat and yogurt. See glossary 3.

180 Even though *bayḍa* generally designates 'egg,' the reference here is to the white cauliflower curd or head. See glossary 12, s.v. *qunnabīṭ*.

181 See glossary 9.2, s.v. *ghalā ghalwatayn*.

these spices together and chop some mint (*naʿnaʿ*), basil (*bādharūj*), and dried thyme on them. If you want to cook the dish with yogurt, then do not put chard in it. Wipe clean the pot, and then remove and ladle.

Kishk as it is cooked nowadays[182]

Cut the meat, wash it in hot water, and then boil it in a pot with enough water to cover it. When the meat is cooked, soak the *kishk* in a small amount of the meat broth [and set it aside].

Add onion and chard to the meat in the pot, and when these are cooked, throw in the *kishk* [that was set aside]. Let the pot come to a boil, ten times (*ʿashr ghalwāt*). Pound some garlic for it and add it, with cumin, to the pot. Season it (*yutabbal*),[183] and then keep it on the smoldering fire to simmer, and then ladle it.

Recipe for _Maʾmūniyya bi-dajāj_ (rice porridge with chicken)[184]

Take 2 *qadaḥs* (4½ pounds) of *Wāḥī* rice,[185] and wash it well to get rid of all traces of salt, dry it in the sun, grind it, and sift it through a fine-meshed sieve.

Weigh 2 *raṭl*s (2 pounds) of sugar and 8 Egyptian *raṭl*s (4 quarts/16 cups) milk for it. Combine all the ingredients [in a pot].

Now, take the breasts of two chickens, boil them until they fall apart, and shred the meat into fine threads after you rinse them well with water and then squeeze out excess moisture. Stir the chicken into the milk and sugar mix, and put the pot on the fire. Continue stirring, never stopping, until its consistency resembles that of *ʿaṣīda* (dense flour-soup). Remove it from the fire and scent it with musk and camphor. When it is ladled [into bowls], pour some sesame oil on top.

Recipe for _aruzz bi-laban_ (rice pudding with milk)[186]

Wash the rice the night before, and spread it on a new piece of cloth. The following morning, crush the rice until it is as fine as flour.

182 This is an interesting example of how old, traditional recipes were preserved by circulation, but they also evolved over time. This recipe only appears in Gotha, fol. 31r. The text states, '*fī hādhā l-zamān*.'

183 See the recipe above for the spices usually added.

184 This recipe appears in DK, appendix 22; Gotha, fol. 31v; and *Zahr*, fol. 10v.

185 Egyptian rice grown in the oases. See glossary 2, s.v. *aruzz Wāḥī*. The rice grains must be washed well to remove any remaining salt used in whitening them.

186 This recipe only appears in DK, appendix 23; and Gotha, fols. 31v–2r.

The amounts used are [as follows], for each 1½ *raṭl*s (1½ pounds) rice, use 10 *raṭl*s (20 cups) milk, which has just been drawn.[187] Put the milk in a pot and when it boils, start sprinkling the rice on it as you do with flour, and continue stirring on moderate heat until it is cooked. Pour walnut oil or ghee of cow's milk (*samn baqarī*) on it. When it is fully done, sprinkle some sugar on it. If you want the dish to be white, then [there is] no need to do anything else. Otherwise, add saffron if you want it to be yellow. Leave the pot on the smoldering fire to simmer, and serve.

(72) *al-Rukhāmiyya* (marblelike chicken dish)[188]

You need *laban rāʾib* (yogurt made without rennet), sugar, pistachios, and scalded and shelled almonds. Pass the yogurt through a flour sieve [to get rid of lumps]. Crush the sugar and continue stirring it with the yogurt until the mix is thick and smooth. **(30r)**

Boil a chicken and fry it.[189] Put the yogurt in a vessel, and place the chicken in it. Crush the pistachios and almonds and sprinkle them all over it. Drizzle the dish with a bit of the [rendered] chicken fat (*duhn al-dajāj*), and serve.

(73) *Mishmishiyya* (chicken with marzipan apricots)[190]

You need ½ *raṭl* (½ pound) almonds, and ½ *raṭl* sugar. Pound the sugar and scald the almonds [to skin them] and pound them until they are fine in texture. Knead them both with sugar cane molasses (*qaṭr*) and a bit of gum arabic (*ṣamgh*) and saffron. Form the mix into [the shape of] apricots (*yushakhkhaṣ*), and place in the heart of each a scalded and skinned almond.[191] Stick in each of these 'apricots' a whole shelled pistachio, to make it look like its stem.

Boil a chicken, fry it, and put it in a vessel. Put the [marzipan] apricots all over it, and pour ½ *raṭl* (½ pound) sugar syrup (*jullāb*) and ½ *raṭl* Egyptian bee honey (*ʿasal naḥl Miṣrī*) all over them.

(74) *Labaniyya* (meat cooked in milk)

Wash the meat and put it aside on a plate. Put the milk in a pot. There should be one-third water and two-thirds milk. Continue stirring the pot with a ladle until it boils, and then add three or four onions [along with the meat that was

---

187 *Ḥalīb ḥārr*, lit., 'hot milk.'

188 Cf. other *rukhāmiyya* recipes, p. 114, and recipe 64 above. Most probably, the dish was named for the color of the yogurt sauce and its smooth texture.

189 DK adds ويطحن, which should be read as ويطجن 'and fry.'

190 The recipe in the edited text is incomplete. I used the copy of Gotha, fol. 32r, to complete it.

191 Here ends the edited recipe. The rest is from Gotha.

set aside] to it.[192] When the meat and milk are cooked well, grind a couple of cumin seeds with garlic and stir them into the pot.[193] Also, throw in mastic gum (*maṣṭakā'*) and whole pieces of cassia (*dār Ṣīnī*). Let the pot simmer on the smoldering fire.

(75) Recipe for *zīrbāj* (delicately sour golden chicken)

You need sugar, saffron, wine vinegar, almonds, *aṭrāf ṭīb* (spice blend), mint, and black pepper.

Boil the chicken (30v) and add the sugar to it, and continue cooking until it reaches the right consistency [of light syrup].

Pound half the amount of the almonds to be used, and add them to the pot. Also add the [rest of] the ingredients (*ḥawā'ij*) along with the remaining whole almonds. You may substitute sugar with honey, and add it to the chicken [as described above].

(76) Recipe for *ward murabbā* (chicken with rose-petal jam)

You need ½ *raṭl* (½ pound) sugar syrup (*jullāb*), ½ *raṭl* rose-petal jam, and ½ *raṭl* bee honey. [Mix them]

Boil the chicken and fry it, and then pour the *ḥawā'ij* (i.e., the above-mentioned ingredients) all over the chicken. Do this when the chicken is still in the pot, or in a vessel.

(77) Recipe for *ṭabīkh bazr rijla* (stewed purslane seeds)

You need ½ *raṭl* (½ pound) purslane seeds, picked over and lightly toasted. Also, take ½ *raṭl* sugar syrup (*jullāb*) or sugar, and ½ *raṭl* bee honey.

Boil the chicken and fry it. Next, boil the *jullāb* in a pot, along with honey and toasted purslane seeds. Add the fried chicken to the pot, and let it boil briefly.

Put the chicken with the syrup in a bowl and scatter pellets (*ḥarābil*)[194] of [crushed] pistachios kneaded with musk and rosewater, and [pellets of] hard bee honey (*'asal yābis*)[195] all over it.

---

192 The meat is not added to the milk until it comes to a boil, based on a recipe of meat cooked in milk, which is included in al-Warrāq, chapter 83, see 'white *tharīda*' in English trans. *Annals* 341.

193 The text states, *sha'ratayn kammūn*, which may be taken literally as 'two cumin seeds,' or it may just indicate a tiny amount.

194 This appears as حرابل, as it is clearly copied in C and Gotha, fol. 32v. See glossary 9.2 for more on this unfamiliar word.

195 This may be solid raw honey or a form of *fānīdh*, which is pulled taffy made with honey or sugar. See glossary 4.

(78) Recipe for *lubābiyya* (chicken with bread crumbs)

You need the pithy inside (*lubāb*) of cold *kumāj* bread.[196] [Take it out,] crumble it and pass it through a sieve, to make 1 *raṭl* (1 pound) of it. Put the crumbs in a pot and brown them in sesame oil. Now take ½ *raṭl* (½ pound) sugar syrup (*jullāb*) and ½ *raṭl* bee honey (**31r**), [and boil them with the browned crumbs].

Boil the chicken and fry it, and then put it in a vessel, and pour the rest of the ingredients (*ḥawāʾij*) all over it.

(79) Recipe for *lawziyya* (chicken with almonds)

You need ½ *raṭl* (½ pound) scalded and skinned almonds (*masmūṭ*), ½ *raṭl* sugar syrup (*jullāb*), ½ *raṭl* bee honey (*ʿasal naḥl*), and saffron. [Boil them]. Boil the chicken and fry it, and then pour the rest of the ingredients (*ḥawāʾij*) on it.

(80) Recipe for *laymūniyya* (lemon chicken)

[You will need] ½ *raṭl* (½ pound) lemon syrup (*sharāb laymūn*).[197] Boil the chicken and fry it, and then add it to the syrup.

(81) Recipe for *bunduqiyya* (chicken with hazelnuts)

You need ½ *raṭl* (½ pound) sugar syrup (*jullāb*), and ½ *raṭl* toasted and coarsely ground hazelnuts. Put them in a pot with ½ *raṭl* bee honey [and boil them together]. Boil the chicken and fry it; fold it into the rest of the ingredients (*ḥawāʾij*) in the pot, and then remove [and serve].

(82) Recipe for *maḥshī bi-māʾ laymūn* (chicken or young pigeons smothered in lemon sauce)[198]

You need some fresh herbs (*ḥawāʾij baql*),[199] sesame oil, lemon, black pepper, tahini, hazelnuts, and coriander.

Finely chop the herbs, put them in a pot, pour in the sesame oil and let them fry in it until they wilt. Add ground black pepper, lemon juice [and tahini], a bit of toasted and ground hazelnuts, and a small amount of broth [from the boiled chicken or young pigeons].

---

196 It is round bread, thick, pithy, and crusty, baked in the commercial *furn* 'brick oven.'

197 For directions on how to prepare this syrup, see, for instance, recipe 361 below.

198 See glossary 9.2, s.v. *maḥshī*, for more on this cooking technique.

199 Such as mint, parsley, and cilantro.

The chicken or the young pigeons (*firākh*)[200] (31v) are boiled and fried, and then the sauce is spread on them. If using red meat instead, boil it, then fry it, and spread the sauce on it, and serve it.[201]

(83) Recipe for *ṭabāhija* (moist dish of fried meat)[202]

You need meat, sheep-tail fat (*duhn*), honey,[203] pistachios, *aṭrāf ṭīb* (spice blend), wheat starch (*nashā*), vinegar, saffron, black pepper, and mint.

After the [thinly sliced] meat boils,[204] brown it [in fat], and then add some of the broth (*maraq*) to it. Burn some honey,[205] and mix it with the vinegar and *aṭrāf al-ṭīb* along with the pistachios, starch, saffron, and black pepper. Add these to the meat and [cook] until it is suitably thickened.

(84) Recipe for *mulūkhiyya* (Jew's mallow stew)[206]

You need meat, sheep-tail fat (*duhn*), and Jew's mallow. You may also use [additional] chicken (*dajāj*), or young pigeons (*firākh ḥamām*). Also, use garlic, onion, and black pepper.

Boil the meat, [and then take it out of the pot, and fry it]. Strain [the broth]. Pound garlic, black pepper, and coriander or caraway, and add them to the meat.

Pound the meat used for making meatballs (*mudaqqaqa*), and mix with it [more of] the above-mentioned spices. In addition, use baked onion. Add it to the *mudaqqaqa* meat along with the spices. [Shape this into balls].

Return the meat and the [strained] broth to the pot [along with the meatballs]. Strip the leaves of the Jew's mallow, and chop them (*yukharraṭ*). When the meat broth comes to a boil, throw in the Jew's mallow, and let it boil until done.

---

200 Generally, *firākh* designates any young birds. However, in the Egyptian context, it is more specifically young pigeons.

201 The last sentence is added based on Gotha, fol. 33r; and DK, n. 1208. The expression the recipe uses to convey the idea of spreading the sauce on the fried meat is ويعمل عليه.

202 Here I amended the edited recipe based on Gotha, fols. 33r–v; and DK notes.

203 In DK, n. 1209, only a few drops are called for, *ʿasal quṭaran*.

204 This is based on similar dishes in al-Warrāq, chapter 86.

205 Based on today's culinary practices, honey is burnt by boiling it until it caramelizes a little and starts to smoke. Using it in dishes would impart a pleasant, slightly burnt flavor.

206 Here I filled in some missing steps, based on what we already know on *mudaqqaqa* from previous recipes, such as recipe 24 above.

Recipe for *summāqiyya* (meat with sumac)[207]

You need meat and sumac. [You also need] taro (*qulqās*), onion, and gourd (*yaqṭīn*); or chard (*silq*), onion, and eggplant; or apples—sour-sweet or sweet.[208] Also use tahini (*ṭaḥīna*), garlic, *ḥawāyij baql*,[209] lime juice (*laymūn akhḍar*) or Damascus citron (*kabbād*),[210] black pepper, hazelnuts, fine-tasting raisins, coriander, and a bit of thyme.

Boil the meat, [take it out of the broth], brown it [in fat], and then pour the broth [back] on it. Throw in the taro and the spices and herbs (*abāzīr*) we mentioned,[211] and let them cook until they are all done.

Pound sumac and sift it. Pound all the *ḥawāyij* [i.e., garlic, black pepper, hazelnuts, raisins, coriander, thyme], each separately. Add them to the sumac, squeeze lemon juice on them, and knead them together [with tahini]. Add this mixture to the pot, and let it boil, and then serve it.

(85) *Aruzziyya* (meat dish with rice)

You need meat, rice, black pepper, coriander, and dill (*shabath*).

Boil the meat, [take it out of the broth,] and brown it. Pound the fat solids attached to it, (**32r**) and return them to the meat.

Pound black pepper and coriander with some meat and a bit of rice, and shape the mix into meatballs (*mudaqqaqa*). After the rest of the meat browns [as mentioned above], pour its broth [back] on it. Add the meatballs, and let them cook until done.

Wash some rice, and add it to the pot along with a bit of dill, [and let them cook] and simmer gently, and serve.

(86) Recipe for *iṭriya* (meat dish with dried noodles)

You need meat and dried noodles (*iṭriya*),[212] black pepper and a bit of coriander for the meatballs (*mudaqqaqa*).

Make meatballs with a small amount of the meat. Pound the meat with a bit of black pepper, coriander, and baked onion.

---

207 This recipe only appears in Gotha, fol. 33v; and DK, appendix 24. Here I followed the more coherent Gotha version.

208 My guess on the two illegible words is *muzzī aw ḥulwī* (مزي او حلوي).

209 See n. 199 above.

210 Al-Anṭākī, *Tadhkira* 50, identifies *kabbād* as a variety of *astabūn*. It is the fruit of a *nāranj* tree (sour orange, *Citrus aurantium*), which has been grafted with branches of the *utrujj* tree (true citron, *Citrus medica*). See glossary 7.

211 Quite probably, the vegetables mentioned at the beginning of the recipe are to be added at this stage, not *abāzīr*, because the latter is mentioned in the following instructions.

212 See glossary 2, for more on this type of noodles.

[As for the rest of the meat,] boil it, strain it, and brown it [in fat]. Pound black pepper and cilantro and add them to the [fried] meat. Pour the [strained] broth on them, and when the pot comes to a boil, throw in the meatballs. [Continue cooking] until done.

Add dried noodles to the pot, along with snippets of dill (*ḥalqat shabath*), and a small amount of soaked chickpeas. [Let the pot cook] and then simmer, and serve.

Recipe for *tamriyya* (meat with dried dates)[213]

You need meat, dried dates (*tamr*), raisins (*zabīb*), jujubes (*ʿunnāb*), scalded and skinned almonds (*qalb lawz masmūṭ*), wine vinegar, honey, poppy seeds, wheat starch, saffron, *aṭrāf ṭīb* (spice blend), and black pepper.

Boil the meat, [strain it,] and then brown it [in fat]. Add to it some of the broth, dates, and raisins. Cook until done. Mix honey, vinegar, and saffron. Add them to the pot along with *aṭrāf al-ṭīb*, black pepper, and mint. Dissolve starch in a little vinegar and add it to the pot last. Let it simmer, and serve.

(87) *al-Labaniyya* (meat with milk)

You need meat, milk, leeks (*kurrāth*) or onion, mastic gum, cassia (*dār Ṣīnī*), and bit of mint. Suspend the milk [pot] on the fire,[214] and add the ingredients to it. Add the meat itself to the pot along with the milk. However, the onion should be added after [the mix has been] cooking a full hour.

If the meat cooks (**32v**) and the milk [sauce] has not thickened yet, throw in a piece of date palm inflorescence spathe (*kūz ṭalʿ*), or a bit of ground rice or wheat starch, [and cook] until it thickens. Let it simmer and then remove.

Recipe for *zabībiyya* (meat with raisins)[215]

You need meat, raisins, vinegar, honey, poppy seeds, wheat starch, saffron, and [skinned] scalded almonds.

Boil the meat, [strain it], and brown it [in fat], and then pour some of the broth on it. Wash the raisins and add them to the pot until they cook. You can pound some of them [before adding them] to thicken the sauce.

Blend vinegar, honey, and saffron, and add them to the pot. When it comes to a boil, throw in *aṭrāf al-ṭīb* (spice blend), black pepper, and mint. Dissolve

---

213 This recipe only appears in Gotha, fol. 34r–v; and DK, appendix 25.

214 The verb used is *yuʿallaq* 'suspended.' Apparently, the pot is not meant to be placed directly on the fire, as milk can easily burn.

215 This recipe only appears in Gotha, fol. 34v; and DK, appendix 26.

the starch in a small amount of vinegar and add it, last, to the pot. [Simmer] and serve.

(88) Recipe for *sitt shanāʿ* (best of the maligned dishes)[216]

You need meat, fried taro (*qulqās*), hazelnuts, tahini (*ṭaḥīna*), cilantro, and black pepper. Boil the meat and fry it with the [chopped] cilantro and black pepper (with some fat). Toast the hazelnuts, pound it and mix it with the tahini. [Add them to the pot] and cook until done. Put the fried taro on a plate and spread the *ḥawāʾij* (i.e., what was prepared above) on it.

(89) Recipe for *Mutawakkiliyya*[217]

You need meat, taro, garlic, black pepper, cilantro, and a small amount of onion.

Boil the meat, [strain it,] and then fry it with the garlic, cilantro, and black pepper, [and onion]. When it is done, add the [strained] broth,[218] and bring it to a boil. When it is done, you have the choice of adding the taro after frying it, or just washing it and adding it without frying. Let the pot simmer on the smoldering fire until it settles, and then ladle it.

(90) Recipe for *sikbāj* (sour vinegar stew)

You need meat. Also, taro with onion, or quince by itself, or gourd (*yaqṭīn*) and onion, or chard (*silq*), or eggplant and onion. You also need vinegar, honey, *aṭrāf al-ṭīb* (spice mix), black pepper, mint, and wheat starch (*nashā*ʾ).

Boil the meat, [strain it,] then fry it, (**33r**) and return the broth to it. Throw in the taro and onion, or whatever you choose to use. When it is cooked, add honey, vinegar, saffron, and *aṭrāf al-ṭīb*. Dissolve the starch in vinegar and add it to the pot along with mint, after you have put all other ingredients in. When done, remove the pot, and serve it as soon as it settles.

216 This is sometimes called *al-shanʿiyya* (al-Warrāq Istanbul MS, fol. 161r); and *sitt al-shanaʿ* (*Wuṣla* ii 569–70; al-Warrāq Istanbul MS, fol. 160r). In Gotha, fol. 34v, it is erroneously copied as *Nashāʿ*. See glossary 5, for more on the name of this dish.

217 This was named after the Abbasid caliph al-Mutawakkil (d. 861), and is said to be another name for *sitt shanaʿ*, as in al-Warrāq Istanbul MS, fol. 160r. See glossary 5, for more on the history of this dish.

218 Referred to as *māʾ*, lit., 'water.' However, in recipes, *māʾ* may refer to any liquid used, depending on context.

Recipe for *aruzz aṣfar* (yellow rice)[219]

You need rice, honey, saffron, pistachios, and *aṭrāf ṭīb* (spice mix). For each *qadaḥ* (2¼ pounds) of rice, use 3 *raṭl*s (3 pounds) honey, along with small amounts of water and sesame oil (*shayraj*).

Let the honey cook in a pot until it starts to boil. Wash the rice three times and after you dye it with saffron, add it to the honey. When it is cooked, stir in a bit of pistachios and a bit of almonds,[220] and then ladle it and serve it.

(91) Recipe for *fuqqāʿiyya* (foamy stew)[221]

You need meat, eggs, chard or lettuce, black pepper, onion, mint, chickpeas, rice, some fresh herbs (*ḥawāʾij baql*),[222] and lemon.

Boil the meat, [drain off its broth], brown it in fat (*yuḥammaṣ*), and return the broth to it.[223] Wash the chard and add it to the meat, along with [the chopped] onion. When it is cooked, season the pot with black pepper and the other ingredients (*ḥawāʾij*). When it boils, squeeze some lemon juice on it and crack open the eggs all over it. Remove the pot, and let it settle.

(92) Recipe for *isbīdbāj* (white stew)

You need meat, chard or lettuce, black pepper, cilantro, eggs, chickpeas, and rice. Boil the meat, [drain off its broth], and then fry it in fat along with cilantro and black pepper. Return the broth to the pot.

---

219 This recipe only appears in Gotha, fol. 35r–v; and DK, appendix 27. *Zahr* version, fols 10v–1r, is briefly described.

220 The expression *fī baṭnihi* 'inside it' indicates that the nuts are to be stirred in and not sprinkled over the rice.

221 The key to the name of this dish is the foam (*fuqqāʿ*) created with the eggs. This recipe does not give any clues on how the cook might create this. *Fuqqāʿiyya* recipe in *Waṣf* 23, however, mentions that a *shabaka* 'network' of egg white and Macedonian parsley (*maqdūnis*) is to be made on top of the dish when all the ingredients are added and it is almost ready to serve. Two more recipes in al-Warrāq Istanbul MS, fols. 148r–9r, provide us with some more clues: egg white is whipped with crushed skinned almonds, fresh white cheese, parsley, cilantro, mint, and rue, all chopped finely, and seasoned with ginger and black pepper. When the dish is cooked, the mix is thrown into the boiling pot. As soon as the egg starts to set, it is lightly stirred to create the characteristic foamy texture described as *muḥabbab* 'formed into tiny balls.'

222 Such as mint, parsley, and cilantro.

223 Here I replaced the word *milḥ* (ملح) 'salt' [clearly written as such in the edited text and Gotha, fol. 35v] with *māʾ* (ماء) 'liquid, broth,' judging from the preceding recipes, like 89. The two handwritten words can easily be mistaken for one another.

Wash the chard, [chop it,] and add it to the pot along with [chopped] onion. When it is cooked, add the rice [and chickpeas], and add the eggs to the pot last, [after all of the above] ingredients.

Throw in a small amount of *jubn Shāmī* (Levantine cheese like mozzarella), a bit of cumin, mastic gum, (**33v**) and Ceylon cinnamon (*qarfa*). Remove and ladle.

(93) Recipe for fried *Būrāniyya*[224]

You need meat, fried eggplant, black pepper, coriander seeds, mint, and onion. Boil the meat and onion and then [drain off the broth], and fry them together along with black pepper, coriander, and mint. Return the broth to the pot [and cook until the moisture evaporates]. Fry the eggplant and put it in a vessel (*wiʿāʾ*), and spread the [cooked] meat mixture all over it.

(94) Recipe for *kammūniyya* (meat dish seasoned with cumin)

You need meat, turnip (*lift*), chickpeas, garlic, black pepper, cilantro, [and cumin]. Boil the meat, [drain off its broth], and fry it with the spices (*abāzīr*) [mentioned above]. Return the broth to it. Cut the turnip into pieces and add it to the pot.[225] [Cook until done].

(95) Recipe for *narjisiyya* (narcissus flower stew)[226]

You need meat, rice, a bit of black pepper, *jubn Shāmī* (Levantine cheese like mozzarella), cumin, cilantro, chickpeas, and onion. Boil the meat, [drain off its broth], and fry it with cilantro and black pepper. Return the broth to it [along with onion and chickpeas].

Cut the washed carrots into pieces and add them to the pot. When cooked, throw in the rice, cumin, [and cheese]. For those who do not wish to use cheese and cumin, they can leave them out.

Recipe for *kurunbiyya* (meat stew with cabbage)[227]

You need meat, black pepper, cabbage, garlic, onion, cilantro, chickpeas, rice, mastic gum, and Ceylon cinnamon (*qarfa*).

---

224 Named after Būrān (d. 884), wife of the Abbasid caliph al-Maʾmūn (d. 833). It is a precursor of what is known today as *musaqqaʿa*. See Nasrallah, "In the Beginning There Was No *musakka*" 595–606.

225 Probably into 1- to 2-inch cubes, see also recipe 113 below.

226 The name may also designate dishes made with eggs, sunny side up; see *Kanz* recipe 203. Nonetheless, this dish still looks like a narcissus flower with its white, green, and yellow colors.

227 This recipe only appears in Gotha, fol. 36r; and DK, appendix 28.

Boil the meat, [drain off its broth], and fry it with garlic, black pepper, and cilantro. Return the broth to it and let it boil very well. Cut the cabbage into pieces, throw it into the pot, and let it boil [with the rest of the ingredients].

Recipe for *bāmiya* (meat stew with okra)[228]

You need meat (*laḥm*) or young pigeons (*firākh ḥamām*). You also need okra, black pepper, and cilantro.

Boil the meat, [drain off its broth], and fry it. When done, finely chop onion on it, and add black pepper, cilantro, and garlic [and fry them together]. Return the broth to the pot.

Cut the okra into pieces, press it and rub it between the fingers,[229] and add it to the pot. Make sure to squeeze the juice of one lime (*laymūna khaḍrā'*) on it so that the broth does not become viscous.[230] Remove and ladle.

Recipe for *fūliyya* (meat with fava beans)[231]

You need meat, fresh fava beans (*fūl akhḍar*), with both skins removed [i.e., the jacket and bean skin], or whatever you usually do with it. You also need black pepper, garlic, cilantro and coriander seeds, and eggs.

Pound some of the meat to make *mudaqqaqa* (meatballs) seasoned with a bit of coriander and black pepper. Boil the rest of the meat, [drain off its broth] and fry it. You also have the choice of not adding *mudaqqaqa*.

When the meat is done frying, add to it the spices [mentioned above], and cilantro. Continue cooking until all of it is done.

Return the broth to the pot and add the fava beans. When all of it is cooked, crack open the eggs on it, [wait until the eggs set with the heat of the pot,] and ladle the dish and serve it.

---

228 This recipe only appears in Gotha, fol. 36r–v; DK, appendix 29; and *Zahr*, fol. 11r.

229 The verb is derived from *ʿarraka*. Most probably, this is done so the okra releases as much of the mucilaginous substance inside as possible. This detail is included in the Gotha version only.

230 In Gotha, the word for viscous is not clear. In DK, it occurs as *yataʿallab* (يتعلّب) 'toughen.' However, *Zahr* is correct: *yatalaʿʿab* (يتلعّب) 'become viscous with viscid substances,' derived from *luʿāb* 'saliva.' Nowadays, the viscid substance in okra is more commonly referred to as *mukhāṭ* 'mucus.'

231 This recipe only appears in Gotha, fol. 36v; DK, appendix 30. Here I followed the version in Gotha as it has more detail.

(96) Recipe for *lūbyā* (meat with black-eyed beans)[232]

You need meat, black-eyed beans [fresh or dried], garlic, black pepper, and cilantro. Boil the meat, [drain off its broth], and fry it with the garlic, cilantro, and black pepper until done. Pour a small amount of the broth back into the pot, (**34r**) throw in the [prepared] beans, and let the pot cook until the beans are done and the broth is all gone except for its fat and spices and herbs.

(97) Recipe for *baṣaliyya* (meat with onion)

You need meat, onion, vinegar, honey, saffron, black pepper, *aṭrāf ṭīb* (spice blend), and mint.

Boil the meat, [drain off its broth], and fry it. Chop the onion finely and boil it by itself. Pass it through a sieve (*ghirbāl*) and add it to the pot along with the broth. Mix honey with vinegar, and add it to the pot along with saffron and the [rest of the] ingredients (*ḥawāʾij*). [Let it cook for a while] and then remove.

(98) Recipe for *ṭaḥīniyya* (meatless tahini dish)

You need carrots, bulbous leeks (*kurrāth abyaḍ*), tahini, wine vinegar, and *aṭrāf ṭīb* (spice blend).

Slice carrots into thin discs and boil them. Chop the white heads of the leeks, boil them separately, and fry them in sesame oil.

Put tahini in a container, and sprinkle it with hot water little by little while beating it by hand until its oil (*shayraj*) separates. [Remove the oil], and dissolve tahini in a container in a small amount of vinegar, with honey and *aṭrāf al-ṭīb*. Put the carrots in a pot, without adding any liquid; also add the leeks, and spread the prepared tahini, and the rest of the ingredients, all over them. Put only the carrots and leeks that the dish needs to suit the amounts of the rest of the ingredients.

(99) Recipe for *farīkiyya* (porridge with *farīk* 'toasted green wheat')

You need meat, black pepper, *farīk*, cheese, and cumin. Boil the meat and add the coarsely ground *farīk* to it. (**34v**) When done, add milk, cheese, cumin, a small amount of dill, mastic gum, and cassia. [Cook for a while] and remove it from the fire.

---

232 The recipe does not specify whether fresh or dried beans are called for. However, in a better copy of this recipe found in *Wuṣla* ii 590, which I used to amend the edited text, the beans are described as fresh and tender. To prepare them for cooking, both ends are cut off, and any tough beans are opened and only the seeds inside them are used. If dried beans are used, they must be soaked first, for several hours, before being added.

Recipe for *harīsa* (beef porridge)[233]
You need beef (*laḥm baqarī*), mastic gum, cassia (*dār Ṣīnī*), cheese, and cumin. Boil the meat and the husked wheat berries (*qamḥ maqshūr*), along with cassia, mastic gum, and dill. Continue feeding the fire until the beef falls apart. Beat the wheat mix until all the ingredients are blended very well, and then remove and ladle.

(100) Recipe for *qamḥiyya* (porridge of wheat berries)
You need meat, husked wheat berries (*qamḥ maqshūr*), mastic gum, cassia (*dār Ṣīnī*), dill, and cumin.

Boil the meat and wheat berries together if beef is used. However, if using mutton (*ḍaʾn*), then let the wheat berries boil first until they start cracking (*yatashaqqaq*), and then add the meat to it. When all of it is cooked, add mastic gum, cassia, dill, and cumin. If you wish, also add milk. Let it cook on a strong fire until it is good to eat, and then take the pot off the heat.

(101) Recipe for *taqliyyat yaqṭīn* (fried dish with gourd)[234]
You need meat, gourd, garlic, black pepper, chickpeas, cilantro, and a small amount of polished rice (*ruzz mubayyaḍ*). Boil the meat, [drain off its broth], and fry it with garlic, black pepper, and cilantro. Return the broth to it, and let it boil on a strong fire. Throw in the gourd and rice, and if preferred, some meatballs (*mudaqqaqa*), and then remove.

(102) Recipe for *kishk* (meat with *kishk*)[235]
You need meat, young pigeons (*firākh ḥamām*), or *buṭūn*.[236] Also, *kishk* and lemon or sour unripe grapes (*ḥiṣrim*) or Damascus citron (*kabbād*) are needed.[237] Use as well, black pepper, garlic, chickpeas, onion, eggplant, chard, the white heads of turnip (*bayāḍ lift*), and mint.

Boil the meat with chickpeas, and then [drain off the broth], and brown them [in some fat]. (**35r**) Return the broth, and throw in the eggplant and the other [vegetables]. Cook until done.

---

233 This recipe only appears in Gotha, fol. 37r; and DK, appendix 31.

234 Such fried dishes were expected to be moist with fat, with very little sauce remaining in them. See glossary 5, s.v. *nawāshif*.

235 *Kishk* are dried balls of crushed wheat and yogurt. They are added to stews to enrich them and enhance their taste.

236 Innards, organs, and bowels in the abdomens of quadrupeds, usually sheep.

237 See n. 210 above.

Soak the *kishk* and let it dissolve in a small amount of the meat broth, add it to the pot and let it boil. Throw in black pepper, garlic, and lemon [juice]. If sour unripe grapes are used, then boil them [in water], press them through a sieve, and add the juice to the pot.

(103) Recipe for *ḥiṣrimiyya* (meat soured with unripe grapes)
You need meat, safflower seeds (*qurṭum*), mastic gum, Ceylon cinnamon (*qarfa*), mint, sour unripe grapes (*ḥiṣrim*), and eggplant.

Pound the safflower seeds finely. Put the unripe grapes in a pot and, without adding water, let them cook well in their own juice (*yuʿarraq*). Mix them well with the [ground] safflower seeds, and pour some of the meat broth from the pot on them.[238] Strain the grape mix through a sieve. Repeat the straining two or three times. Pour [the resulting liquid] on the meat and add the above-mentioned mastic gum, cinnamon, and mint.

If the unripe grapes do not cook following the method described above, then further boil them [with added water].

[Recipes 104–8 deal with grain porridges.]

(104) Recipe for *khayṭiyya* (porridge with thread-like shreds of chicken breasts)[239]
You need milk (*laban ḥalīb*), bee honey (*ʿasal naḥl*), ground rice (*aruzz maṭḥūn*), and parboiled chicken breasts. Shred the chicken breasts or any other parts used. Put the rice and milk in a pot and cook them until they boil. Throw in the chicken breasts, and continue beating until [the chicken] resembles threads, and then remove.

Honey should be added to the dish after you ladle it onto the plates, **(35v)** and not [stirred] into the pot.

(105) Recipe for white *bahaṭṭa* (milky rice porridge)[240]
You need milk, ground rice, and white sugar (*sukkar bayāḍ*). Cook rice and milk in a pot until done. Stir in the finely crushed sugar. Continue stirring the pot, and do not slacken until it is cooked.

---

238 The recipe omits the directions for boiling the meat, frying it, and returning its broth to it.

239 Here I followed Gotha, fol. 38r, where the name of the dish is correctly copied; it is erroneously called *ḥinṭiyya* (cooked with wheat berries) in the edited text.

240 See glossary 5, for more on this dish.

(106) Recipe for yellow *bahaṭṭa* (milky rice porridge)

You need milk, ground rice, sugar, and saffron. Put the milk and rice in a pot and light a fire underneath it until the rice is cooked. Add the saffron and finely crushed sugar, and keep [stirring] the pot for about an hour.

(107) Recipe for *hayṭaliyya* (smooth milky porridge with fresh wheat starch)[241]

You need finely crushed husked wheat (*qamḥ maqshūr*), and milk. Put the wheat in a large earthenware tub (*mājūr*), add water and mash it, and then strain it into a container using a fine meshed flour sieve (*ghirbāl al-daqīq*). Repeat two or three more times. Strain the resulting liquid, and keep it covered until early morning. Pour off the yellowish liquid and use the starch that settled in the bottom. Put it in a pot along with milk, mastic gum, usnea (*shayba*), and bitter ginger (*ʿirq al-kāfūr*).[242] Let it cook and thicken on very low fire, and then ladle it onto plates, and pour some bee honey on it.

Recipe for *ʿadas muṣaffā* (strained lentil porridge)[243]

You need shelled lentils, vinegar, honey, saffron, jujubes, scalded and skinned almonds, and raisins.

Boil the lentils until they are cooked, and then press them through a flour sieve [to mash them]. Clean honey [by boiling and straining it], and add it to the lentils. Continue cooking and stirring; do not slacken.

Add the vinegar, small amounts of jujubes and raisins, black pepper, *aṭrāf al-ṭīb* (spice mix) [according] to what it needs, and a bit of the scalded and skinned almonds—color it with saffron, but leave some uncolored. Ladle it into bowls (*zabādī*),[244] and garnish it with jujubes and raisins.

(108) Recipe for *aruzz bi-laban* (milky rice porridge) (36r)

You need rice, milk, mastic gum, Ceylon cinnamon (*qarfa*), a little bit of usnea (*shayba*) and bitter ginger (*ʿirq kāfūr*). Boil the milk and add the rest of the ingredients (*ḥawāʾij*) to it, but wash the rice before adding it.

---

241 See glossary 5, for more on this dish.

242 This is also called *zurunbād*.

243 This recipe only appears in Gotha, fol. 38v; DK, appendix 32; *Zahr*, fol. 12r.

244 Sg. *zibdiyya*. This dish was most probably served in a decorative manner, with the yellow portion juxtaposed with the uncolored one.

(109) Recipe for *tuṭmāj* (fresh-pasta with meat and yogurt)[245]

You need meat, yogurt (*laban ḥāmiḍ*), garlic, black pepper, coriander, and a small amount of cilantro.

Make meatballs (*mudaqqaqa*) with [some] of the meat and a bit of black pepper, coriander, and baked onion. With [some of] the meat, make thin strips of trimmed meat (*sharāʾiḥ aḥmar*). Boil [the rest of] the meat with the [meatballs], and fry them along with black pepper, cilantro, and garlic, and [then return some of the] broth [and cook them]. As for the meat strips, fry them separately first, and then cook them in hot water.

Put the [prepared] pasta in boiling water, and let it cook, stirring [gently] with a stick until it is done. [Drain the pasta], and place it in the yogurt and arrange the cooked meat, the strips, and meatballs all over it.

Recipe for *aruzz mufalfal* (fluffy rice with separate grains)[246]

You need a lot of meat and *duhn* (sheep-tail fat), rice, mastic gum, Ceylon cinnamon (*qarfa*), and chickpeas.

Boil the meat, [drain off its broth], and fry it. Then return some of the broth to it. Add the rice after you wash it, and cover the pot to help the rice soften and become fluffy (*yanbut*).[247] Pound the sheep-tail fat and render it (*yuslā*), and then pour it all over the rice. Cover the pot with something and remove. Leave it on the ground for a good hour, and then ladle it.

(110) Recipe for *aruzz muḥallā* (sweetened rice)[248]

You need rice, fatty meat or chicken, bee honey, pistachios, *aṭrāf ṭīb* (spice blend), mastic gum, Ceylon cinnamon (*qarfa*), and saffron. If you wish, use neither meat nor chicken. However, if meat or chicken is used, then sheep-tail fat or sesame oil (*shayraj*) must be used.

Boil the meat, [drain off its broth], and brown it lightly. Add the honey to it and let it boil (**36v**) and then add some of the broth (*māʾ*), and continue boiling until it has the consistency of honey. After washing the rice, rub it with saffron, and add it to the pot. Throw in *aṭrāf ṭīb* and the rest of the spices. Feed the rice with fat [and let it cook until it is good to eat].

---

245 *Tuṭmāj* is fresh pasta made with unfermented stiff dough, rolled out into thin sheets and then cut into squares or triangles, based on a recipe in al-Warrāq Istanbul MS, fol. 168r.

246 This recipe only appears in Gotha, fols. 39r–v; DK, appendix 33; and *Zahr*, fol. 12v, which I used to amend the text slightly.

247 This appears as ينبت in Gotha, fol. 39r. In DK, the verb is يطيب 'good to eat.'

248 I used Gotha copy, fol. 39v to slightly amend the edited text.

(111) Recipe for *um nārayn* (bread pudding cooked between two fires)[249]

You need stale excellent (*ʿalāma*) bread,[250] milk, mastic gum, Ceylon cinnamon (*qarfa*), butter (*zubd*), bitter ginger (*ʿirq kāfūr*), and usnea (*shayba*).

Put the milk in a pot along with the *ḥawāʾij* [i.e., the spices mentioned above], and boil. Pull the inside of the bread from its crust, rub it into fine crumbs, and add it to the pot. Let it cook until done.

While it is cooking on the fire, you need to drizzle some of the butter on it, and drizzle it with some more when you ladle it.

(112) Recipe for *ʿIraqiyya* (Iraqi dish)[251]

You need meat, onion, black pepper, mastic gum, and Ceylon cinnamon (*qarfa*). Boil the meat, drain off its broth, [and set it aside], and brown it along with finely chopped onion heads. Let them brown together. Pound the black pepper and sprinkle it over the meat.

Mastic and cinnamon should be added while the meat boils [in the first stage]. After the meat is done frying with the onion, add to it as much of the broth [that was set aside] as needed [and cook it until done].

(113) Recipe for *safarjaliyya* (meat stew with quince)

You need meat, saffron, (**37r**) *aṭrāf al-ṭīb* (spice mix), (**37r**) mint, mastic gum, Ceylon cinnamon (*qarfa*), sugar or bee honey, and wine vinegar.

Boil the meat, [drain off its broth], and brown it and then return the broth to the pot. Cut the quince, core out the centers, and cut it into pieces the way you usually do with turnip for *kammūniyya* dish.[252] Add it to the meat and broth, and continue feeding the fire underneath until it is cooked.

Dissolve saffron in vinegar and add to it the honey or sugar, [and pour it into the pot]. Pound *aṭrāf al-ṭīb* and add them to the pot along with mint. Pound

---

249 Lit., 'mother of two fires.' Cooking between two fires was an ancient technique used to help brown the bottom and top side of a dish cooking on top of a stove; it is done with the help of a coal fire placed on the lid of the pot. The recipe here does not provide details, as it was probably too common to mention. However, both the name of the recipe and the absence of any directions for stirring the pot, point to this technique. See glossary 9.2, s.v. *ṭabkh bayn nārayn*. It was probably served as a side dish with roasted or grilled meat, as a *jūdhāba* dish. See, for instance, recipes 131 and 132 below.

250 In *Zahr*, fol. 12r, it is described as *abyaḍ* (white).

251 This appears as العراقية. This recipe is not distinguished as being distinctly Iraqi by any details or ingredients. The word in DK, n. 1479, occurs as *al-wāfiya* (الوافية) 'sufficient,' perhaps because it is simple and yet satisfying.

252 Probably cut into 1- to 2-inch cubes, see recipe 94 above.

black pepper and add it. Dissolve a small amount of wheat starch in a small amount of the broth and add it to the pot. [Cook until done.]

(114) Recipe for *mā' wardiyya* (meat stew with rosewater)[253]

You need meat, [dried] rosebuds (*zir ward*), lemon, onion, black pepper, mastic gum, and Ceylon cinnamon (*qarfa*). Boil the meat, [drain off its broth], and fry it. Chop a few onion heads on it and fry them until done. Pound black pepper and add it. Squeeze some lemon juice on it, and crumble [by rubbing between fingers] the rosebuds, there is no need to pound them, then add them to the pot. Add as much of the meat broth as it needs. [Cook until done.]

(115) Recipe for sweet *sanbūsak* (filled pastries)

You need sugar, *qaṭr* (sugar cane molasses) or bee honey, rosewater, hazelnuts, sesame oil, and crepes (*ruqāq al-kunāfa*).[254]

Pound the sugar. Toast the hazelnuts, (37v) grind them coarsely, and knead them into paste with molasses, ground sugar, and rosewater. Alternatively, you may use bee honey [instead of molasses] to knead it.

Cut the *kunāfa* sheets (*waraq*) into strips 4-fingers wide. Put a small amount of the stuffing on each of the pieces, as much as you see suitable, and roll them with the stuffing, all the way down.[255] Seal them with a small amount of [thin] dough, and fry them in sesame oil. Arrange them on plates, sprinkle them with pounded sugar, toasted hazelnuts, and rosewater, and serve.[256]

(116) Recipe for sour *sanbūsak* (meat-filled pastries)[257]

You need some herbs (*ḥawā'ij baql*),[258] sesame oil, vinegar, black pepper, hazelnuts or almonds, and *kunāfa* (crepes).[259]

Finely pound all the meat you are using, shape it into a single disc (*qurṣa*) as large as a [round of flat] bread or a bit smaller, depending on how much meat you are using. Boil it in a frying pan (*ṭājin*) and then flip it, and skim the froth.

---

253 Although the name of the dish suggests that rosewater is used in the recipe, in fact rosebuds are used in this dish.

254 See glossary 2.

255 Most probably, folded into a triangle, like folding a flag.

256 *Zahr*, fol. 12v, uses the verb *yuraṣṣ* 'arrange next to each other,' instead of the generic, all-purpose *yuʿmal*. It also mentions sprinkling rosewater on the pastries.

257 Here I slightly amended the recipe based on *Zahr*, fols 12v–3r.

258 Such as mint, parsley, and cilantro.

259 The Arabic phrase is رقاق بتاع الكنافة, which is a colloquial Egyptian expression.

Keep it until it cooks, and then take it out of the pan and pound the meat one more time, remove all blood vessels (*ʿurūq*).[260] (**38r**)

Suspend the frying pan on the fire, and fry the pounded meat in it once again with sesame oil until it browns. Pour the vinegar on it, and finely chop the herbs onto it and continue folding them in until they wilt. Scald and skin the almonds and grind them coarsely. [If using hazelnuts,] toast them and pound them similarly, and add them to the meat. Pound the black pepper and throw it into the pot. Continue cooking until all the vinegar evaporates.

Cut the *kunāfa* sheets into strips 4-fingers wide. Remove the meat mix (*ḥawāʾij*) from the fire, and after it has cooled down, put as much of it as is needed on each thin sheet of dough (*waraqa*), and roll it all the way down.[261] Seal the pieces with a bit of [thin] dough and fry them in sesame oil.

Snip off the tips of some green herbs,[262] spread them on the vessels, and arrange the pastries over them. Sprinkle them with a small amount of jasmine [water] or something else.[263]

(117) Recipe for *shaʿīriyya* (meat dish with orzo)[264]

You need flour, meat, sheep-tail fat (*alya*), mastic gum, and Ceylon cinnamon (*qarfa*). Boil the meat along with *alya* fat and mastic gum. [Drain off the broth], and brown the meat, and then pour the broth back. As for the *alya* fat, pound it, and then render it (**38v**) with an onion.

Make flour into stiff dough, and roll it between the fingers (*yuftal*) into barley like [pasta]. When you are done, add them to the meat and broth and let them boil until done. Pour the rendered fat into the pot. You can tell that the pasta is done when it floats to the surface.

(118) Recipe for *dajāj maḥshī ḥulw* (sweet stuffed chicken)

Take sugar, pistachios or almonds, musk, and rosewater. Make the stuffing with these.

After you fry the chicken and rub it with saffron, stuff it with the mix, and immerse it in sugar syrup (*jullāb*), or bee honey. [Alternatively, use] rose-petal jam (*ward murabbā*), with almonds and rosewater, which have been cooked

---

260 These would be chewy particles, which would not pound well.

261 See n. 255 above.

262 This appears as أطراف البقل الاخضر, or, in DK, n. 1539 as, أطراف البصل الاخضر 'green stalks of scallion.'

263 The recipe only mentions *yāsamīn*, but the verb *tarushsh* 'sprinkle' suggests a liquid.

264 The pasta used in the dish is rolled like barley *shaʿīr*. Orzo is Italian for barley.

FIGURE 25 *Apples, F1954.74r, Muḥammad al-Qazwīnī,* ʿAjāʾib al-makhlūqāt, *detail (Freer Gallery of Art and Arthur M. Sackler Gallery, Smithsonian Institution, Washington, DC: Purchase—Charles Lang Freer Endowment).*

until they are thick enough. You may stuff the chicken with rose-water jam instead. It will be good whichever way you do it.

(119) Recipe for *tuffāḥiyya bi-zaʿfarān* (meat with apple and saffron)
Boil the meat, [drain off its broth], and fry it in lots of fat. Fry with it sweet apple cut into pieces. Return a small amount of the broth to the meat and add a blend (*mizāj*) of vinegar, sugar, and wheat starch. Continue cooking. Throw in *aṭrāf al-ṭīb* (spice mix), black pepper, ginger, mint, and saffron. Rub the [scalded and skinned] almonds to split them, and add them to the pot. Let the pot simmer, and serve it.

(120) Recipe for *ṭabīkh al-mishmish al-akhḍar* (fresh apricot stew)[265]
Chop fatty meat into small pieces, and put it in a pot with a bit of salt and enough water to cover it. (**39r**) Skim the froth. Chop a washed onion and add it to the meat. Throw in the usual spices (*abāzīr maʿrūfa*), finely ground.

265 *Akhḍar* lit., 'green,' is used here to designate freshness as opposed to *yābis* 'dry' as in the following recipe.

FIGURE 26 *Apricots, F1954.80r, Muḥammad al-Qazwīnī,* ʿAjāʾib al-makhlūqāt, *detail (Freer Gallery of Art and Arthur M. Sackler Gallery, Smithsonian Institution, Washington, DC: Purchase—Charles Lang Freer Endowment).*

Take fresh, soft apricots (*akhḍar ṭarī*), bruise them, boil them until they are cooked, and mash them by hand. Strain the apricots, and add the juice to the meat pot. Some people [further] thicken the stew by adding liquid of safflower seeds (*ḥabb al-qurṭum*) extracted from ground safflower seeds steeped in water, which is the recommended thing to do.

Let the pot cook until it comes to a boil, simmer it on the smoldering fire, and then remove.

(121) Recipe for *ṭabīkh al-mishmish al-yābis* (dried apricot stew)

Boil fatty meat in a small amount of water, and skim the froth. Take some dried apricots, remove their stones, and replace them with scalded, skinned almonds. When the meat is done cooking and frying [in its fat], add the apricots, raisins, *aṭrāf al-ṭīb* (spice blend), poppy seeds, a stick of cassia (*ʿūd dār Ṣīnī*),

FIGURE 27
Pigeon, F1954.102v, Muḥammad al-Qazwīnī, ʿAjāʾib al-makhlūqāt, *detail (Freer Gallery of Art and Arthur M. Sackler Gallery, Smithsonian Institution, Washington, DC: Purchase—Charles Lang Freer Endowment).*

mint, mastic gum, Ceylon cinnamon (*qarfa*), saffron, and jujubes (*ʿunnāb*). Sweeten it with sugar,[266] and let it simmer, and then serve.

(122) Recipe for *firākh al-ḥamām* (young pigeons stewed in vinegar)
Slaughter them, clean, and wash them, and then half-boil them, color them with saffron, fry them in sesame oil, and put them aside.

Set the pot on the fire, and put very sour vinegar (*khall ḥādhiq*) in it, after you color it with some saffron. (**39v**) Add to it mint, toasted hazelnuts, black pepper, crushed rosebuds, and *aṭrāf al-ṭīb* (spice blend). Add the pigeons to the pot and let them simmer ever so slowly until the dough [sealing the pot] is cooked.[267] Let the pot settle on the remaining heat, and then take it down and serve the dish.

(123) *Kuskusū* (couscous)[268]
You need meat, sheep-tail fat, flour (*daqīq*), a small amount of sweet olive oil (*zayt ṭayyib*), mastic gum, Ceylon cinnamon (*qarfa*), black pepper, coriander seeds, and chicken.

Boil chicken, meat, and sheep-tail fat with mastic gum and sweet olive oil. Roll the dough between the fingers (*tufattal*), as you do with *mufattala*.[269] Put them in a pot with a perforated bottom, which you put on the meat pot. This

---

266 Or honey, as in DK, n. 1579. We can assume that some of the broth remains in the pot to moisten the fruits while it simmers.

267 Sealing the pot to its lid with dough was a common cooking practice to help trap in steam. See, for instance, al-Tujībī, *Fiḍāla* 87.

268 This appears as *kuskuwā* (كسكوا), in DK, n. 1595; and *Zahr*, fol. 13r. It is incorrectly copied in the edited text as *kishk*. A recipe somewhat similar to this is found in *Wuṣla* ii 608, where it is called *kuskusū Maghribī* 'Moroccan couscous.' It is unclear whether the flour used here is common flour or semolina flour.

269 This is a type of couscous rolled into tiny balls, like peppercorns.

will prevent the boiling liquid from reaching up to them.[270] Continue feeding the fire until the meat is cooked.

Pound the sheep-tail fat, render it with an onion, and fold the couscous into it.[271] Brown the meat [in fat] along with a [chopped] onion, black pepper, and coriander, and arrange them on the couscous. Garnish the top with sour *sanbūsak* filled with meat,[272] and serve it.

(124) Recipe for *laḥm taqliyya* (fried meat)

Take cut-up meat, onion, black pepper, mastic gum, Ceylon cinnamon (*qarfa*), coriander, and a small amount of sweet olive oil (*zayt ṭayyib*) (**40r**) or sesame oil (*shayraj*), and lemon.

Make meatballs with some of the meat. Season them with a bit of black pepper, boil [them along with] the meat, adding mastic gum, cinnamon, and olive oil, and cook until done. [Drain the meat broth], and brown the meat, adding black pepper and coriander. Return some of the broth to the meat. Chop the onion on it and let it boil until done [and the moisture is reduced]. Squeeze lemon juice on it.

Laḥm sharāʾiḥ (fried thin slices of meat)[273]

You need meat, sheep-tail fat (*duhn*) and sesame oil—or just sheep-tail fat, mastic gum, and Ceylon cinnamon (*qarfa*).

Cut the meat into thin slices (*yusharraḥ*) and boil it with mastic gum and cinnamon. Drain its broth, and fry it in sesame oil. If only sheep-tail fat is used, then boil it with the meat, pound it, [render it,] and then fry the meat with it.

(125) Recipe for *mudaqqaqa maqliyya* (fried meat patties)[274]

You need meat, black pepper, cilantro, and coriander seeds, a small amount of sweet olive oil or sesame oil, and a small amount of onion.

Pound the meat with a baked onion and the rest of the *ḥawāʾij* [i.e., black pepper, cilantro, and coriander], and make as many patties (*quraṣ*) as you need. Suspend the frying pan (*ṭājin*) on the fire and put a small amount of water in it. When it boils and bubbles, add the patties to it, and let them boil until they are half done, then take them out. Next put sesame oil in a frying pan

---

270 The couscous will be steamed.

271 The steamed couscous is simply referred to here as *ʿajīn*, lit., 'dough.'

272 See recipe 116 above.

273 This recipe only appears in DK, appendix 34; Gotha, fol. 42v; and *Zahr*, fol. 13r.

274 Here I amended the text based on *Zahr*, fol.13r.

set on the fire. Fry the patties, and put them on plates. Pound a small amount of coriander and sprinkle it on them.

Kharūf Kurdī (Kurdish-style whole lamb roast)[275]

You need a lamb, sheep-tail fat (*duhn*), pistachios, sugar or bee honey or sugar cane molasses (*qaṭr*), aloeswood (*ʿūd*), ambergris (*ʿanbar*), rosewater, and saffron.

Slaughter the lamb, scald it (*yusmaṭ*) [to remove the wool], and slit open its cavity and remove whatever is in it. Wash it very well and rub it with saffron. Pound the sheep-tail fat and render it. Pound pistachios and sugar and knead them with the fat, along with bee honey and rosewater. Stick this mix (*ḥawāʾij*) in a clean vessel after you shape it into a disk. Put the aloeswood and ambergris on the fire [to smoke] and turn the vessel upside down on it so that the mix is infused with the aromatic smoke.[276] Put the [smoked] ingredients in the lamb's cavity and sew it closed with a needle [and thread].

Put the lamb in the *tannūr* (open-topped, bell-shaped clay oven) to roast it, until it is done. [While it is roasting,] put [a pan with layered] thin sheets of *ruqāq* bread under it.[277]

(126) Recipe for *kharūf mamzūj* (whole lamb roast, seasoned with vinegar-based liquid sauce)[278]

You need a lamb, wine vinegar (*khall khamr*), lemon, sesame oil, black pepper, *aṭrāf ṭīb* (spice blend), and saffron. Scald the lamb [to remove the wool], slit open the cavity, (**40v**) and remove whatever is in it.

Squeeze a lemon and mix its juice with vinegar, and the pounded *ḥawāʾij* [i.e., saffron and spice blend], also add a bit of black pepper and sesame oil [this will be its seasoning sauce, or *mizāj*].

Slit the lamb [in several places], but keep it whole.[279] Make a bundle of feathers. Roast the lamb [in the *tannūr*] until it is done. Take it out, dip the bundle of feathers in the *ḥawāʾij* [i.e., seasoning sauce, or *mizāj*, prepared in the

---

275 This recipe only appears in Gotha, fols. 42v–3r.

276 See glossary 9.2, s.v. *tabkhīr*.

277 The recipe is very briefly describing *jūdhāba*, which is a kind of sweet bread pudding usually set under roasting meat or chicken in the *tannūr*, so that it catches all the dripping juices and fat. See glossary 5.

278 This is called *mizāj*, from which the adjectives *mamzūj* (in the edited version) and *mumazzaj* (in Gotha, fol. 43r) derive.

279 At this point, the edited version and Gotha, fol. 43r, seem to continue with another recipe. In their n. 1646 the editors explain, "The last part of the recipe as it is in C is found in DK 41v–2r, under the title '*Sanbūsak*.'" The original *sanbūsak* recipe is provided by *Zahr*,

previous step], sprinkle the lamb all over with it,[280] and then return it to the *tannūr*. Repeat the procedure until all the *ḥawāʾij* is used up, and then take the lamb out of the oven.

[Note:] As usual, put some thin moistened sheets of *ruqāq* bread or *jardaq* (round thick and pithy bread) under the lamb while it is roasting.[281]

Recipe for *sanbūsak* (filled pastries)[282]

Put some pounded meat in a pot and let it sweat (*yuʿarraq*) along with a piece of Ceylon cinnamon (*qarfa*), a bit of mastic gum, and onions sliced but left intact (*mushaqqaq*).[283] When the meat is done sweating, [i.e., all juices released have evaporated], fry it in sesame oil to remove all undesirable greasy odors (*zafar*).

Add sumac juice (*māʾ al-summāq*) to the meat; put enough in to sour it. Let it cook until all the liquids evaporate. Add some chopped lemon preserved in salt (*laymūn mumallaḥ*),[284] mint, and aromatic spices (*afāwīh ʿaṭira*).[285] [Fill and fold as in recipe 116 above], and fry them in fresh sesame oil, but before doing so, smear (*yulaṭṭakh*) the pieces with saffron dissolved in rosewater.

(127) Recipe for making *sanbūsak* filling

Take ½ *raṭl* (½ pound) meat and boil it as described earlier [above recipe]. Pound it again and let it dry out in the open air. [Also take] 4 bunches of Macedonian parsley (*baqdūnis*) and one bunch of fresh mint (*naʿnāʿ akhḍar*), both chopped finely; ½ *ūqiyya* (15 grams/1 tablespoon) black pepper; ½ *ūqiyya* caraway seeds; 3 sticks of Ceylon cinnamon (*qarfa*); a couple of nodes from a ginger rhizome;[286] 2 *dirhams* (6 grams/1 teaspoon) of each of *aṭrāf ṭīb* (spice blend), cardamom (*hāl*), cloves (*qaranful*), spikenard (*sunbul*), and betel leaves (*tunbul*). (**41r**)

---

fol. 13r, where it is called *sanbūsaka*. I complete the recipe using the final missing part provided by DK, n. 1646. Next, I complete the *sanbūsak* recipe based on *Zahr*.

280 And hence the need for slitting the lamb's skin, so that the seasoning soaks into the meat.

281 A dish prepared this way is called *jūdhāba*. It is a kind of bread pudding, usually sweet, set in the *tannūr* under roasting meat—a whole lamb in this case—so that it catches all the dripping juices and fat. See glossary 5.

282 The opening sentence is found only in *Zahr*, fol. 13r; the rest of the recipe was inadvertently annexed to the previous one by the copyist.

283 On sweating the meat, see glossary 9.2, s.v. *taʿrīq*.

284 See chapter 18 below, for recipes.

285 Such as cinnamon, cardamom, and nutmeg.

286 In the recipe, it is called *ʿuṣfūrayn*, lit., 'two sparrows.'

Put the pounded meat in a pot, and add parsley and mint to it. Sift the spices [after grinding them] and stir them in.[287] It would even be better with pounded skinned almonds, pistachios, hazelnuts, or walnuts.

Fill thin sheets of *ruqāq bread* with this filling, and fry the pieces in sesame oil until done, [and take them out, and serve].[288]

(128) Recipe for *ʿadas muṣaffā* (strained lentils)

Take crushed lentils, boil them in a large brass pot (*dast*), and then transfer them into a wide-mouthed earthenware vessel (*mājūr*). Allow them to cool down and then strain them through a sieve (*munkhul*).

Suspend the brass pot (*dast*) on the fire, and put in it *ʿasal mursal* (sugar cane syrup);[289] for each *qadaḥ* (2¼ pounds) of lentils, use 4 *raṭls* (4 pounds) of clean syrup. Add the strained lentils to the pot, and cook.

Moisten the mix with vinegar.[290] For each *qadaḥ* [of lentils], use 1 *raṭl* (2 cups) vinegar. Also, for each *qadaḥ* [of lentils], use ¼ *ūqiyya* (½ tablespoon) each of black pepper, ginger, and *aṭrāf ṭīb* (spice blend), all ground. Add black raisins, jujube, and scalded and skinned almonds colored with saffron. The seeds of raisins need to be removed.

Add all these ingredients to the pot, along with a small amount of butter. Continue cooking until it is done. Ladle it into plates (*ṣuḥūn*), let it cool down, and then eat it.

(129) Recipe for *najmiyya* (star-studded meat dish)[291]

You need meat, sumac, several heads of onion, black pepper, eggs, thyme (*zaʿtar*), lime juice (*laymūn akhḍar*), hazelnuts, and some fresh herbs (*ḥawāʾij baql*).[292]

Boil the meat, [drain off its broth], and brown it [in fat] with black pepper. Sift the sumac after you pound it, (**41v**) and add it to the pot. Finely chop the herbs and add them to the pot. Throw in thyme and the [crushed] hazelnuts

287 'And sift' is written as ونصف instead of وانسف. In this book, س is often written as ص, and vice versa, as in *masbūgh* (مسبوغ) for *maṣbūgh* (مصبوغ) 'colored.' This is one of the examples on the dialectical vocalizations we encounter in this book, see Introduction, pp. 12–3.

288 This sentence وينزل ويهدأ 'remove the pot from the fire and let it settle,' which concludes the recipe, is redundant, because fried foods are usually taken out immediately.

289 This is made by boiling down sugar cane juice when it fails to crystallize into *qand*, as described in al-Nuwayrī, *Nihāyat al-arab* viii 196. It is an Egyptian product not known in the Levant, al-Nuwayrī adds.

290 The word used is *yuṭfā*, lit., 'extinguish.'

291 Gotha does not include this recipe. I amended it in several places based on DK.

292 Such as mint, parsley, and cilantro.

[and lemon juice]. Pour [the drained] broth on the ingredients, enough to cover them, and cook until done. Crack open the eggs on them.[293]

(130) Recipe for *kurunb mumazzaj* (cabbage seasoned with honey-vinegar sauce)[294]

You need cabbage, vinegar, honey, saffron, hazelnuts, and caraway. Cut the cabbage as is commonly done [i.e., cut the leaves off the stems], boil it until it is done, and take it out of the water (*yushāl*). Burn the honey,[295] [and add to it] vinegar with saffron dissolved in it. Add to them *aṭrāf al-ṭīb* (spice blend) and a bit of toasted and crushed coriander seeds along with the *ḥawāʾij* (i.e., hazelnuts and caraway).

Take a cabbage leaf, dip it in the *ḥawāʾij*,[296] and then put it on a plate. Repeat with the rest of the cabbage leaves, and when finished, pour the remaining *ḥawāʾij* (i.e., *mizāj*) all over them.

(131) Recipe for *Asyūṭiyya*[297]

You need sugar, pistachios, bee honey, sheep-tail fat (*alya*), thin sheets of *ruqāq* bread, *tamr* (dried dates) or *ʿajwa* (sweet and soft dried dates),[298] poppy seeds, saffron, sesame oil, and rosewater.

Suspend the honey pot on the fire, and let it boil, and skim its froth. Pound the sugar and add it along with the coarsely pounded pistachios. Also, add poppy seeds, saffron, rosewater, and sesame oil [and dates].

Chop the sheep-tail fat and render it. [The thin sheets of bread should be layered with the honey mix in a casserole-like pan], and then pour the rendered fat over it slowly and in small amounts until it is all used up.[299] Sprinkle its face with pounded sugar and pistachios.

---

293 The eggs are to be left whole, sunny side up; these are the dish's stars (*nujūm*, sg. *najma*).

294 The liquid seasoning sauce is called *mizāj*.

295 See n. 205 above.

296 The reference here is to the prepared liquid sauce, called *mizāj*. The addition appears in DK, n. 1693.

297 Named after Asyūṭ, a city in Upper Egypt. It is meant to be a kind of *jūdhāba*/*jawādhib*, like the following recipe. Cf. recipes 269 and 274 below.

298 ʿAbd al-Laṭīf al-Baghdādī, *Riḥla* 75, mentions that *tamr* in Egypt is the equivalent of *qasb* in Iraq. The latter is a naturally dry date that does not soften and moisten when fully ripe and dried. By contrast, *ʿajwa* in Egypt is the equivalent of *tamr* in Iraq, which is any date variety that softens and moistens when dried, and can be stored pressed into containers.

299 It is not clear whether this casserole is to be further cooked in the oven, but judging from the extant recipes of this type of food, and the following recipe, the casserole is to be baked in the *tannūr* oven.

(132) Recipe for *jawādhib al-khashkhāsh*[300]

You need (**42r**) bee honey, sugar, pistachios, sheep-tail fat (*alya*), poppy seeds, thin sheets of *ruqāq* bread, and *ʿajwa* (sweet and soft dried dates) or *ruṭab* (fresh dates).

Pound sugar and pistachios, and knead them with honey. Render sheep-tail fat, and add it to the honey mix along with poppy seeds and stoned dates. [The thin sheets of bread should be layered with the honey mix in a casserole-like pan], which you put under the roasting lamb (*kharūf al-shawī*).[301] However, you can also make it in the house [kitchen], and dispense with the [roasting] lamb.

When it is done cooking, pound the rest of the sugar, keep it in a container, and sprinkle it on top of the dishes [when served].

[The following, up to recipe 138, are stew recipes.]

(133) Recipe for *firākh maṣūṣ* (young birds stewed in vinegar sauce)[302]

You need meat, young pigeons (*firākh ḥamām*), or young chickens (*farārīj*). Boil the meat, [drain off its broth], fry it, and return the broth to it. Add sugar and vinegar, as well as *aṭrāf al-ṭīb* (spice blend), mint, a small amount of wheat starch, black pepper, mastic gum, and Ceylon cinnamon (*qarfa*), and let it boil [until done]. You may substitute sugar with bee honey.

Recipe for *rummāniyya* (meat stew with pomegranate juice)[303]

You need meat, and dried pomegranate seeds (*ḥabb rummān*),[304] or fresh sour pomegranate [juice] (*rummān ḥāmiḍ*). Also needed are honey; and eggplant, chard, or gourd (*yaqṭīn*); onion; *aṭrāf ṭīb* (spice blend); black pepper; and a small amount of rice.

Boil the meat, [but] pound part of it to make *mudaqqaqa* (meatballs), to which you add black pepper and the rice. Drain the meat and brown it [with the onion]. Return the broth to the meat along with the eggplant [or the alternative vegetable], and let it cook until [the vegetable] is done. Throw in the meatballs with the rest of *ḥawāʾij* [i.e., remaining ingredients of pomegranate juice and *aṭrāf ṭīb*]. [To be cooked further and simmered.]

---

300 See n. 277 above. Cf. recipe 294 below.

301 The lamb is usually roasted in the household *tannūr*, outside the house.

302 See glossary 5, s.v. *maṣūṣ*.

303 This recipe only appears in Gotha, fol. 44v; and DK, appendix 35.

304 Dried pomegranate seeds are first steeped in water, and then mashed to extract their juice, and drained.

Recipe for *rummāniyya* (meat stew with pomegranate juice)[305]

Cut the meat into pieces and add it to the pot. Pour water on it, [let it boil], and remove the scum. Throw in cassia (*dār Ṣīnī*), mastic gum, ginger, sesame oil, and meatballs (*kubab*), made as small as hazelnuts. The amount of water added to the pot should not be much, so that when the meat is done, only a little of it remains.

Take fresh sour pomegranate juice, balance its taste with rosewater and sugar, and add it to the pot along with some mint leaves. Thicken the sauce with pounded pistachios or almonds, and color it with saffron. Add all the spices in *aṭrāf al-ṭīb* (spice blend), and sprinkle the dish with a little bit of rosewater.

(134) Recipe for *mulūkhiyya* (Jew's mallow stew)

Boil the meat until it is cooked and then [drain off its broth] and fry it with cilantro, garlic, and salt, all pounded together. Add also black pepper, coriander, one baked onion, and caraway. When all of it is fried, add a piece of roasted meat (*shawiyya*) pounded thoroughly.[306] Stir the pot for a short while and then return the meat broth to it and let it boil vigorously.

Next, throw in the [finely chopped] Jew's mallow, adding it in small amounts,[307] and let it cook. When it is done, lightly sprinkle the stew with cold water [to stop the boiling] and remove. (**42v**)

Render sheep-tail fat (*alya*) with mastic gum, cassia (*dār Ṣīnī*), and sweet olive oil or sesame oil. Trickle it all over the surface. The dish is even better if eggplant, fried in rendered sheep-tail fat, is also added to it.

(135) Recipe for *mishmishiyya* (apricot dish)[308]

Slice the meat off the bones and pound it very well. Add to it [ground] herbs and spice seeds and aromatics (*abāzīr* and *afāwih*), and enough salt. Shape it into evenly-sized small [apricot-like balls].[309] Arrange them in a frying pan [in one layer], pour the juice of unripe grapes (*māʾ al-ḥiṣrim*) on them, enough

305 This recipe only appears in DK, appendix 36.

306 Both Gotha, fols 44v–5r, and DK, n. 1728, have instead the word *shiwā* (شوا), which is the plural of *shawiyya* (شوية).

307 The verb تدَرّ, a dialectical vocalization of تذَرّ, implies taking small amounts of something with the finger tips and sprinkling them into a pot, container, etc.

308 In fact, there are no apricots in the dish. The recipe describes how to make meatballs that look like apricots.

309 The recipe refers to them as *kayl*, which suggests that the meatballs must be carefully measured so that they all look like evenly-sized apricots.

to cover them. Put the pan on the fire, and continue turning the balls ever so gently until all the moisture evaporates.

Pour fresh sesame oil on the meatballs, and fry them on one side and then flip them. Every time one is fried, dip it in a mix, which you have already prepared, of eggs with saffron dissolved in rosewater, so that it is completely coated with it, and return it to the frying pan. Repeat, dipping them in the eggs two or three times, so that they look as yellow as apricots.

Arrange the balls on plates, pour sugar syrup scented with rosewater on them, perfume them with musk, and use.

(136) Recipe for *sikbāj* (sour vinegar stew)

[This recipe is identical with recipe 7 above, with the exception of minor details.][310]

(137) Recipe for *sitt al-Nūba* (the 'Nubian lady')[311]

Take [seeds of] Iraqi purslane (*rijla ʿIrāqiyya*), and extract their juice.[312] Also, take bee honey or sugar syrup (*jullāb*). [Put it all in a pot and] suspend the pot on the fire. Add shelled [ground] pistachios, musk, and rosewater. Immerse fried chicken (*dajāj muṭajjan*) in it.

(138) Recipe for *tuffāḥiyya* (meat stew with apples)

Cut the meat into small strips (*ṣighār mustaṭīl*), and add them to the pot along with salt and coriander, a bit of each. (**43v**) Boil the pot until it is almost cooked, and skim the froth. Chop the onion into small pieces and add it to the pot along with a stick of cassia (*dār Ṣīnī*), black pepper, mastic gum, finely ground ginger, and sprigs of mint.

Now take sour apples or sweet-sour ones, peel them, remove the seeds, pound them in a stone mortar, extract the juice and add it to the pot. Next, dissolve a small amount of finely crushed almonds in some water and throw it into the pot.[313] Crumble some dried mint (*naʿnāʿ yābis*) into the pot, and if you choose to add garlic, then do so, but add it whole. If you want to add chicken

---

310 At this point, our compiler might have started to copy from another manual, probably unaware of the repetition in recipes.

311 Cf. recipe 59, which is blackened with raisins; and recipe 66, blackened with toasted and crushed purslane seeds.

312 The juice is extracted by crushing the seeds, then steeping them in water, and pressing out the liquid. The verb usually used is *yustaḥlab*.

313 The verb used for dissolving finely crushed almonds in water is *yurabbā*, as it occurs in DK, n. 1783; and Gotha, fol. 46r.

to the pot, you may do so. However, if you are using chicken, then leave out the garlic.

(139) Recipe for *dajāja karnadāj* (chicken grilled on a rotating spit)[314]

The chicken is grilled and moistened [while rotating] with walnut and almond oil mixed with a bit of salt and saffron.

The chicken will be at its best when it is fatigued until it stops and can no longer run. In addition, it has to be fat, and before slaughtering it, it should be fed with vinegar and rosewater. After that, you can scald it to remove the feathers as usual. While grilling it [by rotating it on a spit], put a small amount of sesame oil with salt and saffron [in a bowl] near you, and continue basting the chicken with it. It will come out splendidly tender and delicious.

[The following 10 recipes, which conclude this long chapter, mostly deal with *ʿaṣāfīr* (sparrows).][315]

(140) Recipe (44r) for *ʿaṣāfīr mashwiyya* (roasted sparrows)

Sprinkle the sparrows with [hot] water, pluck their feathers, open them up, and clean them.

If you want them roasted, take olive oil, black pepper, thyme, garlic, saffron, salt, and Ceylon cinnamon (*qarfa*); pound [the spices] finely and mix them with the olive oil. Next, insert the sparrows on sticks, which have been smoothed and sharpened (*manḥūt*). Between each two sparrows, insert a piece of white onion. Brush them with the prepared olive oil [and roast them].[316] The same thing is done when roasting quails (*sammān*) and chicken (*dajāj*).

If you want to fry the sparrows, heat up olive oil or sesame oil and enhance it (*yukhlaʿ*) with a piece of Ceylon cinnamon (*qarfa*), a bit of mastic gum, and

---

314 Copied as كزنداج in the edited text; كرنداج in DK, n. 1788; and كرنذاج in Gotha, fol. 46r. It also occurs as كرنباج and كردناج in other sources. See glossary 5, s.v. *karnadāj*. This recipe is similar to the last part of recipe 48 above, with the exception of minor stylistic differences. This may be because more than one source was used in putting together the present collection of recipes.

315 The large number of sparrow recipes here, a rare find in our extant medieval Arabic cooking documents, indicates that manuals specializing in such recipes abounded at the time. Their popularity can no doubt be attributed to their properties as aphrodisiacs. See glossary 10, s.v. *ʿaṣāfīr*.

316 Skewers prepared in this way were often roasted in the *tannūr* oven, as it kept them nice and moist. See, for instance, recipes in al-Warrāq, chapter 89. Grilling on an open fire, such as that of a brazier, is called *takbīb*, v. كبب, from which the adj. *mukabbab* and n. *kabāb* derive.

black pepper. Throw whichever you are using, quails, sparrows, or chicken, into the oil.

These birds can be fried right away and do not need to be boiled first. However, if you want to cleanse them of blood, immerse them in extremely hot water to which you have added salt and olive oil. After that [take them out] and let them drain well, and then fry them along with onion. Optionally, [after taking them out of the pan], throw *murrī* (liquid fermented sauce), vinegar, and lemon juice on them [to season and moisten them].

[A cautionary note:] Quails with blue eyes should not be eaten because they cause leprosy, due to a peculiarity in their properties. This is known and has been proven to be true.

(141) Recipe for *ʿuṣfūr makbūs* (sparrow preserved in salt)[317]

Choose domesticated (*baytiyya*) fat small-sized sparrows, open them from the chest, clean them, and discard their gall bladders.

Take salt, (**44v**) cassia (*dār Ṣīnī*), and a bit of mastic gum, and crush them all very well. Put some of the mix in the sparrows' cavities, and sprinkle some of it on them. Pack them tightly (*yuraṣṣ*) in a glass jar (*qaṭramīz zujāj*), pour on them a small amount of *shirsh*, which is *māʾ wa-milḥ* (brine), and cover them all (*yukhammar*) with a lot of salt. Set the jar aside until [it is] done, and then eat them.[318] Truly delicious, God willing.

(142) Recipe for *ʿaṣāfīr bi-l-bayḍ* (sparrows with eggs)[319]

Take the sparrows, open them, clean them, boil them in water until they are done, and take them out. Next, fry chopped onion in sesame oil [in a frying pan], add the sparrows to it [and fry them].

Pour eggs seasoned with salt, as well as spices, herbs, and aromatics (*abāzīr* and *afāwih*) all over the sparrows. Fold them with the eggs, and [continue cooking] until they set. Ladle the dish into vessels, and put them away (*yurfaʿ*).[320]

---

317 The only sparrow recipe found in *Waṣf* 147 is identical with this one, with a bit more detail. Here I used it to amend the edited recipe.

318 See, for instance, recipes 144 and 145 below, which describe how such preserved birds are served.

319 Sparrows with eggs (sometimes called *ʿujja* 'omelet') were popular in medieval times: we have one recipe in al-Warrāq, chapter 79; one in the anonymous *Anwāʿ al-ṣaydala* 21; and another in al-Tujībī, *Fiḍāla* 191–2. It is clear that they all drew on different sources.

320 The concluding instruction indicates that it was offered as a cold dish.

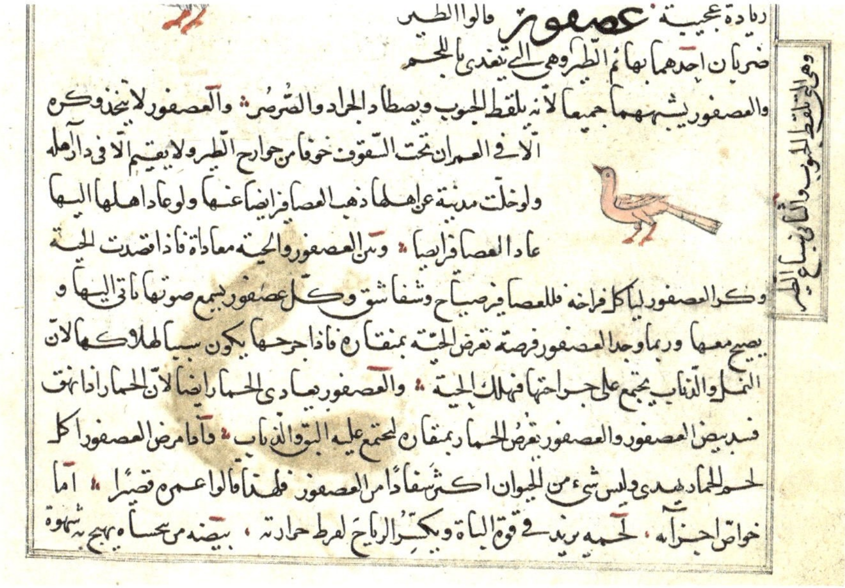

FIGURE 28 *Sparrow, F1954.103v, Muḥammad al-Qazwīnī,* ʿAjāʾib al-makhlūqāt, *detail (Freer Gallery of Art and Arthur M. Sackler Gallery, Smithsonian Institution, Washington, DC: Purchase—Charles Lang Freer Endowment).*

(143) Recipe for fried dishes (*muṭajjan*) of sparrows, young chickens (*farārīj*), and chicken

Take whatever you wish of these, cut them open and clean them [and use them right away] if they are the small kind of birds. Big birds, like young chickens, and chickens, need to be cleaned and cut up into pieces, washed, boiled in water with vinegar and salt—enough to cover them. [After they are cooked,] take them out of the water, drain them, and rub them with saffron dissolved in rosewater.

Fry [whatever you choose of the prepared birds] in sesame oil, sweet olive oil (*zayt muṭayyab*),[321] or chicken fat, and then put them away (*yurfaʿ*), and use [as needed].[322]

---

321 See glossary 6, for details on how olive oil was enhanced.

322 The concluding instruction indicates that it was offered as a cold dish.

(144) Recipe for *ʿuṣfūr māliḥ muṭayyab* (seasoned salt-preserved sparrow)[323]

Take a sparrow [which has been preserved in salt, as in recipe 141], (**45r**) clean it, and wash it with wine vinegar three or four times [to get rid of extra salt]. After that, pour some sweet olive oil (*zayt ṭayyib*) and lime juice (*māʾ laymūn akhḍar*) on it.[324] Keep the sparrow whole.

(145) Another way of doing it

Do it as described first [in the recipe above, i.e., wash the sparrow in vinegar], and then cut it into smaller pieces. Add lime juice (*māʾ laymūn akhḍar*), sweet olive oil, Macedonian parsley (*baqdūnis*), rue (*sadhāb*), and *aṭrāf al-ṭīb* (spice mix) to it; and eat it.

(146) Recipe for a sparrow dish (omelet with sparrows)

Cut open the sparrows from the back, wash them, and put them in a pot to fry in olive oil and bit of salt. When they brown, take a bit of black pepper, caraway, cumin, coriander, cilantro, a sprig of rue,[325] and some common parsley (*karafs*). Chop all these [fresh herbs], mix them with eggs, and spread them on the sparrows. Let the dish cook until it is done, and after it has cooled down, ladle it.

(147) Another recipe for sparrows (fried)

Cut open the sparrows from the back, wash them, and fry them in olive oil. When they brown and fully cook, drizzle some *murrī* (liquid fermented sauce) and vinegar on them, and sprinkle some [ground] spices (*abāzīr yābisa*) on them. Let them cool down and serve them.

(148) Recipe for sparrows eaten with drinks, in Baghdad and Mosul[326]

Clean the sparrows, cut open their bellies, (**45v**) and wash them very well. Cut off the heads after cleaning them thoroughly, and set them aside. Cut off the feet and only the tips of the wings. Then, one after the other, put them on a nice, clean marble slab or a piece of flat wood, and pound them with a stone or

---

323 This recipe and the following are identical with *Wuṣla* recipes ii 695–6. Clearly, both compilers had access to the same source. However, whereas *Wuṣla* takes only these two recipes and moves on, the *Kanz* copies more of them, which is typical of the compiler's method. Here I used the *Wuṣla* version to amend the text slightly.

324 As it occurs in *Wuṣla*.

325 I follow DK, n. 1871, where the word *ṭāqa* 'sprig' is copied instead of *ḥuzma* 'bunch' in the edited text and Gotha, fol. 47v. Rue is always used sparingly due to its strong bitter flavor.

326 This is a *mezza* dish, called *naql* in medieval times, see glossary 5.

a clean piece of wood to break the sparrows' chests. However, keep the [heads with the] brains [untouched]. Now take all the pieces and color them [yellow] with turmeric (*kurkum*).[327]

Put a flat-bottomed frying pan on the fire (*miqlā mabsūṭa*). Put sweet olive oil (*zayt ṭayyib*) or sesame oil in it. Feed the fire under it until the oil is very hot. You can tell this if the oil splatters and sizzles when you put a drop of water in it. At this point, arrange the sparrows in the frying pan so that they lay flat next to each other and are not overlapping each other. Weigh them all down with a solid stone, which you keep for a short while and then remove.[328]

While frying, turn the sparrows over several times until they cook and brown. Prepare a large tub (*ijjāna*) of water with salt dissolved in it, and place it next to the frying pan. The water should be noticeably salty. Now, take a [fried] sparrow out of the pan and drop it into the salty water. (**46r**) Do this with all the sparrows,[329] and set them aside until they cool.

Take the sparrows out of the water, squeeze out any extra moisture, and arrange them on a plate. Sprinkle them with finely ground coriander, caraway, black pepper, and mastic gum, and serve.

(149) Recipe for stewed sparrows (*ʿaṣāfīr maṭbūkha*), eaten with drinks,[330] as prepared in Morocco and Andalusia

This dish must be cooked in a glass pot (*qidr zujāj*). The witty companions (*ẓurafāʾ*) and the dignitaries and kings of Morocco and Andalusia would put this pot in an easy-to-reach place, especially in the winter and the fall, and they would entertain themselves by looking at it, as it reveals the sparrows that are cooking in it, as they move while boiling on the fire. Every now and then, each one of them would have a small bowl (*sukurruja*) of the hot broth and a sparrow as *naql* [eaten between drinks]. They would continue doing this from the beginning of the drinking session until the end.

Description of the pot

The pot is to be made of thin glass, which is used for making bottles and glasses. However, it is not how thin or thick it is that makes it good, as much as the way it is made. It looks like a pot, no difference here, but the glassmaker (*zajjāj*)

327 This is a rare mention of this spice; it is used here to color and flavor the sparrows. It is much cheaper than saffron. See glossary 8.

328 This helps keep the sparrows flattened.

329 It can be assumed that the heads were also being fried.

330 See n. 326 above.

should apply the pontil (*būlīn*) to its bottom (**46v**) while it is still malleable and push it up to two-thirds of its height, without letting it open at the top.[331]

When it is made this way, this pot can be used for cooking any kind of meat and any variety of dishes. The fire must be fueled by charcoal (*faḥm*), it does not matter how hot it gets. However, cooking in this kind of pot must be under these conditions: the liquid in the pot should always be above the level of the tube in the middle because if it is not, the pot breaks. In addition, the pot should not be put on a strong fire suddenly, nor should it be removed from the fire and immediately placed on a cold surface, because this will cause it to break. It should first be put on a fire of low heat and gradually increase its heat. Another thing: no cold water should be added to replenish the pot while it is cooking on the fire; put whatever [water] is needed right from the very beginning.

Describing how to cook the sparrows in this pot

Clean the sparrows but leave the heads attached. Cut open the bellies [discard the entrails] and return the hearts and livers to the cavities. Do not cut off anything from the sparrows except their feet. Wash them very well and put them in the pot. Chop and add onion and leeks (*kurrāth*), (**47r**) chop them as small as possible. Pour in a suitable amount of olive oil, and throw in a handful of soaked chickpeas. Chickpeas are necessary for this dish.[332]

When the dish is almost cooked, add to the pot fresh herbs like cilantro, leeks, scallion (*baṣal akhḍar*), and rue, each cut up into pieces, a half-finger long [about 2 inches]. Add also small—the smallest you can get—tender hearts of fresh fennel heads (*qulūb al-shamar*). They may be put in whole or cut into pieces. Cut the onion the same size as that of the other herbs.

Throw into the pot salt and many dried spices (*abzār yābisa*), which are black pepper, spikenard (*sunbul*), cloves, cassia (*dār Ṣīnī*), galangal (*khulanjān*), coriander, caraway, and whatever you wish to add, as needed. Pound all these spices and divide the amount into two portions. Tie the first portion in a piece of thin fabric and throw it into the pot when you first put it on the fire. Add the other portion, also tied in a cloth bundle, after the sparrows are fully

---

331 The only source where I found the word *būlīn* mentioned is Hassan and Hill, *Islamic Technology* 155. It is somewhat like the punt of a wine bottle, but longer, more like a long blind tube.

332 This is partly for display, as we see later in the recipe, and partly for their properties as aphrodisiacs, which are like those of sparrows.

cooked, to season the pot.[333] Also, when the pot is fully cooked, add as much rosewater as you like and a small amount of musk to enhance the taste of the dish.

So, when everything you need for the dish is already put in the pot, take one part pure water, one part very sour wine vinegar (*khall ḥādhiq*), and one part strained *murrī naqīʿ* (liquid fermented sauce).[334] (**47v**) Combine all three in a separate vessel and taste the liquid and see if it needs more vinegar or more *murrī* or whatever you prefer, depending on how strong the vinegar or *murrī* are, until it tastes moderately sour. Pour this liquid on the sparrows in the pot, along with the vegetables and herbs prepared. Put enough to fill it to no more than the boiling level of the pot.

Now put the stove [called] *nāfikh nafsihi* in an enclosed place,[335] and put a lighted piece of charcoal in the middle of coals used. Leave it for a short while until the coals start catching fire. Now put the pot on the stove and let it boil until all of it is cooked, and then season it with the spices and fresh herbs as well as rosewater and musk.

At this point people can start eating from this dish, as we mentioned earlier, while watching the [cooking] sparrows, with heads attached, moving up and down with all the white and black chickpeas in between and the green fennel heads and the herbs and vegetables; this is even more fantastic and delightful than eating it.

The pot can stay on the fire for a whole day or a whole night. Nothing will happen to it unless the middle tube is revealed. When you want to empty the pot, (**48r**) and the remaining food in it has reached the level of the top of the tube, take out whatever is left of the sparrows and other stuff. However, keep the remaining broth and the chickpeas in the pot until it gradually cools down. At this point, you can take them out [i.e., the broth and chickpeas], and clean the pot and stow it away until needed.

This is one of the most exclusive dishes which kings and dignitaries eat to boost their libido (*quwwat al-bāh*), so know this.

---

333 The verb as written is *yuṭarraʾ* (يطرأ), most probably due to a copyist's spelling mistake; otherwise, the proper spelling is *yuṭarrā* (يطرّى), which, in a cooking context, simply means 'season to enhance the taste of food' (*Lisān al-ʿArab*, s.v. طرأ).

334 See the following chapter for recipes.

335 This refers to a portable self-ventilating stove. See glossary 9.1.

في عمل المرّي وخزن ماء الحصرم والليمون

Making *murrī* (Liquid Fermented Sauce), and Preserving Sour Grape Juice (*māʾ al-ḥiṣrim*) and Lemon Juice (*māʾ al-laymūn*)

(150) Recipe for *murrī naqīʿ* (liquid fermented sauce)

Take 8 *qadaḥ*s (17½ pounds) good recently milled barley flour,[1] knead it into dough, with bran (*nukhāla*), but without salt. Shape it into small cones, similar to the conical molds of sugar (*qawālib al-sukkar*),[2] and press a hole in the middle of each with your finger. Place them on a board covered with bran, and keep them in a shady place for 20 days. Then turn them over and leave them for 20 more days, after which all the bran and dust should be completely scraped off the pieces, and then coarsely crush it into pieces, the size of a fava bean each.

To this [crushed grain] add 1 *rubʿ* (8¾ pounds) barley flour with its bran. Also, add 4 *mudd*s (8 pounds) salt, and put them all (**48v**) in a non-porous large earthenware jar (*khābiya ghayr rashshāḥa*), which has previously been used to store olive oil. Add enough water, and put the jar in a place exposed to sunlight all day long. Using a stick of the caprifig tree (*al-dhukār*),[3] stir the jar four times a day, more if possible, for eight consecutive days.

Next, take 1 *rubʿ* (8¾ pounds) wheat flour (*daqīq qamḥ*) and knead it with its bran, without salt, shape it into flat bread, which you bake in the *furn* (brick oven), just until they firm up. Break them into bite-size pieces and add them to the jar while still hot. Cover the jar and leave it for three days, after which, put your hand into the jar and with your fingers crush whatever remains of

---

1 Likewise, in Gotha, fol. 50r. However, in *Zahr*, fol. 14r and DK, n. 2024, it is *rubʿayn*, lit., 'two quarters,' (sg. *rubʿ*). One *rubʿ* equals approx. 8.8 pounds, in the medieval measuring system. The two *rubʿ*s would be 17½ pounds. The 'quarter' is calculated as a quarter of the weight measure called *wayba* (ويبة), which is 16 kilograms. Al-Suyūṭī, *Ḥusn al-muḥāḍara* 323, mentions that a *rubʿ* equals 4 *qadaḥ*s, and that each *qadaḥ* equals 232 *dirhams*.

2 *Qawālib*, sg. *qālab*, are molded pieces. A comparable recipe in al-Tujībī *Fiḍāla* 262–4, also called *murrī naqīʿ*, calls for the dough to be shaped like *jamājim al-sukkar* 'small rounded masses of sugar.'

3 Caprifig, *Ficus carica sylvestris* (S), is the male, pollen-bearing wild variety of the common fig, used to pollinate the edible fig. See glossary 7, s.v. *dhukār*.

 | DOI 10.1163/9789004349919_009

the solid pieces of bread. Stir the jar with the stick of the caprifig tree (*ʿūd al-dhukār*) four times a day, more if possible, for eight consecutive days.

Next, take 1 *rubʿ* (8¾ pounds) wheat flour and knead it with 1 *mudd* (2 pounds) salt. Shape it into thick disks and [let it bake slowly] overnight in the [remaining heat of] the oven (*furn*), until it firms up; do not leave it until it burns. Pound this bread and add it to the jar, and continue stirring it with the stick for two months. Do not forget to do this [regularly] and do not let an unclean person (*najis*)[4] touch it.

After the two months have elapsed, you will see that the *murrī* has already channeled its way up in streams and can be seen above the watery surface. Now take a *quffa* (large round basket made of date palm fronds) and fill it with the contents of the jar (*khābiya*).[5] Suspend the *quffa*, and put a large earthenware tub (*qaṣriyya*) under it. (**49r**) Let [the liquid] drip down into the tub for a day and a night. Take whatever has accumulated in it, and put it in a green-glazed jar (*ḥantam*). Take whatever was left [of the dregs] in the *quffa* basket and set these aside.

With the remaining contents of the *khābiya* jar, do what you did the first time, as mentioned above, and add [the resulting *murrī* from this second round, called] *al-thānī* (the second), to the first *murrī*.

Now, combine the dregs (*thufl*) resulting from this second round with [the dregs set aside] from the first round, and put them in the *khābiya* jar. Add enough water to them, stir them, and leave them for twenty days. With the [contents of the jar] do what you did in the first round—hanging [it in a basket] and draining it. Combine [the resulting sauce] with the previous batch, and put [the combined sauce] in a large earthenware tub (*qaṣriyya*). Leave it in the sun for three days, and then put it away and use it [as needed].

(151) Recipe for Moroccan *murrī* (liquid fermented sauce) made with barley
Take leaves of citron (*utrujj*), sour orange (*nāranj*), yellow lemon (*laymūn marākibī*),[6] peach (*khawkh*), and lemon balm (*rayḥān utrunjī*). Immerse all these leaves in fine tasting (*ḥulw*, lit., 'sweet') water, put it in large earthenware tubs (*qaṣārī*, sg. *qaṣriyya*), and leave it in the sun for four days.

Now take barley, sift it, pick it over, and then toast it, and finely crush it. Mix it with a quarter of its bulk of crushed salt, knead it very well, and shape it into

4 Such as menstruating women, and men and women who have not bathed after having intercourse.

5 The jar is not completely emptied of its contents, as we learn.

6 Levantine yellow lemons were imported to Egypt via trading ships known as *marākib*, hence the name. See glossary 7.

thin flat unleavened breads (*faṭā'ir*). Bake these breads quite well, so that no moisture remains in them. Let them cool, and then add them to the tubs [with leaves, prepared above]. Cover it well with water, set it aside in the hot sun for a couple of weeks.

After that, press and mash the mix, strain it, and cook it thoroughly. (**49v**) [Before cooking it] you will have added 2 *qadaḥ*s (4½ pounds) caraway seeds, which have been sifted, toasted, and crushed. Stow the sauce away [and use as needed]. It is wonderful.

(152) Recipe for making [preserved juice of] sour unripe grapes (*ḥiṣrim*)

Take sour unripe grapes, sprinkle them with salt, stomp on them, squeeze their juice out, strain them, and then put the [resulting juice] in *qarrābāt* (large flagons).[7] With their tops open, set the flagons aside until the juice begins to ferment (*yaghlī*, lit., 'boil'), and the impurities rise to the surface, and the dregs (*thufl/tufl*) settle in the bottom.

Strain the juice into other flagons, and leave the tops open. Wait until the remaining impurities of the juice rise up and the dregs settle in the bottom.

Now, strain the juice into other flagons and wait until it stops fermenting, and then empty them into other flagons. Add washed olive oil (*zayt maghsūl*),[8] and sprigs of mint. [Close the tops of the flagons and seal them with clay].[9] Leave them in the sun until the clay dries, and then put them away and use [as needed].

(153) Another recipe [for preserved sour grape juice], which keeps for a long time, and does not change or go bad

Press juicy unripe grapes, strain the liquid, and put it in a tin-lined copper pot (*qidr mu'annaka*). Cook the juice until froth starts [accumulating] on the surface; skim off the froth often with a latticed ladle (*mighrafa mushabbaka*). Let the juice boil down until a quarter or a sixth of its volume has evaporated, and then remove it from the fire. Leave the juice in the pot until it settles and cools. Ladle out the clear juice into jars, to which you add mint leaves and washed olive oil (*zayt maghsūl*). Close the tops of the jars, seal them with clay, and set them aside in the sun for ten days. Put them away, and use [as needed].

---

7 As specified in Gotha, fol. 51v.

8 See glossary 6.

9 Based on the following recipe.

(154) Another recipe [for preserved sour grape juice]

Take firm unripe grapes,[10] pick them over, and crush them with a press (*miʿṣara*), or pound them in a wooden bowl until the skins are stripped from the pulp. [Strain the juice and] put it in a new pot and set it aside overnight so that it settles. Ladle out the clear juice, put it in a pot, and let it cook on a high fire until it boils down to half its bulk, and looks reddish-brown (*aḥmar*) like carnelian (*ʿaqīq*).[11]

Add pieces of cassia (*dār Ṣīnī*) to the pot, and stir the juice with large bunches of mint. Do this continuously for a while,[12] and every time a bunch is spoiled [by the heat] replace it with another one.

Remove the pot from the fire, and set it aside so that the dregs settle in the bottom and the juice becomes clear. When it has cooled and all impurities have settled, ladle out the clear juice (**50r**) into glass vessels, and top it with a bit of sesame oil to seal it. If the glass vessels are not filled well, the juice will spoil.

This juice will stay good for years.

(155) Recipe for *māʾ al-laymūn* (preserved lemon juice) used for making *sharāb* (sweet drinks)

Wash the lemons and extract their juice onto pieces of sugar. Keep it in a glass vessel and use it [diluted with water] for making drinks.

(156) Recipe for *māʾ al-nāranj* (preserved sour orange juice)

Put a small amount of salt in a container. Squeeze the oranges. The person who does this should not be the same one who has peeled them. (**50v**) After extracting the juice, leave it aside to let the dregs settle. Ladle out the clear juice, add to it some fresh rue (*sadhāb*), take it up [to the roof], and keep it in the sun. It is delicious. It is best if you let the oranges wither before extracting their juice.[13]

---

10 Described as *ʿajir* in the edited text, and *fujj* in Gotha, fol. 51v.

11 In medieval Arabic, there was no specific word for the color brown. *Aḥmar* 'red' was used to designate red and brown and in-between shades.

12 The expression used is *sāʿa baʿd sāʿa*, lit., 'one hour after the other.'

13 See n. 17 below.

FIGURE 29 *Distilling apparatus, Add. 25724, fol. 36v, detail (The British Library Board).*

(157) Recipe for *khall al-naʿnāʿ* (mint-infused vinegar)[14]

Strip mint leaves from their stems (*yumshaq*) and stuff them in a *qarʿa* (cucurbit), and add enough vinegar to submerge the leaves. Light the fire under it, but keep the joint (*waṣl*) throttled.[15] When the liquid starts to boil gently,[16] loosen the joint and distill the liquid the same way you distill rosewater. Store the [resulting] vinegar in a glass vessel (*inā' zujāj*).

(158) Another recipe, similar to this [one above]

Mix vinegar and mint and stuff the *qarʿ* (cucurbit) with it [and distill as above]. It will become crystal-clear white vinegar. It is also said if roses are sprinkled on it and then it is distilled, the resulting rose vinegar will taste delicious and smell nice.

---

14 The recipe describes how to distill vinegar using the cucurbit, which is the lower part of the distillation apparatus, and the alembic, which is the head of the distilling device. See glossary 9.2, s.v. *taṣʿīd*. Distillation is also referred to as *taqṭīr*. For more recipes on distillation, see recipe 684 and following.

15 This is done to give the vapors enough time to accumulate.

16 The verb used is طبخ, a general term for cooking in liquid.

FIGURE 30 *Sour oranges, F1954.80v, Muḥammad al-Qazwīnī,* ʿAjāʾib al-makhlūqāt, *detail (Freer Gallery of Art and Arthur M. Sackler Gallery, Smithsonian Institution, Washington, DC: Purchase—Charles Lang Freer Endowment Art).*

(159) Another recipe [for distilled white grape vinegar]

Make vinegar with white grapes. Stuff it in the cucurbit (*qarʿ*) with mint, and distill it in alembics (*anābīq*, sg. *inbīq*). It will become fine white vinegar.

(160) Recipe for *māʾ nāranj* (preserved sour orange juice)

Harvest sour oranges (*nāranj*) at the end of the season. Peel off a strip all around the middle of each orange and discard it.[17] The person who peels the orange should be different from the person who squeezes the juice; otherwise, it will taste bitter. (**51r**) Therefore, after you peel an orange, give it to someone else to cut it in half and extract its juice. And the knife used to cut the orange in half should be different from the knife used to peel it, unless it is washed.

After extracting enough of the juice, strain it through a sieve (*munkhul*) or a strainer (*rāwūq*) to filter out the seeds. Empty the juice into glass bottles (*qanānī*), seal the tops with olive oil, and stow them away until needed.

17 From *Wuṣla* ii 514–5 and 600, we learn that the best way to extract orange juice is to wilt the oranges (*nāranj*) first by leaving them in a high well-ventilated place for a week. The cook is also instructed to peel a strip 3-fingers wide around the middle of the *nāranj* so that when it is cut in half and juiced, the bitterness of the peel does not get into the juice.

When you need to use some of it, open a bottle, [invert it] with the mouth [of the bottle] on the palm of your hand, so that the oil goes up, all the way to the bottom of the bottle. Open your hand and take whatever you need of the juice, and then flip the bottle back. Replenish the bottle with more orange juice if you have it, or olive oil. Otherwise, if the bottle is not full, the juice develops a white film on the surface (*yuqaṭṭin*), and this causes it to spoil, and you must throw it away.

(161) Recipe for [preserving] *māʾ al-laymūn* (lemon juice)
Crush excellent sugar and put it in an oiled vessel placed under the lemon press (*miʿṣara*). Press the lemons on the sugar, and then filter it through a strainer (*rāwūq*) or a sieve (*munkhul*). Discard the seeds and empty the juice into jars (*qirab*, sg. *qirba*). Seal the tops with almond oil or sesame oil. When needed, absorb the oil with some cotton, and use the juice for making *sharāb* (sweet diluted drinks), *aqsimā* (digestive drinks),[18] and all sorts of other drinks, except for the salty ones (*mulūḥāt*). (**51v**)

(162) Recipe for *khall mustaqṭar* (distilled vinegar)
[Except for some minor stylistic differences, this is the same as recipe 157.]

(163) Another recipe [for distilled vinegar]
[Except for some minor stylistic differences, this is the same as recipe 158.][19]

(164) Recipe for *murrī naʿnaʿ* (liquid fermented sauce infused with mint)[20]
Take two parts of barley flour and one part salt. Crush the salt, combine it with the flour, knead them [with water], and make unleavened (*faṭīr*) flat bread dough. Let the bread bake overnight, in the [remaining heat of the] oven (*furn*). Take them out the following morning. They should be burnt inside and out; otherwise return them to a hot oven and keep them there until they burn.

Break the bread into pieces, each the size of a fava bean, put them in a clean pot, and cover them with water. Add a handful of thyme, mint, some stalks of fresh fennel (*rāzyānaj*), a bruised pinecone (*raʾs ṣanawbar*), peels of citron (*utrujj*) and quince, along with a few citron leaves. (**52r**) Put the pot in the [remaining heat] of the oven, and leave it there overnight. The following morning, take it out, and strain it. Add good honey to it, enough to make it taste less salty.

---

18 See, for instance, recipes 404 and 405 below.

19 This repetition is quite likely due to the fact that the repeated recipes are given slightly different names.

20 This type of *murrī*, which was not left to ferment, is called *maṭbūkh* (cooked).

FIGURE 31 *Mint, F1954.83r, Muḥammad al-Qazwīnī,* ʿAjāʾib al-makhlūqāt, *detail (Freer Gallery of Art and Arthur M. Sackler Gallery, Smithsonian Institution, Washington, DC: Purchase—Charles Lang Freer Endowment).*

Ladle it into clean containers, and pour good olive oil on it to preserve it. It is wonderful.

(165) Another wonderfully aromatic *murrī* recipe[21]

Take two parts wheat flour (*daqīq al-ḥinṭa*) and add half a part of salt to it.[22] Knead them [with water] and shape the dough into disks of flat bread. Leave them in the [remaining heat of the] oven (*furn*) overnight. Take them out the following morning. If they look burnt, fine and good; if not, then they need to be [further baked until they are] burnt.

Break the bread into small pieces, and put them in a pot with a handful of thyme. Also add leaves of bay laurel (*rand*), citron (*utrujj*), mint, basil (*rayḥān*), and sour orange (*nāranj*), a handful of each. Cover all of it with water, and leave the pot overnight in the [remaining heat of the] oven.

The following morning, strain the contents of the pot, [keep the strained liquid in a container]. Add some more water to the remaining dregs and return the pot to the oven after you press and mash the contents by hand (*yumras*). After you take the pot out of the oven the following morning, strain the pot. If you wish, you can mix the resulting two liquids; or you may keep them separate.

---

21 See n. above.

22 The term used to designate 'part' is *kayla*.

Adding wheat starch [when you add the water], will result in a thick and smooth *murrī*. In addition, if you stir a bit of burnt honey (*ʿasal muḥarraq*) into it,[23] it will be wonderful. (**52v**) So know this.[24]

---

23 Based on today's culinary practices, honey would be boiled down until it caramelizes a bit, and just starts to smoke. Adding it would give the dish a slightly burnt flavor.

24 This must have been the end of the original specialized pamphlet from which this chapter was copied, as revealed in C and DK manuscripts, because it includes the usual explicit that indicates the end of the manuscript. See introduction, section 3, p. 14.

CHAPTER 7

فيما يُعمل من البيض من العجج وغيرها

Eggs Cooked as Omelets and Other Dishes

(166) Recipe for omelet (*ʿujja*)

Take meat [pound it and] boil it, and then pound it again and fry it in fat. Finely chop Macedonian parsley (*baqdūnis*) and put it, along with the meat, in a bowl. Break the eggs on them; add hot spices,[1] cilantro, coriander, pounded bread, and Ceylon cinnamon (*qarfa*). Fry it in a frying pan (*ṭājin*) in olive oil and sesame oil.

The frying pan (*miqlā*) used should be round, with high sides, and a long handle like that of a ladle. It should be set on a low charcoal fire, and a few ladlefuls (*jamjāt*) of olive oil and sesame oil should be poured into it.[2] Wait until it gets very hot, and then pour in the egg mixture.

For each omelet, use 5 eggs, a bit of herbs and spices, and fried meat. Fill the frying pan with this, and cook it until it no longer looks wet. Add a bit of sesame oil and olive oil, and continue flipping it every now and then,[3] until it is cooked.

(167) Another version, with fava beans (*bāqillā*)

Make the omelet as we described earlier, only add fresh fava beans, after shelling them from the jackets and bean skins. Fry it as mentioned in the previous recipe.

(168) Recipe for *ʿujja ḥāmiḍa* (sour omelet)

Prepare the omelet as mentioned earlier, but add chopped lemon preserved in salt (*laymūn māliḥ*). (**53r**) Fry the omelet and when it is almost done, poke it in many places with a knife, and with a spoon, dribble vinegar and lemon

---

1 Such as black pepper and ginger.

2 It is only in *Zahr*, fol. 15v, that the word for ladlefuls is clearly copied as حمجات, with a dot missing from the first letter. The word is *jamjāt* (جمجات), a Turkish loan word. See Abū Ḥayyān al-Andalusī's thirteenth-century Turkish-Arabic dictionary *Kitāb al-Idrāk* 61, where the word occurs as *jamjā* (جمجا).

3 The expression used is *kull sāʿa*, lit., 'every hour.'

 | DOI 10.1163/9789004349919_010

juice on it. Wait for a short while and let it fry,[4] and repeat. Do this six or seven times—be patient with it,[5] and you will get a sour omelet.

(169) Recipe for *ʿujjat qanānī* (bottle omelet)

Take the omelet mixture [as mentioned in the first recipe], fill glass bottles with it and close their tops tightly. Put them in water,[6] and let them boil until the omelet is done. Then [take the bottles out and] break the glass very gently, so that the omelets preserve their shape, and then fry them in olive oil and sesame oil. This kind of omelet is used to decorate dishes.[7]

(170) Recipe for *ʿujja bi-ʿaṣāfīr* (omelet with sparrows)[8]

Take sparrows, clean them, and fry them in some olive oil with salt until they brown. Take 10 eggs, and beat them with a bit of black pepper and chopped cilantro. Pour the eggs on the sparrows and fry until done.

(171) Recipe for omelet without eggs[9]

Boil chickpeas and pound them until they become smooth. Boil onion and pound it with the chickpeas. Pour some olive oil and *murrī* (liquid fermented sauce) on them, and throw on some salt and dried spices (*abzār yābisa*), namely, coriander, caraway, and black pepper. Also, add some gum arabic (*ṣamgh*). Fry it in a pot until it is cooked. (**53v**) Those who eat it will have no doubt it is an egg omelet.

(172) Recipe for *bayḍ maḥshī* (stuffed eggs)[10]

Boil eggs, shell them, and cut them in half. Take out the yolks, put them in a *ṣaḥfa* (large wide bowl), and add to them cilantro, onion juice, Ceylon cinnamon (*qarfa*), spikenard (*sunbul*), betel leaves (*tunbul*), a bit of barley-based

---

4 Addition from *Zahr*, fol. 15v: 'until they are absorbed' (الى أن تنشرب).

5 The phrase "وتطوّل روحك عليه" is easily recognizable as a colloquial Egyptian expression by those familiar with today's Egyptian dialect.

6 Here I have amended the sense; the word is written as في نار, which most probably was a misreading of في ماء, as the following sentence deals with boiling.

7 Here I amended the text. The word is copied as الساهر in the edited text, and الساهير in Gotha, fol. 54v. It is, no doubt, a misreading of التشاهير, which refers to garnishes and decorations for dishes.

8 This recipe is identical to one of al-Warrāq's omelet recipes (chapter 79); this indicates the possibility that both drew on similar manuals, specialized in omelet dishes.

9 Again, this recipe is the same as that in al-Warrāq's copy (chapter 46), except for some stylistic differences. See note above.

10 Similar to deviled eggs, except that the filled halves are further joined and fried.

liquid fermented sauce (*murrī shaʿīr*), and good olive oil. Rub all these together into a mix, form it into clumps, and fill the eggs with it.

Tie the eggs with threads, dust them (*yughabbar*) with powdery wheat flour (*ghubār al-darmak*),[11] and fry them. Make sauce (*maraq*) for the eggs like the one used for the stuffing [without the yolks], and sprinkle spikenard and Ceylon cinnamon on them.

(173) Recipe for *bayḍ makbūs* (pickled eggs)

Take eggs and boil them; shell them, pierce them with a large needle (*misalla*), and then put them in a jar with some salt. Pour honey and vinegar on them, but let the vinegar dominate the taste.

(174) Recipe for *bayḍ mukhallal* (pickled eggs)[12]

Boil eggs, and when done, take them out, shell them, and pierce them in many places with the tip of a thin knife or a large needle (*misalla*). Soak them in salted water for part of a day to get rid of their odor,[13] and then wash them in fresh water (*māʾ ʿadhb*) to get rid of salt, until only traces of it remain. [Set it aside.]

Pour sour vinegar in a clean pot, put [what you estimate will be] enough to cover the eggs. (**54r**) Add cassia (*dār Ṣīnī*), ginger, cumin, coriander, a few whole cloves, rue (*sadhāb*), citron leaves, common parsley (*karafs*) leaves, and mint. Also, add honey or sugar so that it tastes pleasantly sweet and sour (*muzz*). However, if you do not want it to be sweet and sour, but just sour, do not add sweeteners.

Put the pot on the fire and let it boil until the spices and herbs are well cooked. Remove the pot from the fire, and throw in the boiled eggs while the vinegar is still boiling. Leave them in the pot, and set aside.

These eggs are eaten with the cooled meat of *sikbāj* (sour vinegar stew), in which rosewater is liberally added.[14] If you like, color the eggs yellow with saffron, or red with safflower (*ʿuṣfur*). It is scrumptious.

---

11 This powder is the by-product of crushed wheat. Generally, grains crushed with a quern (*raḥā*) or a larger grinder (*ṭāḥūna*) produce a fine powder that falls all over the place. See glossary 2, under *daqīq*.

12 Both *makbūs* and *mukhallal* designate pickling. However, the former denotes the act of packing the food in pickling jars, while the latter denotes the use of vinegar (*khall*) as a preserving agent.

13 The word used is *zuhūma* 'undesirable greasy odor.'

14 See, for instance, recipes 7, 90, and 136 above.

(175) Another recipe [like the above]

Take the eggs, and do with them exactly what you did in the earlier recipe. However, do not cook the spices and herbs. Put the eggs in a large wide-mouthed jar (*barniyya*), either green-glazed (*khaḍrāʾ*) or glass (*zujāj*), and pour the vinegar with the herbs and spices into it, put enough to cover the eggs. If you wish, add honey or sugar. You can also add saffron. However, use safflower if you want it to be red.

It is eaten [sprinkled] with rosewater, with roasted meat, and herbs (*buqūl*). It can be kept for days, and it will still be good to eat. It is delicious.

(176) A variation on this recipe [i.e., no. 174]

(**54v**) The eggs are boiled and shelled as we described earlier. Put [vinegar] in a clean pot, and for the spices and herbs, use leaves of citron (*utrujj*), rue, cassia (*dār Ṣīnī*), sprigs of common parsley (*karafs*), ginger, and whole cloves.

Bring the vinegar to a boil, two or three times,[15] and then remove it from the fire. Immediately, put the eggs in it while it is still boiling—the vinegar should be enough to cover the eggs. Throw in the spices and herbs (*ḥawāʾij*) we mentioned. It is very delicious.

(177) *ʿUjja* (omelet)

You need eggs, some fresh herbs (*ḥawāʾij baql*),[16] some onions, sesame oil or linseed oil (*duhn bazr*),[17] and black pepper. Finely chop the onion, add to it small amounts of water and fine olive oil or sesame oil, and cook until done. Add the herbs and cook until they wilt. Remove the pot from the fire, pound the black pepper and add it to pot, and crack open the eggs on them. Whip them all with a stick.

Suspend the frying pan (*ṭājin*) over the fire, put sesame oil, and when it heats up, put the eggs and *ḥawāʾij* (herbs and spices) in it. [Let it cook] until one side is done, and then flip it. When it is completely done, put it on a round plate.

If, when one side is cooked, you want to turn it over (**55r**) and no sesame oil remains in the frying pan, add some more.

(178) Recipe for *ʿujja bi-l-khall* (omelet seasoned with vinegar)

You need meat, vinegar, eggs, sesame oil, fresh herbs (*ḥawāʾij baql*),[18] black pepper, coriander, and hazelnuts.

---

15 See glossary 9.2, s.v. *ghalya*.

16 Such as mint, parsley, and cilantro.

17 The reference here is to *bazr kattān*, see glossary 6.

18 See n. 16 above.

Pound [the meat very well] with sheep-tail fat (*alya*). Shape it into a disc, which you boil until [one side] is cooked, and then flip it so that the other side cooks as well. Next, pound it [again], spread it out, and remove the blood vessels (*ʿurūq*).[19] Fry the meat in fresh sesame oil, chop the herbs, grind the hazelnuts and add them to it. Pour in the vinegar, and continue boiling it until it all evaporates. Remove the meat, and let it cool.

Add salt to the meat, and crack the eggs into it, and whip the mix. Suspend the frying pan (*ṭājin*) over the fire, put sesame oil in it, and when it gets hot, put the meat and egg mix (*ḥawāʾij*) in it. Cook until one side is done and then flip it; add some more sesame oil and cook it until the other side is done.

(179) Recipe for *madfūna* (the buried)

You need meat, eggs, onion, fresh herbs (*ḥawāʾij baql*),[20] black pepper, mastic gum, and Ceylon cinnamon (*qarfa*).

Boil the meat, drain it, and then fry it until all the moisture is gone. Chop the onion and put it in a separate vessel. Suspend a frying pan (*ṭājin*) over the fire, (55v) put the onion in it along with a small amount of water and salt and let it boil until done. Add to it some sesame oil and fry it. Next, add to it the [chopped] herbs, and cook them until they wilt. Pound the black pepper and add it. Add the [cooked] meat, and crack the eggs over all of it. Whip the mix.

Suspend a frying pan over the fire, put sesame oil in it; and when it gets hot, put all the [whipped] ingredients in it. Cook until done.[21]

(180) Recipe for making *bayḍ maṣūṣ* (poached eggs in vinegar sauce)[22]

Put sesame oil in a frying pan (*ṭājin*). Remove the stalks from common parsley (*karafs*) and add the leaves to the pan. When they fry in it, sprinkle some cassia (*dār Ṣīnī*), mastic gum, and caraway on them.

Pour in as much vinegar as is needed, color it with a bit of saffron, crack the eggs in it, and cover the pot. Remove when done.

(181) Recipe for *bayḍ mukhardal* (eggs seasoned with mustard)

Boil the eggs, shell them, and pierce them with a needle. Season them with a bit of salt, and crushed cumin, put them in a vessel, and set them aside from

---

19 These chewy particles would resist pounding.

20 See n. 16 above.

21 It is my guess that the dish is called 'the buried' because the meat and herbs are all coated with the cooked eggs.

22 See glossary 5, s.v. *maṣūṣ*.

early morning to midday. Take the eggs, color them with saffron, and pour vinegar, mustard seeds (*khardal*), mint, and *aṭrāf al-ṭīb* (spice mix) on them.

(182) Recipe for *bayḍ mukhallal* (eggs pickled in vinegar)

Shell boiled eggs, roll them in crushed cumin and salt, and keep them in a bowl (*zibdiyya*) for half a day (**56r**) until their moisture seeps out. Then mix saffron,[23] *aṭrāf al-ṭīb*, black pepper, ginger, and rosebuds with wine vinegar, and put it [along with the eggs] in a glazed vessel (*wiʿāʾ madhūn*) or a ceramic glazed jar (*qaṭramīz*). Put in some mint and Macedonian parsley (*baqdūnis*), and set it aside until [the eggs are] good to eat.

(183) Recipe for omelet, which comes out great

Take 1 *raṭl* (1 pint) milk (*laban ḥalīb*), vinegar, and chickpeas boiled until very soft. Mix them all and beat them together very well, and press them through a sieve. Take 15 eggs and whip them very well [and add them to the chickpea mix]. Also, add 5 lemons preserved in salt (*laymūnāt māliḥa*), cumin, hazelnuts, walnuts, black pepper, and Macedonian parsley (*baqdūnis*), all chopped.

[In a frying pan,] heat up 1½ *ūqiyyas* (1½ ounce/3 tablespoons) sesame oil, and add 1 chopped onion and 1 *ūqiyya* (1 ounce) olive oil to this. [When the onion is well fried, pour in the egg mixture,] and let it fry on the fire. It will be a delicious omelet.

(184) Recipe for an omelet, easy to make[24]

Take 1 *rubʿ* (8¾ pounds) roasted chickpeas.[25] Pound them thoroughly and beat [the resulting flour] into the milk. Crack 50 eggs onto them,[26] whip the mix well, and then fry it [as omelets] with ghee (*samn*).

---

23 The verb for 'mixing' used here is *tuqattil*. When this verb is used for 'mix' it implies that the added ingredients will help balance the sharp taste of the vinegar. This interpretation is based on the entry in *Lisān al-ʿArab*, s.v. قتل, where the example given is *qattala al-khamr* (mixing it with water to weaken it).

24 The Arabic expression is *qalīlat al-mūna* 'requires little labor.' *Lisān al-ʿArab*, s.v. مان, says that it is derived from *al-ayn* (الأين), 'labor,' 'hardship.'

25 *Ḥimmaṣ mujawhar*. Based on what we know today of how they are prepared, the chickpeas are soaked, parboiled, and then dry-toasted in a large shallow pan containing sand. They are eaten as a snack food today.

26 In the edited text and Gotha, fol. 57v, the number of eggs is five. 'Fifty eggs' is only mentioned in DK, n. 2395. Fifty eggs are more in proportion to the amount of chickpeas used.

(185) Recipe for delicious omelet that enhances and fortifies coitus (*bāh*)

Take 4 onions and bake them in the *furn* (brick oven) until well done.[27] Remove their outer skins, and pound them very well. (**56v**) Also take ½ *raṭl* (½ pound) meat, which has been boiled and completely cooked, [drained of its broth], and then fried. Pound the meat, and mix it with the baked onion and whatever remains of the broth. Add 20 egg yolks and whip all of them together. Add the aforementioned spices,[28] just enough to bring out their flavors. Also, add a bit of salt. However, it would be better if it were salt of scincus (*milḥ saqanqūr*).[29] Fry [the omelets] with sesame oil or ghee.

If carrots are in season, fry them and add them to the pounded meat and onion as described.

(186) Recipe for preparing eggs to garnish *tabāla* dishes[30]

Take the number of egg yolks you want, and omasum (*qibāwa*).[31] Put the yolks inside the omasum and sew it closed. Bring water to a full rolling point and then place the [filled] omasum in it. Let it boil twice, and then take it out of the water, let it cool, and take the yolk [ball] out.

Put the egg whites in a larger omasum, and place the yolk [ball] in it, too. Boil the water even harder than you did earlier, throw in the omasum and after it boils, take it out and let it cool and take the egg out. It is used as a garnish (*tashwīr*).[32]

(187) Omelet recipe for [invigorating] coitus (*bāh*)

Take 3 *ūqiyyas* (3 ounces) cocks' testicles (*khiṣā al-duyūk*) and 20 egg yolks, preferably of pigeon eggs, (**57r**) as well as the spices.[33] Fry them [as omelets] using ghee (*samn*) or sesame oil (*shayraj*).

---

27 Only *Zahr*, fol. 16v, specifies where the baking is to be done.

28 The spices are given in recipe 198, which seems to have been mentioned earlier in the original manual from which these recipes have been copied.

29 It was believed to be a strong aphrodisiac. See glossary 8.

30 *Tabāla* is a variety of *isbīdāj*/*isfidhbāj*, which is white meat stew (see *Kanz* recipe 92). *Tabāla* recipe can be found in al-Warrāq Istanbul MS, fols. 153v–4r, and *Wuṣla* ii 607.

31 Also called *qibba*. It is the third compartment in the stomach of ruminants, a ball-like folded structure of tripe.

32 It will indeed look like the egg of a roc (a mythological bird).

33 See n. 28 above.

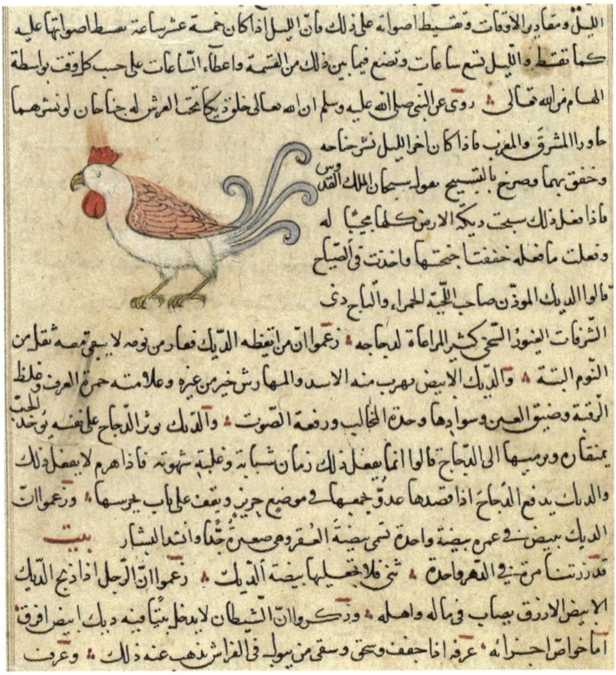

FIGURE 32 *Rooster, F1954.100v Muḥammad al-Qazwīnī,* ʿAjāʾib al-makhlūqāt*, detail (Freer Gallery of Art and Arthur M. Sackler Gallery, Smithsonian Institution, Washington, DC: Purchase—Charles Lang Freer Endowment Art).*

(188) Another recipe, which enhances coitus

Take 7 eggs, 7 onions, 3 *ūqiyya*s (3 ounces) good olive oil, 2 *dirham*s (6 grams) mastic gum, and Ceylon cinnamon (*qarfa*).

Chop the onion, throw it into the frying pan (*ṭājin*), and pour the olive oil on it. Let it fry, then add the eggs and a bit of salt, and stir. Pound the mastic gum and cinnamon, and sprinkle them on the omelet. Remove it from the fire, and eat it.

(189) Recipe for *mubaʿthara* (scrambled omelet) with meat

Boil trimmed meat, and finely shred it with the fingers (*yunassar*); [or] take roasted meat (*shawī*) and finely shred it.[34] Crack the eggs in a bowl (*zibdiyya*), whip them with sufficient spices and salt. Fry [the meat] with fresh sesame oil

34 ʻOrʼ is my addition, as او ʻorʼ could have easily been misread as و ʻandʼ by the copyist. Otherwise, there is no apparent reason for combining boiled and grilled meat.

in a frying pan (*ṭājin*), fold in the eggs, and stir the mix [to scramble it] to your liking, and eat it.[35]

(190) Recipe for omelet, well-liked (*tustaṭāb*)

Take trimmed meat, suet (*shaḥm*), and sumac. Pound them with a stone pestle (*mihrās*), along with the spices.[36] Squeeze lemon juice on the meat, add mint, and then combine all of it with the eggs. Fry it [into omelets] on a low fire. It is a well-liked dish (*yustaṭāb*).

(191) Recipe for *muba'thara ḥāmiḍa* (sour scrambled eggs)

Boil the meat, finely shred it with the fingers (*yunassar*), and put it aside, then moisten it (*yuṭfā*) with a bit of lemon [juice] and wine vinegar.[37] Let the meat remain half-cooked.

Crack the eggs and throw in the spices.[38] Heat the sesame oil [in a frying pan], (57v) and then throw in the meat and eggs. Mix everything well while it is frying and scramble it well, to your liking.

(192) Recipe for *muba'tharat al-baṣal* (scrambled eggs with onion)

Chop onion into fine pieces and squeeze out the juice. Put it in a frying pan (*ṭājin*) and pour enough fresh sesame oil on it to fry the onion. Fold in the eggs, which have been beaten very well, so the yolks are mixed with the whites; throw in some salt and spices.[39] Continue stirring until it is cooked, and then remove.

(193) Recipe for *muba'thara ṣafrā'* (yellow scrambled eggs)

Take only the yolks of the eggs, beat them in a bowl (*zibdiyya*) until they are well mixed. Add a bit of saffron. When you fry it, it will look yellow.

(194) [*Muba'thara*] *bayḍā'* (white scrambled eggs)

Beat the whites of the eggs and throw them into the frying pan (*ṭājin*). Prepare this as you did the previous [recipe], until it is cooked. Fold in the spices, and then remove.

---

35 The last statement, to stir the egg mixture, is only given in DK, n. 2455; it is a key instruction for a dish of scrambled eggs.

36 See n. 28 above.

37 The verb *yuṭfā* means 'extinguish,' or 'douse.'

38 See n. 28 above.

39 See n. 28 above.

(195) Recipe for *muba'thara sādhaja* (plain scrambled eggs)
Heat the frying pan on the fire, with sesame oil in it. Crack the eggs in a bowl and beat then until they are well mixed, throw them into the frying pan, and stir. Add a bit of salt. Continue stirring until the fire dries up all the moisture in it. (**58r**) Add spices to it,[40] and then remove.

(196) Recipe for *bayḍ muṭajjan* (hard-boiled fried eggs)
Shell boiled eggs and fry them in sesame oil until nicely browned, and then take them out of the frying pan (*miqlā*) and dip them in *murrī* (liquid fermented sauce). [Take them out,] sprinkle them with crushed coriander, caraway, and cassia (*dār Ṣīnī*), and serve.

(197) Recipe for *bayḍ maṣūṣ* (eggs poached in vinegar sauce)[41]
Put sesame oil in a frying pan (*miqlā*). Strip the leaves of common parsley (*karafs*) from their stalks and throw them into the pan. When the leaves are fried, sprinkle cassia, mastic gum, coriander, and caraway [all pounded] as needed. Next pour in as much vinegar as needed, and color it with a bit of saffron. When the pan comes to a boil, season it with salt. Crack the eggs, put them in it, and cover the pan with its lid. When the eggs are set, remove the pot from the fire.

(198) Recipe for spices (*abāzīr*) used with omelets and scrambled eggs (*'ujaj* and *muba'tharāt*)
Take one part each of ginger, galangal (*khūlanjān*), rolled bark of Ceylon cinnamon (*qarfat al-laff*), saffron, fennel seeds (*shamar*),[42] black pepper, cumin, and fine-tasting thyme (*za'tar ṭayyib*). Take one quarter of a part of rosebuds (*zir ward*); and one eighth of a part of good spikenard (*sunbul*). Pound all these spices (*ḥawā'ij*) thoroughly, and stow them away and use as needed.

Whenever you want to add these spices to omelets, first throw in a small amount of pounded fresh *jubn Shāmī* (Levantine cheese, like mozzarella), (**58v**) and then add the spices (*ṭīb*).

(199) Recipe for a beautiful [omelet] dish (*malīḥ*)
Take 5 *raṭl*s (5 pounds) trimmed goat meat (*laḥm mā'iz*), and 1 *raṭl* (1 pound) suet (*shaḥm*). Boil the meat until it cooks, and then remove it and shred it with the fingers (*yunassar*).

---

40 See n. 28 above.

41 This recipe is clearly the same as recipe 180, but expressed somewhat differently. It was likely copied from another manual on omelets.

42 الشمر as in DK, n. 2508, and not *al-sha'r* الشعر 'hair', as it occurs in the rest of the copies.

Season the meat with ½ *qadaḥ* (approx. ¾ pound) coriander seeds[43]—toasted, ground, and sifted; ½ *ūqiyyas* (1 tablespoon) black pepper; and ¼ *qadaḥ* (approx. ⅓ pound) caraway seeds—toasted, ground, and sifted. Season the meat with them.

Now, take 60 eggs and crack them into the broth from the boiled meat, after the fat on the surface has been skimmed off. Beat the eggs thoroughly by hand until the broth mixes with the egg yolks and whites,[44] and add the meat to it. Render the pound of suet with half a pound of ghee (*samn*), and set it aside in a bowl.

Put the egg and meat broth mixture in a frying pan (*ṭājin*), bake it in the *furn* (brick oven), and take it out when it is done. [While it is still in the pan,] slice it into squares, pour the fat [that was set aside] over it, and eat it.

When you take it out of the oven, sprinkle ground Ceylon cinnamon (*qarfa*) all over the surface. The dish will be beautiful, and it will have a good texture.

(200) Recipe for *ʿujja bi-kubūd* (omelet with livers)

Take the gizzards (*qawāniṣ*) and livers (*kubūd*) of 20 chickens, and fry them in olive oil until they cook and look golden brown (*tatawarrad*). Crack 20 eggs in a green-glazed bowl (*ghaḍāra*) and add ½ *ūqiyya* (1 tablespoon) *murrī* (liquid fermented sauce) to them.

Sprinkle 1 *ūqiyya murrī* on the livers [and gizzards], (59r) and throw in sprigs of rue (*sadhāb*). Add ½ *dirham* (1½ grams/¼ teaspoon) coriander, 1 *dirham* black pepper, ½ dirham cassia (*dār Ṣīnī*), and 2 *dānaqs* (1 gram) ginger to the eggs. Beat the eggs and mix them with the livers [in the frying pan, and fry them into an omelet]. Remove the pan before the omelet dries out.

(201) Recipe for an omelet with fresh cheese and truffles (*kamʾa*)

Take 3 young pigeons (*firākh*), clean and disjoint them. Wash them, put them in a pot, and then pour on them ⅓ *raṭl* (5 ounces/⅔ cup) olive oil, ¼ *raṭl* (4 ounces/½ cup) chicken fat, ⅓ *raṭl* water, and 2 *dirhams* (1 teaspoon) salt. Boil the young pigeons until they are done [all their moisture evaporates] and brown them [in fat].

Throw ½ *raṭl* (½ pound) peeled truffles into the pot. Also, add 50 *dirhams* (5 ounces) fresh cheese (*jubn raṭb*), cut it into small pieces so that it melts [when cooked]; but first mix it with 1 or 2 *ūqiyyas* (2 or 4 tablespoons) of water

43 I am assuming here that the *qadaḥ* used for the spice is the small one, which is equivalent to approx. 1.5 pounds.

44 Here I replaced *bi-l-milḥ* 'with salt' (بالملح) with *bi-l-muḥḥ* 'with egg yolk' (بالمح); this is a clear misreading on the part of the copyist.

and then add it in. Shell the jackets and skins from 1 *raṭl* (1 pound) fresh fava beans (*bāqillā akhḍar*) and add them to the pot.

Now, take a green-glazed bowl (*ghaḍāra*),[45] and crack 20 eggs into it. Add 2 *dirhams* (1 teaspoon) coriander, and 1 *dirham* each of black pepper, cassia (*dār Ṣīnī*), and ginger. When everything in the pot is well cooked, pour the eggs over it, and keep [it on a low fire] for an hour,[46] and then take the pot off the heat.

(202) Recipe for *ʿujja Muʿtamidiyya* with cheese[47]

Take the breasts of two young chickens and slice them thinly. **(59v)** Also take 1 *raṭl* (1 pound) meat and slice it similarly. Wash the meats, put them in a pot on the fire, and pour 1 *raṭl* (2 cups) olive oil, and 2 *dirhams* (1 teaspoon) salt on them. Let them boil until they are almost done.

Take ¼ *raṭl* (6 ounces) cheese, slice it and add it to the meat in the pot. Season it with 2 *dirhams* (1 teaspoon) coriander, and black pepper and cassia (*dār Ṣīnī*), 1 *dirham* (½ teaspoon) of each. Throw in 10 olives, seeds removed.

Crack 20 eggs in a green-glazed bowl (*ghaḍāra*),[48] and add 1 *ūqiyya* (2 tablespoons) *murrī* (liquid fermented sauce) to them. Beat the eggs very well.

Stir the contents of the pot, and let it cook until the meat browns. Pour the eggs on it. Chop some rue (*sadhāb*) on it, and then remove and serve.

(203) Recipe of *ʿujja narjisiyya* (omelet with eggs sunny side up)[49]

Thinly slice 2 *raṭls* (2 pounds) of fatty meat, then cut it into squares, 3-fingers-wide (about 2 inches). Throw it into a frying pan (*miqlā*) along with 20 cleaned sparrows. Pour ½ *raṭl* (1 cup) water and ⅓ *raṭl* (⅔ cup) olive oil on them. Let them boil until all the moisture evaporates, and fry them until they are brown. Sprinkle on them 3 *dirhams* (1½ teaspoons) coriander, 1 *dirham* (½ teaspoon) cassia (*dār Ṣīnī*), ½ *dirham* ginger, 2 *dānaqs* (1 gram) spikenard (*sunbul*), and 1 *dānaq* cloves (*qaranful*). **(60r)**

---

45 In DK, n. 2560.

46 At this point, the text mentions stirring the pot (وحرّكه); if we follow the directions in the following recipe, this would apply to the meat mixture that is cooked before the eggs are added.

47 Most probably named after Abbasid Caliph al-Muʿtamid (d. 892), who had a cookbook named after him.

48 In DK, n. 2583.

49 'That looks like narcissus.'

When the meat browns, spread it [in a wide frying pan]. Break 30 eggs, sunny side up over the meat.[50] Sprinkle it with 1 *ūqiyya* (2 tablespoons) *murrī* (liquid fermented sauce), and scatter [chopped] rue (*sadhāb*) all over it.[51] It is a wonderful dish, so go for it.

---

50 *ʿUyūnan* (عيوناً) 'eyes.'

51 DK, n. 2605, adds وقدمه في المطابق 'serve it in the frying pan.' I had no luck tracing the meaning of *maṭābiq* in the medieval extant sources. It is highly likely, however, that it was a copyist's misreading of *ṭābaq* (طابق), which is a wide pan or skillet. We know that omelets with eggs sunny side up, called *narjisiyyāt*, were not ladled into serving dishes before they were served to diners. Instead, the entire skillet was carried to the table in a tray to avoid disturbing the narcissus-like formation of the dish. We learn this from a comparable recipe in al-Warrāq's cookbook (chapter 73), which instructs the cook to serve the dish in this way. Interestingly, it also specifies that the frying pan should be skirted with a thin sheet of *ruqāq* bread to hide the blackened sides of the pan.

CHAPTER 8

فيما يتغذى به العليل من مزورات البقول

Vegetarian Dishes (*muzawwarāt al-buqūl*)[1] for the Nourishment of the Sick[2]

(204) Making *muzawwarāt* stews for the sick, such as *ḥiṣrimiyya* (with sour grape juice), *summāqiyya* (with sumac extract), *rummāniyya* (with pomegranate juice) and the like[3]

Fry coriander in sesame oil and make it into stew by adding one of the above-mentioned liquids. When done, add some *lawz farik*,[4] which have been [pounded] and blended with rosewater (*murabbā*). Also add a small lump of salt (*ḥaṣāt*, lit., 'pebble').

If the *muzawwara* is cooked with spinach, then fry the spinach with the coriander. If with a gourd, boil the gourd first,[5] and then throw it into the stew. If it is cooked with sprigs of purslane (*rijla*), just add it to the stew. If it is made for people with diarrhea, add to it pounded almonds, which have been toasted with the skins and blended with rosewater, and sprigs of mint. Also cook mung beans (*māsh*) with almond milk (*mā' al-lawz*) along with a small lump of *milḥ*

---

1 *Muzawwarāt* (simulated, fake) are meatless dishes, which Christians eat during Lent, and physicians prescribe for the sick because they were deemed lighter and easier to digest.

2 The title of this chapter is identical to a title in al-Warrāq's cookbook. In fact, in the course of the chapter, we come across recipes (205, 206, 207, and 224) that are also similar to those of al-Warrāq.

3 This opening segment is identical with a passage in *Waṣf* 181–2, where it is stated that it is copied from chapter 41 of Ibn 'Abdūn's book. He is none other than the Christian physician of Baghdad, Abū Anīs al-Mukhtār b. 'Abdūn b. Sa'dūn b. Buṭlān (d. 1066), whose works include *Taqwīm al-ṣiḥḥa*, *Da'wat al-aṭibbā'*, and *Kunnāsh al-adīra wa-l-ruhbān*. The latter work includes chapter 41, which must have been a widely circulated pamphlet and a valued source of meatless recipes for the sick and fasting Christians. I am grateful to Professor Paulina Lewicka for providing me with this chapter from Jadon, "The Arab Physician ibn Buṭlān" 317–30. See also Lewicka, *Food and Foodways* 37, n. 50.

4 A desirable variety of almonds with easy-to peel skins. The adj. *farik*/*farīk* indicates that the skin can be removed by just rubbing it between the fingers.

5 *Waṣf*, fol. 182, adds ونشّفه 'and drain off extra moisture'; this is the way it occurs in Ibn Buṭlān's *Kunnāsh*, see n. 3 above.

 | DOI 10.1163/9789004349919_011

raṭb (freshly harvested sea salt, still moist). Pour in some almond oil and cook it until it thickens.

If the aim is to reduce the density of the sick person's humors[6] while offering a variety of differently flavored dishes, then cook the *muzawwarāt* dishes the same way you [cook] meat [dishes, just leave out the meat].[7]

(205) *Muzawwara* for a patient with fever (*maḥmūm*)[8]

Take a fresh tender gourd, **(60v)** peel it very well and discard the [fibrous] inside and all the seeds. Cut it into chunks and put it in a clean pot. Chop and add a small onion, a bit of salt, and a stick of cassia (*dār Ṣīnī*). Pour in as much fresh sesame oil as needed, and throw in 1 *ūqiyya* (1 ounce) spinach, boiled and pounded, 2 *ūqiyyas* (¼ cup) fine-tasting water (*māʾ ḥulw*), as well as coriander and cassia, both pounded. Thicken the stew with bread crumbs,[9] and then remove and serve.

(206) *Muzawwara* of *zīrbāj* (delicately sour golden stew) for people with excess yellow bile (*aṣḥāb al-ṣafrāʾ*)

Take the white part of a fresh onion, chop it and fry it in almond oil along with some fresh herbs (*abzār ruṭb*). Take whichever is available, lettuce stems or gourds,[10] peel them, cut them up into large pieces, and fry them with the onion until they brown. Sprinkle them with a small amount of wine vinegar. Also add a bit of saffron and a piece of cassia (*dār Ṣīnī*), and serve.

(207) *Muzawwara* beneficial to patients suffering from fever triggered by excess yellow bile (*ḥummā ṣafrāwiyya*)[11]

Take a gourd, peel it, discard the [fibrous] inside, and dice the flesh. Put it in a pot, pour in enough sour grape juice (*māʾ ḥiṣrim*) to cover it. Also, add a piece

6 Based on the medieval Galenic theory, humors are the elemental bodily fluids, of which there are four types: blood, phlegm, yellow bile, and black bile. Of these, phlegm and black bile are the dense ones. See glossary 11, s.v. *mizāj*, and *talṭīf*.

7 At this point the section borrowed from Ibn ʿAbdūn's chapter 41 ends. The *Waṣf*, however, copies the entire chapter in a couple of places in the book: 34–8, and 181–3. It is quite likely that both al-Warrāq and the *Kanz* drew on a similar source for recipes of meatless dishes for the sick.

8 This recipe is identical with that of al-Warrāq (chapter 105), where it is mentioned that it belongs to Ibn Māsawayh's cookbook. See English trans. *Annals* 433. Here I used it to amend the edited text.

9 *Lubāb al-khubz* is the soft pithy inside of fresh bread.

10 Here I amended the edited text's بماء حصرم مع, using al-Warrāq's version ايما حضر من.

11 This recipe is identical with that of al-Warrāq, English trans. *Annals* 436–7.

FIGURE 33 *Gourd, F1954.83v, Muḥammad al-Qazwīnī,* ʿAjāʾib al-makhlūqāt, *detail (Freer Gallery of Art and Arthur M. Sackler Gallery, Smithsonian Institution, Washington, DC: Purchase—Charles Lang Freer Endowment).*

of galangal (*khūlanjān*), 1 *ūqiyya* (1 ounce) almond or sesame oil, a bit of salt, and the finely chopped white part of a fresh onion. Boil until cooked. Next, add coriander and cassia (*dār Ṣīnī*) [both pounded], and thicken the broth with pounded bread crumbs.[12] Offer it, along with a spoon, (**61r**) to the patient. It is good for people with fevers and those suffering from an excess of hot properties (*aṣḥāb al-ḥarārāt*).

Another way of preparing it

Choose a tender green gourd, peel it, and discard the inside, including the seeds. Chop it, boil it until it is cooked, and then pound it in a mortar until it resembles bone marrow in consistency. Set it aside.

Now take a clean pot,[13] and put in it 1 *dirham* (3 grams) of the diced white part of a fresh onion (*bayāḍ baṣal*), a piece of cassia—leave it whole, 2 *ūqiyyas* (¼ cup) almond or sesame oil, a small amount of chopped fresh herbs (*abzār ruṭb*), and 1 *raṭl* (1 pound) of the prepared gourd. Pour on it sour grape juice and fresh water, ½ *raṭl* (1 cup) of each.

12 The word *madqūq* 'pounded' indicates that dried crumbs are used here.

13 I filled in some missing steps in this section based on al-Warrāq's version.

When the onion cooks, add to the pot 2 *ūqiyyas* (2 ounces) skinned and ground almonds, 1 *ūqiyya* sugar, 1 *dirham* (3 grams) salt, 2 *dirhams* crushed coriander, and 2 *dirhams* bread crumbs (*lubāb khubz*) blended with 5 *dirhams* (1 tablespoon) rosewater.

The final stew should be of medium consistency, neither too thin nor condensed. Offer it to the sick person with a spoon. He will be cured.

(208) *Muzawwarat al-māsh* (mung beans)[14]

Mung bean [juice] is extracted with a piece of cloth. [First] soak them, wash them, boil them, and then strain them with a cloth [by squeezing the liquid through it]. Mash the remaining solids and add them to it.

Take an onion, [chop it] and fry it in almond or sesame oil, and add to it the mung beans. Also, add ½ *ūqiyya* (1 tablespoon) sugar. Let it cook until the stew thickens, and then remove.

(209) *Muzawwarat ḥabb* (61v) *al-rummān* (dried pomegranate seeds), good for nausea (*qaraf*)

Take pomegranate seeds, boil them, and strain their juice (*khāṣṣiyyatahu*). Now take some almonds, and pound them very well [and set them aside]. Take fresh mint and a bit of cilantro, chop with them an onion, and fry them in sesame oil [and set them aside].

Put the pomegranate seed juice on the fire with a small amount of *aṭrāf al-ṭīb* (spice blend). When it comes to a boil, add the [pounded] almonds and the aforementioned herbs (*ḥawāʾij*), with a small amount of sugar. Let it cook until the broth thickens.

(210) *Muzawwarat ḥabb rummān*, good for diarrhea (*jarayān al-jawf*),[15] and heartburn (*wajaʿ al-fuʾād*)

Take dried pomegranate seeds (*ḥabb rummān*), toast them, and then finely pound them. [Boil the pounded seeds,] strain their liquid, and add a bit of dried mint to it. When you ladle it, add to it a small amount of local rosewater (*māʾ ward baladī*).[16]

---

14 The edited recipe is a bit confused. Here I have amended it slightly based on Gotha, fols. 62r–v, and DK, n. 2702.

15 Here I replaced the edited للخوف, which is irrelevant in this context, with Gotha's, fol 62v جريان الجوف.

16 See glossary 8, under s.v. *māʾ ward*.

(211) *Muzawwarat summāq* (sumac)

Toast the sumac berries and then sift them.[17] Take the resulting finely crushed sumac [husks], and set them aside, keeping them dry. Soak the remaining sumac [berries] in clear water. Fry one onion in almond or sesame oil, and after you drain it, pour the sumac juice into it, along with small amounts of dried mint, *aṭrāf al-ṭīb* (spice blend), and pounded hazelnuts. Also, take some *khubz maʿrūk* or *baqsamāṭ*,[18] pound it, and add it to the pot. When you ladle the dish, sprinkle some of the [remaining] crushed sumac on it.

(212) *Muzawwara* of *zīrbāj* (delicately sour golden stew)

Take 1½ *ūqiyyas* (3 tablespoons) white vinegar and add (**62r**) 1 *ūqiyya* (1 ounce) sugar to it. Throw in a sprig of fresh mint, along with 1 *ūqiyya* scalded and skinned almonds, pounded first and then mixed with some hot water. Add this mixture to [a pot where] an onion has been [chopped and] fried in sesame or almond oil. As soon as it boils, add to it 1 *ūqiyya* sugar and a bit of *aṭrāf al-ṭīb* (spice blend), rosewater, and saffron.

(213) *Muzawwarat yaqṭīn* (gourd)

You need gourds, almonds, and small amounts of sesame oil, sugar, mastic gum, cassia (*dār Ṣīnī*), black pepper, and mint.

Put some water in a frying pan, and put a [chopped] onion in it. Boil the gourd separately, and when the onion is cooked, add the gourd to it. Add the sugar, and squeeze some lemon juice all over the ingredients [including those mentioned at the beginning of the recipe].

(214) *Muzawwarat ḥabb al-rummān* (dried pomegranate seeds), cooked with gourd

You need a gourd, almonds, mastic gum, cassia (*dār Ṣīnī*), and pomegranate seeds. First, boil the gourd separately. Pound the almonds, put them in a pot and add to it a small amount of water and a fried [chopped] onion, and let the almonds cook with the onion. Throw in mastic gum and cassia.

Pound the pomegranate seeds and extract their essence using some of the liquid in which the gourd was boiled, and add it to the ingredients in the pot. Add some sugar and (**62v**) the boiled gourd.

If young chickens (*farrūj*) are used, they can replace the gourd.[19]

---

17 Here I read تنشفه as تنسفه, and consider it dialectical vocalization of the 's' sound.

18 The first is bread made from vigorously and thoroughly kneaded dough, which was thought to be easier to digest. *Baqsamāṭ* is twice-baked hard bread and cookies.

19 *Muzawwarāt* are recommended for the sick because they are meatless. However, in this chapter we do come across recipes, such as this one, that call for young chickens (*farrūj*).

(215) *Muzawwarat isfānākh* (spinach)
Spinach and a small amount of coriander are needed. Boil the spinach until it cooks and then drain it and pour some sesame oil on it. Also, add the coriander, along with a bit of salt and a small amount of the boiling liquid from the spinach.

(216) *Muzawwarat al-māsh* (mung beans), good for coughs (*suʿāl*)
You need mung beans, sweet olive oil, an onion, mastic gum, and cassia (*dār Ṣīnī*). Fry the [chopped] onion first in the oil and then add water until it boils. Throw in the mung beans, which have been shelled and pounded. Throw in mastic gum and cassia, and cook until done.

(217) *Muzawwara* with gourd and safflower seeds (*qurṭum*)
You need safflower seeds, a gourd, a bit of mint, sugar, almonds, mastic gum, and cassia (*dār Ṣīnī*). Boil the gourd, and keep just a small amount of its liquid in the pot [set the rest aside]. Add sugar to the pot. Pound the almonds after you scald and shell them, and add them, along with the rest of the ingredients. Pound safflower seeds, steep them in some of the boiling liquid from the gourd, and add them to the pot. You can also make the dish without the gourd.

(218) *Muzawwarat rijla* (purslane)
You need (63r) purslane, dried pomegranate seeds (*ḥabb rummān*), sugar, mastic gum, and cassia (*dār Ṣīnī*). Boil purslane first, and then pound the pomegranate seeds and extract their essence [by steeping them in some of the boiling liquid from the purslane?]. Throw the sugar, mastic gum, and cassia [into the pot of purslane], and add [the extracted pomegranate liquid].

(219) *Muzawwara* with pomegranate seeds and young chickens (*farrūj*)[20]
You need young chickens, dried pomegranate seeds, mastic gum, and cassia (*dār Ṣīnī*). Boil the young chickens; extract the juice of the pomegranate seeds [by soaking them in water, mashing them, and draining the liquid]. Fry the young chickens in a small amount of sesame oil. Put a small amount of fresh herbs (*baql*) in the cavities of the young chickens while they are frying, just to help the inside gather enough heat; remove them after they are done frying. Pour the extracted pomegranate juice over them.

Young chickens were approved by physicians because they were deemed light enough for the sick. In this case, *muzawwara* is used loosely to mean 'a dish suitable for the sick.'.

20 See n. above.

(220) *Muzawwarat mulūkhiyya* (Jew's mallow)

You need Jew's mallow, sesame oil, mastic gum, cassia (*dār Ṣīnī*), an onion, and coriander. Fry the onion in sesame oil, and let it cook with the rest of the ingredients until done.

(221) *Muzawwarat isfānākh* (spinach) with sugar and pomegranate seeds

You need sugar, spinach, dried pomegranate seeds, mastic gum, and cassia (*dār Ṣīnī*). Boil the spinach first, and then add to it juice extracted from the pomegranate seeds [by steeping them in water], along with the rest of the ingredients.

(222) *Muzawwarat qurṭum* (safflower seeds)

Pound safflower seeds, and extract their liquid [by steeping them in water and straining them], then boil it and color it with a bit of saffron. Throw in a sprig of mint and another of cilantro; add sugar as well. Use it as a flavoring sauce (*mizāj*) by adding some lime juice (*laymūn akhḍar*) to it.[21]

(223) *Muzawwarat qarʿ* (gourd)

Take a gourd, peel it, cut it into pieces, boil it, and fry it in almond or sesame oil. Sprinkle a small amount of coriander on it, and leave it on the remaining heat until it settles (*yahdaʾ*). **(63v)**

(224) *Muzawwara* for people suffering from fever triggered by excess of yellow bile (*aṣḥāb al-ḥummā al-ṣafrāʾ*)[22]

Peel a whole gourd (*yaqṭīna*),[23] and discard the inside seeds. Cut it into small pieces and put it in a pot. Pour on it a small amount of fresh sesame oil, the white part of fresh [chopped] onion, fresh herbs (*abzār raṭba*), a small amount of rue (*sadhāb*), and a pinch of salt.

When the stew is done, sprinkle it with a small amount of rosewater, and season it with a bit of coriander.[24] Thicken the stew with bread crumbs (*lubāb al-khubz*),[25] and ladle it out [into bowls]. It will be beneficial.

---

21 See glossary 9.2, for more on *mizāj*.

22 With the exception of some minor stylistic differences and omissions, this recipe is identical with that of al-Warrāq. See English trans. *Annals* 433. Here I used it to amend the edited text.

23 It would seem that this was a large variety of gourd, as only one is needed.

24 Al-Warrāq's version also adds, "Sprinkle it lightly with sour juice of unripe grapes (*māʾ ḥiṣrim*) and add a bit of white sugar to balance its sourness."

25 Al-Warrāq specifies *khubz maʿrūk*, see n. 18 above.

(225) *Muzawwara* made with chard (*silq*)

Take chard stalks (*aḍlāʿ al-silq*) and boil them. When they are done, take them out of the pot and put them in cold water. Next, strain them, and put them in a green-glazed bowl (*ghaḍāra*). Add a handful (*kaff*) of sifted sumac to them and toss the bowl so that the chard absorbs its sourness. Pour over them a small amount of sesame, olive, or almond oil, and serve.

(226) *Zīrbāj* (delicately sour golden stew)

Its properties are almost perfectly balanced.[26] It benefits people whose dominant humor is yellow bile (*aṣḥāb al-ṣafrāʾ*), and those with inflamed livers (*akbād multahiba*), and weak stomachs. It is also good for jaundice (*yaraqān*), blockages (*sudud*) in the liver and spleen (*ṭuḥāl*), and ascites (*istisqāʾ*).

Take some onion, chop the amount you need, and throw it into a small pot placed on low fire. Add almond oil, sesame oil, or olive oil, depending on the temperament (*mizāj*) [of the person who will eat the dish].[27]

When the onion is done frying, add to it (**64r**) a small amount of pounded coriander, a bit of mint, and as much spikenard (*sunbul*), cassia (*dār Ṣīnī*), and mastic gum as it needs. Next, pour in very sour vinegar (*khall thaqīf*) diluted with a suitable amount of water. Then sweeten the stew with sugar, thicken it with finely crushed skinned almonds, and scent it with saffron and rosewater. A bit of wheat starch (*nashāʾ*) added to it is fine, too. Remove the pot [and serve].

(227) *Muzawwarat al-ḥabb rummān* (pomegranate seeds)

Its properties are cold and dry; [this is] beneficial for fevers triggered by a surfeit of yellow bile (*ḥummā ṣafrāwiyya*) and inflamed livers; it alleviates thirst and cures nausea. It suits all ailing bodies.

Take a small amount of pounded coriander; fry it in almond, sesame, or olive oil,[28] and add to it a bit of mint and a bit of spikenard.

Now pour into the pot [fresh] pomegranate juice mixed with water, as needed. Or, you may use [dried whole] pomegranate seeds boiled in water, and then pressed and mashed, and strained—as necessary. The [dried] pomegranate seeds are not pounded first because [if they are] their properties become more astringent (*qābiḍ*) than when the seeds are boiled whole. Moreover, if

26 See glossary 11, s.v. *mizāj*.

27 See glossary 6 for the different types of oils and their properties; and glossary 11 for terms related to temperaments and physical disorders.

28 Depending on the temperament (*mizāj*) of the person who will eat the dish, as recipe 226 explains.

the pomegranate seeds were pounded they would generate more wind (*rīḥ*) in the body.[29]

So, when the broth boils, enhance its flavor (*yuftaq*) with sugar, thicken it with pounded almonds, and scent it with rosewater. If the dish is meant to be astringent, then toast the almonds before pounding them. If you do not want it to be astringent, cook it with stalks (*aḍlāʿ*) of spinach, purslane (*ḥamqāʾ*), and chard (*silq*). (**64v**) [When done,] remove the pot from the heat.

29 For medical terms, see glossary 11.

CHAPTER 9

فيما يعمل من أنواع السمك من سائر ألوانه

All Kinds of Dishes Made with Different Varieties of Fish

(228) Recipe for making *samaka ṭaḥīniyya* (fish with tahini sauce)
[You will need] vinegar, *aṭrāf ṭīb* (spice blend), black pepper, saffron, and onion. Wash the fish, dust it with a bit of flour,[1] and fry it in sesame oil [and set aside].

Pound black pepper and spices, add them to [chopped] onion, and fold them in. Dissolve tahini with vinegar and saffron, add it to the *ḥawāyij* (onion mixture), and let it boil. When it is done, put the [fried] fish in this [sauce].[2]

(229) *Al-samaka al-kuzbariyya* (fish with cilantro sauce)
You need fresh fish, black pepper, garlic, cilantro, sesame oil, and onion. Wash the fish, [cut it into pieces], dust it with flour, and fry the pieces in sesame oil. [Set it aside and] let it cool.

Now, take onion and chop it finely; pound cilantro and garlic; pound black pepper; and put it all in a frying pan, [with water as needed,] and fold it together until it is cooked. The liquid added should make enough [sauce]. Pour the sauce over the fish.

(230) *Al-samak al-zabībiyya* (fish with raisins)
You need fresh fish (*samak ṭarī*), raisins (*zabīb*), wine vinegar, *aṭrāf ṭīb* (spice blend), saffron, black pepper, almonds, and sesame oil. Wash the fish, dust it with flour, fry it, and [set it aside to] cool.

Boil vinegar, and add raisins and black pepper, both pounded, along with the spices. Scald and skin the almonds, daub them with saffron [steeped in water], and add them [together]. Pour this [sauce] all over the fish.

(231) *Al-samak al-laymūniyya* (lemon fish)
(**65r**) You need fresh fish, safflower seeds (*qurṭum*), lemon, mastic gum, cassia (*dār Ṣīnī*), and a sprig of mint. Pound the safflower seeds, [steep them in

---

1 The verb used here is *yutabbal*, usually used when spices (*tawābil*) are added. However, in the recipes in this chapter, this verb is also used when the fish is dusted with flour only.

2 In al-Warrāq's cookbook, such sauces are called *ṣibāgh*, as in chapter 34.

 | DOI 10.1163/9789004349919_012

water and] strain them. Put the [strained liquid] in a pot suspended over the fire. Squeeze the lemon, strain its juice and add it to the safflower [liquid]. Let them boil.

Wash the fish, cut it into pieces, and immerse it in the [sauce] pot while it is still on the fire. Keep the fire going until the fish is done [i.e., poached], at which point you add the mastic gum, cassia, and mint.

(232) *Al-samak al-mudaqqaqa* (patties of pounded fish)

You need fresh fish, black pepper, sesame oil, coriander, a small amount of sweet olive oil, and one onion.

Wash the fish, remove all the small bones (*shawk*), and finely pound it in a mortar (*hāwan*). Pound black pepper and coriander, and add it to the fish, along with a small amount of sweet olive oil. Pound them all and make patties (*mudaqqaqa*) with them, shaped as rings and discs.

Suspend the pot over the fire, put [water] in it and let it boil. Put the patties in it and keep the fire going until they are cooked, and then take them out of the pot. Suspend a frying pan [on the fire], put sesame oil in it, and fry the fish [patties]. Arrange them on plates (*ṣuḥūn*). Pound coriander and salt, and sprinkle them on the patties.

(233) Recipe for *samak maḥshī* (fish smothered in sauce)[3]

Take fresh fish, clean it, and let it drain (**65v**) for an hour. Take vinegar, [pounded] garlic, and coriander. Smear the fish with them, set it aside for an hour, then coat it once again, this time with flour, and fry it in sesame oil.

Pound black pepper and *aṭrāf al-ṭīb* (spice blend), add them to the [chopped] onion [that is frying], and stir them together. Dissolve tahini in vinegar along with saffron, add it to the *ḥawāʾij* (i.e., onion mixture) and let them boil. When [the sauce] is done, immerse the fried fish in it.

(234) Another recipe for *samak maḥshī*

Take the fish, wash it, [and drain it]. Take caraway and coriander, [mix them as in recipe above], rub (*yulaṭṭakh*) the fish with them, and set it aside for an hour. Next, coat it with flour and fry it in sesame or olive oil.

Now, take sumac and the rest of the sauce ingredients (*ḥawāʾij* [mentioned below]) of *samak maḥshī*, and mix them with lemon juice [put just enough to moisten them].[4] Also, add [chopped] lemon preserved in salt (*laymūn māliḥ*),

---

3 See glossary 9.2 for more on *maḥshī*.

4 The recipe uses the verb *latta*, which suggests adding just enough to combine and moisten the ingredients.

a small amount of water, enough to blend the sauce ingredients. Also add a bit of garlic to it. Boil the mix two or three times.[5] Arrange the [fried] fish pieces in a bowl (*zibdiyya*) and pour the [cooked] sauce all over them.

The ingredients of the sauce for smothered fish (*ḥawāʾij al-maḥshī*) are sumac, walnuts, coriander, thyme, caraway, a small amount of garlic, black pepper, chopped lemon preserved in salt, common parsley (*karafs*), and mint.

(235) Section on ways to cook sour fish dishes (*samak ḥāmiḍ*)[6]

Take the fish, scale it, sprinkle it with salt, and set it aside for an hour so that it absorbs the salt, (**66r**) and then wash it very well, roll it in flour, and fry it in olive oil, or if you wish, sesame oil.

With this fried fish, you can make all kinds of fish dishes, such as *sikbāj* (sour vinegar stew), *laymūniyya* (lemon stew), *summāqiyya* (sumac stew), *ṭabāhija* (succulent fried dish), *kuzbariyya* (stew flavored with cilantro), and so on.

If you want to prepare fish as ***sikbāj***, suspend the pot over the fire and fry a [chopped] onion in olive oil or sesame oil. Add vinegar to the fried onion in the pot, color the fried fish with saffron, and after the vinegar boils arrange the pieces of fish in the pot. Season it with aromatics and spice seeds (*afāwīh wa abāzīr*). Add mint, and then remove.

If you want to prepare it as ***laymūniyya*** (with lemon juice), squeeze lime juice (*laymūn akhḍar*) on the onion fried in oil (*taqliyya*), mentioned above.[7] Add some water. When the pot boils, arrange the fish pieces in it, season them with spices and mint, and then take the pot off the heat. If you want to thicken the broth, pound a small amount of safflower seeds [mix them with some water] and add them to the pot.

If you want to prepare it as ***summāqiyya*** (with sumac), add water, as needed, to the *taqliyya* (i.e., the fried onion) in a soapstone pot (*burma*), as mentioned above. When it boils, add sumac to it, and season it with spices (*abāzīr*) and *aṭrāf al-ṭīb* (spice blend). If you want to thicken the broth, pound walnuts and mix them in a bowl (*zibdiyya*) with finely ground sumac. (**66v**) Steep them with some of the broth [and add them to the pot]. When you ladle this dish into serving bowls, garnish the tops with [ground] sumac.

If you want to prepare it as ***ṭabāhija*** (succulent fried dish), add just a small amount of water to the above-mentioned *taqliyya*, and add as much *murrī*

5 See glossary 9.2, s.v. *ghalwa*.

6 This section is called *bāb* 'chapter' in the edited text because it briefly describes the different methods for preparing sour dishes with fish. I follow DK, n. 2989, and Gotha, fol. 66v, where the word الحامض 'sour' is copied, because it is more relevant than the edited الخاص 'special.'

7 See glossary 5, s.v. *taqliyya*.

al-sha'īr (barley fermented sauce) mixed with lime [juice] as needed. Season it with spices and mint, arrange the fried fish pieces in it, and take the pot off the heat.

If you want to prepare it as ***kuzbariyya*** (flavored with cilantro), fry finely pounded garlic—do not fry any onion for it, just pounded garlic and olive oil and nothing else. Also mix pounded spices with it. Pound cilantro, extract its juice, and pour it into the pot. Let it boil, then arrange the [fried] fish pieces in it, and take the pot off the heat.

(236) *Samak mashwī* (oven-baked fish)

Take black pepper, cassia (*dār Ṣīnī*), caraway, ginger, sumac, coriander, thyme, and a bit of cumin. Pound them all with a bit of [dried] mint, and sift them. Peel garlic cloves and pound them in a mortar along with a lump of salt and sweet olive oil. Add enough of the [above] spices (*ḥawā'ij*) to them so that you can knead the mix. After kneading it, take walnuts, pound them, and add them [to the first mixture]. Take lemon [juice], olive oil, and tahini, as needed, add them to the spice mix, (**67r**) and then knead them all together.

Now, take the fish and stuff it well [with the above mix], in the belly and in slits made in its skin.[8] Arrange some thin sticks in the bottom of the frying pan (*ṭājin*) or use a thin wood board to prevent the fish from sticking [to the pan while baking]. [Place the fish in the prepared pan and] send it to the [commercial] *furn* (brick oven).[9] When the top cooks, take the pan out of the oven, let the fish cool on the board for an hour, and then [turn it over],[10] and resume baking it until it is done.

(237) Recipe for *samak maqlī* (fried fish)

Take fresh fish, scale it and remove the prickly bones. Slit open the belly and take out the entrails. Wash the fish very well, sprinkle it with salt and set it aside for a good hour. After that, put it in a *quffa* (basket woven with date palm fronds), and fold it on the fish. Place the basket on a large flat tile (*bilāṭa*), weigh it down with another one, and set it aside until the fish is drained of all its moisture. Then return to it, cut it up into small pieces, and dust them with good flour.

---

8 I opted to replace the word *jawānibihi* (جوانبه) 'its sides' in the edited text with *jawābīhi* (جوابيه) 'slit places' found in DK, n. 3045. See *Lisān al-'Arab*, s.v. جوب.

9 The imperative *waddī* (ودّيه) is a colloquial Arabic expression that means 'send it'; this indicates that the fish was not baked at home.

10 The fish is left to cool off so that it firms up a little and does not fall apart when it is turned over.

Suspend the frying pan (*ṭājin*) over the fire and put sesame oil or sweet olive oil in it, it is up to you. Put a lot of oil so that the fish pieces swim in it.[11] Fry the fish thoroughly so that no moisture remains in it.

Now, take grape vinegar (*khall al-ʿinab*), toasted coriander and caraway, all the ingredients of *aṭrāf al-ṭīb* (spice blend), and saffron. Stir this liquid mix (*mizāj*), and put the fried fish in it. (**67v**) There should be enough to submerge it.

Put the fish in glass vessels (*āniya zujājiyya*) or glazed ceramic jars (*qaṭramīz*), and pour the vinegar mix all over it. Stash the jars aside until needed. It will stay good for days and does not go bad. Some people provision themselves with it when they travel to far-off places and it does not spoil.

(238) Recipe for *samak bi-l-summāq* (fish with sumac)

You need fresh fish, sumac, sweet olive oil, tahini, garlic, thyme, some fresh herbs (*ḥawāʾij baql*),[12] black pepper, coriander, caraway, lemon or Damascus citron (*kabbād*).

Wash the fish in salted water, and then sprinkle it with salt and set it aside for a full hour so that it will taste good. Now, take the sumac and sift it with the sieve used for sifting whole wheat flour (*ghirbāl qamḥī*). Take the stems and husks [remaining in the sieve] and soak them in water for an hour. Finely pound the [sifted] sumac and sift it again, to get rid of any solid particles.

Finely pound the thyme and add it to the pounded sifted sumac. Chop the herbs over them, and add tahini. Now, take lemon, squeeze its juice and strain off the seeds—do likewise if *kabbād* is used. Pound the spices [coriander, caraway, and black pepper] and add them to the sumac mix. Add the rest of the ingredients [olive oil and garlic], and knead all of the sumac mixture with the [extracted] juice of lemon or *kabbād*.

Arrange the fish pieces in a frying pan (*ṭājin*), throw the [above prepared] *ḥawāʾij* (sumac mix) over them, but set aside a small amount of it. Strain the [soaking] sumac stems through a sieve and add this liquid to the sumac mix that was set aside. Pour it (**68r**) over the fish [and cook it on the fire until done.]

(239) Recipe for *samak mashwī* (baked fish)

You need fresh fish, sweet olive oil, coriander, and pounded black pepper. Toast the coriander and grind it, and then mix it with olive oil and black pepper. Sprinkle the fish with salt, set it aside for an hour, and then wash it to get rid of

11 The verb used is *yaʿūm* 'swim' i.e., there must be enough oil for the pieces of fish to move about freely, without overcrowding the pan.

12 Such as mint, parsley, and cilantro.

the salt. Put the prepared *ḥawāʾij* (oil and spice mix) in the belly of the fish, and put it in a frying pan (*ṭājin*), [and bake it in the oven].

(240) Recipe for *samak māliḥ* (salt-cured fish)

You need [salt-cured] fish and sweet olive oil. Soak the fish for an hour to get rid of [the excess] salt, and then wash it, rub it with some linseed oil (*zayt ḥārr*),[13] and wash it [again]. The washing will help rid the fish of its strong smell (*zafar*). Arrange the fish pieces [in a pan], pour olive oil on them, and send them to the [commercial] *furn* (brick oven) [to be baked].

(241) Recipe for *samak mukaffan* (smothered fish)[14]

You need [salt-cured] flathead grey mullet (*samak al-baṭārikh*),[15] sweet olive oil, some fresh herbs (*ḥawāʾij baql*),[16] vinegar, saffron, *aṭrāf ṭīb* (spice blend), coriander, hazelnuts, tahini, and black pepper.

Take the roes (*baṭārikh*) out of the fish, put them in pan and pour sweet olive oil [that was set aside] on them. Soak the fish in water for an hour to get rid of [excess] salt, and then wash it and put it in a pan. Pour some olive oil on it and send it [along with the roe-pan] to the [commercial] *furn* (brick oven) to let them bake until done. When they are brought back from the oven, let them cool.

Now, take onion, finely chop it, and put it in a frying pan (*ṭājin*). Add **(68v)** a bit of water to it and keep the fire going until it boils. Chop the herbs over it, and continue feeding the fire until it is done.

Pound black pepper and add it to the pan; toast coriander, pound it, and add it; also add *aṭrāf al-ṭīb*. Mix saffron with vinegar and tahini, and add them to the onion mixture.

Continue stirring the pan for a while (lit., 'an hour')—but do not let the vinegar dry out, and then remove it and cool it. Spread it all over the fish, which should also be cold, and serve.

---

13 Lit., 'hot oil,' see glossary 6.

14 The general meaning is 'covered'; the word is closely associated with shrouding the dead. In its general sense, it is related to *maḥshī* dishes, see, for instance, recipes 233, and 234 in this chapter.

15 This fish is called *būrī*, *Mugil cephalus*, from which bottarga (*baṭārikh*) 'fish roe' is taken.

16 Such as mint, parsley, and cilantro.

(242) Recipe for *ṣīr muṭayyab* (seasoned anchovies)[17]

Take [salt-cured] *ṣīr* [put them in a bowl, and] add a small amount of the [briny] juice (*maraq*) to them. Also, add lime juice (*māʾ laymūn akhḍar*), sweet olive oil, and thyme. Chop rind of lime (*qishr al-laymūn al-akhḍar*), press it, and rub it with your fingers [to release its essence], and add it to the fish.

(243) Another recipe for *ṣīr muṭayyab*

Peel off (*yuslakh*) the skins of [salt-cured] *ṣīr*,[18] chop them into fine pieces, and add them to olive oil, lime juice (*māʾ laymūn akhḍar*), dried thyme, chopped Macedonian parsley (*baqdūnis*), mint (*naʿnāʿ*), rue (*sadhāb*), and a bit of pounded garlic. Mix all [the ingredients], and eat it.

(244) Recipe for *ṣīr mushakshak* (split-open anchovies)[19]

Take [salt-cured] *ṣīr* (anchovies).[20] Chop cilantro and onion for them. Parboil the onion, press out the excess moisture, color it with saffron, fry it in sweet olive oil, and then take it out of the pan and add it to pounded cilantro. (**69r**)

Next, fry the *ṣīr* in sweet olive oil, remove their thorny bones (*shawk*), and add to them—while they are still on the fire—the [fried] onion with cilantro, along with toasted coriander, caraway, *aṭrāf al-ṭīb* (spice blend), mint, olive oil, and tahini. Fold the ingredients together, and serve.

(245) Another [*ṣīr*] recipe[21]

Take an onion, chop it finely, and fry it in sweet olive oil. Add whole [salt-cured] *ṣīr* (anchovies) to it, and let them fry.[22] Add black pepper, *aṭrāf ṭīb*

---

17 These are also known as *balam* (بلم). This small fish is used already salt-cured. When consumed fresh, it is referred to as *absāriyya* (see, for instance, recipes 246 and 247 below). It looks like a sardine. However, *ṣīr* is sometimes used to designate fresh anchovies, when they are destined for salt curing and made into condiments, as in recipe 255 below.

18 See above note.

19 My interpretation of the name of the dish is based on the Arabic verb *yushaqq* (يشق), *yushaqqaq* (يشقّق), and the adjective *mashqūq* (مشقوق), *mushaqqaq* (مشقّق) and *mushaqshaq* (مشقشق), which is a common variant. The vocalization of q (ق) as k (ك) is a recognized Egyptian dialectical variant. Therefore, *mushakshak* (مشكشك) might well have been an Egyptian variant of *mushaqshaq* (مشقشق). See recipe 250 below, where the same fish, butterflied, is described as *mashqūq*. See glossary 5.

20 See n. 17 above.

21 See n. 17 above.

22 The verb is clearly written as *yughlā* (يغلى) 'boiled,' but the word often appears interchangeably with *yuqlā* (يقلى) 'fried.'

(spice blend), and vinegar to them. If you enjoy it with lemon juice, then add it instead of the vinegar. Add pounded garlic, and eat it.

(246) Recipe for *samak maqlī* (fried fish)

You need fresh fish or *bisāriyya*,[23] and sesame oil or sweet olive oil (*zayt ṭayyib*). You also need coriander, and flour.

Wash the fish with a small amount of linseed oil (*zayt ḥārr*),[24] [rinse it] and let the fish drain for an hour. Cut [large fish] into pieces, and coat it with flour. Put the frying pan (*ṭājin*) on the fire, add sesame oil or whatever you are using, and when it sizzles,[25] fry the floured fish pieces. Do not turn them over to the other side until the first fried side is completely brown; only then can you turn it over.

When it is done, arrange the fish in vessels (*awʿiya*), and sprinkle them with pounded coriander mixed with a bit of salt, and serve. (**69v**)

(247) Recipe for *absāriyya mukaffana* (fresh anchovies smothered in sauce)[26]

You need fresh thick-fleshed anchovies (*absāriyya ghalīẓa*), sesame oil or some other kind [such as sweet olive oil], coriander, garlic, vinegar, saffron, hazelnuts, a small amount of flour, tahini, and black pepper.

Wash the fish with salt, a bit of flour, and linseed oil (*zayt ḥārr*).[27] [Rinse it and set it aside]. Pound garlic with a bit of coriander and salt, and rub this mix all over the fish after you soak and wash it [as described above]. Set the fish aside for a good hour so that it absorbs the garlic flavor.

Put flour in a vessel (*wiʿāʾ*), put the fishes in it, and make them look like combs, as usual.[28] Suspend a frying pan (*ṭājin*) over the fire, add the oil, and

---

23 Written as *absāriyya* in Gotha, fol. 70r. These are fresh anchovies, which, when preserved in brine, are referred to as *ṣīr*. See Maqrīzī, *Khiṭaṭ* i 309–10.

24 See n. 13 above.

25 The expression used is *yaṭīr sharārahu*, lit., 'its sparks fly out.' My guess is that the heat of oil was tested by dropping some water from the fingertips; if the water sizzles and evaporates, it is hot enough to fry in. This test is followed by many cooks today.

26 See notes 14 and 23 above.

27 See n. 13.

28 The verb used is *tumashshiṭ*, lit., 'comb.' The recipe refers to them as fish combs (*amshāṭ al-absāriyya*). Other medieval sources do not describe similar dishes; therefore, the following interpretation is based on today's Egyptian culinary practices: to fry sardine-like small fishes, each three are held from their tails and coated with seasoned flour on both sides, then the process is repeated for the rest of the fishes. These comb-like fish formations are referred to as *amshāṭ al-samak*. See online: http://forums.banat-style.com/arab girlsfashion3285/, accessed 24 Dec. 2016. It is my guess that the name was inspired by

keep a strong fire going until the oil sizzles.[29] Put *amshāṭ al-absāriyya* in it,[30] but do not turn the pieces over until the first side is brown; after that you can turn them over. Take them out of the oil, put them in vessels, and let them cool.

Pound the rest of the garlic, and put it in the frying pan on the fire, into which you have poured a small amount of sweet olive oil (*zayt ṭayyib*) so that garlic fries in it. Pound coriander, black pepper, and toasted [hazelnuts], and add them to the frying pan. Chop some herbs (*ḥawāʾij al-baql*) over them. Dissolve saffron in vinegar mixed with tahini, and throw them into the ingredients in the frying pan.

Arrange the fried fishes (**70r**) in a vessel (*wiʿāʾ*); cover them all with the sauce, and set the dish aside for an hour to allow the flavors to blend (*yukhammar*), and serve.

(248) Recipe for *al-samak al-zīrbāj* (fish in delicately sour golden sauce)

You need fresh fish, vinegar, honey, saffron, *aṭrāf al-ṭīb* (spice blend), tahini, black pepper, raisins (*zabīb*), almonds, sesame oil, and flour.

Wash the fish, cut it into pieces, [drain it well], and dust it with flour. Suspend the frying pan over the fire, [add the oil, and when it is hot enough,] fry the fish in it, and then let it cool.

Now to the vinegar, saffron, onion, spice blend, black pepper, and tahini. First, fry the [chopped] onion in a small amount of sesame oil. Pound the spices, add them to it along with the rest of the ingredients, and stir. When the mixture boils, pour it over the fish [that you have put in dishes]. Scald and skin the almonds, color them with a bit of saffron, and scatter them over the dishes along with [drizzles of] olive oil, and serve.

(249) Recipe for *al-samak al-sikbāj* (fish in vinegar-honey sauce)

You need fresh fish, vinegar, honey, *aṭrāf ṭīb* (spice blend), black pepper, onion, saffron, sesame oil, and flour.

Wash the fish, cut it into pieces, [drain it well], fry it in sesame oil after you dust it with flour, and take it out when done [and set aside]. Chop the onion, and fry it in sesame oil until it browns. Pound black pepper, and add it along with the spice blend. Dissolve saffron in vinegar and honey, and throw it into pan with the onion. When the sauce is done cooking, put the [fried] fish pieces in it. (**70v**)

---

the comb-like formation of the metatarsal bones of the feet, called *amshāṭ al-qadam* in Arabic, see *Lisān al-ʿArab*, s.v. مشط. See also glossary 10, s.v. *absāriyya*.

29 See n. 25 above.

30 See n. 28 above.

(250) Recipe for *samak bi-l-khardal* (fish in mustard sauce)

You need filleted salt-cured fish (*samak māliḥ mashqūq*), sesame oil, mustard seeds, vinegar, raisins, dates, and honey. Wash the fish and fry it. However, the fish needs to dry out completely before frying it; [otherwise, it will splatter].

As soon as the fish is done frying, pick over the mustard seeds, pound them thoroughly, sift them in a flour sieve, and dissolve them in vinegar and honey. [Pound the raisins and dates and add them.] Boil the mix until it thickens somewhat,[31] and then put the fried fish in it.

(251) *Al-samak al-summāqiyya* (fish poached in sumac sauce)

You need fresh fish, sumac, tahini (*ṭaḥīna*), garlic, black pepper, onion, coriander, lemon or Damascus citron (*kabbād*), hazelnuts, and sesame oil.

Finely chop the onion and fry it in sesame oil. Pick over the sumac, pound it, and sift it through a flour sieve twice, to get as much of it as you can, and add it to the chopped onion in the frying pan (*ṭājin*). Pound all the spices [mentioned above] and add them along with tahini and lemon juice [or *kabbād*] after straining the seeds. Keeps the fire going strong until it boils. Wash the fish, cut it into large pieces, and lower it, raw—as it is—into the pot until it cooks, and then ladle it into the vessels (*awʿiya*). Toast hazelnuts, pound them and sprinkle them over the top of it.

(252) Another fish dish [fried fish in nut vinegar sauce]

Cut the [fresh] fish into pieces, and wash it. Put sesame oil in a frying pan, and fry it until it browns, and set it aside.

Now, take the onion, chop it finely, parboil it in salted water, then take it out, squeeze out the moisture, color it with saffron, and fry it in olive or sesame oil until it browns. Add chopped Macedonian parsley (*baqdūnis*) to it, and stir. Moisten (*yuṭfā*) the onion mix with sour vinegar,[32] and throw in pounded toasted nuts (*qulūbāt muḥammaṣa*), and stir it until [moisture evaporates and] the ingredients start frying in their oil.[33] Throw in toasted coriander and caraway; also add cassia (*dār Ṣīnī*), black pepper, mint, and *aṭrāf al-ṭīb* [all pounded]. [Add water and] let the mix boil.

Drop the fried fish into the pot [*qidr*], where the seasoning liquid (*mizāj*) was prepared, and cook until the liquid starts bubbling (*yanbaʿ wa-yashuqq*). Take the pot off the heat, and set it aside to cool. Arrange the fish pieces on a

31 The recipe uses the generic term *yuʿmal*, which in the given context implies boiling.

32 The verb *yuṭfā* literally means 'douse' or 'extinguish.'

33 The expression used is *yalʿabu fī duhnihi* (lit., 'plays in its oil').

plate (*ṣaḥn*), and crumble a bit of dried herbs between your fingers, and sprinkle them on top.

(253) Another fish dish [fried fish in hazelnut tahini sauce]

Take fresh fish, clean it, sprinkle it lightly with salt, rinse it, and then spread it on a *qafaṣ*[34] to drain off all the moisture. Fry it in sesame oil.

Take some herbs (*ḥawāʾij al-baql*) and mint, and chop them all finely. Take pounded toasted hazelnuts, black pepper, cassia (*dār Ṣīnī*), ginger, rosebuds, *aṭrāf ṭīb* (spice blend), toasted coriander, and saffron. Thin the tahini by mixing it with good vinegar, and add it to all the [previously mentioned] ingredients.

Put the fried fish in this sauce; [there should be] enough to cover it. Set it aside overnight to let the flavors blend (*yakhtamir*), and eat it. It is delicious.

(254) Recipe for *būrī mukaffan* (fried flathead grey mullet smothered in sauce)[35]

Bake the onion,[36] and then finely chop it, rinse it in salted water, fry it in sweet olive oil (*zayt ṭayyib*), and set it aside.

Now, take saffron, *aṭrāf ṭīb* (spice blend), shelled hazelnuts, ginger, mint, rue (*sadhāb*), fresh herbs (*ḥawāʾij baql*),[37] and raisins. Add them all, [along with the onion] to the wine vinegar, and boil them and pour all of it over the fried fish [the grey mullet]. Set the fish aside overnight to let the flavors blend (*yakhtamir*), and eat it. It is truly wonderful (*ghāya*).

[The following recipes deal with *ṣaḥna*, a condiment made with salt-cured anchovies (*ṣīr*); four of them are *ṣaḥna kadhdhāba* (false, made without fish)]

(255) Recipe for *ṣaḥna*, outstandingly delicious

Take 5 *raṭl*s (5 pounds) of *ṣīr* (salt-cured anchovies), ½ *raṭl* (½ pound) black pepper, 3 *ūqiyya*s (3 ounces) ginger, ½ *qadaḥ* (approx. 1 pound) coriander, 1 *ūqiyya* (1 ounce) bitter ginger (*zurunbād*),[38] ½ *qadaḥ* (approx. 1 pound) Moroccan caraway (*karāwiya Maghribiyya*), 4 *ūqiyya*s (4 ounces) madder (*fuwwa*), ½ *raṭl*

---

34 A cage-like basket made from the stems of date palm fronds.

35 Cf. recipes 241 and 247 above. The *būrī* fish used in this recipe may be fresh, as there are no instructions to soak it, as in recipes that deal with salt-cured fish.

36 The recipe opens with *yushwā* 'bake.' Some of the recipes do indeed call for baking the onion before using it in a recipe, to mellow its sharpness.

37 Such as mint, parsley, and cilantro.

38 Aromatic rhizome of the ginger family, also called *ʿirq kāfūr*.

(½ pound) garlic, ½ *ūqiyya* (1 tablespoon) Moroccan thyme (*zaʿtar Maghribī*), 1 *raṭl* (2 cups) sweet olive oil (*zayt ṭayyib*), 2 *dirhams* (1 teaspoon) spikenard (*sunbul*), ½ *qadaḥ* (approx. 1 pound) salt, and 1½ *ūqiyyas* (3 tablespoons) *aṭrāf ṭīb* (spice blend). Pound and sift all these spices separately, and set them aside. Crush the garlic in a mortar [and set it aside].

Next, put the anchovies in a large earthenware tub (*qaṣriyya*) and clean it of any grass (*ḥashīsh*) that might be in it. Mix it with ½ *qadaḥ* (approx. 1 pound) salt or coriander. After that, mix it with madder, set it aside for seven days, and then pass it through a flour sieve [to crush it].

Throw the coriander into it, followed by caraway, then black pepper, then cassia (*dār Ṣīnī*), then ginger, then *zurunbād*, then crushed garlic that has been mixed with ½ *raṭl* (1 cup) olive oil, and then, all at once, add all the spices of *aṭrāf al-ṭīb*. (**71r**)

Put the fish mixture in a glass jar (*qaṭramīz*) until it is almost full. Seal the surface with olive oil, and set the jar aside for a whole month, and use [as needed].

(256) Recipe for another *ṣaḥna*[39]

Take 10 *raṭls* (10 pounds) of *ṣīr* (salt-cured anchovies), and put them in a stone jar (*maṭr ḥajarī*).[40] For each *raṭl* of fish, use 2 *ūqiyyas* (2 ounces) finely crushed salt. Thus, [this recipe] would require 1 *raṭl* (1 pound) plus 8 *ūqiyyas* (8 ounces) salt, as well as ½ *raṭl* crushed madder (*fuwwa*), and ½ *raṭl* garlic pounded with olive oil and salt.

Combine all the ingredients in the stone jar [along with the fish], and stir them seven times daily for seven consecutive days. After that, strain the mix through a whole-wheat sieve (*ghirbāl al-qamḥ*).[41] [Set it aside.]

Now, take spikenard (*sunbul*), betel leaves (*tunbul*), green cardamom (*hāl*), cloves (*qaranful*), and nutmeg (*jawz ṭīb*), the total amount of all these combined is 1 *raṭl* (1 pound). Also, take 1 *qadaḥ* (2¼ pounds) caraway, 2 *qadaḥs* (4½ pounds) coriander, ¼ *qadaḥ* (approx. ½ pound) thyme and pound them all.[42]

---

39 The same recipe, with the heading "Making good-quality *ṣaḥna*" (عمل الصحنة الجيدة) can be found in *Waṣf* 146. I used it here to amend the edited text.

40 A non-porous jar with a bulging belly and a narrow mouth, as described in *Kanz* recipe 501 below. They are commonly used for keeping oil or small salt-cured fish (*samak mumallaḥ*), as described by Dozy, *Takmilat al-maʿājim* 1461. From the *Kanz* recipes, we learn they were also handy for keeping cheese, pickles, fermented condiments, and sauces.

41 In DK, n. 3331, at this stage, the sieve was used for sifting coarsely crushed wheat.

42 Here I followed يطحن 'pound' in *Waṣf*, rather than the edited يعجن 'knead,' which is irrelevant in this context.

Add to the spices 1 *raṭl* (1 pound) black pepper, 1 *raṭl* cassia (*dār Ṣīnī*), ½ *ūqiyya* (1 tablespoon) saffron,[43] 1 *raṭl* (1 pound) rosebuds (*zir ward*), ½ *raṭl* (1 cup) olive oil, 3 *dirhams* (9 grams/1½ teaspoons) mastic gum (*maṣṭakā'*), and 3 *ūqiyyas* (3 ounces) usnea (*shayba*).

Strain the *ṣīr* mixture [that was set aside] again, this time using a [fine-meshed] flour sieve (*ghirbāl al-daqīq*). Add the spices (*ḥawā'ij*) to it. Mix it all well, and stow it away [in glass jars] after you seal the surface very well with sweet olive oil (*zayt ṭayyib*).

Another *ṣaḥna*, which excites the appetite, strengthens the stomach, and reduces the density of phlegm[44]

Take whatever you wish of *ṣīr* (salt-cured anchovies),[45] and pour some lemon juice on them,[46] add enough to moisten and soften them, and press all of it through a sieve. Add to it pounded almonds or walnuts. Also add sumac, sweet olive oil (*zayt ṭayyib*), fine-tasting spices and herbs, aromatic spices (*afāwīh 'aṭira*), saffron, and rosewater. Also, extracted juice of salted lemon (*laymūn māliḥ*) should be put in it. For those who wish, add a bit of garlic; it will indeed enhance its taste.

(257) Recipe for another *ṣaḥna*, [called] *kadhdhāba* (false), made without fish[47]

Use raisins, hazelnuts, walnuts, pistachios, sweet olive oil (*zayt ṭayyib*), 10 *dirhams* (30 grams/approx. 1 ounce) of each, [all finely pounded]. Also, use vinegar, lemon [juice], Ceylon cinnamon (*qarfa*), (**71v**) mastic gum, black pepper, caraway, and *aṭrāf al-ṭīb* (spice blend) [all pounded]. Use as much of these spices as the *ṣaḥna* needs to enhance its taste.

Another *ṣaḥna*[48]

Ten *jarwī raṭls* (20 pounds) of *ṣīr*,[49] 1 *qadaḥ* (2¼ pounds) salt, ½ *raṭl* (½ pound) garlic. Mix with them 3 *ūqiyyas* (3 ounces) olive oil, 4 *ūqiyyas* (4 ounces) crushed madder (*fuwwa*), and a handful of lemon balm [leaves] (*rayḥān turunjī*). Mix

43 In *Waṣf*, the amount is 1½ handfuls, كف ونصف.

44 This recipe only appears in appendix 37; Gotha, fol. 73r; and *Zahr*, fol. 18v.

45 *Zahr* calls for any small fish of one's choice.

46 *Zahr* adds *sharāb ṣirf* (undiluted wine).

47 This is also known as *muzawwara* 'imitation.' Here I slightly amended the recipe based on Gotha, fol. 73r.

48 This recipe only appears in DK. appendix 38; and Gotha, fol. 73r–v.

49 The *raṭl jarwī* is a medieval Egyptian weight measure, approx. 2 pounds. See glossary 13.

all these ingredients before you get to the straining stage (*taṣfiya*).[50] Work on this mix for ten days [i.e., put it in a jar, keep it in the sun, and stir it several times a day]. [After that, press the fish mixture through a sieve.]

Now, take ½ *raṭl* (½ pound) black pepper, 3 *ūqiyyas* (3 ounces) rolled bark of Ceylon cinnamon (*qarfa laff*), 3 *ūqiyyas* (3 ounces) ginger, 1 *ūqiyya aṭrāf ṭīb* (spice blend), ¼ *ūqiyya* (½ tablespoon) saffron, 1 *ūqiyya* (1 ounce) Iraqi roses (*ward ʿIrāqī*), 1 *ūqiyya* (1 ounce) bay laurel (*rand Rūmī*), ½ *ūqiyya* (½ ounce) coriander, and 3 *ūqiyyas* (3 ounces) sweet olive oil (*zayt ṭayyib*). [Mix all of these with the strained fish mixture, then store it in a glass jar, and seal the surface with a layer of olive oil.]

(258) Recipe for *ṣaḥnat al-summāq* (with sumac)[51]

Take as many sumac [berries] as needed, pound them finely, sift them, and discard the seeds.[52] Also, take thyme, a quarter of the amount of sumac used. This should also be finely pounded.

Now, add as much garlic as you like, with a bit of salt. Throw in coarsely ground walnuts and mix them, along with a bit of mastic gum and cassia (*dār Ṣīnī*), both finely ground. Put in as much fresh sesame oil as the ingredients can take, and enhance its flavor (*yukhlaʿ*) by throwing several cumin seeds in it and heating it on a low fire. While the oil is still hot, pour it over the mixed ingredients.

Add to the mix black pepper, ginger, caraway, olive oil, tahini (*ṭaḥīna*), and lemon juice or vinegar. Mix all the ingredients thoroughly, and set the condiment aside, covered, to temper the garlic's potency, and then serve it between courses of dishes [as a dipping condiment with bread]. It is superb.

(259) Recipe for *ṣaḥna kadhdhāba* (false, made without fish), beneficial for people whose dominant humor is yellow bile (*aṣḥāb al-ṣafrā*ʾ). It refreshes the stomach (*tunʿish al-maʿida*)[53]

---

50 The condiment is usually left in airy and warm shaded places to ferment for a while before it is strained. See, for instance, recipe 256 above.

51 This is another recipe of *ṣaḥna* without fish, called *kadhdhāba*. Except for few stylistic differences and some details, the same recipe is found in *Waṣf* 146–7. Here I amended the text based on this version, as well as Gotha, fol. 73v.

52 This detail is from the *Waṣf* version; it clearly shows that of the dried sumac berries, the recipe uses only the husky dried fruit of the berry, which the edited text and Gotha refer to as *zahr summāq*. The hard seeds are discarded.

53 This recipe is also in Gotha, fols. 73v–4r; and in *Zahr*, fol. 18v–9r; and *Wuṣla* ii 690–1, where it is described as *baladiyya* 'local.' Here I amended the edited recipe with the help of these other works.

Take sumac berries, pound them with salt, sift them to get their deep-red husk (*zahratuhu*),[54] then soak them in a small amount of water and extract the juice [by pressing it] through a piece of cloth. [Remember to] leave a small amount of pounded sumac-husks unsoaked.

Now, take equal amounts of chopped Macedonian parsley (*baqdūnis*), mint (*naʿnāʿ*), and rue (*sadhāb*). Put them in a bowl and rub them between your fingers (*yufrak/yuʿarrak*) with a little bit of salt to wilt them. Fold into them generous amounts of toasted walnuts, which have been pounded until the oil is released,[55] and tahini (*ṭaḥīna*). Their amounts should be equal. Add also lime juice (*māʾ laymūn akhḍar*) and the [extracted] sumac juice.

Fold all these ingredients together and mix them well, adding a small amount of pounded sumac; use it sparingly; (**72r**) otherwise it will discolor and darken the condiment. Mix everything well, add pounded garlic and pounded dried thyme (*zaʿtar*) to them; add a lot of the latter, because it is this herb that gives the condiment is typical taste.[56]

Season it with toasted and ground coriander and caraway seeds, as well as black pepper, ginger, *aṭrāf ṭīb* (spice blend), salt, and sweet olive oil (*zayt ṭayyib*). Mix them all with the condiment.

To [test for the perfect] consistency, scoop it with a piece of bread. It should keep its shape. You can also mix with it finely chopped lemon preserved in salt (*laymūn māliḥ*). The lighter pink it is, the better, and the more walnuts and tahini are used the lighter and better it will look.

When you scoop the condiment into a *sukurruja*,[57] pour a lot of sweet olive oil on its face. Also, note that this condiment will not taste delicious if you do not use a lot of olive oil in it [i.e., while making it]. For those who want to use hazelnuts instead of walnuts [because they tend toward excess in] black bile (*khalṭ sawdāwī*), they can do so.[58] For those who like to sprinkle some [ground] pistachios on top, they can go ahead and do so.

---

54 Fresh sumac berries are hard seeds with downy outer coverings that become husks when they are dried. This husky part gives sumac spice its deep red color and its tart flavor. It is called *zahrat/zahr al-summāq*, i.e., its intensely deep-red husk. It is still known this way in the Levant. When it is dried, the sumac berries are pounded, and sifted to get the deep-red husk; the hard seeds are discarded.

55 *Yalʿabu fī duhnihi* (lit., 'plays in its oil').

56 *Yuẓhiru ṭaʿmahu.*

57 A small bowl (of half a cup) for serving dips and condiments. Details about the kind of vessel used are only mentioned in the *Wuṣla*.

58 Black bile is one of the four humors of the body, see glossary 11, s.v. *mizāj*. Its properties are cold, dry, and dense, and hazelnuts are more suitable for it than walnuts. While walnuts are hot and moist, hazelnuts are moderately hot and dry (see, for instance, Anṭākī,

(260) Recipe for *ṣīr muṭayyab* (seasoned salt-cured anchovies)[59]
It is made in several ways:

The first one: Take *ṣīr* (salt-cured anchovies), and pour on then a bit of its [salty] liquid, along with lemon juice, thyme, and a lot of sweet olive oil. Chop lemon peel and fold it into it. Arrange the fishes [in a platter].

The second: Take *ṣīr*, peel off their skins, and chop them into small pieces. Fold them with sweet olive oil, lime juice (*māʾ laymūn akhḍar*), dried thyme, chopped Macedonian parsley (*baqdūnis*), mint, rue, and a bit of pounded garlic. Mix very well, and eat it. It is a nice dish (*malīḥ*).

The third: Take an onion, chop it finely, and fry it in sweet olive oil. Add to it whole fried *ṣīr* fishes. Add *aṭrāf ṭīb* (spice blend), black pepper, and vinegar. Also add lemon juice, (**72v**) and pounded garlic if you wish. Let it cool, and eat it. It is truly wonderful (*ʿajīb*).

(261) Recipe for seasoning (*taṭyīb*) *ṣaḥna Iskandarāniyya* (Alexandrian salt-cured anchovy condiment)[60]
[To the prepared salt-cured anchovy condiment recipe below] add and combine sweet oil, lemon juice, hot spices,[61] and garlic, then serve.

Another kind may be made: Add to the *ṣaḥna* [condiment], sumac husks (*zahr summāq*),[62] *aṭrāf ṭīb* (spice blend), finely pounded walnuts, and hot spices (*abzār ḥārra*).

(262) Recipe for *ṣaḥna Iskandarāniyya* (Alexandrian salt-cured anchovy condiment), authentic and regal, prepared in these days for kings and dignitaries[63]
Take 10 *raṭl*s (10 pounds) salt-cured fish preserved in earthenware vessels (*samak dibb*);[64] the best kind are *ṣīr* (salt-cured anchovies). Put them in a large tub (*ijjāna*), and set them aside for two or three days to let them soften.

Tadhkira 92, 120). The idea is that if the body, in its healthy condition, is naturally prone to black bile, then it should be given foods that match its humoral properties.

59 This recipe also appears in *Wuṣla* ii 694–5. The edited text was slightly amended based on the *Wuṣla* and Gotha, fol. 74r–v.

60 This recipe also appears in the *Wuṣla* ii 696.

61 *Abzār ḥārra*, such as black pepper, ginger, and cinnamon.

62 See n. 52 above.

63 The famous Syrian physician Ibn al-Quff (d. 1286) says *ṣaḥna* is made in Egypt and other places, but the Alexandrian *ṣaḥna* is the best (*Jāmiʿ al-gharaḍ* 245).

64 The earthenware vessel is *dabba*; pl. *dibāb*, and apparently *dibb*, as in this text.

Knead the fish by hand very well, adding to it ¾ *qadaḥ* (1½ pounds) salt, and 4 *qadaḥ*s (9 pounds) pounded coriander—it should be mixed with the salt and pounded. Add also 1¼ *qadaḥs* (2¾ pounds) [each of] black pepper and Levantine coriander (*kuzbara Shāmīyya*),[65] ¼ *qadaḥ* (½ pound) thyme, 9 *ūqiyyas* (9 ounces) pounded garlic, 3 *ūqiyyas* (3 ounces) caraway, ½ *raṭl* (½ pound) Ceylon cinnamon (*qarfa*), 1 *ūqiyya* (1 ounce) each of ginger, black pepper, and cloves. Also, add, ½ *ūqiyya* (½ ounce) galangal (*khūlanjān*), ½ *raṭl* (1 cup) sweet olive oil, 2 *dirhams* (1 teaspoon) dried mint and a similar amount of rue, ½ *dirham* (¼ teaspoon) [dried] common parsley (*karafs*)—then intensify its flavor with 1 *qīrāṭ* (¼ gram) musk dissolved in rosewater.

Mix all these ingredients into a soft mass, and store it in *baranī zujāj* (large wide-mouthed glass jars).[66] Cover the condiment, (**63r**) up to the mouths of the jars, with sweet olive oil, and cover their tops with white linen cloth.[67] Eat from them whenever needed, but replenish whatever you take with sweet olive oil [to prevent any contact with air inside the jar].

(263) Recipe for *ṣaḥna* made in Baghdad and Upper Iraq

Take small fishes—leave them unwashed; otherwise, they will spoil. Preserve them by salting them and stow them away.[68]

Whenever you want to make *ṣaḥna*, put the salted fish in a stone mortar (*jurn*), and throw in one-tenth of its amount of each of [the following:] terebinth berries (*ḥabba khaḍrā'*), cumin, fennel seeds (*rāzyānaj*), peeled Levantine apples, and sour quince.

Crush all the ingredients thoroughly until they have the consistency of bone marrow (*mukh*). Combine the mix with olive oil, and dilute it with some of the liquid of the salt-cured fish (*ṣaḥna mumallaḥa*), and stow it away.[69]

---

65 Al-Anṭākī, *Tadhkira* 300, says that there is not much difference between this variety and the Egyptian one.

66 Sg. *barniyya*.

67 I here follow C, n. 3448: "*Wa-tuqawwah al-āniya*" (وتقوه الآنية), i.e., the vessels should be covered with a white linen fabric called *qūhī* (قوهي). See *Lisān al-ʿArab*, s.v. قوه.

68 This is a recipe, from the region itself, for small salt-cured fish used for making *ṣaḥna*: "Add what equals fourth of the small fish's weight of salt. Put them aside in an airy, warm, and shaded place away from direct sunlight. Add to them dried thyme and dried asafetida leaves, a handful of each, and store them away." (al-Warrāq, English trans. *Annals* 207). Note that in Iraq the fish may have been any small river fish that was available in the region. Cf. In Egypt, anchovies were the preferred type of fish. See glossary 10, s.v. *ṣīr*.

69 The word *ṣaḥna* designates the finished condiment of *ṣaḥna* as well as the salt-cured fish that was used to make it. Apparently, this was how the term was used in Iraq. The extant *ṣaḥnāt* recipe in al-Warrāq's Baghdadi cookbook reflects this usage. See above note.

(264) Recipe for another *ṣaḥna* [condiment without fish]

Take 1 *qadaḥ* (2¼ pounds) coriander, 1 *qadaḥ* caraway, ¼ *qadaḥ* (approx. ½ pound) thyme, ¼ *qadaḥ* pennyroyal (*fulayyā*), 1 *raṭl* (1 pound) sumac husks (*zahr summāq*),[70] 1 *ūqiyya* (1 ounce) rolled bark of Ceylon cinnamon (*qarfa laff*), ¼ *ūqiyya* (½ tablespoon/7 grams) mastic gum, and small amounts of spikenard (*sunbul*), betel leaves (*tunbul*), cardamom (*hāl*), and cloves. Also add ¼ *ūqiyya* (½ tablespoon/7 grams) black pepper. Finely pound all the ingredients, adding as much salt as needed. Set it aside.

Take small amounts of mint, rue, and common parsley (*karafs*). Bunch them together, and chop and pound them. Set them aside.

Now, take 5 *raṭl*s (5 pounds) *kusb al-lawz* (sediment that remains after extracting the oil), drench them in very sour good wine vinegar, and let them steep for a day or two. **(73v)** Press and mash them (*yumras*) very well, and combine and stir in all of the [above-mentioned] pounded ingredients. Add to the mixture small amounts of olive oil and tahini, and use.

70 See n. 52 above.

CHAPTER 10

في أعمال الحلوى من سائر أنواعها

Making All Kinds of Sweets (*ḥalwā*)[1]

(265) Recipe for making *fānīdh* (pulled taffy)[2]

Take sugar [for each 2 *raṭl*s/2 pounds of sugar, use 1 *raṭl*/1 pint of water], dissolve it [and let it boil] until it reaches a brittle consistency (*qiwām al-qaṣf*).[3] Take the pot off the heat.

Take fine white flour (*ṭaḥīn nāʿim abyaḍ*),[4] for each 10 *raṭl*s of sugar, use 1 *raṭl* of flour. Fold the flour into the syrup after you remove it from the fire. [By the way,] you should add ½ *raṭl* (½ pound) honey for each 10 *mann*s (20 *raṭl*s/20 pounds) of sugar after you dissolve it [as mentioned at the beginning of the recipe].[5]

Pull the taffy on a nail [hammered into the wall],[6] and then shape it into twisted ropes (*yuftal fatāʾil*), then cut them into pieces with a pair of scissors.

---

1 In *Zahr*, fol. 19v, the chapter is just given the title *al-Ḥalāwāt* and opens with a general remark, found only in this version. It deals with ways to figure out the correct amount of fat to add to desserts. When making pastries, the sign is when flour and fat clump together when they are pressed by hand. When cooking the condensed puddings of *khabīṣ*, for instance, the sign is when the fat starts separating from the cooking *ḥalwā*.

2 Here I amended the recipe with the help of relatively similar recipes found in the following cookbooks: (1) Tujībī *Fiḍāla* 245, *ghubbayṭ majbūd*; (2) Baghdādī 75, *ḥalwāʾ yābisa*; (3) *Waṣf* 154–5, *nāṭif* and *ḥalwāʾ yābisa*; (4) *Wuṣla* ii 638, 639.

3 In *Waṣf* 154, this stage is described thus, "A cooled off piece taken from it should be brittle and break easily." In today's culinary terminology, this would be called 'hard crack point,' 300–310 degrees F.

4 Flour is more commonly referred to as *daqīq*. Judging from today's practices, the addition of fine flour at this stage helps give the pulled taffy a smooth texture. In making the popular medieval Egyptian taffy (*nayda*), flour is similarly added (ʿAbd al-Laṭīf al-Baghdādī, *Riḥla* 118). See glossary 4, s.v. *nayda*.

5 Adding honey prevents the syrup from crystallizing again.

6 The verb used is *tuqṣar*, which describes putting something back in its original place; this applies to repeatedly pulling a sugar strand away from the nail (*mismār*) and hooking it back to it.

 | DOI 10.1163/9789004349919_013

(266) Recipe for *aqrāṣ laymūn* (hard lemon drop candy)[7]

Dissolve and boil sugar on the fire until it reaches a brittle consistency (*qiwām al-qaṣf*),[8] [add lemon juice at this stage]. Remove the pot [from the heat], and then pull the syrup (*yuqṣar*) on the ground [on a slab of marble or something similar, until it looks white].[9]

Have the molds (*qawālib*) already in the water. When ready to use them, take them out of the water, shake off the remaining water, and fill them with the sugar, using a spoon (*milʿaqa*).

(267) Recipe for *dhāt al-katifayn* (fledgling locusts)[10]

Take dates; slit them open halfway through, to remove their stones. Replace the stones with two pistachios. Make sugar syrup (*jullāb*), and cook it until it reaches a brittle stage (*qiwām al-sukkar*) or a little less.[11] Put the prepared dates in the syrup [while it is still hot], and continue folding the dates in the pot until the sugar thickens and sets (*yaʿqud*). Store [the dates] in wide-mouthed jars (*baranī*), covered (**74r**) with very thick sugar syrup (*jullāb sukkar qawī*).

(268) Recipe for making mulberries (*tūt*)[12]

Make stiff dough similar in consistency to that of *tuṭmāj*.[13] Put ghee (*samn*) [and yeast] in it. When it is done fermenting, take a sieve (*ghirbāl*), and put a piece of the dough [size of a mulberry] on its mesh. [Put your finger in the middle of the dough and press and rub it. It will be hollow and the outside will take the impressions of the sieve,] and it will look like a mulberry. [Repeat with

---

7 Recipes 349 and 370 in the following chapter are similar to this one. Most of the information skipped here is provided by the other recipes.

8 See n. 3 above. The ratio of water to sugar is probably similar to the above recipe, i.e., 1:2. Lemon juice is not mentioned here. The other recipes mention adding lemon juice as needed, or juice of one medium lemon, for each *raṭl* /1 pound of syrup. This would be added when the syrup is done cooking and thickening.

9 See n. 6 above.

10 Lit., 'having two shoulders.' The dates stuffed with two pistachios look like fledgling flightless locusts (i.e., when young adult locusts first develop shoulders with wings that are still small and soft at this stage). See al-Jāḥiẓ, *al-Ḥayawān* 498, where a locust at this stage is called *al-kutfān*.

11 The expression that describes the brittle stage is more accurately copied as *qiwām al-sukkar al-qaṣif*, in recipe 383 below. See also n. 3 above.

12 In this recipe, the pastries are shaped like mulberries. A comparable recipe in *Wuṣla* ii 630–1, gives more detail, which I provide in square brackets.

13 It is stiff unfermented dough, usually rolled out until it is thin, cut into squares, and cooked as fresh pasta. See recipe 109 above.

the other pieces,] fry them in sesame oil, then dip them in sugar syrup (*jullāb*), and take them out and sprinkle them with sugar.

(269) Recipe for *Asyūṭiyya* (from Asyūṭ in Upper Egypt)[14]

[Take] 1 *raṭl* (1 pound) sugar, ½ *raṭl* bee honey, 3 *ūqiyya*s (3 ounces) pistachios, and a similar amount of poppy seeds (*khashkhāsh*), 6 sheets of very thin *ruqāq* bread, and as much musk and rosewater as you wish. [Insert the ingredients between the thin sheets of bread in a casserole with handles, drench them in fat and bake them in the *tannūr* oven.]

(270) Recipe for *khudūd al-aghānī* (chanteuses' cheeks)[15]

Make dough with flour, ghee, and sesame oil.[16] Flatten it with a rolling pin (*shawbaq/suwayq*), and cut it into discs using a round cutter like [the one used for] *kalījā*.[17] [Make a dent in the middle of each cookie (*yubkhash fī wasaṭihi*) so that they do not swell (*ḥattā lā yanfur*) while frying.]

Fry the cookies in sesame oil [on low heat, and turn them, and then take them out] and dip them in sugar syrup (*jullāb*) [and take them out].

Make *ḥalāwa* (thick pudding) for the cookies [as follows]:[18] Add a small amount of musk to syrup. Fry flour in sesame oil until it is golden brown, and then cook it [by adding the syrup and letting it boil] until the sesame oil separates.[19] Throw in some poppy seeds, toasted shelled pistachios, and [skinned] almonds, sliced lengthwise.

Remove the *ḥalāwa* from the fire, stuff it between [each two] cookies, and press them together well [to make sandwich cookies], and eat them.

---

14 This recipe is just a list of ingredients. However, recipe 274 below gives more details. Additionally, there is a comparable recipe in *Wuṣla* ii 638, and an identical one in *Waṣf* 153. They all describe a sweet similar in structure to tray baklava.

15 *Aghānī* 'chanteuses,' as used here, is an Egyptian colloquial usage of the term (usually, *aghānī* means 'songs'). To my knowledge, the only other medieval source in which the word is similarly used is the Egyptian al-Maqrīzī, *Khiṭaṭ* i 306. Regarding the recipe's text, similar copies in *Wuṣla* ii 637, and *Waṣf* 151–2, give less and more details. Here I used them to amend and complete the recipe.

16 The amounts given in *Wuṣla* and *Waṣf* are 1 *raṭl* (1 pound) flour, 1 *ūqiyya* (1 ounce) wheat starch, 4 *ūqiyya*s sesame oil, to be kneaded with some *jullāb* 'sugar syrup.'

17 Round cookies, see glossary 2. *Wuṣla* suggests using the rim of a glass (*qadaḥ*).

18 *Wuṣla* recipe uses *ḥalwā ṣābūniyya* (thick wheat starch pudding). For a recipe, see 302 below.

19 *Yaqdhifu shayrajuhu*, lit., 'throws up its sesame oil.'

(271) Recipe for *fustuqiyya Nābulusiyya* (pistachio sweet from the Palestinian city of Nablus)

Knead *daqīq* (wheat flour) or *samīdh* (semolina of durum wheat), with some salt, mastic gum, (**74v**) and a bit of rosewater. Bake it as unleavened bread (*faṭīr*).

When it is brought back from the *furn* (brick oven),[20] crumble it into small pieces. Boil milk and sprinkle it on them, but before doing this, rub the crumbs with butter (*zubd*) or ghee (*samn*), and then sprinkle the boiled milk on them. After that, pour some more ghee or butter on them. Sprinkle sugar and shelled whole pistachios on them, and [sprinkle them with] musk and rosewater.[21]

(272) Recipe for *makshūfa* (open-faced pie)[22]

Take fine wheat flour (*daqīq ṭayyib*), put it in a pot, and add enough ghee so the flour forms a dough-like consistency. Continue [stirring and] toasting the flour until it is golden (*ashqar*), and you see that it has cooked. Put it in the middle of a *ṭabaq nuḥās* (flat-bottomed copper pan), and spread it until it covers the entire base.

Now take all types of nuts (*qulūbāt*), toast them and pound them separately. Take sugar, as much as all the nuts combined, and start layering the nuts and the sugar on the [spread] flour—one layer (*sāf*) of sugar, then one layer of pistachios, another layer of sugar, followed by a layer of almonds, thus putting a layer of sugar each time you add [one of nuts].

When the layering is done, take sugar syrup (*jullāb*), and rosewater and musk dissolved together, and pour them over all of it. The pan should be taken to the *furn* (brick oven)[23] after [the bread baking is done and] its heat is low, and [it should be baked] after it has been sealed (*yuṭayyan*).[24]

---

20 The expression فإذا جاء من 'when it is brought back from' suggests that the pastry was baked at a commercial oven.

21 Musk is usually dissolved in rosewater before adding it.

22 Lit., 'exposed.'

23 The expression يؤدى الى الفرن 'to be taken to the oven,' suggests that the pastry is to be baked at a commercial oven.

24 Although the verb literally means 'to be sealed with mud,' pots and pans were usually sealed with dough.

(273) Recipe for making *Ḥāfiẓiyya* (filled cookies)[25]

Take almonds and sugar, and make them into a stuffing similar to that [used in] *qaṭāʾif*.[26] Now take the dough, which you have kneaded with sesame oil, divide it into small pieces, put some of the stuffing inside, [seal the opening], and bake them in the *furn* (brick oven).

(274) Recipe for *Asyūṭiyya* (from Asyūṭ in Upper Egypt)[27]

Take the soft insides (*lubāb*) of two rounds of fine quality (*muḥassan*) bread. [Break them into pieces,] and throw on them 1½ *raṭl*s (1½ pounds) crushed sugar, 1½ *raṭl*s bee honey, ½ *raṭl* almonds, 3 *ūqiyya*s (3 ounces) pistachios and a similar amount of poppy seeds. Also, take 1 *kharrūba* (0.2 gram) camphor.[28]

Mix all the ingredients and enclose them in thin sheets of *ruqāq* bread, then place this in a *saṭl* (brass kettle with handles). Drench all of it with 2 *raṭl*s (2 pounds) of [rendered] sheep-tail fat, and put it in the *tannūr* [to bake].

(275) Recipe for *makshūfa* (candy brittle)[29]

It is made with four quarters [of the following ingredients, by weight]: one-quarter almonds, one-quarter sesame oil, one-quarter sugar, and one-quarter bee honey.

---

25 A type of *kaʿk* 'cookie,' which used to be made by al-Ḥāfiẓiyya, concubine of the Ayyubid king, al-Malik al-ʿĀdil al-Kabīr (d. 1218), as stated in *Wuṣla* ii 658. The name of this concubine was Arghawān, she died in 1250. In *Wuṣla*, the details of the cookie attributed to her differ from this one.

26 These are pancakes, stuffed with sugar and nuts and drenched in perfumed syrup. Their basic stuffing is composed of equal amounts of chopped nuts and pounded sugar, scented with rosewater and bound with a little almond or walnut oil. See, for instance, recipe 281 below.

27 Cf. recipe 269, and recipes 131 and 132 above. They all deal with a type of sweet bread pudding, which originally, was baked under a chunk of meat roasting in the *tannūr*. This savory sweet dish was called *jūdhāba*. With the passage of time, bread pudding started to be consumed as a dessert, as we have it here. Also, cf. *Wuṣla* ii 638, and *Waṣf* 153.

28 *Kharrūba* is a small dry measure, designating a carob seed. It weighs $^{1}/_{16}$ of a *dirham*. See glossary 13.

29 Generally, the word means 'exposed.' However, it also specifically describes land that is bare and exposed due to dryness, like this dessert, which is dry and brittle. Comparable recipes can be found in *Wuṣla* ii 619; and *Waṣf* 157–9, which includes two recipes. Cf. recipe 272 above, where the dish means open-faced, exposed.

Take the almonds, scald them [to remove their skins], pound them, and throw them into the sesame oil, which is already on the fire. Add honey to them when they start boiling, and continue cooking it until the mix thickens in consistency. Remove it from the fire, and fold in (*yuʿlaf*) the sugar, along with some saffron. Spread it on a platter (*jām*).[30]

(276) Recipe for a wonderful sweet called *mushabbaka* (latticework)[31]
Take semolina flour, which is not too finely crushed,[32] and fine-tasting ghee. Put them in a pot, and fold and rub them together until they clump together when you squeeze a handful of the mix in your hand.

Now take a pan with a lip (*ṭabaq bi-shafa*),[33] put the flour and fat mixture in it, (**75v**) and press it [to bottom and sides] but it should be below the upper edge by a half-finger width (about ⅓ inch). Send the pan to the *furn* (brick oven) after the bread baking is done [and let the pan bake slowly in the remaining heat].

Meanwhile, put bee honey on the fire with a small amount of rosewater added to it [and boil it until it thickens]. Now, take the pan out of the *furn*. If you see that the pastry sides have risen to its top edge, pour in the prepared honey and rosewater syrup. You should also have ready [coarsely crushed] pistachios, hazelnuts, almonds, and fine white sugar (*sukkar sanīnāt*).[34] Sprinkle them on the honey [in latticed strips/rows].[35] Let it cool and then cut it into slices (*shawābīr*).[36]

[When the pan comes from the *furn*, if you see that] the pastry sides have not risen to the top edge of the pan, return it to the oven [to continue baking] until it does so.

---

30 The candy is usually spread into a thin layer and then broken to pieces, as in al-Warrāq's chapter 104, where this candy is called *nāṭif*.

31 I opted to follow DK, n. 3590, *ʿajība* (عجيبة) 'wonderful' rather than the edited *ʿajamiyya* (عجمية) because the recipe does not describe the latter, which is a kind of thick flour pudding, for which recipes will follow.

32 The Arabic expression is الدقيق الذي فيه سمذه. *Samīdh* is granular flour from durum wheat (*Triticum durum*). The pie shell made here is comparable to today's graham cracker pie shells.

33 I amended the text here based on Gotha, fol, 77r. The lip makes handling the pan easier without breaking the pie shell.

34 This is synonymous with *sukkar ṭabarzad*, which is fine brayed/chiseled white sugar. See glossary 4, s.v. *sukkar*.

35 This is the only reason the recipe is called latticed (*mushabbak*).

36 They would look like pie slices. See glossary 9.2, s.v. *shawābīr*.

(277) Recipe for *kunāfa* (enclosed cookies)[37]

Take *samīdh* (semolina of durum wheat), and toast it very well. After it cools down, rub it with a small amount of ghee, knead it very well with bee honey, form it into discs (*aqrāṣ*), and set it aside.

Now take *daqīq* (common wheat flour), rub it with sesame oil, knead it very well with water, and form it into discs. Put the [semolina] discs you made earlier inside the discs you made with sesame oil.[38] Attach the edges of the outer layers by crimping them with the tips of pastry tongs (*minqāsh*), and bake them. They are wonderful.

(278) Recipe for making *makshūfa* (candy brittle)[39]

Take equal amounts [by weight] of sugar, honey, almonds, and sesame oil. Pound the sugar and set it aside, and do likewise with the almonds.

Put a large brass pot (*dast*) on low heat and pour in the sesame oil. (**76r**) When it comes to a boil, add the pounded almonds, and continue stirring it with an *isṭām* (large paddle-like iron spatula) until it is toasted. Add honey, and continue stirring until it thickens. Next, sprinkle the sugar over it, and mix and stir them together. Color the honey mixture with saffron steeped in rosewater and musk.

Continue stirring the pot on a low fire until it is done, and ladle it into vessels.[40] It may also be kept in leather or wooden boxes (*ʿulab*), and carried [when traveling], for it is indeed the best of provisions.

(279) Recipe for *shuʿabiyya* (candy fingers)[41]

Take shelled pistachios, pound them, and mix them with an equal amount of ground sugar. Sprinkle them with rosewater flavored with musk (*māʾ ward mumassak*), and set it aside.

Continue boiling sugar syrup (*jullāb*), which has been skimmed of its froth until it reaches a brittle consistency.[42] [Immediately,] pour it on a marble slab

---

37 *Kunāfa* here is different from *kunāfa* recipes 298, 325, 332, 333 below. The word *kunāfa*, as it occurs here, suggests something that is enclosed, surrounded, embraced. See *Lisān al-ʿArab*, s.v. كنف.

38 Each semolina disc is enclosed between two layers of the flour dough.

39 Cf. recipe 275, above. Cf. Baghdādī 76, which has slightly different details.

40 This type of candy is usually spread in a thin layer; and after it cools, it is broken into pieces, and stored. See, for instance, the following recipe.

41 The name derives from *shuʿab* 'fingers of the hand.'

42 Here I replaced يتسكّر 'crystallize' with يتكسّر 'break,' which is the same as the '*qiwām al-qaṣf*' stage mentioned in recipe 266 above. In addition, see recipe 284 below, where both DK, n. 3701, and Gotha, fol. 78v, use it.

greased with sesame oil, spread it [thinly], and cut it into strips. Spread the pistachio mix on them, and roll each piece to make it look like a finger. Arrange them in layers in containers (*awānī*), and use [as desired].

(280) Recipe for *musayyar al-qarʿ* (paste of gourd strips)[43]

Choose a gourd (*yaqṭīn*),[44] cut it open, discard the inside pulp, peel it, and using a knife, scrape it (*yunḥat*) [into long thin strips], as thin as possible. Mix each *raṭl* (1 pound) of it with 2 *ūqiyyas* (2 ounces/¼ cup) of wheat starch (*nashā*) dissolved in rosewater. Boil it with sugar syrup (*jullāb*), which has been cleansed of its froth, until it becomes thick. Meanwhile, continue feeding it with fresh sesame oil (**76v**) or almond oil.

For those who intend to use to induce sleep, they can add as much poppy seeds as possible. Take the pot off the heat, and use [as needed].

(281) Recipe for *qaṭāʾif maḥshī* (stuffed pancakes)

Take sugar and a similar amount of skinned almonds or pistachios. Pound them separately, and then mix them, sprinkle them with rosewater infused with as much camphor and musk as needed, and knead them all. Stuff and roll the *qaṭāʾif* discs with this mix after you daub them with sesame oil.[45]

Arrange the rolls on plates (*ṣuḥūn*). When ready to eat, drench them in sugar syrup (*jullāb*) or bee honey diluted with some rosewater.

(282) [Fried *qaṭāʾif*]

As for the fried variety, stuff and roll the [*qaṭāʾif*] discs [as described above], seal the edges with wheat starch dissolved in some water (*nashāʾ maḥlūl*), fry them in sesame oil, and then dip them in sugar syrup or bee honey, [take them out] and serve them.

(283) Recipe for *khabīṣ al-ward* (thick rose-petal pudding)

Take *ward Jūrī*,[46] or any other variety of red rose, and discard their hypanthia (*aqmāʿ*). Take 1 *raṭl* (1 pound) of these and boil them in 2 *raṭls* (1 quart) of water. When the rose petals look white, strain them [discard the petals].

---

43 This dessert is like a thick jam or paste made with long shreds of gourd, *suyūr*, adj. *musayyar*. Cf. recipes 312 and 313 below. Also, see al-Anṭākī, *Tadhkira* 329.

44 The two words for gourd—*qarʿ* and *yaqṭīn*—are used interchangeably.

45 The recipe does not explain how to make the pancakes. For *qaṭāʾif* batter, see glossary 2, under *kunāfa*, and al-Warrāq, English trans. *Annals* 422.

46 It is also known as damask rose. See glossary 8, under *ward*.

FIGURE 34 *Damask rose* (ward Jūrī/ward Shāmī), *Elizabeth Blackwell,* A Curious Herbal, *1738, plate 82 (From the New York Public Library: http://digitalcollections.nypl.org/items/510d47dd-c310-a3d9-e040-e00a18064a99).*

To the [strained liquid] add its equal weight in sugar. Let it boil, [continue] skimming the froth until it starts to thicken. Add wheat starch (*nashāʾ*), 2 *ūqiyyas* (¼ cup) for each *raṭl* (1 pound) of the rose-syrup. Let it cook, with sesame oil added to it, until it thickens.

If you wish, (**77r**) it can be thickened with crumbs of *khubz samīdh* (bread made with fine white flour, which is high in starch),[47] indeed it will be better than starch. However, if this bread is chosen [to replace the starch], it should be very well fermented (*shadīd al-khumra*). Stir it into the rose-syrup. Take the pot off the fire [when it is done cooking].

(284) Recipe for *mushāsh* (suckers, lollipops)

Let the sugar syrup boil down until it reaches a brittle consistency.[48] Remove the pot [from the fire], and start beating it with *isṭām* (paddle-like spatula) or a *mihrāsh* (stone pestle).[49] This will make it boil [quickly, and help release the air bubbles]. Pour the syrup on a marble slab and cover it with a piece of cloth (*mindīl*) for half an hour, and then remove it.

For those who like them yellow, add saffron to the mixture before removing the pot from the fire. This is used to make all kinds of figurines (*tamāthīl*). It can be made in different colors by adding all kinds of dyes while it is still boiling on the fire.

(285) Recipe for *aṣābiʿ Zaynab* (cannoli fingers)

Take *samīdh* (semolina of durum wheat), and knead it with thin sugar syrup (*jullāb raqīq*). Also, use some yeast (*khamīra*), or a small amount of natron (*naṭrūn*) or sodium bicarbonate (*būraq*).[50] Use just enough to help the dough ferment.

Now take finger-long pieces of thin reeds.[51] Grease them with sesame oil, and cover each one individually with some of the dough. Partially fry the pieces in sesame oil, take them out, pull out the reeds, and set them aside.

---

47 This was deemed the finest and purest variety of bread made with *daqīq samīdh*, which is fine white flour, high in starch, made from bread wheat (*Triticum aestivum*). In this recipe, it is suggested as a substitute for wheat starch. See glossary 2, for more on this.

48 See recipe 266, and n. 42 above. Here I replaced يتسكّر with يتكسّر used in Gotha, fol. 78v.

49 This is a dialectical vocalization of *mihrās*.

50 These two minerals share similar chemical components, but *naṭrūn* has somewhat stronger properties. See glossary 8.

51 I here follow Gotha, fol. 79r, المبدي في الرقة 'fairly thin,' instead of the incoherent المقدي في الرقة of the edited text.

Take shelled pistachios and almonds, one part of each. Pound them (77v) and mix them with an equal amount of pounded sugar. Sprinkle them with musk-flavored rosewater, knead them to combine, and stuff the mix into the cavities made by the reeds.

Fry the pieces once again until they nicely brown (*yatawarrad*), and throw them[52] into sugar syrup or fine-tasting bee honey. If you wish, color the pieces before frying them. Take them out [of the syrup or honey,] and use [as you wish].

(286) Recipe for *luqaymāt al-qāḍī* (judge's tidbits)[53]

Take the fermented dough you prefer, roll it out until it is thin, cut it into small discs like *dīnārs*,[54] fry them, and set them aside.

For each *raṭl* (1 pound) of sugar syrup, use 1 *ūqiyya* (2 tablespoons) wheat starch and 3 *ūqiyyas* pounded shelled pistachios. Boil them down with sesame oil, and add aromatic spices like nutmeg (*jawza*),[55] cubeb (*kabāba*), cloves (*qaranful*), saffron (*zaʿfarān*), aloeswood (*ʿūd*), and musk (*misk*), as needed.

When the syrup mixture becomes very thick, remove it from the fire, and divide it into portions. Between every two [of the fried dough discs] put 2 *ūqiyyas* (2 ounces) of the thickened syrup mixture.[56] Arrange them on plates (*ṣuḥūn*), and pour syrup, thinned down with musk-infused rosewater, over them and serve.

(287) Recipe for *qāwūt* (toasted wheat granola)[57]

Take as many wheat berries (*ḥinṭa*) as you like, put them in a cool damp place, leave them there until they sprout, and then transfer them to a sunny place

52 Here I amended the text based on context. The copyist's ما was a possible misreading of the original ويرمى 'throw.'

53 They look like dainty sandwich cookies.

54 Gold coins, about an inch in diameter.

55 More commonly called *jawz al-ṭīb* or *jawz bawwa*.

56 The syntax in the text is somewhat obscure (and this is true in all the versions); this is probably because the copyists were unable to read the original text. Clearly, the instruction is to fill the prepared fried discs with the thick syrup mix to make dainty sandwich cookies.

57 The origin of the word is *qāghūt*, a Turkish word related to the Arabic *qūt* 'sustenance.' It is used to designate special foods of toasted and crushed grains mixed with sugar and fat, in Arabic called *sawīq*; these were given to women after labor (Kāshgharī, *Kitāb Dīwān lughāt al-Turk* 122). *Sawīq*, in its basic form, is crushed toasted grains mixed with fat and sugar, mostly used by travelers to make drinks, nourishing foods, and dense *khabīṣ* puddings. In this recipe, it is prepared as a dense granola sweetmeat. See also recipes 304 and 307 below.

to dry out, and crush and sift them. These days, some people (**78r**) make it by using the [sifted] granules of the crushed wheat.[58]

First toast it until it browns, and then pour ghee (*samn*) on it, and fold it together. Add honey, and continue stirring it until the ingredients mix well. Throw in shelled almonds, pistachios, hazelnuts, and white sugar [all crushed]. Take the pot off the heat. Stuff the mix into pieces of tripe (*kurūsh*)—which have been washed and scraped and cleaned, and then sew their openings [closed].[59] This would be stocked in leather or wooden boxes (*ʿulab*),[60] and used as provisions for travelers.

(288) Recipe for *khabīṣ al-ʿunnāb* (thick jujube pudding)

This is recommended for weight gain. Its properties are moderately hot and high in moisture.[61] It nourishes the thin and the weak, provides the bodily system with the needed moisture. It induces euphoria, lightens the skin color, softens the complexion and gives it luster. It strengthens a hot stomach, and helps soften the bowels, and deflates winds. It is diuretic, and beneficial to the kidneys and bladder. It helps women gain weight quickly, which is something they care a lot about. It also helps reduce the density of their humors.[62] However, it is harmful for phlegmatics (*mubalghamīn*) and the old (*ʿajāʾiz*).[63]

Here is the recipe:
Take the kernels (*lubb*) from the seeds of snake cucumbers (*qiththāʾ*),[64] common cucumbers (*khiyār*), gourds (*qarʿ*), muskmelons (*biṭṭīkh Samarqandī*), and watermelons (*biṭṭīkh Hindī*).[65] Also take shelled and skinned pistachios, hazelnuts, and almonds; toasted white poppy seeds (*khashkhāsh abyaḍ*), (**78v**) and shelled and washed purslane (*baqla*) seeds. Use one part of each [of the above].

---

58 The Arabic expression is السميذ من الطحين. *Samīdh* is made from durum wheat, *Triticum durum*.

59 The recipe does not specify what to do with the filled tripe sacks next; we can assume that they would be set aside to dry completely, and then stored and consumed as pressed granola whenever needed.

60 Sg. *ʿulba*.

61 See glossary 11, s.v. *mizāj* 'humoral temperament.'

62 *Yulaṭṭif mizājahunna*, see glossary 11, s.v. *talṭīf*.

63 The word is used to designate both sexes and is not necessarily restricted to women. Both the phlegmatic and the old suffer from excess in cold humoral properties.

64 *Cucumis melo* var. *flexuosus*.

65 See glossary, s.v. *biṭṭīkh*.

Also, take the pulp of [dried] barberries (*amīrbārīs*), toasted coriander (*kuzbara*) and seeds of wild marjoram (*marū*), yeast (*khamīra*),[66] and salep (*mustaʿjala*). Use half a part of each.

Take one part of each of the following: *sawīq al-ghubayrāʾ*,[67] chickpea flour, and gum of the almond tree (*ṣamgh al-lawz*). Also, take a quarter of a part of each of gum of tragacanth tree (*kathīrāʾ*), tamarisk seeds (*ʿadhba*), aniseeds (*anīsūn*), ajowan (*nānkhawāh*), turmeric (*wars*), and black cumin of Kirmān (*kammūn Kirmānī*). Also use one-sixth of a part of each of mastic and Ceylon cinnamon (*qarfa*).

Pound all the above-mentioned ingredients separately, and sift whatever needs to be sifted. Mix them all together. Now, take what equals half of their weight in pounded and toasted crumbs of *khubz samīdh* (bread made with fine white flour, high in starch).[68] Take a similar amount of *ʿunnāb Jurjānī* (jujubes of Jurjān, a city in northern Persia), and a similar amount of white sugar.

Mix the bread crumbs with the above-mentioned herbs and spices (*ḥawāʾij*), and set [the mixture] aside. Boil the jujubes in five times their amount of water. Boil the sugar in it and skim its froth. Throw in the ingredients [*ḥawāʾij*] [set aside], and add almond oil or fresh sesame oil or ghee from cow's milk (*samn baqarī*); add enough to combine all the ingredients. Let it cook until it thickens, and then remove [it from the fire].

(289) Recipe for delicious uncooked confection (*ḥalwā ṭayyiba bilā nār*)[69]

Take white sugar, pounded as fine as possible, and shelled and skinned pistachios.[70] The amount should be two-thirds sugar and one-third pistachios.

Put the [ground] pistachios in a wide container and moisten them with water to help release their oil. (79r) Press and spread the pistachios (*yubsaṭ*), and then press the pounded sugar on top of them, and serve. It is delicious.

---

66 It must be dried yeast, like the rest of the ingredients. There is also the possibility that the ingredient used is *khamīrat al-ʿaṭṭār* (خميرة العطار) mountain meadow saffron (*Colchicum montanum*), which is more commonly known in Arabic sources as *sūranjān* (سورنجان). See Gloss. 8 for more on this ingredient.

67 Meal made of dried sorbus fruit, toasted, ground, and mixed with fat and sugar.

68 See n. 47 above, for more on this bread.

69 This recipe is slightly amended based on Gotha, fol. 80v.

70 When shelled pistachios are blanched first, it makes the skin easy to slip off.

FIGURE 35 *Wild marjoram, Elizabeth Blackwell,* A Curious Herbal, *1738, plate 280 (From the New York Public Library: http://digitalcollections.nypl.org/items/510d47dd-cd6e-a3d9-e040-e00a18064a99).*

(290) Recipe for *Akhmīmiyya* (from Akhmim, city in Upper Egypt)[71]

One *raṭl* (1 pound) of *kunāfa*.[72] Slice it into very thin strips,[73] then throw them into a large brass pot (*dast*) along with 4 *ūqiyyas* (4 ounces) sesame oil, and fry them lightly. Next, throw in 1 *raṭl* coarsely crushed sugar (*sukkar majrūsh*), and continue stirring it until the sesame oil it absorbed begins to separate. This is a sure sign that it has fried well.

Stir in 4 *ūqiyyas* (4 ounces) bee honey, and add 4 *ūqiyyas* toasted and pounded hazelnuts or nuts (*qulūbāt*) of your choice. Take the pot off the heat, and when it cools, perfume it with musk and rosewater [and stir]. Ladle it onto plates (*ṣuḥūn*).

(291) Recipe for *harīsat al-fustuq* (pistachio porridge)[74]

Take crumbs (*lubāb*) from the previous day's bread (*khubz bāʾit*), pass it through a sieve, and throw it into a large brass pot (*dast*). Also, add sesame oil, and continue adding the bread crumbs to it until it is saturated and starts disgorging the excess oil.

Use 1 *raṭl* (1 pound) sugar syrup (*jullāb*) and 1 *raṭl* thinned bee honey, however, add them separately. First throw in the sugar syrup, and stir the pot. Also use ½ *raṭl* pistachios [these are added later in the recipe].

Take [boiled] chicken breasts, [shred them into threads,] and wash them in rosewater. For each *raṭl* (pound) of [sugar syrup], use the breasts of five chickens. After you throw in the chicken breasts, add the honey, (79v) and [continue cooking and stirring] until it thickens, and when it is lifted with a spoon, it makes a hair-like trail (*yaṣīr lahā shaʿra*). After that, throw in the pistachios, and continue stirring as you do with *ṣābūniyya* (thick wheat-starch pudding).[75] Use ½ *raṭl* (½ pound) pistachios.[76]

---

71 This recipe can also be found in *Wuṣla* ii 627–8; I used it, in addition to Gotha, fol. 80v, to amend the edited text slightly. Akhmīm is described as a flourishing city, with its marketplaces and baths, on the eastern side of the Nile in Upper Egypt. Al-Ḥimyarī, *al-Rawḍ al-miʿṭār* 13, describes astonishing archaeological remains of buildings.

72 The recipe expects the cook to have the unleavened sheets of *kunāfa* ready to use. See glossary 2, s.v. *kunāfa*.

73 *Wuṣla* ii 627, states that *kunāfa* sheets should be greased with sesame oil before they are rolled and sliced thinly into long threads of dough.

74 Except for some stylistic differences, the same recipe is found in *Waṣf* 167–8; and *Wuṣla* ii 647. Here I amended the edited text, which was confused in several places, based on these better-copied versions.

75 See recipe 302 below, for instance.

76 This was mentioned earlier.

If the porridge becomes yellowish in hue, color it [green] with chard dye (*silq maqṭūʿ*),[77] or a bit of indigo (*nīl*),[78] [extract its color] in sesame oil [and add it to the cooking pot]. Scent it with musk and rosewater while it is still on the fire, and then remove. Ladle it onto plates, and sprinkle it with sugar.

[By the way,] the chicken breasts should be boiled, and then finely shredded (*mansūla*).

(292) Recipe for *jawādhib al-khubz mukhtamir* (pudding of fermented bread)[79]

Take the crumbs of fermented bread, and soak them in milk for a day until it turns sour (*yakhtamir*). [In a pot,] spread a layer of almonds pounded with sugar both under and over the soaked bread. Color it with saffron, and leave it on the fire until it emits a nice aroma. Stir the pot and then remove.

(293) Recipe for *jawādhib al-qaṭāʾif* (bread-pudding casserole with stuffed pancakes)[80]

[Prepare] pancakes (*qaṭāʾif*) filled with [pounded] almonds and sugar, and then fried. In a large brass pot (*dast*), put these filled *qaṭāʾif* between two large thin sheets of *ruqāq* bread, and then set the pot under a chicken [roasting in the *tannūr* oven].

---

77 Lit., 'separated chard juice'; the recipe in *Wuṣla* ii 583 describes how to obtain this. Chard leaves are first pounded, and then strained to extract the juice. Next, it is boiled, which causes the green particles to separate (*yanqaṭiʿ*). When this happens, it is removed from the heat and set aside for an hour. The clear water on top is poured off, leaving the green particles in the bottom of the pot. This green part is whipped vigorously, and at this point, it can be added to foods and dishes to color them green.

78 The porridge is meant to look green from the crushed pistachio. If prolonged cooking causes the sugar and honey to caramelize and spoil the color, the greenness can be restored by adding chard dye; or blue indigo, which, when mixed with the yellow porridge, would turn it green.

79 The name also occurs as *jūdhāba*. It is a sweet-savory dish of bread pudding baked in the *tannūr* with a chunk of roasting meat, such as a chicken or a whole lamb, suspended above it. In this recipe, however, the dish is considered a sweet by itself, which might or might not be baked under the roasting meat in the oven. It may even have been left on the stove's direct heat to cook. Here I amended the text using similar copies of the recipe, as found in *Wuṣla* ii 633, and *Waṣf* 148.

80 See note above. Here I amended the edited text using similar copies in *Wuṣla* ii 633; and *Waṣf* 149.

[Alternatively,][81] spread layers of the seasoned finely ground almond and sugar filling of *qaṭāʾif*, alternating with thin sheets of *ruqāq* bread. Pour sesame oil all over it. If you wish, also pour milk on it and use more sugar. [Place it on the fire of the stove,] and when it cooks and emits a pleasant aroma, remove it.

(294) Recipe for *jawādhib al-khashkhāsh* (bread pudding with poppy seeds)[82]

Take 2 *raṭl*s (2 pounds) sugar, and mix it with ½ *raṭl* poppy seeds. (**80r**) Color it with saffron, and let it boil [with some added water] until it thickens. Some people use honey [instead of sugar], and when it thickens it is spread between two layers of thin sheets of *ruqāq* bread, [and then placed in the *tannūr* oven] with a [roasting] chicken rubbed with saffron hung above it.

(295) Recipe for *samīdhiyya* (thick semolina pudding)

Take sesame oil and add 1 *raṭl* (1 pound) *samīdh* (semolina of durum wheat) to it. Stir them both until they emit a pleasant aroma. Pour in 4 *raṭl*s sugar syrup, bee honey, or cane-sugar honey (*quṭāra ʿāl*). Cook the pot on low heat, stirring with an *isṭām* (a large paddle-like iron spatula) until the pudding throws up its [excess] oil, and then remove it. [Ladle it into platters,] with fine sugar spread under and over it.

This pudding is seasoned with rosewater flavored with musk (*māʾ ward mumassak*).

(296) Recipe for *khabīṣ al-qarʿ* (thick gourd pudding)

Peel the gourd, remove the seeds, and then boil it in sugar syrup (*jullāb*). Take it out and place it on *ṭabaq mushabbak* (latticed tray of woven date palm fronds). Next, mash it in a stone mortar (*jurn*), squeeze out the extra moisture, put it in a pot, add sugar syrup to it, [and let it cook] until it thickens, and then remove it.

Khabīṣ al-jazar **(thick carrot pudding)** is made similarly.

---

81 At this point, I amended the recipe based on context. Clearly, the dish can be baked under the chicken in the oven, to receive its drippings; or it can be cooked on direct heat using the *qaṭāʾif* filling.

82 Cf. recipe 132 above.

(297) Recipe for *mukhannaqa*[83]

Take 2 *raṭls* (2 pounds) *kunāfa*,[84] 1½ *raṭls* bee honey, [1 *raṭl* sugar,] 4 *ūqiyyas* (4 ounces) sesame oil, and 4 *ūqiyyas* shelled nuts (*qulūbāt*).[85]

Dissolve half of the amount of sugar in water [to make sugar syrup], and pound the other half. Put the honey [and sugar syrup in a pot] on the fire, [and when they boil, add] the *kunāfa*, and feed them with sesame oil. Continue stirring the pot so that they mix well, (**80v**) and then remove the pot from the fire.

Pound the pistachios, mix this with the pounded half of the sugar [that was set aside]. Sprinkle it into the pot, while stirring it and adding [more] sesame oil. Season it with musk and rosewater, and then ladle it onto plates (*ṣuḥūn*).

(298) Recipe for *kunāfa mumallaḥa* (sugar-coated pastry strips)[86]

Take 1 *raṭl* (1 pound) *kunāfa*, 3 *ūqiyyas* (3 ounces) sesame oil, 4 *ūqiyyas* (4 ounces) sugar syrup (*ḥall*)[87] or cane-sugar molasses (*qaṭr*), 3 *ūqiyyas* pounded sugar, 2 *ūqiyyas* pistachios, and musk and rosewater.

[Here is how to slice the *kunāfa* into thin strips:]

[After you make the *kunāfa* crepes,[88]] put one disc on a plate, rub it with sesame oil, and place another single sheet (*waraqa*) over it, all spread flat [and brush it with sesame oil].[89] Repeat this until you stack up enough of them. Roll them together, and slice them with a knife into thin strips (*suyūr ruqāq*), and use them to serve any *kunāfa* dishes.[90]

---

83 Lit., 'the throttled.' In the name of this dish of *kunāfa*, the thin strips cooked in syrup might evoke the practice of boiling silkworm cocoons to extract the silk threads. In Arabic, the process is called تخنيق الشرانق 'throttling the cocoons,' see Dozy, *Takmilat al-maʿājim* 418, s.v. خنّق. Here I slightly amended the text using a comparable recipe in *Wuṣla* ii 636–7.

84 Thin pastry strips. See the following recipe for directions on how to slice *kunāfa* into thin strips; and glossary 2, s.v. *kunāfa*.

85 *Wuṣla* specifies pistachios. Later in this recipe, we learn that it is indeed so.

86 *Mumallaḥa* (lit., 'salted') often describes foods preserved in salt, such as *akbād mumallaḥa* 'livers preserved in salt' as it occurs in Dhahabī, *Tārīkh al-Islām* 1135. However, it was also used metaphorically to designate anything coated with white, such as frost (Dozy, *Takmilat al-maʿājim* 1472). In our case, the *kunāfa* is coated with coarsely-crushed white sugar, as we learn from recipe 332 below. The word occurs as *mamlūḥa*, in the corresponding recipe in *Wuṣla* ii 626–7.

87 The word *ḥall* (حل) is often erroneously written as *khall* (خل) 'vinegar.'

88 The recipe expects the cook to have the unleavened sheets of *kunāfa* ready to use for the recipe. See glossary 2, s.v. *kunāfa*.

89 As mentioned in *kunāfa* recipes in *Wuṣla* ii 626–7, the process of brushing each piece with sesame oil is important.

90 We can assume that the ingredients given at the beginning of the recipe are used to make the dessert. Details are given in recipe 332 below.

(299) Recipe for *Shīrāziyya*[91]

Take 4 *ūqiyyas* (4 ounces) bread crumbs (*lubāb khubz*). Fry them in 1 *ūqiyya* (2 tablespoons) sesame oil, add to it 2 *ūqiyyas* (2 ounces) shelled nuts and ½ *ūqiyya* (½ ounce) poppy seeds. Fry them all and set them aside.

Dissolve sugar in water (*yuḥall*) to make sugar syrup (*jullāb*), and boil it until it becomes thick enough. Throw into it one-sixth of its amount in bee honey, as well as the bread crumb mix that was set aside. Stir the pot, and season it with musk and rosewater, and serve. Some people replace the fried bread crumbs with *manfūsh*,[92] (**81r**) which makes it truly nice.[93]

(300) Recipe for [*nuhūd*] *al-ʿadhārī* (virgins' breasts)[94]

[This recipe calls for] one part flour, one part ghee (*samn*), one part sugar, [and one part almonds].[95] Crush them all together, knead them very well, and make [cookies] like breasts.[96] Water is not used [in making these cookies]. Arrange them in a [yellow copper] tray (*ṭabaq*) and bake them in a *furn* (brick oven).

(301) Recipe for *ḥalwā wardiyya* (thick rose-petal pudding)[97]

Boil rose petals until all their color seeps into the water [and drain it to discard the petals]. Dissolve sugar in water to make syrup (*jullāb*), and boil it until it reaches the desired consistency. Add the rose-infused water bit by bit and continue boiling until the syrup is almost thick.

Dissolve wheat starch in the rosewater as usual, and throw it into the syrup. Also add some fresh rose petals. Stir in 2 *ūqiyyas* (2 ounces) sesame oil and

---

91 A bread pudding named after Shiraz, a city in southeast Persia.

92 Gotha, fol. 82v, refers to it as *al-khubz al-manfūsh*. It is fluffy and brittle fried white bread, served as a sweet pastry drenched in sugar. For more on this sweet bread, see glossary 2, s.v. *al-manfūsh*.

93 Similar copies of this recipe, found in *Wuṣla* ii 638–9 and *Waṣf* 155–6, do not include this *manfūsh* option.

94 The name occurs in a similar recipe in *Waṣf* 163–4 as نهود العذاري. In this same source, another similar recipe is called *nuhūd al-ʿadhrāʾ* 'virgin's breasts.' In *Wuṣla* ii 625, the recipe is not given a name, the details differ slightly, but it is clearly a 'breast' cookie recipe. I amended the edited text slightly with the above-mentioned copies available to us.

95 In the *Wuṣla* version, the flour is toasted in the ghee and rendered sheep-tail fat first and then kneaded with the sugar.

96 From the *Wuṣla* recipe, we learn that the cookies are pressed into molds, perhaps like small round bowls, to make them look like breasts (ويعمل منه قوالب مثل النهود).

97 This recipe is also found in *Wuṣla* ii 640, where it is described as *ladhīdha* 'delicious.' Here I use it, along with Gotha fol. 82v, to slightly amend the edited text.

2 *ūqiyya*s [skinned] almonds. [Stir until it thickens, and then] flavor it with musk (*yumassak*) and rosewater, and then remove.

(302) Recipe for *ṣābūniyya* (thick wheat starch pudding)[98]

Dissolve sugar in water and make sugar syrup [*jullāb*] in a large brass pot (*dast*). Take half of it out and put it aside in a vessel.

Dissolve wheat starch [in some water] and add it to the remaining syrup in the pot. The amount should be a sixth [by weight, of the sugar used]. It is even better if rice starch (*nashāʾ aruzz*) is used instead.

Continue stirring the pot [on the fire], and when it has almost thickened, start adding the remaining sugar syrup bit by bit. While stirring, continue adding sesame oil. Next, stir in bee honey; use 2 *ūqiyya*s (2 ounces) for each *raṭl* (1 pound) of the sugar.

When the pudding is done cooking, remove it, and stir scalded and skinned almonds and pistachios into it; use 2 *ūqiyya*s (2 ounces) for each *raṭl* [of sugar]. Also, stir in 2 *ūqiyya*s (4 tablespoons) of rosewater.

Spread it [on a tray or platter] and sprinkle it with sugar.[99] It will be wonderful.

(303) Recipe for *ʿajamiyya* (thick Persian-style flour pudding)[100]

For each *raṭl* (pound) of flour, take 1 *raṭl* sheep-tail fat (*duhn alya*) or sesame oil.[101] Toast the flour very well, (**81v**) and pour in the fat [and stir it].

For each *raṭl* of flour used, take 2 *raṭl*s bee honey; and saffron and rosewater, 1 *dirham* (½ teaspoon) of each. Heat the honey and set it aside, over burning coals (*nār jamr*), so that it stays hot.

Now, continue toasting the flour on low heat until it looks golden (*yaṣfarr*). To test its doneness, take a bit of the flour and drop it on the [heating] honey. If it splatters (*ṭashṭasha*), it is done. At this point, take the fire from under

98 Lit., 'looking like soap bars.' See glossary 4. With the exception of slight differences, similar copies of this recipe are also found in *Wuṣla* ii 640, and *Waṣf* 156–7. I amended the text slightly based on the latter.

99 It is commonly served in small blocks that look like pieces of soap (*ṣābūn*), hence the name.

100 This is a variety of *khabīṣ* puddings, which were ubiquitous in Abbasid Baghdadi cuisine. See, for instance, al-Warrāq's chapter 94, and Baghdādī's recipes 73–4. It is called *ḥalāwat ṭahīn* 'flour pudding' in modern Iraq. It is still a well-known traditional dessert in modern Egypt, where it is known by the names *ʿajamiyya, sadd al-ḥanak* 'the mouth-shutter,' and *ḥalāwat daqīq* 'flour pudding.' Also see recipes 327 and 345 below. I slightly amended the edited text based on a similar recipe in *Wuṣla* ii 645.

101 In *Wuṣla*, the recipe requires the flour to be extremely fine (*daqīq nāʿim jiddan*).

the pot, and pour the honey into it and stir to mix. Next, take the pot off the heat, cover it with a lid to prevent the steam from escaping the pot, and set it aside, covered, for an hour.[102] After that, remove the lid, and sprinkle some coarsely crushed pistachios and sugar on it.

(304) Recipe for Turkish *qāwūt* (granola)[103]

Take wheat berries (*ḥinṭa*) that have been picked over, wash them in water (*yuṣawwal*),[104] and then boil them until they are one-quarter done. [Drain them, and] let them dry overnight. Then take them to the chickpea-roaster,[105] so that he may roast them for you the same way he usually roasts chickpeas (*quḍāma*), on low heat,[106] and have him crush them for you to a medium grind (*daqīq wasṭ*).

The basic amounts used are, for each *raṭl* (pound) of this flour, use 4 *ūqiyya*s (4 ounces) ghee and sesame oil, and 4 *ūqiyya*s bee honey.

Melt the ghee with sesame oil, and rub (*yufrak*) the flour with them. Next, dissolve honey with saffron, and add to the flour mixture along with the shelled nuts (**82r**) of pistachios, almonds, and hazelnuts, one *ūqiyya* (1 ounce) of each. Also, add 1 *ūqiyya* poppy seeds and 1 *ūqiyya* (2 tablespoons) rosewater.

Mix all the ingredients and put them in a clean traveling sack (*jirāb*) [for provisions].

(305) Recipe for making *al-sitt danif* (the sick lady)[107]

Take 1 *raṭl* (pound) of sugar dissolved to make sugar syrup (*jullāb*).[108] Boil it on the fire, as is done with *aqrāṣ al-laymūn* (lemon-flavored hard candy).[109]

---

102 Detail from *Wuṣla*.

103 For details on the name *qāwūt*, see n. 57 above. Here I added some missing sentences based on *Zahr*, fols. 19v–20r. Cf. recipe 307 below.

104 Legumes and grains are cleaned by putting them in water and stirring them so that all the impurities rise to the surface and can be discarded.

105 The Arabic expression is الذي يعمل القضاضة. See the following note.

106 *Quḍāma* refers to chickpeas and fava beans roasted by professional roasters on a low heat so that they are thoroughly roasted and crunchy. In the Middle East today, chickpeas prepared this way are a popular snack food. To my knowledge, this cookbook is the only medieval source in which *quḍāma* is described in some detail.

107 In Gotha, fol. 83v, it is named *al-shabb danif* 'the sick young man.' *Shabb* is the dialectical vocalization of *shābb*. It is my guess that the sweet is called this because it is brittle and fragile, like young people who are sick, most probably with love. A recipe called al-*danif* in *Wuṣla* ii 650, and *Waṣf* 174 is made differently but is equally fragile.

108 Here I amended the text based on context.

109 I.e., the syrup reaches a brittle consistency. See recipe 266 above for cooking instructions.

Take the pot off heat and stir it until it looks good [i.e., it whitens]. Throw in 3 *ūqiyyas* (3 ounces) pounded pistachios along with rosewater and musk.

Grease a large flat tile (*bilāṭa*) with sesame oil, and pour and spread the cooked syrup on it. Cut it into small pieces (*shawābīr*),[110] and arrange them on plates. Sprinkle the surface with shelled pistachios when you spread the syrup on the tile.

(306) Recipe for making *abū lāsh* ('Nile-tilapia' pastries)[111]

Rub flour with 3 *ūqiyyas* (3 ounces) ghee, and then make it into dough by adding water. Add a small amount of salt, and knead vigorously.

Roll [the dough pieces into discs], like those of *qaṭā'if* (pancakes),[112] each a finger-long in diameter, and very thin. Fry them in sesame oil, and dip them in sugar syrup (*jullāb*) or honey. Color their edges [red] with alkanet (*sāq al-ḥamām*),[113] in a crisscross design (*mushabbak*). Put them on plates and sprinkle sugar on them.

(307) Recipe for *qāwūt baladī* (local-style granola)[114]

Take 1 *raṭl* (1 pound) flour, and toast it very well in 4 *ūqiyyas* (4 ounces) ghee and sesame oil. Fold into it 1¼ *raṭls* bee honey colored with saffron. **(82v)** Also add 1 *ūqiyya* (2 tablespoons) rosewater, 1 *ūqiyya* (1 ounce) shelled hazelnuts, 1 *ūqiyya* poppy seeds, and 3 *ūqiyyas* coarsely ground sugar. Do not store it away until it is completely cold. Keep it in leather or wooden boxes (*'ulab*), or vessels (*aṭbāq*).

---

110 They could be triangles or strips. See glossary 9.2.

111 Or *bū lāsh*, as in DK, n. 4014. *Lāsh* is the name of a Nile River round, red fish of the tilapia species (chromis niloticus); called 'lacha' in Spanish. See Dozy, *Takmilat al-ma'ājim* 1367, s.v. لاش; and Idrīsī, *Nuzhat al-mushtāq* i 34. The thin round pastries, which are red with a crisscross design around the edges for the tail and fins, are made to resemble this fish. There is a recipe by the same name in *Wuṣla* ii 630, but it is very brief and different: "it can be made with milk and sugar, or coarsely crushed toasted pistachio is sprinkled on small *qaṭā'if* discs; and then drenched in syrup."

112 As it occurs in DK, n. 4019. The edited text gives the singular *qaṭīfa*.

113 As it occurs in DK, n. 4026; otherwise it is written as *sham'a* (lit., 'bee-wax candle') in the edited text and Gotha, fol. 83v. *Sham'a* is a misreading of *'āqir sham'ā*, which is another name for *sāq al-ḥamām*, also called *rijl al-ḥamām*. This plant is bugloss, used by dyers; it is also called alkanet (*Alkanna tinctoria*), the root of which is primarily used as a ruby-red coloring agent for fabrics, soaps, lip balm, etc.

114 For details on the name *qāwūt*, see n. 57 above. Cf. the Turkish variety in recipe 304 above.

(308) Recipe for *aṣābiʿ Zaynab* (cannoli fingers)[115]

For each *raṭl* (pound) of flour, use 2½ *ūqiyyas* (2½ ounces) sesame oil and ghee. Rub and press the fat into the flour.[116] Knead well by adding hot water and a bit of salt.

Now get some dry reed stalks (*ʿūd nushshāb*) or sugar cane stalk joints (*ʿuqad qaṣab*). Roll out the dough on the *bilāṭa* (large flat tile), and roll it over the reed or sugar cane joints, which should be less than a finger long.

Fry the pieces until they are half done; after you remove the reeds, fry them again on low heat until the inside is fully cooked. Dip the pieces (*yughaṭṭas*) in sugar syrup (*jullāb*) [flavored with] rosewater and musk.

The filling is made of toasted pistachios, pounded finely with sugar [and moistened and bound] with rosewater and musk. Shape the mix into cylinders (*fatāʾil*), and then stuff them inside [the hollow fried fingers]. Arrange the pieces on plates and sprinkle them with finely pounded sugar.

(309) Recipe for making *qarn Bārūq* (Bārūq's horn)[117]

Take 1 *raṭl* (1 pound) flour and rub it with 2½ *ūqiyyas* (2½ ounces) ghee (*samn*), and knead it vigorously with [some water and] a small amount of salt.[118]

Roll out the dough as you do with thin sheets of fresh pasta (*tuṭmāj*),[119] sprinkling it (**83r**) with [melted] ghee while doing so. Every time you roll out a sheet, wipe off the [excess] fat and make it into a roll, less than two-fingers wide (approx. 1¼ inch). Cut it [crosswise] into slices (*shawābīr*), which you then fry in sesame oil, and dip in sugar syrup (*jullāb*) or honey, [flavored] with rosewater and musk. Arrange the pieces on plates (*ṣuḥūn*) and trays (*aṭbāq*), and sprinkle them with crushed sugar and pounded pistachios.

(310) Recipe for making *ḥalāwa makshūfa* (barefaced thick pudding)[120]

Take ½ *raṭl* (½ pound) shelled almonds, and pound them finely. Also, take ½ *raṭl* sesame oil and brown the almonds in it very well. Throw in ½ *raṭl* flour,

---

115 See another recipe (285 above), which is made with semolina flour.

116 The verb is *yulatt*, usually used when rubbing and mixing fat into flour to moisten it. See glossary 9.2, s.v. *latta*. The general verb designating kneading dough is *ʿajana*.

117 In Ibn Khaldūn's *Tārīkh* 1842, we read that Bārūq was an eleventh-century Turkish leader defeated in Ramla, Palestine. It is highly likely that the 'horny' pastries with their satanic association were made to commemorate his defeat. In the corresponding recipe in *Wuṣla* ii 630, this pastry is called *kul wa-shkur* 'eat and be thankful.' The name is still used today, albeit to designate tiny pieces of baklawa.

118 The recipe also adds "5 *dirhams* (2½ teaspoons)," but does not mention the ingredient.

119 See glossary 2.

120 Several recipes are called *makshūfa* in this chapter, cf. recipes, 272, 275, and 278.

[honey, and rosewater] dyed with saffron.[121] Stir the pot on a low heat until it is thick enough, as usual. Stir in ½ *raṭl* (½ pound) finely crushed sugar.

When you ladle it, garnish (*yushahhar*) the top with 1½ *ūqiyyas* (1½ ounces) pounded pistachios. Rosewater should be added when you add the honey.

(311) Recipe for *lawzīnaj yābis* (almond brittle)

Take sugar and dissolve it [in water] to make sugar syrup (*jullāb*), and let it boil on the fire, as is done with *aqrāṣ al-laymūn* (lemon-flavored hard candy).[122] Add some rosewater and musk, and [away from the heat, beat it] to let it crystallize and whiten. Add to it finely ground almonds. Grease a large flat tile (*bilāṭa*) with sesame oil, and spread the sugar mix on it. Cut it out into small pieces (*shawābīr*), and arrange them on plates.

(312) Recipe for *qarʿiyya* (gourd paste)

Take (83v) a sweet and tender green gourd. Peel off the outer skin and grate the gourd (*yujarrad*) until you get to the pithy white center.[123]

For each *raṭl* (pound) of grated gourd (*qarʿ majrūd*), use 9 *ūqiyyas* (9 ounces) sugar [made into *jullāb* syrup by adding water and boiling it], and ½ *raṭl* honey. Put the gourd in a large brass pot (*dast*) and pour in half the amounts of honey and *jullāb*. Let the pot cook on low heat (*nār layyina*), folding it [frequently] with a wooden pestle (*midaqqa khashab*). Whenever it dries out, add to it [the remaining half of honey and syrup] bit by bit (*qalīlan qalīlan*), until it has the consistency of paste (*maʿjūn*).

[Immediately, spread the paste on a stone slab or a tray,[124] and] sprinkle on it 2 *ūqiyyas* (2 ounces) pistachios and sugar, crushed finely and flavored with musk. You must add some rosewater before removing it from the fire.

(313) Recipe for *qarʿiyyat al-suyūr* (paste of gourd strips)[125]

Take a tender, sweet green gourd. Peel off the outer skin, and cut the gourd into discs [crosswise], each one-finger wide. Discard the center with the white

---

121 Here I provide the missing ingredients, honey and rosewater colored with saffron. At the end of the recipe, we learn that rosewater was to be added with honey.

122 I.e., the syrup reaches a brittle consistency. See recipe 266 above for cooking instructions.

123 The pithy spongy white center is called *bayāḍ* (lit., 'whiteness'). Here I followed the omission of لا in C, n. 4098, to clarify the meaning.

124 As we learn from the following recipe.

125 This dish is also called *musayyar al-qarʿ*, or just *musayyar*. See al-Anṭākī, *Tadhkira* 329, where it is said to be the best of jams (*murabbayāt*).

pithy stuff; just leave the green part. Thinly slice the gourd into strips, the way you do with *rishtā* (thin fresh noodles).

Put the cut gourd in a large brass pot (*dast*) and add sugar syrup (*jullāb*), honey, and rosewater, as you did in the previous recipe, and stir. Whenever it dries out, add [syrup and honey] bit by bit, as you did in the previous recipe. Continue doing this until the gourd has the consistency of carrot paste (*maʿjūn al-jazar*). It must be chewy in texture (*ʿalik*).

Sprinkle it with [crushed] pistachios and sugar flavored with musk [as you did in the previous recipe].

The moment you take the pot off the heat, spread it on a stone slab or a tray, to let it cool.

(314) Recipe for *qarʿiyya* (thick gourd pudding), beneficial for moistening dry humoral properties (*tarṭīb*) and for breaking up dense humors (*taḥlīl*)[126]

Take poppy seeds and draw out their essence (**84r**) with water and a piece of cloth.[127] Take the extracted liquid, and pour it on sugar and make it into syrup, without using egg [white].[128]

Now take a tender, sweet green gourd, peel it, discard its white [pithy center], and grate it as usual [and set it aside].

Next, take almonds, skin them [by scalding them first], pound them, and draw out their milk.[129] Take this milk and dissolve wheat starch in it. For each *raṭl* (pound) of sugar [in this recipe], use 1½ *ūqiyyas* (1½ ounces) starch.

Take the grated gourd and boil it in 3 *ūqiyyas* (3 ounces) honey, and set it aside. Put half of the [above prepared] sugar syrup (*jullāb*) [in a pot,] and add the [dissolved] starch to it. Continue stirring the pot, adding sesame oil, and gradually feeding it [with the other half of the syrup]. Then add the boiled gourd. Stir the pot until it is done,[130] and then remove.

---

126 For more on these Galenic terms, see glossary 11.

127 The poppy seeds had to be crushed, then steeped in water, then their juice was drained by squeezing it through a piece of cloth.

128 Egg whites were cooked with syrup to cleanse it, as the impurities coagulate with the egg, and thus could easily be discarded.

129 This is done by steeping the pounded almonds in hot water and then extracting the milk by squeezing it through a piece of cloth.

130 It should probably have the consistency of a thick pudding, but not as thick as the paste (*maʿjūn*).

(315) Recipe for *shakrīnaj* (almond confection)[131]

Take 1½ *raṭls* (1½ pounds) skinned almonds, pound them finely. Also, take 2 *raṭls* fine white sugar (*sukkar ṭabarzad*), pound it, and sift it.

Put ¼ *raṭl* (½ cup) almond oil (*duhn lawz*) in a frying pan (*ṭājin*), also add 1½ *dirhams* (4½ grams) saffron. Light a low fire under it and keep it until it gets hot. Throw in the almonds, followed by the pounded sugar, and stir it very well. Next, add ¼ *raṭl* honey and 1 *ūqiyya* (2 tablespoons) rosewater. Continue stirring the mix until it becomes one thick mass.

(**84v**) Empty the almond mixture onto a marble slab (*rukhāma*) or a wooden board (*khiwān*), and flatten it with a mallet (*ṣawlaj*) to a medium thickness. Cut it into bite-size rhombuses,[132] arrange the pieces on platters (*jām*), and serve them.

(316) Recipe for *khabīṣat khashkhāsh* (thick poppy seed pudding)[133]

Take ½ *raṭl* (1 cup) almond oil, 1 *raṭl* (1 pound) *daqīq samīdh* (fine white flour, high in starch content),[134] and 2 *raṭls* (2 pounds) pounded and sifted sugar.

Pour the oil into a frying pan (*ṭājin*),[135] and throw in 2 *dirhams* (6 grams/1 teaspoon) saffron. Light a low fire under it, and when it is hot, [gradually] sprinkle in the flour so that it fries in the oil. Next sprinkle about ½ *raṭl* (1 cup) rosewater, and continue stirring until it is cooked and thickened. Stir in 1 *ūqiyya* (1 ounce) white poppy seeds and take the pot off the heat. Allow it to cool, and then stir in the pounded sugar, and mix it well.[136] Spread it on a platter (*jām*) and serve.

---

131 This recipe was also known as *lawzīnaj yābis*. See the recipes in al-Warrāq, chapter 99. The name derives from the Persian *skakar* (Arabic *sukkar*) 'sugar.'

132 The adjective used here is موازياً, and in the other copies مواربا. To my knowledge, this is the earliest evidence that *lawzīnaj* (or *shakrīnaj*, as it is called here) was cut into the characteristic diamond shape.

133 This recipe, as well as recipes 318 and 319, is similar to recipes in al-Warrāq's tenth-century Baghdadi cookbook, English trans. *Annals* 391, 392, and 402. The *Kanz* version, however, differs slightly in style and is somewhat simplified.

134 See glossary 2 on this kind of flour.

135 Or *ṭinjīr*, a copper cauldron with a rounded bottom used for making thick puddings, as in DK, n. 4177.

136 Gotha, fol. 86r, adds the verb *yulatt*, which clearly indicates that the sugar must be mixed thoroughly.

(317) Recipe for *fālūdhajiyya bayḍā'* (white thick pudding of wheat starch)

Take ½ *raṭl* (½ pound) starch, and pound and sift it. Take 1 *raṭl* white honey, strain it [by boiling it and skimming the froth], and let it cool.

Next take a copper cauldron with a rounded bottom (*ṭinjīr*) and pour in 1 *raṭl* (2 cups) [almond] oil (*duhn*). Set the pot on a low heat. When it gets hot, sprinkle in the starch and let it fry. Next, sprinkle in the sugar,[137] and stir the pot (85r) very well until the pudding is cooked and thickened, and it releases the oil [it could not absorb].

Always leave the cooking fire on low, and it will come out truly delicious.

(318) Recipe for *khabīṣa Ma'mūniyya* (thick almond pudding)[138]

Take 1 *raṭl* (1 pound) skinned and pounded almonds. Put 1 *raṭl* (2 cups) [almond] oil in a copper cauldron with a rounded bottom (*ṭinjīr*). Now take 1½ *raṭl*s sugar and ½ *raṭl* bee honey and put them in another *ṭinjīr*. Pour 1 *raṭl* (2 cups) rosewater over them, and let them boil.

Put the pot with oil in it on a low heat, and throw in 1 *dirham* (3 grams/ ½ teaspoon) saffron. When the oil gets hot, sprinkle in 2 handfuls of *daqīq al-samīdh* (fine white flour, high in starch),[139] and stir it. When it is well mixed, pour in the [boiled] sugar and honey, as well as the pounded almonds, and stir.

When it is cooked, and has thickened and released the [extra] oil, remove it, and then spread it on a platter (*jām*), and serve.

(319) Recipe for uncooked *khabīṣa* (thick pudding)[140]

Take 1½ *raṭl*s (1½ pounds) skinned almonds, pound them and sift them through a *munkhul sha'r* (fine meshed sieve made of animal hair). Also, take 1½ *raṭl*s fine white sugar (*sukkar ṭabarzad*), pound and sift it, and keep aside about ¼ *raṭl* of it.

Now, mix the almonds with the sugar, and pour over them ¼ *raṭl* (½ cup) almond oil, (85v) ¼ *raṭl* rosewater, and 1 *dānaq* (½ gram) [pounded] cassia (*dār Ṣīnī*). Mix and knead them all very well until the mix looks like *khabīṣ* (thick pudding). Spread it on a platter (*jām*), sprinkle the sugar [that was set aside], and serve.

---

137 It seems the writer has forgotten that the recipe mentions white honey as a sweetener.

138 Named after the Abbasid caliph, al-Ma'mūn (d. 833). See also n. 133 above.

139 See glossary 2 on this kind of flour.

140 See n. 133 above.

(320) Recipe for a sweet (*ḥalāwa*) called *kāhīn* (ragged)[141]

Take the whites of eggs; for each egg white, use 2 *dirhams* (6 grams/1 teaspoon) wheat starch. Finely crush the starch and whip it very well with the egg white.[142] Fry it into discs in a frying pan (*ṭājin*), and then dip them in sugar syrup (*jullāb*). It will come out wonderfully pretty.

(321) Recipe for *jimāliyya* (melt-in-your-mouth date dessert)[143]

Take butter and throw it into a large brass pot (*dast*), and when it all melts, throw in stoned *ʿajwa* (sweet and soft dried dates), and cook it until it thoroughly disintegrates and melts with the butter. Next, throw in the crumbs from excellent white bread, and stir the pot the way you do when making a thick pudding (*ḥalāwa*). Stir in crushed sugar and pistachios, and then remove. It is very good (*malīḥ*).

(322) Recipe for the perfect *Qāhiriyya* (delicate Cairene ring cookies)[144]

Tale 1 *raṭl* (1 pound) sugar, ¼ *raṭl* almonds, and ¼ *raṭl* fine-tasting top grade flour. Pound (**86r**) the sugar finely, and sift it. Pound the remaining coarse sugar grains, pound them again, and sift them, so that it looks like *samīdh al-qamḥ* (wheat semolina).[145]

Now, take the almonds, scald them and remove their skins. Pound them and sift them, and again pound the remaining coarse almonds and sift the mixture. Combine everything [sugar, almonds, and flour], and knead them with 4 *ūqiyyas* (4 ounces) sesame oil, and then knead them well by adding some water until they look like dough of *kaʿk* (dry cookies).[146] So [after] you add

141 In Hans Wehr, *Dictionary*, *kuhna* means ragged or tattered.

142 A copy of this recipe in *Wuṣla* ii 625–6, gives more details at this point. The egg white and wheat starch are put in a bowl, with just a small amount of rosewater; otherwise, if too much is added, the mix will not bind. A new sweep made of reed leaves is used to whip the mix until it is foamy. A frying pan is put on a low heat, and small dots of the mix are dropped with a spoon into the oil until they brown. They should not stick to each other. They are then put into the thick syrup and eaten warm; it would not taste as good when cold.

143 Similar sweets are called *hays* and *ḥays*, for which we have recipes: In this chapter, recipe 343 below; Baghdādī 82; and al-Warrāq, English trans. *Annals* 402–3. The name *jimāliyya* could be derived from جميل 'melted solid fat' (*Lisān al-ʿArab*, s.v. جمل). However, there is also a possibility that the name was derived from *jimāl* 'camels,' and thus related to the custom of carrying this food as a provision for travelers in camel caravans.

144 Named after the city of al-Qāhira 'Cairo,' which was founded in 969.

145 Semolina, which is somewhat sandy in texture, is made from durum wheat, *Triticum durum*.

146 See, for instance, recipe 4 above. The dough is on the stiff side.

water and knead it, shape it into *Qāhiriyya* rings, which look like *kaʿk* rings. Sprinkle some flour on a wooden board and arrange these rings on it, and let them dry in the air. If you make them in the afternoon, let them dry until the following morning.

Early in the morning, take a large, wide earthenware bowl (*qaṣriyya*), and put 1½ *raṭls* (1½ pounds) fine-tasting fermented dough in it,[147] and whip it by hand [while adding water to it], like you do with dough of *zalābiya* (fried lattice fritters).[148] Add to it 2 *dirhams* (1 teaspoon) natron (*naṭrūn*), and whip. Next, add two egg whites, do not add the yolks, and whip all of it until the mix looks like *zalābiya* dough.[149]

Add as much musk, rosewater, (**86v**) and camphor as you like. However, these should be added to the earlier mentioned sugar [and almond] dough.

Put the bowl [with batter in it] on your right, and put the frying pan (*ṭājin*) on the fire. Add a lot of sesame oil, so that the rings float up to the surface [while frying]. Heat the sesame oil. Also, take fine-tasting honey and pour it into another large, wide bowl (*qaṣriyya*), and put it on your left.

[When you are ready to fry it,] pick up one of the dried-out rings with the help of an iron skewer (*saffūt ḥadīd*),[150] dip it first in the yeast batter in the bowl, and then take it out and put it in the frying pan (*ṭājin*). Repeat the same thing with the other pieces. Let them fry well and then dip them in the honey bowl [and take them out]. Continue frying and dipping in honey until all the pieces are done. Put them in bowls (*zabādī*), and sprinkle them with musk and rosewater, as much as suits you. Also, pound pistachios and sprinkle them on.

This is how true *Qāhiriyya* is made, so understand this.

(323) Recipe for making *qaṭāʾif maqlī* (fried pancakes)

For each *raṭl* (pound) of sugar, take 1 *raṭl* almonds or pistachios,[151] and ¼ *raṭl* fine-tasting excellent flour. (**87r**)

Pound the sugar in a mortar (*hāwan*) and sift it; scald [and skin] the almonds, and pound and sift them; sift the flour as well. Mix them all and knead them with 2 *ūqiyyas* (2 ounces) sesame oil and a bit of water so that they do not crumble (*yatafarfar*). Add as much musk and rosewater or camphor as you like, knead this mix well, and put it in a bowl (*zibdiyya*). Know that these

147 *Khamīra*, a sour dough, was usually used as a leavening agent in yeasted breads.

148 For a good recipe, see al-Warrāq, English trans. *Annals* 414–5.

149 *ʿAjīn al-zalābiya* is more like pancake batter in consistency.

150 A dialectical vocalization of *saffūd*.

151 In DK, n. 4294, the amount is ¼ *raṭl*.

same amounts and this same mixture (*khalṭa*) are also used for making stuffed pancakes (*qaṭāʾif maḥshū*).

Now, take a *qaṭāʾif* disc and set it on something [like a flat board or a plate].[152] Keep a bowl with some fine-tasting yeast [batter] in front of you.[153] Cut a piece of the prepared stuffing and put it on the *qaṭāʾif* [disc], and then fold it and seal its sides with some of the yeast [batter]. Repeat with the other pieces.

Put the frying pan (*ṭājin*) on the fire and put sesame oil in it, as much as needed to fry the *qaṭāʾif* you have made. As soon as the oil is hot enough, start frying the pieces. On your left, put a large, wide bowl (*qaṣriyya*) with fine-tasting good honey, and whenever a *qaṭāʾif* piece is done, pick it up with the skewer (*saffūt*) and dip it in the honey, as you do with *Qāhiriyya* [in the above recipe]. Continue doing this until all the pieces are done, and then put them (**87v**) in bowls (*zabādī*) and sprinkle them with as much musk and rosewater as suits you.

(324) Recipe for *qaṭāʾif maḥshū* (stuffed pancakes)

For each *raṭl* (pound) of sugar, take ¼ *raṭl* almonds—or pistachios if you wish, and ¼ *raṭl* fine flour.

Pound and sift the sugar, scald the almonds or pistachios and remove their skins and pound and sift them, and sift the flour, too. Mix them all and knead them by adding 2 *ūqiyya*s (2 ounces) sesame oil. Add also 2 *ūqiyya*s water after you add the oil; [this will] prevent the mix from crumbling (*yatafarfar*). Add as much musk and rosewater as suits you. Knead the mix vigorously the same way you do with *kaʿk* dough,[154] and after you are done, put it in a bowl (*zibdiyya*).

Now, take the [prepared] *qaṭāʾif* and put them in front of you [on a tray, for instance];[155] also put in front of you a bowl with ½ *raṭl* (1 cup) sesame oil. Lay a *qaṭāʾif* piece flat. Sprinkle it with some sesame oil and let the *qaṭāʾif* absorb [the oil]. [Take a small piece of the prepared stuffing, and] make a small cylinder (*khuwayṭa*),[156] then place it in middle of the piece of *qaṭāʾif*. Roll it up, and dip it in a bowl in front of you, which is filled with sugar syrup flavored with musk and rosewater.[157] Take the roll out [and repeat this process with the rest of the pancakes]. Pack the pieces in bowls, as they are done.

---

152 The recipe does not give directions for making the pancakes, rather it assumes that they are already made. See glossary 2, under *kunāfa*.

153 See n. 147 above.

154 See, for instance, recipe 4 above.

155 For directions on how to make the pancakes, see glossary 2, under *kunāfa*.

156 In CB, n. 4345, it is *ḥarbala* (pl. *ḥarābil*) 'cylinder.' Evidently, both carry the same meaning.

157 *Al-ḥall al-jullāb* (الحل الجلّاب), and not *al-khall* (الخلّ) 'vinegar,' as copied in the edited text.

When you are finished, take sesame oil (**88r**) and drizzle it over the pieces [of *qaṭāʾif*]. Do the same thing with sugar syrup, and sprinkle some musk and rosewater on them, as much as suits you. So, take note of this and follow the recipe.

(325) Amounts for making the usual *kunāfa* (*al-kunāfa al-ʿāda*)

For each *raṭl* (pound) of (*kunāfa* sheets),[158] use 2 *raṭl*s of a sweetener [such as honey or sugar syrup] and ½ *raṭl* sesame oil. Stir them as usual. Fold in hazelnuts (*yukhashkhash*); do not add the *kunāfa* sheets until the sweetener comes to a boil.

(326) *al-Basandūd* (round sandwich cookies)[159]

You need sugar, wheat starch and [or] excellent flour,[160] rosewater, scalded [and skinned] almonds, and sesame oil.

For each 10 *raṭl*s (10 pounds) [of sugar], use 2 *raṭl*s of starch, and 2 *raṭl*s of pistachios or almonds.[161] The cookie crust itself (*qishra*) is made the same way as that of the *khushkanān* crust.[162]

(327) Recipe for *ḥalāwa ʿajamiyya* (thick Persian-style toasted flour pudding)[163]

Take excellent flour, bee honey or other kinds [such as sugar syrup or cane-sugar molasses], sesame oil, saffron, musk, and rosewater.

Toast the flour until it browns, but be careful not to let it burn. Boil honey in a frying pan (*ṭājin*), and add the flour to it [by sprinkling it while stirring], also add the saffron, and stir. Pour in the sesame oil along with musk and rosewater. The oil should be poured bit by bit. When it is fully cooked [and thickened], ladle it onto plates and sprinkle a bit of musk and rosewater on it.[164]

---

158 The recipe calls for prepared *kunāfa* sheets. See recipe 298 above for instructions on how to slice it into thin strips; and glossary 2, s.v. *kunāfa*.

159 See glossary 2 for more details on this cookie. The ingredients and amounts given in the recipe are for the filling only.

160 In the other available recipe in *Wuṣla* ii 656, wheat starch is the ingredient used. It is quite possible that و ‘and’ was miscopied for أو ‘or’.

161 The ingredients are cooked to make a very thick pudding, which is sandwiched between two baked cookie discs, as the recipe in *Wuṣla* ii 656 demonstrates.

162 This is a variant of *khushkanānaj*, cookies stuffed with a mix of pounded sugar and nuts. See al-Warrāq, English trans. *Annals* 418–9; Baghdādī 79; *Wuṣla* ii 656; and *Waṣf* 165–6. See glossary 2.

163 See recipe 303 above, for another recipe for the same dessert.

164 The musk is usually dissolved in the rosewater, then used.

(328) Recipe for *qaṭāʾif maqlī* (fried pancakes)[165]

You need sugar (88v) and bee honey or cane sugar molasses (*qaṭr*), pistachios and hazelnuts—or just hazelnuts, musk, rosewater, aloeswood (*ʿūd*), and ambergris (*ʿanbar*).

Pound sugar and pistachios or hazelnuts, knead them with the bee honey or molasses, and mix them with musk and rosewater. Put the mix in a container and infuse it with the smoke of aloeswood and ambergris (*yubakhkhar*).

Cut a piece [of the nut mixture] and stuff it in the [prepared] *qaṭāʾif*—[166] the amount of the stuffing depends on the size of the pancakes. Seal the edges with a bit of dough (*ʿajīn*). Put the sesame oil in a frying pan (*ṭājin*) and set it on the fire. [When it gets hot,] fry the *qaṭāʾif*, and then dip them in cane-sugar molasses (*qaṭr*), just long enough to moisten them.[167] Sprinkle them with a bit of musk and rosewater.

(329) Recipe for *qaṭāʾif maḥshī* (stuffed pancakes)[168]

You need *qaṭāʾif* (prepared pancakes), pistachios, almonds, sugar, cane-sugar molasses (*qaṭr*), musk, and rosewater.

Pound sugar, pistachios, and almonds. Knead them into dry paste by adding some molasses, and then infuse the paste with smoke [of aloeswood and ambergris].[169] Now take a piece the size of a date stone (*niwāya*),[170] put it in the *qaṭāʾif* disc, and roll it up. Pack the rolls in containers, and drizzle the remaining molasses over them. Pound a bit of pistachios, and sprinkle over them.

(330) Recipe for *mukhannaqa*[171]

For each *raṭl* (pound) of [*kunāfa*] sheets (*waraq*), take 3 *raṭl*s sugar and honey—two-thirds [sugar] and one-third [honey]. Dissolve the sugar in water [to make *jullāb al-sukkar* (sugar syrup)] and when it comes to a full boil, add the [*kunāfa*] sheets, which have been cut [into strips], and stir as usual [i.e., continuously]. Add sesame oil (89r) and stir. For each *raṭl* [of *kunāfa*], use 1½ *raṭl*s (3 cups) oil.

---

165 See recipe 323 above, for another recipe for the same dessert.

166 The recipe assumes that the pancakes are already prepared and ready to stuff and fry. See glossary 2.

167 The verb used is *yutfaʾ* (lit., 'extinguish').

168 See recipe 324 above, for another recipe for the same dessert.

169 See previous recipe.

170 Vernacular for *nawāt*, it designates seeds in general, however, it was originally the name of the date stone (*Lisān al-ʿArab*, s.v. نوي).

171 See recipe 297 above for another version of the dish. Also, see, n. 83 above for more on the name of the dish.

When all the moisture has been absorbed, add the honey, in two batches or three, to the pot and continue adding the oil until it becomes thick enough. Saffron should be added, too. Throw in [pounded] pistachios while stirring. Remove it as soon as it stops absorbing any more [of the added oil and honey]. Stir in musk and rosewater, ladle it [on a plate], flatten the surface (*yubsaṭ*), and serve it.

(331) Recipe for *qaṭāʾif abū lāsh* (layered pancakes)[172]
You need *qaṭāʾif* (pancakes), sesame oil, hazelnuts, cane-sugar molasses (*qaṭr*), and rosewater.

Drizzle the *qaṭāʾif* discs with sesame oil one by one, and stack them in containers. Pound sugar, and toast hazelnuts and pound it coarsely. Sprinkle these on the discs [as you stack them], and when done, pour molasses or bee honey, and a bit of rosewater over them.

(332) Recipe for *kunāfa mumallaḥa* (sugar-coated *kunāfa*)[173]
You need *kunāfa* [crepes] thinly cut [into strips].[174] You also need, sugar, sesame oil, cane-sugar molasses (*qaṭr*) bee honey (*ʿasal naḥl*), and rosewater.

After thinly slicing the *kunāfa*, rub it (*yuʿarrak*) with sesame oil to moisten it, and when you are done with this, pour the molasses or bee honey on the shreds, and rub them with it [to coat them all]. Next, sprinkle them (**89v**) with coarsely ground white sugar and some rosewater. Put the *kunāfa* in containers and sprinkle it with the remaining coarsely ground sugar.[175]

(333) Recipe for *kunāfa maṭbūkha* (cooked *kunāfa*)
For each *raṭl* (pound) of *kunāfa*, use ½ *raṭl* (1 cup) sesame oil. Put the oil in a large brass pot (*dast*), and light the fire under it. As soon as it boils, throw in 1 *raṭl kunāfa*, which has been cut into strips like *rishtā* (fresh noodles).[176] Let

---

172 This is a variation on recipe 306 above. The name of the dish, as I explain in recipe 306, does not apply to this dessert, which seems to have kept the name but strayed from the original dish.

173 Lit., 'salted.' It is sprinkled with a lot of coarsely ground white sugar, which makes it look as if it were salted (*mumallaḥa*). See recipe 298 above, for another version. Here I amended the text based on Gotha, fol. 90v. Both *kunāfa mumallaḥa* and the following *kunāfa maṭbūkha* occur in al-Ḥajjār, *Kitāb al-Ḥarb al-maʿshūq* 118.

174 See recipe 298 above, for details on how this is done. Also, see glossary 2, s.v. *kunāfa*.

175 It is quite possible that *kunāfa* was prepared like this to preserve it so that it could be consumed whenever one wished, as in the following recipe, where it is said that it stays good for a year.

176 See recipe 298 above, for details on how this is done. Also see glossary 2, s.v. *kunāfa*.

them fry in the oil, and then throw in ½ *raṭl* (½ pound) crushed white sugar and stir it in until it dissolves entirely. Next, add 1 *raṭl* honey and continue stirring until the oil separates, and it all looks good.

You will have ready some scalded and skinned almonds and pistachios. Color them with saffron and throw them in the pot, and stir it very well. Add musk and rosewater as needed, while it is still on the fire, and then remove. Store it [after it has cooled]. It will stay good to eat for a whole year.

(334) Recipe for *ḥalāwa* (thick pudding) made with *ʿajwa* (sweet and soft dried dates)

Take sheep-tail fat (*alya*) and render it (*tusalla*ʾ). Remove the stones of *ʿajwa* dates and throw them into the rendered fat. Let them cook [while stirring] until they look like *ḥalāwa.*

Scald [and skin] almonds, and color them with saffron. Throw them into the pot along with some poppy seeds. Stir [the *ḥalāwa*] until it looks good, and then remove. Spread it on plates (*ṣuḥūn*). Sprinkle [crushed] pistachios and white sugar on it, along with musk (**90r**) and rosewater.

(335) Recipe for *qaṭāʾif maḥshī* (stuffed pancakes)[177]

For each 2 *raṭl*s (2 pounds) of *qaṭāʾif* (pancakes), use 1 *raṭl* sugar and ½ *raṭl* [ground] pistachios. Crush the sugar until it is as fine as [the ground] pistachios. Use [this mixture] to fill the *qaṭāʾif,* then pack it [in containers]. Pour sugar syrup (*jullāb*), *qaṭr al-nabāt* (finest molasses),[178] or bee honey, along with musk and rosewater over them. Make sure there is enough syrup to cover them all (*yukhammar*);[179] then eat them.

(336) Recipe for *ḥalāwa* (confection) made with *biṭṭīkh ʿAbdulī* (melon)[180]

Peel the melon, [cut the pulp into small pieces] and leave it in the sun until it becomes dry and leathery in texture (*yataqaddad*), turns brown (*yaḥmarr*),[181] and the pieces stick to each other.

Now take sugar syrup (*jullāb*), let it boil on the fire and skim the froth. Add the dried melon to it and put the mix in a small brass pot (*dast laṭīf*). Using an

---

177 See recipes 324 and 329 for other versions of this dessert. For directions on how to make the pancakes, see glossary 2, under *kunāfa.*

178 This is the purest type of cane-sugar molasses, left over after sprouting sugar crystals make sugar candy (*sukkar nabāt*); it was produced at sugar mills. See glossary s.v. *sukkar.*

179 In DK, n. 4518, the word occurs as *yughmar* (drench).

180 An Egyptian variety of melon (*Cucumis melo* var. *chate*); see glossary 7, s.v. *biṭṭīkh.*

181 Lit., 'turns red,' is used here to designate brown.

isṭām (large paddle-like iron spatula), stir the pot [while it is cooking], until all the moisture evaporates and it becomes as thick as *ḥalāwat al-musayyar*.[182] Fold in [crushed] pistachios.

[The moment you remove the pot from the heat,] empty the *ḥalāwa* onto a large flat tile (*bilāṭ*), and spread it into discs like chewy candy (*ʿaqīd*).[183] Cut them into small pieces (*shawābīr*) and pack them in containers. Alternate layers of [crushed] sugar and *ḥalāwa* pieces [to prevent them from sticking to each other].

Before putting the *ḥalāwa* pieces into the container, you should scent them with rosewater flavored with musk.

This is truly delicious, and it is beneficial for sicknesses related to black bile disorders (*amrāḍ sawdāwiyya*).

(337) Recipe for *ḥalāwa* (confection) made with *malban* (thick and chewy wheat starch pudding)[184]

Take *malban* [pieces], fry them in sesame oil, and sprinkle them with crushed sugar. Prepared thus, it will look like *ṣābūniyya* (thick wheat starch pudding),[185] and serve it. Delicious. (**90v**)

(338) Recipe for another *ḥalāwa* (thick pudding)[186]

In a large brass pot (*dast*), thoroughly render sheep-tail fat (*alya*) with a little of sesame oil, and set it aside in a container. Now, take honey or sugar syrup (*jullāb*) and put it in the *dast*. Remove the stones of fine-tasting *ʿajwa* (sweet and soft dried dates), finely pound them in a stone mortar (*jurn*), adding to them a bit of Levantine rosewater (*māʾ ward Shāmī*).[187] Add it to the honey [in the pot] after it boils and its froth is skimmed off by stirring egg white into it.

Let the mix boil until it becomes thick enough, and then throw in [whole] almonds colored with saffron after they are scalded and skinned. Stir the pot

---

182 Like paste, see, for instance, recipe 313 above.

183 See, for instance, recipe 348 below.

184 Today it is more commonly known as *luqum*/*ḥalqūm*, and in the West, as Turkish delight. A briefer recipe in *Wuṣla* ii 626, mentions that another name for *malban* is *jild al-faras* 'horse's penis.' Ibn Baṭṭūṭa, *Riḥla* 37 and 261, provides similar information. See glossary 4, s.v. *malban*.

185 This confection literally means 'looking like bars of soap.' See recipe 302 above.

186 The recipe is for a variety of thick date pudding, a kind of *khabīṣ*. In *Zahr*, fol. 21v, the same recipe is given the name صفة حلاوة من العجوة 'Recipe for a thick pudding made with *ʿajwa* (sweet and soft dried dates).'

187 *Ward Shāmī* 'Levantine roses' is the variety more commonly known in English as damask roses.

with an *isṭām* (large paddle-like iron spatula), adding rendered sheep-tail fat all the while. When the fat starts to separate [and is no longer absorbed], take the pot off the heat, and immediately season it with the [usual] aromatic spices (*afāwih*), in addition to some poppy seeds and rosewater flavored with musk.

When you ladle it onto the plates, sprinkle their surfaces with crushed toasted hazelnuts, pistachios, and fine white sugar (*sukkar bayāḍ*), and eat it.

The poor may cook it with [the cheaper] sugar cane molasses (*quṭāra*) or sugar cane syrup (*ʿasal al-qaṣab*).[188]

(339) Recipe for another confection (*ḥalāwa*)

Take [crushed] pistachios, [toasted?] flour, and sugar. Knead them all with sugar syrup (*jullāb*), press and shape them into a disc, which you cut into slices (*shawābīr*), and season with musk and camphor.

(340) Recipe for *ruṭab muʿassal* (honeyed fresh dates)[189]

Take fresh dates that have just been harvested. Spread them in a shaded airy place for a couple of days. Pull the stones out of the calyxes using a long needle (*misalla*) (**91r**) or a sharpened stick, and replace them with fine skinned sweet almonds.

For each 10 *raṭl*s (pounds) of dates, use 1 *raṭl* bee honey, in which you dissolve 1 *ūqiyya* (2 tablespoons) rosewater, and then boil this on the fire, skim off its froth and color it with ½ *dirham* (¼ teaspoon) saffron.

Add the dates to the honey, and as it starts boiling, stir it ever so gently to let it absorb the honey, and then remove it. Spread the dates on a heath-wood tray (*ṭabaq khalanj*), and when they are lukewarm, sprinkle them with finely pounded fine-tasting sugar.

Those who want it to have hot properties, can make it with musk, spikenard (*sunbul*), and a small amount of aromatic spices (*afāwih*).[190] For those who want it to have cold properties, they can make it with camphor and poppy seeds.[191]

Store the dates in glass vessels (*awānī zujāj*), and do not eat them until it gets cold and it is past the season of fresh dates.[192]

---

188 See glossary 4, for more on these syrups.

189 Here I amended the edited text based on similar recipes in *Wuṣla* ii 652–3; and *Waṣf* 173–4.

190 These spices are all known for their hot properties.

191 These spices are known for their cold properties, see glossary 11, s.v. *mizāj*.

192 Here I replaced the edited وزمان الرطب 'fresh date season' with وانقضاء زمان الرطب 'past fresh date season' in the version in *Waṣf*. Fresh dates are only available during the hot season.

(341) Recipe for *ruṭab murabbā* (fresh date jam)
Leave fresh dates in the sun [for a while] so that they dry out a little. Remove their stones and replace them with skinned almonds, and then pack them in glass vessels. Pour in bee honey, which has been [boiled], its froth skimmed off, and [colored with] a bit of saffron.

Set the vessels aside, but check on them every week [to make sure that] no moisture has seeped out of the dates [into the syrup], which will cause the jam to go sour [and spoil].

(342) Recipe for *tumūr mulawwaza* (dried dates stuffed with almonds)
Wash dried Iraqi *qaṣb* dates in hot water,[193] and replace their stones with pistachios or scalded [and skinned] almonds.

Boil sugar syrup (*ḥall*) and honey, (**91v**) and skim the froth. Throw in the dates and let them boil just once.[194] Immediately, turn them over into a green-glazed wide-mouthed jar (*barniyya*). Color them with saffron, and season them with musk, rosewater, and camphor. Do not expose it to too much heat [when boiling]. Remove it from the fire, and let it cool completely. If its syrup is adequately thickened, it will be wonderfully good.

(343) Recipe for *hays* (date balls)[195]
Take dried fine bread or *kaʿk* (dry cookies), and finely pound it; for each *raṭl* (pound) of it, use ½ *raṭl* of *ʿajwa* (sweet and soft dried dates). Remove their stones, and mix and mash them with the pounded *kaʿk* [or bread].

Next, take finely chopped shelled walnuts, almonds, and pistachios, as well as toasted sesame seeds. Take one *ūqiyya* (1 ounce) of each. Throw them into the date mixture.

Take sesame oil, and heat it on low heat, and then pour it over [the dates], mix and rub them by hand to combine [them into one mass]. Shape it into balls (*kubab*), sprinkle them with pounded sugar, and stash them away (*yurfaʿ*).

(344) Recipe for *ḥalāwa* (thick pudding) made with dried dates (*tamr*)
Remove the stones from dried dates, and throw them into a large brass pot (*dast*). Add water [and keep mashing and boiling] until they fall apart (*yataharraʾ*).

---

193 *Qaṣb* (قصب) is the Egyptian variant for *qasb* (قسب). It is a naturally dry delicious Iraqi date, usually stored loose because it cannot be pressed together like other moist dried dates.

194 Here I amended the text following the copy of *Wuṣla* ii 653–4.

195 Lit., 'the pounded.' It is also known as *ḥays*, which, besides 'pounding,' suggests the idea of 'being on the road' (*Lisān al-ʿArab*, s.v. حيس). *Hays* was one of the travelers' favorite provision. See recipe 321 above for a variation on this confection.

Take them off the heat, and press them through a sieve. Return them to the pot, and let them cook until the mass of dates thickens.

If you wish to make a thick pudding (*ḥalāwa*) with it, then add bee honey, ghee (*samn*), and toasted and coarsely crushed shelled hazelnuts. Stir the pot, and then remove it and season it with musk and rosewater. Scald almonds [and skin them], color them with saffron and scatter them on top of [the pudding, after you spread it on plates to serve]. It is (**92r**) wonderful.

(345) *Ḥalāwa ʿajamiyya* (thick Persian-style toasted flour pudding)[196]

Take picked over wheat berries (*qamḥ*), lightly toast them in the *furn* (brick oven), and pound them into fine flour. For each *raṭl* (pound) of the wheat, take 2 *raṭl*s of a sweetening syrup, and ½ *raṭl* sesame oil.

Put the wheat flour [in a pot] suspended over the fire, let it brown in a bit of sesame oil, and take it out and set it aside. Now take whatever sweetening syrup you have chosen, add a bit of water and put [it in a pot] suspended over the fire. When it starts to boil, throw in the toasted flour, and continue stirring until it becomes as thick as *ʿaṣīda* (dense flour soup). Next, pour in the [½ *raṭl*] sesame oil, and stir. Add [skinned] almonds and poppy seeds—both colored with saffron. Also, add saffron that has been steeped in rosewater and musk. Continue stirring, and then remove the pot. Let it cool and ladle it onto plates.

(346) Recipe for fine *tamr muʿassal* (honeyed dried dates)

Take dried dates, remove their calyxes, wash them, dry them, and then pull out their stones. Scald the almonds, [remove their skins,] and in place of each stone insert an almond.

Now take bee honey, and boil it [and skim its froth] until it becomes clean. Add the dates to it, and light a low fire under it. When it becomes thick, add all the [commonly used] aromatic spices,[197] and then remove it.[198]

[Recipe for making ghee from milk[199]

Take 10 *raṭl*s (10 pints) cow milk, and take a stick that is as high as the milk in the pot. Mark [the stick] into thirds.

---

196 See recipes 303 and 327 above for other versions of this dessert.

197 See, for instance, recipe 340 above.

198 At this point, Gotha ends its copy of the *Kanz*. However, before the copyist ends the MS, a final recipe is added, one which is not found in any of the extant medieval cookbooks. It deals with making a kind of adulterated ghee with cow milk rather than butter (fol. 94r). Here I include the entire recipe, enclosed in square brackets.

199 This is the concluding recipe in Gotha, see note above.

Light a low fire under the pot, [and let it boil] until two-thirds of it is gone. At this point, take 3 *ūqiyyas* (3 ounces) of yellow Alexandrian beeswax (*shamʿ Iskandrānī aṣfar*), and 1 *dirham* (½ teaspoon) saffron threads (*zaʿfarān shaʿr*). Steep the saffron in a small amount of the hot milk, and add it to the pot. Also, melt the wax and add it.

Empty the milk into a new wide-mouthed earthenware jar (*mājūr aḥmar*); do not rinse it. Leave the vessel outside overnight; it may be left exposed or covered with a piece of light cloth. In the morning, you will find that it has turned into pure ghee (*samn khāliṣ*). Cook with it whatever you wish.]

CHAPTER 11

في الجوارشنات والمعاجن والاشربة التي تقدم قبل الطعام وبعده

Digestive Stomachics (*juwārishnāt*), Electuaries (*maʿājin*), and Drinks (*ashriba*) Offered Before and After the Meal

(347) *Sakanjabīn* (92v) *safarjalī* (quince oxymel)[1]

It is made by taking one part, by weight, of the juice of the delicious and aromatic Aṣfahānī or Barzī quince,[2] a similar amount of pure white sugar, and a quarter the amount of very sour vinegar (*khall thaqīf*). Boil them down to thick syrup.

If preferred, throw in quince, thinly sliced into crescent-shaped pieces. Add these before the syrup thickens. It may also be scented with rosewater into which saffron and musk have been dissolved. Some people make it with honey [instead of sugar], in which case it will be more effective in clearing phlegm (*balgham*) and rarefying humors (*talṭīf al-akhlāṭ*). Others make it without vinegar so that it becomes better and more effective in cases of constipation (*ḥabs al-ṭabīʿa*).

(348) Recipe for *sakanjabīn ʿaqīd* (oxymel of chewy-candy)

This is the best *naql* (*mezze*) to be had with alcoholic drinks for people whose humors are naturally prone to heat (*aṣḥāb al-amzāj al-ḥārra*).[3]

It is made by boiling sugar syrup (*jullāb*) until it thickens, and then throwing in pure, clear, very sour vinegar—for each *raṭl* of *jullāb* use 3 *ūqiyyas* (3 ounces) vinegar. Continue boiling it until it thickens to a brittle stage of consistency.[4]

---

1 *Sakanjabīn* is a sweet and sour syrup, used diluted as a digestive drink. See glossary 11 for medical terms and medicinal preparations. See also glossary 1 for digestive and restorative drinks.

2 Of Isfahan (Persian province), or Barza (Damascene village), respectively. Compared with the quince variety used in recipe 359 below, the flesh of these two types is not dense.

3 For more on *naql*, see glossary 5.

4 The word here occurs as يتسكر (crystallize), which should have been copied as يتكسر (lit., 'break'), descriptive of the brittle stage of the syrup, *qiwām al-qaṣf* (قوام القصف). Based on *Waṣf* 154, this stage is described as, "A cooled off piece taken from it should be brittle and break easily." In today's culinary terms, it is called the 'hard crack point.' See recipes 265, 266, 279 (n. 42), and 284, in the above chapter.

 | DOI 10.1163/9789004349919_014

Spread it on a marble slab (*rukhāma*) after you oil its surface, [shape it into a disc and cut it into triangles],[5] and use [as needed].

(349) Recipe (93r) for *aqrāṣ al-laymūn* (hard lemon drops)

These excite the appetite and strengthen digestion. Make them by boiling sugar syrup (*jullāb*) until it thickens. Then add [lemon juice to it] and continue boiling it down until it almost reaches the brittle stage.[6] Scoop it with a small spoon and drop it into [small] discs (*aqrāṣ*) on a wooden board (*khiwān*). When these become cold and harden, put them in a wide-mouthed glass jar (*barniyya zujāj*) and use them.[7]

(350) Recipe for *mayba* (aromatic restorative quince drink)

This is a seasoned quince drink (*sharāb al-safarjal*) made by taking good quince, which you cut into pieces [after] peeling it and discarding the seeds.

Pound the quince in a marble or wooden mortar, squeeze the juice and strain it, and then add what equals half of its amount of Levantine aged wine (*sharāb ʿatīq rikābī*) or clear cooked wine (*maṭbūkh ṣāfī*), after you soak in it the remaining quince pulp for a whole day.[8]

Cook the juice mixture in a soapstone pot (*qidr birām*), or a glazed earthenware one (*fakhkhār madhūn*) on moderate heat until half of its original amount has evaporated. Next, throw in what equals a quarter of its amount of honey, which you have boiled and skimmed the froth from; or sugar. While it is cooking, put[9] the following [spices], tied in piece of cloth (*khirqa maṣrūra*) into the pot:

> (351)[10] Ginger (*zanjabīl*), cassia (*dār Ṣīnī*), cloves (*qaranful*), cubeb, green cardamom (*hāl*), nutmeg (*jawzat al-ṭīb*), spikenard (*sunbul*), Ceylon cinnamon (*qarfa*), aloeswood (*ʿūd*), mastic (*maṣṭakāʾ*), and saffron—½ dirham (¼ teaspoon) of each. Coarsely crush them.

---

5 As described in recipe 336 above.

6 See n. 4 above.

7 From *Wuṣla* ii 622, we learn that *aqrāṣ laymūn* are sometimes made in other colors and used as garnish in sweet dishes.

8 For more on these wines, see glossary 1.

9 Interestingly, DK, n. 4738, uses the verb *yazaʿ* (put), which we recognize today as a typical Egyptian rendition of the verb *yaḍaʿ*.

10 The editors give this section a number, with the assumption that it is a new recipe, which in fact it is not. The recipe is just giving a list of what spices to put in the cloth bundle. Following DK, n. 4740, the sentence reads,

وينزّل مع الطبيخ في خرقة مصرورة ما هذه صفته.

Now, let the pot with honey [or] sugar cook until (93v) it is reduced [to a consistency of thin honey].[11] When it is all done, perfume it with musk, and store it in glass vessels, and use [as needed].

(352) Recipe for *sharāb ḥummāḍ al-utrujj* (concentrated syrup for a citron pulp drink)[12]

It is made by taking the pulp of Susa citron (*utrujj Sūsī*),[13] discarding its peel, membranes, and seeds. Set it aside.

For each *raṭl* (pound) of citron pulp [used], dissolve [in water] 2 *raṭls* of sugar or more, as preferred, and make it into a sugar syrup (*jullāb*). Skim off the froth and let it boil until it thickens and almost reaches a brittle consistency.[14] Throw in the [prepared] citron pulp,[15] and continue stirring it on low heat until it reaches the consistency of *sharāb* [medium syrup]. Store it [in glass vessels] and use it [diluted in cold water].

(353) Recipe for *sharāb laymūn safarjalī* (concentrated syrup for lemon-quince drink)

Take a quince, peel it, cut it into pieces, and remove the seeds. Boil it in water until it softens and is half cooked. Put the quince pieces aside, and keep the boiling liquid.

Dissolve sugar in the water and boil it until it thickens. Throw in the reserved liquid in which the quince was boiled, and resume boiling it until the syrup is thick enough. Throw in the [boiled] quince and bring it to a boil once or twice, and then remove it. Squeeze one or two lemons on it, and scent it with rosewater.

---

11 In comparable al-Warrāq recipes (English trans. *Annals* 479), there are instructions on how to consume this drink: "Take 1 *ūqiyya* (2 tablespoons) of the syrup and dilute it in cold water."

12 See above note. All the following *sharāb* preparations are consumed diluted in cold water.

13 Susa is a city in the province of Khuzistan, in southwestern Persia, adjoining southern Iraq. This citron variety is known for its huge size and heavy weight. A single citron of this kind might weigh up to 30 pounds, as described in an anecdote in Ibn al-Jawzī, *al-Adhkiyāʾ* 106. See glossary s.v. *utrujj*.

14 The Arabic expression is يقارب أن يتسكر. See n. 4 above.

15 Apparently, the citron pulp is not made into juice, but added in chunks to the boiling syrup. Similarly, in the following recipe, the boiled pieces of quince are added to the syrup.

FIGURE 36 Utrujj (*Citron*), *F1954.72r, Muḥammad al-Qazwīnī,* ʿAjāʾib al-makhlūqāt, *detail (Freer Gallery of Art and Arthur M. Sackler Gallery, Smithsonian Institution, Washington,* DC*: Purchase—Charles Lang Freer Endowment).*

(354) Recipe for *maʿjūn al-utrujj* (electuary of citron), good for the digestion
Take (**94r**) a citron peel and put it in salted water until all its bitterness is gone, and then wash it in sweet water (free of salt) (*māʾ ḥulw*). Spread the peel to dry, and then cut it into pieces.

Now take 1¼ *raṭl*s (1¼ pounds) sugar and 1¼ *raṭl*s bee honey. Combine them in a large brass pot (*dast*), [boil them], and skim the froth. Throw in the citron peel and [let syrup boil] until it thickens.

Take the pot off the heat and add ginger, long pepper (*dār fulful*), cassia (*dār Ṣīnī*), and mastic gum (*maṣṭakāʾ*), 3 *dirhams* (1½ teaspoons /9 grams) of each. Also, add mace (*basbāsa*), black pepper, nutmeg (*jawz ṭīb*), spikenard (*sunbul*), and aloeswood (*ʿūd*), 1 *mithqāl* (⅔ teaspoon/4½ grams) of each. Also add musk, rosewater, raw ambergris (*ʿanbar khām*), and aloeswood incense (*ʿūd bakhūr*). Store it away.

(355) Another recipe [for a digestive]

This is to be taken after [eating] greasy foods (*aṭʿima dasima*).

[Take] 5 *dirhams* (15 grams) black myrobalan (*kābulī*);[16] the same amount of emblic myrobalan (*umluj*);[17] the same amount of Andalusian caraway (*karāwiya Andalusiyya*); the same amount of wild pomegranate blossoms (*jullanār*); and the same amount of *qarfa laff* (rolled barks of Ceylon cinnamon).

Also add, 3 *dirhams* (9 grams) Ceylon sandalwood (*ṣandal Maqāṣīrī*); the same amount of clove stalks (*ḥaṭab qaranful*);[18] the same amount of green cardamom (*hāl*); the same amount of spikenard (*sunbul*); the same amount of betel leaves (*tunbul*); and the same amount of nutmeg (*jawzat ṭīb*).

Add 312 *dirhams* (2 pounds) raisins (*zabīb*), 80 *dirhams* (8½ ounces) tamarind (*tamr Hindī*), and 80 *dirhams* [dried] pomegranate seeds.

Crush together the pomegranate seeds, tamarind, (**94v**) and raisins after their seeds are removed, and add to them 1 *dirham* (½ teaspoon/3 grams) mastic gum. Mix all the ingredients with very sour vinegar (*khall ḥādhiq*), and throw 30 *dirhams* (3 ounces) mint leaves into the mix. Store it away.

(356) Recipe for making [candied] citron (*utrujj*)

Take *utrujj*, peel [the outer skin] and divide it into slices (*shawābīr*), which you fry in sesame oil, and then set aside.

Set a large brass pot (*dast*) on the fire, and put sugar syrup (*jullāb*) or bee honey in it. Boil it and skim its froth, and then add the fried citron pieces to it. Let it boil until the syrup thickens to the consistency of *sharāb*, and the citron is saturated with the syrup.

Add some *aṭrāf al-ṭīb* (spice blend) to the pot, as well as saffron, crushed aloeswood of Khmer (*ʿūd Qamārī*), musk, and rosewater. Take the citron pieces out of the pot, and arrange them on plates. Sprinkle them with sugar and serve.

(357) Recipe for *sharāb al-laymūn al-murammal* (grainy concentrated syrup for lemon drink)[19]

Take as much sugar as you wish, [dissolve it in water, boil it] and clear it of impurities by skimming its froth. Let it boil and when it becomes very thick in consistency, remove the pot, [put it on the ground], and whip it with a cylindrical wooden rod (*dakshāb khashab mabrūm*), adding lime juice as needed.

---

16 Also, chebulic myrobalan. Its full name is *ihlīlaj kābulī*, *Terminalia chebula* (S), see glossary 7.

17 It is also known as Indian gooseberry, *Phyllanthus emblica* (S), see glossary 7.

18 See glossary 8, s.v. *qaranful*.

19 *Murammal* (lit., 'having a sandy texture'), derives from *raml* 'sand.'

[Note] Add the lemon juice only when the pot is [removed from the fire and is] on the ground (*ʿalā al-ṭīn*), and while you are whipping it with the *dakshāb*.

(358) Recipe for *laymūn safarjalī* (concentrated syrup for lemon-quince drink), from another copy[20]

Dilute (**95r**) sugar syrup (*jullāb*) with water, and while it is boiling on the fire, add quince juice to it. For each *raṭl* (pound) of syrup, use 4 *ūqiyyas* (½ cup) quince juice. Also add enough [lemon juice] to give it a sweet and sour taste (*muzz*). Let it boil until it thickens, and then [remove it from the fire] and put it [on the ground]. Add a bit of musk. Crush a small amount of sugar and sprinkle it on it. Whip the mixture [as in the previous recipe], and store it away. However, it is better if you add musk after you empty the syrup into the jar (*barniyya*).[21]

(359) Recipe for quince cooked in sugar[22]

Take good sugar, [add water to it] and boil it until it thickens into sugar syrup (*jullāb*). Throw in *safarjal qaṣbī* (a hard-fleshed variety of quince),[23] which has been sliced neatly. Continue cooking on a low fire until the syrup turn as red as carnelian (*ʿaqīq*) and thickens, and the quince cooks. The [cooking] quince pieces need to be touched [for doneness],[24] and as soon as each one is cooked, take it out [and set it aside]. When the time comes to take the pot off the heat, return the entire cooked quince to it.

If you have used *safarjal Barzī* in making it,[25] it would have fallen apart, and spoiled. If you want to make it taste sour by adding fresh lime juice (*māʾ laymūn akhḍar ṭarī*) to it, then go ahead and do so; otherwise, you can leave it plain (*sādhaj*). It is even better if you pound some [fresh] quince and extract

---

20 Cf. recipe 353 above for another version. As in a recipe in *Waṣf* 181, which is somewhat similar to this one, the amounts used call for one part of the quince boiling liquid, three parts of *jullāb* 'sugar syrup,' and 2 *ūqiyyas* (¼ cup) lemon juice.

21 See the end of recipe 360 below, for an explanation.

22 A similar recipe is found in *Wuṣla* ii 510. I here slightly amended the edited text based on *Wuṣla*.

23 The word قصبي is dialectical vocalization of قسبي 'hard and dry.'

24 Here I replaced *yaḥsun* (يحسن), which means 'looks good' with *Wuṣla's yujass* (يجس), 'to be touched,' as it is more relevant in this context.

25 Here I replaced the edited *bazrī* (بزري) with *Barzī* (برزي), which is a variety grown in Barza (a Damascene village), based on *Wuṣla*. See recipe 347 above. Based on this recipe, we learn that this quince variety is not dense.

and strain its juice, and add it to the sugar syrup. When you take the pot off the heat, season it with musk-flavored rosewater.[26]

(360) Recipe for *sharāb al-ḥummāḍ* (concentrated syrup for citron-pulp drink), from another copy[27]

Take pulp of citron (*ḥummāḍ al-utrujj*, *Citrus medica*) **(95v)** in the month of January (Ṭūba).[28] Extract its juice vesicles (*shuʿayrahu*) with a wooden knife,[29] and mix them with 1 *ūqiyya* (1 ounce) sugar to prevent them from turning bitter.

Put sugar syrup (*jullāb*) on the fire, skim its froth, and let it boil until it thickens. Add the citron pulp mentioned above to the [syrup mixture].[30] For each *raṭl* (2 pounds) [of the syrup] use 4 *ūqiyyas* (8 ounces) of the citron vesicles,[31] follow *jarwī* weight measures.[32]

When it is all well mixed and the syrup is thick enough, take the pot off the heat, and flavor it with musk, and store it in a container. Do not add the musk until you empty the syrup into a vessel, [and this should be done] while it is still hot.[33] [Otherwise,] if you leave the pot in the sun until it gets cold, it will be difficult [to empty the syrup], as it will be hard and stick to the sides of the pot. Do the same thing when you add the musk to the *laymūn safarjalī* (syrup for lemon-quince drink).

---

26 In addition, *Wuṣla* uses raw ambergris (*ʿanbar khām*), and *ʿūd Qāqulla*, also called *ʿūd Qāqullī*, which is an excellent variety of aromatic resinous twigs, see glossary 8, s.v. *ʿūd*.

27 Cf. recipe 352 above, for another version.

28 I.e., when they are completely ripe. Al-Anṭākī, *Tadhkira* 41, says that *utrujj* starts ripening at the end of November, when the sun reaches the ninth zodiac position of *al-qaws* (Sagittarius).

29 Al-Anṭākī, *Tadhkira* 208, observes that using a steel knife will cause fruit juice to flow easily.

30 Here I follow DK, n. 4858, where 'citron pulp' is more accurately written, rather than the edited 'quince.' The latter must have been a copyist's error.

31 Once again, the edited copy inserts the irrelevant 'quince' (سفرجل). In DK, the word occurs as سنغر, which I take as a misreading of شعير 'juice vesicles,' which also occurs as *shaʿr* (شعر), as in Baghdādī BL, fol. 22r.

32 Based on this medieval Egyptian weight measure, 1 *raṭl* = approx. 2 pounds, and *ūqiyya* = 2 ounces.

33 I have resolved the meaning here, following the recommendation given in recipe 358 above, where it states that musk is better added to the syrup after it is put in containers.

(361) Recipe for *sharāb al-laymūn al-sāʾil* (thin syrup for lemon drink)[34]

Put sugar syrup (*jullāb*) in a large brass pot (*dast*) after you clean it of any impurities [by adding water to it, boiling it, and skimming the froth from it]. Let it boil until it is concentrated [into a thin syrup]. Add enough lemon [juice] to give it a sweet-tart taste (*mazāza*), and store it away [in containers].

(362) Recipe for *sharāb al-tūt* (concentrated syrup for mulberry drink)

Take fully ripe mulberries, pound them in a mortar and strain the juice. For each *raṭl* (1 pound/2 cups) of sugar syrup (*jullāb*), use 4 *ūqiyya*s (½ cup) mulberry juice. [Let it boil] until it becomes thick enough.

(363) Recipe for *sharāb sakanjabīn jullābī* (concentrated syrup for oxymel drink, made with sugar syrup)[35]

Take (**96r**) sugar syrup (*jullāb*), which [has been boiled and] its froth skimmed off. While it is still on the fire add to it fine-tasting date vinegar (*khall al-tamr*), and keep cooking it until it thickens in consistency and tastes sweet and sour, and store it away.

Sakanjabīn buzūrī (made with fresh and dried herbs and seeds) is similarly made: Add *jullāb* and the extracted liquid of celery stalks (*aṣl al-karafs*), Macedonian parsley (*baqdūnis*), endives (*hindibāʾ*), and fresh fennel (*rāzyānaj akhḍar*), as well as a bit of dodder seeds (*bazr kashūth*). [To extract the liquids:] Pound them all, strain out the juice, and throw [the strained juice] into the *jullāb* while it is still cooking on the fire.

For each *raṭl* (pound) of *jullāb*, use 1 *ūqiyya* (1 ounce/2 tablespoons) of the liquid extracted from the ingredients.

(364) Recipe for *sharāb sakanjabīn rummānī* (concentrated syrup for oxymel drink made with pomegranate juice)

Take sour pomegranates. For each *raṭl* (pound) of sugar syrup (*jullāb*), use 4 *ūqiyya*s (½ cup) of pomegranate juice. Add the juice to the syrup while it is still [boiling] in a large brass pot (*dast*). Let it boil until it thickens, and then remove it.

---

34 Generally, *sāʾil* designates a fluid consistency.

35 See glossary 1, s.v. *sakanjabīn*. Cf. recipe 347 above, made with white sugar or honey.

FIGURE 37 *Endive, F1954.83v, Muḥammad al-Qazwīnī,* ʿAjāʾib al-makhlūqāt, *detail (Freer Gallery of Art and Arthur M. Sackler Gallery, Smithsonian Institution, Washington, DC: Purchase—Charles Lang Freer Endowment).*

(365) Recipe for *sharāb al-ḥiṣrim al-munaʿnaʿ* (concentrated syrup for drink of minted juice of unripe grapes)

Take sugar syrup (*jullāb*) after it has been dissolved [in water, boiled] and clarified [by skimming its froth], and extract the juice of sour unripe grapes (*ḥiṣrim*); use 4 *ūqiyyas* (½ cup) of it for each *raṭl* (pound) of syrup.

Take a bunch of fresh mint (*naʿnāʿ akhḍar*) and stir the syrup [mix] with it while it is cooking on the fire. If you wish, you can throw the mint bunch into the syrup pot, [and let it cook with the syrup mix] until all of its essence is released, and then remove it. Strain the syrup into a vessel [and store it away].

(366) Recipe for *sharāb al-tuffāḥ* (concentrated syrup for apple drink)

Take sugar syrup (*jullāb*) that has been clarified [by boiling it with added water and skimming its froth]. Also take fresh apples (*tuffāḥ akhḍar*).[36] Pound the apples, extract the juice and add it to the *jullāb* while it is still cooking on the fire. For each *raṭl* (pound) of *jullāb* (**96v**), use 4 *ūqiyyas* (½ cup) of the apple juice.

Sharāb al-safarjal (concentrated syrup for quince drink) is made the same way. Remove it from the fire when the syrup is thick enough.

---

36 *Akhḍar* (lit., 'green') also used to designate the state of being fresh, as opposed to being dry (*yābis*).

(367) Recipe for *sharāb al-ward* (concentrated syrup for rose drink)

Water is added [to the *jullāb* syrup] and then it is [boiled and] clarified by skimming the froth from it. For each *raṭl* (pound) of *jullāb*, throw in the petals of a hundred red roses. Let it boil until all its essence is released, and then strain it in a fine sieve. Return the strained syrup to the fire and let it boil until it becomes thick, and then remove.

When it is not the season of fresh roses, take dried Iraqi red roses, and leave them soaking in water overnight. After that, boil them very well, add the strained liquid to the *jullāb* syrup [and let it cook] until it is thick enough.

(368) Recipe for *sharāb al-ward al-mukarrar* (concentrated syrup for refined rosewater drink)[37]

Cut rose petals into small pieces (*yuqarraṭ*), discard their hypanthia (*aqmāʿ*), and put them in a green-glazed wide-mouthed jar (*barniyya*). Boil water very well, pour it into the *barniyya* and keep it covered for an hour.

Next, strain off the roses, boil the remaining liquid, and pour it into another *barniyya*, in which there are [more cut] rose petals. Repeat what you have just done with the first batch. This should be done three times.

Take the strained rose liquid and add it to sugar syrup (*jullāb*) while it is boiling on the fire. Let it cook until (**97r**) it is thick enough, and then remove it.

(369) Recipe for *sharāb laymūn safarjalī* (concentrated syrup for lemon-quince drink)[38]

[Take] one part quince juice, and three parts sugar syrup (*jullāb*). Let them boil with pieces of quince that you leave in the mixture until they are almost cooked and then take them out. [Set them aside].

Let the syrup boil until it thickens. Next, for each *raṭl* (pound) of the thickened syrup use 2 *ūqiyyas* (¼ cup) lemon juice. Return the quince pieces, and resume cooking until the syrup is thick enough. Season it with musk, saffron, and rosewater, and store it away, and use [as needed].

---

37 This recipe describes how to obtain refined rosewater (*māʾ ward mukarrar*), which should be differentiated from distilled rosewater (*māʾ ward muṣaʿʿad*), as in recipe 695 below, for instance. In Sābūr b. Sahl, *Dispensatory*, recipe 54 describes a similar preparation with specific amounts. In addition, the procedure is repeated up to ten times, and this results in more refined syrup.

38 *Waṣf* 181 has a similar recipe, which I used here to add a detail missing from the *Kanz* version.

(370) Recipe for *aqrāṣ al-laymūn* (lemon flavored hard candy drops), only good as *naql* (foods nibbled while imbibing alcoholic drinks)[39]

For each *raṭl* (pound) of sugar syrup (*jullāb*), which you leave to boil until it thickens, use [the juice of] a medium-size lemon, neither big nor small. [When the syrup boils down to a thick syrup,] beat it with a *dakshāb* (wooden paddle-like stirring utensil) until it looks white and then pour it into molds (*qawālib*).[40]

(371) Recipe for *ʿaqīd al-tamr Hindī* (chewy tamarind candy)

Take 1 *ūqiyya* (1 ounce) tamarind, soak it in water and strain the liquid. Add to it 2 *ūqiyyas* (2 ounces) sugar, and put it in a soapstone pot (*qidr birām*) on a low fire, that is, on smoldering embers (*nār jamr*). Continue stirring it until it reaches the consistency of chewy candy (*qiwām al-ʿaqīd*); this is the brittle state (*yaqṣuf*).[41] Store it in a *jurn* (marble bowl) that has been greased with almond oil.

(372) Recipe for *juwārish al-utrunj* (digestive stomachic of citron)

It is balanced (*muʿtadil*) regarding hot and dry properties. It sweetens the breath (*yuṭayyib al-nakha*), perfumes and strengthens the stomach, improves digestion, and repels winds (*yarudd al-riyāḥ*). It benefits people with cold humoral properties (*aṣḥāb al-amzāj al-bārida*), (**97v**) and breaks down phlegm (*balgham*). However, it is harmful for people whose humoral properties are naturally prone to heat (*aṣḥāb al-amzāj al-ḥārra*).[42]

To make it, take the outer *layer* of the *utrujj* rind, cut it into small pieces, and let it soak in water for 10 days, during which time, change the water once a day to get rid of the bitterness.

Drain the peel and cook it in water and honey—enough to submerge it—until it softens. Also, add mastic. [Next, transfer it into] a twig tray (*ṭabaq ʿīdān*) to drain the liquid,[43] and then cook the peel in bee honey, which has been [boiled, and its] froth skimmed. For each *raṭl* (pound) [of the peel], use 2 *raṭls* [of honey].

---

39 I.e., they have no significant restorative benefits. Lemon was believed to help slow intoxication and prevent hangovers. See recipe 377 below.

40 See recipe 266 above.

41 See recipe 266 above.

42 See glossary 11 for more on the medical terms.

43 Here I replaced the edited يتّصل, which is redundant in this context, with *yanṣul* (ينصل) 'drain.'

Sprinkle it with these aromatic spices (*afāwih*): black pepper, ginger, long pepper (*dār fulful*), cloves, nutmeg, spikenard, Ceylon cinnamon (*qarfa*), and cubeb (*kabāba*)—an equal amount of each; also add half the amount of aloeswood (*ʿūd*), and as much musk as you choose. Also, add enough saffron to color the mix—but first pound it, sift it, and then sprinkle it on [the citron peel mix]. Mix it all well, and store it away.

(373) Recipe for *juwārish al-tuffāḥ* (digestive stomachic of apple)

It is temperate (*muʿtadil*) [in properties]. It sweetens the breath, scents the stomach, invigorates digestion, induces euphoria (*yufarriḥ al-qalb*), and disperses vapors (*yuzīl al-bukhār*). It is beneficial to people whose humoral properties are naturally prone to heat (*aṣḥāb al-amzāj al-ḥārra*).

To make it, take aromatic sweet-sour apples, peel them, cut them into pieces, and remove the seeds. Add to them enough rosewater, vinegar, and borage water (*māʾ lisān al-thawr*) to submerge them.

Cook the apples in an earthenware or soapstone pot until all the moisture is gone, (**98r**) and then put them in a wooden *qaṣʿa* (large wide bowl) and mash them thoroughly. Next, cook them with sugar syrup (*jullāb*) until the mix thickens.

Sprinkle on it aloeswood, spikenard, and saffron, one part of each—pound them and sift them first, and then add them to it.

(374) *Juwārish al-safarjal* (digestive stomachic of quince)

It is temperate in properties (*muʿtadil*), it fortifies the stomach, stimulates the appetite, strengthens the nerves, and aids good digestion (*istimrāʾ*). It enhances the complexion (*yuḥassin al-bashara*), and curbs bowel movements (*yaḥbis al-ṭabʿ*).

To make it, take choice quince (*safarjal mukhtār*), peel it and then cut it with a blunt knife (*sikkīn ghayr ḥadīd*), discard the seeds, and put it in an earthenware or soapstone *dast* (large pot). Add enough juice of unripe sour grapes and rosewater to submerge it. Boil the pot until the quince is cooked and the liquid evaporates.

Put the quince in a wooden *qaṣʿa* (large wide bowl), mash it, and return it to the pot after you wash it. Let the quince cook and thicken with bee honey, which has been [boiled and] skimmed of its froth; use equal amounts of both. When it is thick enough, mix with it these spices (*afāwih*): tamarisk seeds (*ʿadhba*), ajowan (*nānkhawāh*), cumin of Kirman (*kammūn Kirmānī*),[44] spikenard, Ceylon cinnamon (*qarfa*), mastic, saffron, Indian aloeswood (*ʿūd Hindī*),

44 This was fine-tasting black cumin named after the Persian city of Kirman.

cubeb, and aniseeds (*anīsūn*), in equal amounts. Pound and sift the spices and then use them.

When it is all done, spread it on a slab of marble, cut it into small pieces (*shawābīr*) and wrap (*yukaffan*) each (98v) in a citron leaf. Pack them in glass vessels, and use as needed.

(375) Recipe for *juwārish al-muthallath* (digestive stomachic made with three main ingredients)[45]

It is temperate in properties (*muʿtadil*), induces euphoria (*yufarriḥ al-qalb*), sweetens the breath, strengthens the stomach, induces good digestion, stimulates the appetite, improves the mood (*yuḥassin al-akhlāq*), gives the face a glow, clears the mind (*yuṣaffī al-dhihn*), and restores the balance of the humoral properties (*yuʿaddil al-ṭabʿ*). It is beneficial to people suffering from excess in black bile humor (*aṣḥāb al-mālīkhūlyā*).

To make it, take apples, quince, and rose-petal conserve (*ward murabbā*), one part of each. Cut the apples and quince into pieces after you peel them, and discard the seeds. Put them in a soapstone or earthenware pot, and cover them with equal amounts of rosewater, juice of sour unripe grapes, borage water (*māʾ lisān al-thawr*), vinegar, and aged wine (*sharāb ʿatīq*).

Cook the fruits on low heat until all the liquid is gone, and then put them in a stone or wooden vessel, add to them rose-petal conserve, and mix them all. Pound them all with a stone pestle (*mihrāsh*)[46] until they turn to mush, and return them to the pot. Add what equals their weight of [already cooked and] thickened sugar syrup (*jullāb*), and stir [and cook] until the *juwārish* is thick enough.

Sprinkle on it whatever you choose of the *afāwih*, depending on the eaters' humoral properties (*amzija*), such as aloeswood, Ceylon cinnamon (*qarfa*), mint, saffron, and musk, and whatever varieties of aromatic spices (*ṭīb*) you choose (99r).

(376) Recipe for *juwārish al-jazar* (digestive stomachic of carrot)

It is hot in properties, beneficial to people with cold humoral properties and ailing bodies. It invigorates coitus (*yuqawwī al-bāh*), aids digestion, and breaks down phlegm. However, it is harmful for people with hot humoral properties and excessively hot livers (*akbād multahiba*).

45 Namely, apple, quince, and rose-petal conserve.

46 A dialectical vocalization of *mihrās*.

To make it, take fresh and tender red carrots (*jazar aḥmar*), wash them, scrape their [peels], and chop them as small as you can. Throw them into a soapstone or earthenware pot, and add a bit of honey, and enough water to submerge them. Cook the pot until the carrot wilts, and then drain it thoroughly in a sieve.

[Return the carrot to the pot and] add to it what equals its amount of bee honey, which has been [boiled and] skimmed of its froth. Let it cook [and thicken] until it has the consistency of *juwārish*, and then mix in these spices: black pepper, long pepper, ginger, green cardamom (*hāl*), Ceylon cinnamon (*qarfa*), cubeb, spikenard, mace (*basbāsa*), galangal (*khūlanjān*), aloeswood, saffron, and as much musk as you choose.

Store it in a glass vessel, and use it whenever needed. It is very good.

(377) Recipe for *juwārish al-laymūn* (digestive stomachic of lemon)

It is moderately hot in properties, leaning more toward dryness. It is the most beneficial of all the *juwārishnāt*: it sweetens the breath, strengthens the gums, prevents bad breath (*bakhar*), stops the urge to clear the throat (*nuḥūḥa*), removes the brackish taste [of phlegm] in the mouth, and clears the voice. It perfumes the stomach, (**99v**) excites the appetite, alleviates nausea, restrains vomiting, aids good digestion, curbs yellow bile, breaks down phlegm, clears the blood, resists black bile, protects from poisons, strengthens the heart, brings about euphoric feelings, and makes the face look radiantly clean. It slows down intoxication (*sukr*) and is beneficial for hangovers (*khumār*). It opens blockages, dissipates winds, stimulates the sexual appetite, and strengthens the loins. However, it is harmful for people with hot humoral properties (*amzija ḥārra*).

To make it, choose yellow Chinese lemons (*laymūn Ṣīnī aṣfar*), wrap each lemon with fermented dough, arrange them in a copper tray or an earthenware frying pan, then put them on the floor of the *tannūr* (open-topped, bell-shaped clay oven). When the dough bakes and looks golden brown (*yatawarrad*), take the trays out. Wait until they cool down, and then discard the dough, slice the lemons, remove their seeds, and pound them in a stone mortar (*jurn ḥajar*) until the skins mash and mingle with the pulp. Set them aside.

Next, dissolve sugar in rosewater; use double the amount of lemon, by weight (*bi-waznihi*). Boil the sugar, skim its froth, and continue cooking it until it reaches a brittle consistency.[47] Throw in [the lemon] you have prepared, and continue stirring the soapstone pot (*birām*) until it has the [thick] consistency of *juwārish*.

---

47 See n. 4 above.

Sprinkle on it pounded and sifted spices (*ḥawāʾij*), (**100r**), namely, Ceylon cinnamon (*qarfa*), cloves (*qaranful*), long pepper (*dār fulful*), nutmeg (*jawzat ṭīb*), spikenard (*sunbul*), cubeb (*kabāba*), Indian leaf (*sādhaj Hindī*), mace (*basbāsa*), green cardamom (*hāl*), galangal (*khulanjān*), aniseeds (*anīsūn*),[48] ajowan (*nānkhawāh*), *kammūn Kirmānī*,[49] aloeswood (*ʿūd*), and saffron—use an equal amount of each.

Scent it with whatever musk you choose, and store it in glass vessels, and use whenever needed.

(378) Recipe for *juwārish al-ʿūd* (digestive stomachic of aloeswood)[50]

Take 2 *mithqāl*s (9 grams) rosebuds (*ward azrār*) with their hypanthia (*aqmāʿ*) removed. Also, take *sunbul ʿaṣāfīrī* (Indian spikenard), cloves (*kibāsh qaranful*), green cardamom (*hāl*), and nutmeg (*jawz ṭīb*), 1 *mithqāl* (4½ grams) of each; mastic gum (*masṭakāʾ*/*maṣṭakā*), Indian aloeswood (*ʿūd Hindī*)—2 *dirhams* (6 grams) of each. Also add black cardamom (*qāqulla*) and *tabashir*[51]—1 *mithqāl* (4½ grams) of each; as well as wild nard (*asārūn*) and Ceylon sandalwood (*ṣandal Maqāṣīrī*)—1 *dirham* of each (3 grams).

Finely pound all of these spices and knead them with honey, which has been boiled and its froth skimmed; and sugar syrup (*jullāb*), use an equal amount of each. Add enough [honey and sugar syrup] to give the mix the consistency of *juwārish* [i.e., a thick and chewy texture]. Store it away, and [when needed] use ½ *dirham* (¼ teaspoon) to 1 *dirham* of it.

(379) Recipe for *juwārish al-ʿanbar* (digestive stomachic of ambergris)

It heats up the stomach, perfumes it, and dissipates cold and dense winds. Take green cardamom (*hāl*), cassia (*dār Ṣīnī*), long pepper (*dār fulful*), and nutmeg (*jawz ṭīb*)—1 *dirham* (3 grams/½ teaspoon) of each. Also use wild nard (*asārūn*), cloves (*qaranful*), saffron (*zaʿfarān*)—½ *dirham* of each; ambergris, and musk-scented pastilles (*sukk misk*)—2 *dānaq*s (1 gram) of each; (**100v**) and 1 *raṭl* (1 pound) of Egyptian sugar.

Follow the method used to make *juwārishnāt*.[52]

---

48 It also occurs in DK, n. 5064 as *yānsūn*.

49 A variety of cumin named after the Persian city of Kirman.

50 *Waṣf* 180 has a similar recipe, which I used here to fill in some missing details.

51 *Ṭabāshīr* are loose lumps of chalky porous silica, deposited in the stem cavities of reeds and bamboo.

52 As was done in the above recipes.

(380) Recipe for *juwārish al-kammūn* (digestive stomachic of cumin)
It disintegrates dense abdominal winds, improves digestion, and disintegrates winds and phlegm, which cause colic (*qawlanj*). It also induces a mild diarrhea (*ishāl khafīf*) and helps food descend gently from the stomach. It is beneficial in cases of acid belching, and drives away the harms of foods that have cold and dense properties.

Take 100 *dirhams* (10½ ounces) *kammūn Kirmānī* (fine-tasting wild cumin), which has been soaked in wine vinegar. Also take ginger, black pepper, dried leaves of rue (*sadhāb*)—30 *dirhams* (3 ounces) of each; and 10 *dirhams* (1 ounce) of Armenian sodium borate (*būraq Armanī*).

Pound all the ingredients, sift them, and then knead them with three times their weight of bee honey, which has been [boiled and] skimmed of its froth. Store it away. A single dose of it is 4 to 7 *dirhams* (12 to 21 grams/2 to 3½ teaspoons).

(381) Recipe for *maʿjūn al-nāranj* (electuary of sour oranges)
Take orange peels; soak them in salted water for 10 days, change the water once or twice daily, so that they are no longer bitter. Boil them in water until they are utterly free of any bitterness.

Cut the peels into pieces, each the size of a fava bean, and press out all their moisture. For each *mann* (2 pounds) of orange peels use 2 *manns* (4 pounds) of honey. Boil the honey (**101r**) until it has the consistency of the concentrated syrup for the lemon drink (*sharāb al-laymūn*),[53] and throw in the peels. Boil the mix until it becomes noticeably thick. Add to it as much saffron and other spices and herbs (*afāwih*) as needed.

If you want to keep the peels of the oranges whole,[54] then cut out their stem ends—keep the stems attached, [set them aside]. [Keep the oranges intact, but] empty out their pulp. Soak the peels in salted water until they are free of any bitterness, change the salted water [as above]. Boil the peels in water, and keep them exposed to the air to dry.

Prepare *ḥall al-sukkar* (sugar syrup), and let it boil until it has the consistency of the concentrated syrup for lemon drink (*qiwām sharāb al-laymūn*).[55] Throw in the whole peels, and continue boiling the syrup until it is thick again. Take the peels out, and let them air dry.

53 See, for instance, recipes 353, 357, and 358.
54 As prepared below, they will look like candied stuffed oranges.
55 See n. 53 above.

Now take the sugar [syrup] again and make *juwārish al-nāranj* (digestive stomachic of sour orange),[56] adding to it diced orange peels, and spices and herbs as well. Fill the [intact] orange peels with this *juwārish*, and close their openings with the ends that were cut out.

Make *ḥall* (sugar syrup) for it; let it boil until it thickens and has the consistency of *aqrāṣ sharāb al-laymūn* (syrup for hard candy lemon drops),[57] and then stir and pull it (*yuqṣar*) using a *dakshāb* (wooden paddle-like stirring utensil) until it looks white, and then coat the [prepared] *nāranj* with it.

(382) Recipe for *maʿjūn al-zanjabīl al-mahzūl* (soft electuary of ginger)[58]

Take pure honey, boil it until it reaches the brittle stage,[59] and then place the pot on the floor.

[Take dried ginger, briefly soak it, and remove the skins],[60] dry it, [and pound it]. For each *mann* (2 pounds) of it, use 10 *manns* (20 pounds) honey. [Mix it well] and pour the honey mixture on a *bilāṭa* (large flat tile) that has been (**101v**) greased with sesame oil. Let it cool, and then hang it on a large nail (*mismār*) and pull it as you do with pulled-taffy (*nāṭif*).[61] Store it in bowls.[62]

(383) [*Maʿjūn ʿūd* (electuary of aloeswood)]

If you want to make ***maʿjūn al-ʿūd*** (electuary of aloeswood), boil sugar syrup until it reaches the brittle stage (*qiwām al-sukkar al-qaṣif*).[63] Remove the pot from the fire and add the spice [i.e., aloeswood]. Pull it [as in the recipe above] until it starts to firm up (*yathbut*). Spread it on a *bilāṭa* (large flat tile) greased with sesame oil. Cut it into pieces (*yuqaṭṭaʿ*), [and store it away, and use as needed].

(384) Recipe for *maʿjūn al-zanjabīl al-maqṣūṣ* (electuary of [reconstituted and] diced ginger)

Take a bowl (*zibdiyya*) filled with water, and throw in [dried] ginger [rhizomes]. Take them out quickly and peel them. After that, keep them in water for five

56 See recipe 372 for a similar preparation.

57 As in recipe 349.

58 *Mahzūl* designates someone who is gaunt and emaciated. However, it is also used metaphorically to designate a thin and soft consistency.

59 *Yaqṣuf*, see recipe 266 above.

60 Here I provide the missing detail based on the opening sentence in recipe 384 below.

61 See recipe 265 above, n. 2. Also, see glossary 4, s.v. *fānīdh*.

62 *Aḥqāq*, sg. *ḥuqq*, are round bowls made of carved wood, ivory, or other materials. Since the preparation is soft and does not keep its shape if cut into pieces, it is stored as one mass.

63 See recipe 266 above.

days, until they soften. Slice the ginger thinly and dice it finely. Return it to the water and keep it there for two more days, and then take it out. Place it in a *qinnīna* (bowl made of woven esparto grass),[64] squeeze out its moisture, and then weigh it down with stones [to drain all the remaining moisture].

Dissolve sugar [in water] to make syrup (*ḥall*) for it, for each *mann* (2 pounds) of the ginger use one *mann* of sugar. Throw in the ginger before the syrup starts to thicken, and continue cooking it on low heat until the syrup has the consistency of the thin syrup [used] for making lemon drink (*sharāb al-laymūn al-raqīq*). Remove the pot [from the fire], but keep the ginger in it for a whole day, so that it may absorb as much as possible of the syrup and swell (*yarbub*).

Return the pot to the fire. For each *mann* of ginger used, add one *mann* of honey. Let the pot boil until it has the consistency of the ginger [electuary], which is similar to the consistency of thick syrup for making lemon drink (*sharāb al-laymūn al-qawī*).

Take the pot off the heat, (**102r**) and using a *dakshāb* (wooden paddle-like stirring utensil), whip the syrup in the pot itself, and then fill the bowls (*aḥqāq*) with it.

(385) Recipe for *maʿjūn al-kammūn* (electuary of cumin)

Take honey, boil it on the fire, and have the spices and herbs (*afāwih*) ready for it, namely, for each *mann* (2 pounds) of honey, use 10 *dirhams* (1 ounce/30 grams) cumin, and 20 *dirhams* of *afāwih* [spices and herbs].[65]

Let the honey boil until it reaches the brittle stage (*yaqṣuf*) or just a bit less [i.e., before this stage].[66] Take the pot off the heat, add the spices, and store it away in a container.

(386) Recipe for electuary of *al-jazar al-barrī* (wild carrot), which is *shaqāqul* (parsnip)

Take parsnips, slice them and put them in an earthenware jar with some water. Close the opening of the jar and leave it overnight in [the remaining heat of] the *furn* (brick oven). The following day, take the jar out, strain off any remaining water in the jar, and thoroughly mash the parsnips with a marble pestle (*mihrās rukhām*). Squeeze the mashed parsnip very well [to get rid of extra moisture, and set aside].

---

64 See glossary 9.1 for the different types of this vessel.

65 Based on recipe 391 below, these are cloves, green cardamom, spikenard, cassia, ginger, and saffron.

66 See recipe 266 above.

Put honey [in a pot] on the fire. For each *mann* (2 pounds) of parsnips use 2 *manns* (4 pounds) of honey. Boil the honey until it has the consistency of thick syrup used in making lemon drink (*sharāb al-laymūn al-qawī*). Add the parsnips. Continue stirring until [the mix] becomes thick enough, and then remove.

Prepare some pounded ginger; for each *mann* (2 pounds) of parsnips, use 5 *dirhams* (15 grams/2½ teaspoons) ginger. Also, stir in chopped almonds, which have been scalded and skinned.

(387) Recipe for *maʿjūn al-jazar* (electuary of carrot)

Take carrots, peel them, grate them (*yuḥakk*), and then squeeze out the extra moisture very well. Now take honey; for each *mann* (2 pounds) [of carrot] use 2½ *manns* (5 pounds) honey.

Let the honey boil slightly on the fire and then remove it. Now take the carrots (**102v**) after they have been squeezed, and put them in a large brass pot (*dast*) without adding any water. Let them dry out a little and add the honey to them. Continue cooking the pot until the syrup is thick enough, and then remove it and add the spices (*afāwih*) to it.[67]

(388) Recipe for *maʿjūn al-naʿnāʿ* (electuary of mint)

Take sugar, and boil it on the fire [with honey]. For each ½ *mann* (1 pound) of sugar add 1 *mann* (2 pounds) of honey. Mix it and boil it well with the sugar, until the syrup is thick enough.

Throw in crumbled [dried] mint,[68] and continue boiling the syrup, while moistening it with a bit of vinegar every now and then, until the mint [electuary] reaches the right consistency [i.e., very thick]. Take the pot off the heat after you throw the spices (*afāwih*) into it.[69] Store it away.

(389) Recipe for *maʿjūn al-fujl* (electuary of radishes)

Chop [the radishes], boil them, mash them, and squeeze out [the extra moisture] very well. Take honey for it; for each *mann* (2 pounds) [of radishes] use 2 *manns* [of honey].

---

67 See n. 65 above.

68 The verb *mafrūk* (rubbed between the fingers and crumbled) clearly indicates that dried mint should be used.

69 See n. 65 above.

Boil the honey on the fire until it has the consistency of *sharāb al-laymūn* (thick syrup for a lemon drink). Add the squeezed radishes, and cook them on low heat until the syrup is quite thick. Throw the spices (*afāwih*) into it,[70] and store it away.

(390) Recipe for *maʿjūn al-maṣṭakā'* (electuary of mastic gum)

Take sugar, dissolve it in water, and boil it on the fire until it thickens.[71] [Add crushed mastic gum],[72] and continue boiling it until it thickens very well. Pour it onto a large flat tile (*bilāṭa*), wiped [with rosewater], (**103r**), and cut it into pieces.

(391) Recipe for *maʿjūn al-safarjal* (electuary of quince)

Take quince, slice it, discard the seeds, and cut it to resemble the taro (*qulqās*) used in making the *Mutawakkiliyya* dish.[73] Put the quince on the fire with enough water to cover it. Boil it until it is cooked, and then drain it and finely pound it in a mortar. Pass it through a fine sieve.

Now take bee honey, which has been [boiled and] skimmed of its froth. Throw the quince mentioned above into it, and boil it on the fire until it is very thick. Season it with *afāwih* (aromatic spices), namely, cloves, green cardamom, spikenard, cassia (*dār Ṣīnī*), ginger, and saffron. And God knows best.

---

70 See n. 65 above.

71 The rest of the recipe is somewhat confused and missing some steps. With the help of the alternative readings given in DK, notes, 5251–5, I try to straighten the text.

72 Here DK adds a somewhat incoherent instruction, which obviously deals with amounts:
ويكون لكل منّ ورق عشرة مصحونة.
It may be amended to ويكون لكل منّ دوانق عشرة مصحونة.
which translates to, 'For each *mann* (2 pounds) let there be 10 *dānaq*s (5 grams), crushed.' In this case, the former refers to sugar syrup, and the latter to mastic.

73 I.e., the quince should be cut into finger shapes. The type of taro referred to here is called *qulqās aṣābiʿ*, see recipe 69 above.

CHAPTER 12

في عمل الفقّاع وغيره

Making *fuqqāʿ* (Foamy Beer),[1] and Other Drinks[2]

Know that *fuqqāʿ* made with ground malted barley (*daqīq al-shaʿīr*) is harmful to the nerves and causes headaches and flatulence.[3] It is diuretic. It abates excessive heat generated by fever, and subdues yellow bile (*al-ṣafrāʾ*). It cures excessive heat in the stomach.

Fuqqāʿ made with *khubz ḥuwwārā* (bread made with white bran-free flour) and seasoned with mint (*naʿnāʿ*), common parsley (*karafs*), tarragon (*ṭarkhūn*), and rue (*sadhāb*) is better than *fuqqāʿ* made with ground malted barley. However, it is not recommended for people with excessively hot properties (*maḥrūrīn*) or those suffering from fevers (*maḥmūmīn*).

(392) Recipe for making *fuqqāʿ khāṣṣ* (excellent foamy beer)[4]

Take ½ *raṭl* (½ pound) bee honey, (**103v**) 1 raṭl sugar, and 5 *raṭl*s (5 pints) water. Also add 1 *ūqiyya* (1 ounce) [dried] pomegranate seeds (*ḥabb rummān*). Mix in 3 *ūqiyyas* (3 ounces) hot bread, and mash all the ingredients very well. Squeeze in some lime juice, and then strain the mix, and season it with aromatic spices (*ṭīb*), most of which should be nutmeg. Also, add a lump of musk (*ḥabbat misk*). Pour it into the *fuqqāʿ* jars (*kīzān*, sg. *kūz*), and keep them submerged in cold water [to prevent fermentation] for a day, or overnight until it is ready to drink.

1 The beer and similar drinks prepared in this chapter are non-alcoholic, as they only ferment lightly overnight or for a day. Drinks fermented for no more than three days are permissible in Islam.

2 The opening statement of this chapter is almost identical with al-Warrāq's chapter 112, which indicates that both drew on similar sources. I have recently discovered that ultimately, both al-Warrāq's book and the *Kanz* drew on copies of al-Rāzī's *Kitāb al-Manṣūrī* fol. 19r from his section on the properties of non-intoxicating drinks (في قوة الاشربة غير المسكرة). Here I amended the text based on that and al-Warrāq's better-copied version.

3 A recipe for making malted ground barley is provided in al-Warrāq, English trans. *Annals* 454.

4 *Zahr*, fol. 22v, includes this recipe, which I used here to amend the edited text slightly.

 | DOI 10.1163/9789004349919_015

(393) Another recipe for *fuqqāʿ* (foamy beer)

For each *kūz* [of water],[5] soak 1 *dirham* (3 grams) dried pomegranate seeds. Press and mash them in the evening (*ʿashiyya*), and add 10 *dirhams* (1 ounce) sugar. Season it with sprigs of rue and mint and flavor it with musk and rosewater. Pour it into jars (*kīzān*), [tightly close their mouths] and turn them over.[6] [Leave it overnight, and use the drink the following morning].

(394) Another Recipe: *fuqqāʿ shaʿīrī madhkhūr* (foamy beer with malted barley, stored [by replenishing it repeatedly])[7]

Sprout barley (*yubaqqal*), and then dry it and crush it. Add wheat flour (*daqīq al-ḥinṭa*) to it—use twice as much, by bulk measurement (*bi-l-kayl*). Put them in a *khābiya* (large earthenware jar).

Now take a large pot and boil water in it, let it boil vigorously, and then pour it into the jar. Cover the jar so that no steam escapes. Boil another batch of water and pour it into the jar. Repeat until the jar is full to the brim, cover it, and set it aside for 3 days, and then uncover it. You will find the liquid has turned into clear water.

Take whatever you wish from it [and put it in a small jar], and chop some mint into it; squeeze some lemon juice for it; and throw in chopped rue, (**104r**) a small amount of [dried] pomegranate seeds; and lemon peel. Leave it overnight, and the following morning, sweeten it with sugar, raisins, or date syrup, and drink it.

As for the *khābiya* [the large jar, where the rest remains], pour cold water into it, equal to the same amount you took from it, so that it becomes full once again. Continue taking and replenishing until you notice that what was settled in the bottom has surfaced to the top. At this point you need to make a new batch altogether, because this one has been depleted of all its essence (*khāṣṣiyya*).

---

5 The *kūz* has a capacity of 18 cups.

6 In the edited text, the word occurs as *yukabbab*, a variant of *yukabb* (from كبب 'to put something on its face'). The jars are arranged in tubs and sprinkled with water. See the end of recipe 422 below, for similar directions.

7 The same recipe is found in *Waṣf* 189–190; and *Wuṣla* ii 505. I used both versions to amend a few details in the edited recipe.

(395) Another recipe for *fuqqāʿ* (foamy beer)[8]

Soak a [piece of] hot bread in 2½ *ūqiyyas* (5 tablespoons) rosewater. Add to it [later,] ½ *raṭl Miṣrī* (½ pound) sugar,[9] 10 *dirhams* (1 ounce) crushed rock salt (*milḥ Andarānī*), and 1½ *raṭls* (3 cups) sweet-sour pomegranate juice, or sour pomegranate and quince [juices].

Mash the bread with water, strain the liquid, and mix it with the juices and the sugar [and salt]. Throw in spikenard, mastic, nutmeg, black pepper, ginger, and a bit of saffron. Let it ferment (*yukhammar*) and use it.[10]

(396) Another recipe for *fuqqāʿ* (foamy beer)[11]

Take 3 *ūqiyyas* (3 ounces) sugar and a similar amount of [dried] pomegranate seeds; 3 *dirhams* (1½ teaspoons) *aṭrāf ṭīb* (spice blend); and 3 *dirhams* black pepper, *lisān ʿuṣfūr* (fruit of Syrian ash), and ginger; 3 *ūqiyyas* (¼ cup) rosewater, and 1 *qīrāṭ* (¼ gram) musk.

Steep the pomegranate seeds in 1 *raṭl* (2 cups) water, and press and mash them until all of their essence is released into the water. Strain the resulting liquid in a fine-meshed sieve (*ghirbāl daqīq*).

Dissolve the sugar in 1 *raṭl* (2 cups) water. Pound the black pepper (**104v**) in a *ṣallāya*,[12] sift it and tie it in a piece of cloth along with the rest of the spices, all crushed and sifted. Also, add to the bundle 10 lumps of *kaʿk* (dry cookies),[13] or crumbs of bread made with *ḥuwwārā* flour (white bran-free flour).[14] All of it should be crushed and tied in a bundle (*ṣurra*).

Now mix the sugar solution with the pomegranate liquid, and dip and press the bundle in them so that they [i.e., spices and bread] release all their essence.

---

8 This recipe is also found in *Wuṣla* ii 505 (*Waṣf* 190 gives only the first half of the recipe). In both cases, the recipe is named *fuqqāʿ jayyid* 'good beer.' In addition, it is repeated in recipe 409 below, with minor differences. I amended the edited text based on the *Wuṣla* and the *Waṣf*.

9 The version in the *Waṣf* uses the Baghdadi *raṭl*, which is little bit lighter than the Egyptian one.

10 Judging from the rest of the recipes, the duration of the fermentation is brief.

11 A similar recipe can be found in *Wuṣla* ii 506, where it is called *fuqqāʿ khāṣṣ* 'excellent beer.' Here I used it to amend the edited text. In addition, recipes 398 and 399 below, both named *fuqqāʿ khāṣṣ*, are duplicates of this one, with very minor stylistic differences and few misreadings and omissions. All are used to render a comprehensive recipe of this kind of beer.

12 This is a wide stone slab that was used with a large stone (called *fihr*), to crush spices and aromatics.

13 See, for instance, recipes in chapter 2 above.

14 See glossary 2 for more on this kind of flour.

Throw in half the amount of rosewater and musk, and empty the liquid into jars with traces of previous fermentation (*kīzān ḍāriya*).[15] Throw in sprigs of rue (*sadhāb*) and top the jars with the remaining rosewater and musk. Do not fill the jars to the top; you need to leave some empty space [to allow for fermentation]. Leave the jars for a short period and [then] use. It is wonderful.

(397) Another [*fuqqāʿ*] recipe

Take hot bread and soak it in water, as much as needed—use ½ *raṭl* (1 cup), less or more [depending on how much you need]. Add to it ½ *raṭl* (½ pound) sugar, 10 *dirhams* (5 teaspoons) clean rock salt (*milḥ Andarānī*), and 1½ *raṭls* (3 cups) pomegranate juice, either sweet-sour (*muzz*) or sour (*ḥāmiḍ*).

Press and mash the bread in water, [add pomegranate juice] and strain the mix. Add to the [resulting] liquid a bit of excellent spikenard (*al-sunbul al-ṭayyib*),[16] mastic gum, nutmeg, black pepper, and thyme. Also add chopped rue—the amount should be in proportion to the pomegranate juice used. Let it ferment for a day and a night, after which it can be chilled [with ice] and imbibed.

Some people choose to make it with lemon juice rather than pomegranate juice; while others make it with sugar; use whatever is available. (**105r**) However, if pomegranate juice is not available, soaked [dried] seeds of pomegranate of Ṣuḥār may be used.[17]

Pomegranate *fuqqāʿ* extinguishes heat and alleviates thirst. It is beneficial to people whose dominant humor is yellow bile, and those with fevers. Some people make it with ground malted barley (*daqīq al-shaʿīr*), but this is wrong and should be avoided whenever possible because it causes many harms besides the ones we mentioned [at the beginning of the chapter].

(398) Recipe for *fuqqāʿ khāṣṣ* (excellent beer)

[This is a duplicate of recipe 396. See n. 11 above] (**105v**)

(399) Recipe for *fuqqāʿ khāṣṣ* (excellent beer)

[This is a duplicate of recipe 396. See n. 11 above]

---

15 See recipes 407 and 418 below, for directions on how to do this with new jars.

16 This occurs more commonly as *sunbul al-ṭīb*, which is Indian spikenard, see, for instance, recipe 400 below.

17 In the edited text, it occurs as *ḥabb al-rummān al-Suḥārī*, [dried] pomegranate seeds from Suḥār. It is a dialectical vocalization of Ṣuḥār, the Kasbah of Oman.

(400) Recipe for *fuqqāʿ* made with pomegranate juice (*māʾ al-rummān*)

Take 10 pomegranates, either sweet-sour or sour. Take their seeds and press their juice into a *qinnīna* (bowl made of woven esparto grass),[18] or a green-glazed wide-mouthed jar (*barniyya*). Throw in a bunch of (**106r**) angelica (*karafs Nabaṭī*), a bunch of rue, a bunch of mint, and a bunch of tarragon [all fresh]. Pound one sprig of Indian spikenard (*sunbul al-ṭīb*), and 5 cloves; add them, all pounded. Also, add a bit of musk—use half a lump or even less, and throw in sugar.

Cover the opening completely with a clean, tightly woven piece of cloth or paper (*kāghad*) to prevent the aromas from escaping from the vessel. Set it aside from early in the morning, and through the night to the following morning. It is very delicious.

(401) Recipe for *aqsimā* (digestive drink)[19]

Take a vessel with traces of previous fermentation in it (*wiʿāʾ ḍārī*),[20] and put crumbs (*lubāb*) of white *kumāj* bread in it.[21] Pour in hot water and a bit of beer yeast (*khamīr al-fuqqāʿ*),[22] and set it aside overnight. Early in the morning, stir the liquid ever so gently so that you do not mash the bread or even touch it at all.

Pour the clear liquid [only] into a fine-meshed *rāwūq* (strainer for liquids) [and set it on a vessel]. Sweeten it with sugar and add rue, mint, and *aṭrāf al-ṭīb* (spice blend), using only the spices specially used for *aqsimā*, namely ginger, green cardamom (*hāl*), and a tiny amount of cloves; other than these three, the spices of *aṭrāf al-ṭīb* will darken the *aqsimā* color. Add rosewater.

Now, remove the bread from the vessel with traces of fermentation in it, [the one] first used; and return the *aqsimā* liquid to it. Set it aside until it starts to ferment (*yaṭlaʿ*), and [then] use it.

---

18 This vessel is described in Dozy, *Takmilat al-maʿājim* 1296. It is so tightly woven that it is waterproof. *Qinnīna*, as used in this recipe, cannot be a regular narrow-necked glass bottle.

19 An Egyptian variety of beer, like *fuqqāʿ* but a bit more fermented, sweet, and usually offered after the meal to aid digestion; by contrast, *fuqqāʿ* was imbibed on an empty stomach. This recipe is also found in *Wuṣla* ii 509–10, with slight stylistic differences.

20 See n. 15 above.

21 It is white bread, shaped into discs that are thicker than flat breads, and spongy and pithy in texture. They are baked in the commercial *furn* 'brick oven.'

22 In *Wuṣla* ii 509, it is beer yeast from *fuqqāʿ khāṣṣ* 'excellent beer.' For this beer, see recipe 392 above. Beer yeast was most probably what now is called top-fermenting yeast; it is obtained by skimming the yeast-rich froth that gathers at the surface of beer during the first days of fermentation.

For those who are in a place where [fresh] bread is not available, they can use pounded *baqsamāṭ* (dried cookies/biscotti), (**106v**) or cook thin *ḥarīra* (flour-based soup) using fine white flour (*daqīq muthallath*).[23]

(402) Recipe for *khamīrat aqsimā* (distilled *aqsimā*-base for making instant digestive drinks)[24]

Take mint and *aṭrāf al-ṭīb* (spice blend).[25] Pluck the leaves from the mint sprigs, and finely pound the spices. Steep them overnight in distilled water of the bark of Egyptian willow (*māʾ al-khilāf*) and Syrian rosewater (*māʾ al-ward al-Shāmī*).[26] Early in the morning, add enough vinegar to it [to submerge the leaves] and put it in a cucurbit (*qarʿa*), which should be tilted downward a little (*munakkas*). Set the alembic (*inbīq*) on its [opening], and put the receiving receptacle (*qābila*) [at its end, and start distilling it on a very low heat].[27]

Store the distilled liquid in a glass bottle (*qinnīna*), and whenever you want to make an *aqsimā* drink, dissolve sugar in water [in a vessel], squeeze some lemon juice into it, and add a bit of rue and mint leaves and rub them in [to release their flavors]. Mix in a very small amount of the distilled liquid, and you will have a delicious *aqsimā* drink, which can be immediately imbibed.

(403) Recipe for *aqsimā* (digestive drink)

Pick over barley grains, wash them, and then soak them in water for a whole day. Spread the grains in a vessel; cover them with chard leaves weighed down with stones. Check on them day after day, sprinkling them with a bit of water, until they sprout (*yanbut*). Take them from the vessel and let them dry out in a shaded place.

When the grains are dry, take 4 *ūqiyyas* (4 ounces) and finely grind them. Sprinkle the ground barley with water until it has the consistency of ointment (*marham*). Add to it 2 *ūqiyyas* (2 ounces) excellent [wheat] flour. Boil for it 2 *raṭls* (4 cups) water—let it boil well—and dissolve the barley paste in it. (**107r**) Stir it well, and then cover it and set it aside until it cools. Next throw

23 It is made from bread wheat (*Triticum aestivum*), see glossary 2, for more on this kind of flour.

24 *Khamīra* (lit., 'fermenting agent'), is used here to designate an aromatic distilled base for making the digestive drink of *aqsimā*. Slightly modified recipes can be found in *Waṣf* 189, and *Wuṣla* ii 504–5, where the word *iksīr* (elixir, distilled essence) is used instead of *khamīra*.

25 See above recipe for instructions on which spices to use.

26 This also occurs as *al-Dimashqī* 'Damascene' in DK, n. 5484. The *khilāf* tree, also called *ṣafṣāf Miṣrī* (*Salix aegyptiaca*) is an Egyptian species of the willow tree.

27 For distilling, see glossary 9.2, s.v. *taṣʿīd*.

into it 2 *kūzes* (36 cups) of water,[28] and set it aside until the liquid looks clear [after the sediment settles].

Take the clear liquid, and dissolve sugar in it, use 1 *raṭl* (1 pound) sugar for each 2 *raṭl*s (4 cups) of the liquid. Rub a bunch of mint into the sugar [solution], and throw in a whole sprig of rue. Also, add 3 *dirhams* (9 grams) crushed black pepper and *aṭrāf ṭīb* (spice blend).[29] Pour it into a vessel with traces of previous fermentation (*wiʿāʾ ḍārī*),[30] and set it aside overnight, after which you can strain it, and use it.

Chapter on Making *Aqsimā* (Digestive Drinks), *Fuqqāʿ* (Foamy Beer), and *Māʾ al-Shaʿīr* (Malted Barley Drinks)[31]

(404) Recipe for *khamīrat al-aqsimā* (distilled *aqsimā* base for making instant digestive drinks)[32]

Take 1 *ūqiyya* (1 ounce) ginger; and 3 *dirhams* (9 grams/1½ teaspoons) of each of spikenard, *tunbul* (betel leaves), cloves (*kibāsh qaranful*), and rue [fresh leaves]. Also, take two parts [that equal the above spices and herbs combined, by weight] mint leaves; and two parts wine vinegar. Also, use 3 *ūqiyyas* (3 ounces) sugar.

Pound all the [dry] spices (*ʿaqāqīr*), and add them to the vinegar along with mint and rue. Distill them in a cucurbit (*qarʿa*) and alembic (*inbīq*),[33] [and store this distillate in glass bottles]. Whenever you need to make *aqsimā*, dissolve sugar [in water], and add to it [a bit] of this *khamīra* (base), and there you have it, an *aqsimā* drink.

(405) Recipe for making *aqsimā* (digestive drink)

For each *raṭl* (pound) of sugar use 1 large *kūz* (18 cups) of water, 4 lemons, rue, mint, and *aṭrāf ṭīb* (spice blend).[34] [Combine and] dissolve all the ingredients, squeeze in the lemons, and empty the mix into a vessel with traces of previous fermentation (*wiʿāʾ ḍārī*).[35] Let it stay overnight, and use it in the morning.

---

28 See glossary 13, s.v. *kūz*.

29 See recipe 401, for instructions on which spices to use.

30 See recipes 407 and 418 below, for directions on how to do this with new jars.

31 It seems that, from this point, the compiler is copying from another source on drinks.

32 See n. 24 above.

33 For distilling, see glossary 9.2, s.v. *taṣʿīd*.

34 See recipe 401 for instructions on which spices to use.

35 See recipes 407 and 418 below for directions on how to do this with new jars.

(406) Recipe for making *fuqqāʿ* (foamy beer)

(**107v**) For each 10 cups (*kīzān*) of *fuqqāʿ*,[36] use 1 *ūqiyya* (1 ounce) [dried] pomegranate seeds and 10 *ūqiyyas* (10 ounces) sugar. Soak them in 4 *raṭls* (8 cups) of water and 4 *ūqiyyas* (½ cup) rosewater flavored with musk.

Put rue stems in the jars (*kīzān*).[37] After you mash and mix the ingredients and strain them in a *rāwūq* (large strainer for drinks), season the liquid,[38] and pour it into the jars (*kīzān*). [Keep them overnight, and use the drink].

(407) Recipe for lacing new jars with fermentation agents (*taḍriyat al-awʿiya*)[39]

Take a piece of fresh bread yeast, dissolve it in water, and add to it rue, mint, and lemon, which has been cut into pieces. Put the mix in a new jar, tie the mouth [of the jar with a piece of cloth], and keep it in a warm place for three days, and it will be laced with fermenting agents (*ḍārī*).

Chapter (*Bāb*)[40]

Recipe [for an instant drink][41]

Pour some [already made] *fuqqāʿ* from its vessel into a bowl (*zibdiyya*), and add to it an equal amount of *aqsimā*.[42] It is also said that *aṭrāf al-ṭīb* (spice blend) and fresh rue can be added as well. Press and mash them into the liquid, and then strain it in a *rāwūq* (large strainer for drinks). Add some rosewater seasoned with musk, and pour it into glasses and use it.

---

36 Sg. *kūz*, used here to designate a measure of a serving of a drinking glass; otherwise if the fermenting *kūz* 'jar' is meant, the amount of water is 180 cups, which is too much to consider.

37 The verb used is *tusaddab*, derived from *sadāb* 'rue,' as it is correctly written in C, n. 5523.

38 With the usual spices, see recipe 412 below.

39 See also recipe 418 below.

40 Apparently, at this point the compiler switches to another pamphlet on drinks, and copies some additional recipes; this may well be the reason we have two repeated recipes (409, 410), with slight differences.

41 This recipe is not numbered in the edited text.

42 See previous recipes.

(408) Recipe for *shush Yemenī* (Yemeni grain-based beer)[43]

Take 2 *qadaḥ*s (4½ cups) rice and ½ *qadaḥ* (approx. 1 pound) *daqīq ḥuwwārā* (white bran-free flour). Boil them in water until they fall apart (*yataharra'*), and then strain them through a fine sieve. Add sugar and bee honey to them, just enough to sweeten them. Also, add a piece of fresh bread yeast (*khamīrat ʿajīn*).

Pour in 5 *kūz*es (45 pints) *fuqqāʿ khāṣṣ* (excellent beer),[44] as well as musk and rosewater. Pour it into a new jar (*jarra*) or one that was used previously to make the drink. (**108r**) Close the opening with leaves of sour orange (*nāranj*), and bury the jars in straw (*tibn*) for half a day.

(409) Recipe for *fuqqāʿ*

[This is a duplicate of recipe 395 above].

(410) Recipe for *fuqqāʿ khāṣṣ* (excellent beer)

[This is a duplicate of recipes nos. 396, 398, and 399] (**108v**)

(411) Recipe for *mā' al-shaʿīr* (malted barley drink) for the month of Ramadan

Take picked over barley, soak it in water overnight and drain it early the following morning. Spread the grains on a *quffa* (large basket of woven date-palm fronds), weigh them down,[45] and wait until they sprout. Dry them in the sun, and finely grind them into flour.

Next, take ½ *qadaḥ* (approx. 1 pound) of this flour, as well as ¼ *qadaḥ* wheat flour (*daqīq qamḥ*). Put them in an earthenware tub (*mājūr*), and boil water in a large pot. Pour a little of it into the *mājūr* and stir with a ladle. Next, add enough [of the hot water] to cover it, and set it aside for the rest of the day and overnight, so that it sours. Early in the morning, add more cold water to fill the *mājūr*, and set aside for two more days.

On the third day, add to it leaves of citron (*turunj*) and sour orange (*nāranj*), as well as those of rue and mint. Cut 10 lemons in half and add them to the *mājūr*. Add just enough salt to give it a pleasant taste.

---

43 Based on internal evidence, the Yemeni way of preparing the drink was to add other ingredients to an already available *fuqqāʿ khāṣṣ*. This would make it stronger than *fuqqāʿ* by itself, but still within the permissible limits of no more than three days of fermentation. *Wuṣla* ii 504 includes an identical recipe, albeit a better copied one, which I used here to amend the edited text.

44 See recipe 396 above.

45 See recipe 403 above for details on how to do this.

In the evening (*ʿashāʾ*), take the amount you want to serve [from the *mājūr*], (**109r**) strain it, squeeze some lemon juice on it, add sugar, musk, and rosewater to it, and it will be ready to drink.

(412) Another recipe for *māʾ al-shaʿīr* (malted barley drink)

Take 1 *qadaḥ* (2¼ pounds) barley grains that have been cleaned of mud [and other impurities]. Soak them overnight and then drain them and spread them in a *quffa* (large basket of woven date-palm fronds), weigh them down and set them aside for a day and a night, and they will sprout. However, do not let them sprout a lot. Spread the grains in a sunny place until they dry, and then grind them and store [the resulting flour] away.

[To make the drink,] take a jarful of water,[46] and heat it to a rolling boil.[47] Next, take the ground malted barley, vigorously knead it with cold water and add it to the water while it is boiling. Stir it and set it aside for a whole day, during which time the clear liquid will rise, leaving the sediment (*thufl*) in the bottom.

Take the clear liquid, stir in [dried] pomegranate seeds if you like, or lemon [juice], and sweeten it with sugar, to your liking. Take *fuqqāʿ* spices, namely, green cardamom (*hāl*), black pepper (*fulful aswad*), betel leaves (*tunbul*), and spikenard (*sunbul*). Stir them in, and pour the liquid into earthenware jars, season the top of the liquid with whatever you wish (such as, musk and rosewater) [and use].

(413) Recipe for *fuqqāʿ* [easy to make, and quite cheap][48]

Keep bread soaked [in water] from early morning (*bukra*) to the evening (*ʿashāʾ*), after that mash it, strain it, [let the sediment settle, and] take the resulting clear liquid. For each *raṭl* (2 cups) add 1 *ūqiyya* (1 ounce) dried pomegranate seeds (**109v**) or juice of 1 lemon, ½ *ūqiyya* (1 tablespoon) sugar, and *aṭrāf ṭīb* (spice blend),[49] black pepper, and rue. Pour it into jars (*kīzān*), put them together (*yuraṣṣ*),[50] [and set them aside to ferment briefly] and then take them away [and use as needed].

---

46 The vessel is called *jarra*. Another name for it is *qulla*.

47 The verb used to describe this stage of boiling is *yashuqq* (lit., 'split').

48 The Arabic expression is قريب المأخذ رخيص الثمن, as described in the corresponding recipe in *Zahr*, fol. 22v. Here I used it to amend the edited text slightly.

49 See above recipe.

50 In both the edited text and the *Zahr* copy, the verb is copied as ويرص 'put tightly together'; and in C copy, n. 5628, as ويرمى 'and thrown,' which is irrelevant in context. In the directions of the edited text, the jars are expected to be kept in a warm place to ferment

(414) Another recipe for *fuqqāʿ* (foamy beer)[51]

Keep bread soaked in water from early morning (*bukra*) to noon (*ẓuhr*), and then mash it with the water, strain it, [and allow the sediment to settle in the bottom]. Take the clear liquid and add dried pomegranate seeds or lemon juice, and leave it until the afternoon prayer (*ṣalāt al-ʿaṣr*). Next, add sugar and rue, season it with a bit of musk, and pour it into jars (*kīzān*). Tightly close the mouths of the jars, put them in a large and wide earthenware tub (*qaṣriyya*), on their heads, and sprinkle them with water.[52] It will be ready early the following morning (*ghadāt*).

(415) Recipe for an excellent *fuqqāʿ* (foamy beer), flavorful and delicious

Take 1 *kūz* (18 cups) fine-tasting fresh water (*māʾ ḥulw*),[53] and add to it 2 *ūqiyyas* (2 ounces) finely pounded dried pomegranate seeds. Put the water in a large wide bowl (*ṭāsa*),[54] and throw in ½ *raṭl* (½ pound) sugar, and 1 *dirham* (½ teaspoon) beer yeast (*khamīrat al-fuqqāʿī*).[55] Squeeze on it the juice of 1 lemon, and leave it overnight in vessels with traces of previous fermentation (*ḍārī*).[56]

(416) Recipe for *aqsimā* (digestive drink)

Take dried carnation petals (*zahr qaranful*), spikenard, ginger, a bit of black pepper, and dried rosebuds (*zir ward*). Pound all the ingredients. [Mix them] with sugar, lemon juice, [and water]. Keep it [in jars, overnight, and then use as needed].

---

for a short period. The word in C could easily have been a copyist's misreading of ويدفن 'buried.' Indeed, we learn that the jars were often left buried in straw for a while, as in the above recipe 408: ويدفن في تبن.

51 This recipe is included in *Zahr*, too, fols 22v–3r. Here I amended the edited text based on it and that of DK, notes 5631, 5632, and 5634.

52 We can assume that the jars are to be sprinkled with water several times to keep them cool and prevent too much fermentation. Tipping the jars on their heads will indeed make the sprinkling more effective. The directions given imply that the vessels used are the small single-serving size of *kūzes* (see glossary 1).

53 Lit., 'sweet water.'

54 It is a vessel in which water is cooled.

55 See n. 22 above.

56 See recipes 418 below, and 407 above, for directions on how to do this with new jars.

(417) Another [*aqsimā*] recipe

For each *raṭl* (pound) sugar, use 5 *raṭl*s (5 pints) water. Dissolve the sugar in water, and throw in 1 *dirham* (½ teaspoon) *aṭrāf ṭīb* (spice blend).[57] Squeeze the juice of 1 lemon on it, and add a bit of mint and rue [leaves]. (**110r**) Pour it into a vessel with traces of previous fermentation (*wiʿāʾ ḍārī*),[58] [and set it aside overnight and use as needed].

(418) Recipe for lacing [new] vessels with fermentation agents[59]

Take a new earthenware vessel, and bread dough yeast (*khamīrat ʿajīn*). Cook the yeast on the fire [by mixing it with water] to make it resemble *ḥarīra* (i.e., a thin and smooth soup). Mix in a bit of mint and rue [leaves] and some lemon juice. Dissolve it in water and a bit of vinegar. Put it in the above-mentioned vessel and set it aside it for three days.

(419) Recipe for *fuqqāʿ* (foamy beer)

Take 2 *ūqiyya*s (2 ounces) dried pomegranate seeds, soak them in 4 *raṭl*s (4 pints) hot water, and add a bit of mint [leaves]. Strain the liquid and dissolve in it 1 *raṭl* (1 pound) sugar and ¼ *ūqiyya* (½ tablespoon) musk-scented rosewater (*māʾ ward mumassak*). Put the liquid in jars with traces of previous fermentation (*kīzān ḍāriya*),[60] and sprinkle [the top of the liquid with] a bit of Ceylon sandalwood (*ṣandal Maqāṣīrī*). [Leave it overnight and use as needed].

(420) Recipe for good *aqsimā* (digestive drink)[61]

Use 24 *dirhams* (2½ ounces) black pepper, and a similar amount of ginger. Also, use 4 *dirhams* (12 grams) of each of the following: *zir ward munaqqā* (rosebuds with their hypanthia removed), spikenard (*sunbul*), betel leaves (*tunbul*), green cardamom (*hāl*), cloves (*qaranful*), and mace (*basbāsa*). Also use 20 *dirhams* (2 ounces) mint leaves,[62] and 120 *dirhams* (12½ ounces) wine vinegar.[63]

---

57 See recipe 401, for instructions on which spices to use.

58 See n. 56 above.

59 See also recipe 407 above.

60 See n. 56 above.

61 A slightly modified recipe is found in *Waṣf* 189 (called أقسما), and *Wuṣla* ii 5045 (called أكسير اقسما). In all the versions, an *iksīr* (elixir, distilled essence) is used to make the drink *aqsimā*. Cf. recipe 404 above.

62 In *Wuṣla*, the amount is 200 *dirhams* = 42 ounces.

63 In *Wuṣla*, amount is 1,200 *dirhams* = 15½ cups.

Finely pound all the spices (*ḥawāʾij*), and steep them in the vinegar, along with the mint, for two days, then distill the liquid on a very low heat,[64] and store it away.

Whenever you want to drink *aqsimā*, dissolve some sugar in water, squeeze lemon juice on it, add a bit of rue [leaves], (**110v**) and crush them in the liquid [to release their flavor]. Add a very small amount of the distilled liquid, and there you have it, instant *aqsimā*, which is so good for the digestion (*yahḍum al-ṭaʿām*).

(421) Recipe for *fuqqāʿ shaʿīrī* (foamy barley beer)
Take barley grains, soak them, crush them finely, and sift them in a fine-meshed sieve (*munkhul shaʿr*).

Now, take rue [leaves], put them in a clean copper cauldron (*mirjal*), pour water into it, cover it [and light a fire under it to boil] until the rue leaves turn yellow.

Take the [prepared] barley flour, put it in a vessel, and pour in the water boiled with rue, while somebody else stirs vigorously and constantly. Cover the vessel, and set it aside to cool and settle, and then strain it through a fine-meshed sieve (*ghirbāl shaʿr*). Add to it cassia (*dār Ṣīnī*), spikenard, and cloves, all finely crushed and pounded.

Empty the liquid into jars (*jarra* or *kūz*), tightly close their mouths, and bury them in sand (*yurammal*) [overnight].

(422) Recipe for *fuqqāʿ buqūl* (foamy beer with herbs)
Take 2 *qadaḥ*s (4½ pounds) wheat grains (*qamḥ*) and pound them in a stone mortar until they are fine. Put them in a vessel, and add to them an equal amount—by capacity—*daqīq ḥuwwārā* (white bran-free flour of common wheat). Add [enough] cold water to dissolve the flour into a *ḥarīra*-like consistency.[65] Set it aside for a full hour (*sāʿa jayyida*).

Heat up water until it boils very well, and then pour it on the base (*khamīra*) prepared above—pour only 3 small *kūzes* (3 cups).[66] Let it ferment for an hour, (**111r**) and then cover it well, and set it aside for two more hours. Remove the cover, set it aside to cool, and then add cold water—an amount equal to the hot water added, that is 3 *kūzes*. Stir the liquid until it is well mixed, and set it aside until the sediment settles and the liquid looks clear. Take the clear liquid and put it in another vessel.

---

64 For details on how to distill the liquid, see recipe 402 above.

65 *Ḥarīra* is a flour-based soup, silky smooth, and fluid in consistency.

66 These were drinking cups with handles. See glossary 9.1, and 13, s.v. *kūz ṣaghīr*.

Pound ½ *ūqiyya* (1 tablespoon) black pepper; 1 *dirham* (3 grams) green cardamom (*hāl*), 1 *dirham* betel leaves, 1 *dirham* mace (*basbāsa*), and ½ *dirham* cloves (*kibāsh qaranful*). Add them to the vessel along with the peel of two limes (*laymūn akhḍar*), and dissolve a lump of musk (*ḥabbat misk*) in it. Mix all of it well.

Now take the [small] jars (*kīzān*) and put a sprig of rue in each one.[67] Fill them with the clear liquid, [tightly close their mouths], turn them over on their heads, and sprinkle them with water.[68] Leave them overnight, and drink the beer the following day. If you want it made with sugar, then dissolve the needed amount in it.

Tightly close the mouths of the jars, put them in a large, wide earthenware tub (*qaṣriyya*), on their heads, and sprinkle them with water. It will be ready early the following morning (*ghadāt*).

(423) Recipe for *khamīrat al-aqsimā* (distilled *aqsimā*-base for making instant digestive drink)[69]

Use 1 *ūqiyya* (1 ounce) ginger, 3 *dirhams* (1½ teaspoons) spikenard, and a similar amount of betel leaves, a similar amount of cloves (*kibāsh qaranful*), a similar amount of nutmeg, and a similar amount of mace. In addition, use 2 *dirhams* (1 teaspoon) cubeb (*kabāba*) and a similar amount of aloeswood (*ʿūd*), 3 *dirhams*, (1½ teaspoons) green cardamom, ½ *dirham* (¼ teaspoon) saffron, 3 *dirhams* (1½ teaspoons) rosebuds, and a similar amount of black cardamom (*qāqulla*). Also, use two snips (*jazzatayn*) of rue and a similar amount of mint,[70] as well as 3 *ūqiyyas* (6 tablespoons) wine vinegar.

Pound all the dried spices (*ʿaqāqīr*) and add them to the vinegar, along with mint (**111v**) and rue. Distill them in an alembic,[71] and whenever you want to drink *aqsimā*, dissolve sugar [in water] and add [a bit] of this distillate, and you will get an *aqsimā* drink.

---

67 The vessels used must be the serving size of a *kūz*, as only one sprig of rue is put in each one of them. See glossary 1, s.v. *kūz*.

68 As instructed in recipe 414 above, the *kūzes* are arranged in a large tub and sprinkled with water. Tipping the jars on their heads will indeed make the sprinkling more effective.

69 Cf. recipes 404 and 420 above.

70 Based on context, and the following recipe, the word in the edited text should read جزّتين or جرزتين 'two snips,' which amount to approx. 10 snips, rather than جزئين 'two parts' or حزمتين 'two bunches.' See glossary 9.2, s.v. *jarza*.

71 For details on how to distill the liquid, see recipe 402 above.

(424) Recipe for *aqsimā* (digestive drink)

For each 2 *raṭl*s (2 pounds) of sugar used, add 4 *ūqiyya*s (4 ounces) bee honey, and one snip (*jarza*) rue leaves,[72] mint, *aṭrāf ṭīb* (spice blend),[73] a lump of musk, [juice of] 5 or 6 limes, 1 *ūqiyya* (2 tablespoons) rosewater, and a bit of the *aqsimā* base.[74] [Mix them all with water and] put it in jars with traces of a previous fermentation.[75] [Set it aside overnight, and then] strain the liquid and drink it.

(425) Recipe for *sukkar wa-laymūn* (sugar with lemon), made for travelers (*musāfirīn*)

Take sugar, coarsely crush it, spread it on a marble slab or some other thing, and continue adding lemon juice to it in drops until it cannot absorb any more. Spread the sugar again and let it dry, and then gather it, mix it, spread it, squeeze lemon juice on it [in drops], and dry it again. This should be repeated three times.

Pack the sugar in molds like *ublūja* (cone).[76] If this mold is not available, then use something else [comparable to it]. Unmold the sugar [pieces],[77] and hang them in an airy place to dry.

To use the sugar, pour some water [in a vessel] and dissolve in it as much of this sugar as you need—for each *raṭl* (pint) of water use 2 *ūqiyya*s (2 ounces) of this sugar.[78] If it is meant to be used with foods, use more lemon juice when making it.

(426) Recipe for *shush* (Yemeni grain-based beer)[79]

Take [wheat] flour [add water to it] and cook it into *ʿaṣīda* (a dense flour soup). Stir into it *fuqqāʿ kharjī* (ordinary foamy beer),[80] and sweeten it with honey

---

72 I opted to use the word as it occurs in CB, n. 5718, rather than the edited *juzʾ* 'part.' See n. 70 above.

73 See recipe 401 for instructions on which spices to use.

74 The Arabic is خميرة الاقسمة, as prepared in the recipe above, 404, and 420.

75 See recipes 407 and 418 above, for directions on how to do this with new jars.

76 Such molds were used to make the characteristic shape of sugar cones, called *sukkar al-abālīj*. See glossary 4, s.v. *sukkar*.

77 *Wa-tadhurruhu*, from ذرر 'come out,' as in DK, n. 5729.

78 This must be the first documented 'Kool-Aid' preparation in the history of beverages!

79 *Wuṣla* ii 504 includes a similar recipe, where it is called *shush Yemenī*, I used it here to amend the edited text. See also *shush* recipe 408 above.

80 To my knowledge, the name is not explained in any of the existing medieval records. It is my contention that it is related to beer, which used to be made by the Christian Copts

or sugar. Add fresh peel of citron, mint, rue, *aṭrāf ṭīb* (spice blend),[81] and beer yeast.[82] (**112r**) Warm it up (*tudaffaʾ*), [and then empty it into jars,] then bury them in straw (*tibn*) or just keep them in a warm room, until they start to ferment, and drink it.

(427) Recipe for another kind [of *shush*]

Boil water, and mix it with a bit of [wheat] flour and spices (*abzār*). Cool it down, and drink it by mixing it with *fuqqāʿ* (foamy beer) and sugar. The same thing is done with grape juice: press the grapes and take their juice, and do it as described here, but without boiling the juice, and use it. *Sūbiya* (grain-based digestive beer) is made the same way.[83]

(428) Recipe for another kind [of *shush*]

Grind rice, mix it with water and cook it into *ʿaṣīda* (dense flour soup), until it is well done. Put it in a large wide bowl (*ṭāsa*), and add water bit by bit, while you whip it by hand the same way leaves of *sidr* (lotus jujube) are whipped.[84] Whenever you feel the mix is becoming too dense to handle, add some more water, and continue whipping until it increases in bulk, and becomes smooth and thin. [Set it aside to let the sediment settle.] Take the clear liquid, and add sugar. For each *raṭl* (1 pound) of sugar, use 2 *raṭl*s (2 pints) of this liquid. Also add 3 *ūqiyya*s (3 ounces) Egyptian bee honey, and rue.

In wintertime, put the liquid in a glass vessel and bury it in sand or straw (*tibn*). Leave it there overnight, and the following morning, strain it and drink it. However, in summertime, put the liquid in *taljiyya fakhkhār*,[85] there is no need to bury it. You can use it right away.

---

who are indigenous Egyptians, collectively among the *Ahl al-Kitāb* (non-Muslims living in Muslim lands). They had been making similar beers for centuries. The tax imposed on them, which was charged per head, was called *kharj*, and the beer for which they were known was named *fuqqāʿ kharjī*. See also glossary 1.

81 See recipe 401 for instructions on which spices to use.

82 In Arabic خميرة الفقاع الخاص. See n. 22 above.

83 *Sūbiya* recipes follow.

84 Soap-like foam comes up when these leaves are whipped with water. From the following recipes, we learn that the more this drink is whipped the more foam it produces.

85 *Taljiyya* is a dialectical vocalization of *thaljiyya*, which is an earthenware jar used to cool water; the lower part of it was buried in mud. The word is derived from *thalj* 'ice.'

(429) Recipe for *sūbiyat al-aruzz* (rice-based digestive beer), relieves discomforts from overeating (*tukhama*) and indigestion (*imtilāʾ*), and sweetens the breath

Take the rice, boil it until it softens, and mash it and pass it through a sieve. Now take *ʿajwa* (sweet and soft dried dates), soak them in four times their amount of water, leave them overnight, and then boil them and strain them. Dissolve the strained rice in the date juice; and boil them until the liquid thickens a bit.

Add all the spices of *aṭrāf al-ṭīb* (spice blend), and sour orange peel. (**112v**) Throw in ginger, dried rue, and mint. Let the liquid ferment in a jar with traces of previous fermentation (*wiʿāʾ ḍārī*),[86] and drink it. It is beneficial and delicious.

(430) Recipe for delicious *sūbiya* (grain-based digestive beer), good for winter and summer; cooling (*mubarrid*), and helps gain weight (*musammin*)

Take three discs of bread of the finest *khubz ḥuwwārā* (bread made with white bran-free flour), cut them into pieces and pour enough water on them to submerge them, to double the height of the bread in the vessel, and set them aside in a clean earthenware jar (*jarra*), a new pot (*qidr*), or a large earthenware cask (*dann*). Press and mash the bread, and strain it, and when it looks good, return it to the pot [or whatever you choose to use], and put in it a small fistful of very tender citron leaves (*qulūb utrujj*), rue (*sadhāb*), common parsley (*karafs*), mint (*naʿnāʿ*), and tarragon (*ṭarkhūn*).

Set the vessel aside from early morning (*bukra*) to midday (*wasṭ al-nahār*), then strain the liquid and drink it. When served with ice (*thalj*), it will be even better and more beneficial. However, if the vessel is left until the following morning, it will sour and its properties will be like those of *mizr*.[87]

(431) Another recipe for *sūbiya* (grain-based digestive beer)

For each 1½ *raṭl*s (1½ pounds) flour, use 4 *raṭl*s top-quality cane-sugar molasses (*quṭāra ʿāl*). Beat the flour with water; add enough to give it the consistency of thin soup (*ḥasū*).[88] Cook it on the fire, stirring it constantly with a wooden *dakshāb* (stirring utensil), until it is done. [Remove it from the fire and] continue whipping it until it gets cold. Now, while stirring, throw in the molasses;

86 See recipes 418 and 407 above for directions on how to do this with new jars.

87 A drink like *fuqqāʿ*, which contains a high level of alcohol, was said to be a popular drink for commoners in Egypt. See glossary 1.

88 Based on context, I amended two words to straighten out the meaning: بملء to بماء 'with water,' and حشو to حسو 'thin soup.'

and while doing this, add water little by little and taste it; continue doing this until you are satisfied with it sweetness.[89] Strain it.

Now, add ground *aṭrāf al-ṭīb* (spice blend) to it. Mix the spices with water and knead them together first, and then whip them into the liquid, along with a bit of fresh mint. Also, add a small amount of fermented *sūbiya*, set aside from the previous day's batch. Empty the liquid into vessels with traces of a previous fermentation (*awʿiya ḍāriya*).[90]

In the summertime, (**113r**) make it during the daytime: prepare it early in the morning and drink it in the afternoon (*ʿaṣr*). During winter, prepare it in the evening (*ʿashāʾ*) and drink it the following morning.

(432) Recipe for *sūbiya Yamaniyya* (Yemeni grain-based digestive beer)[91]
Take flour and white sugar. [Mix sugar with some water] and boil it to make very thin syrup (*jullāb*)—the thinnest you can get it. Take fine white flour (*muthallath*),[92] and cook it into thick soup [by adding water to it],[93] do not add salt. Let it cool and then put it in a large shallow basin (*ṭasht*), and whip it by hand while adding the syrup to it—do not add all the syrup at once; add it in ladlefuls. The more you whip, the foamier the drink will become. Continue doing this until it has the consistency of not-so-thin *ḥarīra*.[94]

Pour in *fuqqāʿ kharjī* (ordinary foamy beer),[95] do this aggressively.[96] In Egypt, *aqsimā* (digestive drink) is used instead. So, when the mix is thin enough, pour it into a clean vessel with traces of date syrup (*dibs*) or bee honey. Put in a lot of rue—tie it in bunches and add it; do likewise with mint. Add *aṭrāf al-ṭīb* (spice blend) such as cloves, mace, ginger, and nutmeg; also add rosewater and musk.[97] Use lots of *aṭrāf al-ṭīb*. Put the vessels in a warm place, and drape them with large pieces of [heavy warm] cloth. When it is done this way, the drink will be very foamy.

---

89 This sentence is provided by DK, n. 5777.

90 See recipes 418 and 407 above for directions on how to do this with new jars.

91 This recipe is also found in *Wuṣla* ii 503, and al-Ghuzūlī, *Maṭāliʿ* ii 88, where it is called *aqsimā mulūkiyya* 'top quality *aqsimā*.' Here I used these two copies to amend the edited text.

92 This fine white flour is made from bread wheat (*Triticum aestivum*), see glossary 2, for more on this kind of flour.

93 *ʿAṣīda*, dense flour soup.

94 Flour-based soup, with smooth and flowing consistency.

95 See n. 80 above.

96 The word *manfūḍ* (poured in aggressively) suggests that the resulting foam was desired.

97 These spices are mentioned in al-Ghuzūlī, *Maṭāliʿ* ii 89.

When you want to use it, pour into it some *fuqqāʿ kharjī*, other than the one used above—pour it aggressively,[98] and serve it. It is indeed the best of beverages.

[Notes:] Amounts are not given in the recipe because people who make it will tell by tasting when it is sweet enough, or hot enough. [Another thing,] when the drink starts fermenting [and it is good to drink], take an unglazed earthenware vessel (*inā' rashshāḥ*) or *ḥuqq Yemenī* (rounded Yemeni soapstone bowl), infuse it with the aromatic smoke of ambergris (*ʿanbar*), empty the drink into it, and serve it.

(433) Another [*sūbiya*] recipe[99]
This is like the one we described above, except you add rice, which has been boiled and its [drained] liquid is thrown into it [while whipping the ingredients in the *ṭasht*, as in the above recipe]. This will give you another kind of *sūbiya*. Besides, while sipping the *sūbiya*, you can eat the [drained boiled] rice.[100]

Some people make it with rice flour, but fine white flour (*daqīq muthallath*)[101] is better. **(113v)** [A rule of thumb:] the more you whip it, the foamier it will be.

(434) Another [*sūbiya*] recipe[102]
Take 1 *qadaḥ* (2¼ pounds) excellent white wheat flour (*daqīq ʿalāma ʿāl*), cook it into *ʿaṣīda* (dense flour soup), do not add salt to it. Empty it into a large wide tub (*qaṣriyya*) and let it cool down.

Heat up water. [Transfer the cooked flour into a] large, wide serving bowl (*jafna*), and whip it with the hot water until it resembles *sawīq* in consistency.[103] Now, take as much *aṭrāf al-ṭīb* (spice blend) as you need, namely spikenard, betel leaves, clove stalks (*ḥaṭab qaranful*), green cardamom, nutmeg, mace, black pepper, ginger, and rosebuds (*zir ward*). Crush them all and throw them into the prepared mix. For each *qadaḥ* (2¼ pounds) of flour, use 2 *ūqiyya*s

98 Again, the verb انفض suggests this. I assume this increases the amount of foam in the beer served. The foam was a sought-after quality in *fuqqāʿ*; indeed, that is how the beverage acquired its name 'the foamy,' or 'bubbly.'

99 This recipe is also found in *Wuṣla* ii 504. I used it here to amend the edited text.

100 This interesting detail is provided in *Wuṣla* only. The verb used is *yutaḥassā* (to be sipped), which suggests a drink with a somewhat thick consistency, like that of thin soup (*ḥasū*).

101 It is made from bread wheat (*Triticum aestivum*), see glossary 2, for more on this kind of flour.

102 This recipe also appears in *Zahr*, fol. 23r.

103 *Sawīq* is a sweet and somewhat thick drink made with toasted and crushed grains. See glossary 1 and 2.

(2 ounces) *aṭrāf al-ṭīb*. In addition to these spices, crush in 2 *ūqiyyas* (2 ounces) mint. Add a whole bunch of rue—crush half of it and add it to the *sūbiya* mix; add the other half uncrushed. Mix in 2½ *raṭls* (2½ pounds) bee honey or fine-tasting cane-sugar molasses (*quṭāra ṭayyiba*). Mix all these ingredients in a clean vessel, and dissolve ½ *dirham* (¼ teaspoon) saffron in them.

Empty the resulting liquid into a non-porous jar with traces of previous fermentation.[104] Set it aside overnight, and use it [as needed]. Keep these instructions in mind and follow them.

---

104 See recipes 418 and 407 above for directions on how to do this with new jars.

CHAPTER 13

في نقوع المشمش

Dried-Apricot Compote (*naqūʿ al-mishmish*)

(435) Recipe for *naqūʿ al-mishmish al-lawzī* (compote of sweet apricots)[1]
Take [dried] *mishmish lawzī*, wash them very well to get rid of all the dust, and pour over them water of blue Egyptian lotus (*māʾ al-laynūfar*),[2] borage water (*māʾ lisān al-thawr*), and rosewater.[3] Squeeze on them (**114r**) fresh juice of sour pomegranates, and add some sprigs of mint. Sweeten the mix with white sugar, and set it aside until the apricots are moistened and infused with the flavors (*yantaqiʿ*), but still firm. Put the mix in a vessel infused with smoke of ambergris, and it will be delicious.

(436) Another recipe for [dried] *mishmish lawzī*, to be eaten while imbibing alcoholic drinks[4]
Take rosewater and musk, and dissolve excellent sugar and some water in them. Let the washed apricots steep in this liquid, but do not keep them for too long, lest they become mushy (*yataharraʾ*). Take them out while they are still firm, and once again let them dry in a clean vessel—but they should not become too dry. They are the best and the most delicious food to have as *naql* (mezze).

(437) Another recipe for [dried] apricots, stuffed (*maḥshū*)
Wash [dried] apricots, wrap them in a cotton cloth, and set them aside from evening till early morning. Remove their seeds.

Start boiling sugar syrup (*jullāb*) on the fire.

Steep ½ *dirham* (¼ teaspoon) of saffron in rosewater of Nuṣaybīn,[5] along with half a lump of musk.

---

1 Lit., 'almondy apricot,' so-called because the kernels are as sweet as almonds. See also n. 11 below. The first two recipes in this chapter are also available in *Wuṣla* ii 507 and al-Ghuzūlī, *Maṭāliʿ* ii 89. Here I used them to amend the edited text.

2 The flower is more properly known as *naylūfar*.

3 These are all distilled waters. See recipes 684 and following. Also, see glossary 9.2, s.v. *taṣʿīd*.

4 *Yutanaqqalu bihi*. See glossary 5, s.v. *naql*.

5 Nusaybin was a city in upper Mesopotamia, now in the Turkish province of Mardin. It was renowned for its orchards and gardens. Roses named after it are pinkish in hue.

 | DOI 10.1163/9789004349919_016

Continue boiling the *jullāb*; for each *raṭl* (pound) of it, add 1 *ūqiyya* (2 tablespoons) rosewater—other than the rosewater-saffron prepared above. For each *raṭl* (pound) of this *jullāb*,[6] scald and skin (*yusmaṭ*) 1 *ūqiyya* (1 ounce) almonds. Color them yellow with the [steeped] saffron mentioned earlier in the recipe, and set them aside.

[Now back to the boiling *jullāb*.] Skim its froth. When it has boiled enough, add the steeped saffron to it, and let it boil until you feel the stickiness of the syrup between your two fingers.[7] For each *raṭl* (pound) of the *jullāb* used, add 1 *ūqiyya* (2 tablespoons) wine vinegar, which has been distilled in a cucurbit (*qarʿa*) and alembic (*inbīq*).[8] Let the vinegar boil in the syrup, and stir until it is thick enough.

Take the pot off the heat, and sprinkle it with 10 *dirhams* (1 ounce) *aṭrāf al-ṭīb* (spice blend). (**114v**) Continue stirring the pot, [even] while it is on the floor, to prevent the syrup from sticking to the pot. Continue doing this until it is cool enough.

Now, take a wide-mouthed jar (*barniyya*), either porcelain (*ṣīnī*) or ceramic (*qīshānī*); wash it very well, dry it, sprinkle it with musk and rosewater, and then infuse it with the smoke of aloeswood and ambergris—tie the mouth so that the smoke penetrates well into the vessel. Put in it the things you prepared [i.e., the syrup, and the apricots, which have been stuffed with the colored and skinned almonds].[9] Top them with a bit of white sugar, and sprinkle them with musk and rosewater.

Cover the opening of the jar with a clean linen cloth, top it with another layer of a thin sheet of leather (*riqq*), tie it with a thread, and stow it away until needed. Serve it [in a bowl along with other goodies, both imbibed and eaten] in a *sukurdān*.[10]

The cooking [of the syrup] must be done in a soapstone pot (*qidr birām*).

---

6 Here, based on context, I replaced the word 'saffron' in the edited text with '*jullāb*'; otherwise, a pound of saffron sounds quite unrealistic.

7 The Arabic expression is يتدبّق بين الاصابع. One of the ways of testing that the syrup is done is to put a drop of it between the tips of the thumb and the forefinger, to feel its stickiness.

8 For distilling, see glossary 9.2, s.v. *taṣʿīd*. The vinegar is distilled so that it becomes colorless.

9 The recipe's title promises stuffed apricots, but it neglects to mention what is to be done with the softened pitted apricots and the skinned almonds.

10 This is a large tray, in which varieties of delicious small dishes are served as snacks to nibble on during social gatherings, including those involving drinking alcoholic beverages. The word is said to be a combination of the Arabic *sukr* 'imbibing alcoholic drinks,' and the Persian *dān* 'vessel' (al-Khafājī, *Shifāʾ al-ghalīl* 182).

(438) *Naqūʿ mishmish* (apricot compote)

Take dried sweet apricots of Khorasan (*mishmish lawzī Khurāsānī*),[11] wash them, spread them on the back of a sieve, and let them dry in the shade.

Take distilled water of Levantine borage (*māʾ lisān thawr Shāmī*); for each *raṭl* (pound) of apricot use 1 *raṭl* (1 pint) of borage water, 2 *ūqiyyas* (¼ cup) rosewater infused with musk, 3 *ūqiyyas* (3 ounces) high-quality sugar, 4 *ūqiyyas* (½ cup) distilled wine vinegar.[12] For each *raṭl* (pint) of all these liquids [together], use 3 *ūqiyyas* (3 ounces) dried pomegranate seeds (*ḥabb rummān*).

Put all the ingredients [except the apricots] in a clean soapstone pot (*qidr birām*), along with a tied bunch of mint. Let it boil three times,[13] and then remove it, cool it, and strain it through a sieve.

Now, take a bowl (*zibdiyya*), either porcelain (*ṣīnī*) or ceramic (*qīshānī*); wash it, and infuse it with the smoke of aloeswood and ambergris. Pack it with the sweet apricots (*mishmish lawzī*) first mentioned in the recipe, which have been left to dry out. Pour on them (**115r**) the prepared liquid, and add to the surface (*tukhtam*) a bit of musk and rosewater. Cover the opening with a linen cloth and on top of this a sheet of thin leather, and tie it [with a thread] and set it aside until needed. Serve it either by itself or in a *sukurdān* tray [along with many other small dishes of delicious foods and drinks].[14]

(439) Recipe for another [apricot] *naqūʿ*

Take [dried] apricots and wash them with rosewater until all the sand and impurities are removed. Spread them in the sun to dry.

Take a suitable amount of vinegar, and add sugar to it if you want it to be sweet. Also, add ½ *dirham* (¼ teaspoon) saffron, as well as *aṭrāf ṭīb* (spice blend), musk, and rosewater; add what is needed of these. Stir this liquid seasoning mix (*mizāj*) by hand, and then set it aside from early in the morning until noon, all the while keeping the apricots in the sun [to dry].

Now, take a wide-mouthed jar (*barniyya*), either porcelain (*ṣīnī*) or ceramic (*qīshānī*); wash it, dry it, and perfume it with the smoke of aloeswood and ambergris. Close the opening of the jar [while doing this,] so that it is infused with enough smoke (*bakhūr*).

---

11 This variety, from the northeastern Persian region of Khurasan, is intensely sweet, and its pits naturally open (al-Anṭākī, *Tadhkira* 330). See also n. 1 above.

12 See n. 8 above.

13 *Thalāth ghalyāt*, see glossary 9.2, s.v. *ghalā*.

14 See n. 10 above.

Take the apricots, put them in the jar and pour on them the prepared liquid mix (*mizāj*). Top the surface with musk and rosewater, and set it aside for an hour. [The apricots are eaten, and the remaining liquid is] served in small bowls (*sakārij*, sg *sukurruja*) as a drink—it is sweet, strained (*murawwaq*), and clear.

During Ramadan, make it early in the morning and serve it when the night sets [for the *ifṭār* meal]. During non-fasting days, make it at night and serve it the following morning.

(440) Recipe for another [apricot] *naqūʿ*

Take sweet apricots (*mishmish lawzī*);[15] wash them in fine-tasting water [lit., 'sweet'] to remove all the sand. Spread them on the back of a tray or sieve and leave them in a shaded place. Now,[16] take Levantine borage water, Levantine rosewater with musk and mint, and soak the apricots in them. When the apricots are moist enough, pack them in a green-glazed wide-mouthed jar (*barniyya*) or china bowl (*qadaḥ ṣīnī*) that has been perfumed with smoke of aloeswood and ambergris.

Pour on them vinegar which has been distilled (*khall mustaqṭar*) in a cucurbit (*qarʿa*) and alembic (*inbīq*),[17] add enough to cover the apricots. If this is not available, then use *khamīrat aqsimā*[18] instead. Add (**115v**) enough sugar to sweeten it. Top the surface with rosewater infused with musk, cover the vessel with a linen cloth and on top of that a sheet of thin leather (*riqq*), and tie it [with a thread].[19] Leave it overnight and use it the following morning. It is the best food to have as *naql* (mezze) with alcoholic drinks. If you remove the stones of the apricots and replace them with almonds, it will be very good, even better than *qamar al-dīn*, in delaying intoxication.[20]

---

15 See n. 1 above.

16 The following details, up to the mention of perfuming the vessel, are only available in DK, n. 5932.

17 See n. 8 above.

18 This is the distilled base for the digestive drink *aqsimā*, see recipes 404 and 423, in chapter 12 above.

19 The following lines are an addition from DK, n. 5932.

20 The Arabic verb used is *yunjiz* (lit., 'delivers its promise'). *Qamar al-dīn* are sheets of dried pureed apricot. See glossary 7, s.v. *mishmish*.

FIGURE 38 *Green glazed wide-mouthed jar* (barniyya), *thirteenth century, 36.20.47 (MET NY—Rogers Fund, 1936).*

CHAPTER 14

في صفة عمل أدوية القرف

Making Preparations Which Relieve Nausea (*adwiyat al-qaraf*)[1]

(441) Recipe for a preparation to relieve nausea (*dawāʾ qaraf*)
Take raisins, dried pomegranate seeds, and tamarind. Remove the seeds [of the raisins and tamarind] and pound all of them in a stone mortar (*jurn*), along with [dried] mint, black pepper, and Ceylon cinnamon (*qarfa*). Add wine vinegar and saffron, and stir the mix with a bunch of sweet basil (*ḥamāḥim rayḥān*),[2] [while boiling it on the fire].

Season the liquid with aloeswood, ambergris, musk, and rosewater after the pot has finished boiling. Store it away in a green-glazed wide-mouthed jar (*barniyya*), and use whenever needed.

(442) Recipe for *ṣalṣ* (smooth table sauce)[3]
Chop Macedonian parsley (*maqdūnis*),[4] mint, and a bit of rue. Add to them [crushed] walnuts, hazelnuts, almonds, and pistachios, along with black pepper, cassia (*dār Ṣīnī*), mastic, tahini, olive oil, lemon juice, thyme, toasted coriander and caraway seeds, garlic, and vinegar. [Mix well and] set aside to allow the flavors to blend and mellow.[5] It is wonderful.

---

1 *Qaraf* (nausea) is more commonly called *ghathayān* in the medieval sources on medicine and dietetics. In *Lisān al-ʿArab*, *qaraf* is explained as being in a state of near sickness (مداناة المرض).

2 *Ocimum basilicum*. Here I amended بعرق 'with a root of' to بعذق 'with a bunch of,' written as بعذوق 'with bunches' in C, n. 5948. This is more relevant to the context.

3 Pl. *ṣulūṣāt*, were served with the dishes, as they were believed to stimulate the appetite and aid digestion. This might justify the presence of two such recipes in a chapter dealing with queasiness. Otherwise, chapter 16 below is entirely dedicated to similar *ṣulūṣāt*. These two *ṣalṣ* recipes can also be found in *Waṣf* 117, 119, given in a chapter on fish dishes.

4 In this book, the name more frequently occurs as *baqdūnis*.

5 *Yukhammar*. The verb may also designate fermentation, but not in this context.

© KONINKLIJKE BRILL NV, LEIDEN, 2018 | DOI 10.1163/9789004349919_017

(443) Another *ṣalṣ* recipe, white

[Take] walnuts, garlic, cassia (*dār Ṣīnī*), white mustard seeds (*khardal abyaḍ*)[6] [all crushed]; tahini, and lemon juice. [Mix them together, set aside, and serve.]

(444) Recipe for a preparation to relieve nausea (*dawāʾ qaraf*)

Take red raisins, white sugar, wine vinegar, lemon [juice], a bit of black pepper, and sweet basil (*ḥamāḥim rayḥān*).

Remove the seeds from the raisins, pound them into paste and put them in a frying pan (*ṭājin*), and add the sugar—finely pounded, along with black pepper [vinegar and lemon juice]. Stir the pot with [a bunch of] sweet basil until it is done.

(445) Recipe for a preparation to relieve nausea (*dawāʾ qaraf*)

(**116r**) Take raisins and dried pomegranate seeds, pound them, stir them into wine vinegar, and then strain them and put the [resulting liquid] in a soapstone pot (*qidr birām*). Cook it on the fire with a bit of sugar, while stirring continuously with a bunch of mint, myrtle leaves (*marsīn*),[7] and sweet basil (*ḥamāḥim rayḥān*). Continue cooking until it thickens.

Add *aṭrāf ṭīb* (spice mix), a bit of black pepper, rosebuds (*zir ward*), and ginger—all pounded; stir the pot, and then remove. Stir in musk and rosewater, and put it away.

(446) Recipe for an excellent, exquisite preparation to relieve nausea (*dawāʾ qaraf*)

Take 2 *ūqiyyas* (2 ounces) dried seeds of pomegranate of Jūr,[8] Pound them in a stone mortar, along with 7 *ūqiyyas* washed mint leaves. Pound them thoroughly so that they mix well. Add 2 *ūqiyyas* (¼ cup) local rosewater (*māʾ ward baladī*), and squeeze on them the juice of two limes. Add ½ *ūqiyya* sugar, and put them in a pot on a low fire. Stir them until they mix, and then sprinkle on them a bit of crushed Javanese aloeswood (*ʿūd Qāqullī*). Stir the mix with sprigs from the Egyptian willow (*ʿīdān khilāf*),[9] or sprigs of mint (*ʿīdān naʿnāʿ*), until all the ingredients fuse into each other. Add rosewater seasoned with musk, and store it away [in glass jars until needed].

---

6 Also known as *khardal Shāmī* 'Levantine mustard,' and *isfind*.

7 Also known as *ās*.

8 A village in Shiraz, in southeastern Persia. It is known for its fertility and fruit orchards.

9 *Khilāf* tree is also called *ṣafṣāf Miṣrī*, *Salix aegyptiaca* (S). It is an Egyptian species of the willow tree.

(447) Another recipe [for *dawāʾ qaraf*]
[Take] 1 *ūqiyya* (2 tablespoons) lemon juice and 2 *ūqiyyas* (2 ounces) sugar. Put them in a pot on a low fire and stir them with fresh [sprigs] of sweet basil (*ḥamāḥim rayḥān*) until the mix thickens. Sprinkle on them ¼ *dirham* (⅛ teaspoon) *aṭrāf ṭīb* (spice blend) (**116v**). Stir the pot and then remove.

(448) Recipe for a preparation to relieve nausea (*dawāʾ qaraf*)
Take sour orange (*nāranj*),[10] peel it, and extract its pulp in chunks, keeping the juice vesicles unruptured. Sprinkle sugar on it, squeeze on it *nāranj* juice, add borage water (*māʾ lisān al-thawr*), water of blue Egyptian lotus (*māʾ nūfar*),[11] ice cold water (*māʾ thalj*), rosewater, and distilled water of Egyptian willow bark (*māʾ al-khilāf*).[12] It is wonderful. If you also add some rue and a bit of *aṭrāf al-ṭīb* (spice blend), and let it boil with them, it will also be good. And preparing Damascus citron (*kabbād*) the same way as sour orange (*nāranj*) is done, will also be good.

(449) Recipe for *laʿūq* (restorative thick syrup),[13] good for nausea and vomiting (*qayʾ*)
Take flakes from a smoky kitchen wall.[14] Add water to it, drain it, and add water to it again. Throw in the outer shells of fresh pistachios, and set it aside for a day, after which you stir it, and then set it aside until all the sediment settles in the bottom.

Take the clear liquid sitting on the settled flakes, and add lime juice (*māʾ laymūn akhḍar*), local rosewater (*māʾ ward baladī*), juice of unripe grapes, fresh sour pomegranate juice, and sumac molasses (*qaṭr summāq*). Also, add the liquid from the stems of a grape vine (*zarjūn dawālī*), which you get by pounding them and extracting the resulting juice.

Put the liquid in a large brass pot (*dast*), put a lump of sugar in it, enough to sweeten it and balance its acidity. Boil it down on a low fire until it has the right consistency of *laʿūqāt*.[15] [While boiling,] stir the pot with two or three bunches

---

10 Here I replaced *turunj* 'citron' with *nāranj* 'sour orange,' based on context, and on DK, n. 6001 toward the end of the recipe, which indeed mentions the fruit as *nāranj*.

11 More properly called *naylūfar*.

12 See n. 9 above.

13 Pl. *laʿūqāt*. The syrup is sufficiently firm but still soft; therefore, it is usually licked with a spoon. See glossary 4.

14 *Turāb ḥāʾiṭ maṭbakh mudakhkhan*. The mud plaster coated with cooking smoke seems to have some medicinal benefits. It could have been the soot and kaolin 'hydrated aluminum silicate,' which, in traditional medicine, is known for its soothing effects on the stomach.

15 See n. 13 above.

of mint; whenever one bunch wilts, replace it with another fresh one. Use [this preparation] whenever needed.

(450) Recipe made with dried pomegranate seeds, good for treating nauseated people with hot humoral properties (*aṣḥāb al-amzija al-ḥārra*)[16]

Soak dried pomegranate seeds in water of blue Egyptian lotus (*māʾ laynūfar*),[17] borage water (*māʾ al-lisān*),[18] and rosewater. Add mint and rue, squeeze in limes (*laymūn akhḍar*), (**117r**) sweeten it with sugar, and drink it. It will indeed be more delicious than *fuqqāʿ* (foamy beer).[19] However, because water of blue Egyptian lotus (*māʾ al-nūfar*)[20] slackens the stomach and weakens the sexual ability,[21] it does not agree with people with hot humoral properties, and God knows best.

(451) Recipe made with sugar and lemon

Take white sugar, water of blue Egyptian lotus (*māʾ al-nūfar*),[22] borage water (*māʾ lisān*),[23] and *aṭrāf ṭīb* (spice blend) [and combine them all]. Rub and press rue and mint into the liquid, and sprinkle it with rosewater. Perfume a *qarrāba* (large flagon) with smoke of ambergris and aloeswood; repeat three times, and then pour the liquid into it. It will be more delicious than *fuqqāʿ* (foamy beer), and more beneficial.

(452) Recipe made with dried pomegranate seeds

It prevents nausea when drinking medicine, and improves bad taste in the mouth.

Take dried pomegranate seeds, pound them in a mortar (*hāwan*), adding white sugar as well as mint leaves, and continue until they are thoroughly pounded. Sprinkle them with rosewater seasoned with musk, and perfume them with smoke of ambergris; do this twice or thrice, and use.

---

16 See glossary 11, s.v. *mizāj*.

17 More correctly known as *naylūfar*.

18 I.e., *māʾ lisān al-thawr*.

19 For recipes, see chapter 12.

20 See n. 17 above.

21 *Naylūfar* is known for its cold and moist properties, and hence its negative effects on sexual virility, see glossary 8.

22 See n. 17 above.

23 See n. 18 above.

(453) *Al-nāranj* (sour orange drink)

Take *nāranj* and extract the juice vesicles of its pulp.[24] Cook it the same way you do with *sharāb al-ḥummāḍ*.[25] It is good for black bile (*sawdāʾ*). It also curbs yellow bile (*yaqmaʿ al-ṣafrāʾ*). [It is] gorgeous (*nihāya fī ḥusnihi*).

(454) Recipe for a preparation to relieve nausea (*dawāʾ qaraf*)

Take raisins from Upper Egypt (*zabīb Ṣaʿīdī*), wash them in water, [drain them,] and set them aside wrapped in a *miʾzar* (woolen wrapper cloth) overnight. Discard their seeds.

Set a soapstone pot (*qidr birām*) on the fire, put in bee honey, [add some water] and throw in the raisins. Let them cook until the mix has the consistency of *jullāb* (medium sugar syrup).

Now, take a bit of saffron, stir it with rosewater seasoned with musk, and add vinegar to it. Extract the juice of fresh mint by pounding it, (117v) and add it to the vinegar, along with small amounts of water of blue Egyptian lotus (*māʾ nūfar*),[26] and rosewater. Add all this to the raisins and honey, and cook the mix on low heat until it has the consistency of sugar syrup (*jullāb*), and then remove it.

Add to it betel leaves (*tunbul*), spikenard (*sunbul*), clove stalks (*ḥaṭab qaranful*), mace (*basbāsa*), nutmeg (*jawz bawwa*), ginger (*zanjabīl*), black pepper (*fulful*), cassia (*dār Ṣīnī*), rosebuds (*zir ward*), and mastic gum (*maṣṭakāʾ*). Pound them all and whip them into the syrup.

Perfume a green-glazed wide-mouthed jar (*barniyya*) with smoke of aloeswood and ambergris, close its top for about an hour, and then put the syrup in it, and store it away until needed.

(455) Another recipe [for treating nausea]

Take *zabīb Sulṭī* (sultana raisins), choose the excellent ones, which are delicious and plump. Discard the stems, wash the raisin in water, and spread them out in a sunny place. Next, remove their seeds, and pound them in *jurn al-fuqqāʿī*,[27] along with wine vinegar, mint, and *aṭrāf al-ṭīb* (spice blend), until the consistency of the mix resembles ointment (*marham*). Add enough sugar to sweeten it; add sugar and rosewater as needed.

---

24 The juice vesicles are called *shaʿr* and *shuʿayr* (lit., 'hair').

25 See, for instance, recipe 352 above.

26 See n. 17 above.

27 Large stone mortar used by beer-makers to crush grains, herbs, and spices. It is also safe for pounding liquid and acid ingredients. See Ibn Abī Uṣaybiʿa, *ʿUyūn al-anbāʾ* 394.

Perfume a green-glazed wide-mouthed jar (*barniyya*) with smoke of aloeswood and ambergris, [spoon the raisin mix into it], top it with musk and sugar, and store it away until needed.

(456) Recipe for a preparation to relieve nausea (*dawāʾ qaraf*)

Take black cumin of Kirmān (*kammūn Kirmānī*), Andalusian wild caraway (*karāwiya Andalusiyya*),[28] 5 *dirhams* (15 grams/2½ teaspoons) of each. Also, take 1 *dirham* (½ teaspoon) of each of [the following:] mild white potash (*ushnān ʿaṣāfīrī*),[29] *qurṣ Yamānī* (pastille of Yemen),[30] and *qurṣ qurūn* (pastille of coral).[31] Add one *dirham* (3 grams/½ teaspoon) [seeds of] Iraqi couch grass (*najm ʿIrāqī*), myrtle berries (*ḥabb ās*), oak gall (*ʿafṣ*), Levantine wild pomegranate blossoms (*jullanār Shāmī*). Also add 1 *dirham* ginger, ⅛ *dirham* Javanese aloeswood (*ʿūd Qāqullī*), ½ *dirham* cubeb (*kabāba*), and a similar amount of musk-scented pastille (*sukk misk*), 1 *dirham* mace (*basbāsa*), (**118r**) 2 *dirhams* purslane seeds (*bazr rijla*), and one madder berry (*thamarat fuwwa*).[32] Pound all these ingredients and mix them.

Now, take unripe grapes—if not in season, use lime juice instead—pound them and extract the juice, and put it in a soapstone pot. Let it boil.

Take ¼ *raṭl* (4 ounces) white sugar and ½ *raṭl* (8 ounces) tamarind. Soak the tamarind in wine vinegar until it softens, then press and mash it [and strain it to extract its juice]. Now, add sugar and tamarind to the soapstone pot, where you have put the above-mentioned unripe grape juice (*māʾ al-ḥiṣrim*).

Light a low fire under the pot, and when it boils add the above prepared [pounded] spices and herbs (*ḥawāʾij*). Wait until all the ingredients are well combined, and then take the pot off the heat.

---

28 Also known as *qardamānā*, and *karāwiya jabaliyya* 'mountain caraway'; it grows abundantly in the mountains near Granada. See glossary 8.

29 Also known as *ushnān Fārisī*, see glossary 8 and 11.

30 They must have been restorative pills made with frankincense, available for purchase from druggists' shops. Frankincense was believed to be good for the stomach.

31 *Qurūn* must have been a dialectical corruption of *qurūl*, which is also known as *bussadh*. A recipe for making these coral pastilles is available in Sābūr b. Sahl, *al-Aqrabādhīn* 121, which uses coral and frankincense in addition to other ingredients. They are bound with gum Arabic and egg white, and shaped into pastilles.

32 I took the edited text's فواد as a misreading of فوة 'madder'; otherwise, as far as I know, the edited word is not relevant here.

Now take 1 *dirham* (½ teaspoon) of each of tabashir of Tastar (*ṭabāshīr Tashtar*)[33] and dry gum lac (*lukk yebis*);[34] in addition to ½ *dirham* (¼ teaspoon) saffron threads (*zaʿfarān shaʿr*). Crush all these and throw them into the pot when it cools. Add basil seeds (*bazr rayḥān*), use whole ones.

Store it away [in a jar] and use it as needed. It is wonderful.

(457) Recipe for a preparation to relieve nausea (*dawāʾ qaraf*)

Take lemon juice, fresh sour pomegranate juice, local rosewater (*māʾ ward baladī*), and juice of unripe grapes (*māʾ ḥiṣrim*). Also use tamarind, which has been steeped in wine vinegar, and then pressed mashed, and strained [to extract its juice]; and dried pomegranate seeds, which have been pounded and their juice extracted [by steeping them in water and then straining it].

Add sugar to all these ingredients, put them [in a pot] on the fire, and while boiling, use 2 bunches of mint to stir the liquid. [While boiling,] add pieces of quince and *aṭrāf ṭīb* (spice blend). Take limes, slit them lengthwise in four places, stuff the slits with black pepper and *aṭrāf ṭīb*, and throw them into the liquid (*sharāb*).

Let it boil (118v) until it has the consistency of *laʿūq* (restorative thick syrup).[35] It is to be used by those who are nauseated, for it is indeed the best of preparations to treat nausea.

About the mint: every time a bunch wilts, replace it with a fresh one.

(458) Another recipe: [This is a duplicate of the first half of recipe 448.]

(459) Another recipe

Take raisins and soak them in very sour vinegar overnight. The following morning, strain the raisins and pound them thoroughly. Combine honey with the drained vinegar [and the pounded raisins] and let them boil very well until the mix thickens.

Add spices (*afāwih*) to it, namely, spikenard, betel leaves, cloves, nutmeg, black pepper, and Ceylon cinnamon (*qarfa*). Use equal amounts. These spices should be added when you take the pot off the heat. Also, add a bit of rue.

---

33 Tabashir is loose lumps of chalky porous silica deposited in the stem cavities of reeds. Tastar (or the dialectical variant Tashtar) is a city in the Persian province of Khuzistan, bordering Basra in southern Iraq.

34 As it occurs in DK, n. 6080.

35 See n. 13 above.

(460) Recipe for an excellent preparation to relieve nausea (*dawāʾ qaraf khāṣṣ*), it is the best

Take 1 *ūqiyya* (1 ounce) fine-tasting dried pomegranate seeds, pound them in a stone *ṣallāya*,[36] along with 4 bunches of mint; pound them very well so that they mix together.

Add to the mix 1 *ūqiyya* (2 tablespoons) local rosewater (*māʾ ward baladī*), and squeeze the juice of one lime on it. Add 1 *ūqiyya* (1 ounce) sugar to all of it.

Put the pot on a low fire and stir to mix the ingredients. [Remove the pot and] sprinkle in a bit of crushed Javanese aloeswood (*ʿūd Qāqullī*)—add ¼ *dirham* (⅛ teaspoon). Add a similar amount of ambergris, and a lump of musk, too. Stir the pot with a sprig of Egyptian willow (*khilāf*)[37] or sprigs of mint, so that they release their essence and mix the ingredients well. [Store it in glass jars, and] use it [as needed].

(461) Recipe for a preparation to relieve nausea (*dawāʾ qaraf*), (119r) also good for headaches (*ṣudāʿ*) and fever (*ḥummā*)

Take 3 *ūqiyyas* (3 ounces) tamarind and 4 *ūqiyyas* (½ cup) local rosewater (*māʾ ward baladī*). Soak the tamarind in rosewater overnight. The following morning, press and mash the tamarind and strain it through a sieve. Put the [strained] liquid in an earthenware pot (*qidr fakhkhār*) and suspend it over the fire.

Add aloeswood, ambergris, Ceylon sandalwood (*ṣandal Maqāṣīrī*), and 3 *ūqiyyas ʿaqīd sakanjabīn* (chewy oxymel candy) to the pot.[38] Let the pot boil until the mix thickens—add some sugar to it as well. So, when it thickens, stir in a bit of rosewater and store it in a glazed wide-mouthed earthenware jar. Cover it, and store it away [and use whenever needed].

When you boil the pot on the fire, stir it with sprigs of myrtle leaves (*marsīn*) or sweet basil (*ḥamāḥim rayḥān*).

(462) Another recipe

Take red amaranth (*ḥamāḥim rayḥān aḥmar*),[39] soak it in lime juice (*māʾ laymūn akhḍar*) overnight, and then press and mash it, strain the liquid, and

---

36 A *ṣallāya* was a wide stone slab that was used with a large stone (*fihr*) to crush spices and aromatics.

37 See n. 9 above.

38 Here I amended the edited text based on context and on a recipe we already know (see recipe 348 above). *Sakanjabīl* is a variant of *sakanjabīn*.

39 Based on al-Malik al-Muẓaffar, *al-Muʿtamad* 141, and al-Hurawī, *Baḥr al-jawāhir* 121, who identified another type of *ḥamāḥim* as *bustān abrūz*, the amaranth with its terminal vividly red spikes of flowers. See glossary 8.

put it in an earthenware pot suspended over the fire. Add sugar as needed, and also add aloeswood, ambergris, Ceylon sandalwood (*ṣandal Maqāṣīrī*), and a bit of saffron beaten (*yuqtal*) in Damascene rosewater (*mā᾽ ward Shāmī*).

Let the pot cook until the mix thickens [into syrup]. Put it in a green-glazed wide-mouthed jar (*barniyya*), cover the top, and store it away until needed.

(463) Another recipe

Take black raisins; remove their seeds and stems after you wash them. Soak them in vinegar overnight, and then drain them [but keep the drained vinegar], and finely pound them in a mortar, either *hāwan* or *jurn*,[40] along with mint.

Put the [drained] vinegar on the fire [with the pounded raisins], (**119v**) adding sugar as needed. After it is done cooking, add *aṭrāf al-ṭīb* (spice blend), black pepper, ginger, rosebuds, nutmeg, saffron, Levantine rosewater, and *sandal maqāṣīrī* (top quality sandalwood).

Beat (*yuqtal*) a bit of civet (*zabada*) in wine vinegar,[41] and add it to the pot after you remove it from the fire. Stir the mix, empty it into a vessel perfumed with the aromatic smoke of aloeswood and ambergris, and store it away.

(464) Another recipe

Take black raisins, discard the very dry ones among them. Wash them, and then dry them on the back of a sieve. Remove their seeds, wash them, and finely pound them in a stone mortar (*jurn*) with mint and vinegar.[42] Add [more] vinegar and strain them. Strain the vinegar several times until nothing remains of the raisins in it, [set aside the strained raisins].

Now, take the tender tops of fresh mint sprigs (*qulūb naʿnaʿ*), discard their stems. In a glazed ceramic jar (*qaṭramīz*), layer the [strained] raisins alternately with the mint leaves, until the jar is almost full. Pour the strained vinegar into the jar. If it is sour, sweeten it with bee honey or date syrup (*dibs*)—to match the humoral properties (*mizāj*) of the person it is for.[43] Add to the mix a bit of *aṭrāf al-ṭīb* (spice blend) and ginger, and set it aside for six or seven

40 The *jurn* is carved out of a large piece of stone, whereas *hāwan* is molded metal, mostly copper.

41 *Zabada* must be the colloquial Egyptian name for civet; it is more commonly known as *zabād*. Civet, as mentioned in Ibn al-Ukhuwwa, *Maʿālim al-qurba*, fol. 82v, is clearly vowelized as *zabada*.

42 See note 41 above.

43 Based on the tenets of the Galenic theory, while both honey and date syrup are hot, the former is dry and the latter is moist. See glossary 11, s.v. *mizāj*.

days. If you wish, add Nuṣaybīn rose petals,[44] when in season; it will also be good.

(465) Another recipe

It is made like the previous one. Plain vinegar is used, and it is sweetened with whatever you wish. This variety does not contain pounded raisins.

(466) Another one

Take raisins from *jawza* grapes (*zabīb jawzānī*),[45] layer them with mint in a glazed ceramic jar (*qaṭramīz*) as we mentioned above, (**120r**) and pour sweetened wine vinegar on them, along with *aṭrāf ṭīb* (spice blend) and pistachios. It will come out good, and will have a sharp flavor (*ḥirrīf*).

(467) Another one

Take 1 *raṭl* (1 pound) bee honey, 1 *raṭl* (2 cups) aged wine vinegar, and 1 *raṭl* (1 pound) excellent raisins from *jawza* grapes (*zabīb jawzānī*).[46]

Remove the seeds from the raisins and pound them thoroughly. Put honey in a large red copper pot (*dast nuḥās aḥmar*) and suspend it over the fire. Let it boil well, and then add the raisins to it. Add vinegar to the mix while the pot is boiling, until you finish adding all the vinegar, and then remove.

Now, take 1 *ūqiyya* (1 ounce) cloves, 1 *ūqiyya* ginger, ½ *ūqiyya* black pepper, ½ *dirham* (¼ teaspoon) aloeswood, 2 bunches of mint, and one bunch of rue. Chop the herbs, pound the spices, and add them to the pot. Scent it with rosewater, and store it away. And God knows best.

---

44 Nuṣaybīn was a city in upper Mesopotamia, now in the Turkish province of Mardin. It was renowned for its orchards and gardens. Roses named after it are pinkish in hue. See glossary 8, s.v. *ward*.

45 *Jawza* is deemed an excellent Levantine variety of grapes; see Dozy, *Takmilat al-maʿājim* 245. They are not large, and turn intensely yellow when fully ripe.

46 See note above.

CHAPTER 15

في عمل الخردل اللطيف والحارّ الحرّيف

Making Mustard [Condiments], Mild and Pungent Hot[1]

(468) [Recipe for making *khardal* (condiment)][2]

Take mustard seeds, pick them over to remove any small wood chips (*diqq*), any with insect damage (*musawwas*),[3] twigs (*ʿīdān*), and any other impurities. Put the seeds in a *hāwan* (mortar), and pound them finely. If this proves difficult, add a piece of cotton to the seeds and they will crush quickly.

Once you finish pounding, add an equal amount of walnuts to the seeds, and continue pounding. Then pour as much vinegar as you like and strain the mixture in a fine sieve. You will get mustard that is like white sea foam (*zabad*). Take the foam only, and add to it a little salt and serve it. With what's left, make *ṣināb* sauce with pounded raisins.[4] If you prefer, **(120v)** sweeten it with sugar.

If you wish, pound the mustard seeds first, put them in a small tub (*ijjāna*), and pour in enough water to knead them. With the tub facing the wind, whip the mustard mix continuously by hand until it becomes white.[5] Next, knead together [pounded] walnuts, salt, and pleasant-tasting vinegar (*khall ṭayyib*). Add this mixture to the whipped mustard. [Continue whipping, and] skim any

1 Besides mustard condiment, often referred to as *khardal maʿmūl* 'prepared mustard,' this chapter also includes dipping sauces, collectively called *ṣibāgh*; these may or may not contain mustard. They were poured on fish and poultry dishes and were intended to aid in digestion.

2 This detailed recipe for mustard condiment is found in al-Warrāq, chapter 38, where it is titled *ṣifat al-khardal*. Here I used it to amend the edited text. Interestingly, while both compilers must have used a similar source for sauces and condiments, al-Warrāq took one recipe and moved on to other chapters, whereas the compiler of the *Kanz* went on and copied 17 recipes from it.

3 Here I used al-Warrāq's version, which copies the word correctly as مسوس and not سوس, as in the edited text.

4 The edited text replaces the word *ṣināb* 'mustard-raisin sauce' with the non-specific *shay'* 'something.' Quite likely, the name *ṣināb* was not a familiar word at the time the *Kanz* was written.

5 It is my guess that the person whipping the mustard mixture is advised to face the wind to protect him from inhaling the rising fumes of the mix. See, for instance, recipe 518 below, where the person working on chopped green mustard leaves is advised to mask his face.

 | DOI 10.1163/9789004349919_018

foam that rises to the surface and transfer it to another container. [This will be your mustard condiment]. Make *ṣināb* sauce with the remaining mustard mix by adding raisins,[6] sugar, and other ingredients [as above].

If you wish, knead the pounded mustard [with some water] and form it into a disc (*qurṣ*), which you stick into a bowl (*ṭayfūr*). Sprinkle ashes on it and rinse it in water several times until it is clean. Some dirty-looking bitter water will come out [of the mustard disc]. Repeat with the other side of the mustard disc. Then add pounded walnuts and beat the mix hard by hand. Skim whatever froth rises, [this will be your mustard condiment]. The amount of foam depends on how long you beat it, and how many walnuts you use. Make *ṣināb*[7] with the remaining mustard mix using raisins, sugar, pomegranate juice; or whatever you like.

(469) Another recipe [for mustard condiment]

Sift the pounded mustard [seeds]—½ *raṭl* (½ pound) of it. Put it in a *qaṣʿa* (large wide bowl), sprinkle it with a bit of water, knead it so that it releases its oil, and loses its bitterness. Put it in a bowl (*zibdiyya*), and add to it ½ *raṭl* (1 cup) vinegar, ½ *raṭl* (½ pound) bee honey, 1½ *dirhams* (¾ teaspoon) ginger, and 2½ *dirhams* (1¼ teaspoons) salt. [Mix the ingredients well], strain the mustard sauce, and put it in a *sukurruja* (small bowl for dips).

[The following recipes, to recipe 480, deal with *ṣibāgh* (dipping sauces, see n. 1 above)]

(470) Recipe for a dipping sauce (*ṣibāgh*) to be eaten with [cooked] fresh fish (*samak ṭarī*)[8]

Take the extracted juices of onion, *kurrāth* (leaf leaks), and cilantro (*kuzbara raṭba*); and take as much wine vinegar, fresh water (*māʾ ʿadhb*), and salt as needed. (**121r**) Also take olive oil.[9]

---

6 Once again *ṣināb* is referred to as *shayʾ*, see n. 4 above.

7 See n. 4 above.

8 This recipe and the following two (471, 472) are also found in al-Warrāq Istanbul MS, fols. 111r–v, with some stylistic differences and textual variants. Apparently, both drew on a similar source, a pamphlet that perhaps specialized in cold dishes and accompanying sauces. In addition, by examining the sauce recipes in al-Warrāq Istanbul MS, I have discovered that in this recipe our copyist unknowingly combined two recipes; this explains the absence of instructions on what to do with the reduced sauce in the pot. Here I amended the text based on Istanbul recipes.

9 In al-Warrāq Istanbul MS version, the amounts used should be 1 *raṭl* (2 cups) each, of juices of onion, leaf leeks, and cilantro; 1½ *raṭls* each, of vinegar and water; ¼ *raṭl* of olive oil.

Combine all the ingredients in a pot, and put it in the *tannūr* (an open-topped, bell-shaped clay oven) with the fish.[10] Keep it there until the fish bakes, and most of the liquid in the pot evaporates from the heat of the fire—2 *raṭl*s (4 cups) or less of the liquid should be left in it.

Now, take crushed caraway, asafetida leaves (*anjudhān*), thyme, black pepper, cassia (*dār Ṣīnī*), chopped rue, cilantro,[11] and a bit of crushed garlic. Throw all these spices and herbs into the pot when you take it out of the *tannūr*. Stir the pot, and if you wish, put the fish, while it is still hot, in a large wide bowl (*qaṣʿa*) and pour this *ṣibāgh* on it.

[Another recipe [for *ṣibāgh*] from the copy of Kushājim][12]

Take asafetida leaves (*anjudhān*), thyme, caraway, black pepper, galangal, cassia (*dār Ṣīnī*), ginger, *murrī* (liquid fermented sauce), and cilantro juice.[13] Combine the dried spices, and pound them thoroughly, and knead them [along with the rest of the ingredients] with the [crushed] kernels of 23 walnuts, along with olive oil and salt—use as much as needed. Also add crushed cloves of garlic. Knead the paste very well, and spread it in [the bottom of a] glass (*qadaḥ*). Make some smoke by sprinkling olive oil on an ember and turn the glass over it, to infuse the spice paste inside it with smoke. Repeat several times until the paste is sufficiently smoky. Start doing this as soon as you are finished preparing the fish [and it is already in the *tannūr*].

So, take the smoked spice mix, put it in a glass bottle (*qinnīna*), and add to it very sour vinegar (*khall ḥādhiq*), and a glass of *maṭbūkh* (non-alcoholic cooked wine). Whip them vigorously.

When the fish is done baking, take it out of the *tannūr*, put it on a plate, and pour the sauce all over it. You will have added leaves of rue, mint, and thyme to the sauce bottle. If you wish, add them finely chopped.

Knowing these amounts will make more useful the later information, that only 2 *raṭls* or less of the liquid should remain in the pot.

10 In al-Warrāq Istanbul MS, fol. 111r, the pot is placed under a suspended fatty fish that is baking, so that all the melting fats drip into the liquid in the pot.

11 I completed this first recipe based on al-Warrāq Istanbul MS, fol. 111r. See n. 8 above.

12 As it occurs in al-Warrāq Istanbul MS, fol. 217v. Kushājim (d. 961) was a famous Abbasid poet and gourmet cook who wrote several cookbooks; these were referred to as *Kutub al-ṭabāʾikh li-Kushājim* (cookbooks by Kushājim). See al-Ghazālī, *Sirr al-ʿālamayn* 8. See also n. 8 above.

13 Here we continue the rest of the second recipe, as it is copied in the edited text. While it is similar to the al-Warrāq Istanbul MS version, see n. 8 above, it has additional finishing details.

(471) Another recipe [for *ṣibāgh*], to souse (*tunaqqiʿ*) fried fresh fish in[14]

Knead crushed mustard seeds with cold water and press and spread the paste onto a plate (*ṣaḥn*). Wash it with [a solution of] salt, ash (*ramād*) and hot water, and then scrape the paste off the dish after it is thoroughly washed.

Now, take thoroughly crushed walnuts, the same amount as that of mustard,[15] (**121v**) add it to the [washed] mustard, and pound them both in a stone mortar, and make mustard [condiment] with them as usual.[16]

Take 1 *sukurruja* (½ cup) of this mustard and whip it with a similar amount of wine vinegar. Add caraway, black pepper, ginger, cassia (*dār Ṣīnī*), chopped rue, cloves of garlic, and asafetida leaves (*anjudhān*); all crushed. Whip them with the mustard and vinegar. [Finally,] add crushed coriander seeds or chopped fresh cilantro.

Arrange the pieces of fried fresh fish on platters (*jāmāt*), and pour this prepared dipping sauce (*ṣibāgh*) all over them. Sprinkle chopped rue leaves on them, and set them aside to allow the fish to absorb the flavor of the sauce.

Serve this dish along with peeled radishes (*fujl*). It is truly delicious.

(472) Another recipe [for *ṣibāgh*] which gives fried salt-cured fish (*samak māliḥ*)[17] soused (*yunaqqaʿ*) in it a delicious flavor[18]

Take a handful of raisins with the seeds removed. Soak them in wine vinegar for an hour, and then throw them into a stone mortar and pound them thoroughly. Add crushed cloves of garlic, and 1 *sukurruja* (½ cup) mustard condiment (*khardal maʿmūl*), prepared with walnuts and mustard seeds.[19]

Add to the mix a bit of asafetida leaves (*anjudhān*), coriander seeds, cassia (*dār Ṣīnī*), and aniseeds, about ½ *dirham* (¼ teaspoon) of each—or more, depending on the amount of the [fried] fish arranged on platters.

In a glass bottle (*qinnīna*), vigorously whip this mix of spices and vinegar, along with olive oil. Mix in tender tips of stalks of mint, common parsley (*karafs*), and cilantro. When it is all whipped well, pour it on the fish. Set the platters aside for an hour [to allow the fish to soak up the sauce], and then serve it.

---

14 See n.8 above.

15 Here I amended the edited text by replacing مقل وزن الخردل وجوز مدقوق, which makes no sense, with مثل وزن الخردل جوز مسحوق, which means, 'crushed walnuts, same amount as that of mustard,' as it is more accurately copied in al-Warrāq Istanbul MS.

16 See the first recipe in this chapter.

17 See recipe 240 above for directions on how to cook the salt-cured fish.

18 See n. 8 above.

19 See the first recipe in this chapter for directions.

(473) Another [*ṣibāgh*] recipe for young chickens (*farārīj*)

Take (**122r**) black pepper, coriander, cassia (*dār Ṣīnī*), cloves (*qaranful*), caraway, and thyme, 1 *ūqiyya* (1 ounce) of each. Pound them all and sift them.

Take pounded mustard seeds and walnuts, and a bit of salt. Dissolve them in extracted liquid of [pounded] raisins and dried pomegranate seeds [that were steeped in vinegar and their juice pressed out]. Mix them with the pounded spices and herbs. Add as much as needed.

Pour this sauce on [grilled] young chickens, which have been cut into pieces. First, put a layer of the breasts and on top of these a layer of the wings and legs. Pour the *ṣibāgh* all over them, and set the plate aside to let the flavors of the sauce penetrate the meat.

[Garnish the dish with] chopped peeled tender *khiyār* (common cucumber) and some chopped leaves of tarragon (*ṭarkhūn*), in addition to thinly sliced boiled eggs. Spread sweet-smelling sprigs of herbs (*rayḥān*) under it, that is, under the plate itself.[20]

Recipe for a dipping sauce (*ṣibāgh*), to be eaten with *dajāj maḥshī* (stuffed chicken)[21]

Take the kernels of 20 walnuts, finely pound them and put them in a green-glazed bowl (*ghaḍāra*). Add a bit of black pepper, ginger, thyme,[22] galangal (*khūlanjān*), cumin, as well as a *sukurruja* (½ cup) of mustard condiment (*khardal murabbā*), a ladleful of *murrī* (liquid fermented sauce), a bit of pounded cassia bark [?],[23] and garlic cloves pounded in a stone mortar (*mihrasa*). Drizzle sweet and mellow olive oil (*zayt ʿadhb*) over them, and whip them vigorously.

Dip in it whatever you choose of the cooked chicken; or, if you wish, use it as a dipping sauce.[24]

---

20 This is done for the sake of presentation. In addition, the herb will spread a pleasant aroma around the dish. In this context, *rayḥān* generally designates any sweet-smelling herbs, plants, and flowers, such as mint, basil, and myrtle.

21 This recipe only appears in DK, appendix 41. For a stuffed chicken dish, see, for instance, recipe 118 above.

22 Written as زعطر, a dialectical variant of زعتر.

23 Possibly, the meaningless أعداد المدقوق might be a misreading of أعواد الدارصيني المدقوق.

24 The Arabic expression is كلْ منه غمساً. In this case, the sauce is put in a small deep bowl, and the eaters treat themselves to it by dipping pieces of bread or morsels of meat in it.

(474) Another [condiment] recipe, served as table sauce,[25] good with all kinds of food. It aids digestion, dispels winds, and breaks down phlegm (*yuqaṭṭiʿ al-balgham*)

Take 2 *ūqiyyas* (2 ounces) shelled walnuts, crush them in a stone mortar, and blend them (*yurabbab*) with the foamy mustard condiment (*raghwat al-khardal*) that has been extracted, and enhanced with vinegar, honey, and bread crumbs.[26] Season it with a bit of salt, and put it in a bowl (*zibdiyya*). Scatter chopped rue leaves all over the surface, drizzle it with olive oil, sprinkle it with a bit of salt, and put it on the table.

(475) Another [*ṣibāgh*] recipe [used with salt-cured fish]

Take mustard condiment (*khardal maʿmūl*),[27] and dissolve it in the strained extracted liquid of pounded raisins,[28] along with a pounded garlic clove. Season it with thyme, galangal (*khūlanjān*), asafetida root (*maḥrūth*), cumin, coriander, and a bit of aniseeds (*anīsūn*). Mix all these ingredients.

Pour the sauce on the [fried] salt-cured fish (*samak māliḥ*),[29] and chop fresh rue and common parsley (*karafs*) on it. [Set it aside for a while] to let the fish absorb the flavors of the sauce.

(476) Another [*ṣibāgh*] recipe used with fish

(**122v**) Take wine vinegar, common parsley (*karafs*), rue, thyme, mint, black pepper, cumin, caraway, cassia (*dār Ṣīnī*), and salt. [Mix all the ingredients and pour them on fried or grilled fish.]

(477) Recipe for a dipping sauce (*ṣibāgh*) which alleviates the harms of fish when eaten together

[Take] spikenard, cloves, Ceylon cinnamon (*qarfa*), nutmeg, and mastic gum. Use 1 *dirham* (½ teaspoon/3 grams) of each. Crush them all, and dissolve them in equal amounts of vinegar and aged *murrī* (liquid fermented sauce). This should be eaten with fresh fish dishes (*samak ṭarī*).

25 The Arabic expression is يتأدّم به على المائدة.

26 See the first recipe in this chapter for directions on how make this foamy mustard condiment.

27 See above note.

28 Judging from the recipes, the pounded raisins are steeped in vinegar first, and then their juice is pressed out.

29 See recipe 240 above for directions on how to cook salt-cured fish.

(478) Another [*ṣibāgh*] recipe; it helps digest the fish, invigorate coitus, and arouse the desire for intercourse

Take ginger and cassia (*dār Ṣīnī*), 2 *dirhams* (1 teaspoon) of each; ajowan (*nānkhawāh*) and *maḥrūth* (asafetida root), 1 *dirham* (½ teaspoon) of each; and 2 *dirhams* (1 teaspoon) salt of scincus (*milḥ saqanqūr*).[30]

Crush all the ingredients and dissolve them in a liquid of *murrī* (fermented sauce) combined with onion juice. Use it as a dipping sauce (*ṣibāgh*).[31]

(479) Another [*ṣibāgh*] recipe; it prevents fish from changing their elemental properties into harmful ones[32]

[Take] dried thyme, coriander, saffron, and caraway, 1 *dirham* (½ teaspoon) of each. Crush them all, sift them, and then dissolve them in *khall al-ushturghāz*.[33] Use it as a dipping sauce (*ṣibāgh*).

(480) Another [*ṣibāgh*] recipe that excites the appetite

Take mustard seeds, spikenard, cloves, ginger, cassia (*dār Ṣīnī*), black pepper, caraway, coriander, and cumin. Pound them all and sift them, and then dissolve them in honey, vinegar, and *murrī* (liquid fermented sauce). Use it as a dipping sauce (*ṣibāgh*).[34]

[The chapter ends with four recipes on mustard condiments]

(481) Another recipe for *khardal* (mustard condiment), good for those with an excess in moist humoral properties (*ruṭūbāt*), cold winds (*riyāḥ bārida*), joint aches and pains, and acid belching (*jushā' ḥāmiḍ*)

Take 1 *raṭl* (1 pound) good white mustard seeds (*khardal Shāmī*),[35] pound them and sift them through a sieve. Take also 1 *raṭl* black raisins, remove their seeds, pound them, and then pour ¼ *qisṭ* (¾ cup) good very sour vinegar on them. Press and mash the raisins in it very well, (**123r**) and then strain the liquid, then add the [ground] mustard to it. Also add 1 *sukurruja* (½ cup) bee honey, and 2 *dirhams* (1 teaspoon/6 grams) thyme. If you would like to enhance its aroma, add ½ *dirham* (¼ teaspoon) spikenard.

---

30 Believed to be strong aphrodisiacs, see glossary 8.

31 Based on context, I replaced يصطنع به, which is irrelevant here, with يصطبغ به.

32 See glossary 11, s.v. *istiḥāla*.

33 This is vinegar flavored with *ushturghāz* (alhagi, *Alhagi maurorum*). Its rhizome is said to be like that of asafetida (see glossary 8). Here I amended the text by replacing the meaningless بخل الأسمر عال, a copyist's misreading, with بخل الأشتر غاز, based on context.

34 Based on context, I replaced يصنع به, which is irrelevant here, with يصطبغ به.

35 Levantine mustard seeds.

FIGURE 39 *White mustard, Elizabeth Blackwell,* A Curious Herbal, *1738, plate 29 (From the New York Public Library: http://digitalcollections.nypl.org/items/510d47dd-c23a-a3d9-e040-e00a18064a99).*

(482) Another recipe [for mustard condiment]

Take mustard seeds and a bit of black pepper, pound and sift them. Add enough water to knead them, and set them aside to allow them to blend well and mellow (*yakhtamir*). Next, put them in a mortar (*hāwan*) and continue crushing them for a long while (*sāʿa ṭawīla*), with a bit of salt and crushed almonds. If you prefer, just pound all the ingredients together, and use them.

(483) Recipe [for mustard condiment], good to use at home and while traveling

Take as much mustard seeds as you want. Pour enough water on them to submerge them, and set them aside overnight. Pour off the water, and wash the seeds three times.

Pound half of the mustard seeds, and extract their foam using a sieve; do this until no mustard foam can be obtained from it.[36] Season it with a bit of salt.

Let the other half of the seeds dry completely, and then pound them—but first make sure no traces of moisture remain in them. Throw the pounded seeds into the extracted foam, and knead them until they become a whole mass of a ball (*kubba*). Set it aside to dry, and then store it away.

Whenever you want to eat it, take a piece and add vinegar, sugar, and pounded walnuts to it. When it is prepared in this way, it will be much lighter in color and sweeter and milder in taste.

(484) Another recipe [for mustard condiment][37]

Take mustard seeds, finely pound them and sift them in a very fine-meshed sieve.[38] Knead it [with some water] in a large, wide kneading bowl (*jafnat al-ʿajīn*). Let the paste be dry to begin with, but bit by bit soften it by sprinkling it with hot water. [When it is thin enough,] rub it vigorously with your palm until you stir up foam on top, like that of soap. Add a bit of rock salt (*milḥ Andarānī*) (**123v**) and a bit of vinegar to it.

Next, bring some cold water close to you. Dip your hand down to the bottom of the bowl, slowly stir your fingers around the inside of the bowl while the water is being poured into it. The water added must be very cold.[39] Take out your hand, and set the bowl aside for an hour. During this time, the mustard

---

36 See the first recipe in this chapter for instructions on how to extract the foam from the seeds.

37 This recipe is also in *Zahr*, fol. 23v. Based on it, I amended the edited text in several places.

38 *Munkhul ḥuwwārā* was used to sift *ḥuwwārā* flour, which is white bran-free flour of bread wheat, *Triticum aestivum*.

39 This is done to prevent the poured water from deflating the accumulated foam at the top.

will foam, and bubbles will start surfacing. When this happens, sprinkle water on it, bit by bit, to stop the bubbling, and then start scooping the top foam in handfuls, and put whatever you scoop off in a vessel. It will look like hail (*barad*).

If you wish, you can add sugar, [pounded] raisins, or honey. Or, just leave it as it is, and use it.[40]

40 Interestingly, Shihāb al-Dīn in *Zahr*, fol. 23v, adds a general commentary at the end of this recipe, that mustard sauces are made in many ways, but he has refrained from including them because they are labor-intensive and quite costly. He says, "I compiled this inventory of recipes (*taʿlīq*) for my household slave girls, and I accommodated it to my low income."

CHAPTER 16

في الصلوصات

On Making Table Sauces (*ṣulūṣāt*)[1,2]

(485) Recipe for *ṣalṣ* (table sauce)

Coarsely chop Macedonian parsley (*baqdūnis*), and chop a bit of … and rue for it.[3] Pound them in a stone mortar (*jurn*) until they have the consistency of ointment (*marham*). Squeeze out [the extra] juice [and set it aside].

Toast coriander and caraway seeds; toast hazelnuts, as well. Pound them [separately]. Also, take *aṭrāf ṭīb* (spice blend), along with Ceylon cinnamon (*qarfa*), ginger, and rosebuds (*zir ward*). Mix *tahini* with sweet olive oil. A bit of lemon juice and wine vinegar are also used in this *ṣalṣ*.

So, whip tahini with the oil vigorously (*taqtul*), and then add the hazelnuts to it, followed by coriander and caraway [while whipping the mixture]. Next, add pounded and sifted sumac; also add the herbs (*ḥawāʾij al-baql*),[4] which you have pounded [with] rue and mint.

If the sauce turns out to be lacking in acidity, add extra vinegar and olive oil, but just enough so that you can still scoop it up with a piece of bread.[5]

Put the sauce in a glazed vessel (*wiʿāʾ madhūn*), and be sure to cover its top with a piece of cloth after you seal the surface of the sauce with sweet olive oil.

---

1 Sg. *ṣalṣ* and *ṣalṣa*, a precursor of table sauce and pesto, were served in small bowls along with the dishes as condiments. These are unlike the previous chapter's *ṣibāgh* 'dipping sauce,' which was poured over the already cooked meat or the meat was submerged in it before sending it to the table. Several of the *ṣalṣ* recipes in *Wuṣla* ii 697–701 are also found here. I used them to amend the edited text.

2 Editors' n. 6480: C breaks off here and continues at recipe 489. Here begins folio CB64v.

3 There is a lacuna here, but the missing word might well have been *naʿnaʿ* 'mint,' judging from the subsequent instructions in the recipe.

4 *Ḥawāʾij al-baql* is used repeatedly in recipes to designate the familiar fresh herbs that cooks commonly used to prepare the dishes; these include mint, parsley, and cilantro; or whatever herbs the recipe already mentioned.

5 The Arabic expression, على قدر ما يشال على اللقمة, is a key description of the consistency of *ṣalṣ*: it is neither too thin nor too thick, so that it can be neatly scooped with a piece of bread without dripping, while transferring it from the bowl to one's mouth.

 | DOI 10.1163/9789004349919_019

(486) *Ṣalṣ* made with sour grape juice (*māʾ ḥiṣrim*)[6]

Take the juice of unripe grapes. Finely pound shelled and toasted walnuts or hazelnuts, and add garlic, coriander, black pepper, and small amounts of thyme and rue [all crushed]. Add the grape juice to this mix bit by bit, (**CB 65r**) while you continue pounding until the mix has the consistency of sauce (*qiwām al-ṣalṣ*),[7] and it will be good to eat.

(487) Another *ṣalṣ* [with sour grape juice]

Take the juice of fresh unripe grapes, and add a bit of salt. Strain it on finely ground walnuts. Add garlic and hot spices [all crushed],[8] and use it.

(488) Another *ṣalṣ* (table sauce)

Take Macedonian parsley (*baqdūnis*), rue, tarragon (*ṭarkhūn*), and common parsley (*karafs*)….[9] Pound them in a stone mortar (*jurn*) until they have the consistency of ointment (*marham*). Squeeze out the juice thoroughly, and take the extracted juice, and fold into it the [following] mix.

Take walnuts, toast the kernels, and remove the skins. Pound them thoroughly until the oil is released. Toast a bit of caraway seeds, pound them and add them [to the walnut]; also add pounded *aṭrāf al-ṭīb* (spice blend). Mix this with olive oil and tahini; add enough of these to combine them into a smooth mass.[10]

If it is made for a Turk (*Turkī*), use garlic with it; however, if it is for a local (*baladī*), then omit the garlic. If you wish to use vinegar with it, then go ahead and do so; otherwise, you may use lemon juice instead. However, you need to squeeze the lemons on 2 *dirham*s (1 teaspoon) of salt in a bowl. If Damascus citron (*kabbād*) are in season, extract its juice along with that of lemon, and add them to the sauce mix (*mizāj*).

Now throw in the [squeezed juice of] the Macedonian parsley (*baqdūnis*) and the other herbs. Add a bit of salt and olive oil.

If [fresh] almonds are in season, just remove the outer skins, and throw the almonds in. Stir the mix very well, and store it in a glazed ceramic jar (*qaṭramīz*)

---

6 This recipe and the following one are also included in *Wuṣla* ii 700–1. I used them to amend the edited text slightly.

7 See n. 5 above.

8 Such as ginger, cinnamon, and black pepper. See glossary 8, s.v. *abzār ḥārra*.

9 There is a lacuna here. It is probably mint, an herb that was used repeatedly in the sauce recipes.

10 The verb used is *yujbal*, which suggests a thick porridge-like consistency.

or a green-glazed wide-mouthed jar (*barniyya*), after you seal the surface with sweet olive oil. Keep it covered until it is needed.

(489) (CB 65v) *ṣalṣ muḥallā* (sweetened table sauce)

Take raisins from *jawza* grapes (*zabīb jawzānī*),[11] remove their seeds and extract their juice using vinegar.[12] Toast skinned almonds, hazelnuts, and pistachios, and pound them all in a mortar (*hāwan*) until they release their oils. Throw the nuts into the strained vinegar [and raisins].

Take all the components of *aṭrāf al-ṭīb* (spice blend), crush them, and put them, along with the vinegar, in *jurn al-fuqqāʿī*.[13] Crush black pepper as well, and throw it in. Take a bit of mountain meadow saffron (*khamīrat al-ʿaṭṭār*),[14] pound and sift it, and sprinkle it on the mix. Add also a bit of saffron that has been beaten with musk and rosewater.

Stir the mix very well. Perfume a green-glazed wide-mouthed jar (*barniyya*) or glazed ceramic wide-mouthed jar (*qaṭramīz*) with smoke of aloeswood and ambergris, and cover it for an hour. Empty the *ṣalṣ* into the container, seal the top [with fine olive oil], and put it away until it is needed.

(490) Recipe for another *ṣalṣ*, excellent (*khāṣṣ*)[15]

Take scalded almonds (*masmūṭ*), remove the skins, put them in a stone mortar, and crush them along with yellow lemon juice (*laymūn marākibī*)[16] until the mix looks as smooth as ointment (*marham*). Stir in ginger and nutmeg, both crushed, and pound all the ingredients in the stone mortar (*jurn*) until the mix looks like ointment.

If it is prepared for common folk (*ʿawām*), then sugar is added, enough to sweeten it. (**124r**) However, if it is prepared for Turks, crushed garlic moistened with olive oil (*thūm murabbab bi-l-zayt*) should be added instead.

---

11 *Jawza* were deemed to be an excellent Levantine variety of grapes (Dozy, *Takmilat al-maʿājim* 245). At this point, C resumes (editors' note 6484).

12 Raisins are pounded and steeped in vinegar, and then mashed, pressed, and strained.

13 This was a large stone mortar used by beer-makers to crush grains, herbs, and spices. Liquid and acidic ingredients can also be safely pounded into it. See Ibn Abī Uṣaybiʿa, *ʿUyūn al-anbāʾ* 394.

14 This was also known as *sūranjān* (*Colchicum montanum*). The sliced and dried white corms of this plant are used. It was known for enhancing sexual pleasure, see glossary 8.

15 This recipe is also in *Zahr*, fol. 23v; and a shorter, similar version can be found *Wuṣla* ii 698, *Ṣalṣ abyaḍ* (white table sauce).

16 Levantine yellow lemons were imported to Egypt via trading ships (*marākib*), hence the name. See glossary 7.

(491) Recipe for *ṣalṣ Kāmilī*[17]

Take the tender leaves from the tips of citron stems (*qulūb al-utrunj*), soak them in fine-tasting water (*mā' ḥulw*), and then [drain them, and] take one part, and pound them in a *jurn al-fuqqāʿī*.[18] Take a similar amount, by weight, of Macedonian parsley (*baqdūnis*), and another similar amount of lemon balm (*rayḥān turunjī*). Pound them in the same manner, and mix them all; sprinkle crushed rock salt (*milḥ Andarānī*) on them, and squeeze in lime juice (*laymūn akhḍar*), as needed.

Empty the sauce into glass bottles, and seal their surfaces with sweet olive oil. In each bottle, there should be enough for a single table. Before serving the sauce, [a mix of] galangal, ginger, cloves, and black pepper—all crushed, are sprinkled on it to give it a delicious flavor. Some people choose to use it without adding these spices.

(492) Recipe for *ṣalṣ* (table sauce)[19]

This has a cooling effect on an inflamed stomach; it aids digestion and fortifies organs in the belly; it decreases the viscous phlegm in the stomach and pushes it through the system. It extinguishes the blood when it becomes acrid and hot [due to excess in yellow bile], abates it when it boils, and extinguishes its flames. It cuts down whatever [density] is generated by black bile; sweetens the breath and improves the hue of the complexion.[20]

Take ½ *raṭl* (½ pound) lemon balm (*rayḥān turunjī*), and 1 *raṭl* Macedonian parsley (*baqdūnis*) leaves, from which the stems have been removed. Pound them separately in a stone mortal, using a wooden pestle, and then weigh them.[21]

Combine them, and add rock salt (*milḥ Andarānī*), as much as is needed to make it taste noticeably salty. Next, squeeze over them what amounts to 5 *raṭl*s (10 cups) of lime juice (*mā' laymūn akhḍar*). Mix them all very well, and then empty them into a smooth glazed vessel (*inā' amlas madhūn*). Use the sauce while having the food.

---

17 Most probably named after the Ayyubid king, al-Malik al-Kāmil, who suffered from gout. He ruled Egypt from 1218 to 1238.

18 See n. 13 above.

19 A shorter version is included in *Zahr*, fol. 23v.

20 See glossary 11 for more on medical terms.

21 Weighing after pounding ensures that the required amounts are exact.

You may also add ½ *raṭl* (1 cup) liquid of rose petals steeped in water (*khamīrat ward*),[22] and 1 *mithqāl* (4½ grams/⅔ teaspoon) saffron. It is beneficial, by the will of God the Almighty.

(493) Recipe for another *ṣalṣ* (table sauce)[23]

[Take] sumac, coriander, caraway, toasted hazelnuts, black pepper, rolled bark of Ceylon cinnamon (*qarfa luff*), thyme, sweet olive oil, (**124v**) tahini (*ṭaḥīna*), Macedonian parsley (*baqdūnis*), garlic, lemon [juice], rosebuds (*zir ward*), long pepper (*dār fulful*), ginger, cassia (*dār Ṣīnī*), mint, a bit of rue, and *aṭrāf ṭīb* (spice blend).

Pound all the [dry] ingredients, and mix them with olive oil, tahini, and lemon [juice]. Set it aside to allow the flavors to blend (*yukhammar*), and then eat it.

(494) Recipe for *ṣalṣ* (table sauce), eaten with fried salt-cured fish (*samak maqlī mamlūḥ*), and other dishes[24]

Take fine-tasting raisins and scalded [and skinned] almonds, 1 *raṭl* (1 pound) of each. Finely pound them until they have the consistency of bone marrow (*mukh*).

Take 3 *ūqiyyas* (3 ounces) mustard seeds of Acre (*khardal ʿAkkāwī*),[25] [coarsely pound them,] and rub and press them very well in ½ *raṭl* (1 cup) wine vinegar, so that all of their essence is released into the vinegar. [Strain it,] discard the dregs, and add the liquid to the pounded raisins and almonds.

Next, take ½ *ūqiyya* (½ ounce) fine-tasting garlic, skin it, pound it, and fry it in sweet olive oil to remove its sharp taste. Throw in 3 *ūqiyyas* (3 ounces) toasted hazelnuts and a similar amount of walnuts—add them after pounding them. Add this mix to the first mix [i.e., the raisin-almond mixture]; also add 1 *raṭl* (2 cups) wine vinegar.

Boil them in a pot until the mix thickens. Now, take 1 *dirham* saffron (½ teaspoon); along with ginger, Ceylon cinnamon (*qarfa*), galangal (*khūlanjān*),

---

22 Water, with rose petals steeped in it, was usually used for distillation. See Dozy, *Takmilat al-maʿājim* 413, where *khamīr* is said to be a term used by druggists and perfumers to designate ingredients steeped in liquid to release their essence, and then distilled. See also *Kanz* recipes on distilled liquids in chapter 22.

23 This recipe is included in *Zahr*, fol. 24r.

24 This recipe and the following one are found in *Waṣf* 38–9, in the same sequence. I used them here to amend the edited text. Chapter 9 above contains many fish dishes that go with this sauce.

25 This must be a variety of black mustard seeds, whose hard coats are usually discarded, as is done in this recipe.

Indian spikenard (*sunbul ṭīb*), 2 *dirhams* (1 teaspoon) of each. Crush them all and add them to the sauce (*ṣalṣ/ṣalṣa*), along with a handful of mint, a few sprigs of rue, and 3 *ūqiyyas* (3 ounces) bee honey. Let the pot simmer gently, and then remove. Eat this sauce with fish [dishes]. It is wonderful.

(495) Another *ṣalṣ* recipe

Take *ḥawāʾij al-baql*,[26] and chop them finely. Also, take scalded [and skinned] almonds, pound them with the herbs, along with a head of garlic. Throw in black pepper, caraway, thyme, Ceylon cinnamon (*qarfa*), (**125r**) and saffron, as much as needed.

Put them all in a pot, along with rue and mint, as needed. Pour in fine-tasting vinegar—add enough to submerge the ingredients, and let the pot boil on the fire until the vinegar reduces.

Squeeze lemon juice on it, as much as it needs; chop lemon preserved in salt (*laymūn māliḥ*)[27] on it, and then remove. Eat it with fish dishes.

(496) Recipe for *khardal* (mustard sauce)[28]

Take one *qadaḥ* (2¼ pounds) mustard [seeds], 1 to 2 *raṭls* (1–2 pounds) cane-sugar honey (*quṭāra*), and ½ *raṭl* (1 cup) vinegar. Also, take 3 *ūqiyyas* (3 ounces) raisins, and similar amounts of each of [dried] jujubes (*ʿunnāb*) and almonds. Also take 1 *ūqiyya aṭrāf ṭīb* (spice blend), ½ *mithqāl* (⅓ teaspoon) saffron, and one quarter and an eighth [i.e., 3/8 *mithqāl*, less than ⅓ teaspoon] of camphor.

Pound the mustard seeds, sift them twice, and knead them with water into a stiff paste. Shape it into a disc, soak it in water for an hour, and then wash it and rub it with your hand seven times.[29] Pour vinegar on it, and dissolve and press the ground seeds very well until they have the consistency of tahini. Strain it through a sieve, but set aside the dregs. Again, extract the mustard essence by mixing the dregs with a small amount of vinegar, rub and mix them, and then strain the liquid, and add it to the first [extracted] batch.

So, when you are done straining the mustard liquid, add to it cane-sugar honey (*quṭāra*), and stir by hand to mix them well. Throw in the jujubes, and

---

26 These are the fresh herbs, such as basil, parsley, and tarragon, that are usually used.

27 For recipes, see chapter 18 below.

28 This recipe is for a dipping mustard sauce, which more suitably belongs to the previous chapter. The recipe is also found in *Waṣf* 46, which I used to amend the edited text in several places.

29 Here I followed *Waṣf*'s وتحكه 'rub it' rather than the edited وتحله 'dissolve,' which does not accurately describe what is being done at this stage.

stir; throw in raisins and stir; scald the almonds, skin them and split them in half, and add them. Pound *aṭrāf al-ṭīb* and mix them in.

Give the mix a good whip, and empty it into a glazed ceramic jar (*qaṭramīz*) or a green-glazed wide-mouthed jar (*barniyya*).

Fry the [salt-cured] butterflied fish (*mashqūq*) after you soak it in water for a couple of days [to get rid of excessive salt]. Cut it up into portions after you skin it, and then fry it until done, and set it aside to cool. Add saffron to the mustard sauce, mix well, (125v), and then pour it all over the fish. It is wonderful.

(497) Another [*ṣalṣ*]

Take Macedonian parsley (*baqdūnis*), strip the leaves (*yukharraṭ*), pound them, and squeeze out their [extra] moisture. Chop (*yufram*) a bit of rue and mint and mix these with the parsley [and set it aside].

Toast coriander and caraway seeds, as well as walnuts and hazelnuts. Scald almonds, [skin them, and] color them with saffron. [Set them aside.]

Mix tahini with lemon juice and vinegar; mix in sweet olive oil, a bit of *khardal* (mustard condiment),[30] and a bit of garlic, which has been boiled and fried.

Now mix all [the above] ingredients (*ḥawāʾij*); add [the walnuts and hazelnuts] after you coarsely crush them. The almonds should be split in half, and [later] sprinkled on the face of the sauce when it is served. [But for now,] add [to the sauce mix] some sumac, *aṭrāf ṭīb* (spice blend), sweet olive oil, mint, and rosebuds; mix them very well.

Empty the sauce into a glazed (*madhūn*) or glass (*zujāj*) vessel. Seal the surface with sweet olive oil, and put it away until needed.

When the sauce is emptied on a serving plate (*ṣaḥn*), sprinkle broken pistachio nuts, rosebuds (*zir ward*), and the colored almonds on the top. Generously drizzle it with sweet olive oil, and serve it.

(498) Another [*ṣalṣ*] recipe

Take sweet basil (*ḥamāḥim rayḥān*),[31] chop it and then pound it along with rue or mint after you chop it. However, it is better if the rue leaves are just stripped off their stems and added without chopping them.[32]

---

30 See recipes 468 and 469 for directions on how to prepare it.

31 *Ocimum basilicum*, see glossary 8.

32 The Arabic expression used is *kharriṭ al-sadhāb b-ilā farm*. *Kharraṭa* generally designates chopping; *farm* is a dialectical variant on *tharm*. However, it may also refer to stripping the leaves from stems, as the recipe here clearly describes.

Pound toasted hazelnuts along with scalded [and skinned] almonds, toasted coriander and caraway seeds, black pepper, cumin, (**126r**) and Ceylon cinnamon (*qarfa*).

Combine and pound all ingredients together, along with olive oil and tahini. Squeeze some lime juice on a lump of salt (*ḥaṣāt milḥ*) [to prevent it from becoming bitter], and strain it on the sauce. Combine everything into one smooth mass (*yujbal*).[33] [Empty it into a glass jar, seal the surface of the sauce with olive oil, and] stow it away (*yushāl*).

(499) Another [*ṣalṣ*] recipe

Take the usual herbs (*ḥawāʾij al-baql*),[34] [especially] rue, and mint. Wash, chop, finely pound them, and put them in a bowl (*zibdiyya*). [Set it aside.]

Take toasted and coarsely crushed (*muharrash*) hazelnuts; also take toasted and pounded coriander and caraway seeds. Take black pepper, ginger, rolled bark of Ceylon cinnamon (*qarfa laff*), rosebuds (*zir ward*), and *aṭrāf ṭīb* (spice blend). Pound them all thoroughly [and set them aside].

Take sumac berries, wilt them (*yudhabbal*),[35] finely pound them, sift them, and then [put the resulting pounded husks] in a container, and set it aside. Next, squeeze lime juice on a lump of salt (*ḥaṣāt milḥ*) [to prevent it from becoming bitter], and strain it on the sumac [that was set aside], which has been cleaned and pounded (*summāq madqūq muṣawwal*).[36]

Transfer the crushed sumac into a stone mortar, and pound it with sweet olive oil, as needed, along with the rest of the [above-mentioned] ingredients, and a bit of cumin.

Store [this sauce] in a glazed vessel (*wiʿāʾ madhūn*). If you wish, mix in some garlic, which has been skinned and pounded with olive oil, salt, and vinegar. It is delicious (*ṭayyib*), and will stay good for a long while.

---

33 The verb *yujbal* suggests that it should be a thick porridge-like consistency.

34 The fresh herbs, such as mint, basil, parsley, and tarragon, that are usually used.

35 This process, called *taṣwīl*, involves first submerging sumac berries in several changes of water to remove any sticks and impurities, and then draining them, and spreading them to dry out. The sumac husks wilt in the process, and when the berries are pounded, they easily separate from the hard seeds, which are discarded. Legumes and grains are cleaned in the same manner.

36 See above note.

CHAPTER 17

فيما يعمل من الألبان من الكوامخ والجاجق والكبر والزعتر والبراف وغير ذلك

Of Dishes Made with Dairy (*albān*): *kawāmikh* (Fermented Condiments), *jājaq* (Drained-Yogurt Condiment), Condiments with *kabar* (Capers), and *zaʿtar* (Thyme), *bīrāf* (Clotted Cream), and the Like

(500) Delicious *kāmakh* (fermented dairy condiment)

Take [baked] bread after it cools; break it into pieces, put these in a new jar, layering it with fresh fig leaves.[1] **(126v)** Repeat this until the jar is full. Close its top, turn it upside down, and set it aside for twenty or more days, until the bread molds (*yuʿaffin*). Take the bread out of the jar with the mold on it, separate it from the fig leaves, and set it aside to dry out.

Knead an equal amount of unfermented bread (*khubz faṭīr*), immediately divide it into balls, roll them out into thin discs (*ruqāq*), and bake them until done.[2] Dry this bread, as you did with the first bread. When it is as dry as the moldy bread that is already dried, pound both the moldy and the unfermented bread, and knead them with cold milk.

Put the mix in a vessel to which you have added a bit of sweet olive oil. Leave it in a sunny place for three days. On the fourth day, knead it with [more added] milk; however, add only enough so that when you put a stick in the middle, it stays standing. The stick should be taken from a fig tree;[3] peel off its skin [before using it, and keep it standing in it while it is fermenting]

Leave the vessel in a sunny place, day and night; stir the mix [with the stick], once early in the morning and once in the evening. Continue doing this until it matures in the sun.

When you come to knead it on the fourth day, [i.e., after leaving the vessel in a sunny place for three days,] stir in it some salt. It will be wonderful.

---

1 Used to encourage the growth of mold, and for their antiseptic properties.

2 Here I amended the text based on the context and *kāmakh* recipes in al-Warrāq, chapter 40.

3 The branches have the same antiseptic properties as those of the leaves. Besides, the milky latex works like rennet in milk, see glossary 7, s.v. *ʿūd dhukār*, under *tīn*.

 | DOI 10.1163/9789004349919_020

(501) Recipe for another *kāmakh* (fermented dairy condiment)[4]

Take 1 *rubʿ* (8¾ pounds) fine tasting sprouted wheat berries (*qamḥ zarīʿ*). Boil them lightly, and then take them out of the boiling liquid and spread them out to dry.

When the wheat is dry, put it in a large brass pot (*dast*), toast it very well, and coarsely crush it (*jarīsh*). Once it is crushed, separate the finely ground wheat (*daqīq*) from the coarsely ground (*dashīsh*) [by sifting it in a fine-meshed sieve].

Take the finely ground wheat (*daqīq*) and knead it vigorously [with water] into stiff dough, which you divide into balls, and set aside to dry. Next, make holes in these balls, [thread them into necklaces], and hang them on a rope in the sun (**127r**) until they dry completely and become like *iksīr*,[5] which common folk call *qamna*.

Now take the coarsely ground wheat (*dashīsh*), which you separated from the finely ground wheat (*daqīq*), and put it in a vessel with a small mouth and a large belly, such as a *muṭr*.[6] Add milk to it, enough to more than just submerge the wheat in it. Throw in three sticks from a fig tree,[7] cover the opening with a thin sheet of leather (*riqq*), and set it aside for 10 days.

Open the vessel and dip your hand in it. If it feels dry, add more milk; otherwise, just leave it. Take a ball of the *qamna* [you threaded], break it into pieces, and add it to the jar. Cover it with the sheet of leather, and make a hole in it. Remove the [three] fig tree sticks you first put in it, and instead insert a long fig tree stick through this hole—it should be long enough to reach the bottom of the vessel [and stick out of the vessel's hole].

Now, each day, put your hand in the vessel and beat the contents.[8] Do this for three days, after which you can take out the condiment and use it. It will taste like *fuqqāʿ* (foamy beer), and will look as yellow as saffron.

You can tell when the condiment is ready to use because the fig tree stick inserted in it starts to smell like *jubn Shāmī* (Levantine cheese, like mozzarella). [Serve it drizzled with olive oil.][9]

---

4 A slightly shortened version of the recipe is included in *Zahr*, fol. 24r.

5 *Iksīr* is the base for making certain preparations. In this context, it is the base for the *kawāmikh* condiments. Previously we came across *iksīr* as the base for making drinks (see, for instance, recipes 402 and 404), also called *khamīra*.

6 In recipe 256 above, it is described as a non-porous stone jar (*maṭr ḥajarī*). Such vessels were commonly used for keeping oil or small salt-cured fish (*samak mumallaḥ*), as described by Dozy, *Takmilat al-maʿājim* 1461. From the *Kanz* recipes, we learn they were also handy for keeping cheese, pickles, fermented condiments and sauces.

7 See note 3 above.

8 Perhaps once (as in recipe 504 below), or twice (as in recipe 500 above) a day.

9 This detail appears in *Zahr* only.

(502) Making *kāmakh* (fermented condiment) without milk[10]

Take *kaʿk* (dry cookies), pound them and then sift them. Also pound raisins (*zabīb*), after you remove their seeds. Take spikenard, cloves, and cumin, ½ *ūqiyya* (15 grams/1 tablespoon) of each. Also, take 1 *ūqiyya* (1 ounce) cassia (*dār Ṣīnī*), 4 *mithqāl*s (18 grams) cloves, and 1 *ūqiyya* (1 ounce) black pepper. Pound them and sift them.

Combine and mix all the ingredients with honey, vinegar, and a bit of *murrī* (liquid fermented sauce).

(503) Recipe for *kāmakh al-ṭarkhūn* (fermented dairy condiment with tarragon)

Take bread, let it mold in fig leaves, and when it does, spread them out and set them aside until (**127v**) they completely dry.[11]

Next, take sheep milk (*laban ḥalīb ghanamī*). Also, you should have prepared tarragon leaves, stripped from their stems. Knead the moldy bread with the milk and tarragon; it should be noticeably salty so that it does not sour [and go bad].

Put it in a new glazed vessel (*wiʿāʾ madhūn*) in a sunny place. There should be a fig tree stick in it;[12] and continue stirring it [once or twice a day] for 10 days.[13]

(504) [Recipe for *kāmakh* with mint]

If you want to make *kāmakh al-naʿnāʿ* (with mint), take 3 *raṭl*s (3 pints) milk, and dissolve moldy bread (*al-ʿafin*),[14] pounded salt, and saffron in it, until it looks a bit thicker than *ḥarīra* (thin smooth soup) in consistency. Continue tasting it until you like its flavor, but it should be noticeably salty.

Take fresh mint leaves, and stir them into the milk mix using a fig tree stick.[15] You need to make this [condiment] in the season when figs and grapes are ripe. Leave it in the sun, and every time you see that it has thickened, add more milk. If [the salt] is insufficient—you will know this by tasting it—[add some more to it].

---

10 An identical recipe is found in al-Warrāq, chapter 46, where it is included in a collection of dishes suitable for Lent consumption; the recipe there also adds that it can be eaten the same day it is made (يؤكل ليومه). I used it here to slightly amend the edited text.

11 See recipe 500 above for more details.

12 See n. 3 above.

13 See n. 8 above.

14 See recipe 500 above for details on how to mold the bread.

15 See n. 3 above.

Stir it once a day, early in the morning, and always cover [the top of the vessel] with a piece of cloth. Continue doing this until it is done; it will turn brown (*yaḥmarr*) when it matures. Add 3 *ūqiyyas* (3 ounces) sweet olive oil to it, stir it and take it down [from the rooftop].[16]

(505) Recipe for *kāmakh al-ward* (fermented dairy condiment with rose petals)
Take Nuṣaybīn[17] rose petals, dry them, pound them, and add them [to the milk] at the same time you add the moldy bread (*ʿafīn*) [as in the above recipe]. Keep this in mind.

[The following are a series of recipes on non-fermented dairy preparations.]

(506) (128r) Recipes for making *jājaq* (drained yogurt condiment), *kabar* (condiment with capers), *bīrāf* (clotted cream), and the like[18]
You need to know that milk is a great source of food; its benefits are many and surpass its harms. Many dishes can be made with it; people enjoy them for their agreeable flavors and delicious taste. In fact, some people do not relish a meal unless there is cheese on the table.

(507) Recipe for making *bīrāf* (clotted cream)[19]
Take large and wide earthenware vessels that look like wide frying pans (*miqlā*). Bring the milk, which has just been drawn [from sheep], and while it is still lukewarm, strain it into the vessels. This should be done early in the evening when the sheep (*ghanam*) have been herded back from the pastures.

Expose the pans to the sky and night dew (*nadā*), and protect them by putting a *qafaṣ* (cage-like basket) over them. Early the following morning, and before the sun rises, skim whatever [cream] has risen to the surface using an

16 Good sunny spots were usually available on rooftops.

17 Nuṣaybīn (now in the Turkish province of Mardin) was a city in Upper Mesopotamia. It was renowned for its orchards and gardens. Roses named after it are pinkish in hue.

18 This is not a recipe but a kind of introduction to the section dealing with non-fermented dairy products. Although the heading includes capers, there are no recipes in this section that use capers. This is an indication that this part may have come from a larger pamphlet, which included such condiments. We find caper pickles in the following chapter, recipes 601, and DK, appendix 53, p. 372.

19 A shortened version of the recipe can also be found in *Zahr*, fol. 24r, where it starts by defining *bīrāf*: "It is the name of the [cream] skimmed with a shell from the face of milk, which has been left out in the open sky all night long.

elongated shell (*maḥḥāra*), and put whatever you skim in a new, clean earthenware vessel. Continue doing this until nothing remains on top.

Cover the pans and set them aside. However, if you are afraid that the sun might reach them later, put them in a cool place [away from the sun]. During the day, skim whatever [cream] comes up again to the surface, and serve it.

Many people choose to eat *bīrāf* by itself, and it is the best thing one can ever eat. Some people choose to have it with honey, while others crush fine white sugar (*sukkar ṭabarzad*), and mix it with the *bīrāf* and eat it. Aḥmad al-Tīfāshī said,[20] as for me, I choose to eat it with *jullāb* (rosewater scented sugar syrup), as I find eating it in this way makes it more delicious. (**128v**) I once told a group of friends about it, and they liked it. *Jullāb* not only makes it delicious, it also bestows some health benefits upon it, and eliminates its harms. For a person who is afraid to eat *bīrāf* by itself, lest it should change into harmful humors in his stomach (*yastaḥīl*) after eating it, he should take a drink of *sakanjabīn safarjalī*,[21] or suck the juice of a quince or two pears [and spit out the pith].[22] I have also seen people eat *bīrāf* with *zalābiya mushabbaka* (fritters dipped in syrup). I tried it and found it quite delicious.

(508) Recipe for making *qanbarīs* (soft yogurt cheese), as it is made in Damascus

It is made with yogurt; therefore, it becomes sour. They [i.e., Damascenes] store it for wintertime by keeping it in thin leather vessels (*riqāq*). Having it with *tharīd*[23] and *sakhātīr* (stuffed tripe) will remedy [its overly cold properties].[24] It is sour, rich in fat (*dasim*), and delicious.

---

20 He was a scholar, poet, anthologist, and geologist originally from Tīfāsh in Tunisia (1184–1253). He traveled to Baghdad and Damascus, and died in Cairo. The following lines seem to be a continuation of the preceding statements. The entire recipe may be al-Tīfāshī's. Therefore, I opt not to indent the following lines.

21 See, for instance, recipe 347 above.

22 I amended the text here based on *Zahr*, where the edited كمثرا وتين 'pears and figs' is more accurately copied as كمثراتين 'two pears.'

23 Based on context and a possible misreading of the word, here I replaced *tabrīd* 'cooling,' which is irrelevant here, with *tharīd*, a dish of bread sopped in rich meat broth, which is well known for its hot and moist properties. Such dishes are needed to counterbalance the cold properties of *qanbarīs*.

24 Like *tharīd*, *sakhātīr* (stuffed pockets of tripe cooked in broth) are known for their hot properties. A recipe for *sakhātīr* (sg. *sukhtūr*) can be found in Baghdādī 53, see glossary 5, s.v. *sakhātīr*.

To make it, take *laban makhīḍ*,[25] and let it thicken (*yaʿqud*)—but less than when you make *aqiṭ* (sour yogurt cheese).[26] Cool it, [drain it] and store it in *riqāq* or white unglazed earthenware jars (*jirār bīḍ*). It will stay good for a year.

(509) Recipe for making *akhlāṭ* (yogurt condiment)[27]

[This is a] specialty of the mountain people, good for those with an excess in humid properties (*marṭūbīn*), and those whose dominant humor is phlegm (*aṣḥāb al-balgham*).[28] It is eaten with bread, and among the cold dishes, it is a favorite. However, it generates black bile (*sawdāʾ*).

To make it, take a good amount of the fresh and tender tips of mustard greens (*qulūb al-khardal*),[29] chop them into small pieces, sprinkle them with a bit of coarse salt, and rub them between your fingers to let their juices leach out. Next, pour cold water on them to wash them, and then drain the liquid. Spread the cut leaves on something and set them aside (**129r**) to dry.

Throw the leaves into *shīrāz* (drained rennet yogurt), and mix them well. The *shīrāz* needs to be sour. Pour on it *zayt al-māʾ*,[30] and set it aside [for a while to mature].

It can also be made with mustard greens chopped finely and added to the yogurt, without having to rub them [and washing them, as above]. It will be equally delicious.

(510) Another *akhlāṭ* recipe

Take leaves of common parsley (*karafs*) and mint, chop them finely, rub them between your fingers, and add them to *shīrāz* (drained rennet yogurt). Dissolve [in a small amount of the yogurt] 2 *dirhams* (1 teaspoon) [crushed seeds of] mustard, and season the yogurt with it [by stirring it in].

(511) Another [*akhlāṭ*] recipe

Take the tender tops of leaves of tarragon and mint, and tender citron leaves (*qulūb al-utrunj*). Finely chop them and add them to *shīrāz* (drained rennet yogurt). Put the mix in a green-glazed wide-mouthed jar (*barniyya*); pour olive

---

25 It is sour buttermilk, which remains after churning milk and extracting its butter.

26 This is done by boiling the sour milk until it thickens and the separated whey is reduced. *Aqiṭ* is more like sour cream cheese, made with sour yogurt.

27 Sg. *khilāṭ*.

28 See glossary 11, s.v. *mizāj*.

29 As a specialty of the mountain people, this condiment must have been, originally, Levantine. *Khardal* (broadleaf mustard greens, *Brassica juncea*) is called *ḥashīshat al-sulṭān* in Egypt. See recipe 518 below.

30 Lit., 'water olive oil,' extracted by treating it with hot water; it is also called *zayt maghsūl* 'washed olive oil.' See glossary 6.

oil and a bit of crushed salt into it. Set it aside for three days, and then serve it with a drizzle of olive oil. It is quite delicious.

(512) Recipe for cooking *libaʾ* (beestings)[31]

Libaʾ is moist in properties, everybody likes it. It nourishes the body, benefits people whose dominant humor is yellow bile (*aṣḥāb al-ṣafrāʾ*), and people with burnt yellow bile (*aṣḥāb al-iḥtirāqāt*) [due to an excess in yellow bile]. It is also a laxative (*yulayyin al-ṭabīʿa*).[32]

Here is how to prepare it: Take 2 parts milk and 1 part beestings of sheep (*libaʾ al-ghanam*), drawn after the third day she has delivered. Combine the two and put them in a soapstone or earthenware pot. Place the pot on a very low heat or in hot ashes overnight. The following morning, you will find that it has heated up and its top has browned. Take it and serve it.

[Notes:]

The more milk used and the less beestings, the better and more delicious it gets. I have even seen people use one quarter beestings and half and a quarter (i.e., ¾) milk, (**129v**) and it turned out well. If a lot of beestings is used, the milk will spoil and harden, it will be as hard as a rock; devoid of any flavor or delectability.[33]

(513) Another *libaʾ* recipe [using ordinary milk]

Take milk and four egg whites for each *raṭl* (2 cups). Whip them thoroughly in an earthenware pot (*qidr fakhkhār*), and light fire under it until the milk thickens. It will be wonderful if a yolk of one egg is also added.

(514) Another [*libaʾ* recipe][34]

Take a clean stone pot (*qidr ḥajar*) and put it on the fire. Pour into it as much [beestings] milk as you wish.[35] Now take yogurt[36]—a quarter of the amount of *libaʾ* used—and put it next to you.

---

31 Colostrum, the first milk drawn from a mammal which has just delivered its offspring.

32 See glossary 11 for more on these medical terms.

33 Ibn Mubārak Shāh, *Zahr*, fol. 24v, adds at the end of the recipe, "The farmers who used to work at an estate I once owned used to make it for me, but I never liked it until I told them about mixing it with milk."

34 I amended the edited text slightly, based on internal evidence.

35 The following instructions clearly refer to this milk as *libaʾ* (beestings).

36 Although the recipe mentions *laban ḥalīb* (milk), the following instruction clearly refers to it as *laban rāʾib* (yogurt).

Light a low fire under the pot, and when it starts boiling and foaming with the *liba*ʾ milk (beestings) in it, scoop a small amount of the yogurt (*laban rāʾib*), which you put next to you, with your hand and sprinkle it on the milk, and wait.

When the pot starts foaming again, sprinkle it once more [with the yogurt]. Continue doing this, and keep the fire very low, until you use up all the yogurt. As soon as the yogurt is all in, remove the smoldering coals from under the pot. Pour cold water on the [outside] of the pot (*aqrartahā*) so that the *liba*ʾ inside cools. When you take it out, it will be porous in texture.[37]

Eat it with honey, sugar, or dates.

(515) Recipe for making *qanbarīs* (soft yogurt cheese)[38]

Take new pots and put a small amount of very sour vinegar in them. Put them on the fire until the vinegar boils, and then take them away and pour milk into them. Set the pots aside [with their lids on them], and do not disturb them. (**130r**) The following morning, when you lift the lids, you will find that the milk has thickened into *qanbarīs*.

(516) Recipe for making *shamār akhḍar bi-laban* (fresh fennel with yogurt)[39]

Thinly slice fresh fennel,[40] rub it thoroughly with salt until it wilts, and leave it in a large wide bowl (*qaṣʿa*) for a whole day. Leave the bowl tilted sideways to drain the seeping liquid, and then thoroughly squeeze out the extra moisture.[41]

Drain yogurt; and pound garlic and mint with olive oil, and mix them with it. Add the yogurt mix to the fennel. Sprinkle it with [chopped] mint leaves; crumble some dried rosebuds all over it, put black olives on top, and serve it.

---

37 I suspect that the edited word مسعب 'elastic,' or CB, n. 6600, مسقب, a meaningless word, might have originally been منقب 'porous.' Indeed, the famous food poet Kushājim (d. 961) once described *liba*ʾ thus:

*Liba*ʾ on a platter put, as a crescent turned to full moon.
Porous, as if bees have made their home in it. (al-Warrāq, English trans. *Annals* 200).

38 Cf. recipe 508 above.

39 The vegetable is also known as *rāzyānaj* and *basbās*, whose seeds are named similarly. I have found a similar recipe in the book on agriculture *ʿAlam al-malāḥa fī ʿilm al-filāḥa* by al-Nābulusī (d. 1731), which is a concise version of the copy by Raḍiyy al-Dīn al-Ghazzī l-ʿĀmirī (d. 1529), both from Syria. Since the *Kanz* was written before the time of the latter, we can assume that both drew on similar sources dealing with food preservation. Similar recipes are pointed out in the following chapter. I used this source to amend the text.

40 In al-Nābulusī, *ʿAlam al-malāḥa* 266–7, it occurs as *qulūb al-shamar*, i.e., the tender inner layers of fennel; and the instruction is to chop into the smallest pieces possible.

41 The last detail is from al-Nābulusī's addition.

(517) *Kurunb bi-laban* (cabbage with yogurt)

Boil the cabbage, remove it from the water, and sprinkle it with a bit of salt [and set it aside]. Pound garlic with a bit of salt and add olive oil to it. Next, drain the yogurt, chop some rue leaves, and throw them into the yogurt along with the garlic pounded with salt and olive oil.

Dress the cabbage (*yutabbal*) with the yogurt mix, and set it aside for an hour to allow the flavors to blend and mellow (*yukhammar*). [Spread the cabbage on a platter, and] put mint leaves and black olives, as well as a lot of fine-tasting olive oil over it, and eat it.

(518) Recipe for *jājaq* (drained yogurt condiment) with *ḥashīshat al-sulṭān* (broadleaf mustard greens)[42]

Take mustard greens, pick them over and chop them, I mean only the leaves, do not chop the stems. Chop them as is done with *mulūkhiyya* (Jew's mallow) or even finer. Put them in an earthenware tub (*mājūr*) and sprinkle them with salt.

Mask your mouth and nose with *fūṭa*[43] or *mindīl* (towel),[44] and rub the greens with salt very well until the moisture seeps out. [Squeeze out the juice until] none of it remains.

Drain delicious and rich Turkmens' yogurt (*laban Turkumānī*) [made from sheep milk], and whip it well with a bit of salt.[45] Now take the (**130v**) lumps of [chopped mustard greens], (**130v**) which you squeezed out and collected in a vessel. Add them to the *qanbarīs*,[46] and whip the mix very well. If the *qanbarīs* turns out to be dry, mix it with sheep milk (*laban ḥalīb ḍaʾnī*), and whip it the way *jājaq* ought to be whipped.

Add to the yogurt 10 *dirhams* (30 grams) chopped mint along with a bit of sweet olive oil. Leave the vessel aside overnight, and the following morning you can serve it in [small bowls arranged in] a *sukurdān*,[47] to be eaten and enjoyed.

---

42 *Brassica juncea* (S). *Ḥashīshat al-sulṭān* is its name in Egypt; otherwise, *khardal Fārisī*, *khardal akhḍar*, or just *khardal* (as in recipe 509 above).

43 This is an unsewn piece of cloth, used by women as a head cover.

44 To protect the person working on them from inhaling the rising irritating fumes of the pungent mustard leaves.

45 When drained, *laban Turkumānī* is called *qanbarīs Turkumānī*. *Qanbarīs* is generally sour soft cheese.

46 The yogurt is now referred to as *qanbarīs*, as it has been drained and become a kind of soft cheese.

47 This is a tray that holds an array of small dishes in small bowls called *sukurrujāt* (sg. *sukurruja*); the dishes were served as appetizers and *naql* 'mezze.'

It strengthens the back and invigorates coitus (*yuqawwī al-jimāʿ*). It is a fantastic food.

(519) Recipe for *jājaq* (drained yogurt condiment) with wild mustard greens (*labsān*)[48]

Take five bunches or more of *labsān*, pick them over, wash them, and chop them into small pieces. Put them in a bowl (*zibdiyya*) and throw on them 30 *dirhams* (approx. 3 ounces) crushed rock salt (*milḥ Andarānī*). Rub the leaves with the salt.

Put 5 *raṭl*s (5 pounds) of yogurt in a clean sack, and hang it to drain [the whey].[49] Take the thickened yogurt out of the sack and put it in a vessel, along with the chopped *labsān*. Stir them so that they mix well, and add to them the *jājaq* ingredients mentioned earlier [in above recipes].[50] [Leave it overnight, and serve it the following day, as in the above recipe.]

(520) Recipe for *jubn ḥālūm bi-ṣalṣ* (semi-hard white cheese in sauce)[51]

Boil milk with a small amount of salt until a third of it is reduced; put *zaʿtar Shāmī* (Levantine thyme) in it,[52] and then remove. Let it cool and strain it. Mix a few peach leaves with the pieces of cheese, pour the milk all over them, and put them all in a *maṭr*,[53] so that the liquids do not filter through. Keep the cheese thus preserved (*yukbas*).

Whenever you want to eat it, take the cheese [from the jar], and cut it into pieces. Press them to remove extra moisture. They should be added to a vinegar [-mix, described below] and kept in it overnight.

---

48 This recipe can also be found in *Zahr*, fol. 25r. I used it here to amend the edited text slightly. For more on *labsān*, see glossary 12.

49 Hanging the sack to drain appears in *Zahr* only.

50 *Zahr* mentions them as 10 *dirhams* (30 grams) of finely chopped mint and sweet olive oil.

51 The recipe uses already made cheese. The first part describes how to preserve it, and the second deals with a sauce to season it, and serve it with. Lewicka, *Food and Foodways* 240–1, misinterprets the directions in the first part as a recipe for making *ḥālūm*. Al-Isrāʾīlī's text, used to support this interpretation, has been misunderstood. Al-Isrāʾīlī divides the components of cheese into *jawhar al-jubn* 'solids,' *jawhar al-samn* 'fat,' and *jawhar al-ruṭūba* 'moisture.' He says fresh cheese contains the highest percentage of moisture among the varieties of cheese; whereas aged cheese contains the least (*Kitāb al-Aghdhiya* i 317–8).

52 *Origanum syriacum*, also known as 'true thyme.'

53 This is a non-porous stone jar, with a bulging belly and a narrow mouth. See n. 6 above.

Chop *ḥawāʾij al-baql*,[54] (**131r**) [namely] mint and rue, pound them along with [dry] pounded thyme and crushed mustard seeds. Knead them with vinegar,[55] along with black pepper, ginger, crushed rosebuds, garlic pounded with fine-tasting olive oil, salt, and lemon juice. Also, add sweet olive oil, toasted hazelnuts, toasted coriander and caraway seeds, and tahini.

Make sauce (*ṣalṣ*) with these, put the pieces of cheese in it, and toss them [to coat them all with the sauce]. Set it aside overnight to allow the flavors to blend and mellow (*yukhammar*), and eat it.[56]

(521) Recipe for seasoning [and preserving] *ḥālūm* cheese[57]

Boil milk with salt and thyme until a third of it is reduced, and then remove it and cool it.

Now take a small bundle of silk cloth,[58] and tie a small amount of crushed pellitory (*kundus*) in it.[59] This should be put in the *maṭr*,[60] where the cheese [is kept]. Also add tender leaves of sour orange (*nāranj*), Damascus citron (*kabbād*), citron (*turunj*), and lemon (*laymūn*), and fresh thyme.

Fill the *maṭr* with layers of cheese pieces alternating with layers of the tender leaves. Fill the jar with the [cooled] milk, and seal the top with some sweet olive oil. Preserved thus in the jar, the cheese can be stored, and used as needed.

(522) Recipe for seasoning (*tatbīl*) *ḥālūm* cheese

Take *ḥālūm* cheese, cut it into pieces and put it in a vessel. Take garlic, skin it and pound it with a bit of olive oil and salt. Squeeze lime juice (*laymūn akhḍar*) on it, or add wine vinegar. Also add pounded toasted walnuts and ginger. Pound the mix until it has the consistency of ointment (*marham*).

Stir into the mix a small amount of toasted seeds of coriander and caraway, a bit of chopped mint, and a sprig of rue. Season the cheese with it, [spread it] and drizzle the top with sweet olive oil. Crumble [dried] rosebuds on it,

---

54 'The fresh herb usually used'—this was presumably common knowledge among the medieval cooks.

55 Here I amended the text, based on context. Several words are repeated.

56 Since this cheese condiment is called *ṣalṣ*, it must have been offered in small bowls as a table sauce, served with other dishes. Cf. recipes in chapter 16 above.

57 This recipe also appears in *Zahr*, fol. 25r, which I used to amend the edited text. 'Seasoning' (تطييب) in the recipe title is *Zahr*'s addition. Again, the recipe uses already made cheese.

58 Here I replaced *jīr* 'slaked lime' in the edited text with the more accurately copied *ḥarīr* 'silk,' in *Zahr*.

59 This is also known in Arabic as *ʿāqir qarḥā*, and in English, as Spanish chamomile, *Anacyclus pyrethrum*.

60 A non-porous stone jar, with a bulging belly and a narrow mouth. See n. 6 above.

sprinkle a small amount of coarsely crushed toasted hazelnuts, (131v) and eat it. It is delicious.

(523) *Jājaq* (drained yogurt condiment)

Take common cucumbers (*khiyār*), peel them, and make two cross-like slits lengthwise [but not all the way through]. Sprinkle them with a bit of salt. Chop fresh fennel (*shamār*) and mint.

Put *laban Turkumānī* (yogurt of sheep milk) in a sack, [and hang it to drain the whey] from early morning until noontime (*ẓuhr*). Now squeeze out the moisture from the cucumbers and put them in the [drained] yogurt; also add 1 *dirham* (½ teaspoon) crushed mastic gum; [add the chopped fresh fennel and mint as well].

Remove the leafy parts of the stalks of wild mustard greens (*labsān*). [Gather the stalks in bunches] and cut each bunch in half. Put the cut stalks in a *quffa* (large round basket made of date palm fronds), and rub them with salt very well, and take them out.

Soak moldy bread (*ʿafīn*)[61] in yogurt, thoroughly mash it, and then strain the mix through a sieve [to get rid of any lumps], [add this along with] the *labsān* stalks to [the drained yogurt].

Continue stirring the yogurt mix, once in the morning and once in the evening [for several consecutive days] until it [matures and] tastes good. [When you serve it,] drizzle it with sweet olive oil. It is delicious.

(524) Recipe for making Khurāsānī-style[62] *kishk* (dried dough of crushed wheat and yogurt)[63]

Crush wheat berries as you do when you make *harīsa* (wheat porridge). Sift the flour from the crushed wheat and [only] use the coarsely crushed particles. Put these in a pot, and add water [and boil them lightly until they just] soften. Drain the water, and put them in a vessel in a sunny place. Pour in milk or yogurt—whichever you want to use, and also add a bit of salt. Beat the mix well once a day, and keep it covered until the wheat softens, ferments (*yaghlī*), and turns sour (*yaḥmuḍ*).

As soon as it ferments, sours, and tastes good, add onion, leeks (*kurrāth*), purslane (*baqla ḥamqāʾ*), cilantro, common parsley (*karafs*), wild thyme (*nammām*), and mint—all finely chopped.

---

61 See recipes 500 and 503 above, which describe how to grow mold on the bread.

62 Khurasan is a province in northeastern Persia.

63 It is a preparation used to make *kishkiyyāt* dishes, by pulverizing it, and then dissolving it in liquid and adding it to the pot.

Shape it into small discs, arrange them on mats (*ḥuṣr*),[64] and leave them there until they dry. They are very good.

(525) Recipe for [enhancing] *ḥālūm* cheese, delicious and good

Take 1 *raṭl* (1 pound) fresh (*ṭarī*) [*ḥālūm*] cheese, and cut it into small pieces. Take 2 *raṭl*s (4 cups) sheep milk (*laban ḍa'n*), and put it in an unglazed wide-mouthed jar (*barniyya ghayr madhūna*). Put the cheese in it, and add to it 1½ *ūqiyya*s (1½ ounces) salt. Taste it and see if you like it; otherwise, add an extra ½ *ūqiyya* salt. Throw in thyme—do not pound it. (**132r**) Set it aside for 3 days, and then use it.

Preventing milk from going sour in summertime[65]

Take sprigs of fresh or dried mint, and throw them in the milk. This will keep it from going bad, and keep it unchanged. If it is sweet (*ḥulw*, i.e., milk), it will stay as it is; and if it is curdled (*rā'ib*, i.e., yogurt), it will stay as it is.

(526) Recipe for exquisite milk, [the kind that] used to be made for the ruler of Mosul (Ṣāḥib al-Mawṣil)[66]

Take 2 *raṭl*s (4 cups) ewe's milk (*laban ni'āj*), add 1 *ūqiyya* (2 tablespoons) yogurt, and set it aside for an hour to allow it to settle [meanwhile the milk-fat will separate and accumulate at the top].[67]

Put the milk in a large brass pot (*dast*), cover with its lid, and drape it with layers of heavy cloth (*yudaththar*), and start cooking it on very low fire, which is kept hot with small amounts of fuel added bit by bit. Every now and then, uncover the pot and check for doneness. It you see that a [thick] skin has accumulated at the top, it is done. Remove the pot, [skim the thick skin on top] and eat it with sugar, or by itself. Utterly delicious.

(527) Recipe for making yogurt in wintertime

Take dried unripe grapes (*ḥiṣrim mujaffaf*), soak them in hot water and then pound and strain the juice. Pour milk on it, as much as you wish. It will curdle and become *rā'ib* (yogurt made without rennet).

---

64 Sg. *ḥaṣīra*, made with woven reeds or date palm fronds.

65 This recipe only appears in CB, appendix 42.

66 He might have been Sultan Badr al-Dīn Lu'Lu' al-Atābikī (1209–61).

67 The verb used to suggest this is *yurawwaq* (lit., 'filter,' 'make clear').

(528) Recipe for making *laban yāghurt* (cow and water buffalo yogurt with rennet)[68]

Boil cow or water buffalo milk. Remove it from the fire when it starts boiling, and then cool it.

If you are using an Egyptian *qinṭār* (approx. 99 pounds),[69] take 1 *raṭl* (1 pound) of very sour yogurt (*laban maqṭūʿ*), which will be the fermenting agent (*khamīra*). Also, take ½ *ūqiyya* (½ ounce) rennet (*minfaḥa*),[70] which has been whipped in water. Mix all of it in an earthenware tub (*mājūr*), and then empty it into vessels.

If you make it early in the morning, it will be ready in the evening. If you make it in the evening, it will be ready for you early the following morning.

(529) Recipe for *zaʿtar* (dairy condiment with thyme), a specialty of Mosul[71]

Take thyme, strip the leaves from the stems, and wash and drain them. Wash them in salted water, [and drain them]. Next, wash them in cheese whey (*mish al-jubn*), and squeeze out the extra moisture.

You will have already prepared for it delicious *qanbarīs Turkumānī* (sour soft cheese).[72] Stir the *qanbarīs* with a bit of salt, and then add the prepared thyme to it along with 2 [chopped] bunches of mint. Mix all of it well, and eat it with olive oil [drizzled on it].

(530) Recipe for making [dairy condiment] with pounded thyme (*zaʿtar madqūq*)

Take thyme, wilt it [by leaving it exposed to the sun for a while], pick it over [i.e., strip the leaves from the stems], and then pound them and squeeze out the extra moisture. (**132v**)

Take moldy bread (*ʿafīn*),[73] pound it with a bit of salt, and stir it with the thyme. Now, for each 10 *raṭl*s (10 pounds) of thyme, use 2 *raṭl*s sweet olive oil. Mix them with the milk—boil it first for best results.

Put the thyme mix in a glazed pot (*qidr madhūn*), cover it, put it in a sunny place, and stir it with a fig tree stick daily for 10 days.[74] Every time it looks dry,

---

68 The root of the name is the medieval Turkic '*yog*,' which means 'thicken.'

69 Approx. 11½ gallons.

70 It is the fourth stomach (abomasum) of suckling lambs, goats, or calves.

71 A city in northern Iraq.

72 Made with sheep milk. See recipe 518 above, for instructions.

73 See recipes 500 and 503 above, which describe how to grow mold on bread.

74 See n. 3 above.

replenish it with more milk, and stir. When it is done, eat it. Delicious and appetizing.

Recipe for making [dairy condiment] with pounded Levantine thyme (*zaʿtar Shāmī madqūq*)[75]

Strip the leaves from the stems [of thyme], wash them, squeeze out the extra moisture, and pound them in a marble mortar (*jurn rukhām*). You will have already pounded the *ʿafīn* (dried moldy bread),[76] and put it in a vessel close to the mortar. As you pound the thyme, repeatedly add to it a bit of the pounded moldy bread and a bit of salt.

[When you are done pounding,] put the thyme in a vessel. Pound a bit of *jubn Shāmī* (Levantine cheese, like mozzarella) and picked-over *zaʿtar Shāmī* (*Origanum syriacum*), and add them to the thyme along with a bit of sweet olive oil and milk.

Put the thyme mix in a glazed vessel [and keep it in a sunny place]. Put a fig tree stick in it and stir with it once in the morning and once in the evening.[77] If you add a bit of pounded mustard seeds or ginger to it, it will be truly nice. Continue doing this until it is done, and then move the vessel away from the sun to a shaded place, and it will be good to eat.

(531) Recipe for making *qanbarīs* (sour soft cheese)[78]

Take milk, put it on the fire and bring it to a full boil. Empty it into a new pot, and set it aside to cool for an hour. Take *laban yāghurt* (cow milk yogurt with rennet).[79] For each 10 *raṭl*s (10 pints) [of milk], use ½ *raṭl* (½ pound) *laban yāghurt*. [Add it to the milk] and stir it with a ladle. Cover the pot, and put it in a warm place. Put some straw (*tibn*) underneath it, and leave it there from evening to the following morning. It will look like one solid disc.

When you put the yogurt in a sack and drain it, it becomes *qanbarīs* (sour soft cheese). Take it out of the sack, and add a bit of salt to it. Stir it and store it away in a vessel, which has traces of previous fermentation (*wiʿāʾ ḍārī*).[80]

---

75 This recipe only appears in CB, appendix 43. It uses more ingredients, and gives more detailed instructions than the above recipe. The thyme called for in this recipe is *Origanum syriacum*, also known as 'true thyme.' See glossary 8, s.v. *zaʿtar*.

76 See n. 73 above.

77 On the use of fig tree sticks, see n. 3 above.

78 This recipe can also be found in *Zahr*, fol. 25v, which I used here to amend the edited text.

79 See recipe 528 above.

80 See, for instance, recipes 407 and 418 above.

[Serve it by] mixing it with mace (*basbāsa*), *bāzār*,[81] common cucumber (*khiyār*), eggplant, or whatever you wish.[82] It will come out truly nice.

(532) Recipe for making [dairy condiment] with thyme (*zaʿtar*)

Strip the leaves of thyme, and wash them and squeeze out the extra moisture. Put them in an earthenware tub (*mājūr*), rub them with salt, leave them in the salt for an hour, and then squeeze out the juice.

You will have ready moldy bread (*ʿafīn*),[83] which has been soaked in milk and a bit of salt. Mash it by hand once a day for three days, (**133r**) after which, put it through a sieve [to get rid of any lumps], and then add thyme to it. Stir the mix, and add a bit of Syrian thyme (*zaʿtar Shāmī, Origanum syriacum*), from which the leaves have been stripped and pounded, as well as a bit of pounded *jubn Shāmī* (Levantine cheese like mozzarella). Stir the mix, and put it in a glazed vessel. Seal the top with sweet olive oil.[84]

(533) Recipe for making [a condiment] with thyme (*zaʿtar*)

Take thyme, [strip the leaves,] clean them, wash them, and then rub them with salt and squeeze out the extra moisture. Add sweet olive oil to them. For each 10 *raṭl*s (10 pounds) of thyme, use 1 *raṭl* olive oil. Put them in a green-glazed

---

81 The only source where *bāzār* is explained, but not identified, is Dozy, *Takmilat al-maʿājim* 70, where it is described as a Levantine plant, used in yogurt condiments of *khilāṭ* (pl. *akhlāṭ*). It is also added that the Levantines prefer it to *khilāṭ* with capers (*kabar*), although they eat the latter as well. It is my guess that the vegetable in question is white/cnicus thistle (*Picnomon acarna*). The name given in Arabic sources (e.g., al-Anṭākī, *Tadhkira* 73) is *bādhāward*, which also occurs as *bāzāward*, as in Ibn Sīnā, *al-Qānūn* 752, 1194. It might have been corrupted to *bāzār*. This wild plant is a variety of *ʿakkūb*/*kharshaf* (gundelia, *Gundelia tournefortii*), which is ubiquitous in the Levant and the surrounding regions. Al-Ḥajjār, *Kitāb al-Ḥarb al-maʿshūq* 100, mentions *bāzār* along with *basbāsa* as ingredients added to Lebanese *qanbarīs*, as in our recipe. He also mentions *ʿakkūb* in relation to the yogurt condiment of *jājaq*. See glossary 12.

82 The version in *Zahr* adds this bit of information at the beginning of the recipe. Unfortunately, it does not help us in identifying the vegetable *bāzār*, because only eggplant is mentioned.

83 See n. 73 above.

84 We expect the vessel to be treated as described in the above recipes, such as in CB, appendix 43, see n. 75 above.

wide-mouthed jar (*barniyya madhūna*), smooth out the surface of the mix (*yukallas*),[85] and [sprinkle it] with some crushed salt.

If you want to eat it seasoned, pound skinned garlic with a bit of salt and olive oil until it looks like ointment (*marham*); also, pound walnuts for it, and eat the condiment [mixed with them]. It is wonderful.

85 Since no *kils* 'slaked lime' is involved in making this condiment, I take the word to mean 'smoothen,' as given in *Lisān al-ʿArab*, s.v. كلس. However, some of the pickling recipes in the following chapter do indeed require *kils*.

CHAPTER 18

في سائر أصناف المخللات من اللفت والبصل وتخليل الفواكه
والبقول على سائر أصنافه وتمليح الليمون والكبّاد وغيره

All Kinds of Pickled Turnips and Onions, Pickling Fruits and Vegetables of All Kinds, and Preserving Lemons, Damascus Citron and the Like, in Salt[1]

[Recipes 534–56 are all about pickling turnips.]

(534) Making *lift bi-l-khamīra* (turnip pickles, with yeast)[2]
Take turnips, peel them, cut them into pieces, and let them boil once in a large brass pot (*dast*).[3] Put them in whatever vessel you want to use. Dissolve bread yeast and salt in water, and pour it onto the turnips—there should be enough liquid to submerge them.

Take mustard seeds, pound them finely and extract their juice with a piece of cloth, the way you extract juice of purslane seeds (*bazr baqla*).[4] Pour the juice on the vessel contents [do not stir it in]. Cover the vessel, and put it aside, untouched and undisturbed for a while.

The amounts of yeast and mustard seeds should suit the amount of turnip used.

1 Pickles are *mukhallalāt*, pickling is *takhlīl*, which commonly use *khall* 'vinegar' as a preserving agent. Preserving in salt is *tamlīḥ*.

2 *Wuṣla*, which shares several similar turnip recipes with the *Kanz*, as is indicated in the following recipes, confirms the importance of turnip pickles among the rest of the pickled vegetables and fruits. In *Wuṣla* ii 665, it is described as *'umdat al-mukhallal* 'the best and most essential of all pickles.'

3 I.e., take the pot off the heat the moment it starts to boil.

4 The pounded seeds are tied in a piece of cloth, which is dipped and stirred in water, so that the seeds release their essence. The bundle is then squeezed out and discarded.

 | DOI 10.1163/9789004349919_021

(535) Another turnip [pickle]

Take tender and sweet turnips, (133v) peel them and slit them in half with a knife, but do not let the halves separate. Sprinkle crushed salt on them, and set them aside overnight so that their juices seep out. Next, put them in a clean green-glazed wide-mouthed jar (*barniyya*). If you want them to look yellow, use saffron. Submerge the turnips with clear wine vinegar. However, if you want them to look red, then dye them with safflower (*ʿuṣfur*) instead. If you want to add mustard seeds, then go ahead and do so.

(536) Turnip pickles, which can be eaten the following day

Peel turnips, parboil them (*niṣf ṣalqa*), and then take them out and set them aside until they drain thoroughly. Put them in a vessel with vinegar, and dye them as we described above.

(537) Recipe for turnip [pickles], which stay good for a whole year[5]

Take turnips, peel them, cut them into large cubes (*murabbaʿ ghilāẓ*), sprinkle them with salt, and leave them overnight in a vessel so that their juices seep out and wilt. Next, take them and add vinegar and the necessary spices and herbs (*ḥawāʾij*) to them;[6] this is how all kinds of turnip pickles are made.

(538) Recipe for preparing mustard, used with turnips and other pickles[7]

Take white mustard seeds (*khardal abyaḍ*);[8] pound them with a bit of salt so that they do not become bitter.

Prepare the turnips or other vegetables for pickling. Hazelnuts added to pickles should be toasted, cooled, and have their skins removed, so that they look white. Pound them finely. The same is done with walnuts [i.e., toast them and remove the skins].[9] Mix the nuts with the mustard and use it with whatever turnip pickles or other kinds you choose.

---

5 This recipe and the following three are also found in al-Nābulusī's *ʿAlam al-malāḥa fī ʿilm al-filāḥa*. See recipe 516, n. 39 above, for more details on this source.

6 See above recipes for more details on this.

7 This recipe, dealing with mustard, is also found in *Wuṣla* ii 665; *Zahr*, fols. 25v–26r; and al-Nābulusī, *ʿAlam al-malāḥa* 260. See n. 5 above. Both *Wuṣla* and al-Nābulusī add that mustard is indispensable in pickling (الخردل عمدة المخلل).

8 This is also known as *khardal Shāmī* (Levantine mustard), and *isfind*.

9 In recipe 546 below, the walnuts should not be pounded, but added in pieces; otherwise, they turn the pickling juice blue (*yuzarriq*).

(539) Recipe for turnip [pickles], which stay good for a month (134r)
Cut turnips as we mentioned earlier. Put water in a large brass pot (*dast*), and bring it to a rolling boil (*ḥattā yaqlib*). Throw in the turnips, [let them blanch] and take the pot off the heat. Put the turnips in a strainer; press them by hand to get rid of all the extra moisture. Sprinkle them with the mustard and salt while they are still lukewarm (*fātir*). Add vinegar and other ingredients (*ḥawāʾij*) as mentioned [in earlier recipes].

(540) Another recipe [for pickled turnips], which can be eaten in a few days[10]
Peel turnips and boil them until they are fully cooked, and prepare them as mentioned earlier. This is the established rule for pickling the turnips this way.

Eggplant, likewise, may be kept for a year by soaking it in brine overnight and then keeping it submerged in vinegar. As for pickles consumed within a month, the vegetables are first wilted in boiled water (*yukhaddar*). For pickles eaten the same day they are made, the vegetables are boiled until they fully cook, and then they are seasoned, as we mentioned earlier.

(541) Another recipe for *lift abyaḍ muḥallā* (sweetened white pickled turnips)[11]
Take turnips, peel them and cut them into large cubes (*murabbaʿ kibār*), use as many as you want. If you want them to last for a whole year, do it as mentioned above; if for a month, also do as above.

[With pickles to be kept for a year,] sprinkle turnips with salt and set them aside until they absorb the salt, and then wilt (*yadhbul*) and release their moisture. [For those to be kept for a month, half boil them; and for those to be eaten right away, boil them completely.]

Sprinkle mustard, which has been pounded with salt, on the turnips. Pour wine vinegar sweetened with honey on them, and season them with *aṭrāf ṭīb* (spice blend); put enough vinegar to submerge the turnips; the vessel you use should be large and wide.

Add to it leaves of mint and rue, as well as *qulūb*.[12] Those who like to sweeten it with sugar [instead of honey] may go ahead and do so. Some people sprinkle *aṭrāf ṭīb* and husked sesame seeds (*simsim muqashshar*) on it.

---

10 Here I used the corresponding recipe in *Wuṣla* ii 666 to amend the edited text.

11 Here I used the corresponding recipe in *Wuṣla* ii 667 to amend the edited text.

12 Judging from previous recipes, such as recipe 521 above, this refers to the tender leaves of citron, orange, and lemon.

(542) Recipe for *lift Rūmī* (Byzantine-style turnip pickles)

Take small and large turnips, as many as you want, cut off their stalks, leaving attached only a knob (*ʿiqṣa*), (**134v**) 1–finger long;[13] no stems (*ʿurūq*) and no leaves (*waraq*) should remain.

Peel the turnips,[14] and make seven or eight slits lengthwise and widthwise [but not all the way up, to keep the turnips in one piece]. Sprinkle them with salt, and pour water on them. Set them aside for two days and two nights, after which you take them out of the salt and water.

Stuff the slits with mustard [seeds pounded] with salt. Pour on them wine vinegar, and set them aside. They will stay good for a whole year.

(543) Recipe for yellow turnip pickles[15]

Cut turnips into small and large pieces after you peel them. Dye them with safflower (*ʿuṣfur*). Give them a nice color, which you like. To prepare the dye, pound safflower, rub it with some vinegar, and color the turnips with it. Pour vinegar sweetened with honey or sugar on them, and add mint, rue, *aṭrāf ṭīb* (spice blend), and husked sesame seeds (*simsim maqshūr*).

(544) Another recipe for yellow turnip pickles

Cut turnips into small pieces, and color them yellow with saffron. When they are yellow enough, pour on them vinegar, which has been sweetened with honey, sugar, or date syrup (*dibs*). Also add mint, rue leaves, and *aṭrāf ṭīb* (spice blend).

(545) Recipe for *lift maḥshī* (turnips coated in vinegar sauce)[16]

Take turnips, wilt them as mentioned [above, e.g., recipe 541], and then sprinkle [pounded seeds of] mustard on them. Take black raisins, pound them thoroughly, and then strain their juice by adding wine vinegar to them—do this several times until nothing remains of the raisins. The liquid should be somewhat thick (*khāthir*). If it tastes sour, sweeten it with some date syrup or honey,[17] and add mint, rue, *aṭrāf ṭīb* (spice blend), husked sesame seeds, and

13 In the corresponding recipe in *Wuṣla* ii 667: 3–fingers long.

14 The recipe in *Wuṣla* says not to peel them.

15 *Wuṣla* ii 668 combines this recipe and the following one.

16 *Wuṣla* ii 668 adds that this type of pickle is called *al-muqawwara*, which literally means coated with pine tar (*qaṭirān*), see *Tāj al-ʿarūs*, s.v. قور. The pickle is called *muqawwara* (in the preceding statement) because the turnips are coated with a blackish mix of vinegar, as if by tar.

17 *Wuṣla*'s addition.

toasted hemp seeds (*shahdānaq*).[18] There should be enough of this vinegar to cover all the turnips.

(546) Recipe for *ʿajamī* (Persian-style) [pickles][19]

Take turnip leaves that have been cut from the turnip roots. Discard the long stems, (**135r**) which are bare of any leafy parts. Keep the leaves with their stems [in the middle], and cut them [widthwise] into pieces 3–fingers wide. The very small turnips are left as they are [with their leaves attached]. Discard the tough and yellow leaves.

[For the ones left with small turnip heads], slit their heads into four sections [lengthwise], but do not slice through, so the pieces are intact]. Leave the stalks attached to the heads as they are.

Boil water and add the leaves [and the small slit turnips with their stalks]. Then remove the pot, and drain off the liquid. While they are still hot, sprinkle salt and mustard seeds on them, and set them aside to cool.

Take vinegar, and add pounded toasted hazelnuts, as mentioned earlier [see recipe 538 above]—add a good amount. Also, add sweet olive oil, toasted and pounded coriander seeds, caraway, *aṭrāf ṭīb* (spice blend), pounded garlic, husked sesame seeds, and hemp seeds (*shahdānaq*). Fold all these together into the turnip leaves, put them away, and store them in a vessel after you add a lot of olive oil to them.

For those who want to eat the pickles right away, let them cook on the fire as mentioned above. As for those who want to keep them good for a year, they should not be put in boiled water.[20] Those who want to sweeten them with sugar or honey can do so. Walnut halves, which have been toasted [and their brown skins removed], can also be added, but beware of adding pounded walnuts, because it will turn the vinegar and hazelnuts blue (*yuzarriq*). Hazelnuts are much better [to use] in terms of taste, and they do not change the color of the vinegar.

(547) Recipe for *lift bi-ḥabb rummān* (turnip pickles with dried pomegranate seeds)[21]

Pound pomegranate seeds and strain their juice using wine vinegar. Do this several times until nothing substantial remains in the seeds. Add honey or

18 This also occurs as *shāhdānaj*.

19 This recipe also appears in *Wuṣla* ii 668–9, and *Zahr*, fol. 26r. Here I used both versions to amend the edited text at several places in the recipe.

20 See, for instance, recipe 540 for more details.

21 This recipe also appears in *Wuṣla* ii 671; *Zahr*, fol. 26v; and al-Nābulusī, *ʿAlam al-malāḥa* 261. Here I used them to amend the edited text.

sugar, (**135v**) and boil it on the fire until it thickens into syrup. Add mint, rue, *aṭrāf ṭīb* (spice blend), black pepper, ginger, poppy seeds, sesame seeds, hemp seeds, and pieces of toasted walnuts.

When the syrup thickens, take skinned garlic, which has been cut into pieces with a knife, fry them in sesame oil until they brown and throw them into the syrup.

Peel and cut the turnips into small pieces, and wilt them as described earlier [see recipe 541 above]. Boil them to your liking,[22] and add them to the pomegranate seed [syrup], and bring them to a boil several times.[23] These will indeed be the best of pickles.

As for coloring the turnip [for pickling], if you want it yellow, use saffron after you cut the turnip into pieces; if blue, then use indigo (*nīl*); for red, use hibiscus flowers (*khubbāza*).[24] If you want it white, do not add anything.

(548) Recipe for *lift ʿajamī* (Persian-style pickled turnips), eaten right away
You need turnips, pounded seeds of coriander, caraway, and mustard, use as much as needed. Boil the turnips and cool them. Add enough of the abovementioned spices (*ḥawāʾij*).

(549) Another recipe for [pickled turnips]
Peel the turnips and chop them into pieces the size of a fava bean (*fūl*) each. Soak them in salted water for two days, and then take them out, squeeze out the extra moisture, and put them in [a solution of] wine vinegar and bee honey seasoned with *aṭrāf al-ṭīb* (spice blend) and mint. Store them away.

(550) Recipe for white pickled turnips made with yeast (*khamīra*)[25]
Take barley flour; knead it with bread yeast, hot water, and a bit of salt. Set it aside until it becomes very sour. (**136r**)

When the barley dough is sour enough [dissolve it in] hot water in which turnips have been boiled [and taken out] and set aside. Strain the liquid, and continue adding water to it until it becomes thin, so that it is suitable for drinking [when the pickles are done].

---

22 See recipe 540 above, for the rules.

23 See glossary 9.2, for details on this cooking technique, s.v. *yaghlī*.

24 *Carcade, Hibiscus sabdariffa*, known as roselle. Today in Egypt, it is more commonly known as *karkadeh*.

25 Compared with the corresponding recipe in al-Nābulusī, *ʿAlam al-malāḥa* 260, this version has more details.

Throw into this liquid the turnips, which have been peeled, cut crosswise[26] into thin slices, and half-boiled in water [and taken out].[27] The yeast [mentioned above] is dissolved in this boiling liquid. As for the turnips, they are sprinkled with [ground] mustard seeds, and then are left to cool and added to the liquid with yeast.

Add a lot of mint and rue, as well as leaves of sour orange (*nāranj*), and sprinkle *aṭrāf al-ṭīb* (spice blend) on it. Keep the yeast solution with the turnips in it in a warm place [to mature], and then take them out and eat them.

(551) Another recipe [for turnip pickles], very tasty[28]

Take ½ *qinṭār* (approx. 49½ pounds) turnips. Peel them, [put them in a pot,] and add enough water to submerge them—this should be done once or several times [depending on the size of the pot].

Light the fire under the pot until the water is quite warm, but do not let it boil, and then remove [the pot from the fire]. Pour cold water on it, and when the turnips cool, transfer them to a *dann* (large earthenware cask). [Keep the liquid.]

Now, take 2½ *raṭls* (2½ pounds) wheat flour bread yeast, dissolve it in the cooled liquid in which the turnips were put. Pour the liquid over the turnips [in the *dann*], enough to submerge them. Add cold water if needed.

Take $^{1}/_{16}$ *qadaḥ* (2 ounces)[29] mustard seeds; extract their essence with water [by pounding and steeping them in water, and straining the liquid]. Do this several times to extract all of their essence. Add the liquid to the turnips, and mix all of it by hand, so that what is on top goes down to bottom.

Set the vessel aside until its taste matures, and then use it.

(552) Another [pickled turnip] recipe

Peel the turnips, cut them into pieces and boil them in salted water. Take them out while they are still firm.

Take wine vinegar, (**136v**) white bee honey or fine white sugar (*sukkar ṭabarzad*), and crushed coriander seeds. Divide the mix among wide-mouthed jars (*barānī*),[30] and color it differently: some with saffron, and some with a mix of safflower and saffron. Do this in the jars themselves. Seal the mouths

26 This detail is from the corresponding version in *Wuṣla* ii 670.

27 Or boiled to a quarter of their doneness, as in *Wuṣla*.

28 Here I used the corresponding recipe in *Zahr*, fol. 27r, to amend the edited text.

29 'Half an eighth,' as copied in *Zahr*, fol. 26v.

30 Sg. *barniyya*.

of the jars, and set them aside until the dye colors the turnips, and their taste matures. It is served with rosewater.[31]

(553) Recipe [for pickled turnips][32]

Peel the turnips, and cut them into small and large pieces. Bring them to a boil twice;[33] they should still be firm when they are removed from the fire. Season them with [crushed] mustard seeds and salt.

Put the turnips in a bowl (*ḥuqq*) and chop rue leaves on them. Now, take bread yeast, which has been souring for five days, dissolve it in hot water, and set it aside until the liquid looks clear. Take the clear liquid and pour it onto the turnips. Set it aside for four days and use.

(554) Recipe [for pickled turnips]

Peel and cut the turnips into pieces, and sprinkle them with a bit of salt, *aṭrāf al-ṭīb* (spice blend), some aromatic spices (*afāwih*), cassia (*dār Ṣīnī*), and crushed mastic gum. Rub and mix all the ingredients, and put them in a wide-mouthed glass jar (*barniyya zujāj*). Pour good vinegar on them, enough to submerge them. If you wish, add bee honey as well; and dye them with saffron.

(555) Recipe for *lift ʿajamī* (Persian-style pickled turnips)

Take *ʿiqaṣ al-lift* (small heads of turnips with stems 1–finger long).[34] Boil them until they are half-done, and then put them in [a sauce of] vinegar, mustard, tahini (*ṭaḥīna*), hazelnuts, walnuts, coriander, sweet olive oil, and caraway seeds.

(556) Another recipe for pickled turnips

Take turnips, boil them, drain them, and rub them well with mustard and cardamom (*hāl*), so that their flavors penetrate the turnips. Next, take sugar, wine vinegar, cardamom, and saffron threads (*zaʿfarān shaʿr*). Add these to the turnips, and set them aside, covered, for three days. They will become as yellow as gold.

---

31 This is the only place where rosewater is mentioned in relation to serving pickles.

32 Here I used the corresponding recipe in *Zahr*, fol. 27r to amend the edited text.

33 *Yaghlī ghalwatayn*, see glossary 9.2.

34 As described in recipe 542 above.

(556)[35] Another recipe for pickled turnips with yeast

Soak white turnips, which have been peeled and cut into fingers and discs (*mudawwar*), in salted water for three days. Rinse them, and then soak them in unsalted water for a couple of days.

Take 4 *raṭl*s (4 pounds) bread yeast (*khamīra*), dissolve it in water until the liquid is extremely thin. Leave it until the sediment settles on the bottom, and remove the clear liquid.

Take the turnips out of the water, and throw them into a green-glazed wide-mouthed jar (*barniyya*). Pour on them the clear yeast liquid, and add 3 *ūqiyya*s (3 ounces) mustard seeds that have been crushed and washed in natron (*naṭrūn*). Also add rue, mint, and a bit of rosebuds (*zir ward*). Leave the pickles in the jar for five days, and then replace the rue and mint leaves with some fresh ones. Also, refresh the yeast by adding more, and stir in sugar or honey.

Every time you want to eat some, stir the jar [before taking some out of it]. It is wonderful.

[The following, up to recipe 568, are all about olives.]

(557) Recipe for *zaytūn mukallas* (preserved olives treated with slaked lime)[36]

Take picked over olives that are free of any blemishes. Wash large earthenware jars (*khawābī*),[37] and put the olives in them.

Take *kils* (quicklime), slake it (*yuṭfa'* i.e., mix it with water) and set it aside overnight. Now, take potash (*qilī*), pound it thoroughly, sift it, and for each *mudd* of olives, use 1 *ūqiyya* (7 ounces) slaked lime and 1 *ūqiyya* potash.[38] The Levantine *mudd* equals 10 Egyptian *raṭl*s (approx. 10 pounds).

Now take water [which you estimate is] enough to submerge the olives, and pour it into a copper pot. Add the slaked lime and potash, and boil the water until one-third of it is reduced. When this happens, take the pot off the heat, (**137v**) and empty the water into an earthenware vessel, and leave it overnight. The following morning, it will look as clear as sesame oil. Pour the clear water

35 This is the editors' numbering. It should be 557, but I have maintained it, to avoid confusion.

36 The compiler of *Wuṣla* ii 677 explains that he does not include any such recipes in his book because they are very well known. Fortunately, the compiler of the *Kanz* thought otherwise.

37 Sg. *khābiya*.

38 The modern measures I give here are based on the assumption that all the recipe measures follow the Levantine weights system. Recipe 559 below specifies the Damascene *ūqiyya*. See n. 42 below.

over the olives [that were put in the large earthenware jars]; add enough to cover the olives. Also, cover the top of the olives with whatever leaves you have, and weigh them down so that the olives will not come up to the surface of the water and become discolored.

Keep the olives in these jars for three days, and then take an olive and crack it open. If you see that the seed has turned black and the olive does not taste bitter any more, take the olives out of the liquid, put them in vessels, and wash them until they are clean. Immediately, lest they should discolor, take them out and put them in salt-free water, and keep them in it for three days. Next, put them in water to which a good amount of salt has been added, and the olives will be good to eat.

(559)[39] Another recipe for *zaytūn mukallas* (preserved olives treated with slaked lime)

Take good [black] olives when they are still green but have some oil content in them,[40] choose the ones that are free of any bruises or surface blemishes. Put the olives in a vessel with enough water to submerge them, and leave them there for a couple of days. Then, take them out of the water and pour water and slaked lime (*kils*)[41] on them—for each *mudd* of olives (approx. 10 pounds), use 2 Damascene *ūqiyyas* (14 ounces) slaked lime.[42] Keep the olives in the slaked lime solution until they are good to eat. Then take them out, wash them and keep them in brine, and use them as needed.

(560) Recipe for *zaytūn murammad* (olives cured with ashes)

For each *mudd* (approx. 10 pounds) of olives, use 1 *ūqiyya* (7 ounces) slaked lime and 1 *mudd* sifted ashes (*ramād*).[43] Mix the slaked lime with the ashes and knead them with water until they have the consistency of *ʿaṣīda* (thick flour soup). Add this mix to the olives, and stir them so that all the olives are smeared with the lime ash, as if by mud.

---

39 Apparently, the editors inadvertently skipped the number 558. Here I followed their numbering to avoid confusion. See also n. 35 above.

40 I.e., picked, when they have obtained full size, however, before their ripening cycle has begun and they have turned black.

41 See the previous recipe for more information on slaked lime.

42 Cf. the Egyptian *ūqiyya* = 1 ounce, and 1 *raṭl* = approx. 1 pound. The Levantine *raṭl* is approx. 3¾ pounds, and 1 *ūqiyya* = approx. 7 ounces.

43 The modern measures I give here are based on the assumption that all the recipe measures follow the Levantine/Damascene weights system, like the two previous recipes. See note above.

Set the vessel aside for three days, (**138r**) and take one olive and crack it open, if you see that the stone has darkened, add potash (*qilī*) to water,[44] and wash the olives in it. Take them out and keep them in a fresh change of [just] water for three days. After that, take them out and keep them in brine. Whenever you wish, take some out and eat them.

(561) Another similar recipe (i.e., olives cured with ashes)
Take green olives[45] that are firm and free of any blemishes. Put them in a vessel and pour salted water on them, and set them aside for a week. Then, sift the ashes and add it to olives, as much as needed, so that they are coated with it like a layer of mud. Keep the olives like this for a month or longer. Whenever you want to eat the olives, take the amount you need out of the vessel and wash them and eat them.[46]

(562) Recipe for preparing *zaytūn aswad* (black olives)
Take black Palmyra olives (*Zaytūn Tadmurī*),[47] remove their pits, and put them on the back of a sieve, and infuse them with the smoke of Javanese aloeswood (*ʿūd Qāqullī*) and dried walnut shells that are burning under [the upside-down sieve]. When the olives are thoroughly smoked, sprinkle coriander seeds on them, and add chopped Macedonian parsley (*baqdūnis*), sweet olive oil, toasted and crushed walnuts, and fine chopped lemon preserved in salt (*laymūn māliḥ*). [Mix well and] keep them in a clean vessel that has been infused with aromatic smoke (*mubakhkhar*).

(563) Another recipe for black olives
Take [already cured] olives and remove their pits. Pound toasted walnuts, and add lemon juice, *aṭrāf ṭīb* (spice blend), tahini, lemon preserved in salt (*laymūn māliḥ*) and cut into pieces, chopped Macedonian parsley (*baqdūnis*), mint, and rue. [Mix all of these and add them to the olives]; the mix [should

44 The verb used is *tuqill al-māʾ*.

45 In the corresponding recipe in *Zahr*, fol. 27v, the text adds,

الزيتون الاخضر الذي يعصر منه الزيت.

i.e., black olives used for extracting oil, harvested when still green and firm.

46 The last sentence is an addition from *Zahr*, which clearly indicates that the olives remain in the ashes, and are used as needed.

47 These are black olives of Palmyra, they are large and elongated in shape, and low in oil content, used as table olives. In this recipe, they are already cured and good to eat.

be thick enough to] coat the olives, so that they can be scooped with a piece of bread. Also, add some coriander,[48] caraway, and a bit of black pepper.

(564) Recipe for delicious olives

Take cured olives (*zaytūn mustawī*), and remove their pits. (**138v**) Pound garlic and add it to the olives, use enough to give them a noticeable garlicky taste. Shell walnuts free of any rancidity (*zanakh*). Finely pound them and rub them with the olives thoroughly so that they mix well.

Now, take fine fresh sesame oil, add a good amount of it to the olives, and resume rubbing the olives [with the ingredients added]. Skin almonds, dye them in different colors, and add them to the olives as garnishes (*yuzayyan bihi*). Sprinkle them with a bit of sesame seeds, finely ground sumac, thyme, and mint. Pack the olives in a green-glazed wide-mouthed jar (*barniyya*) or *bāṭiya* (large wide bowl). Use a lot of sesame oil [with these olives], they are wonderful.

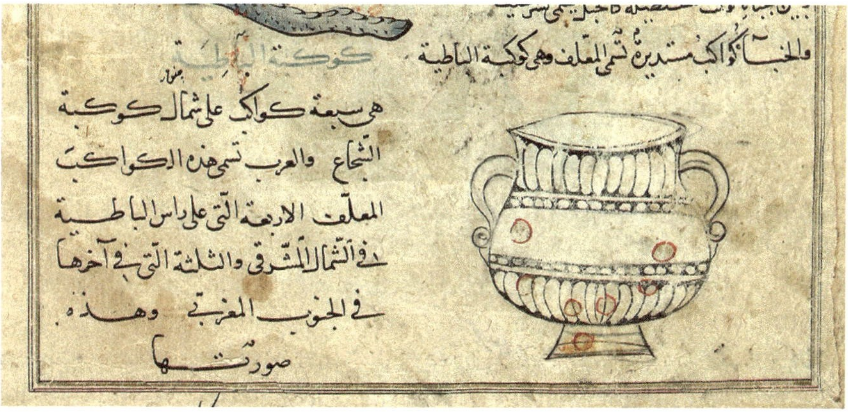

FIGURE 40 Bāṭiya, *F1954.47v, Muḥammad al-Qazwīnī,* ʿAjāʾib al-makhlūqāt, *detail (Freer Gallery of Art and Arthur M. Sackler Gallery, Smithsonian Institution, Washington, DC: Purchase—Charles Lang Freer Endowment).*

48 The corresponding recipe in *Wuṣla* ii 677 correctly copies the preposition phrase 'in it' (فيه), rather than the edited 'on' (على).

(565) Recipe for *zaytūn mutabbal* (seasoned olives)

Take [fully ripe raw] olives, crack them (*yufshakh*), remove their pits, and extract half of their oil. Keep them in several changes of water until they lose their bitterness. Squeeze them out [to remove extra moisture].

Take toasted seeds of caraway and coriander, as much as needed, also take enough *aṭrāf ṭīb* (spice blend), hazelnuts, tahini, and very sour wine vinegar. Season the olives with this [mixture] and set them aside in a vessel for three days. Fold the mix with the olive oil, and use.

(566) Another recipe for *mutabbal* (seasoned) olives[49]

Take [cured] black olives, remove their pits, and pound them in a wooden mortar (*jurn khashab*) or *hāwan* (brass mortar), pound them very well.

Pound sumac and sift it. Take lemon preserved in salt (*laymūn māliḥ*) and chop it into small pieces. Pound walnuts, caraway seeds, and a bit of black pepper. [Mix them all with the pounded olives] and add sesame oil to the mix.

The more you add of the ingredients we mentioned, the better it will be; except for sumac; it should be used sparingly. [Finally,] take as much garlic as you like, finely pound it in a stone mortar and mix it with the rest of the ingredients. (139r) Stow it away and use whenever needed.

If green olives are used, [do not pound them, but] chop them as fine as lentils.

Another recipe for *zaytūn mutabbal muṭayyab* (seasoned and flavored olives)[50]

These are appetizing and quite delicious, they aid digestion, and sweeten the breath.

Take the excellent fleshy olives of Fayyūm[51] that have been already cured in salt (*mumallaḥ*). Crack them open, remove their pits, and split each one in half. Wash them in cold water, squeeze them thoroughly by hand to get rid of all the moisture, and then put them in a vessel and cover them with fine-tasting water (*māʾ ḥulw*). Set them aside, covered, [for a couple of hours].

Again, squeeze out their moisture, cover them with a fresh change of water, and keep them in it for two to three hours. Continue doing this until the olives no longer taste salty. Thoroughly squeeze them out by hand until they feel spongy and no moisture remains in them.

49 This preparation results in olive paste.

50 This recipe only appears in CB, appendix 44.

51 A district in central Egypt.

Put the olives in a vessel, pour vinegar on them and fold them together. The olives should be tightly packed in it (*tukayyituhu*). The following morning, wash the olives [and press out the extra moisture] as you did earlier, until no vinegar remains. Spread them on a tray, or anything you want, to expose them to the air.

Toast coriander and caraway seeds [and pound them]. Also, toast hazelnuts, and set them aside along with the other two ingredients mentioned.

Take cloves (*qaranful*), [dried] carnation petals (*zahr qaranful*), black pepper, Ceylon cinnamon (*qarfa*), spikenard (*sunbul*), betel leaves (*tunbul*), nutmeg (*jawzat ṭīb*), rosebuds (*zir ward*), green cardamom (*hāl*), and mace (*basbāsa*). Pound them all and sift them [and set them aside].

Season the olives with the pounded caraway and coriander. Coarsely crush the hazelnuts and season the olives with them [and set the olives aside].

Now take tahini, put it on a plate or any wide vessel, add to it 1½ *ūqiyya*s (3 tablespoons) fine-tasting Levantine rosewater, and dissolve the tahini in it. Take clear white wine vinegar, and add it in drops to the tahini and rosewater; mix them until they all combine. Make enough of it to suit the amount of olives used.

Finely chop rue, Macedonian parsley (*baqdūnis*), and mint—make enough of these, using equal amounts of each. Add them [to the tahini mix], followed by the spices we mentioned earlier. Stir the mix by hand. Add to this a suitable amount of sweet olive oil, which does not taste sharp; it is better to use washed olive oil (*zayt maghsūl*).[52] Stir the ingredients very well.

Now take the olives you prepared, mentioned earlier, and add them to this *mizāj* (seasoning mix), and put them all in a glazed wide-mouthed jar (*barniyya madhūna*). Seal the surface with olive oil, and tie the opening of the jar with a piece of cloth. Put it away, and use as needed.

Another [olive] recipe[53]

Crack [already cured] olives, and season them with toasted and pounded coriander and caraway seeds [and set them aside].

Lightly toast walnuts, and pound them, adding [lemon] juice,[54] while they are being pounded in the stone mortar (*jurn*), so that it blends with them. The same is done with the garlic, which is skinned and pounded with olive oil along with lemon preserved in salt, after removing their seeds.

---

52 See glossary 6.

53 This recipe only appears in CB, appendix 45.

54 Due to a hole in the CB, the word is missing. Based on some of the olive recipes in this chapter, the juice might well be that of lemon.

Pound all the ingredients thoroughly until the mix is as smooth as ointment (*marham*). Add to the mix a bit of black pepper and Ceylon cinnamon (*qarfa*), both pounded, and combine it with the olives, along with a bit of rue, Macedonian parsley (*baqdūnis*), and [chopped] mint. Also add sweet olive oil and as much tahini as needed. Let the entire mix be seasoned well, set it aside overnight [to mature], and then it will be good to eat. Bowls can be filled with it and served in *sukurdānāt*.[55]

(567) Another recipe for olives that is quite delicious (*ṭayyib*)
Take whole [cured] black olives, as much as you want. Take walnuts and hazelnuts, toast them, remove their skins, and pound them finely. Toast coriander seeds and pound them. Cut lemon preserved in salt (*laymūn māliḥ*) into small pieces. Take sesame oil or washed olive oil (*zayt maghsūl*),[56] and fold it in with the olives [and the rest of the ingredients] so that they all mix well. Store it away and use as needed.

(568) Recipe for *zaytūn mubakhkhar* (smoked olives)[57]
Take fully ripe olives, either black or green, but the latter are more conducive to smoking.

Bruise the olives, put enough salt on them, and continue folding them in salt every day until they are no longer bitter. Meanwhile, whenever they release any moisture, pour it off. When they are no longer bitter, spread them on a latticed tray (*ṭabaq mushabbak*) until they dry thoroughly.

Pound skinned garlic along with rue, and picked over thyme leaves, use as much as needed. Take 1 *dirham* (½ teaspoon) of this mix, along with a piece of walnut shell with the kernel inside it, 1 *dirham* wax (*shamʿ*), a piece of cotton dipped in sesame oil, and a date pit. Put all these ingredients on a very low fire [lit] in a brazier (*kānūn*), and shut the door. Put the tray with the olives in it on the top of the brazier,[58] and cover it with a tray to let the smoke permeate the olives. Leave them undisturbed for a whole day, and then transfer them to a vessel large enough to contain them.

---

55 Sg. *sukurdān*, a large tray on which a variety of appetizing small dishes are arranged and served.

56 See glossary 6.

57 Except for some minor differences in details, *Waṣf* 142–3 includes a copy of this recipe, which I used here to amend the edited text in several places.

58 The brazier as described here is like a box with a door and a perforated top that allows smoke to escape upwards.

الوسخة وخلط بالعسل وضمد به فيحلل الاورام
الحارة ويلين حدة الدمامل اذا انقلع واذامضغ
اوراقه الغض والاضلاع واذا نصد با لورق
مع دقيق الشعير كان صالحا للاسهال المزمن
وعصارته وطبخه يفعلان ضد ذلك وعصارته
اذا احتملت قطعت الرطوبات السايلة من الرحم
المزمنة ونزف الدم وردعت والعين وينفع من
قرحة

FIGURE 41   *Olives*, al-ʿUmarī, Masālik al-abṣār, *fol. 171v (BnF, Department of manuscripts, Arab 2771).*

Mix the olives with the [remaining] pounded garlic and thyme, along with some bruised walnuts and a handful of toasted sesame seeds. (**139v**) Heat up sesame oil with some caraway seeds, and toss the olives into it. Take a green-glazed wide-mouthed jar (*barniyya madhūna*) and infuse it with the same smoke used [in smoking the olives]. Put the olives in this vessel, cover the top, and set it aside for several days so that the sharp taste of the garlic mellows, and use.

[Here begins a series of recipes for pickling fruits and vegetables, but mostly onion and lemon]

(569) Recipe for [pickled] onions

Take dried round onions free of any mold (*ʿafan*), clean them and discard the unwanted parts.[59] Keep them in very sour vinegar until they mature. Some people keep them in brine first, for a while, and then they rinse them, weigh them down with something to get rid of the extra moisture, and then put them in vinegar.

(570) Another recipe [for pickled onions]

These do not stay good for long. Take large onions,[60] remove the outer skins, make two cross-like slits lengthwise, but keep them intact. Add a lot of salt and water, and set them aside for a day and a night. After that, squeeze out their moisture, and stuff the cross-like slits with the tender leaves of mint, common parsley (*karafs*), Macedonian parsley (*baqdūnis*), and rue. Also use toasted and pounded coriander seeds and caraway. Pack the onions in a glazed ceramic jar (*qaṭramīz*), pour very sour vinegar and olive oil on them. Set the jar aside for several days, and it will be good to eat.

(571) Another recipe [for pickled onions]

Cut the onion into large pieces, rinse them in salted water, and add vinegar, lemon juice, chopped Macedonian parsley (*baqdūnis*), mint, coriander, caraway, and *aṭrāf al-ṭīb* (spice blend). It can be eaten the following day.

---

59 As suggested by the verb *yunaqqā*. Both ends were trimmed off and the inedible outer layers removed.

60 The corresponding recipe in *Wuṣla* ii 687–8 specifies *baṣal salmānī*. However, the identical recipe in al-Nābulusī, *ʿAlam al-malāḥa* 265 only specifies their size.

(572) Another recipe [for pickled onions] that stay good and do not spoil for a whole year[61]

Take small onions, leave their skins on, but discard any that are already separating from them. Put them in a vessel, and soak them for 20 days. (**140r**) For the first 10 days, soak them in lightly salted water. During this period, continue changing the salted water so that the onions lose their pungency. Next, replace the salted water with slightly salted wine vinegar [and keep them in that for 10 more days].

Drain the onions, [put them in a jar,] and add [a new batch of] very sour vinegar, enough to submerge them, and store them away.

Before serving them in a *sukurdān*,[62] peel them first. They are delicious when added to *sikbāj* (sour vinegar stew).

(573) Recipe for *baṣal makbūs* (pickled onions)

Take clean round onions that are free of any mold (*ʿafan*). Pack a jar with them, and pour enough vinegar [with salt] to submerge them. Cover them from the inside of the jar with date palm fronds (*khūṣ*) or its fibrous sheath (*līfa*).[63] This will allow the vapors that form to escape, so the pickles do not spoil.

They can be eaten after 15 days, and when all the onions are gone, and you want to make another batch, add more onions and more of the vinegar-salt solution, as you did earlier.

(574) Recipe for pickling onions and eggplant

Take as many round onions and small eggplants as you like. Slit the eggplants and stuff them with *aṭrāf al-ṭīb* (spice blend). Leave the onions unpeeled.

[In a jar,] arrange the onions in alternate rows with the eggplant. Pour vinegar [with some salt] on them, [set them aside to allow them to mature], and then eat them. They are delicious.

---

61 This recipe also appears in *Wuṣla* ii 687; and al-Nābulusī, *ʿAlam al-malāḥa* 265. Additionally, it is repeated in recipe 583 below. All of the versions are a bit confused with regard to the details of soaking the onions for 20 days. Here I used them to amend the edited text.

62 A large tray on which a variety of delicious small dishes are served as appetizers and *naql* 'mezze.'

63 Both are resistant to mold.

(575) Recipe for pickling fresh green walnuts (*jawz akhḍar*)[64]

Take green walnuts in April, when their kernels are fully grown, and pierce them in many places with a long needle (*misalla*). Soak them in salted water for 20 days or a bit less, until the liquid that seeps out of them is no longer black, (**140v**) and they start to taste sweet [i.e., no longer acrid]. Take them out, and wash and drain them. Do this fast.

Next, pour very sour vinegar on them; add spices and herbs (*abāzīr*) and whole garlic cloves, and it will taste quite delicious. Also, add mint and common parsley (*karafs*). It will look very nice. These pickles are good for [purging excess] phlegm.

(576) Recipe for pickling Damascus citron (*kabbād*), called *maskal mankal*;[65] it used to be made by the [Fatimid] caliphs' concubines (*al-jawārī al-quṣūriyyāt*)[66]

Take Damascus citron (*kabbād marākibī*), which are large and fully ripe, and have thick pithy peels. Take the peels, cut them into pieces (*shawābīr*), and fry them in sesame oil until they are fully cooked.

Now take the pulp, separate the sections, but keep their skins intact. Put them in a vessel; pour very sour wine vinegar sweetened with honey or sugar on

---

64 This recipe can also be found in al-Nābulusī, *ʿAlam al-malāḥa* 265. Here I used it to amend the edited text, particularly the first sentence. Cf. recipe 590 below, also dealing with pickling fresh green walnuts.

65 In *Wuṣla* ii 689–90, a duplicate recipe is given the name *sankal mankal*. The writer/compiler Ibn al-ʿAdīm claims that he learnt it at the palace of al-Malik al-ʿĀdil (Ayyubid king, d. 1218) from the Fatimid caliphs' slave girls (جواري الخلفاء). This is a pickle name that is only found in these two cookbooks. This recipe is also found in al-Nābulusī, *ʿAlam al-malāḥa* 266, but it has none of the interesting historical details or the enigmatic name bestowed on it in the other two versions. Therefore, there is no way even to verify its pronunciation at the time. Nonetheless, I find the name to be curiously evocative of the story of Joseph and the wife of Potiphar.

First, the k sound in the two words might well have been the written form of the Egyptian and Levantine dialectical vocalization of g sound, which is, in turn, a variant of the j sound. Based on this, the name might well have been the local pronunciation of *sanjal manjal*.

Now, Sanjal, a Palestinian town, was believed to be the location of the well Joseph was thrown into by his brothers. *Manjal* is derived from *najl* 'cutting,' which could be an allusion to the Egyptian episode of the story as it occurs in the Qur'an (12:31). When Potiphar's wife Zulaykha heard the women gossip about her lust for Joseph, she prepared a banquet for them, gave each of them a knife and a citron *mutk*, and called for Joseph. When the women saw him, they cut their hands instead of the citron.

66 Al-Nābulusī, *ʿAlam al-malāḥa* 266, calls for *kabbād*, which is an indication that *kabbād* and *kabbād marākibī* may designate the same variety of the fruit.

them. Add a good amount of toasted and shelled hazelnuts, coarsely crushed. Also add *aṭrāf ṭīb* (spice blend), mint, and the fried peel—add these while they are still hot. Use enough [sugar or honey] to give it a sweet taste. Set the vessel aside for [a few] days and eat it.

(577) Recipe for *kabbād mumallaḥ* (Damascus citron preserved in salt)

Cut *kabbād* into pieces (*shawābīr*). Crush salt, color it with saffron, and coat the *kabbād* with it. Squeeze the juice of more *kabbād* and color it with the saffron-colored salt.

Put the pieces in a green-glazed wide-mouthed jar (*barniyya*) and pour the extracted juice on them. Seal the surface with sweet olive oil, cover the jar, and then store it away, and take some out of it whenever needed.

(578) Another recipe for [salt-preserved *kabbād*]

Cut the *kabbād* into halves (*aflāq*). Color salt with saffron. (**141r**) Toast caraway seeds; pound ginger, cloves, and rosebuds; and mix them with the salt. Chop some rue.[67]

[Combine *kabbād* pieces with the salt mix, fold in the rue,] and add sweet olive oil. Season them with some spices (*yutabbal*), and pack them in a glazed ceramic jar (*qaṭramīz*). Seal the surface with sweet olive oil.

(579) Recipe for *baṣal mukhallal* (pickled onions), ready to eat the following day

Take whole small onions; remove the roots and the [outer] skins sprouting out of them.[68] For each 10 *raṭl*s (10 pounds) of onions, use ½ *raṭl* date syrup (*dibs*), which you whip with water and pour on the onions, add enough to submerge them. Put them in an earthenware vessel (*fakhkhāra*), light a fire under it, and let it boil. The onions will come out darkened in hue.

Pierce each onion from the top and bottom with a sharp needle, make seven holes or more, and make sure to get to the core of the onion. Clean the earthenware vessel and put the onions [back] in it. Pour very sour wine vinegar on them, enough to submerge them. Lightly boil the earthenware vessel.

Take the onions out of the vinegar, drain them of excess moisture, put them in a green-glazed wide-mouthed jar (*barniyya*), cover them with vinegar, and set them aside overnight. They will be wonderful when eaten the following day; they will taste as if they were aged for a year.

---

67 I took the incoherent بقدوم of the edited version to be a copyist's misreading of the original ويفرم 'and chop.'

68 I replaced الثابتة عنه with النابتة عنه 'sprouting,' based on context.

(580) A recipe for pickling onions, a specialty of Egypt (*diyār Miṣr*)

Take excellent (*rafīʿ*) dried onions, and spread them out in a high, well-ventilated place.[69] Keep them there for 20 days until they are no longer dense, and then remove their loose [outer] skins and the scraggly roots growing from them (*ʿarāmīsh*).[70]

Pack the onions in large earthenware jars (*khawābī*),[71] and pour vinegar on them, fill the jars almost to the top, to a level where a sparrow could almost drink from it.[72] Next, cover the entire surface with pieces of broken fired pottery jars.[73] Set these [pieces] directly on the onions (*yushaffaf*). Wait until the vinegar rises above the fragments of pottery by a space of 4–fingers [put together].[74] Cover (**141v**) the opening of the jar with something like a large, wide earthenware tub (*qaṣriyya*) [turned upside down on it],[75] and tie it securely to the opening of the jar. Set it aside for two months until the pickling is done, and then use it. It can even be used to treat nausea.

[**To use it:**] Take the onion, after you remove the outer skins and cut off both ends, cut it in half. Repeat with as many onions as you need, squeeze out the extra moisture, and color them with saffron. Prepare a mix of wine vinegar, sugar, mint, and *aṭrāf al-ṭīb* (spice blend). Put the onions in a green-glazed wide-mouthed jar (*barniyya*) or a glazed ceramic jar (*qaṭramīz*), and pour as much of this liquid as they can take. Set them aside for five days and serve them in a *sukurdān*,[76] or for other purposes.

---

69 I replaced فيقشر 'and they are peeled' with فينشر 'and they are spread,' based on context. Spreading out the onions at the highest level of the house would spare people the constant smell of wafting onions.

70 Sg. *ʿurmūsh*.

71 Sg. *khābiya*.

72 Not that they want sparrows to drink it; this is merely to give us an idea of how close to the top the vinegar should be.

73 I amended the text here, and read بشفاف الجرار المرقية as بشقاف الجرار الحرقية, based on context. These jars, baked in fire, were usually used for cooking purposes, as they can stand the heat, though they break easily with use. However, they are ideal for this purpose, as they remain intact and do not disintegrate in the vinegary liquid.

74 While they are pressed down with the pottery fragments, the onions wilt and settle, thus increasing the level of vinegar between them and the surface of the vinegar.

75 The enclosed dome that is created here allows the vinegar-onion fumes to escape and dissipate.

76 A large tray on which a variety of delicious small dishes are served as appetizers or *naql* (mezze).

[**Another way of using them;**] take some of the onions prepared earlier, peel them and cut them as we mentioned above, and squeeze out the extra moisture very well. Take drained yogurt (*laban munashshaf*), and add a bit of crushed ginger, mint, and rue. If basil thyme (*rayḥān qaranfulī*) is in season,[77] take the leaves only, and chop them and add them [to the yogurt]. If it is not available, then coarsely crush stalks of Indian clove (*ḥaṭab al-qaranful al-Hindī*),[78] add them, and stir all the ingredients. It will stay good for more than a couple of days, after which, make a new batch. It is an exotic dish that aids digestion and whets the appetite.

(581) [Pickled] onions, eaten the same day

Take onions, cut cones out of their root ends (*yuqawwar min asāfilihi*) [and discard]. Put them in a pot, and pour enough vinegar to submerge them all. Add iron nails,[79] bring the pot to a brief boil, and take it off the fire. (**142r**) [Pour off the vinegar in which the onions were boiled and] replace it with some other vinegar, and use the pickles.

(582) Recipe for delicious pickled onions

Take onions, and spread them on the ground to dry for two to three days, and then clean them [remove the outer skins, cut off both ends] and layer them in a vessel, alternating with a layer of salt and nigella seeds (*shūnīz*). When you are done tightly packing the onions, pour in enough wine vinegar to cover all of them. If the vinegar is too sour, add water to it until it tastes moderately sour. There should be an arm's length space between the onions' surface and the top of the jar, because the onions will moisten [and puff up] and fill the jar.

The pickles are good to eat when the onions taste sour and absorb the flavor of the vinegar.

(583) Another [onion recipe]

[This is the same as recipe 572 above; repeated here probably from another pickling manual.]

---

77 This is also called *ḥabaq qaranfulī* and *faranjamushk*, *Calamintha acinos* (S).

78 Here I replaced the edited فزهر, which is redundant, with مرص from C, n. 6847, but I read it as (فرضّ) 'then coarsely crush.'

79 The nails react with the vinegar and form iron acetate, which fixes the vinegar's dye to the onions.

(584) Recipe for making radishes with vinegar; they aid digestion, and are quite delicious

Take large, tender radishes, slice them lengthwise into fingers (*aṣābiʿ*), and put them in a wide-mouthed glass vessel (*qārūra*). Pour enough good wine vinegar to submerge them. Throw on them asafetida leaves (*anjudhān*), nigella seeds (*shūnīz*), a bit of pounded chickpeas, and mustard condiment (*khardal maʿmūl*) that has been pounded and [treated and] is no longer bitter.[80] Also, add pounded thyme and salt. Let the flavor of the asafetida leaves overpower the others, but it needs to be pounded before adding it in.

Eat it [with other foods] because it helps them digest well.

(585) Recipe for Damascus citron (*kabbād*) [preserved in seasoned salt]

Cut *kabbād* into slices (*shaqqāt*). (**142v**) Take salt, toasted caraway seeds, rue, sweet olive oil, pieces of ginger—keep them whole—pieces of Ceylon cinnamon (*qarfa*), and whole pieces of stalks of clove (*ḥaṭab qaranful*).

Season the *kabbād* with salt and the [above-mentioned] spices (*āla*).[81] Put them in a vessel, and seal the surface with sweet olive oil. Cover the vessel, and tie a piece of cloth on top of this cover. Put it away until needed. It will mature in three days.

This condiment needs to be taken care of and be checked on. If the solution in the vessel decreases, replenish it with olive oil, and transfer it to a smaller vessel. It is fantastic.

(586) Recipe for [sweet pickles of] *ḥummāḍ al-utrujj* (citron pulp)[82]

Take the citron pulp (*ḥummāḍ*), and pull out the pulp vesicles (*shuʿayrahu*) [discard the membranes, and set them aside].

Take sugar, and toasted pistachios and hazelnuts. Also, take rose-petal jam (*ward murabbā*), cooked and ready to use, and add it to the [sugar and nuts], along with saffron, musk, and rosewater. Put the mix on the fire, add rosewater, and let it cook until it has the consistency of sugar syrup (*jullāb*).

Infuse a green-glazed wide-mouthed jar (*barniyya*) with the smoke of aloeswood and ambergris, and put the citron [that was set aside] in it. Cover it tightly, so that none of its aroma escapes the jar. It is the best.

---

80 See, for instance, recipe 483 above.

81 This is another handy word, like *ḥawāʾij*, that was used to designate the ingredients called for in the recipe.

82 This preserved variety is sweet and sour. The sourness of citron replaces the vinegar.

القديم ووجع الاذن والشرب منه التي تمسك البطن

ليموا

هذا النوع من اشجار بلاد الروم وخاصية الليموا وشجرها
وقشرها وحماضها شبيه بالاترج وقد مر فلا نعيده
ولليموا خاصية عجيبة في دفع ضرر سم الحيات والافاعي
ومن عجيب حكاياته ما ذكره ابو جعفر بن عبد الله وكان
من

FIGURE 42 *Lemons, al-ʿUmarī,* Masālik al-abṣār, *fol. 202v (BnF, Department of manuscripts, Arab 2771).*

(587) Recipe for [a condiment with] *laymūn māliḥ* (salt-preserved lemons)
Take lemons [preserved in salt], cut them into pieces and throw them into vinegar. Drain the vinegar, and again throw them into another portion of vinegar to get rid of the salt. Drain the lemons from this vinegar, and color [and scent] the pieces with saffron and rosewater.

Take [fresh] lemons and squeeze the juice onto crushed fine sugar. Pound good walnuts, and a bit of ginger (**143r**) along with a small amount of green cardamom (*hāl*), betel leaves (*tunbul*), mint, rue, and a bit of toasted caraway seeds.

Discard any seeds in the lemon [pieces], and add the prepared ingredients (*ḥawāʾij*), along with 1 *ūqiyya* (1 ounce) fine-tasting almond oil. Infuse a vessel with the smoke of aloeswood and ambergris, and put the lemon mix in it. Seal the surface with almond oil, cover the vessel, and store it away. Whenever needed, serve it [in small bowls] arranged in a *sukurdān*.[83] Put the amount [you need] in a glazed ceramic jar (*qaṭramīz*), add very sour wine vinegar to it, and when you put it [in the small bowls] in the *sukurdān*, sweeten it with sugar, bee honey, or date syrup (*dibs*).

(588) Another recipe[84]
Take the tender hearts (*qulūb ghaḍḍa*) [of fresh fennel]. Keep them in vinegar until they mature. The same thing can be done with garlic; do not do anything to them, just keep the small heads of garlic, with their skins on, in vinegar.

(589) Pickling celery (*karafs*)[85]
Take celery stalks (*uṣūl al-karafs*), with their tender hearts and green leaves. Put them in a vessel, pour vinegar on them, set them aside for several days, and they will be good to eat. It is wonderful.

(590) Recipe for pickling fresh walnuts (*jawz akhḍar*)[86]
Take green walnuts before the kernels fully ripen; do this in April. Chop a lot of them with a knife, and soak them in salted water for 20 days, until the liquid

---

83 See n. 76 above.

84 The only clue to what is being pickled here is قلوبه الغضة 'their tender hearts,' which applies to fresh fennel. The expression is similarly used in recipe 591 below, dealing with pickling fennel.

85 Clearly, the recipe is not dealing with the herb, common parsley (*karafs*), which is used mainly for its tender leaves. See glossary 8, s.v. *karafs*.

86 Recipe 575 above has the same name, and the opening lines are similar, but this one is sweet and sour.

that seeps out is no longer blackish. Alternatively, put it in many changes of water until it loses its acridity, and the liquid it soaks in is no longer discolored.

Squeeze them [by hand] very well to get rid of excess moisture, and color [and scent them] with saffron and rosewater.

Cook sugar, wine vinegar, and *aṭrāf ṭīb* (spice blend) together, and throw in two bunches of mint. After the sugar mix boils, (**143v**) but before it thickens (*yaʿqud*), take out the mint, cool it and squeeze out its juice. Return this juice to the pot and continue boiling it until the mix is the consistency of sugar syrup (*jullāb*).

Cool the syrup and then pour it on the [prepared] walnuts in a green-glazed wide-mouthed jar (*barniyya*) that has been infused with the smoke of aloeswood and ambergris. Cover the top, store it away, and use it as needed.

Recipe for pickling fine fresh walnuts[87]

Peel fresh walnuts, and grate them (*yunḥat*), discarding their insides [and set them aside]. Next, take honey, ginger, *aṭrāf ṭīb* (spice blend) and some aromatic spices (*afāwih*). Pound all [the spices and aromatics] including the ginger.[88] Extract [the acrid and bitter substances of the walnuts] with vinegar.

Pound some caraway for it, along with a bit of fresh mint and almonds. Rub and mash (*yuqtal*) a bit of saffron with rosewater [to extract all its essence]. Add the aromatics and the spices along with the other ingredients (*ḥawāʾij*) [to the vinegar]. Sweeten it with sugar, and put the [grated] walnuts in it. Empty the mix into a glass jar (*qaṭramīz*), and store it away, covered, and use it whenever needed.

[Another way of making it.] Chop the walnuts, parboil them in vinegar, then take them out and set them aside to cool. Take another portion of fine-tasting vinegar; add enough bee honey to sweeten it.

Now, take *aṭrāf ṭīb* (spice blend), mint, rue, some [dried] carnation petals (*zahr qaranful*), mace, Levantine mint,[89] and a bit of galangal and nutmeg (*jawz bawwā*). Put all these ingredients in a *jurn fuqqāʿī*,[90] and crush them

87 This recipe only appears in DK, appendix 50.

88 The text is a bit confused at this point. Based on context, I take يستخرج بالخل to refer to the procedure of extracting the acrid and bitter substances of fresh walnuts by parboiling them in vinegar, as is done in the second part of this recipe.

89 *Naʿnaʿ Shāmī, Origanum dictammus*, also known as hop marjoram, and dittany of Crete.

90 A large stone mortar used by beer-makers to crush grains, spices, and dried and fresh herbs.

as with beer spices and herbs (*abāzīr al-fuqqāʿ*).[91] When they are thoroughly crushed,[92] add them to vinegar and honey [mentioned above].

Squeeze the walnuts between your hands to get rid of all the moisture. Dissolve saffron in rosewater and musk, and color the walnuts with it. Take aloeswood and ambergris, and infuse a glazed ceramic jar (*qaṭramīz*) with their smoke and smear the inside with the ashes.[93]

Pour the prepared seasoning solution (*mizāj*) into the jar and add the walnuts. Stir the contents well, cover the jar, and stow it away.

(591) Recipe for pickling fresh fennel (*shamār akhḍar*)[94]

Cut the tender hearts [of fresh fennel] into medium-sized pieces. Boil them in wine vinegar until they are half done. Squeeze out the extra moisture, and then add a seasoning mix (*mizāj*) of wine vinegar, sugar, *aṭrāf ṭīb* (spice blend), toasted caraway seeds, mint, and a bit of rosewater. Combine them very well.

Take a green-glazed wide-mouthed jar (*barniyya*), infuse it with the smoke of aloeswood and ambergris. Put the fennel mix in it, [cover it,] store it, and use as needed. It is delicious, and is recommended for dispelling winds [in the digestive system].[95] It can be nibbled on after meals to aid digestion and prevent bloating.[96]

(592) Recipe for [pickled] quince (*safarjal*)[97]

It is made in two ways:

The first: If you want to load a *sukurdān*,[98] and you do not have quince, take the quince pieces found in *sharāb laymūn safarjalī* or *sakanjabīn safarjalī*

---

91 The spices and herbs are pounded finely and sifted, or if there is some moisture from the fresh herbs, they should be smooth like ointment (*marham*). See chapter 12 above for recipes.

92 Here I replaced the redundant انضجت 'cooked' with انصحنت 'crushed,' based on context.

93 The verb used is تدمنه, derived from دمان 'ashes'; see *Lisān al-ʿArab*, s.v. دمن.

94 Al-Nābulusī, *ʿAlam al-malāḥa* 266 includes a much shorter version of this recipe, where it is mentioned that the vegetable is cut into medium pieces.

95 The Arabic expression used is *taṣrīf al-riyāḥ*.

96 The expression *yutanaqqal bihi* derives from *naql*, which are small dishes and foods consumed with alcoholic drinks, comparable to today's mezze dishes. See glossary 5, s.v. *naql*. However, it is also loosely used to designate snacks in general, as in this recipe.

97 This recipe and the following one are found in *Wuṣla* ii 675–6, where it is mentioned that there are two ways of doing it. In the *Kanz*, however, we have two more recipes. Here I used the version in *Wuṣla* to make sense of a largely confused recipe.

98 A large tray on which a variety of delicious small dishes are arranged and served as *naql* 'mezze' and appetizers.

FIGURE 43 *Quince, al-ʿUmarī,* Masālik al-Abṣār, *fol. 177r, detail (BnF, Department of manuscripts, Arab 2771).*

[and set them aside].[99] Add some vinegar to the syrup [from which the quince pieces were taken], add enough to thin it down (*yamruq*). Boil it on the fire, and throw in the pieces of quince, adding a bit of *aṭrāf al-ṭīb* (spice blend). This replaces the pickled quince; it is even more delicious.

(593) The second way to prepare [pickled quince][100]

Take vinegar and bee honey or sugar. Put them on the fire and boil them several times. Cut [fresh] quince and add it to the liquid after the seeds and the scraggly hairy fibers at their bases (*ʿarāmīsh*)[101] are discarded. Let them boil until the mix starts to condense (*yaʿqud*), while the quince cooks and the pickling liquid thickens. (**144r**) Throw in *aṭrāf ṭīb* (spice blend) as well as pistachios

99 See recipes 347 and 353 above.

100 I amended the text slightly, based on *Wuṣla*. See n. 97 above.

101 This addition is in *Wuṣla* only. The *ʿarāmīsh* refer to the remnants of flower petals, stigmas and stamens attached to the base of the ripe quince.

and scalded and skinned almonds that have been colored with saffron. Take the pot off the heat, put the pickled quince in a vessel, and use it.

(594) The third way for preparing [pickled quince]

Take quince that have been cut into pieces, peel them, and color them with saffron. Pound raisins from *jawza* grapes (*zabīb jawzānī*),[102] and extract their juice using vinegar and a sieve.[103] Add sugar to the [raisin juice], as well as saffron, *aṭrāf ṭīb* (spice blend), mint, finely pounded walnuts, and a bit of musk and rosewater. [Add this raisin-juice mix to the quince pieces.] Put all of it in a green-glazed wide-mouthed jar (*barniyya*) that has been infused with smoke of aloeswood and ambergris. Seal the surface [with olive oil], and store it away. It is the ultimate in deliciousness (*nihāya*).

(595) Recipe for pickling quince, the way common people do it (*takhlīl safarjal ʿāmmī*)

Cut quince and color it with saffron. Put enough sugar-cane molasses (*quṭāra*) in a soapstone pot (*birām*),[104] throw in the quince and boil it until the syrup starts to condense. Throw in *aṭrāf ṭīb* (spice blend), a bit of mint, and fine-tasting wine vinegar. Continue boiling until its consistency thickens, and then remove [it from the fire].

Allow [the quince mixture] to cool, and then put it in a green-glazed wide-mouthed jar (*barniyya*), seal the surface [with olive oil], and store it away.

Another very nice recipe [for pickling quince][105]

Pick quince off the trees, while the down is still on them.[106] Sprinkle them with a bit of distilled water of Egyptian willow bark (*māʾ al-khilāf*) and rosewater.[107] Pack them—leave them whole—in a glazed ceramic jar (*qaṭramīz*).

Now, get very sour white vinegar. If [white] wine vinegar is not available, take [any] clear vinegar, and add to it *aṭrāf ṭīb* (spice blend) and sweeten it with a bit of honey. Put it in a cucurbit (*qarʿa*) and set the alembic (*inbīq*) on

102 *Jawza* were deemed an excellent variety of grapes, see Dozy, *Takmilat al-maʿājim* 245.

103 The raisins are pounded first, steeped in vinegar, and then strained through a sieve repeatedly.

104 Cane-sugar molasses was cheaper than honey.

105 This recipe only appears in DK, appendix 47.

106 This indicates that the quince is picked before it is fully ripe.

107 The *khilāf* tree, also called *ṣafṣāf Miṣrī* (*Salix aegyptiaca*), is an Egyptian species of the willow tree.

it. Distill the vinegar on low heat.[108] Pour the distilled vinegar into the quince jar. [Put enough to submerge them,] close the top of the jar, and store it away.

(596) Recipe for pickling cucumber (*khiyār*)[109]

Take cucumbers harvested in September (*khiyār Tishrīn*).[110] Pick the small ones. Soak them in brine for two days and two nights, and then take them out of the brine, and put them in a glazed ceramic jar (*qaṭramīz*) and pour wine vinegar on them. Throw in the tender top leaves of common parsley (*karafs*), mint, and rue. There should be more rue than parsley.

Set the jar aside for several days, and then use it. It is delicious. It will stay good for a year or perhaps a bit less.

The second method [for pickling cucumber][111]

This is done the same as the above, except that cucumber juice is added to the vinegar. Pound the cucumbers, strain their juice, and mix it with the vinegar, which you pour onto the cucumbers along with spices and herbs as above. Only few spices are used in this pickling [process].

Add large heads of garlic to it, and it can be made without using vinegar. If tarragon is in season, add a few sprigs to the pickles. It will be delicious. This kind of pickles does not keep well for long.[112]

The third method [for using cucumber][113]

[It is] beautiful and elegant (*ẓarīf*).

Take small cucumbers and slice them thinly. Take fenugreek (*ḥulba*) [seeds], keep them soaked in water for two days and two nights to get rid of their bitterness, and then mix them with the cucumbers. Drain yogurt in a sack until it has thoroughly thickened, and mix it with the cucumbers and fenugreek. Add tender tips of mint stems (*qulūb naʿnaʿ*) to these.

---

108 For more on the process of distilling, see glossary 9.2, s.v. *taṣʿīd*.

109 This recipe, as well as 597 and 598, are also found in al-Nābulusī, *ʿAlam al-malāḥa* 264, 266, and 261, respectively.

110 That is, at the end of their season.

111 This recipe only appears in DK, appendix 48; and *Wuṣla* ii 684. Here I amended the edited text based on the latter. The first method [in *Wuṣla*] is the previous recipe in our edited text.

112 This last paragraph is an addition from *Wuṣla*.

113 This recipe only appears in DK, appendix 49. It is also found in *Wuṣla* ii 685; and al-Nābulusī, *ʿAlam al-malāḥa* 264. Here I amended the text based on these other recipes. The food described here is more like the dishes of *jājaq* and *akhlāṭ* we encountered in chapter 17 above.

Put the yogurt mix in a pot,[114] and add a bit of salt. Set the pot aside for two days, after which they can be eaten. They do not stay good more than four days. In addition, the vessel used should be a new earthenware pot.

However, if pickled cucumbers (*khiyār mukhallal*) are used [instead of the fresh ones used above], they will stay good for a year and even more if the vessel is taken good care of by regularly washing it from the outside, constantly keeping it clean, and stowing it in a cool place.[115]

(597) Recipe for pickling carrots (*takhlīl al-jazar*)[116]

Take tender, nice-looking carrots, peel them and cut them into small pieces. (**144v**) Discard the central part of the carrots.

Take bee honey, wine vinegar, ginger, and *aṭrāf ṭīb* (spice blend). Put them [in a pot] on the fire, and let them boil several times.[117] Add the carrots to it, and continue cooking on a low heat until the mix becomes as thick as condensed pudding (*ḥalāwa*).[118]

Serve it in [small bowls arranged on a] *sukurdān*.[119] It is very good. Small amounts of saffron and musk may also be used with it.

(598) Recipe for [pickling] eggplant (*bādhinjān*)[120]

Take sprigs of common parsley (*karafs*), mint, and Macedonian parsley (*baqdūnis*). Strip the leaves [from the stems] and keep some of their tender tips (*qulūb*). Put them in a vessel, and sprinkle on them toasted and pounded coriander and caraway seeds, *aṭrāf ṭīb* (spice blend), black pepper, skinned cloves of garlic—leave them whole.

Take eggplants, cut off the [tip of the] calyx of each eggplant and around its edges, so that only part of the calyx remains. Make a cross-like slit [lengthwise] in each eggplant. Next, peel them, and stuff [the slits] with the herbs and spices. Pack them in a vessel, and pour vinegar on them [enough to submerge them].

---

114 In both *Wuṣla* and al-Nābulusī the pot is said to be *qidr Zabadānī*, an earthenware pot for which al-Zabadānī, a city in southwestern Syria, must have been known.

115 Here I replaced the unintelligible edited text احفظ وعاد وعسل من ظاهر بماء بارد with the correct version found in *Wuṣla*: اذا حفظ وعاؤه وغسل ظاهره ونظف وكان في مكان بارد.

116 This recipe also appears in *Wuṣla* ii 693; I amended the text based on it.

117 *Yaghlī ghalyāt*, see glossary 9.2 s.v. *yaghlī*.

118 In al-Nābulusī, *'Alam al-malāḥa* 266, musk and saffron are added.

119 A large tray on which a variety of delicious small dishes are arranged and served as snacks and *naql* 'mezze.'

120 This recipe also appears in *Wuṣla* ii 671; I amended the edited text slightly, based on *Wuṣla*.

Another kind [of pickled eggplant][121]

Cut the eggplants into pieces, and fry them well in sesame oil, in a large brass pot (*dast*), until they brown. Leave the pot on the ground to cool.

Thoroughly pound together dried pomegranate seeds and black raisins. Add these to the eggplant along with vinegar. Mix in almonds, walnuts, sesame seeds, and *aṭrāf ṭīb* (spice blend). Put them in a glazed ceramic jar (*qaṭramīz*), and it is ready to eat [whenever desired].

(599) Recipe for *yaqṭīn mukhallal* (pickled gourd)

Take a gourd, scrape the skin, cut it into pieces, and remove the pulpy inside. Next, cut it into small wedges (*shawābīr*), boil them in vinegar to a quarter of their doneness or even less than that [i.e., lightly blanch them]. Take them out, cool them, and then squeeze out the extra moisture, and color [and scent] them with saffron and rosewater.

Put sugar and wine vinegar [in a pot] on the fire, and let them boil until the liquid starts to thicken to the consistency of sugar syrup (*jullāb*).[122] When it gets to this point, throw in a bunch of mint before the syrup gets any thicker. When the mint releases its essence into the syrup, take it out before the syrup thickens. Squeeze it out, and return the remaining liquid to the pot. (**145r**) [Continue cooking until the syrup thickens.] Season it with the usual spices, and set it aside to cool.

Infuse a green-glazed wide-mouthed jar (*barniyya*) with the smoke of aloeswood and ambergris. Put the prepared gourd in it, and pour in the syrup. Stir the jar, wipe all around the jar so it is clean, and seal the surface of the jar that has pickles in it with sugar, rosewater, and musk. Store the jar, and use as needed.

(600) Another recipe for *yaqṭīn mukhallal* (pickled gourd)

Take gourds, which are harvested at the end of their season, put them in a pitched vessel (*wiʿāʾ muzaffat*) or a glass vessel, and pour enough vinegar on them to submerge them. Put a clean piece of glass or a flat piece of broken pottery (*shaqfa*) on top of them, and [set it aside for a few days] until the vinegar is above [the pickling gourd] by a width of 2- to 3-fingers.[123] Cover the mouth of the jar, and store it until needed.

---

121 This recipe only appears in DK, appendix 52.

122 I.e., medium syrup.

123 See recipe 580 above for similar instructions.

(601) Recipe for *qubbār bi-l-khall* (capers with vinegar)[124]

Take capers preserved in salt (*qubbār mumallaḥ*); wash them in water repeatedly, until all the salt is gone. Cover them with vinegar sweetened with sugar or honey, add a small amount of pounded garlic, coriander, and pour sweet olive oil on top.

The second method, using capers with sumac[125]

Take capers preserved in salt, and soak them until all the salt is gone. Take vinegar and lemon juice, and extract the sumac juice by putting ground sumac tied in a piece of cloth in the liquid. [Squeeze the soaked cloth bundle to extract the sumac essence]. Add the [resulting] juice to the capers, and sprinkle a bit of finely pounded sumac on them. Also, add garlic, coriander, caraway, and dried thyme. Finely chop lemon preserved in salt (*laymūn māliḥ*), and mix it in. Pour sweet olive oil all over the top.

(602) Recipe for *thūm mukhallal* (pickled garlic)

Take as much garlic as you want, and put them—keep the heads whole—in a pitched vessel (*inā' muzaffat*). Pour on them enough water to submerge them. Also add a handful of salt and a handful of barley.[126] Seal the top of the vessel with clay, and set it aside until the garlic tastes sour and delicious.

Bulbous leeks (*kurrāth Shāmī*) and the pungent small yellow onions may be prepared similarly.[127]

(603)[128]

Binn is hot and dry.[129] Even though it induces thirst, (**145v**) it is beneficial [because it] purges phlegm from the stomach and cures bad breath (*bakhar*).

---

124 *Kabar* is another name for capers. The resulting dish is more like a condiment to be served as soon it is done. Likewise, with the following recipe.

125 This recipe only appears in DK, appendix 53; *Wuṣla* ii 678; and *Zahr*, fol. 28v. An identical recipe is also found in al-Nābulusī, *ʿAlam al-malāḥa* 263.

126 *Kaff* is what the cupped hand can hold.

127 The Arabic expression used to describe the onion is *al-baṣal al-ḥirrīf al-raqīq al-aṣfar*.

128 The following segment is not a recipe but a list of the various types of condiments, pickles and vinegar, and their properties (*ṭabʿ*) and benefits. In *Zahr*, fol. 29r, it is given as a separate section at the end of the chapter. This whole section is found as chapter 24 in al-Warrāq. Interestingly, all versions start with the same misreading of the condiment *binn* as *laban* (yogurt). This clearly indicates that both books drew on a similar copy, the original source of which was al-Rāzī's *Kitāb al-Manṣūrī* fols. 25v–6r. Here I used al-Warrāq's and al-Rāzī's better-copied versions to amend the text (see English trans. *Annals* 152–3).

129 It is a fermented condiment, like *kāmakh*, albeit less salty and non-dairy. In al-Rāzī's copy, the word is correctly copied as البن and not اللبن.

Ṣaḥnāt is hot and dry.[130] It induces thirst and purges phlegm from the stomach. However, addiction to it spoils the blood and causes mange (*jarab*).

Kāmakh al-kabar (fermented condiment of capers) is hot and dry. It is bad for the stomach. It induces thirst and weakens the body.

Kāmakh al-thūm (fermented condiment of garlic) is good for phlegmatic people and those suffering from ague fits (*ḥummā al-nāfiḍ*). It is also beneficial [because it] dissolves kidney stones (*ḥaṣāt*).

Kāmakh al-marzanjūsh (fermented condiment of marjoram) is good for flatulence, coldness in the stomach, and heavy-headedness caused by colds and phlegm.

While all kinds of *kāmakh* (dairy-based fermented condiments) have the properties of the ingredients from which they are made, they acquire other properties from the salt and mold (*ʿafan*) added to them.

Rabīthā is hot and dry.[131] It stimulates the appetite and arouses coitus.

Mukhallalāt (vegetables pickled in vinegar) in general become less coarse and dense as a result of the vinegar used in making them.

Capers pickled in vinegar (***kabar mukhallal***) are less hot than capers cured in salt (***makbūs bi-l-milḥ***). They are good for opening obstructions in the liver and spleen.

Baṣal mukhallal (pickled onion) has neither heating nor cooling effects, nor does it induce thirst. It whets the appetite.

Pickled khiyār (common cucumbers) and ***qiththāʾ*** (snake cucumbers) acquire excessively cold properties. Nevertheless, they become less dense (*laṭīf*) [with pickling].

All kinds of salty *kawāmikh* (dairy-based fermented condiments) and pickles (*mukhallalāt*) are bad for sore throats. The overly salty ones among them are particularly harmful for people with an itch (*ḥakka*),[132] mange (*jarab*), and all other similar diseases that are caused from burning of the blood (*iḥtirāq al-damm*).

---

130 A condiment of small fish, such as *ṣīr*, see the recipes in chapter 9 above.

131 Incorrectly copied as الربليا in the edited text. This is most probably due to the copyists' unfamiliarity with *rabīthā*, the Iraqi shrimp condiment. The *Kanz* does not have any recipes for this condiment, but al-Warrāq does, in chapter 40.

132 Here I replaced the edited تعثر به, which is redundant in this context, with تعتريه 'afflicted with,' based on the other sources, see n. 128 above.

Saljam mukhallal (pickled turnips)[133] are cold, and do not cause bloating. They extinguish yellow bile.

Olives (*zaytūn*) preserved in brine are hot and dry.[134] They loosen the bowels (*yuṭliq al-baṭn*) when consumed before the meal, (**146r**) and strengthen the top gate of the stomach (*fam al-maʿida*, lit., 'mouth of the stomach'). On the other hand, oil olives (*zaytūn al-zayt*) generate a lot of heat.[135] They are less effective in strengthening the top gate of the stomach and are less laxative [in their effect].[136]

Pickled *ushturghāz* (alhagi)[137] has the power to heat and assist digestion. However, it generates a poor-quality substance in the stomach.[138] The salted variety has a stronger heating property.[139]

It is said that regularly eating pickles after meals will bestow radiance to one's complexion (*tuẓhir al-lawn*).

[Here begins the last part of the chapter; it deals with preserving lemons.]

(604) Recipe for [seasoning] *laymūn māliḥ* (salt-preserved lemons)[140]

Take lemons preserved in salt,[141] cut them into small pieces, and put them in a vessel. Squeeze lime juice (*laymūn akhḍar*) or juice of sour orange (*nāranj*) on them, but these are not as good as lemon. When enough is added to cover the lemon pieces, add sweet olive oil, *aṭrāf ṭīb* (spice blend), toasted and crushed coriander seeds, chopped Macedonian parsley (*baqdūnis*), mint, and rue.

It is the best and most delicious.

---

133 The Levantine and Egyptian name for turnip is *lift*, as used in the recipes in the *Kanz*. *Shaljam*/*saljam* is an Iraqi name of Persian origin. Nowadays in Iraq, it is *shalgham*.

134 Olives low in fat and high in moisture content are usually preserved in brine and consumed as pickles. They are called *zaytūn al-māʾ* 'water olives.' See glossary 5.

135 *Zaytūn al-zayt* 'oil olives' are rich in oil content, usually used for extracting olive oil, but also cured and eaten.

136 I amended the paragraph dealing with olives in several places, based on the other sources (see n. 128 above), to make it more meaningful.

137 *Alhagi maurorum* (S). The rhizome of this thorny plant is said to be like that of asafetida, but smaller, with no resin.

138 This is sometimes referred to as *kaylūs* 'chyme,' the thick semi-fluid, partially digested substance in the stomach before it is fully digested in the liver.

139 Here ends the corresponding portion in al-Warrāq.

140 This recipe also appears in *Wuṣla* ii 673; and *Zahr*, fol. 28v and 37r. I slightly amended the edited text based on the former.

141 For directions on how to preserve lemons in salt, see recipes 605–9.

(605) Another recipe [for salt-preserved lemons][142]

Peel off the outer skin of [fresh] lemons, taking care not to injure the thin inner layer with the knife. Color the lemons with saffron and sugar dissolved [in water], use just enough to give the faintest yellow hue.

Put the lemons in a glazed ceramic jar (*qaṭramīz*); pour enough lemon juice on them to submerge them. Also, add a good amount of salt to prevent the lemons from going bad. Seal the surface with olive oil [and stow it away until the lemons mature]. Delicious and exotic (*gharīb*).

(606) Another recipe [for enhancing salt-preserved lemons]

Take wine vinegar, sweeten it with honey, and fold sweet olive oil into it. Pour this mix on whole salted lemons, and they will be ready to eat. [It is] fantastic (*ʿajīb*).

(607) Recipe for preserving lemons (by packing them in salt)[143]

Many people use honey, saffron, and *kathīrāʾ* (gum taraganth) to make it; but it will not come out good. What we have seen come out good is [the following]:

Slit each lemon crosswise and stuff the slits with coarsely ground salt (*milḥ jarīsh*). Tightly pack the stuffed lemons in a porcelain bowl (*zibdiyya*), and leave them there for two nights to allow them to wilt. [Take them out and] put them in a glass vessel, and pack them very tightly. Squeeze lemon juice on them to submerge them all. Seal the surface with olive oil, and stow the vessel away [to let the lemons mature]. It will develop a lovely yellow color.

Another Recipe[144]

After you pack the lemons with salt [as above], add a fistful (*qabḍa*) of rue, a bit of bee honey, sweet olive oil, and saffron to each [pickling] vessel. Use lemons harvested in the month of Ṭūba (Jan. 9–Feb. 7) or Amshīr (Feb. 8–March 9).[145] It will be wonderful.

---

142 This recipe also appears in *Wuṣla* ii 674; *Zahr*, fol. 37r, and al-Nābulusī, *ʿAlam al-malāḥa* 262. I slightly amended the edited text based on them.

143 *Kabs* literally designates salting and packing lemons tightly in jars. However, the term may also be used in the general sense of 'pickling.' The first part of the recipe can also be found in *Wuṣla* ii 674, which I used here to make sense of the opening statement. Interestingly, *Zahr*, fol. 28v provides the second part only, which turns out to be the beginning of a new recipe. This is confirmed by DK, n. 7124 addition صفة اخرى 'another recipe.'

144 See note above.

145 The reference here must be to domestically grown limes, which at the end of their growing season turn yellow and are fully ripe. The names of the months are from the Egyptian Coptic calendar, which has 13 months.

(608) Recipe for *laymūn māliḥ* (salt-preserved lemons)

Slit each lemon crosswise. Stuff the slits with salt and pack the lemons tightly [in a vessel] for two days. Next, press out the extra moisture, [set it aside], remove the seeds, and put a [dried] ginger root (*ʿirq zanjabīl*), a sprig of mint, and rue in each lemon.

Pack the lemons in a vessel, to which you add bee honey and saffron. [Pour the set aside lemon juice on them. If it is not enough to submerge them, add some more.][146] Seal the surface with sweet olive oil, [and set it aside to allow the lemons to mature].

(609) Another recipe [for salt-preserved lemons][147]

Slit each lemon crosswise. Stuff the slits with salt, and pack the lemons in a large, wide earthenware tub (*qaṣriyya*). Weigh down the lemons with stones, cover the vessel, and set it aside for three days.

Next, remove the lemons and put them in a glazed ceramic jar (*qaṭramīz*). Collect the juice of the lemons [which came out while they were pressed in the tub], color it with saffron and strain out the seeds. If this juice is not enough, add more lemon juice.

Tightly pack the lemons in *muṭr*,[148] [add the lemon juice] and let it submerge the lemons. Seal the surface with sweet olive oil, cover the jar, and stow it [until the lemons mature].

Recipe for *laymūn sukkarī* (sugary pickled lemons)[149]

Peel the lemons [slit them into intact four sections, lengthwise] and discard the seeds. Mash and beat (*yuqtal*) saffron with musk and rosewater, and color the lemons with the mix. Do this fast, before the lemons become bitter (*yatamarrar*).

The lemon should be slit into intact four sections, lengthwise; and the sugar crushed with musk should be close to you, ready to use. Stuff the lemons with

---

146 I added this information based on the following recipe, which is similar to this one.

147 This recipe also appears in *Zahr*, fol. 29r. Here I slightly amended the text based on it.

148 Sg. *maṭara* and *maṭṭār* are jars with bulging bellies and narrow mouths, as described in *Kanz* recipe 501 above. They were commonly used for keeping oil or salt-cured small fish (*samak mumallaḥ*), as described by Dozy, *Takmilat al-maʿājim* 1461. From the *Kanz* recipes, we learn that they were also useful for keeping cheese, dairy condiments, pickles, and fermented sauces.

149 This recipe only appears in DK, appendix 46. The pickles are sweet and sour. Here the lemon juice replaces the vinegar usually used in pickling.

this sugar, add [skinned] almonds, which have been colored with saffron and infused with the smoke of aloeswood and ambergris.

Pack the lemons tightly in a glazed ceramic jar (*qaṭramīz*); put them in layers with sugar. Infuse the vessel with the smoke of aloeswood and ambergris. If it turns out that the vessel needs more lemon juice, crush sugar, put it in a porcelain bowl (*zibdiyya*), squeeze lemon juice on it, and pour it into the *qaṭramīz*; add enough to cover the lemons.

With a piece of glass weigh down the top of [the lemons packed in] the *qaṭramīz*, and seal the surface with some almond oil. Cover the jar, stow it away, and use as needed.

Another recipe [for sweet and sour pickled rose petals][150]

Take [the petals of] white roses of Nuṣaybīn,[151] put them in honey, and leave them in the sun until they wilt. Fold wine vinegar and a bit of mint into them, and put them [in a jar], and use [as needed].

Those who do not have fresh roses can take ready-made rose-petal honey jam and add vinegar to it. If it turns out to be too sour, sweeten it [with sugar or honey]. This will be as fine as the one first mentioned. It will look nice, and it is quite easy to make.[152]

---

150 This recipe only appears in DK, appendix 40; and *Wuṣla* ii 690.

151 Nuṣaybīn was a city in upper Mesopotamia, now in the Turkish province of Mardin. It was renowned for its orchards and gardens. Roses named after it are pinkish in hue. This recipe, however, calls for white roses. It is my guess that this variety of roses might have fleshier petals, though they are less aromatic than the pinkish ones.

152 *Wuṣla*'s addition.

CHAPTER 19

في عمل البوارد

Making Cold Dishes (*bawārid*)

[The following recipes, up to 619, and recipe 624, are all chickpea dips.][1]

(610) *Ḥimmaṣ kassā* (mashed chickpeas)[2]
Mash the [boiled] chickpeas and pass them through a sieve. Take toasted walnuts, pound them until the oil is released, and add tahini (*ṭaḥīna*) [and the mashed chickpeas]. Add enough olive oil, *aṭrāf ṭīb* (spice blend), toasted and finely pounded seeds of coriander and caraway, rue, mint, and enough wine vinegar. Beat these ingredients together by hand until they mix well.

Next add lemon preserved in salt (*laymūn māliḥ*) after you cut it into very small pieces. Also add [pounded] pistachios.

Put the mix in a porcelain bowl (*zibdiyya*), and garnish as usual.[3] Sprinkle [crushed] pistachios on it, drizzle it with olive oil, and serve.

(611) Another recipe [for *ḥimmaṣ kassā*]
Fry the *ḥimmaṣ kassā* [chickpeas boiled, mashed, and passed through a sieve] in rendered sheep-tail fat (*duhn alya*). Set it aside.

Take onion, chop it finely, and start boiling it. When it is half boiled, [take it out and] put it in a vessel and squeeze it [by hand] to get rid of all the moisture. Color it with saffron, fry it in rendered sheep-tail fat, and add it to the chickpeas. Also add rue, mint, Macedonian parsley (*baqdūnis*) [all chopped finely], and toasted and pounded caraway and coriander. Chop on them one lemon preserved in salt, and add *aṭrāf al-ṭīb* (spice blend) as needed.

---

1 Chickpeas were believed to be highly aphrodisiac, which may justify the prominence they are given in this chapter on cold dishes.

2 *Kassā* (كسّا) is derived from كسس 'pound something hard' (see *Tāj al-ʿarūs*). The mashed chickpeas recipes in this chapter—along with a copy of recipe 613 in *Wuṣla* ii 718–9, a copy of recipe 618 in *Waṣf* 113, and a new one in DK, appendix 54—(a total of 14 recipes) are the earliest precursors of the dips known today as *ḥummuṣ bi-ṭaḥīna* and *mutabbal*. The consistency of this dip is good if it holds its shape when picked up with a piece of bread.

3 Based on the following recipes, these could be chopped herbs, nuts, black olives, cinnamon, olive oil. The word for garnish occurs as شهر/تشاهير and شهّل/تشاهيل, though none of these words, with this sense, appear in the medieval dictionaries, only in their cookbooks.

 | DOI 10.1163/9789004349919_022

Return all [the above] to the frying pan (*ṭājin*), and when the mix is halfway browned (*niṣf muḥammaṣ*), moisten it with a bit of lemon juice.[4] The frying pan used should be made of soapstone (*birām*).

Put [the chickpea mash] in a porcelain bowl (*zibdiyya*), sprinkle on it toasted and coarsely crushed (*muharrash*) hazelnuts, and serve it, and eat it.

(612) **Another recipe [for *ḥimmaṣ kassā*], invigorates coitus**

Take boiled chickpeas, press them [through a sieve] to mash them. Put the mash in a porcelain bowl (*zibdiyya*), (**147v**) sprinkle on it crushed salt, cumin, cassia (*dār Ṣīnī*), and aniseeds, all crushed. Also add olive oil, and *murrī* (liquid fermented sauce), and serve it.

It is even more delicious if you add to it leaf leeks (*kurrāth*), mint, and salt-preserved lemon (*laymūn makbūs*).

(613) Recipe for *ḥimmaṣ kassā* (mashed chickpeas)[5]

Take already boiled chickpeas, mash them with [the back of] a spoon until not a single chickpea remains whole. However, leave some chickpeas whole and set them aside.

Thoroughly dissolve tahini in very sour vinegar, and add it to the [mashed] chickpeas. Finely grind toasted walnuts, dissolve them in lime juice and a bit of vinegar, and add the mix to the chickpeas. Finely pound rue and add it to the chickpeas. Chop Macedonian parsley (*baqdūnis*) and mint and add them to chickpeas. Use a lot of these so that they give the chickpeas a lovely [green] color.

Add to the chickpeas sweet olive oil, *aṭrāf ṭīb* (spice blend), coriander seeds, caraway, cassia (*dār Ṣīnī*), black pepper, and ginger. Mix them very well. Add a good amount of finely chopped lemon preserved in salt (*laymūn māliḥ*).

[In making this dip,] use more lemon juice than vinegar. Put [the finished dip] in a porcelain bowl (*zibdiyya*), and sprinkle the surface with [crushed] pistachios. For those who want to use some of these pistachios in the chickpea mix itself, they can go ahead and do so.

[To garnish,] put a lot of olive oil on top, and sprinkle chopped Macedonian parsley and rue on it. Decorate it with cassia and [crushed dried] rosebuds.

---

4 The verb used is *yuṭfā* (lit., 'douse,' 'extinguish').

5 This recipe is identical with *Wuṣla* ii 718–9 *Ḥimmaṣ akhḍar kassā*, except for a few stylistic differences. The herbs used in the recipe give the mashed chickpeas dip its green color.

[The mix should be thick enough so that when it is scooped up with a piece of bread, it stays on the bread.][6]

(614) Another chickpea recipe

Boil the chickpeas, press and mash them in a bowl (*ṣaḥfa*).[7] Pour on them vinegar and *murrī* (liquid fermented sauce), [and add] caraway, olive oil, black pepper, cassia (*dār Ṣīnī*), and rosebuds (*zir ward*). Chop some rue and sprinkle it on the chickpea mix, and serve.

Ḥimmaṣ kassā[8]

Boil the chickpeas, pound them in a mortar (*hāwan*) until they look like paste (*ʿajīn*), and press them through a whole wheat flour sieve.[9] However, if the chickpeas are already smooth and mushy (*nāʿim*), there is no need to do this.

Knead the chickpeas with wine vinegar and pith of [the peel of] lemon preserved in salt (*shaḥm al-laymūn al-māliḥ*). Add Ceylon cinnamon (*qarfa*), black pepper, and ginger. Finely chop some Macedonian parsley (*baqdūnis*) along with mint and rue, and sprinkle them on top of [the chickpea mix when you spread it in] the porcelain bowls (*zabādī*). Add a generous amount of olive oil as well.

(615) Recipe for *ḥimmaṣ kassā*

For each *mudd* (2 pounds) of chickpeas, use 6 *dirhams* (18 grams/3 teaspoons) natron (*naṭrūn*). Put them in a jar [with water to cover], close the top and put it in the *tannūr* (open-topped, bell-shaped clay oven).[10] (**148r**) It will come out nicely.

[To serve,] mix some vinegar, thyme, dried rue, tahini, and linseed oil (*duhn al-bazr*) with the chickpeas.

---

6 The Arabic expression is وليكن خلطه بحيث أن ينقطع منه على الخبز عند الاكل. In other words, it should hold its shape. This addition only appears in *Wuṣla* version. It clearly describes the ideal consistency of the dip: not too thick, not too thin.

7 This would be done by hand as the verb يعجن (lit., 'knead') suggests. *Ṣaḥfa* is a wide, shallow bowl.

8 This recipe only appears in DK, appendix 54.

9 *Ghirbāl al-qamḥ.*

10 The jar is put on the floor of the oven after the baking is done, so it is left to cook in the remaining heat, usually overnight.

(616) Recipe for *ḥimmaṣ kassā*

Boil the chickpeas, and pick out the fine-tasting and tender ones.[11] Put them in a huge wide bowl (*jafna*), and beat them well with a ladle until they disintegrate into each other.[12] Next, press them through a sieve, and discard the remains, [like the skins, which do not pass through the sieve].

When the chickpeas are ready to use, take salt-preserved lemons (*laymūn māliḥ*), chop it into small pieces (*yufram rafīʿ*), and pound it in a stone mortar; but take care to remove all of the seeds. Add sweet olive oil and tahini to this lemon, and stir well. Next, add to them a bit of wine vinegar, *aṭrāf ṭīb* (spice blend), rue, mint, and a bit of pounded and sifted cumin. Stir all these ingredients, and add the chickpeas to them. Stir all of it well.

Spread the mix in a porcelain bowl (*zibdiyya*),[13] garnish (*yushahhal*) with [salt-cured] black olives and olives preserved in brine (*mukhallal*),[14] toasted hazelnuts, *aṭrāf al-ṭīb*, and a bit of rue and mint.

(617) Another recipe for *ḥimmaṣ kassā*

Take boiled chickpeas and pound them into fine mush. Add vinegar, sweet olive oil, tahini, black pepper, *aṭrāf ṭīb* (spice blend), mint, Macedonian parsley (*baqdūnis*), and a bit of dried rue. Also add, walnuts, almonds, pistachios, and hazelnuts—all pounded, as well as Ceylon cinnamon (*qarfa*), toasted caraway seeds, coriander, salt, lemon preserved in salt (*laymūn māliḥ*), and olives.

[Mix it all,] spread the mix [in a bowl or plate] (*yubsaṭ*), set it aside for a day and then serve.

(618) Another recipe for [*ḥimmaṣ kassā*][15]

Pound chickpeas until they become mushy after boiling them. (**148v**) Take vinegar, olive oil, tahini, *aṭrāf ṭīb* (spice blend), black pepper, mint, Macedonian parsley (*baqdūnis*), a bit of dried thyme, walnuts, hazelnuts, almonds, pistachios, toasted coriander and caraway seeds, lemon preserved in salt (*laymūn māliḥ*), olives, and salt as needed.

---

11 Tenderness of chickpeas is described in terms of being feminine (*unthā*).

12 The verb used in the edited text is *yuqtal*, which implies thorough beating; and DK, n. 7223, *yuḍrab* 'beaten.'

13 The verb *yubsaṭ* indicates that the *hummus* mix should be spread in a somewhat thin layer, as is done nowadays.

14 Olives low in fat and high in moisture content are usually the ones preserved in brine and served as pickles. They are called *zaytūn al-māʾ* 'water olives.' See glossary 5.

15 This recipe also appears in *Waṣf* 113. Aside from some minor differences, this recipe is another copy of the previous one.

Knead all these ingredients to mix them, and spread them (*yubsaṭ*) [on a plate]. Sprinkle the surface with cassia (*dār Ṣīnī*) and drizzle it with olive oil. Set it aside overnight, and serve it. It will come out good, God willing.[16]

(619) Recipe for *ḥimmaṣ kassā*

Thinly slice roasted fatty lamb on a wooden board (*qirma*)—slice the meat with its sheep-tail fat (*alya*).[17] Put the meat in a large brass pot (*dast*) and fry it, and when the fat is released, throw in [boiled and mashed] chickpeas.[18]

When the chickpeas are frying, take *aṭrāf ṭīb* (spice blend), finely chopped Macedonian parsley (*baqdūnis*), mint, and a bit of rue, and throw them into the pot and stir.

Squeeze 2 large lemons—squeeze them on salt first [to prevent the juice from turning bitter] and then add it to the pot. Also add 1 *dirham* (½ teaspoon) crushed cumin, 1 *dirham* galangal (*khūlanjān*), and 2 *dirhams* [ground] *qarfa laff* (rolled bark of Ceylon cinnamon)—add half of it to the pot and leave the other half for the garnish. Do not let the pot cook for a long time; otherwise, it will be ruined.

Put the meat mix in a *zibdiyya* (bowl), and spread the usual herbs and seasonings (*ḥawāʾij*) on top. The *zibdiyya* must be ceramic (*qīshānī*) or china (*ṣīnī*).

Put the *zibdiyya* on a large platter (*ṭabaq*), and garnish it with the usual fresh herbs and greens (*buqūl*) after you pick them over and wash them.[19] The vegetables and herbs (*khuḍar*) can be radishes when in season, leaf vegetables (*baql*),[20] and some fresh herbs (*ḥawāʾij al-baql*), and mint, rue, leaf leeks, and common parsley (*karafs*).[21]

Serve this platter with a small bowl (*sukurruja*) on the side, (**149r**) filled with a preparation to prevent and cure nausea (*dawāʾ qaraf*).[22] If it is the season for fresh fava beans (*fūl akhḍar*), also put some [boiled ones] on this platter, and rub the hands with them to remove greasy odors (*zafar*).

---

16 The last two sentences are added in *Waṣf*.

17 This looks like today's thinly shaved *shawarma* meat.

18 I.e., *ḥimmaṣ kassā*, as indicated in the recipe's name, and the rest of the recipes.

19 The herbs and greens used should be scattered around the bowl on the platter.

20 Such as lettuce, and arugula (*jirjīr*).

21 It is my guess that the last four herbs enumerated are listed as suggested varieties of 'the usual herbs' used to garnish the tray. The recipe seems to be aimed at making the dish sound as festive as possible.

22 For recipes, see chapter 14 above.

Recipe for *fūl akhḍar* (fresh fava beans)[23]

Remove the outer skins of the fava beans and then boil them, and after they cool, squeeze out the extra moisture.

Whip tahini with sweet olive oil, and add vinegar, *aṭrāf ṭīb* (spice blend), mint, toasted caraway seeds with a bit of toasted and pounded hazelnuts. Chop Macedonian parsley (*baqdūnis*), mint, and a sprig of rue. Add all these to the vinegar mix.

Color the fava beans with a bit of saffron, and combine them with the vinegar sauce (*mizāj*). Keep them in containers. It is delicious and aromatic.

For those who crave boiled **dried fava beans** (*fūl yābis*), take the amount they want of the boiled beans, remove their skins, season them with vinegar, caraway, sweet olive oil, a bit of sumac, and thyme, and then serve.

(620) Recipe for *tatbīl al-qunnabīṭ* (seasoned cauliflower)[24]

Take boiled cauliflower, cut it into very small pieces, and squeeze out the extra moisture. Take olive oil, tahini, walnuts, vinegar, mustard [seeds], mint, caraway, and *aṭrāf al-ṭīb* (spice blend).

Season the cauliflower with this mix (*mizāj*), and put in platters [on a tray] along with other cold dishes (*bawārid*).

(621) Another recipe [with cauliflower]

Take the juice of Damascus citron (*kabbād*) and lemon [and set it aside]. Take a bit of rue, and the usual fresh herbs (*ḥawā'ij baql*),[25] ginger, black pepper, and hazelnuts. Pound these and add them to the sour juices,[26] along with olive oil, and as much tahini as needed. Mix them all [with the prepared cauliflower, as in the recipe above]. Set it aside to allow flavors to mature (*yukhammar*), and eat it.

(622) Another recipe [with cauliflower][27]

Boil cauliflower, and split it into smaller pieces [and set it aside].

---

23 This recipe only appears in DK, appendix 55.

24 The name of this vegetable occurs as *qarnabīṭ* in DK, n. 7292, which, in *Tāj al-ʿarūs*, is said to be an Egyptian variant. See glossary 12.

25 Such as leaf leeks, mint, parsley, and cilantro.

26 Here I read the edited الحمّص 'chickpeas' as الحمض 'the sour ingredients,' which is more relevant to the context.

27 This recipe also appears in *Wuṣla* ii 711–2. Here I used it to amend the edited text, which is incoherent as several places.

Take walnuts, and pound them finely until the oil is released.[28] Add chopped rue, and toasted and coarsely crushed pistachios.

Now, take olive oil and a bit of hot water, dissolve in them the walnut mix, along with garlic. Let the mix boil once, and season (*yutabbal*) the cauliflower with it. Put it in containers, with the florets facing upwards.[29] Pour sweet olive oil over them, and sprinkle them with shelled pistachios, chopped rue, and caraway seeds, which have been toasted and pounded; and serve it.

(623) Another recipe [for cauliflower][30]

Boil it, and drench it in sumac, which has been steeped in water, strained through a piece of cloth, and then thickened [by boiling it] with finely pounded almonds, and [seasoned with] *aṭrāf ṭīb* (spice blend), black pepper, garlic, and chopped rue. The sumac sauce (*marqat al-summāq*) should be thick (*thakhīna*); and serve the dish.

(624) Another recipe [for cauliflower][31]

(**149v**) Take tahini, sprinkle it with rosewater, and rub and mix the two (*yumʿak*) very well until the tahini releases its oil (*shayraj*). Dissolve the mix with vinegar, which has been sweetened with honey. Add to it enough [crushed] mustard seeds to make it taste sharp and pungent (*ḥirrīf*).

Now, fry a [chopped] onion in sesame oil, and put the [boiled] cauliflower in it.[32] Sprinkle it with chopped rue.

(625) Recipe for *ḥimmaṣ kassā,* a Byzantine specialty[33]

Take [boiled] chickpeas, mash them, pass them through a sieve, and color them with saffron whipped with musk and rosewater.

Put bee honey on the fire, the amount should be enough for the chickpeas used. Let it boil until it thickens and becomes very sticky (*yatadabbaq*). Skim off the froth, and throw in musk and rosewater, but you must add these before it starts to boil. Moisten (*yutfā*) the honey with clear white vinegar, and add

28 The expression used is يلعب في دهنه (lit., 'plays in its oil').

29 The expression used is يجعل زهره الى فوق (lit., *zahr* is flower, used here to designate florets).

30 This recipe also appears in *Wuṣla* ii 712, where it clearly identifies the vegetable as cauliflower. The edited text refers to the vegetable as 'it.'

31 See above note.

32 At this point, we assume that the cauliflower has been drenched with the prepared sauce.

33 The main difference between this dish of mashed chickpeas and the previous ones is that this one is a sweet preparation.

to it [dried] jujubes, raisins from *jawza* grapes (*zabīb jawzānī*),[34] pitted Iraqi *qaṣb* dates,[35] pistachios and almonds—scalded, skinned, and colored with saffron. Boil the mix, and then add the chickpeas, which have been colored with saffron [prepared earlier]. Cook the mix until it resembles a thick pudding (*ḥalāwa*) in consistency.

Take the pot off the heat, and ladle the mix onto plates. Sprinkle on them [crushed] pistachios, almonds, and sugar. Garnish the plates with pieces of *ḥalāwa ʿalika* (chewy thick pudding) colored red and yellow.[36] It is the ultimate [cold dish].

(626) Recipe for roasted lamb (*shawī*)

Take fine roasted fatty lamb with its sheep-tail fat (*alya*). (**150r**) Slice it thinly with a cleaver (*sāṭūr*) as is usually done.[37] Put the meat in a soapstone frying pan (*ṭājin birām*), and set it on the fire.

Add toasted walnuts to it, and throw in toasted and pounded coriander and caraway seeds, along with Macedonian parsley (*baqdūnis*) and mint. Add one chopped lemon [preserved in salt], and fry the meat until it browns. Squeeze on it the juice of two limes, and stir in a bit of *aṭrāf al-ṭīb* (spice blend).

Put the meat in a dish, and eat it while it is still hot.[38] It is delicious.

(627) Recipe for purslane (*rijla*)[39]

Take purslane, discard the stems, and use the [stripped] leaves and the tender tips. Boil it until it is done, and then dress it with yogurt mixed with [crushed] garlic, [pounded] mustard seeds, and sweet olive oil.

---

34 *Jawza* were deemed an excellent variety of grapes (Dozy, *Takmilat al-maʿājim* 245), see glossary 7.

35 Egyptian variant for *qasb*. It is a naturally dry delicious Iraqi date, usually stored loose because it cannot be pressed together like other moist dried dates.

36 The Arabic is حلاوة حمراء وصفراء علكة; it is similar to the candy known in the West as Turkish delight.

37 This looks like today's thinly shaved *shawarma* meat.

38 Unlike the other vegetable dishes, which are usually served cold. It is accompanied by cold vegetable dishes.

39 This recipe also appears in *Wuṣla* ii 709.

FIGURE 44
Purslane, Elizabeth Blackwell, A Curious Herbal, *1738, plate 287 (From the New York Public Library: http://digitalcollections.nypl.org/items/510d47dd-cd75-a3d9-e040-e00a18064a99).*

(628) Another [purslane] recipe[40]

Clean the purslane as mentioned above,[41] and boil it. Fry a [chopped] onion in sesame oil, and add the purslane to it.[42] Fold in vinegar sweetened with sugar or bee honey. If you like, in place of the vinegar use the juice of sour unripe grapes (*māʾ ḥiṣrim*) or lemon juice.[43]

40 This recipe also appears in *Wuṣla* ii 709–10, with some stylistic differences. Here I used it to amend the text slightly.

41 This addition appears in *Wuṣla*.

42 The purslane in this recipe is called *farfaḥīn*.

43 *Wuṣla* specifies that the grape juice used is aged (*ʿatīq*); and gives pomegranate juice as another alternative.

Recipe for chard (*silq*)[44]
Take chard, cut it into small pieces [as follows]:[45] take a whole leaf with its spine, and slice it [crosswise] into pieces one-finger wide. Boil the chard, squeeze out the extra moisture, [spread it on a plate] and cover it with [the sauce of] drained yogurt mixed with [crushed] garlic.

(629) Another [chard] recipe[46]
Boil the chard and fry it in sesame oil [set it aside].

Take sumac, which has been steeped in water, and its juice extracted with a piece of cloth. Finely pound walnuts, and add the sumac juice to them. Add lots of lemon juice, as well as black pepper, garlic, ginger, and *aṭrāf ṭīb* (spice blend).

Pour the [sumac sauce] on the chard, [which has been spread on a dish], and drizzle the top with sweet olive oil, and [chopped] Macedonian parsley (*baqdūnis*), rue, and mint.

If you want to make it with the sour juice of unripe grapes (*māʾ ḥiṣrim*) [instead of sumac juice], then go ahead and do so.

(630) Recipe for *ʿajjūr* (variety of unripe melon)[47]
(**150v**) Take *ʿajjūr*, peel it, split it (*yushaqqaq*), [boil it,] squeeze out the extra moisture, fry it in a mix of olive oil and sesame oil [and set it aside].

Chop onion, and fry it (*yuṭajjan*). Add chopped Macedonian parsley (*baqdūnis*), and continue frying until they wilt. Fold these into the fried *ʿajjūr*. Add also very sour vinegar, and let the mix boil several times.[48] Season it with *aṭrāf ṭīb* (spice blend), sprigs of mint, black pepper, and coriander.

---

44 This recipe only appears in DK, appendix 56; *Wuṣla* ii 710; and *Zahr*, fol. 37v. I slightly amended the text based on *Wuṣla*.

45 As explained in *Wuṣla*.

46 This recipe also appears in *Wuṣla* ii 710–1; and *Zahr* 37v. Here I amended the text based on these; both copies clearly identify the vegetable as chard (*silq*).

47 *Cucumis melo* var. *chate*, Egyptian chate. Here I used *Zahr*, fol. 37v–8r copy to make sense of the recipe. This recipe and the following one are also found in *Wuṣla* ii 701–2, where *yushaqqaq* clearly involves slitting the vegetable crosswise into four sections, but not going all the way through it, that is, leaving it intact.

48 The Arabic phrase is يغلي غلوات, see glossary 9.2, s.v. *yaghlī*.

(631) Another [*ʿajjūr*] recipe[49]

Peel the *ʿajjūr*, split it (*yushaqqaq*),[50] boil it, and then fry it in sesame oil. Fry some chopped onion until it is cooked, and add it [to the *ʿajjūr*]. Dissolve pounded walnuts and a bit of tahini in vinegar, and add them [to the *ʿajjūr*]. Fry all of it together, and season the dish with a small amount of *aṭrāf ṭīb* (spice blend).

If you like, you may sweeten it with sugar, or add a bit of garlic to it; and eat it.

(632) Recipe for *lūbyā* (fresh black-eyed peas in the pod)[51]

Pound walnuts until the oil is released, and then dissolve them in sweet olive oil mixed with caraway and coriander seeds. Pour this on the [boiled] black-eyed peas, and eat them.

(633) Another [*lūbyā*] recipe

Mix the walnuts [mentioned above] with lemon juice, sweet olive oil, caraway, and garlic [and use as above].

(634) Another [*lūbyā*] recipe

Take lime juice. Finely pound walnuts [and add them to the juice]. Also, add chopped Macedonian parsley (*baqdūnis*), mint, and rue; and season with coriander, caraway, *aṭrāf ṭīb* (spice blend), **(151r)** and garlic. Add the boiled black-eyed peas to the mix. Give it a boil, and then let it cool, and eat it.

(635) Another [*lūbyā*] recipe

Extract the juice of sumac steeped in water by squeezing it through a piece of cloth. Add enough lemon juice to make it taste sour. Thicken it with pounded walnuts mixed with black pepper and garlic. Pour this [sauce] on the [boiled] black-eyed peas.

---

49 Additions and amendments made in this recipe are based on DK, n. 7409.

50 See n. 47 above.

51 This recipe and the following one are also found in *Wuṣla* ii 703, which I used to slightly amend the edited text. From the *Wuṣla* instructions given in the recipe that precedes these two, we know that the beans used are fresh. In this recipe, both ends of the fresh green *lūbyā* pods are snipped off, and the yellowed ones are opened and only their seeds are used. To preserve the green color of the beans while boiling them, the recipe recommends using ash (*ramād*), a piece of potash (*qilī*), or ammonia (*nashādir*).

(636) Recipe for gourd (*qarʿ*)

Scrape the skin of a gourd (*yunḥat*), and cut [its flesh] into *shawābīr* (small pieces). Roll the pieces in flour—as is done with fish, and fry them in sesame oil.

[Put the fried gourd pieces on a plate, and] pour on them [sauce of] tahini dissolved in a mix of vinegar, lemon juice, pounded walnuts, chopped Macedonian parsley (*baqdūnis*), mint, pounded coriander and caraway seeds, *aṭrāf ṭīb* (spice blend), a bit of saffron, and garlic. Sweeten the mix with sugar, and spread it on the gourd, and serve.

Recipe for gourd (*qarʿ*)[52]

Take gourd and lightly scrape the skin. Cut [the gourd flesh] into long pieces and discard the pithy core attached to them. Chop it into small pieces, boil it until it is cooked, and then take it out of the water. Pour cold water on it, and put it in a colander (*miṣfāt*). When it cools, squeeze out the extra moisture by hand.

Now, take *qanbarīs* (soft yogurt cheese),[53] whip it, press it through a sieve (*munkhul*), add [pounded] mustard [seeds] to it, and combine it with the gourd and mix them well. Do not use a lot of *qanbarīs*. Spread the mix in a dish, and pour sweet olive oil on it.

There should be chopped rue in the cheese-gourd mix. Garlic may also be added to it, but it will be much better if only mustard is used.

Another gourd recipe[54]

Prepare it as above, but instead of *qanbarīs* (soft yogurt cheese) use strained yogurt (*laban muṣaffā*) because when sugar is used, the dish will not taste good with *qanbarīs* due to it saltiness.

Pounded sugar is used in this gourd dish. However, neither olive oil nor garlic are used;[55] only mustard seeds and yogurt.

---

52 This recipe only appears in DK, appendix 59; and *Wuṣla* ii 707, which I used to amend the text.

53 See recipe 515 above, for instance. *Wuṣla* specifically mentions *qanbarīs* cheese from Baalbeck in Lebanon.

54 This recipe only appears in DK, appendix 60; and *Wuṣla* ii 707, which I used to amend the text slightly.

55 Here I replaced mustard with olive oil, based on *Wuṣla* text.

Recipe for *yaqṭīn bi-laban* (gourd with yogurt)[56]

You need gourd, sour yogurt, garlic, sweet olive oil, and a bit of black cumin (*kammūn aswad*).[57]

Cut a gourd into thin pieces as usual, boil it, and then squeeze out the extra moisture. Pound garlic after removing the skin, and then whip it with yogurt, along with a bit of sweet olive oil. Add the [prepared] gourd to the yogurt [sauce], spread the mix in dishes, and sprinkle them with [black] cumin.

Recipe for eggplant (*bādhinjān*)[58]

Slice eggplant and cut it into small pieces. Mix with it peeled small onions—keep them whole. Put them in a large brass pot (*dast*), pour on them sesame oil or olive oil and a bit of water. Let them cook on low heat until all of it is cooked and the moisture evaporates.

[Ladle the eggplant and onion into a dish,] and spread sour yogurt (*laban ḥāmiḍ*) on them and [garnish it with] chopped *baqdūnis* (Macedonian parsley). The [yogurt] should be pressed through a sieve [first]; and a bit of garlic is added to it.

Another eggplant recipe[59]

Chop the eggplant into small pieces, boil it, and squeeze out the extra moisture. Take sesame oil and fry the chopped onion in it. Add the eggplant and let them cook until done.

Add Macedonian parsley (*baqdūnis*), rue, and mint [all chopped]. Also add coriander, caraway, *aṭrāf ṭīb* (spice blend), garlic, a small amount of olive oil, and vinegar. Let them boil once,[60] and then serve the dish.

(637) Recipe for *kurunb bi-l-ṭaḥīna* (cabbage with tahini)

You need cabbage, tahini, vinegar, and mustard. Cut the cabbage leaves into pieces;[61] boil them with the [cut off] stems under them in the pot [for protection]. Take them off the heat when done [and set this aside].

---

56 This recipe only appears in DK, appendix 62; and *Zahr*, fol. 38r. *Yaqṭīn* and *qarʿ* are both used to designate gourd. See glossary 12.

57 This is a wild variety of black cumin, which also goes by the name *kammūn Ḥabashī* 'Abyssinian cumin.'

58 This recipe only appears in DK, appendix 57; and *Wuṣla* ii 706, which differs slightly in the details.

59 This recipe only appears in DK, appendix 58; and *Wuṣla* ii 706.

60 The added herbs release some moisture, which should boil and evaporate.

61 The pieces should still be large, judging from the word *ghuṣn* 'branch,' used later in the recipe. The leaves growing from the central stem are like branches stemming from the trunk of the tree.

Take tahini, sprinkle it with a bit of hot water, and whip it until its oil (*shayraj*) separates, [set this oil aside,] and dissolve the [remaining] tahini with vinegar. Pound mustard seeds and add them to it.

Now, take the cabbage leaves, and one by one dip them in the prepared tahini mix (*ḥawāʾij*), (**151v**) and put them in vessels. When you are finished with the leaves, pour the remaining tahini mix all over the leaves. In addition, pour all over them the oil extracted [and set aside] from the tahini itself.

Recipe for cabbage (*kurunb*)[62]

You need cabbage, sweet olive oil, garlic, and caraway. Boil the cabbage, and remove it when it is done.

Pound garlic with caraway and some sweet olive oil. Take the cabbage pieces,[63] and coat them with the garlic mix (*ḥawāʾij*). Leave them in containers for a full hour (*sāʿa jayyida*), with some water under them.[64] Pour sweet olive oil on top of them.

---

62 This recipe only appears in DK, appendix 61.

63 The phrase *aghṣān al-kurunb* (lit., 'cabbage branches') indicates that the leaves are in large pieces, and not chopped. See n. 61 above.

64 Based on context, I read the edited ترعى, which is irrelevant here, as ترمي (lit., 'throw'). The water is added to prevent the cabbage leaves from drying out.

CHAPTER 20

في الطيب وطبع الخلال من الصفصاف ومن عيدان الخلاف

On Aromatics (*ṭīb*), and the Properties of Toothpicks (*khilāl*) Made from Willow Wood (*ṣafṣāf*) and Egyptian Willow Twigs (*ʿīdān al-khilāf*)[1]

(638) [On toothpicks and their properties][2]
Willow wood (*ṣafṣāf*) is cold and dry [in properties] and causes little harm to the teeth. Using it has many benefits. It is the best kind ever to use for picking the teeth to get rid of unpleasant greasy odors (*zuhūmāt*). It is safe and beneficial to the teeth.

Khilāl maʾmūnī (toothpicks from esparto grass stems) is a desert plant with long, slender stems. [Its properties] are hot and dry. The seeds of the wild variety of this plant can purge intestinal worms (*dūd*) when taken [internally] as a medicinal compound powder (*safūf*).[3] These toothpicks are called *maʾmūnī* because they cause little harm to the teeth. Toothpicks made from it are usually used by the common folk (*ʿawām*).[4]

Any cold and dry wood may be used for making toothpicks. These have more benefits than hot and dry varieties.

---

1 In addition, the chapter includes recipes for handwashing compounds (*ushnān*), scented soaps, and aromatic compounds and oils to remove greasy odors from hands. The *khilāf* tree, also called *ṣafṣāf Miṣrī* (*Salix aegyptiaca*) is an Egyptian species of the willow tree.

2 Except for a few stylistic differences, this passage is identical to al-Warrāq's chapter 128. I complete the edited text here using the addition given in DK, n. 7461, which is also found in al-Warrāq's cookbook.

3 Here begins the additional text from DK, 7461, see n. above.

4 These must have been cheaper than the choice varieties that had cold and dry properties.

The best way to use these toothpicks is to soak the sticks in water for a night or two so that they become flexible and do not break. Otherwise, they will leave splinters between the teeth, which can only be pulled out with tweezers.[5]

Egyptian willow twigs (*ʿīdān al-khilāf*) are cold and moderate with regard to [their properties of] humidity and dryness. Only middle-class people (*awsāṭ al-nās*) use them, especially to replace the made toothpicks (*khilāl maʿmūl*), when they are not available.

Manners (*adab*) observed when using toothpicks

It is good manners to use toothpicks. One needs to clean the teeth and remove the tiny pieces of meat between them. If meat stays in the mouth it rots, especially the solid particles.

Now that we have mentioned toothpicks, we must also mention *ushnān* (handwashing compounds made with *ushnān* (potash)

(639) *Ushnān* (handwashing compound made with potash) for kings, princes, and the wealthy[6]

Take 3 *raṭl*s (3 pounds) pure white *ushnān Fārisī ʿaṣāfīrī*,[7] **(152r)** 4 *ūqiyya*s (4 ounces) fine-tasting Kufan cyperus (*suʿd Kūfī*),[8] 4 *ūqiyya*s crushed and sifted white, pure usnea (*shayba*),[9] 3 *ūqiyya*s grated yellow sandalwood (*ṣandal aṣfar*) dissolved in rosewater, 3 *ūqiyya*s crushed pure white rose petals, 2 *ūqiyya*s finely crushed citronella of Mecca (*idhkhir Makkī*),[10] and a similar amount of cloves.

---

5 Here ends DK addition.

6 This recipe also appears in *Wuṣla* ii 721. Both the *Kanz* and *Wuṣla* seem to have drawn from similar sources, which must have been copied, originally, from *Ṭīb al-ʿarūs* by Muḥammad b. Aḥmad al-Tamīmī (d. ca. 1000). Al- Tamīmī's original recipes are a bit more elaborate, with more ingredients added to the compounds. The ones in hand are simplified versions. For this recipe, see al-Tamīmī, recipe 265, which I used here to amend the edited text. Al-Tamīmī calls it *ushnān Ḥamdūnī*, which he himself concocted.

7 This was an excellent-quality white potash, deemed the most delicate and gentle, that was used particularly for washing the hands. See glossary 11, under *ushnān* 2.

8 This was also called tigernut, a rhizome, from Kufa, a city south of Baghdad.

9 This was also called *shaybat al-ʿajūz* (lit., 'old man's hair'). Its English name is 'old man's beard.' See glossary 8.

10 *Cymbopogon schoenanthus* (S), also known as camel's hay or straw, and sweet-smelling rush.

Also take 1½ *ūqiyyas* of spikenard (*sunbul*) and Ceylon cinnamon (*qarfa*), and 8 *ūqiyyas* finely pounded pure white rice.

After you pound and sift the *ushnān*, add to it the rest of the ingredients. Knead them with rosewater, and scent the mix with ambergris for a day and a night. After that, enhance its scent (*yuftaq*) with 1 *mithqāl* (4½ grams) strongly scented camphor (*kāfūr rayyāḥī*).[11]

This is the way to make excellent *Ḥamdūnī ushnān*,[12] [the kind] with which the caliphs and the viziers of their inner circles used to wash their hands.

(640) Another *ushnān* recipe (handwashing compound made with potash), that used to be made for Caliph al-Maʾmūn for washing his hands[13]

Take 1 *mann* (2 pounds) pure white *ushnān Fārisī* known as *ʿaṣāfīrī*,[14] and ½ *mann* dried peel of *shammām*, which is *biṭṭīkh aṣfar*, with yellow stripes.[15] Also take ¼ *mann* pounded and sifted skinned sweet almonds, **(152v)** 1 *ūqiyya* (1 ounce) crushed saffron, and 2 *ūqiyyas* [dried] carnation petals (*al-qaranful al-zahr*).

Pound all the ingredients, sift them and knead them with rosewater. Spread the mix in a porcelain bowl (*zibdiyya*) and infuse it with the smoke of aloeswood, and then let it dry in a shaded place. When it is completely dry, pound and sift the mix, and store it in wide-mouthed jars (*baranī*).[16]

---

11 This was also called *kāfūr Rabāḥī*; it is an excellent-quality camphor, said to have been named after an Indian king known by the name Rabāḥ.

12 This was named after Ḥamdūna, daughter of Caliph Harūn al-Rashīd (d. 809).

13 This recipe also appears in *Wuṣla* ii 722; and al-Tamīmī, recipe 267. Al-Maʾmūn was an Abbasid caliph, d. 833. Al-Tamīmī says that Ibn al-Bawwāb (Abū Bakr al-Murandij) told him about it. Aside from al-Tamīmī's references to him, he is not mentioned in the sources. I used al-Tamīmī's version to amend the text slightly.

14 See n. 7 above.

15 *Shammām* is *Cucumis dudaim*. As the recipe explains, it is a variety of yellow melon (muskmelon), which is striped with yellow. *Makhlūṭ* 'mixed with' in the edited text must have been a misreading of *mukhaṭṭaṭ* 'striped.' Al-Tamīmī's corresponding recipe 266 better describes it as

البطيخ الخراساني اللطاف الحُمر المخططة بالصفرة 'الذي يسمّى شمّام البطيخ.

(It is a variety of melon of Khurasan, which is small and red, striped with yellow. It is called *shammām al-biṭṭīkh*.).

16 Sg. *barniyya*.

(641) Here is a recipe for [preparing] pure rice flour used in making *ushnān*[17]
Thoroughly wash picked over rice three times, and then [drain it and] spread it in the sun until it is somewhat dried. Pound it and sift it with a fine-meshed sieve.

Recipe for *ushnān* (handwashing compound made with potash) that used to be made for al-Rashīd[18]
Take cloves, *salīkha* (bark similar to cassia), black cardamom (*qāqulla*), and *falanja*;[19] one part of each. Also, take what equals one part altogether of mastic, citronella (*idhkhir*), cyperus (*su'd*), and *may'a yābisa*.[20] Also take three parts of marjoram (*marzanjūsh*), five parts of white Meccan clay (*ṭīn abyaḍ Makkī*), and white potash (*ushnān Fārisī*)[21]—double or triple the amount of clay. Use white rice, which has been soaked, dried, crushed and sifted;[22] its amount is equal to that of potash.

Pound each of these ingredients separately, and then mix them all together.

Another recipe for a lesser *ushnān*[23]
Finely grind together equal amounts of potash (*ushnān*) and white clay (*ṭīn abyaḍ*). Mix with them one-sixth of their amount pounded and sifted citronella (*idhkhir*), and one-fourth of their amount ground and sifted cyperus (*su'd*). Also mix in one-twelfth of their amount grated sandalwood.

Pour on them distilled camphor water (*mā' al-kāfūr*), and knead them with it into an integrated mass and use, God willing.

Another recipe for a lesser *ushnān*[24]
Take picked over white potash (*ushnān abyaḍ*),[25] pound it, sift it, and set it aside. Take grated white clay (*ṭīn abyaḍ*)—half the amount of the potash used.

---

17 This recipe also appears in *Wuṣla* ii 724; and al-Tamīmī, recipe 272.

18 This is a reference to the Abbasid caliph, Hārūn al-Rashīd (d. 809). This recipe is in DK, appendix 63; and al-Ghuzūlī, *Maṭāli'* ii 66. This recipe and the following two are also found in al-Warrāq's chapter 129. I used al-Warrāq's version to amend the text.

19 This is a small variety of cubeb (*kabāba*) used mainly in perfume compounds.

20 This is a dry fragrant resin of the storax tree (*lubnā*).

21 This is also known as *'aṣāfīrī*, see n. 7 above.

22 See recipe 641 above.

23 This recipe only appears in DK, appendix 64. Here I amended the text based on al-Warrāq's corresponding version, See n. 18 above.

24 This recipe only appears in DK, appendix 65. Here I amended the text based on al-Warrāq's corresponding version, See n. 18 above.

25 See n. 7 above.

Also, take pounded and sifted citronella (*idhkhir*)—a quarter of the amount of potash; and cyperus (*suʿd*)—a quarter of the potash used.

Mix them all with distilled camphor water (*māʾ al-kāfūr*), and then rub the mix between the hands to crumble it, and use.[26]

(642) Recipe for scented yellow soap (*ṣābūn aṣfar muṭayyab*)[27] (DK 128r)
Take a slab of pure soap (*lawḥ ṣābūn*), finely grate it, and knead it gently while sprinkling it with rosewater until it becomes as smooth as ointment (*marham*) and all the solid particles dissolve.

Pound safflower (*ʿuṣfur*) and *maḥlab* kernels.[28] Add these to the soap, knead them together, and set them aside overnight to allow the ingredients to blend (*yakhtamir*). Early in the morning, spread this soap mix on a large flat dish (*ṭabaq*), cut it into small pieces (*shawābīr*),[29] and impress each one in the middle with a beautifully-carved wooden stamp. Alternatively, shape the soap into flat polygons (*muḍallaʿ*), snail-like shapes (*ḥalazūnī*), cones like *abālīj al-sukkar*,[30] using copper molds (*qawālib nuḥās*). Line the molds with a very thin piece of cloth first, and then stuff them very well with the soap, and impress them with the carved wooden stamp. [Take the formed soaps out of the molds with the help of the cloth.] When you gently peel off the cloth, you will have decorated soaps. Put them on the back of a sieve for a day to dry out. (DK 128v) Then, smooth the soaps with your hand after wetting it with a bit of rosewater, and set them aside to dry.

Do not use safflower with white soap; use only *maḥlab* and a bit of ceruse (*isfīdāj*).[31] For green soap, use a bit of verdigris (*zinjār*);[32] and for blue ones, use indigo (*nīl*). Whatever colors you make, do not leave out *maḥlab*. To color soap pink (*wardī*), use a bit of red lead (*sayraqūn*); for carnelian red soap (*aḥmar ʿaqīqī*),[33] use a bit of vermilion (*zunjufr*); and for pure yellow, use saffron.

26 *Yufrak*, al-Warrāq's addition.

27 This recipe also appears in *Wuṣla* ii 724–5. Here I used it to amend the edited text slightly. In addition, the first part of this recipe is missing from C but available in DK, as explained by the editors, n. 7509.

28 Aromatic kernels of the pit of a variety of small black cherry (*Prunus mahaleb*). See glossary 8.

29 *Shawābīr* (lit., 'triangles') are often used to designate small cut pieces. See glossary 9.2.

30 Solid conical masses of white cane sugar. See glossary 4, s.v. *sukkar*.

31 White lead pigments. See glossary 8, for this and the rest of the coloring agents mentioned in the recipe.

32 This was a green powder obtained by rusting copper.

33 In *Wuṣla*, it is said to be *aḥmar ʿamīq* 'dark red.'

(643) Another [soap] recipe

Make soap as described above, but in addition, use green cardamom (*hāl*), mace (*basbāsa*), and cloves (*kibāsh qaranful*), all pounded and sifted through a piece of silk cloth. Add to them enough rosewater to combine them, and knead them with the soap mix [described at the beginning of the above recipe]. (**153r**) It will come out very good and utterly fragrant. Also, add a bit of *maḥlab*.[34] It is the best.

(644) Recipe for *ushnān muṭayyab* (scented washing compound made with potash)

[Take] potash (*ushnān*), myrtle [leaves] (*ās*), bitter ginger (*ʿirq al-kāfūr*), Kufan cyperus (*suʿd Kūfī*),[35] and Indian spikenard (*sunbul al-ṭīb*), and crush all these ingredients and use as a cleansing compound (*ghasūl*).[36]

(645) Recipe for *ushnān mulūkī* (top quality handwashing compound), mentioned by ʿAlī b. Rabban al-Ṭabarī in his book *Firdaws al-ḥikma*[37]

[Take] 2 *raṭl*s (2 pounds) potash (*ushnān*), 1 *ūqiyya* (1 ounce) each, of cloves, Ceylon cinnamon (*qarfa*), top-quality yellow sandalwood (*ṣandal aṣfar*), cyperus (*suʿd*), dry storax resin (*mayʿa yābisa*), mace (*basbāsa*), cubeb, green cardamom (*hāl*), and Indian aloeswood (*ʿūd Hindī*).

Crush each spice separately, and sift it through a piece of silk cloth. Mix them with *ushnān* after you pound it and sift it. Add to them 2 *ūqiyya*s (2 ounces) fava bean flour to replace the rice flour used in the previous recipes.[38]

Knead the ingredients with rosewater and strongly scented camphor (*kāfūr rayyāḥī*).[39] Infuse them with smoke of aloeswood and camphor until they are saturated with their scents, and then enhance their scent (*yuftaq*) with *kāfūr rayyāḥī*, use 1 *mithqāl* (4½ grams/⅔ teaspoon) for each *raṭl* of the mix.

---

34 See n. 28 above.

35 This was also called tigernut, a rhizome, from Kufa, a city south of Baghdad.

36 This was commonly used for washing the hair and body. See glossary 11.

37 He was a famous scholar, physician, and scientist who served in the courts of the Abbasid caliphs, d. 861. This recipe is found in *Wuṣla* ii 723; and al-Tamīmī, recipe 268. I used both copies to amend the edited text.

38 In his version, al-Tamīmī, at this point, comments (referring to himself as Muḥammad b. Aḥmad) that rice flour is much superior to fava bean flour.

39 See n. 11 above.

(646) Another recipe for *ushnān mulūkī*[40]

[Take] potash (*ushnān*), rice flour, citronella (*idhkhir*), top-quality yellow sandalwood (*ṣandal aṣfar*), cyperus (*su'd*), and *maḥlab*.[41]

Gently pound the *maḥlab* so that its oil does not separate. Sift all the ingredients [after pounding them], and mix and knead them with rosewater and strongly scented camphor (*kāfūr rayyāḥī*).[42] Then dry out the mix, and sift it [again].

Maḥlab pounded with the *ushnān* will go rancid if kept for long.[43] **(153v)** Therefore, make only the amount needed for a week.[44]

(647) Another [*ushnān*] recipe[45]

Use equal parts of wheat starch, potash (*ushnān*)—either *Bāriqī* or *Fārisī*,[46] and white *maḥlab* kernels. Mix with them cloves, *qaṣab dharīra* (*Acorus calamus*), sweet costus (*qusṭ ḥulw*), nutmeg (*jawz bawwa*), use one part of these ingredients taken all together. Enhance its scent (*yuftaq*) with crushed strongly scented camphor (*kāfūr rayyāḥī*).[47]

(648) Another [*ushnān*] recipe[48]

One part potash (*ushnān*); one part rice flour; and a half part of each of nutmeg, cloves, and pounded white *maḥlab* kernels. Pound each ingredient separately, and sift them through a piece of silk cloth. Mix them all, and add a bit of saffron to them, enough to give the mix a yellow color.

---

40 This recipe also appears in *Wuṣla* ii 723; and al-Tamīmī, recipe 271. The latter credits Muḥammad b. al-'Abbās al-Khushshakī with it. The name is erroneously copied in *Wuṣla* as al-Ḥalabī. I used both copies to amend the edited text.

41 See n. 28 above.

42 See n. 11 above.

43 The verb for 'go rancid' is *zannakha* or *rayyaḥa*.

44 *Jum'a* (Friday) is used here to designate 'a whole week.' This last statement is al-Tamīmī's comment (referring to himself as Muḥammad b. Aḥmad), based on al-Tamīmī's and copies of the *Wuṣla*.

45 This recipe can also be found in *Wuṣla* ii 724, where it is credited to Ibn al-'Abbās. See n. 40 above.

46 *Ushnān Bāriqī* is a pure and excellent variety brought from Bāriq, a place near Kufa in Iraq. For *ushnān Fārisī*, see n. 7 above.

47 See n. 11 above.

48 Largely similar copies of this recipe are found in *Wuṣla* ii 724, and al-Tamīmī, recipe 272, where it is credited to Ibn al-'Abbās. See n. 40 above.

Muḥammad b. Aḥmad said,[49] The domestic variety also adds 2 *ūqiyyas* (2 ounces) crushed mild white potash (*ushnān ʿaṣāfīrī*),[50] as this will enhance it and make it a better cleansing agent.

(649) Another recipe for *ushnān mulūkī* (top quality potash compound)
Take 1 *qadaḥ* (2¼ pounds) mild white potash (*ushnān ʿaṣāfīrī*),[51] 1 *qadaḥ* cyperus of Kufa (*suʿd Kūfī*), ½ *qadaḥ* (approx. 1 pound) cyperus of Quṣār (*suʿd Quṣārī*),[52] 3 *dirhams* (9 grams/1½ teaspoons) dwarf violet iris (*qazmat banafsaj*),[53] 3 *dirhams* Iraqi rosebuds, and 1 *qīrāṭ* (¼ gram) musk.

Pound and sift them all, and then add potash (*ushnān*) to them. This will make an excellent aromatic *ushnān Mulūkī*.

(650) Recipe [for an aromatic compound], to remove greasy odors (*zafar*) from hands
Take sticky fleabane (*barnūf*);[54] crush and sift it after you dry it, and then mix it with ground [dried] lupine beans (*turmus*),[55] and wash your hands with it (**154r**) to remove their greasy odors. It can still remove greasy odors even when used while still moist (*raṭb*).

[Here follow recipes for *adhān* (sg. *duhn*) 'aromatic oils.']

(651) Recipe for *duhn* (aromatic oil), which removes the greasy odors on hands[56]
Keep *nisrīn* flowers (dog rose) steeped in sesame oil in a sunny place for 40 days, and then add a bit of camphor to it and store it. The same is done with

---

49 I used al-Tamīmī's version to straighten out the edited text, where the name is given as محمد بن أحمد البلدي. Al-Tamīmī constantly refers to himself as Muḥammad b. Aḥmad (محمد بن أحمد). Therefore, *al-baladī* (البلدي) here simply means 'the local variety.'

50 This was also known as *ushnān Fārisī*, see n. 7 above.

51 See n. 7 above.

52 Cyperus of Kufa (a city south of Baghdad) and cyperus of Quṣār (a place between India and China, as described in al-Qalqashandī, *Ṣubḥ al-aʿshā* 239), respectively. The first variety is deemed the best, with white rhizomes, large, dense, heavy, and fragrant.

53 It is قزمة, written as قرمة in DK, n. 7575, and not حزمة 'bundle,' as in the edited text, which is irrelevant in the context, considering the small amount called for in the recipe. Dozy, *Takmilat al-maʿājim* 137, mentions قرم بنفسج to designate *sawsan* 'iris,' s.v. قرم, which should have been قزم 'dwarf.'

54 *Dittrichia viscosa*, a bitter, heavy-smelling plant, with downy sticky leaves; it grows abundantly in Egypt.

55 See glossary 12.

56 This recipe also appears in *Wuṣla* ii 497.

FIGURE 45 *Dog-rose, F1954.83r, Muḥammad al-Qazwīnī,* ʿAjāʾib al-makhlūqāt, *detail (Freer Gallery of Art and Arthur M. Sackler Gallery, Smithsonian Institution, Washington, DC: Purchase—Charles Lang Freer Endowment).*

almonds: if you mix it with the oil of sour orange blossoms (*zahr al-nāranj*), it will come out good, and can be used right away. Besides, the hands can be wiped with [just] oil extracted from almonds. Indeed, this will be the best.

(652) Recipe for *duhn* (aromatic oil)[57]

Take almond oil stirred with rose petals,[58] infuse cotton with aromatic smoke, and then add the rose oil to it.

Here is the recipe for infusing cotton with aromatic smoke:[59] Take spinning-cotton and fluff it. Oil the inside of a china vessel (*ināʾ ṣīnī*), stick the cotton all over the surface, and infuse it with the smoke of aloeswood and ambergris. Repeat six or seven times, after which add the rose oil to the vessel. Sprinkle it with [crushed] ambergris and musk, and use. It is very fragrant.

57 This recipe also appears in *Wuṣla* ii 495. However, here I followed *Wuṣla* SOAS 16, to amend the edited text, as it is a better copy.

58 Here I followed *Wuṣla* SOAS معلوف 'stirred with,' rather than the irrelevant مصلوق, مغلوف, and معلوق in the other versions. Rose petals stirred into the oil infuse it with their aroma.

59 The term used is *tabkhīr*, see glossary 9.2.

(653) Recipe for oil infused with fragrant smoke, known as *duhn al-zafar* (oil for removing greasy odors)[60]

It is beneficial for cold winds (*aryāḥ bārida*) and bloating (*nafkh*), and for all cold-related illnesses, and for those with swollen hands due to cold exposure. It is also effective in removing greasy odors, even those of fish, from hands. It smells quite aromatic, very nice, and only few people know about it.[61]

Take nutmeg, green cardamom, Indian mace (*basbāsa Hindiyya*), cloves, spikenard, betel leaves, bay laurel leaves (*waraq rand*); use one part of each. (154v) Also take 2 parts of *zir ward Mizzī*—[62] remove their hypanthia (*aqmāʿ*), and 2 parts usnea (*shaybat ʿajūz*).

Pound all the ingredients, and sift them through a *jābūniyya*.[63] The ingredients need to be crushed thoroughly. Add to them crushed ambergris and Ceylon sandalwood (*ṣandal Maqāṣīrī*). Mix them all and crush them. This will be your ***dharūr*** (perfumed powder compound).

Now, take 3 parts aloeswood, 2 parts sugar candy (*sukkar nabāt*), and sweet and bitter costus (*qusṭ*)—one part of each. Also take *ẓufr* (onycha), leave them soaking overnight in henna [powder] kneaded into water. In the following morning, boil them and scrape off whatever dirt is stuck on them with a knife—use one part of this. In addition, use 1½ parts of the best ladanum resin (*lādhan ʿanbarī*); roll it between the fingers into small pieces. Also use one part of [dried] myrtle leaves snipped [into small pieces] with a pair of scissors, and one part of saffron threads (*zaʿfarān shaʿr*) crushed in a mortar (*hāwan*). This will be your ***bakhūr*** (incense).

Now, take spinning cotton and fluff it into thin layers. Oil a large porcelain bowl (*zibdiyya*) with fresh sesame oil, and stick the cotton to its inner walls, but do not put any of it in the bottom because it will burn. Put two or three burning coals on a plate and put a good amount of the incense prepared above (*bakhūr*) on top of the burning coals. Turn the bowl lined with cotton over

---

60 Here I used copies of the recipe in *Wuṣla* ii 495–6, and *Wuṣla* SOAS 16–7, to amend the edited text.

61 This addition is from *Wuṣla*.

62 These are dried rosebuds from Mizza, a district in Damascus. I opted to use *Wuṣla* SOAS version Mizzī مزّي rather than مربّى 'made into jam' in the *Kanz* edited text and that of the edited version of *Wuṣla*. All the ingredients called for here should be dry, and using jam would make sifting them impossible.

63 The word جابونية is not used anywhere else in our sources, to my knowledge. *Wuṣla*'s خاتونية does not help here either. Based on context, we know that it must be a piece of silk cloth of the kind usually used in recipes to sift ingredients into fine powder. It could be a variety of silk from India; the word could have been named after Jāba, a kingdom in India (see Ibn Khurradādhbih, *al-Masālik* 4, 15, 16).

the plate and it will be infused with the aromatic smoke. When no more smoke is produced, [remove the bowl] and add more of the incense to make more smoke. Turn over the cotton that was in the bowl; stick it again on the sides of the bowl; sprinkle it lightly with sesame oil; and infuse it with the aromatic smoke [as done earlier]. Repeat [this process] seven times, (**155r**) and then infuse the cotton once more with the smoke of ambergris. When the cotton turns yellow, sprinkle it generously with the perfumed powder compound (*dharūr*) prepared earlier, and throw it into fresh sesame oil—let it cover the cotton and a little bit more.

Now infuse the vessel [that will be used to keep the oil in] with the smoke of the incense [you prepared above] along with ambergris. Put the cotton and the oil in this vessel, and scent the surface with musk and civet (*zabād*);[64] add as much as you can afford, and use it.

When you add *dharūr* (powdery mix) to the cotton [see above paragraph], also add usnea (*shaybat ʿajūz*), a bit of crushed ambergris, and rose petals, as these will enhance it and make it even more aromatic.

(654) Recipe for *duhn mubakhkhar* (oil infused with fragrant smoke)
[Take] spikenard, betel leaves (*tunbul*), cloves, green cardamom, nutmeg, khat leaves (*waraq al-Qumārī*),[65] sandalwood, aloeswood, and rosebuds. Add also usnea (*shayba*), which has been washed seven times. These ingredients will give the oil its aroma (*ṭīb*).

As for its incense (*bakhūr*), use sweet costus, bitter costus, the best ladanum resin (*lādhan ʿanbarī*), aloeswood, and ambergris. Infuse it [i.e., the cotton, see previous recipe] with the smoke of these ingredients, seven times. After that, infuse it with the smoke of aloeswood and ambergris, two times with each. [Next, add the aromatic mix, prepared in the first paragraph, to the cotton, and mix all of it with the sesame oil in a vessel]. Enhance the sesame oil with some ambergris and civet (*zabada*).[66]

64 Here I replaced the edited وزيادة 'and more' with وزباد 'and civet,' based on *Wuṣla* ii 496, which copies it correctly. *Zabād* is an aromatic secretion of the perineal gland of the African civet.

65 This was also known as *qāt* (*Catha edulis*); the leaves are chewed, like betel (*tunbul*). It was brought from Qumr in east Africa. See glossary 8.

66 *Zabada* must be the Egyptian variant for *zabād*. It also occurs in Ibn al-Ukhuwwa, *Maʿālim al-qurba*, fol. 82v, where it is clearly vowelized as *zabada*.

CHAPTER 21

في أنواع البخورات المطيّبة المقوّية للنفس والقلب
والحبوب المطيّبة وأدوية العرق وغير ذلك

Varieties of Aroma-Diffusing Incense, Which Fortify Spirit and Heart; Aromatizing Pills; Deodorants; and Other Preparations

(655) Recipe for incense (*bakhūr*)

[Take the] peel of one *laymūna balsīmī*[1] (155v), the peel of one sour orange (*nāranja*), myrtle leaves (*marsīn*),[2] *ẓufr* (onycha),[3] resin of arar tree (*sandarūs*), mastic, saffron threads, sandalwood, and sugar candy (*sukkar nabāt*).

Pound them separately, and take an equal amount of each. Knead them with rosewater of Nuṣaybīn,[4] shape them into discs (*yuqarraṣ*), and let them dry in the air, and stow them away.

(656) Recipe for *fatāʾil al-ʿanbar* (ambergris incense wicks)[5]

Take 1 *qīrāṭ* (¼ gram) musk. Also take 1 *dirham* (3 grams) ambergris crushed in olive oil and rosewater of Nuṣaybīn, and add the musk to them. Add also ¼ *dirham* camphor.

---

1 Here I have chosen the version given in DK, n. 7674, where it is copied as بلسيمي. It is indeed close to the name ʿAbd al-Laṭīf al-Baghdādī gives in his *Riḥla* 75, where he mentions a variety of Egyptian lemon called *laymūn al-balsam*. He says it is the size of the thumb, and looks rather like an elongated egg. Al-Suyūṭī, in his account of Egypt, *Ḥusn al-muḥāḍara* 364, excerpts verses in which the lemon is compared to a chicken egg, smeared with saffron.

In the edited text, the word occurs as تلمسي, which may be a reference to the city of Tlemcen, in northwestern Africa (today in Algeria), famous for its fruit orchards, especially orange, lemon, and grapes; or it is quite likely that it was a misreading of the word.

2 This is also known as *ās*.

3 This is also known as *aẓfār al-ṭīb*, see glossary 8.

4 Nuṣaybīn was a city in upper Mesopotamia, now in the Turkish province of Mardin. It was renowned for its orchards and gardens. Roses named after it are pinkish in hue.

5 Sg. *fatīla*, see glossary 11. Incense *fatīla* may sometimes be made by just rolling the aromatic compound into solid cylinders; this was done when the ingredients have a paste-like consistency. This recipe's oil-based mix requires the use of linen wicks.

 | DOI 10.1163/9789004349919_024

Cook the mix well on the fire, and then mix it with 1 *dirham* of burnt vinewood (*ḥaṭab karam*). Combine all the ingredients well. Make linen tapers (*fatā'il kattān*) and use [them to diffuse the aromatic smoke].

(657) Recipe for aloeswood incense[6]

Split aloeswood into splinters. Soak them in rosewater for 6 to 7 days, and use them for incense [by putting them directly on burning coals].

Recipe for incense[7]

1 *ūqiyya* (1 ounce) aloeswood, ½ *dirham* (1½ grams) saffron, 1 *ūqiyya* rosewater, and 2 *dirhams* (6 grams) white sugar.

FIGURE 46 *Incense burner, early fourteenth century, 17.190.1716 (MET NY—Gift of J. Pierpont Morgan, 1917).*

6 In the following recipes, and to the end of this chapter, *Wuṣla* ii 482–9 shares most of the recipes with the *Kanz*. I will refer to it wherever amendments are made using it.

7 This recipe only appears in DK, appendix 69.

Dissolve sugar in rosewater on the fire. Add saffron and aloeswood. When the mix boils, and the syrup sticks to the aloeswood, take them out and let them dry in the air. This is how to make excellent coated aloeswood (*ʿūd muʿallā*).

Recipe for aloeswood incense, called *al-muʿallā* (the coated)[8]
Split aloeswood into splinters. Take sugar candy (*sukkar nabāt*), dissolve it in rosewater and cook it into sugar syrup (*jullāb*) until it thickens and has the consistency of [syrup prepared for] oxymel chewy candy (*ʿaqīd al-sakanjabīn*).[9]

Add kneaded ambergris (*ʿanbar maʿjūn*),[10] and a bit of musk. Wait until the ambergris melts and then throw in the aloeswood pieces, and stir the pot so that they are all coated. Take them out and let them dry in the air. However, be careful not to under-boil the syrup, or it will not stick to the pieces. This kind [of incense] is marvelously aromatic.

(658) Recipe for *bakhūr muʿallā bi-ʿanbar* (aloeswood incense coated with ambergris), better than the previous one[11]
Split aloeswood into splinters. Finely crush candy sugar (*sukkar nabāt*). Put a vessel on the fire, and melt raw ambergris (*ʿanbar khām*), kneaded ambergris (*ʿanbar maʿjūn*),[12] and a bit of musk. When these melt, add the sugar candy, and stir.

When all the ingredients are well mixed, add the aloeswood, and stir, so that all the splinters are well coated with the ambergris mix. Take them out of the vessel. They will look white and will have a very nice aroma when used as incense.

---

8 This recipe only appears in DK, appendix 70; and *Wuṣla* ii 482, with some stylistic differences.

9 See recipe 348 above.

10 Made by mixing ambergris, aloeswood, and musk; it was also called *nidd*. Al-Nuwayrī, *Nihāyat al-arab* xii 38–9, says (to his fourteenth-century contemporaries) that what was called *nidd* is now called *ʿanbar*. When the ingredient ambergris itself is meant, it is called *ʿanbar khām*. The best of this aromatic compound is called *nidd muthallath* or *ʿanbar muthallath*. It is composed of three equal parts of ambergris, aloeswood, and musk, kneaded together (*maʿjūn*).

11 "Better than the previous one" refers to another recipe for aloe incense coated with ambergris, which only appears in DK (see above recipe). The edited C manuscript does not include it, and hence "better than the previous one" sounds rather confusing. For this recipe, I used *Wuṣla* ii 483 to amend the edited text slightly.

12 See n. 10 above.

Recipe for *bakhūr Yemenī* (Yemeni incense)[13]

[This is] good for wintertime, and for incensing furs, except those of ermines (*sinjāb*). Take two parts aloeswood, one and a half parts Ceylon sandalwood (*ṣandal maqāṣīrī*), and one-half part each of sweet costus, bitter costus, and *ẓufr* (onycha).

Crush all [costus]. Split aloeswood and sandalwood into small splinters (*yushaẓẓā*). Boil *ẓufr*, and clean off all dirt and fatty solids from it with a knife. After that, pound all the ingredients.

Now take dried but still green myrtle leaves (*marsīn*), and [dried] sour orange peel, one-half part of each, and pound them, too.

Take rosewater, and dissolve sugar and honey in it. Boil it on the fire until it becomes very thick syrup. Add to it the best ladanum resin (*lādhan ʿanbarī*), kneaded ambergris (*ʿanbar maʿjūn*),[14] and saffron. Stir the rest of the ingredients into it until they all mix well. Cool it on a tray. Mix with it ¼ *mithqāl* (approx. 1 gram) civet (*zabād*).[15]

(659) Recipe for *fatāʾil nidd* (slim hand-rolled cylinders of incense)

Take 1 *mithqāl* (4½ grams) ambergris [compound][16] and ⅛ *mithqāl* (½ gram) wax. (**156r**) Dissolve them on the fire, and roll the mix into slim cylinders (*fatāʾil*). When you want to use the incense, light one end and put it out. It will continue diffusing smoke the whole night.

Recipe for good *fatāʾil al-nidd* (slim hand-rolled cylinders of incense)[17]

Take aromatic *ʿanbar muthallath*,[18] and mix with it coals of vine branches (*faḥm al-zarjūn*) or the down of unripe quince (*zaghab al-safarjal*). However, [vine] coal is better. Scrape the coal—choose the black ones, [and mix the scrapings with the ambergris], and shape it into slim cylinders (*fatāʾil*).

---

13 This recipe only appears in DK, appendix 71; and *Wuṣla* ii 484, where the title of the recipe is written as: بخور يمني يصلح في الشتا وللفراء ما خلا السنجاب.
Here I used it to amend the edited text.

14 See n. 10 above.

15 This is an addition from *Wuṣla*. In the *Kanz*'s recipes calling for *zabād*, it is often copied as *zabada*, which must be an Egyptian variant. It also occurs in Ibn al-Ukhuwwa, *Maʿālim al-qurba*, fol. 82v, where it is clearly vowelized as *zabada*.

16 Composed of ambergris, aloeswood, and musk, also called *nidd*. See n. 10 above.

17 This recipe only appears in DK, appendix 72; and *Wuṣla* ii 485. I used the latter to amend the edited text.

18 Composed of ambergris, aloeswood, and musk, also called *nidd muthallath*. See n. 10 above.

Whenever you want to use the incense, light a cylinder (*fatīla*) first and then blow it out. It will continue giving out aromatic smoke. I have also seen some people put them in a silver-cast *ihlīlaj* (shaped like myrobalan plum, *Prunus cerasifera*), or in pierced [silver-cast] balls (*ukar*),[19] and put them in their pockets. The smoke will continue emitting [the fragrance] from their pockets. Pretty and elegant.

FIGURE 47 *Pierced globe incense burner, diam. 6.25 in., early fourteenth century, 17.190.2095a, b (MET NY—Gift of J. Pierpont Morgan, 1917).*

---

19 Sg. *ukara*, most popularly shaped like apples.

Recipe for perfume of Yemen (*ṭīb ahl al-Yemen*)[20]

Take musk, dissolve it in rosewater, and pour it on a flat stone grater (*miḥakka*),[21] and grate and crush in it some camphor and a bit of raw ambergris (*ʿanbar khām*), white sandalwood (*ṣandal abyaḍ*), and sweet-smelling aloeswood. Combine all the ingredients in a vessel and mix them well, and use it as perfume (*ṭīb*).

(660) Recipe for a deodorant (*dawāʾ ʿaraq*), like no other[22]

Take 2 *ūqiyyas* (2 ounces) tutty (*tūtyā*),[23] and finely crush it. Take 15 *dirhams* (1½ ounces) dwarf violet iris (*qazmat banafsaj*). Take also 7 *dirhams* (21 grams/ ¾ ounce) usnea (*shaybat al-ʿajūz*), first soak it in rosewater for a whole day, and then drain it and pound it until it falls apart.

Put all the ingredients in a mortar, and pour the rosewater in which the usnea was soaked, add more if needed [to cover them all]. Keep them there until all the moisture evaporates. Once again pour rosewater on them, keep them in it until they dry. Repeat this [procedure] five times. After that, put them in a glass vessel until they are dry enough to stick to a bowl.

Next, stick the mix in [the bottom of] a porcelain bowl (*zibdiyya*), and infuse it with the smoke of aloeswood of Khmer (*ʿūd Qamārī*). Repeat this ten times. After that, infuse it with smoke of ambergris; between each two smoke infusions, knead the mix, stick it to the bowl as we mentioned earlier, and sprinkle it with rosewater.

When the mix is filled with smoke, finely crush it until it looks like fine dust (*habāʾ*), and then use it. It will stop armpit odors (*ṣunān*) and make you smell nice.

(661) Recipe for pills (*ḥabb*) to sweeten the breath (*yuṭayyib al-nakha*)[24]

These also strengthen teeth, and aid digestion when taken after food. They keep the breath smelling nice when kept in the mouth at bedtime; they can

---

20 This recipe only appears in DK, appendix 66; and *Zahr*, fol. 38r.

21 The ingredients are put in a flattish stone (called a saddle quern), and grated and crushed with a handheld rubbing stone.

22 Here I slightly amend the edited text based on *Wuṣla* ii 494. Both DK, n. 7701, and *Wuṣla* copy the name of the recipe as *dawāʾ ʿaraq* 'deodorant' and not *fatāʾil* 'incense cylinders' as in the edited text.

23 It is finely powdered impure zinc oxide. *Wuṣla* specifies its variety as *marāzibī*, which al-Anṭākī (*Tadhkira* 106) describes as delicate white thin sheets. He adds that the pharmacists call it *shaqfa*. Al-Bīrūnī, *Ṣaydana* 120, compares this variety of *marāzibī* to eggshells, and says it is the best.

24 This recipe also appears in *Zahr*, fol. 38v; *Wuṣla* ii 740; and al-Tamīmī, recipe 262.

be used as incense, or as *dharīra* (perfumed powder) when used dry. They can be used as *ghāliya* (compound perfume) to anoint the body with, when crushed and dissolved in ben oil (*duhn bān*).[25] (**156v**) In addition, when dissolved in rosewater, it will be good for wiping the body.

Take 7 *dirhams* (21 grams/¾ ounce) Indian aloeswood (*ʿūd Hindī*), 4 *dirhams* (12 grams) cloves, 4 *dirhams* mace, 3 *dirhams* (9 grams) cubeb (*kabāba*), 5 *dirhams* (15 grams) white cyperus of Kufa (*suʿd abyaḍ Kūfī*),[26] and a similar amount of sandalwood. Also take 3 *dirhams* (9 grams) black cardamom (*qāqulla*), ½ *ūqiyya* (½ ounce) musk-scented pastilles (*sukk al-misk*),[27] and ½ *mithqāl* (2 grams) camphor.

Crush all these ingredients, and knead them with Persian rosewater, but rosewater of Nuṣaybīn is better.[28] Shape the mix into pills the size of a chickpea each, or a little bit bigger, and let them dry in a shaded place.

Take a pill in the mornings and after meals. Slowly and continually roll it in your mouth, swallowing whatever dissolves from it. Repeat at bedtime.

(662) Recipe for pills (*ḥabb*) that sweeten the breath and stop bad breath (*bakhar*) when they are kept in the mouth

Take nutmeg and black cardamom (*qāqulla*), 1 *dirham* (3 grams) of each, and two lumps of pure musk. Combine all these ingredients and pound them. Then sift them all, except for the musk. Take one pill in the mouth as needed.

Another recipe [for aromatic pills][29]

Take Javanese aloeswood (*ʿūd Qāqullī*), spikenard, betel leaves, and a bit of Iraqi musk. Put all the ingredients [in a vessel] at a breeze catcher (*mahabbāt*),[30] and continue adding rosewater to them for three days. After that, spread them to dry, and form them into pills, each as small as a black peppercorn.

[When having a bath],[31] put one pill in your mouth, chew it a little [just to break it, do not swallow], drink some water [do not swallow], swish it in your

---

25 Oil extracted from the kernels of seeds of the moringa tree (*Moringa oleifera*).

26 Kufa is a city in Iraq, south of Baghdad. This white variety is deemed the best.

27 See glossary 8.

28 Nuṣaybīn was a city in upper Mesopotamia, now in the Turkish province of Mardin. It was renowned for its orchards and gardens. Roses named after it are pinkish in hue.

29 This recipe only appears in DK, appendix 75.

30 The breeze catchers were shafts, built in walls for ventilation and to decrease indoor temperatures. In this recipe, the ingredients are placed in front of such an opening to keep them ventilated. It is also known as *bādhāhanj*.

31 This paragraph clearly deals with bathing, like the one in recipe 666 below.

mouth and squirt it (*yunajjā*) [into the water basin];[32] the water will smell exactly like pure rosewater scented with musk. Also, put another pill in the upper basin; but this one should be kept in a loosely woven piece of cloth, which is tied to a piece of lead, so that it stays there and does not get pushed into the water [in the lower basin] by the [force of the] water [flowing into the lower basin].

Another recipe for pills to sweeten the breath (*yuṭayyib al-nakha*)[33]
These can also be used as incense (*bakhūr*), finely crushed as scented powder (*dharīra*), and dissolved in rosewater as *ghāliya* (compound perfume). It is also good as a food spice, and a digestive.

Take ambergris, sugar, and musk; 1 *dirham* (3 grams) of each. Take also 1 *dirham* strongly scented camphor (*kāfūr rayyāḥī*),[34] and a similar amount of cloves. Combine these after crushing and sifting them. Ambergris should be crushed and sifted with aloeswood first, and then added to the other spices.

Knead them all with rosewater of Nuṣaybīn.[35] Form them into pills each the size of a chickpea, and let them dry in a shaded place on the back of a sieve.

Take one pill in the morning and another in the evening. Taking it after the meal will facilitate digestion. It is also beneficial for heart palpitations (*khafaqān*) and [other] heart-related ailments.

Recipe for pills to cure bad breath (*bakhar*)[36]
Take aloeswood, cloves, and mastic. Pound them all and knead them with gum arabic (*ṣamgh*) that has been dissolved in clear *khall rayḥānī*.[37] Form this into pills, and dry them in the shade. Put one in the mouth whenever needed.

(663) Recipe for a deodorant (*dawāʾ ʿaraq*)
1 *ūqiyya* (1 ounce) tutty (*tūtyā*),[38] 5 *dirhams* (15 grams) fragments (*shaqaf*) of earthenware beer jars (*kīzān al-fuqqāʿ*),[39] 2 *dirhams* (6 grams) silver slag (*khabath fiḍḍa*),[40] 2½ *dirhams* (7½ grams) fragments of china (*ṣīnī*), 1 *ūqiyya*

32 From which bowlfuls of water will be scooped to wash the body.
33 This recipe only appears in DK, appendix 76.
34 Also called *kāfūr Rabāḥī*, see glossary 8.
35 See n. 28 above.
36 This recipe only appears in DK, appendix 77.
37 Vinegar made from *rayḥānī* wine, named for its pleasant aroma.
38 See n. 23 above.
39 See glossary 1, s.v. *kūz*.
40 Here I amended it, based on context, to replace the irrelevant *khabar* in the edited text.

(2 tablespoons) domestic rosewater (*māʾward baladī*), and ½ *ūqiyya* rosewater of Nuṣaybīn.[41]

Dissolve the ingredients in rosewater and use.[42] It is the best for blocking perspiration.

(664) Recipe for *zahriyya* (aromatic compound with sour orange blossoms)

Put sour orange blossoms (*zahr al-nāranj*) in a piece of cloth—only use the white blossoms.[43] Infuse them from underneath, and while still fresh, with the smoke of aloeswood, ambergris, sandalwood, and sugar. Let them dry in a shaded place and stow them.

Take 1 *ūqiyya* (1 ounce) Iraqi rosebuds, from which the hypanthia have been removed; also take 1 *ūqiyya* spikenard, and green cardamom and cloves, ½ *ūqiyya* of each.

Now, take ½ *raṭl* (½ pound) of the dried orange blossoms [prepared above], and crush them along with the rest of the ingredients using a grinder (*ṭāḥūn*). Put them together [in a vessel]. Take rosewater, musk, and civet (*zabada*)[44]—use 2 *ūqiyyas* (¼ cup) rosewater and as much musk and civet as you like. Moisten and knead the ingredients with these, and then let the mix dry in a shaded place, covered, and store it in a glass vessel.[45]

(665) Recipe for *Barmakiyya*[46]

Take ½ *raṭl* (½ pound) bitter costus, 1 *ūqiyya* (1 ounce) of the best ladanum resin (*lādhan ʿanbarī*), ½ *ūqiyya* boiled *ẓufr* (onycha), 1 *ūqiyya* crumbled aloeswood, ½ *ūqiyya* rosebuds, 2 *ūqiyyas aṭrāf ṭīb* (spice blend)—use all its components; use more spikenard than the rest. Also use 2 *dirhams* (6 grams/1 teaspoon) saffron threads, ½ *ūqiyya* mastic, 2 *dirhams* resin of arar tree (*sandarūs*), and 1 *ūqiyya qishr mayʿa* (resinous bark of storax tree).[47]

---

41 See n. 28 above.

42 It is to be assumed that they are finely crushed first.

43 I.e., only use blossoms in their prime. The not so fresh ones start to lose their whiteness.

44 More commonly known as *zabād* (زباد). *Zabada* must be an Egyptian variant. It also occurs in Ibn al-Ukhuwwa, *Maʿālim al-qurba*, fol. 82v, where it is clearly vowelized as *zabada*.

45 The recipe does not specify how this aromatic compound is to be used. However, judging from medieval Arabic sources on making fragrant preparations, *zahriyya* would have been thinned down with liquid, such as rosewater, and used as *nuḍūḥ* to be sprinkled around the house; or used as a primary ingredient in making *lakhlakha* 'potpourri.'

46 Named after the Barmakids, an influential Persian family during the early Abbasid rule. Here I amended the text based on *Wuṣla* ii 493.

47 This was also called *mayʿa yābisa* 'dry storax resin.'

Also use 2 *ūqiyyas* (¼ cup) rosewater; *nuḍūḥ*,[48] and myrtle water (*māʾ al-ās*)—2 *ūqiyyas* of each; ½ *raṭl* (½ pound) bee honey, (157v) 1 *dirham* (3 grams/ ½ teaspoon) camphor, and ½ *dirham* civet (*zabada*).[49]

Finely pound and crush the ingredients (*ḥawāʾij*),[50] and mix them well.[51] Boil *nuḍūḥ*, honey, and myrtle water. Dissolve ladanum in them, and throw the [pounded] ingredients into them. Stir the pot with a spoon (*milʿaqa*) on a very low fire.

Dissolve camphor and civet (*zabada*) in rosewater, and when the pot is removed from the fire, knead its contents with this rosewater mix. Store it in a glass vessel.[52]

(666) Another kind [of aromatic preparation]

Take ½ *dirham* (¼ teaspoon) musk, and 3 *ūqiyyas* (6 tablespoons) rosewater. Put a piece of cotton in a small bowl (*sukurruja*) and pour rosewater and musk on it. Set it aside until the cotton dries out.

[When you go to the bath] with whomever you wish, once you get there, use this piece of cotton to stop up the water pouring into the tub, but put a piece of wood crosswise to keep the cotton from falling. The entire water [in the tub] will smell like pure rosewater, and whoever takes water from this tub for his bath will not doubt that it is rosewater.

(667) Recipe for *nisrīniyya* (incense with dog rose)

Take 2 *ūqiyyas* (2 ounces) fresh dog rose (*nisrīn akhḍar*), 1 *ūqiyya* cloves, and ½ *ūqiyya* of each of spikenard and green cardamom.

Pound the [dry] ingredients, sift them and pound them with the dog rose. Infuse them with the smoke of aloeswood and ambergris, and enhance their scent (*yuftaq*) with civet (*zabada*),[53] camphor, and rosewater.

This can be used as incense even when it is freshly made and still moist.

---

48 *Nuḍūḥ* is an aromatic preparation, prepared as in the above recipe, kept dried in jars and used as needed.

49 See n. 44 above.

50 I.e., the dry ingredients in the first paragraph.

51 Except for *lādhan*, as it will be added separately.

52 *Wuṣla* adds that weights in this recipe follow the Egyptian *raṭl*, a clear indication that the recipe originated in Egypt. Again, the recipe does not specify how this aromatic compound is to be used. See n. 45 above for possibilities. However, it was most likely used as incense, given the amount of honey used in making it. See also recipes 670, 672 below.

53 See n. 44 above.

(668) Recipe for *banafsajiyya* (aromatic compound with violets) (158r)
Finely crush violet petals, and mix them with rosewater scented with musk and civet (*zabada*).[54] Let them dry in a shaded place covered with *shaʿriyya* (a cloth loosely woven with horsehair). After that put the mix in a glass vessel and use [as incense].

(669) Recipe for *maʿshūqa* (the beloved incense)[55]
Take 1 *ūqiyya* (1 ounce) aloeswood, 2 *dirhams* (6 ounces/1 teaspoon) Ceylon sandalwood (*ṣandal Maqāṣīrī*), 3 *dirhams* ladanum resin (*lādhan*), 1 *mithqāl* (4½ grams) sugar candy (*sukkar nabāt*), 1 *dirham* camphor, and ½ *dirham* (1½ grams) sour orange peel.

Crush all the ingredients. Dissolve ladanum in rosewater, [and add the rest of the ingredients], using just enough rosewater to knead them together. Add a bit of musk.

Form the mix into discs, set them aside to dry in a shaded place, and cover them with *shaʿriyya* (cloth loosely woven with horsehair). Store them in glass vessels, and use them [as incense].

(670) Recipe for another *zahriyya* (aromatic preparation with sour orange blossoms)[56]
Let sour orange blossoms dry in the sun and finely pound them. With each *raṭl* (1 pound) of the pounded blossoms, pound 1 *ūqiyya* (1 ounce) bitter ginger (*ʿirq kāfūr*), 1 *ūqiyya* cyperus (*suʿd*), 1 *ūqiyya* rosebuds, and ½ *ūqiyya* marjoram (*mardaqūsh*). Combine them all with rosewater.

Now, put the mix in a *qinnīna* (vessel made of woven esparto grass),[57] and infuse it with aromatic smoke by putting it in two pots tightly joined with mud, with a small opening (*ṭāq laṭīf*) at the top of the upper pot to allow smoke to escape through it.[58]

54 See n. 44 above.
55 The recipe contains sugar, an ingredient usually included in incense preparations.
56 I used *Wuṣla* ii 493 to amend the edited text.
57 This vessel allows the fumes to penetrate the ingredients, see glossary 9.1 for other vessels called by the same name.
58 The *qinnīna* would be placed on a trivet above the burning coals and incense, which are placed in the bottom of the lower pot. A small hole is made in the bottom of the upper pot, which is upside down over the lower pot to allow the accumulated smoke to escape through it. Both tightly sealed with mud.

For incense [to put in the bottom of the lower pot], use *Barmakiyya* [see recipes 665, 672] and ¼ *ūqiyya* (½ tablespoon) *muʿassala*.[59] When the mud sealing the two pots dries out, it is a sign that the preparation is done.

(671) Recipe for *lakhlakha* (potpourri)

Take a *fayyāsha* with a long neck,[60] and pour into it 1 *ūqiyya* (2 tablespoons) rosewater, 1 *ūqiyya* distilled water of Egyptian willow bark (*māʾ khilāf*),[61] **(158v)** 1 *ūqiyya* distilled water of Levantine borage (*māʾ lisān thawr Shāmī*), ¼ *ūqiyya* (½ tablespoon) distilled water of cloves (*māʾ qaranful*), and ¼ *ūqiyya* distilled water of sour orange blossoms (*māʾ zahr nāranj*) if available.

Also, add 3 *dirhams* (9 grams/1½ teaspoon) coarsely crushed aloeswood, 1 *mithqāl* (4½ grams/⅔ teaspoon) ambergris, and 1 lump of musk. Add also a piece of peeled *tuffāḥa fatḥiyya* (aromatic variety of apple),[62] which has been chopped into small pieces. Do likewise with a piece of quince. Also add ½ *dirham* (¼ teaspoon) black cardamom (*qāqulla*) and a similar amount of cubeb (*kabāba*).

Put this bottle on a very low fire placed in a blowing breeze. A wonderfully aromatic scent will emit from it. Replenish the liquids in the bottle as they decrease, and keep the fire under it very low.

(672) Recipe for *bakhūr Barmakiyya* (incense of the Barmakids)[63]

Those who sit in corridors (*dahālīz*) or toilets (*buyūt al-rāḥa*) can use it to incense themselves. It is very good.

Take sweet costus and bitter costus, one part of each; and one part *ẓufr* (onycha). Also use half a part of each of these: snipped dried myrtle leaves (*marsīn*); the best ladanum resin (*lādhan ʿanbarī*)—rolled between the fingers into small pieces; dried peels of sour orange (*nāranj*) and lemon (*laymūn*). Also add saffron threads.

Coarsely crush all the ingredients [separately, and set them aside]. Mix bee honey with rosewater and wine vinegar. Put the pot on the fire, adding a good amount of the ladanum, and saffron.

---

59 It must have been another aromatic compound with honey, for which I could not find a recipe, here or elsewhere.

60 A glass bottle with a flattish wide lower part, and a long neck. See glossary 9.1.

61 *Khilāf* tree, also called *ṣafṣāf Miṣrī* (*Salix aegyptiaca*), is an Egyptian species of the willow tree.

62 This was also called *tuffāḥ Shāmī* 'Levantine apple'; it was valued for its balanced properties and great aroma.

63 See n. 46 above.

Let the pot cook until the mix is concentrated into thick syrup. [Away from the heat,] add the spices (*ḥawāʾij*) [that were set aside], stir them well, and then spread the mix in a shaded place until it dries.

Recipe for *aqrāṣ* (incense tablets)[64]

Take 6 *dirhams* (18 grams/approx. ¾ ounce) Javanese aloeswood (*ʿūd Qāqullī*), 3 *dirhams* Ceylon sandalwood (*ṣandal Maqāṣīrī*), 1 *mithqāl* (4½ grams) kneaded ambergris (*ʿanbar maʿjūn*),[65] ½ *mithqāl* raw ambergris (*ʿanbar khām*), and ¼ *mithqāl* musk. Also take ¼ *dirham* (approx. 1 gram) dried peel of lemon; and a similar amount of each: sour orange peel, cloves, and mace (*basbāsa*); and ½ *dirham* (1½ grams) saffron. Pound all these ingredients, but not too finely.

Take 6 *dirhams* (18 grams) sugar candy (*sukkar nabāt*), add to it 10 *dirhams* (1 ounce) refined white sugar (*sukkar abyaḍ mukarrar*), and boil them down into sugar syrup (*jullāb*) by adding Nuṣaybīnī rosewater.[66] Let the syrup boil until it becomes very thick. Mix in it the [above-mentioned] ingredients, along with ¼ *dirham* (approx. 1 gram) civet (*zabād*).

Spread the syrup on a large flat plate (*ṭabaq*) to let it cool. Then blend it with a *mifrāk*,[67] so that the particles stick to each other. Take fleawort seeds (*bazr qaṭṭūna*),[68] and soak them in rosewater. When they are done soaking, extract their mucilage (*luʿāb*) by squeezing it out through a piece of cloth. Knead the *ḥawāʾij* (i.e., spice-sugar mix prepared) with it.

Form the mix into tablets (*aqrāṣ*), and spread them on the back of a sieve to dry. Be careful when making the syrup; do not let it become thin; it must have the consistency of syrup prepared for chewy candy (*ʿaqīd*) or even thicker.[69]

---

64 This recipe only appears in DK, appendix 73; and *Wuṣla* ii 486, which I used here to slightly amend the edited text.

65 See n. 10 above.

66 See n. 28 above.

67 It is a simple wooden blender, see glossary 9. It must have been a traditional kitchen tool exclusive to Egypt. The corresponding Aleppan *Wuṣla* recipe uses a *fihr*, which is a round stone that fits into the hand, usually used for crushing spices and the like.

68 Rather than *bazr quṭn* 'cottonseeds' in the edited text. I believe that *bazr qaṭṭūna* (as it occurs in *Wuṣla*) is the intended item, because it produces jelly-like mucilage (*luʿāb*) when soaked in water.

69 See, for instance, recipe 348 above.

FIGURE 48 *Ancient Egyptian* mifrāk *(hand mixer/blender), Graeco-Roman Period (Bibliotheca Alexandrina Antiquities Museum, photo by Christoph Gerigk).*

Recipe for *aqrāṣ* (incense tablets)[70]

Take peels of citron (*utrujj*), sour orange (*nāranj*), and Damascus citron (*kabbād*), as well as apple peel and myrtle leaves [all dried]. Pound them all very well, sift them, and take one *dirham* (3 grams of each).

Also, take aloeswood of Khmer (*ʿūd Qamārī*) and Ceylon sandalwood (*ṣandal Maqāṣīrī*), 2 *mithqāls* (9 grams) of each; and 1 *mithqāl* each of the best ladanum resin (*lādhan ʿanbarī*), mastic, saffron threads, camphor, the down of unripe quince (*zaghab safarjal*), and costus. Also take 2 *mithqāls* ambergris.

Take sugar candy (*sukkar nabāt*), and make it into thick syrup with rosewater, distilled water of Egyptian willow bark (*māʾ khilāf*),[71] and distilled water of cloves (*māʾ qaranful*). Make the syrup very thick as we mentioned earlier [in the recipes above], mix it with the rest of the ingredients. Form it into tablets, spread them on [the back of] a sieve, and use [them as incense].

---

70 This recipe only appears in DK, appendix 74; and *Zahr* version, fol. 38r–v. This recipe combines two different preparations; they were mistakenly combined into one by the copyists of both versions. Here I amended and completed the recipe based on the corresponding copy in *Wuṣla* ii 486–7. The second part deals with a preparation for *dharīra* 'scented powder,' which I provide in the following segment.

71 See n. 61 above.

[Recipe for *dharīra* (scented powder)[72]]

Take equal parts of spikenard, betel leaves, cloves, nutmeg, bay leaves, cardamom, mace, rosebuds—hypanthia removed, sweet and bitter costus, and usnea (*shaybat ʿajūz*). Pound them all very well and sift them to powder.

Soak fleawort seeds (*bazr qaṭṭūna*) in rosewater,[73] and then extract its mucilage [*luʿāb*] by pressing it through a piece of cloth. Knead the ingredients with it, form the mix into large discs, and stick them onto [the inner wall of] a new earthenware pot.

Now, take sugar candy (*sukkar nabāt*), aloeswood of Khmer (*ʿūd Qamārī*), sandalwood, and *ẓufr* (onycha), which have been boiled and cleaned of any solid fatty substances. Also, take the best ladanum resin (*lādhan ʿanbarī*), sweet costus, bitter costus, sour orange peel, dried myrtle leaves snipped into small pieces with scissors, mastic, and saffron threads. Crush them all, and put them in the bottom of another pot. Use equal parts of these ingredients. Turn the pot with the discs stuck in it over this pot. It should fit on it completely. Seal them both with mud so that neither scent nor smoke escapes from them.

Put the pot with the incense ingredients on a very low fire to let it burn and produce smoke for a whole night or a whole day. Be careful not to let the fire become strong, lest it should burn the incense ingredients. It should be very low to allow it to produce [aromatic] smoke.

When all the incense ingredients are burnt out, open the pot, take out the discs, and let them dry in a shaded place. Then, crush them thoroughly, add the ambergris, as well as crushed aloeswood and a bit of musk. Add also a bit of civet (*zabād*), or use as much as you want.

(673) Recipe for *nidd murakkab* (scenting pastilles coated with ambergris), used as incense. Wonderful[74]

Use ¼ *ūqiyya* (7½ grams/½ tablespoon) Indian aloeswood (*ʿūd Hindī*), ¼ *mithqāl* (1 gram) musk-scented pastilles (*sukk misk*),[75] **(159r)** ½ *mithqāl* saffron, 1 *mithqāl* oily ambergris (*ʿanbar dasim*), ½ *mithqāl* musk, ¼ *mithqāl*

---

72 This is the second half of DK recipe, appendix 74, see n. 70 above. Here I amended and completed the recipe using *Wuṣla* ii 491–2, where the recipe is called *dharīra* 'scented powder,' see chapter 22 below, for similar recipes.

73 See n. 68 above.

74 Here I used *Wuṣla* ii 488–9 to amend the edited text. *Murakkab* could simply mean 'compound,' or judging from the last detail in the recipe, it may mean 'coated with.'

75 See glossary 8 for more on *sukk*.

strongly scented camphor (*kāfūr rayyāḥī*),[76] and ¼ *mithqāl* of the best ladanum resin (*lādhan*).

Crush all the ingredients [separately]. Knead them with the juice of Levantine apples (*tuffāḥ Shāmī*), and juices of fresh wild thyme (*nammām*) and marjoram (*marzanjūsh*). The amount of apple juice should be double the amount of that of wild thyme. Knead the mix into a stiff dough. However, do not knead ambergris, musk, and camphor with the rest [at this point]. Set the mix aside for a day and a night to allow the flavors to blend (*yukhammar*) [and set it aside].

Pinch the ambergris into small pieces, heat up a *ṭabaq* (large flat pan) [on the fire], and when the ambergris melts, add to it fair-colored honey,[77] which has been skimmed of its froth.[78] Also, add ladanum to the ambergris. When they melt and mix well, remove the pan and add the ingredients (*ḥawāʾij*) [that were set aside]. Knead the mix hard and well, and then put it on a stone slab (*ṣallāya*),[79] which has been wiped with rosewater. Finely crush the dough with a stone (*fihr*) coated with rosewater[80] until it all blends well.

Flatten the dough on a large flat tile (*bilāṭa*), and cut it into small pieces (*shawābīr*), in any shape you like.[81] Put the pieces [in one layer] on a sieve, and set it aside in a ventilated place, clear of dust, for 15 days [and use it as incense].

If you wish to coat the pieces with ambergris, then take ambergris, melt it in a large flat pan (*ṭabaq*) on a low fire, and dip the [dried] pieces in it. Turn the pieces over [to coat both sides], and return them to the sieve, (**159v**) and set them aside to dry [and use as coated incense, *bakhūr murakkab*].

Recipe for *nidd* (scenting pastilles)[82]

Take 1 *ūqiyya* (1 ounce) Indian aloeswood (*ʿūd Hindī*) or any other kind, ⅓ *ūqiyya* (10 grams) sea costus (*qusṭ baḥrī*),[83] ¼ *ūqiyya* (7½ grams) sandalwood, and 1 *dirham* (3 grams) *aẓfār* (sg. *ẓufr*, onycha). Pound them all.

---

76 This also occurs as *kāfūr Rabāḥī*, an excellent camphor, said to have been named after an Indian king known by the name Rabāḥ.

77 *ʿAsal abyaḍ* (lit., 'white honey').

78 This is done by boiling the honey to cleanse it of all impurities.

79 A wide stone slab that was used with a large stone, called *fihr*; it was used mainly to crush spices and aromatics.

80 A *fihr* is a stone large enough to fill the hand.

81 This clearly indicates that *shawābīr* (lit., 'triangles') may designate any flattish small pieces.

82 This recipe only appears in DK, appendix 78.

83 It is white, light in weight, and strongly fragrant.

Take also ⅓ *ūqiyya* musk, 2 *dirham*s saffron, ⅓ *dirham* camphor, and 1 *dirham* mastic. Combine all the ingredients, pound them coarsely with a stone pestle (*mihrās*), and sift them in a sieve with relatively large holes (*munkhul wāsiʿ*).

Now, take coarsely crushed almonds,[84] and [fresh] peels of citron and apples, pound them all, and squeeze out their juice. Pour on them a bit of apple juice, rosewater, and other similar waters. [Add enough of it to the above-mentioned ingredients] so that the mix looks like dough.

Pound this dough thoroughly, press and knead it with your fingers (*yughmaz*) so that the ingredients mix well and their aromas blend with each other. [Roll it out and cut it into small pieces, and] spread them [on a sieve] in the shade until they dry. Store them in a thoroughly clean vessel.

Recipe for *nidd* (scenting pastilles), even better than the above[85]

[Take] 1 *ūqiyya* (1 ounce) Indian aloeswood (*ʿūd Hindī*), ⅓ *ūqiyya* (10 grams) sea costus (*qusṭ baḥrī*),[86] 1 *dirham* (3 grams) sandalwood, and 1 *dirham azfār* (sg. *ẓufr*, onycha), ½ *ūqiyya* (15 grams) musk, ½ *mithqāl* (approx. 2 grams) camphor, 1 *dirham* (3 grams) mastic, 2 *dirham*s ladanum resin (*lādhan*), and 2 *dirhams* resin of storax tree (*mayʿat lubnā*), which is *iṣṭarak*.[87]

Combine all the ingredients,[88] and pour on them a bit of concentrated grape juice (*ʿaqīd al-ʿinab*) scented with an equal amount of rosewater. Combine and knead them all until they have the consistency of dough.

If you like, press it into a mold (*qālab*) so that it takes on the decorative impressions, and then [take it out and] dry it in a shaded place and store it away. Otherwise, you can just form it into small balls (*banādiq*), if you prefer.

You can also [play tricks with it:] Fill your mouth with plain water, and when you spritz it at friends around you, it will come out rosewater. [Here is how to do it:] Moisten 1 large *ūqiyya* (7 ounces)[89] of it [i.e., the above *nidd* mix]

---

84 Here I replaced the edited word موز 'banana' with لوز 'almond,' which can indeed be coarsely crushed (*yujrash*).

85 This recipe only appears in DK, appendix 79.

86 See n. 83 above.

87 Here I amended the edited text based on what we know of the listed ingredients. Thus, I read, ميعة وبان وهو الاصطرك as ميعة لبنى وهو الاصطرك because *mayʿa* is resin of *lubnā* tree 'storax,' and *iṣṭarak* is another name for this tree. *Bān*, on the other hand, is oil extracted from the kernels of seeds of the moringa tree (*Moringa oleifera*).

88 Here I deleted ويعصرماؤه 'and their juice pressed out,' as the combined ingredients are all dry, unless the copy misses a line or two with more instructions, or it is simply a copyist's mistake.

89 This reads أوقية كبيرة. This could be the Levantine *ūqiyya*, known to be larger than the Egyptian and Baghdādī *ūqiyya*.

with 3 *ūqiyyas* (10½ ounces/1⅓ cups) rosewater, 3 lumps of fine musk, and a bit of wheat starch (*nashā'*). [Mix and knead them, and then] form them into small balls (*banādiq*). Let them dry in the shade, and then store them, and use as needed.

Take one of these balls, put it under your tongue, fill your mouth with plain water, and squirt it [at friends around you]. It will come out as fragrant pure rosewater, the best.

Besides, if you finely crush tutty (*tūtyā*) on a large stone slab (*ṣallāya*),[90] with a bit of musk [and combine it with the above *nidd* mix], nothing will compare to it as a deodorant (*dawā' al-ʿaraq*).

Recipe for [*ʿanbarī*], magnificently aromatic and aphrodisiac[91]

Grate and crush (*yuḥakk*) aloeswood with rosewater on an ironstone (*ḥajar ṣandal*)[92] until you have a good amount of it. Squeeze it out through a piece of cloth until nothing remains of the rosewater in it. Put it in a porcelain bowl (*zibdiyya*).

Grate and crush Ceylon sandalwood (*ṣandal maqāṣīrī*), as you did with aloeswood until you have a similar amount. Combine them both with rosewater and spread them in a vessel in a thin layer. Infuse them with the smoke of aloeswood several times, then smoke them with ambergris several times. Between each two or three times of incensing, sprinkle the mix with rosewater, and then knead it again, spread it as was done earlier, and incense it again.

When the mix takes on enough of the smoke, add to it a bit of civet (*zabād*), and a bit of musk. Let it dry in the vessel. Next, add to it *kathīrā'* (gum of the taraganth tree) dissolved in rosewater, and knead them into paste. Make *ʿanbarī* with it.[93]

Whenever the pieces are no longer fragrant, sprinkle them with rosewater and infuse them with aromatic smokes. It is a great scent indeed.

---

90 For more on *tūtyā*, see n. 23 above. A *ṣallāya* is a wide stone slab used with a large stone, called *fihr*, mainly used to crush spices and aromatics.

91 This recipe only appears in DK, appendix 68; and *Wuṣla* ii 481–2, which I used here to slightly amend the edited text. The aromatic preparation in this recipe is clearly a type of *ʿanbarī*, as the recipe itself refers to it toward the end. In *Wuṣla*, it is called *ʿanbarīnā*; both designate solid pieces of perfume compounds, shaped artistically and worn as ornaments, such as necklaces, bracelets, and girdles.

92 It is also called *khumāhān*, *ḥajar ḥadīdī* 'ironstone,' and *ṣandal ḥadīdī* 'iron sandal.' It is very hard reddish stone.

93 See note 91 above.

CHAPTER 22

في الذرائر الملوكية وغيرها

Top Quality Perfumed Powders (*dharāʾir mulūkiyya*) and Other Preparations[1]

(674) Recipe for *dharīra* (scented powder)[2]

Take 1 *ūqiyya* (1 ounce) spikenard, pound it finely and sift it. Also, pound [and sift] cloves and mace, 2 *dirhams* (6 grams/1 teaspoon) of each. Mix them with rosewater into paste, spread it in a china bowl (*zibdiyya ṣīnī*), and infuse it three times with smoke of Yemeni musk (*misk Yemenī*), seven times with aloeswood, and five times with ambergris. Every time you incense the paste twice or thrice, turn it over, knead it, sprinkle it with rosewater [and resume]. The more you incense the paste the more aromatic it gets.

When the time comes to divide it into discs, mix ¼ *dirham* (¾ gram/⅛ teaspoon) civet (*zabād*) with it. Divide it into discs, and put them on the back of a sieve to dry in a shaded place. Next, crush them and mix the powder with ambergris—this should be used crushed—and aloeswood, 5 *dirhams* (15 grams/2½ teaspoons) of each. Store it in a vessel and use it. It is very good.

(675) Recipe for *dharīra bārida* (scented powder with cold properties), for summertime[3]

Take Ceylon sandalwood (*ṣandal Maqāṣīrī*), and grate it with rosewater on a stone (*ḥajar*),[4] and then put it in a piece of cloth and squeeze out all the moisture. Spread it in a ceramic bowl (*zibdiyya*), and infuse it with the smoke of aloeswood and ambergris. Next, mix with it 1 *mithqāl* (4½ grams) of musk and

---

1 Besides the perfumed powders, the chapter includes 31 preparations for scented distilled water.

2 I slightly amended the edited text using the same recipe given in *Wuṣla* ii 489. *Wuṣla* also has corresponding copies of *Kanz's* recipes 675–8. In this chapter, recipes 674–8 deal with perfumed and incensed powders used topically. After taking a bath and drying the body, such scented powders were sprinkled all over the body.

3 For details on the Galenic theory of the properties, see glossary 11, s.v. *mizāj*.

4 Based on DK recipe, appendix 68, above p. 420, the stone (*ḥajar*) should be ironstone (*ḥajar ḥadīdī*), also called *khumāhān*, and *ṣandal ḥadīdī* 'iron-sandal.' It is a very hard reddish stone.

 DOI 10.1163/9789004349919_025

ambergris, and ¼ *dirham* (¾ gram/⅛ teaspoon) civet (*zabād*), and [then dry, and crush it, and] use it.

(676) Recipe for *dharīra suʿdiyya* (scented powder with cyperus)[5]

Take one part cyperus (*suʿd*), one part aloeswood of Khmer (*ʿūd Qamārī*), and one part Ceylon sandalwood (*ṣandal Maqāṣīrī*). Pound them, sift them, and knead them with rosewater. (**160r**) After that, dry the mix in a shaded place. When it is dry, do the same thing with it the following day. Repeat this three times.

When it is dry, pound it, and for each 10 *dirhams* (30 grams) of it, mix in 1 *dānaq* (½ gram) camphor and 1 *dānaq* musk [all crushed].

(677) Recipe for *dharīra wardiyya* (scented powder with rosebuds)[6]

Take 15 *dirhams* (1½ ounces) rosebuds, 1 *mithqāl* (4½ grams) aloeswood of Khmer (*ʿūd Qamārī*), 3 *dirhams* (9 grams) Ceylon sandalwood (*ṣandal Maqāṣīrī*), and 1 *dirham* (3 grams) black cardamom (*qāqulla*).

Pound and sift all the ingredients, knead them with rosewater, and infuse them with the smoke of costus, *ẓufr* (onycha), and sandalwood; repeat this five times. Next, infuse them with the smoke of aloeswood six to seven times. When you finish two or three rounds of incensing, knead the mix and then spread it in the bowl as you did the first time.

After you let it dry, crush it, and use it.

(678) Recipe for *dharīrat utrunj* (scented powder with citron peel)

Take 10 *dirhams* (30 grams) *salīkha* (bark similar to cassia), 1 *mithqāl* (4½ grams) usnea (*ushna*),[7] and 10 *mithqāls* (4½ ounces) citron peel, take only the thin outer layer of the peel.

Pound the ingredients finely with the citron peel until they are all mixed well. Knead them with rosewater, and infuse them with the smoke of costus and aloeswood—seven times with each one. Let the mix dry, finely pound it, and use it.

---

5 Here I amended the text using the copy of *Wuṣla* ii 490.

6 Here I amended the text using the copy of *Wuṣla* ii 491.

7 This was also known as *shaybat al-ʿajūz* 'old man's hair.' Cf. the English, 'old man's beard.' See glossary 8.

(679) Recipe for *dharūr al-māʾ ward* (restorative powder with rosewater)[8]

It has amazing properties; it boosts the libido in the elderly (*miḥrāq li-l-mashāʾikh*), invigorates intercourse,[9] and brings joy (*hanāʾ*).

Take 3 *dirhams* (9 grams/1½ teaspoons) white gum of tragacanth tree (*kathīrāʾ bayḍāʾ*) and put it in a clean vessel. Now, take 1½ *ūqiyyas* (3 tablespoons) excellent Levantine rosewater, along with a bit of musk. Add the *kathīrāʾ* to it over three days. Next, let it dry, [pound it] and keep it as *dharūr* (powder compound). (**160v**)

Know that if you take what amounts to the weight of a wheat berry of this *dharūr*, put it under your tongue, drink a small amount of water, and then spray it after keeping it in your mouth for a short while (*suwayʿa laṭīfa*), it will come out smelling like pure, fragrant rosewater.

This powder can be put in a lot of drinks and exquisite pickles, like those of apples, quince, pears, and top-quality colored turnips. It can also be added to boiled dishes (*masālīq*), meatless dishes (*muzawwarāt*), and top-quality dishes (*aṭbikha rafīʿa*), so know this.

(680) Recipe for *dharūr al-ʿanbar* (restorative powder with ambergris)

This is beneficial for pain in the heart (*wajaʿ al-qalb*) and excess in the brain's moist humoral properties (*ruṭūbāt al-damāgh*). It sweetens odors in the mouth and the breath. It is also used in refined drinks, compotes (*naqūʿāt*), and meatless dishes (*muzawwarāt*), which are beneficial for aches and pains. It also has some fantastic properties (*khawāṣ ʿajība*).[10]

Take 3 *dirhams* (9 grams/1½ teaspoons) white gum of tragacanth tree (*kathīrāʾ bayḍāʾ*), and soak it in excellent rosewater. When it dissolves, add to it 1 *dirham* (3 grams) finely crushed *ʿanbar muthallath*.[11] Mix them very well, dry them [in a shaded place], crush them, and store them [and use] as *dharūr*.

---

8 Recipes 679–82, 716–7 all deal with powders to be taken internally and not used as body powders. They are not infused with incense, and they all include white gum of tragacanth tree (*kathīrāʾ bayḍāʾ*), which, besides its medicinal benefits, is also valued for boosting libido in both sexes. Note the consistent difference in their nomenclature in this book: *dharīra* for scented body powder, and *dharūr* for ingested restorative powders.

9 *Asrār* (lit., 'secrets,' 'pleasures'), is used to convey intercourse, see *Lisān al-ʿArab*, s.v. سرر.

10 These must be related to boosting sexual activities. For *muzawwarāt* dishes, see chapter 8 above.

11 This is a combination of three equal parts of ambergris, aloeswood, and musk (al-Nuwayrī, *Nihāyat al-arab* xii 38–9).

(681) Recipe for *dharūr al-zaʿfarān* (restorative powder with saffron)

This gladdens the heart, invigorates coitus (*muqawwī li-l-bāh*), and unblocks any chronic obstructions.[12] It is used with some of the drinks that go with it, and some dishes, (**161r**) such as simple yellow rice with chicken (*aruzz al-dajāj al-aṣfar al-sādhaj*), and some fine pickles. Here is how to make it:

Take 3 *dirhams* (9 grams/1½ teaspoon) white gum of tragacanth tree (*kathīrāʾ bayḍāʾ*). Soak it in the water of the blue Egyptian lotus (*māʾ nanūfar*).[13] When it dissolves, throw in fine-tasting saffron, mix them very well, dry them [in a shaded place], [crush them,] and store them [and use] as *dharūr*.

(682) Recipe for *dharūr al-dār ṣīnī* (restorative powder with cassia)

Know, may God bring you prosperity, that this powder can do wonderful things. Take 1 *raṭl* (2 cups) fresh milk, add to it 4 *ūqiyyas* (4 ounces) sugar, boil it on the fire, and add 5 *dirhams* (15 grams/2½ teaspoons) of this powder. Leave it for one hour and a half,[14] and you will find that it has become as thick as clotted cream (*bīrāf*).[15] It is the best you can have in taste, aroma, and benefits.

If you want to add it to rice dishes or green wheat (*farīk*),[16] and many kinds of fine grilled dishes, it is beneficial and even more effective than monitor lizards (*awrāl*).[17] Add it to some pickles, and it is beneficial in helping the bodily

---

12 Such obstructions, called *sudud*, may result from dense mucilaginous cold humors.

13 A variant of *naylūfar*.

14 In this recipe, time is measured by the system of the equal hour (*sāʿa mustawiya*), also called *sāʿa falakiyya*. In this system, the 24 hours of the day are divided into 15 equal periods (*darajāt*); each period contains 4 minutes. The other system, which was also followed, measures the 24 hours of the day by the unequal hour called *sāʿa muʿwajja*, also known as *sāʿa zamāniyya*, and *sāʿa zawāliyya*. Sunrise marks the beginning of the day, which is 12 hours. Sunset begins the night, which is also 12 hours. The length of the hours varies with the changing seasons.

15 See recipe 507 above.

16 From this point to "some pickles," the edited text is incoherent due to several obscure words; this is quite likely due the original copyist's inability to read some of the words properly, because of bad handwriting or damage to the paper. I tried to make sense of it to the best of my knowledge. The edited text reads:

والنماص الشاوان اللطيفة فإنه ينفع ويؤثر أحسن الاوران العسه على بعض المخللات.

Cf. my version of what it might have been:

وأنماط الشوايا اللطيفة فإنه ينفع ويؤثر أحسن من الاورال والقيه على بعض المخللات.

17 *Sg. waral* (ورل) was valued for its aphrodisiac properties.

humoral properties to blend well (*mumāzij*). It is also used with refined table sauces (*ṣulūṣāt rafīʿa*).[18]

To make it, take 3 *dirhams* (9 grams/1½ teaspoon) white gum of tragacanth tree (*kathīrāʾ bayḍāʾ*), and soak it in liquid, in which nutmeg has been steeped to extract its essence. Keep the gum there for three days, and when it dissolves, (**161v**) add a similar amount of the best rolled bark of Ceylon cinnamon (*qarfa*),[19] which has been finely pounded and sifted through a tightly woven piece of cloth. Mix them very well, and then dry the mix and stow it [and use it] as *dharūr*.

(683) Making incense of aloeswood (*bakhūr al-ʿūd*)[20]

Take pieces of Indian aloeswood (*ʿūd Hindī*), dip them in very thick sugar syrup (*jullāb qawī*), and then roll them in crushed camphor, and put them on a sheet of paper (*kāghad*) [to dry]. If you melt the camphor and dip the aloeswood pieces in it, you do not need to use syrup.

[The following recipes, up to 715, are on distilled waters.][21]

(684) Distilling saffron water (*taṣʿīd māʾ al-zaʿfarān*)

Take the amount of crushed saffron you want. Keep it moistened throughout the night by covering it. Early the following morning, and while it is still moist, put it in a cucurbit (*qarʿa*),[22] and distill it by steam.[23] It will come out white [i.e., colorless], smelling like pure saffron, but it is clear and white, and does not stain or show on the clothes.

---

18 See chapter 16 above, for recipes.

19 In the name of the recipe, it is cassia.

20 This is the only incense recipe in a chapter dedicated to powders and distilled waters.

21 Here begins a long section of recipes on distillations. The source for recipes 684–94 is to be found in ninth-century *al-Taraffuq fi-l-ʿiṭr* by al-Kindī, whose recipes on distillation (80–2, 86, 88, 93, 95, 100, 103–8) correspond with the *Kanz*'s recipes above, albeit with some textual stylistic variations. I used al-Kindī's corresponding versions to amend the edited text wherever needed.

22 It is the boiling flask.

23 (*Tuṣāʿiduhu bi-l-ruṭūba*). The boiling flask is placed in a large pot of boiling water. The flask itself is heated by steam. See glossary 9.2, s.v. *taṣʿīd*.

ثم اغوزه في الوسط وركب الغطا عليها وطينها واجعلها في بنيه مثل عمل
النشادر واوقد عليه بنار لينه نصف يوم حتى تذهب الرطوبه ثم قوي
عليها النار تمام ثلاثه ايام بلياليها ثم اضعها تبرد يوم اخر وافتحها تجد
قد صعد على الوجه جوهرا كانه الخفية البيضا فخذها واعلم انك قد حزت
ملك الدنيا فاخزنها في اناء زجاج واحكم الوصل بكلما تقدر عليه فان
الحكمه بالشد الجيد ليلا يروحن ويفر منك فاعلم ذلك ثم خذ
من الجز الاول طري فاغسله واجعله في قرعه وانبيق الى ثلثها او نصفها بلا زياده
وركب عليها الانبيق الواسع المزراب واحكم وصلها واوقد عليها بنار لينه
مثل حرارة الشمس يطلع الما صافيا

فاعلم يا ولدي ان كانت نارك
شديده طلع الما اصفر مطرب الى الحمره فيكون مفسد
فيكون نارك برشد تنال ما تريد بسرعه بمشية الله وعونه
حتى اعزل الثفل حتى تحتاج اليه ثم خذ من ذلك الما
الابيض عشر دراهم التي منها ثلاثة دراهم ونصف من ذلك النشادر فانه ينحل فيه
ويصير في اشد بياض من اللبن الحليب وهو الذي يقال له لبن العذرى فاجعله في
قدح العقد واحكم وصلها باللطف ثلاثة ايام بلياليها بالين ما تقدر عليه وعلامة
انعقاده ليس يطلع في القدح الفوقاني عرق البته فاعلم انه انعقد ثم ضعه

FIGURE 49 *Distilling apparatus, Add. 25724, fol.36v (The British Library Board).*

(685) Recipe for musk water (*māʾ al-misk*)

Take 1 *dānaq* (½ gram) good musk,[24] and 1 Baghdadi *raṭl* (1 pound) good water of Jūr roses.[25] Mix the musk with rosewater, and set them aside for an hour or two. Put them in the cucurbit and alembic, and distill the water by steam.[26] The resulting musk water will be pure and wonderful.

(686) Recipe for distilling camphor

Take 1 *mithqāl* (4½ grams) fine strongly scented camphor (*kāfūr rayyāḥī*),[27] (**162r**) and add to it ½ [*raṭl*/pound] pure *māʾ ward mukarrar*.[28] Distill them in the cucurbit and alembic by steam.[29] The resulting liquid will be camphor water (*māʾ kāfūr*).

(687) Recipe for distilling clove water (*māʾ al-qaranful*)

Take cloves, as much as you wish; and pour rosewater on them, in an equal amount, by weight, after you bruise the cloves.[30] Keep them in rosewater, covered, overnight. The following morning, press and mash the cloves in this liquid, and distill it in a cucurbit and alembic. The resulting liquid will be good clove water.

(688) Recipe for distilling spikenard water (*māʾ al-sunbul*)

Choose good spikenard [roots] and remove the tufted fibers attached to their tops.[31] Pound them, pour on them an equal amount of fresh water (*māʾ ʿadhb*),

---

24 Al-Kindī's version, recipe 93, specifies *musk Ṣughdī* (مسك صغدي), i.e., from Ṣughd in Khurasan. The merchants of that region bought high-quality musk from Tibet and distributed it to other parts of the world.

25 *Ward Jūrī* (intensely fragrant roses) were used mostly for distillation; they were named after the Persian village of Jūr. See glossary 8, s.v. *ward*. The Baghdadi *raṭl* is a little bit lighter than the Egyptian.

26 See n. 23 above.

27 In al-Kindī's version, recipe 95, the camphor needs to be crushed.

28 This rosewater is produced by steeping rose petals in boiling water and straining the liquid, then repeating the process three times, as described in recipe 368 above.

29 See n. 23 above.

30 Here I read the edited *yuraṣṣ* (يرصّ) 'pack' as *yuraḍḍ* (يرضّ) 'bruise.' Al-Kindī's version, recipe 100, uses ground or whole cloves.

31 Based on what we know of the spikenard plant, I amended the opening sentence in the edited text, which is incoherent due to a couple of obscure words. I read المها آخر أتلامه as المهاديب آخر أكمامه 'their top tufted hairy fibers.' Unfortunately, al-Kindī's corresponding version, recipe 103, does not contain this opening direction. It only says to take cleaned spikenard.

and let them soak in it for a day and a night. Then mash them, strain the liquid, and distill it in a cucurbit and alembic as you did with the clove water [above]. The resulting liquid will be splendid spikenard water.

(689) Distilling aloeswood water (*māʾ al-ʿūd*)

Take 1 *ūqiyya* (1 ounce) pounded Indian aloeswood (*ʿūd Hindī*),[32] 2 *dānaq*s (1 gram) musk, and 3 *raṭl*s (6 cups) pure rosewater. Mix all the ingredients and distill them.

(690) Recipe for distilling sandalwood water (*māʾ al-ṣandal*)

Take 1 *ūqiyya* (1 ounce) good crushed sandalwood, dissolve it in 3 *raṭl*s (6 cups) rosewater, and distill it as you did with the aloeswood.

(691) Distilling red rosewater

You cannot get red rosewater unless you stuff both the cucurbit and the alembic itself well with the rose petals. (**162v**) Put the alembic on the cucurbit, distill them by steam (*fī ruṭūba*),[33] and the condensed water will look red as we described above.[34]

If you want the rosewater to be as red as gazelle's blood, take some pieces of alkanet (*ʿāqir shamʿā*)[35]—make sure it is good and not moldy—soak it in water for an hour, wrap it in a piece of cotton, and stuff it inside the alembic attached to the cucurbit.[36] Distill the liquid in steam as we said earlier, and as

32 Al-Kindī's version, recipe 104, requires that the aloeswood be *ʿūd nayʾ* 'moistened aloeswood.'

33 See n. 23 above.

34 'As we described above' is a clear indication that the recipe is incomplete. Fortunately, al-Kindī's version, recipe 106, provides this opening missing part:

"Take as many petals of red roses as you like, and remove their hypanthia. Use fresh and tender red roses. Spread the petals and set them aside for a short while. Next, stuff the cucurbit up to its neck with them, put the alembic on it, and distill the liquid by steam. Do this if you want your rosewater to be as red as the red roses themselves. When you pour it on someone's [white] clothes, it will dye them red at first, but as the clothes start to dry, the red color gradually fades, and when the clothes are fully dry, the color vanishes altogether, leaving behind white clothes redolent with fragrance of rosewater."

35 Here I amended the edited text based on al-Kindī's version, recipe 106, and replaced *summāq* 'sumac' with *ʿāqir shamʿā*, which al-Kindī's recipe explains as *shinkār*. This ingredient is alkanet, which is a common red-ruby dye, also called *shinjār*, and *rijl al-ḥamām* or *sāq al-ḥamām*.

36 In al-Kindī's recipe, the cotton is stuffed inside the tube (called *aḥlīl* or *bilbula*) attached to the head of the alembic.

the rosewater passes through the cotton and soaks it, it will be colored with it, and it will look red. It will do to the clothes as was done by the first rosewater [earlier prepared].[37] [I.e., it will infuse the clothes with the aroma of rosewater and leave them unstained.]

If you replace the alkanet (*shamʿā*) in the cotton with purple amaranth (*bustān abrūz*),[38] you will get a similar color.

If you put saffron threads in the cotton [when distilling rosewater], the resulting water will be yellow. If you put pounded, fresh leaves of alfalfa (*raṭba*) in the cotton, the resulting water will be green. They will all affect the clothes the same way the red rosewater mentioned [above] does.[39]

(692) Distilling water of dried roses

Take 3 *raṭl*s (3 pounds) of dried petals from red roses, and soak them in an equal amount of water. Set them aside for three days, and then rub them with your hands to release their flavor into the water. Strain them, and distill the resulting liquid by steam, as we said before.[40]

(693) Distilling flowers of dog rose (*nisrīn*) and jasmine (*yāsamīn*)

Remove their hypanthia (*aqmāʿ*) and [distill] them as you [distill] the roses.[41]

(694) Recipe for distilling [rind of] citron (*utrunj*)

Take good red or yellow citron.[42] (**163r**) Slice off the outer layer of the peel, put it in the cucurbit [along with water], and distill it the same way you distill rosewater.

---

37 See n. 34 above.

38 The text here is confused. The word سمقا has no meaning, but might have been a misreading of شمعا 'alkanet,' see n. 35 above. The incoherent phrase سنان ايران in the edited text and سارارون in the other copies must have been a misreading of بستان ابروز 'purple amaranth,' as it occurs in al-Kindī's version.

39 See n. 34 above.

40 See n. 23 above.

41 Al-Kindī's version, recipe 108, gives more details. The flowers are spread out for a short while at first, and then they are stuffed in the cucurbit, enough to fill two-thirds of it. They are distilled by steam for a day and a night, and then poured into glass bottles.

42 *Aḥmar* 'red' is used here to designate orange, for which there was no specific word. This might not be an indication that two kinds of citron are meant, but rather it may refer to two stages of ripeness. Cf. al-Kindī's version, recipe 80, where the peel called for is *aṣfar* (yellow, ripe) or *akhḍar* (green, not fully mature).

The same is done with large **apples,**[43] which are first chopped into small pieces, after they are cored and their seeds are removed.

As for **myrtle** (*ās*), strip the green, fresh leaves from the stems,[44] pound them while sprinkling them with a bit of the liquid you use to distill them with.

Do the same thing if you want to distill **marjoram** (*marzanjūsh*),[45] **wild thyme** (*nammām*),[46] **violet** (*banafsaj*), **iris** (*sawsan*), and **narcissus** (*narjis*).

(695) Recipe for distilling water of fresh roses[47]

Take fresh red roses, strip off the petals (*yufarraṭ*) and remove the hypanthia (*aqmāʿ*). Pour boiling water on the petals and set them aside, thus submerged, one day and one night.

Stuff two-thirds of the cucurbit well with the petals, and for each *raṭl* (pound) of roses used, pour 3 *ūqiyyas* (¼ cup) of the liquid in which the hypanthia have been soaked. It is very good; and it is even better if you add camphor to it.

(696) Another recipe [for distilling fresh roses]

Take 1 *raṭl* (1 pound) of fresh rose petals from which the hypanthia have been removed. Submerge them in a tub (*ijjāna*) containing ½ *raṭl* (1 cup) water with 2 *dānaqs* (1 gram) musk and a lump of camphor (*ḥabbat kāfūr*). Whip them together very well, and stuff them in the cucurbit, set it aside overnight, without applying any heat, to allow the essences to blend (*yakhtamir*).

Light the fire under it and distill the liquid. However, do not overdo it with the distilling. Take the cucurbit off the heat while there is still some liquid in it. It is marvelous.

(697) Recipe for another kind of rosewater, which is blue (*azraq*)[48] **(163v)**

Take 1 Baghdadi *raṭl* (approx. 1 pound) of red rose petals,[49] and stuff them in a cucurbit. Also take 100 *dirhams* (10½ ounces) recently dried deep blue violets (*banafsaj shadīd al-zurqa*) that have been kept in the sun just enough to

---

43 In al-Kindī's corresponding recipe 81, Levantine apples are specified.

44 In al-Kindī's corresponding recipe 82, the fresh and tender tips of the myrtle branches are stripped.

45 In al-Kindī's recipe 82, *marmāḥūz* (*Origanum maru*) is mentioned instead.

46 Al-Kindī, recipe 82, also mentions gillyflower (*khīrī*).

47 Here begins a series of recipes (695–715) that are almost identical with those in *Wuṣla* ii 728–37. Four of them (695, 702, 706, 707) are also found in al-Tamīmī, *Ṭīb al-ʿarūs* (recipes 129, 124, 140, 146). I used the duplicate versions to amend the edited text wherever needed.

48 I amended the edited text based on *Wuṣla* ii 729.

49 The Baghdadi *raṭl* is a little bit lighter than the Egyptian one.

preserve their color. Sprinkle them with rosewater to moisten them, put them in the distilling apparatus, and distill them.

The distilled water will look as blue as indigo (*nīl*), but it will not stain clothes when it is sprinkled on them. Do not overdo it with the distilling, [stop while there is still liquid in the cucurbit], just take the best part of it.

(698) Recipe for distilling red rosewater[50]

Take [only the petals of] red and white roses, and stuff them in the cucurbit. Put 4 *ūqiyya*s (4 ounces) of petals of intensely red roses and 2 *dirham*s (6 grams) of the flowers called *bustān abrawīz* (amaranth)—either fresh or dried—in the alembic.

The distilled water will look like distilled sapanwood (*baqqam*),[51] and those who see it will be too scared to use it on their clothes. In fact, it does not spoil the clothes or leave any stains on them.

(699) Another recipe for [red rosewater]

Stuff the alembic with rose petals. Also add fresh petals from poppy anemones (*shaqāʾiq al-Nuʿmān*), for they will make it look red. The resulting color will be a beautiful red that does not stain white clothes when it is sprinkled on them.

(700) Recipe for another kind of rosewater [yellow]

To make yellow rosewater (*māʾ ward aṣfar*) which does not stain white clothes: Along with the roses you stuff in the alembic, add saffron threads, about 2 *dānaq*s (1 gram). When it is distilled, the rosewater will look yellow.

(701) Recipe (164r) for distilling rosewater from dried roses (*ward yābis*)

Use soaked (*murabbā*) good dried red roses; take 1 *raṭl* (1 pound) of the roses, discard their hypanthia, and soak them in rosewater of Nuṣaybīn.[52] Put them in green-glazed wide-mouthed jars (*barānī*, sg. *barniyya*), and keep their tops covered for two days and two nights.

Next, pour on them fresh water (*māʾ ʿadhb*), four times their weight. Crush 1 *mithqāl* (4½ grams) camphor, 3 *dirham*s (9 grams) cloves, and 2 *qīrāṭ*s (½ gram) musk. Add them to the rose petal mix and whip them all very well. Blend this mix with rosewater, stuff it into the cucurbit, and distill it through the alembic.

---

50 I slightly amended the edited text here based on *Wuṣla* ii 729–30.

51 Red dye is obtained from it.

52 Nuṣaybīn was a city in upper Mesopotamia, now in the Turkish province of Mardin. It was renowned for its orchards and gardens. Roses named after it are pinkish in hue.

To the remaining dregs (*thufl*), add water, about 3 *raṭls* (3 pints), and distill it again. The resulting liquid will be the second batch of rosewater (*māʾ ward thānī*), which will be comparable to the first batch (*al-awwal*) in quality.

(702) Recipe for distilling saffron

It is amazing how wonderfully aromatic this is: Take 2 *ūqiyyas* (2 ounces) saffron threads, put them in a green-glazed wide-mouthed jar (*barniyya*), pour rosewater on them, cover the top, and set the jar aside for a day and a night.

Crush 1 *mithqāl* (4½ grams) [dried petals of] carnation flowers (*zahr al-qaranful*), and 1 *mithqāl* strongly scented camphor (*kāfūr rayyāḥī*). Blend these with the saffron [liquid], and whip them very well.

Distill the mix in a cucurbit and alembic by water [-steam] as is usually done with rosewater.[53] It will come out as wonderfully aromatic water. To the remaining dregs, add plain water (*māʾ qurāḥ*), and distill a second batch from it, but it will be inferior to the first batch.

(703) Recipe for distilling musk with rosewater

Take 1 *dānaq* (½ gram) sweet-smelling musk (*misk adhfar*), and 1 Baghdadi *raṭl* (approx. 1 pint) good rosewater of Nuṣaybīn.[54] **(164v)** Crush the musk, whip it with the rosewater, and set it aside for an hour. Next, pour it into the cucurbit, set the alembic on it, and distill it with steam. It will become musk water of unsurpassed quality.

[These are the basic amounts used,] those who want more may increase the amounts, and those who want less may decrease them. After you are done distilling this, pour into the cucurbit rosewater [by itself], and it will also become musk water, but it will be inferior to the first one.

(704) Recipe for distilling water of Javanese aloeswood (*ʿūd Qāqullī*)

Take Javanese aloeswood, pound it or crush it, and soak it in a similar amount of rosewater in a wide-mouthed glass jar (*barniyya*). Leave it there for two days and two nights, [with a covering on it]. After that, open the jar, take the rosewater [with the aloeswood] out and put it all in a cucurbit, along with ¼ *mithqāl* (approx. 1 gram) musk, and ¼ *mithqāl* camphor. Add more rosewater to it, and distill it on very low heat.

---

53 See n. 23 above.

54 See n. 52 above.

(705) Recipe for distilling Ceylon sandalwood (*ṣandal maqāṣīrī*)

Take ¼ *raṭl* (4 ounces) Ceylon sandalwood, crush it in a quern (*raḥāʾ*), and soak it in an equal amount of rosewater in a green-glazed wide-mouthed jar (*barniyya*). Leave it there for two days and two nights, [with a covering on it].

Open the jar, take out the sandalwood liquid and put it all in a cucurbit, along with ¼ *mithqāl* (approx. 1 gram) musk, and a similar amount of camphor. Set the alembic on it and distill the liquid on very low heat.

If you add to [this distilled water] half its amount of distilled saffron water and another half of distilled clove water (*māʾ al-qaranful*), its aroma will be splendid.

(706) Recipe for distilling water of Indian spikenard (*sunbul ʿaṣāfīrī*)

Take red Indian spikenard, remove all the roots and leaves,[55] (**165r**) pound it, and knead it with rosewater and water of wild thyme (*nammām*). Set it aside for the night to let the flavors blend. Early in the morning, stir it and whip it with rosewater; for each 2 *ūqiyya*s (2 ounces) of spikenard use 1 *mann* (2 pounds) rosewater.

Stuff the mix in a cucurbit, set the alembic on it, and distill the liquid on very low heat. Do not rush it. To the remaining dregs, add plain water and distill it again. The resulting liquid can be used to season food (*li-l-ḥawāʾij*) and for washing purposes (*ghasūlāt*).

(707) Recipe for distilling carnation water (*māʾ al-qaranful*)[56]

Take [the petals of] carnations (*qaranful zahr*). Use 2 *ūqiyya*s (2 ounces) for each cucurbit. Steep them in 1½ *raṭl*s (3 cups) rosewater, and set it aside for two days and two nights. Put the carnations with the rosewater in the cucurbit, set the alembic on it, and distill it on very low heat until the liquid evaporates.

If you want it to be more aromatic, add 1 *ūqiyya* (1 ounce) rose petals to the steeped carnation and rosewater. In addition, crush 1 *qīrāṭ* (¼ gram) musk, and whip it into the mix and distill it. It will be aromatic and have cooling effects.

[When you are done distilling,] take the carnation out of the cucurbit, rinse it in cold water, dry it, and store it. It can be used in cooking, or it can be added to handwashing compounds (*ushnān*), and other things.

---

55 These roots would be the threadlike minor roots entangled and wound around the spikenard rhizomes. As al-Nuwayrī, *Nihāyat al-arab* xii 24, explains, when bared this way, they are called *musallal* (lit., 'stripped').

56 This is described as plain (*sādhaj*) in *Wuṣla* ii 734–5, and al-Tamīmī, recipe 145. I amended the edited text slightly based on al-Tamīmī.

(708) Recipe for distilling the water of sour orange blossoms (*mā᾿ zahr al-nāranj*)

Stuff the blossoms in the cucurbit [along with water], set the alembics (*anābīq*) on it,[57] distill the water on very low heat, and keep it in a glass vessel (*inā᾿ zujāj*).[58]

Loosely roll together some woolen threads to make a cord, [lower the cord into the bottle until it touches the top of the distilled orange blossom water], and secure its end at the top of the bottle (*ra᾿s al-qinnīna*) by crushing some ceruse (*isfīdāj*) and sticking it to the bottle.[59] Some oil will accumulate on the surface of these distilled flowers, (165v) and the woolen thread will pick it up. [It will eventually be gathered separately as oil of sour orange blossoms]. Meanwhile keep the distilled water exposed to the sun for two or three weeks.

(709) Recipe for distilling basil (*rayḥān*) and common cucumbers (*khiyār*), to be used in bathrooms

The bathrooms are sprinkled with it when cucumber and basil are not in season. Very nice.

Take fresh basil, remove the stems and sprinkle it with rosewater. Chop the cucumbers into small pieces. Stuff them both in a cucurbit, [add water or rosewater] and distill them on very low heat, as is done to distill rosewater. Store it in bottles.

(710) Recipe for distilling myrtle (*ās*)

This is used in making potpourris (*lakhālikh*),[60] and hair dyes (*khiḍāb al-shaʿr*), it also promotes hair growth and prevents it from falling out while combing it.

Take the fresh tips of myrtle branches, strip the leaves from the stems, pound them, and sprinkle them with rosewater. Pour hot water on them; use 2 *raṭl*s (2 pounds) of it for each *raṭl* of myrtle. Set it aside overnight, then put it in the cucurbit, and distill it on very low heat. Set the distilled water in a sunny place for two weeks, after that it is good for the purposes we mentioned above.

(711) Recipe for distilling cloves (*qaranful*)

Take as many cloves as you like, pick them over, discard any small twigs (*ʿīdān*), and soak them in rosewater for a day and a night. Distill them through an

---

57 The recipe seems to be describing a distilling apparatus with several alembics attached to the cucurbit.

58 The following paragraph calls it a *qinnīna* 'bottle.'

59 *Isfīdāj* has a sticky, glue-like property. See glossary 8.

60 Sg. *lakhlakha*, see glossary 11.

alembic on very low heat. The remaining dregs are used in cooking [as a spice] and in handwashing compounds (*ushnān*).

(712) Recipe for distilling Ceylon cinnamon water (*māʾ al-qarfa*)
Take 1 *raṭl* (1 pound) excellent Ceylon cinnamon, pound it, sift it, and then pour 3 *raṭl*s hot water on it. (**166r**) Steep the cinnamon in this water for three days. After that, mash and press it very well by hand (*yumras*), and put it in the cucurbit, [add water,] and distill it. If the liquid added is half water and half rosewater, it will be even more aromatic.

(713) Recipe for distilling water of wild thyme (*nammām*)
Strip the fresh leaves of wild thyme stems, also strip their tender tops. Put them on platters (*jāmāt*), sprinkle them with rosewater, and sprinkle on them pounded aloeswood, Ceylon sandalwood (*ṣandal maqāṣīrī*), and a lump of musk. Cover all of it with peels of apple and citron. Set them aside, covered, for a day and a night.

Put the wild thyme with the added *dharīra* [i.e., the pounded aloeswood, sandalwood, and musk),[61] and the peels in the cucurbit. Pour on them rosewater that has been whipped with ¼ *mithqāl* (approx. 1 gram) camphor and a similar amount of crushed cloves. Distill it on very low heat, do not rush it with higher heat.

[Distill what remains in the cucurbit again] by adding plain water and rosewater.

(714) Recipe for distilling marjoram (*marzanjūsh*)
This is done exactly like the wild thyme [recipe above], except that camphor should be replaced with musk.

(715) Recipe for distilling citron peel (*qushūr al-utrunj*)
Take fresh and tender (*ghaḍḍ*) citron peels, rub them with rosewater and sprinkle them with aloeswood (*ʿūd*) and Ceylon sandalwood (*ṣandal Maqāṣīrī*). [These two ingredients] must be pounded first, sifted, kneaded with rosewater, infused with the smoke of aloeswood and ambergris, enhanced with musk and a bit of civet (*zabād*), and then dried and crushed. (**166v**) Sprinkle them on the citron peels.

61 *Dharīra* is perfumed powder, here it is used loosely to designate the pounded aromatic ingredients. See recipes at the beginning of this chapter.

Set them aside covered for a day and a night to let the flavors blend and mellow (*yukhammar*). Next, add leaves of wild thyme (*nammām*) and set the mix aside again to let the flavors mellow.

Put the mix in the cucurbit, and pour equal amounts of water and rosewater on it. Also add ½ *qīrāṭ* (⅛ gram) camphor, and ½ *mithqāl* (approx. 2 grams) saffron water (*mā' zafarānı*), and then distill it.

Recipe for wonderful water, fit for kings[62]
Take blossoms of sour orange (*zahr*), lilies (*zanbaq*),[63] dog rose (*nisrīn*), and *Nuṣaybīnī* and *ʿĀṣimī* roses.[64] Distill them, and put the distilled water in a vessel and seal it with musk. It is very aromatic.

[The chapter ends with two more recipes on restorative powders (*dharūr*).]

(716) Recipe for *dharūr qaranfulī* (restorative powder with cloves)
This is beneficial for nausea and gastric winds, and it improves digestion. It is good for expelling bad excretions (*faḍalāt radīʾa*), and preventing intestinal worms (*dūd*) and the excessive accumulation of bodily fat and flesh (*rabāl*). Its properties are low in density.[65]

Take 3 *dirhams* (9 grams) white gum of tragacanth tree (*kathīrā' bayḍā'*), and soak it for several days in water that has been infused with clove essence. When the gum dissolves, add to it 1 *dirham* finely crushed fruit of Syrian ash (*lisān ʿuṣfūr*). Mix the ingredients well, [let them dry, crush them] and store the mix, and use as *dharūr* [as follows]:

It can be added to *sawābī*,[66] fine pickles, and *aqsimā* (digestive drinks). You can make quick *aqsimā* with it: sweeten water with a quarter of its weight of refined sugar (*sukkar*), unrefined sugar (*qand*), or bee honey (*ʿasal*). Add some

62 This recipe only appears in DK, appendix 67; and *Zahr*, fol. 38r.

63 Here I read the incoherent edited word وثيق as وزنبق (lilies), based on context. In *Zahr*, it is written as ونبق, which is irrelevant in context.

64 *Nuṣaybīnī* roses are named after Nuṣaybīn, a city in upper Mesopotamia, now in the Turkish province of Mardin. It was renowned for its orchards and gardens. Roses named after it are pinkish in hue. As for the *ʿĀṣimī* roses, they could be a variety of white mountain roses named after the mountainous province in northeast Syria between Aleppo and Antioch, called al-ʿAwāṣim. The area was praised for the quality of its air, water, and the abundance of its crops (see Yāqūt al-Ḥamawī *Muʿjam al-buldān* 182).

65 *Khawāṣ laṭīfa*, such properties will generate thin blood, which is dominated by yellow bile.

66 Sg. *sūbiya*, a grain-based digestive drink, see chapter 12 above, for recipes.

of the *dharūr* (powder) to it, and set it aside for an hour. It will be the best *aqsimā* ever made.

(717) Recipe for *dharūr al-ṣandal* (restorative powder with sandalwood)

This is beneficial for hemoptysis (*ramī l-damm*),[67] diarrhea caused by too much black bile (*ishāl al-sawdāʾ*), and pain in the liver. It is used particularly in drinks.

Soak 3 *dirhams* (9 grams) white gum of tragacanth tree (*kathīrāʾ bayḍāʾ*) in 1 *ūqiyya* (2 tablespoons) fine-tasting distilled water of Egyptian willow bark (*māʾ khilāf*).[68] When it dissolves, add to it 1½ *dirhams* (4½ grams) finely crushed red sandalwood (*ṣandal aḥmar*). Mix them well, (**167r**) and then dry them, [crush them into powder], and store them as *dharūr* (to be used as a restorative powder).

Now, if you take 1 *raṭl* (2 cups/1 pound) water sweetened with a quarter of its amount of refined or unrefined sugar (*sukkar* or *qand*), and add ½ *dirham* (1½ grams) of this *dharūr* to it, after an hour you will find it has turned it into blood-red *aqsimā* (digestive drink). Add to it *khamīrat al-aqsimā*,[69] and it will be the best made.

---

67 This is also called *nafth al-damm* 'bloody sputum from the chest.'

68 The *khilāf* tree, also called *ṣafṣāf Miṣrī* (*Salix aegyptiaca*) is an Egyptian species of the willow tree.

69 The distilled *aqsimā* base used for making instant digestive drinks. See recipes 404 and 423 above.

CHAPTER 23

في خزن الفواكه وادّخارها إلى غير أوانها

Storing Fresh Fruits and Keeping Them to Use After Their Season

(718) [Storing fresh peaches (*khawkh*)]

If you want to keep peaches fresh when they are out of season, put them in a vessel, pour sweet wine on them, and then cover the vessel, and seal its opening with clay. Place the vessel on a layer of dry grass until the peaches shrink a little, and then take them out and put them in a pitched jar (*ināʾ muzaffat*). They will stay good for a long time.

(719) [Storing fresh grapes (*ʿinab*)][1]

To store grapes and keep them fresh so that whoever eats them will have no doubt, from their taste or their smell, that they are indeed [fresh], take sumac juice (*māʾ al-summāq*) and boil it until one-third of its bulk is gone.[2] Cool it and put it in a glass or earthenware vessel. Put the fresh grapes in it, and seal the opening with gypsum (*jaṣṣ*).

The liquid in which the grapes are kept will turn into vinegar, which is aged and very sour, and has curative properties. The grapes themselves will stay nice and tender, and those who eat them will have no doubt, from their taste or their smell, (**167v**) that they are fresh, as if they have just been picked from the vine.

1 Four recipes in this chapter (719, 721, 722, and 733) are also included in *Zahr*, fols. 29r–30r; recipe 726 is similar to Baghdādī 82; and recipe 740 is found in al-Warrāq's last recipe in chapter 95. In these three sources, the recipes have some minor stylistic differences. I have also found out that the entire segment numbered 723 in the edited text is found in al-Nābulusī, *ʿAlam al-malāḥa* 246–9. For more on this source, see recipe 516, n. 39 above.

2 Sumac juice is obtained by soaking sumac berries in warm water for a while and then draining them.

 | DOI 10.1163/9789004349919_026

(720) [Storing fresh quince (*safarjal*) and apples (*tuffāḥ*)]

To keep [fresh] quince good to eat for a long time, store it in a large earthenware jar full of unfermented grape wine (*ṭilā*).[3] Alternatively, moisten each quince with a fig leaf,[4] and then store them in a cool corner of the house, they will stay good for a long time.

Also, you can wipe the bottoms of the quinces with sweet olive oil, put them in a new earthenware vessel, and fill it with sweet unfermented grape wine, [and seal it].

If you wrap the quince [individually] in fig leaves, coat them with clay, dry them in the sun, and then store them hanging [in the shade], they will stay [good] for a long time.

The same thing can be done with apples.

(721) Recipe for fresh roses when not in season

Take a new shallow, wide bowl (*ṣaḥfa*), fill it with pure clay,[5] and place it in a wide-mouthed earthenware tub (*mājūr*) with water in it. Leave the bowl floating on the surface of the water for an hour; do not add any water to it.

Now, take [dried] Iraqi rosebuds and stick them in the mud. Leave them there for a couple of days, with the large tub covered. On the third day, when you lift off the cover, you will find that the rosebuds have retained their original [fresh state], what was red is now red, and what was green is now green. You may offer them as fresh roses that have just been picked.

Alternatively, take whole dried rosebuds, soak them in rosewater for three days, and they will open [like fresh roses].

(722) Another recipe [for roses]

Take whole [dried] rosebuds; (**168r**) put them in a Persian reed (*qaṣaba Fārisiyya*),[6] in single row. Seal the ends of the reed with wax, tie one end with a string, and dangle it in the hot water tank of the bath (*khizānat al-ḥammām*), and leave it exposed to the steam for a day and a night. When you take the buds out of the reed, you will find them fresh.

---

3 See glossary 1, s.v. *ṭilā*.

4 This would have been done by rubbing the outside of the quince to smear it with the milky juice of the fig leaf. See glossary 8, s.v. *tīn*.

5 *Ṭīn quḥḥ*. Here I amended the word قمح 'wheat,' which is irrelevant in the context, to قح 'pure,' which designates clay free of sand or stones, also called *ṭīn ḥurr*.

6 The reed is thick, long, and sturdy.

[General remarks on storing various kinds of foods][7]

The best places to store fruits, and other foods like grains and pulses (*ḥubūb*), spice seeds and dried herbs (*buzūr*), roasted legumes (*quḍāmā*),[8] and flour (*daqīq*) are cool, clean places that are not close to kitchens, smoke, or unpleasant odors. In addition, do not keep them in the same place quince is stored.[9]

(723) Ways of storing grapes[10]

If you burn fig leaves and branches, and scatter their ashes on the grape bunches, they will stay good for a long while.

If you dip the grape bunches in the juice extracted from purslane (*baqla ḥamqā*ʾ) [and then take them out and hang them], they will stay good. If you dip them in dill juice,[11] and then take them out and hang them, they will stay good for a year.

If you whip the sawdust of teak wood (*ṣāj*)[12] or male cedar (*arz*), or ashes of vine wood (*ramād al-karam*), whichever is available, with water, the way you do with the marshmallow plant (*khiṭmī*),[13] and then dip the grape bunches in it, take them out, and keep them in a clean temperate place, either spread or hanging, they will stay good.

If you make a vessel with cow dung (*akhthāʾ al-baqar*) mixed with a small amount of white clay[14]—make [the vessel] well so that it will not crack, put the grape bunches in it, seal the opening with clay, and put it in a clean, cool place, (**168v**) the grapes will stay good till Nayrūz.[15]

---

7 In the edited text, this paragraph appears as part of recipe 722, but actually deals with a new topic.

8 Mostly chickpeas and fava beans. See glossary 5.

9 *Ḥabb al-safarjal*. Quince should be stored separately because its smell was believed to be harmful to stored foods near it. See, for instance, al-Nābulusī, *ʿAlam al-malāḥa* 246, who says the smell is particularly harmful to the stored fresh and dried grapes.

10 This entire segment is found in al-Nābulusī, *ʿAlam al-malāḥa* 246–9. Here I used it to amend the edited text.

11 Dill juice (ماء الشبث) was usually extracted by pounding dill, and then adding water to it, and extracting the liquid. However, in al-Nābulusī the word occurs as *māʾ al-shabb* (ماء الشب), or 'alum dissolved in water,' which is used in pickles for its preservative qualities.

12 It occurs in al-Nābulusī as ساج; it is written as عاج 'ivory' in the edited text.

13 This mucilaginous plant was whipped with water by hand to generate soapy foam, and used to wash the hair, *Lisān al-ʿArab*, s.v. خطم.

14 A variety of *ṭīn ḥurr* 'pure clay' free of any sand and stones.

15 This is the celebration of the new year. In the Coptic calendar, the Nayrūz festival occurs in the month of Tūt 'September,' which is the beginning of winter; the Persians celebrate it in spring, see al-Maqdisī, *Aḥsan al-taqāsīm* 68. The text refers to the time of the Persian Nayrūz, in which the grapes preserved are summer grapes.

As for the delicious thick-skinned winter grapes, they will stay fresh for a whole year if you take them when they are fully ripe and at their sweetest, which would be in the second half of the month of November,[16] or at its end, depending on how early or late the season the crops matured.[17] The bunches should be cut off the vine with a sharp iron utensil, on a sunny day and when the sun is high enough to dry the dew from the grapes. Do it in the period of the waning moon (*nuqṣān al-shahr*) [of the lunar month].

Discard all the imperfect and rotting grapes.[18] Spread the bottoms of large new earthenware jars (*khawābī*, sg. *khābiya*) with a layer of hay of spelt (*ishqāliyya*) or rye (*sult*),[19] followed by a layer of grapes. Continue layering them like this until the jars are full. Seal the mouths of the jars with clay after you completely cover the contents with clay to prevent them from having any contact with air. Keep the jars in a shaded place, which the sun never reaches, and the grapes will stay fresh for a whole year.

You may also dip the grape bunches in brine, and spread them apart on a bed of hay of lupine beans (*turmus*), fava beans (*fūl*), or barley, use whichever is available. The place they are kept should be cool, [a place] where the sun does not shine, and where fire is not lighted. The grapes will stay good for a long while.

If you put a bunch in a new earthenware jar, tie the top tightly with a piece of leather, and bury it in the ground, then you can take it out any time you want and it will still be perfect. (**169r**) In addition, if you keep the jar in water submerged up to its mouth; or if you cut off the grape bunch along with its branch and leaves, dip the cut place in dissolved bitumen (*qār*), and hang the bunches apart from each other, the grapes will remain fresh all winter long.

If you spread the grape bunches on a bed of hay of fava beans, the rats will not get near them so long as they are kept there—with the bunches set apart, they will stay good for a while.

Grapes remain fresh if you take sumac juice (*māʾ al-summāq*),[20] boil it until one-third of its bulk is gone, and then cool it and put it in a glass or green-glazed

---

16 Nūnabar, as it was called in the Arabized Byzantine calendar. The edited Nūnabrā must be a copyist's misreading or a variant of Nūnabar. The latter occurs in *Zahr*, fol 29v; and al-Ṭaghnarī, *Zahrat al-bustān* 74.

17 Here I amended the irrelevant *takbīr* to *tabkīr* 'coming early,' based on al-Nābulusī's text.

18 The following edited lines are incoherent. I straighten out the sense based on al-Nābulusī's text.

19 Here I amended the incoherent الجلائيين السلّية, based on al-Nābulusī's الاشقالية أو السلت. *Ishqāliyya* is also known as *ʿalas*, and the other name for *sult* is *shaylam*.

20 Sumac juice is obtained by soaking sumac berries in warm water for a while and then straining them.

earthenware vessel. Put in it as many grape bunches, which have been cleaned of any bad grapes among them, as it can take. Store the grapes submerged in the liquid, and they will stay fresh. It is also said that the mouth of the jar should be sealed with gypsum (*jaṣṣ*) and then stored in a place the sun does not reach, away from the heat of fire or smoke.[21]

If you bury the grape bunches in barley, they will not go bad.

If you pick the grape bunch with its stem or many bunches sharing one branch, dip them in unfermented grape wine (*ṭilā*), and hang each from a string, the grapes will not go bad.

If you want to keep the grape bunches on their own vine (*dāliya*) so that you may cut them off whenever you wish, then make linen drawstring bags (*kharā'iṭ*, sg. *kharīṭa*), and insert each bunch in one of these bags so that they stay intact, and then tie the bags around the branch or the stem of the grape bunch. The grapes will stay fresh for a long time. (**169v**) In addition, the bunches may be wrapped with fluffed wool, as this will keep wasps (*zanābīr*) and bees (*naḥl*) away, and the grapes will stay good for a while. In fact, this method is much better than the drawstring bags, and cheaper. It is also said that if this wool is first soaked in garlic water, it will be even more effective in driving away wasps and bees.

(724) Recipe for obtaining fresh roses when not in season

Take Levantine rosebuds [with stems], soak them in fine-tasting water (*mā' ḥulw*) for an hour, and then change the water and soak them again for an hour. Repeat this five times during the day. When night comes, fill an earthenware cup (*kūz*) with water, and put the buds in it through a lattice (*shubbāka*), and leave them under the night sky until the following morning. The buds will open during the night and look even better than the fresh ones.

[Recipe for writing on fruits]

If you want to write words that will look beautiful in green on apples, sour oranges (*nāranj*), or citron (*utrujj*), and serve them on fruit platters, and be in your master's good graces,[22] mix slaked lime (*kils*), ochre (*maghra*), and vinegar. Write with them on the fruits while they are still green on the trees. When the fruits are fully ripe, wipe off what you have written on the fruits. The place

21 Except for some differences, mostly stylistic, this paragraph is similar to recipe 719 above; this may be an indication that the chapter drew on several sources that contained similar information.

22 I read the edited وتخطّى 'pass by' as وتحظي 'to be in someone's good graces.'

where the writing was will look green whereas the rest of the citron, or whatever fruit you used, will be yellow.

(725) Recipe for fresh dates (*ruṭab*) when not in season

Take a piece of cloth lining (*biṭāna*),[23] wet it with water, wring it out, and use it to wrap whole dates (dried with calyxes attached) overnight. Next, take a new water bucket (*naʿʿāra*) and soak the dates in water overnight. (**170r**) The following morning, change the water and soak the dates overnight again, after which the dates will be good, [as good as fresh].

(726) Another recipe for out-of-season fresh dates[24]

Take *qaṣb* dates;[25] choose the large and meaty ones with the calyxes still attached. Soak them in hot water for an hour, and then wash them and spread them out to dry.

Take a watermelon (*biṭṭīkha khaḍrāʾ*),[26] and cut a cone out of its top [making an opening as wide as your hand].[27] Take out the pulp, but keep the liquid in. Put the dates in it, put the [cored out] top back, and set it aside for a day, after which you can check on the dates to see if they are done. If not, then leave them for another night to absorb more liquid, so that they become soft and delicious.

Take the dates out and spread them on a latticed tray to drain.[28] [To serve, put them in vessels, and] arrange them on trays (*ṣawānī*), and sprinkle them with rosewater and sesame oil.

(727) Another recipe [for out-of-season fresh dates]

Boil milk, and when it foams up, skim off the foam. Throw in the dried dates (*tamr*). The dates will look better if they are washed first, and the calyxes are kept attached. Let them boil once, and then leave them in the milk for a couple of days, and take them out [and use].

---

23 Usually made of cotton.

24 This recipe is similar to Baghdādī 82, with the exception of some minor differences.

25 This is a dialectical vocalization of *qasb*. It is a naturally dry, delicious Iraqi date, usually stored loose because it cannot be pressed together like other moist dried dates.

26 Lit., 'green melon.' See glossary 7.

27 This detail is provided by Baghdādī.

28 *Ṭabaq mushabbak*. Such trays are usually made of woven date palm fronds.

(728) Another recipe [for out-of-season fresh dates]

Take [dried] *qaṣb* dates,[29] gently pierce them with a needle, and then soak them in milk for an hour so that they may soften to your liking. After that, keep them submerged in honey in a cold place. They will be fresh and nobody will doubt this.

(729) Recipe (170v) for keeping fruits fresh by submersion (*taghmīr*)
Submerging grapes (*taghmīr al-ʿinab*)

Take good grapes. The harvested amount should not have among them any grapes that have fallen on the ground (*mahwī*) or been bitten into [by birds or bees].[30] Shake the bunches with your hand [to make sure all the grapes are firmly attached], and then seal the stems of the bunches with wax.

Now, take vinegar and date syrup (*dibs*), and combine them, adding enough amounts of each to make a mix balanced [in sweetness and sourness].

Put the grapes in a glazed ceramic vessel (*inā' muzajjaj*) such as a *qaṭramīz* (wide-mouthed jar), and pour on them the liquid you have mixed. Let the liquid submerge the grapes by a width of 4–fingers.

Whenever you want to use them, take out the amount you need, hold each bunch by its stem and dip it in cold water. Serve the grapes [in vessels arranged] on trays (*ṣawānī*), and they will be the best grapes eaten out of season.

(730) Another recipe [on keeping grapes fresh]

Cut the grape bunches from the vine. Tie a cord for them in the storage house.[31] Open each bunch with both hands and hang it on this cord. Now, pluck a single grape from each bunch and stick it into the bunchstem, and keep it there but check on it every day. If you find that it has deteriorated, replace it with another fresh grape.

Thus, the grape bunches will remain fresh and whenever you want, remove them from the string, and serve them out of season.

29 See n. 25 above.

30 The verb used is *maghmūs*, which generally means 'dipped.' However, in the context, I believe it must be the dialectical vocalization of *maghmūz* 'bitten into' or *maghmūṣ* 'defective.'

31 The phrase reads, ويعمل له خيط في البيت. The cord would be tied from both ends, like a clothesline.

(731) Recipe for submerging all kinds of figs (*taghmīr al-tīn*)

Take good dried *Maʿarrī* figs.[32] Soak them in a small amount of water overnight, (**171r**) and then mash them [with the water] with your hands very well, press out the juice and strain it. Be careful; do not leave any of the seeds in the juice.

Now, take chard leaves, pound them, squeeze out their juice, and boil it with the fig juice on a low fire until it thickens [and cool it].

Put the [fresh] figs in a glazed ceramic vessel (*inā' muzajjaj*) after you pick them over, but do this gently so that their skins remain intact; otherwise, they will go bad. So, when you are done arranging the figs in the vessel, pour on them the liquid you boiled, and make sure that the opening of the vessel is tightly closed. The figs will stay fresh for as long as you want them.

FIGURE 50 *Figs, F1954.74v, Muḥammad al-Qazwīnī,* ʿAjā'ib al-makhlūqāt, *detail (Freer Gallery of Art and Arthur M. Sackler Gallery, Smithsonian Institution, Washington, DC: Purchase—Charles Lang Freer Endowment).*

32 These were named after the Syrian city Maʿarrat al-Nuʿmān, famous for its figs and olives.

(732) Another recipe, which turns dried figs (*tīn yābis*) into fresh ones (*akhḍar*)[33]

Take fine-tasting dried figs, stuff them with honey mixed with a bit of crushed saffron, and arrange them on the back of a sieve. Put the sieve on the opening of a pot with boiling water, and let the figs swell (*yanfuj*) with the steam (*bukhār*). Next, arrange the figs on a platter (*ṭabaq*), and set them aside covered, overnight. The following morning, they will look as if they have just been picked from the tree.

(733) Recipe for submerging apricots (*taghmīr al-mishmish*)

Put [fresh] apricots in [a liquid] of crushed saffron, and they will stay fresh for as long as you want them. Safflower (*ʿuṣfur*) may be substituted for saffron. However, with saffron the apricots will retain their sweetness, whereas with safflower they will lose their flavor, and their color will change somewhat. **(171v)**

(734) Recipe for submerging pears (*taghmīr al-kummathrā*)[34]

Take firm pears, put them in a new earthenware jar (*jarra fakhkhār*), cover the opening very well, and bury it in the ground. Take out the pears whenever you need them, and they will come out safe and sound.

In addition, if you take a wide vessel, sprinkle its base with salt and arrange the pears on it in one layer, they will stay good for a long time.

(735) Recipe for submerging cherry plums (*qarāṣiyā*) and peaches (*khawkh*)

Take bee honey with its wax (*ʿasal al-shahd*), and strain it, but do not boil it on the fire. Put in it whatever cherry plums and peaches you wish and they will stay good for a whole year.

Whenever you want to use the fruits, take them out of the honey, and spread them on the back of a sieve for an hour. Take some lukewarm water, [dip them in it] and wash them gently so that their skins stay intact. Take them out of the water and put them on the sieve [again] for an hour, after which you can arrange them on trays (*ṣawānī*) and plates (*aṭbāq*), and offer them to whomever you wish.

---

33 In this context, *akhḍar* (lit., 'green') designates freshness.

34 In this recipe, the pears are not submerged in liquid, but by burying them in the ground, a technique also known as *ṭamr*. See glossary 9.2, s.v. *taghmīr*.

(736) Recipe for submerging various kinds of mulberry (*tūt*), but not the Levantine variety, which is done differently[35]

If you want to submerge mulberries, take as many mulberries as you want, put them in a tightly woven woolen wrapper cloth (*miʾzar ṣūf ṣafīq*), and squeeze out their juice, but be careful not to leave any seeds in it. (**172r**)

After you squeeze out the juice, let it boil on a low fire until half of it is gone, and then remove it, and let it cool.

Now, take the mulberries [you want to submerge], and put them in a glazed ceramic vessel (*wiʿāʾ muzajjaj*). Pour the prepared liquid on them, and submerge them by a width of 4–fingers. Make sure the vessel is tightly covered, and set it aside.

Whenever you need to use them, take them out of the vessel and spread them on [the back of] a sieve, overnight, after which you can offer them [on platters] on trays (*ṣawānī*) to whomever you want. You will blow their minds away with it, especially if it is offered when the sun is at the [low] zodiac sign of Sagittarius (*shams al-qaws*).[36]

FIGURE 51 *Zodiac sign of Sagittarius, F1954.45r, Muḥammad al-Qazwīnī,* ʿAjāʾib al-makhlūqāt, *detail (Freer Gallery of Art and Arthur M. Sackler Gallery, Smithsonian Institution, Washington, DC: Purchase—Charles Lang Freer Endowment).*

---

35 *Tūt Shāmī* 'Levantine mulberries' are a sweet-sour black variety.

36 I.e., the beginning of winter. The bow zodiac sign is from 22nd November to 21st December.

(737) Recipe for submerging apples (*taghmīr al-tuffāḥ*)
If you want to submerge apples, which do not propagate from offshoots (*lā yanbut*),[37] such as *budayris*,[38] *biṭṭīkhī*, *ḥalawānī*, *ḥayyāfī*,[39] and the like, take good grape [juice] that has been cooked on a low fire until it thickens, and then remove it and cool it.

Now, take any of the apples we mentioned, and put them in the grape juice; they should be submerged by a width of 4–fingers. Avoid letting them have any contact with air until you need to use them. When they are taken out, they will look as if they have just been picked from the tree.

[General remark] Know that for any fruits you want to submerge, you must seal their stems with wax, so that the fruits do not absorb any of the honey [or any other liquid] in which they are kept. (**172v**)

(738) Recipe for out-of-season fresh dates (*ruṭab*)
Take as many fine-tasting [dried] *qaṣb* dates as you want,[40] wipe off any dirt or dust, and then pack them in a glazed ceramic vessel (*inā' muzajjaj*).

Submerge the dates in milk that has just been drawn. Cover the vessel, and set it aside overnight. The following morning, pour off the milk, but keep the dates in the vessel to absorb the remaining liquids. Do not touch the dates with your hands.

Take a plate (*ṭabaq*), pack the dates well, and leave them there for an hour before serving them.

(739) Another recipe [for keeping dates fresh and using them out of season]
If you want to keep fresh dates (*ruṭab*) fresh, put them in a new earthenware jar, close the opening tightly, and bury it in the ground [and leave it there]. Whenever you wish, take the jar out and you will find the dates still fresh. Alternatively, you can submerge the jar in water up to a little below its mouth [and keep it there]. Take it out whenever you wish, and you will find the dates are still fresh.

---

37 Hence, there are not too many of them. *Nabāt* designates the offshoots growing around the mother tree.

38 The word is بديرس, but could be read as *barīrī* (بريري), a variety of Damascene apple mentioned in al-Badrī, *Nuzhat al-anām* 201. It was probably so called because its color resembles the ripe, bright red fruit of the *arāk* tree (*Salvadora persica*).

39 The word occurs as حيافي. It could have been a misreading of *jinānī* (جناني), a variety of Damascene apple mentioned in al-Badrī, *Nuzhat al-anām* 201. Both *ḥalawānī* and *biṭṭīkhī* are mentioned in al-Badrī's book as well.

40 See n. 25 above.

(740) Recipe [for out-of-season fresh dates][41]

Take [dried] *qaṣb* dates[42] that are chewy and fleshy (*layyin laḥim*), and soak them in milk overnight. When they are well soaked, take them out and put them in smooth, thin white honey (*ʿasal mādhī*). Those who eat them will not have any doubts that they are fresh. If you wish, replace the stones with skinned almonds, and they will be even more delicious.

The most delicious way to eat *ruṭab* (fresh dates) and *tamr* (dried dates) is to put them on a platter (*jām*) and scatter broken pieces of ice over them. (**173r**) They will be scrumptious eaten chilled this way. Al-Maʾmūn used to do this with *tamr, ruṭab,* and other sweet foods (*ḥalwā*).[43] Al-Wāthiq used to have his *qaṭāʾif* (pancakes) always served chilled with ice around them.[44]

(741) [How to keep narcissus flowers (*narjis*) fresh, and how to change their color]

If you want narcissus flowers to stay fresh for a long time, slit each bulb in several places and then enclose the entire bulb with ash.[45] Then, put them in water [in a vessel], and they will stay fresh. Avoid exposing narcissus flowers to smoke because it is not good for them.

If you want to make white narcissus flowers red, before the flower stalks open, wrap them in woolen cloth (*kisāʾ*),[46] which you keep partially drenched in water with safflower steeped in it all day long.[47] When the night comes, hang the flowers upside down using a string tied to a post, and leave them there overnight. Continue doing this for several days until the stalks open. You will find that the flowers have turned from white to red.

(742) Recipe for submerging roses (*taghmīr al-ward*)

If you want to keep roses and offer them fresh and fragrant when the sun is at the [lowest] zodiac sign of Capricorn (*shams al-jadī*),[48] take the stems of roses with large, firm unopened buds (*azrār*). Take as many as you wish a couple of days before they open, and put them in a new earthenware bucket (*naʿʿāra*

---

41 With the exception of minor stylistic differences, this recipe is identical to that in al-Warrāq, English trans. *Annals* 398. Here I used it to amend the edited text slightly.

42 See n. 25 above.

43 Al-Maʾmūn was an Abbasid caliph, son of Hārūn al-Rashīd (d. 833).

44 Al-Wāthiq was an Abbasid caliph known for his big appetite and love for food (d. 847).

45 The phrase is فحزّزه حززاً; this was usually done with a sharp knife, and the bulbs are supposed to stay intact.

46 *Kisāʾ* may designate many kinds of outer garments, usually made of thick fabrics.

47 The verb used is *sābiḥ* (lit., 'swimming').

48 I.e., the first part of winter. The goat zodiac sign is from 22nd December to 20th January.

Zabadāniyya)[49] that has been kept wet in water for a whole day, and then emptied and left to dry. (**173v**)

Put the rosebuds you have gathered into this vessel, but do not pack them in it. Close the opening with a sheet of leather (*riqq*), but make sure that it is tied tightly, so that no air can get in and spoil the buds. Keep the bucket hanging near the water.[50] Whenever you wish, take out the bucket, open it up, and take fresh roses out of it.

However, if you are in a hurry, and need fresh roses, take good [dried] buds of Iraqi roses (*ward ʿIrāqī*), soak them in rosewater overnight, and then remove the outer leaves (sepals). Return the buds to the rosewater, and they will open as if fresh and their hypanthia (*aqmāʿ*) will turn green.[51] Whoever sees them will have no doubt whatsoever that they have just been picked.

FIGURE 52 *Zodiac sign of Capricorn, F1954.45r, Muḥammad al-Qazwīnī,* ʿAjāʾib al-makhlūqāt, *detail (Freer Gallery of Art and Arthur M. Sackler Gallery, Smithsonian Institution, Washington,* DC*: Purchase—Charles Lang Freer Endowment).*

---

49 Earthenware vessels, such as this one, must have been named after al-Zabadānī, a city in southwest Syria.

50 Such as in a well, a little above its water level.

51 I read ويحضر in the edited text, and وتحفر in DK, which are irrelevant here, as وتخضر 'turn green,' based on context.

(743) Another way [to have fresh roses out of season]

Fill a jar with dried roses, seal its opening with wax, and keep it submerged in water overnight. The following morning, take them out, and they will look like fresh roses.

(744) Recipe for out-of-season roses

Take dried roses that are in perfect condition, soak them in rosewater for three days. After that, you will find that they have been restored, and look like fresh roses, and you can give them as a gift to whomever you wish.

(745) Recipe for submerging common cucumbers (*khiyār*),[52] snake cucumbers (*qiththā'*),[53] *'ajjūr* (variety of unripe melon),[54] *faqqūs* (small variety of *qiththā'*), melons (*biṭṭīkh*),[55] and the like

If you want to submerge any of the vegetables mentioned above, (174r) take white sand (*raml abyaḍ*), wash it thoroughly, and put it in a deep hole in the ground. Put whatever you want of *khiyār, qiththā', 'ajjūr, faqqūs*, and *biṭṭīkh* in it.[56] There should be plenty of sand and the place should be cool.

(746) Recipe for submerging carrots (*jazar*), turnips (*lift*), taro (*qulqās*), onion (*baṣal*), and the like

Regarding vegetables (*khuḍar*): if you want to submerge any of these varieties [mentioned above], make a big hole in the ground, then take red clay (*ṭīn aḥmar*), and alternate each layer of this clay with a layer of whatever you want to submerge. Do not put the vegetables on top of each other.

Whenever you want, take out the amount you need, wash it with lukewarm water, and cook it, eat it, or gift it to whomever you wish. It is very good.

(747) Recipe for submerging eggplant (*bādhinjān*)

Take raw red soil (*turāb aḥmar ḥayy*), mix it with water as is done with pottery soil (*turāb al-fawākhīr*), and stir it well so that the sand and stone separate and settle in the bottom of the container.[57] Set it aside to dry in its own place, and

52 *Cucumis sativus*.

53 *Cucumis melo* var. *flexuosus*.

54 *Cucumis melo* var. chate, also called Egyptian chate.

55 *Cucumis melo*.

56 As we see in the following recipe, the fruits and vegetables are not put on top of each other; rather, they are placed next to each other with alternating layers of sand.

57 This is done to cleanse the used soil of any impurities.

then take it out, crush it and mix it with very sour vinegar, add enough of it to make it resemble henna paste.

Smear the outside of the eggplants with this clay paste, (**174v**) after you cover their stems with wax. Give each one a good coating of clay and cover it entirely, and pack them [in containers] on top of each other.

Whenever you want to use some, take them out and wash them with lukewarm water. They will come out as if they have just been picked from the vine.

(748) Recipe for keeping fresh grapes (*ṣiyānat al-ʿinab*) beyond their season

Take a glass (*zujāj*) or glazed earthenware (*fakhkhār madhūn*) vessel. Fill one-third of it with bunches of sweet grapes. Pour on them water that has been boiled until one-third of it is gone. [Fill the vessel with it], and cover its opening. The grapes will be good to use beyond their season, and the remaining liquid is beneficial for all sorts of sicknesses.

(749) Recipe for [keeping] quince (*safarjal*)

Take clean shavings of wood (*nishārat al-khashab*), and place the quince on it, bottoms down. They will stay for a long time and even become more flavorful.

You can also keep quince in barley straw (*tibn al-shaʿīr*), or keep them in a place where there is a fresh fruit.

If quince is wrapped in fig leaves, smeared with clay—which has been kneaded with barley straw, and then dried, it will stay fresh as long as it is thus covered. The same may be done with apples.

However, you must know that quince does not agree with raisins and grapes. If you store quince with them or even close to them, they will go bad.[58]

(750) [How to keep and store fruits]

It you coat citron (*utrujj*) with gypsum (*jaṣṣ*), (**175r**) it will stay fresh. Burying it in barley [straw] will also keep it fresh. In addition, if you bury it in moist sand or good soil, it will stay fresh even longer, beyond its season.

If you want to keep fresh dates, which are sweet and ripe and still crunchy (*busr*), put them in a green-glazed wide-mouthed jar (*barniyya*), and fill it with bee honey. They will stay fresh for a long time.

58 In al-Nābulusī, *ʿAlam al-malāḥa* 246, the smell of quince is said to be particularly harmful to stored fresh and dried grapes.

If you take small *tamr Wāḥī*[59] and soak them in citron pulp juice (*mā' ḥummāḍ al-utrujj*), they will become fresh dates (*balaḥ*). Also, if you take the fresh red dates (*balaḥ aḥmar*), and soak them in the juice of Damascus citron (*kabbād*) or lemon, they will stay fresh for a whole year.

If you want fresh dates when not in season, take *usṭarūs*,[60] add Levantine rosewater to it, and boil it in a soapstone pot (*qidr birām*). Remove the calyxes from *tamr Wāḥī*, and add them to the syrup that has been boiling on a low fire. Remove the pot and let it cool. Store [the dates with the syrup] in glass vessels, and use whenever needed. To serve, put the dates on plates, and drizzle some sesame oil and rosewater over them.

If *usṭarūs* is not available, use instead cane-sugar molasses (*qaṭr*) or sugar syrup (*ḥall sukkar*). The dates [described above] are cooked on the fire because *Wāḥī* dates are thick-skinned. Otherwise, when other dried dates (*qaṣb*) are used,[61] just dissolve the cane-sugar molasses with rosewater and musk, (175v) and keep the dried dates in the syrup overnight. After this, the dates can be put on plates, sprinkled with musk [dissolved in] rosewater, and served.

If you want to store lemon, take ripe ones that still have green skins.[62] Leave their stalks attached. Bury them in granular ground (*batānī*),[63] with moist sandy clay soil (*ṭīn murammal*). Arrange the lemons in alternate layers with this soil, and they will stay fresh for two to three months.

If you want to store grapes, as soon as they ripen, and while they are still on the vine,[64] take a thin hemp thread (*khayṭ qinnab*) and cut it into strings. Tie [one end of each string] tightly to the middle of a bunch, and tie [the other

---

59 These are dried dates harvested from the date palms in the Egyptian western oases (*al-Wāḥāt*). They do not moisten and soften when dried.

60 This lesser sugar-cane molasses was produced at the sugar mills from the collected left-overs of cooked sugar. This sugar was scraped from the tops of the conical earthenware molds (*abālīj*, sg. *ublūj*) to level-off the surface after sugar has been cooked and poured into them. It was also collected from whatever was left on the reed mats, when the cones were unmolded. As explained by al-Nuwayrī, *Nihāyat al-arab* viii 202, who calls it *usṭarūsh*.

61 *Qasb* dates are naturally dry, and do not soften and moisten when dried like most date varieties.

62 The phrase is يؤخذ نضجاً وهو أخضر. Green, as used in this sentence, is literally descriptive of the color. Lemon pulp usually ripens before the skin.

63 This is a dialectical vocalization of *bathānī*, sg. *bathna* 'granular soil with little cohesive-ness,' *Lisān al-ʿarab*, s.v. بثن.

64 The expression is على امّه (lit., 'on their mother').

end] to the reeds (*kaʿb*) [supporting the vine]. Leave them there overnight. The following morning, cut the grape bunches, and put them in a glass vessel. Pour on them wine vinegar mixed with date syrup, cover the vessel, and store it until needed. They will be fresh grapes out of season, and God knows best.

The book *Kanz al-fawāʾid fī tanwīʿ al-mawāʾid* is finished. All praise is due to Allah.
May He bless our Master Muhammad, his family, and companions;
and grant them salvation until the Day of Judgment.
Amen

Glossary

The main sections in this glossary and the English transliteration of the Arabic entries are arranged alphabetically. Information in the following sections is mainly based on medieval Arabic sources.

Contents

1. Beverages for Pleasure and Health

aqsimā (أقسما) ***aqsima*** (اقسمة) ***aqsām*** (اقسام) sweet-sour digestive drink which is made in three ways, based on the recipes given in *Kanz* chapter 12. We learn from Ibn al-Ukhuwwa, *Maʿālim al-qurba*, fol. 80r, that *aqsimā* is *fuqqāʿ khāṣṣ* (excellent foamy beer, see below). He mentions its main ingredients, which are sugar, pomegranate seeds, and special spice blends (*afāwī l-ṭīb*).

Now, in the collection of *fuqqāʿ* recipes in *Kanz* chapter 12, there are recipes for *fuqqāʿ khāṣṣ* and others for *aqsimā*. Although there is not a single indication that the names are synonymous, some of the preparations called *aqsimā* are indeed like *fuqqāʿ khāṣṣ*, such as recipes 401, and 403;[1] otherwise the majority of the *aqsimā* recipes are for light and refreshing sweet-sour preparations, non-frothy, and may be imbibed as digestives after meals. Recipes 405, 417, and 424 are prepared as sweetened water, herbed and spiced, and kept overnight in jars with traces of previous fermentation (*wiʿāʾ ḍārī*). Other *aqsimā* recipes deal with a preparation called *khamīrat al-aqsimā*, also called *iksīr*, made by distilling herbed and spiced vinegar. It is a kind of base kept in bottles, and used for making instant *aqsimā*. Whenever needed, sugar is dissolved in water, and herbs, like mint and rue, along with a small amount of this base, are added to make an *aqsimā* drink.

It is my guess that etymologically the name *aqsimā* might have its roots in oxymel, the ancient drink of vinegar and honey.

ashriba (أشربة) drinks; sg. *sharāb* (شراب) see entry below.

daqīq al-shaʿīr (دقيق الشعير) lit., 'barley flour.' It is ground malted barley used in making *fuqqāʿ* (foamy beer), see entry below.

fuqqāʿ (فقاع) foamy beer, for which *Kanz* chapter 12 offers the largest extant medieval collection of recipes, with varying degrees of complexities and flavors. Ibn al-Ukhuwwa, *Maʿālim al-qurba*, fol. 80r, mentions two types of *fuqqāʿ* beer that were sold in the markets: *fuqqāʿ kharjī*, ordinary beer, made with sugar-cane molasses; and *fuqqāʿ khāṣṣ*, excellent beer, made with sugar, pomegranate seeds and spice blends (see below).

In medieval Egypt, *fuqqāʿ* was an affordable, favorite summer drink purchased chilled from the beer makers (*fuqqāʿiyyūn*) in the marketplaces, which were once beautifully described by al-Maqrīzī as a stretch of about 20 stores that sold *fuqqāʿ*, aligned on both sides of the street. The stores were all built of colorful marble; they

1 Another instance may be found in al-Ghuzūlī, *Maṭāliʿ* ii 88, where a recipe for *aqsima mulūkiyya* (lit. 'royal,' top quality) resembles *Kanz* recipe 432, called *sūbiya Yamaniyya*, which is a type of digestive beer.

 | DOI 10.1163/9789004349919_027

had fountains, which sprayed water on this marble where the sealed beer jars (*kīzān al-fuqqāʿ*) were arranged in lines on both sides of the street for passersby to look at.[2]

Besides its cooling effect, *fuqqāʿ* was also believed to have other benefits, provided it was imbibed on an empty stomach. It cools down heat in the stomach and treats acute thirst due to hangovers. It was also said to purge the chest and lungs, and when it was chilled with ice, it was said to extinguish the heat of yellow bile. However, having it on a full stomach does not benefit the body, as it putrefies the digesting food (Ibn al-Bayṭār, *al-Jāmiʿ* iii 225). All the drinker would gain from it would be a few enjoyable burps (al-Ghuzūlī, *Maṭāliʿ* ii 88).

The commonly used beer with malted barley was not encouraged by physicians because it causes bloating, generates bad humors, and fills the brain with dense vapors. Al-Rāzī, *Manāfiʿ* 89, 91, describes it as a cause of bloating and as harmful to the stomach and digestion because of its cold properties. But this can be remedied by seasoning it with cloves, spikenard, and mastic (al-Kāzarūnī, *al-Sadīdī* 295). The best is made with good wheat bread or malted wheat. In *Kanz* chapter 12, only two *fuqqāʿ* recipes use barley, and the rest are made with wheat and wheat bread.

The recommended aromatics and spices used to improve the properties of *fuqqāʿ*, as given by Ibn al-Bayṭār, *al-Jāmiʿ* iii 225–6, are spikenard, mastic, Ceylon cinnamon, long pepper, mace, and cloves. For each 20 beer-brewing jars (see *kūz* below), 1 *mithqāl* (4½ grams) or 2 *dirhams* (6 grams) of these spices are used. Small amounts of rue, mint, tarragon, and tender citron leaves enhance its deliciousness.

The overall religious opinion was that *fuqqāʿ* was permissible as long as it was not allowed to ferment more than three days. All of those described in the *Kanz* recipes in chapter 12 are left to ferment overnight or a day. However, a good portion of what was sold in the medieval markets indeed must have been alcoholic. See also *kūz* below.

Besides *fuqqāʿ*, *Kanz* chapter 12 offers other varieties, consumed after the meals as digestives; see *aqsimā*, *sūbiyā*, and *shush* in this section.

fuqqāʿ kharjī (فقاع خرجي) common foamy beer, was the most prevalent variety sold in the medieval Egyptian markets. To my knowledge, the name is not explained in any of the existing medieval records. It is my contention that it is related to beer, which used to be made by the Christian Copts, the indigenous Egyptians, collectively called *Ahl al-Kitāb* (non-Muslims living in Muslim lands), who had been making similar beers for centuries. Tax imposed on them, which was charged per head, was called *kharj* (خرج),[3] and the beer for which they were known must have been named after them.

---

2 Al-Maqrīzī, *Khiṭaṭ* ii 435–6.

3 Cf. tax imposed on Muslims (charged on cultivated land), which was called *kharāj* (خراج). See *Tāj al-ʿarūs*, s.v. خرج.

It was also consumed in the Levant. Al-Ghuzūlī, *Maṭāliʿ* ii 88, says that the Damascenes call it *al-musaddab* (المسدب) instead, because it was fermented in jars (*kīzān*) stuffed with *sadhāb barrī* (wild rue).[4] This herb was believed to improve the quality of beer and so it caused less bloating. It must have been a popular affordable drink. As we learn from Ibn al-Ukhuwwa, *Maʿālim al-qurba*, fol. 80r, it was made with sugar-cane molasses, which was cheaper than sugar or honey.[5] The standard proportions of its main ingredients, which Ibn al-Ukhuwwa provides, are for each 100 *kūz*es of beer, 8⅓ *raṭl*s (8⅓ pounds) of *quṭāra* are used along with spices and aromatics.

The *Kanz* does not include recipes for making it, perhaps it was too basic and common to mention. However, it was used as an ingredient to make more elaborate beers, such as in recipes 426 and 432.

fuqqāʿ khāṣṣ (فقاع خاص) excellent foamy beer, sold in the medieval Egyptian markets as a higher-grade drink than *fuqqāʿ kharjī* (see above). Ibn al-Ukhuwwa, *Maʿālim al-qurba*, fol. 80r, mentions its main ingredients, which are sugar, pomegranate seeds, and special spice blends (*afāwī l-ṭīb*).[6] Most of the *fuqqāʿ* recipes in chapter 12 include these ingredients, some are particularly called *fuqqāʿ khāṣṣ*, such as 392, 393, 396, 397, and 415; and others are just called *fuqqāʿ* but they do use pomegranate seeds and are not substantially different from the *khāṣṣ* beer, see recipes 400, 406, 413, and 419.

Fuqqāʿ khaṣṣ offers more variety in flavor and adds more complexity to the basic beer with all the spices and herbs added; in addition, it can be manipulated so that the drink may agree with the disposition (*mizāj*) of the drinker.

iksīr (إكسير) elixir, see *khamīrat aqsimā* below.

jullāb (جلاّب) syrup made with rosewater and sugar or honey. Ibn Sīnā, *al-Qānūn* 1229, provides a recipe in which 2 pounds of sugar are simmered with ½ cup water. Just before the pot is removed from the fire, ¼ cup rosewater is added.

The syrup was diluted with water, sometimes chilled with ice, and served as a refreshing drink. Medicinally, it was valued for its cooling effects. It was believed to benefit the stomach, chest, and lungs; but people with diarrhea should avoid it. Due to its cold properties, it was recommended for hangovers (al-Thaʿālibī *Yatīmat al-dahr* 535).

---

4 Pronounced *sadāb* in the vernacular. See glossary 8, s.v. *sadhāb*.

5 Ibn al-Ukhuwwa's manual for market inspectors insists that the best grade of molasses should be used, which is *quṭāra ʿāl*. Neither *ʿasal qaṣab* nor *ʿasal mursal*, which are lower grades of sugar-cane molasses, should be used because of the sharpness and astringency in their tastes. See glossary 4, for types of molasses.

6 According to Ibn al-Kutubī, *Mā lā Yasaʿ al-ṭabīb jahlahu*, s.v. *fuqqāʿ*, *fuqqāʿ* made with pomegranate seeds is deemed the best.

khamīra (خميرة) lit., 'fermenting agent,' was sometimes used to designate an aromatic distilled base for making digestive drinks, such as *khamīrat aqsimā*.

khamīrat aqsimā (خميرة اقسمة), also called *iksīr* (اكسير) elixir. It is a distilled liquid base used for making instant *aqsimā*, which is a digestive drink, see above. The liquid is vinegar mixed with spices and herbs and then distilled and stored in glass vessels and used as needed, see *Kanz* recipes 402, 404, 420, 423. To make an instant *aqsimā* drink, a small amount of this liquid is added to water mixed with sugar and lemon juice.

***khamīr fuqqā*ʿ** (خميرفقاع) beer yeast, most probably what now is called top-fermenting yeast, was obtained by skimming the yeast-rich froth that gathers at the surface of beer during the first days of fermentation.

***kīzān al-fuqqā*ʿ** (كيزان الفقاع) large and small jars used for brewing and drinking *fuqqā*ʿ, see *kūz* below.

kūz (كوز) earthenware drinking cup or pitcher, made glazed and unglazed, ranging in size from small to large.[7] The larger ones were used for brewing *fuqqā*ʿ (foamy beer). They have handles and a spout called *bulbul*, and could hold 6 *qisṭs* (18 cups).[8] The small ones have no spouts, and were used for drinking liquids. The ones used for storing and drinking *fuqqā*ʿ were specially made: they were spheroconical vessels which could easily be held and kept in the palm of the hand.[9] In al-Azdī, *Gharāʾib al-tanbīhāt* 150, it is described thus:

Embraced by the palm of the hand,
As if it were the firm breast of a beauty.

The earthenware ones, glazed and unglazed, were made with thick walls to resist the pressure from the foamy drink. Their necks are short and mouths are narrow, which help reduce the surface from which the foam may escape. Their openings are tightly sealed with leather fastened with a thread. The vessels were kept in ice until they were ready to drink. When the seal was removed, the beer would gush out of the vessel. In an enigma-poem (*lughz*) by al-Ibshīhī, *Mustaṭraf* 436, a *fuqqā*ʿ *kūz* is described thus:

---

7 Porcelain varieties are also reported in al-Maqrīzī, *Ittiʿāẓ al-ḥunafā* 195; and ones made of *qaṣdīr* (tin) are mentioned in Ibn al-Ukhuwwa, *Maʿālim al-qurba* fol. 80r.

8 As calculated by al-Khawārizmī, *Mafātīḥ* 33.

9 For a description of this type of vessel, see Ghouchani and Adle, "A Sphero-Conical Vessel" 70–92; elaborated on by Lewicka, *Food and Foodways* 466–7.

FIGURE 53
Spheroconical fuqqāʿ *drinking vessel, unglazed earthenware, c. tenth century, 40.170.232, (MET NY—Rogers Fund, 1940).*

Imprisoned, but for no wrongs committed.
In captivity clad in a garment of lead.[10]
Set him free, and he will jump up high,
Happy to be released, and kiss your lips.

Following the regulations for the *fuqqāʿ*-makers and sellers in medieval Egyptian markets, the inside of the earthenware ones must be brushed with a fibrous *miswāk* brush,[11] before the beer is poured into them; and they must be replaced as soon as they start to smell. The tin ones (made of *qaṣdīr*) should be replaced every three months. Additionally, the vessels must be scented with aromatic smoke before they are filled (Ibn al-Ukhuwwa, *Maʿālim al-qurba*, fol. 80r).

10 This might be metaphorically suggestive of the heavy pottery vessel, or literally, of the vessels made of tin (*qaṣdīr*), also called *raṣāṣ qalʿī* (رصاص قلعي), which in medieval times was deemed good-quality lead.

11 Fibrous sweet-smelling sticks taken from the *arāk* tree (*Salvadora persica*). They were usually used as tooth-brushes.

kūz fuqqāʿ ḍārī (كوز فقاع ضاري) jar with traces of previous fermentation, used for brewing the foamy beer called *fuqqāʿ*. See *Kanz* recipes 407 and 418 for directions on how to do this with new jars.

māʾ ʿadhb (ماء عذب) fresh water.

māʾ bi-l-thalj al-maḍrūb (ماء بالثلج المضروب) water chilled with crushed ice, believed to be better for the stomach than having *thalj* (natural ice) or *jalīd* (made ice) alone, because they induce thirst. It is harmful for the elderly, and those with phlegmatic blood. The best *thalj* should be free of any sand, and the best *jalīd* should be made with pure fine-tasting water (al-Malik al-Muẓaffar, *al-Muʿtamad* 88; al-Anṭākī, *Tadhkira* 109).

māʾ ḥulw (ماء حلو) lit., 'sweet water,' fine tasting water.

māʾ mubarrad fi-l-hawāʾ (ماء مبرّد في الهواء) air-cooled water.

māʾ muzammal (ماء مزمّل) water cooled in *muzammala*, a glazed earthenware vessel wrapped in coarse cloth, such as sackcloth or canvas, for insulation, then the space between the cloth and the sides of vessel was filled with hay.

māʾ al-shaʿīr (ماء الشعير) drink of malted barley, particularly consumed during the fasting month of Ramadan as it was believed to aid digestion and quench thirst. See *Kanz* recipes 411–2.

māʾ al-thalj (ماء الثلج) ice-cold water.

maṭbūkh (مطبوخ) non-alcoholic cooked wine, permissible because the grape juice is boiled down on the fire rather than letting it ferment in the heat of the sun.

maṭbūkh ṣāfī (مطبوخ صافي) clear cooked wine.

mayba (ميبة) aromatic restorative drink of quince that is made by diluting a specially prepared quince syrup, which has the consistency of thin honey. See *Kanz* recipe 350.

mizr (مزر) a drink related to *fuqqāʿ* and *sūbiyā*. It contains a high level of alcohol, and was popular in Egypt among the commoners (ʿAbd al-Laṭīf al-Baghdādī, *Riḥla* 123). As described in Ibn al-Bayṭār, *al-Jāmiʿ* iv 443–4, it is made with sprouted wheat, barley, or millet (*jāwars*), and people drink it instead of wine. However, it does not have the same pleasant effects upon its drinker that *fuqqāʿ* has. Drinking too much *mizr* may cause nausea, vomiting, and bloating. It causes headaches, and is bad for the nervous system.

naqūʿ al-mishmish (نقوع المشمش) apricot compote, the liquid of which was enjoyed as a digestive thirst-quenching drink. See also entry in glossary 4 below. For recipes, see *Kanz*, chapter 13.

sakanjabīn (سكنجبين) ***sakanjabīl*** (سكنجبيل) oxymel drink, valued for its digestive properties, was prepared by diluting syrup made with vinegar and honey or sugar. In Ibn Sīnā *al-Qānūn* 1229, a basic recipe calls for putting fine sugar in a pot, where it is leveled with a spoon, and then gently pouring strong vinegar in until bubbles are seen on the sugar surface. The pot is cooked on a gentle fire until the sugar dissolves and the scum is removed. After this, water is added until the mixture looks thin. It is then boiled further, until it thickens into syrup. When needed, the syrup is diluted with water, and sometimes chilled with ice. For recipes, see *Kanz*, chapter 11.

sakanjabīn buzūrī (سكنجبين بزوري) made with fresh and dried herbs and seeds.
sharāb sakanjabīn jullābī (شراب سكنجبين جلابي) concentrated syrup for oxymel drink, made with *jullāb* 'sugar syrup.'
sharāb sakanjabīn rummānī (شراب سكنجبين رماني) concentrated syrup for oxymel drink made with pomegranate juice.

sharāb (شراب) pl. *ashriba* (أشربة) generic for beverages, including wines and non-alcoholic refreshing drinks. The following entries describe the latter (wines are entered separately):

qiwām al-sharāb (قوام الشراب) This term describes the consistency of syrups flavored with fruit juice, and imbibed after diluting them with cold water. The standard proportions of sugar and fruit juice are, for each 10 *raṭl*s (10 pounds) of sugar, 3⅓ *raṭl*s of fruit juice were used (Ibn al-Ukhuwwa, *Maʿālim al-qurba*, fol. 76v). Sugar is mixed with water and cooked into *jullāb* (sugar syrup), and then the fruit juice is added, and boiling is resumed until it becomes syrup of medium consistency.

The fruity concentrated syrups were kept in jars or bottles, and when needed, the required amount was diluted in cold water chilled with ice (*thalj*). In al-Ghuzūlī, *Maṭāliʿ* ii 88, 2 *ūqiyya*s (¼ cup) of the syrup are used for a single serving.

sharāb al-ḥiṣrim al-munaʿnaʿ (شراب الحصرم المنعنع) concentrated syrup for sour grape drink flavored with mint.
sharāb ḥummāḍ al-utrujj (شراب حماض الاترج) concentrated syrup for citron-pulp drink.
sharāb laymūn (شراب ليمون) concentrated syrup for lemon drink.
sharāb al-tuffāḥ (شراب التفاح) concentrated syrup for apple drink.
sharāb al-tūt (شراب التوت) concentrated syrup for mulberry drink.
sharāb al-ward al-mukarrar (شراب الورد المكرر) concentrated syrup made with the refined liquid of rose petals. See *Kanz* recipe 368.

These sweetened chilled drinks were believed to be refreshing in the hot season. They were also offered at the end of the meals as an aid to digestion. With the addition of spices and herbs, they could also serve as tonic drinks with curative properties.

sharāb ʿatīq rikābī (شراب عتيق ركابي) Levantine aged wine, it was called *rikābī* because it was transported on backs of camels.
sharāb rayḥānī (شراب ريحاني) sweet-smelling wine, served undiluted.
shush (شش) sweetened grain-based drink related to beer (*fuqqāʿ*) and *sūbiyā* (سوبيا). See recipes in chapter 12 (408, 426–428), where it is described as a Yemeni drink.

shush Yemenī (شش يمني) Yemeni sweetened grain-based beer. Based on internal evidence, the Yemeni way of preparing the drink involved adding other ingredients to an already available *fuqqāʿ khāṣṣ* (see above). This made it stronger than *fuqqāʿ* by itself, but still within the permissible limits of no more than three days of fermentation. See *Kanz* recipe 408.

sūbiya (سوبية) ***sūbiyā*** (سوبيا) sweetened grain-based digestive beer (*fuqqāʿ*), said to be popular in Egypt (*Lisān al-ʿarab*, s.v. سوب; al-Hurawī, *Baḥr al-jawāhir* 214).[12] The best was made with rice. The *Kanz* offers six recipes, two of which are made with rice; the rest are made with bread and with flour cooked into thick porridge and then used to make the drink.

The drink was kept in jars overnight to ferment a little, or for a day or two and perhaps a little longer but not more than five days. It was said to be useful for the digestion, and with the addition of spices, it could be aphrodisiac (al-Anṭākī, *Tadhkira* 224). See *Kanz* recipes 429–34.
sukkar wa-laymūn (سكر وليمون) sugar-lemon cones, used by travelers as provisions. Whenever they were needed, a piece was dissolved in water and imbibed as a refreshing lemon drink; the first 'Kool-Aid' in the history of beverages, indeed! See *Kanz* recipe 425.
ṭilā (طلا) unfermented grape wine. Grape juice is cooked down to one-third of its original amount. Prepared this way, it becomes like *rubb* (concentrated juice), and was imbibed diluted in water as permissible wine.
yukhammar (يخمّر) 'left to ferment,' said in relation to drinks.

---

12 Chalabī (d. 1682), *Riḥla* i 465, mentions it as an exclusively Egyptian drink. He compares it to the Ottoman *būza*/*būẓa* (بوظة/بوزة), which was made with rice, and looks like milk; it is seasoned with cinnamon, cloves, and nutmeg, and sweetened with sugar. He adds that it causes a very slight intoxication, and it refreshes the body. See also Lane, *Manners and Customs* 324, where he says that *sūbiya* is also made with melon seeds, and sold in the streets of nineteenth-century Cairo. In today's Egypt, *sūbiya* is still popular, especially in the fasting month of Ramadan. Professionals make it with crushed barley and bread broken into pieces, drenched in water and left to ferment for a couple of days. It is strained, and the resulting liquid is spiced with cinnamon and cardamom and sweetened with sugar. After setting it aside for a day, it is good to drink, chilled, http://vb.elmstba.com/t106025.html, accessed Jan. 5, 2017. There are also home recipes using rice flour.

2. Breads, Grains, Pasta, Noodles, and Sweet and Savory Pastries[1]

Introductory Remarks

This section untangles the confusing terminology related to breads and flours in the eastern (al-Mashriq) and western (al-Maghrib) medieval Arabo-Islamic world (see also related entries in the section itself).

This section deals with foods that incorporate wheat products. Given the topographical and cultural diversities of the medieval Arabo-Islamic world in its eastern region (al-Mashriq), which includes Iraq, the Levant and Egypt; and the western one (al-Maghrib), which includes North Africa and Andalusia, the terminology related to wheat products was not always uniform. This factor has been a cause of confusion among modern researchers in regard to determining types of flour, especially the ingredient *samīd/samīdh*, which was used in making foods included in the extant medieval Arabic cookbooks; some of which were written in the Mashriq, and some in the Maghrib.[2]

1. The breads and flours used in Mashriqī cookbooks, such as those by al-Warrāq and al-Baghdādī, used the types of flour from what is now called common wheat or bread wheat (*Triticum aestivum*). It was hard wheat, which was high in gluten, and which was characterized by its elasticity (*ʿulūka*) and adhesivity (*luzūja*). The resulting bread was porous and chewy in texture, and these were sought after qualities.
2. Based on two principal medieval sources, Ibn Waḥshiyya, *al-Filāḥa* i 432–70; and al-Isrāʾīlī, *al-Aghdhiya* 2–60, flour types of al-Mashriq were discussed in the following terms:

    2.1 *Daqīq al-samīdh* (دقيق السميذ) was deemed the finest. It is bran-free white flour, high in starch content.[3]

---

1 The syrupy pastries are in glossary 4 below.

2 For instance, my interpretation of *samīdh* as fine white flour in al-Warrāq, *Annals*, English translation, was unjustifiably 'revised' to semolina, in two citations, which occur in Sato, *Sugar* 144, 145.

3 This type of flour contains the inner parts of the wheat endosperm, where the starch is most concentrated, and which is easier to grind into fine flour. Al-Isrāʾīlī calls this portion *lubāb* (لباب) and *samīdh* (سميذ). The rest of the endosperm he calls *daqīq* (دقيق).

 | DOI 10.1163/9789004349919_028

2.2 *Ḥuwwārā* (حُوّارى) was also a fine type of flour, comparable to *daqīq al-samīdh*; it is white and bran-free, but it contains the entire endosperm.[4]

2.3 *Khushkār* (خشكار), also called *daqīq ḥinṭī* (دقيق حنطي). This is whole wheat flour, from which nothing has been removed.

2.4 *Daqīq nukhālī* (دقيق نخالي) was mostly bran (*nukhāla*) and the outer portions of the endosperm (*daqīq*)

Now, in the medieval lexicons, *ḥuwwārā* was satisfactorily explained as whitened flour (from *taḥwīr* تحوير 'whitening,' *Lisān al-ʿarab*, s.v. حور). Regarding *samīdh*, however, except for al-Isrāʾīlī's information, we do not find any explanations as to why such a fine flour, almost as fine as starch, is called *samīdh*; a name which, today, we associate with semolina, the gritty sandy wheat flour from durum wheat.

It is my contention that the term *samīdh* as used in the eastern region was an indigenous term that could be traced back to the ancient Akkadian *samīdu*, which means 'grind finely' (Black, *Concise Dictionary of Akkadian*).

3. Almost all al-Warrāq's and al-Baghdādī's recipes use the term *daqīq samīdh* (sometimes just *daqīq*), which should be interpreted based on 2.1 above. In Iraq, there is no indication that semolina from durum wheat (*Triticum durum*) was used in making bread, the same way the different types of flour from common wheat (*Triticum aestivum*) were used in baking breads and pastries.[5]

Common wheat is hard and high in gluten; but durum wheat (*Triticum durum*) is even harder, and its gluten is poor in elasticity but high in protein.[6] It grows more successfully in dry climates, and the wheat berries it produces are tough to grind, hence their characteristic gritty sandy texture. The flour produced from it is not white but yellowish in hue, and bread made from it tends to be dense in texture due to the lack of the elastic gluten, which characterizes bread wheat.

4. Confusingly, when al-Isrāʾīlī discusses semolina of durum wheat, as we know it today, he also calls it *samīdh* (سميذ), and he mentions it along with *jashīsh* (جشيش), which is coarsely crushed grain.

Now, the term *samīdh* as used here cannot possibly have the same connotations as those of *samīdh* described in point 2.1 above. It is not explained anywhere, but it is my contention that the word may stem, etymologically, from the

4 That is, both *lubāb* and *daqīq*, see note above.

5 Based on Watson, *Agricultural Innovation* 20–3, durum wheat may have originated in Abyssinia (Ethiopia) and then reached the lower Nile valley and Fayyūm during the time of Byzantine Egypt. By the eighth century, Muslim Arabs played a role in its diffusion to other parts of the region, such as North Africa.

6 It is more suitable for making pasta.

root صمد (*ṣ-m-d*). In *Tāj al-ʿarūs*, *muṣammad* (مصمّد) designates solid objects, as opposed to brittle ones. Pronouncing ṣ as s is quite common in Arabic dialects. Therefore, etymologically, *musammad* (مسمّد), *simda* (سمدة), and *samīd* (سميد), also pronounced *samīdh* (سميذ), can be taken to describe a physical characteristic of the crushed hard grains.

5. Recipes calling for *samīd*/*samīdh*, which is semolina as we know it today, abound in the two surviving cookbooks from the thirteenth-century Maghribī region.[7] Two grades of grinds are mentioned:

   5.1 *Samīdh nāʿim* (سميذ ناعم) finely ground, which is sandy in texture, was used in making bread and couscous.
   5.2 *Samīdh kabīr al-ḥabb* (سميذ كبير الحب) coarsely ground, was used in making porridges and the like (Anon., *Anwāʿ al-ṣaydala* 190).

   The recipes require that *samīd* flour be moistened with warm water (in winter) or cold (in the summer) and set aside for a while before kneading it, to soften the grains. Fine flour in the Maghrib, comparable to eastern *ḥuwwārā* flour (see point 2.2 above), was called *darmak* (درمك). When it is used in a recipe, the instruction is to use it right away, like any other regular fine flour. The term *darmak* designates the physical characteristic of this fine flour.[8]

6. In relation to the Egyptian cookbook *Kanz al-fawāʾid*, flour-related terminology, interestingly, reflects the diversity of the country itself. Besides the generic term for flour (*daqīq*), we come across *daqīq samīdh* (see point 2.1 above) of the eastern region (e.g., *Kanz* recipe 316), as well as *samīdh*, the gritty sandy flour of semolina, ubiquitous in the Maghrib (see points 4 and 5 above).

ʿajīn (عجين) dough.

ʿajīn yābis (عجين يابس) stiff dough.

ʿajīn al-tuṭmāj (عجين التطماج) fresh pasta. Stiff unfermented dough is rolled out into thin sheets, cut into strips, and left out in the air for half a day, after which they are cut into pieces 2-fingers long, and then cooked as fresh pasta (as described in al-Warrāq Istanbul MS, fol. 168r).

akhbāz (أخباز) general term for regular bread as well as sweet and savory pastries and cookies.

aqrāṣ (أقراص) of bread and cookies, discs.

---

7 Al-Tujībī, *Fiḍālat al-khiwān*; and the anonymous *Anwāʿ al-ṣaydala*.

8 In *Tāj al-ʿarūs*, درمك is anything, which is ground until it becomes as fine as dust.

aqrāṣ mamlūḥa (اقراص مملوحة) ***aqrāṣ mumallaḥa*** (أقراص مملّحة) salted cookies offered with sweet ones in case the eater's appetite dulls from having sweet foods, as explained in *Kanz*, chapter 2.

aruzz (أرز) *ruzz* (رز) rice. As described in al-Anṭākī, *Tadhkira* 45, white rice is the best, yellow rice is next, and the worst is the black variety. Rice, called *marʿishī* (مرعشي) grown in the area around Aleppo, he adds, is better than Egyptian rice; the worst is grown around Damascus; and the best by far is the Indian variety.

The hot and dry properties of rice do not suit people with excessively hot temperaments. It lingers in the stomach, and the best way to balance its properties is to cook it with milk, almond oil, and sugar. This way it will nourish the body and generate pleasant dreams.

aruzz abyaḍ (أرز أبيض) husked white rice.
aruzz aḥmar (أرز أحمر) lit., 'red rice,' unhusked rice.
aruzz maṭḥūn (أرز مطحون) ground rice.
aruzz mubayyaḍ (أرز مبيض) polished whitened rice. *Kanz* recipe DK, appendix 22, p. 125, clearly indicates that rice has been whitened and polished with salt. The recipe specifies that it should be washed very well until all traces of salt are gone. The whitening effect of salt on rice is evident in the fifteenth-century *Mufākharat al-ruzz wa-l-ḥabb rummān*,[9] which is a boasting debate between rice and pomegranate seeds. The seeds tell the rice that it would not have looked white but for being beaten with rocks, and fiercely rubbed with sea salt.
aruzz Wāḥī (أرز واحي) Egyptian rice grown in the oases (*wāḥāt*). The rice grains must be washed well to remove any remaining salt used in whitening them.

aṣābiʿ Zaynab (أصابع زينب) cannoli fingers, stuffed and decorated, see *Kanz* recipes 285 and 308.

baqsamāṭ (بقسماط), also known as *khubz Rūmī* (خبز رومي) Byzantine bread, which al-Anṭākī, *Tadhkira* 149, describes as *maḥrūq* (lit., 'burnt'), overbaked. It is a variety of twice-baked bread, a kind of savory biscotti. Ibn al-Bayṭār, *al-Jāmiʿ* ii 316, describes it as a variety of the dry cookies of *kaʿk*. With its dry properties, it is beneficial for diarrhea, and can dry up humidities in the stomach. See *Kanz* recipe 211.

basandūd (بسندود) round sandwich cookies. Discs of cookie dough are baked in the oven first and then stuffed with simple starch confection called *ṣābūniyya* (see glossary 4); sometimes with nuts added to it. A poet singing its praises describes it thus (al-Ghuzūlī, *Maṭāliʿ* ii 84):

---

9 Geries, *Mufākhara* 70.

Round and brittle discs, as pure as camphor.
Stacked on a platter, like silver *dirhams* layered with gold dinars.

buzūr (بزور) generic term for seeds. However, in cooking contexts, it designates spice seeds and dried herbs.

daqīq (دقيق) generic term for flour of pulses and grains. If not specified, it designates wheat flour. All bread and cookie recipes in *Kanz*, chapter 2, use the term *daqīq*, which must have been white flour from common wheat (*Triticum aestivum*), also known as bread wheat. Al-Anṭākī, *Tadhkira* 149, says that the Egyptians use fine white flour, called *ḥuwwārā* (see entry below), in making cookies (*kaʿk*) for their religious feasts. Sometimes, the quality of *daqīq* is qualified with adjectives like:

Abyaḍ (white), ***ʿalāma*** (finely milled white flour), ***ʿalāma ʿāl*** (the best, excellent white flour), ***ḥadīth*** (freshly milled), ***nāʿim*** (finely crushed), ***nāʿim jiddan*** (very fine), and ***ṭayyib*** (fine-tasting flour). Bread made with fine white flour, for instance, is called *khubz ʿalāma abyaḍ* (*Kanz* recipe 321).

Other terms related to flour, mentioned a few times in the *Kanz* are the following:

daqīq fīhi simda (دقيق فيه سمدة) semolina flour from durum wheat (*Triticum durum*), which is not too finely crushed. See *Kanz* recipe 276, which deals with a pie shell comparable to today's graham cracker pie shells.

daqīq samīdh (دقيق سميذ) ***daqīq al-samīdh*** (دقيق السميذ) fine white flour, high in starch content, made from common wheat (*Triticum aestivum*), from which the finest quality of bread, *khubz samīdh*, was made in the eastern region of the medieval Arabo-Islamic world. This type of flour appears in *Kanz* recipes 283, 316, and 318, the last two of which are based on recipes from medieval Baghdad, from al-Warrāq's tenth-century cookbook (English trans. *Annals* 391, 402).

darmak (درمك) bran-free fine white flour.[10] Etymologically, it refers to anything that is pounded finely; even fine dust is called *darmak*.

ghubār al-darmak (غبار الدرمك) powdery flour. Generally, any grains crushed with a quern (*raḥā*) or the larger grinder (*ṭāḥūna*) produce fine powder, which falls all over the place. It is called *ghubār al-daqīq*; it was collected and used to make glues, and to dust foods before frying them. See Ibn Waḥshiyya, *al-Filāḥa* i 421.

10 As described by the fourteenth-century Andalusian scholar al-Arbūlī, *al-Kalām ʿalā l-aghdhiya* 124.

ḥuwwārā (حوارى) bran-free fine white flour, made from common wheat (*Triticum aestivum*), comparable to *darmak*, above. See entry below

muthallath (مثلث) fine white flour which has been washed three times. As described in Ibn Waḥshiyya, *al-Filāḥa* i 420 and 432–3, after removing the husks from the wheat berries, they are washed and dried, and then washed again and dried. He says washing wheat three times will result in the whitest and finest flour. *Muthallath* is also related to the practice of sifting the crushed wheat three times. The third sifting yields the finest flour.

samīdh al-daqīq (سميذ الدقيق) fine semolina, which is granular flour of durum wheat (*Triticum durum*). The term occurs in *Kanz* recipe 61, where toasted hazelnuts are pounded in a mortar and sifted so that they resemble fine semolina.

dashīsh (دشيش) coarsely ground grains and pulses.

farīk al-ḥinṭa (فريك الحنطة), or just *farīk*, toasted green wheat. Wheat stalks are harvested when they are still green, and then they are bundled into sheaves and burnt, until they are toasted, in a flaming fire free of any smoke. To remove the husks, they are rubbed between the fingers, for which the Arabic word is *yufrak*, and hence the name *farīk*. If the wheat berries need more heat, they are further toasted in stone pans to get rid of all moisture in the grains.[11] It is stored as whole grains, or cracked. In the case of the latter, it would be similar in texture to *burghul* (برغل) bulgur, made from fully grown wheat berries.

faṭā'ir (فطائر) unleavened bread.

ḥinṭa (حنطة) wheat, also called *burr* (بُرّ) and *qamḥ* (قمح). See *qamḥ* below.

ḥubūb (حبوب) general term for dried grains, legumes, and seeds.

ḥuwwārā (حُوّارى) lit., 'whitened.' It is fine bran-free white flour of common wheat (*Triticum aestivum*). The term is mostly used in the eastern region of the medieval Arabo-Islamic world. Because of the gluten it contains, it is suitable for making good chewy bread. As described by al-Hurawī, *Baḥr al-jawāhir* 137, *ḥuwwārā* bread is made with wheat, which has been husked, washed repeatedly to whiten it, dried in the shade, and then crushed into flour.

In *Kanz* recipes, the name *ḥuwwārā* occurs only in the chapter for making beer (*fuqqāʿ*) and similar drinks (recipes 391, 396, 408, 422, and 430). In the western region (the Maghrib) of the Arabo-Islamic world, its counterpart is *darmak*. See entry under *daqīq* above.

---

11 As described in the thirteenth-century *Milḥ al-malāḥa* by ʿUmar b. Yūsuf (sultan of Yemen), 55.

irnīn (إرنين) cookies stuffed with nuts or dates and shaped into rounds using wooden molds. See *Kanz* recipe DK, appendix 3, p. 80.[12]

iṭriya (إطرية) thin dried strings of noodles, purchased from the market and measured by cooks in handfuls. *Kanz* recipe 86 uses it in a meat dish.

jardaq (جردق) round thick and pithy bread. The name was said to derive from Persian *garda*, which means 'round' (*Tāj al-ʿarūs*, s.v. جردق).

jūdhāba (جوذابة) pl. *jawādhib* (جواذب) and *jawādhīb* (جواذيب) sweet bread pudding, originally baked under a suspended chunk of meat roasting in a *tannūr* (an open-topped, bell-shaped clay oven), as described in *Kanz* recipe 294. However, in recipes like 292 and 293, they are prepared as desserts, without the meat.

kaʿk (كعك) generic term for simple dry cookies, like crackers. However, it was also used to designate more refined cookies (see chapter 2), such as:

kaʿk bi-l-ʿajwa (كعك بالعجوة) date cookies.
kaʿk maltūt (كعك ملتوت) cookies enriched with fat.
kaʿk sukkarī (كعك سكري) sugary cookies.

kalījā (كليجة) round cookies, cut out with a special round cutter called *qālab al-kalījā* (قالب الكليجا). Alternatively, *Wuṣla* ii 658 suggests using the rim of a glass (*qadaḥ*).[13]

khamīra (خميرة) bread yeast. Usually a piece of the day's bread dough is kept in a bowl for the following day's dough. To make dough yeast from scratch, flour is kneaded with some oil and water, and is kept aside overnight to ferment (al-Hurawī, *Baḥr al-jawāhir* 17).

khubz (خبز) bread. In the eastern region (the Mashriq) of the Arabo-Islamic world, common wheat, also known as bread wheat (*Triticum aestivum*) was the most commonly used wheat variety. Based on al-Ghuzūlī, *Maṭāliʿ* ii 41:

1) The finest bread was called *samīdh*, and was described as the food of kings. It was made with the finest and whitest flour, called *daqīq al-samīdh*, which was fine white flour, high in starch content and bran free, made from common wheat (*Triticum aestivum*). It was said to be finer and more expensive than *ḥuwwārā* bread (al-Maqrīzī, *Ittiʿāẓ al-ḥunafā* 150), which comes next in excellence.
2) *Ḥuwwārā* was also made with fine bran-free flour of common wheat, but it was less starchy. It was said to be fit for the elite (*khawāṣ*).

---

12 For more on these cookies, see al-Warrāq, English trans. *Annals* 571–2.

13 Such references, in addition to the one made by Ibn Baṭṭūṭa, *Riḥla* 178, are the earliest citations of today's traditional cookies called *kleicha* (as pronounced in Iraq) and *koloocheh* in Iran. For more on this, see Nasrallah, "The Iraqi Cookie" 4–10.

3) As for the commoners (*ʿawām*), they had the less refined *khushkār* bread to eat, made with whole wheat flour. *Shaʿīr* bread made with barley flour, on the other hand, was the food of the esoteric.

In the western (the Maghrib) region of the Arabo-Islamic world, bread was predominantly made with durum wheat (*Triticum durum*), where it was more abundantly cultivated due to the general dry conditions of the region. The crushed flour from durum wheat is called *samīd*/*samīdh*, which is characterized by its yellowish hue and gritty sandlike texture. As displayed in the extant medieval Andalusian/Moroccan cookbooks, breads and pastries are made with it, but not before it is moistened with water and kept aside for a while to soften, and then kneaded like regular flour. Bread made with it is just called *khubz*, and sometimes qualified with adjectives like *faṭīr* (unleavened), depending on whether it was baked in a *tannūr*, *furn*, *malla* (buried in sand), or *ṭājin al-ḥadīd* (iron plate).[14] See *samīd* below.

fatāt khubz (فتات خبز) crumbs of bread.
lubāb khubz (لباب خبز) crumbs of the soft inner part of the fresh bread. It is often used crushed in recipes, either fresh or toasted.

khubz al-abāzīr (خبز الابازير) ***khubz mubazzar*** (خبز مبزّر) rich bread enhanced with sesame seeds, as in *Kanz* recipe DK, appendix 2, p. 80.
khubz abyaḍ ʿalāma (خبز أبيض علامة) excellent bread, made with fine white flour from common wheat (*Triticum aestivum*).
khubz bāʾit (خبز بائت) previous day's bread, stale.
khubz faṭīr (خبز فطير) unleavened bread.
khubz ḥuwwārā (خبز حوّارى) bread made with *ḥuwwārā*, which is fine bran-free flour of common wheat (*Triticum aestivum*). It was said to be the most balanced of all breads, being in the middle—neither too refined nor too dense. It was favored by physicians (al-Ghuzūlī, *Maṭāliʿ* ii 41). Based on al-Maqdisī, *Aḥsan al-taqāsīm* 199, it was deemed the best variety of bread in Egypt.
khubz manfūsh (خبز منفوش) fried fluffy and brittle white bread, served as sweet pastry sprinkled with sugar, see *al-manfūsh* below.
khubz maʿrūk (خبز معروك) bread made with dough which has been kneaded vigorously by rubbing and pressing it. Due to the prolonged kneading and perfect fermentation, the bread is praised as being nourishing and easy to digest. In the bread market, it was more expensive than other types of bread (see for instance, Ibn Ṭūlūn, *Mufākaha* 214). It is often mentioned as the bread to eat with the *muzawwarāt* stews

14 See, for instance, al-Tujībī, *Fiḍālat al-khiwān* 36–7.

for the sick. See for instance *Kanz* recipe 84. A recipe for making *khubz maʿrūk* is found in al-Warrāq, English trans. *Annals*, chapter 13.

khubz mukhtamir (خبز مختمر) well-fermented bread.

khubz shadīd al-khumra (خبز شديد الخمرة) very well fermented bread.

khubz muṭayyab (خبز مطيّب) enhanced bread made delicious and aromatic by adding spices, herbs and the like.

khubz samīdh (خبز سميذ) the most refined bread made with flour called *daqīq al-samīdh*, as it is called in the eastern (the Mashriq) region of the Arabo-Islamic world. It is fine white flour, high in starch content and bran free, made from common wheat (*Triticum aestivum*). It is finer and more expensive than *ḥuwwārā* (al-Maqrīzī, *Ittiʿāẓ al-ḥunafā* 150).

khubz ṭayyib (خبز طيّب) delicious bread, sweet, rich and delicate. See *Kanz* recipe DK, appendix 1, p. 79.

khudūd al-aghānī (خدود الاغاني) chanteuses' cheeks, sumptuous round sandwich cookies. See *Kanz* recipe 270.

kumāj (كماج) round white bread, made thick, spongy and pithy; unlike the thin sheets of *ruqāq* bread. It is baked in the commercial *furn* 'brick oven.'

kunāfa (كنافة), *waraq kunāfa* (ورق الكنافة), *ruqāq kunāfa* (رقاق كنافة), *khubz al-kunāfa* (خبز الكنافة), crepes for making *kunāfa* sweets (see glossary 4 below), or used as wrappers for making *sanbūsak* (see below). *Kunāfa* recipes in the *Kanz* use ready-made crepes, but do not give directions on how to make them. They were probably available to purchase from the food market.

We do find, however, some useful guidelines in *Wuṣla* ii 648 for making batter for *kunāfa* and *qaṭāʾif* (pancakes):

1) Batter for *qaṭāʾif* is prepared by first making unleavened firm dough (*faṭīr*) and setting it aside. Next, a leaven is prepared by mixing some of the unleavened dough with hot water and *būraq* (sodium bicarbonate) or *naṭrūn mashwī* (baked natron).[15] This mix, along with water, is worked into the dough until it becomes like batter in consistency, and left to rest for an hour.
2) Batter for *kunāfa* is made by preparing unleavened dough first, and then thinning it down with water until it has the consistency of batter.

Al-Tujībī, in his Andalusian cookbook *Fiḍāla* 69–70, provides details, using the prevalent semolina flour. He says firm dough is made with two pounds of best *samīd*

15 Al-Anṭākī, *Tadhkira* 95, says that the best natron is that which has been baked in earthenware vessels. For borax and natron, see glossary 8 below.

flour,[16] and then water is poured on it, and it is worked with the hand until it thins down, as is done when making starch solution for starching clothes (*talbīna li-l-thiyāb*), al Tujībī explains. The solution is strained so that nothing remains of the wheat particles. It is then left to settle, after which the liquid is poured off, leaving the starch in the bottom. Enough water is added to this starch until it is neither too thin nor too thick. It is then used by pouring some of it in a very thin layer on a large heated plate set on flameless coal fire.

kuskusū (كسكوا) (كسكسو) dish of meat and home-made couscous. In *Kanz* recipe 123, the dough is made with flour (*daqīq*),[17] and then rolled into small balls, like *mufattal*. The couscous particles are also referred to as *ʿajīn* (dough), which are steamed by placing them in a perforated pot fitted tightly on another pot of boiling stew. In *Wuṣla* ii 608, a comparable dish, called *kuskusū Maghribī* (Moroccan couscous), describes making couscous by sprinkling water on flour (*daqīq*) and rubbing it between the fingers like *mufattala*, and then sifting it. The Andalusian couscous recipes in al-Tujībī, *Fiḍāla* 87–90 call for semolina (*samīd*).[18]

lubāb al-khubz (لباب الخبز) bread crumb, see under *khubz* above.

lubāb al-ḥinṭa (لباب الحنطة) starchy portion of the wheat grain (al-Hurawī, *Baḥr al-jawāhir* 218). See p. 465, n. 3 above.

al-manfūsh (المنفوش) fried fluffy and brittle white bread, served as sweet pastry sprinkled with sugar, as I gathered from the frequent allusions to it in fifteenth-century Ibn Sūdūn, *Nuzhat al-nufūs*, 150, 179, 182, 188, 200, 221, and 233. In addition, from a reference to it in *Mufākharat al-ruzz wa-l-ḥabb rummān*,[19] which is a fifteenth-century boasting debate between rice and pomegranate seeds, we also gather that it was made with rice flour. This indeed explains the repeated references to its whiteness in Ibn Sūdūn's *Nuzhat al-nufūs*.

However, from Ibn al-Ukhuwwa, *Maʿālim al-qurba*, fol. 76r, we learn that other fine white flours were used to make it. In his specifications for the properly made *manfūsh*, with each 10 *raṭl*s (10 pounds) of flour, 5 *raṭl*s of wheat starch must be used. They are kneaded with egg whites, but Ibn al-Ukhuwwa cautions against using too much of it, lest the pastry should smell of eggs (*zafar*). He also recommends adding aromatics to help mask any eggy smell. The dough is shaped into discs and then fried in fresh sesame oil, and drenched in white sugar.

---

16 In North Africa and Andalusia, it is semolina flour of durum wheat.

17 The recipe does not specify the variety of flour used.

18 On the history of couscous, which is generally believed to be of Berber origin, see Wright, *Mediterranean Feast* 660–4.

19 Geries, *Mufākhara* 67.

mufattal (مفتّل) couscous rolled into tiny balls like peppercorns. See *kuskusū* above.
nashā (نشا) ***nashāʾ qalb*** (نشاء قلب) wheat starch.

nashāʾ maḥlūl (نشاء محلول) starch dissolved in liquid.

nuhūd al-ʿadhārī (نهود العذاري), *nuhūd al-ʿadhrāʾ* (نهود العذراء) lit., 'virgins' breasts,' delicate and aromatic cookies shaped like breasts, see *Kanz* recipe 300.
nukhāla (نخالة) wheat bran.
qamḥ (قمح) *Triticum* (S) wheat, also called *ḥinṭa* (حنطة) and *burr* (بُرّ), as we learn from medieval lexicons like *Lisān al-ʿarab.* The differences were regional and linguistic. *Ḥinṭa* was the term preferred in the eastern regions, like Iraq; whereas *qamḥ* was common in the Levant, Egypt, and North Africa; and *burr* was considered a purer Arabic term (*afṣaḥ*) than the other two. The best wheat variety is smooth, large, and heavy (*razīn*); neither too dense (*mulazzaz*) nor too brittle (*sakhīf*), and wax-yellow (*aṣfar*) in color—between red wheat (*qamḥ aḥmar*) and white wheat (*qamḥ abyaḍ*).[20] Its properties are moderate, leaning toward heat and moisture, and it was deemed superior to other grains. Al-Anṭākī, *Tadhkira* 146, says that in Egypt it is sown in October and harvested in June.
qamḥ madshūsh (قمح مدشوش) coarsely crushed wheat.

qamḥ madshūsh rafīʿ (قمح مدشوش رفيع) wheat crushed into fine grains.
qamḥ maqshūr (قمح مقشور) husked wheat berries.
qamḥ zarīʿ (قمح زريع) sprouted wheat berries, used in *Kanz* recipe 501 to make a fermented condiment.

qaṭāʾif (قطائف) pancakes, drenched in syrup, see glossary 4 below.

ʿajīn al-qaṭāʾif (عجين القطائف) batter used in making sweet dishes of *kunāfa* and *qaṭāʾif.* See *kunāfa* above.
waraq qaṭāʾif (ورق القطائف) pancakes used to make this dessert. See *kunāfa* above.

qāwūt (قاووت) granola. The name was originally *qāghūt* (قاغوت), a Turkish word related to the Arabic *qūt* (sustenance, provisions), used to designate special food of toasted and crushed grains mixed with sugar and fat. In Arabic, it is called *sawīq*, and was given to women after labor (Kāshgharī, *Kitāb Dīwān lughāt al-Turk* 122). In its basic form, *sawīq* is crushed toasted grains and seeds, mixed with fat and sugar; used to

20 As described in Ibn Jazla, *Minhāj al-bayān* 78r; and al-Isrāʾīlī, *Kitāb al-Aghdhiya* ii 3–4.

make drinks, nourishing foods, and thick *khabīṣ* puddings. It was a favorite provision of travelers. See *Kanz* recipes 287, 304, 307 for the different ways it is prepared.

qāwūt Baladī (قاووت بلدي) local-style granola.
qāwūt Turkī (قاووت تركي) Turkish-style granola.

quḍāmā (قضاما) crunchy roasted legumes, such as chickpeas and fava beans.
raghīf muḥassan (رغيف محسّن) refined bread.
rishtā (رشتا) fresh thin noodles. See also *iṭriya* above.

FIGURE 54
Cook making rishtā, *detail from a detached folio, S1986.221 (Freer Gallery of Art and Arthur M. Sackler Gallery, Smithsonian Institution, Washington, DC: Purchase—Charles Lang Freer Endowment).*

ruqāq (رقاق) large malleable thin sheets of bread (*labiq*), made from leavened dough and baked on a round heated plate or in the *tannūr* (open-topped, bell-shaped clay oven), one at a time. They are like today's *lawāsh* (lavash) bread, also called *marqūq*. It is convenient for scooping morsels of food.

Besides eating it as baked bread, it was used to wrap—baked or unbaked—the fried pastries of *sanbūsak*, see entry below. It was also used in making *jūdhāba*, see entry in glossary 5. Huge sheets of this kind of bread were used to line the tray in which the food was served. When used in this manner, it was referred to as *ṣabīr al-khiwān* (صبير الخوان), *Tāj al-ʿarūs*, s.v. صبر.

samīdh (سميذ) *samīd* (سميد) semolina, commonly made from durum wheat (*Triticum durum*).[21] It was known for its gritty sandlike texture. In Ibn al-Mujāwir, *Tārīkh al-mustabṣir* 82, sand is compared to *samīdh* which has not been ground finely. In fact, this distinctive gritty texture of the crushed grains of this type of hard wheat—the hardest of all cultivated wheat varieties—led to its name *samīd*.[22]

It is the major type of wheat flour used in the western (Maghrib) region of the Arabo-Islamic world. This is well-attested in the recipes included in the two surviving thirteenth-century Andalusian cookbooks, where *samīd* is often called for in making bread, porridges, sweet condensed puddings, couscous, and some pastries. However, before kneading *samīd* flour, the cook is often instructed to moisten it first with some water—cold water in the summer, and warm in winter—and set it aside for a while, after which it can be kneaded like regular flour.[23]

samīdh al-qamḥ (سميذ القمح) semolina from durum wheat (*Triticum durum*).

sanbūsak (سنبوسك) sweet and savory deep-fried filled pastries, often folded into triangles. The rolled ones are called *mukaffan* (shrouded). Wrappers used in making *sanbūsak* include sheets of thin dough, or pieces of already baked thin sheets of bread that were cut out, called *ruqāq*; or *kunāfa* sheets. See entries in this section. See for instance *Kanz* recipes 115, 116, and 127.

sawīq (سويق) toasted and crushed seeds and grains, mixed with fat and sugar, and stored and used as needed to make drinks, nourishing foods, and thick *khabīṣ* puddings. It was a favorite provision of travelers. See also *qāwūt* above.

shaʿīriyya (شعيرية) orzo. Flour is made into stiff dough, and then rolled (*yuftal*) between the fingers into barley-like pasta. See *Kanz* recipe 117.

shishbarak (ششبرك) raviolis. It is made with flattened unleavened dough, filled with a meat mixture, shaped into rolls, triangles or half-moons, and then fried and simmered in yogurt or sumac sauce. See *Kanz* recipe 37.

tuṭmāj (تطماج) *ṭuṭmāj* (ططماج) fresh noodle strips, called *lakhsha* (lit., 'slippery') in Persian, made with stiff unfermented wheat dough. It is flattened into a thin sheet, cut into strips, and then spread outside to dry in the air for half a day. Next, it is cut into pieces 2-fingers long (as described in al-Warrāq Istanbul MS, fol. 168r). In *Kanz*, recipe 109, *tuṭmāj* is cooked in boiling water, and stirred with a stick so that the noodles do not stick to each other, and to avoid breaking the pasta pieces.

---

21 Cf. different usage of the term *samīdh* in the eastern (Mashriq) regions of the Arabo-Islamic world in *daqīq samīdh* under *daqīq* entry above. See also the introductory notes in this section.

22 See the introductory note in this section, point 4.

23 Al-Tujībī, *Fiḍālat al-khiwān*; and anonymous *Anwāʿ al-ṣaydala*.

3. Dairy

akhlāṭ (أخلاط) sg. *khilāṭ* (خلاط) condiment of drained yogurt infused with chopped tender vegetables and herbs. See *Kanz* recipes 509 and 510.

aqiṭ (أقط) sourish yogurt cheese, made by heating yogurt and leaving it until the whey separates from the solids, and then draining it. See *Kanz* recipe 508.

bīrāf (بيراف) clotted cream, see *Kanz* recipe 507.

ḥālūm (حالوم) semi-hard white cheese, smooth in texture, indigenous to Egypt. Etymologically, the name is said to have a Coptic origin.[1] It is not as chewy and compact as *jubn Shāmī* (see below). It is stored in brine over a period of months; the longer it is kept, the saltier it becomes (al-Anṭākī, *Tadhkira* 113). See *Kanz* recipes 520–2, which do not give a recipe for making it, but describe ways for serving it with seasoned sauces.

jājaq (جاجق) condiment of drained yogurt, see *Kanz* recipes 518, 519, and 523.

jubn Shāmī (جبن شامي) Levantine cheese, like mozzarella cheese in texture. Al-Anṭākī, *Tadhkira* 113, says that in Egypt what is known as *jubn Shāmī* is imported from Cyprus. He describes its texture as being semi-hard, compact, and chewy. It is kept by salting and draining it of its moisture. *Kanz* recipe 198 uses it pounded (*madqūq*), which does indeed verify al-Anṭākī's description of it. Otherwise, with hard aged cheeses, the usual instruction is to grate it (*yuḥakk*).

jubn ṭarī (جبن طري), ***jubn akhḍar*** (جبن أخضر) lit., 'green cheese,' fresh cheese.

khamīra (خميرة) fermenting agent for making yogurt; it is usually a small amount of sour yogurt. *Kanz* recipe 527 suggests a way to help milk ferment well in the cold days of winter. Dried unripe sour grapes are soaked in hot water, and then pounded and their strained juice is added to the milk.

kishk (كشك) dried dough of crushed wheat and sour yogurt. It is used to make *kishkiyyāt* dishes, first it is pulverized, then dissolved in liquid, and added to the pot. In *Waṣf* 194–5, it is said that peasants in villages prepare *kishk* with crushed wheat and yogurt. The Turkmen (Turkumān), however, only make it with sour yogurt. It is shaped into discs, and left in the sun to dry.

> ***kishk Khurāsānī*** (كشك خراساني) named after the northeastern province in Persia. See *Kanz* recipe 524 for directions on how to prepare it.

laban (لبن) pl. *albān* (ألبان) may designate milk or yogurt. To differentiate between the two, sometimes milk is called *laban ḥulw* (sweet milk), or *laban ḥalīb*. Yogurt is referred to as *laban rā'ib* (curdled milk), or *laban ḥāmiḍ* (sour milk).

---

1 See for instance, Hinds and Badawi, *Dictionary of Egyptian Arabic*, s.v. حلوم.

 | DOI 10.1163/9789004349919_029

laban Fārisī (لبن فارسي), also called *laban Shīrāz* (لبن شيراز) thick drained yogurt, see *Shīrāz* below.

laban ḥalīb (لبن حليب) sometimes referred to just as *laban*, milk.

laban baqarī (لبن بقري) cow's milk.
laban ḥalīb ḍa'nī (لبن حليب ضأني) sheep's milk.
laban ḥāmiḍ (لبن حامض) yogurt.
laban jāmūsī (لبن جاموسي) water buffalo milk.
laban makhīḍ (لبن مخيض) buttermilk.
laban maqṭūʿ (لبن مقطوع) very sour yogurt.
laban munashshaf (لبن منشف) drained yogurt.
laban niʿāj (لبن نعاج) ewe's milk.
laban rā'ib (لبن رائب) yogurt made without rennet. After churning the butter and removing it, the remaining milk is left for a day or two to curdle into yogurt. It was believed to be easier to digest than thick and drained varieties of yogurt (Ibn al-Bayṭār, *al-Jāmiʿ* iv 373).
laban Shīrāz (لبن شيراز) see *Shīrāz* below.
laban Turkumānī (لبن تركماني) Turkmens' yogurt, made from sheep milk, described in *Kanz* recipe 518 as rich and delicious.
laban yāghurt (لبن ياغرت) cow or water buffalo yogurt, made with rennet. See *Kanz* recipe 528.

liba' (لبأ) beestings, colostrum, the first milk drawn from a mammal which has just delivered. See *Kanz* recipe 512.

minfaḥa (منفحة) rennet, which is the fourth stomach (abomasum) of suckling sheep, goats, or calves.

mish al-jubn (مش الجبن) cheese whey. See *Kanz* recipe 529, where it is used in preparing a thyme condiment.

qanbarīs (قنبريس) somewhat salty soft yogurt cheese, described as sour, rich, and delicious. It was kept in unglazed jars or thin leather containers; it can stay good to use for a whole year. See *Kanz* recipes 508 and 515.

qanbarīs Turkumānī (قنبريس تركماني) sour soft cheese, made with sheep milk.

rakhbīn (رخبين) dried buttermilk, made from whey. It is used in a meat dish named after it, *rakhbīniyya*. When needed, a small amount of it is dissolved in water or broth and added to the pot. It is the precursor of what is now known as *jamīd* (جميد) in the Levant. In Jordan today, it is an essential ingredient in the traditional dish of *minsaf* (منسف).

samn (سمن) ghee, used as cooking fat, see glossary 6 below.

Shīrāz (شيراز), also called *laban Fārisī* (لبن فارسي) drained yogurt which has been made with rennet. It is used as a condiment served with bread. Al-Hurawī, *Baḥr al-jawāhir* 320, compares its consistency to very thick *ḥasū* (thick flour-based soup), and says it is served as a condiment. A recipe in al-Tujībī, *Fiḍāla* 217, describes how to make it and suggests ways to serve it.

zubd (زبد) ***zubda*** (زبدة) butter, mostly consumed fresh with dates and bread. In the *Kanz*, few recipes require butter. *Samn* (ghee) is used instead as cooking fat. See *samn* in glossary 6 below.

4. Desserts, Sweeteners, and Conserves for Pleasure and Health

abū lash (أبو لاش), *bū lāsh* (بو لاش) pastries shaped like Nile-tilapia fish. *Lāsh* is the name of a Nile River fish; it is a round, red fish of the tilapia species (*Chromis niloticus*); called 'lacha' in Spanish (Dozy, *Takmilat al-maʿājim* 1367, s.v. لاش). The thin round pastries are made to resemble this fish. They are colored red with a crisscross design around the edges for tail and fins.

There is a recipe by the same name in *Wuṣla* ii 630, but it is very brief and different, described as follows: "It can be made with milk and sugar; or coarsely crushed toasted pistachios are sprinkled on small *qaṭāʾif* discs; and then drenched in syrup."

ʿajamiyya (عجمية) thick flour-based pudding, whose name implies that it is made in the Persian style. It is a variety of *khabīṣ* pudding, ubiquitous in the Abbasid Baghdadi cuisine. See, for instance, al-Warrāq's chapter 94, and recipe in Baghdādī 73–4. In modern Iraq, it is known as *ḥalāwat ṭahīn* (حلاوة طحين).[1]

It is still a well-known traditional dessert in modern Egypt; known by the names *ʿajamiyya, sadd al-ḥanak* (سد الحنك) 'the mouth-shutter', and *ḥalāwat daqīq* (حلاوة دقيق) 'flour pudding.' It is not known exactly why the dessert is called *sadd al-ḥanak*. Some speculate that the dessert is so filling that its eater just 'shuts up' and stops asking for more food. See *Kanz* recipes 303, 327, 345.

ʿaqīd (عقيد) syrups and juices, which are boiled down to a thick and chewy consistency.

> ***ʿaqīd sakanjabīn*** (عقيد سكنجبين) chewy oxymel candy, see *Kanz* recipe 348.
> ***ʿaqīd al-tamr Hindī*** (عقيد التمر هندي) chewy tamarind candy, see *Kanz* recipe 371.

aqrāṣ laymūn (أقراص ليمون) hard lemon drop candy. They were recommended as *naql*, which are nibbles, enjoyed while having alcoholic drinks. Such foods were believed to slow down intoxication and prevent hangovers. See *Kanz* recipe 349.

ʿasal (عسل) *ʿasal naḥl* (عسل نحل) bee honey, which is touted as very nourishing food. The best is the spring harvest, which is sweet and pleasant smelling, and somewhat thick in consistency. It is purified by mixing it with some water, and boiling it until water evaporates, and meanwhile skimming the resulting froth. Its properties are hot and dry, it generates good blood, strengthens the stomach, and keeps the body in good health; and it is the best cure for cold-related illnesses. It is highly

---

1 This dessert was in fact known in the Near Eastern region from ancient times. A surviving Akkadian text tells of a sweet dish called 'muttaqu,' made with flour, sesame oil, honey, and water. See Levey, *Chemistry* 49.

 | DOI 10.1163/9789004349919_030

aphrodisiac, boosts erection, and increases semen. In short, it is the most beneficial food for the body. It is the best medium for combining medicinal herbs and spices because it preserves them. Due to its excessively hot properties, it was deemed fit for the elderly and the phlegmatic. To reduce its heat, the recommendation was to have sour drinks after eating it (al-Rāzī, *Manāfiʿ al-aghdhiya* 240; al-Malik al-Muẓaffar, *al-Muʿtamad* 377–9).

ʿasal abyaḍ (عسل أبيض) white (i.e., light-colored) bee honey.
ʿasal mādhī (عسل ماذي) smooth and thin white honey.
ʿasal muḥarraq (عسل محرّق) burnt honey, obtained by boiling it until it is slightly caramelized, turns medium to dark brown, and starts to smoke. Adding it in small amounts gives a sauce like *murrī* a pleasant slightly burnt flavor. See *Kanz*, recipe 165.
ʿasal naḥl Miṣrī (عسل نحل مصري) Egyptian bee honey.
ʿasal al-shahd (عسل الشهد) bee honey with its wax.

In addition, the name *ʿasal* may also designate other syrupy products, such as:

ʿasal mursal (عسل مرسل) sugar cane syrup made by reducing sugar cane juice, as described by al-Nuwayrī, *Nihāyat al-arab* viii 196. He further explains that this is done when the boiling cane juice fails to crystallize (*yataqannad*).[2] He also adds that it is an Egyptian product, not known in the Levant.
ʿasal qaṣab (عسل قصب) sugar cane syrup, a by-product of the first boiling of cane juice. It is less refined than *qaṭr* (entry below), which is produced in the repeated rounds of refining sugar.
ʿasal tamr (عسل تمر) date syrup, also called *dibs*, see entry below.

dhāt al-katifayn (ذات الكتفين) (lit., 'having two shoulders'), date candy. Each date is stuffed with two pistachios to make it look like a fledgling locust. See *Kanz* recipe 267.
dibs (دبس) date syrup, produced by extraction. Piles of dried dates with high syrup content are pressed with weights until their syrup oozes out. Another way of producing *dibs* is by cooking the dates with water and straining and boiling it down to the consistency of syrup.
fānīdh (فانيذ) pulled taffy made with sugar or honey, and stretched and aerated by pulling it repeatedly by means of a large nail (*mismār*) hammered into the wall. The verb used to describe this method is *yuqṣar*, which describes putting a thing back to its original place; this applies to pulling a sugar strand away from the nail and hooking it back to it. This is done when the boiling sugar reaches a stage described thus:

2 The verb derives from *qand* 'crystallized sugar.'

"A cooled off piece taken from it should be brittle and break easily" (بحيث انه اذا اخذ منه شئ وبرد تكسر وتقصف), as described in *Waṣf* 154. In today's culinary terminology, this would be called the 'hard crack point,' 300–310 degrees F. See *Kanz* recipe 265.

In the medieval Arabo-Islamic world, *fānīdh* had several names:

ghubbayṭ majbūd (غبيط مجبود) pulled taffy made with honey, described in al-Tujībī *Fiḍāla* 245. Other variants on the name are *qubayṭā'* (قبيطاء), *qubbāṭ* (قباط), and *qubbayṭā* (قبيطى).[3]

ḥalwā' yābisa (حلواء يابسة) 'hard sweets' made with sugar. See the recipes in Baghdādī 75; *Waṣf* 154–5; and *Wuṣla* ii 639.

nāṭif (ناطف) hard candy, mentioned in *Wuṣla* ii 638; and *Waṣf* 154.

nāṭif al-mismār (ناطف المسمار) taffy, pulled and stretched by means of a nail (*mismār*), in al-Warrāq, chapter 94.

qurāḍiyya (قراضية) lit., 'the clipped.' As described in al-Hurawī, *Baḥr al-jawāhir* 295, it is hard, sticky candy, made with and without nuts and seeds. It is clipped into small balls (*banādiq*) using a *miqrāḍ* (مقراض), hence the name.

Fānīdh is hard and chewy in texture. It is left plain or colored, and shaped in a variety of ways, some are simply shaped into discs, some are formed into figurines (*tamāthīl*), as suggested in *Wuṣla* ii 639, and some are molded into rings, and triangles, as in *Waṣf* 155.

Al-Hurawī, in *Baḥr al-jawāhir* 357, calls this chewy candy *nāṭif murakkab* (ناطف مركب) if it is kneaded with a variety of nuts; and *nāṭif mubazzar* (ناطف مبزر) if it is kneaded with seed spices.

ḥall (حلّ) *ḥall al-sukkar* (حل السكر) simple sugar syrup, made by dissolving sugar in water and boiling it to the consistency of syrup. The only other medieval source where *ḥall al-sukkar* is used in recipes and correctly copied is al-Warrāq Istanbul MS, fol. 238v. Copyists of *Kanz* erroneously write it as *khall* (خلّ) 'vinegar,' probably a term with which they were more familiar. In *Kanz*, recipe 63, we learn that this simple syrup could also be purchased from the marketplace, in which case it was just heated up, and used as directed in the recipe. See also *jullāb* below.

ḥalwā (حلوى) and *ḥalāwa* (حلاوة) thick puddings; these may also designate sweets in general.

ḥalāwa ʿajamiyya (حلوى عجمية) see *ʿajamiyya* above.

ḥalāwa makshūfa (حلوى مكشوفة) three recipes in *Kanz* chapter 10 carry this name: 272, which is an open-faced pie; and 275 and 278, which describe candy brittle.

3 *Lisān al-ʿarab*, s.v. قبط.

ḥalwā ṣābūniyya (حلوى صابونية) dense wheat starch pudding, usually colored red, yellow, and green, so that the cut pieces look like colored soap bars.[4] *Kanz* recipe 302 of *ṣābūniyya*, however, does not call for coloring the dessert.

ḥalwā ṭayyiba bilā nār (حلوى طيبة بلا نار) uncooked confection made with sugar and pistachios, see *Kanz* recipe 289.

ḥalwā wardiyya (حلوى وردية) thick rose-petal pudding.

hays (هيس) date balls, a favorite provision for travelers, see *Kanz* recipe 343.

jamājim al-sukkar (جماجم السكر) rounded masses of white sugar, from which pieces are broken as needed. The phrase occurs in al-Tujībī *Fiḍāla* 262, where small pieces of dough are shaped like *jamājim al-sukkar*. Generally, *jamājim* was used in medieval times to designate rounded masses, such as those of ambergris (*jamājim al-ʿanbar*) found floating in the sea, or opium poppy pods (*jamājim al-khashkhāsh*). Reciting verses in praise of sweet muskmelons, a poet compares them to *jamājim al-sukkar* coated with rough leather to prevent their being dissolved by water (al-Suyūṭī, *Bughyat al-wuʿāt* 171).

jullāb (جلاّب), *jullāb maḥlūl* (جلاّب محلول) *ḥall jullāb* (حل جلاّب) sugar syrup, used for cooking purposes. The term is used loosely to designate simple syrups, which are not necessarily perfumed with rosewater. However, *jullāb* used for making refreshing restorative drinks must be true to its name (rosewater). See *ḥall* above; and *jullāb*, glossary 1, above.

Ready-to-use syrup was expected to be available to cooks. *Kanz* recipe 63, for instance, gives the option of buying it from the market place. In this case, the instruction is only to heat it up very well. Otherwise, as this recipe shows, it must be made from scratch, starting with sugar and water.

jullāb maʿqūd (جلاب معقود) sugar syrup thickened by boiling it down.

jullāb raqīq (جلاب رقيق) sugar syrup, thin in consistency.

jullāb sukkar qawī (جلاب سكر قوي) sugar syrup, thick in consistency.

In addition, recipes sometimes refer to the proper consistency of the cooking syrup, in terms of its *qiwām* (consistency):

qiwām al-mayba (قوام الميبة) thin consistency, like thin honey.

qiwām qawī (قوام قوي) syrup should be thick enough to fall from the spoon in sheets, as explained in one of the almond candy recipes in *Wuṣla* ii 646.

---

4 As detailed by ʿAbd al-Laṭīf al-Baghdādī, *Riḥla* 118.

qiwām al-qaṣf (قوام القصف) descriptive of syrup that has reached a brittle stage, see entry below.

jimāliyya (جمالية) melt-in-your-mouth date dessert, see *Kanz* recipe 321.

juwārish (جوارش) syrupy preparations consumed as digestive stomachic after the meals. See *Kanz* recipes 372–80.

khabīṣ (خبيص) thick pudding made with toasted flour or crushed almonds, with fat and sugar, see *Kanz* recipes 326, 318, and 319. See also *ʿajamiyya* above.

kunāfa (كنافة) thin strips are made by slicing baked thin sheets of dough, and then cooking them in syrup. See *kunāfa* in glossary 2 above.

kunāfa maṭbūkha (كنافة مطبوخة) *kunāfa* shreds cooked in syrup, See *Kanz* recipe 333.

kunāfa mumallaḥa (كنافة مملحة) lit., 'salted *kunāfa*.' *Kunāfa* shreds are sprinkled with a lot of coarsely ground white sugar which makes them look as if they were salted (*mumallaḥ*). See *Kanz* recipes 298, 332.

laʿūq (لعوق) pl. *laʿūqāt* (لعوقات) restorative thick syrup, sufficiently firm but still soft, so that it can be licked with a spoon. See *Kanz* recipe 449.

lawzīnaj yābis (لوزينج يابس) almond brittle, see *Kanz* recipe 311.

luqaymāt al-qāḍī (لقيمات القاضي) judge's tidbits, which are delicate small sandwich cookies doused in syrup, see *Kanz* recipe 286.

maʿjūn (معجون) pl. *maʿājīn* (معاجين) restorative electuary with a paste-like consistency, see *Kanz* recipes 354, 355, 381–2, 384–91.

malban (ملبن) thick and chewy starch pudding. Today, it is more commonly known as *luqum*/*ḥalqūm*, and in the West, as Turkish delight. Another name for it is *jild al-faras* (جلد الفرس) 'horse's penis' (*Wuṣla* ii 626; Ibn Baṭṭūṭa, *Riḥla* 37, 261). Ibn Baṭṭūṭa explains that it is a Damascene confection made with *rub al-ʿinab* (grape molasses), starch, and nuts, and apparently shaped like sausages, the way they are made today. See *Kanz* recipe 337, which uses it in making dessert.

mukhannaqa (مخنّقة) lit., 'throttled.' This dish of *kunāfa*, which consists of thin strips cooked in syrup, might be evocative of the practice of boiling silkworm cocoons to get the silk threads. In Arabic, the process is called (تخنيق الشرانق) 'throttling the cocoons' (See Dozy, *Takmilat al-maʿājim* 418, s.v. خنّق). See *Kanz* recipe 297.

musayyar al-qarʿ (مسيّر القرع) paste of gourd strips. It is like a thick jam or paste made with long shreds of gourd, *suyūr*. See *qarʿiyyat al-suyūr* below.

mushāsh (مشاش) suckers, or lollipops, see *Kanz* recipe 284. The name is derived from *mushāsh*, the soft ends of bones, such as chicken thighbones, which can be sucked and chewed.

naqūʿ (نقوع) compote made with dried fruits such as apricots, prunes, raisins, jujubes, tamarinds, and pomegranate seeds, eaten for their delicious taste and for their health benefits.[5] Ibn Sīnā calls it *naqūʿ al-qadīd* because the fruits are dried (*al-Qānūn* 552).

naqūʿ al-mishmish (نقوع المشمش) compote with apricots is the most prevalent, offered at the end of meals to aid digestion and quench thirst. See the *Kanz* recipes in chapter 13.

nāṭif (ناطف) pulled taffy made with sugar or honey, also called *ghubbayṭ majbūd* (غبيط مجبود), *ḥalwā' yābisa* (حلواء يابسة), and *fānīdh*. See *fānīdh* above.

nayda (نيدة) popular medieval Egyptian taffy, which al-Maqdisī, *Aḥsan al-taqāsīm* 75, says is *samnawā* (سمنوا).[6] He marvels at the unusual way it is made, adding that it is spread on mats to dry, and is chewy in texture. The *Kanz* does not include any recipes for making it, perhaps because it was more likely to be made by professional confectioners.

ʿAbd al-Laṭīf al-Baghdādī, *Riḥla* 118, says it looks dark brown, and it is not overly sweet. He briefly describes how it is made: Wheat grains are first sprouted and then boiled, so that they release all their starch into the water, which is strained, and boiled until it thickens. It is sprinkled with flour and stirred until it is very thick. When prepared this way, it is called *naydat al-bosh* (نيدة البوش).[7] Alternatively, it is left to boil without flour until it thickens into paste. When it is done this way, it is called *nayda maʿqūda* (نيدة معقودة), which is superior to the former. It is to be assumed that it is divided into taffy-like pieces and left to dry.[8]

qand (قند) crystallized unrefined sugar, see *sukkar* below.

qarʿiyyat al-suyūr (قرعية السيور), also called *musayyar al-qarʿ* (مسير القرع) thick jam of gourd, which has been cut into thin strips, hence the name *suyūr* (strips).

Besides eating it for its delicious taste, it is also consumed for its restorative properties, a kind of cure-all food. It invigorates coitus, helps weight gain, and opens obstructions. It also blocks vapors from going up to the head, thus preventing melancholy, dizziness, and all kinds of mental disorders. It cures chest pains,

---

5 See, for instance, al-Kāzarūnī, *al-Sadīdī* 327.

6 Possibly a corruption of *mann wa-salwā* (من وسلوى), which is originally made with manna. Imitation *mann wa-salwā* tastes and looks like nougat.

7 *Bosh* (بوش) is a Turkish word, which means 'of little value' (Redhouse, *Turkish and English Lexicon*).

8 Note that no sugar is used in making this taffy. However, malting the grains releases the starch and facilitates its turning into sugar. The prolonged boiling of the liquid causes the sugar it contains to caramelize, which indeed explains its final dark-brown color.

and strengthens the stomach. By adding poppy seeds to it, it can cure insomnia. Al-Anṭākī, *Tadhkira* 329, says it is so well known in all countries that people just call it *musayyar*. Sandalwood and mastic are among the essential spices added to it. See for instance *Kanz* recipes 313, 314.

qarn Bārūq (قرن باروق) Bārūq's horn are pastries shaped into small horn-like rolls, and then fried and dipped in syrup (*Kanz* recipe 309). Possibly, the pastry was named after Bārūq, an eleventh-century Turkish leader who was defeated in Ramla, Palestine.[9] It is likely that the 'horny' pastries with their satanic association were made to commemorate his defeat. In the corresponding recipe in *Wuṣla* ii 630, this pastry is called *kul wa-shkur* (كل واشكر) 'eat and be thankful.' The name is still used today to designate tiny pieces of baklawa.

Wuṣla gives this pastry the alternative name *qarn yārūq* (قرن ياروق). Isin, *Sherbet and Spice* 180–1, takes this as an originally Turkish name, and links it to *karni yarik* (split belly), which is indeed more descriptive of the slit and stuffed eggplant dish known by this name today than of this medieval pastry. In addition, the horn, as a form of pastry, was common during the time of the *Kanz*. For instance, al-Ḥajjār, *Kitāb al-Ḥarb al-maʿshūq* 118, mentions *qarn Bārūq* and another pastry called *qarn al-fīl* (elephant's horn, i.e., its tusk).

We should mention, however, that a medieval Turkman leader named Yārūq Asralān once lived in Aleppo, but he was a revered chief, after whose name the Aleppan village Yārūqiyya was named, and there is no reason to link his name to some 'horny' pastries. Unless perhaps the horn was an allusion to *Dhū l-Qarnayn* (one with two horns), who, in Arabo-Islamic culture, was a legendary example of the perfect ruler and is sometimes identified as Alexander the Great.

qaṭāʾif (قطائف) pancakes drenched in syrup, see *kunāfa* in glossary 2 above.

qaṭāʾif maḥshī (قطائف محشي) stuffed pancakes, see *Kanz* recipes 323 and 324.

qaṭr (قطر), also called *ʿasal al-qaṭr* (عسل القطر) cane-sugar molasses, collected from the drippings of the boiled-down juice of sugar cane, left in pottery vessels perforated with three holes.

qaṭr al-nabāt (قطر النبات) the purest variety of cane-sugar molasses, left over after growing sugar crystals to make sugar candy (*sukkar nabāt*), which was produced at the sugar mills (al-Nuwayrī, *Nihāyat al-arab* viii 197).

quṭāra ʿāl (قطارة عال) top-quality cane-sugar molasses. This is the drippings gathered during the final stage of refining white sugar.

usṭarūs (أسطروس) cane-sugar molasses, see entry below.

9 Ibn Khaldūn, *Tārīkh* 1842.

qawālib al-sukkar (قوالب السكر) sugar cones, which take their shape from the clay vessels in which the reduced cane-sugar juice is left to crystallize and refine.

qiwām al-qaṣf (قوام القصف) related to sugar syrup, when it is reaches a brittle consistency. In *Waṣf* 154, this stage is described thus, "A cooled off piece taken from it should be brittle and breaks easily" (بحيث انه اذا اخذ منه شئ وبرد تكسر وتقصف). In today's culinary terms, it is called 'hard crack point,' 300–310 degrees F.

ruṭab mu'assal (رطب معسل) fresh dates cooked in honey, see *Kanz* recipe 346.

ṣābūniyya (صابونية) see *ḥalwā ṣābūniyya* above.

sakanjabīn 'aqīd (سكنجبين عقيد) oxymel of chewy-candy, said to be the best *naql* (*mezze*) to be had with alcoholic drinks. See *Kanz* recipe 348.

shakrīnaj (شكرينج) almond confection, also known as *lawzīnaj*, see *Kanz* recipe 315, which instructs the cook to cut it into bite-size rhombuses. The word the recipe uses to convey this instruction is (موازياً) and (مواربأ), as in the other *Kanz* copies, 'on the diagonal.' To my knowledge, this is the earliest evidence of *lawzīnaj* (or *shakrīnaj*, as it is called here) being cut into the characteristic diamond shape.

shu'abiyya (شعَبية) candy fingers. The name derives from *shu'ab* (شُعَب) 'fingers of the hand.' See *Kanz* recipe 279.

sukkar (سكّر) sugar extracted from *qaṣab al-sukkar* (قصب السكر) sugar cane. Writing in the sixteenth century, al-Anṭākī, *Tadhkira* 212–3, gives a brief description of how sugar was produced:[10]

1) The first stage of processing: After boiling down the juice of sugar cane and filtering it several times, it is poured into huge pottery vessels with wide tops and narrower bases, with three holes in them, loosely covered with cane husk. They are left in a somewhat warm place for about a week, with vessels under them to catch the dripping syrup, which at this first stage is called *'asal qaṣab* (عسل قصب) cane syrup, unrefined, very sweet, and dark in color. The resulting crystallized unrefined sugar is called *sukkar aḥmar*,[11] which is brown sugar. The verb *yataqannad* (يتقنّد) is used to describe sugar when it crystallizes, it is derived from *qand* (قند) 'crystallized sugar.'
2) In the second stage, the crystallized brown sugar is broken to pieces, dissolved in water, and cooked again to a certain reduced amount. Next, it is emptied into conical pottery vessels, like the ones used in the first stage, but smaller. The narrow bottom is sucked to draw out impurities, and then

10 The most detailed account by far is found in al-Nuwayrī, *Nihāyat al-arab* viii 194–7, discussed in Sato, *Sugar* 34–48. There is also some useful information regarding the names of types of sugar and their properties in Ibn al-Kutubī, *Mā lā Yasa' al-ṭabīb jahlahu*, s.v. سكر. For a discussion of sugar and honey, see, Marín and Waines, "The Balanced Way" 125–31.

11 Lit., 'red sugar.' In medieval times, there was no special word for brown.

left to drain the molasses, until the sugar is dry. The crystallized sugar in the lower, narrow part of the vessel is not as good as the rest of it. The resulting sugar is called *sukkar Sulaymānī*,[12] which is light in color, but still not quite white.

3) Sugar resulting from the second cooking is further cooked a third time. If it is poured into rectangular molds and is cooked no more, the resulting sugar is called *fānīdh*.[13] The rectangular mold is cut into pencil-like fingers or bars, called *aqlām*, sg *qalam* (pencils).

   However, if it is further treated by boiling it with milk, which rids it of all the remaining impurities, and then it is poured into smaller conical molds, which allow sugar to filter through more molasses, it is called *ublūj* (pl. *abālīj*),[14] named after the shape of the mold. It is also called *ṭabarzad*, after the custom of chiseling the required amounts with a *tabar* (Persian for hatchet). The resulting sugar is coarse granules, which are white but not translucent. *Ublūj*, also *ṭabarzad*, and *sanīnāt* is finer than *qalam*.

4) The finest of all sugars, one that is translucent and pure, can be obtained by treating sugar in a fourth stage. The sugar is further cooked, and then poured into glass containers with hay blades or splinters of reeds put inside, so that sugar may crystallize around them. The resulting sugar is called *sukkar nabāt* (sugar candy, rock candy), or as al-Anṭākī calls it *nabāt qazāzī* (sugar candy, which looks like pieces of glass).

Al-Anṭākī observes that except for sugar refineries in the Levant and Egypt, most sugar makers do not go beyond the second stage of refining it. All the same, sugar is consumed in all of its different stages of refinement.

In addition, molasses is obtained with each stage of refining sugar, and the more refined the sugar is, the better the quality of the molasses. The purest molasses, called *qaṭr nabāt*, is obtained in the fourth stage. See *qaṭr* above.

sukkar bayāḍ (سكر ابيض) fine white sugar.
sukkar majrūsh (سكر مجروش) coarsely crushed sugar.
sukkar Miṣrī (سكر مصري) Egyptian sugar, known for its fine and pure quality.

---

12 So-called because King Solomon was believed to have been the first to use it. Hard sugar candy, which was shaped into fingers, rings, and tablets, was also called *sukkar Sulaymānī*. See, for instance, al-Warrāq, English trans. *Annals* 412, 413.

13 Based on al-Anṭākī. *Fānīdh* may also designate sugar candy (entry above), which is made with the resulting *qand* 'crystallized sugar.'

14 This also occurs as *iblīj* (ابليج).

sukkar nabāt (سكر نبات) sugar candy, also called rock candy, often compared to crystal (*billawr*) and *qazāz* (glass).

sukkar sanīnāt (سكر سنينات) fine white cane sugar, the Arabic etymological equivalent of the Persian *ṭabarzad*, see below.[15]

sukkar ṭabarzad (سكر طبرزد), also called *sukkar ublūj*, and *sukkar sanīnāt*. It is fine white cane sugar, usually sold in solid cone-shaped masses which take their shape from the clay vessels in which the cooked sugar syrup is left to crystallize and refine. The name *ṭabarzad* comes from the practice of chiseling the required amounts with a *tabar*, a Persian loan word for hatchet.

sukkar ublūj (سكر ابلوج) pl. *sukkar abālīj* (سكر اباليج), also called *sukkar ṭabarzad*, refined white sugar processed in conical pottery molds with three holes in the bottom to allow the remaining molasses and impurities to drip down, leaving behind molded fine white sugar.

Sugar is hot in its properties, albeit moderately so in comparison with bee honey (*ʿasal naḥl*, see above). It is also moist in its properties, unlike honey, which is dry. The heat and moistness of sugar vary depending on how refined it is. *Sukkar ṭabarzad*, for instance, is moderate leaning toward heat; whereas *sukkar Sulaymānī* (light brown sugar) is hot and moist. Even the most refined and purest of all sugars, sugar candy (*sukkar nabāt*), is still considered hot, but dry.[16] However, its qualities are modified by what is added to its syrup; with rosewater, it becomes lighter and cooler and moderately purging; with violet-petal water, it becomes more effective in softening and purging the system.

Sugar is praised as nourishing food, gentle on the stomach, and as an aid to weight gain. It revives the soul, strengthens the liver, and dispels black bile, which is to be blamed for all kinds of anxieties and mental illnesses. It is the best medium for taking medicine; it makes it more palatable, and enables the medication to reach the deepest places in the body because it flows into the blood stream fast.

Sugar is recommended for cold-related sicknesses. Dissolving it in hot water or sucking a piece of sugar candy soothes a sore throat and raw chest, and relieves coughs. Unrefined sugar was said to be good for tremors and palpitations caused

---

15 *Sanīnāt*, sg. *sanīn* (سنين) is whatever falls when a solid object is brayed or chiseled; and *sinna* (سنّة) is a hatchet (*Lisān al-ʿarab*, s.v. سنن). The word *sanīnāt* (سنينات) is incorrectly read as *sīnatāb* (سينتاب) in a citation from Ibn al-Nafīs by Sato, *Sugar* 98, where it is left unidentified.

16 According to al-Anṭākī, it is a common folk misconception (من غلط العامة) to describe this type of sugar as having cold properties; it is still reflected even in today's research. See for instance, Lewicka, "Diet as Culture" 609, 611, where sugar, described as cold, is said to be given to sick people with fevers, to counterbalance their heat.

by having too much sex. Eating it slows down aging, and overall it is the best for invigorating coitus. However, the recommendation was to eat it with almond oil and milk; or drink it as lemonade (al-Anṭākī, *Tadhkira* 213; Ibn al-Kutubī, *Mā lā Yasaʿ al-ṭabīb jahlahu*, s.v. سكر).[17]

tūt (توت) small pastries shaped like mulberries, and then fried and dipped in syrup. See *Kanz* recipe 268.

usṭarūs (أسطروس) cane-sugar molasses produced at the sugar mills from the collected leftovers of cooked sugar. This sugar was scraped from the tops of the conical earthenware molds (*abālīj*, sg. *ublūj*) to level-off the surface after the sugar has been cooked and poured into them. It was also collected from whatever was left on the reed mats, when the cones were unmolded.[18]

ward murabbā (ورد مربّى) rose-petal jam, also called *jalanjabīn* (جلنجبين), believed to strengthen the stomach and aid digestion.

yaʿqud (يعقد) to thicken, used in relation to cooking syrup.

yuḥall (يحلّ) of sugar, to be dissolved in water to make sugar syrup (*ḥall*).

zalābiya mushabbaka (زلابية مشبكة) latticed fried fritters dipped in syrup. The *Kanz* does not give a recipe for making it. It is only mentioned in recipe 507. For a good recipe, see al-Warrāq, English trans. *Annals* 414–5.

---

17 See also Sato, *Sugar* 91–113, where sugar as medicine is discussed.

18 As described by al-Nuwayrī, *Nihāyat al-arab* viii 202, who calls it *usṭarūsh* (أسطروش). The only other document that mentions it is al-Ḥajjār, *Kitāb al-Ḥarb al-maʿshūq* 105, where it occurs as *ushṭarūsh* (اشطروش), a typical Egyptian dialectical variant.

5. Dishes and Prepared Foods: Main and Side Dishes, Snacks, Condiments, Pickles, Dips, and Table Sauces

alwān (الوان) dishes.

> ***alwān kibār*** (الوان كبار) main dishes, such as stews.
> ***alwān ṣighār*** (الوان صغار) side dishes, such as omelets, and cold and fried dishes.

aruzziyya (ارزية) meat dish with rice (*aruzz*), as in *Kanz* recipe 85. It may also designate rice porridges cooked with meat.

ʿaṣāfīr maṭbūkha (عصافير مطبوخة) stewed sparrows, nibbled on during drinking sessions. See *Kanz* recipe 149. The sparrows are simmered with vegetables and chickpeas in a specially designed glass pot, which allows the onlookers to see through the pot and enjoy the sight of the sparrows, with heads attached, moving up and down in the boiling broth. For more sparrow dishes, see the last ten recipes in *Kanz*, chapter 5. Sparrows were favorite mezza dishes (*naql*). They were also valued for their aphrodisiac properties.

ʿaṣīda (عصيدة) flour-based soup, thick in consistency.

aṭbikha rafīʿa (أطبخة رفيعة) refined dishes.

bahaṭṭa (بهطة) sweetened meatless porridge made with rice flour and milk, and without using water. The name was said to be of Indian origin (*Lisān al-ʿArab*, s.v. بهط). See *Kanz* recipes 105, 106. It was also known as *muhallabiyya*. See, for instance, al-Warrāq's chapter 78. The variety made with wheat starch is called *hayṭaliyya*, see below.

bāmiya (بامية) meat stew cooked with okra cut into pieces, onion, and cilantro. It is soured with fresh lemon juice, which prevents the stew from getting too viscous. See *Kanz* recipe DK, appendix 29, p. 135.

banādiq (بنادق) ***bunduqiyyāt*** (بندقيات) small meatballs added while cooking meat stews to enrich their flavor, and possibly to offer an easier option to eat meat.

bārida (باردة) pl. *bawārid* (بوارد) cold dishes of cooked vegetables seasoned with souring agents, oils, along with herbs and spices. See chapter 19 for recipes, many of which deal with mashed chickpea preparations like today's hummus dip. From Ibn al-Ukhuwwa, *Maʿālim al-qurba*, fol. 64v, we learn that such cold dishes were popular food-market fares. To make them appealing to customers, the boiled vegetables were immediately dipped in cold water to preserve their green color. This market inspection manual considers it a harmful practice, which causes leprosy (*baraṣ*).

 | DOI 10.1163/9789004349919_031

bayḍ makbūs (بيض مكبوس), *bayḍ mukhallal* (بيض مخلل) pickled eggs; see *Kanz* recipes 173–6. Both *makbūs* and *mukhallal* designate pickling. However, whereas *makbūs* suggest the act of packing the food in pickling jars, *mukhallal* denotes the use of vinegar (*khall*) as a preserving agent.

binn (بنّ) fermented condiment, similar to *kāmakh* (see entry below), albeit less salty and non-dairy.

Būrāniyya maqliyya (بورانية مقلية) a casserole-like dish of fried slices of eggplant layered with a spicy mix of ground meat and onion, see *Kanz* recipe 93. It is a variety on what was known, originally, as *Būrāniyya*, an Abbasid dish of fried eggplant, said to have been invented by, or made for, Būrān (d. 884), wife of Caliph al-Maʾmūn.[1] It is a precursor of what is known today as *musaqqaʿa*.[2]

dajāja ḥulwiyya (دجاجة حلوية) chicken dish sweetened with sugar syrup or honey, and colored with saffron. The recipe cautions against using garlic and onion with this dish. Spices used are cinnamon, black pepper, and a bit of coriander. The *Kanz* provides several recipes for this type of dish (see recipes 47, 62 and 118). When ʿAbd al-Laṭīf al-Baghdādī visited Egypt around the turn of the thirteenth century, he was not familiar with the local Egyptian dishes, especially the sweet chicken dishes, which to him were like dessert (*Riḥla* 119).

dajāja mamqūra (دجاجة ممقورة) fried chicken, soused in a mix of vinegar and *murrī* (liquid fermented sauce), as in *Kanz* recipe 43. Such dishes were consumed cold, and the resulting liquid served as their dipping sauce (*ṣibāgh*). See also *mamqūr* below.

dajāja maṣūṣ (دجاجة مصوص) stew of fried chicken simmered in vinegar sauce; see *Kanz* recipe 42, See also *maṣūṣ* below. A comparable dish cooked with red meat is usually called *sikbāj*, see below.

fālūdhajiyya (فالوذجية), also called *māwardiyya* (ماوردية) chicken or meat dish named after the popular starch-based thick puddings of *fālūdhaj*, see *Kanz* recipes 33 and 46.

farīkiyya (فريكية) porridge of green wheat, cooked with meat and milk; see *Kanz* recipe 99.

firākh al-ḥamām (فراخ الحمام) young pigeons; half-boiled, fried, and simmered in vinegar and crushed hazelnuts. See *Kanz* recipe 122.

fuqqāʿiyya (فقاعية) lit., 'foamy stew,' containing meat, eggs, chard, rice, and lemon. The key to the name of this dish is the mock foam created with eggs. See *Kanz* recipe 91 for details.

ḥarīra (حريرة) flour-based soup, silky-smooth and fluid in consistency.

---

1 See al-Warrāq, chapter 45.

2 See Nasrallah, "In the Beginning There Was No *musakka*."

harīsa (هريسة) smooth porridge cooked with meat (either beef or mutton) and grains, particularly wheat. See, for instance, *Kanz* recipe DK, appendix 31, p. 137.

ḥasū (حسو) thin soup.

hayṭaliyya (هيطلية) porridge made with milk and freshly extracted wheat starch, served drizzled with honey. See *Kanz* recipe 107, which includes directions on how to extract the wheat starch. The name of this dish associates it with the central Asian city of Hayṭaliyya in Khwarazm region (Maqdisī, *Aḥsan al-taqāsīm* 17).

ḥimmaṣ kassā (حمص كسّا) dish of boiled and mashed chickpeas, mixed with tahini along with other ingredients. It is the precursor of today's hummus (*ḥummuṣ bi-ṭaḥīna*). See *Kanz* recipes in chapter 19.

ḥiṣrimiyya (حصرمية) stew soured with juice of unripe grapes. See, for instance, recipes 18, 25, and 103.

Ibrāhīmiyya (إبراهيمية) white stew named after the Abbasid gourmet prince Ibrāhīm b. al-Mahdī (d. 839); see *Kanz* recipe 8.

isbīdbāj (اسبيدباج) ***isfīdbāj*** (اسفيدباج) white stew, highly recommended by physicians for its balanced properties. In its most basic form, it is meat cooked in its broth, called *mā' wa milḥ* (ماء وملح) 'water and salt' (al-Rāzī, *Manāfiʿ* 140). See *Kanz* recipe 92.

iṭriya (إطرية) meat dish cooked with thin dried noodles; see *Kanz* recipe 86.

jūdhāba (جوذابة) pl. *jawādhīb* (جواذيب) sweet-savory dish, composed of two parts: 1) A sweet bread pudding, in which either no seasonings are used, or they are kept to a minimum, perhaps rosewater and/or saffron, or a bit of aromatics like cinnamon and cloves. This pudding is arranged in a casserole, called *jūdhābadān* (جوذابدان), or just referred to as *saṭl*, which is a brass kettle with handles. 2) A large fatty chunk of meat, an entire sheep, a chicken, or even a chunk of cheese. The bread casserole was placed inside the *tannūr* oven, and the meat was secured in a large skewer and suspended horizontally above the casserole, so that it catches the dripping juices and fat of the grilling meat. The dish was served by slicing the meat into thin shreds and offering it with the bread casserole. It was believed that the sweet bread aids the digestion of the grilled meat.

We see that some *Kanz* recipes include the *jūdhāba* proper with meat and bread, and others include just the bread part, and were served as a sweet dish. More variety is seen in recipe 44, where a disjointed chicken is boiled and fried, and then placed on rice cooked with milk, without sugar, but with a lot of chicken fat added, then it is covered and left to simmer for an hour. The dish has obviously been evolving into a simpler fare. See *Kanz* recipes 131, 132, 269, 274, 294. See also al-Warrāq, chapter 92, which contains 19 recipes.

kabar (كبر) capers, see *qubbār* below.

kabbād mumallaḥ (كبّاد مملح) Damascus citron preserved in salt; see *Kanz* recipe 577. See also *kabbād* in glossary 7 below.

kaftāwāt (كفتاوات) meatballs, see *kubab* below.

kāmakh (كامخ) dairy-based fermented condiment, sour and salty. See *Kanz*, recipes 500–5

> ***kāmakh bi-l-kabar*** (كامخ بالكبر) dairy-based fermented condiment made with salt-cured capers. See also *qubbār* below.
> ***kāmakh al-marzanjūsh*** (كامخ مرزنجوش) dairy-based fermented condiment, flavored with marjoram.
> ***qamna*** (قمنة) the base for making *kāmakh*. See *Kanz* recipe 501.

karnadāj (كرنداج) poultry grilled on a rotating spit, see *Kanz* recipe 139.

khardal maʿmūl (خردل معمول) mustard condiment, see *Kanz* recipe 468.

kharūf mamzūj (خروف ممزوج) a whole sheep roasted and seasoned with vinegar-based liquid sauce, see *Kanz* recipe 126.

kibrīkiyya (كبريكية) moderately sour meat stew, praised for its temperate properties. The name is a corruption of *dīkabrīka*, see *Kanz* recipe 13.

kishkiyya (كشكية) meat dish enriched with *kishk*, which is the dried dough of crushed wheat and yogurt. See *Kanz* recipes 53, 54, and 524.

kubab (كُبب) and ***mudaqqaqāt*** (مدقّقات) ground meat formed into patties and balls, often added to dishes which already have meat in them. When formed into balls, they are sometimes referred to as *bunduqiyyāt* and *banādiq*, i.e., round like hazelnuts. In the thirteenth-century Aleppan *Wuṣla* ii 550 and the fifteenth-century Egyptian al-Ḥajjār, *Kitāb al-Ḥarb al-maʿshūq* 108, 113, 114, 115, they are called *kaftāwāt*, the origin of today's *kafta* (ground meat patties).

lawn abyaḍ (لون أبيض) white dish, which is a meat stew, with uncolored broth, such as *isbīdbāj*, see entry above.

laymūn makbūs (ليمون مكبوس), *laymūn mumallaḥ* (ليمون مملح), *laymūn māliḥ* (ليمون مالح) lemons preserved by slitting them and stuffing them with salt and packing them in jars with herbs, spices, honey, saffron; then topping the jar with olive oil to seal them. See for instance *Kanz* recipes 607–9.

maḍīra (مضيرة) white stew cooked with meat and sour milk. It was believed to heal all maladies, and be the perfect dish for a hot summer day.

mamqūr (ممقور)[3] dish of chicken or fish, steeped in seasoned vinegar. It was a way of preserving such meats, for short-term storage, to be served whenever needed, along with their vinegar, as a dipping sauce. See for instance *Kanz* recipe 43, and al-Warrāq's chapter 37.

The name *mamqūr* (adj.) derives from the verb مقر 'steep in liquid' (*Lisān al-ʿArab*).

3 This sometimes occurs as *manqūr* (منقور), which reflects the ungrammatical spoken rendition of the word.

Ma'mūniyya (مأمونية) sweetened rice-based porridge, named after Abbasid Caliph al-Ma'mūn (d. 833), who favored it.

marwaziyya (مروزية) delicate golden lamb stew, which is sweet and sour. It is cooked with dried cherry plums and raisins. A dish by this name is also found in the thirteenth-century anonymous Andalusian cookbook *Anwāʿ al-ṣaydala* 19, where the recipe calls for chicken, prunes, jujubes, and pounded almonds. The anonymous writer says that it is a favorite Egyptian and North African dish, comparable to the eastern *zīrbāja* stew. *Zīrbāja* was highly praised for its balanced properties, and was deemed the perfect dish for convalescents who need to gain strength (Ibn Sīnā, *al-Qānūn* 730, 1166).

Dozy, *Takmilat al-maʿājim* 1446, traces the name of the dish to the Latin *amorusia*, which must have, originally, designated meat juice or bouillon, the perfect food for the recuperating sick. He adds that in Granada, the dish was also named *al-ʿĀṣimī* (العاصمي). Most probably, the name was an adaptation of the eastern nickname *Um ʿĀṣim*, given to a comparable sweet and sour stew called *sikbāja*, see below.

masālīq (مساليق), also called *ṣalīq* (صليق) boiled dishes of meat or vegetables.

mashwī (مشوي) ***shiwā*** (شوا) large chunks of meat roasted in the *tannūr*. Cf. *kabāb* (كباب)/*mukabbab* (مكبب), which are smaller pieces of meat grilled on the brazier's open fire. See glossary 9.2, s.v. *shawī*.

maṣūṣ (مصوص) sour stew, usually cooked with meat other than that of quadrupeds, such as birds (as explained in al-Warrāq Istanbul MS, fols. 200v–1r; and *Tāj al-ʿarūs*, s.v. مصص). The souring agent is usually vinegar, but other sour fruit juices were also used. See *Kanz* recipes 42, 133, 180, and 197—the last two are with eggs.

It was deemed a light dish fit for the sick. Ibn Sīnā, *al-Qānūn* 1034, especially recommends it for people suffering from palpitations. Indeed, from al-Jāḥiẓ, *al-Bayān* 6, we learn that another name for it is *muzawwar*, which is a light dish for the sick, see below. Similar dishes cooked with red meat are called *sikbāj*, see entry below.

mubaʿtharāt (مبعثرات) dishes of scrambled eggs, see *Kanz* chapter 7.

mudaqqaqa (مدققة) sometimes written as *muḍaqqaqa* (مضققة), a dialectical variant. It is usually used to designate dishes cooked with pounded meat; either left loose, or shaped into patties (*aqrāṣ*) or meatballs, called *kubab* (كبب) and *bunduqiyyāt* (بندقيات). See entry above.

mukhallalāt (مخللات) pickles, which were believed to arouse the appetite and facilitate the digestion of dense foods. In particular, pickled turnips (*lift mukhallal*) are described as *ʿumdat al-mukhallal* 'the best and most essential of all pickles' (*Wuṣla* ii 665). *Kanz* chapter 18 includes 75 recipes on pickling foods.

mulūkhiyya (ملوخية) meat stew with Jew's mallow, see *Kanz* recipes DK, appendix 15, p. 115; 84 and 134.

muzawwarat mulūkhiyya (مزورة ملوخية) Jew's mallow dish without meat.

mumazzaj (ممزج) designates a dish in which liquid seasonings are added to it while it is cooking, to enhance its flavor. See, for instance, *Kanz* recipes 48 and 130.

murrī (مري) liquid fermented sauce, see *Kanz* chapter 6 for recipes, which are grain-based. The sauce is sour, salty, and bitterish. With its hot and dry properties, it can excite the appetite, dissipate phlegmatic humors in the stomach, and facilitate good digestion of dense and coarse foods. However, it induces thirst.

It was offered in small bowls as a table sauce by itself, to aid digestion of coarse dishes, such as wheat porridge of *harīsa*; it was also incorporated into other sauces and condiments, such as *ṣibāgh* (dipping sauces). It was added as a seasoning to the cooking dishes, with little or no sauce in them, such as omelets, and fried and grilled sparrows, young chicken, and fish.

murrī maṭbūkh (مري مطبوخ) fast method of preparing liquid fermented sauce.

murrī naqīʿ (مري نقيع) liquid fermented sauce which has been left to ferment over a period of months.

Mutawakkiliyya (متوكلية) meat dish cooked with *qulqās* (taro). It is named after Abbasid Caliph al-Mutawakkil (d. 861); see *Kanz* recipes 89, and DK, appendix 10, p. 110. It is another name for a dish called *sitt shanāʿ*, see below.

muzawwarāt (مزورات) lit., 'counterfeit,' 'false.' They are vegetarian dishes, which Christians cooked during the fasting days of Lent, and physicians recommended for the sick. They were cooked to imitate the original meat dishes. See *Kanz*, chapter 8. The name *muzawwarāt* sometimes included light dishes for invalids, even though they may contain meat, as in *muzawwara* recipe 219, which uses young chickens.

muzawwarāt al-buqūl (مزورات البقول) vegetarian dishes.

naql (نقل) small dishes and foods served during drinking sessions, comparable to today's mezza. They include salted and roasted nuts, raisins and fruits, small dishes of stewed sparrows, chewy candy, hard lemon drops, and apricot compote. See, for instance, *Kanz* recipes, 149, 349, 370, and 436. The benefit of such dishes is that they either induce thirst, slow down intoxication or prevent hangovers. Recipe 149, for stewed sparrows (*ʿaṣāfīr maṭbūkha*), is particularly interesting for its entertaining element and the aphrodisiac properties it offers to the nightlong drinkers. There is an indication in some *Kanz* recipes, however, that the term *naql* was beginning to describe any small dishes which are nibbled on, such as recipe 591.

narjisiyya (نرجسية) lit., 'looking like narcissus flower.' In *Kanz* recipe 95, the dish is cooked with rice; whereas in recipe 203, it is an omelet cooked with eggs, sunny side up.

nawāshif (نواشف) fried meat dishes which are described as dry (*nāshif*). They are sauceless, but still moist enough with their own fats and oils; see *Kanz* recipe 21, for instance.

qalāyā (قلايا) sg. *qaliyya* (قليّة) fried dishes. See *Kanz* recipes 21, and 35.

qamḥiyya (قمحية) porridge of shelled whole wheat berries cooked with beef or mutton, see *Kanz* recipe 100.

qubbār (قبّار), *kabar* (كبر) capers, of which the berries, called *thamar* (ثمر), are used. They are either cured in salt and used in making condiments, or preserved in vinegar (*mukhallal*). The latter was deemed better due to its colder properties.

> ***kāmakh bi-l-kabar*** (كامخ بالكبر) dairy-based fermented condiment made with salt-cured capers (see *qubbār mumallaḥ* below). It was said to be harmful for the stomach because it induces thirst and inflames the body with its heat. Of its benefits, it stimulates the appetite and cleanses the digestive system.
>
> ***qubbār mumallaḥ*** (قبّار مملح), *mamlūḥ* (مملوح), or *makbūs bi-l-milḥ* (مكبوس بالملح) salt-cured capers, which are rinsed in water repeatedly to eliminate the extra salt before using them in condiments with vinegar, called *qubbār bi-l-khall* (قبار بالخل); or with sumac, as in *kabar bi-summāq* (كبر بسماق). See *Kanz* recipes 601, and DK, appendix 53, p. 372. They revive the appetite, and are best eaten before the main dishes (al-Anṭākī, *Tadhkira* 294).

rakhbīniyya (رخبينية) meat stew flavored with *rakhbīn*, which is dried buttermilk; see glossary 3 above, s.v. *rakhbīn*.

rummāniyya (رمانية) meat stew flavored and soured with pomegranate juice, and thickened with nuts, see *Kanz* recipes 10, and DK, appendix 36, p. 153.

sādhaj (ساذج) pl. *sawādhij* (سواذج) simple plain dishes that are neither sweet (*ḥulw*) nor sour (*ḥāmiḍ*). See, for instance, *Kanz* recipes 30, and 193.

ṣaḥna (صحنة), called *ṣaḥnāt* (صحناة) in Iraq, and in Syriac *ṣaḥnīthā* (صحنيثا), see al-Bīrūnī, *Ṣaydana* 246. It is a condiment made with salt-cured small fish—*ṣīr* (anchovies) in Egypt, crushed with herbs and spices. It was believed to aid digestion when taken with heavy foods. For more, see glossary 10 below, s.v. *ṣaḥna*, under *ṣīr*.

> ***ṣaḥna Iskandariyya*** (صحنة اسكندرية) *ṣīr* condiment, a specialty of Alexandria. The famous Syrian physician Ibn al-Quff (d. 1286) says that *ṣaḥna* is made in Egypt and many other countries, but the Alexandrian is the best (*Jāmiʿ al-gharaḍ* 245), see *Kanz* recipe 262.
>
> ***ṣaḥna kadhdhāba*** (صحنة كذّابة) false condiment made without fish, see *Kanz* recipes 257, and 259. See also glossary 10 below, s.v. *ṣaḥna*

ṣalīq (صليق), also called *masālīq* (مساليق) boiled vegetables or meats.

ṣalṣ (صلص) pl. *ṣulūṣāt* (صلوصات) table sauce, which is smooth with ointment-like texture. Some of these sauces can be stored in vessels, such as bottles, good for one use.

Generally, this type of condiment is offered in small bowls, along with the dishes. See also *ṣibāgh* (dipping sauce) below. For recipes, see *Kanz*, chapter 16.

samak maḥshī (سمك محشي) fish, which is grilled or fried first and then smothered in sauce (*ṣibāgh*). Al-Warrāq Istanbul MS, fol. 63r, explicitly confirms the dish's concept and the related terminology. See also *maḥshī* in glossary 9.2 below.

samak maqlī (سمك مقلي) fried fish, as in recipe 237. See also *Kanz* chapter 9, for more fish dishes.

sanbūsak (سنبوسك) deep-fried filled pastries, sweet and savory. See glossary 2 above.

shaʿīriyya (شعيرية) meat stew cooked with orzo, which is made by kneading stiff dough and rolling it into small pieces of pasta, like barley (*shaʿīr*). See *Kanz* recipe 117.

shishbarak (ششبرك) raviolis, filled with a meat mix, shaped into rolls or triangles and fried. Alternatively, they are shaped into half-moons, and then boiled and served with yogurt or sumac sauce. See *Kanz* recipe 37.

ṣibāgh (صباغ) unfermented dipping sauce, mostly vinegar-based. It is consumed right after it is prepared, served in small bowls, in which the eaters dip their morsels of food. Alternatively, it is poured on fried, boiled, or grilled meats and vegetables before they are served. See *Kanz* recipes 471–80.

sikbāj (سكباج) *sikbāja* (سكباجة) meat stew soured with vinegar, said to be the perfect summer dish due to is cold properties, see *Kanz* recipes 7, 90. The best meat cooked with it is beef; however, it is also cooked with fish, as in *Kanz* recipe 249. Similar dishes cooked with poultry and eggs are called *maṣūṣ*, see above.

ṣināb (صناب) a variety of *ṣibāgh* sauce, made with ground mustard seeds and raisins. The color *ṣinābī*, 'yellowish red,' derives from the color of this sauce.

ṣīr mushakshak (صير مشكشك) a refined dish of salt-cured split-open-anchovies, fried in sweet olive oil and tossed in herbs, spices, and tahini, see *Kanz* recipe 244. My interpretation is that the name of the dish, *mushakshak*, is based on the Arabic verb *yushaqq* (يشق), *yushaqqaq* (يشقّق), and the adjective *mashqūq* (مشقوق), *mushaqqaq* (مشقّق), and *mushaqshaq* (مشقشق), which is a common variant. Vocalizing *q* (ق) as *k* (ك) is recognized today as an Egyptian dialectical variant. Therefore, *mushakshak* (مشكشك) might well have been an Egyptian variant of *mushaqshaq* (مشقشق). In addition, in *Kanz* recipe 250, the same fish, used butterflied, is called *mashqūq* (split open).

To my knowledge, the only document that includes a fish dish by the name *mushakshak*, occurs in al-Shirbīnī, *Hazz al-quḥūf* 218–9. In al-Shirbīnī's book, it is a very humble fare, which poor Egyptian villagers prepared using the skins of *fasīkh* fish (salt-dried *būrī* 'grey mullet') after they eat the meat. The skins are washed, put in a *ṭājin*, along with chopped onion and linseed oil. They are baked in the oven and eaten with bread. Al-Shirbīnī adds that they sometimes added to it a bit of the dregs from the extracted sesame oil, thinned down with water; instead of tahini. He says the villagers love it, it is to them like roast lamb. As for why it is called *mushakshak*, he says this may have stemmed from the custom of the women-cooks who tested its doneness by piercing the skins (شكشك *shakshaka*) with a stick or a spoon.[4]

sitt shanāʿ (ست شناع) 'the best of the maligned dishes.' Sometimes it is copied as *al-shanʿiyya* (الشنعية), as in al-Warrāq Istanbul MS, fol. 161r; and *sitt al-shanaʿ* (ست الشنع), as in *Wuṣla* ii 569–70 and al-Warrāq Istanbul MS, fol. 160r. From the latter, we learn that it is also called *al-Mutawakkiliyya* (المتوكلية), named after Abbasid Caliph al-Mutawakkil (d. 861).

I suspect that the details al-Maqrīzī, *Khiṭaṭ* iii 385, gives on some of the actions of the eccentric Fatimid Caliph al-Ḥākim bi-Amrillāh (985–1021), a Shii Ismāʿīlī, provide us with a clue as to why this dish has these two names. It is said that al-Ḥākim prohibited the Egyptians from eating their beloved *mulūkhiyya* (Jew's mallow) because it was favored by the Sunni Umayyad Caliph Muʿāwiya (d. 680). He also prevented them from eating *jirjīr* (arugula) because it was associated with the Prophet's wife ʿĀʾisha, who was favored by the Sunnis. As for al-Mutawakkiliyya dish, he prohibited it because it was named after the Abbasid Caliph al-Mutawakkil, a Sunni. After the death of Caliph al-Ḥākim, people resumed eating their favorite foods and dishes. It is my guess that *al-Mutawakkiliyya* came to be called, in jest, *sitt al-shanaʿ* (the best of the maligned dishes). See *al-Mutawakkiliyya* above, and *Kanz* recipe 88.

summāqiyya (سماقية) meat stew soured with sumac, see *Kanz* recipes 56 and DK, appendix 24, p. 130. It is also cooked with fish, as in recipe 251.

ṭabāhija (طباهجة) In its basic form, it is a succulent fried dish of thinly sliced red meat. See, for instance, *Kanz* recipe 83. As mentioned in *Waṣf* 14, Egyptian cooks were used to adding taro (*qulqās*), which has been fried in sesame oil.

tabāla (تبالة) a variety of *isbīdāj/isfidhbāj*, which is a simple white meat stew (entry above). Recipes for making it can be found in al-Warrāq Istanbul MS, fols. 153v–4r; and *Wuṣla* ii 607. The one in al-Warrāq's is stew of young pigeons or chickens, or mutton, cooked in plain water and seasoned with mastic, cinnamon, dill, olive oil, and salt.

taqliyya (تقليّة) pl. *taqālī* (تقالي) moist dish of sliced fried meat, with spices and herbs and some vegetables. See *Kanz* recipes 101 and 128. It was one of the main dishes in medieval Egypt, as we learn from Ibn Iyās, *Badāʾiʿ al-zuhūr* i 574. The dish is also mentioned in al-Ḥajjār, *Kitāb al-Ḥarb al-maʿshūq* 113; and *Mufākharat al-ruzz wa-l-ḥabb rummān*.[5]

However, *taqliyya* was also used to designate chopped onion fried in oil, used to enhance the flavor of the stew, as in *Kanz* recipe 235. Today's Egyptian tradition

---

4 Al-Shirbīnī offers other interpretations, but they are not meant to be taken seriously.

5 Geries, *Mufākhara* 104.

of the *taqliyya*, of frying onion and/or garlic along with cilantro and other spices to garnish or enrich an already cooked dish, is largely a continuation of such old culinary practices. Indeed, al-Shirbīnī, *Hazz al-quḥūf* 198, refers to *taqliyya* of finely chopped onion fried in sesame oil and added to a pot of *kishk* before serving it.

tharīd (ثريد) broken pieces of bread sopped in the rich broth of stew, served with the stew meat and vegetables. The *Kanz*, however, does not offer recipes for dishes which are specifically called *tharīd*, contrary to what we see in other medieval cookbooks, such as tenth-century al-Warrāq's chapters 61 and 83; and the ones in the two thirteenth-century Andalusian cookbooks, the anonymous *Anwāʿ al-ṣaydala* 156–69, and the second chapter in al-Tujībī's *Fiḍāla* 39–57.

The first chapter of the *Kanz* (p. 75) describes how best to serve the cooked stews as *tharīd*: bread must be given enough liquid and fat to saturate it, and then it is set aside for a short while to give it enough time to absorb the liquid and soften. A dent is made in the middle, in which is poured the necessary amount of the accumulated fat of the stew. The most delicious, the *Kanz* adds, is *tharīd* made with the sour vinegar stew (*sikbāj*).

Tharīd was a dish loved and praised by all as the perfect food, nutritious and easy to digest due to its hot and moist properties.

thūm mukhallal (ثوم مخلل) pickled garlic, see *Kanz* recipe 602.

tuṭmāj (تطماج) boiled fresh noodle strips, served in yogurt sauce with fried meat strips and meatballs. See *Kanz*, recipe 109, and *tuṭmāj* (the noodle) in glossary 2 above.

ʿujaj (عجج) omelets, shaped as discs and scrambled, renowned for their aphrodisiac properties. See *Kanz* chapter 7, for recipes.

umm nārayn (أم نارين) lit., 'cooked between two fires.' It is a bread pudding, with crispy brown top and bottom, cooked on the stove. The recipe does not give details on how this was made, as it was probably too common to mention. However, both the name of the recipe and the absence of any directions for stirring the pot, point to the technique of cooking between two fires. The pot is put directly on a low heat, with lighted coals arranged all over the lid. See also glossary 9.2, s.v. *ṭabkh bayn nārayn*; and *Kanz* recipe 111.

ʿuṣfūr makbūs (عصفور مكبوس) sparrow preserved in salt, see *Kanz* recipe 141.

zaytūn (زيتون) olives, both green (*akhḍar*) and black (*aswad*) olives were preserved in brine after treating them to leach their bitterness; or curing them in salt. They were eaten as table olives, or used with other ingredients to create delicious condiments. They were believed to stimulate the appetite, strengthen the stomach, and open blockages (al-Anṭākī, *Tadhkira* 200). The olive varieties destined for the table were usually low in fat content. They are called *zaytūn al-māʾ* (زيتون الماء) lit., 'water olives,' because their moisture content is high. See *Kanz* recipes 557–68. Black olives high in oil content were also cured when still green (see *Kanz* recipe 561).

zaytūn al-Fayyūm (زيتون الفيوم) table olives of Fayyūm, a district in central Egypt, described in the *Kanz* as excellent fleshy olives (CB, appendix 44, p. 352).

zaytūn mubakhkhar (زيتون مبخر) smoked olives, see *Kanz* recipe 568 for instructions.

zaytūn mukallas (زيتون مكلس) green olives preserved in brine after being pre-treated with slaked lime to leach out their bitterness and prevent discoloration. The olives preserved this way must be in perfect condition, with no bruises. See *Kanz* recipe 557.

zaytūn mumallaḥ (زيتون مملح) table olives cured in salt.

zaytūn murammad (زيتون مرمد) green olives cured with ashes, to leach out their bitterness and prevent discoloration. Olives treated this way must be firm in flesh and free of any blemishes or bruises. See *Kanz* recipes 560 and 561.

zaytūn mustawī (زيتون مستوي) ready to eat cured olives; either eaten as they are, or made into delicious condiments.

zaytūn mutabbal (زيتون متبل) condiment of seasoned olives, see, for instance, *Kanz* recipes 565 and 566.

zaytūn Tadmurī (زيتون تدمري) excellent black olives of Palmyra; they are large and elongated in shape, low in oil content. They were used as table olives.

6. Fats and Oils

alya (ألية) sheep-tail fat, sometimes referred to as *duhn al-alya* (دهن الالية), often used rendered. To render it, it is chopped into small pieces and then cooked in a pot with some oil until it melts. The remaining sediment is discarded. When used with cookies, it is sometimes enhanced (*yukhlaʿ*) with aromatics like mastic, cinnamon, musk, and camphor, as in *Kanz* recipe DK, appendix 4, p. 81.

duhn (دهن) used loosely to designate rendered sheep-tail fat *alya*; otherwise it is oil extracted from plants and seeds other than olive oil (*zayt*).

duhn bazr (دهن بزر) and *duhn bazr al-kattān* (دهن بزر الكتان) linseed oil. *Bazr* by itself designates seeds in general. However, it is also recognized as an abbreviated reference to *bazr kattān* (بزر كتّان) linseed. In *Kanz* recipes 240, 246, and 247, it is used to rub the prepared fish with before further cooking it, as it was believed to remove the fishy smells.

duhn dajāj (دهن دجاج) chicken fat, used to fry sparrows, as in *Kanz* recipe 143.

duhn lawz (دهن لوز) oil of sweet almonds. It is a delicate oil used in dishes for the sick, refined porridges, and desserts. It is also used as the base for making aromatic oils. Because of its moderately cold and moist properties, it is usually recommended for headaches. It can also weaken women's appetite, for those who want to lose weight (al-Anṭākī, *Tadhkira* 314).

samn (سمن) ghee, used in *Kanz* recipes for making cookies, condensed puddings, fine dishes of rice with milk (*aruzz bi-laban*), and omelets (*ʿujaj*). It is usually obtained by cooking butter until all the liquid evaporates and nothing remains but pure fat and sediment in the bottom of the pot, which are discarded. See the last recipe of *Kanz* chapter 10, for an interesting way of obtaining ghee directly from milk. Besides its culinary uses, *samn* is believed to have medicinal benefits, such as soothing dryness of throat and mouth, and purging brain and chest. It is also recommended as a facial cream (al-Anṭākī, *Tadhkira* 218).

> ***samn baqarī*** (سمن بقري) ghee from cow's milk, said to be the best. Gee from milk of sheep is second best.
>
> ***samn khāliṣ*** (سمن خالص) pure ghee.

shaḥm (شحم) solid animal fat, suet.

shayraj (شيرج) ***shīrāj*** (شيراج) sesame oil, used as an all-purpose fat, for example, for frying and baking cookies.

> ***shayraj makhlūʿ*** (شيرج مخلوع) enhanced sesame oil, which is made by heating the oil with small amounts of spices, such as a cinnamon stick, mastic, black

 | DOI 10.1163/9789004349919_032

pepper, and cumin; the spices are all used whole so that they can be removed from the oil. Olive oil is enhanced similarly, see for instance *Kanz* recipe 140.

shayraj ṭarī (شيرج طري) fresh sesame oil.

FIGURE 55 *Olive tree, al-ʿUmarī,* Masālik al-abṣār, *fol. 171v, detail (BnF, Department of manuscripts, Arab 2771).*

zayt (زيت) olive oil. The word derives from *zaytūn* (olives). Oils extracted from other plants are more accurately called *adhān* (sg. *duhn*), such as *duhn al-lawz* (almond oil). This rule, however, is not always followed. See *zayt ḥārr*, below.

As described by al-Anṭākī, *Tadhkira* 200, on varieties of olive oil:

1) The olives are harvested as they first start to change color (not fully ripe), they are pounded, mixed with hot water, and then rubbed and pressed until the oil floats up to the surface and is collected.[1] This, he says is called

1 As described in Hassan and Hill, *Islamic Technology* 224, this oil is commercially produced: The olive pulp left from the first cold pressing is soaked in hot water and pressed again to

zayt maghsūl (زيت مغسول) 'washed olive oil,' also called *zayt anfāq* (زيت انفاق). Its properties are cold and moderately dry.

2) The fully ripe olives are first crushed, then cooked on the fire, and their oil is pressed out in the oil presses; this, he says, is called *zayt ʿadhb* (زيت عذب) 'sweet olive oil.' Its properties are hot and dry.

He further adds that the Iraqis call both *zayt rikābī* (زيت ركابي) because they were transported to them on backs of camels from the Levant.

zayt ḥārr (زيت حار) 'hot oil,' which has hot properties. In Egypt, it designates linseed (al-Maqrīzī, *Khiṭaṭ* i 292), see *duhn bazr* above. In addition, Nāṣir Khusrū, *Safarnāma* 26, mentions that *zayt ḥārr* is used in Egypt to designate oils extracted from seeds of turnip and radish. These oils were used mainly for lighting purposes.

zayt ḥulw (زيت حلو) sweet olive oil, see *zayt ṭayyib* below.

zayt maghsūl (زيت مغسول) lit., 'washed olive oil.' It is made from olives harvested when they first start to change color (not fully ripe). See *zayt* above, point 1, on how it is extracted. Washing the oil this way improves its properties and eliminates its acidity and astringency.

zayt makhlūʿ (زيت مخلوع) olive oil enhanced by heating it up with small amounts of spices, such as a cinnamon stick, mastic, black pepper, and cumin; all used whole so that they may be removed from the oil. The flavor of sesame oil is enhanced similarly, see *Kanz* recipe 140. See also *shayraj makhlūʿ* above.

zayt muṭayyab (زيت مطيب) olive oil enhanced by eliminating its acridity and sweetening its taste. It is first mixed with a small amount of sesame oil and water—double the amount of olive oil used. The mix is then whipped and boiled until all the water evaporates. The process is repeated four times, after which the oil is cooled, strained, and stored (as described in al-Warrāq Istanbul MS, fol. 253v).

zayt ṭayyib (زيت طيب) also called *zayt ʿadhb* (زيت عذب), and *zayt ḥulw* (زيت حلو) fine, sweet, and mellow olive oil, made with fully ripe olives, which are free of astringency and acidity. See also *zayt* above.

zaytūn al-zayt (زيتون الزيت) lit., 'oil olives,' descriptive of varieties of olives high in oil content, usually used for extracting olive oil. Cf. *zaytūn al-māʾ* 'water olives,' which are high in moisture content and low in fat. They were usually used as table olives, after being cured in salt and preserved in brine (see glossary 5 above, s.v. *zaytūn*).

zubd (زبد) ***zubda*** (زبدة) butter, mostly eaten fresh with dates and bread. Few recipes in the *Kanz* use it, for example, see recipe 111 for making a pudding, and 321, for a date-based confection.

---

extract the remaining oil in it. To separate it from water and wash it from impurities, it is passed through running streams of water to allow the oil to float, and then it is collected.

7. Fruits and Nuts

ʿajwa (عجوة) sweet and soft variety of dried dates. See *tamr* below.

amīrbārīs (اميرباريس) also occurs as *barbārīs* (برباريس) *anbarbārīs* (انبرباريس) and *zirishk* (زرشك) *Berberis* (S) barberries. They are small sour berries used as a souring agent in stews. They were said to be cold and dry in properties, and as such, they were applied medicinally to strengthen the stomach, liver, and heart. They were used to aid digestion and stop nausea. Al-ʿUmarī, *Masālik* xxi 31, specifies the Levantine variety as being the best.

balaḥ (بلح) fresh ripe dates, when they are still yellow, very firm, and crunchy, and not so sweet, see *tamr* below.

balaḥ aḥmar (بلح أحمر) fresh ripe red dates, still very firm and crunchy, and not so sweet.

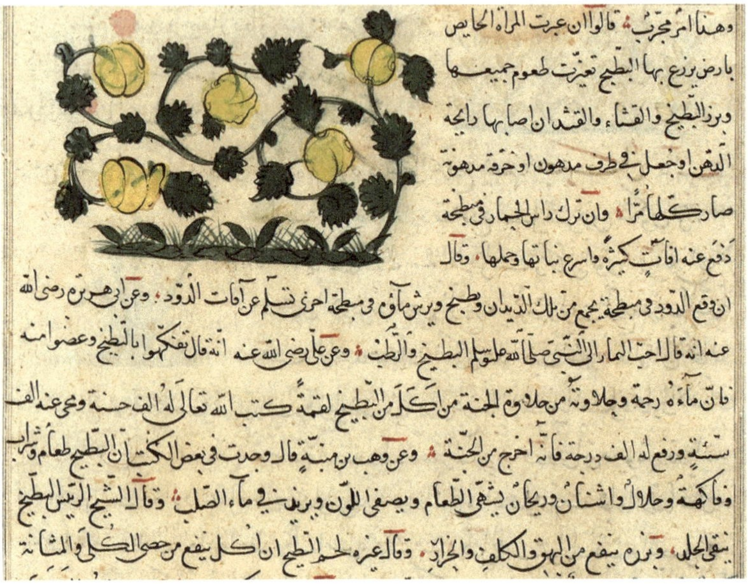

FIGURE 56 *Muskmelon, F1954.82v, Muḥammad al-Qazwīnī,* ʿAjāʾib al-makhlūqāt, *detail (Freer Gallery of Art and Arthur M. Sackler Gallery, Smithsonian Institution, Washington, DC: Purchase—Charles Lang Freer Endowment).*

biṭṭīkh (بطيخ) The reference is rather confusing in Arabic, as it generally applies to watermelon (*Citrullus lanatus/vulgaris*) and muskmelon (common melon, *Cucumis melo*). Sometimes a difference arises and muskmelon is called *biṭṭīkh aṣfar* (بطيخ اصفر) yellow melon, and watermelon *biṭṭīkh akhḍar* (بطيخ اخضر) is called green

 | DOI 10.1163/9789004349919_033

melon, or *biṭṭīkh aḥmar* (بطيخ احمر) red melon, depending on whether the peel or the pulp, respectively, is being described.

biṭṭīkh ʿAbdulī (عبدلي), also occurs as *ʿAbdulāwī* (عبدلاوي) *Cucumis melo* var. *chate* (S), also called Egyptian chate. It is an Egyptian variety of melon which ʿAbd al-Laṭīf al-Baghdādī describes in his *Riḥla* 77–8. He says it was named after ʿAbdallāh b. Ṭāhir al-Khurāsānī when the Abbasid Caliph al-Maʾmūn appointed him governor in Egypt in 826. However, he says that Egyptian farmers call it *biṭṭīkh Dumayrī* (بطيخ دميري) after the Egyptian village of Dumayra in the Delta region, where it grows. The melon is intensely yellow, and has a belly and a twisted neck; it looks like an Iraqi gourd. The peel is somewhat rough and thin. Its taste is generally insipid. In weight, it averages between one pound and ten pounds. The Egyptians prefer it to other non-native varieties, *biṭṭīkh muwallad*, which they call *Khurāsānī* (خراساني) and *Ṣīnī* (صيني), originally from Khurasan and China, respectively. They claim it has health benefits, and eat it with sugar. When it is still small, green, and unripe, some of them are harvested and sold as *faqqūs* (فقوس), which tastes like *qiththāʾ* (قثاء) snake cucumber, see entries in glossary 12 below.

biṭṭīkh akhḍar (بطيخ اخضر) *Citrullus lanatus/vulgaris* (S) lit., 'green melon,' watermelon. ʿAbd al-Laṭīf al-Baghdādī, *Riḥla* 8, says this type of melon is not sold by weight. He gives its other names: *dillāʿ* (دلّاع) in the western Arabo-Islamic region, *biṭṭīkh ranshī* (رنشي) in the Levant, and *biṭṭīkh raqqī* (بطيخ رقي) in Iraq. It is also called *biṭṭīkh Filasṭīnī* (بطيخ فلسطيني) Palestinian, *Hindī* (هندي), and *Sindī* (سندي).

biṭṭīkh Hindī (بطيخ هندي) Indian melon, which is a variety of watermelon, see *biṭṭīkh akhḍar* above.

biṭṭīkh Samarqandī (بطيخ سمرقندي) melon of Samarqand, as it is called in the Levant. In Egypt, it is called *biṭṭīkh Ṣīnī* (بطيخ صيني); otherwise known as *biṭṭīkh Maʾmūnī* (بطيخ مأموني), a variety of muskmelon, named after the Abbasid Caliph al-Maʾmūn. It has an extremely sweet, somewhat reddish (i.e., orange) pulp, which is grown in Maru in Persia (al-Isrāʾīlī, *Aghdhiya* iii 6–7). Ibn Baṭṭūṭa, *Riḥla* 179, says it looks greenish from the outside and reddish (more like orange) from the inside, with an intensely sweet and firm flesh; it was eaten fresh and dried.

biṭṭīkh Ṣīnī (بطيخ صيني) Chinese melon. The Egyptians call it *biṭṭīkh aṣfar* (بطيخ اصفر) yellow melon. It is a variety of muskmelon which has a rough outer skin. It is heavy for its size, with a yellow, smooth, and buttery pulp.

qishr al-biṭṭīkh (قشر البطيخ) melon peel, which may apply to muskmelon and watermelon if unspecified. For tenderizing tough cuts of meat and cooking them fast, *Kanz*, chapter 1, recommends the peel of *biṭṭīkh akhḍar* (green melon), which is watermelon. However, al-Anṭākī, *Tadhkira* 85, particularly mentions the peel of *biṭṭīkh aṣfar* (yellow melon), which is muskmelon, *Cucumis melo* (S). Apparently, all melon peels were utilized the same way.

shammām al-biṭṭīkh (شمام البطيخ) *Cucumis dudaim* (S) a variety of muskmelon, called Queen Ann's pocket melon in English. Al-Tamīmī, *Ṭīb al-ʿarūs*, recipe 266, calls it *biṭṭīkh Khurāsānī* (melon of Khurasan), and describes it as being small and red, and striped with yellow. Because of its striped peel, it is also called *biṭṭīkh ʿitābī* (بطيخ عتابي), after the fashionable striped cloth of *al-ʿitābiyya*. Even when it is still green and unripe, it is consumed as *faqqūs ʿitābī* (فقوس عتابي), see *faqqūs*, glossary 12 below. It is the size of an orange, extremely aromatic, with a smooth peel and thin pulp. It is valued more for its scent than its flavor (Ghālib, *Mawsūʿa*, s.v. *shammām ʿajamī* 'Persian melon').

FIGURE 57 *Melon seller, fol. 49r from* Manṭiq al-ṭayr, *63.210.44, detail (MET NY—Fletcher Fund, 1963).*

bunduq (بندق) *Corylus avellana* (S) hazelnuts, frequently used toasted and crushed in *Kanz* recipes for savory and sweet dishes. Its shells were said to be effective in absorbing the unpleasant odors of the not-so-fresh cooking meat, and the burning stench of boiling pulses and beans. According to al-Anṭākī, *Tadhkira* 92, the best are brought from the Mosul region in northern Iraq.

Its properties are moderately hot and dry, and it was believed to have the power to arouse coitus, which indeed might explain its dominance over the rest of the nuts in preparing the dishes in *Kanz*. Having it with sugar or honey was said to cure coughs. Of its other non-culinary benefits: placing it around the house discourages scorpions from frequenting the place—this is tried and true, al-Anṭākī says; likewise, when it is carried in one's pocket. However, it generates dense winds, and slows the digestion, and it is the least nourishing of all nuts.

busr (بسر) fresh dates, ripe and sweet, but still crunchy, see *tamr* below.

dhukār (ذكار) *Ficus carica sylvestris* (S) caprifig, the male, pollen-bearing wild variety of the common fig, used to pollinate the edible fig. Several of these figs are hung close to edible figs to allow the fig wasp (*Blastophaga psenes*) to transfer the pollen to the female flowers. Ibn al-ʿAwwām, *Kitāb al-Filāḥa* 572–4, gives a detailed description on the pollination process, and compares the wasp to the insect *baʿūḍ* (بعوض) mosquito.

fustuq (فستق) *Pistacia vera* (S) pistachios, popularly eaten as a snack food and used in cooking savory and sweet dishes. Its properties are hot and dry, with some astringency and bitterness in its taste. It stops palpitations, and generates good blood; it nourishes the brain and improves memory and mental faculties. It sweetens the breath and strengthens the stomach.

ghubayrāʾ (غبيراء) *Sorbus domestica* (S) sorbus fruit. The tree is said to be quite common in the eastern region (Bilād al-Mashriq) of the Islamic world, especially in Iraq, which produces larger and meatier fruit. It is described as the size of a medium olive, bright red, with a palatable sweet taste mixed with an agreeable, slight astringency.

It was said to be good for headaches. Having it as *naql* (*mezza*) with alcoholic drinks could slow down intoxication considerably. In some parts of the Mashriq, women were said to be sexually aroused by the fragrance of its blossoms, so much so that men would keep them under lock and key to protect their virtue until the end of the blossoming season (Ibn al-Bayṭār, *al-Jāmiʿ* iii 202–3; al-Anṭākī, *Tadhkira* 269). In addition to its fruit, the tree was also valued for the quality of its wood, which is highly resistant to mold. This may be the reason it was the preferred wood for bathroom doors. Besides, its branches could be used against annoying flies, which tend to congregate on the branches (al-ʿUmarī, *Masālik* xx 255–6).

sawīq al-ghubayrāʾ (سويق الغبيراء) meal of dried sorbus fruit, toasted, ground, and mixed with fat and sugar.

ṭaḥīn al-ghubayrāʾ (طحين الغبيراء) is just dried and ground sorbus fruit.

Both of the above preparations were used to control diarrhea, and stop nausea. See *Kanz* recipe 288, which uses it along with other ingredients.

ḥabba khaḍrāʾ (حبة خضراء) *Pistacia terebinthus* (S) green berries of the terebinth tree. The fruit was used as food and medicine (see *Kanz* recipe 263). When the berries are still green and brittle, that is, before they mature and develop a hard shell, bunches of them are pickled in vinegar and salt, or just cured in salt, as is done with capers (Ibn al-Bayṭār, *al-Jāmiʿ* i 134–5, s.v. *buṭm*). The entire plant is astringent, and hot and dry in properties. It is diuretic, and can dispel winds, and aid menstruation.

ḥummāḍ al-utrujj (حماض الاترج) pulp of citron (*utrujj*), see entry below.

FIGURE 58 *Plum tree, F1954.72v, Muḥammad al-Qazwīnī,* ʿAjāʾib al-makhlūqāt, *detail (Freer Gallery of Art and Arthur M. Sackler Gallery, Smithsonian Institution, Washington, DC: Purchase—Charles Lang Freer Endowment).*

ijjāṣ (إجّاص) ***injāṣ*** (إنجاص) *Prunus domestica* (S) plums, prunes; known as such in Iraq; also identified as *ijjāṣ Dimashqī* (إجاص دمشقي) *P.d subsp. insititia* (S) Damson plum. Its names in the Maghrib and Andalusia are *ʿAnbaqar* (عنبقر) and *ʿuyūn al-baqar* (عيون البقر). These names designate a variety of black plum, said to be similar in shape to pigeons' eggs. The white variety called *shāhlūj* (شاهلوج) is described as huge, white, dense in texture and not so juicy, and sweet; this causes it to lack the laxative property for which plums are known (al-Bīrūnī, *Ṣaydana* 24–6; al-Isrāʾīlī, *Aghdhiya* ii 174–7; al-Ṭaghnarī, *Zahrat al-Bustān* 164–5).

For other varieties of the genus *Prunus*, see *qarāṣiyā* (قراصيا), *mishmish* (مشمش), *khawkh* (خوخ), and *khawkh al-dubb* (خوخ الدب).

ʿinab (عنب) grapes. Chapter 23 offers ways for storing fresh grapes so that they may be used off season. The grape vine is called *dāliya* (دالية) and *karm* (كرم).

ʿaqīd al-ʿinab (عقيد العنب) concentrated grape juice, also called *rubb al-ʿinab* (رب العنب)

faḥm al-zarjūn (فحم الزرجون) coals of burnt vine branches.

ḥiṣrim (حصرم) sour unripe grapes, see *māʾ ḥiṣrim* in glossary 8 below.

jawzānī (جوزاني) excellent variety of grapes (Dozy, *Takmilat al-maʿājim* 245). Raisins made from it are called *zabīb jawzānī*, see below.

Sulṭī (سلطي) fair-colored grapes, named after the city of Sulṭ, in the Jordan Valley. Raisins made from it are called *zabīb Sulṭī*, from which the sultana raisins took their name.

zarjūn al-dawālī (زرجون الدوالي) stems and branches of grape vines.

Grapes are hot and moist in their properties; the white variety is the hottest, the red and black are a little less so. They were deemed the best of fruits in that they nourish, arouse the appetite, help with weight gain, and cleanse the blood. However, they should not be eaten after a meal (al-Anṭākī, *Tadhkira* 264).

jawz (جوز) walnuts, which the Egyptians call *al-Shawbakī* (الشوبكي), as al-Anṭākī mentions in *Tadhkira* 120, adding that it was brought from the Levant. Its properties are hot and moist. Eating it toasted and while still hot can prevent discomforts resulting from overeating. Cooks were advised to add several pierced walnuts to the pot to get rid of the unpleasant stench of burnt pulses and grains. It was also recommended to improve the smell of not-so-fresh meat.

jawz akhḍar (جوز اخضر) fresh green walnuts, used in *Kanz* recipes 575 and 590 to make pickles beneficial for curing excess phlegm and other chest-related ailments. Women use the outer skins to color their lips and cheeks red.

jummayz (جميز) sycomore fig, see *tīn barrī* below.

kabbād (كبّاد) Damascus citron (Kharna sour orange hybrid, *Citrus aurantium* var. *khatta*).[1] Al-Anṭākī, *Tadhkira* 50, describes *kabbād* as a variety of *astabūn* (أستبون).[2] He says it is the fruit of a *nāranj* tree (sour orange, *Citrus aurantium*), which has been grafted with branches of the *utrujj* tree (true citron, *Citrus medica*).

---

1 For more on this variety, see http://www.citrusvariety.ucr.edu/citrus/kharna.html, accessed Dec. 12, 2016. The Latin name was first suggested in 1888 by Bonavia, *The Cultivated Oranges and Lemons* 17. He says it makes "a good sweet jelly, and also a good marmalade."

2 Al-Anṭākī adds that the other variety of *astabūn* is produced by grafting branches of true citron (*Citrus medica*) into a lemon tree. The resulting fruit is the size of a lemon with an elongated shape like a true citron. He says it grows abundantly in Egypt, where it is called *ḥummāḍ shuʿayrī* (حماض شعيري). See *laymūn murakkab* under *laymūn* entry, below.

In modern sources, it was identified for the first time and described in detail in 1963 by Chapot.[3] It is a hybrid between true citron and orange, and originated in Damascus, where it is "found almost exclusively as isolated plants in the homes and palaces." It looks like a large sour orange. Its rind is thick and firm, with a bumpy golden-yellow surface, and the pulp is sour and somewhat juicy.[4] Indeed, this confirms al-Anṭākī's sixteenth-century identification of it, mentioned above (*Tadhkira* 50).

Al-ʿUmarī, *Masālik*, iii 279, 285, points out that *kabbād* trees grow in the Levant and Egypt. It seems, however, that some of Egypt's supplies were also imported. Once in *Kanz* (recipe 521), *kabbād marākibī* is mentioned. It must have been transported in ships from the Levant to Egypt, as was done with *laymūn marākibī* (see entry below).

In other medieval sources, the name *utrujj* only designates citron (*Citrus medica*). *Kabbād*, if ever mentioned, was thought to be the commoners' word for *utrujj* (*Muḥīṭ al-muḥīṭ*, s.v. كبد). In *Tāj al-ʿarūs*, s.v. كبد, we even come across the word *kabbāj* [sic], and it was said to be a variety of lemon.

However, based on the recipes in the *Kanz*, *kabbād* is certainly not another name for *utrujj*, as both are called for in the same recipe a couple of times (recipes 521, and DK, appendix 74, p. 416). To my knowledge, the only other sources where the name *kabbād* occurs are *Wuṣla* ii 486, 689; and al- Nābulusī, *ʿAlam al-malāḥa* 266, and that is because their recipes are similar to those of *Kanz*. Apparently, they all drew on the same source. Today, the only region where the name *kabbād* is used is the Levant.

Judging from the *Kanz* recipes, *kabbād* seems to have been more commonly used in daily preparations of dishes than *utrujj* (*Citrus medica*). It has more juice than *utrujj*, and as such, it sometimes complements or replaces lemon juice. In addition, it is the type of citron to use in making varieties of pickles (*Kanz* recipes 576, 577, 578). For other uses, such as making perfumed and digestive preparations and drinks, *utrujj* is the citron to go to, as it has much stronger properties. See also *utrujj* below.

---

3 "Le cedrat kabbad" 61. It is certainly not trifoliate orange (*Poncirus trifoliata*), as identified in Maxime Rodinson's 1948 "Studies in Arabic Manuscripts" 144; and Lewicka, *Food and Foodways* 267, 278. The trifoliate, also known as hardy orange, looks like a very small downy orange (about 1½ inches), and is very bitter. The tree itself is recognizable by its three leaflets and long thorns.

4 Based on information provided by a Damascene writer, who has several *kabbād* trees in his garden. He calls *kabbād* the twin-sister of *nāranj* (see al-Sibāʿī, "*Kabbād al-Shām*").

kabbād marākibī (كباد مراكبي) Damascus citron, shipped to Egypt from the Levant.[5]

Kābulī (كابلي), also called *ihlīlaj kābulī* (إهليلج كابلي) *Terminalia chebula* (S) black myrobalan, also known as chebulic myrobalan, named after Kabul. Of all the varieties of myrobalan, *Kābulī* was deemed the most beneficial. It was said to be moderately cold and astringent. Of its uses, it treats diarrhea, invigorates the mental powers, improves memory, and prevents hair from going grey when several are taken daily. It is most effective when taken pickled or preserved in sugar or honey (al-Anṭākī, *Tadhkira* 68; al-Malik al-Muẓaffar, *al-Muʿtamad* 27). In *Kanz* recipe 355 it is used in preparing a digestive to be taken after a heavy meal.

FIGURE 59 *Peach tree, F1954.76r, Muḥammad al-Qazwīnī,* ʿAjāʾib al-makhlūqāt, *detail (Freer Gallery of Art and Arthur M. Sackler Gallery, Smithsonian Institution, Washington,* DC*: Purchase—Charles Lang Freer Endowment).*

khawkh (خوخ) *Prunus persica* (S) peach. Al-Bīrūnī, *Ṣaydana* 186, gives its Byzantine Greek name as *dūraqīnī* (دورقيني), from which the Levantine name *durrāqin* (دُرّاقن) and *durrāq* (دُرّاق) for peach must have come. He also adds that peach varieties with loose and easy to remove pits are called *falīq* (فالق), and these are recommended because they are easy to digest. Peach varieties with hard to remove pits are called *lazīq* (لزيق); they are dense and not easily digested.

5 *Marākibī* (adj.) is derived from *marākib* (ships).

khawkh aqraʿ (خوخ اقرع) bald beach, smooth-skinned, also called *khawkh Miṣrī* (خوخ مصري) Egyptian peach, and *khawkh shatawī* (خوخ شتوي) early winter peach.

khawkh Baylaqānī (خوخ بيلقاني) peach of southern Azerbaijan, said to be very large and round (Ibn Waḥshiyya, *al-Filāḥa* ii 1191).

khawkh miskī (خوخ مسكي), lit., 'smells like musk,' was said to be the best variety.

khawkh shaʿrī (خوخ شعري) downy peach, said to be the common peach (Dozy, *Takmilat al-maʿājim* 419).

Fully ripe peaches are good for the stomach, but the best time to have them is before the meal. It excites the appetite and coitus and cools people with hot properties. Dried peach, however, is not as good in this respect. Leaves of the peach tree are particularly useful in preparations used to eliminate unpleasant odors from hands and clothes.

khawkh al-dubb (خوخ الدب) *Prunus ursina* (S) bear's plum,[6] which is a wild variety of *qarāṣiyā* (cherry plum, see entry below). Al-Warrāq in his cookbook (chapter 40) identifies it as *ijjāṣ ṣighār ḥāmiḍ* (إجّاص صغار حامض) small sour plum; and in the Levantine cookbook *Wuṣla* ii 545, it is said to be a variety of *qarāṣiyā* (cherry plum), used both fresh and dried.

Ibn Waḥshiyya, *al-Filāḥa* ii 1198, mentions it as a mountain variety (*ijjāṣ jabalī*). He says it is not large (the size of a hazelnut each), it is rounded in shape with rounded pits, very sour and astringent; it was used by first cooking it in water and straining it. The resulting juice, he explains, is more delicious in dishes than juices of apple, mulberry, unripe grapes, or pomegranate.

lawz (لوز) *Prunus dulcis* (S) almonds, used in cooking and desserts after rubbing off the brown skin by scalding them first in water. Almonds are used extensively in stews. They may be added whole or split; the milk may be extracted by dissolving pounded almonds in liquid and staining it. Added thus, it enhances the flavor and thickens the sauce and enriches it. To further enhance the flavor, its oil may be added. It is also popular as a stuffing for pastries when mixed with sugar and moistened with rosewater.

---

6 Although this fruit is in fact a variety of plum (*ijjāṣ*), it is named peach (*khawkh*) because *ijjāṣ* is called *khawkh* in the Levant. Even more confusingly, the Levantines call *kummathrā* 'pear' *ijjāṣ*. As for *khawkh* 'peach,' they call it *durrāqin*. See ʿAbd al-Laṭīf al-Baghdādī, *Riḥla* 79. The Andalusian al-Ṭaghnarī, *Zahrat al-bustān* 165 and 231, mentions that in his region *kummathrā* 'pear' is called *ijjāṣ*; and apricot '*mishmāsh*,' they call it *burqūq*, which in the Levant designates a small variety of plum (*ijjāṣ ṣaghīr*). See Ibn al-Bayṭār, *al-Jāmiʿ* i 18–9.

lawz akhḍar (لوز اخضر) fresh almonds with their outer skins.

lawz farik (لوز فرك) desirable variety of almonds with thin skin, which is easily peeled by just rubbing it between the fingers (Yāqūt al-Ḥamawī, *Muʿjam al-buldān* 1499).

lawz ghaḍḍ ṭarī (لوز غض طري) fresh and tender almonds.

kusb al-lawz (كسب اللوز) almond sediment after extracting the oil.

Sweet almonds have hot and moist properties; the bitter variety is dry and much hotter than the sweet. They were believed to be good for the chest and asthma, when combined with sugar. They relieve coughs, and help with weight gain. Almond oil, on the other hand, was said to suppress the appetite of women, to help them lose weight (al-Anṭākī, *Tadhkira* 314). It was believed to increase semen, and nourish the mind. Eating salted and toasted almonds was said to slow down intoxication; and eating fifty bitter almonds before drinking wine can prevent intoxication (Ibn Sīnā *al-Qānūn* 302; Ibn Jazla, *Minhāj al-bayān* fol. 186v1).

laymūn (ليمون) generic name for lemon, which is one of the basic souring agents used in the *Kanz* in savory dishes. Al-Maqrīzī, *Khiṭaṭ* ii 69, mentions that both *laymūn akhḍar* (lime) and *laymūn aṣfar* (common lemon) are abundant in Egypt.

laymūn akhḍar (ليمون اخضر) lime, lit., 'green lemon.' It is the domestic Egyptian variety (*Citrus limonum pusilla*), also called *laymūn baladī* (local lemon), *laymūn Miṣrī* (Egyptian), and the Persian *banzahīr*.[7] Al-Anṭākī, *Tadhkira* 316, describes this variety as *aṣlī* (original, ungrafted), round and small, and having a very thin peel.

This variety of lemon was common in the medieval Arabo-Islamic world. The tenth-century Ibn Waḥshiyya, *al-Filāḥa* i 182, gives the Chaldean name of the lime tree as *ḥasbanā* (حسبنا), and its Persian name as *līmū* (ليمو), but adds that the tree was originally Indian. He describes the edible grown fruit as round and green, which eventually turns yellow. It has sour pulp and a pleasant scent.

laymūn aṣfar (ليمون اصفر) *Citrus limon* (S) lit., 'yellow lemon,' common yellow lemon. Al-Maqrīzī, *Khiṭaṭ* ii 69, mentions that it is abundant in Egypt. It is also called *laymūn marākibī*, see below.

laymūn al-balsam (ليمون البلسم) mentioned by ʿAbd al-Laṭīf al-Baghdādī in his *Riḥla* 75. He says it is the size of the thumb, and looks like a rather elongated egg. In al-Suyūṭī's account of Egypt, *Ḥusn al-muḥāḍara* 364, excerpted verses describe a variety of lemon, which is compared to a chicken egg smeared with

7 See Waines, *Food Culture* 194.

saffron. In *Kanz* recipe 655, a variety of lemon is called *balsīmī* (بلسيمي), which indeed could be a variant of the name *balsam*.

laymūn māliḥ (ليمون مالح), ***laymūn mumallaḥ*** (ليمون مملح), ***laymūn muṣayyar*** (ليمون مصيّر) whole lemons, packed with salt and preserved as pickles, see for instance recipes 607–9. It was consumed as an appetizing relish, but also used chopped to season and garnish cold dishes, appetizers, and sauces, see, for instance, *Kanz*, chapter 19.

laymūn marākibī (ليمون مراكبي) *Citrus limon* (S), common yellow lemon. Levantine yellow lemon imported to Egypt via trading ships (*marākib*), hence the name. In some parts of the Levant today, it is still called *marākibī*. Al-Anṭākī, *Tadhkira* 316, points out that *laymūn marākibī* is the result of grafting the original lemon trees (lime, *Citrus limonum pusilla*) with *nāranj* (sour orange, *Citrus aurantium*). From his account, we understand that this variety did not seem to grow abundantly in Egypt. It was shipped to them in abundance from the Levant.

laymūn mukhattam (ليمون مختّم) mentioned by ʿAbd al-Laṭīf al-Baghdādī in his *Riḥla* 75. He describes it as being orange-red, even more so than *nāranj* (sour orange). He says it is very round, oblate, with a depression at each end.[8]

laymūn murakkab (ليمون مركب) lemon from lemon trees grafted with branches of the *utrujj* tree (*Citron medica*). Al-Anṭākī, *Tadhkira* 50, says it is a variety of *astabūn*, which is a Persian name. He adds that the resulting fruit is the size of a lemon, but elongated in shape like the regular citron (*utrujj*); and that it is plentiful in Egypt, where it is called *ḥummāḍ shuʿayrī*.

laymūn Ṣīnī aṣfar (ليمون صيني اصفر) yellow Chinese lemon, which could be Meyer lemon, *Citrus meyeri* (S), known to be native to China. See *Kanz*, recipe 377.

laymūn tuffāḥī (ليمون تفاحي) apple-like lemon. Al-Maqrīzī mentions it in *Khiṭaṭ* i 757. He says it is an Egyptian variety which ripens in August, and it is delicious and sweet enough to be eaten without sugar.

māʾ laymūn (ماء ليمون) lemon juice.

māʾ laymūn akhḍar (ماء ليمون اخضر) lime juice.

māʾ laymūn ʿatīq (ماء ليمون عتيق)[9] preserved lemon juice.

qishr laymūn yābis (قشر ليمون يابس) dried lemon peel.

shaḥm al-laymūn (شحم الليمون) white pith of the lemon peel.

---

8 It would seem to be a description of a tangerine (*Citrus tangerina*).

9 It occurs in *Zahr*, fol. 35r.

Besides its culinary benefits, lemon was also a handy medicinal asset. It was valuable as a breath freshener, and was recommended for a weak stomach, and as an aid to digesting coarse foods. It has the power to cleanse the digestive system after eating fatty and rich foods. In addition, it was used to treat nausea, headaches, and vertigo. Sweet lemon drinks and lemon drops were enjoyed for their refreshing taste, but more significantly for their medicinal benefits. When consumed as *naql* (mezza) with alcoholic drinks, they were believed to combat hangovers (Ibn al-Bayṭār, *al-Jāmiʿ* iv 395–400). See *Kanz*, recipes 349, 369, and 370, for instance.

lubb (لب) kernels of seeds.

FIGURE 60 *Banana tree, F1954.80v, Muḥammad al-Qazwīnī,* ʿAjāʾib al-makhlūqāt, *detail (Freer Gallery of Art and Arthur M. Sackler Gallery, Smithsonian Institution, Washington, DC: Purchase—Charles Lang Freer Endowment).*

mawz (موز) banana, consumed raw and cooked. The sweet large ones were deemed the best. They were not left to ripen on the trees. The cut bunches were hung in cellars for a few days until ready to eat (al-Bīrūnī, *Ṣaydana* 181). Bananas were said to be hard to digest, and better eaten with sugar or honey. When fully digested, they can be very nourishing (Ibn Sīnā, *al-Qānūn* 317).

mawz akhḍar (موز اخضر) may literally designate green unripe bananas; or fresh ones.

mawz aṣfar (موز اصفر) yellow ripe bananas.

mishmish (مشمش) *Prunus armeniaca* (S) apricot, used in *Kanz* recipes to make stews (recipes 120, 121) and compotes (chapter 13). The compotes were particularly popular as *naql* (mezza) taken during drinking sessions as they were believed to delay intoxication. Apricot is cold and moist in its properties; therefore, it was recommended for heat related ailments, and to quench heat. It should be avoided by cold-tempered people and the old. It has a tendency to sour and putrefy in the stomach; therefore, *sakanjabīn* drinks of vinegar and honey must be taken immediately after eating it to facilitate its fast purging.

mishmish akhḍar (مشمش اخضر) may designate green unripe apricot; or fresh apricot.

mishmish lawzī (مشمش لوزي) sweet apricot, because the kernel of its seed is as sweet as almonds (*lawz*). Al-Anṭākī, *Tadhkira* 330, mentions a variety called *ḥāzimī* (حازمي) or *Armawī* (ارموي), as recorded in ancient books, named after the northwestern city in Persia. It is larger, juicier, and less sweet than *lawzī*.

mishmish lawzī Khurāsānī (مشمش لوزي خراساني) sweet apricot of Khurasan, a region in northeastern Persia. As al-Anṭākī describes it, it is excessively sweet with pits that open up naturally when the fruit ripens.

mishmish yābis (مشمش يابس) dried apricot.

qamar al-dīn (قمر الدين) dried sheets of pureed apricot. Al-Anṭākī, *Tadhkira* 330, mentions that it is made by first soaking the fresh apricots, and then mashing them. The pits are removed, the pulp is spread in thin layers on boards oiled with sesame oil, and then it is left to dry in the sun.

Ibn Baṭṭūṭa, *Riḥla* 91 and 136, mentions that *qamar al-dīn* is the name of a wonderful large variety of apricot he encountered in Isfahan and the northern coast of Syria. He praises its sweet pits, and mentions that Egyptians import it dried. Therefore, the dried leathery sheet of apricot might well have gotten its name from the apricots it was originally made from.

nāranj (نارنج) *Citrus aurantium* (S) sour orange, said to be of Indian origin. The name is of a Persian origin meaning 'red' or 'red pomegranate' (red here designates a deep orange color). We learn from Ibn Khalṣūn's *Kitāb al-Aghdhiya* 100, that large sweet *nāranj* were also available. His general recommendation, however, is to eat the fruit with sugar. According to al-Anṭākī, *Tadhkira* 358, the best variety was said to be deep orange and round, with a dimpled and relatively thin peel.

The peel is known for its bitterness, and when the juice is called for in recipes, the cook is advised to have different people handle the peeling and the juicing (see for instance *Kanz* recipe 160). From *Wuṣla* ii 514–5 and 600, we learn that the best way to extract *nāranj* juice is to wilt the oranges by leaving them in a high well-ventilated place for a week and then use them. The cook is also instructed to peel a strip 3-fingers wide from around the middle of the *nāranj*, so that when it is cut in half and juiced, the peel's bitterness does not get into the juice.

The peel was said to have tremendous antidepressant properties. When stored dried with clothes, it can protect them from insects. The leaves are valued for their scent. The distilled water of its blossoms is described as bitter.

duhn al-nāranj (دهن النارنج) oil of the rind or blossoms of sour orange, which was said to have the power to purge winds and strengthen joints and nerves with its heat (Ibn Waḥshiyya, *al-Filāḥa* i 177–8).

laḥm al-nāranj (لحم النارنج), also called *ḥummāḍ al-nāranj* (حماض النارنج)[10] sour orange pulp, was said to have properties similar to those of citron (*utrujj*). It can alleviate heat and thirst, and reduce excess in yellow bile.

māʾ zahr al-nāranj (ماء زهر النارنج) distilled water of sour orange blossoms. *Kanz* recipe 708 describes how to distill it and how to extract its oil. Apparently, due to its bitterness, *Kanz* recipes only use it in preparations for topical use, such as oils for washing the hands, perfume compounds, and potpourri (recipes 651, 664, 670, and 671).

zahr al-nāranj (زهر النارنج) sour orange blossoms, see above.

In *Kanz* recipes, the juice, pulp, peel, and leaves are often used to make stews, drinks, jams, pastes, stomachics, and anti-nausea preparations (see, for instance, recipes 19, 20, 160, and 381). However, when the juice and pulp are used, the recipes include cautionary remarks on how to handle the bitter peel to prevent it from spoiling the dish, as in recipe 19.

niwāya (نواية) of fruits, pits, kernels, stones. The word is a dialectical variant of *nawāt* (نواة).

qamar al-dīn (قمر الدين) sheets of dried pureed apricot; see entry under *mishmish* above.

qarāṣiyā (قراصيا) *Prunus cerasifera* (S) cherry plums, also known as myrobalan plums, described as round, green when unripe and then red and dark red when fully ripe. It looks somewhat like a cherry but it is not the same (see next entry). It is sweet-sour and succulent in texture. Its cold properties can curb yellow bile, relieve nausea, and alleviate thirst. The gummy sap of the tree was said to treat coughs, and invigorate coitus (al-Anṭākī, *Tadhkira* 282).

---

10 *Ḥummāḍ* is more commonly used to designate citron pulp. Nonetheless, we do come across medieval texts in which, for instance, sour orange pulp (*ḥummāḍ al-nāranj*) is substituted for citron pulp (*ḥummāḍ al-utrujj*), as in Ibn Sīnā, *al-Qānūn* 1154.

qarāṣiyā Baʿlabakī (قراصيا بعلبكي) in the Levant, *ḥabb al-mulūk* (حب الملوك) in the Maghrib and Andalusia, and *jarāshiyā* (جراشيا) in Sicily. These are cherries (*Cerasus*), of which there are several varieties, consumed fresh and dried. The fruit is compared to round grapes, which dangle in pairs from green threadlike-stems. The black cherries (*Prunus avium*) are sweet; the red ones (*Prunus cerasus*) are sour; and there are sweet-sour ones, described as *muzz*. The sweet ones were said to glide through the digestive system fast, they have the properties of a laxative, and an aphrodisiac. The sour ones bind the stomach, and help alleviate thirst (Ibn al-Bayṭār, *al-Jāmiʿ* ii 253, iv 249; al-Anṭākī, *Tadhkira* 282).

qaṣb (قصب) Egyptian variant of *qasb* (قسب). It is a naturally dry variety of dates, the best of which was said to grow in Iraq, described as large light-brown dates, very delicious, with small pits. When dried they do not moisten and soften like other dates but keep their shape and become chewy and rather brittle (Ibn al-Bayṭār, *al-Jāmiʿ* i 191). It was said to be better for the body than the soft and moist dry dates due to its relatively cold properties (al-Rāzī, *al-Ḥāwī* 1826). ʿAbd al-Laṭīf al-Baghdādī, *Riḥla* 75, says that what is called *tamr* in Egypt is the equivalent of *qasb* in Iraq. On the other hand, what is called *ʿajwa* in Egypt is the equivalent of *tamr* in Iraq, which is any date variety that softens and moistens when dried, and can be stored pressed into containers.

qulūb (قلوب) pl. *qulūbāt* (قلوبات) nuts, kernels of seeds.

qulūb utrujj (قلوب الاترج) tender citron leaves.

ra's ṣanawbar (رأس صنوبر) pinecone. In *Kanz* recipe 164, the entire head is bruised and added to a preparation of fermented liquid sauce of *murrī*. The cones with the seeds inside them are harvested from the female pine tree. Its properties are hot and moist, and deemed beneficial to the elderly and people with cold properties. They can snack on the seeds (*ḥabb al-ṣanawbar*) while imbibing alcoholic drinks. It can excite the two appetites (sex and food), but it is slow to digest (al-Anṭākī, *Tadhkira* 245).

rummān (رمّان) *Punica granatum* (S) pomegranates, which can be sweet (*ḥulw*), sweet-sour (*muzz*), and sour (*ḥāmiḍ*). The ideal pomegranates are the large juicy ones, with intensely-red smooth peels. Sweet pomegranates are mostly eaten as fruit, but are also used in cooking, mixed with sour pomegranates to balance its taste. The sour variety was believed to stimulate the appetite and curb yellow bile. It was used in making savory dishes and drinks.

ḥabb al-rummān (حبّ الرمّان) pomegranate seeds. When in season, the juice of the fresh seeds is extracted and used in dishes. When out of season, dried seeds are used. Some dried varieties were imported, as we learn from *Kanz*, recipe 397, which calls for pomegranate seeds of Suḥār, Kasbah of Oman. The dried seeds are used whole or pounded, and are then boiled in water, strained, and used.

rummān Jūrī (رمّان جوري) it must be an excellent variety of pomegranate, which grows in Jūr, a Persian village in the Shiraz area of southeastern Persia. The area is known for its fertility and fruit orchards.

ruṭab (رطب) fresh ripe dates, when they soften and moisten. See *tamr* below.

safarjal (سفرجل) *Cydonia oblonga* (S) quinces. The large, sweet, and crisp ones were deemed the best. They were believed to excite the appetite, energize the body, and gladden the soul even by just smelling them. Having the fruit with alcoholic drinks was said to prevent hangovers. It was also believed that if a pregnant woman started eating quince regularly from the third month of pregnancy, she would give birth to a beautiful smart child. Sharp steel knives were better avoided in cutting it, as they were believed to cause it to lose its juice fast (al-ʿUmarī, *Masālik*, xx 201; al-Anṭākī, *Tadhkira* 208), see *Kanz* recipe 374. The following varieties are mentioned in the *Kanz*:

safarjal Aṣfahānī (سفرجل اصفهاني) of Isfahan, the Persian province. Based on *Kanz* recipe 347, this variety is delicious, aromatic, and soft-fleshed.

safarjal Barzī (سفرجل برزي) of Barza, a Damascene village. It is like *safarjal Aṣfahānī*, in that it is aromatic and soft-fleshed.

safarjal qaṣbī (سفرجل قصبي) based on *Kanz* recipe 359, this variety is hard-fleshed.

tamr (تمر) generic name for dates. However, it may also designate this fruit at the stage of its final ripeness, when they can be stored as dried dates. Depending on their moisture content, they can either be pressed into containers, such as *ʿajwa*, or stored loose, such as *qasb*.

ʿAbd al-Laṭīf al-Baghdādī, *Riḥla* 75, says that *tamr* in Egypt is the equivalent of *qasb* in Iraq. The latter is a naturally dry date that does not soften and moisten when fully ripe and dried. On the other hand, *ʿajwa* in Egypt is the equivalent of *tamr* in Iraq, which is any date variety that softens and moistens when dried, and can be stored pressed into containers.

Dates have different names depending on their stages of ripeness:

ṭalʿ (طلع) when dates first sprout.

khalāl (خلال) at the earliest stage of ripeness when dates are still green and sour.

balaḥ (بلح) when dates turn yellow, but are still very firm and not so sweet.

busr (بسر) when dates are sweet and ripe but still crunchy.

ruṭab (رطب) when fresh ripe dates start to moisten and soften until finally the entire fruit is soft and highly moist in texture.

tamr (تمر) dates in the last stage of ripeness. They are fully ripe, sweet and soft, and contain the least amount of moisture. At this stage, dates can be safely stored.

With their moist and hot properties, dates were believed to increase semen and cause headaches. The recommendation was to eat them with almonds and poppy seeds. They were said to be hard to digest and cause teeth and gums to spoil. *Qasb* dates, which are naturally dry, were said to be relatively colder than the moist sticky variety. That is why they were deemed to cause less bloating and be gentler on the digestive system (Ibn Sīnā, *al-Qānūn* 373; Ibn al-Bayṭār, *al-Jāmiʿ* i 191–2).

ʿajwa (عجوة) excellent quality dark and sweet date of the Hijaz. It was said to be the Prophet's favorite date. In Egypt, however, the name *ʿajwa* is also used to designate *tamr*, the dried moist and sticky dates, which can be stored pressed into containers.

tamr maʿjūn (تمر معجون) soft and moist dried dates pressed into paste, and stored as blocks in containers. See *ʿajwa* above.

nawā l-tamr (نوى التمر) date seeds.

qimʿ al-tamr (قمع التمر) calyx of the date.

tamr Wāḥī (تمر واحي) a variety of *qasb* (naturally dry dates) harvested from the date palms in the western Egyptian oases (al-Wāḥāt). In *Kanz*, recipe 750, they are described as having thick skins, which renders them harder than the Iraqi *qasb* variety.

tamr Hindī (تمر هندي) *Tamarindus indica* (S) lit., 'Indian date.' The pulp of the pod-like fruit of this tree is used as a souring agent in cooking (*Kanz* recipe, DK, appendix 17, p. 120). Such dishes are recommended for the summertime (al-Warrāq, Istanbul MS, fols. 140r–v) It is also an essential ingredient in preparations to cure nausea (*Kanz*, chapter 14), and digestives and chewy candy, called *ʿaqīd* (*Kanz* recipes 355, 371). With its cold and dry properties, it can relieve the symptoms of heat-related ailments, and stop vomiting and nausea. It is a thirst quencher and a laxative (al-Anṭākī, *Tadhkira* 104).

tīn (تين) *Ficus carica* (S) common fig, of which the white or yellow variety was deemed the best. The red and black varieties are not as sweet.

dhukār (ذكار) *Ficus carica sylvestris* (S) caprifig, the male, pollen-bearing wild variety of the common fig, used to pollinate the edible fig. See entry above.

laban al-tīn (لبن التين) milky sap, latex, of the fig tree, which acts like rennet in curdling milk into yogurt and cheese, and helps hasten the cooking and tenderizing of meat.

tīn Maʿarrī (تين معري) figs named after the Syrian city Maʿarrat al-Nuʿmān, famous for its figs and olives.

tīn Wazīrī (تين وزيري) the sweetest of all kinds of figs; it has thin skin and tiny seeds, named after Wazīriyya, a district in the city of Sāmarrā, north of Baghdad (Masʿūdī, *Murūj* 561).

waraq tīn (ورق تين) fig leaves, which have antiseptic properties. They are used to encourage bread pieces to mold in *Kanz* recipe 500 for making the fermented condiment of *kāmakh*.

tīn yābis (تين يابس) dried figs.

ʿūd al-dhukār (عود الذكار) sticks from *dhukār* (ذكار), see above. They are left in the large jars of *murrī*, the fermenting sauce, and used to stir the mix for several months, as in *Kanz* recipe 150. Wood of wild fig trees, including *jummayz* (see below), is known for its resistance to rot, and its antiseptic properties. However, any fig sticks will do when used to stir the condiments of *kāmakh*, as they do not take long to ferment (see *Kanz* chapter 17).

tīn barrī (تين بري) *Ficus sycomorus* (S), also known as *jummayz* (جميز) sycomore fig. It is a wild fig variety. The tree produces a profuse amount of latex. The Levantine variety of the fig is described as large and red, and much sweeter and more digestible than the Egyptian variety, though it grows abundantly in Egypt. To make it lighter on the digestion, the Egyptians habitually drink water after having it, as they think this will make it float in their stomachs. However, al-Anṭākī, *Tadhkira* 118, disapproves of this.

From this variety of fig, very sour vinegar and strong wine are made (ʿAbd al-Laṭīf al-Baghdādī, *Riḥla* 65). It was also believed to be medicinally beneficial in treating chest pains and coughs, and other respiratory ailments. The leaves can abort fetuses and stimulate menstruation. The latex has antiseptic properties and can seal wounds. In addition, its wood is valued for its durability and resistance to rot.

tuffāḥ (تفاح) apples, of which there are many varieties ranging from the sweet, sweet-sour (*muzz*), sour, and insipid (*tafih*). Apples were valued as good food, especially the sweet ripe ones, and the large aromatic varieties with crisp flesh and thin skins. They have the power to strengthen and gladden the heart, and when enclosed in dough and baked, they were said to excite poor appetites. Sniffing aromatic apples was believed to fortify the heart and brain (Ibn Sīnā, *al-Qānūn* 373). The following varieties are mentioned in the *Kanz*:

tuffāḥ fatḥī (تفاح فتحي), also called *tuffāḥ Shāmī* (Levantine apple) large variety of apple valued for its balanced properties and great aroma, used in scented preparations like potpourri (*lakhlakha*).

tuffāḥ rayḥānī (تفاح ريحاني) aromatic variety of apple, used in cooking.

tuffāḥ Shāmī (تفاح شامي) Levantine apple, see *tuffāḥ fatḥī*.

Other varieties of apple are mentioned in *Kanz* recipe 737. This recipe deals with methods for storing fresh apples for use when not in season. Based on internal evidence, these varieties seem to be valued types that were in limited supply in Egypt, as they could not be propagated by means of offshoots. They are

budayris (بديرس) unidentified, but could have been a misreading of *barīrī* (بريري), a Damascene apple variety mentioned in al-Badrī, *Nuzhat al-anām* 201. Probably called so because in color it resembles the ripe bright red fruit of the *arāk* tree (*Salvadora persica*).

ḥayyāfī (حيافي) unidentified, but could have been a misreading of *jinānī* (جناني), a Damascene apple variety mentioned in al-Badrī's book.

ḥalawānī (حلواني) and ***biṭṭīkhī*** (بطيخي), both are included in al-Badrī, *Nuzhat al-anām* 201, in his list of Damascene apple varieties.

Apples were also used as ornamental fruits on which words were written (see *Kanz*, recipe 724), and even their shape was manipulated. An unripe apple was enclosed in a mold, so that it takes the shape of the mold as it ripens and grows larger.[11]

tūt (توت) *Morus* (S) mulberry, the best of which are the large and sweet ones.

tūt abyaḍ (توت ابيض) *Morus alba* (S) sweet white mulberry, known as *Nabaṭī* in Iraq, and *Ḥalabī* (Aleppan) in the Levant.

tūt aḥmar (توت احمر) red mulberry of the Levantine variety (*Shāmī*), see below. In *Kanz* recipe 23, it is used in a meat dish called *Yāqūtiyya* (carnelian), where chunks of gourd are cooked and colored with its juice, which is sweetened with sugar or honey. The cooked chunks of gourd will look like carnelian gemstones.

tūt Shāmī (توت شامي) *Morus nigra* (S) Levantine mulberry is a large variety, black or red, and sour. It was said to be appetizing, and good for quenching intense thirst and reducing heat.

---

11 This was also done with other fruits like pears, pomegranates, quinces, and citron. See al-Ṭaghnarī, *Zahrat al-bustān* 246–7.

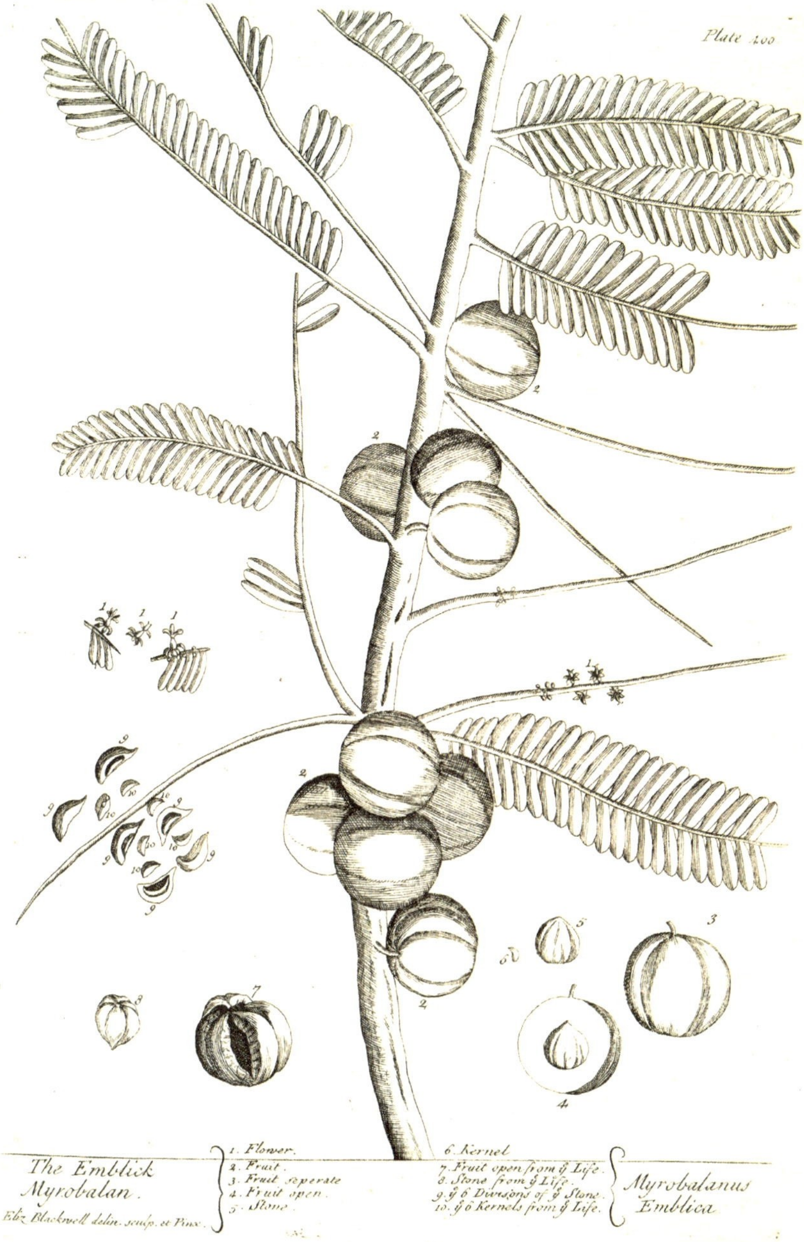

FIGURE 61 Umluj (*emblic myrobalan*), *Elizabeth Blackwell,* A Curious Herbal, *1738, plate 400 (From the New York Public Library: http://digitalcollections.nypl.org/items/510d47dd-cd07-a3d9-e040-e00a18064a99).*

umluj (املج), called ***sanānīr*** in Egypt (سنانير) *Phyllanthus emblica* (S) emblic myrobalan, also known as Indian gooseberry. When this fruit is steeped in milk before drying it to eliminate some of its astringency, it is called *shīr umluj* (*shīr* is milk in Persian). The best looks yellowish; dark ones are not good. With its cold and dry properties and astringency, it is beneficial in stopping diarrhea, improving the odor of sweat, and strengthening the stomach (al-Anṭākī, *Tadhkira* 62–3; al-Malik al-Muẓaffar, *al-Muʿtamad* 27). In *Kanz* recipe 355, it is used along with *Kābulī* (entry above) in a digestive preparation to be taken after a heavy meal.

ʿunnāb (عُنّاب) *Ziziphus jujuba* (S) jujubes, which look like olives, with a rather dry and dense texture. The large red ones were deemed the best. In cooking, they are used to flavor and garnish the dishes. Medicinally, they were valued for their hot and moist properties. Steeped and cooked, they were believed to be good for coughs and raw chests. The recommendation was to have them before the meals and to nibble on them during drinking sessions. The wood of the tree was used in making small household objects.

ʿunnāb Jurjānī (عُنّاب جرجاني) jujube of Jurjān, a city in northern Persia. This variety was said to be the best (al-Malik al-Muẓaffar, *al-Muʿtamad* 396).

FIGURE 62 Utrujj (*citron*), *al-ʿUmarī,* Masālik al-abṣār, *fol. 142r, detail* (*BnF, Department of manuscripts, Arab 2771.*

utrujj (أترج), ***turunj*** (ترنج) *Citrus medica* (S) citron. See also *kabbād* above. The entire fruit is highly valued for its restorative and digestive properties, especially the leaves. It strengthens the stomach, and stimulates the appetite. It is beneficial for palpitations, and alleviates thirst and hangovers (*khumār*).

ḥummāḍ al-utrujj (حماض الاترج) sour citron pulp, used in cooking dishes of *ḥummāḍiyyāt*, and in refreshing restorative drinks (see for instance, *Kanz* recipes 11 and 360). The juice was also deemed the best pacifier for women's lust (Ibn al-Bayṭār, *al-Jamiʿ* i 13–5; al-Bīrūnī, *Ṣaydana* 21–3).

qiddāḥ al-utrujj (قداح الاترج) citron blossoms, highly aromatic, used mostly in distilled waters.

qishr al-utrujj (قشر الاترج) citron peel. Due to its thickness and density, the peel is used in making jams. The outer skin is valued for its aromatic oil and distilled waters. It was believed to have a euphoric property when sniffed. It sweetens the breath if kept in the mouth; it was also used as an air freshener. The dried peel was kept between layers of clothes to protect them from moths. Zesting the peel to extract its oil was done with a sharp piece of iron or a thin shard of glass. To extract the oil without injuring the outer skin, a thin silver spoon or a potsherd with blunt edges was used (Ibn al-Bayṭār, *al-Jāmiʿ* ii 401–2, s.v. *duhn al-utrujj*).

shuʿayr al-utrujj (شعير الاترج), ***shaʿr al-utrujj*** (شعر الاترج) juice vesicles of the citron pulp, see, for instance, *Kanz* recipes 360, 586. A chunk of vesicles is called *fuṣṣ* (pl. *fuṣūṣ*).

waraq al-utrujj (ورق الاترج) citron leaves used fresh and dried, in dishes, preserved foods, and in curative and aromatic preparations.

utrujj Sūsī (اترج سوسي) Susa citron. Susa is a city in the province of Khuzestan, in southwestern Persia. This variety of citron is known for its huge size and heavy weight; a single citron of this kind might weigh up to 30 pounds, as mentioned in an anecdote in Ibn al-Jawzī, *al-Adhkiyāʾ* 106. Its pulp is used in *Kanz* recipe 352 to make syrup for a citron drink.

zabīb (زبيب) large raisins with seeds, the best of which are described as meaty, with thin skins and few seeds. Al-Anṭākī says that this variety is called *darbalī* (دربلي) in his time (sixteenth century), and *Khurāsānī* (خراساني) in the past. Next in excellence, he adds, is the large black variety, called *ṣubayʿ* (صبيع) 'little finger' in Egypt. It tastes a bit sour, and is often used in making *aqsimā* (sweetened digestive drinks). Next come *zabīb aḥmar* (زبيب احمر) 'red raisins,' which are truly sweet. The fair-colored ones are not as good, and are slightly bitter. The worst variety, as described by al-Anṭākī, does not have meaty flesh, and contains lots of seeds. This, he says, is what is called *al-zabīb al-ʿUbaydī* (الزبيب العبيدي) in Egypt.

Zabīb was enjoyed as dried fruit. It was also incorporated into dishes and drinks. It was highly praised by physicians, believed to be good for the stomach, kidneys, liver, and bladder (Ibn al-Bayṭār, *al-Jāmiʿ* ii 454–5; al-Anṭākī, *Tadhkira* 190–1).

zabīb aḥmar (زبيب احمر) red raisins, used only once in the *Kanz* in a preparation for nausea (recipe 444).

zabīb aswad (زبيب اسود) black raisins, the most common variety used in cooking.

zabīb jawzānī (زبيب جوزاني) raisins made from *jawza/jawzānī*, which were deemed an excellent Levantine variety of grapes (Dozy, *Takmilat al-maʿājim* 245). They are not large, and turn intensely yellow when fully ripe.

zabīb Ṣaʿīdī (زبيب صعيدي) raisins of Upper Egypt, used in *Kanz*, recipe 454, in a preparation for curing nausea. It must be a hard-skinned variety because the recipe requires them to be washed in water, and then left overnight wrapped in a woolen cloth before removing their seeds.

zabīb Sulṭī (زبيب سلطي) sultana raisins, which is a variety of Levantine raisins made from *Sulṭī* grapes growing in the city of Sulṭ in the Jordan Valley. It is used only once in *Kanz* recipes in a preparation for nausea (recipe 455).

zaytūn (زيتون) olives, see glossary 5 above, for table olives; and glossary 6 above, for oils extracted from them.

8. Ingredients Used in Foods and Medicinal Preparations: Herbs, Spices, Aromatics, Minerals, Food Colors, and Seasoning Sauces

abāzīr (أبازير), ***abzār*** (أبزار) seasoning herbs, spices, seeds, and aromatics. See below for spice blends of *aṭrāf al-ṭīb*; *abāzīr al-sūbiyā;* and *abāzīr al-ʿujaj*.

abāzīr ʿatīqa (أبازير عتيقة) old, expired herbs and spices.

abāzīr ḥadītha (أبازير حديثة) newly dried herbs and spices.

abāzīr ḥārra (أبازير حارة) spices with hot properties, such as black pepper, cinnamon, ginger, caraway, spikenard, cumin, and mastic.

abāzīr al-sūbiyā (أبازير السوبيا) spice blend provided in *Kanz* recipe 434, used with grain-based digestive beer. It is a special blend of *aṭrāf al-ṭīb* (see below) containing the following:

> Spikenard, betel leaves (*tunbul*), clove stalks (*ḥaṭab qaranful*), green cardamom, nutmeg, mace, black pepper, ginger, and rosebuds (*zir ward*),

abāzīr al-ʿujaj (أبازير العجج) spice blend used with omelets (*ʿujaj*) and scrambled eggs (*mubaʿtharāt*). Its components, as provided in *Kanz* recipe 198, are the following:

> One part of each of the following: ginger, galangal (*khūlanjān*), rolled Ceylon cinnamon bark (*qarfat al-laff*), saffron, fennel (*shamar*), black pepper, cumin, and fine-tasting thyme (*zaʿtar ṭayyib*). Add one quarter of a part of rosebuds (*zir ward*), and one eighth of a part of good spikenard (*sunbul*). Pound all these spices (*ḥawāʾij*) thoroughly, and stow them away and use as needed.

abāzīr yābisa (أبازير يابسة), *abzār yābisa* (أبزار يابسة) dried spices in general, such as black pepper, spikenard (*sunbul*), cloves, cassia (*dār Ṣīnī*), galangal (*khulanjān*), coriander, and caraway.

abzār ruṭb (أبزار رطب) fresh herbs, such as parsley, cilantro, and dill.

ʿadhba (عذبة) tamarisk seeds, also known as *ḥabb al-athal* (حب الاثل), and *kazmāzaj* (كزمازج), seeds of *Tamarix Articulata* (S) tamarisk tree. The seeds, a bit bitter and astringent, are mostly used in digestives, and preparations which help with weight gain and add glow and luster to the complexion. See *Kanz* recipe 288.

afāwih (أفاوه), ***afāwīh*** (أفاويه) spices in general, particularly the aromatic ones.

afāwīh ʿaṭira (أفاويه عطرة), ***afwāh ṭayyiba*** (أفواه طيبة) aromatic spices, such as cardamom, nutmeg, mace, spikenard, cinnamon, and cloves.

 | DOI 10.1163/9789004349919_034

afāwih al-fuqqāʿ (أفاوه الفقاع) spice blend used for making beer; these include:

Green cardamom, black pepper, betel leaves (*tunbul*), and spikenard (*sunbul*), as provided in *Kanz* recipe 412.

ʿafṣ (عفص) oak gall, best taken when still green and unripe, and dense and heavy. Its properties are cold and dry, and it is extremely astringent. It can firm up any slackening organs, and is good for all kinds of swelling in the rectum. It is also good for stomach ulcers and diarrhea. Of its other non-medicinal uses, black ink and hair dye are produced from it (al-Malik al-Muẓaffar, *al-Muʿtamad* 384–5).

āla (آلة) general term for 'spices and herbs used.'

amīr bārīs (أمير باريس) also called *barbārīs* (برباريس), and the Persian *zirishk* (زرشك) *Berberis vulgaris* (S) barberry, used in *Kanz* recipe 17 to make a sour stew, thickened with almonds. With its cold and dry properties, it was believed to quench thirst and strengthen the stomach. It is beneficial for people with excess hot properties. It was said to be good for palpitations, nausea, and weak appetites (al-Anṭākī, *Tadhkira* 63).

ʿanbar (عنبر) *Ambra grisea* (S) ambergris, greyish substance located in the intestines of the sperm whale (*Bilaenopetra musculus*), valued for its aroma. The best is the Indian, described as chewy in texture, yellowish, and oily; and black ambergris is the worst.

Medicinally, it is recommended for the elderly, as its dry and hot properties can heat up their bodies. Inhaling its fumes can break down dense winds and phlegm in the head. Generally, it is good for the entire nervous system. Drinking it repeatedly with honey drinks can restore sexual appetite lost in old age. Adding a small piece of it to one's wine will induce fast intoxication (al-Anṭākī, *Tadhkira* 263; al-Malik al-Muẓaffar, *al-Muʿtamad* 395).

ʿanbar dasim (عنبر دسم) oily ambergris.
ʿanbar khām (عنبر خام) raw ambergris.

anīsūn (أنيسون), ***yānsūn*** (يانسون) *Pimpinella anisum* (S) aniseeds. The plant is mainly cultivated for its seeds. It was believed to be good for cold-related ailments; it strengthens the stomach, and helps with flatulence.

anjudhān (أنجذان) leaves of the asafetida plant (*Ferula assa-foetida*), used in *Kanz* recipes with dipping sauces called *ṣibāgh*, such as 470–3; and digestive pickles, such as recipe 584. With its hot and dry properties, it was believed to dispel dense winds, break down dense phlegm, and digest foods. It was also said to be good for chest-related ailments and coughs (al-Anṭākī, *Tadhkira* 64).

ʿaqāqīr (عقاقير) in culinary contexts, it generally designates dried spices.

ʿāqir shamʿā (عاقر شمعا), also called *shinkār* (شنكار), *shinjār* (شنجار) and *rijl al-ḥamāma* (رجل الحمامة) and *sāq al-ḥamām* (ساق الحمامة) *Alkanna tinctoria* (S) dyer's bugloss, alkanet. Its root is primarily used as a ruby-red coloring agent for fabrics, soaps, lip balm, and the like.

asārūn (أسارون) also called *nārdīn barrī* (ناردين بري) *Asarum europaeum* (S) wild spikenard, a mountainous plant with rhizomes and lots of minor roots, which have an aromatic smell and a hot sharp taste. The roots are used in medicinal preparations to treat sciatica, strengthen kidneys and the bladder, and dissolve kidney stones. It is also said to increase semen (Ibn al-Bayṭār, *al-Jāmiʿ* i 31–3).

aṭrāf al-ṭīb (أطراف الطيب), also called *afwāh al-ṭīb* (أفواه الطيب). It was a widely-used blend of aromatic spices. Ibn al-ʿAdīm's thirteenth-century cookbook *al-Wuṣla ilā l-ḥabīb* ii 518 gives its components:

> *Sunbul* (spikenard), *tunbul* (betel-leaf), *waraq rand* (bay leaves), *jawz al-ṭīb* (nutmeg), *basbāsa* (mace), *hāl* (green cardamom), *kibāsh qaranful* (cloves), *zir ward* (rosebuds), *lisān al-ʿaṣāfīr* (fruit of Syrian ash),[1] *dār fulful* (long pepper), *zanjabīl* (ginger), and *fulful* (black pepper).

All these spices are ground separately and then mixed and stored, to be used as needed. The cooks are sometimes asked to use all the components of this spice blend, such as in *Kanz* recipes 15, 70, and 429; or some of them, as in recipe 434 (see *abāzīr al sūbiyā* above).

aṭrāf al-ṭīb al-mukhtaṣṣa bi-l-aqsimā (أطراف الطيب المختصة بالاقسما) spice blend specially used with the digestive drink of *aqsimā*. It includes the following:

> Ginger, green cardamom (*hāl*), and a tiny amount of clove. These spices will not discolor the drink, as provided in *Kanz* recipe 401.

awrāl (أورال) sg. *waral* (ورل) monitor lizards, valued for their properties as aphrodisiacs. See *waral* below.

bādharūj (باذروج), also called *ḥawak* (حوك), and ***rayḥān*** (ريحان) *Ocimum* (S) basil, see *rayḥān* below.

banafsaj (بنفسج) *Viola* (S) violet, hot and dry in properties, usually shade-dried and used. It was believed to be good for coughs and the stomach. Cooked with sugar as jam, it was used to induce sleep. However, it does not have a pleasant taste (Ibn al-Bayṭār, *al-Jāmiʿ* i 156–7).

---

1 See *lisān al-ʿuṣfūr* below.

banafsaj shadīd al-zurqa (بنفسج شديد الزرقة) deep-blue violet, added to distilled rose petals to color them blue.

qazmat al-banafsaj (قزمة البنفسج) *Iris verna* (S) dwarf violet iris, used in the *Kanz* in handwashing preparations, deodorants, incense, and distilled waters. Dozy, *Takmilat al-maʿājim* 137, mentions *qarm banafsaj* (قرم بنفسج) to designate *sawsan* (iris), s.v. *q-r-m* (قرم) [sic].

FIGURE 63 Baqdūnis (*Macedonian parsley*), *Elizabeth Blackwell,* A Curious Herbal, *1738, plate 382 (From the New York Public Library: http://digital collections.nypl.org/items/510d47dd-ccf5-a3d9-e040-e00a18064a99).*

baqdūnis (بقدونس) *maqdūnis* (مقدونس) *Petroselinum macedonicum* (S) Macedonian parsley, which is a variety of *karafs* (see entry below).

It was originally called *karafs Maqdūnī* (كرفس مقدوني), named after Macedonia; its other names include *karafs Rūmī* (كرفس رومي) Byzantine parsley, and *karafs jabalī* (كرفس جبلي) mountain parsley. It was said to be plentiful in Andalusia; it was described as having a sharp taste, flavorful, and pleasantly aromatic (al-Ishbīlī, *'Umdat al-ṭabīb* i 315). Ibn Waḥshiyya, *al-Filāḥa* ii 781, adds that *karafs Rūmī* is the greenest of all varieties of parsley, and has the most flavor. Ibn al-Jazzār, *Kitāb al-I'timād*, fol. 86v, in his entry on *karafs*, mentions two types of cultivated parsley (*bustānī*): the common *karafs* and *ma'dūnis*, described as having smaller leaves, which are more aromatic and sharper in taste than parsley.[2] See also *karafs* below.

baqqam (بقّم) *Caesalpinia sappan* (S) sapanwood, from which red dye is obtained.

barnūf (برنوف) *Dittrichia viscosa* (S) sticky fleabane, which grew abundantly in Egypt. It has downy sticky leaves, tastes bitter, and has a somewhat aromatic heavy smell. With its hot and dry properties, it opens blockages in the head and nose caused by colds (Ibn al-Bayṭār, *al-Jāmi'* i 122). In *Kanz* recipe 650, it is used dried and crushed, along with crushed lupine beans, for handwashing, and to remove unpleasant greasy odors. It is equally effective when used fresh.

FIGURE 64
Barnūf (*sticky fleabane*), *Elizabeth Blackwell,* A Curious Herbal, *1738, plate 103* (*From the New York Public Library: http://digitalcollections.nypl.org/items/510d47dd-c6c9-a3d9-e040-e00a18064a99*).

2 The earliest pictorial presentation of *baqdūnis* I found is in Elizabeth Blackwell's *Curious Herbal* in 1739.

baṣal (بصل) *Allium cepa* (S) onion, described as hot and pungent, but pickling it improves its properties. It was said to excite the two appetites (food and sex), especially when cooked with meat. It induces thirst, and the best way to get rid of its odor in the mouth is to chew on toasted walnuts, fried cheese, or over-toasted bread. Al-Anṭākī, *Tadhkira* 83, says onion is abundant in Egypt. The best variety is white onion, especially the longish ones. The worst, he adds, is red onion, especially the round variety.

ʿarāmīsh (عراميش) sg. *ʿurmūsh* (عرموش) loose outer skins and scraggly roots growing from the onion.

baṣal abyaḍ (بصل أبيض), ***bayāḍ baṣal*** (بياض بصل) white onion, especially the long variety, is said to be the best in Egypt.

baṣal akhḍar (بصل اخضر) scallion; *aṭrāf al-baṣal al-akhḍar* (أطراف البصل الاخضر) green leaves of scallion.

baṣal ḥirrīf raqīq aṣfar (بصل حرّيف رقيق اصفر) yellow and thin skinned pungent onion, used in pickling.

baṣal mudawwar (بصل مدور) round onion, used in pickling (see *Kanz* recipes, chapter 18).

baṣal ramlī (بصل رملي) onion grown in sandy soil. I have not encountered it in medieval sources other than *Kanz*, recipe 65. However, from our common knowledge of growing onion, sandy soil allows the onion bulbs to expand. Therefore, the onion called for in a fruity meat stew (*Kanz* recipe 65) could have been large white onion, juicy and sweet, neither sharp nor pungent.

baṣal ṣighār (بصل صغار) small onion, used in pickling (see *Kanz* recipes, chapter 18).

basbāsa (بسباسة) mace, the lacy covering of the nutmeg, whose properties are like those of nutmeg (see *jawz ṭīb* below). It has a pleasant sharp aroma, which can sweeten the breath. It aids digestion and drives out gas. It also removes the smell of sweat, especially under the arms. It was used in cooking dishes as well as in restorative and digestive preparations (al-Anṭākī, *Tadhkira* 81).

basbāsa Hindiyya (بسباسة هندية) Indian mace.

bazr baqla (بزر بقلة) seeds of common purslane, see *bazr rijla* below.

bazr qaṭṭūna (بزر قطونة) *Plantago psyllium* (S) fleawort, of which the seeds are the most used part. They produce jelly-like mucilage when soaked in water, which is beneficial in binding ingredients. Medicinally, it was valued for its laxative and cooling properties.

bazr rijla (بزر رجلة) seeds of common purslane (*Portulaca oleracea*), which is its most common name in Egypt. Its other names include *baqla ḥamqāʾ* (بقلة حمقاء) or just *baqla as* in the Levant, *farfakh* (فرفخ), and *barbahīn* (بربهين) and *barbīn* (بربين). It is a succulent sprawling plant, with tiny fruit capsules, filled with tiny round black seeds. In *Kanz* recipe 66, the seeds are toasted, crushed, and then added to a chicken dish called *sitt al-Nūba* (Nubian lady), to give it a darkish hue. The essence of the seeds is extracted (*yustaḥlab*) by crushing the seeds first and then tying them in a piece of cloth, which is dipped in liquid several times to help the seeds release their essence.

būraq (بورق) sodium bicarbonate, a mineral, of which there are many varieties. The two major ones are the Armenian (see entry below); and the Egyptian, obtained from the saline oases in western Egypt (Wādī Naṭrūn).

Of this Egyptian natural mineral, there are two kinds:

1) *Naṭrūn* (نطرون), obtained from saline rocks. It is reddish in hue, and tastes salty and sour, mingled with slight bitterness, which is an indication of its being exposed to excess heat. See entry below.
2) *Būraq al-khubz* (بورق الخبز) looks like white flour, tastes salty and sour, but not bitter. It is called this because it is used as a leavening agent in making bread. The Egyptian bakers dissolve it in water and wipe the already shaped breads in its solution,[3] to make it look bright and glossy (Ibn al-Bayṭār, *al-Jāmiʿ* i 170–3).

These two minerals—*naṭrūn* and *būraq*—are similar in their chemical components. However, the former was deemed somewhat stronger in its functions. For instance, Ibn Waḥshiyya, *al-Filāḥa* i 436, says he prefers to use *naṭrūn* rather than yeast in making bread because it makes it rise and fluff more effectively. He adds that *būraq* can be used instead, and it will have the same effect; however, more of it should be used. Al-ʿUmarī, *Masālik* xxii 216, mentions that kneading *naṭrūn* with the bread dough makes it look white and enhances its taste; and that adding it to a pot of boiling meat makes it cook faster.[4]

Judging from the *Kanz* recipes, the two can indeed be used interchangeably. *Būraq*, for instance, is the mineral specified to hasten the cooking of meat, where-

3 The verb used is *yughsal* (يغسل), lit., 'wash.'

4 The same observation has been documented by the seventeenth-century Awliyā Chalabī, *Riḥla* i 497. He says that due to the scarcity of firewood in Egypt, Egyptians often use *naṭrūn* to replace salt in cooking their foods. That is why, he observes, their food does not taste like much.

as *naṭrūn* is added to boiling chard, turnips, cabbage, and beans. In recipe 285 for cookies, either one is said to be good to use.

būraq Armanī (بورق ارمني) Armenian sodium borate, described as the best and purest variety, and strongest in properties, generated from saline rocks. It is white, soft, and brittle. It is also called *būraq al-ṣāgha* (بورق الصاغة) 'jewelers' borax' because it can be used to clean and polish silver (al-Anṭākī, *Tadhkira* 94–5). Even though it was said to be bad for the stomach, it was used in small amounts medicinally, to relieve colic, improve the color of the complexion, help purge intestinal worms; and when rubbed on the male organ and the area around it, it was claimed to cause a powerful and prolonged erection (Ibn al-Bayṭār, *al-Jāmiʿ* i 173). In *Kanz* recipe 380, it is used in a digestive preparation.

bustān abrawīz (بستان ابرويز), ***bustān afrūz*** (بستان افروز), ***bustān abrūz*** (بستان ابروز) *Amaranthus* (S) amaranth. The name is originally Persian. It means 'inflaming the garden' (Steingass Persian/English *Dictionary*). Ibn al-Bayṭār, *al-Jāmiʿ* i 129, describes the plant's beautifully bountiful pink (*firfīrī*) and velvety spikes of flowers, which grow out of the leaves' axils. The plant is not fragrant, but the flowers, fresh and dried, were used as food dye. Their cold and dry properties meant that they were also useful medicinally. A drink of their juice boiled with syrup or honey was believed to cool hot liver and stomach. It is also called *ḥamāḥim rayḥān aḥmar*, see *ḥamāḥim* below.

dār fulful (دار فلفل) *Piper longum* (S) long pepper, a close relative of the black pepper (*fulful*) *Piper nigrum*. Al-Anṭākī, *Tadhkira* 164, says that the Egyptians call it *ʿirq al-dhahab* (عرق الذهب) 'gold stem.' Most of the medieval Arab herbalists describe it as the black pepper capsules picked before they ripen. Its properties are like those of black pepper, albeit stronger. Due to its hot and dry properties, it was used in digestives and electuaries (as in *Kanz* recipes 354, 372, 376, 377, and 379) to dissipate winds and arouse the two appetites, food and sex.

dār Ṣīnī (دارصيني) *Cinnamomum cassia* (S) cassia, lit., 'tree of China.' It is related to, and often confused with *qarfa* (Ceylon cinnamon), see entry below. It was available as a dried red-brown bark, which breaks into pieces easily; it was said that it stays good to use for more than fifteen years. Apparently, it was more expensive than *qarfa*, because it was often adulterated with it (al-Anṭākī, *Tadhkira* 163).

Its properties are hot and dry, and in this respect, it is stronger than *qarfa*. However, it is less sweet than the latter, which is why its use is mostly limited to savory food preparations. It appears only once in the *Kanz*, for instance, in chapter 10 on desserts, which contains more than 80 recipes. However, due to its heat, dryness, and aroma, it was extensively used in medicinal preparations, digestives, and aromatic compounds. It was also believed to energize the brain, induce a state of euphoria, and arouse coitus.

ʿūd dār Ṣīnī (عود دارصيني) stick of cassia.

duhn bān (دهن بان) oil of moringa seed, also known as ban oil. It was extracted from the seeds of *shajarat al-bān* (شجرة البان) moringa tree, which is also known as benzoil tree. The scientific name of the tree is *Moringa oleifera* (S). The oil is extracted by first bruising the seeds on a marble slab, and then crushing the kernels and extracting their aromatic and slightly bitter oil. It was used in perfume compounds, and was believed to sweeten the odor of sweat. Medicinally, it was used to induce vomiting and diarrhea.

falanja (فلنجة) small variety of cubeb (*kabāba*) used mainly in perfume and handwashing compounds. With its hot and dry properties, it can dissipate dense winds. It is also effective in relieving head blockages.

fawfal (فوفل) seed of the areca palm (*Areca catechu*), betel nut, also called areca nut. It is an Indian spice, red and brittle, and looks like nutmeg. Indians use it for the aroma, but it dyes the teeth red (Ibn Sīnā, *al-Qānūn* 3430; Ibn al-Bayṭār, *al-Jamiʿ* iii 232). In the *Kanz*, this spice is used to make fish bones fall apart while the fish are being grilled (see p. 77).

fulayyā (فليا) *Mentha pulegium* (S) Egyptian name for *fūtanaj/fūdhanaj barrī* (wild mint), pennyroyal. Its leaves are small and round, like those of thyme. In fact, people of the Levant call it *ṣaʿtar* (thyme). It smells and tastes somewhat like *fūtanaj nahrī* (river mint). See Ibn al-Bayṭār, *al-Jāmiʿ* iii 232, s.v. *fūdanaj*.

It helps purge dense and mucilaginous humors through the lungs and chest. It can dislodge the placenta and abort fetuses (al-Anṭākī, *Tadhkira* 432–3).

fulful (فلفل) *Piper* (S) peppercorns. Black peppercorns are fully grown, and white peppercorns are harvested while they are still unripe. The latter were believed to be less hot than the black ones. It was indispensable in cooking, and it was believed to remove the unpleasant greasy odors of the cooking meat, and facilitate its digestion.

fuwwa (فوة), also called *ʿurūq al-ṣabbāghīn* (عروق الصباغين) *Rubia tinctorum* (S) dyer's madder, common madder, valued for its red roots, from which orange-red dye is extracted. It was sometimes added to red berry wines and ink to color them red (al-Bīrūnī, *Ṣaydana* 295–6). It is described in al-Anṭākī, *Tadhkira* 277, as a sweet-smelling plant with hot and dry properties. It improves the hue of the complexion, and is good for the stomach. In the *Kanz*, it is used in making *ṣaḥna* (condiment of salt-cured anchovies), to give it an attractive reddish hue (recipes 255, 256, DK, appendix 38, p. 205). In recipe 456, the *fuwwa* berries are used in a preparation for nausea.

ḥabb al-qurṭum (حب القرطم) or just *qurṭum* (see entry below) seeds of the safflower plant (*Carthamus tinctorius*). The flower of the plant is called *ʿuṣfur*, see the entry below.

hāl (هال) *Elettaria cardamomum* (S) green or true cardamom is related to larger *qāqulla* (قاقلة) *Amomum subulatum* (S) black cardamom. *Hāl* is described as much superior, nicer, less astringent, and gentler in taste than *qāqulla*. It was commonly used in making women's liquid perfumes. Medicinally, it was considered good for the liver and kidneys, due to its rarefying qualities (*laṭīf*). It is good for headaches caused by dense winds, and it was highly recommended as a digestive (Ibn al-Bayṭār, *al-Jāmiʿ* iv 241; Ibn Sīnā, *al-Qānūn* 259). In *Kanz* recipes, it is almost exclusively used in digestive drinks, handwashing preparations, soaps, and incense.

ḥamāḥim rayḥān (حماحم ريحان) *rayḥān al-ḥamāḥim* (ريحان الحماحم), also called *ḥabaq ḥamāḥimī* (حبق حماحمي) *Ocimum basilicum* (S), sweet basil. Its other names include wide-leaf *ḥabaq Kirmānī* (حبق كرماني), and *ḥabaq Nabaṭī* (حبق نبطي) in the Levant. It is also called *ḥabaq al-zawānī* (حبق الزواني) 'harlots' basil,' because they used it a lot (al-Ishbīlī, *ʿUmdat al-ṭabīb* i 162).

It is a cultivated variety of basil, described as having brittle square-shaped stems, white blossoms, with wide leaves like those of common basil. With its hot and dry properties, it opens blockages when one smells it and eats it, and improves the mood. It is good for curing ailments related to excess in phlegm and humidities. It sweetens the breath and induces aromatic belching. It was also used in cooking (Ibn al-Bayṭār, *al-Jāmiʿ* ii 292; al-Malik al-Muẓaffar, *al-Muʿtamad* 421–2).[5]

We also read in al-Malik al-Muẓaffar, *al-Muʿtamad* 141, and al-Hurawī, *Baḥr al-jawāhir* 121, that *ḥamāḥim* may also be identified as *bustān abrūz* (بستان أبروز), the amaranth (*Amaranthus*), with its terminal red spikes of flowers.[6] This might well be a reference to another *ḥamāḥim*, which is mentioned as *ḥamāḥim rayḥān aḥmar* (حماحم ريحان احمر) red *ḥamāḥim* (recipe 462) in the *Kanz*.[7] It is said that this variety has cold and dry properties, and is beneficial in cooling the stomach and liver when it is taken in the form of a drink made with syrup from its juice reduced with sugar syrup or honey. In fact, the *Kanz* recipe mentioned above does indeed describe a similar preparation to treat nausea. See *bustān abrawīz* above.

ḥawāʾij al-baql (حوائج البقل), also called *ḥawāʾij al-māʾida* (حوائج المائدة), and *buqūl al-māʾida* (بقول المائدة) 'table herbs.' They are fresh herbs, which can be eaten raw with the foods served at the table; these herbs include mint, basil, parsley, leaf leeks, and tarragon (al-Maqrīzī, *Khiṭaṭ* ii 583). In *Kanz* recipes, references to *ḥawāʾij al-baql* may generally be taken to designate the fresh herbs that cooks usually use in preparing a given dish; or, whatever herbs the recipe has already mentioned, to avoid repetition.

---

5 Al-Anṭākī, *Tadhkira* 189, briefly mentions that *ḥamāḥim* is *ḥabaq al-Sūdān* (حبق السودان), which may mean that it is what was grown in the Sudan.

6 Ibn Jazla, *Minhāj al-bayān* 77v identifies it first as the cold and dry *bustān abrūz*, and then associates it with a hot *rayḥān* variety.

7 In al-Suyūṭī, *Ḥusn al-muḥāḍara* 358, verses on *ḥamāḥim* compare the red terminal spikes of the flowers to the combs of fighting cocks. In addition, in al-Tamīmī, *Ṭīb al-ʿarūs* 100, the description of it as *ruʾūs ḥamāḥim ḍakhma* (رؤوس حماحم ضخمة) 'large heads of *ḥamāḥim*,' and the instruction to pick them before they start seeding, also point to amaranth.

ḥinnāʾ (حنّاء) *Lawsonia inermis* (S) henna plant with leaves, like those of the olive tree, and white blossoms, called *fāghiya* (فاغية). Henna designates the leaves, which are used as a dye for the hair, skin, and nails. It is called *sayyid al-khiḍāb* (سيد الخضاب) 'master of all hair dyes.'

Henna was believed to sweeten the body odor and invigorate coitus. The blossoms are put between woolen clothes to drive away insects. Pounded henna mixed with water is used in *Kanz* recipe 653, to soak *ẓufr*, which are the horny operculums from sea snails (onycha).

ḥiṣrim (حصرم) sour unripe grapes.

ḥiṣrim mujaffaf (حصرم مجفف) dried sour unripe grapes, used in *Kanz* recipe 527 to curdle milk into yogurt.

māʾ ḥiṣrim (ماء حصرم) sour juice of unripe grapes, used as a souring agent in savory dishes. When fresh, their juice was extracted by boiling the grapes and straining them. However, when not in season, the preserved juice was used. See *Kanz* recipes 152–4, for recipes on how to preserve it.

FIGURE 65
Ḥulba (*fenugreek*), *Elizabeth Blackwell,* A Curious Herbal, *1738, plate 384 (From the New York Public Library: http://digitalcollections.nypl.org/items/510d47dd-ccf7-a3d9-e040-e00a18064a99).*

ḥulba (خلبة) *Trigonella foenum-graecum* (S) fenugreek, which commonly designates the seeds. The leaves of the plant are usually referred to as *baql al-ḥulba* (بقل الحلبة), both share the same properties and uses. Due to its hot and dry properties, it causes nausea and headaches when consumed in excess. The plant is especially good for coughs and asthma. It stimulates the appetite and coitus. However, it changes the odor of the breath, perspiration, and urine (al-Malik al-Muẓaffar, *al-Muʿtamad* 133). In *Kanz* recipe 596 for a cucumber yogurt condiment, the seeds are soaked in water for two days to eliminate their bitterness.

idhkhir (إذخر) *Cymbopogon* (S) citronella, sweet-smelling reed-like rush with small, thin stems and aromatic flowers which look like fluffed cotton. Both stems and flowers are used in handwashing compounds and medicinal preparations. With their hot astringent properties, they help stop bleeding. An overdose may induce sleep. The fine stems were used as toothpicks, called *khilāl maʾmūnī* (safe toothpicks). The stems were also used in making brooms and baskets (Ibn al-Bayṭār, *al-Jāmiʿ* i 21; al-Bīrūnī, *Ṣaydana* 27–8; Ibn Jazla, *Minhāj al-bayān*, fol. 20r).

idhkhir Makkī (إذخر مكي) *Cymbopogon schoenanthus* (S), Meccan citronella, also known as camel's hay or straw, and sweet-smelling rush.

ʿirq al-kāfūr (عرق الكافور) also called *kāfūr al-kaʿk* (كافور الكعك), *ʿirq al-ṭīb* (عرق الطيب), and *zurunbād* (زُرنباد). It is *Zingiber zerumbet* (S) a variety of ginger, called bitter ginger, shampoo ginger, and pinecone ginger. It resembles ginger in taste and color. It is exported as dried slices from its country of origin, China.

The truly bitter ones were deemed best for medicinal purposes, whereas the relatively sweeter ones were weaker in their medicinal properties. It is to be assumed that the latter variety was used in cookies and other food preparations, and handwashing compounds (see *Kanz* recipes 6, 107, 108, 255, 644, and 670).

It was believed to stimulate the appetite, relieve flatulence, aid digestion, and check vomiting and diarrhea. It also helps with weight gain. It can rid the breath of the unpleasant odors of garlic, onion, and wine (Ibn Sīnā, *al-Qānūn* 262–3; al-Anṭākī, *Tadhkira* 194).

isfīdāj (إسفيداج) ***isbīdāj*** (إسبيداج) ceruse, used for its white lead pigments in *Kanz* recipe 642, and for its gluing property in recipe 708.

jaṣṣ (جَصّ) gypsum, used as a sealant. For instance, citron coated with it stays fresh for a long time (*Kanz* recipe 750). Fresh grapes stored in jars and sealed with it stay good for months (*Kanz* recipe 719).

jawz ṭīb (جوز طيب) also called *jawz bawwa* (جوز بوة) *Myristica fragrans* (S) nutmeg, brought from India. Good nutmeg is described as heavy and brownish-reddish. It was believed to freshen the odor of mouth and stomach; and to be good for cold-related ailments. It can prevent nausea and vomiting because it strengthens the upper gate of the stomach. *Basbāsa* (mace) can replace it (al-Anṭākī, *Tadhkira* 120–1).

jīr (جير) slaked lime (calcium hydroxide), also called *kils* (كلس), see entry below.

jullanār (جلّنار) blossoms of the wild pomegranate tree, which is called *al-maẓẓ* (المظ). It is considered a male tree (*dhakar al-rummān*) because its blossoms do not develop into pomegranates. It grows in the mountains, and is said to blossom a large number of red flowers, containing honey-like nectar, which people like to suck and bees feed on. With its cold and dry properties, as well as astringency, it can decrease diarrhea, reduce bleeding, and firm up the gums and teeth.

jullanār Shāmī (جُلّنار شامي) Levantine wild-pomegranate blossoms.

kabāba (كبابة) *Piper cubeba* (S) cubeb, dark brown berries of the pepper family. It is aromatic and slightly bitter, close in flavor to allspice. It was said to be good for gum diseases.

The large variety of this spice is called *ḥabb al-ʿarūs* (حب العروس) 'the bride's seeds.' According to Ibn Sīnā, *al-Qānūn* 291, the saliva of the groom who has chewed cubeb, will pleasure his bride while having sex.

kāfūr (كافور) camphor, white and aromatic crystalline resinous sap of the camphor tree (*Cinnamomum camphora*), native to India and China. White camphor is extracted directly from the tree by slitting it and collecting the seeping resin. This is called *kāfūr makhlūq* (naturally extracted). Camphor may also be extracted from the cut wood by boiling it so that it releases the remaining resin. This is called *kāfūr maʿmūl* (made).

Camphor is cold and dry in properties, and hence it was thought to be beneficial in treating heat-related ailments. In the summertime, it was used in flavoring dishes, instead of the hot ambergris. It induces euphoria, but has a negative effect on libido.

kāfūr rayyāḥī (كافور ريّاحي), also occurs as *kāfūr Rabāḥī* (كافور رباحي), excellent strongly-scented camphor, said to have been named after an Indian king by the name of Rabāḥ. The alternative name *rayyāḥī* describes its diffused aroma.

māʾ al-kāfūr (ماء الكافور) distilled camphor water.

kammūn (كمون) *Cuminum cyminum* (S) cumin seeds, of which many varieties are known. The most dominant is the so-called white cumin, which is the tan-colored common cumin. When cumin occurs in recipes unspecified, it is more likely to be this common type. It is known by the name *kammūn Nabaṭī* (Nabatean cumin). With its hot and dry properties, it can dissipate gastric winds, aid digestion, and warm the body.

kammūn aswad (كمون اسود) black cumin, which is a wild variety, was also identified by the name *kammūn Ḥabashī* (Abyssinian cumin).

kammūn Kirmānī (كمون كرماني) fine-tasting darkish cumin, named after the Persian city Kirman. It has the strongest properties of all the other varieties. It was said to be black. However, this could be a reference to its darkish hue, compared with the other tan and yellow varieties.

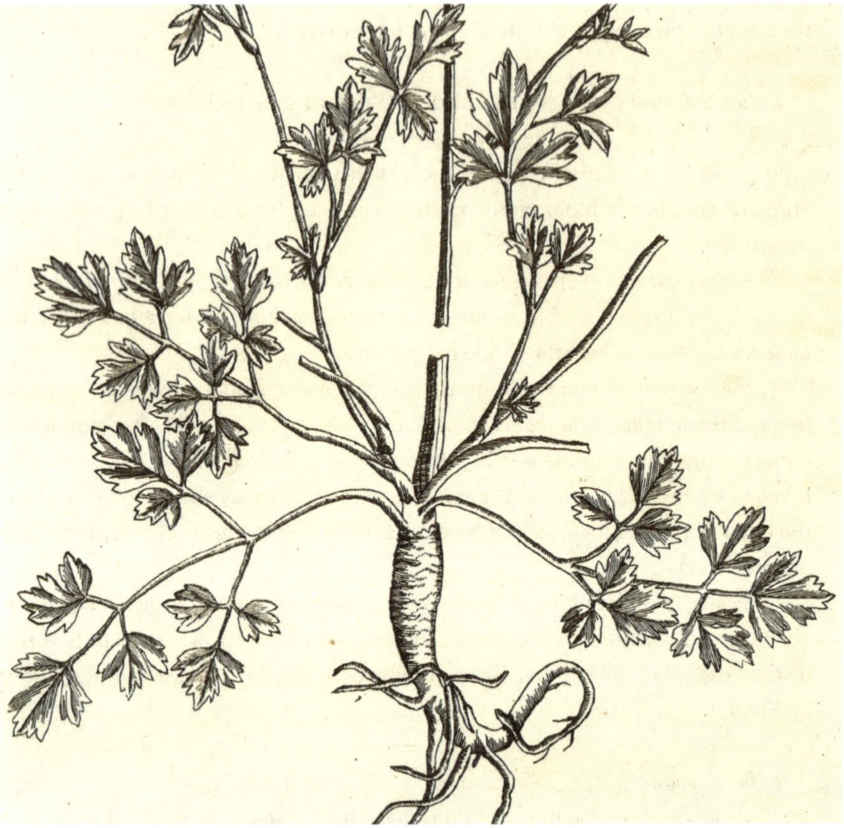

FIGURE 66 Karafs (*common parsley*), *Elizabeth Blackwell*, A Curious Herbal, *1738, plate 172 (From the New York Public Library: http://digitalcollections.nypl .org/items/510d47dd-c746-a3d9-e040-e00a18064a99).*

karafs (كرفس) In the medieval Arabo-Islamic world, it designated both common parsley (*Petroselinum sativum*) and stalk celery (*Apium graveolens* var. *dulce*).

In *Kanz* recipes, *karafs* (common parsley) was used in making *fuqqāʿ* (beer) and digestive drinks, as well as cooked dishes, mostly those with fish, pickles (*mukhallalāt*), table sauces and condiments of *ṣibāgh* and *ṣulṣ*, and vinegar-soured poultry stews (*maṣūṣ*). *Baqdūnis* (Macedonian parsley) was used in a similar manner, albeit more ubiquitously (see entry above).

In *Kanz* recipes 363 and 589, celery stalks (*uṣūl al-karafs*) are pickled and their juice is extracted to make a digestive drink.

karafs Nabaṭī (كرفس نبطي) 'celery indigenous to Iraq,' also called *karafs 'aẓīm* (كرفس عظيم) 'huge celery,' *karafs Mashriqī* (كرفس مشرقي) 'eastern celery,' and *karafs shatawī* (كرفس شتوي) 'winter celery.' It is angelica (*Angelica archangelica*), which, as stated by Ibn Waḥshiyya, *al-Filāḥa* ii 781, is the strongest of all celery varieties, with the sturdiest stalks and most delicious taste.

Al-Isrā'īlī, *Aghdhiya* iii 34–5, describes it as being much larger than the cultivated variety of celery. The stalk is white and tubular, and looks as if it is striped. The larger leaves are tinged with red, and have a sharp taste and a pleasant aroma. The whole plant—its tender root, stalks, and leaves—is aromatic, and it is used in cooking as well as eaten raw. It grows in shaded areas, along streams. In the kitchen, it has the same uses as the cultivated varieties. It is cooked with fish and vinegar or pickled in brine. In the *Kanz*, it occurs only once in recipe 400, for making *fuqqā'* (beer).

All the varieties of *karafs* share the same properties. Of its medicinal benefits, it is used as a diuretic, and it can control diarrhea and relieve flatulence. *Karafs* is recommended as a powerful aphrodisiac for both men and women. It also works as a breath freshener (Ibn al-Bayṭār, *al-Jāmi'* iv 310–4; al-Bīrūnī, *Ṣaydana* 315–6).

karāwiya (كراوية) *Carum carvi* (S) caraway. The entire plant is aromatic, but the seeds are the most commonly used part. Its properties are hot and dry, and it is useful in relieving bloating and dissipating gastric winds. It is especially good with beans. It stimulates the appetite, aids digestion, and induces burping.

karāwiya Andalusiyya (كراوية اندلسية) Andalusian caraway, which is also known as *qardamānā* (قردمانا), and *karāwiya jabaliyya* (كراويا جبلية) 'mountain caraway.' It grows abundantly in the mountains near Granada. Its properties are stronger than those of common caraway.

karāwiya Maghribiyya (كراوية مغربية) Moroccan caraway, which must be the same variety as that of the Andalusian (see above).

kathīrā' (كثيراء) *Astragalus gummifer* (S) gum of tragacanth tree, of which the white variety is edible. Its properties are moderate; they were deemed good for coughs and chest ailments. Eating white tragacanth mixed with equal amounts of wheat starch and sugar is useful for weight gain (see for instance, *Kanz* recipe 288). It was believed to boost libido in both sexes (al-Anṭākī, *Tadhkira* 295). It is viscous, odorless, and tasteless; and when dissolved in water, it can treat split hairs and straighten it. Gum arabic may be a substitute for it.

khall (خلّ) vinegar, a liquid spice, made from different fruits, such as dates, grapes, figs, and apples. It is sometimes used with bread as a dip by itself. With its cold and dry properties, it can cool the body and dry it. It also helps hot-tempered people lose weight. When cold-tempered people take it, they are advised to heat its elemental properties by using it with hot spices and vegetables, like caraway and onion.

khall ṭayyib (خل طيب) fine-tasting vinegar.
khall abyaḍ (خل ابيض) white vinegar.
khall ʿinab (خل عنب) grape vinegar.
khall ushturghāz (خل اشترغاز) vinegar flavored with *ushturghāz* (alhagi), see entry below.
khall tamr (خل تمر) date vinegar.
khall ḥādhiq (خل حاذق) very sour vinegar.
khall khamr (خل خمر) wine vinegar.
khall khamr ʿatīq (خل خمر عتيق) aged wine vinegar.
khall khamr ṭayyib (خل خمر طيب) fine-tasting wine vinegar.
khall mustaqṭar (خل مستقطر) distilled vinegar.
khall rayḥānī (خل ريحاني) vinegar made from *rayḥānī* wine, named for its pleasant aroma.
khall thaqīf (خل ثقيف) very sour vinegar.

khamīrat al-ʿaṭṭār (خميرة العطار) *Colchicum montanum* (S) mountain meadow saffron. It is more commonly known in Arabic sources as *sūranjān* (سورنجان).[8] The sliced and dried white corms of this wild plant were deemed edible; the black and red ones were said to be poisonous. Al-Anṭākī, *Tadhkira* 223, says that young men in the mountainous Levantine regions pick it, and eat it baked. They call it *abzāz* (ابزاز).[9] Its properties are hot and dry, and medicinally it was deemed to be effective in relieving rheumatic pain and gout. It was also extolled for enhancing sex, especially when it is consumed with ginger and black pepper.

khamīrat al-ward (خميرة الورد) liquid of rose petals steeped in water, usually destined for distillation. See Dozy, *Takmilat al-maʿājim* 413, where *khamīr* was said to be a term used by druggists and perfumers to designate any ingredients steeped in liquid for a while to release their essence, and then distilled. See also *Kanz* recipes on distilled liquids in chapter 22. The distilled rosewater resulting from distilling *khamīrat al-ward* is purer.

8 To my knowledge, the *Kanz* is the only medieval source in which the plant is called *khamīrat al-ʿaṭṭār*. In Ghālib, *al-Mawsūʿa*, s.v. سورنجان الجبل, the corm of this plant is clearly identified as *khamīrat al-ʿaṭṭār* and *abzāz*. Associating this name with *sūranjān* can also be found in today's Arabic sources, in which the plant's corm is touted as an effective enhancement to sex. See al-Tallaʿfarī, *Mawsūʿat al-ṭibb al-badīl* 724; and Rizq and ʿAlāma, *Asrār al-takhalluṣ min al-ʿajaz al-jinsī* 80.

9 Colloquial for nipples and udders. The Egyptian Ibn Sūdūn, *Nuzhat al-nufūs* 146, refers to the cow's udder as *bizbiz* (بزبز).

khardal (خردل) *Brassica* (S) mustard seeds, of which there are several varieties. Good seeds are described as light in color, large and plump, and when pounded, their insides look yellow, and feel somewhat moist.

With its hot and dry properties, mustard was said to be good for all cold-related maladies. It is also offered with dense foods, to aid in digestion. It is usually consumed as a condiment, called *khardal maʿmūl* 'prepared mustard,' see *Kanz* recipes, chapter 15. Al-Anṭākī observes that Egyptians particularly like to eat it with grilled meat during ʿĪd al-Aḍḥā.[10] It was also used as an aphrodisiac (al-Malik al-Muẓaffar, *al-Muʿtamad* 157–8; al-Anṭākī, *Tadhkira* 150–1; Ibn al-Bayṭār, *al-Jāmiʿ* ii 318–9).

khardal abyaḍ (خردل ابيض) *Brassica alba* (S) white mustard seeds, also known as *isfind* (إسفند). The seeds are not exactly white, but can be light brown, yellow, or beige. The yellow ones are the best; they are big, and feel heavy. Their taste is milder than those of the black variety.

khardal ʿAkkāwī (خردل عكاوي) mustard seeds of Acre. These must be a variety of black mustard seeds (*Brassica nigra*), whose hard outer skins are usually discarded, as is done in *Kanz* recipe 494.

khardal Shāmī (خردل شامي) lit., 'Levantine mustard seeds,' which must be the white variety (*Brassica alba*), see above.

khashkhāsh (خشخاش) poppy seeds obtained from the opium plant (*Papaver somniferum*), known in Egypt as *abū l-nawm* (أبو النوم) 'sleep-inducer.' The best is the white variety (*khashkhāsh abyaḍ*), whereas the black has stronger properties. It is often used to cure chest ailments. Having it twice a day, for example, kneaded with bread, is useful for weight gain (al-Anṭākī, *Tadhkira* 158).

khashkhāsh abyaḍ (خشخاش ابيض) white poppy seeds, see above.

khilāf (خلاف), also known as *ṣafṣāf Miṣrī* (صفصاف مصري) *Salix aegyptiaca* (S). It is an Egyptian species of the willow tree (*Salix*). The catkins (*sanābil*) of the tree were said to be very fragrant, soft, smooth, and downy. The name of the tree, which means 'deviating from the norm,' stems from the fact that despite its bitterness (usually a hot property), it is cold.

The blossoms themselves benefit people with excessively hot humoral properties, by inhaling them, they can open blockages and relieve severe headaches. This must be an effect of the aspirin they contain. Their oil, *duhn al-khilāf*, obtained by steeping the fresh catkins in sesame oil, is aromatic. The leaves and water distilled from the bark of the tree, called *māʾ khilāf* have the same effect (al-Malik al-Muẓaffar, *al-Muʿtamad* 172–3; al-Bīrūnī, *Ṣaydana* 183–4).

---

10 Many Muslims sacrifice sheep and cows and distribute the meat to the needy to celebrate the end of the hajj to Mecca.

In *Kanz* recipes, the distilled water of the bark is used in digestive drinks. Its leafy stems are whipped in preparations to treat nausea, which also use its distilled water. The twigs are used as toothpicks, which can benefit the gums. It is also used in potpourris, incense tablets, and restorative body powders.

ʿīdān khilāf (عيدان خلاف) twigs of the willow tree.
māʾ khilāf (ماء خلاف) distilled water of willow bark.

khīrī (خيري) *Cheiranthus cheiri* (S) gillyflower. In Egypt and the Levant, it is called *manthūr* (منثور), which means 'scattered,' because of the custom of strewing them in places where social gatherings take place. Al-Nābulusī, *ʿAlam al-malāḥa* 207, mentions that it comes in eight varieties and colors, such as white, pink, red, dark red, blue, and yellow. The uncultivated variety, *khīrī l-barr* (خيري البر), is lavender (*khuzāmā*). The yellow variety has the strongest properties. Due to its heat and dryness, it is used medicinally to promote menstruation, kill fetuses, and purge phlegm from those with head colds.

khubbāza (خبّازة) *Hibiscus sabdariffa* (S) hibiscus flowers, carcade, known as roselle. Today in Egypt, it is more commonly known as *karkadeh* (كركديه). In *Kanz* recipe 547, it is used to color pickled turnips red.

khūlanjān (خولنجان) *Alpinia galangala* (S) galangal, a rhizome, which belongs to the ginger family. It is dried as a spice and used in cooking and in medicinal preparations. It is especially recommended as a digestive and dispeller of gases, breath-sweetener, and aphrodisiac.

kils (كلس), also called *jīr* (جير), may designate quicklime (calcium oxide) and slaked lime (calcium hydroxide). Sometimes, the adjectives *muṭfaʾ* (مطفأ) 'slaked' and *ghayr muṭfaʾ* (غير مطفأ) 'unslaked' are added. *Kils* is slaked (*yuṭfaʾ*) by adding water to it.

In *Kanz* recipes, it is used in preserving green olives in brine (recipes 557, 559, 560), as it helps leach out their bitterness, prevent their discoloration, and keep them firm. Lime is also used in cleaning tripe.

kundus (كندس) also called *ʿāqir qarḥā* (عاقر قرحا) *Anacyclus pyrethrum* (S) pellitory, Spanish chamomile. Its properties are hot and dry, and it is capable of purging and cleansing the digestive system, and breaking down foods to facilitate the digestion (al-Anṭākī, *Tadhkira* 305).

kurkum (كركم) *Curcuma longa* (S) turmeric, a rhizome of the ginger family. Most of the medieval sources identify it as saffron, or they are not sure what it is.

Al-Malik al-Muẓaffar, *al-Muʿtamad* 486–7, mentions that it is a root imported from India, and that it is called *hurd* (هرد) in Persian. He says that people in Basra (southern Iraq) started calling *hurd kurkum* because they likened it to *zaʿfarān* (saffron) due to its yellow dye, and *kurkum* is *zaʿfarān*.[11]

11 See also Ibn al-Bayṭār, *al-Jāmiʿ* ii 367, iv 325.

To my knowledge, of all the extant recipes in medieval cookbooks, *Kanz* recipe 148 is the only one that mentions turmeric. The recipe gives instructions on how to prepare fried sparrows as it is done in Baghdad and Mosul. This proves that turmeric was indeed used in cooking at the time, when the more expensive and delicate saffron would have been wasted had it been used. In the recipe, the cleaned sparrows are first colored with turmeric, and then flattened with weights and fried. From what we know of modern-day cooking, saffron would lose its delicate flavor with intense frying, whereas frying brings out the aroma of turmeric and enhances the flavor of the cooked meat.

Apart from its culinary uses, turmeric was used in ointments to cure mange (*jarab*) and dry wounds, sharpen eyesight, and treat cataract (*bayāḍ al-ʿayn*).

kurrāth (كراث) leeks, of which there are two main varieties:

kurrāth Shāmī (كراث شامي) *Allium porrum* (S) Levantine leeks, a variety cultivated for its bulb. It is also called *kurrāth abyaḍ* (كراث ابيض) white leeks, descriptive of the onion-like bulbous head, which is the only part consumed. It is always served cooked.

kurrāth Nabaṭī (كراث نبطي) 'Nabatean leeks' (cultivated in Iraq), *Allium ampeloprasum* var. *persicum* (S) leaf leeks, also called salad leeks, and Persian leeks. It does not produce bulbous heads; only leaves, which are mostly consumed raw. *Qirṭ* (قرط) is another name for it.[12] It is also known as *kurrāth al-māʾida* (كراث المائدة) 'table leeks,' which al-Anṭākī, *Tadhkira* 299, says is its name in Egypt; he adds that it is the most ubiquitous type of leeks in the region. It is called *kurrāth al-baql* (كراث البقل) 'herb leeks,' because the leaves are eaten raw as a fresh herb.[13]

FIGURE 67 Kurrāth Nabaṭī (*leaf leeks*), *photo by Kate Robin, Rotterdam.*

---

12 As explained in one of the recipes in *Waṣf* 18.

13 Unlike tubular chive leaves, *kurrāth* leaves are flat.

All varieties of leeks have hot and dry properties, but leaf leeks are the hottest and most pungent of all. The plant, and especially its seeds, was believed to be an aphrodisiac. Due to its strong properties, it was blamed for causing dimness of the eyesight and heavy-headedness.

kūz ṭalʿ (كوز طلع) inflorescence spathe of the date palm. In *Kanz* recipe 87, a piece of it is added to a meat stew cooked with yogurt, to thicken it. This is done when the meat is cooked and the broth has not thickened yet. Substitutes given are rice flour and wheat starch.

kuzbara (كزبرة), ***kusbara*** (كسبرة), ***kusfara*** (كسفرة) *Coriandrum sativum* (S) coriander seeds and fresh cilantro leaves:

kuzbara raṭba (كزبرة رطبة) ***kuzbara khaḍrāʾ*** (كزبرة خضراء) fresh cilantro leaves.
kuzbara yābisa (كزبرة يابسة) coriander seeds.

The seeds and the leaves have hot and moist properties. The seeds were believed to strengthen the heart and delight the soul. However, they can dry up semen and prevent erection if the liquid in which they have been steeped is taken sweetened with sugar. The fresh leaves of cilantro were said to improve digestion and induce sleep. It was believed that chewing the seeds or the fresh leaves would remove the unpleasant breath odors of onion and garlic (al-Malik al-Muẓaffar, *al-Muʿtamad* 488–9; al-Anṭākī, *Tadhkira* 300–1).

kuzbara Shāmīyya (كزبرة شامية) Levantine coriander, which al-Anṭākī, *Tadhkira* 300, says is no different from the Egyptian variety.

FIGURE 68
Kuzbara raṭba (*fresh cilantro leaves*), *Elizabeth Blackwell,* A Curious Herbal, *1738, plate 176 (From the New York Public Library: http://digitalcollections.nypl.org/items/510d47dd-c74d-a3d9-e040-e00a18064a99).*

lādhan (لاذن) ladanum, a fragrant sticky resin which covers leaves of shrubs of *qasūs* (قسوس) *Cistus ladanifer creticus*, a species of rockrose. The resin is collected directly from the shrub by gatherers using pieces of wool or other things to stick to them and then extracting it. Alternatively, it is combed from the hair and wool of goats and sheep, which have been grazing on the shrubs. The first method yields pure, clean, excellent ladanum, called *lādhan ʿanbarī*. In *Kanz*, chapter 20, ladanum is used in perfumed oils, and incense compounds.

lādhan ʿanbarī (لاذن عنبري) best ladanum resin, very aromatic, collected directly from the shrub, see above.

laymūn mumallaḥ (ليمون مملح) lemon preserved in salt, see chapter 18 for recipes. It was often chopped and used to season and garnish cold dishes, appetizers, and sauces; see, for instance, *Kanz*, chapter 19, and recipes 495, and 601.

laynūfar (لينوفر), **naylūfar** (نيلوفر), **nūfar** (نوفر) *Nymphaea caerulea* (S) blue Egyptian lotus, an aquatic plant. Its flowers are used in making distilled water, called *māʾ al-laynūfar* (ماء اللينوفر). It was used in medicinal preparations to relieve nausea and headaches, quench the thirst, and soften the bowels. It is also said to help people sleep (al-Anṭākī, *Tadhkira* 354).

FIGURE 69
Lisān al-thawr (*borage*), *Elizabeth Blackwell,* A Curious Herbal, *1738, plate 36 (From the New York Public Library: http://digitalcollections.nypl.org/items/510d47dd-c28e-a3d9-e040-e00a18064a99).*

lisān al-thawr (لسان الثور) *Anchusa azurea* (S) borage, whose leaves look like cows' tongues, and hence the name. It is a species of *marū* (see entry below). It is also called *marū abyaḍ* (مرو ابيض) after its white seeds.

It is not particularly aromatic. Its properties are moderate, and it was believed to have a euphoric effect when mixed and cooked with drinks (al-Malik al-Muẓaffar, *al-Muʿtamad* 525; Ibn Jazla, *Minhāj al-bayān*, fol. 195v).

lisān al-thawr al-Shāmī (لسان الثور الشامي) Levantine borage, believed to be the best, distinguished by its thick leaves, with spots on top.

māʾ lisān al-thawr (ماء لسان الثور) distilled borage water.

lisān al-ʿuṣfūr (لسان العصفور) fruit of a variety of *dardār* tree, which could be *dardār Sūrī*, also called *murrān Sūrī* (*Fraxinus syriaca*) Syrian ash tree. The leaves of the tree resemble those of the almond tree, albeit smaller. The trunk and the branches look reddish. The fruit (*thamar*) is elongated, with pointed ends. It looks like a sparrow's tongue, with a skin resembling that of the almond kernel. The fruits grow in loose bunches.

Its properties are hot and moist, it is somewhat bitter and astringent, and has a pleasant aroma. It was valued for its medicinal and restorative properties, as it was believed to be good for the stomach and palpitations. More importantly, it was highly regarded as an aphrodisiac (al-Malik al-Muẓaffar, *al-Muʿtamad* 526; al-Ishbīlī, *ʿUmdat al-ṭabīb* i 351).

lukk yebis (لك يَبِس) dry gum lac, sweet-smelling deep red secretion of lac insects, especially the species *Kerria lacca*. In medieval Arabic books on botany, it is assumed to be the secretion of a tree like that of myrrh.

The gum is valuable primarily as a dye; however, it also has some medicinal benefits. Its hot and dry properties open blockages in the liver and stomach. It fortifies the organs, and helps fat people lose weight.

māʾ al-kāfūr (ماء الكافور) distilled liquid of camphor, an oily liquid exuded from the trunk of the camphor tree, or obtained by boiling and straining camphor tree bark with the camphor stuck to it. See *kāfūr* above.

māʾ al-khilāf (ماء الخلاف) distilled water of the bark of the *khilāf* tree (*Salix aegyptiaca*), see *khilāf* above.

māʾ al-laymūn (ماء ليمون) lemon juice, see *laymūn* in glossary 7 above.

māʾ lisān al-thawr (ماء لسان الثور) distilled borage water, see *lisān al-thawr* above.

māʾ al-nūfar (ماء النوفر) distilled water of blue Egyptian lotus, see *laynūfar* above.

māʾ ward (ماء ورد) rosewater, mostly used in distilled form in cooking, medicinal, and aromatic preparations. It is valued for its moderately cold, dry, and astringent properties, which strengthen the brain, liver, and stomach, and ease hangover symptoms. See also *ward*, below.

mā' ward baladī (ماء ورد بلدي) distilled water of roses grown domestically in Egypt, also called *ward Dimashqī* and *ward Shāmī*. See *mā' ward Shāmī* below.

mā' ward mumassak (ماء ورد ممسك) rosewater flavored with musk.

mā' ward Nuṣaybīnī (ماء ورد نصيبيني) rosewater of Nusaybin roses, a city in upper Mesopotamia, now in Turkish province of Mardin. The region was renowned for its orchards and gardens. Roses named after it are typically pinkish in hue.

mā' ward Shāmī (ماء ورد شامي) distilled water of the Levantine rose, more commonly known in English as damask rose (*Rosa damascene*), renowned for its fine fragrance. It is medium pink and relatively small. The roses grow in groups.

mā' ward mukarrar (ماء ورد مكرر) rosewater was sometimes obtained by soaking the rose petals in boiling water, and then straining out the petals. The resulting liquid was used to steep a new batch of rose petals and then straining it again. The procedure is repeated several times. This results in a refined liquid of roses, called *mā' ward mukarrar*, used in making restorative and digestive drinks, see, for instance, *Kanz* recipe 368. It was believed that this way of preparing liquid of roses (*takrīr*) improves its properties.

mā' ward muṣa''ad (ماء ورد مصعّد) rosewater obtained by *taṣ'īd* (تصعيد) distillation, see entry in glossary 9.2 below. Distillation is also called *taqṭīr* (تقطير), see, for instance, *Kanz* recipe 695. This is the most commonly used method to obtain distilled rosewater, it is usually just referred to as *mā' ward*. Distilled rosewater is used extensively in cooking and in medicinal preparations.

maghra (مغرة) ochre, a natural earth pigment, described as clay which has been thoroughly cooked by the sun. This prolonged exposure to the sun was believed to increase the clay's viscidity and make it look reddish. It was brought from the Byzantine regions, and used as dye (see *Kanz* recipe 724). The best was said to be red, dense, and free of sand.

With its cold and dry properties, it was believed to be beneficial in stopping bleeding and diarrhea, and killing intestinal worms. To help them gain weight, women of the Levant used to take it with water and sugar (al-Anṭākī, *Tadhkira* 342).

maḥlab (محلب) aromatic kernels of the small stones of a variety of cherry tree (*Prunus mahaleb*). White *maḥlab* kernels were deemed the best, and used in the *Kanz* in making aromatic soap (*ṣābūn*) and handwashing preparations (*ushnān*), as they were believed to remove undesirable body odors. Its properties are hot and dry. They were often used in breads to facilitate digestion. They can purify the stomach and dissipate dense winds (al-Anṭākī, *Tadhkira* 322–3).

maqdūnis (مقدونس) parsley, a variety of *karafs*. See *baqdūnis* above.

marsīn (مرسين) Egyptian name for myrtle, also called *ās* (آس) and *rayḥān* (ريحان) *Myrtus communis* (S). It is a sweet-smelling evergreen shrub, highly valued for its aroma and medicinal benefits. The leaves—fresh and dried, the bitterish-sweet blackberries—called *ḥabb ās* (حب آس), and the distilled water of the leaves are all used internally and externally.

Marsīn strengthens the organs, checks diarrhea, and controls hair loss. It was also believed to induce feelings of joy when used in perfumed oils, powders, and incense. It was believed that a concoction made with the syrup of its berries (*rubb al-ās*) would delay intoxication. Branches of the plant's leaves are customarily spread around sitting areas as an air freshener (Ibn al-Bayṭār, *al-Jāmiʿ* i 37–40, s.v. *ās*; al-Anṭākī, *Tadhkira* 48).

marū (مرو) *Origanum maru* (S) wild marjoram, of which there are seven species. The best is *marūmāḥūz* (مروماحوز) or *marmāḥūz* (مرماحوز), it is the most aromatic of them all. See also *lisān al-thawr* (entry above), which is another species of *marū*.

Generally, the taste of *marū* is described as not quite pleasant, and somewhat bitter. However, it is valued for its properties, which ease flatulence. It is also said to strengthen the stomach and liver, and eliminate any symptoms of weakness caused by overeating and drinking a lot of cold water (al-Malik al-Muẓaffar, *al-Muʿtamad* 558–9).

marzanjūsh (مرزنجوش) *Origanum majorana* (S), also called *mardaqūsh* (مردقوش), and *ādhān al-fār* (آذان الفار) 'mouse ears.' It is marjoram, described as very sweet smelling, with fuzzy leaves. Its properties are hot and so it was recommended for treating colds and nasal congestion, and opening blockages. Its strong properties were said to speed up intoxication if it is inhaled while imbibing wine (al-Malik al-Muẓaffar, *al-Muʿtamad* 557).

maṣṭakāʾ (مصطكاء), *maṣṭakā* (مصطكا), *mistika* (مستكة), also known as *ʿilk Rūmī* (علك الروم) 'Byzantine gum.' It is mastic gum, resin of the mastic tree (*Pistacia lentiscus*), valued for its refreshing aroma and medicinal benefits. The best was said to be white, heavy, dry, and brittle.

Mastic has complex properties, which are at once astringent, hot, laxative, and desiccative. It is chewed as gum and taken internally to freshen the breath, induce aromatic belching, heat the stomach, and improve digestion.

In *Kanz* recipes, it is used more in savory meat dishes than in sweet ones, as it was believed to remove the unpleasant smell of meat (*zafar*) while cooking, and aid the digestion. Egyptian cooking today is still distinguished for the way mastic is used with savory dishes, such as soups and stews, unlike the rest of the Arab regions, where it is reserved for seasoning sweets.

mayʿa (ميعة), also called *mayʿat lubnā* (ميعة لبنى) sweet-smelling benzoin resin of a tree called *lubnā* (لبنى) and *iṣṭarak* (إصطرك) *Styrax* (S) storax tree, also known as benzoin tree.

The resin is available in two forms:

mayʿa sāʾila (ميعة سائلة) resin with honey-like consistency. The light-yellow resin collected directly from the tree is top quality. Another way of collecting it is by boiling the tree bark, and pressing and extracting the resin. This also has a honey-like consistency, but it is reddish in hue.

mayʿa yābisa (ميعة يابسة) dry storax resin. This is the rest of the resin that remains in the bark after it is boiled to extract the fluid resin. It is too thick to separate from the bark. This is also called *qishr mayʿa* (قشر ميعة) bark of the storax resin.

The aromatic resin is used in perfumes and incense. With its hot and dry properties, it is medicinally beneficial for cold-related ailments, just by inhaling it.

milḥ (ملح) salt, usually used loose. However, some recipes mention adding lumps of salt (*ḥaṣāt milḥ*). With its hot and dry properties, it is beneficial in purging excretions, and preventing the blood from putrefying. It also helps check tooth decay, and cure cold-related stomachaches. It has the power to stimulate the appetite and aid digestion. It is also beneficial in preserving foods, by drying up their moisture. In cooking meat dishes, it is essential in eliminating the unpleasant greasy odors (*zafar*) of meat.

ḥaṣāt milḥ (حصاة ملح) lump of salt.

milḥ Andarānī (ملح اندراني), also called *dārānī* (داراني), *darrānī* (درّاني) rock salt. It is also referred to as *milḥ maʿdanī* (ملح معدني) mineral salt. It is high quality salt distinguished by its pure white color and translucent crystals.

milḥ jarīsh (ملح جريش) coarsely ground salt.

milḥ raṭb (ملح رطب) freshly harvested sea salt which is still moist and unrefined.

milḥ saqanqūr (ملح سقنقور) salt of the scincus (*Scincus*) a genus of skinks; it was believed to have the same effect as today's Viagra.

The scincus is a small reptile that Arabic medieval sources say was widely used in Egypt, Sudan, and other countries. The best was said to be Indian. In Egypt, it is found in sandy areas along the Nile and the desert, but Ibn al-Bayṭār, *al-Jāmiʿ* iii 27–30, says that the best is caught in al-Fayyūm district, cured, and brought to Cairo. The reptiles were slaughtered right after they were caught, then their heads, limbs, and tails were cut off, their bellies were slit lengthwise, and then they were cleaned and stuffed with salt. They were left in a shaded place to dry, and then stored in baskets.

The salt inside them, because it had hot and dry properties, was commonly used to invigorate coitus. Ibn Sīnā, *al-Qānūn*, 857, says only a small amount of it should suffice. Indeed, al-Anṭākī, *Tadhkira* 212, mentions that it is so effective that it might cause death due to prolonged erection. Its fat and its navel were also used to treat joint pain, hemiplegia (*fālaj*), facial paralysis (*laqwa*) and the like. In *Kanz* recipe 185, *saqanqūr* salt is used in an aphrodisiac omelet dish.

misk (مسك) musk, greasy secretion produced in a glandular sac beneath the skin of the abdomen, behind the navel of the male musk deer (*Moschus*). The best was said to be the Tibetan, because the deer feed on the aromatic spikenard plant. The musk pod itself is called *nāfijat al-misk*, or *fa'r al-misk*, because it looks like a mouse. Good musk was kept in its pod and transported; unlike Chinese musk, which was taken out of the pods, and as such was easily adulterated. However, we are told that Chinese musk could be as good as the Tibetan, when it is not mixed with anything, and kept tightly sealed in glass bottles (*qawārīr*). This would be called *misk qārūrī* (مسك قارورِي), and as such, it was transported by land and sea to Persia, Oman, Iraq, and other regions.

Musk was used in cooking and perfume preparations. Medicinally, because of its hot and dry properties, it was used in treating cold-related ailments. It sweetens the odor of sweat, induces euphoria, and invigorates coitus. Its heat is sometimes tempered with cold camphor, and its dryness with rose oil (*duhn al-ward*) (al-Bīrūnī, *Ṣaydana* 345–6; al-Malik al-Muẓaffar, *al-Muʿtamad* 564–7).

misk adhfar (مسك أذفر) sweet-smelling musk.

misk ʿIrāqī (مسك عراقي) Iraqi musk, named after the regions it was brought from, east of Iraq, as far as India, as Ibn al-Bayṭār, *al-Jāmiʿ* ii 425, explains. This implies that it was transported by land via the Silk Road.

misk Yemenī (مسك يمني) musk of Yemen, which was brought to its harbors by sea via the Indian Ocean.

mizāj (مزاج) vinegar-based flavoring and seasoning sauce, prepared with spices and herbs, see, for instance, *Kanz* recipes 126, 237, 252, and 439. A dish seasoned this way may be called *mumazzaj* (ممزّج) as in recipe 48, and *mamzūj* (ممزوج) as in recipe 126.

murrī (مرّي) liquid fermented sauce, salty, sour, and a bit bitter. With its hot and dry properties, it is beneficial in breaking down dense foods and facilitating digestion. It was often praised as being the 'essence of food' (*jawhar al-ṭaʿām*), because of its power to stimulate the appetite, digest food, and cure bad breath. See *Kanz* recipes in chapter 6.

murrī naqīʿ (مرّي نقيع) cereal-based liquid sauce which has been fermented over several months. It is also called *murrī Nabaṭī* (مري نبطي), named after the Nabateans, the indigenous Iraqis. The sauce is a strong tasting darkish liquid.

murrī shaʿīr (مرّي شعير) barley-based liquid fermented sauce, also called *murrī naqīʿ*, see above.

mustaʿjala (مستعجلة) *Orchis mascula* (S) Satyrion, salep. In Arabic, it is also called *khuṣā l-thaʿlab* (خصى الثعلب) 'fox's testicles,' *khuṣā l-kalb* (خصى الكلب), 'dog's testicle,' and *qātil akhīhi* (قاتل اخيه) 'brother killer.' Al-Anṭākī, *Tadhkira* 329, also reports that it was called *ʿirq inṭirāb* (عرق انطراب) in Egypt during his time (sixteenth century).

The root of the plant begins as two egg-like soft tubers, and as one grows, the other one gets smaller. The root is yellowish white, sticky, with a sweetish, somewhat sharp taste. It has a faint semen-like odor. It is principally used as an aphrodisiac (Ibn al-Bayṭār, *al-Jāmiʿ* iv 447; Ibn Sīnā, *al-Qānūn* 380). Al-Malik al-Muẓaffar, *al-Muʿtamad* 167, says that if a man eats the larger tuber, he will have a boy; and if the woman eats the smaller tuber, she will have a girl. He further adds that it is a well-known plant in Egypt; it grows in Alexandria, and from thence, it is exported to the Levant. He says women cook the tubers with milk to help them gain weight and improve the color of their complexion.

najm (نجم), also known as *theyyel* (ثيّل) *Elymus repens* (S) couch grass. Its properties are cold and astringent. The grass, rhizomes, and seeds are used to break up kidney stones, help wounds heal, and relieve colic. The seeds are said to be good for treating nausea (al-Malik al-Muẓaffar, *al-Muʿtamad* 90–1).

najm ʿIrāqī (نجم عراقي) this must have had stronger properties than the other varieties. It is used in *Kanz* recipe 456, in a preparation to relieve nausea.

nammām (نمّام) *Thymus serpyllum* (S), wild thyme, also known as creeping thyme, and mother of thyme. It has a marjoram-like scent that is so pronounced that the whole area becomes redolent with it. In this respect, it is like a *nammām*, a gossipy person who cannot keep a secret. With its hot properties, it is beneficial as a diuretic and antiseptic. It promotes menstruation and causes miscarriages. Having a drink with *nammām* steeped in it was said to stop hiccups (al-Malik al-Muẓaffar, *al-Muʿtamad* 599–600).

naʿnaʿ (نعنع) ***naʿnāʿ*** (نعناع) *Mentha* (S) mint, which has a refreshingly sharp taste. Its hot and dry properties were believed to stimulate the appetite, aid digestion, relieve bloating, and stop hiccups and vomiting.

ʿīdān naʿnāʿ (عيدان نعناع) sprigs of mint.
naʿnāʿ akhḍar (نعناع أخضر) fresh mint.
naʿnāʿ Shāmī (نعناع شامي) *Origanum dictammus* (S) Levantine mint, known as hop marjoram and dittany. It is a wild variety of mint described as having

round leaves, like those of thyme. In taste and aroma, it is like river mint (*fūdhanaj nahrī*). See Ibn al-Bayṭār, *al-Jāmiʿ* iii 232–3.

naʿnaʿ yābis (نعنع يابس) dried mint.

nānkhawāh (نانخواه) *Trachyspermum ammi* (S) ajowan. Al-Anṭākī, *Tadhkira* 357, says Egyptians call it ***nakhwa Hindiyya*** (نخوة هندية); also called *kammūn mulūkī* (كمون ملوكي) royal cumin. It is a seed the size of mustard seed, with a strong scent and sharp taste. With its hot and dry properties, it was believed to be effective in deflating winds, and easing bloating and hiccups. Ibn al-Bayṭār, *al-Jāmiʿ* iv 469, explains that the Persian name *nānkhawāh* means *ṭālib al-khubz* 'demanding bread' because bread sprinkled with it before it is baked becomes appetizing.

narjis (نرجس) *Narcissus tazetta* (S) narcissus. Medieval cooks compare their sunny side up egg omelets (*narjisiyyāt*) to it. Medicinally, it was used to relieve headaches and cold symptoms. It was also believed to enlarge the male organ if it is rubbed with a narcissus bulb. Al-Anṭākī adds that it can abort fetuses when needed, "but let's not spread the word about this," he cautions (*Tadhkira* 360).

naṭrūn (نطرون) natron, sodium bicarbonate, a mineral component, closely related to *būraq*. It is used in *Kanz* recipes in small amounts to boil vegetables and beans, such as turnips, cabbage, beans, and chickpeas. It is also used as a leavening agent with pastries (recipe 322). See *būraq* above.

naylūfar (نيلوفر) water lilies, see *laynūfar* above.

nīl (نيل) *nīlaj* (نيلج) *Indigofera tinctoria* (S) indigo, a plant valued for its blue dye, which was obtained by rinsing the leaves in hot water, then removing them; the indigo dye pigments would settle like mud in the water. The sediment is taken out and dried.

This plant has cold properties, which renders it good for all types of swelling (al-Malik al-Muẓaffar, *al-Muʿtamad* 603). In *Kanz* recipes, it is used to color food, distilled water, and soap. See, for instance, recipes 291, 547, 642, and 697.

nisrīn (نسرين) *Rosa canina* (S) dog rose grows in the mountains and is cultivated in orchards. It has a strong aroma. The farther it grows from water sources, the stronger its scent becomes. Its aroma induces pleasant feelings, and fortifies the intellect and senses. It drives away winds and relieves nausea and cold symptoms. In *Kanz* recipe 651, oil infused with it is used to wipe the hands after washing them, to get rid of the greasy odors of food.

nisrīn akhḍar (نسرين أخضر), lit., 'green;' it is fresh dog rose.

qāqulla (قاقلة) *Amomum subulatum* (S) black cardamom, greater cardamom. It is a large variety of cardamom, related to *hāl* (هال), see entry above. It is described as the fruit of an Indian plant called *kakūlā* (ككولا) in Hindi (al-Bīrūnī, *Ṣaydana* 299).

It might have been named after Qāqula, which Ibn Baṭṭūṭa, *Riḥla* 313, describes as a place somewhere around Java Island.

It is an aromatic spice with a sharp burning taste, like that of cubeb, with a camphoric overtone. It is much coarser and more astringent than *hāl* (green cardamom), and this renders it more suitable for savory dishes.

With their hot and dry properties, all varieties of cardamom are used in cooking and medicine. They were recommended as a digestive because they open blockages in the liver and kidneys, and cure nausea, vomiting, and colds. Additionally, they were said to induce euphoria. In *Kanz* recipes, *qāqulla* is used in digestive drinks and stomachics, as well as handwashing compounds and perfumed preparations.

qaranful (قرنفل) ***kibāsh qaranful*** (كباش قرنفل) *Syzygium aromaticum* (S) cloves, unopened flower buds of a small evergreen tree indigenous to China and India. This spice is bitingly hot, and slightly bitter. Besides its culinary uses, it is a valued medicinal item. It sweetens the breath, strengthens the internal organs and gladdens the soul. It arouses coitus however it is used.

ḥaṭab qaranful (حطب قرنفل) clove stalks, said to be stronger and more pungent than the cloves themselves (Grieve, *Modern Herbal* i 208).

qaranful zahr (قرنفل زهر), *zahr qaranful* (زهر قرنفل) *Dianthus caryophyllus* (S) carnation flower, valued for its aroma and medicinal properties. The petals are used dried or in distilled form in preparing handwashing compounds, digestive drinks, and pickles. It was believed to aid digestion, control bowel movements, stop vomiting and nausea, and sweeten the breath (al-Ghassānī, *Ḥadīqat al-azhār* 249).

qarfa (قرفة) *Cinnamomum verum* (S) Ceylon cinnamon, which is true cinnamon, is characterized by its rolled bark. It is related to cassia (*dār Ṣīnī*), and is often confused with it, see entry above. It seems to have cost less than cassia, because it was often used to adulterate it (al-Anṭākī, *Tadhkira*, 163). Its hot and dry properties are weaker than those of cassia. However, it is sweeter than cassia, which renders it more suited to sweet and savory dishes alike.

qarfa laff (قرفة لف) rolled bark of Ceylon cinnamon.
qarfa laff ḥurra (قرفة لف حرّة) top-quality rolled bark of Ceylon cinnamon.

qaṣab dharīra (قصب ذريرة) *Acorus calamus* (S) sweet flag, which has scented leaves and rhizomes. It is astringent and sharp in taste, used in the *Kanz* in a handwashing preparation, as it was believed to help remove undesirable odors. Medicinally, it is good for chronic coughs and chest pain, and was recommended for relieving pain in the womb (Ibn al-Bayṭār, *al-Jāmiʿ* iv 268).

qazmat banafsaj (قزمة بنفسج) dwarf violet iris. Dozy, *Takmilat al-maʿājim* 137 mentions *qarm banafsaj* (قرم بنفسج) to designate *sawsan* (iris), s.v. قرم.[14] See *banafsaj* above.

qiddāḥ (قداح) blossom of citrus fruits, used in cooking and in distillations.

qilī (قلي), also called *ushnān* (أشنان) potash, made by first producing ashes from the *ushnān* plant, also called *qāqullā* (قاقلّى) and *qāqullī* (قاقلّي), which is saltwort (*Salsola kali*); in Arabic *ḥurḍ* (حُرض). See also glossary 11, s.v. *ushnān* 2.

qirṭ (قِرط) leaf leeks, also known as *kurrāth*, see entry above.

qishr mayʿa (قشر ميعة) bark of storax tree; also called *mayʿa yābisa* (ميعة يابسة) dry storax, and *lubnā* (لبنى). See *mayʿa* above.

qurṭum (قرطم), also called *ḥabb al-qurṭum* (حب القرطم), and *ḥabb al-ʿuṣfur* (حب العصفر) seeds of safflower (*Carthamus tinctorius*), used to thicken stews by first grinding them, and then steeping them in liquid and extracting their juice. See *ʿuṣfur* below.

qurūn (قرون) coral, the best of which was said to be the red. *Qurūn* must have been a dialectical corruption of *qurūl* (قرول), which was also known by the name *bussadh* (بسذ), and *marjān* (مرجان).

A recipe for making *aqrāṣ qurūn* (اقراص قرون) coral pastilles, which is an ingredient used in *Kanz* recipe 456, is available in Sābūr b. Sahl, *al-Aqrabādhīn* 121. It uses coral and frankincense in addition to other ingredients. They are bound with gum arabic and egg white, and shaped into pastilles.

Coral has cold and dry properties. It was deemed beneficial for the eyes, the heart, teeth, gums, and stomach.

qusṭ (قُسط) *Saussurea costus* (S) costus, kuth, the root of which is used in aromatic preparations. It looks like licorice but is much more fragrant. It is used in *Kanz* recipes (chapters 20, 21, and 22) dealing with handwashing compounds and incense. It is often just referred to as *qusṭ*; however, some recipes require specific varieties, the sweet, the bitter, and sea costus:

qusṭ baḥrī (قسط بحري) sea costus, also called *qusṭ ḥulw* (قسط حلو) sweet costus, and *qusṭ ʿArabī* (قسط عربي) Arabian costus. It is described as white, lightweight, and strongly fragrant. It looks like a peeled and dried carrot, and it is brought from Abyssinia, as stated by al-Bīrūnī, *Ṣaydana* 307–8. The Abyssinian is rated as high quality costus, next in excellence is the Indian costus.

qusṭ ḥulw (قسط حلو) sweet costus, see above.

qusṭ murr (قسط مر) bitter costus, also called *qusṭ Hindī* (قسط هندي) Indian costus, next in excellence to sea costus (entry above). It is described as black, thick, and bitter.

14 It could have been a typographical error or a misreading of قزم 'dwarf.'

All costus varieties have hot and dry properties, and as such they can dry phlegm in the head, and remedy cold-related ailments, when inhaled and taken internally.

ramād (رماد) ashes, used with and without slaked lime to preserve olives in brine (*Kanz* recipes 560, 561). It helps leach out their bitterness and prevents their discoloration.

rand (رند), also called *rand Rūmī* (رند رومي) *Laurus nobilis* (S) bay laurel. *Rand* is its Levantine name; otherwise, it is called *ghār* (غار). In *Kanz* recipes, it is incorporated into condiments and scented handwashing compounds. With its hot and dry properties, it is beneficial medicinally to cure phlegmatic headaches, induce sneezing, and relieve colic. It was said that sprinkling the floor with water in which its leaves have been steeped will keep flies away. Ibn Waḥshiyya, *al-Filāḥa* i 150, claims that sticking a clean fresh leaf behind the ear can prevent intoxication and hangovers.

rand Rūmī (رند رومي) 'Byzantine bay laurel,' see above entry.

raṭba (رطبة) *Medicago sativa* (S) fresh alfalfa. Al-Anṭākī, *Tadhkira* 275, calls this plant *fiṣfiṣa* (فصفصة), which Egyptians call *birsīm* (برسيم).

The plant is recognized as the best forage for cattle. For humans, it helps with weight gain if taken with almonds. It also stimulates milk production. In *Kanz* recipe 691, it is used to dye the distilled water green, due to its high chlorophyll content.

rayḥān (ريحان), also called *bādharūj* (باذروج) *Ocimum* (S) basil. Its properties are hot and dry. It induces sneezing, and strengthens the sense of smell because it opens blockages, and induces feelings of euphoria with its fragrance. However, it was said to be bad for the digestion, as it putrefies in the stomach fast, and may breed worms in the digestive system (al-Anṭākī, *Tadhkira* 73).

Besides basil, the name *rayḥān* was often be applied to designate other sweet-smelling herbs. In Egypt and the western region of the Arabo-Islamic world, it designates *marsīn* (مرسين), called *ās* (myrtle) in the eastern region.

bazr rayḥān (بزر ريحان) basil seeds.

rayḥān qaranfulī (ريحان قرنفلي), also called *ḥabaq qaranfulī* (حبق قرنفلي) and *faranjamushk* (فرنجمشك) *Calamintha acinos* (S) basil thyme, described as having small leaves which look like those of basil, slightly yellowish and furry. They emit a pleasant clove-like aroma. Al-Anṭākī says it grows abundantly in Egypt.

It was said to induce feelings of euphoria, and stimulate comforting and pleasant-smelling burping. Putting a few sprigs of it in wine was believed to keep it from going bad. It strengthens the heart and a cold stomach, and aids in the digestion of dense foods.[15] It is used in *Kanz* recipe 580 for pickling onions.

---

15 Ibn al-Bayṭār, *al-Jāmiʿ* i 53, iii 220; al-Anṭākī, *Tadhkira* 274; al-Malik al-Muẓaffar, *al-Muʿtamad* 421.

rayḥān utrujjī (ريحان اترجي), *rayḥān turunjī* (ريحان ترنجي), and *turunjān* (ترنجان) *Melissa officinalis* (S) lemon balm, balm mint, whose leaves have a gentle scent of citrus. Al-Suyūṭī, *Ḥusn al-muḥāḍara* 358, composed the following verses on this aromatic herb:

Never have I known before passing by *turunjān*,
That emerald can indeed grow into stems and leaves,
Marvelously fragrant; from *utrujj* it must have stolen its scent.
What's going on people? Even plants now have become thieves!

The herb induces euphoria and feelings of well-being. In fact, Ibn al-Bayṭār, *al-Jāmiʿ* i 103, offers a magic recipe for success: put in your pocket some dried bits of the root, stems, and seeds of this plant, all tied with a thread of silk, and you will feel happy, and confident. Of its other benefits, it can relieve colic pain, aid digestion, and induce fragrant belching.

rāzyānaj (رازيانج) *Foeniculum vulgare* (S) fennel. Other names for it are *shamar* (شمر) *shamra* (شمرة), *shūmer* (شومر), *ḥabbat ḥulwa* (حبة حلوة). In Andalusia and the Maghrib, it is called *basbās* (بسباس). It is an aromatic seed, a bit larger than aniseed, beneficial for deflating gastric winds, and aiding digestion.

FIGURE 70
Rijl al-ḥamāma (*alkanet*), *Elizabeth Blackwell,* A Curious Herbal, *1738, plate 112 (From the New York Public Library: http://digitalcollections.nypl.org/items/510d47dd-c6d5-a3d9-e040-e00a18064a99).*

rijl al-ḥamāma (رجل الحمامة), also called *sāq al-ḥamāma* (ساق الحمامة), *ʿāqir shamʿā* (عاقر شمعا), *shinkār* (شنكار), *shinjār* (شنجار) *Alkanna tinctoria* (S) dyer's bugloss, alkanet. Its root is primarily used as a ruby-red coloring agent for fabrics, soaps, lip balm, and the like. See *Kanz* recipes 306 and 691.

FIGURE 71
Sadhāb (*rue*), *Elizabeth Blackwell,* A Curious Herbal, *1738, plate 7 (From the New York Public Library: http://digitalcollections.nypl.org/items/510d47dd-c207-a3d9-e040-e00a18064a99).*

sadhāb (سذاب) *sadāb* (سداب) is a dialectical variant; called *fayjan* (فيجن) in Andalusia. It is *Ruta graveolens* (S), rue, bitter and acrid herb with an unpleasant smell. Nonetheless, it was an important herb in medieval cooking and was valued for its power to deflate flatulence and wind, and remove garlic and onion odors when chewed after the meal. It was used as a contraceptive and abortive when inhaled. It was believed to work as an antidote to poison. Small quantities were recommended, because having an excess of it dulls the mind and heart and weakens the eyes.

sadhāb barrī (سذاب بري) wild rue. It has the same qualities as the garden rue, albeit much stronger.

sādhaj Hindī (ساذج هندي), also called *waraq al-Hind* (ورق الهند) Indian leaf. There was confusion among medieval botanists concerning the identification of this plant. It was said to be *tānbūl* (betel pepper, *Piper betel*), *waraq al-ghār al-Hindī* (Indian bay leaf, *Cinnamomum tamala*), leaves of *al-sunbul al-Hindī* (Indian spikenard,

Nardostachys jatamansi). In fact, it is often adulterated with the latter because it smells like it.

True *sādhaj* is described as a free-floating aquatic plant with small leaves, which grows in wetlands in India. Its leaves are green, long and wide, with no visible veins or midribs, hence the name *sādhaj* (simple). The plant has neither stems nor branches, just the threadlike roots hanging in the water, growing the way *ʿadas al-māʾ* (water lentil, Lemna minor) and Egyptian *bishnīn* (blue Egyptian water lily) grow. The leaves are soft, smell like spikenard, and do not break or crumble easily. It is gathered and tied in bundles with thread, and left to dry, and then stored and used as needed.

Its properties are hot and dry; it was believed to be useful in comforting the bereaved, and easing the mental conditions of anxiety, delusions, and solitude. It was incorporated into restorative preparations that aid digestion, and stimulate the appetite (see *Kanz* recipe 377). It was also put between clothes to protect them from insects. See al-Anṭākī, *Tadhkira* 203; and Ishbīlī, *ʿUmdat al-ṭabīb* ii 528.

salīkha (سليخة) bark, like cassia (*dār Ṣīnī*) but it is not the same plant. The Indian variety was said to be the best. The tree is described as having a short thick trunk, with thick bark covering the trunk and the branches. The reddish bark is like open seam tubes. They are aromatic, and smell almost like wine, with a biting pungent taste. Cassia bark is often used as a substitute for it, because of the similarities they share in aroma and properties (Ibn Waḥshiyya, *al-Filāḥa* ii 1252; al-Anṭākī, *Tadhkira* 214). In the *Kanz*, it is used in handwashing preparations and scented powders.

ṣamgh (صمغ) natural hardened sap of several varieties of trees, of which *ṣamgh ʿArabī* (gum arabic) is the most frequently used, see below.

ṣamgh ʿArabī (صمغ عربي) or just *ṣamgh* (صمغ) acacia gum, also called gum arabic. It is the hardened sap of *sanṭ ʿArabī* (سنط عربي), *shawka Qibṭiyya* (شوكة قبطية) *Acacia arabica* (S) Egyptian acacia, also called gum-arabic tree. It has a neutral taste and no aroma; therefore, it is used mostly in preparing dishes that need a thickening and binding agent, as in *Kanz* recipes 73 and 171. Medicinally, it was incorporated into many compounds for eye treatments. It was also used to fix fractures. Internally, it was taken to control bowel movements.

ṣamgh al-lawz (صمغ اللوز) gum of the almond tree, valued for its strong heating and rarefying properties, used in *Kanz* recipe 288.

ṣandal (صندل) *Santalum* (S) sandalwood, an aromatic wood brought from regions of southern India, used in incense and other aromatic compounds and medicinal preparations. Its three major varieties, white, red, and yellow, are all used.

Sandalwood has cold and dry properties, and as such, it was used to sooth headaches caused by excess heat. It was also used in the bathrooms as a rub to mask the odors of depilatory *nūrā* (Ibn al-Bayṭār, *al-Jāmiʿ* iv 340, s.v. *kils*).

ṣandal aḥmar (صندل احمر) red sandalwood, which is heavy, looks good, but has no aroma. See, for instance, *Kanz* recipe 717, where it is used as a restorative powder (*dharūr*).

ṣandal abyaḍ (صندل ابيض) white sandalwood is a sweet-smelling variety of *ṣandal Maqāṣīrī* (see below), it only differs in color. Some say this white sandalwood is the outer bark of the tree, and *ṣandal Maqāṣīrī* is the inner layer of the wood.

ṣandal aṣfar (صندل اصفر) yellow sandalwood smells good, but its aroma is not rich.

ṣandal Maqāṣīrī (صندل مقاصيري) Ceylon sandalwood. It is a high-quality variety, which al-Bīrūnī, *Ṣaydana* 248, says is brought from *Arḍ al-dhahab* ('gold region,' Serendib, Ceylon, today's Sri Lanka). It is yellow, dense, resinous, and very fragrant. Regarding its name, some say it is named after a place called Maqāṣīr, whereas others claim that some of the Abbasid caliphs used it in building *maqāṣīr* (private quarters) for some of their favored wives and slave girls (al-Nuwayrī, *Nihāyat al-Arab* xii 21–3; al-Qalqashandī, *Ṣubḥ al-aʿshā* ii 123–4).

sandarūs (سندروس) sweet-smelling resin of arar tree, also called sandarac tree (*Tetraclinis articulata*). It is like *kahrabā* (كهربا) amber, albeit less solid. The best resin is yellow, heavy, pure, and transparent.

Its properties are hot and dry. Medicinally it is beneficial in soothing toothaches, and easing symptoms of colds and asthma. Wrestlers infused drinks with it to maintain their physical and mental strength. In *Kanz* recipes 655 and 665, it is used in preparations for incense.

sāq al-ḥamāma (ساق الحمامة) dyer's bugloss, see *rijl al-ḥamām* above.

sayraqūn (سيرقون) *sārqan* (سارقن), also known as *isrinj* (اسرنج) red lead, also called minium, a vivid red dye. Al-Bīrūnī, *Ṣaydana* 42, mentions that it is obtained by burning *ānak* (lead) and reddening it with *kibrīt* (sulfur). In *Kanz* recipe 642, it is used to color soap light red (*wardī*).

shabath (شبث) *Anethum graveolens* (S) dill, eaten fresh and dried. It was believed to deflate wind, which explains its inclusion in the grain dishes in *Kanz*. Other benefits include its ability to induce sleep and stop hiccups (Ibn al-Bayṭār, *al-Jāmiʿ* iii 66).

shahdānaq (شهدانق) also occurs as *shāhdānaj* (شاهدانج) hemp seeds, of the plant *qinnab* (قنّب) *Cannabis sativa sativa* (S).[16] They were used the same way sesame seeds

16 It is not a narcotic like *Cannabis sativa indica* (*qinnab Hindī*/*ḥashīsha*), which is marijuana. The plant fiber is used to make rope and hemp clothes, and oil is extracted from its seeds.

were used, toasted and untoasted. Physicians cautioned against overindulgence, as they tend to dry semen with their powerful heating properties. They are also said to be difficult to digest. However, they are quite effective in dispelling wind (al-Malik al-Muẓaffar, *al-Muʿtamad* 462–3).

shamʿ Iskandrānī aṣfar (شمع اسكندراني اصفر) yellow beeswax of Alexandria. Another name for beeswax is *mūm* (موم). It is used in a *Kanz* recipe for making ghee using milk, as it helps thicken the consistency (see last recipe in chapter 10). This excellent variety of beeswax might well have been a product of Alexandria, which was renowned for its many beekeepers, who sold their products in the Cairene markets (al-Idrīsī, *Nuzhat al-mushtāq* i 319); or it was imported via this Mediterranean coastal city. Al-Bīrūnī, *Ṣaydana* 415, for instance, mentions that the best is brought from the island of Crete.

The best beeswax was taken from the honey cells themselves or the walls of the hive. It is yellowish in hue, lightweight, and sweet smelling. In addition, it should be easy to knead, and does not crumble.

shamar (شمر) fennel, see *rāzyānaj* above.

shaqāʾiq al-Nuʿmān (شقائق النعمان) *Anemone coronaria* (S) poppy anemone, of which there are several colors, but the red is the most dominant. In *Kanz* recipe 699, the flowers are added to the roses being distilled to give the resulting rosewater a vivid red color.

shayba (شيبة) as it is called in Egypt, *Usnea florida* (S), a variety of lichen. Other names for it are *shaybat al-ʿajūz* (شيبة العجوز) 'old man's hair,' *liḥyat al-ʿajūz* (لحية العجوز) 'old man's beard,' and *ushna* (أشنة).

It is composed of hairy strands attached to branches of trees. The best lichen was said to be white and grow on pine, oak, and walnut trees. It is beneficial for the eyes, stomach, liver, kidneys, and spleen. In the kitchen, it was used as a spice, and was known for being an aphrodisiac. Al-Hurawī, *Baḥr al-jawāhir* 24, describes how it is pounded first, and then soaked in water, kneaded with flour and other ingredients, and baked as bread. Recipe 6 in the *Kanz* verifies his description. Dozy, *Takmilat al-maʿājim* 208, mentions that balls of lichen are dipped in scented powders, and then taken out and used as perfumed balls, which do not stain the clothes with the perfume dyes.

shirsh (شرش) described as *māʾ wa-milḥ* (ماء وملح) salt and water, brine, as stated in *Kanz* recipe 141.

shūnīz (شونيز) *Nigella sativa* (S) nigella seeds, also known as *ḥabba sawdāʾ* (حبة سوداء) 'black seed.' With its hot and dry properties, it was recommended for cold-related ailments. Its smoke was used as an insect repellant. Using it with baked breads was believed to combat flatulence (al-Bīrūnī, *Ṣaydana* 421–2).

simsim (سمسم) sesame seeds, used toasted in small amounts sprinkled on olive and pickle condiments. It was also added to breads and date sweets.

simsim muqashshar (سمسم مقشر) husked sesame seeds, which are used with pickled turnips in *Kanz* recipes.

suʿd (سعد) Cyperus, also called tigernut, a grass-like aquatic plant; the rhizomes are used. Al-Anṭākī, *Tadhkira* 206, says it grows abundantly in Egypt, even in household gardens. Its properties are hot and dry. Its astringency has a tannic effect on the stomach. It was used to treat hemorrhoids, heat a cold stomach and liver, and remove bad odors in mouth and nose.

suʿd abyaḍ Kūfī (سعد ابيض كوفي), ***suʿd Kūfī*** (سعد كوفي) white cyperus of Kufa, a city south of Baghdad. This was deemed the best and most fragrant of all varieties. The white rhizomes are large, dense, heavy, and fragrant (al-Malik al-Muẓaffar, *al-Muʿtamad* 272).

suʿd Quṣārī (سعد قُصاري) cyperus of Quṣār, a place between India and China (al-Qalqashandī, *Ṣubḥ al-aʿshā* 239). This must be the Indian variety, sometimes referred to in other sources. It is good cyperus, but cyperus of Kufa surpasses it in excellence. However, we read in al-Anṭākī, *Tadhkira* 206, that this variety is called *rayḥān al-qaṣārī* (ريحان القَصاري) because Egyptians grow it in pots (*qaṣārī*) in their home gardens. He adds that it is ubiquitous in Egypt.

sukk misk (سك مسك) pastilles of an aromatic musk compound used to flavor foods and drinks. It was also used in aromatic and restorative preparations, such as incense, breath fresheners, and stomachics (see *Kanz* recipes 379, 456, 661, and 673). Of its medicinal benefits, it fortifies internal organs, and curbs bowel movements. It helps to narrow a woman's female passage by fumigation (Ibn al-Bayṭār, *al-Jāmiʿ* iii 32; Ibn Sīnā, *al-Qānūn* 323).

The basic component for making *sukk* is a preparation called *rāmak* (رامك). *Rāmak* is a dark-colored mix of *ʿafṣ* (gall) and *umluj* (emblic myrobalan).[17] Fresh dates can be substituted for the latter. In a complex and time-consuming operation, the *rāmak* is made into small discs of dough, threaded, and set aside to dry, to be used as needed in making *sukk* (al-Nuwayrī, *Nihāyat al-arab* xii 40–2).

To make *sukk al-misk*, *rāmak* is pounded, and then kneaded with water, and set aside overnight. It is then mixed with crushed musk. The mix is kneaded well, and then shaped into discs, which are left on the back of the sieve to dry for about a year (Ibn al-Bayṭār, *al-Jāmiʿ* iii 32–3).

summāq (سماق) *Rhus* (S) sumac. For cooking purposes, only the husk of the berries is used. It was an essential spice in medieval Arabo-Islamic cooking; it was used

17 It is also known as Indian gooseberry (*Phyllanthus emblica*), see glossary 7 above.

as an appetite stimulator. Its astringent properties were used to treat diarrhea and bleeding.

mā' al-summāq (ماء السماق) sumac juice, obtained by soaking sumac berries in hot water, or boiling them in water with a piece of bread, and then straining the liquid.

qaṭr summāq (قطر السماق) also called *rubb al-summāq* (رُب السماق) sumac molasses, produced by reducing sumac juice into syrup consistency.

taṣwīl al-summāq (تصويل السماق) a process which involves first submerging sumac berries in several changes of water to remove any sticks and impurities. Next, they are drained and spread on mats to dry. After this process, the outer skins of the berries wilt and become brittle, and can be easily husked by pounding them. The hard seeds themselves are usually discarded.

zahr summāq (زهر سماق) deep-red sumac husk. Fresh sumac berries are hard seeds with downy outer coverings that become husks when they are dried. This husky part gives the sumac spice its characteristic color and tartness. That is why the bunches of sumac berries should be harvested before they are rained on; otherwise, the rain washes away their downy covering. This part of the sumac is called *zahr summāq*, for its intensely deep-red husk. It is still called this in the Levant. When they are dried, the sumac berries are pounded, and sifted to get this husk, and the hard seeds are discarded.

sunbul (سنبل) also called *nārdīn* (ناردين) *Nardostachys jatamansi* (S) spikenard; the rhizomes are the most valued parts used. The sweet-smelling rhizomes (called *ʿaṣāfīr*, lit., 'sparrows') are oblong, woody in texture, with lots of hairy minor roots entangled around them. Each rhizome is crowned with tufted fibers.

They are harvested by pulling out the entire plants and tying them in bundles. When they are almost dry, the rhizomes are collected, dried, and stored. Whenever needed, the rhizomes are cleaned of the dried mud attached to them—this sweet-smelling mud is used in handwashing preparations. The hairy roots surrounding them are also removed, and in this state, the rhizome can be described as *musallal* (stripped). When held in the hand for a while, this stripped rhizome smells like an apple (al-Nuwayrī, *Nihāyat al-arab* xii 24–5).

The most important of its varieties are

sunbul al-ṭīb (سنبل الطيب), also called *sunbul Hindī* (سنبل هندي) Indian spikenard, and *sunbul ʿaṣāfīrī* (سنبل عصافيري), because the rhizomes look like sparrows (see above). Their dark-red rhizomes are described as shorter than other varieties, with the most aroma and the strongest properties.

Nārdīn Rūmī (ناردين رومي), also called *nārdīn iqlīṭī* (ناردين اقليطي) a variety of spikenard which has the same aroma and properties as those of the Indian variety described above, albeit in lesser degrees.

Spikenard is used as a food spice, and in this case, it is usually added with cloves. In the *Kanz*, the dish recipes do not specify the variety of spikenard. However, in recipes for distillations, digestive drinks, and stomachics, the Indian variety is required. We assume that for dishes any other good varieties will do. It was also incorporated in digestives, handwashing compounds, and medicinal preparations, as it was believed to be good for the stomach, liver, and spleen. It has the power to bring pleasure to the soul, and boost memory and sexual desires (al-Bīrūnī, *Ṣaydana* 236–7; Ibn al-Bayṭār, *al-Jāmiʿ* iii 48–51; al-Ishbīlī, *ʿUmdat al-ṭabīb* ii 528–9).

ṭabāshīr (طباشير) tabashir, loose lumps of chalky porous silica deposited in the cavities of the stems of reeds. Indian reed (*Canna Indica*), called *qaṣab Hindī* (قصب هندي) was said to be its main source. The reeds are described as thick, long, and sturdy. They were used to make arrows (*nushshāb*). The best tabashir is distinguished by its intense whiteness. With its cold and dry properties, it can relieve feelings of thirst and heat, and stop diarrhea.

ṭabāshīr Tashtar (طباشير تشتر) tabashir from reeds grown in the city of Tastar (Tashtar, a dialectical variant) in the Persian province of Khuzestan, bordering Basra, Iraq. The reeds are the same size as those of the Indian variety, albeit less sturdy (al-Nābulusī, *ʿAlam al-malāḥa* 37).

ṭaḥīna (طحينة) tahini, sesame paste made by grinding sesame seeds. It is used in many *Kanz* recipes, both for hot dishes and cold side dishes. See, for instance, chapter 19, where it is used to make dips comparable to today's hummus (*ḥummuṣ bi-ṭaḥīna*). It was said to cause satiety when eaten as a dip by itself with bread. The recommendation was to have it along with honey or date syrup (Ibn Jazla, *Minhāj al-bayān*, fol. 110r).

ṭarkhūn (طرخون) *Artemisia dracunculus* (S) tarragon, described as having hot and dry properties. It is slightly bitter, and its sharp taste has a slight numbing effect on the tongue. It weakens libido. The fresh and tender leaves are served with other herbs (like mint, basil, and leaf leeks) as table herbs (*buqūl al-māʾida*), to excite the appetite and sweeten the breath. It is sturdy enough to be preserved in brine and incorporated into yogurt condiments. It is slow to digest. Of its benefits, it strengthens the stomach and helps check gum plaque when chewed and kept in the mouth for a while (al-Anṭākī, *Tadhkira* 254; al-Malik al-Muẓaffar, *al-Muʿtamad* 358–9).

taṣʿīdāt (تصعيدات) distilled waters, see *Kanz* recipes 684–715; see also *taṣʿīd* in glossary 9.2 below.
tawābil (توابل) sg. *tābil* (تابل) dried herbs and spices, used to season the dishes (al-Hurawī, *Baḥr al-jawāhir* 79).
thūm (ثوم) garlic.

kanāfish al-thūm (كنافش الثوم) hairy garlic roots which look like a bushy beard.
ra's thūm (راس ثوم) garlic head.
sin thūm (سن ثوم) garlic clove.

Al-Anṭākī, *Tadhkira* 110, mentions three varieties of garlic:

1) mountain garlic, whose bulb comes out as one head.
2) Levantine garlic, whose bulb comes out as two large conjoined heads.
3) Egyptian garlic, whose cloves are small, and the skins are hard to rub off.

The best garlic, al-Anṭākī adds, has large cloves which are easy to separate and skin. In taste, it is not sharp; and when cut, it feels somewhat sticky, like honey. This he says was called Nabatean garlic (i.e., indigenous to Iraq) in the old books, and it was imported from Cyprus in his time (sixteenth century). The eleventh-century Andalusian al-Ṭaghnarī mentions in his horticultural book *Zahrat al-bustān* a variety, which he saw in the Maghrib. He says it has one large and solid clove, and is round like an apple. What al-Ṭaghnarī describes here sounds like what we call today solo garlic, *Allium ampeloprasum* (S).

Garlic has hot and dry properties, and as such, it was believed to help dispel flatulence and thin the blood. The recommendation was to cook it with coarse dishes like *kishkiyya* and *maḍīra*,[18] to help break down their densities. It was also deemed beneficial to the elderly, whose humors are dominantly cold. People with hot humors can eat it pickled.

thūm bustānī (ثوم بستاني) *Allium sativum* (S), common garlic.
thūm kurrāthī (ثوم كراثي), also called *kurrāth al-thūm* (كراث الثوم), *thūm Shāmī* (ثوم شامي), and *kurrāth Andalusī* (كراث اندلسي) *Allium ascalonicum* (S) shallots, also known as Ascalonian garlic, named after the ancient Phoenician coastal city of Ascalon (عسقلان). They are said to taste like garlic and leeks combined. Its leaves are like those of leeks, and the bulb looks like a red onion from the outside, but it is composed of three or four conjoined bulbs (Ibn al-Bayṭār, *al-Jāmiʿ* iv 322–3).
thūm Shāmī (ثوم شامي) Levantine garlic, is shallots, see *thūm kurrāthī* above.

18 See glossary 5 above.

tunbul (تنبل) ***tānbūl*** (تانبول) *Piper betle* (S) betel leaves, which grow on a climbing plant, are abundant in India. The leaves are used when fresh and sweet smelling. The fresh leaves used in southern Arabia were brought from Oman.

The leaves are popular for their pleasant taste, which is somewhat like cloves. In India, they are chewed with *fawfal* (فوفل) betel nut, to sweeten the breath and strengthen the gums, stomach, and liver. They have the power to dispel gases and sweeten burping. People put some leaves next to them when they sleep so that as soon as they wake up they can chew them to sweeten their morning breath. It is slightly intoxicating, and has euphoric effects (*mufarriḥ*) upon its chewers (Ibn Baṭṭūṭa, *Riḥla* 124). In *Kanz* recipes, it must have been used dried in dishes and pickles, but more often in digestive drinks and aromatic compounds.

tūtyā (توتيا) tutty, finely powdered impure zinc oxide, which in *Kanz* recipes 660 and 663 is only used in deodorants (*dawāʾ ʿaraq*).

tūtyā marāzibī (توتيا مرازبي) tutty, which looks like delicate white thin sheets, as described by al-Anṭākī, *Tadhkira* 106. He adds that the pharmacists call it *shaqfa* (شقفة). Al-Bīrūnī, *Ṣaydana* 120, compares it to eggshells, and says it is the best.

ʿūd (عود) aloeswood, dark resinous heartwood of *Aquilaria* and *Gyrinops* trees in Southeast Asia. The best wood is described as blackish, heavy, bright, bitter and aromatic.

Due to its bitter and acrid taste, *ʿūd* is added in very small amounts to dishes like sweets. However, it is most useful when used as incense for general purposes, as well as in the kitchen to infuse foods and utensils with its aromatic smoke. Its dry and hot properties render it effective in medicinal preparations, which aid digestion, curb excess in phlegm, relieve asthma symptoms, and improve coitus (al-Anṭākī, *Tadhkira* 265).

Before burning the chips for incense, they are first soaked in water, or steamed in a kind of double boiler, which al-Nuwayrī describes in *Nihāyat al-arab* xii 21. Moistened aloeswood is called *ʿūd ṭarī* (عود طري) and *ʿūd nayʾ* (عود نيء).

ʿūd Hindī (عود هندي), also called *ʿūd Mandalī* (مندلي) Indian aloeswood, said to be the best of all varieties of aloeswood and the most expensive. A variety of it, called *qāmirūnī* (قامروني), is brought from a mountainous region in India, called Qāmirūn. However, some say, *qāmirūn* is the name of the tree from which the wood is taken. It is very moist, black, and heavy. It sinks when put in water (al-Nuwayrī, *Nihāyat al-arab* xii 17–8). In *Kanz* recipes, it is used in aromatic preparations and incense, as well as in handwashing compounds, digestives, and pills to sweeten the breath. Its bitter aroma is appreciated as it was said to discourage generating lice in the clothes, unlike the sweeter varieties (see below).

ʿūd Qamārī (عود قماري) excellent aloeswood of Khmer, in southeast of India, which is described as a huge and prosperous kingdom (al-Wardī, *Kharīdat al-ʿajāʾib* 36). The best quality was said to be black, dense, and moist, and continues burning for a good while. In *Kanz* recipes, it is used in deodorants, incense, and perfumed powders.

ʿūd Qāqullī (عود قاقلّي) Javanese aloeswood, named after the seacoast city named Qāqulla (Ibn Baṭṭūṭa, *Riḥla* 313). It is good quality, moist, sweet and aromatic, and keeps clothes smelling nice for a good while. However, at the end of its burning it might give off an unpleasant aroma; therefore, it should be put out before it reaches this point. Even though it might look like *Qamārī* aloeswood, it is in fact a lesser variety, but still good (al-Nuwayrī, *Nihāyat al-arab* xii 17–8). In *Kanz* recipes, it is used in smoking olives, in preparations to treat nausea, distillations, and incense.

ʿuṣārāt (عصارات) juices of herbs extracted by pounding them in a mortar and squeezing out the liquid.

ʿuṣfur (عصفر) *Carthamus tinctorius* (S) safflower. The seeds of the flower are called *qurṭum*, see entry above. Crushed safflower is called *abū mulayḥ* (أبو مليح). The flower is often compared to saffron, and is sometimes given as a substitute for it, even though it lacks its flavor and subtle scent (see *Kanz* recipe 174). Its yellow dye is more intense than that of saffron. It is added to meat dishes to work as a tenderizer.

Medicinally, it is used as a diuretic. The seeds have the power to expel wind, increase semen, and improve the voice. The flower and the seeds must be taken in moderation; otherwise, they induce drowsiness and spoil digestion (Ibn al-Bayṭār, *al-Jāmiʿ* iii 170, iv 259).

ushna (أُشنة) usnea, a variety of lichen. See *shayba* (شيبة) above.

ushnān ʿaṣāfīrī (أشنان عصافيري) pure and mild white potash, called *ʿaṣāfīrī* because it looks like sparrows' droppings, also called *ushnān Fārisī* (أشنان فارسي). It is the mildest of all potash varieties. In *Kanz* recipe 456, it is one of the ingredients included in a preparation for nausea. See glossary 11 below, s.v. *ushnān* 2.

ushturghāz (أشترغاز) *Alhagi maurorum* (S) alhagi. The name *ushturghāz* is said to be Persian for 'camel thorns' (شوك الجمال), also known as *al-marīr* (المرير), and *zanjabīl al-ʿajam* (زنجبيل العجم) Persian ginger. Its rhizome is like *anjudhān* (asafetida rhizome), albeit smaller, softer in texture, sharper in taste, with no resin (Ibn al-Bayṭār, *al-Jāmiʿ* i 48–9; al-Anṭākī, *Tadhkira* 51).

ushturghāz mukhallal (أشترغاز مخلل) pickled *ushturghāz*. With its heating properties, it can aid digestion and strengthen the top gate of the stomach.

khall al-ushturghāz (خل الاشترغاز) vinegar flavored with *ushturghāz* was believed to whet the appetite and purge and strengthen the stomach (Ibn al-Bayṭār, *al-Jāmiʿ* i 48).

waral (ورل) pl. *awrāl* (أورال) monitor lizard, whose generic name *Varanus* is derived from the Arabic. Al-Anṭākī, *Tadhkira* 212, says that it is like *saqanqūr* (see entry *milḥ saqanqūr* above), and adds that most of what is found and used in Egypt is in fact *waral*. For invigorating coitus, the males are particularly sought after. All parts of the creature were deemed beneficial, especially their fat and meat. They help women gain weight, even when applied topically. As al-Anṭākī, *Tadhkira* 371, explains, putting slices of its meat on whatever part of the body needs it, such as the hips, will enlarge them tremendously.

waraq al-Qumārī (ورق القُماري), also known as *qāt* (قات) and *qat* (قت)[19] *Catha edulis* (S) khat. They are bay-like leaves that are chewed, like betel (*tunbul*). They are brought from Qumr in east Africa (Comoros Islands). In *Kanz* recipe 654, it is used in an aromatic oil preparation.

Most medieval sources are not quite clear on what it is. They know it as a chewed leaf with a pleasant aroma, and say it is betel (*tunbul*). However, Ibn al-Bayṭār, *al-Jāmiʿ* i 182, is quite clear on this: "It is wrong to think that betel leaves are the same as the leaves available to us today, which are like bay leaves in shape and aroma, and which herbalists in Basra call *waraq al-Qumārī* because they are brought from a country called Qumr."

ward (ورد) roses, used extensively in distillations. Fresh ones are valued for their pleasant refreshing aroma; and the dried ones, especially their petals (*waraq al-ward*) and rosebuds (*azrār al-ward*), are used in cooking dishes and making aromatic preparations. Their hypanthia (*aqmāʿ*) are usually discarded. The *Kanz* includes recipes for storing fresh roses and using them when out of season (such as recipe 742).

We come across a variety of roses in *Kanz* recipes:

ward aḥmar (ورد أحمر) red roses, used fresh (*ṭarī*) in *Kanz* recipe 695.

ward aḥmar ʿIrāqī (ورد أحمر عراقي) red roses grown in Iraq. In *Kanz* recipe 367 they are used dried (*yābis*).

19 This is its name in Yemen (al-Malik al-Muẓaffar, *al-Muʿtamad* 423). Some medieval botanists identify khat as *fiṣfiṣa* (فصفصة), but this is incorrect. Al-Anṭākī, *Tadhkira* 275, identifies *fiṣfiṣa* with *raṭba* (رطبة), and adds that its Egyptian name is *birsīm* (برسيم), which is alfalfa. In addition, *Kanz* recipe 691 uses *raṭba* to dye distilled water green, which indeed applies more to the chlorophyll-rich alfalfa.

ward ʿĀṣimī (ورد عاصمي) mountain variety of white roses, named after al-ʿAwāṣim, the mountainous province in northeastern Syria between Aleppo and Antioch; it was praised for the quality of its air, water, and abundance of crops (Yāqūt al-Ḥamawī *Muʿjam al-buldān* 182).

ward baladī (ورد بلدي) *Rosa damascene* (S) roses grown locally in Egypt, pink and intensely fragrant, also known as *ward Jūrī*, see below.

ward Dimashqī (ورد دمشقي) Rosa damascene (S) damask rose, also known as *ward Jūrī*, see below.

ward Jūrī (ورد جوري) *Rosa damascene* (S) intensely fragrant pink roses, with lots of thorns, named after Jūr, a village in Shiraz in southeastern Persia, famous for its fertility and fruit orchards. It is also known as *ward Dimashqī* and *ward Shāmī* (see below). The roses are used extensively for distilling rosewater and rose oil (*duhn al-ward*).

ward naqī al-bayāḍ (ورد نقي البياض) pure white roses.

ward Nuṣaybīnī (ورد نصيبيني) roses named after Nusaybin, a city in upper Mesopotamia, now the Turkish province of Mardin. The area was renowned for its orchards and gardens. Roses named after it are typically pinkish, although white roses of Nusaybin are also mentioned in one of *Kanz*'s recipes (DK, appendix 40, p. 377)

ward Shāmī (ورد شامي) *Rosa damascene* (S) Levantine rose, more commonly known in English as damask rose, renowned for its fine fragrance. It is medium pink, with relatively small flowers, which grow in groups.

ward yābis (ورد يابس) dried roses.

wars (ورس) turmeric (*kurkum*), based on al-Anṭākī, *Tadhkira* 371, who points out that this is how it is identified in Egypt, see *kurkum* above.[20]

yāsamīn (ياسمين) *Jasminum officinale* (S) white jasmine. With its hot and dry properties, it was deemed beneficial in relieving headaches, breaking down phlegm, opening obstructions, and driving out dense winds. It induces feelings of euphoria, it is an aphrodisiac, and when mixed with wine, even in small amounts, it causes extreme intoxication.

full (فلّ) *Jasminum sambac* (S) double-flowered jasmine, brought to Egypt from Yemen.

---

20 There are some conflicting reports of this plant, its description, and which parts of it are used. However, it is known and appreciated for its saffron-like yellow dye and healing properties. Ghālib, *al-Mawsūʿa*, s.v. ورس, identifies it as the Ceylon cornel tree (*Memecylon tinctorium*).

yāsamīn aṣfar (ياسمين أصفر) *Jasminum humile* (S) yellow jasmine, from which *duhn al-zanbaq* (دهن الزنبق) 'jasmine oil' is extracted (al-Anṭākī, *Tadhkira* 373).

zabād (زباد)[21] civet musk, aromatic secretion of the perineal gland of *sinnawr al-zabād* (سنّور الزباد) African civet cat (*Civettictis civetta*). It is abundant in Abyssinia (Ethiopia), and feeds on fresh spikenard. The animals are kept in iron cages, and when petted, they secrete *zabād* from glands between their thighs, which is collected with silver or gold spoons.

The best *zabād* looks reddish black and glistens. When rubbed between the fingers, it does not feel sticky, and even when washed, the fingers will still smell of its aroma. The worst looks white.

Its properties are hot and moist, and it was deemed effective in treating nausea, and soothing heartburn. When taken with saffron, it removes anxiety, mania, melancholy, and induces euphoria. It also eases labor. In *Kanz* recipes in chapter 21, it is used in aromatic preparations, oils, scented powders, and incense.

zaʿfarān (زعفران) *Crocus sativus* (S) saffron, used in the recipes for its vibrant color and delicate flavor. When ground, it is easily adulterated with safflower mixed with sugar. Genuine saffron threads are described as brittle but not crumbly, and when steeped in liquid, they should dye the fingers almost immediately.

It was believed to be good for the digestive and respiratory systems; however, it may cause a loss of appetite. It also has the power to stimulate coitus and ease labor. It strengthens the potency of alcoholic drinks when added to them, and drinkers were said to experience euphoria. The most one should use is 1 *dirham* (3 grams/ ½ teaspoon), as overdosing might prove fatal. See al-Anṭākī, *Tadhkira* 196; al-Malik al-Muẓaffar, *al-Muʿtamad* 247–9.

zaʿfarān Janawī (زعفران جنوي) good-quality saffron imported from Genoa.

zaʿfarān shaʿr (زعفران شعر) saffron threads.

zahr nāranj (زهر نارنج), also called *qiddāḥ nāranj* (قداح نارنج) orange blossoms, see *nāranj* in glossary 7 above.

zahr qaranful (زهر قرنفل) carnation flower, also occurs as *zahr* (زهر) and *qaranful Shāmī* (قرنفل شامي) Levantine carnation. It is valued for its aroma, especially in making scented preparations. Al-Anṭākī says it grows everywhere, and people like to stick it behind their ears. With its hot and dry properties, it is used medicinally to

---

21 In the *Kanz* recipes, it is often copied as *zabada*, which must be an Egyptian variant of the name. It also occurs in Ibn al-Ukhuwwa, *Maʿālim al-qurba*, fol. 82v, where it is clearly vocalized as such.

dissipate dense winds, and relieve colic when ingested as a drink. It can also bring sleep to insomniacs.

zanjabīl (زنجبيل) *Zingiber officinale* (S) ginger, described as having a pleasant smell but not particularly aromatic. It has a sharp taste, which is as hot as black pepper. Ginger is usually used in its dried form because it rots quickly. The Chinese variety is praised for its white color and the numerous number of its rhizome nodes, that look like hands (*kufūf*). It is at its best preserved in brine or honey, called *zanjabīl murabbā* (زنجبيل مربّى), which is touted as an aphrodisiac and digestive. It prevents fish from inducing thirst if it is eaten with it (al-Anṭākī, *Tadhkira* 198).

ʿirq zanjabīl (عرق زنجبيل) dried ginger root.

ʿuṣfūr al-zanjabīl (عصفور الزنجبيل) node of the ginger rhizome.

zaʿtar (زعتر) *Thymus* (S) thyme, of which there are many varieties. In sources other than the *Kanz*, the name also occurs as *saʿtar* (سعتر) and *ṣaʿtar* (صعتر). When fresh thyme is required in the recipes, it is referred to as *raṭb*. The following varieties of thyme are mentioned in the *Kanz*:

zaʿtar Maghribī (زعتر مغربي) *Thymus maroccanus* (S) Moroccan thyme, a wild variety. It is most probably the same as *zaʿtar jabalī* (زعتر جبلي) mountain thyme, also called *arīghānūn* (أريغانون). Its properties are stronger and more pungent than the cultivated ones. This herb is mentioned only once in the *Kanz* (recipe 255), in a condiment made with salt-cured anchovies, in which another Moroccan wild mountain herb (*karāwiya Maghribiyya* 'Moroccan caraway') is required.

zaʿtar Shāmī (زعتر شامي) *Origanum syriacum* (S) Levantine thyme, also known as 'true thyme.' It is harvested in the wild, and is stronger than the cultivated varieties. It is used in *Kanz* recipes dealing with yogurt condiments, which are often specialties of the mountainous regions.

When *zaʿtar* is mentioned in *Kanz* recipes and the type is not specified, it is to be assumed that the cultivated variety (*bustānī*) is intended. It is rendered more suitable for cooking purposes, as it is less sharp and pungent that the wild ones. Thyme was said to be good for the stomach, as it aids digestion, and diffuses gastric winds. It soothes toothaches, heals ailing gums, improves memory, and sharpens eyesight.

zinjār (زنجار) verdigris, a green powder obtained by rusting copper, used to color soap green

zir ward (زر ورد) rosebuds, see *ward* above.

zir ward ʿIrāqī (زر ورد عراقي) Iraqi rosebuds.
zir ward Mizzī (زر ورد مِزّي) dried rosebuds from Mizza, a district in Damascus.

ẓufr (ظفر), also called *ẓufr al-ṭīb* (ظفر الطيب) pl. *aẓfār al-ṭīb* (أظفار الطيب) *Unguis odoratus* (S) onycha, which are the aromatic horny operculums from certain groups of sea snails, such as those belonging to the family of muricidae, Arabic *dawlaʿ* (دولع). Ibn al-Bayṭār, *al-Jāmiʿ* i 54, mentions several sea varieties, some red and others black, found along the shores between the Indian Ocean and the Red Sea. All these varieties were deemed good enough to be added to aromatic preparations of incense.

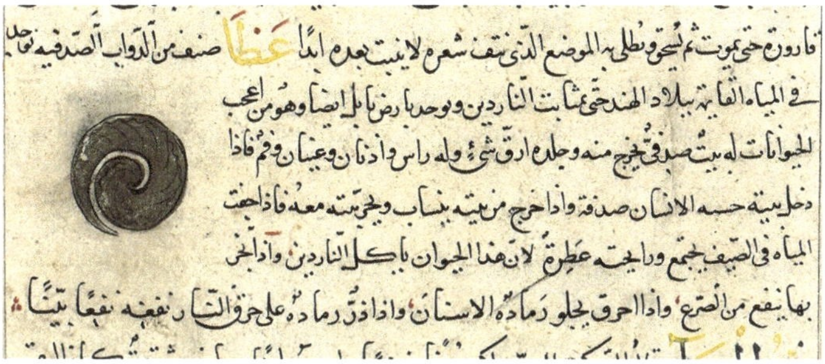

FIGURE 72 Ẓufr (*onycha*), *F1954.71v, Muḥammad al-Qazwīnī,* ʿAjāʾib al-makhlūqāt, *detail (Freer Gallery of Art and Arthur M. Sackler Gallery, Smithsonian Institution, Washington,* DC*: Purchase—Charles Lang Freer Endowment*).

zunjufr (زنجفر) vermilion, dark red pigments made from crushed cinnabar, which is a bright red mineral consisting of mercury sulfide. In *Kanz* recipe 642, it is used to color soap dark red (*aḥmar ʿamīq*) or carnelian red (*aḥmar ʿaqīqī*).

zurunbād (زرنباد) *Zingiber zerumbet* (S) a variety of ginger, called bitter ginger, shampoo ginger, and pinecone ginger. Another name for it is *ʿirq al-kāfūr* (عِرق الكافور), see entry above.

9. Kitchen and Cooking Implements, and Culinary Techniques and Terms

9.1 Kitchen and Cooking Implements

akhthāʾ al-baqar (أخثاء البقر) cow dung, used in *Kanz* recipe 723 to make a vessel, after mixing it with white clay. These vessels were used to store fresh grapes, so that they may be used out of season.

awānī (أواني) sg. *āniya* (آنية) vessels (in general).

bardī (بردي) papyrus, of which a small piece is thrown into the pot to absorb smoky odors or excess salt (*Kanz*, p. 70).

barniyya (برنية) pl. *barānī* (براني) wide-mouthed jar, short necked, like *qaṭramīz*, see entry below.

> ***barniyya billawr*** (برنية بللور) wide-mouthed crystal jar.
>
> ***barniyya ghayr madhūna*** (برنية غير مدهونة) unglazed wide-mouthed jar.
>
> ***barniyya khaḍrāʾ*** (برنية خضراء), *barniyya ghaḍār* (برنية غضار) green-glazed wide-mouthed jar.
>
> ***barniyya madhūna*** (برنية مدهونة) glazed wide-mouthed jar. See *wiʿāʾ madhūn* below.
>
> ***barniyya qīshānī*** (برنية قيشاني) wide-mouthed ceramic jar.
>
> ***barniyya ṣīnī*** (برنية صيني) wide-mouthed porcelain jar.
>
> ***barniyya zujāj*** (برنية زجاج) wide-mouthed glass jar.

bāṭiya (باطية) large wide bowl, commonly made of glass, used as a punch bowl, filled with wine for drinkers to scoop from (*Lisān al-ʿArab*, s.v. بطا). It was also used in the kitchen, as in *Kanz* recipe 564, for keeping seasoned olives.

bilāṭa (بلاطة) large flat tile.

biṭāna (بطانة) lining cloth, usually made of cotton, used in *Kanz* recipe 725 to keep the dates moist throughout the night.

burma (برمة) pl. *birām* (برام) soapstone pot.

bustūqa (بستوقة) large earthenware jar.

 | DOI 10.1163/9789004349919_035

FIGURE 73
Bustūqa, *F1902.190, c. twelfth century (Freer Gallery of Art and Arthur M. Sackler Gallery, Smithsonian Institution, Washington, DC: Gift of Charles Lang Freer).*

dabba (دبّة) pl. *dibāb* (دِباب) and *dibb* (دِبّ) earthenware vessels in which salt-cured fish were preserved. Fish preserved this way are called *samak dibb* (سمك دب).

dakshāb (دكشاب) paddle-like stirring utensil.

dakshāb khashab mabrūm (دكشاب خشب مبروم) cylindrical wooden rod, used for stirring a pot, as in *Kanz* recipe 357.

dann (دنّ) large earthenware cask.

dast (دست) large brass pot, also called *ṭinjīr* (طنجير). A *dast* could also be made of soapstone (*birām*) or earthenware (*fakhkhār*).

dast laṭīf (دست لطيف) small brass pot.

dast nuḥās aḥmar (دست نحاس احمر) large red copper pot.

dast nuḥās mu'annak (دست نحاس مؤنّك) tinned copper pot, primarily used for making thick puddings (*ḥalāwāt*), because it can stand the rigorous stirring and beating involved in making them.

faḥm (فحم) charcoal, preferred for fueling the fire because it does not generate smoke.

fakhkhār (فخار) earthenware pots and utensils.

fayyāsha (فياشة) a glass bottle with a flattish wide lower part and a long neck, used in *Kanz* recipe 671 for a potpourri preparation.

FIGURE 74
Fayyāsha, *long-necked glass bottle, c. fourteenth century, 36.33 (MET NY—Purchase, Joseph Pulitzer Bequest, 1936).*

fihr (فهر) round stone that fits into the hand; it was used for crushing spices and the like.

furn (فرن) brick oven, built with a front opening and a flat horizontal baking surface. The fuel was first lighted on the side of the baking chamber. When it was heated, the ashes were swept away and the baking could begin.[1] Alternatively, fuel was put in another chamber below the baking surface. A *furn* was used for baking bread and pastries, as well as casserole dishes prepared in wide clay vessels called *ṭājin*, and the like.

1 See Hassan and Hill, *Islamic Technology* 219.

Besides the commercially operated *furns*, it is safe to assume that this type of oven, albeit simpler and smaller, was available at the time the *Kanz* was written for the use of private households, at least outside the city centers and in rural areas. Writing about the daily lives of Egyptian peasants, the seventeenth-century al-Shirbīnī, *Hazz al-quḥūf* 194, mentions that household *furns* were used for baking the daily bread and simmering pots of beans, as well as baking modest fish and pigeon *ṭājins*. In Lane's account of nineteenth-century Egyptian customs and manners, a detailed description is given of a peasant's household in Lower Egypt, where the oven is said to "resemble ... a wide bench or seat, and is about breast-high: it is constructed of brick and mud; the roof arched within, and flat on the top."[2]

Some *Kanz* recipes direct the cook to put the prepared food in the *furn*, which might or might not be the household oven; it was probably not critical where it was done. Such instances occur in recipes for baking bread and simple cookies. Similarly, in recipes like 386, where a jarful of parsnips with water is left overnight in the oven to cook slowly, and in 185 and 199, where onions are baked.

However, directions to take the prepared food to the *furn* or bring it back point to the use of a commercial *furn*. This was more often used in baking fish dishes, as in recipes 236, 240, and 241; and for some delicate pastries that needed more controlled heat, as in recipes 271, and 272.

farrān (فران) professional baker who operates the *furn*.

ghaḍāra (غضارة) pl. *ghaḍā'ir* (غضائر) deep dish bowl, usually green-glazed. Imported Chinese *ghaḍā'ir* are described as white, transparent, and opaque (al-Qazwīnī, *Āthār al-bilād* 20). Al-Bīrūnī, *al-Jamāhir* 97, says the best of the Chinese ones are apricot-colored, thin, and clear.

ghirbāl (غربال) round sieve which looks like a tambourine. Sometimes, soft chunky ingredients are mashed by pressing and passing them through it.

ghirbāl al-daqīq (غربال الدقيق) fine-meshed flour sieve.

ghirbāl ḍayyiq (غربال ضيق) fine-meshed sieve.

ghirbāl qamḥī (غربال قمحي) ***ghirbāl al-qamḥ*** (غربال القمح) sieve for sifting whole wheat flour, used in *Kanz* recipe 238 to sift crushed sumac; and DK, appendix 54, p. 380, to press the mashed boiled chickpeas through it.

---

2 Lane, *Manners and Customs* 21. Even though the two sources cited are a few centuries later than the *Kanz*, it is unlikely that such basic activities and age-old apparatuses should be any different from those available during the era of our book, and even much earlier.

ḥajar ṣandal (حجر صندل), also called *khumāhān* (خماهان), and *ḥajar ḥadīdī* (حجر حديدي) ironstone, and *ṣandal ḥadīdī* (صندل حديدي) iron sandalwood. It is a very hard reddish stone used for grating and crushing aromatics, such as aloeswood mixed with rosewater.

ḥantam (حنتم) green-glazed jar.

ḥaṣīra (حصيرة) pl. *ḥuṣr* (حصر) reed mats, also woven with date palm fronds.

ḥaṭab (حطب) firewood, such as dry olive wood and oak (*sindiyān*). These were preferred because they do not emit smoke profusely. In addition, burning the dried stems of date clusters (*ʿarājīn al-balaḥ*) produced a very pleasant aroma (Ibn Mubārak Shāh, *Zahr al-ḥadīqa*, fol. 1v). Trees with milky saps (*ashjār yatūʿiyya/tuyūʿiyya*) and oleander (*diflā*) were better avoided.

> ***ḥaṭab raṭb*** (حطب رطب) wood which is not fully dry. It produces a lot of smoke, and must be avoided.

hāwan (هاون) mortar; made of stone (*ḥajar*) for meat, and of copper (*nuḥās*) for spices.

FIGURE 75
Bronze mortar, c. twelfth century, 13.81 (MET NY—Rogers Fund, 1907).

ḥuqq (حُقّ) pl. *aḥqāq* (أحقاق) rounded bowl made of carved wood, ivory, or other materials. It was made in different sizes.

> ***ḥuqq Yemenī*** (حق يمني) rounded Yemeni soapstone bowl.

ḥuzmat kibrīt (حزمة كبريت) bunch of sulfur-tipped matchsticks, used in the medieval kitchens to light fire by striking them on a granite stone. In *Kanz* recipe 64, their tips are discarded and the remaining sticks are added to a pot of rice pudding to get rid of the smoke odors that the food picked up.

Apparently, the matchsticks were usually kept in bundles. In one of al-Ḥarīrī's *Maqāmāt* 99 (*al-Maqāma al-najrāniyya*), there is a riddle about *ṭāqat kibrīt* (طاقة كبريت) 'bundle of sulfured matchsticks.' From Ibn Waḥshiyya, *al-Filāḥa* i 519, we learn that the slender stems of *qinnab* (hemp, *Cannabis sativa*), were cut into shorter pieces, and their tips were then dipped in sulfur, and left to dry, which was important as damp sulfur does not ignite easily.[3]

ijjāna (إجانة) large tub.

inā' ḥantam (إناء حنتم) green-glazed vessel.

inā' muzaffat (إناء مزفت) pitched vessel, used for storing pickles, and keeping fresh fruits good to eat out of season.

inā' muzajjaj (إناء مزجج) glazed ceramic vessel.

inā' rashshāḥ (إناء رشاح) unglazed earthenware vessel that allows for filtration.

inā' ṣīnī (إناء صيني) china vessel.

inā' zujāj (إناء زجاج) glass vessel.

inbīq (إنبيق) pl. *anābīq* (أنابيق) alembic, used in distilling liquids, see ***taṣʿīd*** in glossary 9.2 below.

isṭām (إسطام) large paddle-like iron spatula.

jābūniyya (جابونية) a piece of silk cloth, used in recipes to sift ingredients into fine powder. This may have been an Indian variety of silk. The word could have been named after Jāba, a kingdom in India (Ibn Khurradādhbih, *al-Masālik* 4, 15, 16).

jafna (جفنة) pl. *jifān* (جفان) large, wide serving bowl, said to be large enough to feed ten people (*Lisān al-ʿArab*, s.v. صحف).

jafnat al-ʿajīn (جفنة العجين) large, wide bowl used for kneading bread dough.

jām (جام) serving platter, like *ṭabaq* (طبق).

jamjā (جمجا) ladle.[4]

jamra (جمرة) small live piece of coal.

jarra (جرّة) pl. *jirār* (جرار), also known as *qulla* (قُلّة), pl. *qulal* (قلل), earthenware jar. The term *jarra* was also used as a measuring unit, the capacity of which is approx. 27 pints.

---

3 As specified in the *ḥisba* manuals for market inspectors. See Ibn al-Ukhuwwa, *Maʿālim al-qurba*, fol. 156r.

4 The word occurs as *jamjā* in the thirteenth-century Turkish-Arabic dictionary *Kitāb al-Idrāk li-lisān al-atrāk* 61 by Abū Ḥayyān al-Andalusī, who spent most of his life in Cairo, and died there in 1344. In Steingass *Persian/English Dictionary*, the word occurs as *chamcha*, which is still used in Iraq today to designate the same tool.

jarra bayḍāʾ (جرة بيضاء) white unglazed earthenware jar.
jarra fakhkhār (جرة فخار) earthenware jar.

jāwlī (جاولي) winnowing fan made of reeds. It is a Persian loan word,[5] the Arabic for which is *minsaf*. It was used to take boiled raviolis out of a pot, as it allows liquid to drip down easily. See *Kanz* recipe 37.

jirāb (جراب) traveling sack or bag used for storing provisions.

jurn (جرن) stone mortar, made from a hollowed-out stone.

jurn al-fuqqāʿī (جرن الفقاعي) large stone mortar used by beer-makers to crush grains, herbs, and spices. It was also rendered safe to grind acid and liquid ingredients. Table sauces, called *ṣulṣ*, were crushed and smoothed into the consistency of ointment by using it (see *Kanz* recipes in chapter 16). See Ibn Abī Uṣaybiʿa, *ʿUyūn al-anbāʾ* 394.
jurn ḥajar (جرن حجر) stone mortar.
jurn rukhām (جرن رخام) marble mortar.

kaʿb (كعب) reeds, used to support grape vines.

kāghad (كاغد) paper made from the fiber of the hemp plant, *Cannabis sativa* (S). See Ibn Waḥshiyya, *al-Filāḥa* i 520. Paper made from *bardī* (بردي) *Cyperus papyrus* (S) is called *qirṭās* (قرطاس).

kānūn (كانون) brazier, generally used as a portable heating and cooking device. *Kanz* recipe 568, which deals with smoking olives, calls for a somewhat elaborate *kānūn*, which might have looked like a box with a perforated top and a door. During the smoking process the door is kept closed.

khābiya (خابية) pl. *khawābī* (خوابي) large cylindrical earthenware jar with a tapered rounded bottom.

khābiya ghayr rashshāḥa (خابية غير رشاحة) large non-porous earthenware jar.

kharīṭa (خريطة) pl. *kharāʾiṭ* (خرائط) linen drawstring bags.

khayṭ qinnab (خيط قنب) hemp thread.

khirqa (خرقة) piece of cloth.

khirqa kattān (خرقة كتان) piece of linen cloth.
khirqa maṣrūra (خرقة مصرورة) piece of cloth tied into a bundle to enclose herbs and spices.

---

5 The word occurs as *chāwlī* in Steingass *Persian/English Dictionary*.

khirqa muhalhala (خرقة مهلهلة) loosely woven piece of fabric.
khirqa rafīʿa (خرقة رفيعة) piece of thin fabric.

khiwān (خوان) cutting board; but may also designate a low table on which the dishes served along with bread are spread.
khizānat al-ḥammām (خزانة الحمام) hot-water tank of the bath.
khūṣ (خوص) date palm fronds. The fibrous sheath of the frond is called ***līfa*** (ليفة). Both parts are resistant to mold.
kibrīt (كبريت) sulfur, see *ḥuzmat kibrīt* above.
kisāʾ (كساء) may designate many kinds of outer garments, usually made of thick fabrics, such as wool.
kīzān ḍāriya (كيزان ضارية) jars with traces of previous fermentation. See *Kanz* recipes 407 and 418, for directions on how to do this with new jars.
kurūsh (كروش) cases made of dried tripe, used for storing.
kūz (كوز) pl. *kīzān* (كيزان) earthenware drinking cup or pitcher, made glazed and unglazed, ranging in size from small to large.[6] The larger ones were used for brewing *fuqqāʿ* (foamy beer). See glossary 1, s.v. *kūz*.

FIGURE 76
Kūz (*earthenware drinking cup*), *c. thirteenth century, 28.72* (*MET NY—Rogers Fund, 1928*).

6 Porcelain varieties are also reported in al-Maqrīzī, *Ittiʿāẓ al-ḥunafā* 195; and ones made of *qaṣdīr* 'tin' are mentioned in Ibn al-Ukhuwwa, *Maʿālim al-qurba* fol. 80r.

mahabbāt (مهبّات) breeze catchers, which were shafts built in walls for ventilation and to cool indoor temperatures. Cooks found such cool, ventilated places ideal for drying ingredients, as in *Kanz* recipe DK, appendix 75, p. 409. It is also known as *bādhāhīj* (باذاهيج) or *bādhāhanj* (باذاهنج). ʿAbd al-Laṭīf al-Baghdādī, *Riḥla* 113, says that almost all houses in Egypt have them, and they are efficiently built.

maḥḥāra (محارة) shell used for scooping cream (called *bīrāf*), in *Kanz* recipe 507.

mājūr (ماجور) pl. *mawājīr* (مواجير) large wide-mouthed tub, usually made of earthenware, used for making dough.

mājūr fakhkhār (ماجور فخار) large wide-mouthed earthenware tub.

maṭara (مطرة), ***maṭṭār*** (مطّار) pl. *muṭr* (مُطر) stone jar, with bulging belly and a narrow mouth, as described in *Kanz* recipe 501. Recipe 256 describes it as being made of stone (*maṭr ḥajarī*), a non-porous material. They were commonly used for keeping oil or salt-cured small fish (*samak mumallaḥ*), as described by Dozy, *Takmilat al-maʿājim* 1461. From *Kanz* recipes 256, 501, 520, and 521, we learn that they were also handy for keeping cheese, pickles, fermented condiments and sauces.

maṭara ḥajar (مطرة حجر) stone jar, see description above. The stone from which such jars were made is *marū* (flint stone), described as a thin, white, and bright stone (*Lisān al-ʿArab*, s.v. مرو).

midaqqa khashab (مدقة خشب) wooden pestle, used in *Kanz* recipe 312 to fold the gourd paste.

mifrāk (مفراك) wooden blender/mixer used in *Kanz* recipe (DK appendix 73, p. 415) to blend ingredients into one mass. It was made in different lengths with a variety of heads. It must have been a traditional kitchen utensil exclusive to Egypt. The corresponding recipe in the Aleppan *Wuṣla* ii 486 uses a *fihr* instead, which is a rounded stone that fits into the hand and was usually used for crushing spices and the like.

The main part of the *mifrāk* is a rounded dowel. A small rounded wooden stick is inserted closer to its end, to make it look like the letter T. Alternatively, a couple of the small sticks are inserted crosswise; some have several rows of such crosses; or the dowel may end with a crescent-like piece of wood. It was operated by rolling the handle back and forth between the open palms of the hand.

The above information is based on the excavated *mifrāk*s of ancient Egypt and the ones still used today in the Sudan and Upper Egypt (Ṣaʿīd), where, for instance, the traditional stew of *mulūkhiyya* (Jew's mallow) or the okra dish *wīka* (ويكة) are mashed with a *mifrāk*. The fragrant and durable wood of acacia (*sanṭ*, *ṭalḥ*) was used to make this kitchen utensil.

FIGURE 77 *Ancient Egyptian* mifrāk (*hand mixer/blender*), *Graeco-Roman Period* (*Bibliotheca Alexandrina Antiquities Museum*).
PHOTO BY CHRISTOPH GERIGK.

mighrafa (مغرفة) ladle, also known as *kifkīr* (كفكير), as it occurs in al-Hurawī, *Baḥr al-jawāhir* 346.

mighrafa muqaʿʿara (مغرفة مقعرة) concave ladle.
mighrafa mushabbaka (مغرفة مشبكة) latticed ladle.
mighrafa muthaqqaba (مغرفة مثقبة) perforated ladle.

miḥakka (محكة) flat stone grater. Ingredients were put on a flattish stone (called a saddle quern), and grated and crushed with a handheld rubbing stone. The rotary hand-quern was called a *mijrasha* (مجرشة).

mihrāsh (مهراش) dialectical vocalization of *mihrās* (مهراس), a pestle made of a large, heavy long stone or hardwood, used to crush seeds and the like.

milʿaqa (ملعقة), sometimes written as *miʿlaqa* (معلقة) spoon.

FIGURE 78
Silver spoons, fourteenth century, 07. 228.85a, b, d (MET NY—*Rogers Fund, 1907*).

milqāṭ (ملقاط), also called *minqāsh* (منقاش) tweezers.
mindīl (منديل) piece of cloth.
miqlā (مقلى) pl. *maqālī* (مقالي) frying pan, used for making *qalāyā* (fried dishes) and *nawāshif* (dry meat dishes, i.e., sauceless dishes). The frying pan for making omelets (*ʿujaj*) is described as round, with high sides, and a long handle like that of a ladle.

miqlā wāsiʿ (مقلى واسع) wide, level-bottomed frying pan.

miqṭaʿ mudawwar (مقطع مدور) round cookie cutter.
mirjal (مرجل) large copper cauldron.
misalla (مسلة) long needle.
miʿṣarat māʾ al-laymūn (معصرة ماء الليمون) lemon juicer.
miṣfāt (مصفاة) colander.
miʾzar (مئزر) woolen cloth worn as a wrapper or a loincloth. In the *Kanz*, it is used to wrap pieces of not-so-fresh meat, which has been dusted with fenugreek. Wrapped thus, the meat was parboiled to freshen it up.

miʾzar ṣūf ṣafīq (مئزر صوف صفيق) tightly woven woolen wrapper cloth, used to extract mulberry juice in *Kanz* recipe 736.

munkhul ḥuwwārā (منخل حوارى) sieve used for sifting fine white flour.
munkhul ṣafīq (منخل صفيق) fine-meshed sieve.
munkhul shaʿr (منخل شعر) fine-meshed sieve made of animal hair.
munkhul wāsiʿ (منخل واسع) sieve with relatively large holes.
muqaʿʿara (مقعّرة) concave ladle.
muzammala (مزمّلة) water-cooling green-glazed crock; used for cooling drinking water. It was wrapped with a coarse cloth, such as sackcloth or canvas, and the space between the cloth and the vessel was filled with hay, which served as insulation.
naʿʿāra Zabadāniyya (نعّارة زبدانية) earthenware bucket, named after al-Zabadānī, a city in southwest Syria.
nāfikh nafsihi (نافخ نفسه), also called *nāfikh rūḥihi* (نافخ روحه) a portable self-ventilating stove. As described by al-Khawārizmī, *Mafātīḥ al-ʿulūm* 48, it had three legs with a base and sides all pierced with holes. In the middle was a clay platform, under which a coal fire was lit, and on top of which the cooking pot was put. This stove was placed in an open area, exposed to the breeze so that the coals continued burning gently with the circulation of the air. Luckily, *Kanz* recipe 149 provides more details. The stove was first put in an enclosed place (موضع مقفل). The coals were put in it, and a single burning coal (*jamra*) was placed in the middle; as soon as the coals became hot, the cooking would start.

This kind of cooking device seems to have been relatively popular among the affluent. It was especially handy when a dish needed to cook on low heat for many hours without spoiling its flavor, as in al-Warrāq's recipe for cooking a delicate green stew (see English trans. *Annals* 283–4); or when the cooking pot itself was made of glass, as in *Kanz* recipe 149. The stove was also used in the distilling process (*taṣʿīd*) because it allowed for prolonged low-heat burning of the coals.

nishārat al-arz (نشارة الارز) sawdust of a male cedar tree, used in *Kanz* recipe 723, which deals with the process of storing fresh grapes.

nishārat al-ṣāj (نشارة الصاج) sawdust of teak wood, see above.

qadaḥ (قدح) may designate a drinking glass, available in different sizes, the smallest of which was said to be enough for two people. In wine-drinking contexts, it refers to an empty glass, whereas *ka's* (كأس) is a filled glass. A large *qadaḥ* was used for collecting drawn milk, and a small one was used as a cup. It can also be used for keeping butter (Dozy, *Takmilat al-maʿājim* 1167). *Qadaḥ* is also an Egyptian weight measure (see glossary 13 below).

FIGURE 79
Glass drinking beaker with fish motif, fourteenth century, 17.190.1039 (MET NY—Gift of J. Pierpont Morgan, 1917).

qafaṣ (قفص) cage-like basket made with stems of date palm fronds.
qālab (قالب) mold or cutter.
qār (قار) bitumen, used in *Kanz* recipe 723, which deals with storing fresh grapes. The tips of the stems of grape bunches are sealed with it.
qarʿa (قرعة) cucurbit, used along with *inbīq* (alembic) to distill liquids, see *taṣʿīd* in glossary 9.2 below.
qarāṭīs (قراطيس) sg. *qirṭās* (قرطاس) sheets of paper made from *bardī* (بردي) *Cyperus papyrus* (S).
qarrāba (قرّابة) large flagon with two handles and a spout (Steingass *Persian/English Dictionary*), used for fermenting wine in the sun over long periods of time.
qārūra (قارورة) flask or bottle made of glass.

> ***qārūra wāsiʿat al-fam*** (قارورة واسعة الفم) wide-mouthed flask or bottle.

qaṣʿa (قصعة) large, wide serving bowl.
qaṣʿa muqaʿʿara (قصعة مقعّرة) large, wide rounded bowl.
qaṣab (قصب) reeds.
qaṣaba Fārisiyya (قصبة فارسية), also called *ʿūd nushshāb* (عود نشاب) thick, long, and sturdy reed, used in the *Kanz* to make cannoli-like pastries; and in recipe 722, to store fresh rosebuds in their cavities.
qaṣriyya (قصرية) large, wide earthenware tub.
qaṭramīz (قطرميز) wide-mouthed jar, like *barniyya*, see entry above.

> ***qaṭramīz muzajjaj*** (قطرميز مزجج) wide-mouthed glazed ceramic jar.
> ***qaṭramīz zujāj*** (قطرميز زجاج) wide-mouthed glass jar.

qidr (قدر) pot.

> ***qidr birām*** (قدر برام) soapstone pot.
> ***qidr fakhkhār*** (قدر فخار) earthenware pot.
> ***qidr fakhkhār madhūn*** (قدر فخار مدهون) glazed earthenware pot.
> ***qidr nuḥās mubayyaḍ*** (قدر نحاس مبيض) tinned-copper pot.
> ***qidr Zabadānī*** (قدر زبداني), earthenware pot named after Zabadānī, a city in southwest Syria. Zabadānī was particularly famous for its rosewater and good pottery, used locally and exported.
> ***qidr zujāj*** (قدر زجاج) cooking pot made of glass, described and used in *Kanz* recipe 149.

qinnīna (قنينة) pl. *qanānī* (قناني) glass bottle. It may also designate a bowl made of tightly woven esparto grass, or a rounded wooden bowl, carved out of a date palm trunk (Dozy, *Takmilat al-maʿājim* 1265); see *Kanz* recipes 384 and 400.

FIGURE 80
Glass bottle, twelve century, 2005.318 (MET NY—Purchase, Friends of Islamic Art Gifts, 2005).

qirba (قربة) pl. *qirab* (قِرب) large leather bags for keeping liquids.
qirma (قرمة) piece of wood, usually a slice of a tree trunk, used for cutting meat.
quffa (قفة) large round basket made of woven date palm fronds.
raḥāʾ (رحاء) more commonly written as ***raḥā*** (رحى) quern.
ramād al-karam (رماد الكرم) ashes of grapevine wood, used in *Kanz* recipe 723, which deals with the process of storing fresh grapes.
rāwūq (راووق) large strainer, used mostly for straining wine into smaller vessels.
riqq (رق) pl. *riqāq* (رقاق) thin sheet of leather. Vessels made with this kind of leather were also called *riqāq*.
saffūd (سفّود) spit. *Saffūt* is a dialectical variant.

saffūt ḥadīd (سفّود حديد) iron skewer.

ṣaḥfa (صحفة) wide, shallow serving bowl.
ṣaḥn (صحن) pl. *aṣḥun* (أصحن) plate.

ṣaḥn mabsūṭ (صحن مبسوط) flat plate.

FIGURE 81
Flat glass plate, fourteenth century, 91.1.1533 (MET NY—Edward C. Moore Collection, Bequest of Edward C. Moore, 1891).

FIGURE 82
Plate, twelfth century, 1979.210 (MET NY—Purchase, Gifts in memory of Richard Ettinghausen, 1979).

ṣallāya (صلّاية) wide stone slab, used with a large stone (*fihr*) to crush spices and aromatics.

saṭl (سطل) brass kettle with handles, used for baking cookies in the *tannūr* (open-topped, bell-shaped clay oven). The handles made it easy for the baker to lower the pan and take it out of the oven.

sāṭūr (ساطور) cleaver.

ṣawānī (صواني) sg. *ṣīniyya* (صينية) metal serving trays. The expensive ones were made of shiny gold or silver, beautifully etched and inlaid with other metals.
shaqaf (شقف) broken fragments of pottery, used in *Kanz* recipe 580 to weigh down the pickling onions in a jar.
shaʿriyya (شعرية) cloth loosely woven with horsehair.
shawbaq (شوبق), also called *suwayq* (سويق) rolling pin.
shawka (شوكة) large pitchfork.
shubbāka (شباكة) lattice, used in *Kanz* recipe 724, which deals with the process of reviving stored fresh rosebuds.
sikkīn (سكين) knife.

> ***sikkīn ḥādd*** (سكين حادّ) sharp knife.
> ***sikkīn ghayr ḥadīd*** (سكين غير حديد) blunt knife used in *Kanz* recipe 374 to cut quinces into pieces. It was believed that sharp steel knives should be avoided in cutting it because they cause it to lose its juice fast. (al-ʿUmarī, *Masālik*, xx 201; al-Anṭākī, *Tadhkira* 208).
> ***sikkīn khashab*** (سكين خشب) wooden knife, required in *Kanz* recipe 360 to carefully extract the juice vesicles of citron pulp without breaking them.
> ***sikkīn raqīq*** (سكين رقيق) knife with a thin blade used to slice meat.

sukurdān (سكردان) large tray, on which varieties of delicious small dishes were served as appetizers and snacks, such as seasoned olives, pickles, and dairy condiments. They were served during social gatherings, including those involving drinking alcoholic beverages. The word is said to be a combination of the Arabic *sukr* (سكر) imbibing alcoholic drinks, and the Persian *dān* (دان) vessel (al-Khafājī, *Shifāʾ al-ghalīl* 182).[7]
suwayq (سويق) rolling pin for pastries, also called *shawbaq* (شوبق).
ṭabaq (طبق) large platter, tray, or large flat-bottomed pan.

> ***ṭabaq bi-shafa*** (طبق بشفة) pan with a lip used for baking a pie shell in *Kanz* recipe 276. The lip made handling the pan easier without breaking the pie shell.

---

7 We find a good example of what might have been loaded on such trays in al-Ḥajjār, *Kitāb al-Ḥarb al-maʿshūq* 102, who mentions many varieties of pickles, cured olives and capers, lemon preserved in salt, varieties of salted fish dishes, such as Alexandrian *ṣaḥna*, salt-cured sparrows and fishes of batoids (*rāi*), anchovies (*ṣīr*), tilapia (*balṭī*), and Nile carp (*labīs*).

FIGURE 83
Lipped pan, fourteenth century, 07.228.84 (MET NY—Rogers Fund, 1907).

ṭabaq mushabbak (طبق مشبك) latticed tray woven with date palm fronds, used as a strainer.

ṭabaq nuḥās (طبق نحاس) flat-bottomed copper pan or tray, used for baking delicate cookies and pastries.

ṭabaq nuḥās mubayyaḍ (طبق نحاس مبيض) flat-bottomed tinned-copper pan or tray.

ṭāḥūn (طاحون) grinder.

ṭājin (طاجن) frying pan, which was also used as a casserole pan. The best ones were made of soapstone (*birām*), and were suspended on the fire for fried dishes, or sent to the commercial *furn* 'brick oven' for baked ones.

As described in the thirteenth-century Istanbul MS of al-Warrāq's cookbook, fols 125v, 171r, it is a wide pan with low sides, either green-glazed (*ḥantam*), soapstone (*ḥajar* or *birām*), or tinned copper (*nuḥās mubayyaḍ*). In the seventeenth-century *Hazz al-quḥūf* 218, al-Shirbīnī describes the *ṭājin* as a familiar earthenware vessel, round and wide, where fish, rice, red meat, and poultry are baked in the *furn*.

ṭājin birām (طاجن برام) soapstone frying pan.

tannūr (تنّور) immobile open-topped, bell-shaped clay oven, the best of which were built with a large interior and walls of medium thickness, based on the specifications given in al-Warrāq's tenth-century Baghdadi cookbook. It had a small opening in the bottom, called *rawwāj*, which facilitated air circulation in the *tannūr*, and was used to sweep out the ashes of burnt wood. It was closed, along with the top opening, when a low fire was required; and kept open when stronger heat was needed to brown the baking foods. The *tannūr* was built outside the living quarters and the kitchen, in an open space, which faces the opposite direction of the wind, as this would help blow the smoke away from the kitchen and the house.[8]

The *tannūr* was used for baking flat breads, roasting sheep and large chunks of skewered meat, simmering jarfuls of chickpeas, and pots of stews overnight.

ṭāsa (طاسة) a metal bowl for scooping drinking water. It may also designate a large bowl in which water was cooled.

ṭasht (طشت) large shallow basin.

ṭayfūr (طيفور) bowl.

thaljiyya (ثلجية) an earthenware jar to cool water, the lower part of which was buried in mud. The word is derived from *thalj* 'ice.'

tibn (تبن) straw used for burying jars of *fuqqāʿ* (beer) to allow for light fermentation, as in *Kanz* recipe 408.

tibn al-shaʿīr (تبن الشعير) barley straw used in the process of storing fresh fruits, as in *Kanz* recipes 749 and 750.

ṭīn (طين) clay, which had many uses in the medieval kitchen. In the *Kanz*, it is used to clean pots and remove their greasy odors. The boiling pots were sometimes sealed with it, so that they function as steam pots. Clay was also added to handwashing compounds to help remove grease from fingers and mouth.

ṭīn abyaḍ (طين ابيض) white clay, a variety of *ṭīn ḥurr* (طين حر) pure clay, used in *ushnān* (handwashing preparations). It was deemed effective in removing grease from hands and mouth because it does not dissolve quickly in water, and when it does, it becomes sticky (see *Kanz* recipes in chapter 20). In *Kanz* recipe 723, white clay is mixed with cow dung to make the vessels used to store fresh dates, so that they stay good beyond their season.

ṭīn abyaḍ Makkī (طين ابيض مكي) white clay of Mecca, a variety of *ṭīn ḥurr* (see above). It can be crushed easily, and does not contain any stones or sand. It was also known as *ṭīn Ḥijzāī* (طين حجازي) from the western region of the Arabian Peninsula. In Andalusia, it was called *al-khiyār* (الخيار) i.e. 'the best' (al-ʿUmarī, *Masālik* xxii 178). It was a valued commodity that visitors to Mecca used to take back home with them. It was mainly used in handwashing compounds (*ushnān*), as in *Kanz* recipe DK, appendix 63, p. 395.

ṭīn aḥmar (طين احمر) red clay used in *Kanz* recipe 746 to store fresh vegetables.

ṭīn ḥurr (طين حر), also called *ṭīn quḥḥ* (طين قح) pure red clay free of sand and stones, and very low in organic matter. The best was said to be Egyptian,

---

8 See al-Warrāq, English trans. *Annals* 88–9.

obtained from the basin of the Nile River, after it floods and the soil settles (al-Anṭākī, *Tadhkira* 255). In *Kanz* recipes 721 and 746, it is used in storing fresh roses and vegetables.

ṭīn murammal (طين مرمّل) sandy clay soil, used in *Kanz* recipe 750, to store fresh lemons by keeping them between its layers.

turāb aḥmar ḥayy (تراب احمر حي) raw red soil in its natural state; it was washed to get rid of all impurities, and then used to make earthenware pottery.

turāb al-fawākhīr (تراب الفواخير) red soil, which was taken raw from the river banks, and then washed to eliminate its impurities, and used to make pottery utensils.

ublūja (ابلوجة) conical mold, usually used to make the characteristic shape of sugar cones, called *sukkar al-abālīj*.

ʿūd al-dhukār (عود الذكار) sticks from *dhukār* (ذكار) *Ficus carica sylvestris* (S) caprifig, the male, pollen-bearing wild variety of the common fig, used to pollinate the edible fig (see entry in glossary 7 above).

The sticks were left in large jars of the fermenting sauce of *murrī*, and were used to stir the mix for several months, as in *Kanz* recipe 150. Wood of wild fig trees, including *jummayz* (see glossary 7 above, s.v. *tīn*) was known for its resistance to rot, and antiseptic properties.

ʿūd nushshāb (عود نشاب) thick, long, and sturdy reeds.

ʿulba (علبة) pl. *ʿulab* (علب) wooden or leather boxes, often used by travelers for storing provisions.

waqūd (وقود), also occurs as *waqīd* (وقيد) fuel, such as *faḥm* 'coal,' which was deemed the cleanest and the best fuel. Dried firewood (*ḥaṭab*), which is not moist or sappy, was recommended, as it does not produce a lot of smoke.

wiʿāʾ madhūn (وعاء مدهون) glazed vessel. Following the rules set by the market inspectors, the potters were required to apply three coats of glaze, so that the vessel was completely saturated with it. If they cheated by only applying it once or twice, the glaze would peel off and spoil the vessel used to hold liquids and foods (Ibn Bassām, *Nihāyat al-rutba* 363).

wiʿāʾ muzaffat (وعاء مزفت) vessel coated on the inside with black resinous pitch (*zift*), so that it becomes non-porous. In *Kanz* recipes, such vessels were used in making pickles and keeping fresh fruits for use out of season.

zibdiyya (زبدية) pl. *zabādī* (زبادي) bowls. Typically, they were porcelain bowls imported from China, made in different sizes and colors. However, *zabādī* were also made by the local potters. From Ibn al-Ukhuwwa, *Maʿālim al-qurba*, fol. 148r, we learn that these bowls were supposed to be made with crushed stones and not sand. However, sand could be used in making bowls used for serving wedding feasts.[9] In addition, the potters were required to glaze the *zabādī* thoroughly (see *wiʿāʾ madhūn* above);

9 These would be comparable to today's disposable containers.

otherwise, the glaze would flake and peel off when the bowl was used to carry liquids or foods.

zibdiyya qīshānī (زبدية قيشاني) ceramic bowl.
zibdiyya ṣīnī (زبدية صيني) china bowl.

FIGURE 84
Set of bowls, fourteenth century, 11.61.1 (MET NY—Rogers Fund, 1911).

FIGURE 85
Zibdiyya *(bowl), c. fourteenth century, F1905.277 (Freer Gallery of Art and Arthur M. Sackler Gallery, Smithsonian Institution, Washington, DC: Gift of Charles Lang Freer).*

9.2 Culinary Techniques and Terms

abrāj shamsiyya (أبراج شمسية) sg. *burj* (برج) astrological signs, beginning with *burj al-kabsh* (Aries) and ending with *burj al-ḥūt* (Pisces).

ʿafan (عفن) mold (in the context of bread).

ʿafiṣ (عفص) astringent.

ʿajir (عجر), also occurs as *fujj* (فجّ) unripe (in the context of vegetables and fruits).

āla (آلة) a general term that designates ingredients, especially herbs and spices, needed to make a specific dish. It is a conveniently brief term used by cooks describing their dishes, counting on common knowledge. The term *ḥawāʾij* (حوائج) is used similarly.

ʿalik (علك) chewy.

ʿarraka (عرّك) of dough, the act of pressing and rubbing it while kneading it; this was done more effectively by working it with the heel of the hand.

ashqar (أشقر) light gold, in relation to toasting flour.

aṭbikha (أطبخة), also *ṭabīkh* (طبيخ) dishes cooked in liquid, such as stew.

> ***maṭbūkh marratayn*** (مطبوخ مرّتين) twice cooked in liquid, by draining the boiled food, and cooking it again with a new batch of water.

aṭʿima dasima (أطعمة دسمة) greasy foods.

bakhkhara (بخّر) perfume with the smoke of aromatics, like aloeswood and ambergris.

baladī (بلدي) adj. domestic, indigenous, local; opposite of *majlūb* (مجلوب) brought from other places;[10] *baladī* (n.) Indigene, local. Cf. *ʿawām* (عوام) which designates the social class of the common folk.

banādiq (بنادق) small balls, which look like *bunduq* (hazelnuts).

bāqa (باقة) a bunch (in the context of herbs).

bayyata (بيّت) keeping, or leaving (something) overnight.

bukhār (بخار) steam; *bakhara* (بخّر) to steam.

dahin (دَهِن) fatty.

dakhkhana (دخّن) develop undesirable smoky odors (in the context of cooking food).

dallaka (دلّك) rub and press.

daqq mujarrash (دق مجرّش) coarsely ground (e.g., grains).

daqqa (دقّ) pound in a mortar.

dasam (دسَم) grease of cooking meat and animal fat.

---

10 These terms are used in this sense by Ibn Riḍwān, *Dafʿ maḍār al-abdān* (in Dols, *Medieval Islamic Medicine*, Arabic text 8).

dharra (ذرّ) sprinkle.
falaja (فلج) split, cleave.
farraka (فرّك) crumble between fingers (in the context of dried herbs).
fumm (فم), also *dufʿa* (دفعة) doing something once.

> ***fummayn*** (فمّين) ***dufʿatayn*** (دفعتين) doing something twice.
> ***thalāth afmām*** (ثلاث افمام) *thalāth dufūʿ* (ثلاث دفوع) doing something three times.

ghaḍḍ (غضّ) fresh and tender (e.g., herbs).
ghalā (غلا), also *fāra* (فار) boil, n. *ghalayān* (غليان), *fawarān* (فوران). As described by al-Nābulusī, *ʿAlam al-malāḥa* 270, prolonged boiling was maintained by removing the pot from the fire for a while and then returning it. This was repeated until the right consistency of the boiling liquid was reached. Number of boils was often used to measure cooking time.

> ***ghalā ʿashr ghalwāt*** (غلا عشر غلوات) boil ten times.
> ***ghalā ghalwatayn*** (غلا غلوتين) boil twice.
> ***thalāth ghalyāt*** (ثلاث غليات) three boils.

gharafa (غرف) to ladle.
gharbala (غربل) sift, from which *ghirbāl* (غربال) 'sieve' is derived.
ḥalaq (حلق) ring-shaped (cookies).
ḥalqa (حلقة) snippet (of herbs).
ḥāmiḍ (حامض) sour.
ḥār (حار) hot (temperature); spicy hot (taste); having hot elemental properties.
ḥarābil (حرابل) sg. *ḥarbala* (حربلة) small, thin cylinders, pellets. The medieval dictionaries do not have an entry for this word. I spotted it in fourteenth-century Ibn Mankalī, *Uns al-malā bi-waḥsh al-falā* 49, where instructions are given for making *ḥarābil* used to get rid of house mice. In today's North African dialects, *ḥarābil* is used to designate the cylindrical shape.
ḥarraka (حرّك) stir.
ḥawāʾij (حوائج) the spices and seasonings needed, or the ones usually used. It is a versatile term used extensively in the *Kanz*. Sometimes the reference is to ingredients mentioned earlier in the recipe. However, in several places, the writer of the recipe assumes that the cook will know what to use; this sometimes forces modern readers to guess what may be intended.

> ***ḥawwāj*** (حوّاج) synonymous with *ʿaṭṭār* (عطّار) seller of herbs and spices (i.e., *ḥawāʾij*).

ḥirrīf (حرّيف) sharp and pungent (taste).

> ***ḥirrīfiyya*** (حريفية), also *ḥarāfa* (حرافة) sharpness and pungency.

ḥulw (حلو) not bitter (in terms of gourds and turnips); fine-tasting and free of salinity (in relation to water); sweet (taste).

ḥuzma (حزمة) bunch (of herbs or sticks).

jamr layyin (جمر ليّن) embers, smoldering fire of coals or firewood.

jamuda (جَمُدَ) lit., 'freeze'; set (in relation to cooking eggs).

jarrada (جرّد) scrape with a knife (of carrots or gourds).

> ***jurāda*** (جرادة) n. the resulting grated flesh.
> ***majrūd*** (مجرود) adj. grated.

jarza (جرزة) ***jazza*** (جزّة) a snip (of herbs).

khalaʿa (خلع) enhance (fat) by heating it up with some spice seeds.

khalṭa (خلطة) mixture of ingredients.

khuwayṭa (خويطة) small, thin cylinder.

lahīb (لهيب) flames of fire.

laṭīf (لطيف) mild (taste); small (utensil).

latta (لتّ) rub and mix fat into dry ingredients; cf. *bassa* (بسّ), which is suggestive of more vigorous mixing. The general verb for kneading is *ʿajana* (عجن).

lāẓī (لاظي) dense (texture, such as that of bread).

māʾ fātir (ماء فاتر) lukewarm water.

madhūn (مدهون) glazed (roasting lamb).

madqūq (مدقوق) pounded (in relation to nuts and meat).

> ***madqūq nāʿim*** (مدقوق ناعم) finely pounded.

madshūsh (مدشوش), also *marḍūḍ* (مرضوض) coarsely crushed. *Dashīsha* (دشيشة), which is soup made with coarsely crushed grains, is derived from this term.

maḥshī (محشي) depending on the prepared foods, this may designate dishes smothered or dressed in seasoned sauce, such as *Kanz* recipes 82, 233, 234, 545. Alternatively, it may designate stuffed foods, such as *Kanz* recipes 118, 172, 281.

maʿjūn (معجون) having a paste-like consistency.

makbūs (مكبوس) packed and preserved in brine or vinegar, i.e., pickled (vegetables, eggs, or fruits).

makhrūṭ (مخروط) (herbs and leaf vegetables) stripped from their stems. It may also designate fine chopping.

māliḥ (مالح) too salty.

mamlūḥ (مملوح) salted, as needed.

mamzūj (ممزوج), also *mumazzaj* (ممزج) seasoned with *mizāj*, which is a vinegar-based liquid sauce (used in relation to cooking food, such as meat roast). See *Kanz* recipe 126.

maqlī (مقلي) fried.

marasa (مرس) press and mash between the fingers.

maratha (مرث), also *marata* (مرت), and *marada* (مرد), see *marasa* above.

marḍūḍ (مرضوض) bruised, coarsely crushed (nuts).

mariq (مَرِق) of food cooked in liquid, soupy in consistency (like *maraq*); opposite of *yābis* (يابس) or *nāshif* (ناشف).

marraqa (مرّق) adding liquid to (cooking food).

masḥūq (مسحوق) crushed.

maska laṭīfa (مسكة لطيفة) nicely firm to the touch, al dente (boiled vegetables and fruits).

maṣlūq (مسلوق) boiled.

maṭḥūn (مطحون) finely crushed.

milḥ muʿtadil (ملح معتدل) salt added in a moderate amount.

milḥ ẓāhir (ملح ظاهر) salt, which has been added to make food taste noticeably salty, as in *Kanz* recipe 1, for salted cookies.

mizāj (مزاج) vinegar-based liquid mix used to season cooking dishes. See *mamzūj* above.

muʿarraq (معرّق) lit., 'sweated' (meat), descriptive of an initial stage of cooking meat cut into pieces. See *taʿrīq* below.

muḥabbab (محبب) lumpy.

mujawhar (مجوهر) roasted (chickpeas). See *ḥimmaṣ* in glossary 12.

mukabbab (مكبب) grilled on open fire (e.g., meat); see *shawī* below.

mukaffan (مكفن) lit., 'shrouded,' used to designate wrapped foods, as in *Kanz* recipe 37; or dishes smothered in sauce, as in *Kanz* recipes 241, 247, 254.

mukhallal (مخلل) ***makbūs*** (مكبوس) pickled.

muntin (منتن) does not smell good (in relation to raw meat).

muqaʿʿar (مقعّر) concave (utensils).

murabbā (مربّى) adj., depending on context, it may designate fruits and vegetables preserved as jam or pickled; it may describe a solution in which finely crushed ingredients, such as almonds, are blended and dissolved; or it may simply describe an ingredient soaked in liquid.

murr (مرّ) bitter.

muṣaffā (مصفّى) strained (cooked grains and pulses).

musawwas (مسوّس) insect-damaged (spices).

mushabbak (مشبّك) latticed.

mustaqṭar (مستقطر) distilled (liquids).

muʿtadil al-muzūza (معتدل المزوزة) balanced (taste, in terms of sweetness and sourness).

muṭayyab (مطيّب) enhanced (food), by seasoning with spices, aromatics, herbs, etc.; scented, perfumed.

muzz (مزّ) adj. sweet-sour (taste); ***mazāza*** (مزازة) n.
nār layyina (نار لينة), ***nār hādiʾa*** (نار هادئة) low heat, slow burning fire.
nassala (نسّل) loosened into threads (in relation to boiled chicken).
niṣf ṣalqa (نصف صلقة) half-boiled, parboiled (vegetables or meat).
qaraṣa (قرص) become ***qarīṣ*** (قريص) very sour; or gel and become like aspic.
qiwām (قوام) consistency.
qurṣ (قُرْص) pl. *quraṣ* (قُرَص) disc; round patty (in relation to meat).
rafīʿ (رفيع) excellent quality (ingredients).
raghwa (رغوة) foam, mostly used to designate the frothy layer, which accumulates on the surface of the boiling meat and needs to be skimmed off.
rāʾiq (رائق) clear (liquid).
rakhṣa (رخصة) fresh and tender (vegetables).
ramād sukhn (رماد سُخن) hot ashes.
rāq (راق), also *sāf* (ساف) layer.
raqīq (رقيق) thin (in consistency).
rawwaḥa (روّح) keeping bread in the air for a short while to aerate.
rayyaḥa (ريّح) descriptive of raw meat when it loses its freshness.
rīm (ريم) scum of boiling food.
sāʿa (ساعة) an hour.

> ***kull sāʿa*** (كل ساعة), lit., 'every hour,' i.e., every now and then.
> ***sāʿa baʿd sāʿa*** (ساعة بعد ساعة) lit., 'one hour after another,' i.e., continue doing something for a while.
> ***sāʿa jayyida*** (ساعة جيدة) for a full hour.
> ***suwayʿa laṭīfa*** (ساعة لطيفة) for a short while.

sāʿa falakiyya (ساعة فلكية), also called *sāʿa mustawiya* (ساعة مستوية) an 'equal hour,' which follows the equal hour timing system. In this system, the 24 hours of the day are divided into 15 equal periods (*darajāt*); each period contains 4 minutes.

The other system, which was also followed, measures the 24 hours of the day by the 'unequal hour,' called *sāʿa miʿwajja* (ساعة معوجة), also known as *sāʿa zamāniyya* (ساعة زمانية), and *sāʿa zawāliyya* (ساعة زوالية). Sunrise marks the beginning of the day, which is 12 hours. Sunset begins the night, which is also 12 hours. The length of the hours varies with the changing seasons.

sādhaj (ساذج) plain, neither sweet nor sour (dishes).
sāf (ساف) layer.
ṣalīq (صليق) boiled food.
salqa (سلقة) a boil.

> ***niṣf salqa*** (نصف سلقة) boil food until half done.
> ***rubʿ salqa*** (ربع سلقة) boil food to a quarter of its doneness.

samaṭa (سمط) scald (a slaughtered animal) in boiling water to remove hair, wool, feathers, and clean tripe; scald (almonds) so that their skins may be easily removed.
sharāʾiḥ (شرائح) thin slices.
shawābīr (شوابير) thin small pieces, which may be triangular, cut out of thinly rolled-out paste or dough; or anything thin and flat. The term may have derived from the Persian *shāhpar*, which is the longest feather in a bird's wing. In medieval times, it was the name of a hairstyle: the front hair was parted in the middle, and pushed to both sides, like the spread-out wings of a bird.
shawī (شوي), ***shay*** (شي) roasting meat—whole animals, large chunks, or skewered pieces—in an enclosed place, such as a clay oven (*tannūr*), or a brick oven (*furn*). They help keep the meat nice and moist, see for instance al-Warrāq's chapter 89.

Grilling on an open fire, such as that of a brazier, is called *takbīb* (تكبيب); v. كبب, from which the adj. *mukabbab* (مكبب) and n. *kabāb* (كباب) derive.

mashwī (مشوي) roasted (meat). See above.

ṣighār mustaṭīl (صغار مستطيل) (food) cut into small thin strips, i.e., julienned.
sukhn (سُخْن), also *ḥārr* (حار) hot (liquid).
ṭabkh bayn nārayn (طبخ بين نارين) lit., 'cooking between two fires,' an ancient technique used to brown the bottom and the top of the dish without having to use an oven.

In a nineteenth-century Lebanese cookbook, cooking between two fires is described as keeping a pot on low heat, with lighted coals put all over its tight lid (Sarkīs, *Ustādh al-ṭabbākhīn*).[11] Recipe 111 in the *Kanz*, for a sweet bread pudding called *um nārayn* (lit., 'mother of two fires,' 'having two fires') does not give such details. Perhaps it was too familiar to mention. However, absence of any directions for stirring the pot and the name of the dish do indeed point to this way of cooking.

Interestingly, in al-Ibshīhī, *Mustaṭraf* 180, we learn that a reheated stew is called *bint nārayn* (daughter of two fires), and it was not deemed proper to serve it at the tables of the affluent.
tabkhīr (تبخير) infusing (food or utensils) with aromatic smoke of ambergris and aloeswood.
tadakhkhana (تدخّن) pick up a disagreeable smoky taste (in relation to cooking food).
tafih (تفِه) insipid (taste).
tafṣīl (تفصيل) disjointing (meat).
taghayyara (تغيّر) no longer fresh (in terms of raw meat).

---

11 The page is not numbered. A similar cooking technique was frequently used in the late sixteenth-century Safavid cookbook *Madatolhayat* (The substance of life) by Nurollah, head chef of the Persian king, Shah Abbas I. For instance, a delicate pastry dish of stuffed layered thin sheets of dough, called *buraq*, was cooked in a tray that was covered with another tray and positioned with fire on top and underneath it (12).

taghmīr (تغمير) keeping fruits fresh by submerging them in liquids. However, submersion was sometimes performed by burying the fruit in the ground, a technique also known as *ṭamr* (طمر). See *Kanz*, chapter 23, for recipes.
ṭaḥana (طحن) crush
tahdaʾ (تهدأ) settles (in relation to a cooking pot).

tihtidī (تهتدي) (a cooking pot that) stops boiling and starts to simmer.

tamāthīl (تماثيل) figurines.
ṭamr (طمر) submerging by burying in the ground, as a means of preserving and storing fresh fruits and vegetables. See *taghmīr* above.
ṭāqa (طاقة) stem or sprig (of herbs).
taqṭīr (تقطير) distillation, also called *taṣʿīd* (تصعيد), see entry below.
ṭarī (طري) fresh (used in relation to fruits and vegetables).
taʿrīq (تعريق) 'sweating' (meat), descriptive of an initial stage of cooking cut-up meat. It is first fried in rendered sheep-tail fat (*alya*) mixed with sesame oil (*shayraj*), along with some herbs like cumin and coriander. The meat would release its juices first (i.e., sweat), which would then evaporate in the process, and let meat brown in the fat. This method was specifically recommended in *Kanz*, chapter 1, as necessary with dishes of *sawādhij* (plain meat stews) and *qalāyā* (fried meat), as it helps remove the unpleasant greasy odor of meat (*zafar*) before it is boiled.
tarushsh (ترشّ) sprinkle (liquid).
tashāhīr (تشاهير) garnishes and decorations for dishes.
tashayyaṭa (تشيّط), also occurs as *tadakhkhana* (تدخن) burn with a stench (in the context of cooking food).
tashrīḥ (تشريح) slicing (e.g., meat) thinly.
ṭashṭasha (طشطش) splatter (e.g., cooking oil).
tashwīr (تشوير) garnishing.
taṣʿīd (تصعيد) distillation, also called *taqṭīr* (تقطير). The *Kanz* includes many recipes for making perfumed distilled waters (recipes 684–715). The distillation apparatus includes *qarʿa* 'cucurbit' and *inbīq* 'alembic.' The liquid to be distilled is put in the lower part, which is the cucurbit, and is left to heat up. The distillate forms in the alembic and passes through the delivering tube to the *qābila* 'receiving vessel.'

The best way to distill the essences of delicate ingredients, such as flowers, is to heat the liquid in the cucurbit not by placing it on direct heat but by means of steam as follows: A huge pot with water is placed on the burning fire—preferably fueled by coal, and the cucurbit is placed above the water level, to let it heat with steam.
taṣwīl (تصويل) cleaning (legumes and grains) by putting them in several changes of water and stirring them so that all impurities rise to the surface and can be discarded.

tatbīl (تتبيل) n. ***tabbala*** (تبّل) v. seasoning food with spices (*tawābil*). See also *yutabbal* below.
tatjīn (تطجين) braising, which involves an initial stage of frying the meat and then letting it slowly cook in a small amount of liquid; also used to designate frying in general.
thufl (ثفل) dregs.
tudaffa' (تُدفأ) warm (food).
tufattal (تفتّل) roll (dough) between the fingers.
tunaqqaʿ (تنقّع) souse food in liquid, such as vinegar.
yudās bi-l-arjul (يداس بالارجل) stomp on (unripe grapes) to facilitate the extraction of their juice.
yadhbul (يذبل) wilt (vegetables).
yafishsh (يفشّ) shrivel (e.g., garlic).
yaghlī (يغلي) boil (cooking liquids); ferment (drinks).

> ***yaghlī ghalwāt*** (يغلي غلوات), ***yaghlī ghalyāt*** (يغلي غليات) boil a lot.
> ***yaghlī ghalwatayn*** (يغلي غلوتين) boil twice. The cooking pot is removed from the fire until boiling subsides, and then it is returned to resume boiling.[12] Number of boils was often used to measure cooking time.

yahda' (يهدأ) simmer and settle (food in a cooking pot).
yaḥdhū al-lisān (يحذو اللسان) tongue-biting (taste).
yaḥmarr (يحمر) brown (in the context of frying or baking food).
yaḥmuḍ (يحمض) turn sour (e.g., milk).
yakhtamir (يختمر) ferment.
ya'khuḍ qiwāmahu (يأخذ قوامه) thicken and reach the expected consistency (e.g., boiled syrup).
yaksir al-mulūḥa (يكسر الملوحة) make (food) less salty.
yalʿabu fī duhnihi (يلعب في دهنه) lit., 'plays in its oil.' when all liquids evaporate (from frying meat) and only the fat remains.
yaʿluq (يعلق) stick to the pot (of cooking food).
yanʿaqid (ينعقد), also *yaʿqud* (يعقد) thicken (e.g., syrup).
yanbaʿ wa yashuqq (ينبع ويشق) start bubbling, which is a sign of the beginning of fermentation (of a liquid).
yanbut (ينبت) soften and fluff (e.g., of cooking rice); sprout (grains).
yarshaḥ (يرشح) filter through (e.g., liquids in jars).
yashuqq (يشقّ) reach the point of a rolling boil.

---

12 See, for instance, al-Nābulusī, *ʿAlam al-malāḥa* 270, where he describes how to reduce syrups used for making drinks.

yaskun fawarānuhu (يسكن فورانه) stop boiling vigorously.
yastawī (يستوي) done and ready to eat.
yatadabbaq (يتدبق) thicken and become too sticky (e.g., boiling syrup).
yatafarfar (يتفرفر) (dough that) does not bind, and hence crumbles.
yataharra' (يتهرأ) (cooking food that) falls apart.
yatala''ab (يتلعّب) derives from *lu'āb* (لعاب) 'saliva.' For example, okra stew becomes viscous due to the viscid substances inside it.
yataqaddad (يتقدد) become dry in texture (in relation to drying food, such as sliced fruits and meat). The dried food is called *qadīd* (قديد).
yataṣarraf (يتصرف) steam dissipates (from hot bread).
yatashaḍḍā (يتشظّى) splinter (in relation to bones).
yatawarrad (يتورّد) nicely brown (in relation to frying meat or chicken); turn golden brown (in relation to baking pastries).
yu'affin (يعفّن)[13] mold (in relation to bread). Makers of fermented sauces and condiments deliberately cause bread to mold and use it in making them. See *Kanz* recipe 500, where instructions are given to cause bread to mold.
yu'allaq (يعلّق) suspend (a pot) above the fire.

FIGURE 86 *Pot suspended on the fire, detail from Arabic Translation of* De Materia Medica *of Dioscorides, 13.152.6 (MET NY—Rogers Fund, 1913).*

13 Most of the following entries beginning with *yu-* are actions in the passive form, some are in the third-person singular, as given in *Kanz* recipes. My explanations use the infinitive form.

yubaqqal (يبقّل), also *yunabbat* (يُنبّت) sprout (wheat or barley).
yubkhash (يبخش) make a dent (in dough) with the finger.
yubsaṭ (يبسط) spread food in a thin layer.
yudāf (يداف) dissolve a dry ingredient into liquid to let it release its essence, as when saffron is mixed with water to bring out its color.
yudarr (يدرّ) dialectical vocalization for ***yudharr*** (يذرّ) sprinkle.
yudhāb (يذاب) dissolve.
yudīr (يدير) stir (a cooking pot) in a circular movement.
yuḍrab (يضرب) beat (cooking puddings) with a large spatula, called *isṭām*.
yufarraṭ (يفرّط) strip off the petals (of roses); release the seeds from the pith (of pomegranates).
yufrak (يفرك) rub and crush (dried herbs) between the fingers; crumble.
yufram (يفرم) chop.
yufshakh (يفشخ) crack them by hitting them with a large stone (e.g., olives).
yuftaq (يفتق) allow the flavor of an ingredient to emerge by mixing it with a small amount of liquid or oil; season the sauce of a dish to enhance its flavor.
yughabbar (يغبّر) dust food, such as boiled eggs, with fine flour before frying them, as in *Kanz* recipe 172.
yughaṭṭ (يغطّ), also *yughaṭṭas* (يغطّس) dip.
yughlā (يغلى) bring (liquids) to a boil.
yughmaz (يغمز) knead with fingers only.
yughraz (يغرز) insert.
yuḥakk (يحك) grate and crush (e.g., aloeswood).
yuḥall (يحلّ) dissolve (sugar) by adding water and boiling it into syrup, which is called *ḥall* (حلّ).
yuḥammaṣ (يحمّص) dry toast (nuts or seeds); brown and crisp (fried foods).
yuḥarrak (يحرّك) stir (cooking food).

yuḥarrak muttaṣilan (يحرّك متّصلا) stir it constantly.

yujbal (يجبل) mix into porridge-like consistency; bind dry ingredients with some liquid.
yukallas (يكلس) smooth the surface of a condiment to serve it, as in *Kanz* recipe 533.
yukhaddar (يخدّر) wilt (vegetables) by keeping them in boiled water for a short while
yukhammar (يخمّر) allow (flavors) to mellow and blend by setting the dish aside for a while. Cover (food containers) with a piece of cloth, thin leather, and the like.
yukharraṭ (يخرّط) strip (vegetables and herbs) off their stems. In addition, it is also used to designate the chopping of vegetables, such as *mulūkhiyya* (Jew's mallow). For fine chopping, a special knife with two handles, called *mukharriṭa* (mezzaluna rocking knife), was used.
yukhaththar (يخثّر) thicken (liquids) with starchy ingredients.

yukhbaṣ (يخبص) stir (the cooking pudding) thoroughly until it thickens. The pudding is called *khabīṣ*.
yukhlaʿ (يخلع) improve the flavor of oil and rendered sheep-tail fat by heating them with aromatic spices, such as cinnamon, mastic, cumin, black pepper, musk, and camphor. See, for instance, *Kanz* recipe 140, and DK. appendix 4, p. 81.
yuʿlaf (يعلف) fold and mix solid ingredients into a liquid.
yulaṭṭakh (يلطّخ) smear, rub.
yumarrāgh (يمرّغ) coat (e.g., food before it is fried) with flour by rolling it in it.
yumraq (يمرق) add liquid, to thin down consistency.
yumshaq (يمشق) strip the leaves from their stems (e.g., herbs).
yunaqqā (ينقّى) picking over grains and whole spices.
yunassar (ينسّر), ***yunshar*** (ينشر) finely shred (boiled meat) with the fingers.
yunḥat (ينحت) grate (carrots, cinnamon sticks, gourds, hard cheese etc.); scrape with a knife.

> ***manḥūt raqīq*** (منحوت رقيق) adj. thinly or finely grated.

yuqarraṣ (يقرّص) shape (dough) into discs.
yuqarraṭ (يقرّط) cut into small pieces.
yuqaṭṭin (يقطّن) develop a white film on the surface (of vinegar and pickles).
yuqawwar (يقور) cut a cone out of a piece of fruit or vegetable, for instance. In *Kanz* recipe 581, the onions are prepared for pickling by cutting a cone out of the root end of each onion.
yuqtal (يقتل) descriptive of mixing ingredients, to be beaten vigorously to mix, mash, or blend well. See for instance *Kanz* recipes 182, 616.
yurabbā (يربّى) dissolve and blend (as when ground almonds are mixed with water and stirred before adding them to a boiling pot). In the *Kanz*, the verb *yudhāb* (يذاب) 'dissolve' is sometimes used instead. In another context, *yurabbā* means 'thicken,' as when a fruit juice is boiled down to thick syrup, called *rubb* (رُبّ).
yuraḍḍ (يرضّ) bruise, coarsely crush.
yurakhkhī (يرخّي) release moisture while cooking.
yuraṣṣ (يرصّ) arrange next to each other; pack tightly.
yurawwaq (يروّق) filter and make (a liquid) clear.
yusakhkhan (يسخّن) heat (a food or liquid).
yuṣawwal (يصوّل) n. *taṣwīl* (تصويل) clean (legumes or grains) by putting them in water and stirring them so that the impurities rise to the surface and can be discarded.
yushaddakh (يشدّخ) crack with a large stone or similar things (e.g., olives).
yushakhkhaṣ (يشخّص) shape food into forms, e.g., marzipan into the shape of apricots, as in *Kanz*, recipe 74.
yushaẓẓā (يشظّى) split into small splinters (e.g., aloeswood and sandalwood).
yuslā (يسلا) render (e.g., sheep-tail fat).

yuslakh (يسلخ) peel the skins (from something).
yusmaṭ (يسمط) immerse (a slaughtered sheep or chicken) briefly in boiling water to pluck the wool or feathers; briefly boil (whole almonds) in water to remove the skins.
yustaḥlab (يستحلب) extract liquid of pounded seeds and nuts by dissolving them in water first and then straining the juice.
yutabbal (يتبّل) season (dishes) with spices and herbs (*tawābil*), used synonymously with *yubazzar* (يبزّر); as in *Kanz* recipes 517 and 578. In another context, it describes dusting fish, for instance, with flour before frying it, as in recipe 228.
yuṭajjan (يطجّن) fried in a *ṭājin*, which is a frying pan (e.g., meat and vegetables); as used in the *Kanz*. More specifically, this way of cooking, *tatjīn*, is descriptive of braising disjointed poultry dishes or tender cuts of red meat, which are simmered in a lot of oil and a small amount of water with some herbs and spices, resulting in juicy fried food. See, for instance, al-Warrāq's chapter 32. The name of *ṭājin*, the dish, is derived from the cooking vessel itself, *ṭājin*; see glossary 9.1 above.
yuṭarrā (يطرّى) seasoning (cooking food) to enhance its taste.
yuṭayyab (يطيّب) improve quality, aroma, or taste of food and aromatic preparations, such as soap.
yuṭayyan (يطيّن) lit., 'seal with clay.' However, it may also be used when a cooking pot or baking pan is sealed with dough to trap in steam, as in *yuṭayyan bi-ʿajīn* (يطين بعجين).
yuṭbakh (يطبخ) cook (food) in liquid.

FIGURE 87 *Cooking in liquid, detail from Arabic translation of* De Materia Medica *of Dioscorides, thirteenth century, 57.51.21* (*MET NY—Bequest of Cora Timken Burnett, 1956*).

yuṭfā (يطفى) lit., 'extinguish,' moisten a cooking dish with vinegar or lemon juice.

yuṭḥan (يطحن), also *yuṣḥan* (يصحن) grind by crushing.

yuṭlā (يطلى) smear to coat.

zabad (زبد) foam and scum that rise to the top of the cooking pot, and need to be skimmed off.

zafar (زفر), also occurs as *zufra* (زفرة) undesirable greasy odors of foods, especially meat. It is also used to designate the froth accumulating on the surface of boiling meat, which needs to be removed. See *zabad* and *raghwa* above.

FIGURE 88
Sheep to be slaughtered for the feast of Sada, fol. 22v from Shahnama of Shah Tahmasp, *c. sixteenth century, 1970.301.2, (MET NY—Gift of Arthur A. Houghton Jr., 1970).*

10. Meat

absāriyya (ابسارية) and *bisāriyya* (بسارية), also called *balam* (بلم) *Engraulidae* (S) fresh anchovies. They look like sardines. When salt-cured, they are referred to as *ṣīr* (صير). However, the name *ṣīr* is sometimes used to refer to fresh anchovies to be cured with salt (al-Maqrīzī, *Khiṭaṭ* i 310). Al-Anṭākī, *Tadhkira* 218, says what is called *bisāriyya* in Egypt is in fact *raḍrāḍ* (رضراض), deemed the best type of fish, they inhabit clear waters with rocky sea floors. Their properties tend toward heat, more than other fishes, and they generate good blood. See *Kanz* recipes 246–7, and *ṣīr* below.

aghshiya (اغشية) membranes of red meat, which need to be removed before cooking it.

alya (الية) sheep-tail fat, a delicate moist fat highly valued by medieval cooks. To render it, it is chopped and cooked with some sesame oil. The remaining particles called *ḥumam* (حمم) are discarded. In some *Kanz* recipes this type of fat is also called *duhn* (دهن).[1]

ʿaṣāfīr (عصافير) sg. *ʿuṣfūr* (عصفور) *Passer domesticus* (S), also called *dūrī* (دوري) sparrows, associated with human habitat, in rural and urban areas. The best are the fat ones caught in winter. Their meat is hot and dry, it is highly aphrodisiac, and increases semen, especially when prepared with eggs in omelets. Those who eat sparrows are advised not to eat the bones as they may scratch the esophagus or the stomach (al-Dumayrī, *Ḥayāt al-ḥayawān* 487; al-Anṭākī, *Tadhkira* 261). For sparrow dishes, see *Kanz* recipes 140–9.

> ***ʿaṣāfīr baytiyya*** (عصافير بيتية) house sparrows.

baqar (بقر) cows. Meat of adult cows, beef, has cold and dense properties, it is hard to digest, and generates black bile. It is only good for physically active people. It takes longer to cook than mutton (see *Kanz* recipe 100).

1 See *Wuṣla* ii 517–8 for other ways to melt the fat, enhance it, and store it for future use.

 | DOI 10.1163/9789004349919_036

Meat of calves, veal, is cold but somewhat moist. Therefore, it was deemed more useful than beef for generating better humors. Meat of suckling calves is temperate and generates good blood. In this respect, it is comparable in goodness to lamb. Meat of female calves is better than that of the male ones (al-Arbūlī, *Kalām* 131–2).

baṭārikh (بطارخ) bottarga, roe taken from *būrī* (بوري) flathead grey mullet (*Mugil cephalus*). See *būrī* below.

bayḍ (بيض) eggs, when not specified, this usually designates chicken eggs. Eggs, which are not fertilized during their formation are considered poor in nutrition. The best are the fertilized ones obtained the day they are laid. Some of them might contain two yolks.

The egg white was said to be slow to digest, generating undercooked humors and lots of phlegm. The yolk, on the other hand, is nutritious, and generates wholesome humors. Eggs are best cooked as *nīmrisht* (نيمرشت) soft-boiled, prepared by adding the eggs to boiling water and counting to 100. When added to cold water, the count is to 300. Frying eggs in sesame oil is the least favorable. It was recommended to eat from 5 to 15 eggs per serving (al-Anṭākī, *Tadhkira* 96–7).

bayḍ ḥamām (بيض حمام) pigeon eggs.

būrī (بوري) flathead grey mullet (*Mugil cephalus*), named after a village called Būra, close to Tinnīs (al-Maqrīzī, *Khiṭaṭ* i 310). Al-Idrīsī, *Nuzhat al-mushtāq* i 36–7, describes it as a fine-colored flavorful fish which weighs two to three pounds. It enters the Nile River from the sea. It is eaten fresh and dried. *Kanz* recipe 254 uses it fresh, and recipe 241, dried.

In Egypt, it is particularly loved and valued for its roe, called *baṭārikh* (بطارخ) bottarga. Judging from *Kanz* recipe 241, and al-Shirbīnī, *Hazz al-quḥūf* 251–3, the fish is salt-dried with the eggs inside, and kept to dry thoroughly in the air. When cured this way, it is called *fasīkh al-baṭārikh* (فسيخ البطارخ).[2] Al-Shirbīnī praises it as food of high society (*ma'kūl al-akābir*), unlike the humbler, eggless *fasīkh*, which is made with another variety of mullet called *ṭūbār* (طوبار) thinlip grey mullet (*Chelon ramada*). It is made into *fasīkh* by stacking the fresh fishes in piles alternating with layers of salt, and leaving it until all the moisture drains and the fishes dry out. Al-Shirbīnī says it is quite popular among the common folk.

In both *Kanz* recipe 241 and al-Shirbīnī's account, the dried roe is taken out, and put in a separate vessel with a drizzle of olive or sesame oil. As for the dried *būrī*, it is soaked in water to get rid of excess salt and then oven-fried and smothered in vinegar-based tahini sauce.

2 The *Kanz* recipe calls it *samak al-baṭārikh*.

buṭūn (بطون) innards, organs, and bowels in the abdomens of ruminants. See *Kanz* recipe 102, which uses it in a dish of *kishk*.

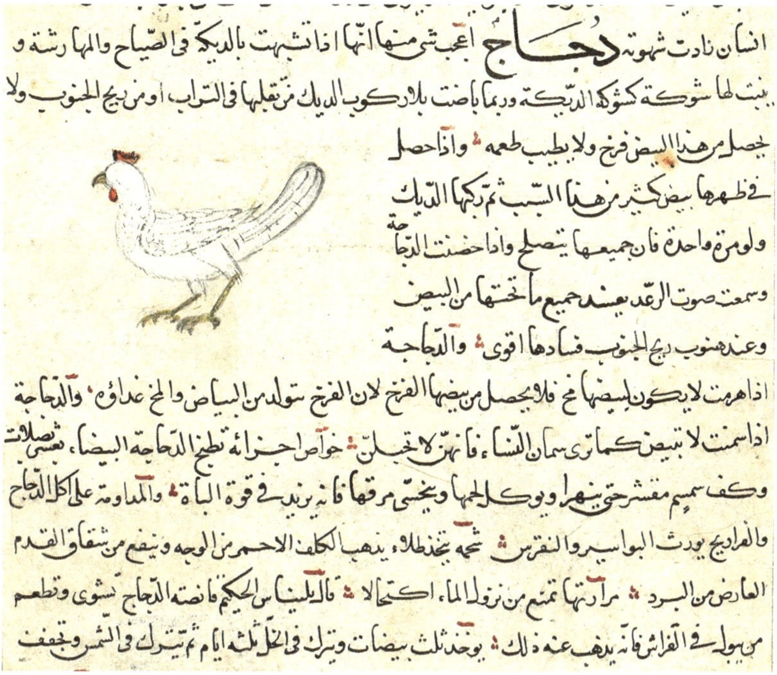

FIGURE 89 *Chicken, F1954.101r, Muḥammad al-Qazwīnī,* ʿAjāʾib al-makhlūqāt, *detail (Freer Gallery of Art and Arthur M. Sackler Gallery, Smithsonian Institution, Washington, DC: Purchase—Charles Lang Freer Endowment).*

dajāj (دجاج) chicken. In medieval Egypt, most of the chicken sold in the poultry markets was supplied by what they called *maʿmal al-farrūj* (chicks' factory).[3] Al-Anṭākī, *Tadhkira* 165, says that they are not any different from the ones hatched under their mothers' wings. The worst chicken, he adds, are the castrated ones, which are fattened by force-feeding.

Chicken is hot and moist in its properties, and agrees with all eaters, especially those leading leisurely lives. Stew of aged cocks (*dīk harim*), cooked with almonds, mastic, and *kaʿk* (crackers) was believed to rejuvenate body and soul, and improve the mind's power.

ḍaʾn (ضأن) adult sheep, which is known as the 'blessed animal,' and whose meat is the best of all red meats. It is at its best when the animal is fat and is no more than two years old.

3 See introduction, pp. 41–2.

Ḍa'n was deemed to be most nourishing and most temperate of all meats, and best suits people with temperate humors. Generally, the younger the animal is, the moister and better its meat is. Meat of a sheep older than four years is not considered top-quality mutton. See al-Anṭākī, *Tadhkira* 247; and al-Malik al-Muẓaffar, *al-Muʿtamad* 347.

The mature female sheep, the ewe, is called *shāt* (شاة), and the mature male sheep, the ram, is *kabsh* (كبش). When they are still in their first year the male lamb is called *kharūf* (خروف) or *ḥamal* (حمل), and the ewe lamb is *kharūfa* (خروفة) or *naʿja* (نعجة).

When the sheep reach their second year, and they have no more than two permanent incisors in each of their jaws, the young sheep (both female 'maiden ewe' and the male 'hogget') are called *thanī* (ثني) 'yearlings.'

FIGURE 90 *Fat-tailed sheep, the source for the rendered cooking fat* alya, *F1954.89r, Muḥammad al-Qazwīnī,* 'Ajā'ib al-makhlūqāt, *detail (Freer Gallery of Art and Arthur M. Sackler Gallery, Smithsonian Institution, Washington,* DC*: Purchase—Charles Lang Freer Endowment).*

dīk (ديك) pl. *duyūk* (ديوك) rooster, see *dajāj* above.

khiṣā al-duyūk (خصى الديوك) testicles of roosters, used in *Kanz* recipe 187 to make an aphrodisiac omelet.

farārīj (فراريج) young chickens. They were recommended for convalescents. They nourish the body, and enhance the intellect. See also *dajāj* above.

dasam (دسم) grease of cooking meat and animal fat.

firākh ḥamām (فراخ حمام) sometimes only referred to as *firākh* (فراخ) young pigeons, the lightest of which were said to be the fledglings, called *nawāhiḍ* (نواهض) and *zaghālīl* (زغاليل). The domesticated house pigeons were not usually used for food. The pigeons came from cotes, called *abrāj al-ḥamām*, which were built by peasants in rural areas. These were built like towers with holes to which were attached pottery vessels (*qawādīs*). The wild pigeons (*ḥamām barrī*) would remain in those cotes for a while to hatch their eggs there.[4]

Pigeon meat was said to be the hottest of all poultry, and hard to digest. The recommendation for people with excess hot properties (*maḥrūrīn*) was to eat it cooked with sour juice of unripe grapes, coriander seeds, and cucumber pulp (Ibn al-Bayṭār, *al-Jāmiʿ* iii 221; al-Rāzī, *Manāfiʿ* 105–6). In *Kanz* recipes, they are used as the main meat in the dish, and to supplement other meats. See, for instance, recipes 82, 84, 102, 122, 133, and 201.

FIGURE 91 Burj al-ḥamām (*pigeon cotes*).
PHOTO BY MOHAMMED MOUSSA, SIWA OASIS, EGYPT (https://commons.wikimedia.org/w/index.php?curid=35564449).

4 Al-Shirbīnī, *Hazz al-quḥūf* 255.

ghanam (غنم), also called *shāʿ* (شاء) generic name for sheep (*ḍaʾn*) and goat (*māʿiz*), see respective entries.

ghudad (غدد) nodules (of red meat). They could be glands, lymph nodes, or any stiff growths found in meat, tallow, or between the skin and meat. They were believed to be harmful because they are susceptible to infections and should be removed before cooking the meat.

ḥumam (حمم) solid particles left after rendering sheep-tail fat (*alya*). They are discarded.

ʿijl (عجل) calf, whose meat, veal, was said to be easier on the digestion than beef, see *baqar* above.

jadī (جدي) kid, young male goat less than one year old. With regard to the properties of its meat, it was deemed to be the most balanced. It was recommended for people leading leisurely lives (al-Rāzī, *Manāfiʿ* 99). See also *māʿiz* below.

karsh (كرش) pl. *kurūsh* (كروش) tripe of ruminants, believed to have cold and dry properties. It is slow to digest, and has little nutritional value. The recommendation was to cook it well, and season it with vinegar (Ibn Khalṣūn, *Kitāb al-Aghdhiya* 88).

kharūf (خروف), *khārūf* (خاروف) lamb, male sheep in their first year, when their meat has hot and moist properties—moister than meat of yearling male sheep (*kabsh thanī*), the hoggets. Their meat is still viscous (*lazij*) and needs to be fully cooked and seasoned with coriander, so that it digests well in the stomach (al-Arbūlī, *al-Kalām* 130–1).[5]

> ***kharūf samīn*** (خروف سمين) fatty lamb in its first year.
>
> ***Kharūf thanī*** (خروف ثني) *kabsh thanī* (كبش ثني) yearling, young male sheep in their second year. See also *ḍaʾn* above.

kubūd (كبود) livers, hot and moist in properties. It was believed to be nutritious, generating a lot of good blood. However, it is slow to digest. The best way to eat it is grilled, dusted with cinnamon and mastic, with a vinegar dip and fermented sauce (*murrī*). It must be chewed well (Ibn Khalṣūn, *Kitāb al-Aghdhiya* 87).

labīs (لبيس) fresh water Nile carp (*Labeo niloticus*), described as delicious fish, which does not smell fishy. It has firm white flesh, and can be cooked like red meat (al-Idrīsī, *Nuzhat al-mushtāq* 8).

laḥm (لحم) meat. If it is not specified in the recipes, lamb or mutton, which was deemed top quality meat, is meant. Next in excellence is meat of *jadī* (جدي), which is a male kid, less than one year old; and next is veal of a *calf* (عجل), which is less than one year old. In any case, veal is better than mutton from sheep, which are older than

5 Coriander is known to linger in the stomach longer than other herbs, which gives the lamb time to digest well.

four years. Fetuses are considered bad because they are not fully grown (al-Anṭākī, *Tadhkira* 310).

As described by Ibn al-Ḥājj, *al-Madkhal* i 126, in Egypt mutton has a strong gamey smell (*dhafar*), unlike mutton in Iraq, the Maghrib, and the Hijaz. Therefore, the hands should be washed thoroughly after eating it. Finely pounded meat was believed to digest easily and well. Generally, combining meat with bread or yogurt was believed to slow down its digestion (al-Anṭākī, *Tadhkira* 310).

aḍlāʿ al-laḥm (أضلاع اللحم) meat ribs.
laḥm afkhādh (لحم أفخاذ) meat of the upper leg.
laḥm aḥmar (لحم أحمر) meat trimmed of its fat.
laḥm baqarī (لحم بقر) beef, see *baqar* above.
laḥm ghalīẓ (لحم غليظ) dense, tough meat.
laḥm hazīl (لحم هزيل) lean meat.
laḥm khirāf (لحم خروف) lamb, see *kharūf* above.
laḥm māʿiz (لحم ماعز) goat meat. It is denser than mutton, but lighter than beef, see *māʿiz* below.
laḥm muntin (لحم منتن) meat which smells putrid.
laḥm murawwaḥ (لحم مروّح) meat, which does not smell fresh, but is not yet putrid.
laḥm samīn (لحم سمين) fatty meat.
laḥm thanī (لحم ثني) meat of yearling sheep, see *ḍaʾn* above.
laḥm ʿujūl (لحم عجول) veal, which was said to be better and more beneficial than beef, see *baqar* above.

lāsh (لاش) Nile River fish, which is of the tilapia species (*Chromis niloticus*); called 'lacha' in Spanish (Dozy, *Takmilat al-maʿājim* 1367, s.v. لاش). Al-Idrīsī, *Nuzhat al-mushtāq* i 34, describes it as a rare Nile River fish, round with a red tail, meaty, and quite flavorful.

māʿiz (ماعز) goat in general. The grown female is called *ʿanz* (عنز) and the young one is *miʿza* (معزة). The grown male goat is *tays* (تيس), and the young one is *jadī* (جدي).

The best meat of grown goats is that of castrated males. The meat of old goats is not favored because it generates disorders related to black bile. Goat meat in general is hard to digest due to its cold and dry properties. The way to remedy this is to cook it with lots of suet (*shaḥm*), along with oils and hot spices (al-Arbūlī, *al-Kalām* 132). In the *Kanz*, recipe 199 is the only one in the book that specifically requires goat meat, and it does indeed call for a pound of suet.

Overall, the meat of immature goats is almost balanced in its properties, generating temperate blood leaning toward dryness, which is why it must be cooked with a lot of suet. Meat of suckling kids (*jadī raḍīʿ*) is perfect. It is delicious and nourishing, generating good balanced blood. It was the recommended food for convalescents (al-Arbūlī, *al-Kalām* 132–3).

marāra (مرارة) pl. *marā'ir* (مرائر) gall bladder.

qawāniṣ (قوانص) gizzards of chickens.

qibāwa (قباوة), also called *qibba* (قبة) omasum, which is the third compartment in the stomach of ruminants, a folded structure of tripe, which looks like a ball. It is stuffed with a spicy mix of meat and rice, and then sewn and boiled.[6] See *Kanz* recipe 186, where it is used to create a huge egg.

samak (سمك) fish,[7] consumed fresh and cured in salt. For recipes, see *Kanz*, chapter 9. The anonymous Andalusian work, *Anwāʿ al-ṣaydala* 51, mentions that the Egyptians in the port city of Tinnīs (Tinnis) cook dishes with fish the same way red meat is cooked in other places. *Kanz* recipe 235 does indeed prove this to be true, not only in Tinnīs.

Due to its cold and moist properties, certain measures must be taken to avoid its harms. It is best eaten fresh, baked with vinegar-based dips and sauces. Sweets, such as dates or honey, were recommended after eating it. Drinking water is to be avoided with it; otherwise, it will be like bringing the fish back to life and killing oneself. Also to be avoided is eating red meat, eggs, and milk the same day as fish.

samak al-baṭārikh (سمك البطارخ) salted *būrī* (بوري) flathead grey mullet (*Mugil cephalus*), from which bottarga (*baṭārikh*) 'fish roe' is taken. Al-Anṭākī, *Tadhkira* 86, gives *baṭrākhiyūn* (بطراخيون) as another name for the cured roe, which are described as having hot and dry properties. They putrefy in the stomach fast, but this can be remedied by having olive oil and sour ingredients with them. Eating them with ginger prevents them from inducing thirst. See also *būrī* above.

samak dibb (سمك دبّ) salt-cured fish preserved in earthenware vessels, called *dibāb* (دِباب) and *dibb* (دِبّ) sg. *dabba* (دَبّة).

samak māliḥ (سمك مالح) salted fish, preserved in its dried state, the most popular of which is *būrī* (بوري) flathead grey mullet, from which bottarga (*baṭārikh*) 'fish roe' is taken, see *būrī* above. In *Kanz* recipes 240–1, which use salted fish, the instruction is to soak it in water for an hour, and then wash it to get rid of the salt.

samak mashqūq (سمك مشقوق) butterflied fish.

samak ṭarī (سمك طري) fresh fish.

---

6 For the recipe, see al-Warrāq, English trans. *Annals* 245–6.

7 For a discussion of fish in medieval Egypt, see Lewicka, *Food and Foodways* 209–25.

sammān (سمّان), also known as *sumānā* (سمانى), and *salwā* (سلوى) quail. It is also called *qatīl al-raʿd* (قتيل الرعد) 'casualty of thunder' because it is believed that its noise kills it. It is a migrating bird, which comes to Egypt from the Mediterranean Sea in autumn.

It is described as a plump bird, a bit larger than the sparrow. Its meat is tasty and nourishing; it fertilizes the body and arouses women's sexual appetites. It is praised as being good for those who are healthy and the convalescents. Because it is slow to digest, it should be cooked with lots of spices. See Ibn al-Bayṭār, *al-Jāmiʿ* iii 42; al-Anṭākī, *Tadhkira* 217. In *Kanz* recipe 140 on roasting and frying sparrows and quails, the cook is cautioned against using quails with blue eyes because they cause leprosy due to a peculiarity in their properties. This has been known and proven true, the recipe says.

shaḥm (شحم) solid animal fat, suet.

shawk (شوك) lit., 'thorns,' the prickly fine bones of fish.

ṣīr (صير) salt-cured anchovies. In its fresh state, the fish is called *absāriyya*, see entry above. However, fresh anchovies destined for salt curing may also be called *ṣīr*. In the Levant, it is used to make *murrī l-samak* (fermented fish sauce), see al-Rāzī, *al-Ḥāwī* 1718.

Al-Maqrīzī, *Khiṭaṭ* i 309–10, very briefly describes how it is caught and cured. After trapping the fish in nets, it is spread on reed mats (*ankhākh*),[8] and then kept in large stone jars (*amṭār*).[9] When done, the fish is sold; and in this state, it is called *mulūḥa* (ملوحة) and *ṣīr*. He adds that this is done only with fishes that are 1-finger long and smaller.

The ready to use salt-cured anchovies, or any small fish cured in a similar manner, were stored in a briny liquid, referred to in *Kanz* recipes as *maraq* and *māʾ*. This liquid is a by-product of the preserving process. After spreading the salted fishes on mats, and leaving them away from direct sunlight for a period, and then letting them cure in non-porous stone jars, as described above, the preserved fishes release the remaining juices, which melt the salt into brine.[10]

8 Sg. *nakhkh* (نخّ), also called *ḥaṣīra* (حصيرة).

9 A variant on *muṭr*; sg. *maṭara*, *maṭṭār*, characterized by its bulging belly and narrow mouth, see glossary 9.1 above.

10 Kurlansky, *Salt* 160, in his account of anchovy curing in the medieval Mediterranean region, describes the resulting brine as being pink, and the cured meat around the bones as deep pink. He adds that the "unscrupulous anchovy makers dyed their brine pink." This might indeed explain the addition of madder (*fuwwa*) in *Kanz* recipes for making the *ṣīr* condiment of *ṣaḥna*, to give it the desirable color associated with good-quality cured anchovies.

Delicious small dishes of *ṣīr muṭayyab* are made with salt-cured *ṣīr*, see *Kanz* recipes 424–5. *Ṣīr* is also the principal ingredient in a condiment called *ṣaḥna*, see below.

ṣaḥna (صحنة) condiment made with salt-cured anchovies (*ṣīr*), see *Kanz* recipes 255–9, 261–4. They all use madder (*fuwwa*) to give the condiment a reddish color. Even the adulterated ones, those made without fish, called *ṣaḥna kadhdhāba*, use sumac to imitate the color of the true *ṣaḥna*, see *Kanz* recipes 258, 259, 264.[11]

ṣaḥna mumallaḥa (صحنة مملحة) salt-cured small fish, which is the equivalent of *ṣīr* in Egypt. It is used to make the *ṣaḥna* condiment. The expression is used with this meaning in *Kanz* recipe 263, which is said to be from Baghdad and the upper region of Iraq. Apparently, this was the case in Iraq, and the extant *ṣaḥnāt* (صحناة) recipe in al-Warrāq's Baghdadi cookbook reflects this usage. See the above-mentioned *Kanz* recipe for more details.

thanī (ثني) yearling sheep and goats, see *ḍa'n* and *laḥm* above.

ʿurqūb (عرقوب) lamb hock, used in *Kanz* recipe 36 for a simple dish of boiled meat, to enrich the flavor of the sauce.

ʿurūq (عروق) blood vessels (of red meat), which are removed before cooking the meat, as they become chewy when cooked.

---

11 See above note.

11. Medical Terms, Medicinal Preparations, and Personal Hygiene and Perfumes[1]

The medical terms and expressions in this section are based on the tenets of the Galenic humoral theory, which was prevalent in medieval times. See *mizāj* below for explanatory notes on the main principles of the theory. See also introduction, section 10.

adhān (أدهان) aromatic oils.

> ***adhān mubakhara*** (أدهان مبخرة) oils scented with aromatic smoke.

adwiyat al-ʿaraq (أدوية العرق) deodorants.
akbād multahiba (اكباد ملتهبة) inflamed livers.
akhlāṭ (اخلاط) sg. *khalṭ* (خلط) the four humors: blood, phlegm, yellow bile, and black bile; see *mizāj* below.
amrāḍ sawdāwiyya (امراض سوداوية) sicknesses related to excess in black bile, see *mizāj* below.
amzija (امزجة) sg. *mizāj* (مزاج) elemental properties or temperaments, see *mizāj* below.
ʿanbar (عنبر) *Ambra grisea* (S), greyish substance formed in the intestines of sperm whales, see glossary 8 above.

> ***ʿanbar khām*** (عنبر خام) raw ambergris.
> ***ʿanbar maʿjūn*** (عنبر معجون) kneaded ambergris. Al-Nuwayrī, *Nihāyat al-arab* xii 38–9, comments that to his fourteenth-century contemporaries, what used to be called *ʿanbar* (عنبر) is now *nidd* (ندّ), the best of which is *nidd muthallath* (ندّ مثلث), also called *ʿanbar muthallath* (عنبرمثلث). It is composed of three equal parts of ambergris, aloeswood, and musk, kneaded together (*maʿjūn*).

ʿanbarī (عنبري), also called *ʿanbarīnā* (عنبرينا) solid pieces of perfumed compounds of ambergris, musk, and aloeswood, shaped artistically. They were worn as ornaments, such as necklaces, bracelets, beads, and girdles, especially during the summertime because they had a cooling effect on the wearer's temperament. They were also carried in pockets (al-Nuwayrī, *Nihāyat al-arab* xii 38). See recipe in *Kanz* DK, appendix 68, p. 420.
ʿaqīd sakanjabīn (عقيد السكنجبين) chewy candy made with oxymel, which is a digestive syrup of sugar and vinegar. See *Kanz* recipe 348.

---

1 For single ingredients, see glossary 8.

 | DOI 10.1163/9789004349919_037

FIGURE 92 *Preparing medicine from honey, folio from Arabic translation of* De Materia Medica *of Dioscorides, thirteenth century, 57.51.21 (MET NY—Bequest of Cora Timken Burnett, 1956).*

aqrāṣ (أقراص) tablets.
aqrāṣ al-laymūn (أقراص الليمون) lemon-flavored hard candy drops. See *Kanz* recipe 349.
ās (آس) myrtle, see *marsīn*, glossary 8 above.
aṣḥāb al-amzāj al-bārida (أصحاب الامزاج الباردة) people whose humoral properties are naturally prone to cold.
aṣḥāb al-amzāj al-ḥārra (أصحاب الامزاج الحارة) people whose humoral properties are naturally prone to heat
aṣḥāb al-balgham (أصحاب البلغم) people whose dominant humor is phlegm.
aṣḥāb al-ḥarārāt (أصحاب الحرارات) people suffering from excess in hot properties.
aṣḥāb al-ḥummayyāt (أصحاب الحميات) people with fevers.
aṣḥāb al-iḥtirāqāt (أصحاب الاحتراقات) people with burnt yellow bile.
aṣḥāb al-ishāl (أصحاب الاسهال) people with diarrhea.
aṣḥāb al-mālīkhūliyā (أصحاب الماليخوليا) people suffering from excess black bile, causing *mālīkhūliyā*, which interferes with the faculty of thinking.
aṣḥāb al-ṣafrā' (أصحاب الصفراء) people whose dominant humor is yellow bile.
ashriba (أشربة) designates both ordinary beverages and tonics with curative properties. See glossary 1 above.
asrār wa-hanā' (أسرار وهناء) lit., 'secrets and pleasures,' used to convey intercourse (*Lisān al-ʿArab*, s.v. سرر). See, for instance, *Kanz* recipe 679, which promises such joys.
ʿaṭash (عطش) thirst.
bāh (باه) coitus.
bakhar (بخر) bad breath.
bakhūr (بخور), ***bakhūrāt*** (بخورات) incense.
baraṣ (برص) leprosy.
damm (دم) blood.
dawā' qaraf (دواء قرف) preparations to treat nausea. See *Kanz*, chapter 14.
dharīra (ذريرة) pl. *dharā'ir* (ذرائر) scented body powder; perfumed and incensed powders used topically. After taking a bath and drying the body, such scented powders were sprinkled all over the body. See *Kanz*, chapter 22.
dharūr (ذرور) restorative powder to be ingested. It is not used topically like *dharīra*, and it is not infused with incense. All *dharūr* recipes include white gum of tragacanth tree (*kathīrā' bayḍā'*), which, besides its medicinal benefits, was also valued for boosting libido in both sexes. The *Kanz* text is consistent in calling scented body powder *dharīra*, and the ingested variety *dharūr*.
dūd (دود) intestinal worms.
duhn (دهن) pl. *adhān* (أدهان) aromatic oil, see *Kanz* recipes 651–4.
duhn al-zafar (دهن الزفر) oil for removing greasy odors from the hands.
duhn mubakhkhar (دهن مبخّر) oil infused with fragrant smoke.
faḍalāt radī'a (فضلات رديئة) bad excretions.

fam al-maʿida (فم المعدة) lit., 'mouth of the stomach,' that is, the top gate of the stomach.
fatāʾil (فتائل) slim cylinders, such as those used as candles.

> ***fatāʾil kattān*** (فتائل كتان) linen tapers.
> ***fatāʾil nidd*** (فتائل ند) hand-rolled slim cylinders of incense, see *Kanz* recipe 659. See *nidd* below.

ghāliya (غالية) highly aromatic perfume compound, popular in medieval times, but known to the Arabs even in pre-Islamic times (al-Tamīmī, *Ṭīb al-ʿarūs* 80, n. 1). The basic components are musk, ambergris, and ben oil (*duhn al-bān*), which is oil extracted from the kernels of seeds of the moringa tree (*Moringa oleifera*). See al-Nuwayrī, *Nihāyat al-arab* xii 29–35.
ghasūl (غسول) pl. *ghasūlāt* (غسولات) cleansing compounds, such as soaps and perfumed water, commonly used for washing the hair and body.
ḥabb (حبّ) *ḥubūb* (حبوب) pills. See, for instance, *Kanz* recipes 661–2, for pills which sweeten the breath.
ḥabs al-ṭabīʿa (حبس الطبع) constipation.
hāḍim (هاضم) spices or medicinal preparations which aid good digestion.
haḍm (هضم) digestion.
ḥakka (حكّة) itch.
ḥaṣāt (حصاة) kidney stone.
ḥummā (حمّى) fever.

> ***ḥummā al-nāfiḍ*** (حمّى النافض) ague fit.
> ***ḥummā ṣafrāwiyya*** (حمّى صفراوية) fever triggered by surfeit of yellow bile.

iḥtirāq al-damm (إحتراق الدم) burning of the blood, due to excess in yellow bile.
imtilāʾ (إمتلاء) indigestion due to surfeit.
ishāl al-sawdāʾ (إسهال السوداء) diarrhea caused by an excess in black bile.
istiḥāla (إستحالة) changing of the elemental properties (of the digesting food) into harmful ones, such as when eating fish, which has cold and moist properties, without the dipping sauces (*ṣibāgh*), to aid its digestion. These dipping sauces, with their hot and dry properties, prevent the digested food from generating excess in black bile, which is harmful to the body (see *Kanz* recipe 479).
istimrāʾ (إستمراء) good digestion.
istisqāʾ (إستسقاء) ascites.
iʿtidāl (إعتدال) humoral temperance, see *mizāj* below.
jarab (جرب) mange.
jarayān al-jawf (جريان الجوف), also called *ishāl* (إسهال) diarrhea.

jushāʾ ḥāmiḍ (جشاء حامض) acid belching.

juwārish (جوارش)[2] pl. *juwārishnāt* (جوارشنات) digestive stomachics, see *Kanz* recipes in chapter 11. Al-Hurawī, *Baḥr al-jawāhir* 109, says that *juwārish* preparations always taste and smell good, unlike those for *maʿjūn* (electuaries), which may be sweet or sour, and may smell good or not. For recipes, see *Kanz*, chapter 11.

khabath fiḍḍa (خبث فضة) silver slag, which is the waste of silver-working processes, such as smelting and smithing, used in *Kanz* recipe 663 in a deodorant preparation. It was deemed beneficial for curing wounds. Taken internally with egg yolk, it was believed to be an aphrodisiac. Silver slag is especially good for the eyes (al-Anṭākī, *Tadhkira* 148).

khafaqān (خفقان) heart palpitations.

khawāṣ ʿajība (خواص عجيبة) fantastic properties, mostly related to boosting sexual activities.

khawāṣ laṭīfa (خواص لطيفة) humoral properties which are low in density.

khiḍāb al-shaʿr (خضاب الشعر) hair dye.

khilāl (خلال) toothpicks.

> ***khilāl maʾmūnī*** (خلال مأموني) toothpicks from esparto grass stems. They are called *maʾmūnī* because they cause little harm to the teeth. Toothpicks made from it are usually used by the common folk (*ʿawām*), apparently because they are cheaper than the choice varieties with cold and dry properties. See *Kanz* recipe 638.

khumār (خمار) hangover.

lakhlakha (لخلخة) potpourri, aromatic ingredients mixed with aromatic liquids, put in a long-necked bottle, called *fayyāsha*, and set on very low heat. It is usually put in places around the house, such as bedrooms, toilets, and guestrooms. It is also put near the wind-catcher (*bādhāhanj*) of the house. See *Kanz* recipe 671.

laṭīf (لطيف) low density (food properties).

laʿūq (لعوق) pl. *laʿūqāt* (لعوقات) thick medicinal syrup, sufficiently firm but still soft. It was licked with a spoon, (*milʿaqa*) and hence the name. See *Kanz* recipe 449, for a *laʿūq* beneficial for curing nausea.

maḥmūm (محموم) patient with fever.

maḥrūrīn (محرورين) people with excessively hot properties.

maʿjūn (معجون) electuary, a restorative and digestive preparation, which has a paste-like consistency. See recipes in *Kanz*, chapter 11.

marṭūbīn (مرطوبين) people with an excess in humid properties.

---

2 I follow the pronunciation provided by al-Hurawī, *Baḥr al-jawāhir* 109.

mayba (ميبة) aromatic medicinal drink of quince, see *Kanz* recipe 350.

miḥrāq li-l-mashāʾikh (محراق للمشائخ) boosting libido in the elderly. See *Kanz* recipe 679, for a restorative preparation which promises such effects.

mizāj (مزاج) humoral temperament or property. Based on the Galenic theory of the humors, all objects in nature, animate and inanimate, are composed of four elements (*arkān*): fire, air, water, and earth; each of which possesses its own innate quality, called a property, temperament or nature; in Arabic, *mizāj* (pl. *amzija*) or *ṭabʿ* (pl. *ṭabāʾiʿ*). There are four basic types of properties: hot, cold, dry, and moist; and each entity in nature is composed of a blend of these elements.

In regard to the human body, these elements are described in terms of humors, or elemental fluids, called *akhlāṭ* or *ruṭūbāt khalṭiyya*, and there are four of them: blood (*damm*), hot and moist; phlegm (*balgham*), cold and moist; yellow bile (*ṣafrāʾ*), hot and dry; and black bile (*sawdāʾ*), cold and dry. All these are generated by the digested food in the stomach and liver.

Each individual human body has its own combination of these humors, which in a healthy state is considered normal. For instance, some people are naturally prone to having an excess in phlegm, described as *aṣḥāb al-ruṭūbāt* or *aṣḥāb al-balgham*. To maintain health, they should eat foods that match their natures, that is, foods with moist and cold properties. People who are naturally prone to heat, *aṣḥāb al-amzāj al-ḥārra*, should eat foods with hot properties. People who are naturally prone to cold, *aṣḥāb al-amzāj al-bārida*, should eat foods with cold properties. People whose humors are balanced, *aṣḥāb al-amzāj al-muʿtadila*, should eat foods with balanced properties. However, having balanced humors does not imply a perfect balance of the humors, which is more a theory than a real state. Rather, balance (*iʿtidāl*) may be within a wide range (leaning toward less or more) of proportions that are considered healthy.

Sometimes the normal balanced state of the humors is altered, to either excess or deficiency, due to internal or external causes, such sicknesses or being exposed to acute conditions of heat or cold. This imbalanced state in the innate elements is called *mizāj ghayr muʿtadil*. It is an unhealthy state, which can be corrected and brought back to health by manipulating the properties of the foods consumed. A person suffering from fevers, and hence having excess in hot properties, can be relieved by consuming foods with cold properties, such as gourd.[3]

Foods themselves are manipulated in the same manner. Coarse and dense foods, for instance, which are hard to digest, such as grain porridges, can be balanced by eating them with *murrī* (liquid fermented sauce), black pepper, and cinnamon. The

3 The basics of the humoral Galenic theory explained here are lucidly discussed in the thirteenth-century *Kitāb al-Aghdhiya* by Ibn Khalṣūn, 43–5. Ibn Khalṣūn summarizes the concept as maintaining health with similars, and curing with opposites:
حفظ الصحة بالمثل وزوال المرض بالضد.

hot and dry properties of these ingredients can break down the densities of these porridges and facilitate their digestion.[4]

muʿaṭṭish (معطّش) inducing thirst (in relation to foods).

mubalghamīn (مبلغمين) phlegmatic people.

mubarrid (مبرّد) having a cooling effect (in relation to foods).

muhaḍḍimāt (مهضّمات) digestives.

muqawwī (مقوي) fortifying, having restorative powers.

musammin (مسمن) foods and medicinal preparations which help with weight gain.

muṭayyab (مطيّب) scented.

nafkh (نفخ) bloating.

nafth al-damm (نفث الدم) ***ramī l-damm*** (رمي الدم) hemoptysis, expectoration of blood or blood-stained sputum from the chest

nakha (نكهة) breath odor.

nidd (ندّ) scented pastilles, the basic ingredients of which are ambergris, aloeswood, and musk. The ingredients are kneaded together, shaped into small balls and discs, or *fatāʾil* (thin cylinders). They are left in the shade to dry completely, and then stored and used as needed. *Nidd* is mainly used for burning as incense (see *Kanz* recipes 674; DK, appendix 79, p. 419. The fragrant pastilles can also be carried in pockets, and placed between layers of clothes.

Al-Nuwayrī, *Nihāyat al-arab* xii 38–9, says that to his contemporaries (in the fourteenth century), what used to be called *nidd* (ندّ) in the past, is now called *ʿanbar* (عنبر). When the ingredient ambergris itself is meant, it would be called *ʿanbar khām* (عنبر خام).

fatāʾil nidd (فتائل ندّ) hand-rolled slim cylinders of incense, made with *nidd*, as in *Kanz* recipes 659; DK, appendix 72, p. 406. Al-Nuwayrī, *Nihāyat al-arab* xii 39–40, describes how these incense cylinders are rolled: a piece of the kneaded *nidd* mix is rolled into a cylinder between the fingers, and then a small hole is made in one end by gently piercing the roll with a large needle. Next, the surface of the cylinder is decorated by rolling it, while pressing it gently, on a wooden stamp corrugated lengthwise. This stamp is called *mishṭāb* (مشطاب). The undecorated ones are simply rolled on a marble slab (*rukhāma*).

nidd muthallath (ندّ مثلث) deemed the best of the *nidd* compounds, it is composed of the three basic ingredients of ambergris, aloeswood, and musk, which are kneaded together. It is also called *ʿanbar muthallath* (عنبر مثلث), see *nidd* above.

nidd murakkab (ندّ مركب) scented pastilles, coated with ambergris.

---

4 For a more detailed account of the Galenic theory of the humors, see al-Warrāq, English trans. *Annals* 55–64; Dols, *Medieval Islamic Medicine* 3–14; Waines, "Dietetics in Medieval Islam" 228–40; and Waines, "'Luxury Foods' in Medieval Islamic Societies" 571–80.

nuḍūḥ (نضوح) aromatic liquids, sprinkled around the house to sweeten its smell.
nuḥūḥa (نحوحة) having to clear one's throat.
qābiḍ (قابض) astringent in properties (e.g., in relation to food); causing constipation.
qaraf (قرف) more commonly known as *ghathayān* (غثيان) nausea, see *Kanz*, chapter 14 for recipes to cure it.
qawlanj (قولنج) colic.
qay' (قيء) vomiting.
rabāl (ربال) excessive accumulation of bodily fat and flesh.
rīḥ (ريح) wind, which, based on the Galenic theory, is present in all parts of the human body. According to Ibn Sīnā, *al-Qānūn* 108, disorder in its properties can be detected by pain and swelling in the affected areas. Arthritis, for instance, is caused by cold and dense winds in the joints, and excess of such winds in the digestive system cause stomach rumbles (*qarāqir*), bloating, and flatulence. Such disorders were treated with herbal preparations and foods to help thin the density of the wind and purge it.

riyāḥ bārida (رياح باردة) cold winds in the body caused by cold and dense humors. Gastric cold winds are counterbalanced with foods that are hot and dry in properties, such as mustard condiments (see, for instance, *Kanz* recipe 481).

ruṭūbāt (رطوبات) excess in moist elemental properties.
ruṭūbāt al-damāgh (رطوبات الدماغ) excess in the brain's moist elemental properties.
ṣābūn (صابون) soap. See *Kanz* recipes 642 and 643.
ṣābūn muṭayyab (صابون مطيّب) scented soap.
ṣafṣāf (صفصاف) willow wood, used for making toothpicks. See *Kanz* recipe 638.
safūf (سفوف) compound medicinal powder, taken internally.
shaqaf kīzān al-fuqqā' (شقف كيزان الفقاع) fragments from earthenware jars, which are used for making beer. The shards are crushed and incorporated into preparations for deodorants, as in *Kanz* recipe 663.

shaqaf ṣīnī (شقف صيني) fragments of china, crushed and incorporated into preparations for deodorants, as in *Kanz* recipe 663.

su'āl (سعال) coughs.
ṣudā' (صداع) headache.
sudud (سدد) blockages, as in the liver and spleen, due to thick, dense, and mucilaginous humors, or an excess of any kind of humors.
ṣunān (صنان) armpit odors.
taḥlīl (تحليل) breaking up dense humors (of food properties).

talṭīf al-mizāj (تلطيف المزاج) reducing density of humors.

taṣʿīdāt (تصعيدات) aromatic distilled waters. See *Kanz* recipes 684–715.

taṣrīf al-riyāḥ (تصريف الرياح) dispelling winds in the digestive system to prevent bloating.

ṭīb (طيب) perfume compounds.

ṭuḥāl (طحال) spleen.

tukhama (تخمة) eating to surfeit.

tunʿish al-maʿida (تنعش المعدة) refreshing the stomach.

turāb ḥāʾiṭ maṭbakh mudakhkhan (تراب حائط مطبخ مدخن) dust from a smoky kitchen wall, used in *Kanz* recipe 449, for a preparation to cure nausea and vomiting. It could have been used for the kaolin (hydrated aluminum silicate), which the mud plaster coated with cooking smoke contains. In traditional medicine, it is known for its soothing effects on the stomach.

tūtyā (توتيا) tutty, finely powdered impure zinc oxide, which in *Kanz* recipes 660 and 663 is used in deodorants (*dawāʾ ʿaraq*).

> ***tūtyā marāzibī*** (توتيا مرازبي) tutty, which, al-Anṭākī (*Tadhkira* 106), describes as delicate white thin sheets. He adds that the pharmacists call it *shaqfa* (شقفة). Al-Bīrūnī, *Ṣaydana* 120, compares it to eggshells, and says it is the best.

tuẓhir al-lawn (تظهر اللون) bestowing radiance to one's complexion (with restorative preparations).

ʿūd (عود) aloeswood, see glossary 8 above.

> ***ʿūd muʿallā*** (عود معلّى) incense of aloeswood coated with aromatics, see *Kanz* recipes DK, appendix 69 and 70, pp. 404–5.

ukar maṣūgha mukharrama (أكر مصوغة مخرّمة) pierced cast silver balls, used for keeping small pieces of perfumed incense, to be carried in pockets. See *Kanz* recipe DK, appendix 72, p. 406. They were most popularly shaped like apples and myrobalan plum (*ihlīlaj*) *Prunus cerasifera* (S).

ushnān 1 (أشنان) handwashing compound, made with potash, which is also called *ushnān*, see *ushnān* 2 below. For handwashing compounds, see *Kanz* recipes in chapter 20.

> ***ushnān mulūkī*** (أشنان ملوكي) top-quality aromatic handwashing compound.
> ***ushnān muṭayyab*** (أشنان مطيب) scented handwashing compound.

ushnān 2 (أشنان), also called *qilī* (قلي) potash, made by first producing ashes from the *ushnān* plant, also called *qāqullā* (قاقلّى) and *qāqullī* (قاقلّي), which is saltwort (*Salsola* *kali*), in Arabic *ḥurḍ* (حُرض). While still fresh, the branches are burnt to ashes and collected, and then continuously sprinkled with water to allow the ashes to leach. The solution of the ashes and water is put in a large pot and boiled until all moisture evaporates, and only a white residue is left, which becomes potash.

ushnān Bāriqī (أشنان بارقي) the purest and best potash, brought from Bāriq, a place near the city of Kufa in Iraq.

ushnān Fārisī ʿaṣāfīrī (أشنان فارسي عصافيري) excellent white potash, deemed the most delicate and gentle, used particularly for handwashing compounds. In *Kanz*, it is referred to as *ushnān abyaḍ* (أشنان أبيض) 'white potash,' *ushnān Fārisī* (أشنان فارسي) 'Persian potash,' and *ushnān ʿaṣāfīrī* (أشنان عصافيري) lit., 'potash of sparrows,' because the potash looks like sparrows' droppings, as explained in al-Bīrūnī, *Ṣaydana* 46.

wajaʿ al-fuʾād (وجع الفؤاد) heartburn, feeling pain and pressure in the upper part of the stomach.

yafishsh al-riyāḥ (يفش الرياح) deflate winds (medicinally).

yaḥbis al-ṭabʿ (يحبس الطبع) control bowel movements.

yajlū al-balgham (يجلو البلغم) purge phlegm.

yaraqān (يرقان) jaundice.

yarudd al-riyāḥ (يرد الرياح) repel winds.

yastaḥīl (يستحيل) (ingested food that) generates harmful humors.

yuʿaddil al-ṭabʿ (يعدل الطبع) restore balance of humoral properties.

yuʿaṭṭir al-maʿida (يعطر المعدة) perfume the stomach.

yubṭiʾ bi-l-sukr (يبطيء بالسكر) slow down intoxication.

yudirr al-bawl (يدر البول) diuretic.

yufarriḥ al-qalb (يفرح القلب) induce euphoria.

yuḥallil al-riyāḥ (يحلل الرياح) cause winds to dissipate.

yuḥassin al-akhlāq (يحسن الاخلاق) improve the mood.

yuḥassin al-bashara (يحسن البشرة) enhance the complexion.

yulaṭṭif al-balgham (يلطف البلغم) reduce the density of phlegm.

yulayyin al-baṭn (يلين البطن) soften the bowels.

yulayyin al-ṭabīʿa (يلين الطبيعة) laxative.

yunabbih al-shahwa (ينبّه الشهوة) excite the appetite.

yuqawwī al-bāh (يقوي الباه) invigorate coitus.

yuqawwī al-jimāʿ (يقوي الجماع) invigorate coitus.

yuqawwī al-ṣulb (يقوي الصلب) strengthen the loins for good sex.

yuṣaffī al-dhihn (يصفي الذهن) clear the mind.

yusakkin al-ghathayān (يسكن الغثيان) alleviate nausea.

yusakkin al-ṣafrāʾ (يسكن الصفراء) subdue yellow bile.
yushahhī al-jimāʿ (يشهي الجماع) stimulate the libido.
yuṭayyib al-nakha (يطيب النكهة) sweeten the breath.
yuṭliq al-baṭn (يطلق البطن) loosen the bowels.
yuzīl al-bukhār (يزيل البخار) disperse vapors.

12. Vegetables and Legumes

ʿadas (عدس), also known as *bulsun* (بلسن) *Lens culinaris* (S) lentils. Good lentils are described as light colored and flat, they cook fast, and do not discolor the broth.

With their dry and cold properties, they are known for causing flatulence, and are suspected of generating dense blood, high in black bile. However, cooking them thoroughly improves their qualities. There is also the caution that lentils may induce bad dreams; this can be averted by mixing it with barley in a dish called *kishk al-ʿadas* (كشك العدس). This makes it a perfectly balanced food, provided the amount of barley is half the amount of lentils used. To avert their harms, it is also suggested that they be cooked with vinegar, sesame oil, and chard (al-Isrāʾīlī, *Aghdhiya* ii 93–103; al-Anṭākī, *Tadhkira* 258–9).

ʿadas maqshūr (عدس مقشور) shelled lentils.

ʿajjūr (عجّور) unripe *Cucumis melo* var. *chate* (S) Egyptian chate. Unlike *faqqūs* (see below), it is not eaten raw. In Egypt, this native variety of melon is called *biṭṭīkh ʿAbdulī* (see glossary 7 above, under *biṭṭīkh*). ʿAbd al-Laṭīf al-Baghdādī, *Riḥla* 78, compares its shape to an Iraqi gourd, with bellies and necks. The Egyptian farmers told him that they would make daily visits to their farms, and harvest a portion of the small and green melons, which were in fact *ʿajjūr*, and would sell them as *faqqūs*. He says they taste like *qiththāʾ* (snake cucumber), see below.

In the *Kanz*, it only shows up in cold dishes, recipes 630 and 631, where it is peeled, slit into four sections, boiled, fried, and made into vinegar-based cold dishes. In recipe 745, it is stored fresh along with melon and cucumber.

bādhinjān (باذنجان) *Solanum melongena* (S) eggplant, of which al-Anṭākī, *Tadhkira* 74, says there are two kinds: the white and oblong that is about 9 inches long (1 *shibr*); and the black and round. The first variety was deemed better and tastier.

Eggplant is described as a familiar food with hot and dry properties. It is highly recommended for sweetening the odor of sweat, removing the underarm odor. It strengthens the stomach, and dries up humidities not generated by the body itself. Eggplant, however, is maligned for its bitterness. It is blamed for generating black bile and causing ailments like cancer, melasma (*kalaf*), and blockages. To remedy these, it is first slit and soaked in salted water, boiled, and then cooked with meat, sesame oil, and vinegar. The *Kanz* recommends that it be cooked with sour-based stews, such as *sikbāja* (recipes 7, 90). It is best eaten fried as *Būrāniyya* (recipe 93), with yogurt sauces (recipe 531), and pickled (such as recipe 598).

qimʿ al-bādhinjān (قمع الباذنجان) eggplant calyx.

 | DOI 10.1163/9789004349919_038

bāmiya (بامية) *Abelmoschus esculentus* (S) okra. Ibn al-Bayṭār, *al-Jāmiʿ* i 111, describes it as an Egyptian vegetable with pointed tips and hairy skin, with small round and white seeds. He says people in Egypt cook it with meat while it is still small and tender.

In terms of its properties, okra is classified as the coldest and moistest of all vegetables. It was believed to generate bad blood, and it was said to be lacking in nutritional value. To drive away its harmful effects, Ibn al-Bayṭār recommends cooking it with *murrī* (liquid fermented sauce) and many spices. ʿAbd al-Laṭīf al-Baghdādī, *Riḥla* 60, describes okra in the same manner.[1] See *Kanz* DK recipe, appendix 29, p. 135.

bāqilā (باقلى) *Vicia faba* (S) fava beans. It is also called *fūl* (فول) and *baysār* (بيسار) in Andalusia and Egypt, see *fūl* below.

baqla ḥamqā' (بقلة حمقاء) common purslane, see *rijla* below.

bāzār (بازار) a vegetable mentioned in *Kanz* recipe 531, which deals with a yogurt condiment. In the recipe, yogurt cream cheese (*qanbarīs*) is mixed with chopped vegetables, and *bāzār* is given as an option.

The only source where *bāzār* is explained, albeit not identified, is Dozy, *Takmilat al-maʿājim* 70, where it is described as a Levantine plant used in a yogurt condiment (*khilāṭ* pl. *akhlāṭ*). He adds that the Levantines prefer it to *khilāṭ* with capers (*kabar*), although they do eat the latter as well. It is my guess that the vegetable in question is white/cnicus thistle (*Picnomon acarna*), Arabic *bādhāward* (باذاورد), also occurs as *bāzāward* (بازاورد),[2] and *shawka bayḍā'* (شوكة بيضاء). *Bāzār* must have been a corrupted form of *bāzāward*.

This wild plant is a variety of *ʿakkūb/kharshaf* (gundelia, *Gundelia tournefortii*), which is ubiquitous in the Levant and the surrounding regions. Al-Ḥajjār, *Kitāb al-Ḥarb al-maʿshūq* 100, mentions *bāzār* along with *basbāsa* as ingredients added to Lebanese *qanbarīs*, as in the *Kanz* recipe mentioned above.

bisillā (بسلّا) *Pisum arvense* (S), field peas, a large variety of grass peas, closely related to garden peas (*Pisum sativum*), eaten cooked only. It is the kind of vegetable that only hard workers and farmers can digest because it generates crude blood and bloating gases (Ibn al-Bayṭār, *al-Jāmiʿ* i 130).

buqūl (بقول) vegetables in general.

faqqūs (فقوس) *faqqūṣ* (فقوص) a small variety of *qiththā'* (قثّاء) snake cucumber (entry below). ʿAbd al-Laṭīf al-Baghdādī, *Riḥla* 77–8, says it does not grow larger than a

---

1 We learn from Mehdawy and Hussein, *Pharaoh's Kitchen* 89, that its ancient Egyptian name was *bano*. They also point out that the French Egyptologist, Gaston Maspero "briefly mentions finding the remains of this plant."

2 In Ibn Sīnā, *al-Qānūn* 752, 1194.

fitr (7 inches); and most of them are 1-finger long. He adds that they are softer and sweeter than *qiththāʾ*. He also reports that Egyptian farmers used to harvest the unripe *biṭṭīkh ʿAbdulī* melons (see glossary 7 above, under *biṭṭīkh*), and sell them as *faqqūs*.

Faqqūs ʿitābī (فقوس عتابي) is another unripe *ʿajjūr* melon, which passed for *faqqūs*. It is the muskmelon variety, called *biṭṭīkh ʿitābī* and *shammām al-biṭṭīkh* (see glossary 7, under *biṭṭīkh*).

Faqqūs is consumed raw and pickled, like cucumber. The recommendation was to eat it while it is still small and tender. It is not easy to digest, especially when it becomes large and tough and causes abdominal pain and bloating in the lower intestines (al-Rāzī, *Manāfiʿ* 229).

fujl (فجل) *Raphanus sativus* (S) radish, the best of which is the tender cultivated variety. The roots and the leaves are mostly eaten raw, offered with the meals, and as garnishes, as in *Kanz* recipe 619 of a mashed chickpea dip. *Kanz* recipe 471 directs the cook to serve a fish dish with peeled radish. In other recipes, radishes are made into a digestive electuary (recipe 389), and a pickle, as an aid to digestion (recipe 584).

Eating it after meals, especially the leaves, was said to stimulate digestion. With its hot and moist properties, it induces burping, and expels winds (al-Malik al-Muẓaffar, *al-Muʿtamad* 416–7; al-Anṭākī, *Tadhkira* 273).

fūl (فول), also called *bāqillā* (باقلى) and *baysār* (بيسار) *Vicia faba* (S) fava beans, eaten fresh and dried. It was said to be good for expelling humidities from the lungs; its broth is especially good for this. The broth is also beneficial in preventing kidney and bladder stones. On the negative side, it induces feelings of lethargy and laziness; it causes intense bloating, and causes nightmares.

fūl akhḍar (فول أخضر) fresh fava beans. When eaten spiced with ginger, it was said to induce strong erection. However, it is hard on the digestion because it is not fully mature.

fūl yābis (فول يابس) dried fava beans. To reduce their bloating effect, prolonged soaking and cooking were recommended to facilitate its digestion. Cooking it with pepper, salt, asafetida, thyme, caraway, rue, and oil, would help too (al-Malik al-Muẓaffar, *al-Muʿtamad* 37–8).

Most *Kanz* recipes call for the fresh green fava beans. They are incorporated into stews (DK, appendix 30, p. 135), in omelets (recipes 167, 201), and in sour-based cold dishes. Interestingly, recipe 619 suggests that fresh fava beans boiled in the jacket are to be served along with the offered dishes to wipe the hands with after the meal to remove greasy odors.

ḥashīshat al-sulṭān (حشيشة السلطان) as it is called in Egypt; otherwise, *khardal Fārisī* (خردل فارسي) or just *khardal* (خردل) *Brassica juncea* (S) broadleaf mustard greens. For wild mustard greens, see *labsān* below.

Al-Malik al-Muẓaffar, *al-Muʿtamad* 157, says that the cultivated variety is best. It is characterized by its wide leaves, with their extremely pungent and sharp taste. It was said to be a well-known vegetable which grew abundantly in the orchards of Alexandria, Cairo, and even more so in the Levant (Ibn al-Bayṭār, *al-Jāmiʿ* ii 319, s.v. *khardal Fārisī*). It shares the same medicinal benefits as those of the seeds (see *khardal*, glossary 8 above).

Due to their extreme pungency, when the leaves are used uncooked, they must be repeatedly treated by rubbing them with salt and washing and rinsing them before using them. In *Kanz* recipe 518, which involves a yogurt condiment with leaves of *ḥashīshat al-sulṭān*, the cook is instructed to mask his nose and mouth with a piece of cloth while rubbing the finely chopped leaves with salt. This was undoubtedly necessary to protect the person doing this from inhaling the rising irritating fumes. We notice that no such instructions are given in recipe 509, which also deals with a yogurt condiment with mustard greens, because it uses only the tender tips of the leaves.

ḥimmaṣ (حمّص) *Cicer arietinum* (S) chickpeas, deemed the best of all pulses. With their hot and dry properties, they were said to be the best cure for cold-related headaches and chest ailments. They are slow to digest and cause extreme bloating. However, they are valued as an aphrodisiac.

ḥimmaṣ abyaḍ (حمص ابيض) lit., 'white chickpeas'; these are the light-yellow ones, deemed the best of all varieties of chickpeas, especially the large ones with smooth skins.

ḥimmaṣ aswad (حمص اسود) black chickpeas, next to the white variety in quality, and they have the strongest properties.

ḥimmaṣ mablūl (حمص مبلول) chickpeas soaked for a while in water before using them.

ḥimmaṣ mujawhar (حمص مجوهر) roasted chickpeas, brittle in texture, sold as snack food. In *Kanz* recipe 184, it is pounded, and then beaten with eggs for an easy omelet. Apparently, it was as popular during the fourteenth century as it is now. Al-Muḥibbī, *Khulāṣat al-athar* 700, writes about one of the famous Egyptian *walī*s (men of God), who, at the beginning of his residence in Cairo, used to earn his living by selling *ḥimmaṣ mujawhar* while roaming the markets of the city. Judging from traditional practices today, it is prepared by soaking and parboiling the chickpeas, and then slowly dry roasting them in a large shallow pan containing sand.

ḥimmaṣ unthā (حمص انثى) fine-tasting tender chickpeas, described in terms of being feminine (*unthā*), as in *Kanz* recipe 616.

hindibāʾ (هندباء), ***hindabā*** (هندبا)[3] *Cichorium endivia* (S) endive. Al-Anṭākī, *Tadhkira* 366, says it is a widely-known leaf vegetable in Egypt. Of the cultivated variety (*bustānī*), there are two types:

hindabā shatawī (winter endive) also called *hindabā Shāmī* (Levantine endive). It is escarole or broad-leaved endive (*Cichorium endivia* var *latifolia*), described as having wide leaves. Although the leaves feel rough in texture, they are in fact quite tender (*rakhṣ*), only slightly bitter, and tasty. It was deemed the best type. The wild variety of this type is somewhat similar in the shape of the leaves and low level of bitterness.

hindabā ṣayfī (summer endive), also known as *hindabā al-baql*, can be eaten fresh as a salad vegetable. It is curly endive (*Cichorium endivia* var *crispum*), described as having small and narrow leaves, which are not as tender as those of winter endive, and more bitter. The wild variety of this type is even more bitter and coarser.

All types of endive have cold and dry properties, but the cultivated varieties are less dry and cooler than the wild ones. They all have a cooling and astringent effect on the stomach, and can curb bowel movements. They strengthen the weak stomach and heart, open liver obstructions, and extinguish heat generated by excess yellow bile. However, it is less effective in extinguishing thirst than lettuce (al-Anṭākī, *Tadhkira* 366–7; al-Malik al-Muẓaffar, *al-Muʿtamad* 612–4).

ḥubūb (حبوب) generic term for seeds, grains, and pulses.

isfānākh (إسفاناخ), also occurs as *isfānakh* (إسفانخ) *Spinacia oleracea* (S) spinach, the best of which was said to be dark green, and freshly cut. With its balanced properties, it was considered a good food, raw and cooked, for the sick suffering from chest ailments (al-Anṭākī, *Tadhkira* 46). In the *Kanz*, it only appears in *muzawwarāt* dishes (vegetarian) that are prepared for the sick (recipes, 204, 215, 221, 227).

jazar (جزر) *Daucus carota subsp. sativus* (S) carrot, of which there are several sizes and colors: *aḥmar* (red), *aṣfar* (yellow), *mujazzaʿ* (with two colors), *aswad* (black), which is the dark purple, *aḥmar ḍārib ilā l-ṣufra* (orange), and *abyaḍ* (white), which could be a kind of parsnip. Orange carrots with their sweet taste are the preferred variety.

---

3 The vocalization of the two forms is clearly described in al-Bīrūnī, *Ṣaydana* 378.

Carrots have hot and dry properties, they are slow to digest, and cause bloating. However, they were valued for their aphrodisiac properties. Wine made with them was said to cause headaches. To make carrot wine, the extracted carrot juice is boiled, strained, boiled again until only a quarter of its amount remains, and then honey is added, the amount of which is a quarter of the reduced carrot juice. It is then kept in jars, whose tops are tightly covered, until it ferments (al-Anṭākī, *Tadhkira* 115).

jazar barrī (جزر بري) wild carrots, also called *shaqāqul* (شقاقل) *Pastinaca schekakul* (S). It is parsnip, described as roots the size of small carrots, which have a sweetish taste. With their hot and dry properties, they can arouse coitus, induce early miscarriages, open blockages, and excite the appetite. Parsnips preserved in honey (*murabbā*) were deemed stronger in properties as an aphrodisiac than carrots (al-Anṭākī, *Tadhkira* 236; al-Ishbīlī, *ʿUmdat al-ṭabīb* ii 587). See *Kanz* recipe 386.

jirjīr (جرجير) *Eruca sativa* (S) rocket, arugula.[4] It was said to grow abundantly in Alexandria, where it was called *baqlat ʿĀʾisha*.[5] It has the following varieties:

jirjīr bustānī (جرجير بستاني) garden rocket, of which there are two varieties: the first has wide pistachio green leaves, which are mildly piquant, tender, and delicious. The second type has narrow jagged leaves, which are aggressively piquant but still bearable, and its seeds are used in cooking.[6]

jirjīr barrī (جرجير بري), also called *kharsā* (خرسا) and *khardal barrī* (خردل بري) wild rocket, with leaves like those of radishes, it is intensely piquant. It is usually eaten raw combined with other leaf vegetables, like lettuce, to alleviate its peppery heat[7] (Ibn al-Bayṭār, *al-Jāmiʿ* i 219).

This leaf vegetable is eaten raw, as it is believed to aid digestion. It is also cooked in dishes, like spinach. Eating a lot of it excites coitus and encourages the production of semen, due to its hot properties. The seeds have the same effect.

---

4 What is known as *jirjīr al-māʾ* (جرجير الماء) is in fact another species, *Nasturtim officinale* (S), watercress. Ibn al-Bayṭār, *al-Jāmiʿ* ii 271, iv 250, says it is sharp in taste like garden cress (*ḥurf*/ *rashshād*), and the leaves look somewhat like those of arugula (*jirjīr*).

5 She was the Prophet's favorite wife. This leaf vegetable was her favorite.

6 This second variety could be the species *Eruca vesicaria* (S).

7 It may be similar to today's Mediterranean wild vegetable called *ḥārra* (حارة) *Diplotaxis harra* (S), which is a species of wall rocket.

jullubān (جلّبان) *Lathyrus sativus* (S), chickling vetch, grass pea. When it comes out in springtime, its fresh green peas are tender and eaten raw. As suggested in al-Warrāq Istanbul MS, fol. 223r, the best way to cook the dried peas is to skin and boil them, with a small amount of *naṭrūn* (sodium carbonate) added.

khardal (خردل) mustard greens, see *ḥashīshat al-sulṭān* above.

khass (خس) *khaṣṣ* (خص) *Lactuca sativa* (S) lettuce, valued for its cooling properties. It was said to be good for the stomach, it excites the appetite, and puts the body to sleep. It is diuretic; helps stop wet dreams and weaken coitus (al-Malik al-Muẓaffar, *al-Muʿtamad* 163).

qulūb al-khass (قلوب الخس) tender lettuce hearts, eaten raw with the main dishes.

uṣūl al-khass (أصول الخس) lettuce stems, cooked in stews, or chopped raw and used in cold dishes. See, for instance, *Kanz* recipes 91, 92, 206

khiṭmī (خطمي) *Alththaea officinalis* (S) marshmallow. ʿAbd al-Laṭīf al-Baghdādī, *Riḥla* 61, identifies it as a variety of wild *khubbāzī* (mallows) *Malva pusilla* (S). The entire plant is mucilaginous, and it is used like shampoo for washing the hair. The ground dried leaves and white flowers are whipped with water by hand to arouse a soapy foam, and then used. In addition, when the crushed white root is dissolved in water and exposed to cool night air, it sets like aspic (*qarīṣ*).

khiyār (خيار) *Cucumis sativus* (S) common cucumber; *qathad* (قثد) is its Arabic name. Compared with *qiththāʾ* (snake cucumber), it has more moisture, which makes its flesh crisper and less dense.

Al-Anṭākī, *Tadhkira* 161, describes two varieties available in Egypt:

khiyār Shāmī (خيار شامي) Levantine cucumber, which is long.

khiyār baladī (خيار بلدي) the local variety, which is short, rounded, and curved.

The best cucumber, he adds, is long, thin, smooth, and tender. The entire plant is cold and moist, and hence it is beneficial for heat-related ailments, and to alleviate thirst. Cucumber is eaten raw and pickled. In *Kanz* recipe 523, it is incorporated into a yogurt condiment, called *jājaq*.

khiyār Tishrīn (خيار تشرين) cucumber harvest of September, i.e., at the end of its season, used for pickling, see *Kanz* recipes in chapter 18.

kurunb (كرنب) *Brassica oleracea* var. *capitata* (S) cabbage. The leaves are boiled first, drained, and then used in meat stews (DK, appendix 28, p. 134) and in cold dishes with yogurt and tahini sauces (recipes 517, 637).

Kurunb was recommended for cold-related ailments. In addition, dishes cooked with it were believed to delay intoxication if they were eaten before imbibing alcoholic drinks, and helped relieve hangover symptoms (Ibn al-Bayṭār, *al-Jāmiʿ* iv 215–9).

labsān (لبسان) *Sinapis arvensis* (S), wild mustard greens, also known as charlock mustard. It was said to be more nutritious and better for the stomach than *ḥummāḍ* (sorrel).[8] In addition, it is not as pungent as the cultivated variety (Ibn al-Bayṭār, *al-Jāmiʿ* iv 362). This explains why it is just chopped and added to the yogurt condiment in *Kanz* recipe 519.[9]

lift (لفت), also called *saljam* (سلجم) and *shaljam* (شلجم) *Brassica rapa* (S), turnips, of which there are several varieties, the most common of which are the oblong (*mustaṭīl*) and the round (*mustadīr*). The best turnips are described as large, round, tender, and sweet. They were said to invigorate coitus because they generate a lot of bloating winds (al-Anṭākī, *Tadhkira* 237).

Ibn Waḥshiyya, *al-Filāḥa* i 550, says that the Levantine turnips (*shaljam Shāmī*) are the largest. They are round (*murawwas*), completely white, but dense in texture, and have a sharp taste. Pickled turnips were believed to excite the appetite, but have no significant nutritional value. Incidentally, we learn from al-Nābulusī, *ʿAlam al-malāḥa* 256, that turnips were usually peeled in spirals.

lift abyaḍ (لفت ابيض) and *bayāḍ lift* (بياض لفت) white turnips.
lift ṭarī ḥulw (لفت طري حلو) tender and sweet turnips.

lūbiya (لوبية) ***lūbyā*** (لوبيا) *Vigna unguiculata* (S) cowpeas, also known as black-eyed peas, used both fresh in the pod and dried. Before boiling the fresh black-eyed beans, both ends of the pods are snipped off. The yellowed ones are opened and only their seeds are used. To preserve the green color of the beans while boiling, recipes recommend using either ash (*ramād*), a small lump of potash (*qilī*), or ammonia (*nashādir*). In the *Kanz*, they are prepared as cold dishes (recipes 632, 634, 635).

---

8 The name of this vegetable is not to be confused with another *ḥummāḍ*, which is citron pulp (حماض الاترج), see glossary 7 above.

9 Cf. other *Kanz* recipes 509 and 518, which use cultivated mustard greens. These must be pretreated before adding them to yogurt condiments. See *ḥashīshat al-sulṭān* above.

FIGURE 93 *Fresh* lūbiya (*black-eyed peas*).
PHOTO BY NAWAL NASRALLAH.

māsh (ماش) *Vigna radiate* (S) mung beans. It is also called *kusharī* (كشري) in al-Anṭākī, *Tadhkira* 319, where the Indian variety is deemed the best; the next best comes from Yemen, and the worst are grown in the Levant.

They are lighter than lentils, and with their cold properties, they alleviate fever symptoms. Its *muzawwara* (vegetarian dish made for the sick) was deemed the best. Its soup was recommended for coughs and colds (Ibn al-Bayṭār, *al-Jāmiʿ* iv 405). However, it is slow to digest and significantly weakens the libido, which indeed explains why its use in the medieval times was quite limited. In the *Kanz* it features only in *muzawwarāt* recipes 204, 208, and 216, cooked for the nourishment of the invalid.

mulūkhiyya (ملوخية), also called *mulūkiyya* (ملوكية) *Corchorus olitorius* (S) Jew's mallow, also known as jute mallow. It is the cultivated variety of *khubbāzī* (mallows) *Malva pusilla* (S). It is a widely-known vegetable in Egypt (Ibn al-Bayṭār, *al-Jāmiʿ* iv 459; and ʿAbd al-Laṭīf al-Baghdādī *Riḥla* 61).

All varieties of *khubbāzī* are insipid, high in liquid content, mucilaginous, and cause bloating. From the *mulūkhiyya* recipes in the *Kanz*, we learn that before adding it to the pot, the leaves are stripped from the stems, and then left in the sun to wilt. Then they are good to chop, finely—as fine as sesame seeds, as specified in al-Warrāq Istanbul MS, fol. 160v. See also *khiṭmī* (marshmallow) above.

***qar*ʿ** (قرع), also called *yaqṭīn* (يقطين) *Curcubita* (S) gourd, the best of which is medium-size, free of any bitterness, tender, and green. Some are long, and others are round with thick skins. Recipes instruct the cooks to peel them, and remove the white pithy center with the seeds. It is always eaten cooked. Fully grown gourds, which develop woody skins, are dried and made into containers.

ʿAbd al-Laṭīf al-Baghdādī, *Riḥla* 8, describes the local Egyptian gourds as being long, similar in shape to *qiththāʾ* (snake cucumber). They may grow to be 2 *dhirā*ʿs long (42 inches) and one span (9 inches) wide. Incidentally, from his account, we also learn that the Iraqi gourd had a rounded belly with a twisted neck.

With its cold properties and neutral flavor, *qar*ʿ is the perfect food for the sick, especially those with fevers. Oil extracted from its seeds was believed to induce sleep. Its jam was exemplary for its benefits. See, for instance, *Kanz* recipes 313–4.

***jurādat al-qar*ʿ** (جرادة القرع) the grated flesh of gourd.

qiththāʾ (قثّاء) *Cucumis melo* var. *flexuosus* (S) snake cucumber. Al-Anṭākī, *Tadhkira* 281, says the best is the long fleshy variety, harvested when young. The worst is the *Nīsābūrī* variety,[10] which is ridged and rough-skinned. It is eaten raw and pickled.

Qiththāʾ has cold and moist properties, and can alleviate thirst, extinguish heat in the stomach and liver, and dissolve kidney stones. It is easier to digest than *khiyār* (common cucumbers, see entry above) and other fruits eaten while unripe. However, it causes stomach rumbles (*qarāqir*) and dense gastric winds. At any rate, it does not generate good humors, and must be peeled or wiped well before eating it.

qulqās (قلقاس) *Colocasia esculenta* (S) taro. It is a tuber described as resembling a coconut from the outside, with a white interior, said to grow in the Levant but more abundantly in Egypt, where it is consumed mostly in wintertime. The best are the oval ones and those like fingers, called *qulqās ṣawābi*ʿ (قلقاس صوابع) or *qulqās aṣābi*ʿ (قلقاس أصابع), because they cook fast and digest well. ʿAbd al-Laṭīf al-Baghdādī, *Riḥla* 67, says some are the size of cucumbers and others are as small as fingers. The opposite of these are the round ones, which are not quite white (al-Shirbīnī, *Hazz al-quḥūf* 212). These never cook well. Al-Anṭākī, *Tadhkira* 289, calls them *dhakar* (male taro); cf. *qulqās ināth* (قلقاس إناث) female taro, which is another name for *qulqās aṣābi*ʿ (finger-like taro), see above.

ʿAbd al-Laṭīf al-Baghdādī says taro tastes like unripe green bananas, slightly astringent, and noticeably sharp in taste. Boiling rids it of its sharpness but releases its viscidity. That is why it is heavy on the digestion. The best way to remedy this, he

---

10 From Nishapur, in northeastern Persia.

suggests, is to drain it after boiling it, and then fry it until it browns. With its hot and moist properties, *qulqās* was deemed the best food to gain weight and arouse coitus.

qunnabīṭ (قنّبيط) *Brassica oleracea* var. *Botrytis* (S) cauliflower. Like cabbage, it is boiled first and used in stews and seasoned cold dishes, as in *Kanz* recipes 620–4. However, cabbage was said to be milder and more tender than cauliflower (*Tāj al-ʿarūs*, s.v. كرنب).

bayḍat al-qunnabīṭ (بيضة القنبيط) white curd or head of cauliflower.

rāzyānaj akhḍar (رازيانج أخضر), also called *shamār akhḍar* (شمار أخضر) *Foeniculum vulgare* var. *azoricum* (S) bulb fennel, fresh fennel. It is a plant with a bulbous base, large stalks, and feathery fronds. In *Kanz* recipes, it is used in stews, yogurt condiments, and pickling. See, for instance, recipes 516, 523, and 591.

qulūb al-shamār (قلوب الشمار) tender inner layers of fennel bulbs.
quḍbān rāzyānaj (قضبان رازيانج) stalks of bulb fennel.[11]

rībās (ريباس) *Rheum ribes* (S) Levantine rhubarb. It is a wild plant which grows abundantly in the Levantine mountainous region. Its stalks and leaves were said to be like those of chard. It tastes sourish sweet, like two pomegranates—one sweet and the other sour—combined. The stalks are described as reddish green, tender and juicy in texture.

With its astringent, cold, and dry properties, *rībās* is used to strengthen the stomach, stop vomiting and thirst. The condensed juice of its stalks (*rubb al-rībās*) is used to cool down heat-related sicknesses, excite the appetite, stop heart palpitations, and induce euphoria (al-Anṭākī, *Tadhkira* 189; al-Malik al-Muẓaffar, *al-Muʿtamad* 235). In *Kanz* recipe 16, meat stew is soured with the juice of its stalks.

rijla (رجلة) *Portulaca oleracea* (S) common purslane. This is its most common name in Egypt. Its other names are *baqla ḥamqāʾ* (بقلة حمقاء), or just *baqla* (بقلة) as it is called in the Levant; also, *farfakh* (فرفخ) and *barbahīn* (بربهين) and *barbīn* (بربين).

It is a succulent sprawling plant, with tiny fruit capsules filled with tiny round black seeds. Because of its cold properties, it is used to quench thirst and relieve symptoms of fever.

rijla ʿIrāqiyya (رجلة عراقية) Iraqi purslane. This must have been a desirable variety, since its good black seeds are needed in a dish like *sitt al-Nūba* (Nubian lady), see *Kanz* recipe 137.

---

11 The dried seeds of this plant are fennel seeds (see glossary 8 above). It is not to be confused with the anise plant (*anīsūn*/*yānsūn*), which is mainly cultivated for its seeds.

shamār akhḍar (شمار أخضر) bulb fennel, also called *rāzyānaj akhḍar*, see entry above.

shaqāqul (شقاقل), also called *jazar barrī* (جزر بري) wild carrot, and *jazar abyaḍ* (جزر أبيض) white carrot. It is parsnip (*Pastinaca schekakul*), see *jazar* above.

silq (سلق) *Beta vulgaris subsp. vulgaris* (S) chard, which is cultivated for its leaves and roots. However, in *Kanz* recipes only the leaves and their stalks are used, mostly in sour stews, such as those cooked with sumac, pomegranate seeds, and *kishk* (dried balls of crushed wheat and yogurt); for instance, see recipes 55, 56, 92, and 102. It also features in vegetarian *muzawwarāt* dishes for the nourishment of the sick (recipe 227), and cold side dishes (*bawārid*), as in recipe 629. A green dye is extracted from it and used to color stews green. See *silq maqṭūʿ* below.

> ***qulūb al-silq*** (قلوب السلق) lit., 'hearts of chard,' tender inner leaves of chard.
> ***aḍlāʿ al-silq*** (أضلاع السلق) chard stalks.
> ***silq akhḍar*** (سلق أخضر) green chard. Other shades of green are also available, such as *silq abyaḍ* (white chard), which is pale green; and *silq aswad* (black chard), which is dark green.[12]

silq maqṭūʿ (سلق مقطوع) lit., 'separated chard juice,' chard green dye. *Wuṣla* ii 583 recipe describes how to obtain it. Chard leaves are first pounded, and then strained to extract the juice, which is then boiled. This causes the green particles to separate (*yanqaṭiʿ*). When this happens, it is taken off the heat, and set aside for an hour. The separated clear water on top is poured off, and the green particles in the bottom of the pot are taken, whipped vigorously, and immediately added to foods and dishes to color them green.

turmus (ترمس) *Lupinus albus* (S) lupine beans. It is also called *bāqillā Miṣrī* (باقلى مصري) Egyptian beans. In *Kanz*, recipe 650, they are used ground with other components to wash the hands and remove greasy odors. For consumption, the recommendation was to boil them thoroughly, then soak them in water for many days to remove their bitterness. It is applied as hair softener. Medicinally, it is used to clear blockages in the liver and spleen (Ibn Sīnā, *al-Qānūn* 372; Ibn al-Bayṭār, *al-Jāmiʿ* i 184).

yaqṭīn (يقطين) gourd, used synonymously with *qarʿ* (قرع), see entry above.

---

12 See Ibn Waḥshiyya, *al-Filāḥa* i 607–14; and al-Isrāʾīlī, *Kitāb al-Aghdhiya* iii 91–4.

13. Weights and Measures

Modern equivalents of medieval weights and measures are approximate. Some of the medieval weights had different values in different parts of the Islamic world. In giving modern equivalents, ounces and pounds are used. Small weights measuring less than an ounce are more conveniently given in grams. Liquid measurements are given in terms of a pint (= 2 cups), and a cup (= 16 tablespoons).

The following guideline for modern equivalents of small weights is approximate because ingredients vary slightly in weight when measured by spoons.

1 ounce = 30 grams = 6 teaspoons = 2 tablespoons
½ ounce = 15 grams = 3 teaspoons = 1 tablespoon
2½ grams = ½ teaspoon
1¼ grams = ¼ teaspoon
1 gram = $^1/_5$ teaspoon
¾ gram = ⅛ teaspoon
½ gram = $^1/_{10}$ teaspoon
⅓ gram = $^1/_{15}$ teaspoon
¼ gram = $^1/_{20}$ teaspoon

Weight Measures

1 ***kharrūba*** (خروبة) literally 'a carob seed' = $^1/_{16}$ *dirham* = approx. 0.20 gram
1 ***ḥabba*** (حبّة) literally, 'a grain' = $^1/_{12}$ gram[1]
1 ***qīrāṭ*** (قيراط) = ¼ gram
1 ***dānaq*** (دانق) = ½ gram
1 ***dirham*** (درهم) = 3 grams = ½ teaspoon
1 ***mithqāl*** (مثقال) = 4½ grams = ⅔ teaspoon
1 ***dīnār*** (دينار) = 4½ grams = ⅔ teaspoon
1 ***ūqiyya*** (أوقيّة) = (Baghdādī) 11 *dirhams* = 34 grams = 2 tablespoons[2]
1 ***ūqiyya*** (أوقيّة) = (Egyptian) 12 *dirhams* = 37 grams = approx. 2 tablespoons

---

1 It also designates a small piece of anything such as a lump of salt or musk.

2 I base my calculations in the following weight measures on Shayzarī, *Nihāyat al-Rutba* 15–6, who explains that the commonly used *qinṭār* is 100 *raṭls*. The Damascene *raṭl* is 600 *dirhams*, and its *ūqiyya* has 50 *dirhams*. The Egyptian *raṭl* has 144 *dirhams*, and its *ūqiyya* has 12 *dirhams*. The Baghdadi *raṭl* equals ½ *mann*, which has 132 *dirhams*.

 | DOI 10.1163/9789004349919_039

1 ***ūqiyya kabīra*** (أوقية كبيرة) lit. large *ūqiyya*, could be the Levantine/Damascene *ūqiyya* (اوقية دمشق) known to be larger than the Egyptian and Baghdādī *ūqiyya*.[3] It is equal to 200 grams = 7 ounces.

1 ***raṭl Miṣrī*** (رطل مصري) Egyptian = 144 *dirhams* = 450 grams = approx. 1 pound (0.99)

1 ***raṭl ʿIrāqī/Baghdādī*** (رطل عراقي/بغدادي) Iraqi/Baghdadi = 132 *dirhams* = 408 grams = approx. 1 pound (0.90 pound).[4]

1 ***raṭl jarwī*** (رطل جروي) = approx. 2 pounds.[5]

1 ***raṭl Shāmī/Dimashqī*** (رطل شامي و دمشقي) Levantine/Damascene = 600 *dirhams* = 1.85 kg. = 4.1 pounds

1 ***raṭl*** (liquid) = 1 pint = 2 cups[6]

1 ***qisṭ*** (قسط) = 24 *ūqiyyas* = 1½ pounds = 3 cups

1 ***mann*** (من) = 2 *raṭls* = 2 pounds

1 ***mudd*** (مد) = 2 *raṭls* = 2 pounds[7]

1 ***mudd Shāmī*** (مد شامي) = 10 Egyptian *raṭls* = 10 pounds[8]

1 ***qadaḥ*** (قدح) = 2¼ pounds[9]

1 ***rubʿ*** (ربع) = 8¾ pounds[10]

1 ***ghumr*** (غمر) = approx. 7 pounds = 14 cups

1 ***qinṭār Miṣrī*** (قنطار مصري) Egyptian = 100 *raṭls*[11] = Approx. 99 pounds = approx. 11½ gallons (of milk)

niṣf thumn (نصف ثمن) half an eighth = $^1/_{16}$

niṣf wa rubʿ (نصف وربع) lit. 'half and a quarter' = ¾

---

3 The *ūqiyya* even weighs more in other Syrian regions, like Aleppo, Ḥimṣ and Ḥamāt.

4 The difference between the Egyptian and the Iraqi *raṭl* is 42 grams (approx. 1½ ounces).

5 The name *jarwī* could have originated from the practice of using an earthenware jar called *jarra* (pl. *jarr* and *jirār*) in weighing olive oil, during the time of the Crusades. Later, its use extended to weigh other commodities, such as rosewater, honey, dried fruits, nuts, cheese, onion, and garlic. See Ibn Mammātī, *Qawānīn* 361; and Ashtor, Levantine weights and standard parcels 473.

6 *Raṭl* is also a mug (1-pint capacity) used for serving wine.

7 It is said to be a capacity measurement (*mikyāl*), which equals what both hands, put together, would hold.

8 Based on *Kanz*, recipe 557.

9 The small *qadaḥ* (قدح صغير) is approx. 1½ pounds.

10 Lit. 'quarter,' calculated as a quarter of the weight measure *wayba* (ويبة, which is 16 kilograms). Al-Suyūṭī, *Ḥusn al-Muḥāḍara* 323, mentions that *rubʿ* equals 4 *qadaḥs*, and that each *qadaḥ* equals 232 *dirhams*.

11 See n. 2 above.

Measuring Containers

kūz (كوز) pl. *kīzān* (كيزان) an earthenware cup with handles, sometimes glazed; it came in various sizes. The large one was used to scoop drinks, and as a measuring unit = 18 cups. It also designated a measure of a serving of a drinking glass = approx. 1 cup.

mighrafa (مغرفة) ladle = ½ cup

qadaḥ (قدح) drinking glass enough for two people. However, in the Egyptian measuring system, it equals 8 cups = 2 liters.

sukurruja (سكرجة) a small bowl for serving table condiments; it measures ½ cup; and the large one measures 1½ cups.

FIGURE 94
Measuring cup, sealed with a capacity of 50 cc (1.70 fluid ounces), which must have been used by pharmacists, 10.130.2648 (MET NY—Gift of Helen Miller Gould, 1910).

Approximate Length and Weight Measures

arbaʿ aṣābiʿ (اربع اصابع) a width of 4 fingers, put together.

arbaʿ aṣābiʿ maftūḥa (اربع اصابع مفتوحة) a width of 4 fingers, spread apart.

iṣbaʿayn (اصبعين) a width of 2 fingers, put together.

thalāthat aṣābiʿ (ثلاثة اصابع) a width of 3 fingers, put together.

dhirāʿ (ذراع) the length of an extended arm, approx. 20.5 inches.

fitr (فتر) a small span, the distance between the tips of the stretched index finger and thumb; approx. 7 inches.

ghumra (غمرة) adding enough liquid to submerge a given ingredient.

juzʾ (جزء) part, ratio.

kaff (كف) handful, what the cupped hand can hold.

kayl (كيل) designates a dry measure by volume, as opposed to weight (*wazn*). It is also the container itself, made of metal or wood, used for measuring dry ingredients, such as grains. It is also used to designate 'part' or 'ratio,' like ***juzʾ*** (جزء).

qabḍa (قبضة) fistful.

qabḍa ṣagīra (قبضة صغيرة) a scant fistful.

qaṭra (قطرة) drop.

shayʾ min (شيء من) some, a little.

shaʿra (شعرة) lit., 'a hair,' this may be taken literally, as in a saffron thread; or just to indicate a tiny amount.

shibr (شبر) a span, the distance between the tips of the stretched little finger and thumb; approx. 9 inches.

Appendix

A Taste of Time: Modern Adaptations of Twenty-Two Recipes from the Kanz Al-Fawāʾid

Grilled quails.
FOOD PHOTOGRAPHY BY NAWAL NASRALLAH.

 | DOI 10.1163/9789004349919_040

Sūbiya
Grain-based Digestive Beer (Recipe 430)
Makes 4 servings

A refreshing nutritious drink, good for winter and summer. The name survives in Egypt to this day to designate comparable drinks; it is especially popular during the month of Ramadan.

5 slices of a plain white loaf of bread
5 cups warm water
A sprig of parsley
¼ teaspoon crushed cardamom
A stick of cinnamon
Optional: a few tender citron leaves, washed; a sprig of tarragon, and a sprig of mint
....

Put the pieces of bread in a bowl along with the water. Set aside for about 30 minutes to allow the bread to soften. Mash the mix with your fingers, and strain it through a fine-meshed sieve.

Pour the resulting liquid into a container with a lid. Add parsley, cardamom, cinnamon stick, and the optional ingredients, if used. Cover the container, and set it aside for a day or two at room temperature. Strain it again, and use it chilled with ice cubes, and sweetened to taste.

Laymūn Māliḥ
Lemon Preserved in Salt (Recipe 609)
(Makes about 8 servings)

The salted lemons can be enjoyed as a delicious relish with other foods. They are also used as an ingredient in many *Kanz* recipes.

6 lemons, washed thoroughly
About ¼ cup pickling salt
4 pieces of fresh ginger, each the size of an almond
4 sprigs of parsley
¼ teaspoon saffron

....

Cut off both ends of four of the lemons, slit them like a cross, lengthwise, but do not separate the quarters. Stuff the slits with salt, and pack the lemons tightly in a container. Cover it, and set it aside for three days (at room temperature).

Take the lemons out of the container, and set aside the remaining liquid. Press them by hand to extract some of their juice, which is to be added to the liquid that was set aside. Discard all the seeds. Stuff each lemon with a piece of ginger and a sprig of parsley. Pack them tightly in a container.

Extract the juice of the remaining two lemons, and add it to the juices that were set aside. Add saffron to it, and pour it all over the lemons. There should be enough juice to cover the lemons completely, add more if needed.

Cover the container, and put it away, at room temperature, preferably in a dark place, for a week or so, and use. Refrigerate the remaining amount.

Ḥimmaṣ Kassā
Green Condiment of Mashed Chickpeas (Recipe 613)
(Makes 4 servings)

This is the precursor of today's condiment of *hummus bi-ṭaḥīna*, which is made in a much simpler way today.

1 cup boiled chickpeas
2 tablespoons tahini, stirred with water and wine vinegar, 2 tablespoons of each
¼ cup finely ground walnuts, stirred with 2 tablespoons lemon juice, and 1 teaspoon wine vinegar
½ cup chopped parsley
¼ cup chopped mint
3 tablespoons olive oil
¼ teaspoon each of caraway, coriander, black pepper, ginger, and cinnamon, all crushed
½ teaspoon salt
A quarter of a salted lemon (see recipe, p. 649 above), cut into small pieces
For garnish: olive oil, chopped pistachios, chopped parsley, cinnamon, and rose petals (optional)

……………………………

Put all the ingredients, except the salted lemon, in a food processor, and pulse the mix until it looks smooth. The mix should look green. Add more of the herbs if needed. The consistency of the mix should be thick enough to pick up with a piece of bread. Add a bit more lemon juice if needed.

Fold in the chopped salted lemon, and use. To serve a dish, spread the condiment on a plate, drizzle a generous amount of olive oil over the face of it, garnish it with chopped parsley, and give it a light sprinkle of cinnamon and crushed rose petals if you like.

Zaytūn Mutabbal
Seasoned Olives (Recipe 567)
(Makes 6 to 8 servings)

Always handy and delicious as an appetizer.

1 cup black olives
¼ cup toasted walnuts, finely crushed
¼ cup toasted hazelnuts, finely crushed
1 tablespoon coriander seeds, toasted whole, and then crushed
Half a salted lemon (see recipe, p. 649 above), finely chopped
¼ cup olive oil

....

Combine all the ingredients in a bowl, and mix them well. If the mix looks a bit dry, add more olive oil. Cover the bowl and set it aside for an hour or two, to allow the flavors to blend, and use.

Jubn Ḥālūm Mutabbal
Seasoned Halloumi Cheese (Recipe 522)
(Makes about 6 servings)

A tasty way to serve this variety of mild white cheese.

½ pound halloumi cheese, cut into cubes
¼ cup red wine vinegar or lime juice
1 clove of garlic, mashed with a bit of salt
¾ cup toasted and crushed walnuts
2 tablespoons olive oil
½ teaspoon each of caraway and coriander seeds, toasted and then crushed
¼ teaspoon ground ginger
¼ cup finely chopped mint
1 teaspoon rose petals, crumbled
For garnish: 1 tablespoon olive oil, 1 teaspoon toasted and coarsely crushed hazelnuts, a bit of chopped mint, and coarsely crumbled rose petals

....

Put the cubed cheese in a bowl. In a food processor, combine the wine vinegar (or lime juice), mashed garlic, walnuts, olive oil, caraway, coriander, and ginger. Pulse the mixture until it has the consistency of pesto. Toss it with the cheese in the bowl, along with the chopped mint and rose petals. Taste it to see if it needs more salt. Cover the bowl and set it aside for about an hour, to allow flavors to blend. Serve it drizzled with olive oil, with a sprinkle of crushed hazelnuts and rose petals.

Ṣaḥna Kadhdhāba
False Fish Condiment (Recipe 259)
(Makes about 6 servings)

This condiment is an imitation of the real *ṣaḥna* made in Egypt with salt-cured anchovies (*ṣīr*). The sumac juice used in this false *ṣaḥna* is meant to mimic its characteristic pinkish hue.

¼ cup finely chopped parsley
½ cup finely chopped mint
½ cup walnuts, toasted and ground
½ cup tahini
¼ cup sumac juice, obtained by soaking 1/3 cup water with ¼ cup ground sumac, and straining it
1 tablespoon lime juice
1 tablespoon crushed sumac
1 clove of garlic, crushed
1 teaspoon crushed dried thyme
¼ teaspoon each of caraway seeds, coriander, black pepper, and ginger, all crushed
2 tablespoons olive oil
Half a salted lemon (see recipe, p. 649 above), chopped into small pieces
For garnish: chunks of salted lemon, olive oil, and crushed pistachios (optional)

....

Put parsley and mint in a bowl and rub them between the fingers, with a bit of salt, to crush them. Fold into them the ground walnuts, along with the tahini, sumac juice, lime juice, crushed sumac, crushed garlic, thyme and the rest of the spices, and olive oil.

Fold in the chopped salted lemon, and taste it to see if it needs more salt. In consistency, the condiment should be thick enough to pick up with a piece of bread. Serve the condiment in small bowls, with a chunk of salted lemon on top, sprinkled with pistachios (if used), with a drizzle of olive oil. Delicious with warm bread.

Takhlīl al-Shamār al-Akhḍar
Sweet and Sour Pickle of Fresh Fennel (Recipe 591)
(Makes about 6 servings)

An unusual pickle, refreshingly sweet and sour, and scented with rosewater. The recipe recommends eating it after heavy meals because it aids digestion and dispels gastric winds.

1 bulb of fresh fennel, cut into medium pieces (use only the tender parts)
1 cup red wine vinegar
3 tablespoons sugar
¼ teaspoon each of toasted whole coriander and caraway seeds
A sprig of mint
1 teaspoon rosewater
....

Boil the cut fennel in wine vinegar until it is half-cooked. Drain it, and squeeze out the extra moisture (keep the drained vinegar). Prepare the vinegar liquid as follows: Mix the remaining vinegar with sugar, toasted seeds, mint, and rosewater.

Put the drained fennel in a container, and pour the prepared vinegar liquid on it. There should be enough to cover the fennel pieces. Cover the container, and set it aside for a week, at room temperature, and use. Refrigerate the remaining amount.

Kurunb bi-Laban
Yogurt Condiment with Cabbage (Recipe 517)
(Makes about 6 servings)

This is an interesting variation on today's yogurt cucumber condiment of *jājīk* (called *jājaq* in the *Kanz*, see recipes 518 and 519). Cabbage may be substituted with fresh fennel, as in *Kanz* recipe 516, which uses only the tender parts of the bulb, very thinly sliced, rubbed with salt, left aside to drain its liquids, and then used as in this recipe.

Half a small head of cabbage, thinly sliced
1 clove of garlic, crushed with a bit of salt
¼ cup olive oil
1 cup drained yogurt

1 tablespoon finely chopped fresh dill
For garnish: chopped mint leaves, black olives, and olive oil

....

Boil the cabbage until done. Drain it and sprinkle it with salt, and set it aside to cool. In a bowl, mix the rest of the ingredients (except the garnishes). Fold in the cabbage that was set aside.

Spread the mixture in a plate, and garnish it with chopped mint and black olives. Give it a generous drizzle of olive oil, and serve.

Lūbyā
Succulent Fried Lamb and Black-Eyed Peas (Recipe 96)
(Makes 2 servings)

A very tasty small dish of *lūbyā* beans.

½ pound lamb, cut into 1-inch cubes
3 tablespoons oil
1 cup cooked black-eyed peas (canned may be used)
¼ cup chopped cilantro
1 clove of garlic, sliced
¼ teaspoon of each of black pepper and salt

....

Boil lamb in a small amount of water along with the oil. Let the meat cook gently until all the water evaporates and the lamb starts to fry in its oil. Toss in the rest of the ingredients, and continue stirring gently, until all the moisture is gone and the ingredients brown lightly in the oil. Remove from heat and serve with warm bread.

Qaliyyat al-Shawī
Succulent Fried Roasted Meat (Recipe 35)
(Makes 2 servings)

Meat of roasted lamb or kid was relished when still hot and fresh. Leftovers from the previous day's roast had to be served differently, as in this succulent fry. Nowadays, this reminds me of Fridays' sandwiches made with leftovers from Thanksgiving's roasted turkey.

½ pound roasted meat (leftovers)
3 tablespoons oil
Your choice of spices and herbs (I used 1 tablespoon chopped cilantro, and coriander, tarragon, black pepper, and ginger, ¼ teaspoon of each)
1 tablespoon lime juice or wine vinegar
4 eggs (optional)
A bit of cinnamon for garnish
....

Cut the roasted meat into thin slices, and in a wide skillet, fry it in the oil, along with the herbs and spices and lime juice or vinegar. Continue stirring until the meat is nicely browned and the seasonings start to emit a pleasant aroma. Taste it to see if it needs more salt, and give it a light sprinkle of cinnamon and serve it with bread.

If using eggs, crack them open on the meat mixture, keep them whole, cover the skillet, lower the heat, and let the eggs set, sunny side up. Sprinkle the eggs with salt and another sprinkle of cinnamon, and serve.

Fūliyya
Fava Bean Stew with Meatballs and Eggs Sunny Side up
(DK, Appx. 30, p. 135)
(Makes 4 small servings)

A delicious way to serve the green fava beans.

6 ounces lamb, cut into 1-inch cubes
3 tablespoons oil, divided
½ pound ground meat
¾ teaspoon black pepper, divided

¾ teaspoon crushed coriander seeds, divided
1 teaspoon salt, divided
1 clove of garlic, sliced
¼ cup chopped cilantro
2 cups (10 ounces) fresh fava beans, (frozen may be used), remove their skins
4 eggs

....

Fry the lamb cubes in 1 tablespoon of oil, and set it aside.

Mix ground meat with ½ teaspoon each of black pepper, coriander, and salt. Shape it into small meatballs, about 1 inch in diameter. Put them in a skillet wide enough to hold them all comfortably in a single layer, along with the remaining oil, and about ½ cup hot water. Let them boil, turning gently to allow all sides to cook, until all the water evaporates and only the fat remains. Add the fried meat that was set aside.

Add garlic, cilantro, fava beans, and the remaining black pepper, coriander, and salt. Stir the pot for a few minutes, and then add ½ cup of hot water. Let it cook gently until most of the liquid evaporates, and the fava beans are cooked.

Crack open the eggs over it, cover the skillet and let it simmer gently until the eggs are set. Serve the dish with warm bread.

Iṭriya
Meatballs with Pasta (Recipe 86)
(Makes 4 servings)

Iṭriya is strips of dried pasta noodle, about one-finger long. This dish tastes scrumptious and looks quite modern.

6 ounces lamb, cut into 1-inch cubes
3 tablespoons oil, divided
½ pound ground meat
¾ teaspoon black pepper, divided
¾ teaspoon crushed coriander seeds, divided
1 teaspoon salt, divided
1 small onion, baked and finely chopped
¼ cup chopped cilantro
½ cup boiled chickpeas (canned may be used)
4 ounces ribbon pasta noodles (such as bavette)
2 sprigs of dill, coarsely chopped

Fry the lamb cubes in 1 tablespoon of oil, and set it aside.

Mix the ground meat with ½ teaspoon each of black pepper, coriander, and salt, along with the chopped onion. Shape it into small meatballs, about 1 inch in diameter. Put them in a pot wide enough to hold them all comfortably in a single layer. Add the remaining oil, and about ½ cup water. Let them boil, turning gently, to allow all sides to cook, until all the water evaporates and only the fat remains.

Add the fried meat that was set aside, the remaining black pepper, coriander, and salt, along with cilantro. Stir the ingredients gently for a few minutes. Add chickpeas, pasta (uncooked), and dill. Pour on them 3½ cups hot water, there should be enough water to cover the pasta. Bring to a boil, cover the pot, and let it simmer gently, until the pasta has cooked and absorbed most of the liquid in the pot (about 20 minutes). Stir the pot gently twice while cooking.

Bāmiya
Okra Stew with Lamb (Recipe DK, Appx. 29, p. 135)
(Makes 4 small servings)

This is the only okra recipe which survived from the medieval Arabo-Islamic world. Nowadays, it is prepared more or less the same way, with the addition of the New World tomato.

1 pound lamb on the bone, or cubed boneless lamb
2 tablespoons oil
1 medium onion, thinly sliced
½ teaspoon black pepper
½ teaspoon salt
¼ cup chopped cilantro
2 cloves of garlic, sliced
1 pound fresh okra, cut off both ends of each okra, and cut it into 1-inch pieces (frozen may be used)
¼ cup lime juice
....
Boil the meat until cooked. Drain any remaining broth, which is to be strained and set aside. Fry the meat in a pot until it starts to brown. Add onion, black pepper, salt, cilantro, and garlic. Gently stir the ingredients for about five minutes.

Meanwhile, prepare the okra. After cutting it, parboil it, strain it, and set it aside. If frozen okra is used, it only needs to be rinsed.

Add the okra to the pot, along with the lime juice. Pour in the broth that was set aside, there should be enough to cover the ingredients, add more hot water if needed. Bring the pot to a boil, and then reduce the heat and let it simmer until the okra is cooked and the sauce is reduced (about 15 minutes).

Ṭabīkh al-Mishmish al-Yābis
Dried Apricot Stew (Recipe 121)
(Makes about 4 small servings)

An enticing dish, delicately sweet and lusciously moist.

½ pound lamb cubes
2 tablespoons oil
½ cup dried apricots
Blanched and skinned whole almonds (the number should match that of apricots)
¼ cup raisins
1 tablespoon poppy seeds
1 piece of cinnamon, plus ¼ teaspoon cinnamon powder
1 tablespoon chopped mint

1 tablespoon sugar
½ teaspoon salt
¼ teaspoon saffron

....

Boil the lamb cubes until done, and then take them out of the broth, and put them in a pot along with oil, and fry them.

Insert an almond inside each apricot and add them to the pot, along with the rest of the ingredients. Fold them gently with the meat, and pour about ¾ cup hot water on them. There should be enough liquid to just cover the ingredients. Bring the pot to a quick boil, and then lower the heat and let it simmer, covered, until the sauce is nicely thickened and reduced (about 15 minutes).

ʿAṣāfīr Mashwiyya
Grilled Sparrows (Recipe 140)
(Makes 3 servings)

Instead of sparrows, I used the optional quails (*sammān*), suggested in the recipe. Quails are a little bit larger than sparrows and available, frozen, at most Middle Eastern grocery stores.

6 quails, defrosted and ready to use
For the marinade: ¼ cup olive oil, ¼ teaspoon black pepper, ¼ teaspoon cinnamon, ½ teaspoon salt, ½ teaspoon dried thyme, 1 crushed clove of garlic, a pinch of saffron.
2 onions, cut in half

………………………………

Tie the legs of the quails, and rub them with the prepared marinade. Set them aside for an hour or so. When ready to grill, rub them once again with the marinade, and thread them through two parallel skewers to keep them from turning around while grilling. Between each two quails, thread an onion half. Grill the birds, or broil them in the oven, as I did. You also have the option of frying them. They may be served as snack food. Offer them with small bowls of sauce made by combining soy sauce (to replace the *murrī* of medieval times) whipped with a bit of lime juice and/or wine vinegar.

Lubābiyya
Sweet Chicken with Crumbs of Fresh Bread (Recipe 78)

This is an unusual chicken dish, a specialty of medieval Egypt, which tastes almost like a dessert. The recipe calls for crumbs of fresh white bread; dried breadcrumbs may not be substituted for this. Use only the pithy inside of the bread.

1 whole chicken, boiled and fried, or use store bought rotisserie chicken
2 cups of crumbs from fresh bread, obtained by pulsing it in a food processor
¼ cup oil
1½ cups sugar syrup (see instructions below), or half sugar syrup and half honey

....

Fry the crumbs in oil, until golden, and stir them into the hot syrup. Put the chicken in a slightly deep platter, and pour the hot syrup all over it. It should be thick enough to stay on the chicken and give it a glazed look. Skip dessert when you have this dish.

To make the syrup:
In a medium pot, combine 1½ cups sugar, 1¼ cups water, 1 tablespoon honey, 1 tablespoon lemon juice, and 1 tablespoon rosewater. Boil the sugar mix until it reaches the right consistency (about 10 minutes). The syrup is done if you put a drop of it in a saucer and it keeps its domed shape and does not go flat. Remove the pot from the heat immediately, and use.

Samak Maḥshī
Fried Fish Smothered in Tahini Sauce (Recipe 233)
(Makes 2 servings)

A flavorful fish dish which offers a delicious way to use tahini, other than in the familiar hummus condiment.

½ pound firm white fish, such as cod, cut into two pieces

For the fish rub: 2 tablespoons wine vinegar, 1 crushed garlic clove, 1 teaspoon crushed coriander, and ½ teaspoon salt
Flour for dusting the fish pieces
Oil for frying the fish (½-inch deep)

For the tahini sauce:
1 medium onion, finely chopped
1 tablespoon oil
¼ teaspoon each of black pepper, ginger, nutmeg, cardamom, cloves, rose petals, all pounded
¼ teaspoon salt, or as needed
¼ cup of each of tahini, wine vinegar, and water
¼ teaspoon saffron or turmeric

………………………………

Combine the rub ingredients and smear the pieces of fish with it. Put the fish in a colander set above a bowl, and set it aside for about an hour. When ready to fry, dust the fish pieces with flour, and fry them in the hot oil. Brown them on both sides, and keep them in a colander to get rid of the extra fat.

Fry onion in one tablespoon oil, until nicely browned. In a small bowl, combine the spices and salt. In another bowl, whip together tahini, vinegar, water, and saffron or turmeric. Add the contents of both bowls to the fried onion, and bring the mix to a boil while stirring.

Place the fried fish pieces on a platter, and pour the prepared tahini sauce all over them, and serve.

Another Recipe for *Samak Maḥshī*
Fried Fish Smothered in Sumac Sauce (Recipe 234)
(Makes 2 servings)

A pretty fish dish. The savory and sour sumac sauce, enriched and thickened with walnuts, is quite flavorful.

½ pound firm white fish, such as cod, cut into two pieces

For the fish rub: 2 teaspoons crushed coriander, 1 teaspoon ground caraway seeds, and ½ teaspoon salt
Flour for dusting the fish pieces
Oil for frying the fish (½-inch deep)

For the sumac sauce:
1 tablespoon each of sumac, oil, lime juice, chopped parsley, and chopped mint
¼ cup crushed walnuts
1 teaspoon crushed coriander
½ teaspoon each of dried thyme and ground caraway

¼ teaspoon black pepper
½ clove of garlic, crushed (*Kanz* recipe says to add a small amount only)
Half lemon preserved in salt (see recipe, p. 649 above), chopped into small pieces
About ¼ cup water

……………………………

Combine the rub ingredients and smear the pieces of fish with it. Put the fish in a colander set above a bowl, and set aside for about an hour. When ready to fry, dust the fish pieces with flour, and fry them in hot oil. Brown them on both sides, and keep them in a colander to get rid of extra fat.

In a small pot, combine all the sumac sauce ingredients, there should be enough water to moisten the mix well. Add a bit more if needed. Let it boil, for 4 or 5 minutes. Taste it to see if it needs more salt.

Place the fried fish pieces on a platter, and pour the prepared sumac sauce all over them, and serve.

Bahaṭṭa Bayḍā' and *Bahaṭṭa Ṣafrā'*
White and Yellow Rice Pudding (Recipes 105 and 106)
(Makes 2 to 4 servings)

This is a meatless pudding included in the chapter for main dishes. It is to be assumed that such dishes were served alongside the familiar stews and porridges, or as a sweet finale to a meal. On our modern tables, it is still served as a light refreshing snack food, served warm or chilled.

3 cups milk
3 tablespoons rice flour
2 tablespoons butter
3½ to 4 tablespoons sugar (or to taste)
1 tablespoon rosewater
A stick of cinnamon
¼ teaspoon saffron, steeped in a small amount of hot water (for the yellow pudding)
Coarsely crushed pistachios for garish

....

Combine all the ingredients (except for the saffron and garnish) in a medium pot. Whisk the mix to remove all lumps, and then boil it gently on medium heat, stirring constantly, until it thickens nicely (about 5 minutes).

Take half of it and put it in another pot, and stir in the steeped saffron with its water. Stir the pudding on medium heat until it comes to a boil, and remove.

Immediately spread the pudding in somewhat deep plates, and garnish the surface with pistachio. You may serve the two colors in the same plate, in a decorative manner.

Naqūʿ al-Mishmish
Dried Apricot Compote (Recipe 436)
(Makes about 3 servings)

A very refreshing snack food, simple, light, and luscious. The dried apricots will taste moist, as if fresh, delicately sweet, and redolent of rosewater. The recipe recommends it as a fine mezze (*naql*) snack.

12 dried apricots
½ cup rosewater
2 tablespoons sugar
Coarsely crushed pistachio, for garnish

……………………………

In a bowl, dissolve sugar in rosewater. Add the apricots to the liquid, there should be enough to cover them. Cover the bowl, and set it aside for a day, at room temperature.

Take the apricots out and arrange them in one layer in a sieve, and let them drain for an hour or two. To serve, put the apricots in a bowl and garnish them with the pistachio.

Qarn Bārūq
Bārūq's Horn (Recipe 309)
(Makes about 20 small pieces)

We have no certain information on who Bārūq was and why his name was associated with these 'horny' syrupy pastries (see the recipe for possibilities). The way the pastries are rolled, as described in the *Kanz* recipe, indeed makes them resemble small cut horns.

2 cups white all-purpose flour
¼ teaspoon salt
2 tablespoons butter, melted
About $^2/_3$ cup water, room temperature
Oil for brushing the flattened dough
Oil for frying the rolls (1-inch deep)
One recipe of sugar syrup, see recipe, p. 666 above
Coarsely crushed pistachios, for garnish
....

Mix flour with salt. Combine melted butter with water, pour them on the flour, and knead into a stiff dough—like pasta dough—and let it rest for about 15 minutes.

Divide the dough into 4 portions, and roll out each one thinly with a rolling pin. Brush the surface with oil, and roll the flattened sheet loosely, about three times or until the roll is about one inch in diameter. Rolling loosely is important because this will allow the inside of the pastry to cook well while frying. Separate the rolled part with a knife, and cut the roll into about 3-inch long pieces, and arrange them on a tray, repeat with the rest of the dough.

Heat the oil in a frying pan, and prepare a colander set over a bowl, and another bowl to put the syrup. When ready to fry (on medium heat), carefully add the pieces, making sure that the lengthwise ends are stuck to the dough so that they do not open while frying. Put the finished ones in the colander to drain the extra fat, and as the others fry, dip the finished ones in the syrup (at room temperature). Keep them there for a minute or so, making sure all parts are coated with the syrup, and then take them out and put them in another colander set over a bowl, to let the extra syrup drain (which may be returned to the syrup bowl and re-used).

Arrange the finished pieces on a platter, and garnish them with pistachios. It is best when enjoyed freshly made.

Nuhūd al-ʿAdhārī
Virgins' Breasts (Recipe 300)
(Makes 20 pieces)

Scrumptious cookies, which seemed to have been quite popular in medieval times, as they featured in other medieval Arabic cookbooks, with slight variations. The recipe does not explain how they are shaped exactly. Studding them with raisins is my interpretation of it.

1 cup white all-purpose flour
1 cup finely ground almonds (almond flour may be used)
¾ cup sugar
1 teaspoon baking powder
½ teaspoon ground cardamom
A pinch of salt
½ cup oil (such as canola)
3 tablespoons rosewater
20 raisins

…………………………………

Put the dry ingredients (the first six) in a food processor, and pulse once or twice to mix them.

Add oil slowly through the tube, and pulse a few more times. Add the rosewater, and pulse several times until the mix clumps together. Add a bit more if needed.

Take a walnut-size piece, roll it by hand into a ball and place it on a lightly oiled cookie sheet. Slightly moisten your hands with a bit of rosewater while handling the mix. Repeat with the rest of pieces, leaving a space between them. Press a raisin in the middle of each piece, and bake them in the middle shelf of a preheated oven (375 F.) for about 13 minutes (do not let them overbake). Finish the baking in the top shelf of the oven for the last two minutes.

Works Cited

ʿAbd al-ʿAzīz, Nabīl. *al-Maṭbakh al-sulṭānī fī zaman al-Ayyūbiyyīn wa-l-Mamālīk*. Cairo, 1989.

ʿAbd al-Laṭīf al-Baghdādī. *Riḥlat ʿAbd al-Laṭīf al-Baghdādī fī Miṣr*. Edited by ʿAbd al-Raḥmān al-Shaykh. Cairo, 1998.

Abū Ḥayyān al-Andalusī. *Kitāb al-Idrāk li-lisān al-atrāk*. Istanbul, 1891.

al-ʿĀmilī, Bahāʾ al-Dīn. *al-Kashkūl*. Online: http://www.alwaraq.net/Core/waraq/coverpage?bookid=155. Accessed 20 March 2017.

Anonymous. *Anwāʿ al-ṣaydala fī alwān al-aṭʿima*. Edited by ʿAbd al-Ghanī Abū al-ʿAzm. Rabat, 2003.

Anonymous. *Kitāb Kanz al-fawāyid wa-tanwīʿ al-mawāyid*. MS orient. A 1345, Gotha Research Library. (See also Marín and Waines below.)

Anonymous. *Kitāb Waṣf al-aṭʿima al-muʿtāda*. MS Taymūr Ṣināʿa 11. Cairo: Dār al-Kutub al-Qawmiyya.

Anonymous. *Kitāb Waṣf al-aṭʿima al-muʿtāda*. Translated by C. Perry (based on MSS Taymūr Ṣināʿa 51 and 52, Cairo: Dār al-Kutub al-Qawmiyya). In *Medieval Arab Cookery*, M. Rodinson, A.J. Arberry, and C. Perry, 275–464. Totnes, UK, 2001.

al-Anṭākī, Dāwūd b. ʿUmar al-Baṣīr. *Tadhkirat ulī l-albāb al-jāmiʿ li-l-ʿajab al-ʿujāb*. Beirut, n.d.

al-Arbūlī, ʿAbd al-ʿAzīz. *al-Kalām ʿalā l-aghdhiya*. Edited by Amador Diaz Garcia. Granada, 2000.

Ashtor, E., "Levantine Weights and Standard Parcels: A Contribution to the Metrology of the Later Middle Ages." *Bulletin of the School of Oriental and African Studies* 45 (1982): 421–88.

al-Azdī, ʿAlī b. Ẓāfir al-Miṣrī. *Gharāʾib al-tanbīhāt ʿalā ʿajāʾib al-tashbīhāt*. Online: http://www.alwaraq.net/Core/waraq/coverpage?bookid=3116. Accessed 20 March 2017.

al-Badrī, Abū l-Baqāʾ ʿAbdallāh al-Miṣrī l-Dimashqī. *Nuzhat al-anām fī maḥāsin al-Shām*. Baghdad, 1922.

al-Baghdādī, Ibn al-Karīm Muḥammad b. al-Ḥasan al-Kātib. *Kitāb al-Ṭabīkh*. Edited by Dāwūd al-Chalabī. Mosul, 1934; reprint, edited by Fakhrī l-Bārūdī. Beirut, 1964.

al-Baghdādī, Ibn al-Karīm Muḥammad b. al-Ḥasan al-Kātib. *Kitāb al-Ṭabīkh*. MS or. 5099 BL.

al-Baghdādī, Ibn al-Karīm Muḥammad b. al-Ḥasan al-Kātib. *Kitāb al-Ṭabīkh*. Translated by A.J. Arberry. "A Baghdad Cookery Book." *Islamic Culture* 13, nos. 1 and 2 (1939): 21–47, 189–214.

al-Baghdādī, Ibn al-Karīm Muḥammad b. al-Ḥasan al-Kātib. *Kitāb al-Ṭabīkh*. Translated by C. Perry. *A Baghdad Cookery Book*. Totnes, UK, 2005.

al-Bīrūnī, Abū l-Rayḥān. *al-Jamāhir fī maʿrifat al-jawāhir*. Online: http://www.alwaraq.net/Core/waraq/coverpage?bookid=512. Accessed 20 March 2017.

al-Bīrūnī, Abū l-Rayḥān. *Kitāb al-Ṣaydana*. Edited and translated by Ḥakīm Muḥammad Saʿīd. Karachi, 1973.

Black, Jeremy, et al. *A Concise Dictionary of Akkadian*. Wiesbaden, 2000.

Blackwell, Elizabeth. *A Curious Herbal*. London, 1739.

Bonavia, E. *The Cultivated Oranges and Lemons etc. of India and Ceylon*. London, 1888.

Chalabī, Awliyā. *al-Riḥla ilā Miṣr wa-l-Sūdān wa-l-Ḥabasha*. Arabic translation by Ḥusayn al-Miṣrī, et al., 2 vols. Cairo, 2006.

Chapot, Henri. "Le cedrat kabbad: et deux autres variétés de cédrat du moyen-orient." *al-Awamia* 8 (1963): 39–61. Online: webagris.inra.org.ma/doc/awamia/00803.pdf. Accessed 12 Dec. 2016.

al-Dhahabī, Shams al-Dīn Muḥammad. *Tārīkh al-Islām*. Online: http://www.alwaraq.net/Core/waraq/coverpage?bookid=141. Accessed 20 March 2017.

Dols, Michael, trans. *Medieval Islamic Medicine: Ibn Riḍwān's Treatise "On the Prevention of Bodily Ills in Egypt."* Arabic text *Dafʿ Maḍār al-Abdān*. Edited by Adil Galal. Berkeley, 1984.

Dozy, Reinhart. *Takmilat al-maʿājim al-ʿArabiyya*. Online: http://www.alwaraq.net/Core/waraq/coverpage?bookid=1119. Accessed 20 March 2017.

al-Dumayrī, Muḥammad b. Mūsā. *Ḥayāt al-ḥayawān al-kubrā*. Online: http://www.alwaraq.net/Core/waraq/coverpage?bookid=118. Accessed 20 March 2017.

Finkel, Joshua. "King Mutton: A Curious Tale of the Mamluk Period." *Zeitschrift für Semitistik und verwandte Gebiete* 8 (1932): 122–48 (part 1); 9 (1933–4): 1–18 (part 2).

Fischel, Walter J. "The Spice Trade in Mamluk Egypt: A Contribution to the Economic History of Medieval Islam." *Journal of the Economic and Social History of the Orient* 1 (1958): 157–74.

Gelder, Geert van. *God's Banquet: Food in Classical Arabic Literature*. New York, 2000.

Geries, Ibrahim (ed.). *Mufākharat al-ruzz wa-l-ḥabb rummān*. Wiesbaden, 2002.

Ghālib, Edwār. *al-Mawsūʿa fī ʿulūm al-ṭabīʿa*. Beirut, 1986.

al-Ghassānī, Muḥammad b. Ibrāhīm al-Wazīr. *Ḥadīqat al-azhār fī māhiyyat al-ʿushb wa-l-ʿiqār*. Edited by Muḥammad al-Khaṭṭābī. Beirut, 1990.

al-Ghazālī, Abū Ḥāmid. *Sirr al-ʿālamayn wa-kashf mā fī l-dārayn*. Online: http://www.alwaraq.net/Core/waraq/coverpage?bookid=561. Accessed 20 March 2017.

al-Ghuzūlī, ʿAlāʾ al-Dīn al-Bahāʾi. *Maṭāliʿ al-budūr fī manāzil al-surūr*. 2 vols. Cairo, 1881.

Ghouchani, A. and C. Adle. "A Sphero-Conical Vessel as *fuqqāʿa*, or a Gourd for 'Beer.'" *Muqarnas* 9 (1992): 72–92.

Goitein, S.D. *Studies in Islamic History and Institutions*. Leiden, 2010.

Grieve, M. *The Modern Herbal*. 2 vols. New York, 1981.

al-Ḥajjār, Aḥmad b. Yaḥyā. *Kitāb al-Ḥarb al-maʿshūq bayn laḥm al-ḍān wa-ḥawāḍir al-sūq*. Edited by Manuela Marín, "On Food and Society." *al-Qantara* 13 (1992): 83–122.

al-Ḥarīrī, Muḥammad. *Maqāmāt*. Online: http://www.alwaraq.net/Core/waraq/coverpage?bookid=96. Accessed 20 March 2017.

al-Hassan, Ahmad Y. and Donald Hill. *Islamic Technology: An Illustrated History*. UNESCO, 1992.

Herodotus. *The Histories*. New York, 2004.

al-Ḥimyarī, Muḥammad b. ʿAbd al-Munʿim. *al-Rawḍ al-miʿṭār fī khabar al-aqṭār*. Online: http://www.alwaraq.net/Core/waraq/coverpage?bookid=316. Accessed 20 March 2017.

Hinds, Martin and Badawi El-Said. *A Dictionary of Egyptian Arabic*. Beirut, 1986.

al-Hurawī, Muḥammad b. Yūsuf. *Baḥr al-jawāhir*. Calcutta, 1871.

Ibn Abī Uṣaybiʿa. *ʿUyūn al-anbāʾ fī ṭabqāt al-aṭibbāʾ*. Online: http://www.alwaraq.net/Core/waraq/coverpage?bookid=79. Accessed 20 March 2017.

Ibn al-ʿAdīm, Kamāl al-Dīn. *al-Wuṣla ilā-l-ḥabīb fī waṣf al-ṭayyibāt wa-l-ṭīb*. MS 90913, SOAS, London.

Ibn al-ʿAdīm, Kamāl al-Dīn. *al-Wuṣla ilā-l-ḥabīb fī waṣf al-ṭayyibāt wa-l-ṭīb*. Edited by Sulaymā Maḥjūb and Durriyya al-Khaṭīb. 2 vols. Aleppo, 1986.

Ibn al-ʿAwwām, Ibn Zakariyyā Yaḥyā. *Kitāb al-Filāḥa*. Madrid, 1802.

Ibn Bassām, Muḥammad b. Aḥmad. *Nihāyat al-rutba fī ṭalab al-ḥisba*. Edited by Muḥammad Ḥasan Ismāʿīl and Aḥmad al-Muzīdī. Beirut, 2003.

Ibn Baṭṭūṭa. *Riḥlat Ibn Baṭṭūṭa*. Online: http://www.alwaraq.net/Core/waraq/coverpage?bookid=67. Accessed 20 March 2017.

Ibn al-Bayṭār. *al-Jāmiʿ li-mufradāt al-adwiya wa-l-aghdhiya*. 4 vols. Beirut, 1992.

Ibn al-Ḥājj, Abū ʿAbdallāh al-Mālikī. *al-Madkhal*. 4 vols. Cairo, n.d.

Ibn al-ʿImād al-Ḥanbalī. *Shadharāt al-dhahab fī akhbār man dhahab*. Online: http://www.alwaraq.net/Core/waraq/coverpage?bookid=3183. Accessed 20 March 2017.

Ibn Iyās, Abū l-Barakāt al-Nāṣirī. *Badāʾiʿ al-zuhūr fī waqāʾiʿ al-duhūr*. Edited by Muḥammad Muṣṭafā. 6 vols. Mecca, 1984.

Ibn al-Jawzī, ʿAbd al-Raḥmān b. ʿAlī. *al-Adhkiyāʾ*. Online: http://www.alwaraq.net/Core/waraq/coverpage?bookid=106. Accessed 20 March 2017.

Ibn Jazla, Yaḥyā b. ʿĪsā l-Baghdādī. *Minhāj al-bayān fīmā yastaʿmiluhu al-insān*. MS British Library, no. ADD 5934.

Ibn al-Jazzār, Aḥmad b. Ibrāhīm, *Kitāb al-Iʿtimād fī-l-adwiya al-mufrada*. Aya Sofia Library MS 3563. Online: www.alukah.net/library/0/89029/. Accessed 10 Jan. 2017.

Ibn Khaldūn. *Tārīkh Ibn Khaldūn*. Online: http://www.alwaraq.net/Core/waraq/coverpage?bookid=116. Accessed 20 March 2017.

Ibn Khalṣūn, Muḥammad b. Yūsuf. *Kitāb al-Aghdhiya*. Edited by Suzanne Gigndet. Damascus, 1996.

Ibn Khurradādhbih, Abū l-Qāsim ʿUbaydallāh. *al-Masālik wa-l-mamālik*. Online: http://www.alwaraq.net/Core/waraq/coverpage?bookid=54. Accessed 20 March 2017.

Ibn al-Kindī, Abū ʿAmr, *Faḍāʾil Miṣr al-maḥrūsa*. Online: http://www.alwaraq.net/Core/waraq/coverpage?bookid=404. Accessed 20 March 2017.

Ibn al-Kutubī, Yūsuf b. Ismāʿīl. *Mā lā yasaʿ al-ṭabīb jahlahu.* MS, Library of Congress. Online: lcweb2.loc.gov/service/amed/amed0001/2001/200149140/200149140.pdf. Accessed 11 Sept. 2016.

Ibn Mammātī, al-Asʿad. *Kitāb Qawānīn al-dawānīn.* Edited by ʿAzīz ʿAṭiyya. Cairo, 1991.

Ibn Mankalī, Muḥammad. *Uns al-malā bi-waḥsh al-falā.* Online: http://www.alwaraq.net/Core/waraq/coverpage?bookid=3274. Accessed 20 March 2017.

Ibn Mubārak Shāh, Shihāb al-Dīn Aḥmad. *Zahr al-ḥadīqa fi l-aṭʿima al-anīqa.* MS orient A. 1344, Gotha Research Library.

Ibn al-Mujāwir, Jamāl al-Dīn al-Dimashqī. *Tārīkh al-mustabṣir.* Online: http://www.alwaraq.net/Core/waraq/coverpage?bookid=2027. Accessed 20 March 2017.

Ibn al-Quff, Abū l-Faraj b. Yaʿqūb. *Jāmiʿ al-gharaḍ fī ḥifẓ al-ṣiḥḥa wa-dafʿ al-maraḍ.* Wellcome Library, Arabic Medicine 116. Online: www.wdl.org/ar/item/16762/. Accessed 10 Feb. 2017.

Ibn Sīnā. *al-Qānūn fi-l-ṭīb.* Online: http://www.alwaraq.net/Core/waraq/coverpage?bookid=30. Accessed 20 March 2017.

Ibn Sūdūn, ʿAlī l-Yashbaghāwī. *Nuzhat al-nufūs wa-muḍḥik al-ʿabūs.* Edited by Maḥmūd Sālim. Damascus, 2001.

Ibn Taghrī Birdī, Jamāl al-Dīn. *al-Nujūm al-zāhira fī mulūk Miṣr wa-l-Qāhira.* Edited by Muḥammad Shams al-Dīn. 16 vols. Beirut, 1992.

Ibn Ṭūlūn, Shams al-Dīn al-Ṣāliḥī. *Mufākahat al-khillān fī ḥawādith al-zamān.* Online: http://www.alwaraq.net/Core/waraq/coverpage?bookid=195. Accessed 20 March 2017.

Ibn al-Ukhuwwa, Muḥammad b. Muḥammad. *Maʿālim al-qurba fī ṭalab al-ḥisba.* MS 5023, Library of the University King Saʿūd. Online: www.al-mostafa.info/data/arabic/depot/gap.php?file=m014108.pdf. Accessed 11 Sept. 2016.

Ibn Waḥshiyya, Abū Bakr al-Kisdānī. *al-Filāḥa al-Nabaṭiyya.* Edited by Tawfīq Fahd. 3 vols. Damascus, 1995.

al-Ibshīhī l-Maḥallī, Shihāb al-Dīn. *al-Mustaṭraf fī kull fann mustaẓraf.* Online: http://www.alwaraq.net/Core/waraq/coverpage?bookid=78. Accessed 20 March 2017.

al-Idrīsī, Abū ʿAbdallāh al-Sharīf. *Nuzhat al-mushtāq fī ikhtirāq al-āfāq.* Edited by Roberto Rubinacci et al. 2 vols. Cairo, 2002

al-Ishbīlī, Abū l-Khayr. *ʿUmdat al-ṭabīb fī maʿrifat al-nabāt.* Edited by Muḥammad al-Khaṭṭābī. 2 vols. Beirut, 1995.

Işin, Mary. *Sherbet and Spice: The Complete Story of Turkish Sweets and Desserts.* London, 2013.

al-Isrāʾīlī, Isḥāq b. Sulaymān. *Kitāb al-Aghdhiya.* 4 vols. Frankfurt, 1986.

Jadon, Samira Yousef. "The Arab Physician ibn Butlan's (d. 1066) Medical Manual for the Use of Monks and Country People." PhD Dissertation, University of California, Los Angeles, 1968.

al-Jāḥiẓ, Abū ʿUthmān. *al-Bayān wa-l-tabyīn.* http://www.alwaraq.net/Core/waraq/coverpage?bookid=65. Accessed 20 March 2017.

al-Jāḥiẓ, Abū ʿUthmān. *al-Ḥayawān*. Online: http://www.alwaraq.net/Core/waraq/coverpage?bookid=16. Accessed 20 March 2017.

al-Jazzār, Abū al-Ḥusayn. "Fawāʾid al-mawāʾid," edited by Ibrāhīm al-Sāmarrāʾī. *al-Majmāʿ al-ʿilmī al-ʿIrāqī* 27 (1976): 204–35, and 28 (1977): 153–71.

al-Kāshgharī, Maḥmūd b. al-Ḥusayn. *Kitāb Dīwān lughāt al-Turk*. Istanbul, 1914.

al-Kāzarūnī, Sadīd al-Dīn. *al-Sadīdī* (*al-Mughnī fī sharḥ al-mūjaz*). Calcutta, 1832.

al-Khafājī, Shihāb al-Dīn. *Shifāʾ al-ghalīl fī-mā fī kalām al-ʿarab min al-dakhīl*. Edited by Muḥammad Kashshāsh. Beirut, 1998.

al-Khawārizmī, Abū ʿAbdallāh. *Mafātīḥ al-ʿulūm*. Online: http://www.alwaraq.net/Core/waraq/coverpage?bookid=132. Accessed 20 March 2017.

Kindersley, Dorling. *Ultimate Food Journeys: The World's Best Dishes and Where to Eat Them*. Norfolk, UK, 2011.

al-Kindī, Yaʿqūb b. Isḥāq. *al-Taraffuq fī l-ʿiṭr*. Edited by Sayf b. Shāhīn al-Mirrīkhī. Doha, 2010.

Kurlansky, Mark. *Salt: A World History*. New York, 2002.

Lane, Edward. *An Account of the Manners and Customs of the Modern Egyptians*. New York, 1973.

Levanoni, Amalia. "Food and Cooking During the Mamluk Era: Social and Political Implications." *Mamlūk Studies Review* 9 (2005): 201–22.

Levey, Martin. *Chemistry and Chemical Technology in Ancient Mesopotamia*. Amsterdam, 1959.

Lewicka, Paulina. "Diet as Culture: On the Medical Context of Food Consumption in the Medieval Middle East." *History Compass* (2014): 607–17.

Lewicka, Paulina. *Food and Foodways of Medieval Cairenes: Aspects of Life in an Islamic Metropolis of the Eastern Mediterranean*. Leiden, 2011.

al-Maghribī, Yūsuf. *Dafʿ al-iṣr ʿan kalām ahl Miṣr*. Facsimile of MS no. M.s.O.788 (1606) at the Library of the University of Leningrad. Edited by ʿAbd al-Salām ʿAwwād. Moscow 1968.

Maḥjūb, Sulaymā and Durriyya al-Khaṭīb (eds.). *al-Wuṣla ilā-l-ḥabīb fī waṣf al-ṭayyibāt wa-l-ṭīb*. 2 vols. Aleppo 1986.

al-Malik al-Muẓaffar, Yūsuf b. ʿUmar b. Rasūl al-Ghassānī. *al-Muʿtamad fi l-aʿshāb al-ṭibbiyya wa-l-adwiya al-Mufrada*. Edited by Nabīl al-ʿArqāwī. Damascus, 2010.

Manniche, Lise. *An Ancient Egyptian Herbal*. London, 1989.

al-Maqdisī, Muḥammad b. Aḥmad Shams al-Dīn. *Aḥsan al-taqāsīm fī maʿrifat al-aqālīm*. Online: http://www.alwaraq.net/Core/waraq/coverpage?bookid=0. Accessed 20 March 2017.

al-Maqrīzī, Taqī l-Dīn Aḥmad. *Ittiʿāẓ al-ḥunafā bi-akhbār al-aʾimma al-fāṭimiyyīn al-khulafā*. Online: http://www.alwaraq.net/Core/waraq/coverpage?bookid=144. Accessed 20 March 2017.

al-Maqrīzī, Taqī l-Dīn Aḥmad. *al-Khiṭaṭ li-maqrīziyya*. Edited by Muḥammad Zīnhum and Madīḥa al-Sharqāwī. 3 vols. Cairo, 1997.

al-Maqrīzī, Taqī l-Dīn Aḥmad. *al-Sulūk li-maʿrifat duwal al-mulūk*. Edited by Muḥammad ʿAṭā. 8 vols. Beirut, 1997.

Marín, Manuela. "Beyond Taste: The Complements of Color and Smell in the Medieval Arab Culinary Tradition." In *A Taste of Thyme*, edited by Sami Zubaida and Richard Tapper, 205–14. London, 1994.

Marín, Manuela and David Waines. "The Balanced Way: Food for Pleasure and Health in Medieval Islam." *Manuscripts of the Middle East* 4 (1989): 123–32.

Marín, Manuela and David Waines (eds.). *Kanz al-fawāʾid fī tanwīʿ al-mawāʾid*. Beirut, 1993.

al-Masʿūdī, Abū l-Ḥasan. *Murūj al-dhahab wa-maʿādin al-jawhar*. Online: http://www.alwaraq.net/Core/waraq/coverpage?bookid=91. Accessed 20 March 2017.

Mehdawy, Magda and Amr Hussein. *The Pharaoh's Kitchen*. Cairo, 2010.

al-Muḥibbī, Muḥammad Amīn Faḍlallāh. *Khulāṣat al-athar*. Online: http://www.alwaraq.net/Core/waraq/coverpage?bookid=288. Accessed 20 March 2017.

al-Nābulusī, ʿAbd al-Ghanī b. Ismāʿīl. *ʿAlam al-malāḥa fī ʿilm al-filāḥa*. MS Damascus 1882. Online: ia800500.us.archive.org/3/items/kitbalamalmalahfoonbul/kitbalamalmalahfoonbul.pdf. Accessed 10 Sept. 2016.

Nāṣir Khusrū, ʿAlawī. *Safarnāma*. Arabic translation by Yaḥyā l-Khashshāb. Cairo, 1993.

Nasrallah, Nawal. "In the Beginning, There Was No *musakka*." *Food, Culture and Society* 13 (2010): 595–606.

Nasrallah, Nawal. "The Iraqi Cookie, *kleicha*, and the Search for Identity." *Repast* 4 (Fall 2008): 4–10.

Nurollah. *Madatolhayat*. English translation by M.R. Ghanoonparvar. *Dining at the Safavid Court*. Costa Mesa, CA, 2017.

al-Nuwayrī, Shihāb al-Dīn. *Nihāyat al-arab fī funūn al-adab*. Edited by Mufīd Qumayḥa, et al. 33 vols. Beirut, 2004.

al-Qalqashandī, Aḥmad. *Ṣubḥ al-aʿshā*. Online: http://www.alwaraq.net/Core/waraq/coverpage?bookid=77. Accessed 20 March 2017.

al-Qazwīnī, Zakariyyā b. Muḥammad. *Āthār al-bilād wa-akhbār al-ʿibād*. Online: http://www.alwaraq.net/Core/waraq/coverpage?bookid=105. Accessed 20 March 2017.

al-Rāzī, Abū Bakr Muḥammad b. Zakariyyā. *al-Ḥāwī fī l-ṭibb*. Online: http://www.alwaraq.net/Core/waraq/coverpage?bookid=14. Accessed 20 March 2017.

al-Rāzī, Abū Bakr Muḥammad b. Zakariyyā. *Kitāb al-Manṣūrī*, MS Majmūʿat al-Manṣūrī, Library of Congress. Online: www.wdl.org/ar/item/4276/. Accessed 12 Jan. 2017.

al-Rāzī, Abū Bakr Muḥammad b. Zakariyyā. *Manāfiʿ al-aghdhiya wa-dafʿ maḍārrihā*. Beirut, 1982.

Redhouse, J.W. *Turkish and English Lexicon*. London, 1880.

Riolo, Amy. *Nile Style: Egyptian Cuisine and Culture*. New York, 2013.

Rizq, Hayām and Maʿṣūma ʿAlāma. *Asrār al-takhalluṣ min al-ʿajaz al-jinsī*. Lebanon, n.d.

Rodinson, Maxime. "Studies in Arabic Manuscripts Relating to Cookery." In *Medieval Arab Cookery*, M. Rodinson, A.J. Arberry, and C. Perry, 91–163. Totnes, UK, 2001.

Sābūr b. Sahl. *al-Aqrabādhīn al-ṣaghīr*. Translated by Oliver Kahl. *Sābūr Ibn Sahl: Dispensatorium Parvum*. Leiden, 1994.

Sarkīs, Khalīl. *Kitāb Tadhkirat al-khawātīn wa-ustādh al-ṭabbākhīn*. Beirut, 1900.

Sato, Tsugitaka. *Sugar in the Social Life of Medieval Islam*. Leiden 2014.

al-Shayzarī, ʿAbd al-Raḥmān b. Naṣr. *Nihāyat al-rutba fī ṭalab al-ḥisba*. Edited by Muḥammad Muṣṭafā Ziyāda. Cairo 1946.

al-Shirbīnī, Yūsuf b. Muḥammad. *Hazz al-quḥūf fī sharḥ qaṣīd Abī Shadūf*. Alexandria, 1872.

al-Sibāʿī, Fāḍil, "*Kabbād al-Shām*." Online: www.albahethon.com/?page=show_det&id=853. Accessed 11 Sept. 2016.

Steingass, F.A. *A Comprehensive Persian-English Dictionary*. New Delhi, 2000.

al-Suyūṭī, Jalāl al-Dīn. *Bughyat al-wuʿāt fī ṭabaqāt al-lughawiyyīn wa-l-nuḥāt*. Online: http://www.alwaraq.net/Core/waraq/coverpage?bookid=3180#authorbooks. Accessed 20 March 2017.

al-Suyūṭī, Jalāl al-Dīn. *Ḥusn al-muḥāḍara fī akhbār Miṣr wa-l-Qāhira*. Online: http://www.alwaraq.net/Core/waraq/coverpage?bookid=3150. Accessed 20 March 2017.

al-Suyūṭī, Jalāl al-Dīn. *Manhal al-laṭāyif fī al-kunāfa wa-l-qaṭāyif*. Edited by Aḥmad ʿAwaḍ. Cairo, n.d.

al-Ṭaghnarī l-Ghirnāṭī, Abū ʿAbdallāh Muḥammad. *Zahrat al-bustān wa-nuzhat al-adhhān*. Edited by Muḥammad al-Mashhadānī. Cairo, 2005.

al-Tallaʿfarī, Ayād ʿAbd al-Qādir. *Mawsūʿat al-ṭibb al-badīl*. Cairo, 2009–13.

al-Tamīmī, Muḥammad b. Aḥmad. *Ṭīb al-ʿarūs wa-rayḥān al-nufūs fī ṣināʿat al-ʿuṭūr*. Edited by Luṭfallāh al-Qārī. Cairo, 2014.

al-Tujībī, Ibn Razīn. *Fiḍālat al-khiwān fī ṭayyibāt al-ṭaʿām wa-l-alwān*. Edited by Muḥammad b. Shaqrūn. Beirut, 1984.

ʿUmar b. Yūsuf b. ʿUmar b. Rasūl. *Milḥ al-malāḥa fī maʿrifat al-filāḥa*. Edited by ʿAbdallāh al-Mujāhid. Damascus, 1987.

al-ʿUmarī, Ibn Faḍlallāh. *Masālik al-abṣār fī mamālik al-amṣār*. Edited by Kāmil al-Jubūrī. 27 vols. Beirut, 2010.

Usāma b. Munqidh, *Kitāb al-Iʿtibār*. Online: http://www.alwaraq.net/Core/waraq/coverpage?bookid=86. Accessed 20 March 2017.

Waines, David. "Dietetics in Medieval Islamic Culture." *Medical History* 43 (1999): 228–40.

Waines, David (ed.). *Food Culture and Health in Pre-modern Islamic Societies*. Leiden, 2011.

Waines, David. "'Luxury Foods' in Medieval Islamic Societies." *World Archaeology* 34, no. 3 (2003): 571–80.

al-Wardī, Sirāj al-Dīn. *Kharīdat al-ʿajāʾib wa-farīdat al-gharāʾib*. Online: http://www.alwaraq.net/Core/waraq/coverpage?bookid=337. Accessed 20 March 2017.

al-Warrāq, Abū Muḥammad al-Muẓaffar b. Naṣr b. Sayyār. *Annals of the Caliphs' Kitchens*. Translated by Nawal Nasrallah. Leiden, 2007.

al-Warrāq, Abū Muḥammad al-Muẓaffar b. Naṣr b. Sayyār. *Kitāb al-Ṭabīkh*. Edited by Kaj Öhrnberg and Sahban Mroueh. Helsinki, 1987.

al-Warrāq, Abū Muḥammad al-Muẓaffar b. Naṣr b. Sayyār. *Kitāb al-Wuṣla ilā-l-ḥabīb li-yughtanā bihi ʿan jahd al-ṭabīb/Kitāb al-Ṭabāyikh* (adapted and augmented copy). MS 7322 A. 2143. Topkapi Sarayi, Istanbul.

Watson, Andrew M. *Agricultural Innovation in the Early Islamic World*. London, 1983.

Wilson, Hilary. *Egyptian Food and Drink*. London, 2001.

Wright, Clifford. *A Mediterranean Feast*. New York, 1999.

Yāqūt al-Ḥamawī. *Muʿjam al-buldān*. Online: http://www.alwaraq.net/Core/waraq/coverpage?bookid=94. Accessed 20 March 2017.

Yāqūt al-Ḥamawī. *Muʿjam al-udabāʾ*. Online: http://www.alwaraq.net/Core/waraq/coverpage?bookid=93. Accessed 20 March 2017.

al-Yūnīnī, Quṭb al-Dīn. *Dhayl mirʾāt al-zamān*. Online: http://www.alwaraq.net/Core/waraq/coverpage?bookid=250. Accessed 20 March 2017.

Zack, Liesbeth. *Egyptian Arabic in the Seventeenth Century: A Study and Edition of Yūsuf al-Maghribī's* Dafʿ al-Iṣr ʿan Kalām Ahl Miṣr. Utrecht 2009.

al-Zarkalī, Khayr al-Dīn. *al-Aʿlām*. Online: http://www.alwaraq.net/Core/waraq/coverpage?bookid=511. Accessed 20 March 2017.

Zayyāt, Ḥabīb. "*Fann al-ṭabkh wa iṣlāḥ al-aṭʿima fī al-Islām*." *al-Mashriq* 41 (1947): 1–26.

General Index

In this index, entries marked with asterisks are not given full page citations.

ʿAbdallāh b. Ṭāhir al-Khurāsānī (governor) 507
ʿAbd al-Laṭīf al-Baghdādī (*Riḥla*) 9, 33, 41, 50, 462, 486, 493, 507, 515, 516, 520, 521, 523, 584, 630, 631, 636, 638, 639
abrāj ḥamām (pigeon cotes) 10, 11, 21, 42, 613
Abū Bakr al-Mādrānī 28
Aḥmad al-Tīfāshī 7, 19, 327
Alexandria 12n31, 23, 26, 51n143, 208, 249, 498, 555, 564, 591n7, 633, 635
ʿAlī b. Rabban al-Ṭabarī (*Firdaws al-ḥikma*) 397
ʿAlī b. al-Ṭabbākh (cook) 35
aphrodisiacs 32n86, 49, 54, 56, 155n315, 160n332, 177n29, 263, 298, 311n30, 317n14, 379n1, 420, 423n10, 424n17, 464, 482, 492, 497, 501, 509, 520, 530, 531, 543, 545, 546, 548, 550, 555, 554, 564, 567, 572, 574, 609, 612, 617, 623, 633, 635
  See also *bāh*; libido
Apicius 23
al-Babbāwī (cook, later vizier) 35
*al-Baghdādī (*Kitāb al-Ṭabīkh*) 8, 17, 18, 94n39, 465, 466

bāh (coitus) 54, 161, 177, 262, 424
  See also aphrodisiacs; libido
bardī (papyrus) 70, 576, 582, 588
barniyya (wide-mouthed jar) 174, 247, 255, 259, 274, 291, 293, 294, 295, 299, 300, 303, 317, 321, 328, 339, 341, 348, 351, 359, 360, 362, 365, 366, 368, 371, 431, 432, 433, 452, 576
  billawr (crystal) 576
  ghayr madhūna (unglazed) 335, 576
  madhūna (glazed) 339, 353, 356, 576
  qīshānī (ceramic) 291, 292, 382, 376, 595
  ṣīnī (porcelain) 292
  zujāj (glass) 251, 347
bāṭiya (large wide bowl) 351, 576
bilāṭa (flat tile) 196, 232, 233, 234, 266, 269, 418, 576
birām, qidr (soapstone pot) 66, 251, 260, 263, 291, 292, 296, 299, 368, 354, 577
  ṭājin (frying pan) 379, 385, 577
Būrān 134n224, 493
bustūqa (jar) 76, 576, 577

Cairo 23, 26–33, 553, 633
  Bayn al-Qaṣrayn 39
  marketplaces 38–44
chicks' factories 41–2, 611

dakshāb (stirring utensil) 254, 260, 266, 267, 286, 277
dann (earthenware cask) 286, 346, 577
dast (large brass pot) 71, 96, 108, 150, 217, 225, 226, 230, 234, 235, 238, 243, 244, 245, 247, 253, 254, 257, 268, 297, 324, 335, 340, 342, 371, 382, 390, 577
  birām (soapstone) 261
  nuḥās aḥmar (red copper) 304
  nuḥās muʾannak (tinned copper) 66, 577

Egypt 8–13
  ancient 20–1, 22
  annual flooding 21, 24, 25, 32, 33, 50, 594
  Arab rule 23–6
  Ayyubids 7, 23, 33, 34, 35, 81n11, 215n25, 318n17, 358n65
  Copts 10n27, 12n31, 29, 284n80, 458, 478
    calendar 25n60, 375n145, 440n15
  famines 33
  Fatimids 23, 25–6, 29–31, 33–5, 45, 49, 358, 500
  Fusṭāṭ 23, 26–7, 36
  Fayyūm 26, 352, 466n5, 502, 553
  High Dam of Aswan 21
  Lower Egypt xi, 10, 47, 507, 579
  Mamluks 1, 19, 23, 33, 34, 35, 36, 37
  Nile River 10, 21, 24–5, 26, 27, 32, 33, 48, 50, 466n5, 553, 594
  Roman Empire 23
  Tulunids 23, 27–8
  Upper Egypt xi, 9, 52, 151, 213, 215, 225, 299, 528, 584
Egyptian Arabic dialect xi, 12–3, 32, 72n38, 75n47, 116n134, 150n287, 153n307, 172n5,

Egyptian Arabic dialect (cont.) 188n17, 199n19, 231n107, 239n150, 255n23, 273n17, 285n85, 301n33, 309n22, 444n30, 453n63, 491n18, 496, 499, 519, 558, 561, 567, 585, 589
al-Maghribī (*Dafʿ al-iṣr ʿan kalām ahl Miṣr*) xi, 12n33

faḥm (charcoal) 119, 160, 406, 511, 577, 594
fayyāsha (long-necked bottle) 414, 578, 623
firewood 20, 32, 66, 67, 535n4, 580, 594, 598
furn (brick oven) 23, 31, 40, 43, 45, 47, 50, 51, 80, 162, 168, 168, 177, 181, 196, 198, 214, 216, 229, 248, 267, 472, 473, 578–9, 592, 601
farrān (oven operator) 40, 43

Galenic humoral theory 53–6, 185n6, 303n43, 619, 624–5, 626
ghaḍāra (deep dish bowl) 181, 182, 191, 309, 579
al-Ghazzī, Raḍiyy al-Dīn 18, 330n39
ghirbāl (sieve) 108, 110, 123, 136, 139, 197, 204, 205, 212, 272, 282, 579
al-Ghuzūlī, ʿAlāʾ al-Dīn (*Maṭāliʿ al-budūr*) 18, 287n91, 395n18, 457n1, 458, 459, 463, 471

al-Ḥāfiẓiyya, Arghawān 7, 35, 215
ḥajar ṣandal (iron sandalwood) 420, 580
al-Ḥajjār (*Kitāb al-Ḥarb al-maʿshūq*) 9, 36, 51n143, 243n173, 338n81, 487, 491n18, 495, 500, 591n7, 631
al-Ḥākim bi-Amrillāh (Fatimid caliph) 31, 500
Ḥamdūna 394n12
hangovers, see *khumār*
ḥantam (green glazed vessel) 163, 580, 581, 592
Hārūn al-Rashīd (Abbasid caliph) 394n12, 395n18
ḥaṣīra (reed mat) 335n64, 580, 617n8
hāwan (mortar) 45, 94, 105, 120, 194, 239, 298, 303, 305, 313, 317, 352, 380, 401, 580
Herodotus (*History*) 21
ḥisba/*muḥtasib* (market inspection) 12, 40, 42, 43, 48, 459n5, 581n3, 594
ḥuqq (rounded bowl) 80n8, 266n62, 347, 580
Yemenī 288
ḥuzmat kibrīt (bundle of matchsticks) 119, 581, 583

Ibn ʿAbdūn, *see* Ibn Buṭlān
Ibn al-Bawwāb 394n13
Ibn Buṭlān (*Kunnāsh al-adīra wa-l-ruhbān*) 16, 54, 185n3
Ibn al-Jazzār (*Kitāb al-Iʿtimād*) 533
*Ibn Mubārak Shāh (*Zahr al-ḥadīqa fī l-aṭʿima al-anīqa*) 19–20, 44, 66n5, 580
Ibn Shāhīn al-Ẓāhirī 31–2
Ibn Sūdūn (*Nuzhat al-nufūs wa-muḍḥik al-ʿabūs*) 12n36, 37–8, 474, 544n9
Ibn Ṭūlūn (amir) 27
ʿĪd Shamm al-Nasīm 10
ijjāna (large tub) 159, 208, 305, 430, 581
ināʾ/*wiʿāʾ* (vessel) 200, 201
ḍārī (with traces of fermentation) 274, 276, 281, 286, 337, 458
madhūn (glazed) 176, 315, 318, 322, 325, 594
muzaffat (pitched) 371, 372, 439, 447, 448, 594
muzajjaj (glazed ceramic) 444, 445
rashshāḥ (unglazed) 288
ṣīnī (porcelain) 400
zujāj (glass) 166, 343
inbīq (alembic) 166n14, 167, 275, 276, 283, 291, 293, 368, 427, 428, 431, 432, 433, 435, 581, 588, 602
iṣṭām (large iron spatula) 217, 220, 227, 245, 246, 581, 605

jafna (large wide serving bowl) 71, 288, 381, 581
jām (serving platter) 216, 236, 237, 308, 435, 449, 581
jamjā (ladle) 171, 581
jāwlī (winnowing fan) 104, 582
al-Jazzār, Abū l-Ḥusayn (*Fawāʾid al-mawāʾid*) 36
jirāb (traveling sack) 231, 582
jurn (stone mortar) 45, 209, 227, 245, 260, 263, 296, 303, 316, 317, 353, 582
fuqqāʿī (used by beer makers) 299, 317, 318, 365
khashab (wooden) 352
rukhām (marble) 337

kāghad (hemp paper) 274, 425, 582
kānūn (brazier) 45, 354, 582
Kārimī merchants 26
khabbāz (bread maker) 40, 42
khābiya (large earthenware jar) 163, 271, 348, 360, 441, 582

ghayr rashshāḥa (non-porous) 162
kharīṭa (linen drawstring bag) 442, 582
khiwān (wooden board) 69, 236, 251, 583
khumār (hangovers) 260n39, 263, 458, 459, 481, 497, 517, 521, 527, 559
Khumārawayh (Egyptian ruler) 28
*al-Kindī, Yaʿqūb b. Isḥāq (*al-Taraffuq fi-l-ʿiṭr*) 14, 425n21
kīzān/kūz (earthenware cup, pitcher) 39, 270, 271, 277, 279, 280, 283, 410, 458, 459, 460, 644
ḍāriya (with traces of fermentation) 273, 281, 583

libido 56, 161, 423, 541, 543, 567, 621, 624, 629, 638
See also aphrodisiacs; *bāh*

mahabbāt (breeze catchers) 44, 409, 584
mājūr (large tub) 71, 139, 150, 249, 278, 331, 336, 338, 439, 584
al-Malik al-ʿĀdil (Ayyubid king) 34, 35, 215n25, 358n65
al-Malik al-Saʿīd b. al-Malik al-Ṣāliḥ (Ayyubid king) 33
al-Malik al-Ṣāliḥ Najm al-Dīn Ayyūb (Ayyubid king) 33
al-Maʾmūn (Abbasid caliph) 16, 121, 123, 237, 394, 449, 507
Marín, Manuela 1, 3, 6n15, 13
maṭara/muṭr (stone jar) 324, 376, 584, 617
mifrāk (mixer) xi, 415, 584
mighrafa (ladle) 69, 585, 644
muqaʿʿara (concave) 75
mushabbaka (latticed) 164
muthaqqaba (perforated) 73
milʿaqa (spoon) 171, 186, 187, 212, 225, 238n142, 251, 379, 412, 463, 484, 485, 500, 527, 585, 623
miqlā wāsiʿ (wide frying pan) 326, 586
miʿṣarat māʾ al-laymūn (lemon press) 168, 586
miṣfāt (colander) 94, 389
Mufākharat al-ruzz wa-l-ḥabb rummān 37, 468, 474, 500
Muḥammad b. al-ʿAbbās al-Khushshakī 398n40
al-Musabbiḥī (Fatimid historian) 33–4
mustawqad (stove) 45
al-Mutawakkil (Abbasid caliph) 31, 110, 132, 497, 500
muzammala (water-cooling crock) 63n6, 83n1, 462, 586

naʿʿāra (bucket) 443, 449–50, 586
*al-Nābulusī (*ʿAlam al-malāḥa fī ʿilm al-filāḥa*) 18, 330n39, 358, 452n58, 512, 546, 597, 637
nāfikh nafsihi (portable stove) 50, 161, 586
al-Nāṣir b. Qalāwūn (Mamluk sultan) 35
Nāṣir Khusrū (*Safarnāma*) 25, 26–7, 45, 505
New Year festival (Nawrūz) 10, 25n60, 29, 440
nuḥās muʾannak/mubayyaḍ (tinned copper) 45, 66, 81, 103, 577, 588, 592

al-Qāḍī l-Fāḍil (Saladin's counselor) 8, 81
qālab (cutter, mold) 80, 162, 419, 471, 588
qarʿa (cucurbit), see *inbīq*
qarrāba (large flagon) 298, 588
qārūra (glass flask or bottle) 362, 554, 588
qaṣʿa (large wide bowl) 73, 261, 306, 307, 330, 588
qaṣab (reeds) 220, 233
Fārisī 439, 588
Qāsim Shaghīta (baker, later vizier) 35
qaṣriyya (large wide tub) 163, 204, 239, 240, 280, 283, 288, 360, 376, 588
qaṭramīz (wide-mouthed jar) 176, 197, 303, 304, 316, 317, 321, 356, 359, 360, 364, 366, 368, 369, 371
zujāj (glass) 156, 204, 365
qidr (pot) 99, 100, 202, 286, 588
birām (soapstone) 251, 260, 291, 292, 296, 299, 453
fakhkhār (earthenware) 103, 302, 329,
ḥajar (stone) 329
madhūn (glazed) 336
nuḥās mubayyaḍ (tinned copper) 164
Zabadānī (earthenware) 370n114
zujāj (glass) 154
qinnīna (glass bottle) 275, 307, 308, 434, 588
(tightly woven bowl) 267, 274, 413, 588
qirba (leather vessel, jar) 168, 589
qirma (tree stump, cutting board) 382, 589
quffa (large basket) 163, 196, 278, 279, 334, 589

raḥāʾ (quern) 173n11, 433, 469, 589
Ramadan 29, 39, 52, 278, 293, 462, 464n12, 648

raṭl jarwī (Egyptian weight) 8, 121, 205n49, 256, 643n5
rāwūq (strainer for liquids) 167, 168, 274, 277, 589
al-Rāzī, Abū Bakr (*Kitāb al-Manṣūrī*) 15, 84n1
riqq (thin leather sheet) 291, 293, 324, 450, 589
Rodinson, Maxime 3, 512n3

sā'a falakiyya (equal hour) 424n14, 600
saffūd (spit, skewer) 77, 589
ṣaḥfa (wide shallow bowl) 172, 380, 439, 589
Ṣalāḥ al-Dīn (Ayyubid sultan) 8, 34, 81n11
al-Ṣāliḥ Ṣāliḥ (Mamluk sultan) 34
ṣallāya (stone slab) 272, 302, 418, 420, 590
saṭl (brass kettle with handles) 215, 494, 590
sāṭūr (cleaver) 69, 88, 385
ṣawānī (metal serving trays) 443, 444, 446, 447, 591
shawbaq/suwayq (rolling pin) 81, 213, 591
shawka (large pitchfork) 76, 591
al-Shirbīnī (*Hazz al-quḥūf*) 9n24, 10, 32, 42, 47n132, 499–500, 501, 579, 592, 610, 639
sikkīn (knife) 45, 69, 74, 167, 171, 218, 228, 341, 345, 358n65, 364, 375, 401, 406, 591
  ghayr ḥadīd (blunt) 261
  khashab (wooden) 256
  raqīq (thin) 173
sukurdān (large tray loaded with appetizers) 51, 291, 292, 331, 354, 357, 360, 364, 366, 370, 591
al-Suyūṭī, Jalāl al-Dīn (*Manhal al-laṭāyif fī-l-kunāfa wa-l-qaṭāyif*) 35–6

ṭabaq (large platter, tray) 229, 382, 396, 415, 446, 448, 591
  bi-shafa (with a lip) 216
  'īdān (twig-tray) 260
  khalanj (heath-wood) 246
  mushabbak (latticed) 224, 254, 443
  nuḥās (copper) 214
  nuḥās mubayyaḍ (tinned copper) 81
ṭābaq (wide pan/skillet) 183n51, 418
ṭabkh bayn nārayn (cooking between two fires) 141n249, 501, 601
ṭāḥūn (grinder) 173n11, 411, 469
**ṭājin* (frying pan, casserole) 45, 96, 592, 607
  birām (soapstone) 385
  ḥadīd (iron) 472
*al-Tamīmī, Muḥammad b. Aḥmad (*Ṭīb al-'arūs*) 16, 393n6, 399n49, 508, 538n7
tannūr (domed clay oven) 42, 47, 52, 61n4, 148, 152n301, 155n316, 213, 215, 226, 227, 263, 307, 380, 471, 472, 476, 494, 496, 590, 592–3, 601
ṭāsa (metal scooping bowl) 280, 285, 593
ṭasht (large shallow basin) 287, 288
ṭayfūr (bowl) 306
thaljiyya (water-cooling vessel) 285, 593
ṭīn (clay) 164, 372, 438, 439, 440, 441, 452, 593
  abyaḍ (white) 395, 440, 577
  abyaḍ Makkī 395
  aḥmar (red) 451
  ḥurr (pure) 67, 439n5
  murammal (sandy clay soil) 453
toothpicks (*khilāl*) 15, 56, 392–3, 540, 546, 623, 626
  'īdān khilāf (willow twigs)
  ma'mūnī 393
  manners observed 393
turāb, aḥmar ḥayy (raw red soil) 451, 594
  al-fawākhīr (potters red soil) 451, 594

ublūja/abālīj (conical pottery mold) 453n60, 489, 490, 491, 594
'ūd dhukār (stick from caprifig) 162, 509, 594
'ūd nushshāb (thick sturdy reed) 233, 567, 588, 594
'ulba (wooden/leather box) 217, 222, 232, 594
Usāma b. Munqidh 34–5

Waines, David 1, 3, 6n15, 13
*al-Warrāq, Ibn Sayyār (*Kitāb al-Ṭabīkh*) 13, 15–6, 270n3, 305n2, 465
  *Istanbul MS 18, 306n8, 477, 483, 499, 500
**Waṣf al-aṭ'ima al-mu'tāda* 9, 13, 14n39, 16, 17–8, 85n1
**al-Wuṣla ilā-l-ḥabīb* (Ibn al-'Adīm) 9, 10, 16–7, 229n77

Zayyāt, Ḥabīb 3, 34n91
**zibdiyya* (bowl) 45, 108, 110, 594–5
  qīshānī (ceramic) 292
  ṣīnī (porcelain) 292, 421

Index of Ingredients, Dishes, Beverages, Aromatics, and other Preparations

In this index, page numbers in bold type designate recipes. Entries marked with asterisks are not given full page citations.

**abāzīr/afāwīh* (spices) 67, 529
aṭrāf al-ṭīb (spice blend) **531**
fuqqāʿ (spice blend) **530**
ḥārra (having hot properties) 115, 208, 316, 529
sūbiyā (spice blend) **529**
ʿujaj (spice blend) **529**
ʿadas (lentils) 21, 26, 630
aswad (black) 31
maqshūr (shelled) 139
muṣaffā (strained) **150**
adhān (oils), *see under* odor removers
ʿadhba (tamarisk seeds) 223, 261, 529
afāwīh, see *abāzīr*
ʿafṣ (oak gall) 300, 530
ʿajjūr (Egyptian chate) **387**, **388**, 451, 630, 632
akhlāṭ (yogurt condiments) 51, **328**, 338n81, 478
aloeswood, see *ʿūd*
**alya* (sheep-tail fat) 48, 68, 606, 609, 614
amīrbārīs (barberries) **91**, 223, 506
**ʿanbar* (ambergris) 70, 405n10, 530
khām (raw) 253, 405, 408, 415
maʿjūn (kneaded), see *muthallath* below
muthallath 405, 405n10, 406, 415, 423, 619
ʿanbarī/ʿanbarīnā (ornamental solid perfume) **420**, 619
anīsūn (aniseeds) 223, 262, 264, 308, 310, 379, 530
apples, see *tuffāḥ*
apricots, see *mishmish*
ʿaqīd sakanjabīn, see under candies
ʿāqir shamʿā/sāq al-ḥamāma (alkanet, colorant) 232, 428, 531, 561
aqsimā (digestive drink) 52, 168, **274**, **275**, **276**, **277**, **280**, **281**, **284**, 287, 436, 437, 457, 527
khamīra/iksīr (distilled base) **275**, **276**, **283**
spice blend for **531**
aruzz/ruzz (rice) 24, 37, 45, 52, 91, 101, 107, 114, 115, 119, 121, 133, 134, 152, 278, 285, 468, 474, 603, 616
abyaḍ/mubayyaḍ (white, polished) 137, 394, 395, 468
aruzziyya, see under porridges
aṣfar (yellow) **133**, 424
bahaṭṭa bayḍāʾ (white pudding) **138**, **669**
bahaṭṭa ṣafrāʾ (yellow pudding) **139**, **669**
bi-laban (pudding, with milk) **125–6**, 139
būza (drink) 464n12
daqīq/madqūq (ground) 72, 85, 121123, 125, 131, 138, 139, 285, 394, 397, 398, 648
how to grind **395**
labaniyya (with milk) **131**
madqūq/ maṭḥūn (ground) 72, 85, 121, 123, 125, 131, 138, 139, 285, 394, 397, 398, 648
Maʾmūniyya, see under porridges
mufalfal (pilaf) **140**
muḥallā (sweetened) **140**
nashā (starch) 230
sūbiya (digestive beer) **286**, **288**, 464
Wāḥī 9, 122, 125
ās, see *marsīn*
asafetida, leaves (*anjudhān*) 209n68, 307, 308, 362, 530, 632
root (*maḥrūth*) 310, 311
ʿaṣāfīr (sparrows) 39, 41, 609
fried **157**, **158**, **172**, **182**
makbūs/māliḥ (salt-preserved) **156**, **158**
omelet 56, **158**
mashwiyya (roasted) **155**
maṭbūkha (stewed) 7, 49–50, **159–61**
with eggs **156**
ʿasal mursal (sugar cane syrup) 8, 150, 459n5, 482

ʿasal qaṣab (sugar-cane honey) 459n5, 482, 488
**ʿasal naḥl* (bee honey) 31, 481–2
Egyptian 8, 126, 285
asārūn (wild spikenard) 264, 531
ashriba (beverages)
aqsimā (digestive), *see entry*
būza 464n12
fuqqāʿ (foamy beer), *see entry*
jullāb 459
**māʾ* (water) 5, 14, 15, 41, 43, 44, 48, 52, 56, 69, 83–4
māʾ shaʿīr (with malted barley) 276, 278, 279, 462
mayba (restorative, quince) **251**, 462, 484, 624
mizr 32, 286, 462
naqūʿ mishmish (liquid of apricot compote) 290–3
sharāb (sweet drinks), *see entry*
sharāb ʿatīq (aged wine) 251, 262
sharāb rayḥānī (sweet-smelling wine) 419, 464, 544
shush (grain-based beer) **278, 284, 285**, 464
sūbiyā (digestive beer), *see entry*
sukkar wa-laymūn (lemon-flavored sugar) 53, **284**, 464
ṭilā (unfermented grape wine) 439, 442, 464
See also *sakanjabīn*
ʿĀṣimī (stew), see *marwaziyya*
Asyūṭiyya (bread pudding) 52, **151, 213, 215**
aṭrāf/afwāh ṭīb* (spice blend) **531
awrāl (monitor lizards), see *waral*

**bādhinjān* (eggplant) 24, 26, 72, 630
bawārid (cold dishes) **390**
Būrāniyya (fried, with meat) 134, **493**
pickled 342, **357, 370, 371**
storing **451**
bāmiya (okra) xi, 9, 21, 31, 492, 584, 604, 631
stew **135, 662**
banafsaj (violets) 413, 430, 531
qazmat (dwarf violet iris) 399, 408, 532, 558
bananas, see *mawz*
baqar (cow, beef) 21, 71, 137, 494, 499, 609–10
dung 440
ʿijl (calf, veal) 71, 610, 614, 615
baqdūnis (Macedonian parsley) 105, 113, 149, 158, 171, 176, 199, 202, 207, 208, 257, 316, 318, 319, 321, 350, 353, 354, 356, 370, 374, 378, 379, 380, 381, 382, 383, 385, 387, 388, 389, 390, 532
See also *maqdūnis*; *karafs* (common parsley)
bāqilā (fava beans), see *fūl*
baqla (purslane), see *rijla*
baqqam (red dye) 431, 533
baqsamāṭ, *see under* breads
barnūf (sticky fleabane) 399, 533
**baṣal* (onion) 21, 26, 45, 50, 70, 74, 534
baṣaliyya (meat dish) **136**
pickled **356, 357, 359, 360, 361, 372**, 373
basbās/shamar (fennel), see *rāzyānaj*
basbāsa (mace) 253, 263, 264, 281, 283, 287, 288, 299, 300, 338, 353, 365, 397, 401, 409, 415, 417, 421, 458, 529, 531, 534, 540
bawārid (cold dishes) 38, 328, 492, 516, 549, 630, 632, 636, 637, 640
ʿajjūr **387, 388**
black-eyed peas (*lūbyā*) **388**, 637
cabbage (*kurunb*) 77, **331, 390, 391**, 556, 636, **656**
cauliflower (*qunnabīṭ*) **383, 384**
chard (*silq*) 77, **387**
eggplant (*bādhinjān*) **390**
fava beans (*fūl*) 74, 382, **383**
gourd (*qarʿ*) **389, 390**
ḥimmaṣ kassā (chickpea dip) xi, 51, **378–82, 384, 650**
purslane (*rijla*) 334, **385, 386**
roasted lamb (*shawī*) **385, 658**
bayḍ (eggs) 40, 41, 76, 97, 99, 100, 103, 107, 133, 135, 154, 154, 610, 658, 659
bayāḍ (egg white) 108, 117, 118, 119, 235, 238, 239, 245, 329
for garnishing 177, 309
madfūna (buried) **175**
maḥshī (stuffed) **172**
maṣūṣ (poached in vinegar sauce) **175, 180**, 496
mukhallal/makbūs (pickled) **173, 174, 176**, 493
mukhardal (with mustard) **175**
muṭajjan (fried) **180**
ʿujja (omelet) **156, 158, 171, 172, 174, 176, 177, 178, 179, 180, 181, 182**

bāzār 338, 631
bazmāward (pinwheel sandwiches) 29, 31
beverages see *ashriba*
binn (fermented condiment) 372, 493
bīrāf (clotted cream) 7, 19, **326**
bisillā (grass pea, large variety) 26, 78, 631
biṭṭīkh (melon) 39, 451, 506–8
  qishr (peel) 70, 73, 77, 507 70, 73, 77, 507–8
  seeds 222, 464n12,
biṭṭīkh akhḍar/aḥmar/Hindī (watermelon) 222, 443n26, 507
biṭṭīkh aṣfar (muskmelon)
  ʿAbdulī/Dumayrī (Egyptian chate) 9, **244**, 507
  shammām/ʿitābī/Khurāsānī 394, 508
  Ṣīnī/Samarqandī/Maʾmūnī 10, 222, 507
breads, cookies, and pastries:
  abū lāsh **232**, **243**, 481
  aqrāṣ mamlūḥa (salted cookies) **80**, 468
  Asyūṭiyya (bread pudding) 52, **213**, **215**
  baqsamāṭ (twice-baked cookies) 188, 275, 468
  basandūd (sandwich cookies) 29, 32, 39, **241**, 468
  bread, see *khubz*
  fustuqiyya Nābulusiyya (sweet crumble) **271**
  Ḥāfiẓiyya (filled cookies) 7, 35, **215**
  ifṭilū (gold-stuffed cookies) 28–9
  irnīn (stuffed cookies) **80**
  kaʿk (dry cookies) 29, 75, 80n10, **81**, 239, 240, 247, 272, 325, 468, 471
    bi-l-ʿajwa (with dates) **82**
    maltūt (enriched with fat) **82**
    sukkarī (sweetened) **81**
  kalījā (round cookies) 213, 471
  khubz abāzīr (seeded sugarless cookies) **80**
  khubz manfūsh (sweet fluffy bread) 10, 229, 474
  khubz ṭayyib (sweet and delicate cookies) **79**
  khudūd al-aghānī (chanteuses' cheeks) 6, 52, **213**
  khushkanānaj (filled cookies) 29, 32, 39, 81n10, 241
  kunāfa (enclosed cookies) **217**
  makshūfa (open-faced pie) **214**
  mushabbaka (latticed honey pie) **216**
  nuhūd al-ʿadhārī (virgins' breasts) 6, **229**, **673**
  Qāhiriyya (ring cookies) **238**
  qāwūt (toasted wheat granola) **221**, 475
    baladī (local-style) **232**
    Turkish **231**
    See also *sawīq*
breath fresheners 54, 56, 260, 261, 262, 263, 286, 318, 352, 372, **408**, **409**, **410**, 423, 509, 517, 534, 540, 543, 548, 561, 565
bunduq* (hazelnuts) 26, 70, 77, **105, 108, **117**, **128**, 508
bunduqiyya (small meatballs) **102**, 492, 495, 496
Būrāniyya (eggplant dish) **134**, 493, 630
būraq (sodium bicarbonate) 70, 73, 220, 473, 535
  Armenian (sodium borate) 265, 536
  See also *naṭrūn*
bustān abrūz (amaranth) 302n39, 429, 431, 536, 538
  See also *ḥamāḥim rayḥān aḥmar*
butter, see *zubd*
buṭūn (innards of ruminants) 137

cabbage, see *kurunb*
candies, confections, and jams:
  ʿaqīd tamr Hindī (chewy tamarind candy) **260**
  aqrāṣ al-laymūn (hard lemon drops) **251**, **260**
  fānīdh (pulled taffy) 32, 109n108, 211, 127n195, **265**, 482–3, 486, 489
  ḥalāwa with *malban* **245**, 485
  ḥalwā bilā nār (uncooked) **223**
  hays (date balls) 238n143, **247**
  kaʿb al-ghazāl (taffy) 29
  lawzīnaj yābis (almond brittle) **234**, 236n131
  makshūfa (candy brittle) **215**, **217**
  mushāsh (lollipops) 39, 52, 71, **220**
  nāṭif (pulled-taffy) 211n2, 216n30, 266, 483
  nayda (Egyptian taffy) 26, 32, 211n4, 486
  qurāḍiyya (hard sticky candy) 109n108, 483
  ruṭab muʿassal (honeyed fresh dates) **246**
  ruṭab murabbā (date jam) **247**
  sakanjabīn ʿaqīd (oxymel chewy-candy) **250**, 302, 405
  shakrīnaj (almond confection) **315**, 488

candies, confections, and jams (cont.)
shuʿabiyya (candy fingers) **217**
sitt danif **231**
tumūr mulawwaza (almond-filled dates) **247**
See also pastes *under* desserts (*ḥalwā*)
caraway, see *karāwiya*
cassia, see *dār Ṣīnī*
celery, see *karafs*
chard, see *silq*
cheese, see *jubn*
cherries, see *qarāṣiyā*
chicken dishes, see *dajāj*
chickpeas, see *ḥimmaṣ*
cilantro, see *kuzbara*
clay, see *ṭīn*
cold dishes, see *bawārid*
condiments 10, 20, 32, 40, 50, 51, 53, 54
dairy (*albān*), see *akhlāṭ, bīrāf, jājaq; kabar; kāmakh; zaʿtar*
dipping sauce, see *ṣibāgh*
fermented, see *murrī; kāmakh; binn*
mustard, see *khardal*
ṣaḥna (small fish) **203, 204, 205, 208, 209**
ṣaḥna kadhdhāba (without fish) **205, 206, 210**
table sauces, see *ṣalṣ*
coriander seeds, see *kuzbara*
cumin, see *kammūn*

dajāj (chicken) 9, 28, 29, 31, 38, 39, 41, 42, 50, 90, 94, 129, 140, 146, 154, 155, 611
bunduqiyya (with hazelnuts) **105, 117, 128**
duhn (fat) 81, 112, 126, 157, 181
fālūdhajiyya (sweet) **108**
fustuqiyya (sweet, with pistachio) **108, 116, 121**
general cooking tips 109
gizzards (*qawāniṣ*) 181
ḥāmiḍa (sour) **107**
harīsat fustuq (pistachio porridge) **225**
ḥiṣrimiyya (with unripe grapes) **93, 112**
ḥulwiyya (sweet) **108**
ḥummāḍiyya (with citron pulp) **88**
jawādhib **107**, 226, 227
jullābiyya (with syrup) **117**
Jurjāniyya (with yogurt sauce) **124**
karnadāj (rotisserie) **155**
khayṭiyya (porridge) **116, 138**
lawziyya (with almonds) **128**
laymūniyya **118, 128**
livers (*kubūd*) 181
lubābiyya (with bread crumbs) **123, 128, 665**
maḥshī (stuffed) **105**, 309
maḥshī bi-māʾ laymūn (smothered in lemon sauce) **128**
maḥshī ḥulw (stuffed, sweet) **105, 143**
mamqūra (steeped in vinegar) **107**
Maʾmūniyya (rice porridge) **125**
maṣlūq (boiled) **103, 105**
maṣūṣ (cooked in vinegar) **107**
mishmishiyya (with marzipan apricots) **126**
muṭajjan (fried) **157**
qarāṣiyā (with cherry plums) **110**
rukhāmiyya (marble-like) **126**
rummāniyya (with pomegranate juice) **110**
safarjaliyya (with quince) **112**
sitt al-Nūba **116, 121, 154**
ṭabīkh bazr rijla (stewed purslane seeds) **127**
tamr-Hindiyya (with tamarind) **120**
ward murabbā (with rose-petal jam) **127**
with yellow rice **424**
zīrbāj (sour golden stew) **106, 112, 118, 127**
See also *farārīj; dīk*
ḍaʾn (mutton) 137, 611–2
**daqīq* (wheat flour) 50, 81, 82
darmak 173, 467, 469, 470
ḥuwwārā 271, 272, 278, 282, 286, 466, 467, 469, 470, 472
muthallath 275, 287, 288, 470
samīdh (fine white flour) 220, 223, 236, 466, 465, 471
samīdh (semolina) 117n142, 214, 217, 220, 227, 466, 467, 472
daqīq shaʿīr (barley flour) 162, 168, **282**, 345, 472
daqīq shaʿīr (malted barley), see under *fuqqāʿ*
dār fulful (long pepper) 235, 261, 264, 319, 531, 536
darmak, see *daqīq*
**dār Ṣīnī* (cassia) 50, 67, 72, 536
dates see *tamr*
dawāʾ qaraf (nausea remedies) 54, 187, **295–304**

deodorants 56, **408**, **410**, 526, 532, 537, 554, 570, 569, 623, 626
desserts (*ḥalwā*), thick puddings and pastes:
ʿajamiyya (with toasted flour) **230**, **241**, **248**, **281**
fālūdhaj (with wheat starch) 27, 28, 102n77
fālūdhajiyya bayḍāʾ (white) 20, **237**
ḥalāwa with *biṭṭīkh ʿAbdulī* (muskmelon paste) **244**
ḥalāwat ʿajwa (with soft dried dates) **244**, **245**
ḥalāwa with dates (thick pudding) **247**
ḥalwā wardiyya (with rose petals) **229**
harīsat al-fustuq (with pistachio) **225**
jawādhib (bread pudding) **226**, **227**
jimāliyya (with dates) **238**
khabīṣ, see entry
musayyar/suyūr al-qarʿ, qarʿiyyat al-suyūr (gourd paste) 109n108, **218**, **234**, 486
qarʿiyya (gourd paste) **234**, **235**
ṣābūniyya (with starch) 37, 213n18, 225, **230**, 245, 468, 484
samīdhiyya (with semolina) **227**
See also *maʿjūn* (electuary)
desserts, syrup-drenched:
aṣābiʿ Zaynab (cannoli fingers) **220**, **233**
ḥalāwa makshūfa (barefaced) **233**
kunāfa, see entry
kāhīn **238**
luqaymāt al-qāḍī **221**
mulberries **212**
qarn Bārūq **233**, 487, **672**
qaṭāʾif, see entry
Shīrāziyya **229**
zalābiya (latticed fritters) 239, 327, 491
dharīra (scented body powder) 409, 410, **417**, **421**, **422**, 435, 621
dharūr (scented edible powder, restorative) 56, 401, **423**, **424**, 425, **436**, **437**, 621
dhukār (caprifig), see under *tīn*
dīk (rooster) 611, 612
khiṣā (testicles) **177**
dīnāriyya (stew with meat patties) **100**
distilled waters **425–436**
māʾ khilāf (of Egyptian willow) 275, 297, 368, 414, 416
duhn bān (ben oil) 409, 537, 622
eggplant, see *bādhinjān*

falanja 537, 595
fālūdhajiyya (sweet stew) 20, 50, **102**, **108**, 493
fānīdh, see under candies
faqqūs 451, 507, 508, 631–2
farārīj/farrūj (young chickens) **109**, 152, *157*, **182**, 188, **189**, **309**, 613
chicks' factory 41–2
farīk (toasted green wheat) 424, 470
farīkiyya (porridge) 71, **136**
fatāʾil ʿanbar (incense tapers) **403**
nidd (incense tapers) **406**, 622, 625
See also *nidd*
fats and oils
alya (sheep tail fat) 48, 68, 81, 93, 97, 99, 103, 123, 143, 151, 152, 153, 175, 230, 244, 245, 379, 382, 385, 503, 614
duhn bazr (linseed oil) 174, 198, 200, 380, 499, 503, 505
duhn dajāj (chicken fat) 52, 81, 112, 126, 157, 181, 494, 503
duhn lawz (almond oil) 116, 155, 168, 185, 188, 191, 218, 223, 236, 237, 260, 364, 377, 400, 491, 515
samn (ghee) 4, 32, 76, 81, 126, 176, 177, 181, 212, 214, 222, 223, 229, 233, **248**, 503
shaḥm (suet) 75, 97, 99n60, 179, 180, 615
**shayraj* (sesame oil) 9, 68, 71, 503, 505, 545, 602, 609, 610, 630
zayt (olive oil), *see entry*
zayt ḥārr (hot oil) 26, 32, 198, 200, 505
zubd (butter) 4, 141, 150, 214, 238, 479, 480, 503, 505, 587
fava beans, see *bāqillāʾ*
fawfal (betel nut) 77, 537, 569
fennel, see *rāzyānaj*
fenugreek, see *ḥulba*
figs, see *tīn*
fish, see *samak*
flour (wheat), see *daqīq*
fujl (radishes) 21, 71, **268**, 308, **362**, 382, 632
fūl/bāqillā (fava beans) 31, 32, 74, 78, 231n106, 441, 632
akhḍar (fresh) **172**, 182, 382, **383**
fūliyya (meat dish) **135**, **659**
mudammas 32
fulayyā (pennyroyal) 210, 537

fulful (black pepper) 50, 72, 82, 529, 530, 531, 536, 537
fuqqāʿ (foamy beer) 15, 31, 39, 47, 52, 270, **271**, **272**, **277**, **279**, **280**, **281**, 285, 457–9
afāwih (spice blend) **530**
buqūl (herbed) **282**
daqīq al-shaʿīr (malted barley) 270, 271, 273, 276, 278, 279, 457, 458
kharjī (common) 284, 287
khāṣṣ (excellent) **270**, 278, **280**
kīzān (cups, jars) 39, 270, 271, 279, 280, 283, 410, 458, 459, 460, 583
kīzān ḍāriya (with traces of fermentation) 273, 281, 583
māʾ rummān (pomegranate juice) **273**, **274**
musaddab (with rue) 459
shaʿīrī (with malted barley) 270, **282**
shaʿīrī madhkhūr **271**
fustuq (pistachio) 6, 12, 26, 80, 81, 87, 94, 105, 116, 509
fustuqiyya (stew) **90**, **108**, **116**, **117**, **121**
fuwwa (madder) 203, 204, 205, 300, 537, 617n10, 618

galangal (*khūlanjān*) 72, 85,112, 124, 160, 180, 186, 209, 263, 264, 307, 309, 310, 318, 319, 365, 382, 529, 546
ghāliya (perfume) 409, 410, 622
ghasūl (cleansing compound) 397, 433, 622
ghee (*samn*), *see under* fats and oils
ghubayrāʾ (sorbus fruit) 2223, 509
ginger, see *zanjabīl*
gourd, see *qarʿ*
grapes, see *ʿinab*

ḥabb (breath-freshening pills) 56, **408**, **409**, **410**
See also breath fresheners
ḥabba khaḍrāʾ (terebinth berries) 209, 509
ḥabb qurṭum, see *qurṭum*
hāl (green cardamom) 149, 204, 210, 251, 254, 263, 264, 274, 279, 281, 283, 347, 353, 364, 397, 531, 537
ḥamāḥim rayḥān (sweet basil) 295, 296, 297, 302, 321, 536, 538
ḥamāḥim rayḥān aḥmar (red amaranth) 302, 536, 538
ḥamām (pigeons) 10, 21, 42, 47n132, 579, 613
eggs **177**
firākh (young pigeons) 10, 39, 42, **128**, 129, 135, 137, **146**, **152**, 181, 493, 613
ḥashīsh (grass) 204
ḥashīsh (marijuana) 37, 38, 563n16
ḥashīshat al-sulṭān/khardal Fārisī (broadleaf mustard greens) 6, 328, 331, 633
See also *labsān* (wild mustard)
hazelnuts, see *bunduq*
henna (*ḥinnāʾ*) 401, 539
ḥimmaṣ (chickpeas) 21, 32, 47, 50, 51, 56, 72, 75, 78
aswad (black) 50, 161, 633
kassā (dip), see under *bawārid*
mujawhar (roasted) 176n25, 633
unthā (feminine) 381
honey, see *ʿasal naḥl*
ḥulba (fenugreek) 21, 77, 369, 540
ḥummāḍiyya (citron pulp stew) **88**, 527
ḥuwwārā, see *daqīq*

Ibrāhīmiyya (stew) **86**
idhkhir (citronella) 395, 396, 398, 540
Makkī 393
ijjāṣ/injāṣ (plums) 510, 514
ʿijl, see under *baqar*
ʿinab (grapes) **167**, **285**, 439, 440–2, 444, 452, 453, 510
ʿaqīd/rubb (concentrated juice) 419, 485, 511
See also *māʾ ḥiṣrim*; *zabīb*
incense (*bakhūr*) 52, 56, 401, 404
aloeswood 253, **404**, **405**, 683
aqrāṣ (tablets) **415**, **416**
banafsajiyya **413**
Barmakiyya **414**
fatāʾil, see entry
maʿshūqa **413**
nidd (pastilles) **417**, **418**, **419**
nisrīniyya **412**
Yemenī **406**
zahriyya **413**
ʿIraqiyya (meat dish) **141**
ʿirq kāfūr/zurunbād (bitter ginger) 82, 139, 141, 203, 397, 413, 540, 575
isbīdbāj (white meat stew)
isfanākh (spinach) **133**, 494, 495
isfīdāj (ceruse) 396, 434, 540

jājaq (yogurt condiment) 51, **326**, **331**, **332**, **334**, 656
jaṣṣ (gypsum) 439, 442, 452, 540
jawādhib/*jūdhāba* (bread pudding) 52, 148n277, 149n281, 215n27, 471, 494
khashkhāsh (with poppy seeds) **152**, **227**
khubz mukhtamir (with fermented bread) **226**
qaṭā'if (with stuffed pancakes) **226**
**jawz* (walnuts) 26, 73, 75, 76, 86
fresh **364**, **365**
jawz ṭīb/*bawwa* (nutmeg) 204, 221, 251, 253, 254, 261, 264, 270, 272, 273, 283, 287, 288, 299, 301, 303, 310, 317, 353, 365, 398, 401, 540
jazar (carrots) 26, 51, 85, 93, 100, 134, 136, 177, **227**, **262**, **268**, **370**, 451, 634
shaqāqul/*barrī* (wild, parsnips) **267**, 635
Jew's mallow, see *mulūkhiyya*
jīr/*kils* (slaked lime) 70, 348, 349, 541, 546
jirjīr (arugula) 31, 71, 72, 500, 635
jubn (cheese) 21, 29, 36, 38, 136, 137, 182, 326, 534, 584
aqiṭ (sour yogurt cheese) 478, 328
ḥālūm (semi-hard white cheese) 26, 32, 51, **332**, **333**, **335**, 478, **652**
mish (whey) 336
qanbarīs (cream cheese) 51, **327**, **330**, 336, **337**, 389, 479
qanbarīsiyya (dish) **124**
raṭb/*akhḍar* (fresh) 181
Shāmī (semi hard, compact and chewy) 134, 180, 324, 337, 338, 478
jullanār (blossoms, wild pomegranate) 254, 300, 541
jullubān (grass peas) 78, 636
jummayz (sycomore fig), see under *tīn*
Jurjāniyya (stew) **86**, **124**
juwārish (digestive stomachics) 34, 54, **260–5**, 623

kabāba (cubeb) 221, 251, 261, 262, 263, 264, 283, 300, 397, 409, 414, 541
kabbād (Damascus citron) 64n9, 130, 137, 194, 197, 202, 297, 316, 333, **359**, **362**, 383, 416, 453, 511
marākibī **358**
Kābulī (black myrobalan) 254, 513, 526
kaftāwāt (meatballs) 494,495
kāfūr (camphor) 81, 89, 102, 106, 110, 112, 113, 120, 121, 122, 125, 215, 218, 239, 246, 247, 320, 399, 403, 408, 409, 412, 413, 416, 419, 422, 425, 430, 431, 432, 433, 435, 436, 503, 541, 554
mā' (distilled water) 395, 396, **427**, 550
rayyāḥī/*Rabāḥī* 394, 397, 398, 410, 418, 432
ka'k (dry cookies), *see under* breads
kāmakh (dairy fermented condiment) 51, **323**, **324**, 373
'afin (moldy bread) 323, 325, 326, 334, 336, 337, 338
kabar (capers) 373, 498
marzanjūsh (marjoram) 373
na'na' (mint) 325
qamna (base for) **324**, 495
ṭarkhūn (tarragon) **325**
thūm (garlic) 373
ward (rose petals) **326**
without milk **325**
kammūn (cumin) 21, 67, 88, 93, 103, 104, 124, 125, 127, 134, 136, 137, 158, 173, 175, 176, 180, 196, 206, 209, 309, 310, 311, 322, 325, 379, 381, 382, 504, 529, 541
aswad (black) 390
juwārish (digestive) **265**
kammūniyya (dish) **134**
Kirmānī 223, 261, 264, 300
ma'jūn (electuary) **267**
karafs (celery) 257, **364**, 542, 543
Nabaṭī (angelica) 274, 543
karafs (common parsley) 72, 102, 158, 173, 174, 175, 180, 195, 209, 210, 270, 286, 308, 310, 316, 328, 334, 356, 358, 369, 370, 382, 542
See also *baqdūnis* (Macedonian parsley)
**karāwiya* (caraway) 67, 529, 543, 544, 632
Andalusiyya 254, 300
Maghribiyya 203
karsh/*kurūsh* (tripe) 40, 70, 177n31, 222, 546, 583, 614
qibāwa/*qibba* (stuffed omasum) **177**, 616
sakhātīr (stuffed pieces of) 327
kathīrā' (tragacanth) 223, 423, 424, 425, 436, 437, 543, 621
khabath fiḍḍa (silver slag) 410, 623
khabīṣ 34, 211n1, 230n100, 245n186, 476, 477, 481, 485

khabīṣ (cont.)
jazar (carrots) **227**
khashkhāsh (poppy seeds) **236**
Ma'mūniyya (almonds) 28, 37, **237**
qar' (gourd) **227**
uncooked (almonds)
'unnāb (jujube) **222**
ward (rose petals) **218**
**khall* (vinegar) xii, 32, 49, 53, 71, 74, 543–4
distilled/white 86, 123, **166**, **167**, **168**, 188
flavored with *ushturghāz* (alhagi) 311
from dates 257
from white grapes **167**
mamqūr (cooked meat steeped in) **107**
maṣūṣ (meat cooked in) **107**, **152**, **175**, **146**, **180**
mint infused **166**
sakanjabīn (digestive drink) **250**, **257**, 311, 462
sikbāj (stew) 72, 75, **85**, **132**, **201**
See also *mukhallalāt*
khamīrat al-'aṭṭār (mountain meadow saffron) 223n66, 317, 544
khardal (condiments, sauces) 53, 202, **305**, **306**, 310, **311**, **313**, **320**, 321, 499
ṣināb 306, 499
khardal (mustard greens), see *ḥashīshat al-sulṭān*
labsān (wild), *see entry*
khardal (mustard seeds) 75, 124, 175, 202, 308, 309, 310, 311, 319, 328, 333, 337, 340, 341, 342, 343, 344, 345, 346, 347, 348, 362, 383, 384, 385, 389, 390, 391, 545, 626
abyaḍ/Shāmī (white) 296
'Akkāwī 319
kharūf (lamb) 94n39, 103, 612, 614
thanī (yearling) 71, 110, 115, 612, 614
Kurdī (whole lamb roast) **148**
mumazzaj (seasoned whole lamb roast) **148**
al-shawī (roasted lamb) 152
qaliyyat al-shawī (fried lamb roast) **103**, **658**
khashkhāsh (poppy seeds) 123, 131, 145, 151, 213, 215, 218, 222, 229, 231, 232, 235, 244, 246, 248, 345, 487, 522, 545
jawādhib (bread pudding) **152**, **227**
khabīṣa (thick pudding) **236**
khashkhāshiyya (stew) **101**, **108**
white 236
khass (lettuce) 12, 72, 133, 636
uṣūl (stems) 185
khawkh (peaches) 439, 446, 513–4
leaves 163, 332
khawkh al-dubb (bear's plums) 514
khayṭiyya, see under porridges
khilāf (willow) 95n43, 296, 302, 393, 545
mā', see under distilled waters
khīrī/manthūr (gillyflower) 430n46, 546
khiṭmī (marshmallow) 440, 636
khiyār (common cucumber) 26, 451, 636
distilled 434
garnish 309
pickled 369, 373
seeds 222
with dairy condiments 334, 338
khubbāza (hibiscus) 345, 546
khubz (bread) 23, 27, 28, 29, 32, 38, 51, 75, 79, 93, 207, 270, 272, 273, 279, 280, 315, 324, 325, 351, 380, 458, 464, 465–7, 471
abyaḍ (fine, white) 32, 215, 238, 469
bā'it (stale) 75, 141, 225
baytūtī (home-prepared dough) 43
faṭīr (unleavened) 164, 168, 214, 323,
ḥuwwārā (fine, white) 270, 272, 278, 282, 286, 466, 470, 471
jardaq (round and pithy) 75, 149, 471
khamīra (yeast) 277, 278, 281, 341, 345, 346, 347, 348, 471
kumāj (round, white and pithy) 128, 274
lubāb (crumbs) 88n13, **123**, **128**, 141, 185, 186, 187, 190, 220, 223, 225, 226, 229, 238, 272, 274, 310, 472, **665**
ma'rūk (well-kneaded) 188, 190n25
mukhtamir (well-fermented) 226
ruqāq (lavash) 51, 75, 96, 148, 149, 150, 151, 152, 183n51, 213, 215, 226, 227, 476, 477
salā'iṭ (large, elongated) 29–30
samīdh (fine, white) 220, 223, 473
khubz sha'īr (barley bread) 31, 32
khūlanjān (galangal) 72, 95, 110, 112, 124, 160, 180, 186, 209, 263, 264, 307, 309, 210, 318, 319, 365, 382, 546
kibrīkiyya (stew) **89**

kils, see *jūr*
kishk (dried yogurt-wheat product) 21, 31
Khurāsānī **334**, 478
kishk (stew) **96**, **113**, **124**, **125**, **137**, 501, 611
kishkiyya (stew) 71, 72, **113**, 495, 568
kishk al-ʿadas (lentil-barley dish) 630
kubūd (livers) 40, **181**, 614
kunāfa (shredded dough) 36, 52, 96, 142, 225, **241**, 473, 477
Akhmīmiyya **225**
maṭbūkha **243**
mukhannaqa **228**, **242**
mumallaḥa **228**, **243**
kundus (pellitory) 333, 546
kurkum (turmeric) 159, 546, 572
kurrāth (leeks) 131, 160, 334, 547
baql/Nabaṭī/qirṭ (leaf leaks) 89, 306, 379
Shāmī (bulbous) 85, 94, 136, 372, 547
kurunb (cabbage) 26, 77, **391**, 536, 556, 636
kurunbiyya (meat dish) **134**
mumazzaj (seasoned) **151**
with tahini **390**
with yogurt **331**, **656**
kusharī (mung beans) 638
See *māsh*
kuskusū (couscous) 467, 474, 475, 477
kuskusū (dish) 49, **146**, 474
**kuzbara raṭba* (fresh cilantro) 73, 492, 501, 548
**kuzbara yābisa* (coriander seeds) 48n135, 50, 67, 493, 548, 602, 613, 614
kūz ṭalʿ (inflorescence spathe of dates) 131, 548

laban (milk) 79, 107, 114, 115, 119, 122, 123, 124, 125, 126, 127, 131, 136, 137, 138, 139, 141, 176, 214, 323, 324, 325, 326, 329, 330, 332, 333, 334, 335, 336, 337, 338, 424, 443, 444, 448, 449, 479, 489, 503, 526, 539, 555, 559, 587, 616
baqarī (cow) 248
ḍaʾnī/ghanamī (sheep) 325, 331, 335
jāmūsī (water buffalo) 336
libaʾ (beestings), *see entry*
niʿāj (ewe) 335
See also *bīrāf*; *kāmakh*
laban (yogurt) 29, 36, 38, 39, 40, 51, 104, 113, **124**, 125, **140**, 327, 329, 334, 335, 385, 389, **390**
makhīḍ (buttermilk) 328
minfaḥa (rennet) 336, 479, 523
munashshaf (drained) 326, 330, **331**, **332**, **334**, 361, 369, 387, 478, 479, 480
rāʾib (without rennet) **126**, 330, 335
rakhbīn (dried buttermilk) 72n35, 479, 498
Shīrāz/Fārisī (drained, with rennet) 93, **328**
Turkumānī (sheep) 331, 334
yāghurt (water buffalo/cow, with rennet) **336**, 337
See also *akhlāṭ*; *jājaq*
labaniyya (meat cooked in milk) 124, 126, 131
labsān (wild mustard greens) 77, 332, 334, 637
See also *ḥashīshat al-sulṭān*
lādhan (ladanum) 413, 418, 419, 549
ʿanbarī (best quality) 401, 402, 406, 411, 414, 416, 417
**laḥm* (red meat) 614–5
aḍlāʿ (ribs) **113**
aḥmar (trimmed of fat) 97, 98, 99, 100, 101, 102, 103, 115, 140, 178, 179, 180
See also *baqar*; *ḍaʾn*; *kharūf*; *māʿiz*
lakhlakha (potpourri) 52, 56, 411n45, **414**, 519, 524, 578, 623
lamb, see *kharūf*
laʿūq (restorative thick syrup) **297**, 301, 485
**lawz* (almond) 80, 514–5
akhḍar (fresh) 316
duhn (oil) 116, 155, 168, 185, 188, 191, 218, 223, 236, 237, 260, 364, 377, 400, 468, 491, 515
farik (easily skinned) 184, 515
lawzīnaj/shakrīnaj (almond confection) 28, 31, **234**, **236**, 488
laymūn* (lemon) 26, 32, 48, 49, 81n12, **128, 453, 515 32, 48, 49, 81n12, 128, 453, 515–7
aqrāṣ (hard drop candy) **212**, 231, **251**, **260**, 497
juwārish (digestive stomachic) **263**
laymūniyya (stew) **118**, **122**, **128**, **143**, 195
māʾ (preserved juice) 89, **165**, **168**
māliḥ/mumallaḥ (salt-preserved) 51, 114, 171, 176, 195, 205, 207, 320, 350, 352, 353, 354, **364**, 372, **374**, **375**, **376**, 377, 378, 379, 380, 381, 385, **649**

laymūn (lemon) (cont.)
marākibī 163, 317, 512, 516
qishr (peel) 208, 271, 403, 414, 415
sharāb (sweet drink) 53, 71, **252**, **254**, **255**, **257**, **259**, **284**, 464
Ṣīnī aṣfar (Chinese, yellow) 263
laynūfar/naylūfar, mā' (distilled water of Egyptian lotus) 290, 7, 298, 299, 424, 549
leeks, see *kurrāth*
lemon, see *laymūn*
lentils, see *ʿadas*
lettuce, see *khass*
liba' (beestings) 20, 329, 330
lift (turnips) 26, 77, 137, 451, 637
kammūniyya (stew) **134**
pickled **341–8**
seeds 26, 32, 505
lisān al-thawr, mā' (distilled water of borage) 261, 262, 290, 297, 298, 550
Shāmī (Levantine) 292, 293, 414
lisān al-ʿuṣfūr/ʿaṣāfīr (fruit of Syrian ash tree) 531, 550
lubābiyya (bread-crumb stew), see under *dajāj*
lūbyā (black-eyed beans) **136**, **388**, 637, **657**
lukk yebis (dry gum lac) 301, 550

maghra (ochre) 442, 551
mā' ḥiṣrim (juice of unripe grapes) 48, 72, 74, 88, 89, 107, 137, 153, 262, 300, 301, 316, 386, 387
from dried sour grapes 335
ḥiṣrimiyya (stew) **93**, **99**, **112**, **138**, **184**
preserved **164**, **165**
sharāb ḥiṣrim munaʿnaʿ (drink with mint) **258**
maḥlab 396, 397, 398, 551
māʿiz (goat) 21, 180, 615
maʿjūn (electuary, paste) 485, 623
jazar (carrots) **268**
jazar barrī/shaqāqul (parsnips) **267**
kammūn (cumin) **267**
maṣṭakā' (mastic gum) **269**
naʿnāʿ (mint) **268**
nāranj (sour orange) **265**
safarjal (quince) **269**
ʿūd (aloeswood) **266**
utrujj (citron) **253**
zanjabīl (ginger) **266**
makhfiyya (egg-yolk stuffed meatballs) **97**
manbūsha (meat dish) **99**
manfūsh, see under breads
maqdūnis (Macedonian parsley) 95, 133n221, 295
See also *baqdūnis*; *karafs* (common parsley)
marijuana, see *ḥashīsha*
marsīn (myrtle) 296, 302, 397, 401, 403, 406, 414, 416, 417, 430, 551
berries 300
distilled water 412, **434**
marū (wild marjoram) 223, 552
marwaziyya (dish) 24, **120**, 496
marzanjūsh (marjoram) 373, 395, 413, 418, 430, 552
distilled water **435**
māsh (mung beans) 78, 184, 638
muzawwara (meatless dish) **187**, **189**
maṣlūqa (boiled meat) **103**
**maṣṭakā'* (mastic gum) 48, 67, 487, 503, 529, 552, 611, 614
maʿjūn (electuary) **269**
**mā' ward* (rosewater) 56, 459, 484, 490, 494, 514, 550, 564, 572
baladī (domestic) 187, 296, 297, 301, 302, 411, 551, 572
mā' wardiyya (stew) 20, 102n77, **142**
mukarrar (refined) 259, 551
muṣaʿʿad (distilled) **428**, **429**, **430**, **431**
Nuṣaybīnī 415, **436**
Shāmī 245, 293, 303, 353, 423
See also *ward*
mawz (bananas) 26, 37, 39, 517
mawziyya (dish) **103**
mayʿa (benzoin resin) 419, 552–3
yābisa/qishr (resinous bark of storax tree) 395, 397, 411, 558
meat, see *laḥm*
**milḥ* (salt) 69, 70, 73, 74, 75, 78, 80
Andarānī (rock salt) 67, 113, 272, 273, 313, 318, 332, 553
raṭb (freshly harvested) 185, 553
saqanqūr (scincus) 54, 117, 311, 553, 571
milk, see *laban*
mint, see *naʿnaʿ*
mishmish (apricots) 128, 518
akhḍar (fresh) 144
lawzī 290, 292, 293, 518

naqūʿ (compote) **290–3**, 671
ṭabīkh (stew) **144**, **145**, 663
qamar al-dīn (leather) 293, 518
yābis (dried) 145
**misk* (musk) 8, 47, 56, 554
ʿIrāqī 409, 554
Yemenī 422, 554
mudaqqaqāt (pounded-meat dishes) 12, 495, 496
ḥāmiḍa (sour) **98**
kubab (meatballs) 87, 113, 129, 130, 135, 137, 140, 152
maqliyya (fried patties) **147**
Miṣriyya (Egyptian style) **90**
sādhaja (plain) **101**
samak (fish) **194**
mukhallalāt (pickles) 8, 44, 341n1, 373, 374
capers **372**, 373
carrots **370**
celery (*karafs*) **364**
cucumbers **369**, 373
eggplants **357**, **370**, **371**
fennel, fresh **366**
garlic **372**
gourd **371**
kabbād (Damascus citron) **358**, **359**, **362**
lemons **364**, **374**, **375**, **376**
onions **356–7**, **359**, **360**, **361**, 373
quince **366**, **367**, **368**
radishes **362**
rose petals **377**
turnips **340–8**, 374
ushturghāz (alhagi) 374
utrujj (citron) **362**
walnuts, fresh **358**, **364**, **365**
See also *zaytūn*
mulūkhiyya (Jew's mallow) 9, 21, 31, 78, **115**, **129**, **153**, 496, 500, 584, 605, 638
muzawwara (meatless) **190**
mung beans, see *māsh*
murrī (liquid fermented sauce) 48, 89, 97, 100, 107, 109, 156, 158, 172, 180, 181, 182, 183, 195, 307, 311, 325, 379, 380, 482, 497, 523, 523, 54, 624, 631
ʿatīq (aged) 310
ʿiṭrī (aromatic) **169**
Maghribī (Moroccan) **163**
naʿnaʿ (mint-infused) **168**
naqīʿ/Nabaṭī (fermented) 161, **162**
samak (fish-based) 617
shaʿīr (barley-based), see *naqīʿ* above
thānī (second fermentation) 163
muskmelon see *biṭṭīkh*
mustaʿjala (salep) 223, 555
mustard, see *khardal*
Mutawakkiliyya (taro stew) 31, **110**, **132**, 269, 497, 500
See also *sitt al-shanaʿ*
mutton, see *ḍaʾn*
muzawwarāt (meatless dishes) 54, **184–92**, 205n47, 423, 472, 497, 634, 638, 641

najm (couch grass) 300, 555
najmiyya (meat dish) **150**
nammām (wild thyme) 334, 418, 430, 433, **435**, 436, 555
**naʿnaʿ* (mint) 39, 72, 555
kāmakh (fermented condiment) **325**
khall (vinegar) **157**
maʿjūn (electuary) **268**
murrī (liquid fermented sauce) **168**
Shāmī (Levantine) 365, 555
sharāb ḥiṣrim munaʿnaʿ **258**
nānkhawāh (ajowan) 223, 261, 264, 311, 556
naqūʿ, see under *mishmish*
nāranj (sour orange) 48, 49, 163, 442, 511, 518–9
drink **299**
duhn (oil) 400, 519
leaves 67, 169, 278, 333, 346
māʾ (fresh juice) 374
māʾ (preserved) **165**, **167**
maʿjūn (electuary) **265**
māʾ zahr (distilled water of blossoms) 411, 413, 414, **434**, **436**
nāranjiyya (stew) **94**
peel 286, 297, 403, 406, 413, 414,415, 416, 417
zahriyya (aromatic preparation) **411**, **413**
nārdīn, see *sunbul*
narjis (narcissus) 430, **449**, 559
narjisiyya (dish) 72, **134**, **182**, 183n51
nashā (wheat starch) 27, 28, 37, 50, 79, 86, 108, 112, 117, 118, 129, 131, 132, 142, 144, 152, 170, 191, 218, 220, 221, 225, 229, 230, 235, 237, 238, 241, 245, 398, 420, 475, 485
fresh **139**
nashā aruzz (rice starch) 230

naṭrūn (natron/sodium bicarbonate) 77, 220, 239, 348, 380, 473, 535, 556, 636
See also *būraq*
nawāshif (sauceless dishes) 68, **97–104**, 137n234, 497, 586
nayda, see under candies
nidd (scenting pastilles) 405n10, **418**, **419**, 619, 625
fatā'il (tapers) **406**, 622, 625
murakkab (coated with ambergris) **417**, 625
See also *muthallath* under *ʿanbar*
nīl (indigo, colorant) 226, 345, 396, 556
nisrīn (dog rose) **339**, **429**, 436, 556
nisrīniyya (incense) **412**
nuḍūḥ (aromatic liquid) 411n45, 412, 626
nukhāla (bran) 75, 162, 466

odor removers 5, 56, 70, 382, 392, **399**, 514, 533
oils, aromatic (*adhān*) **399**, **400**, **401**, **402**, 539, 551, 557, 562, 630, 641
See also breath fresheners; deodorants; *ushnān* (handwashing compounds)
oils, edible, *see* fats and oils
oils, inedible, *see under* odor removers
okra, see *bāmiya*
olives, see *zaytūn*
omelets, see *ʿujja*
onion, see *baṣal*
oxymel, see *sakanjabīn*

parsley, see *karafs* (common parsley)
Macedonian, see *baqdūnis*
pasta and noodles
iṭriya (dried noodles) 71, **130**, 471, **660**
rishtā (fresh noodles) 235, 243, 476
shaʿīriyya (orzo) **143**, 477
shishbarak (raviolis) **104**, 477
tuṭmāj (fresh pasta) **104**, **140**, 143, 233, 466n6, 467, 477
peaches, see *khawkh*
perfume compounds (inedible)
ʿanbarī/*ʿanbarīnā* **420**, 619
bathtub scents 56, **409**, **412**
dharīra, see entry
ṭīb ahl al-Yemen **408**
zahriyya **411**, **413**
pickles, see *mukhallalāt*
pigeons, see *ḥamām*
pistachio, see *fustuq*
pomegranates, see *rummān*
porridges 28, 31n77, 41, 45, 49, 53, 71, 74, 75, 467, 477, 497, 503, 624
aruzziyya (rice) 71, 74, 75, **130**, 492
bahaṭṭa (milky rice) **138**, **139**, 492, **669**
farīkiyya (green-wheat) 71, **136**
harīsa (wheat) 31, 71, 74, **137**, **225**, 497
hayṭaliyya (fresh wheat starch) **139**, 492, 494
khayṭiyya (rice) **115**, **116**, **122**, **138**
Ma'mūniyya (rice) **121**, **123**, **125**
qamḥiyya (wheat berries) **104**, **137**
potash, see *ushnān*
purslane, see *rijla*

qaliyya (fried dish) **97**
qaliyyat al-shawī **103**, **658**
See also *taqālī*
qamar al-dīn, see under *mishmish*
qamḥiyya, see under porridges
qanbarīs, see under *jubn*
qāqulla (black cardamom) 264, 283, 395, 409, 414, 422, 556
qāqullā/*qāqullī* (saltwort) 558, 627
qarʿ/*yaqṭīn* (gourd) 26, 53, 54, 72, 98, 124, 130, 132, 152, 184, 185, 186, 188, 190, 222, 624, 639
bawārid (cold dishes) **389**, **390**
khabīṣ (thick pudding) **227**
mukhallal (pickled) **371**
musayyar/*suyūr* (sweet paste) **218**, **234**, **235**, 486
muzawwara (meatless dish) **188**, **189**, **190**
taqliyyat yaqṭīn (fried) **137**
**qaranful* (cloves) 529, 531, 557, 567
ḥaṭab (stalks) 254, 288, 299, 361, 362, 529, 557
mā' (distilled water) 414, 416, **427**, 428, 433, **434**
dharūr (restorative powder) **436**
qaranful zahr (carnation flower) 280, 353, 365, 394, 432, **433**, 557, 573
qarāṣiyā (cherry plum) **110**, 120, 446, 496, 514, 519
Baʿlabakī/*ḥabb al-mulūk* (cherries) 520
**qarfa* (Ceylon cinnamon) 529, 536, 557
mā' (distilled water) **435**
qarīṣ (aspic) 72, 600, 636
qaṣab dharīra (sweet flag) 398, 557
qaṣb/*qasb*, see under *tamr*

qāt, see *waraq Qumārī*
qaṭā'if (pancakes) 28, 31, 36, 52, 215, 449, 473, 475
  abū lāsh (layered) 243
  jawādhib **226**
  maḥshū/maḥshī (stuffed) **218, 240, 242, 244**
  maqlī (fried) **218, 239, 242**
qaṭr/ʿasal qaṭr (sugar cane molasses) 121, 126, 142, 148, 228, 242, 243, 453, 482, 487
  nabāt (finest quality) 244, 487, 489
  quṭāra (sugar-cane molasses) 13n37, 47, 246, 289, 320, 368, 459
  quṭāra ʿāl (top quality) 224, 286, 459n5, 487
  usṭarūs (lesser quality) 8, 453, 491
qazmat banafsaj (dwarf violet iris) 399, 408, 532, 558
qibāwa (omasum, tripe), see under *karsh*
qiddāḥ/zahr (blossoms of citrus fruits) 88, 400, 527, 558, 573
  duhn (oil) 519
  mā' (distilled water) 414, **434**, 436, 519
  zahriyya (aromatic compound) **411, 413**
qilī, see *ushnān* (potash)
qirṭ (leaf leaks), see *kurrāth*
qiththā' (snake cucumber) 26, **451**, 507, 631, 636, 639
  pickled 373
  seeds 222
quails, see *sammān*
quḍāmā (crunchy roasted legumes) 231, 440, 476
  See also *ḥimmaṣ mujawhar* under *ḥimmaṣ*
quince see *safarjal*
qulqās (taro) 9, 31, **114**, 130, 132, 451, 500, 639
  aṣābiʿ (fingers) 9, 122, 269n73
qunnabīṭ (cauliflower) 124, **383, 384**, 640
qurṭum (safflower seeds) 94, 122, 138, 145, 193, 537, 558, 570
  muzawwara (meatless dish) **189, 190**
qurūn (coral) 300, 558
qusṭ (costus) 416, 422, 558
  baḥrī/ḥulw (sea/sweet) 398, 402, 406, 414, 417, 418, 419
  murr/Hindī (bitter/Indian) 401, 402, 406, 411, 414, 417

radishes, see *fujl*
raisins, see *zabīb*
ramād (ashes) 122, 308, 388n51, 440, 559
rand/ghār (bay laurel) 169, 206, 401, 417, 531, 559
raṭba (fresh alfalfa) 429, 559, 571n19
rayḥān/bādharūj (basil) 125, 169, 559
  bazr (seeds) 301, 559
  distilled water for bathrooms **434**
  ḥamāḥim rayḥān (sweet basil), *see entry*
  qaranfulī/faranjamushk (basil thyme) 361, 559
  utrujjī (lemon balm) 163, 205, 318, 560
rāzyānaj/shamar akhḍar (fresh fennel) 39, 50, 160, 168, 257, 640
  bi-laban (with yogurt) **330**
  pickled **364, 366, 655**
rāzyānaj/shamar/basbās (fennel seeds) 180, 209, 529, 560
rībās (Levantine rhubarb) 640
  rībāsiyya (stew) **91**
rice, see *aruzz*
rijla/baqla ḥamqā' (fresh purslane) 93, 124, 192, 334, **385, 386**, 440, 640
  muzawwara (meatless stew) **184, 189**
rijla, bazr (purslane seeds) 121, 222, 300, 340, 535
  ʿIrāqiyya 154
  ṭabīkh bazr (stew) **127**
rijl al-ḥamāma, see *ʿāqir shamʿā*
rishtā, *see under* pasta and noodles
roses, see *ward*
rosewater, see *mā' ward*
rue, see *sadhāb*
rukhāmiyya (dish) **114, 119, 126**
rummān (pomegranates)
  ḥabb (seeds) 37, 48, 86, 104, 107, 110, 152, **187, 188, 189, 190, 191**, 254, 270, 271, 272, 277, 279, 280, 281, 292, 296, 298, 301, 302, 309, **344**, 345, 371, 457, 45486, 520
  mā' (juice) 87, **152, 153**, 184, 189, 191, 257, 272, 273, 274, 297, 301, 306
  jullanār (blossoms of wild pomegranate) 254, 300, 541
  Jūrī 296, 521
  muzawwara (meatless stew) **187, 188, 189, 190, 191**
  rummāniyya (stew) 72, 87, **110, 152, 153**, 184
  sharāb (sweet drink) 257
ruqāq, *see under* breads
ruṭab, see under *tamr*

ṣābūn (soap) 56, 313, **396**, **397**, 551
**sadhāb* (rue) 39, 72, 75, 457, 458, 459, 561
sādhaj Hindī (Indian leaf) 264, 561–2
safarjal (quince) 8, 26, 27, 51, 112, 132, 141, 209, 250, 251, 252, 255, 258, 259, 261, 262, 269, 272, 301, 327, 414, 521
  Aṣfahānī 250
  Barzī 250, 251, 255, 521
  cooked in sugar **255**
  maʿjūn (electuary) **269**
  mayba (restorative drink) **251**
  mukhallal (pickled) **366**, **367**, **368**, 423
  peel 168
  qaṣbī 255, 521
  safarjaliyya (stew) **112**, **141**
  sakanjabīn (oxymel) **250**, 327
  sharāb (sweet drink) **252**, **255**, 256, **259**, 366
  storing **439**, 440, **452**
  zaghab (down) 406, 416
safflower, see *ʿuṣfur*
  seeds, see *qurṭum*
saffron, see *zaʿfarān*
ṣafṣāf, *see under* toothpicks
safūf (medicinal powder) 392,
ṣaḥna (small-fish condiment) 10, 32, 50, 51n143, **203**, **204**, **205**, **209**, 373, 498, 537, 618
  Iskandarāniyya **208**
  kadhdhāba (false) **205**, **206**, **210**, **653**
  with sumac **206**
sakanjabīn (oxymel) 327, 462–3, 518
  ʿaqīd (chewy-candy) **250**, 302, 405, 481, 488, 619
  buzūrī (with herbs and spices) **257**
  jullābī (with sugar syrup) **257**
  rummānī (with pomegranate) **257**
  safarjalī (with quince) **250**, 366
salīkha 395, 422, 562
ṣalṣ (table sauce) 8, 47, **295**, **315**, **316**, **318**, **319**, **320**, **321**, **322**, 498
  abyaḍ (white) **296**
  Kāmilī **318**
  khāṣṣ (excellent) **317**
  māʾ ḥiṣrim (sour-grape juice) **316**
  muḥallā (sweetened) **317**
  with *ḥālūm* cheese **332**
salt, see *milḥ*
samak (fish) 10, 18, 20, 21, 41n117, 43, 47, 50, 53, 54, **193–210**
  absāriyya/*bisāriyya* (fresh anchovies) 10, 199n17, **200**, 609, 617
  baṭārikh (bottarga) 198n15, 610, 616
  bi-l-khardal (in mustard sauce) **202**
  būrī/*samak al-baṭārikh* (flathead grey mullet) 10, 198n15, **203**, 499, 610, 616
  dallīnas/*umm al-khulūl* (river mussels) 31, 32
  fasīkh (salt-dried) 10, 499, 610
  ḥāmiḍ (sour dish) **195**
  kuzbariyya (with cilantro sauce) **193**
  labīs (Nile carp) 10, 77, 591n7, 614
  lāsh (Nile tilapia) 243, 232n111, 615
  laymūniyya (with lemon sauce) **193**
  maḥshī (smothered in sauce) **194**, **666**, **668**
  māliḥ (salt-cured) **198**, **202**, 308, 310, 616
  maqlī (fried) **196**, **200**
  mashqūq (butterflied) 199n19, 202, 321, 499
  mashwī (oven-baked) **196**, **197**
  mudaqqaqa (patties) **197**
  mukaffan (wrapped) **198**, 203
  rabīthā (shrimp condiment) 373
  ṣaḥna (condiment), *see entry*
  samak al-baṭārikh, see *būrī* above
  ṣīr (salt-cured anchovies), *see entry*
  summāqiyya (poached in sumac sauce) **202**
  ṭaḥīniyya (with tahini sauce) **193**
  ṭarī (fresh) 10, 50, 193, 194, 196, 197, 200, 201, 202, 203, 306, 308, 310
  ṭūbār (thinlip grey mullet) 610
  zabībiyya (with raisins) **193**
  zīrbāj **201**
ṣamgh, *ʿArabī* (gum arabic) 126, 172, 410, 562
  lawz (almond) 223, 562
samīdh, see *daqīq*
sammān (quails) 21, 155, 156, 617, **664**
samn (ghee), *see under* fats and oils
ṣanawbar (pine) 168, 520
sanbūsak 31, 102, 104, **149**, 473, 476, 477
  filling **149**
  sour **94**, **142**
  sweet **96**, **142**
ṣandal (sandalwood) 395, 402, 404, 409, 411, 417, 418, 419, 422, 487, 562–3
  abyaḍ (white) 408
  aḥmar (red) 437
  aṣfar (yellow) 393, 397, 398

dharūr (restorative powder) **437**
māʾ (distilled water) **428**, **433**
Maqāṣīrī (Ceylon) 254, 264, 281, 302, 303, 401, 406, 413, 415, 416, 420, 421, 422, 433, 435
sandarūs (resin of arar tree) 403, 411, 563
saqanqūr (scincus), see under *milḥ*
sawīq (toasted and crushed grains) 221n57, 223, 288, 475, 477, 509
See also *qāwūt*
sayraqūn (red lead, colorant) 396, 563
sesame, see *simsim*
shabath (dill) 104, 105, 130, 131, 136, 137, 440, 563
shahdānaq (hemp seeds) 344, 345, 563
shaḥm (suet), *see under* fats and oils
shaʿīr (barley), bread 31, 32, 472
flour 162, 163, 168, 282, 345
malted 270 271, 273, 275, 276, 278, 279
murrī (liquid fermented sauce) 172–3
tibn (straw) 452
shaʿīriyya (meat with orzo) **143**
shamʿ (beeswax) 249, 564
shamar/basbās (fennel), see *rāzyānaj*
shaqāʾiq al-Nuʿmān (poppy anemone) 431, 564
shaqāqul (wild carrots), see under *jazar*
sharāb (sweet drinks from syrups) 71, 463–4
ḥiṣrim munaʿnaʿ (unripe grapes and mint) **258**
ḥummāḍ al-utrujj (citron pulp) 71, **252**
laymūn (lemon) 71, 128, 165, 168, **254**, **257**
laymūn safarjalī (lemon-quince) **252**, **259**, 366
safarjal (quince) **258**
sakanjabīn, see entry
tuffāḥ (apples) **258**
tūt (mulberry) **257**
ward (rose petals) **259**
ward mukarrar (refined rose liquid) **259**
shayba/ushna (lichen, usnea) 82, 139, 141, 205, 393, 402, 422, 564
shayraj (sesame oil), see under *simsim*
shirsh (brine) 156
shishbarak (ravioli dish) **104**, 477, **499**, 582
shūnīz (nigella seeds) 361, 362, 564
ṣibāgh (dipping sauces) 54, 1932, **306**, **307**, **308**, **309**, **310**, **311**, 315n1, 497, 499
sidr (lotus jujube) 285
sikbāj (sour vinegar stew) 71, 72, 73, **85**, **132**, **154**, 173, 195, 201, 357, 493, 496, 499, 630
silq (chard) 72, 77, 113, 114, 122, 124, 125, 130, 132, 133, 137, 152, 192, 275, **387**, 445, 641
maqṭūʿ (colorant) 226
muzawwara (meatless stew) **191**
simsim (sesame seeds) 80, 247, 342, 343, 344, 345, 351, 356, 371, 472, 564
*shayraj (oil) 9, 68, 71, 80, 81, 82, 399, 401, 402, 503, 505, 545, 609, 610, 630
ṭaḥīna (tahini), *see entry*
ṣīr (salt-cured anchovies) 10, 32, 50, **199**, **203–6**, **208–9**, 498, 499, 609, 617, 618
See also *absāriyya* under *samak*
sitt al-Nūba (purslane-seed stew) **116**, **121**, **154**, 535, 640
sitt al-shanaʿ/shanāʿ (taro stew) 31, **132**, 500
See also *Mutawakkiliyya*
soap, see *ṣābūn*
sparrows, see *ʿaṣāfīr*
spinach, see *isfanākh*
storing fresh produce and flowers 5, 16, 44
apples 439, **448**, 452
apricots **336**
cherry plums (*qarāṣiyā*) **446**
cucumbers and melons **451**
dates **443**, **444**, **448**, **449**, 452, 453
eggplant **451**
figs **445**, **446**
grapes **438**, 440, **444**, **452**, 453
mulberry **447**
narcissus flowers (*narjis*) **449**
peaches **438**, **446**, 514
pears **446**
quince **439**, **440**, 452
root vegetables **451**
roses **439**, **442**, **449**, 450, **451**
sūbiyā (digestive beer) 52, **286**, **288**, 464, **618**, **648**
abāzīr (spice blend) 529
Yamaniyya **287**
suʿd (cyperus) 395, 396, 397, 398, 413, 565
dharīra (scented body powder) **422**
Kūfī 393, 397, 399, 409
Quṣārī 399
sugar, see *sukkar*
sugar-cane molasses, see *qaṭr*
sugar syrups 9, 37, 52,71
ḥall xii, 108, 116, 117, 118, 122, 228, 247, 265, 266, 267, 453, 483
*jullāb 6, 7, 71, 81, 484
jullābiyya (chicken dish) **117**

sugar syrups (cont.)
sharāb (sweet drink) **257**, 459, 463
See also *ʿasal mursal*; *ʿasal qaṣab*
**sukkar* 7, 8, 24, 25, 27, 28, 29, 33, 37, 39, 47, 53, 463, 464, 488–91
kaʿk sukkarī **81**
laymūn sukkarī **376**
Miṣrī 8, 264, 489
mukarrar 26, 415
nabāt 244n178, 401, 404, 405, 413, 489, 416, 417, 487, 489, 490
qand 150n289, 436, 437, 482n2, 488
sanīnāt/ṭabarzad 216, 489, 490
shakrīnaj **236**, 488
ṭabarzad/ublūj 89, 216n34, 236, 237, 327, 346, 489, 490
sukk misk (musk-scented pastilles) 264, 300, 409, 417, 565
sumac, see *summāq*
sumānā al-ghayṭ (dormice) 32
summāq (sumac) 105, 150, 179, 191, 194, 195, 196, 205, 208, 210, 315, 319, 321, 322, 351, 352, 382, 383, 384, 565–6
māʾ (juice) 79, 107, 149, 387, 388, 438, 441, 477, 498
muzawwara (meatless stew) **188**
qaṭr/rubb (molasses) 297
ṣaḥna (small-fish condiment) **206**
summāqiyya (stew) 72, **91**, **113**, **114**, **130**, 184
with capers **372**
with fish **197**, **202**
**sunbul/nārdīn* (spikenard) 458, 529, 530, 531, 554, 566–7, 573
māʾ (distilled water) **427**
sunbul ṭīb/ʿaṣāfīrī (Indian spikenard) 320, 397
māʾ (distilled water) **433**

ṭabāhija (succulent fried meat) 31, 72, 73, **129**, 195, 500
ṭabāshīr (tabashir) 264, 301, 567
ṭaḥīna (tahini) 93, 105, 128, 130, 132, 136, 193, 194, 196, 197, 198, 199, 200, 201, 202, 203, 206, 207, 210, 295, 296, 315, 316, 319, 320, 321, 322, 333, 347, 350, 352, 353, 354, 374, 379, 380, 381, 383, 384, 388, 389, 390, 391, 494, 499, 567
ṭaḥīniyya (meatless dish) **136**, **193**
tamr (dates) 8, 21, 26, 29n73, 80, 82, 151, 152, 202, 330, **443**, **444**, **448**, **449**, 452, 453, 521–2
ʿajwa **82**, 151, 152, 238, **244**, 245, 247, 286, 521, 522
balaḥ 20, 453, 521
busr 452, 521
dhāt al-katifayn (sweet) **212**
dibs (molasses) 85, 271, 787, 303, 343, 359, 364, 444, 482
ḥalāwa (thick pudding) **244**, **245**, **247**
hays (balls) **247**
jimāliyya (sweet) **238**
maʿjūn (pressed into paste) 114, 522
muʿassal (honeyed) **246**, **248**
mulawwaz (stuffed with almonds) **247**
murabbā (jam) **247**
qasb 151n298, 247, 385, 443, 444, 448, 449, 453, 520, 521, 522
ruṭab 26, 152, **443**, **448**, 449, 522
ruṭabiyya (stew) **100**
tamriyya (stew) **101**, **114**, **131**
Wāḥī 9, 453, 522
tamr Hindī (tamarind) **120**, 254, 522
ʿaqīd (chewy candy) **371**
taqālī/taqliyya (fried meat dishes) 34, 50, **137**, **147**, 195, 500
laḥm sharāʾiḥ (fried thin slices) **147**
See also *qaliyya*
ṭarkhūn (tarragon) 72, 271, 274, 286, 309, 316, 328, 369, 458, 538, 567
kāmakh (fermented condiment) **325**
taro, see *qulqās*
tarragon, see *ṭarkhūn*
thanī (yearling sheep), see under *kharūf*
tharīd (bread dish) 45, 75, 327, 501
thūm* (garlic) 8, 20, 26, 45, 47, 50, 72, 74, 77, **372, 373, 442, 568
thyme, see *zaʿtar*
tīn (figs) 21, 85, **445**, **446**, 522
barrī/ jummayz (sycomore) 21, 523
dhukār (caprifig) 162, 163, 509, 522, 523, 594
laban (milky sap) 73, 523
leaves 323, 325, 439, 440, 452
Maʿarrī 445, 52
tuffāḥ (apples) 26, 27, 48, 72, 130, 261, 262, 423, 430, 439, **448**, 452, 523–4, 543

fatḥī 414
juwārish (digestive stomachic) **261**
peel 419
rayḥānī 112
Shāmī 209, 418
sharāb (sweet drink) **258**
tuffāḥiyya (dish) **154**
tuffāḥiyya bi-zaʿfarān (dish) **119**
tunbul (betel leaves) 149, 172, 204, 210, 254, 276, 276, 281, 283, 288, 299, 301, 333, 364, 401, 402, 409, 417, 529, 530, 531, 569, 571
turmus (lupine beans) 21, 399, 441, 641
turnips, see *lift*
tūt (mulberry) 447, 524
mock **212**
sharāb (sweet drink) **257**
yāqūtiyya (stew) **98**
tuṭmāj, see under pasta and noodles
tūtyā (tutty) 408, 410, 420, 569

ʿūd (aloeswood) 67, 85, 86, 148, 221, 242, 251, 253, 261, 262, 263, 264, 283, 291, 292, 293, 295, 298, 299, 300, 302, 303, 304, 317, 362, 364, 365, 366, 368, 371, 377, 394, 397, 400, 401, 402, 406, 408, 410, 411, 412, 413, 414, 420, 421, 422, 435, 569–70
bakhūr (incense) **404, 405, 425**
Hindī 261, 264, 397, 409, 417, 419, 425, 428
juwārish (digestive stomachic) **264**
māʾ (distilled water) **428, 432**
maʿjūn (electuary) **266**
Qamārī (from Khmer) 254, 408, 416, 417, 422
Qāqullī (Javanese) 296, 300, 302, 350, 409, 415
ʿujja (omelet) 40, 50, 56, **171, 172, 174, 175, 176, 179, 180, 182**
abāzīr (spice blend) **180**
aphrodisiac **177, 178**
bottle **172**
mubaʿthara (scrambled) **178, 179, 180**
with cheese and truffles **181**
with chicken livers **181**
without eggs **172**
with sparrows **156, 158, 172**
umluj (emblic myrobalan) 254, 526, 565
um nārayn (bread pudding) **141**, 601
ʿunnāb (jujubes) 53, 85, 87, 112, 116, 120, 131, 139, 146, 150, 320, 385, 486, 496, 526
Jurjānī 223
khabīṣ (thick pudding) **222**
ʿunnābiyya (stew) **102**
ʿurqūb (lamb hock) 104. 618
ʿuṣfur (safflower, colorant) 26, 173, 174, 341, 343, 346, 396, 446, 449, 570, 537
See also *qurṭum*
ushna (lichen), see *shayba*
ushnān (handwashing compounds) 56, **398**, 433, 435, 551, 593, 627
fava bean flour 397
lesser quality (*dūn*) **395**
muṭayyab (perfumed) **397**
rice flour **395**, 398
top-quality (*mulūkī*) **393, 394, 395, 397, 398, 399**
ushnān (potash) 395, 397, 558, 627
ʿaṣāfīrī 300, 393, 394, 399, 570
Bāriqī 398
white 395, 399
ushturghāz (alhagi) 311, 374, 570
usṭarūs/*ushṭarūsh*, see under *qaṭr*
utrujj/*turunj* (citron) 48, 64, 442, 452, 511, 512, 516, 527
candied **254**
ḥummāḍ (pulp) 88, **362**, 453
leaves 67, 88, 163, 169, 174, 286
maʿjūn (electuary) **253**
peel 168, 260, 416
qiddāḥ (blossoms) 88
sharāb (sweet drink) **252, 256**
Sūsī 252

vinegar, see *khall*

waral (monitor lizard) 424n17, 571
See also *saqanqūr* under *milḥ*
waraq Qumārī/*qāt* (khat) 402, 571
ward (roses) 67, 571–2
ʿĀṣimī 436
dharīra wardiyya **422**
Dimashqī 218n46, 245, 275, 303, 551, 572
distilling **428, 429, 430, 431**
duhn (oil) 400, 554, 572
ḥalwā wardiyya (thick pudding) **229**

ward (roses) (cont.)
ʿIrāqī 206, 450
Jūrī 218, 427
kāmakh (fermented condiment) **326**
khabīṣ (thick pudding) **218**
murabbā (jam) 87, 103, 105, **127**, 262, 362
Nuṣaybīnī 304, 326, 377, 436
sharāb (sweet drink) **259**
storing **439, 442, 449**
zir ward (buds), *see entry*
See also *māʾ ward*
wars, see *kurkum*
watermelon, see *biṭṭīkh*
writing on fruits 8, 442, 524

yaqṭīn, see *qarʿ*
yāqūtiyya (mulberry stew) 6, **98**, 524
yāsamīn (jasmine) 26, 143, 572–3
distilled water **429**
yogurt, see *laban*

zabād/zabada (civet musk) 47, 303, 402, 406, 411, 412, 413, 415, 417, 420, 421, 422, 435, 573
zabīb (raisins) 85, 120, 130, 131, 139, 145, 194, 201, 202, 203, 205, 254, 271, 295, 301, 306, 308, 309, 310, 314, 319, 320, 325, 511, 577
aḥmar 296
aswad 86, 116, 150, 303, 311, 343, 371
jawzānī 304, 317, 368, 385
Ṣaʿīdī 9, 299
Sulṭī 299
zabībiyya (stew) **131**
**zaʿfarān* (saffron) 42, 78, 446, 493, 494, 495, 529, 546, 570, 573
dharūr (restorative powder) **424**
distilled **425**, 431, **432**, 433, 436
Janawī 119
with aromatics 396, 398, 401, 403, 404, 405, 406, 411, 414, 415, 416, 417, 419
**zanjabīl* (ginger) 67, 82, 529, 531, 574
ʿirq (dried root) 376
maʿjūn (electuary) **266**
ʿuṣfūr (node of rhizome) 149
**zaʿtar* (thyme) 12, 72, 168, 169, 180, 195, 529, 574, 632
dairy condiments **336, 337, 338**
Maghribī 204, 574
Shāmī (Levantine) 332, 574
**zayt* (olive oil) 73, 74, 504–5
maghsūl/al-māʾ (washed) 164, 328, 353, 354, 505
makhlūʿ (enhanced) 505
muṭayyab (sweet) 74, 157, 505
rikābī 505
ṭayyib/ʿadhb/ḥulw (good, fine, sweet) 32, 78, 146, 147, 158, 159, 169, 173, 174, 178, 200, 201, 203, 104, 105, 106, 207, 309, 317, 505
zayt ḥārr, see under fats and oil
zaytūn (olives) 26, 38, 45, 51, 182, 330, 331, 374, 381, 501–2
mubakhkhar (smoked) **354**
mukallas (cured with slaked lime) **348, 349**
murammad (cured with ashes) **349, 350**
mutabbal (seasoned) **350, 351, 352, 353, 354, 651**
zinjār (verdigris, colorant) 396, 574
zir/azrār ward (rosebuds) 142, 146, 176, 180, 203, 205, 264, 280, 281, 283, 288, 296, 299, 303, 315, 319, 321, 322, 330, 333, 348, 353, 359, 379, 380, 399, 401, 402, 411, 413, 417, 422, 439, 450, 530, 531, 571, 574
ʿIrāqī 411, 439
Mizzī 401
Shāmī 442
zīrbāj (delicate golden stew) **90, 106, 112, 118, 123, 127**, 496
muzawwara (meatless) **185, 188, 191**
with fish **201**
zubd (butter), see under fats and oils
ẓufr/aẓfār ṭīb (onycha) 401, 403, 406, 411, 414, 417, 418, 419, 422, 575
zunjufr (vermilion, colorant) 396, 575
zurunbād (bitter ginger), see *ʿirq kāfūr*